View a guided tour of MyAccountingLab at
http://www.myaccountinglab.com/support/tours

For Students

Interactive Tutorial Exercises

- Homework and practice exercises with additional algorithmic–generated problems for more practice.

- Personalized interactive learning—guided solutions and learning aids for point-of-use help and immediate feedback.

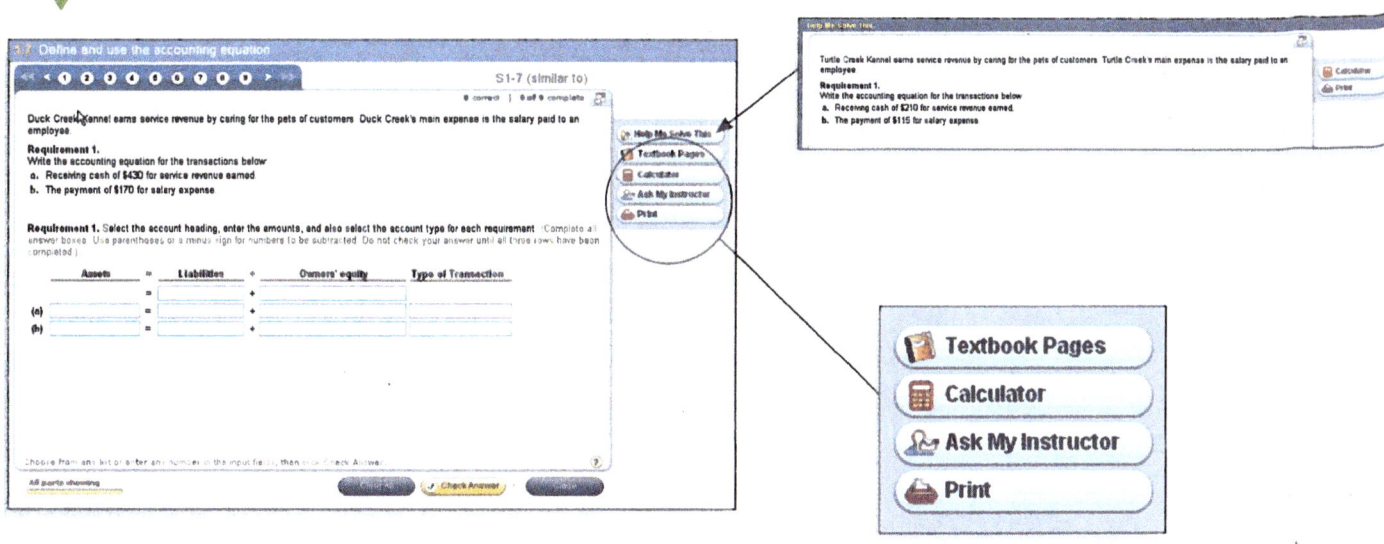

Study Plan for Self-Paced Learning

- Assists students in monitoring their own progress by offering them a customized study plan based on their test results.

- Includes regenerated exercises with new values for unlimited practice and guided multimedia learning aids for extra guidance.

Charles T. Horngren • Srikant M. Datar • Madhav Rajan

Cost Accounting
A Managerial Emphasis

Custom Edition for Oakland University

Taken from:
Cost Accounting: A Managerial Emphasis, Fourteenth Edition
by Charles T. Horngren, Srikant M. Datar, and Madhav Rajan

Cover Art: Courtesy of Stockbyte/Getty Images

Taken from:

Cost Accounting: A Managerial Emphasis, Fourteenth Edition
by Charles T. Horngren, Srikant M. Datar, and Madhav Rajan
Copyright © 2011, 2009, 2006, 2003 by Pearson Education, Inc.
Published by Prentice Hall
Upper Saddle River, New Jersey 07458

This special edition published in cooperation with Pearson Learning Solutions.

Pearson Learning Solutions, 501 Boylston Street, Suite 900, Boston, MA 02116
A Pearson Education Company
www.pearsoned.com

Printed in the United States of America

2 3 4 5 6 7 8 9 10 V092 16 15 14 13 12

000200010270754070

KB

ISBN 10: 1-256-36958-6
ISBN 13: 978-0-256-36958-5

Brief Contents

Contents

About the Authors

Charles T. Horngren is the Edmund W. Littlefield Professor of Accounting, Emeritus, at Stanford University. A Graduate of Marquette University, he received his MBA from Harvard University and his PhD from the University of Chicago. He is also the recipient of honorary doctorates from Marquette University and DePaul University.

A certified public accountant, Horngren served on the Accounting Principles Board for six years, the Financial Accounting Standards Board Advisory Council for five years, and the Council of the American Institute of Certified Public Accountants for three years. For six years, he served as a trustee of the Financial Accounting Foundation, which oversees the Financial Accounting Standards Board and the Government Accounting Standards Board. Horngren is a member of the Accounting Hall of Fame.

A member of the American Accounting Association, Horngren has been its president and its director of research. He received its first Outstanding Accounting Educator Award. The California Certified Public Accountants Foundation gave Horngren its Faculty Excellence Award and its Distinguished Professor Award. He is the first person to have received both awards.

The American Institute of Certified Public Accountants presented its first Outstanding Educator Award to Horngren.

Horngren was named Accountant of the Year, Education, by the national professional accounting fraternity, Beta Alpha Psi.

Professor Horngren is also a member of the Institute of Management Accountants, from whom he received its Distinguished Service Award. He was also a member of the Institutes' Board of Regents, which administers the Certified Management Accountant examinations.

Horngren is the author of other accounting books published by Prentice Hall: *Introduction to Management Accounting*, 15th ed. (2011, with Sundem and Stratton); *Introduction to Financial Accounting*, 10th ed. (2011, with Sundem and Elliott); *Accounting*, 8th ed. (2010, with Harrison and Bamber); and *Financial Accounting*, 8th ed. (2010, with Harrison).

Horngren is the Consulting Editor for the Charles T. Horngren Series in Accounting.

Srikant M. Datar is the Arthur Lowes Dickinson Professor of Business Administration and Senior Associate Dean at Harvard University. A graduate with distinction from the University of Bombay, he received gold medals upon graduation from the Indian Institute of Management, Ahmedabad, and the Institute of Cost and Works Accountants of India. A chartered accountant, he holds two master's degrees and a PhD from Stanford University.

Cited by his students as a dedicated and innovative teacher, Datar received the George Leland Bach Award for Excellence in the Classroom at Carnegie Mellon University and the Distinguished Teaching Award at Stanford University.

Datar has published his research in leading accounting, marketing, and operations management journals, including *The Accounting Review, Contemporary Accounting Research, Journal of Accounting, Auditing and Finance, Journal of Accounting and Economics, Journal of Accounting Research*, and *Management Science*. He has also served on the editorial board of several journals and presented his research to corporate executives and academic audiences in North America, South America, Asia, Africa, Australia, and Europe.

Datar is a member of the board of directors of Novartis A.G., ICF International, KPIT Cummins Infosystems Ltd., Stryker Corporation, and Harvard Business Publishing, and has worked with many organizations, including Apple Computer, AT&T, Boeing, Du Pont, Ford, General Motors, HSBC, Hewlett-Packard, Morgan Stanley, PepsiCo, TRW,

Visa, and the World Bank. He is a member of the American Accounting Association and the Institute of Management Accountants.

Madhav V. Rajan is the Gregor G. Peterson Professor of Accounting and Senior Associate Dean at Stanford University. From 2002 to 2010, he was the area coordinator for accounting at Stanford's Graduate School of Business.

Rajan received his undergraduate degree in commerce from the University of Madras, India, and his MS in accounting, MBA, and PhD degrees from the Graduate School of Industrial Administration at Carnegie Mellon University. In 1990, his dissertation won the Alexander Henderson Award for Excellence in Economic Theory.

Rajan's primary area of research interest is the economics-based analysis of management accounting issues, especially as they relate to internal control cost allocation, capital budgeting, quality management, supply chain, and performance systems in firms. He has published his research in leading accounting and operations management journals including *The Accounting Review*, *Review of Financial Studies*, *Journal of Accounting Research*, and *Management Science*. In 2004, he received the Notable Contribution to Management Accounting Literature Award.

Rajan has served as the Departmental Editor for Accounting at *Management Science*, as well as associate editor for both the accounting and operations areas. From 2002 to 2008, Rajan served as an editor of *The Accounting Review*. He is also currently an associate editor for the *Journal of Accounting, Auditing and Finance*. Rajan is a member of the management accounting section of the American Accounting Association and has twice been a plenary speaker at the AAA Management Accounting Conference.

Rajan has won several teaching awards at Wharton and Stanford, including the David W. Hauck Award, the highest undergraduate teaching honor at Wharton. Rajan has taught in a variety of executive education programs including the Stanford Executive Program, the National Football League Program for Managers, and the National Basketball Players Association Program, as well as custom programs for firms including nVidia, Genentech, and Google.

Preface

Studying Cost Accounting is one of the best business investments a student can make. Why? Because success in any organization—from the smallest corner store to the largest multinational corporation—requires the use of cost accounting concepts and practices. Cost accounting provides key data to managers for planning and controlling, as well as costing products, services, even customers. This book focuses on how cost accounting helps managers make better decisions, as cost accountants are increasingly becoming integral members of their company's decision-making teams. In order to emphasize this prominence in decision-making, we use the "different costs for different purposes" theme throughout this book. By focusing on basic concepts, analyses, uses, and procedures instead of procedures alone, we recognize cost accounting as a managerial tool for business strategy and implementation.

We also prepare students for the rewards and challenges they face in the professional cost accounting world of today and tomorrow. For example, we emphasize both the development of analytical skills such as Excel to leverage available information technology and the values and behaviors that make cost accountants effective in the workplace.

Hallmark Features of *Cost Accounting*

- Exceptionally strong emphasis on managerial uses of cost information
- Clarity and understandability of the text
- Excellent balance in integrating modern topics with traditional coverage
- Emphasis on human behavior aspects
- Extensive use of real-world examples
- Ability to teach chapters in different sequences
- Excellent quantity, quality, and range of assignment material

The first thirteen chapters provide the essence of a one-term (quarter or semester) course. There is ample text and assignment material in the book's twenty-three chapters for a two-term course. This book can be used immediately after the student has had an introductory course in financial accounting. Alternatively, this book can build on an introductory course in managerial accounting.

Deciding on the sequence of chapters in a textbook is a challenge. Since every instructor has a unique way of organizing his or her course, we utilize a modular, flexible organization that permits a course to be custom tailored. *This organization facilitates diverse approaches to teaching and learning.*

As an example of the book's flexibility, consider our treatment of process costing. Process costing is described in Chapters 17 and 18. Instructors interested in filling out a student's perspective of costing systems can move directly from job-order costing described in Chapter 4 to Chapter 17 without interruption in the flow of material. Other instructors may want their students to delve into activity-based costing and budgeting and more decision-oriented topics early in the course. These instructors may prefer to postpone discussion of process costing.

New to This Edition
Greater Emphasis on Strategy

This edition deepens the book's emphasis on strategy development and execution. Several chapters build on the strategy theme introduced in Chapter 1. Chapter 13 has a greater discussion of strategy maps as a useful tool to implement the balanced scorecard and a simplified presentation of how income statements of companies can be analyzed from the strategic perspective of product differentiation or cost leadership. We also discuss strategy considerations in the design of activity-based costing systems in Chapter 5, the preparation of budgets in Chapter 6, and decision making in Chapters 11 and 12.

Deeper Consideration of Global Issues

Business is increasingly becoming more global. Even small and medium-sized companies across the manufacturing, merchandising, and service sectors are being forced to deal with the effects of globalization. Global considerations permeate many chapters. For example, Chapter 11 discusses the benefits and the challenges that arise when outsourcing products or services outside the United States. Chapter 22 examines the importance of transfer pricing in minimizing the tax burden faced by multinational companies. Several new examples of management accounting applications in companies are drawn from international settings.

Increased Focus on the Service Sector

In keeping with the shifts in the U.S. and world economy this edition makes greater use of service sector examples. For example, Chapter 2 discusses the concepts around the measurement of costs in a software development rather than a manufacturing setting. Chapter 6 provides several examples of the use of budgets and targets in service companies. Several concepts in action boxes focus on the service sector such as activity-based costing at Charles Schwab (Chapter 5) and managing wireless data bottlenecks (Chapter 19).

New Cutting Edge Topics

The pace of change in organizations continues to be rapid. The fourteenth edition of *Cost Accounting* reflects changes occurring in the role of cost accounting in organizations.

- We have introduced foreign currency and forward contract issues in the context of outsourcing decisions.
- We have added ideas based on Six Sigma to the discussion of quality.
- We have rewritten the chapter on strategy and the balanced scorecard and simplified the presentation to connect strategy development, strategy maps, balanced scorecard, and analysis of operating income.
- We discuss current trends towards Beyond Budgeting and the use of rolling forecasts.
- We develop the link between traditional forms of cost allocation and the nascent movement in Europe towards Resource Consumption Accounting.
- We focus more sharply on how companies are simplifying their costing systems with the presentation of value streams and lean accounting.

Opening Vignettes

Each chapter opens with a vignette on a real company situation. The vignettes engage the reader in a business situation, or dilemma, illustrating why and how the concepts in the chapter are relevant in business. For example, Chapter 1 describes how Apple uses cost accounting information to make decisions relating to how they price the most popular songs on iTunes. Chapter 3 explains how the band U2 paid for their extensive new stage by lowering ticket prices. Chapter 7 describes how even the NBA was forced to cut costs after over half of the league's franchises declared losses. Chapter 11 shows how JetBlue uses Twitter and e-mail to help their customers make better pricing decisions. Chapter 12 discusses how Tata Motors designed a car for the Indian masses, priced at only $2,500. Chapter 14 shows how Best Buy boosts profits by analyzing its customers and their buying habits. Chapter 18 describes how Boeing incurred great losses as it reworked its much-anticipated Dreamliner airplane.

Concepts in Action Boxes

Found in every chapter, these boxes cover real-world cost accounting issues across a variety of industries including automobile racing, defense contracting, entertainment, manufacturing, and retailing. New examples include

- How Zipcar Helps Reduce Business Transportation Costs p. 33
- Job Costing at Cowboys Stadium p. 108
- The "Death Spiral" and the End of Landline Telephone Service p. 319
- Transfer Pricing Dispute Temporarily Stops the Flow of Fiji Water p. 793

Streamlined Presentation

We continue to try to simplify and streamline our presentation of various topics to make it as easy as possible for a student to learn the concepts, tools, and frameworks introduced in different chapters. Examples of more streamlined presentations can be found in

- Chapter 3 on the discussion of target net income
- Chapter 5 on the core issues in activity-based costing (ABC)
- Chapter 8, which uses a single comprehensive example to illustrate the use of variance analysis in ABC systems
- Chapter 13, which has a much simpler presentation of the strategic analysis of operating income
- Chapter 15, which uses a simpler, unified framework to discuss various cost-allocation methods
- Chapters 17 and 18, where the material on standard costing has been moved to the appendix, allowing for smoother transitions through the sections in the body of the chapter

Selected Chapter-by-Chapter Content Changes

Thank you for your continued support of Cost Accounting. In every new edition, we strive to update this text thoroughly. To ease your transition from the thirteenth edition, here are selected highlights of chapter changes for the fourteenth edition.

Chapter 1 has been rewritten to focus on strategy, decision-making, and learning emphasizing the managerial issues that animate modern management accounting. It now emphasizes decision making instead of problem solving, performance evaluation instead of scorekeeping and learning instead of attention directing.

Chapter 2 has been rewritten to emphasize the service sector. For example, instead of a manufacturing company context, the chapter uses the software development setting at a company like Apple Inc. to discuss cost measurement. It also develops ideas related to risk when discussing fixed versus variable costs.

Chapter 3 has been rewritten to simplify the presentation of target net income by describing how target net income can be converted to target operating income. This allows students to use the equations already developed for target operating income when discussing target net income. We deleted the section on multiple cost drivers, because it is closely related to the multi-product example discussed in the chapter. The managerial and decision-making aspects of the chapter have also been strengthened.

Chapter 4 has been reorganized to first discuss normal costing and then actual costing because normal costing is much more prevalent in practice. As a result of this change the exhibits in the early part of the chapter tie in more closely to the detailed exhibits of normal job-costing systems in manufacturing later in the chapter. The presentation of actual costing has been retained to help students understand the benefits and challenges of actual costing systems. To focus on job costing, we moved the discussion of responsibility centers and departments to Chapter 6.

Chapter 5 has been reorganized to clearly distinguish design choices, implementation challenges, and managerial applications of ABC systems. The presentation of the ideas has been simplified and streamlined to focus on the core issues.

Chapter 6 now includes ideas from relevant applied research on the usefulness of budgets and the circumstances in which they add the greatest value, as well as the challenges in administering them. It incorporates new material on the Beyond Budgeting movement, and in particular the trend towards the use of rolling forecasts.

Chapters 7 and 8 present a streamlined discussion of direct-cost and overhead variances, respectively. The separate sections on ABC and variance analysis in Chapters 7 and 8 have now been combined into a single integrated example at the end of Chapter 8. A new appendix to Chapter 7 now addresses more detailed revenue variances using the existing Webb Company example. The use of potentially confusing terms such as 2-variance analysis and 1-variance analysis has been eliminated.

We have rewritten Chapter 9 as a single integrated chapter with the same running example rather than as two distinct sub-parts on inventory costing and capacity analysis. The material on the tax and financial reporting implications of various capacity concepts has also been fully revised.

Chapter 10 has been revised to provide a more linear progression through the ideas of cost estimation and the choice of cost drivers, culminating in the use of quantitative analysis (regression analysis, in particular) for managerial decision-making.

Chapter 11 now includes more discussion of global issues such as foreign currency considerations in international outsourcing decisions. There is also greater emphasis on strategy and decision-making.

Chapter 12 has been reorganized to more sharply delineate short-run from long-run costing and pricing and to bring together the various considerations other than costs that affect pricing decisions. This reorganization has helped streamline several sections in the chapter.

Chapter 13 has been substantially rewritten. Strategy maps are presented as a way to link strategic objectives and as a useful first step in developing balanced scorecard measures. The section on strategic analysis of operating income has been significantly simplified by focusing on only one indirect cost and eliminating most of the technical details. Finally, the section on engineered and discretionary costs has been considerably shortened to focus on only the key ideas.

Chapter 14 now discusses the use of "whale curves" to depict the outcome of customer profitability analysis. The last part of the chapter has been rationalized to focus on the decomposition of sales volume variances into quantity and mix variances; and the calculation of sales mix variances has also been simplified.

Chapter 15 has been completely revised and uses a simple, unified conceptual framework to discuss various cost allocation methods (single-rate versus dual-rate, actual costs versus budgeted costs, etc.).

Chapter 16 now provides a more in-depth discussion of the rationale underlying joint cost allocation as well as the reasons why some firms *do not* allocate costs (along with real-world examples).

Chapters 17 and 18 have been reorganized, with the material on standard costing moved to the appendix in both chapters. This reorganization has made the chapters easier to navigate and fully consistent (since all sections in the body of the chapter now use actual costing). The material on multiple inspection points from the appendix to Chapter 18 has been moved into the body of the chapter, but using a variant of the existing example involving Anzio Corp.

Chapter 19 introduces the idea of Six Sigma quality. It also integrates design quality, conformance quality, and financial and nonfinancial measures of quality. The discussion of queues, delays, and costs of time has been significantly streamlined.

Chapter 20's discussion of EOQ has been substantially revised and the ideas of lean accounting further developed. The section on backflush costing has been completely rewritten.

Chapter 21 has been revised to incorporate the payback period method with discounting, and also now includes survey evidence on the use of various capital budgeting methods. The discussion of goal congruence and performance measurement has been simplified and combined, making the latter half of the chapter easier to follow.

Chapter 22 has been fully rewritten with a new section on the use of hybrid pricing methods. The chapter also now includes a fuller description (and a variety of examples) of the use of transfer pricing for tax minimization, and incorporates such developments as the recent tax changes proposed by the Obama administration.

Chapter 23 includes a more thorough description of Residual Income and EVA, as well as a more streamlined discussion of the various choices of accounting-based performance measures.

Resources

In addition to this textbook and MyAccountingLab, the following resources are available for students:

- Student Study Guide—self study aid full of review features.
- Student Solutions Manual—solutions and assistance for even numbered problems.
- Excel Manual—workbook designed for Excel practice.
- Companion website—www.pearsonhighered.com/horngren.

The following resources are available for Instructors:

- Solutions Manual
- Test Gen
- Instructors Manual
- PowerPoint Presentations
- Image Library
- Instructors Resource Center—www.pearsonhighered.com/horngren

Acknowledgments

We are indebted to many people for their ideas and assistance. Our primary thanks go to the many academics and practitioners who have advanced our knowledge of cost accounting. The package of teaching materials we present is the work of skillful and valued team members developing some excellent end-of-chapter assignment material. Tommy Goodwin, Ian Gow (Northwestern), Richard Saouma (UCLA) and Shalin Shah (Berkeley) provided outstanding research assistance on technical issues and current developments. We would also like to thank the dedicated and hard working supplement author team and GEX Publishing Services. The book is much better because of the efforts of these colleagues.

In shaping this edition, we would like to thank a group of colleagues who worked closely with us and the editorial team. This group provided detailed feedback and participated in focus groups that guided the direction of this edition:

Wagdy Abdallah
Seton Hall University

David Alldredge
Salt Lake Community College

Felicia Baldwin
Richard J. Daley College

Molly Brown
James Madison University

Shannon Charles
Brigham Young University

David Franz
San Francisco State University

Anna Jensen
Indiana University

Donna McGovern
Custom Business Results, Inc.

Cindy Nye
Bellevue University

Glenn Pate
Florida Atlantic University

Kelly Pope
DePaul University

Jenice Prather-Kinsey
University of Missouri

Melvin Roush
Pitt State University

Karen Shastri
Pitt University

Frank Stangota
Rutgers University

Patrick Stegman
College of Lake County

We would also like to extend our thanks to those professors who provided detailed written reviews or comments on drafts. These professors include the following:

Robyn Alcock
Central Queensland University

David S. Baglia
Grove City College

Charles Bailey
University of Central Florida

Robert Bauman
Allan Hancock Joint Community College

David Bilker
University of Maryland, University College

Marvin Bouillon
Iowa State University

Dennis Caplan
Columbia University

Donald W. Gribbin
Southern Illinois University

Rosalie Hallbauer
Florida International University

John Haverty
St. Joseph's University

Jean Hawkins
William Jewell College

Rodger Holland
Francis Marion University

Jiunn C. Huang
San Francisco State University

Zafar U. Khan
Eastern Michigan University

Larry N. Killough
Virginia Polytechnic Institute & State University

Keith Kramer
Southern Oregon University

Jay Law
Central Washington University

Sandra Lazzarini
University of Queensland

Gary J. Mann
University of Texas at El Paso

Ronald Marshall
Michigan State University

Maureen Mascha
Marquette University

Pam Meyer
University of Louisiana at Lafayette

Marjorie Platt
Northeastern University

Roy W. Regel
University of Montana

Pradyot K. Sen
University of Cincinnati

Gim S. Seow
University of Connecticut

Rebekah A. Sheely
Northeastern University

Robert J. Shepherd
University of California, Santa Cruz

Kenneth Sinclair
Lehigh University

Vic Stanton
California State University, Hayward

Carolyn Streuly
Marquette University

Gerald Thalmann
North Central College

Peter D. Woodlock
Youngstown State University

James Williamson
San Diego State University

Sung-Soo Yoon
UCLA at Los Angeles

Jennifer Dosch
Metro State University

Joe Dowd
Eastern Washington University

Leslie Kren
University of Wisconsin-Madison

Michele Matherly
Xavier University

Laurie Burney
Mississippi State University

Mike Morris
Notre Dame University

Cinthia Nye
Bellevue University

Roy Regel
University of Montana

Margaret Shackell-Dowel
Notre Dame University

Marvin Bouillon
Iowa State University

Kreag Danvers
Clarion University of Pennsylvania

A.J. Cataldo II
West Chester University

Kenneth Danko
San Francisco State University

T.S. Amer
Northern Arizona University

Robert Hartman
University of Iowa

Diane Satin
California State University East Bay

John Stancil
Florida Southern College

Michael Flores
Wichita University

Ralph Greenberg
Temple University

Paul Warrick
Westwood College

Karen Schoenebeck
Southwestern College

Thomas D. Fields
Washington University in St. Louis

Constance Hylton
George Mason University

Robert Alford
DePaul University

Michael Eames
Santa Clara University

We also would like to thank our colleagues who helped us greatly by accuracy checking the text and supplements including Molly Brown, Barbara Durham, and Anna Jensen.

We thank the people at Prentice Hall for their hard work and dedication, including Donna Battista, Stephanie Wall, Christina Rumbaugh, Brian Reilly, Cindy Zonneveld, Lynne Breitfeller, Natacha Moore, and Kate Thomas and Kelly Morrison at GEX Publishing Services. We must extend special thanks to Deepa Chungi, the development editor on this edition, who took charge of this project and directed it across the finish line. This book would not have been possible without her dedication and skill.

Alexandra Gural, Jacqueline Archer, and others expertly managed the production aspects of all the manuscript preparation with superb skill and tremendous dedication. We are deeply appreciative of their good spirits, loyalty, and ability to stay calm in the most hectic of times. The constant support of Bianca Baggio and Caroline Roop is greatly appreciated.

Appreciation also goes to the American Institute of Certified Public Accountants, the Institute of Management Accountants, the Society of Management Accountants of Canada, the Certified General Accountants Association of Canada, the Financial Executive Institute of America, and many other publishers and companies for their generous permission to quote from their publications. Problems from the Uniform CPA examinations are designated (CPA); problems from the Certified Management Accountant examination are designated (CMA); problems from the Canadian examinations administered by the Society of Management Accountants are designated (SMA); and problems from the Certified General Accountants Association are designated (CGA). Many of these problems are adapted to highlight particular points.

We are grateful to the professors who contributed assignment material for this edition. Their names are indicated in parentheses at the start of their specific problems. Comments from users are welcome.

CHARLES T. HORNGREN
SRIKANT M. DATAR
MADHAV V. RAJAN

To Our Families
The Horngren Family (CH)
Swati, Radhika, Gayatri, Sidharth (SD)
Gayathri, Sanjana, Anupama (MVR)

1 The Manager and Management Accounting

All businesses are concerned about revenues and costs.

Whether their products are automobiles, fast food, or the latest designer fashions, managers must understand how revenues and costs behave or risk losing control. Managers use cost accounting information to make decisions related to strategy formulation, research and development, budgeting, production planning, and pricing, among others. Sometimes these decisions involve tradeoffs. The following article shows how companies like Apple make those tradeoffs to increase their profits.

iTunes Variable Pricing: Downloads Are Down, but Profits Are Up[1]

Can selling less of something be more profitable than selling more of it? In 2009, Apple changed the pricing structure for songs sold through iTunes from a flat fee of $0.99 to a three-tier price point system of $0.69, $0.99, and $1.29. The top 200 songs in any given week make up more than one-sixth of digital music sales. Apple now charges the higher price of $1.29 for these hit songs by artists like Taylor Swift and the Black Eyed Peas.

After the first six months of the new pricing model in the iTunes store, downloads of the top 200 tracks were down by about 6%. While the number of downloads dropped, the higher prices generated more revenue than before the new pricing structure was in place. Since Apple's iTunes costs—wholesale song costs, network and transaction fees, and other operating costs—do not vary based on the price of each download, the profits from the 30% increase in price more than made up for the losses from the 6% decrease in volume.

To increase profits beyond those created by higher prices, Apple also began to manage iTunes' costs. Transaction costs (what Apple pays credit-card processors like Visa and MasterCard) have decreased, and Apple has also reduced the number of people working in the iTunes store.

---

[1] *Sources:* Bruno, Anthony and Glenn Peoples. 2009. Variable iTunes pricing a moneymaker for artists. *Reuters,* June 21. http://www.reuters.com/article/idUSTRE55K0DJ20090621; Peoples, Glenn. 2009. The long tale? *Billboard,* November 14. http://www.billboard.biz/bbbiz/content_display/magazine/features/e3i35ed869fbd929ccdcca52ed7fd9262d3?imw=Y; Savitz, Eric. 2007. Apple: Turns out, iTunes makes money Pacific Crest says; subscription services seems inevitable. *Barron's* "Tech Trader Daily" blog, April 23. http://blogs.barrons.com/techtraderdaily/2007/04/23/apple-turns-out-itunes-makes-money-pacific-crest-says-subscription-service-seems-inevitable/

The study of modern cost accounting yields insights into how managers and accountants can contribute to successfully running their businesses. It also prepares them for leadership roles. Many large companies, such as Constellation Energy, Jones Soda, Nike, and the Pittsburgh Steelers, have senior executives with accounting backgrounds.

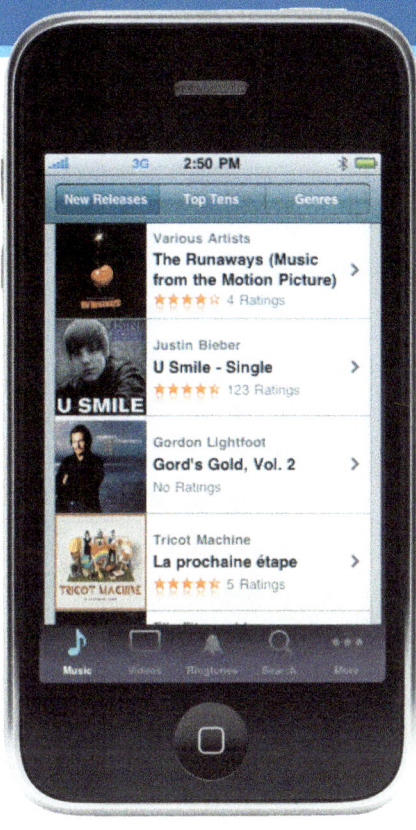

Financial Accounting, Management Accounting, and Cost Accounting

As many of you have already seen in your financial accounting class, accounting systems take economic events and transactions, such as sales and materials purchases, and process the data into information helpful to managers, sales representatives, production supervisors, and others. Processing any economic transaction means collecting, categorizing, summarizing, and analyzing. For example, costs are collected by category, such as materials, labor, and shipping. These costs are then summarized to determine total costs by month, quarter, or year. The results are analyzed to evaluate, say, how costs have changed relative to revenues from one period to the next. Accounting systems provide the information found in the income statement, the balance sheet, the statement of cash flow, and in performance reports, such as the cost of serving customers or running an advertising campaign. Managers use accounting information to administer the activities, businesses, or functional areas they oversee and to coordinate those activities, businesses, or functions within the framework of the organization. Understanding this information is essential for managers to do their jobs.

Individual managers often require the information in an accounting system to be presented or reported differently. Consider, for example, sales order information. A sales manager may be interested in the total dollar amount of sales to determine the commissions to be paid. A distribution manager may be interested in the sales order quantities by geographic region and by customer-requested delivery dates to ensure timely deliveries. A manufacturing manager may be interested in the quantities of various products and their desired delivery dates, so that he or she can develop an effective production schedule. To simultaneously serve the needs of all three managers, companies create a database—sometimes called a data warehouse or infobarn—consisting of small, detailed bits of information that can be used for multiple purposes. For instance, the sales order database will contain detailed information about product, quantity ordered, selling price, and delivery details (place and date) for each sales order. The database stores information in a way that allows different managers to access the information they need. Many companies are building their own Enterprise Resource Planning (ERP) systems, single databases that collect data and feed it into applications that support the company's business activities, such as purchasing, production, distribution, and sales.

Financial accounting and management accounting have different goals. As many of you know, **financial accounting** focuses on reporting to external parties such as investors, government agencies, banks, and suppliers. It measures and records business transactions and provides financial statements that are based on generally accepted accounting principles (GAAP). The most important way that financial accounting information affects managers' decisions and actions is through compensation, which is often, in part, based on numbers in financial statements.

Learning Objective 1

Distinguish financial accounting

. . . . reporting on past performance to external users

from management accounting

. . . helping managers make decisions

Management accounting measures, analyzes, and reports financial and nonfinancial information that helps managers make decisions to fulfill the goals of an organization. Managers use management accounting information to develop, communicate, and implement strategy. They also use management accounting information to coordinate product design, production, and marketing decisions and to evaluate performance. Management accounting information and reports do not have to follow set principles or rules. The key questions are always (1) how will this information help managers do their jobs better, and (2) do the benefits of producing this information exceed the costs?

Exhibit 1-1 summarizes the major differences between management accounting and financial accounting. Note, however, that reports such as balance sheets, income statements, and statements of cash flows are common to both management accounting and financial accounting.

Cost accounting provides information for management accounting and financial accounting. **Cost accounting** measures, analyzes, and reports financial and nonfinancial information relating to the costs of acquiring or using resources in an organization. For example, calculating the cost of a product is a cost accounting function that answers financial accounting's inventory-valuation needs and management accounting's decision-making needs (such as deciding how to price products and choosing which products to promote). Modern cost accounting takes the perspective that collecting cost information is a function of the management decisions being made. Thus, the distinction between management accounting and cost accounting is not so clear-cut, and we often use these terms interchangeably in the book.

We frequently hear business people use the term *cost management*. Unfortunately, that term has no uniform definition. We use **cost management** to describe the approaches and activities of managers to use resources to increase value to customers and to achieve organizational goals. Cost management decisions include decisions such as whether to enter new markets, implement new organizational processes, and change product designs. Information from accounting systems helps managers to manage costs, but the information and the accounting systems themselves are not cost management.

Cost management has a broad focus and is not only about reduction in costs. Cost management includes decisions to incur additional costs, for example to improve

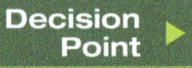

Decision Point

How is management accounting different from financial accounting?

Exhibit 1-1 Major Differences Between Management and Financial Accounting

	Management Accounting	Financial Accounting
Purpose of information	Help managers make decisions to fulfill an organization's goals	Communicate organization's financial position to investors, banks, regulators, and other outside parties
Primary users	Managers of the organization	External users such as investors, banks, regulators, and suppliers
Focus and emphasis	Future-oriented (budget for 2011 prepared in 2010)	Past-oriented (reports on 2010 performance prepared in 2011)
Rules of measurement and reporting	Internal measures and reports do not have to follow GAAP but are based on cost-benefit analysis	Financial statements must be prepared in accordance with GAAP and be certified by external, independent auditors
Time span and type of reports	Varies from hourly information to 15 to 20 years, with financial and nonfinancial reports on products, departments, territories, and strategies	Annual and quarterly financial reports, primarily on the company as a whole
Behavioral implications	Designed to influence the behavior of managers and other employees	Primarily reports economic events but also influences behavior because manager's compensation is often based on reported financial results

customer satisfaction and quality and to develop new products, with the goal of enhancing revenues and profits.

Strategic Decisions and the Management Accountant

Strategy specifies how an organization matches its own capabilities with the opportunities in the marketplace to accomplish its objectives. In other words, strategy describes how an organization will compete and the opportunities its managers should seek and pursue. Businesses follow one of two broad strategies. Some companies, such as Southwest Airlines and Vanguard (the mutual fund company) follow a cost leadership strategy. They have been profitable and have grown over the years on the basis of providing quality products or services at low prices by judiciously managing their costs. Other companies such as Apple Inc., the maker of iPods and iPhones, and Johnson & Johnson, the pharmaceutical giant, follow a product differentiation strategy. They generate their profits and growth on the basis of their ability to offer differentiated or unique products or services that appeal to their customers and are often priced higher than the less-popular products or services of their competitors.

Deciding between these strategies is a critical part of what managers do. Management accountants work closely with managers in formulating strategy by providing information about the sources of competitive advantage—for example, the cost, productivity, or efficiency advantage of their company relative to competitors or the premium prices a company can charge relative to the costs of adding features that make its products or services distinctive. **Strategic cost management** describes cost management that specifically focuses on strategic issues.

Management accounting information helps managers formulate strategy by answering questions such as the following:

- Who are our most important customers, and how can we be competitive and deliver value to them? After Amazon.com's success in selling books online, management accountants at Barnes and Noble presented senior executives with the costs and benefits of several alternative approaches for building its information technology infrastructure and developing the capabilities to also sell books online. A similar cost-benefit analysis led Toyota to build flexible computer-integrated manufacturing (CIM) plants that enable it to use the same equipment efficiently to produce a variety of cars in response to changing customer tastes.

- What substitute products exist in the marketplace, and how do they differ from our product in terms of price and quality? Hewlett-Packard, for example, designs and prices new printers after comparing the functionality and quality of its printers to other printers available in the marketplace.

- What is our most critical capability? Is it technology, production, or marketing? How can we leverage it for new strategic initiatives? Kellogg Company, for example, uses the reputation of its brand to introduce new types of cereal.

- Will adequate cash be available to fund the strategy, or will additional funds need to be raised? Proctor & Gamble, for example, issued new debt and equity to fund its strategic acquisition of Gillette, a maker of shaving products.

The best-designed strategies and the best-developed capabilities are useless unless they are effectively executed. In the next section, we describe how management accountants help managers take actions that create value for their customers.

Value Chain and Supply Chain Analysis and Key Success Factors

Customers demand much more than just a fair price; they expect quality products (goods or services) delivered in a timely way. These multiple factors drive how a customer experiences a product and the value or usefulness a customer derives from the product. How then does a company go about creating this value?

Learning Objective 2

Understand how management accountants affect strategic decisions

. . . they provide information about the sources of competitive advantage

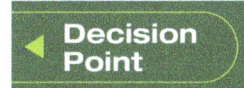

Decision Point

How do management accountants support strategic decisions?

Value-Chain Analysis

Value chain is the sequence of business functions in which customer usefulness is added to products. Exhibit 1-2 shows six primary business functions: research and development, design, production, marketing, distribution, and customer service. We illustrate these business functions using Sony Corporation's television division.

1. **Research and development (R&D)**—Generating and experimenting with ideas related to new products, services, or processes. At Sony, this function includes research on alternative television signal transmission (analog, digital, and high-definition) and on the clarity of different shapes and thicknesses of television screens.

2. **Design of products and processes**—Detailed planning, engineering, and testing of products and processes. Design at Sony includes determining the number of component parts in a television set and the effect of alternative product designs on quality and manufacturing costs. Some representations of the value chain collectively refer to the first two steps as technology development.[2]

3. **Production**—Procuring, transporting and storing (also called inbound logistics), coordinating, and assembling (also called operations) resources to produce a product or deliver a service. Production of a Sony television set includes the procurement and assembly of the electronic parts, the cabinet, and the packaging used for shipping.

4. **Marketing (including sales)**—Promoting and selling products or services to customers or prospective customers. Sony markets its televisions at trade shows, via advertisements in newspapers and magazines, on the Internet, and through its sales force.

5. **Distribution**—Processing orders and shipping products or services to customers (also called outbound logistics). Distribution for Sony includes shipping to retail outlets, catalog vendors, direct sales via the Internet, and other channels through which customers purchase televisions.

6. **Customer service**—Providing after-sales service to customers. Sony provides customer service on its televisions in the form of customer-help telephone lines, support on the Internet, and warranty repair work.

In addition to the six primary business functions, Exhibit 1-2 shows an administrative function, which includes functions such as accounting and finance, human resource management, and information technology, that support the six primary business functions. When discussing the value chain in subsequent chapters of the book, we include the administrative support function within the primary functions. For example, included in the marketing function is the function of analyzing, reporting, and accounting for resources spent in different marketing channels, while the production function includes the human resource management function of training front-line workers.

Each of these business functions is essential to companies satisfying their customers and keeping them satisfied (and loyal) over time. Companies use the term *customer relationship management (CRM)* to describe a strategy that integrates people and technology in all business functions to deepen relationships with customers, partners, and distributors. CRM initiatives use technology to coordinate all customer-facing activities

Exhibit 1-2   Different Parts of the Value Chain

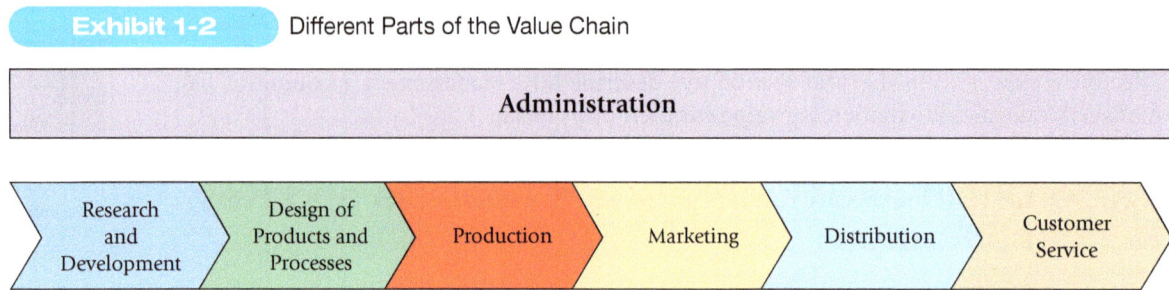

[2] M. Porter, *Competitive Advantage* (New York: Free Press, 1985).

(such as marketing, sales calls, distribution, and post sales support) and the design and production activities necessary to get products to customers.

At different times and in different industries, one or more of these functions is more critical than others. For example, a company developing an innovative new product or operating in the pharmaceutical industry, where innovation is the key to profitability, will emphasize R&D and design of products and processes. A company in the consumer goods industry will focus on marketing, distribution, and customer service to build its brand.

Exhibit 1-2 depicts the usual order in which different business-function activities physically occur. Do not, however, interpret Exhibit 1-2 as implying that managers should proceed sequentially through the value chain when planning and managing their activities. Companies gain (in terms of cost, quality, and the speed with which new products are developed) if two or more of the individual business functions of the value chain work concurrently as a team. For example, inputs into design decisions by production, marketing, distribution, and customer service managers often lead to design choices that reduce total costs of the company.

Managers track the costs incurred in each value-chain category. Their goal is to reduce costs and to improve efficiency. Management accounting information helps managers make cost-benefit tradeoffs. For example, is it cheaper to buy products from outside vendors or to do manufacturing in-house? How does investing resources in design and manufacturing reduce costs of marketing and customer service?

Supply-Chain Analysis

The parts of the value chain associated with producing and delivering a product or service—production and distribution—is referred to as the *supply chain*. **Supply chain** describes the flow of goods, services, and information from the initial sources of materials and services to the delivery of products to consumers, regardless of whether those activities occur in the same organization or in other organizations. Consider Coke and Pepsi, for example; many companies play a role in bringing these products to consumers. Exhibit 1-3 presents an overview of the supply chain. Cost management emphasizes integrating and coordinating activities across all companies in the supply chain, to improve performance and reduce costs. Both the Coca-Cola Company and Pepsi Bottling Group require their suppliers (such as plastic and aluminum companies and sugar refiners) to frequently deliver small quantities of materials directly to the production floor to reduce materials-handling costs. Similarly, to reduce inventory levels in the supply chain, Wal-Mart is asking its suppliers, such as Coca-Cola, to be responsible for and to manage inventory at both the Coca-Cola warehouse and Wal-Mart.

Key Success Factors

Customers want companies to use the value chain and supply chain to deliver ever improving levels of performance regarding several (or even all) of the following:

■ **Cost and efficiency**—Companies face continuous pressure to reduce the cost of the products they sell. To calculate and manage the cost of products, managers must first understand the tasks or activities (such as setting up machines or distributing

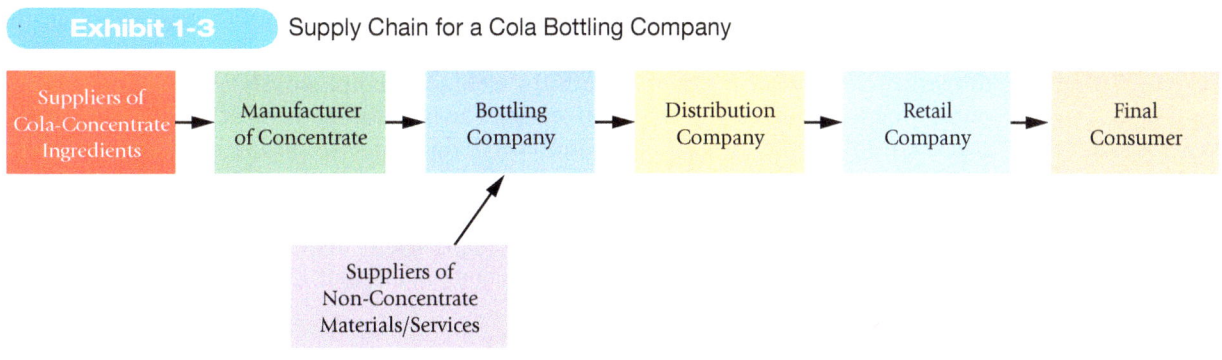

Exhibit 1-3 Supply Chain for a Cola Bottling Company

products) that cause costs to arise. They must also monitor the marketplace to determine prices that customers are willing to pay for products or services. Management accounting information helps managers calculate a target cost for a product by subtracting the operating income per unit of product that the company desires to earn from the "target price." To achieve the target cost, managers eliminate some activities (such as rework) and reduce the costs of performing activities in all value-chain functions—from initial R&D to customer service.

Increased global competition places ever-increasing pressure on companies to lower costs. Many U.S. companies have cut costs by outsourcing some of their business functions. Nike, for example, has moved its manufacturing operations to China and Mexico. Microsoft and IBM are increasingly doing their software development in Spain, eastern Europe, and India.

■ **Quality**—Customers expect high levels of quality. Total quality management (TQM) aims to improve operations throughout the value chain and to deliver products and services that exceed customer expectations. Using TQM, companies design products or services to meet the needs and wants of customers and make these products with zero (or very few) defects and waste, and minimal inventories. Managers use management accounting information to evaluate the costs and revenue benefits of TQM initiatives.

■ **Time**—Time has many dimensions. New-product development time is the time it takes for new products to be created and brought to market. The increasing pace of technological innovation has led to shorter product life cycles and more rapid introduction of new products. To make product and design decisions, managers need to understand the costs and benefits of a product over its life cycle.

Customer-response time describes the speed at which an organization responds to customer requests. To increase customer satisfaction, organizations need to reduce delivery time and reliably meet promised delivery dates. The primary cause of delays is bottlenecks that occur when the work to be performed on a machine, for example, exceeds available capacity. To deliver the product on time, managers need to increase the capacity of the machine to produce more output. Management accounting information helps managers quantify the costs and benefits of relieving bottleneck constraints.

■ **Innovation**—A constant flow of innovative products or services is the basis for ongoing company success. Managers rely on management accounting information to evaluate alternative investment and R&D decisions.

Companies are increasingly applying the key success factors of cost and efficiency, quality, time, and innovation to promote sustainability—the development and implementation of strategies to achieve long-term financial, social, and environmental performance. For example, the Japanese copier company Ricoh's sustainability efforts aggressively focus on energy conservation, resource conservation, product recycling, and pollution prevention. By designing products that can be easily recycled, Ricoh simultaneously improves efficiency, cost, and quality. Interest in sustainability appears to be intensifying. Already, government regulations, in countries such as China and India, are impelling companies to develop and report on their sustainability initiatives.

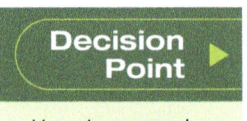

Decision Point

How do companies add value, and what are the dimensions of performance that customers are expecting of companies?

Management accountants help managers track performance of competitors on the key success factors. Competitive information serves as a *benchmark* and alerts managers to market changes. Companies are always seeking to *continuously improve* their operations. These improvements include on-time arrival for Southwest Airlines, customer access to online auctions at eBay, and cost reduction on housing products at Lowes. Sometimes, more-fundamental changes in operations, such as redesigning a manufacturing process to reduce costs, may be necessary. However, successful strategy implementation requires more than value-chain and supply-chain analysis and execution of key success factors. It is the decisions that managers make that help them to develop, integrate, and implement their strategies.

Decision Making, Planning, and Control: The Five-Step Decision-Making Process

We illustrate a five-step decision-making process using the example of the *Daily News*, a newspaper in Boulder, Colorado. Subsequent chapters of the book describe how managers use this five-step decision-making process to make many different types of decisions.

The *Daily News* differentiates itself from its competitors based on in-depth analyses of news by its highly rated journalists, use of color to enhance attractiveness to readers and advertisers, and a Web site that delivers up-to-the-minute news, interviews, and analyses. It has substantial capabilities to deliver on this strategy, such as an automated, computer-integrated, state-of-the-art printing facility; a Web-based information technology infrastructure; and a distribution network that is one of the best in the newspaper industry.

To keep up with steadily increasing production costs, Naomi Crawford, the manager of the *Daily News*, needs to increase revenues. To decide what she should do, Naomi works through the five-step decision-making process.

1. **Identify the problem and uncertainties.** Naomi has two main choices:
   a. Increase the selling price of the newspaper, or
   b. increase the rate per page charged to advertisers.

   The key uncertainty is the effect on demand of any increase in prices or rates. A decrease in demand could offset any increase in prices or rates and lead to lower overall revenues.

2. **Obtain information.** Gathering information before making a decision helps managers gain a better understanding of the uncertainties. Naomi asks her marketing manager to talk to some representative readers to gauge their reaction to an increase in the newspaper's selling price. She asks her advertising sales manager to talk to current and potential advertisers to assess demand for advertising. She also reviews the effect that past price increases had on readership. Ramon Sandoval, the management accountant at the *Daily News*, presents information about the impact of past increases or decreases in advertising rates on advertising revenues. He also collects and analyzes information on advertising rates charged by competing newspapers and other media outlets.

3. **Make predictions about the future.** On the basis of this information, Naomi makes predictions about the future. She concludes that increasing prices would upset readers and decrease readership. She has a different view about advertising rates. She expects a market-wide increase in advertising rates and believes that increasing rates will have little effect on the number of advertising pages sold.

   Naomi recognizes that making predictions requires judgment. She looks for biases in her thinking. Has she correctly judged reader sentiment or is the negative publicity of a price increase overly influencing her decision making? How sure is she that competitors will increase advertising rates? Is her thinking in this respect biased by how competitors have responded in the past? Have circumstances changed? How confident is she that her sales representatives can convince advertisers to pay higher rates? Naomi retests her assumptions and reviews her thinking. She feels comfortable with her predictions and judgments.

4. **Make decisions by choosing among alternatives.** When making decisions, strategy is a vital guidepost; many individuals in different parts of the organization at different times make decisions. Consistency with strategy binds individuals and timelines together and provides a common purpose for disparate decisions. Aligning decisions with strategy enables an organization to implement its strategy and achieve its goals. Without this alignment, decisions will be uncoordinated, pull the organization in different directions, and produce inconsistent results.

   Consistent with the product differentiation strategy, Naomi decides to increase advertising rates by 4% to $5,200 per page in March 2011. She is confident that the *Daily News*'s distinctive style and Web presence will increase readership, creating value for advertisers. She communicates the new advertising rate schedule to the sales department. Ramon estimates advertising revenues of $4,160,000 ($5,200 per page × 800 pages predicted to be sold in March 2011).

Learning Objective 4

Explain the five-step decision-making process

. . . identify the problem and uncertainties, obtain information, make predictions about the future, make decisions by choosing among alternatives, implement the decision, evaluate performance, and learn

and its role in management accounting

. . . planning and control of operations and activities

Steps 1 through 4 are collectively referred to as *planning*. **Planning** comprises selecting organization goals and strategies, predicting results under various alternative ways of achieving those goals, deciding how to attain the desired goals, and communicating the goals and how to achieve them to the entire organization. Management accountants serve as business partners in these planning activities because of their understanding of what creates value and the key success factors.

The most important planning tool when implementing strategy is a budget. A **budget** is the quantitative expression of a proposed plan of action by management and is an aid to coordinating what needs to be done to execute that plan. For March 2011, budgeted advertising revenue equals $4,160,000. The full budget for March 2011 includes budgeted circulation revenue and the production, distribution, and customer-service costs to achieve sales goals; the anticipated cash flows; and the potential financing needs. Because the process of preparing a budget crosses business functions, it forces coordination and communication throughout the company, as well as with the company's suppliers and customers.

5. **Implement the decision, evaluate performance, and learn.** Managers at the *Daily News* take actions to implement the March 2011 budget. Management accountants collect information to follow through on how actual performance compares to planned or budgeted performance (also referred to as scorekeeping). Information on actual results is different from the *pre-decision* planning information Naomi collected in Step 2, which enabled her to better understand uncertainties, to make predictions, and to make a decision. The comparison of actual performance to budgeted performance is the *control* or *post-decision* role of information. **Control** comprises taking actions that implement the planning decisions, deciding how to evaluate performance, and providing feedback and learning to help future decision making.

Measuring actual performance informs managers how well they and their subunits are doing. Linking rewards to performance helps motivate managers. These rewards are both intrinsic (recognition for a job well-done) and extrinsic (salary, bonuses, and promotions linked to performance). A budget serves as much as a control tool as a planning tool. Why? Because a budget is a benchmark against which actual performance can be compared.

Consider performance evaluation at the *Daily News*. During March 2011, the newspaper sold advertising, issued invoices, and received payments. These invoices and receipts were recorded in the accounting system. Exhibit 1-4 shows the *Daily News*'s performance report of advertising revenues for March 2011. This report indicates that 760 pages of advertising (40 pages fewer than the budgeted 800 pages) were sold. The average rate per page was $5,080, compared with the budgeted $5,200 rate, yielding actual advertising revenues of $3,860,800. The actual advertising revenues were $299,200 less than the budgeted $4,160,000. Observe how managers use both financial and nonfinancial information, such as pages of advertising, to evaluate performance.

The performance report in Exhibit 1-4 spurs investigation and learning. **Learning** is examining past performance (the control function) and systematically exploring alternative ways to make better-informed decisions and plans in the future. Learning can lead to changes in goals, changes in strategies, changes in the ways decision alternatives are identified,

	Actual Result (1)	Budgeted Amount (2)	Difference: (Actual Result – Budgeted Amount) (3) = (1) – (2)	Difference as a Percentage of Budgeted Amount (4) = (3) ÷ (2)
Advertising pages sold	760 pages	800 pages	40 pages Unfavorable	5.0% Unfavorable
Average rate per page	$5,080	$5,200	$120 Unfavorable	2.3% Unfavorable
Advertising revenues	$3,860,800	$4,160,000	$299,200 Unfavorable	7.2% Unfavorable

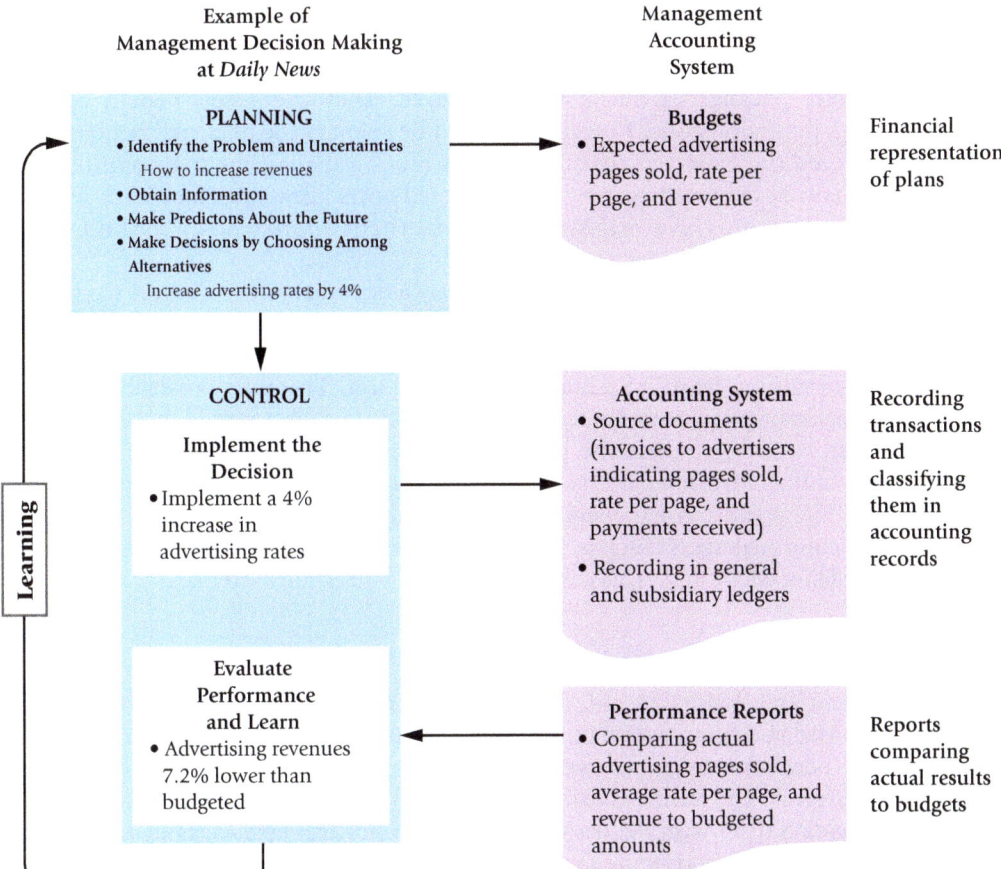

Exhibit 1-5

How Accounting Aids
Decision Making,
Planning, and Control
at the *Daily News*

changes in the range of information collected when making predictions, and sometimes changes in managers.

The performance report in Exhibit 1-4 would prompt the management accountant to raise several questions directing the attention of managers to problems and opportunities. Is the strategy of differentiating the *Daily News* from other newspapers attracting more readers? In implementing the new advertising rates, did the marketing and sales department make sufficient efforts to convince advertisers that, even with the higher rate of $5,200 per page, advertising in the *Daily News* was a good buy? Why was the actual average rate per page $5,080 instead of the budgeted rate of $5,200? Did some sales representatives offer discounted rates? Did economic conditions cause the decline in advertising revenues? Are revenues falling because editorial and production standards have declined? Answers to these questions could prompt the newspaper's publisher to take subsequent actions, including, for example, adding more sales personnel or making changes in editorial policy. Good implementation requires the marketing, editorial, and production departments to work together and coordinate their actions.

The management accountant could go further by identifying the specific advertisers that cut back or stopped advertising after the rate increase went into effect. Managers could then decide when and how sales representatives should follow-up with these advertisers.

The left side of Exhibit 1-5 provides an overview of the decision-making processes at the *Daily News*. The right side of the exhibit highlights how the management accounting system aids in decision making.

Key Management Accounting Guidelines

Three guidelines help management accountants provide the most value to their companies in strategic and operational decision making: Employ a cost-benefit approach, give full recognition to behavioral and technical considerations, and use different costs for different purposes.

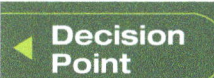
Decision Point

How do managers make decisions to implement strategy?

Learning Objective 5

Describe three guidelines management accountants follow in supporting managers

. . . employing a cost-benefit approach, recognizing behavioral as well as technical considerations, and calculating different costs for different purposes

Cost-Benefit Approach

Managers continually face resource-allocation decisions, such as whether to purchase a new software package or hire a new employee. They use a **cost-benefit approach** when making these decisions: Resources should be spent if the expected benefits to the company exceed the expected costs. Managers rely on management accounting information to quantify expected benefits and expected costs although all benefits and costs are not easy to quantify. Nevertheless, the cost-benefit approach is a useful guide for making resource-allocation decisions.

Consider the installation of a company's first budgeting system. Previously, the company used historical recordkeeping and little formal planning. A major benefit of installing a budgeting system is that it compels managers to plan ahead, compare actual to budgeted information, learn, and take corrective action. These actions lead to different decisions that improve performance relative to decisions that would have been made using the historical system, but the benefits are not easy to measure. On the cost side, some costs, such as investments in software and training are easier to quantify. Others, such as the time spent by managers on the budgeting process, are harder to quantify. Regardless, senior managers compare expected benefits and expected costs, exercise judgment, and reach a decision, in this case to install the budgeting system.

Behavioral and Technical Considerations

The cost-benefit approach is the criterion that assists managers in deciding whether, say, to install a proposed budgeting system instead of continuing to use an existing historical system. In making this decision senior managers consider two simultaneous missions: one technical and one behavioral. The technical considerations help managers make wise economic decisions by providing them with the desired information (for example, costs in various value-chain categories) in an appropriate format (such as actual results versus budgeted amounts) and at the preferred frequency. Now consider the human (the behavioral) side of why budgeting is used. Budgets induce a different set of decisions within an organization because of better collaboration, planning, and motivation. The behavioral considerations encourage managers and other employees to strive for achieving the goals of the organization.

Both managers and management accountants should always remember that management is not confined exclusively to technical matters. Management is primarily a human activity that should focus on how to help individuals do their jobs better—for example, by helping them to understand which of their activities adds value and which does not. Moreover, when workers underperform, behavioral considerations suggest that management systems and processes should cause managers to personally discuss with workers ways to improve performance rather than just sending them a report highlighting their underperformance.

Different Costs for Different Purposes

This book emphasizes that managers use alternative ways to compute costs in different decision-making situations, because there are different costs for different purposes. A cost concept used for the external-reporting purpose of accounting may not be an appropriate concept for internal, routine reporting to managers.

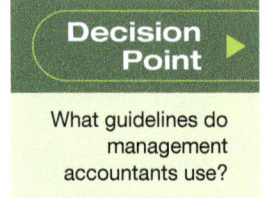

Decision Point ▶

What guidelines do management accountants use?

Consider the advertising costs associated with Microsoft Corporation's launch of a major product with a useful life of several years. For external reporting to shareholders, television advertising costs for this product are fully expensed in the income statement in the year they are incurred. GAAP requires this immediate expensing for external reporting. For internal purposes of evaluating management performance, however, the television advertising costs could be capitalized and then amortized or written off as expenses over several years. Microsoft could capitalize these advertising costs if it believes doing so results in a more accurate and fairer measure of the performance of the managers that launched the new product.

We now discuss the relationships and reporting responsibilities among managers and management accountants within a company's organization structure.

Organization Structure and the Management Accountant

We focus first on broad management functions and then look at how the management accounting and finance functions support managers.

Learning Objective 6

Understand how management accounting fits into an organization's structure

. . . for example, the responsibilities of the controller

Line and Staff Relationships

Organizations distinguish between line management and staff management. **Line management**, such as production, marketing, and distribution management, is directly responsible for attaining the goals of the organization. For example, managers of manufacturing divisions may target particular levels of budgeted operating income, certain levels of product quality and safety, and compliance with environmental laws. Similarly, the pediatrics department in a hospital is responsible for quality of service, costs, and patient billings. **Staff management**, such as management accountants and information technology and human-resources management, provides advice, support, and assistance to line management. A plant manager (a line function) may be responsible for investing in new equipment. A management accountant (a staff function) works as a business partner of the plant manager by preparing detailed operating-cost comparisons of alternative pieces of equipment.

Increasingly, organizations such as Honda and Dell are using teams to achieve their objectives. These teams include both line and staff management so that all inputs into a decision are available simultaneously.

The Chief Financial Officer and the Controller

The **chief financial officer (CFO)**—also called the **finance director** in many countries—is the executive responsible for overseeing the financial operations of an organization. The responsibilities of the CFO vary among organizations, but they usually include the following areas:

- **Controllership**—includes providing financial information for reports to managers and shareholders, and overseeing the overall operations of the accounting system
- **Treasury**—includes banking and short- and long-term financing, investments, and cash management
- **Risk management**—includes managing the financial risk of interest-rate and exchange-rate changes and derivatives management
- **Taxation**—includes income taxes, sales taxes, and international tax planning
- **Investor relations**—includes communicating with, responding to, and interacting with shareholders
- **Internal audit**—includes reviewing and analyzing financial and other records to attest to the integrity of the organization's financial reports and to adherence to its policies and procedures

The **controller** (also called the *chief accounting officer*) is the financial executive primarily responsible for management accounting and financial accounting. This book focuses on the controller as the chief management accounting executive. Modern controllers do not do any controlling in terms of line authority except over their own departments. Yet the modern concept of controllership maintains that the controller exercises control in a special sense. By reporting and interpreting relevant data, the controller influences the behavior of all employees and exerts a force that impels line managers toward making better-informed decisions as they implement their strategies.

Exhibit 1-6 is an organization chart of the CFO and the corporate controller at Nike, the leading footwear and apparel company. The CFO is a staff manager who reports to and supports the chief executive officer (CEO). As in most organizations, the corporate controller at Nike reports to the CFO. Nike also has regional controllers who support regional managers in the major geographic regions in which the company operates, such

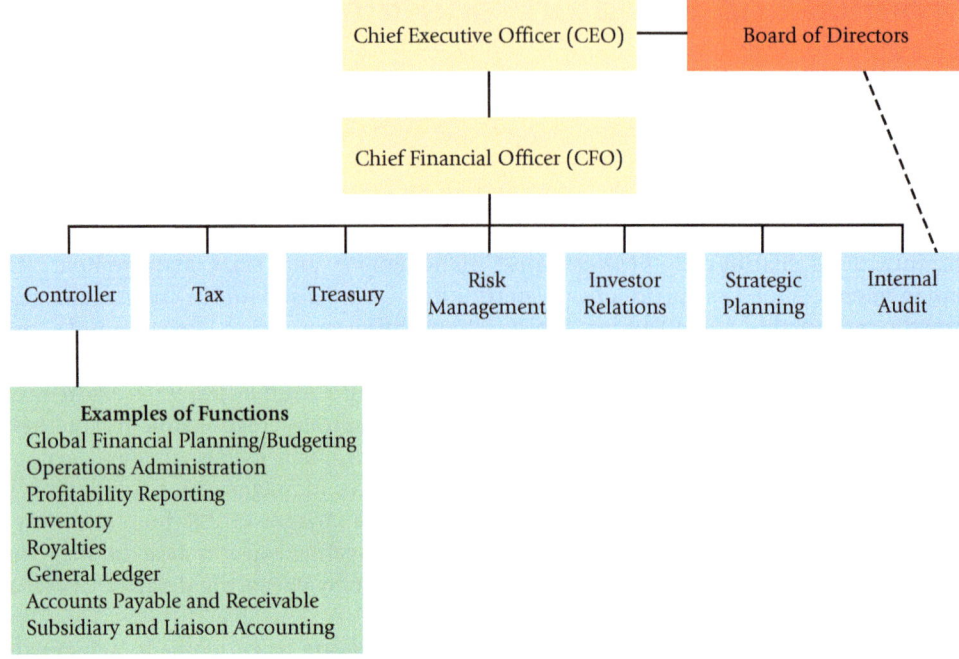

Exhibit 1-6

Nike: Reporting
Relationship for the
CFO and the Corporate
Controller

as the United States, Asia Pacific, Latin America, and Europe. Individual countries sometimes have a country controller. Organization charts such as the one in Exhibit 1-6 show formal reporting relationships. In most organizations, there also are informal relationships that must be understood when managers attempt to implement their decisions. Examples of informal relationships are friendships among managers (friendships of a professional or personal kind) and the personal preferences of top management about the managers they rely on in decision making.

Ponder what managers do to design and implement strategies and the organization structures within which they operate. Then think about the management accountants' and controllers' roles. It should be clear that the successful management accountant must have technical and analytical competence *as well as* behavioral and interpersonal skills. The Concepts in Action box on page 15 describes some desirable values and behaviors and why they are so critical to the partnership between management accountants and managers. We will refer to these values and behaviors as we discuss different topics in subsequent chapters of this book.

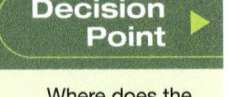

Decision Point

Where does the management accounting function fit into an organization's structure?

Professional Ethics

At no time has the focus on ethical conduct been sharper than it is today. Corporate scandals at Enron, WorldCom, and Arthur Andersen have seriously eroded the public's confidence in corporations. All employees in a company, whether in line management or staff management, must comply with the organization's—and more broadly, society's—expectations of ethical standards.

Learning Objective 7

Understand what professional ethics mean to management accountants

. . . for example, management accountants must maintain integrity and credibility in every aspect of their job

Institutional Support

Accountants have special obligations regarding ethics, given that they are responsible for the integrity of the financial information provided to internal and external parties. The Sarbanes–Oxley legislation in the United States, passed in 2002 in response to a series of corporate scandals, focuses on improving internal control, corporate governance, monitoring of managers, and disclosure practices of public corporations. These regulations call for tough ethical standards on managers and accountants and provide a process for employees to report violations of illegal and unethical acts.

Concepts in Action
Management Accounting Beyond the Numbers

When you hear the job title "accountant," what comes to mind? The CPA who does your tax return each year? Individuals who prepare budgets at Dell or Sony? To people outside the profession, it may seem like accountants are just "numbers people." It is true that most accountants are adept financial managers, yet their skills do not stop there. To be successful, management accountants must possess certain values and behaviors that reach well beyond basic analytical abilities.

Working in cross-functional teams and as a business partner of managers. It is not enough that management accountants simply be technically competent in their area of study. They also need to be able to work in teams, to learn about business issues, to understand the motivations of different individuals, to respect the views of their colleagues, and to show empathy and trust.

Promoting fact-based analysis and making tough-minded, critical judgments without being adversarial. Management accountants must raise tough questions for managers to consider, especially when preparing budgets. They must do so thoughtfully and with the intent of improving plans and decisions. In the case of Washington Mutual's bank failure, management accountants should have raised questions about whether the company's risky mortgage lending would be profitable if housing prices declined.

Leading and motivating people to change and be innovative. Implementing new ideas, however good they may be, is seldom easy. When the United States Department of Defense sought to consolidate more than 320 finance and accounting systems into a centralized platform, the accounting services director and his team of management accountants made sure that the vision for change was well understood throughout the agency. Ultimately, each individual's performance was aligned with the transformative change and incentive pay was introduced to promote adoption and drive innovation within this new framework.

Communicating clearly, openly, and candidly. Communicating information is a large part of a management accountant's job. A few years ago, Pitney Bowes Inc. (PBI), a $4 billion global provider of integrated mail and document management solutions, implemented a reporting initiative to give managers feedback in key areas. The initiative succeeded because it was clearly designed and openly communicated by PBI's team of management accountants.

Having a strong sense of integrity. Management accountants must never succumb to pressure from managers to manipulate financial information. They must always remember that their primary commitment is to the organization and its shareholders. At WorldCom, under pressure from senior managers, members of the accounting staff concealed billions of dollars in expenses. Because the accounting staff lacked the integrity and courage to stand up to and report corrupt senior managers, WorldCom landed in bankruptcy. Some members of the accounting staff and the senior executive team served prison terms for their actions.

Sources: Dash, Eric and Andrew Ross Sorkin. 2008. Government seizes WaMu and sells some assets. *New York Times,* September 25. http://www.nytimes.com/2008/09/26/business/26wamu.html; Garling, Wendy. 2007. Winning the Transformation Battle at the Defense Finance and Accounting Service. *Balanced Scorecard Report,* May–June. http://cb.hbsp.harvard.edu/cb/web/product_detail.seam?R=B0705C-PDF-ENG; Gollakota, Kamala and Vipin Gupta. 2009. *WorldCom Inc.: What went wrong.* Richard Ivey School of Business Case No. 905M43. London, ON: The University of Western Ontario. http://cb.hbsp.harvard.edu/cb/web/product_detail.seam?R=905M43-PDF-ENG; Green, Mark, Jeannine Garrity, Andrea Gumbus, and Bridget Lyons. 2002. Pitney Bowes Calls for New Metrics. *Strategic Finance,* May. http://www.allbusiness.com/accounting-reporting/reports-statements-profit/189988-1.html

Professional accounting organizations, which represent management accountants in many countries, promote high ethical standards.[3] Each of these organizations provides certification programs indicating that the holder has demonstrated the competency of technical knowledge required by that organization in management accounting and financial management, respectively.

In the United States, the Institute of Management Accountants (IMA) has also issued ethical guidelines. Exhibit 1-7 presents the IMA's guidance on issues relating to competence,

---

[3] See Appendix C: Cost Accounting in Professional Examinations in MyAccountingLab and at www.pearsonhighered.com/horngren for a list of professional management accounting organizations in the United States, Canada, Australia, Japan, and the United Kingdom.

Exhibit 1-7

Ethical Behavior for
Practitioners of
Management
Accounting and
Financial Management

Practitioners of management accounting and financial management have an obligation to the public, their profession, the organizations they serve, and themselves to maintain the highest standards of ethical conduct. In recognition of this obligation, the Institute of Management Accountants has promulgated the following standards of ethical professional practice. Adherence to these standards, both domestically and internationally, is integral to achieving the Objectives of Management Accounting. Practitioners of management accounting and financial management shall not commit acts contrary to these standards nor shall they condone the commission of such acts by others within their organizations.

IMA STATEMENT OF ETHICAL PROFESSIONAL PRACTICE

Practitioners of management accounting and financial management shall behave ethically. A commitment to ethical professional practice includes overarching principles that express our values and standards that guide our conduct.

PRINCIPLES

IMA's overarching ethical principles include: Honesty, Fairness, Objectivity, and Responsibility. Practitioners shall act in accordance with these principles and shall encourage others within their organizations to adhere to them.

STANDARDS

A practitioner's failure to comply with the following standards may result in disciplinary action.

COMPETENCE

Each practitioner has a responsibility to:
1. Maintain an appropriate level of professional expertise by continually developing knowledge and skills.
2. Perform professional duties in accordance with relevant laws, regulations, and technical standards.
3. Provide decision support information and recommendations that are accurate, clear, concise, and timely.
4. Recognize and communicate professional limitations or other constraints that would preclude responsible judgment or successful performance of an activity.

CONFIDENTIALITY

Each practitioner has a responsibility to:
1. Keep information confidential except when disclosure is authorized or legally required.
2. Inform all relevant parties regarding appropriate use of confidential information. Monitor subordinates' activities to ensure compliance.
3. Refrain from using confidential information for unethical or illegal advantage.

INTEGRITY

Each practitioner has a responsibility to:
1. Mitigate actual conflicts of interest. Regularly communicate with business associates to avoid apparent conflicts of interest. Advise all parties of any potential conflicts.
2. Refrain from engaging in any conduct that would prejudice carrying out duties ethically.
3. Abstain from engaging in or supporting any activity that might discredit the profession.

CREDIBILITY

Each practitioner has a responsibility to:
1. Communicate information fairly and objectively.
2. Disclose all relevant information that could reasonably be expected to influence an intended user's understanding of the reports, analyses, or recommendations.
3. Disclose delays or deficiencies in information, timeliness, processing, or internal controls in conformance with organization policy and/or applicable law.

Source: Statement on Management Accounting Number 1-C. 2005. *IMA Statement of Ethical Professional Practice.* Montvale, NJ: Institute of Management Accountants. Reprinted with permission from the Institute of Management Accountants, Montvale, NJ, www.imanet.org.

confidentiality, integrity, and credibility. To provide support to its members to act ethically at all times, the IMA runs an ethics hotline service. Members can call professional counselors at the IMA's Ethics Counseling Service to discuss their ethical dilemmas. The counselors help identify the key ethical issues and possible alternative ways of resolving them, and confidentiality is guaranteed. The IMA is just one of many institutions that help navigate management accountants through what could be turbulent ethical waters.

Typical Ethical Challenges

Ethical issues can confront management accountants in many ways. Here are two examples:

- **Case A:** A division manager has concerns about the commercial potential of a software product for which development costs are currently being capitalized as an asset rather than being shown as an expense for internal reporting purposes. The manager's bonus is based, in part, on division profits. The manager argues that showing development costs as an asset is justified because the new product will generate profits but presents little evidence to support his argument. The last two products from this division have been unsuccessful. The management accountant disagrees but wants to avoid a difficult personal confrontation with the boss, the division manager.

- **Case B:** A packaging supplier, bidding for a new contract, offers the management accountant of the purchasing company an all-expenses-paid weekend to the Super Bowl. The supplier does not mention the new contract when extending the invitation. The accountant is not a personal friend of the supplier. The accountant knows cost issues are critical in approving the new contract and is concerned that the supplier will ask for details about bids by competing packaging companies.

In each case the management accountant is faced with an ethical dilemma. Case A involves competence, credibility, and integrity. The management accountant should request that the division manager provide credible evidence that the new product is commercially viable. If the manager does not provide such evidence, expensing development costs in the current period is appropriate. Case B involves confidentiality and integrity.

Ethical issues are not always clear-cut. The supplier in Case B may have no intention of raising issues associated with the bid. However, the appearance of a conflict of interest in Case B is sufficient for many companies to prohibit employees from accepting "favors" from suppliers. Exhibit 1-8 presents the IMA's guidance on "Resolution of Ethical Conflict." The accountant in Case B should discuss the invitation with his or her immediate supervisor. If the visit is approved, the accountant should inform the supplier that the

---

Exhibit 1-8

Resolution of Ethical Conflict

In applying the Standards of Ethical Professional Practice, you may encounter problems identifying unethical behavior or resolving an ethical conflict. When faced with ethical issues, you should follow your organization's established policies on the resolution of such conflict. If these policies do not resolve the ethical conflict, you should consider the following courses of action:

1. Discuss the issue with your immediate supervisor except when it appears that the supervisor is involved. In that case, present the issue to the next level. If you cannot achieve a satisfactory resolution, submit the issue to the next management level. If your immediate superior is the chief executive officer or equivalent, the acceptable reviewing authority may be a group such as the audit committee, executive committee, board of directors, board of trustees, or owners. Contact with levels above the immediate superior should be initiated only with your superior's knowledge, assuming he or she is not involved. Communication of such problems to authorities or individuals not employed or engaged by the organization is not considered appropriate, unless you believe there is a clear violation of the law.
2. Clarify relevant ethical issues by initiating a confidential discussion with an IMA Ethics Counselor or other impartial advisor to obtain a better understanding of possible courses of action.
3. Consult your own attorney as to legal obligations and rights concerning the ethical conflict.

Source: Statement on Management Accounting Number 1-C. 2005. *IMA Statement of Ethical Professional Practice.* Montvale, NJ: Institute of Management Accountants. Reprinted with permission from the Institute of Management Accountants, Montvale, NJ, www.imanet.org.

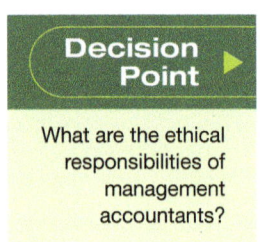

**Decision
Point** ▶

What are the ethical
responsibilities of
management
accountants?

invitation has been officially approved subject to following corporate policy (which includes maintaining information confidentiality).

Most professional accounting organizations around the globe issue statements about professional ethics. These statements include many of the same issues discussed by the IMA in Exhibits 1-7 and 1-8. For example, the Chartered Institute of Management Accountants (CIMA) in the United Kingdom identifies the same four fundamental principles as in Exhibit 1-7: competency, confidentiality, integrity, and credibility.

Problem for Self-Study

Campbell Soup Company incurs the following costs:

a. Purchase of tomatoes by a canning plant for Campbell's tomato soup products
b. Materials purchased for redesigning Pepperidge Farm biscuit containers to make biscuits stay fresh longer
c. Payment to Backer, Spielvogel, & Bates, the advertising agency, for advertising work on Healthy Request line of soup products
d. Salaries of food technologists researching feasibility of a Prego pizza sauce that has minimal calories
e. Payment to Safeway for redeeming coupons on Campbell's food products
f. Cost of a toll-free telephone line used for customer inquiries about using Campbell's soup products
g. Cost of gloves used by line operators on the Swanson Fiesta breakfast-food production line
h. Cost of handheld computers used by Pepperidge Farm delivery staff serving major supermarket accounts

Required | Classify each cost item (**a–h**) as one of the business functions in the value chain in Exhibit 1-2 (p. 6).

Solution

a. Production
b. Design of products and processes
c. Marketing
d. Research and development
e. Marketing
f. Customer service
g. Production
h. Distribution

Decision Points

The following question-and-answer format summarizes the chapter's learning objectives. Each decision presents a key question related to a learning objective. The guidelines are the answer to that question.

Decision	Guidelines
1. How is management accounting different from financial accounting?	Financial accounting reports to external users on past financial performance using GAAP. Management accounting provides future-oriented information in formats that help managers (internal users) make decisions and achieve organizational goals.

2. How do management accountants support strategic decisions?

Management accountants contribute to strategic decisions by providing information about the sources of competitive advantage.

3. How do companies add value, and what are the dimensions of performance that customers are expecting of companies?

Companies add value through R&D; design of products and processes; production; marketing; distribution; and customer service. Customers want companies to deliver performance through cost and efficiency, quality, timeliness, and innovation.

4. How do managers make decisions to implement strategy?

Managers use a five-step decision-making process to implement strategy: (1) identify the problem and uncertainties; (2) obtain information; (3) make predictions about the future; (4) make decisions by choosing among alternatives; and (5) implement the decision, evaluate performance, and learn. The first four steps are the planning decisions, which include deciding on organization goals, predicting results under various alternative ways of achieving those goals, and deciding how to attain the desired goals. Step 5 is the control decision, which includes taking actions to implement the planning decisions and deciding on performance evaluation and feedback that will help future decision making.

5. What guidelines do management accountants use?

Three guidelines that help management accountants increase their value to managers are (a) employ a cost-benefit approach, (b) recognize behavioral as well as technical considerations, and (c) identify different costs for different purposes.

6. Where does the management accounting function fit into an organization's structure?

Management accounting is an integral part of the controller's function in an organization. In most organizations, the controller reports to the chief financial officer, who is a key member of the top management team.

7. What are the ethical responsibilities of management accountants?

Management accountants have ethical responsibilities that relate to competence, confidentiality, integrity, and credibility.

Terms to Learn

Each chapter will include this section. Like all technical terms, accounting terms have precise meanings. Learn the definitions of new terms when you initially encounter them. The meaning of each of the following terms is given in this chapter and in the Glossary at the end of this book.

budget (**p. 10**)
chief financial officer (CFO) (**p. 13**)
control (**p. 10**)
controller (**p. 13**)
cost accounting (**p. 4**)
cost-benefit approach (**p. 12**)
cost management (**p. 4**)
customer service (**p. 6**)

design of products and processes (**p. 6**)
distribution (**p. 6**)
finance director (**p. 13**)
financial accounting (**p. 3**)
learning (**p. 10**)
line management (**p. 13**)
management accounting (**p. 4**)
marketing (**p. 6**)

planning (**p. 10**)
production (**p. 6**)
research and development (R&D) (**p. 6**)
staff management (**p. 13**)
strategic cost management (**p. 5**)
strategy (**p. 5**)
supply chain (**p. 7**)
value chain (**p. 6**)

Assignment Material

Questions

1-1 How does management accounting differ from financial accounting?

1-2 "Management accounting should not fit the straitjacket of financial accounting." Explain and give an example.

1-3 How can a management accountant help formulate strategy?

1-4 Describe the business functions in the value chain.

1-5 Explain the term "supply chain" and its importance to cost management.

1-6 "Management accounting deals only with costs." Do you agree? Explain.

1-7 How can management accountants help improve quality and achieve timely product deliveries?

1-8 Describe the five-step decision-making process.

1-9 Distinguish planning decisions from control decisions.

1-10 What three guidelines help management accountants provide the most value to managers?

1-11 "Knowledge of technical issues such as computer technology is a necessary but not sufficient condition to becoming a successful management accountant." Do you agree? Why?

1-12 As a new controller, reply to this comment by a plant manager: "As I see it, our accountants may be needed to keep records for shareholders and Uncle Sam, but I don't want them sticking their noses in my day-to-day operations. I do the best I know how. No bean counter knows enough about my responsibilities to be of any use to me."

1-13 Where does the management accounting function fit into an organization's structure?

1-14 Name the four areas in which standards of ethical conduct exist for management accountants in the United States. What organization sets forth these standards?

1-15 What steps should a management accountant take if established written policies provide insufficient guidance on how to handle an ethical conflict?

Exercises

1-16 Value chain and classification of costs, computer company. Compaq Computer incurs the following costs:

a. Electricity costs for the plant assembling the Presario computer line of products

b. Transportation costs for shipping the Presario line of products to a retail chain

c. Payment to David Kelley Designs for design of the Armada Notebook

d. Salary of computer scientist working on the next generation of minicomputers

e. Cost of Compaq employees' visit to a major customer to demonstrate Compaq's ability to interconnect with other computers

f. Purchase of competitors' products for testing against potential Compaq products

g. Payment to television network for running Compaq advertisements

h. Cost of cables purchased from outside supplier to be used with Compaq printers

Required Classify each of the cost items (**a–h**) into one of the business functions of the value chain shown in Exhibit 1-2 (p. 6).

1-17 Value chain and classification of costs, pharmaceutical company. Merck, a pharmaceutical company, incurs the following costs:

a. Cost of redesigning blister packs to make drug containers more tamperproof

b. Cost of videos sent to doctors to promote sales of a new drug

c. Cost of a toll-free telephone line used for customer inquiries about drug usage, side effects of drugs, and so on

d. Equipment purchased to conduct experiments on drugs yet to be approved by the government

e. Payment to actors for a television infomercial promoting a new hair-growth product for balding men

f. Labor costs of workers in the packaging area of a production facility

g. Bonus paid to a salesperson for exceeding a monthly sales quota

h. Cost of Federal Express courier service to deliver drugs to hospitals

Required Classify each of the cost items (**a–h**) as one of the business functions of the value chain shown in Exhibit 1-2 (p. 6).

1-18 Value chain and classification of costs, fast food restaurant. Burger King, a hamburger fast food restaurant, incurs the following costs:

a. Cost of oil for the deep fryer

b. Wages of the counter help who give customers the food they order

c. Cost of the costume for the King on the Burger King television commercials

d. Cost of children's toys given away free with kids' meals

e. Cost of the posters indicating the special "two cheeseburgers for $2.50"

f. Costs of frozen onion rings and French fries

g. Salaries of the food specialists who create new sandwiches for the restaurant chain

h. Cost of "to-go" bags requested by customers who could not finish their meals in the restaurant

Classify each of the cost items (**a–h**) as one of the business functions of the value chain shown in Exhibit 1-2 (p. 6).

Required

1-19 Key success factors. Grey Brothers Consulting has issued a report recommending changes for its newest manufacturing client, Energy Motors. Energy Motors currently manufactures a single product, which is sold and distributed nationally. The report contains the following suggestions for enhancing business performance:

- **a.** Add a new product line to increase total revenue and to reduce the company's overall risk.
- **b.** Increase training hours of assembly line personnel to decrease the currently high volumes of scrap and waste.
- **c.** Reduce lead times (time from customer order of product to customer receipt of product) by 20% in order to increase customer retention.
- **d.** Reduce the time required to set up machines for each new order.
- **e.** Benchmark the company's gross margin percentages against its major competitors.

Link each of these changes to the key success factors that are important to managers.

Required

1-20 Planning and control decisions. Conner Company makes and sells brooms and mops. It takes the following actions, not necessarily in the order given. For each action (**a–e**) state whether it is a planning decision or a control decision.

- **a.** Conner asks its marketing team to consider ways to get back market share from its newest competitor, Swiffer.
- **b.** Conner calculates market share after introducing its newest product.
- **c.** Conner compares costs it actually incurred with costs it expected to incur for the production of the new product.
- **d.** Conner's design team proposes a new product to compete directly with the Swiffer.
- **e.** Conner estimates the costs it will incur to sell 30,000 units of the new product in the first quarter of next fiscal year.

1-21 Five-step decision-making process, manufacturing. Garnicki Foods makes frozen dinners that it sells through grocery stores. Typical products include turkey dinners, pot roast, fried chicken, and meat loaf. The managers at Garnicki have recently introduced a line of frozen chicken pies. They take the following actions with regard to this decision.

- **a.** Garnicki performs a taste test at the local shopping mall to see if consumers like the taste of its proposed new chicken pie product.
- **b.** Garnicki sales managers estimate they will sell more meat pies in their northern sales territory than in their southern sales territory.
- **c.** Garnicki managers discuss the possibility of introducing a new chicken pie.
- **d.** Garnicki managers compare actual costs of making chicken pies with their budgeted costs.
- **e.** Costs for making chicken pies are budgeted.
- **f.** Garnicki decides to introduce a new chicken pie.
- **g.** To help decide whether to introduce a new chicken pie, the purchasing manager calls a supplier to check the prices of chicken.

Classify each of the actions (**a–g**) as a step in the five-step decision-making process (identify the problem and uncertainties, obtain information, make predictions about the future, choose among alternatives, implement the decision, evaluate performance, and learn). The actions are not listed in the order they are performed.

Required

1-22 Five-step decision-making process, service firm. Brite Exteriors is a firm that provides house painting services. Robert Brite, the owner, is trying to find new ways to increase revenues. Mr. Brite performs the following actions, not in the order listed.

- **a.** Mr. Brite calls Home Depot to ask the price of paint sprayers.
- **b.** Mr. Brite discusses with his employees the possibility of using paint sprayers instead of hand painting to increase productivity and thus revenues.
- **c.** The workers who are not familiar with paint sprayers take more time to finish a job than they did when painting by hand.
- **d.** Mr. Brite compares the expected cost of buying sprayers to the expected cost of hiring more workers who paint by hand, and estimates profits from both alternatives.
- **e.** The project scheduling manager confirms that demand for house painting services has increased.
- **f.** Mr. Brite decides to buy the paint sprayers rather than hire additional painters.

Classify each of the actions (**a-f**) according to its step in the five-step decision-making process (identify the problem and uncertainties, obtain information, make predictions about the future, choose among alternatives, implement the decision, evaluate performance, and learn).

Required

1-23 **Professional ethics and reporting division performance.** Marcia Miller is division controller and Tom Maloney is division manager of the Ramses Shoe Company. Miller has line responsibility to Maloney, but she also has staff responsibility to the company controller.

Maloney is under severe pressure to achieve the budgeted division income for the year. He has asked Miller to book $200,000 of revenues on December 31. The customers' orders are firm, but the shoes are still in the production process. They will be shipped on or around January 4. Maloney says to Miller, "The key event is getting the sales order, not shipping the shoes. You should support me, not obstruct my reaching division goals."

Required

1. Describe Miller's ethical responsibilities.
2. What should Miller do if Maloney gives her a direct order to book the sales?

Problems

1-24 **Planning and control decisions, Internet company.** WebNews.com offers its subscribers several services, such as an annotated TV guide and local-area information on weather, restaurants, and movie theaters. Its main revenue sources are fees for banner advertisements and fees from subscribers. Recent data are as follows:

Month/Year	Advertising Revenues	Actual Number of Subscribers	Monthly Fee Per Subscriber
June 2009	$ 415,972	29,745	$15.50
December 2009	867,246	55,223	20.50
June 2010	892,134	59,641	20.50
December 2010	1,517,950	87,674	20.50
June 2011	2,976,538	147,921	20.50

The following decisions were made from June through October 2011:

a. June 2011: Raised subscription fee to $25.50 per month from July 2011 onward. The budgeted number of subscribers for this monthly fee is shown in the following table.

b. June 2011: Informed existing subscribers that from July onward, monthly fee would be $25.50.

c. July 2011: Offered e-mail service to subscribers and upgraded other online services.

d. October 2011: Dismissed the vice president of marketing after significant slowdown in subscribers and subscription revenues, based on July through September 2011 data in the following table.

e. October 2011: Reduced subscription fee to $22.50 per month from November 2011 onward.

Results for July–September 2011 are as follows:

Month/Year	Budgeted Number of Subscribers	Actual Number of Subscribers	Monthly Fee per Subscriber
July 2011	145,000	129,250	$25.50
August 2011	155,000	142,726	25.50
September 2011	165,000	145,643	25.50

Required

1. Classify each of the decisions (**a–e**) as a planning or a control decision.
2. Give two examples of other planning decisions and two examples of other control decisions that may be made at WebNews.com.

1-25 **Strategic decisions and management accounting.** A series of independent situations in which a firm is about to make a strategic decision follow.

Decisions:

a. Roger Phones is about to decide whether to launch production and sale of a cell phone with standard features.

b. Computer Magic is trying to decide whether to produce and sell a new home computer software package that includes the ability to interface with a sewing machine and a vacuum cleaner. There is no such software currently on the market.

c. Christina Cosmetics has been asked to provide a "store brand" lip gloss that will be sold at discount retail stores.

d. Marcus Meats is entertaining the idea of developing a special line of gourmet bologna made with sun dried tomatoes, pine nuts, and artichoke hearts.

1. For each decision, state whether the company is following a low price or a differentiated product strategy. Required
2. For each decision, discuss what information the management accountant can provide about the source of competitive advantage for these firms.

1-26 Management accounting guidelines. For each of the following items, identify which of the management accounting guidelines applies: cost-benefit approach, behavioral and technical considerations, or different costs for different purposes.

1. Analyzing whether to keep the billing function within an organization or outsource it
2. Deciding to give bonuses for superior performance to the employees in a Japanese subsidiary and extra vacation time to the employees in a Swedish subsidiary
3. Including costs of all the value-chain functions before deciding to launch a new product, but including only its manufacturing costs in determining its inventory valuation
4. Considering the desirability of hiring one more salesperson
5. Giving each salesperson the compensation option of choosing either a low salary and a high-percentage sales commission or a high salary and a low-percentage sales commission
6. Selecting the costlier computer system after considering two systems
7. Installing a participatory budgeting system in which managers set their own performance targets, instead of top management imposing performance targets on managers
8. Recording research costs as an expense for financial reporting purposes (as required by U.S. GAAP) but capitalizing and expensing them over a longer period for management performance-evaluation purposes
9. Introducing a profit-sharing plan for employees

1-27 Role of controller, role of chief financial officer. George Perez is the controller at Allied Electronics, a manufacturer of devices for the computer industry. He is being considered for a promotion to chief financial officer.

1. In this table, indicate which executive is *primarily* responsible for each activity. Required

Activity	Controller	CFO
Managing accounts payable		
Communicating with investors		
Strategic review of different lines of businesses		
Budgeting funds for a plant upgrade		
Managing the company's short-term investments		
Negotiating fees with auditors		
Assessing profitability of various products		
Evaluating the costs and benefits of a new product design		

2. Based on this table and your understanding of the two roles, what types of training or experiences will George find most useful for the CFO position?

1-28 Pharmaceutical company, budgeting, ethics. Eric Johnson was recently promoted to Controller of Research and Development (R&D) for PharmaCor, a *Fortune* 500 pharmaceutical company, which manufactures prescription drugs and nutritional supplements. The company's total R&D cost for 2012 was expected (budgeted) to be $5 billion. During the company's mid-year budget review, Eric realized that current R&D expenditures were already at $3.5 billion, nearly 40% above the mid-year target. At this current rate of expenditure, the R&D division was on track to exceed its total year-end budget by $2 billion!

In a meeting with CFO, James Clark, later that day, Johnson delivered the bad news. Clark was both shocked and outraged that the R&D spending had gotten out of control. Clark wasn't any more understanding when Johnson revealed that the excess cost was entirely related to research and development of a new drug, Lyricon, which was expected to go to market next year. The new drug would result in large profits for PharmaCor, if the product could be approved by year-end.

Clark had already announced his expectations of third quarter earnings to Wall Street analysts. If the R&D expenditures weren't reduced by the end of the third quarter, Clark was certain that the targets he had announced publicly would be missed and the company's stock price would tumble. Clark instructed Johnson to make up the budget short-fall by the end of the third quarter using "whatever means necessary."

Johnson was new to the Controller's position and wanted to make sure that Clark's orders were followed. Johnson came up with the following ideas for making the third quarter budgeted targets:

a. Stop all research and development efforts on the drug Lyricon until after year-end. This change would delay the drug going to market by at least six months. It is also possible that in the meantime a PharmaCor competitor could make it to market with a similar drug.

b. Sell off rights to the drug, Markapro. The company had not planned on doing this because, under current market conditions, it would get less than fair value. It would, however, result in a onetime gain that could offset the budget short-fall. Of course, all future profits from Markapro would be lost.

c. Capitalize some of the company's R&D expenditures reducing R&D expense on the income statement. This transaction would not be in accordance with GAAP, but Johnson thought it was justifiable, since the Lyricon drug was going to market early next year. Johnson would argue that capitalizing R & D costs this year and expensing them next year would better match revenues and expenses.

Required
1. Referring to the "Standards of Ethical Behavior for Practitioners of Management Accounting and Financial Management," Exhibit 1-7 on page 16, which of the preceding items (**a–c**) are acceptable to use? Which are unacceptable?
2. What would you recommend Johnson do?

1-29 Professional ethics and end-of-year actions. Janet Taylor is the new division controller of the snack-foods division of Gourmet Foods. Gourmet Foods has reported a minimum 15% growth in annual earnings for each of the past five years. The snack-foods division has reported annual earnings growth of more than 20% each year in this same period. During the current year, the economy went into a recession. The corporate controller estimates a 10% annual earnings growth rate for Gourmet Foods this year. One month before the December 31 fiscal year-end of the current year, Taylor estimates the snack-foods division will report an annual earnings growth of only 8%. Warren Ryan, the snack-foods division president, is not happy, but he notes that "the end-of-year actions" still need to be taken.

Taylor makes some inquiries and is able to compile the following list of end-of-year actions that were more or less accepted by the previous division controller:

a. Deferring December's routine monthly maintenance on packaging equipment by an independent contractor until January of next year

b. Extending the close of the current fiscal year beyond December 31 so that some sales of next year are included in the current year

c. Altering dates of shipping documents of next January's sales to record them as sales in December of the current year

d. Giving salespeople a double bonus to exceed December sales targets

e. Deferring the current period's advertising by reducing the number of television spots run in December and running more than planned in January of next year

f. Deferring the current period's reported advertising costs by having Gourmet Foods' outside advertising agency delay billing December advertisements until January of next year or by having the agency alter invoices to conceal the December date

g. Persuading carriers to accept merchandise for shipment in December of the current year although they normally would not have done so

Required
1. Why might the snack-foods division president want to take these end-of-year actions?
2. Taylor is deeply troubled and reads the "Standards of Ethical Behavior for Practitioners of Management Accounting and Financial Management" in Exhibit 1-7 (p. 16). Classify each of the end-of-year actions (**a–g**) as acceptable or unacceptable according to that document.
3. What should Taylor do if Ryan suggests that these end-of-year actions are taken in every division of Gourmet Foods and that she will greatly harm the snack-foods division if she does not cooperate and paint the rosiest picture possible of the division's results?

1-30 Professional ethics and end-of-year actions. Deacon Publishing House is a publishing company that produces consumer magazines. The house and home division, which sells home-improvement and home-decorating magazines, has seen a 20% reduction in operating income over the past nine months, primarily due to the recent economic recession and the depressed consumer housing market. The division's Controller, Todd Allen, has felt pressure from the CFO to improve his division's operating results by the end of the year. Allen is considering the following options for improving the division's performance by year-end:

a. Cancelling two of the division's least profitable magazines, resulting in the layoff of twenty-five employees.

b. Selling the new printing equipment that was purchased in January and replacing it with discarded equipment from one of the company's other divisions. The previously discarded equipment no longer meets current safety standards.

c. Recognizing unearned subscription revenue (cash received in advance for magazines that will be delivered in the future) as revenue when cash is received in the current month (just before fiscal year end) instead of showing it as a liability.

d. Reducing the division's Allowance for Bad Debt Expense. This transaction alone would increase operating income by 5%.

e. Recognizing advertising revenues that relate to January in December.

f. Switching from declining balance to straight line depreciation to reduce depreciation expense in the current year.

1. What are the motivations for Allen to improve the division's year-end operating earnings?

2. From the point of view of the "Standards of Ethical Behavior for Practitioners of Management Accounting and Financial Management," Exhibit 1-7 on page 16, which of the preceding items (a–f) are acceptable? Which are unacceptable?

3. What should Allen do about the pressure to improve performance?

Required

Collaborative Learning Problem

1-31 **Global company, ethical challenges.** Bredahl Logistics, a U.S. shipping company, has just begun distributing goods across the Atlantic to Norway. The company began operations in 2010, transporting goods to South America. The company's earnings are currently trailing behind its competitors and Bredahl's investors are becoming anxious. Some of the company's largest investors are even talking of selling their interest in the shipping newcomer. Bredahl's CEO, Marcus Hamsen, calls an emergency meeting with his executive team. Hamsen needs a plan before his upcoming conference call with uneasy investors. Brehdal's executive staff make the following suggestions for salvaging the company's short-term operating results:

a. Stop all transatlantic shipping efforts. The start-up costs for the new operations are hurting current profit margins.

b. Make deep cuts in pricing through the end of the year to generate additional revenue.

c. Pressure current customers to take early delivery of goods before the end of the year so that more revenue can be reported in this year's financial statements.

d. Sell-off distribution equipment prior to year-end. The sale would result in one-time gains that could offset the company's lagging profits. The owned equipment could be replaced with leased equipment at a lower cost in the current year.

e. Record executive year-end bonus compensation for the current year in the next year when it is paid after the December fiscal year-end.

f. Recognize sales revenues on orders received, but not shipped as of the end of the year.

g. Establish corporate headquarters in Ireland before the end of the year, lowering the company's corporate tax rate from 28% to 12.5%.

1. As the management accountant for Brehdahl, evaluate each of the preceding items (a–g) in the context of the "Standards of Ethical Behavior for Practitioners of Management Accounting and Financial Management," Exhibit 1-7 on page 16. Which of the items are in violation of these ethics standards and which are acceptable?

2. What should the management accountant do with respect to those items that are in violation of the ethical standards for management accountants?

Required

Cost-Volume-Profit Analysis

▶ Learning Objectives

1. Explain the features of cost-volume-profit (CVP) analysis

2. Determine the breakeven point and output level needed to achieve a target operating income

3. Understand how income taxes affect CVP analysis

4. Explain how managers use CVP analysis in decision making

5. Explain how sensitivity analysis helps managers cope with uncertainty

6. Use CVP analysis to plan variable and fixed costs

7. Apply CVP analysis to a company producing multiple products

All managers want to know how profits will change as the units sold of a product or service change.

Home Depot managers, for example, might wonder how many units of a new product must be sold to break even or make a certain amount of profit. Procter & Gamble managers might ask themselves how expanding their business into a particular foreign market would affect costs, selling price, and profits. These questions have a common "what-if" theme. Examining the results of these what-if possibilities and alternatives helps managers make better decisions.

Managers must also decide how to price their products and understand the effect of their pricing decisions on revenues and profits. The following article explains how the Irish rock band U2 recently decided whether it should decrease the prices on some of its tickets during its recent world tour. Does lowering ticket price sound like a wise strategy to you?

How the "The Biggest Rock Show Ever" Turned a Big Profit[1]

When U2 embarked on its recent world tour, *Rolling Stone* magazine called it "the biggest rock show ever." Visiting large stadiums across the United States and Europe, the Irish quartet performed on an imposing 164-foot high stage that resembled a spaceship, complete with a massive video screen and footbridges leading to ringed catwalks.

With an ambitious 48-date trek planned, U2 actually had three separate stages leapfrogging its global itinerary—each one costing nearly $40 million dollars. As a result, the tour's success was dependent not only on each night's concert, but also recouping its tremendous fixed costs—costs that do not change with the number of fans in the audience.

To cover its high fixed costs and make a profit, U2 needed to sell a lot of tickets. To maximize revenue, the tour employed a unique in-the-round stage configuration, which boosted stadium capacity by roughly 20%, and sold tickets for as little as $30, far less than most large outdoor concerts.

The band's plan worked—despite a broader music industry slump and global recession, U2 shattered attendance records in most of the venues it played. By the end of the tour, the band played to over

---

[1] *Source*: Gundersen, Edna. 2009. U2 turns 360 stadium into attendance-shattering sellouts. *USA Today*, October 4. *www.usatoday.com/life/music/news/2009-10-04-u2-stadium-tour_N.htm*

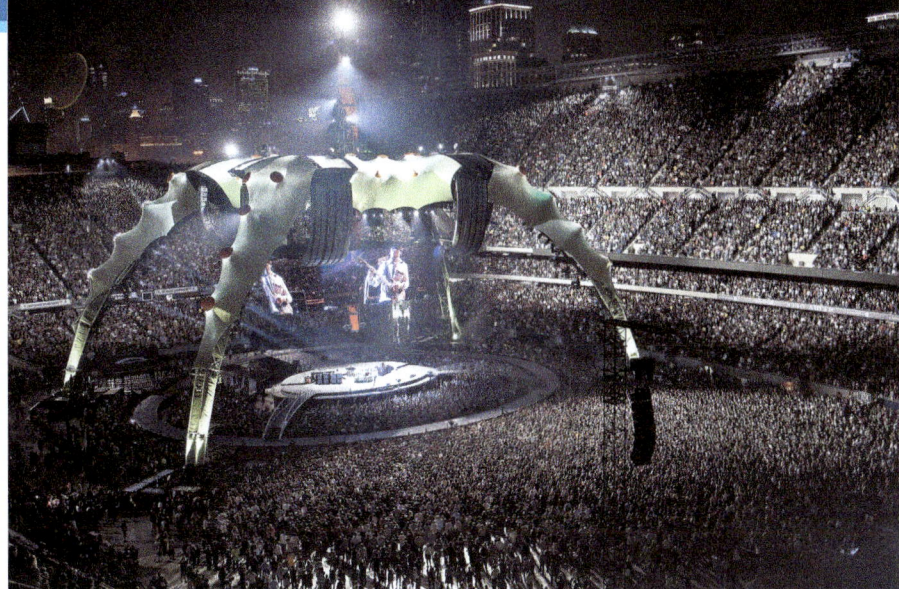

3 million fans, racking up almost $300 million in ticket and merchandise sales and turning a profit. As you read this chapter, you will begin to understand how and why U2 made the decision to lower prices.

Many capital intensive companies, such as US Airways and United Airlines in the airlines industry and Global Crossing and WorldCom in the telecommunications industry, have high fixed costs. They must generate sufficient revenues to cover these costs and turn a profit. When revenues declined at these companies during 2001 and 2002 and fixed costs remained high, these companies declared bankruptcy. The methods of CVP analysis described in this chapter help managers minimize such risks.

Essentials of CVP Analysis

In Chapter 2, we discussed total revenues, total costs, and income. **Cost-volume-profit (CVP) analysis** studies the behavior and relationship among these elements as changes occur in the units sold, the selling price, the variable cost per unit, or the fixed costs of a product. Let's consider an example to illustrate CVP analysis.

Learning Objective 1

Explain the features of cost-volume-profit (CVP) analysis

. . . how operating income changes with changes in output level, selling prices, variable costs, or fixed costs

> Example: Emma Frost is considering selling GMAT Success, a test prep book and software package for the business school admission test, at a college fair in Chicago. Emma knows she can purchase this package from a wholesaler at $120 per package, with the privilege of returning all unsold packages and receiving a full $120 refund per package. She also knows that she must pay $2,000 to the organizers for the booth rental at the fair. She will incur no other costs. She must decide whether she should rent a booth.

Emma, like most managers who face such a situation, works through a series of steps.

1. **Identify the problem and uncertainties.** The decision to rent the booth hinges critically on how Emma resolves two important uncertainties—the price she can charge and the number of packages she can sell at that price. Every decision deals with selecting a course of action. Emma must decide knowing that the outcome of the chosen action is uncertain and will only be known in the future. The more confident Emma is about selling a large number of packages at a good price, the more willing she will be to rent the booth.

2. **Obtain information.** When faced with uncertainty, managers obtain information that might help them understand the uncertainties better. For example, Emma gathers information about the type of individuals likely to attend the fair and other test-prep packages that might be sold at the fair. She also gathers data on her past experiences selling GMAT Success at fairs very much like the Chicago fair.

3. **Make predictions about the future.** Using all the information available to them, managers make predictions. Emma predicts that she can charge a price of $200 for GMAT Success. At that price she is reasonably confident that she will be able to sell at least 30 packages and possibly as many as 60. In making these predictions, Emma like most managers, must be realistic and exercise careful judgment. If her predictions are excessively optimistic, Emma will rent the booth when she should not. If they are unduly pessimistic, Emma will not rent the booth when she should.

   Emma's predictions rest on the belief that her experience at the Chicago fair will be similar to her experience at the Boston fair four months earlier. Yet, Emma is uncertain about several aspects of her prediction. Is the comparison between Boston and Chicago appropriate? Have conditions and circumstances changed over the last four months? Are there any biases creeping into her thinking? She is keen on selling at the Chicago fair because sales in the last couple of months have been lower than expected. Is this experience making her predictions overly optimistic? Has she ignored some of the competitive risks? Will the other test prep vendors at the fair reduce their prices?

   Emma reviews her thinking. She retests her assumptions. She also explores these questions with John Mills, a close friend, who has extensive experience selling test-prep packages like GMAT Success. In the end, she feels quite confident that her predictions are reasonable, accurate, and carefully thought through.

4. **Make decisions by choosing among alternatives.** Emma uses the CVP analysis that follows, and decides to rent the booth at the Chicago fair.

5. **Implement the decision, evaluate performance, and learn.** Thoughtful managers never stop learning. They compare their actual performance to predicted performance to understand why things worked out the way they did and what they might learn. At the end of the Chicago fair, for example, Emma would want to evaluate whether her predictions about price and the number of packages she could sell were correct. Such feedback would be very helpful to Emma as she makes decisions about renting booths at subsequent fairs.

How does Emma use CVP analysis in Step 4 to make her decision? Emma begins by identifying which costs are fixed and which costs are variable and then calculates *contribution margin*.

Contribution Margins

The booth-rental cost of $2,000 is a fixed cost because it will not change no matter how many packages Emma sells. The cost of the package itself is a variable cost because it increases in proportion to the number of packages sold. Emma will incur a cost of $120 for each package that she sells. To get an idea of how operating income will change as a result of selling different quantities of packages, Emma calculates operating income if sales are 5 packages and if sales are 40 packages.

	5 packages sold	**40 packages sold**
Revenues	$ 1,000 ($200 per package × 5 packages)	$8,000 ($200 per package × 40 packages)
Variable purchase costs	600 ($120 per package × 5 packages)	4,800 ($120 per package × 40 packages)
Fixed costs	2,000	2,000
Operating income	$(1,600)	$1,200

The only numbers that change from selling different quantities of packages are *total revenues* and *total variable costs*. The difference between total revenues and total variable costs is called **contribution margin**. That is,

Contribution margin = Total revenues − Total variable costs

Contribution margin indicates why operating income changes as the number of units sold changes. The contribution margin when Emma sells 5 packages is $400 ($1,000 in total revenues minus $600 in total variable costs); the contribution margin when Emma sells

40 packages is $3,200 ($8,000 in total revenues minus $4,800 in total variable costs). When calculating the contribution margin, be sure to subtract all variable costs. For example, if Emma had variable selling costs because she paid a commission to salespeople for each package they sold at the fair, variable costs would include the cost of each package plus the sales commission.

Contribution margin per unit is a useful tool for calculating contribution margin and operating income. It is defined as,

$$\text{Contribution margin per unit} = \text{Selling price} - \text{Variable cost per unit}$$

In the GMAT Success example, contribution margin per package, or per unit, is $200 − $120 = $80. Contribution margin per unit recognizes the tight coupling of selling price and variable cost per unit. Unlike fixed costs, Emma will only incur the variable cost per unit of $120 when she sells a unit of GMAT Success for $200.

Contribution margin per unit provides a second way to calculate contribution margin:

$$\text{Contribution margin} = \text{Contribution margin per unit} \times \text{Number of units sold}$$

For example, when 40 packages are sold, contribution margin = $80 per unit × 40 units = $3,200.

Even before she gets to the fair, Emma incurs $2,000 in fixed costs. Because the contribution margin per unit is $80, Emma will recover $80 for each package that she sells at the fair. Emma hopes to sell enough packages to fully recover the $2,000 she spent for renting the booth and to then start making a profit.

Exhibit 3-1 presents contribution margins for different quantities of packages sold. The income statement in Exhibit 3-1 is called a **contribution income statement** because it groups costs into variable costs and fixed costs to highlight contribution margin. Each additional package sold from 0 to 1 to 5 increases contribution margin by $80 per package, recovering more of the fixed costs and reducing the operating loss. If Emma sells 25 packages, contribution margin equals $2,000 ($80 per package × 25 packages), exactly recovering fixed costs and resulting in $0 operating income. If Emma sells 40 packages, contribution margin increases by another $1,200 ($3,200 − $2,000), all of which becomes operating income. As you look across Exhibit 3-1 from left to right, you see that the increase in contribution margin exactly equals the increase in operating income (or the decrease in operating loss).

Instead of expressing contribution margin as a dollar amount per unit, we can express it as a percentage called **contribution margin percentage** (or **contribution margin ratio**):

$$\text{Contribution margin percentage (or contribution margin ratio)} = \frac{\text{Contribution margin per unit}}{\text{Selling price}}$$

In our example,

$$\text{Contribution margin percentage} = \frac{\$80}{\$200} = 0.40, \text{ or } 40\%$$

Contribution margin percentage is the contribution margin per dollar of revenue. Emma earns 40% of each dollar of revenue (equal to 40 cents).

	A	B	C	D	E	F	G	H
1				**Number of Packages Sold**				
2				0	1	5	25	40
3	Revenues	$ 200	per package	$ 0	$ 200	$ 1,000	$5,000	$8,000
4	Variable costs	$ 120	per package	0	120	600	3,000	4,800
5	Contribution margin	$ 80	per package	0	80	400	2,000	3,200
6	Fixed costs	$2,000		2,000	2,000	2,000	2,000	2,000
7	Operating income			$(2,000)	$(1,920)	$(1,600)	$ 0	$1,200

Exhibit 3-1

Contribution Income Statement for Different Quantities of GMAT Success Packages Sold

Most companies have multiple products. As we shall see later in this chapter, calculating contribution margin per unit when there are multiple products is more cumbersome. In practice, companies routinely use contribution margin percentage as a handy way to calculate contribution margin for different dollar amounts of revenue:

$$\text{Contribution margin} = \text{Contribution margin percentage} \times \text{Revenues (in dollars)}$$

For example, in Exhibit 3-1, if Emma sells 40 packages, revenues will be $8,000 and contribution margin will equal 40% of $8,000, or $0.40 \times \$8,000 = \$3,200$. Emma earns operating income of $1,200 ($3,200 − Fixed costs, $2,000) by selling 40 packages for $8,000.

Expressing CVP Relationships

How was the Excel spreadsheet in Exhibit 3-1 constructed? Underlying the Exhibit are some equations that express the CVP relationships. To make good decisions using CVP analysis, we must understand these relationships and the structure of the contribution income statement in Exhibit 3-1. There are three related ways (we will call them methods) to think more deeply about and model CVP relationships:

1. The equation method
2. The contribution margin method
3. The graph method

The equation method and the contribution margin method are most useful when managers want to determine operating income at few specific levels of sales (for example 5, 15, 25, and 40 units sold). The graph method helps managers visualize the relationship between units sold and operating income over a wide range of quantities of units sold. As we shall see later in the chapter, different methods are useful for different decisions.

Equation Method

Each column in Exhibit 3-1 is expressed as an equation.

$$\text{Revenues} - \text{Variable costs} - \text{Fixed costs} = \text{Operating income}$$

How are revenues in each column calculated?

$$\text{Revenues} = \text{Selling price } (SP) \times \text{Quantity of units sold } (Q)$$

How are variable costs in each column calculated?

$$\text{Variable costs} = \text{Variable cost per unit } (VCU) \times \text{Quantity of units sold } (Q)$$

So,

$$\left[\left(\begin{array}{c}\text{Selling}\\\text{price}\end{array} \times \begin{array}{c}\text{Quantity of}\\\text{units sold}\end{array}\right) - \left(\begin{array}{c}\text{Variable cost}\\\text{per unit}\end{array} \times \begin{array}{c}\text{Quantity of}\\\text{units sold}\end{array}\right)\right] - \begin{array}{c}\text{Fixed}\\\text{costs}\end{array} = \begin{array}{c}\text{Operating}\\\text{income}\end{array} \quad \textbf{(Equation 1)}$$

Equation 1 becomes the basis for calculating operating income for different quantities of units sold. For example, if you go to cell F7 in Exhibit 3-1, the calculation of operating income when Emma sells 5 packages is

$$(\$200 \times 5) - (\$120 \times 5) - \$2,000 = \$1,000 - \$600 - \$2,000 = -\$1,600$$

Contribution Margin Method

Rearranging equation 1,

$$\left[\left(\begin{array}{c}\text{Selling}\\\text{price}\end{array} - \begin{array}{c}\text{Variable cost}\\\text{per unit}\end{array}\right) \times \left(\begin{array}{c}\text{Quantity of}\\\text{units sold}\end{array}\right)\right] - \begin{array}{c}\text{Fixed}\\\text{costs}\end{array} = \begin{array}{c}\text{Operating}\\\text{income}\end{array}$$

$$\left(\begin{array}{c}\text{Contribution margin}\\\text{per unit}\end{array} \times \begin{array}{c}\text{Quantity of}\\\text{units sold}\end{array}\right) - \begin{array}{c}\text{Fixed}\\\text{costs}\end{array} = \begin{array}{c}\text{Operating}\\\text{income}\end{array} \quad \textbf{(Equation 2)}$$

In our GMAT Success example, contribution margin per unit is $80 ($200 − $120), so when Emma sells 5 packages,

$$\text{Operating income} = (\$80 \times 5) - \$2{,}000 = -\$1{,}600$$

Equation 2 expresses the basic idea we described earlier—each unit sold helps Emma recover $80 (in contribution margin) of the $2,000 in fixed costs.

Graph Method

In the graph method, we represent total costs and total revenues graphically. Each is shown as a line on a graph. Exhibit 3-2 illustrates the graph method for GMAT Success. Because we have assumed that total costs and total revenues behave in a linear fashion, we need only two points to plot the line representing each of them.

1. **Total costs line.** The total costs line is the sum of fixed costs and variable costs. Fixed costs are $2,000 for all quantities of units sold within the relevant range. To plot the total costs line, use as one point the $2,000 fixed costs at zero units sold (point A) because variable costs are $0 when no units are sold. Select a second point by choosing any other convenient output level (say, 40 units sold) and determine the corresponding total costs. Total variable costs at this output level are $4,800 (40 units × $120 per unit). Remember, fixed costs are $2,000 at all quantities of units sold within the relevant range, so total costs at 40 units sold equal $6,800 ($2,000 + $4,800), which is point B in Exhibit 3-2. The total costs line is the straight line from point A through point B.

2. **Total revenues line.** One convenient starting point is $0 revenues at 0 units sold, which is point C in Exhibit 3-2. Select a second point by choosing any other convenient output level and determining the corresponding total revenues. At 40 units sold, total revenues are $8,000 ($200 per unit × 40 units), which is point D in Exhibit 3-2. The total revenues line is the straight line from point C through point D.

   Profit or loss at any sales level can be determined by the vertical distance between the two lines at that level in Exhibit 3-2. For quantities fewer than 25 units sold, total costs exceed total revenues, and the purple area indicates operating losses. For quantities greater than 25 units sold, total revenues exceed total costs, and the blue-green area indicates operating incomes. At 25 units sold, total revenues equal total costs. Emma will break even by selling 25 packages.

Decision Point

How can CVP analysis assist managers?

Exhibit 3-2

Cost-Volume Graph for GMAT Success

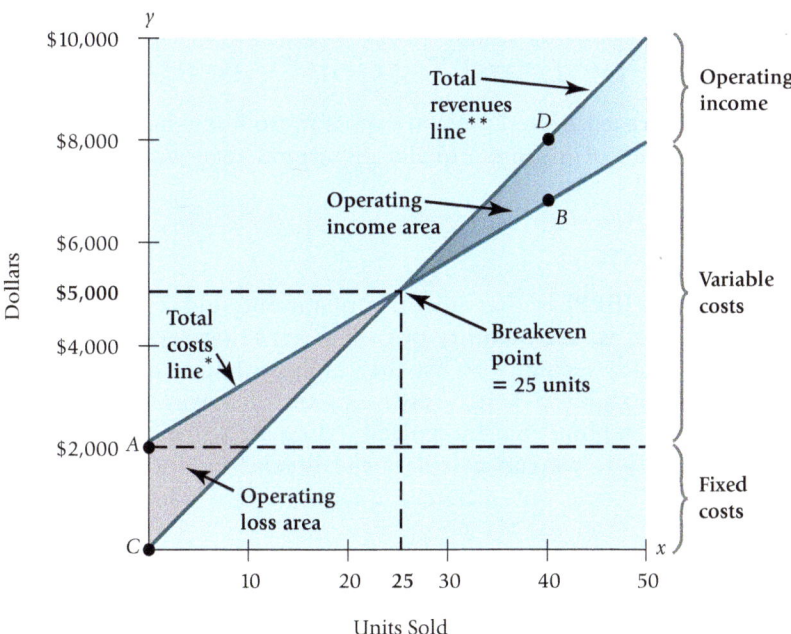

* Slope of the total costs line is the variable cost per unit = $120
** Slope of the total revenues line is the selling price = $200

Cost-Volume-Profit Assumptions

Now that you have seen how CVP analysis works, think about the following assumptions we made during the analysis:

1. Changes in the levels of revenues and costs arise only because of changes in the number of product (or service) units sold. The number of units sold is the only revenue driver and the only cost driver. Just as a cost driver is any factor that affects costs, a **revenue driver** is a variable, such as volume, that causally affects revenues.

2. Total costs can be separated into two components: a fixed component that does not vary with units sold and a variable component that changes with respect to units sold.

3. When represented graphically, the behaviors of total revenues and total costs are linear (meaning they can be represented as a straight line) in relation to units sold within a relevant range (and time period).

4. Selling price, variable cost per unit, and total fixed costs (within a relevant range and time period) are known and constant.

As the CVP assumptions make clear, an important feature of CVP analysis is distinguishing fixed from variable costs. Always keep in mind, however, that whether a cost is variable or fixed depends on the time period for a decision.

The shorter the time horizon, the higher the percentage of total costs considered fixed. For example, suppose an American Airlines plane will depart from its gate in the next hour and currently has 20 seats unsold. A potential passenger arrives with a transferable ticket from a competing airline. The variable costs (such as one more meal) to American of placing one more passenger in an otherwise empty seat is negligible At the time of this decision, with only an hour to go before the flight departs, virtually all costs (such as crew costs and baggage-handling costs) are fixed.

Alternatively, suppose American Airlines must decide whether to keep this flight in its flight schedule. This decision will have a one-year planning horizon. If American Airlines decides to cancel this flight because very few passengers during the last year have taken this flight, many more costs, including crew costs, baggage-handling costs, and airport fees, would be considered variable. That's because over this longer horizon, these costs would not have to be incurred if the flight were no longer operating. Always consider the relevant range, the length of the time horizon, and the specific decision situation when classifying costs as variable or fixed.

Breakeven Point and Target Operating Income

Managers and entrepreneurs like Emma always want to know how much they must sell to earn a given amount of income. Equally important, they want to know how much they must sell to avoid a loss.

Learning Objective 2

Determine the breakeven point and output level needed to achieve a target operating income

. . . compare contribution margin and fixed costs

Breakeven Point

The **breakeven point** (**BEP**) is that quantity of output sold at which total revenues equal total costs—that is, the quantity of output sold that results in $0 of operating income. We have already seen how to use the graph method to calculate the breakeven point. Recall from Exhibit 3-1 that operating income was $0 when Emma sold 25 units, the breakeven point. But by understanding the equations underlying the calculations in Exhibit 3-1, we can calculate the breakeven point directly for GMAT Success rather than trying out different quantities and checking when operating income equals $0.

Recall the equation method (equation 1):

$$\left(\begin{array}{c}\text{Selling} \\ \text{price}\end{array} \times \begin{array}{c}\text{Quantity of} \\ \text{units sold}\end{array}\right) - \left(\begin{array}{c}\text{Variable cost} \\ \text{per unit}\end{array} \times \begin{array}{c}\text{Quantity of} \\ \text{units sold}\end{array}\right) - \begin{array}{c}\text{Fixed} \\ \text{costs}\end{array} = \begin{array}{c}\text{Operating} \\ \text{income}\end{array}$$

Setting operating income equal to $0 and denoting quantity of output units that must be sold by Q,

$$(\$200 \times Q) - (\$120 \times Q) - \$2,000 = \$0$$
$$\$80 \times Q = \$2,000$$
$$Q = \$2,000 \div \$80 \text{ per unit} = 25 \text{ units}$$

If Emma sells fewer than 25 units, she will incur a loss; if she sells 25 units, she will break even; and if she sells more than 25 units, she will make a profit. While this breakeven point is expressed in units, it can also be expressed in revenues: 25 units × $200 selling price = $5,000.

Recall the contribution margin method (equation 2):

$$\left(\begin{matrix} \text{Contribution} \\ \text{margin per unit} \end{matrix} \times \begin{matrix} \text{Quantity of} \\ \text{units sold} \end{matrix} \right) - \text{Fixed costs} = \text{Operating income}$$

At the breakeven point, operating income is by definition $0 and so,

$$\text{Contribution margin per unit} \times \text{Breakeven number of units} = \text{Fixed cost} \quad \textbf{(Equation 3)}$$

Rearranging equation 3 and entering the data,

$$\frac{\text{Breakeven}}{\text{number of units}} = \frac{\text{Fixed costs}}{\text{Contribution margin per unit}} = \frac{\$2,000}{\$80 \text{ per unit}} = 25 \text{ units}$$
$$\text{Breakeven revenues} = \text{Breakeven number of units} \times \text{Selling price}$$
$$= 25 \text{ units} \times \$200 \text{ per unit} = \$5,000$$

In practice (because they have multiple products), companies usually calculate breakeven point directly in terms of revenues using contribution margin percentages. Recall that in the GMAT Success example,

$$\frac{\text{Contribution margin}}{\text{percentage}} = \frac{\text{Contribution margin per unit}}{\text{Selling price}} = \frac{\$80}{\$200} = 0.40, \text{ or } 40\%$$

That is, 40% of each dollar of revenue, or 40 cents, is contribution margin. To break even, contribution margin must equal fixed costs of $2,000. To earn $2,000 of contribution margin, when $1 of revenue earns $0.40 of contribution margin, revenues must equal $2,000 ÷ 0.40 = $5,000.

$$\frac{\text{Breakeven}}{\text{revenues}} = \frac{\text{Fixed costs}}{\text{Contribution margin \%}} = \frac{\$2,000}{0.40} = \$5,000$$

While the breakeven point tells managers how much they must sell to avoid a loss, managers are equally interested in how they will achieve the operating income targets underlying their strategies and plans. In our example, selling 25 units at a price of $200 assures Emma that she will not lose money if she rents the booth. This news is comforting, but we next describe how Emma determines how much she needs to sell to achieve a targeted amount of operating income.

Target Operating Income

We illustrate target operating income calculations by asking the following question: How many units must Emma sell to earn an operating income of $1,200? One approach is to keep plugging in different quantities into Exhibit 3-1 and check when operating income equals $1,200. Exhibit 3-1 shows that operating income is $1,200 when 40 packages are sold. A more convenient approach is to use equation 1 from page 66.

$$\left[\left(\begin{matrix} \text{Selling} \\ \text{price} \end{matrix} \times \begin{matrix} \text{Quantity of} \\ \text{units sold} \end{matrix} \right) - \left(\begin{matrix} \text{Variable cost} \\ \text{per unit} \end{matrix} \times \begin{matrix} \text{Quantity of} \\ \text{units sold} \end{matrix} \right) \right] - \begin{matrix} \text{Fixed} \\ \text{costs} \end{matrix} = \begin{matrix} \text{Operating} \\ \text{income} \end{matrix} \quad \textbf{(Equation 1)}$$

We denote by Q the unknown quantity of units Emma must sell to earn an operating income of $1,200. Selling price is $200, variable cost per package is $120, fixed costs are

$2,000, and target operating income is $1,200. Substituting these values into equation 1, we have

$$(\$200 \times Q) - (\$120 \times Q) - \$2,000 = \$1,200$$
$$\$80 \times Q = \$2,000 + \$1,200 = \$3,200$$
$$Q = \$3,200 \div \$80 \text{ per unit} = 40 \text{ units}$$

Alternatively, we could use equation 2,

$$\left(\begin{array}{c} \text{Contribution margin} \\ \text{per unit} \end{array} \times \begin{array}{c} \text{Quantity of} \\ \text{units sold} \end{array} \right) - \begin{array}{c} \text{Fixed} \\ \text{costs} \end{array} = \begin{array}{c} \text{Operating} \\ \text{income} \end{array} \qquad \textbf{(Equation 2)}$$

Given a target operating income ($1,200 in this case), we can rearrange terms to get equation 4.

$$\begin{array}{c} \text{Quantity of units} \\ \text{required to be sold} \end{array} = \frac{\text{Fixed costs} + \text{Target operating income}}{\text{Contribution margin per unit}} \qquad \textbf{(Equation 4)}$$

$$\begin{array}{c} \text{Quantity of units} \\ \text{required to be sold} \end{array} = \frac{\$2,000 + \$1,200}{\$80 \text{ per unit}} = 40 \text{ units}$$

Proof:

Revenues, $200 per unit × 40 units	$8,000
Variable costs, $120 per unit × 40 units	4,800
Contribution margin, $80 per unit × 40 units	3,200
Fixed costs	2,000
Operating income	$1,200

The revenues needed to earn an operating income of $1,200 can also be calculated directly by recognizing (1) that $3,200 of contribution margin must be earned (fixed costs of $2,000 plus operating income of $1,200) and (2) that $1 of revenue earns $0.40 (40 cents) of contribution margin. To earn $3,200 of contribution margin, revenues must equal $3,200 ÷ 0.40 = $8,000.

$$\text{Revenues needed to earn operating income of } \$1,200 = \frac{\$2,000 + \$1,200}{0.40} = \frac{\$3,200}{0.40} = \$8,000$$

The graph in Exhibit 3-2 is very difficult to use to answer the question: How many units must Emma sell to earn an operating income of $1,200? Why? Because it is not easy to determine from the graph the precise point at which the difference between the total revenues line and the total costs line equals $1,200. However, recasting Exhibit 3-2 in the form of a profit-volume (PV) graph makes it easier to answer this question.

A **PV graph** shows how changes in the quantity of units sold affect operating income. Exhibit 3-3 is the PV graph for GMAT Success (fixed costs, $2,000; selling price, $200; and variable cost per unit, $120). The PV line can be drawn using two points. One convenient point (M) is the operating loss at 0 units sold, which is equal to the fixed costs of $2,000, shown at –$2,000 on the vertical axis. A second convenient point (N) is the breakeven point, which is 25 units in our example (see p. 69). The PV line is the straight line from point M through point N. To find the number of units Emma must sell to earn an operating income of $1,200, draw a horizontal line parallel to the *x*-axis corresponding to $1,200 on the vertical axis (that's the *y*-axis). At the point where this line intersects the PV line, draw a vertical line down to the horizontal axis (that's the *x*-axis). The vertical line intersects the *x*-axis at 40 units, indicating that by selling 40 units Emma will earn an operating income of $1,200.

Decision Point ▶

How can managers determine the breakeven point or the output needed to achieve a target operating income?

Target Net Income and Income Taxes

Learning Objective 3

Understand how income taxes affect CVP analysis

. . . focus on net income

Net income is operating income plus nonoperating revenues (such as interest revenue) minus nonoperating costs (such as interest cost) minus income taxes. For simplicity, throughout this chapter we assume nonoperating revenues and nonoperating costs are zero. Thus,

$$\text{Net income} = \text{Operating income} - \text{Income taxes}$$

Until now, we have ignored the effect of income taxes in our CVP analysis. In many companies, the income targets for managers in their strategic plans are expressed in terms of

Exhibit 3-3

Profit-Volume Graph for
GMAT Success

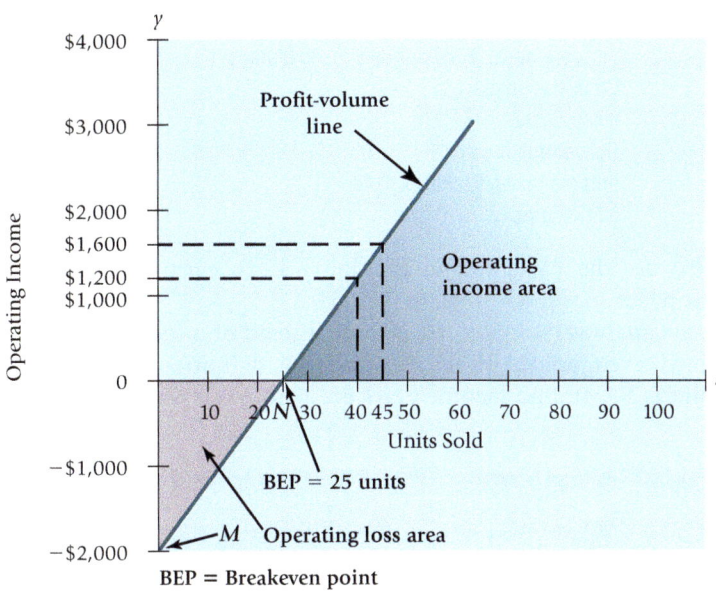

BEP = Breakeven point

net income. That's because top management wants subordinate managers to take into account the effects their decisions have on operating income after income taxes. Some decisions may not result in large operating incomes, but they may have favorable tax consequences, making them attractive on a net income basis—the measure that drives shareholders' dividends and returns.

To make net income evaluations, CVP calculations for target income must be stated in terms of target net income instead of target operating income. For example, Emma may be interested in knowing the quantity of units she must sell to earn a net income of $960, assuming an income tax rate of 40%.

$$\text{Target net income} = \left(\begin{array}{c}\text{Target}\\\text{operating income}\end{array}\right) - \left(\begin{array}{c}\text{Target}\\\text{operating income}\end{array} \times \text{Tax rate}\right)$$

$$\text{Target net income} = (\text{Target operating income}) \times (1 - \text{Tax rate})$$

$$\text{Target operating income} = \frac{\text{Target net income}}{1 - \text{Tax rate}} = \frac{\$960}{1 - 0.40} = \$1{,}600$$

In other words, to earn a target net income of $960, Emma's target operating income is $1,600.

Proof:

Target operating income	$1,600
Tax at 40% (0.40 × $1,600)	640
Target net income	$ 960

The key step is to take the target net income number and convert it into the corresponding target operating income number. We can then use equation 1 for target operating income and substitute numbers from our GMAT Success example.

$$\left[\left(\begin{array}{c}\text{Selling}\\\text{price}\end{array} \times \begin{array}{c}\text{Quantity of}\\\text{units sold}\end{array}\right) - \left(\begin{array}{c}\text{Variable cost}\\\text{per unit}\end{array} \times \begin{array}{c}\text{Quantity of}\\\text{units sold}\end{array}\right)\right] - \begin{array}{c}\text{Fixed}\\\text{costs}\end{array} = \begin{array}{c}\text{Operating}\\\text{income}\end{array} \quad \text{(Equation 1)}$$

$$(\$200 \times Q) - (\$120 \times Q) - \$2{,}000 = \$1{,}600$$

$$\$80 \times Q = \$3{,}600$$

$$Q = \$3{,}600 \div \$80 \text{ per unit} = 45 \text{ units}$$

Alternatively we can calculate the number of units Emma must sell by using the contribution margin method and equation 4:

$$\begin{array}{c}\text{Quantity of units}\\\text{required to be sold}\end{array} = \frac{\text{Fixed costs} + \text{Target operating income}}{\text{Contribution margin per unit}} \quad \text{(Equation 4)}$$

$$= \frac{\$2{,}000 + \$1{,}600}{\$80 \text{ per unit}} = 45 \text{ units}$$

Proof:

	Revenues, $200 per unit × 45 units	$9,000
	Variable costs, $120 per unit × 45 units	5,400
	Contribution margin	3,600
	Fixed costs	2,000
	Operating income	1,600
	Income taxes, $1,600 × 0.40	640
	Net income	$ 960

Emma can also use the PV graph in Exhibit 3-3. To earn target operating income of $1,600, Emma needs to sell 45 units.

Focusing the analysis on target net income instead of target operating income will not change the breakeven point. That's because, by definition, operating income at the breakeven point is $0, and no income taxes are paid when there is no operating income.

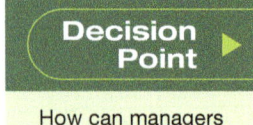

Decision Point ▶

How can managers incorporate income taxes into CVP analysis?

Using CVP Analysis for Decision Making

Learning Objective *4*

Explain how managers use CVP analysis in decision making

. . . choose the alternative that maximizes operating income

We have seen how CVP analysis is useful for calculating the units that need to be sold to break even, or to achieve a target operating income or target net income. Managers also use CVP analysis to guide other decisions, many of them strategic decisions. Consider a decision about choosing additional features for an existing product. Different choices can affect selling prices, variable cost per unit, fixed costs, units sold, and operating income. CVP analysis helps managers make product decisions by estimating the expected profitability of these choices.

Strategic decisions invariably entail risk. CVP analysis can be used to evaluate how operating income will be affected if the original predicted data are not achieved—say, if sales are 10% lower than estimated. Evaluating this risk affects other strategic decisions a company might make. For example, if the probability of a decline in sales seems high, a manager may take actions to change the cost structure to have more variable costs and fewer fixed costs. We return to our GMAT Success example to illustrate how CVP analysis can be used for strategic decisions concerning advertising and selling price.

Decision to Advertise

Suppose Emma anticipates selling 40 units at the fair. Exhibit 3-3 indicates that Emma's operating income will be $1,200. Emma is considering placing an advertisement describing the product and its features in the fair brochure. The advertisement will be a fixed cost of $500. Emma thinks that advertising will increase sales by 10% to 44 packages. Should Emma advertise? The following table presents the CVP analysis.

	40 Packages Sold with No Advertising (1)	44 Packages Sold with Advertising (2)	Difference (3) = (2) − (1)
Revenues ($200 × 40; $200 × 44)	$8,000	$8,800	$ 800
Variable costs ($120 × 40; $120 × 44)	4,800	5,280	480
Contribution margin ($80 × 40; $80 × 44)	3,200	3,520	320
Fixed costs	2,000	2,500	500
Operating income	$1,200	$1,020	$(180)

Operating income will decrease from $1,200 to $1,020, so Emma should not advertise. Note that Emma could focus only on the difference column and come to the same conclusion: If Emma advertises, contribution margin will increase by $320 (revenues, $800 − variable costs, $480), and fixed costs will increase by $500, resulting in a $180 decrease in operating income.

As you become more familiar with CVP analysis, try evaluating decisions based on differences rather than mechanically working through the contribution income statement. Analyzing differences gets to the heart of CVP analysis and sharpens intuition by focusing only on the revenues and costs that will change as a result of a decision.

Decision to Reduce Selling Price

Having decided not to advertise, Emma is contemplating whether to reduce the selling price to $175. At this price, she thinks she will sell 50 units. At this quantity, the test-prep package wholesaler who supplies GMAT Success will sell the packages to Emma for $115 per unit instead of $120. Should Emma reduce the selling price?

Contribution margin from lowering price to $175: ($175 − $115) per unit × 50 units	$3,000
Contribution margin from maintaining price at $200: ($200 − $120) per unit × 40 units	3,200
Change in contribution margin from lowering price	$ (200)

Decreasing the price will reduce contribution margin by $200 and, because the fixed costs of $2,000 will not change, it will also reduce operating income by $200. Emma should not reduce the selling price.

Determining Target Prices

Emma could also ask "At what price can I sell 50 units (purchased at $115 per unit) and continue to earn an operating income of $1,200?" The answer is $179, as the following calculations show.

	Target operating income	$1,200
	Add fixed costs	2,000
	Target contribution margin	$3,200
	Divided by number of units sold	÷ 50 units
	Target contribution margin per unit	$ 64
	Add variable cost per unit	115
	Target selling price	$ 179
Proof:	Revenues, $179 per unit × 50 units	$8,950
	Variable costs, $115 per unit × 50 units	5,750
	Contribution margin	3,200
	Fixed costs	2,000
	Operating income	$1,200

Emma should also examine the effects of other decisions, such as simultaneously increasing advertising costs and lowering prices. In each case, Emma will compare the changes in contribution margin (through the effects on selling prices, variable costs, and quantities of units sold) to the changes in fixed costs, and she will choose the alternative that provides the highest operating income.

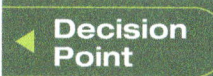

Decision Point

How do managers use CVP analysis to make decisions?

Sensitivity Analysis and Margin of Safety

Before choosing strategies and plans about how to implement strategies, managers frequently analyze the sensitivity of their decisions to changes in underlying assumptions. **Sensitivity analysis** is a "what-if" technique that managers use to examine how an outcome will change if the original predicted data are not achieved or if an underlying assumption changes. In the context of CVP analysis, sensitivity analysis answers questions such as, "What will operating income be if the quantity of units sold decreases by 5% from the original prediction?" and "What will operating income be if variable cost per unit increases by 10%?" Sensitivity analysis broadens managers' perspectives to possible outcomes that might occur *before* costs are committed.

Electronic spreadsheets, such as Excel, enable managers to conduct CVP-based sensitivity analyses in a systematic and efficient way. Using spreadsheets, managers can conduct sensitivity analysis to examine the effect and interaction of changes in selling price, variable cost per unit, fixed costs, and target operating income. Exhibit 3-4 displays a spreadsheet for the GMAT Success example.

Using the spreadsheet, Emma can immediately see how many units she needs to sell to achieve particular operating-income levels, given alternative levels of fixed costs and variable cost per unit that she may face. For example, 32 units must be sold to earn an

Learning Objective 5

Explain how sensitivity analysis helps managers cope with uncertainty

. . . determine the effect on operating income of different assumptions

Exhibit 3-4

Spreadsheet Analysis
of CVP Relationships
for GMAT Success

	Home	Insert	Page Layout	Formulas	Data	Review	View
	D5	▼	*fx* =($A5+D$3)/(F1-$B5)				

	A	B	C	D	E	F
1			**Number of units required to be sold at $200**			
2			**Selling Price to Earn Target Operating Income of**			
3		**Variable Costs**	**$0**	**$1,200**	**$1,600**	**$2,000**
4	**Fixed Costs**	**per Unit**	**(Breakeven point)**			
5	$2,000	$100	20	32[a]	36	40
6	$2,000	$120	25	40	45	50
7	$2,000	$150	40	64	72	80
8	$2,400	$100	24	36	40	44
9	$2,400	$120	30	45	50	55
10	$2,400	$150	48	72	80	88
11	$2,800	$100	28	40	44	48
12	$2,800	$120	35	50	55	60
13	$2,800	$150	56	80	88	96
14						
15	[a]Number of units	$=$	Fixed costs + Target operating income	$=$	$2,000 + $1,200	$= 32$
16	required to be sold		Contribution margin per unit		$200 – $100	

operating income of $1,200 if fixed costs are $2,000 and variable cost per unit is $100. Emma can also use Exhibit 3-4 to determine that she needs to sell 56 units to break even if fixed cost of the booth rental at the Chicago fair is raised to $2,800 and if the variable cost per unit charged by the test-prep package supplier increases to $150. Emma can use information about costs and sensitivity analysis, together with realistic predictions about how much she can sell to decide if she should rent a booth at the fair.

Another aspect of sensitivity analysis is **margin of safety**:

$$\text{Margin of safety} = \text{Budgeted (or actual) revenues} - \text{Breakeven revenues}$$
$$\text{Margin of safety (in units)} = \text{Budgeted (or actual) sales quantity} - \text{Breakeven quantity}$$

The margin of safety answers the "what-if" question: If budgeted revenues are above breakeven and drop, how far can they fall below budget before the breakeven point is reached? Sales might decrease as a result of a competitor introducing a better product, or poorly executed marketing programs, and so on. Assume that Emma has fixed costs of $2,000, a selling price of $200, and variable cost per unit of $120. From Exhibit 3-1, if Emma sells 40 units, budgeted revenues are $8,000 and budgeted operating income is $1,200. The breakeven point is 25 units or $5,000 in total revenues.

$$\text{Margin of safety} = \frac{\text{Budgeted}}{\text{revenues}} - \frac{\text{Breakeven}}{\text{revenues}} = \$8,000 - \$5,000 = \$3,000$$

$$\frac{\text{Margin of}}{\text{safety (in units)}} = \frac{\text{Budgeted}}{\text{sales (units)}} - \frac{\text{Breakeven}}{\text{sales (units)}} = 40 - 25 = 15 \text{ units}$$

Sometimes margin of safety is expressed as a percentage:

$$\text{Margin of safety percentage} = \frac{\text{Margin of safety in dollars}}{\text{Budgeted (or actual) revenues}}$$

In our example, margin of safety percentage $= \dfrac{\$3,000}{\$8,000} = 37.5\%$

This result means that revenues would have to decrease substantially, by 37.5%, to reach breakeven revenues. The high margin of safety gives Emma confidence that she is unlikely to suffer a loss.

If, however, Emma expects to sell only 30 units, budgeted revenues would be $6,000 ($200 per unit × 30 units) and the margin of safety would equal:

$$\text{Budgeted revenues} - \text{Breakeven revenues} = \$6,000 - \$5,000 = \$1,000$$

$$\frac{\text{Margin of}}{\text{safety percentage}} = \frac{\text{Margin of safety in dollars}}{\text{Budgeted (or actual) revenues}} = \frac{\$1,000}{\$6,000} = 16.67\%$$

The analysis implies that if revenues decrease by more than 16.67%, Emma would suffer a loss. A low margin of safety increases the risk of a loss. If Emma does not have the tolerance for this level of risk, she will prefer not to rent a booth at the fair.

Sensitivity analysis is a simple approach to recognizing **uncertainty**, which is the possibility that an actual amount will deviate from an expected amount. Sensitivity analysis gives managers a good feel for the risks involved. A more comprehensive approach to recognizing uncertainty is to compute expected values using probability distributions. This approach is illustrated in the appendix to this chapter.

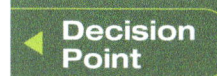

◄ Decision Point

What can managers do to cope with uncertainty or changes in underlying assumptions?

Cost Planning and CVP

Managers have the ability to choose the levels of fixed and variable costs in their cost structures. This is a strategic decision. In this section, we describe various factors that managers and management accountants consider as they make this decision.

Alternative Fixed-Cost/Variable-Cost Structures

CVP-based sensitivity analysis highlights the risks and returns as fixed costs are substituted for variable costs in a company's cost structure. In Exhibit 3-4, compare line 6 and line 11.

Learning Objective 6

Use CVP analysis to plan variable and fixed costs

. . . compare risk of losses versus higher returns

	Fixed Cost	Variable Cost	Number of units required to be sold at $200 selling price to earn target operating income of	
			$0 (Breakeven point)	$2,000
Line 6	$2,000	$120	25	50
Line 11	$2,800	$100	28	48

Compared to line 6, line 11, with higher fixed costs, has more risk of loss (has a higher breakeven point) but requires fewer units to be sold (48 versus 50) to earn operating income of $2,000. CVP analysis can help managers evaluate various fixed-cost/variable-cost structures. We next consider the effects of these choices in more detail. Suppose the Chicago college fair organizers offer Emma three rental alternatives:

Option 1: $2,000 fixed fee

Option 2: $800 fixed fee plus 15% of GMAT Success revenues

Option 3: 25% of GMAT Success revenues with no fixed fee

Emma's variable cost per unit is $120. Emma is interested in how her choice of a rental agreement will affect the income she earns and the risks she faces. Exhibit 3-5 graphically depicts the profit-volume relationship for each option. The line representing the relationship between units sold and operating income for Option 1 is the same as the line in the PV graph shown in Exhibit 3-3 (fixed costs of $2,000 and contribution margin per unit of $80). The line representing Option 2 shows fixed costs of $800 and a contribution margin per unit of $50 [selling price, $200, minus variable cost per unit, $120, minus variable rental fees per unit, $30, (0.15 × $200)]. The line representing Option 3 has fixed costs of $0 and a contribution margin per unit of $30 [$200 − $120 − $50 (0.25 × $200)].

Option 3 has the lowest breakeven point (0 units), and Option 1 has the highest breakeven point (25 units). Option 1 has the highest risk of loss if sales are low, but it also has the highest contribution margin per unit ($80) and hence the highest operating income when sales are high (greater than 40 units).

The choice among Options 1, 2, and 3 is a strategic decision that Emma faces. As in most strategic decisions, what she decides now will significantly affect her operating

Exhibit 3-5

Profit-Volume Graph for
Alternative Rental
Options for GMAT
Success

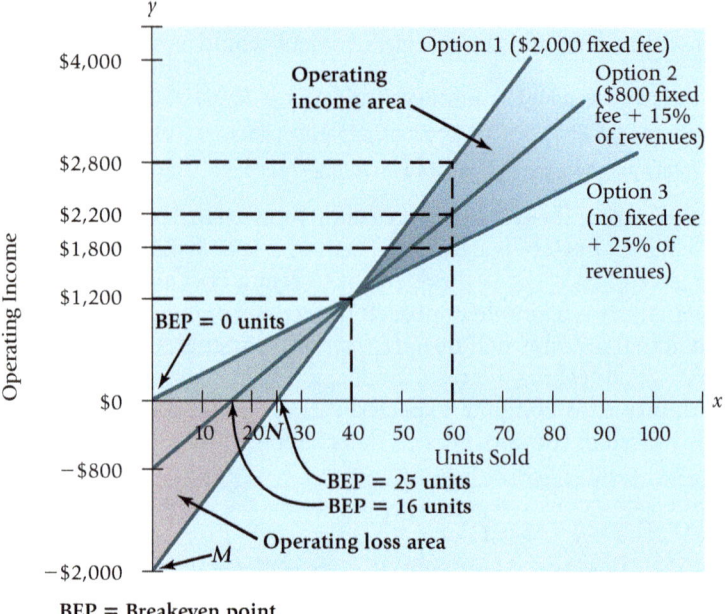

BEP = Breakeven point

income (or loss), depending on the demand for GMAT Success. Faced with this uncertainty, Emma's choice will be influenced by her confidence in the level of demand for GMAT Success and her willingness to risk losses if demand is low. For example, if Emma's tolerance for risk is high, she will choose Option 1 with its high potential rewards. If, however, Emma is averse to taking risk, she will prefer Option 3, where the rewards are smaller if sales are high but where she never suffers a loss if sales are low.

Operating Leverage

The risk-return trade-off across alternative cost structures can be measured as *operating leverage*. **Operating leverage** describes the effects that fixed costs have on changes in operating income as changes occur in units sold and contribution margin. Organizations with a high proportion of fixed costs in their cost structures, as is the case under Option 1, have high operating leverage. The line representing Option 1 in Exhibit 3-5 is the steepest of the three lines. Small increases in sales lead to large increases in operating income. Small decreases in sales result in relatively large decreases in operating income, leading to a greater risk of operating losses. *At any given level of sales,*

$$\frac{\text{Degree of}}{\text{operating leverage}} = \frac{\text{Contribution margin}}{\text{Operating income}}$$

The following table shows the **degree of operating leverage** at sales of 40 units for the three rental options.

	Option 1	Option 2	Option 3
1. Contribution margin per unit (p. 75)	$ 80	$ 50	$ 30
2. Contribution margin (row 1 × 40 units)	$3,200	$2,000	$1,200
3. Operating income (from Exhibit 3-5)	$1,200	$1,200	$1,200
4. Degree of operating leverage (row 2 ÷ row 3)	$\frac{\$3,200}{\$1,200} = 2.67$	$\frac{\$2,000}{\$1,200} = 1.67$	$\frac{\$1,200}{\$1,200} = 1.00$

These results indicate that, when sales are 40 units, a percentage change in sales and contribution margin will result in 2.67 times that percentage change in operating income for Option 1, but the same percentage change (1.00) in operating income for Option 3. Consider, for example, a sales increase of 50% from 40 to 60 units. Contribution margin will increase by 50% under each option. Operating income, however, will increase by 2.67 × 50% = 133% from $1,200 to $2,800 in Option 1, but it will increase by only $1.00 \times 50\% = 50\%$ from \$1,200 to \$1,800 in Option 3 (see Exhibit 3-5). The degree of operating leverage at a given level of sales helps managers calculate the effect of sales fluctuations on operating income.

Keep in mind that, in the presence of fixed costs, the degree of operating leverage is different at different levels of sales. For example, at sales of 60 units, the degree of operating leverage under each of the three options is as follows:

	Option 1	Option 2	Option 3
1. Contribution margin per unit (p. 75)	\$ 80	\$ 50	\$ 30
2. Contribution margin (row 1 × 60 units)	\$4,800	\$3,000	\$1,800
3. Operating income (from Exhibit 3-5)	\$2,800	\$2,200	\$1,800
4. Degree of operating leverage (row 2 ÷ row 3)	$\dfrac{\$4,800}{\$2,800} = 1.71$	$\dfrac{\$3,000}{\$2,200} = 1.36$	$\dfrac{\$1,800}{\$1,800} = 1.00$

The degree of operating leverage decreases from 2.67 (at sales of 40 units) to 1.71 (at sales of 60 units) under Option 1 and from 1.67 to 1.36 under Option 2. In general, whenever there are fixed costs, the degree of operating leverage decreases as the level of sales increases beyond the breakeven point. If fixed costs are \$0 as in Option 3, contribution margin equals operating income, and the degree of operating leverage equals 1.00 at all sales levels.

But why must managers monitor operating leverage carefully? Again, consider companies such as General Motors, Global Crossing, US Airways, United Airlines, and WorldCom. Their high operating leverage was a major reason for their financial problems. Anticipating high demand for their services, these companies borrowed money to acquire assets, resulting in high fixed costs. As sales declined, these companies suffered losses and could not generate sufficient cash to service their interest and debt, causing them to seek bankruptcy protection. Managers and management accountants should always evaluate how the level of fixed costs and variable costs they choose will affect the risk-return trade-off. See Concepts in Action, page 78, for another example of the risks of high fixed costs.

What actions are managers taking to reduce their fixed costs? Many companies are moving their manufacturing facilities from the United States to lower-cost countries, such as Mexico and China. To substitute high fixed costs with lower variable costs, companies are purchasing products from lower-cost suppliers instead of manufacturing products themselves. These actions reduce both costs and operating leverage. More recently, General Electric and Hewlett-Packard began outsourcing service functions, such as post-sales customer service, by shifting their customer call centers to countries, such as India, where costs are lower. These decisions by companies are not without controversy. Some economists argue that outsourcing helps to keep costs, and therefore prices, low and enables U.S. companies to remain globally competitive. Others argue that outsourcing reduces job opportunities in the United States and hurts working-class families.

◄ **Decision Point**

How should managers choose among different variable-cost/ fixed-cost structures?

Effects of Sales Mix on Income

Sales mix is the quantities (or proportion) of various products (or services) that constitute total unit sales of a company. Suppose Emma is now budgeting for a subsequent college fair in New York. She plans to sell two different test-prep packages—GMAT Success and GRE Guarantee—and budgets the following:

Learning Objective 7

Apply CVP analysis to a company producing multiple products

. . . assume sales mix of products remains constant as total units sold changes

	GMAT Success	GRE Guarantee	Total
Expected sales	60	40	100
Revenues, \$200 and \$100 per unit	\$12,000	\$4,000	\$16,000
Variable costs, \$120 and \$70 per unit	7,200	2,800	10,000
Contribution margin, \$80 and \$30 per unit	\$ 4,800	\$1,200	6,000
Fixed costs			4,500
Operating income			\$ 1,500

Concepts in Action

Fixed Costs, Variable Costs, and the Future of Radio

Building up too much fixed costs can be hazardous to a company's health. Because fixed costs, unlike variable costs, do not automatically decrease as volume declines, companies with too much fixed costs can lose a considerable amount of money during lean times. Sirius XM, the satellite radio broadcaster, learned this lesson the hard way.

To begin broadcasting in 2001, both Sirius Satellite Radio and XM Satellite Radio—the two companies now comprising Sirius XM—spent billions of dollars on broadcasting licenses, space satellites, and other technology infrastructure. Once operational, the companies also spent billions on other fixed items such as programming and content (including Howard Stern and Major League Baseball), satellite transmission, and R&D. In contrast, variable costs were minimal, consisting mainly of artist-royalty fees and customer service and billing. In effect, this created a business model with a high operating leverage—that is, the companies' cost structure had a very significant proportion of fixed costs. As such, profitability could only be achieved by amassing millions of paid subscribers and selling advertising.

The competitive disadvantage of this highly-leveraged business model was nearly disastrous. Despite amassing more than 14 million subscribers, over the years Sirius and XM rang up $3 billion in debt and tallied cumulative operating losses in excess of $10 billion. Operating leverage, and the threat of bankruptcy, forced the merger of Sirius and XM in 2007, and since then the combined entity has struggled to cut costs, refinance its sizable debt, and reap the profits from over 18 million monthly subscribers.

While satellite radio has struggled under the weight of too much fixed cost, Internet radio had the opposite problem—too much variable costs. But "How?" you ask. Don't variable costs only increase as revenues increase? Yes, but if the revenue earned is less than the variable cost, an increase in revenue can lead to bankruptcy. This is almost what happened to Pandora, the Internet radio service.

Pandora launched in 2005 with only $9.3 million in venture capital. Available free over the Internet, Pandora earned revenue in three ways: advertising on its Web site, subscription fees from users who wanted to opt-out of advertising, and affiliate fees from iTunes and Amazon.com. Pandora had low fixed costs but high variable costs for streaming and performance royalties. Over time, as Pandora's popular service attracted millions of loyal listeners, its costs for performance royalties—set by the Copyright Royalty Board on a per song basis—far exceeded its revenues from advertising and subscriptions. As a result, even though royalty rates were only a fraction of a cent, Pandora lost more and more money each time it played another song!

In 2009, Pandora avoided bankruptcy by renegotiating a lower per-song royalty rate in exchange for at least 25% of its U.S. revenue annually. Further, Pandora began charging its most frequent users a small fee and also started increasing its advertising revenue.

Sources: Birger, Jon. 2009. Mel Karmazian fights to rescue Sirius. *Fortune*, March 16; Clifford, Stephanie. 2007. Pandora's long strange trip. *Inc.*, October 1; Pandora: Royalties kill the web radio star? (A). Harvard Business School Case No. 9-310-026; Satellite radio: An industry case study. Kellogg School of Management, Northwestern University. Case No. 5-206-255; XM satellite radio (A). Harvard Business School Case No. 9-504-009.

What is the breakeven point? In contrast to the single-product (or service) situation, the total number of units that must be sold to break even in a multiproduct company depends on the sales mix—the combination of the number of units of GMAT Success sold and the number of units of GRE Guarantee sold. We assume that the budgeted sales mix (60 units of GMAT Success sold for every 40 units of GRE Guarantee sold, that is, a ratio of 3:2) will not change at different levels of total unit sales. That is, we think of Emma selling a bundle of 3 units of GMAT Success and 2 units of GRE Guarantee. (Note that this does not mean that Emma physically bundles the two products together into one big package.)

Each bundle yields a contribution margin of $300 calculated as follows:

	Number of Units of GMAT Success and GRE Guarantee in Each Bundle	Contribution Margin per Unit for GMAT Success and GRE Guarantee	Contribution Margin of the Bundle
GMAT Success	3	$80	$240
GRE Guarantee	2	30	60
Total			$300

To compute the breakeven point, we calculate the number of bundles Emma needs to sell.

$$\text{Breakeven point in bundles} = \frac{\text{Fixed costs}}{\text{Contribution margin per bundle}} = \frac{\$4,500}{\$300 \text{ per bundle}} = 15 \text{ bundles}$$

Breakeven point in units of GMAT Success and GRE Guarantee is as follows:

GMAT Success: 15 bundles × 3 units of GMAT Success per bundle	45 units
GRE Guarantee: 15 bundles × 2 units of GRE Guarantee per bundle	30 units
Total number of units to break even	75 units

Breakeven point in dollars for GMAT Success and GRE Guarantee is as follows:

GMAT Success: 45 units × $200 per unit	$ 9,000
GRE Guarantee: 30 units × $100 per unit	3,000
Breakeven revenues	$12,000

When there are multiple products, it is often convenient to use contribution margin percentage. Under this approach, Emma first calculates the revenues from selling a bundle of 3 units of GMAT Success and 2 units of GRE Guarantee:

	Number of Units of GMAT Success and GRE Guarantee in Each Bundle	Selling Price for GMAT Success and GRE Guarantee	Revenue of the Bundle
GMAT Success	3	$200	$600
GRE Guarantee	2	100	200
Total			$800

$$\text{Contribution margin percentage for the bundle} = \frac{\text{Contribution margin of the bundle}}{\text{Revenue of the bundle}} = \frac{\$300}{\$800} = 0.375 \text{ or } 37.5\%$$

$$\text{Breakeven revenues} = \frac{\text{Fixed costs}}{\text{Contribution margin \% for the bundle}} = \frac{\$4,500}{0.375} = \$12,000$$

$$\text{Number of bundles required to be sold to break even} = \frac{\text{Breakeven revenues}}{\text{Revenue per bundle}} = \frac{\$12,000}{\$800 \text{ per bundle}} = 15 \text{ bundles}$$

The breakeven point in units and dollars for GMAT Success and GRE Guarantee are as follows:

GMAT Success: 15 bundles × 3 units of GMAT Success per bundle = 45 units × $200 per unit = $9,000

GRE Guarantee: 15 bundles × 2 units of GRE Guarantee per bundle = 30 units × $100 per unit = $3,000

Recall that in all our calculations we have assumed that the budgeted sales mix (3 units of GMAT Success for every 2 units of GRE Guarantee) will not change at different levels of total unit sales.

Of course, there are many different sales mixes (in units) that result in a contribution margin of $4,500 and cause Emma to break even, as the following table shows:

Sales Mix (Units)		Contribution Margin from		
GMAT Success (1)	GRE Guarantee (2)	GMAT Success (3) = $80 × (1)	GRE Guarantee (4) = $30 × (2)	Total Contribution Margin (5) = (3) + (4)
48	22	$3,840	$ 660	$4,500
36	54	2,880	1,620	4,500
30	70	2,400	2,100	4,500

If for example, the sales mix changes to 3 units of GMAT Success for every 7 units of GRE Guarantee, the breakeven point increases from 75 units to 100 units, comprising 30 units of GMAT Success and 70 units of GRE Guarantee. The breakeven quantity increases because the sales mix has shifted toward the lower-contribution-margin product, GRE Guarantee ($30 per unit compared to GMAT Success's $80 per unit). In general, for any given total quantity of units sold, as the sales mix shifts toward units with lower contribution margins (more units of GRE Guarantee compared to GMAT Success), operating income will be lower.

How do companies choose their sales mix? They adjust their mix to respond to demand changes. For example, as gasoline prices increase and customers want smaller cars, auto companies shift their production mix to produce smaller cars.

The multi-product case has two cost drivers, GMAT Success and GRE Guarantee. It shows how CVP and breakeven analysis can be adapted to the case of multiple cost drivers. The key point is that many different combinations of cost drivers can result in a given contribution margin.

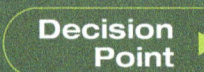

Decision Point

How can CVP analysis be applied to a company producing multiple products?

CVP Analysis in Service and Nonprofit Organizations

Thus far, our CVP analysis has focused on a merchandising company. CVP can also be applied to decisions by manufacturing companies like BMW, service companies like Bank of America, and nonprofit organizations like the United Way. To apply CVP analysis in service and nonprofit organizations, we need to focus on measuring their output, which is different from the tangible units sold by manufacturing and merchandising companies. Examples of output measures in various service and nonprofit industries are as follows:

Industry	Measure of Output
Airlines	Passenger miles
Hotels/motels	Room-nights occupied
Hospitals	Patient days
Universities	Student credit-hours

Consider an agency of the Massachusetts Department of Social Welfare with a $900,000 budget appropriation (its revenues) for 2011. This nonprofit agency's purpose is to assist handicapped people seeking employment. On average, the agency supplements each person's income by $5,000 annually. The agency's only other costs are fixed costs of rent and administrative salaries equal to $270,000. The agency manager wants to know how many people could be assisted in 2011. We can use CVP analysis here by setting operating income to $0. Let Q be the number of handicapped people to be assisted:

$$\text{Revenues} - \text{Variable costs} - \text{Fixed costs} = 0$$
$$\$900,000 - \$5,000\,Q - \$270,000 = 0$$
$$\$5,000\,Q = \$900,000 - \$270,000 = \$630,000$$
$$Q = \$630,000 \div \$5,000 \text{ per person} = 126 \text{ people}$$

Suppose the manager is concerned that the total budget appropriation for 2012 will be reduced by 15% to $900,000 × (1 − 0.15) = $765,000. The manager wants to know how many handicapped people could be assisted with this reduced budget. Assume the same amount of monetary assistance per person:

$$\$765,000 - \$5,000\,Q - \$270,000 = 0$$
$$\$5,000\,Q = \$765,000 - \$270,000 = \$495,000$$
$$Q = \$495,000 \div \$5,000 \text{ per person} = 99 \text{ people}$$

Note the following two characteristics of the CVP relationships in this nonprofit situation:

1. The percentage drop in the number of people assisted, $(126 - 99) \div 126$, or 21.4%, is greater than the 15% reduction in the budget appropriation. It is greater because the $270,000 in fixed costs still must be paid, leaving a proportionately lower budget to assist people. The percentage drop in service exceeds the percentage drop in budget appropriation.

2. Given the reduced budget appropriation (revenues) of $765,000, the manager can adjust operations to stay within this appropriation in one or more of three basic ways: (a) reduce the number of people assisted from the current 126, (b) reduce the variable cost (the extent of assistance per person) from the current $5,000 per person, or (c) reduce the total fixed costs from the current $270,000.

Contribution Margin Versus Gross Margin

In the following equations, we clearly distinguish contribution margin, which provides information for CVP analysis, from gross margin, a measure of competitiveness, as defined in Chapter 2.

$$\text{Gross margin} = \text{Revenues} - \text{Cost of goods sold}$$
$$\text{Contribution margin} = \text{Revenues} - \text{All variable costs}$$

Gross margin measures how much a company can charge for its products over and above the cost of acquiring or producing them. Companies, such as branded pharmaceuticals, have high gross margins because their products provide unique and distinctive benefits to consumers. Products such as televisions that operate in competitive markets have low gross margins. Contribution margin indicates how much of a company's revenues are available to cover fixed costs. It helps in assessing risk of loss. Risk of loss is low (high) if, when sales are low, contribution margin exceeds (is less than) fixed costs. Gross margin and contribution margin are related but give different insights. For example, a company operating in a competitive market with a low gross margin will have a low risk of loss if its fixed costs are small.

Consider the distinction between gross margin and contribution margin in the context of manufacturing companies. In the manufacturing sector, contribution margin and gross margin differ in two respects: fixed manufacturing costs and variable nonmanufacturing costs. The following example (figures assumed) illustrates this difference:

Contribution Income Statement Emphasizing Contribution Margin (in 000s)			Financial Accounting Income Statement Emphasizing Gross Margin (in 000s)	
Revenues		$1,000	Revenues	$1,000
Variable manufacturing costs	$250		Cost of goods sold (variable manufacturing costs, $250 + fixed manufacturing costs, $160)	410
Variable nonmanufacturing costs	270	520		
Contribution margin		480	Gross margin	590
Fixed manufacturing costs	160		Nonmanufacturing costs	
Fixed nonmanufacturing costs	138	298	(variable, $270 + fixed $138)	408
Operating income		$ 182	Operating income	$ 182

Fixed manufacturing costs of $160,000 are not deducted from revenues when computing contribution margin but are deducted when computing gross margin. Cost of goods sold in a manufacturing company includes all variable manufacturing costs and all fixed manufacturing costs ($250,000 + $160,000). Variable nonmanufacturing costs (such as commissions paid to salespersons) of $270,000 are deducted from revenues when computing contribution margin but are not deducted when computing gross margin.

Like contribution margin, gross margin can be expressed as a total, as an amount per unit, or as a percentage. For example, the **gross margin percentage** is the gross margin divided by revenues—59% ($590 ÷ $1,000) in our manufacturing-sector example.

One reason why gross margin and contribution margin are confused with each other is that the two are identical in the case of merchandising companies. That's because cost of goods sold equals the variable cost of goods purchased (and subsequently sold).

Problem for Self-Study

Wembley Travel Agency specializes in flights between Los Angeles and London. It books passengers on United Airlines at $900 per round-trip ticket. Until last month, United paid Wembley a commission of 10% of the ticket price paid by each passenger. This commission was Wembley's only source of revenues. Wembley's fixed costs are $14,000 per month (for salaries, rent, and so on), and its variable costs are $20 per ticket purchased for a passenger. This $20 includes a $15 per ticket delivery fee paid to Federal Express. (To keep the analysis simple, we assume each round-trip ticket purchased is delivered in a separate package. Thus, the $15 delivery fee applies to each ticket.)

United Airlines has just announced a revised payment schedule for all travel agents. It will now pay travel agents a 10% commission per ticket up to a maximum of $50. Any ticket costing more than $500 generates only a $50 commission, regardless of the ticket price.

Required

1. Under the old 10% commission structure, how many round-trip tickets must Wembley sell each month (a) to break even and (b) to earn an operating income of $7,000?
2. How does United's revised payment schedule affect your answers to (a) and (b) in requirement 1?

Solution

1. Wembley receives a 10% commission on each ticket: 10% × $900 = $90. Thus,

$$\text{Selling price} = \$90 \text{ per ticket}$$
$$\text{Variable cost per unit} = \$20 \text{ per ticket}$$
$$\text{Contribution margin per unit} = \$90 - \$20 = \$70 \text{ per ticket}$$
$$\text{Fixed costs} = \$14,000 \text{ per month}$$

a. $$\frac{\text{Breakeven number}}{\text{of tickets}} = \frac{\text{Fixed costs}}{\text{Contribution margin per unit}} = \frac{\$14,000}{\$70 \text{ per ticket}} = 200 \text{ tickets}$$

b. When target operating income = $7,000 per month,

$$\frac{\text{Quantity of tickets}}{\text{required to be sold}} = \frac{\text{Fixed costs + Target operating income}}{\text{Contribution margin per unit}}$$
$$= \frac{\$14,000 + \$7,000}{\$70 \text{ per ticket}} = \frac{\$21,000}{\$70 \text{ per ticket}} = 300 \text{ tickets}$$

2. Under the new system, Wembley would receive only $50 on the $900 ticket. Thus,

$$\text{Selling price} = \$50 \text{ per ticket}$$
$$\text{Variable cost per unit} = \$20 \text{ per ticket}$$
$$\text{Contribution margin per unit} = \$50 - \$20 = \$30 \text{ per ticket}$$
$$\text{Fixed costs} = \$14,000 \text{ per month}$$

a. $$\frac{\text{Breakeven number}}{\text{of tickets}} = \frac{\$14,000}{\$30 \text{ per ticket}} = 467 \text{ tickets (rounded up)}$$

b. $\dfrac{\text{Quantity of tickets}}{\text{required to be sold}} = \dfrac{\$21,000}{\$30 \text{ per ticket}} = 700 \text{ tickets}$

The $50 cap on the commission paid per ticket causes the breakeven point to more than double (from 200 to 467 tickets) and the tickets required to be sold to earn $7,000 per month to also more than double (from 300 to 700 tickets). As would be expected, travel agents reacted very negatively to the United Airlines announcement to change commission payments. Unfortunately for travel agents, other airlines also changed their commission structure in similar ways.

Decision Points

The following question-and-answer format summarizes the chapter's learning objectives. Each decision presents a key question related to a learning objective. The guidelines are the answer to that question.

Decision	Guidelines
1. How can CVP analysis assist managers?	CVP analysis assists managers in understanding the behavior of a product's or service's total costs, total revenues, and operating income as changes occur in the output level, selling price, variable costs, or fixed costs.
2. How can managers determine the breakeven point or the output needed to achieve a target operating income?	The breakeven point is the quantity of output at which total revenues equal total costs. The three methods for computing the breakeven point and the quantity of output to achieve target operating income are the equation method, the contribution margin method, and the graph method. Each method is merely a restatement of the others. Managers often select the method they find easiest to use in the specific decision situation.
3. How can managers incorporate income taxes into CVP analysis?	Income taxes can be incorporated into CVP analysis by using target net income to calculate the corresponding target operating income. The breakeven point is unaffected by income taxes because no income taxes are paid when operating income equals zero.
4. How do managers use CVP analysis to make decisions?	Managers compare how revenues, costs, and contribution margins change across various alternatives. They then choose the alternative that maximizes operating income.
5. What can managers do to cope with uncertainty or changes in underlying assumptions?	Sensitivity analysis, a "what-if" technique, examines how an outcome will change if the original predicted data are not achieved or if an underlying assumption changes. When making decisions, managers use CVP analysis to compare contribution margins and fixed costs under different assumptions. Managers also calculate the margin of safety equal to budgeted revenues minus breakeven revenues.
6. How should managers choose between different variable-cost/fixed-cost structures?	Choosing the variable-cost/fixed-cost structure is a strategic decision for companies. CVP analysis highlights the risk of losses when revenues are low and the upside profits when revenues are high for different proportions of variable and fixed costs in a company's cost structure.
7. How can CVP analysis be applied to a company producing multiple products?	CVP analysis can be applied to a company producing multiple products by assuming the sales mix of products sold remains constant as the total quantity of units sold changes.

Appendix

Decision Models and Uncertainty

This appendix explores the characteristics of uncertainty, describes an approach managers can use to make decisions in a world of uncertainty, and illustrates the insights gained when uncertainty is recognized in CVP analysis.

Coping with Uncertainty[2]

In the face of uncertainty, managers rely on decision models to help them make the right choices.

Role of a Decision Model

Uncertainty is the possibility that an actual amount will deviate from an expected amount. In the GMAT Success example, Emma might forecast sales at 42 units, but actual sales might turn out to be 30 units or 60 units. A decision model helps managers deal with such uncertainty. It is a formal method for making a choice, commonly involving both quantitative and qualitative analyses. The quantitative analysis usually includes the following steps:

Step 1: Identify a choice criterion. A **choice criterion** is an objective that can be quantified such as maximize income or minimize costs. Managers use the choice criterion to choose the best alternative action. Emma's choice criterion is to maximize expected operating income at the Chicago college fair.

Step 2: Identify the set of alternative actions that can be taken. We use the letter a with subscripts $_1$, $_2$, and $_3$ to distinguish each of Emma's three possible actions:

$$a_1 = \text{Pay \$2,000 fixed fee}$$
$$a_2 = \text{Pay \$800 fixed fee plus 15\% of GMAT Success revenues}$$
$$a_3 = \text{Pay 25\% of GMAT Success revenues with no fixed fee}$$

Step 3: Identify the set of events that can occur. An **event** is a possible relevant occurrence, such as the actual number of GMAT Success packages Emma might sell at the fair. The set of events should be mutually exclusive and collectively exhaustive. Events are mutually exclusive if they cannot occur at the same time. Events are collectively exhaustive if, taken together, they make up the entire set of possible relevant occurrences (no other event can occur). Examples of mutually exclusive and collectively exhaustive events are growth, decline, or no change in industry demand, and increase, decrease, or no change in interest rates. Only one event out of the entire set of mutually exclusive and collectively exhaustive events will actually occur.

Suppose Emma's only uncertainty is the number of units of GMAT Success that she can sell. For simplicity, suppose Emma estimates that sales will be either 30 or 60 units. This set of events is mutually exclusive because clearly sales of 30 units and 60 units cannot both occur at the same time. It is collectively exhaustive because under our assumptions, sales cannot be anything other than 30 or 60 units. We use the letter x with subscripts $_1$ and $_2$ to distinguish the set of mutually exclusive and collectively exhaustive events:

$$x_1 = \text{30 units}$$
$$x_2 = \text{60 units}$$

Step 4: Assign a probability to each event that can occur. A **probability** is the likelihood or chance that an event will occur. The decision model approach to coping with uncertainty assigns probabilities to events. A **probability distribution** describes the likelihood, or the probability, that each of the mutually exclusive and collectively exhaustive set of events will occur. In some cases, there will be much evidence to guide the assignment of probabilities. For example, the probability of obtaining heads in the toss of a coin is 1/2 and that of drawing a particular playing card from a standard, well-shuffled deck is 1/52. In business, the probability of having a specified percentage of defective units may be assigned with great confidence on the basis of production experience with thousands of units. In other cases, there will be little evidence supporting estimated probabilities—for example, expected sales of a new pharmaceutical product next year.

Suppose that Emma, on the basis of past experience, assesses a 60% chance, or a 6/10 probability, that she will sell 30 units and a 40% chance, or a 4/10 probability, that she will sell 60 units. Using $P(x)$ as the notation for the probability of an event, the probabilities are as follows:

$$P(x_1) = 6/10 = 0.60$$
$$P(x_2) = 4/10 = 0.40$$

The sum of these probabilities must equal 1.00 because these events are mutually exclusive and collectively exhaustive.

---

[2] The presentation here draws (in part) from teaching notes prepared by R. Williamson.

Exhibit 3-6 Decision Table for GMAT Success

	A	B	C	D	E	F	G	H	I
		Home Insert Page Layout Formulas Data Review View							
1	Selling price =	$200				Operating Income			
2	Package cost =	$120				Under Each Possible Event			
3			Percentage						
4		Fixed	of Fair	Event x_1: Units Sold = 30			Event x_2: Units Sold = 60		
5	Actions	Fee	Revenues	Probability(x_1) = 0.60			Probability(x_2) = 0.40		
6	a_1: Pay $2,000 fixed fee	$2,000	0%	$400^l			$2,800^m		
7	a_2: Pay $800 fixed fee plus 15% of revenues	$ 800	15%	$700^n			$2,200^p		
8	a_3: Pay 25% of revenues with no fixed fee	$ 0	25%	$900^q			$1,800^r		
9									
10	^{l}Operating income = ($200 – $120)(30) – $2,000	=	$ 400						
11	^{m}Operating income = ($200 – $120)(60) – $2,000	=	$2,800						
12	^{n}Operating income = ($200 – $120 – 15% × $200)(30) – $800	=	$ 700						
13	^{p}Operating income = ($200 – $120 – 15% × $200)(60) – $800	=	$2,200						
14	^{q}Operating income = ($200 – $120 – 25% × $200)(30)	=	$ 900						
15	^{r}Operating income = ($200 – $120 – 25% × $200)(60)	=	$1,800						

Step 5: Identify the set of possible outcomes. Outcomes specify, in terms of the choice criterion, the predicted economic results of the various possible combinations of actions and events. In the GMAT Success example, the outcomes are the six possible operating incomes displayed in the decision table in Exhibit 3-6. A **decision table** is a summary of the alternative actions, events, outcomes, and probabilities of events.

Distinguish among actions, events, and outcomes. Actions are decision choices available to managers—for example, the particular rental alternatives that Emma can choose. Events are the set of all relevant occurrences that can happen—for example, the different quantities of GMAT Success packages that may be sold at the fair. The outcome is operating income, which depends both on the action the manager selects (rental alternative chosen) and the event that occurs (the quantity of packages sold).

Exhibit 3-7 presents an overview of relationships among a decision model, the implementation of a chosen action, its outcome, and a subsequent performance evaluation. Thoughtful managers step back and evaluate what happened and learn from their experiences. This learning serves as feedback for adapting the decision model for future actions.

Expected Value

An **expected value** is the weighted average of the outcomes, with the probability of each outcome serving as the weight. When the outcomes are measured in monetary terms, expected value is often called **expected monetary value.** Using information in Exhibit 3-6, the expected monetary value of each booth-rental alternative denoted by $E(a_1)$, $E(a_2)$, and $E(a_3)$ is as follows:

Pay $2,000 fixed fee: $E(a_1) = (0.60 \times \$400) + (0.40 \times \$2,800) = \$1,360$

Pay $800 fixed fee plus 15% of revenues: $E(a_2) = (0.60 \times \$700) + (0.40 \times \$2,200) = \$1,300$

Pay 25% of revenues with no fixed fee: $E(a_3) = (0.60 \times \$900) + (0.40 \times \$1,800) = \$1,260$

Exhibit 3-7 A Decision Model and Its Link to Performance Evaluation

Decision Model
1. Choice criterion
2. Set of alternative actions
3. Set of relevant events
4. Set of probabilities
5. Set of possible outcomes

→ Implementation of Chosen Action → Uncertainty Resolved* → Outcome of Chosen Action → Performance Evaluation

Feedback

*Uncertainty resolved means the event becomes known.

To maximize expected operating income, Emma should select action a_1—pay the fair organizers a $2,000 fixed fee.

To interpret the expected value of selecting action a_1, imagine that Emma attends many fairs, each with the probability distribution of operating incomes given in Exhibit 3-6. For a specific fair, Emma will earn operating income of either $400, if she sells 30 units, or $2,800, if she sells 60 units. But if Emma attends 100 fairs, she will expect to earn $400 operating income 60% of the time (at 60 fairs), and $2,800 operating income 40% of the time (at 40 fairs), for a total operating income of $136,000 ($400 × 60 + $2,800 × 40). The expected value of $1,360 is the operating income per fair that Emma will earn when averaged across all fairs ($136,000 ÷ 100). Of course, in many real-world situations, managers must make one-time decisions under uncertainty. Even in these cases, expected value is a useful tool for choosing among alternatives.

Consider the effect of uncertainty on the preferred action choice. If Emma were certain she would sell only 30 units (that is, $P(x_1) = 1$), she would prefer alternative a_3—pay 25% of revenues with no fixed fee. To follow this reasoning, examine Exhibit 3-6. When 30 units are sold, alternative a_3 yields the maximum operating income of $900. Because fixed costs are $0, booth-rental costs are lower, equal to $1,500 (25% of revenues = 0.25 × $200 per unit × 30 units), when sales are low.

However, if Emma were certain she would sell 60 packages (that is, $P(x_2) = 1$), she would prefer alternative a_1—pay a $2,000 fixed fee. Exhibit 3-6 indicates that when 60 units are sold, alternative a_1 yields the maximum operating income of $2,800. Rental payments under a_2 and a_3 increase with units sold but are fixed under a_1.

Despite the high probability of selling only 30 units, Emma still prefers to take action a_1, which is to pay a fixed fee of $2,000. That's because the high risk of low operating income (the 60% probability of selling only 30 units) is more than offset by the high return from selling 60 units, which has a 40% probability. If Emma were more averse to risk (measured in our example by the difference between operating incomes when 30 versus 60 units are sold), she might have preferred action a_2 or a_3. For example, action a_2 ensures an operating income of at least $700, greater than the operating income of $400 that she would earn under action a_1 if only 30 units were sold. Of course, choosing a_2 limits the upside potential to $2,200 relative to $2,800 under a_1, if 60 units are sold. If Emma is very concerned about downside risk, however, she may be willing to forgo some upside benefits to protect against a $400 outcome by choosing a_2.[3]

Good Decisions and Good Outcomes

Always distinguish between a good decision and a good outcome. One can exist without the other. Suppose you are offered a one-time-only gamble tossing a coin. You will win $20 if the event is heads, but you will lose $1 if the event is tails. As a decision maker, you proceed through the logical phases: gathering information, assessing outcomes, and making a choice. You accept the bet. Why? Because the expected value is $9.50 [0.5($20) + 0.5(−$1)]. The coin is tossed and the event is tails. You lose. From your viewpoint, this was a good decision but a bad outcome.

A decision can be made only on the basis of information that is available at the time of evaluating and making the decision. By definition, uncertainty rules out guaranteeing that the best outcome will always be obtained. As in our example, it is possible that bad luck will produce bad outcomes even when good decisions have been made. A bad outcome does not mean a bad decision was made. The best protection against a bad outcome is a good decision.

Terms to Learn

This chapter and the Glossary at the end of the book contain definitions of the following important terms:

breakeven point (BEP) (**p. 68**)

choice criterion (**p. 84**)

contribution income statement (**p. 65**)

contribution margin (**p. 64**)

contribution margin per unit (**p. 65**)

contribution margin percentage (**p. 65**)

contribution margin ratio (**p. 65**)

cost-volume-profit (CVP) analysis (**p. 63**)

decision table (**p. 85**)

degree of operating leverage (**p. 76**)

event (**p. 84**)

expected monetary value (**p. 85**)

expected value (**p. 85**)

gross margin percentage (**p. 82**)

margin of safety (**p. 74**)

net income (**p. 70**)

operating leverage (**p. 76**)

outcomes (**p. 85**)

probability (**p. 84**)

probability distribution (**p. 84**)

PV graph (**p. 70**)

revenue driver (**p. 68**)

sales mix (**p. 77**)

sensitivity analysis (**p. 73**)

uncertainty (**p. 75**)

---

[3] For more formal approaches, refer to Moore, J. and L. Weatherford. 2001. *Decision modeling with Microsoft Excel*, 6th ed. Upper Saddle River, NJ: Prentice Hall.

Assignment Material

Note: To underscore the basic CVP relationships, the assignment material ignores income taxes unless stated otherwise.

Questions

3-1 Define cost-volume-profit analysis.

3-2 Describe the assumptions underlying CVP analysis.

3-3 Distinguish between operating income and net income.

3-4 Define contribution margin, contribution margin per unit, and contribution margin percentage.

3-5 Describe three methods that can be used to express CVP relationships.

3-6 Why is it more accurate to describe the subject matter of this chapter as CVP analysis rather than as breakeven analysis?

3-7 "CVP analysis is both simple and simplistic. If you want realistic analysis to underpin your decisions, look beyond CVP analysis." Do you agree? Explain.

3-8 How does an increase in the income tax rate affect the breakeven point?

3-9 Describe sensitivity analysis. How has the advent of the electronic spreadsheet affected the use of sensitivity analysis?

3-10 Give an example of how a manager can decrease variable costs while increasing fixed costs.

3-11 Give an example of how a manager can increase variable costs while decreasing fixed costs.

3-12 What is operating leverage? How is knowing the degree of operating leverage helpful to managers?

3-13 "There is no such thing as a fixed cost. All costs can be 'unfixed' given sufficient time." Do you agree? What is the implication of your answer for CVP analysis?

3-14 How can a company with multiple products compute its breakeven point?

3-15 "In CVP analysis, gross margin is a less-useful concept than contribution margin." Do you agree? Explain briefly.

Exercises

3-16 CVP computations. Fill in the blanks for each of the following independent cases.

Case	Revenues	Variable Costs	Fixed Costs	Total Costs	Operating Income	Contribution Margin Percentage
a.		$500		$ 800	$1,200	
b.	$2,000		$300		$ 200	
c.	$1,000	$700		$1,000		
d.	$1,500		$300			40%

3-17 CVP computations. Garrett Manufacturing sold 410,000 units of its product for $68 per unit in 2011. Variable cost per unit is $60 and total fixed costs are $1,640,000.

Required

1. Calculate (a) contribution margin and (b) operating income.
2. Garrett's current manufacturing process is labor intensive. Kate Schoenen, Garrett's production manager, has proposed investing in state-of-the-art manufacturing equipment, which will increase the annual fixed costs to $5,330,000. The variable costs are expected to decrease to $54 per unit. Garrett expects to maintain the same sales volume and selling price next year. How would acceptance of Schoenen's proposal affect your answers to (a) and (b) in requirement 1?
3. Should Garrett accept Schoenen's proposal? Explain.

3-18 CVP analysis, changing revenues and costs. Sunny Spot Travel Agency specializes in flights between Toronto and Jamaica. It books passengers on Canadian Air. Sunny Spot's fixed costs are $23,500 per month. Canadian Air charges passengers $1,500 per round-trip ticket.

Calculate the number of tickets Sunny Spot must sell each month to (a) break even and (b) make a target operating income of $17,000 per month in each of the following independent cases.

Required

1. Sunny Spot's variable costs are $43 per ticket. Canadian Air pays Sunny Spot 6% commission on ticket price.
2. Sunny Spot's variable costs are $40 per ticket. Canadian Air pays Sunny Spot 6% commission on ticket price.
3. Sunny Spot's variable costs are $40 per ticket. Canadian Air pays $60 fixed commission per ticket to Sunny Spot. Comment on the results.
4. Sunny Spot's variable costs are $40 per ticket. It receives $60 commission per ticket from Canadian Air. It charges its customers a delivery fee of $5 per ticket. Comment on the results.

3-19 CVP exercises. The Super Donut owns and operates six doughnut outlets in and round Kansas City. You are given the following corporate budget data for next year:

Revenues	$10,000,000
Fixed costs	$ 1,800,000
Variable costs	$ 8,000,000

Variable costs change with respect to the number of doughnuts sold.

Required

Compute the budgeted operating income for each of the following deviations from the original budget data. (Consider each case independently.)

1. A 10% increase in contribution margin, holding revenues constant
2. A 10% decrease in contribution margin, holding revenues constant
3. A 5% increase in fixed costs
4. A 5% decrease in fixed costs
5. An 8% increase in units sold
6. An 8% decrease in units sold
7. A 10% increase in fixed costs and a 10% increase in units sold
8. A 5% increase in fixed costs and a 5% decrease in variable costs

3-20 CVP exercises. The Doral Company manufactures and sells pens. Currently, 5,000,000 units are sold per year at $0.50 per unit. Fixed costs are $900,000 per year. Variable costs are $0.30 per unit.

Required

Consider each case separately:
1a. What is the current annual operating income?
 b. What is the present breakeven point in revenues?

Compute the new operating income for each of the following changes:
2. A $0.04 per unit increase in variable costs
3. A 10% increase in fixed costs and a 10% increase in units sold
4. A 20% decrease in fixed costs, a 20% decrease in selling price, a 10% decrease in variable cost per unit, and a 40% increase in units sold

Compute the new breakeven point in units for each of the following changes:
5. A 10% increase in fixed costs
6. A 10% increase in selling price and a $20,000 increase in fixed costs

3-21 CVP analysis, income taxes. Brooke Motors is a small car dealership. On average, it sells a car for $27,000, which it purchases from the manufacturer for $23,000. Each month, Brooke Motors pays $48,200 in rent and utilities and $68,000 for salespeople's salaries. In addition to their salaries, salespeople are paid a commission of $600 for each car they sell. Brooke Motors also spends $13,000 each month for local advertisements. Its tax rate is 40%.

Required

1. How many cars must Brooke Motors sell each month to break even?
2. Brooke Motors has a target monthly net income of $51,000. What is its target monthly operating income? How many cars must be sold each month to reach the target monthly net income of $51,000?

3-22 CVP analysis, income taxes. The Express Banquet has two restaurants that are open 24-hours a day. Fixed costs for the two restaurants together total $459,000 per year. Service varies from a cup of coffee to full meals. The average sales check per customer is $8.50. The average cost of food and other variable costs for each customer is $3.40. The income tax rate is 30%. Target net income is $107,100.

Required

1. Compute the revenues needed to earn the target net income.
2. How many customers are needed to break even? To earn net income of $107,100?
3. Compute net income if the number of customers is 170,000.

3-23 CVP analysis, sensitivity analysis. Hoot Washington is the newly elected leader of the Republican Party. Media Publishers is negotiating to publish Hoot's Manifesto, a new book that promises to be an instant best-seller. The fixed costs of producing and marketing the book will be $500,000. The variable costs of producing and marketing will be $4.00 per copy sold. These costs are before any payments to Hoot. Hoot negotiates an up-front payment of $3 million, plus a 15% royalty rate on the net sales price of each book. The net sales price is the listed bookstore price of $30, minus the margin paid to the bookstore to sell the book. The normal bookstore margin of 30% of the listed price is expected to apply.

Required

1. Prepare a PV graph for Media Publishers.
2. How many copies must Media Publishers sell to (a) break even and (b) earn a target operating income of $2 million?
3. Examine the sensitivity of the breakeven point to the following changes:
   a. Decreasing the normal bookstore margin to 20% of the listed bookstore price of $30
   b. Increasing the listed bookstore price to $40 while keeping the bookstore margin at 30%
   c. Comment on the results

3-24 CVP analysis, margin of safety. Suppose Doral Corp.'s breakeven point is revenues of $1,100,000. Fixed costs are $660,000.

1. Compute the contribution margin percentage.
2. Compute the selling price if variable costs are $16 per unit.
3. Suppose 95,000 units are sold. Compute the margin of safety in units and dollars.

3-25 Operating leverage. Color Rugs is holding a two-week carpet sale at Jerry's Club, a local warehouse store. Color Rugs plans to sell carpets for $500 each. The company will purchase the carpets from a local distributor for $350 each, with the privilege of returning any unsold units for a full refund. Jerry's Club has offered Color Rugs two payment alternatives for the use of space.

■ Option 1: A fixed payment of $5,000 for the sale period

■ Option 2: 10% of total revenues earned during the sale period

Assume Color Rugs will incur no other costs.

1. Calculate the breakeven point in units for (a) option 1 and (b) option 2.
2. At what level of revenues will Color Rugs earn the same operating income under either option?
   a. For what range of unit sales will Color Rugs prefer option 1?
   b. For what range of unit sales will Color Rugs prefer option 2?
3. Calculate the degree of operating leverage at sales of 100 units for the two rental options.
4. Briefly explain and interpret your answer to requirement 3.

3-26 CVP analysis, international cost structure differences. Global Textiles, Inc., is considering three possible countries for the sole manufacturing site of its newest area rug: Singapore, Brazil, and the United States. All area rugs are to be sold to retail outlets in the United States for $250 per unit. These retail outlets add their own markup when selling to final customers. Fixed costs and variable cost per unit (area rug) differ in the three countries.

Country	Sales Price to Retail Outlets	Annual Fixed Costs	Variable Manufacturing Cost per Area Rug	Variable Marketing & Distribution Cost per Area Rug
Singapore	$250.00	$ 9,000,000	$75.00	$25.00
Brazil	250.00	8,400,000	60.00	15.00
United States	250.00	12,400,000	82.50	12.50

1. Compute the breakeven point for Global Textiles, Inc., in each country in (a) units sold and (b) revenues.
2. If Global Textiles, Inc., plans to produce and sell 75,000 rugs in 2011, what is the budgeted operating income for each of the three manufacturing locations? Comment on the results.

3-27 Sales mix, new and upgrade customers. Data 1-2-3 is a top-selling electronic spreadsheet product. Data is about to release version 5.0. It divides its customers into two groups: new customers and upgrade customers (those who previously purchased Data 1-2-3, 4.0 or earlier versions). Although the same physical product is provided to each customer group, sizable differences exist in selling prices and variable marketing costs:

	New Customers		Upgrade Customers	
Selling price		$275		$100
Variable costs				
Manufacturing	$35		$35	
Marketing	65	100	15	50
Contribution margin		$175		$ 50

The fixed costs of Data 1-2-3, 5.0 are $15,000,000. The planned sales mix in units is 60% new customers and 40% upgrade customers.

1. What is the Data 1-2-3, 5.0 breakeven point in units, assuming that the planned 60%:40% sales mix is attained?
2. If the sales mix is attained, what is the operating income when 220,000 total units are sold?
3. Show how the breakeven point in units changes with the following customer mixes:
   a. New 40% and Upgrade 60%
   b. New 80% and Upgrade 20%
   c. Comment on the results

3-28 Sales mix, three products. Bobbie's Bagel Shop sells only coffee and bagels. Bobbie estimates that every time she sells one bagel, she sells four cups of coffee. The budgeted cost information for Bobbie's products for 2011 follows:

	Coffee	Bagels
Selling Price	$2.50	$3.75
Product ingredients	$0.25	$0.50
Hourly sales staff (cost per unit)	$0.50	$1.00
Packaging	$0.50	$0.25
Fixed Costs		
Rent on store and equipment	$5,000	
Marketing and advertising cost	$2,000	

Required

1. How many cups of coffee and how many bagels must Bobbie sell in order to break even assuming the sales mix of four cups of coffee to one bagel, given previously?
2. If the sales mix is four cups of coffee to one bagel, how many units of each product does Bobbie need to sell to earn operating income before tax of $28,000?
3. Assume that Bobbie decides to add the sale of muffins to her product mix. The selling price for muffins is $3.00 and the related variable costs are $0.75. Assuming a sales mix of three cups of coffee to two bagels to one muffin, how many units of each product does Bobbie need to sell in order to break even? Comment on the results.

3-29 CVP, Not for profit. Monroe Classical Music Society is a not-for-profit organization that brings guest artists to the community's greater metropolitan area. The Music Society just bought a small concert hall in the center of town to house its performances. The mortgage payments on the concert hall are expected to be $2,000 per month. The organization pays its guest performers $1,000 per concert and anticipates corresponding ticket sales to be $2,500 per event. The Music Society also incurs costs of approximately $500 per concert for marketing and advertising. The organization pays its artistic director $50,000 per year and expects to receive $40,000 in donations in addition to its ticket sales.

Required

1. If the Monroe Classical Music Society just breaks even, how many concerts does it hold?
2. In addition to the organization's artistic director, the Music Society would like to hire a marketing director for $40,000 per year. What is the breakeven point? The Music Society anticipates that the addition of a marketing director would allow the organization to increase the number of concerts to 60 per year. What is the Music Society's operating income/(loss) if it hires the new marketing director?
3. The Music Society expects to receive a grant that would provide the organization with an additional $20,000 toward the payment of the marketing director's salary. What is the breakeven point if the Music Society hires the marketing director and receives the grant?

3-30 Contribution margin, decision making. Lurvey Men's Clothing's revenues and cost data for 2011 are as follows:

Revenues		$600,000
Cost of goods sold		300,000
Gross margin		300,000
Operating costs:		
Salaries fixed	$170,000	
Sales commissions (10% of sales)	60,000	
Depreciation of equipment and fixtures	20,000	
Store rent ($4,500 per month)	54,000	
Other operating costs	45,000	349,000
Operating income (loss)		$ (49,000)

Mr. Lurvey, the owner of the store, is unhappy with the operating results. An analysis of other operating costs reveals that it includes $30,000 variable costs, which vary with sales volume, and $15,000 (fixed) costs.

Required

1. Compute the contribution margin of Lurvey Men's Clothing.
2. Compute the contribution margin percentage.
3. Mr. Lurvey estimates that he can increase revenues by 15% by incurring additional advertising costs of $13,000. Calculate the impact of the additional advertising costs on operating income.

3-31 Contribution margin, gross margin, and margin of safety. Mirabella Cosmetics manufactures and sells a face cream to small ethnic stores in the greater New York area. It presents the monthly operating income statement shown here to George Lopez, a potential investor in the business. Help Mr. Lopez understand Mirabella's cost structure.

	A	B	C	D
	Home	Insert	Page Layout	Formulas	Data	Review	View
1	Mirabella Cosmetics			
2	Operating Income Statement, June 2011			
3	Units sold			10,000
4	Revenues			$100,000
5	Cost of goods sold			
6	Variable manufacturing costs		$55,000	
7	Fixed manufacturing costs		20,000	
8	Total			75,000
9	Gross margin			25,000
10	Operating costs			
11	Variable marketing costs		$ 5,000	
12	Fixed marketing & administration costs		10,000	
13	Total operating costs			15,000
14	Operating income			$ 10,000

Required

1. Recast the income statement to emphasize contribution margin.
2. Calculate the contribution margin percentage and breakeven point in units and revenues for June 2011.
3. What is the margin of safety (in units) for June 2011?
4. If sales in June were only 8,000 units and Mirabella's tax rate is 30%, calculate its net income.

3-32 Uncertainty and expected costs. Foodmart Corp, an international retail giant, is considering implementing a new business to business (B2B) information system for processing purchase orders. The current system costs Foodmart $2,500,000 per month and $50 per order. Foodmart has two options, a partially automated B2B and a fully automated B2B system. The partially automated B2B system will have a fixed cost of $10,000,000 per month and a variable cost of $40 per order. The fully automated B2B system has a fixed cost of $20,000,000 per month and $25 per order.

Based on data from the last two years, Foodmart has determined the following distribution on monthly orders:

Monthly Number of Orders	Probability
350,000	0.15
450,000	0.20
550,000	0.35
650,000	0.20
750,000	0.10

Required

1. Prepare a table showing the cost of each plan for each quantity of monthly orders.
2. What is the expected cost of each plan?
3. In addition to the information systems costs, what other factors should Foodmart consider before deciding to implement a new B2B system?

Problems

3-33 CVP analysis, service firm. Lifetime Escapes generates average revenue of $5,000 per person on its five-day package tours to wildlife parks in Kenya. The variable costs per person are as follows:

Airfare	$1,400
Hotel accommodations	1,100
Meals	300
Ground transportation	100
Park tickets and other costs	800
Total	$3,700

Annual fixed costs total $520,000.

1. Calculate the number of package tours that must be sold to break even.
2. Calculate the revenue needed to earn a target operating income of $91,000.
3. If fixed costs increase by $32,000, what decrease in variable cost per person must be achieved to maintain the breakeven point calculated in requirement 1?

3-34 CVP, target operating income, service firm. Snow Leopard Daycare provides daycare for children Mondays through Fridays. Its monthly variable costs per child are as follows:

Lunch and snacks	$150
Educational supplies	60
Other supplies (paper products, toiletries, etc.)	20
Total	$230

Monthly fixed costs consist of the following:

Rent	$2,150
Utilities	200
Insurance	250
Salaries	2,350
Miscellaneous	650
Total	$5,600

Snow Leopard charges each parent $580 per child.

1. Calculate the breakeven point.
2. Snow Leopard's target operating income is $10,500 per month. Compute the number of children who must be enrolled to achieve the target operating income.
3. Snow Leopard lost its lease and had to move to another building. Monthly rent for the new building is $3,150. At the suggestion of parents, Snow Leopard plans to take children on field trips. Monthly costs of the field trips are $1,300. By how much should Snow Leopard increase fees per child to meet the target operating income of $10,500 per month, assuming the same number of children as in requirement 2?

3-35 CVP analysis, margin of safety. (CMA, adapted) Technology Solutions sells a ready-to-use software product for small businesses. The current selling price is $300. Projected operating income for 2011 is $490,000 based on a sales volume of 10,000 units. Variable costs of producing the software are $120 per unit sold plus an additional cost of $5 per unit for shipping and handling. Technology Solutions annual fixed costs are $1,260,000.

1. Calculate Technology Solutions breakeven point and margin of safety in units.
2. Calculate the company's operating income for 2011 if there is a 10% increase in unit sales.
3. For 2012, management expects that the per unit production cost of the software will increase by 30%, but the shipping and handling costs per unit will decrease by 20%. Calculate the sales revenue Technology Solutions must generate for 2012 to maintain the current year's operating income if the selling price remains unchanged, assuming all other data as in the original problem.

3-36 CVP analysis, income taxes. (CMA, adapted) R. A. Ro and Company, a manufacturer of quality handmade walnut bowls, has had a steady growth in sales for the past five years. However, increased competition has led Mr. Ro, the president, to believe that an aggressive marketing campaign will be necessary next year to maintain the company's present growth. To prepare for next year's marketing campaign, the company's controller has prepared and presented Mr. Ro with the following data for the current year, 2011:

Variable cost (per bowl)	
Direct materials	$ 3.25
Direct manufacturing labor	8.00
Variable overhead (manufacturing, marketing, distribution, and customer service)	2.50
Total variable cost per bowl	$ 13.75
Fixed costs	
Manufacturing	$ 25,000
Marketing, distribution, and customer service	110,000
Total fixed costs	$135,000
Selling price	25.00
Expected sales, 20,000 units	$500,000
Income tax rate	40%

1. What is the projected net income for 2011?
2. What is the breakeven point in units for 2011?
3. Mr. Ro has set the revenue target for 2012 at a level of $550,000 (or 22,000 bowls). He believes an additional marketing cost of $11,250 for advertising in 2012, with all other costs remaining constant, will be necessary to attain the revenue target. What is the net income for 2012 if the additional $11,250 is spent and the revenue target is met?
4. What is the breakeven point in revenues for 2012 if the additional $11,250 is spent for advertising?
5. If the additional $11,250 is spent, what are the required 2012 revenues for 2012 net income to equal 2011 net income?
6. At a sales level of 22,000 units, what maximum amount can be spent on advertising if a 2012 net income of $60,000 is desired?

3-37 CVP, sensitivity analysis. The Brown Shoe Company produces its famous shoe, the Divine Loafer that sells for $60 per pair. Operating income for 2011 is as follows:

Sales revenue ($60 per pair)	$300,000
Variable cost ($25 per pair)	125,000
Contribution margin	175,000
Fixed cost	100,000
Operating income	$ 75,000

Brown Shoe Company would like to increase its profitability over the next year by at least 25%. To do so, the company is considering the following options:

1. Replace a portion of its variable labor with an automated machining process. This would result in a 20% decrease in variable cost per unit, but a 15% increase in fixed costs. Sales would remain the same.
2. Spend $30,000 on a new advertising campaign, which would increase sales by 20%..
3. Increase both selling price by $10 per unit and variable costs by $7 per unit by using a higher quality leather material in the production of its shoes. The higher priced shoe would cause demand to drop by approximately 10%.
4. Add a second manufacturing facility which would double Brown's fixed costs, but would increase sales by 60%.

Evaluate each of the alternatives considered by Brown Shoes. Do any of the options meet or exceed Brown's targeted increase in income of 25%? What should Brown do?

3-38 CVP analysis, shoe stores. The WalkRite Shoe Company operates a chain of shoe stores that sell 10 different styles of inexpensive men's shoes with identical unit costs and selling prices. A unit is defined as a pair of shoes. Each store has a store manager who is paid a fixed salary. Individual salespeople receive a fixed salary and a sales commission. WalkRite is considering opening another store that is expected to have the revenue and cost relationships shown here:

	A	B	C	D	E
	Home Insert Page Layout Formulas Data Review View				
1	Unit Variable Data (per pair of shoes)			Annual Fixed Costs	
2	Selling price	$30.00		Rent	$ 60,000
3	Cost of shoes	$19.50		Salaries	200,000
4	Sales commission	1.50		Advertising	80,000
5	Variable cost per unit	$21.00		Other fixed costs	20,000
6				Total fixed costs	$360,000

Consider each question independently:

1. What is the annual breakeven point in (a) units sold and (b) revenues?
2. If 35,000 units are sold, what will be the store's operating income (loss)?
3. If sales commissions are discontinued and fixed salaries are raised by a total of $81,000, what would be the annual breakeven point in (a) units sold and (b) revenues?
4. Refer to the original data. If, in addition to his fixed salary, the store manager is paid a commission of $0.30 per unit sold, what would be the annual breakeven point in (a) units sold and (b) revenues?
5. Refer to the original data. If, in addition to his fixed salary, the store manager is paid a commission of $0.30 *per unit in excess of the breakeven point*, what would be the store's operating income if 50,000 units were sold?

3-39 CVP analysis, shoe stores (continuation of 3-38). Refer to requirement 3 of Problem 3-38. In this problem, assume the role of the owner of WalkRite.

Required

1. Calculate the number of units sold at which the owner of WalkRite would be indifferent between the original salary-plus-commissions plan for salespeople and the higher fixed-salaries-only plan.
2. As owner, which sales compensation plan would you choose if forecasted annual sales of the new store were at least 55,000 units? What do you think of the motivational aspect of your chosen compensation plan?
3. Suppose the target operating income is $168,000. How many units must be sold to reach the target operating income under (a) the original salary-plus-commissions plan and (b) the higher-fixed-salaries-only plan?
4. You open the new store on January 1, 2011, with the original salary-plus-commission compensation plan in place. Because you expect the cost of the shoes to rise due to inflation, you place a firm bulk order for 50,000 shoes and lock in the $19.50 price per unit. But, toward the end of the year, only 48,000 shoes are sold, and you authorize a markdown of the remaining inventory to $18 per unit. Finally, all units are sold. Salespeople, as usual, get paid a commission of 5% of revenues. What is the annual operating income for the store?

3-40 Alternate cost structures, uncertainty, and sensitivity analysis. Stylewise Printing Company currently leases its only copy machine for $1,000 a month. The company is considering replacing this leasing agreement with a new contract that is entirely commission based. Under the new agreement Stylewise would pay a commission for its printing at a rate of $10 for every 500 pages printed. The company currently charges $0.15 per page to its customers. The paper used in printing costs the company $.03 per page and other variable costs, including hourly labor amount to $.04 per page.

Required

1. What is the company's breakeven point under the current leasing agreement? What is it under the new commission based agreement?
2. For what range of sales levels will Stylewise prefer (a) the fixed lease agreement (b) the commission agreement?
3. Do this question only if you have covered the chapter appendix in your class. Stylewise estimates that the company is equally likely to sell 20,000; 40,000; 60,000; 80,000; or 100,000 pages of print. Using information from the original problem, prepare a table that shows the expected profit at each sales level under the fixed leasing agreement and under the commission based agreement. What is the expected value of each agreement? Which agreement should Stylewise choose?

3-41 CVP, alternative cost structures. PC Planet has just opened its doors. The new retail store sells refurbished computers at a significant discount from market prices. The computers cost PC Planet $100 to purchase and require 10 hours of labor at $15 per hour. Additional variable costs, including wages for sales personnel, are $50 per computer. The newly refurbished computers are resold to customers for $500. Rent on the retail store costs the company $4,000 per month.

Required

1. How many computers does PC Planet have to sell each month to break even?
2. If PC Planet wants to earn $5,000 per month after all expenses, how many computers does the company need to sell?
3. PC Planet can purchase already refurbished computers for $200. This would mean that all labor required to refurbish the computers could be eliminated. What would PC Planet's new breakeven point be if it decided to purchase the computers already refurbished?
4. Instead of paying the monthly rental fee for the retail space, PC Planet has the option of paying its landlord a 20% commission on sales. Assuming the original facts in the problem, at what sales level would PC Planet be indifferent between paying a fixed amount of monthly rent and paying a 20% commission on sales?

3-42 CVP analysis, income taxes, sensitivity. (CMA, adapted) Agro Engine Company manufactures and sells diesel engines for use in small farming equipment. For its 2012 budget, Agro Engine Company estimates the following:

Selling price	$ 3,000
Variable cost per engine	$ 500
Annual fixed costs	$3,000,000
Net income	$1,500,000
Income tax rate	25%

The first quarter income statement, as of March 31, reported that sales were not meeting expectations. During the first quarter, only 300 units had been sold at the current price of $3,000. The income statement showed that variable and fixed costs were as planned, which meant that the 2012 annual net income projection would not be met unless management took action. A management committee was formed and presented the following mutually exclusive alternatives to the president:

a. Reduce the selling price by 20%. The sales organization forecasts that at this significantly reduced price, 2,000 units can be sold during the remainder of the year. Total fixed costs and variable cost per unit will stay as budgeted.

b. Lower variable cost per unit by $50 through the use of less-expensive direct materials. The selling price will also be reduced by $250, and sales of 1,800 units are expected for the remainder of the year.

c. Reduce fixed costs by 20% and lower the selling price by 10%. Variable cost per unit will be unchanged. Sales of 1,700 units are expected for the remainder of the year.

1. If no changes are made to the selling price or cost structure, determine the number of units that Agro Engine Company must sell (a) to break even and (b) to achieve its net income objective.   **Required**

2. Determine which alternative Agro Engine should select to achieve its net income objective. Show your calculations.

3-43 Choosing between compensation plans, operating leverage. (CMA, adapted) Marston Corporation manufactures pharmaceutical products that are sold through a network of external sales agents. The agents are paid a commission of 18% of revenues. Marston is considering replacing the sales agents with its own salespeople, who would be paid a commission of 10% of revenues and total salaries of $2,080,000. The income statement for the year ending December 31, 2011, under the two scenarios is shown here.

	A	B	C	D	E
	Home	Insert	Page Layout	Formulas	Data	Review	View
	A	B	C	D	E
1	Marston Corporation				
2	Income Statement				
3	For the Year Ended December 31, 2011				
4		Using Sales Agents		Using Own Sales Force	
5	Revenues		$26,000,000		$26,000,000
6	Cost of goods sold				
7	Variable	$11,700,000		$11,700,000	
8	Fixed	2,870,000	14,570,000	2,870,000	14,570,000
9	Gross margin		11,430,000		11,430,000
10	Marketing costs				
11	Commissions	$ 4,680,000		$ 2,600,000	
12	Fixed costs	3,420,000	8,100,000	5,500,000	8,100,000
13	Operating income		$ 3,330,000		$ 3,330,000

1. Calculate Marston's 2011 contribution margin percentage, breakeven revenues, and degree of operating leverage under the two scenarios.   **Required**

2. Describe the advantages and disadvantages of each type of sales alternative.

3. In 2012, Marston uses its own salespeople, who demand a 15% commission. If all other cost behavior patterns are unchanged, how much revenue must the salespeople generate in order to earn the same operating income as in 2011?

3-44 Sales mix, three products. The Ronowski Company has three product lines of belts—A, B, and C— with contribution margins of $3, $2, and $1, respectively. The president foresees sales of 200,000 units in the coming period, consisting of 20,000 units of A, 100,000 units of B, and 80,000 units of C. The company's fixed costs for the period are $255,000.

1. What is the company's breakeven point in units, assuming that the given sales mix is maintained?   **Required**

2. If the sales mix is maintained, what is the total contribution margin when 200,000 units are sold? What is the operating income?

3. What would operating income be if 20,000 units of A, 80,000 units of B, and 100,000 units of C were sold? What is the new breakeven point in units if these relationships persist in the next period?

3-45 Multiproduct CVP and decision making. Pure Water Products produces two types of water filters. One attaches to the faucet and cleans all water that passes through the faucet. The other is a pitcher-cum-filter that only purifies water meant for drinking.

The unit that attaches to the faucet is sold for $80 and has variable costs of $20.
The pitcher-cum-filter sells for $90 and has variable costs of $25.

Pure Water sells two faucet models for every three pitchers sold. Fixed costs equal $945,000.

Required

1. What is the breakeven point in unit sales and dollars for each type of filter at the current sales mix?
2. Pure Water is considering buying new production equipment. The new equipment will increase fixed cost by $181,400 per year and will decrease the variable cost of the faucet and the pitcher units by $5 and $9 respectively. Assuming the same sales mix, how many of each type of filter does Pure Water need to sell to break even?
3. Assuming the same sales mix, at what total sales level would Pure Water be indifferent between using the old equipment and buying the new production equipment? If total sales are expected to be 30,000 units, should Pure Water buy the new production equipment?

3-46 Sales mix, two products. The Stackpole Company retails two products: a standard and a deluxe version of a luggage carrier. The budgeted income statement for next period is as follows:

	Standard Carrier	Deluxe Carrier	Total
Units sold	187,500	62,500	250,000
Revenues at $28 and $50 per unit	$5,250,000	$3,125,000	$8,375,000
Variable costs at $18 and $30 per unit	3,375,000	1,875,000	5,250,000
Contribution margins at $10 and $20 per unit	$1,875,000	$1,250,000	3,125,000
Fixed costs			2,250,000
Operating income			$ 875,000

Required

1. Compute the breakeven point in units, assuming that the planned sales mix is attained.
2. Compute the breakeven point in units (a) if only standard carriers are sold and (b) if only deluxe carriers are sold.
3. Suppose 250,000 units are sold but only 50,000 of them are deluxe. Compute the operating income. Compute the breakeven point in units. Compare your answer with the answer to requirement 1. What is the major lesson of this problem?

3-47 Gross margin and contribution margin. The Museum of America is preparing for its annual appreciation dinner for contributing members. Last year, 525 members attended the dinner. Tickets for the dinner were $24 per attendee. The profit report for last year's dinner follows.

Ticket sales	$12,600
Cost of dinner	15,300
Gross margin	(2,700)
Invitations and paperwork	2,500
Profit (loss)	$(5,200)

This year the dinner committee does not want to lose money on the dinner. To help achieve its goal, the committee analyzed last year's costs. Of the $15,300 cost of the dinner, $9,000 were fixed costs and $6,300 were variable costs. Of the $2,500 cost of invitations and paperwork, $1,975 were fixed and $525 were variable.

Required

1. Prepare last year's profit report using the contribution margin format.
2. The committee is considering expanding this year's dinner invitation list to include volunteer members (in addition to contributing members). If the committee expands the dinner invitation list, it expects attendance to double. Calculate the effect this will have on the profitability of the dinner assuming fixed costs will be the same as last year.

3-48 Ethics, CVP analysis. Allen Corporation produces a molded plastic casing, LX201, for desktop computers. Summary data from its 2011 income statement are as follows:

Revenues	$5,000,000
Variable costs	3,000,000
Fixed costs	2,160,000
Operating income	$ (160,000)

Jane Woodall, Allen's president, is very concerned about Allen Corporation's poor profitability. She asks Max Lemond, production manager, and Lester Bush, controller, to see if there are ways to reduce costs.

After two weeks, Max returns with a proposal to reduce variable costs to 52% of revenues by reducing the costs Allen currently incurs for safe disposal of wasted plastic. Lester is concerned that this would expose the company to potential environmental liabilities. He tells Max, "We would need to estimate some of these potential environmental costs and include them in our analysis." "You can't do that," Max replies. "We are not violating any laws. There is some possibility that we may have to incur environmental costs in the future, but if we bring it up now, this proposal will not go through because our senior management always assumes these costs to be larger than they turn out to be. The market is very tough, and we are in danger of shutting down the company and costing all of us our jobs. The only reason our competitors are making money is because they are doing exactly what I am proposing."

1. Calculate Allen Corporation's breakeven revenues for 2011.
2. Calculate Allen Corporation's breakeven revenues if variable costs are 52% of revenues.
3. Calculate Allen Corporation's operating income for 2011 if variable costs had been 52% of revenues.
4. Given Max Lemond's comments, what should Lester Bush do?

Required

Collaborative Learning Problem

3-49 Deciding where to produce. (CMA, adapted) The Domestic Engines Co. produces the same power generators in two Illinois plants, a new plant in Peoria and an older plant in Moline. The following data are available for the two plants:

	A	B	C	D	E
			Peoria		**Moline**
2	Selling price		$150.00		$150.00
3	Variable manufacturing cost per unit	$72.00		$88.00	
4	Fixed manufacturing cost per unit	30.00		15.00	
5	Variable marketing and distribution cost per unit	14.00		14.00	
6	Fixed marketing and distribution cost per unit	19.00		14.50	
7	Total cost per unit			135.00		131.50
8	Operating income per unit			$ 15.00		$ 18.50
9	Production rate per day	400 units		320 units	
10	Normal annual capacity usage	240 days		240 days	
11	Maximum annual capacity	300 days		300 days	

All fixed costs per unit are calculated based on a normal capacity usage consisting of 240 working days. When the number of working days exceeds 240, overtime charges raise the variable manufacturing costs of additional units by $3.00 per unit in Peoria and $8.00 per unit in Moline.

Domestic Engines Co. is expected to produce and sell 192,000 power generators during the coming year. Wanting to take advantage of the higher operating income per unit at Moline, the company's production manager has decided to manufacture 96,000 units at each plant, resulting in a plan in which Moline operates at capacity (320 units per day × 300 days) and Peoria operates at its normal volume (400 units per day × 240 days).

1. Calculate the breakeven point in units for the Peoria plant and for the Moline plant.
2. Calculate the operating income that would result from the production manager's plan to produce 96,000 units at each plant.
3. Determine how the production of 192,000 units should be allocated between the Peoria and Moline plants to maximize operating income for Domestic Engines. Show your calculations.

Required

10 | Determining How Costs Behave

What is the value of looking at the past?

Perhaps it is to recall fond memories you've had or help you understand historical events. Maybe your return to the past enables you to better understand and predict the future. When an organization looks at the past, it typically does so to analyze its results, so that the best decisions can be made for the company's future. This activity requires gathering information about costs and how they behave so that managers can predict what they will be "down the road." Gaining a deeper understanding of cost behavior can also spur a firm to reorganize its operations in innovative ways and tackle important challenges, as the following article shows.

Management Accountants at Cisco Embrace Opportunities, Enhance Sustainability[1]

Understanding how costs behave is a valuable technical skill. Managers look to management accountants to help them identify cost drivers, estimate cost relationships, and determine the fixed and variable components of costs. To be effective, management accountants must have a clear understanding of the business's strategy and operations to identify new opportunities to reduce costs and increase profitability. At Cisco Systems, management accountants' in-depth understanding of the company's costs and operations led to reduced costs, while also helping the environment.

Cisco, makers of computer networking equipment including routers and wireless switches, traditionally regarded the used equipment it received back from its business customers as scrap and recycled it at a cost of about $8 million a year. As managers looked at the accumulated costs and realized that they may literally be "throwing away money," they decided to reassess their treatment of scrap material. In 2005, managers at Cisco began trying to find uses for the equipment, mainly because 80% of the returns were in working condition. A value recovery team at Cisco identified groups within the company that could use the returned equipment. These included its customer service group, which supports warranty claims and service

[1] *Source:* Nidumolu, R., C. Prahalad, and M. Rangaswami. 2009. Why sustainability is now the key driver of innovation. *Harvard Business Review,* September 2009; Cisco Systems, Inc. 2009. *2009 corporate social responsibility report.* San Jose, CA: Cisco Systems, Inc.

contracts, and the labs that provide technical support, training, and product demonstrations.

Based on the initial success of the value recovery team, in 2005, Cisco designated its recycling group as a company business unit, set clear objectives for it, and assigned the group its own income statement. As a result, the reuse of equipment rose from 5% in 2004 to 45% in 2008, and Cisco's recycling costs fell by 40%. The unit has become a profit center that contributed $153 million to Cisco's bottom line in 2008.

With product returns reducing corporate profitability by an average of about 4% a year, companies like Cisco can leverage management accountants' insight to reduce the cost of these returns while decreasing its environmental footprint. Not only can this turn a cost center into a profitable business, but sustainability efforts like these signals that the company is concerned about preventing environmental damage by reducing waste.

As the Cisco example illustrates, managers must understand how costs behave to make strategic and operating decisions that have a positive environmental impact. Consider several other examples. Managers at FedEx decided to replace old planes with new Boeing 757s that reduced fuel consumption by 36%, while increasing capacity by 20%. At Clorox, managers decided to create a new line of non-synthetic cleaning products that were better for the environment and helped create a new category of 'green' cleaning products worth about $200 million annually.

In each situation, knowledge of cost behavior was needed to answer key questions. This chapter will focus on how managers determine cost-behavior patterns—that is, how costs change in relation to changes in activity levels, in the quantity of products produced, and so on.

Basic Assumptions and Examples of Cost Functions

Learning Objective 1

Describe linear cost functions

. . . graph of cost function is a straight line

and three common ways in which they behave

. . . variable, fixed, and mixed

Managers are able to understand cost behavior through cost functions. A **cost function** is a mathematical description of how a cost changes with changes in the level of an activity relating to that cost. Cost functions can be plotted on a graph by measuring the level of an activity, such as number of batches produced or number of machine-hours used, on the horizontal axis (called the x-axis) and the amount of total costs corresponding to—or, preferably, dependent on—the levels of that activity on the vertical axis (called the y-axis).

Basic Assumptions

Managers often estimate cost functions based on two assumptions:

1. Variations in the level of a single activity (the cost driver) explain the variations in the related total costs.
2. Cost behavior is approximated by a linear cost function within the relevant range. Recall that a relevant range is the range of the activity in which there is a relationship between total cost and the level of activity. For a **linear cost function** represented graphically, total cost versus the level of a single activity related to that cost is a straight line within the relevant range.

We use these two assumptions throughout most, but not all, of this chapter. Not all cost functions are linear and can be explained by a single activity. Later sections will discuss cost functions that do not rely on these assumptions.

Linear Cost Functions

To understand three basic types of linear cost functions and to see the role of cost functions in business decisions, consider the negotiations between Cannon Services and World Wide Communications (WWC) for exclusive use of a videoconferencing line between New York and Paris.

■ **Alternative 1:** $5 per minute used. Total cost to Cannon changes in proportion to the number of minutes used. The number of minutes used is the only factor whose change causes a change in total cost.

   Panel A in Exhibit 10-1 presents this *variable cost* for Cannon Services. Under alternative 1, there is no fixed cost. We write the cost function in Panel A of Exhibit 10-1 as

$$y = \$5X$$

where X measures the number of minutes used (on the x-axis), and y measures the total cost of the minutes used (on the y-axis) calculated using the cost function. Panel A illustrates the $5 **slope coefficient**, the amount by which total cost changes when a one-unit change occurs in the level of activity (one minute of usage in the Cannon example). *Throughout the chapter, uppercase letters, such as X, refer to the actual observations, and lowercase letters, such as y, represent estimates or calculations made using a cost function.*

■ **Alternative 2:** Total cost will be fixed at $10,000 per month, regardless of the number of minutes used. (We use the same activity measure, number of minutes used, to compare cost-behavior patterns under the three alternatives.)

   Panel B in Exhibit 10-1 presents this *fixed cost* for Cannon Services. We write the cost function in Panel B as

$$y = \$10,000$$

Exhibit 10-1 Examples of Linear Cost Functions

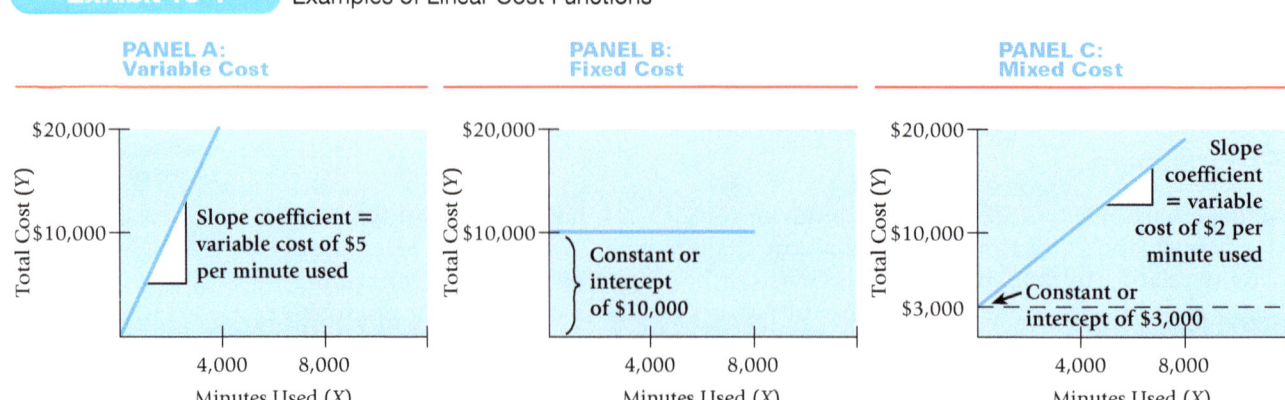

PANEL A: Variable Cost

PANEL B: Fixed Cost

PANEL C: Mixed Cost

The fixed cost of $10,000 is called a **constant**; it is the component of total cost that does not vary with changes in the level of the activity. Under alternative 2, the constant accounts for all the cost because there is no variable cost. Graphically, the slope coefficient of the cost function is zero; this cost function intersects the y-axis at the constant value, and therefore the *constant* is also called the **intercept**.

■ **Alternative 3:** $3,000 per month plus $2 per minute used. This is an example of a mixed cost. A **mixed cost**—also called a **semivariable cost**—is a cost that has both fixed and variable elements.

Panel C in Exhibit 10-1 presents this *mixed cost* for Cannon Services. We write the cost function in Panel C of Exhibit 10-1 as

$$y = \$3,000 + \$2X$$

Unlike the graphs for alternatives 1 and 2, Panel C has both a constant, or intercept, value of $3,000 and a slope coefficient of $2. In the case of a mixed cost, total cost in the relevant range increases as the number of minutes used increases. Note that total cost does not vary strictly in proportion to the number of minutes used within the relevant range. For example, with 4,000 minutes of usage, the total cost equals $11,000 [$3,000 + ($2 per minute × 4,000 minutes)], but when 8,000 minutes are used, total cost equals $19,000 [$3,000 + ($2 per minute × 8,000 minutes)]. Although the usage in terms of minutes has doubled, total cost has increased by only about 73% [($19,000 – $11,000) ÷ $11,000].

Cannon's managers must understand the cost-behavior patterns in the three alternatives to choose the best deal with WWC. Suppose Cannon expects to do at least 4,000 minutes of videoconferencing per month. Its cost for 4,000 minutes under the three alternatives would be as follows:

■ **Alternative 1:** $20,000 ($5 per minute × 4,000 minutes)
■ **Alternative 2:** $10,000
■ **Alternative 3:** $11,000 [$3,000 + ($2 per minute × 4,000 minutes)]

Alternative 2 is the least costly. Moreover, if Cannon were to use more than 4,000 minutes, as is likely to be the case, alternatives 1 and 3 would be even more costly. Cannon's managers, therefore, should choose alternative 2.

Note that the graphs in Exhibit 10-1 are linear. That is, they appear as straight lines. We simply need to know the constant, or intercept, amount (commonly designated a) and the slope coefficient (commonly designated b). For any linear cost function based on a single activity (recall our two assumptions discussed at the start of the chapter), knowing a and b is sufficient to describe and graphically plot all the values within the relevant range of number of minutes used. We write a general form of this linear cost function as

$$y = a + bX$$

Under alternative 1, $a = \$0$ and $b = \$5$ per minute used; under alternative 2, $a = \$10,000$ and $b = \$0$ per minute used; and under alternative 3, $a = \$3,000$ and $b = \$2$ per minute used. To plot the mixed-cost function in Panel C, we draw a line starting from the point marked $3,000 on the y-axis and increasing at a rate of $2 per minute used, so that at 1,000 minutes, total costs increase by $2,000 ($2 per minute × 1,000 minutes) to $5,000 ($3,000 + $2,000) and at 2,000 minutes, total costs increase by $4,000 ($2 per minute × 2,000 minutes) to $7,000 ($3,000 + $4,000) and so on.

Review of Cost Classification

Before we discuss issues related to the estimation of cost functions, we briefly review the three criteria laid out in Chapter 2 for classifying a cost into its variable and fixed components.

Choice of Cost Object

A particular cost item could be variable with respect to one cost object and fixed with respect to another cost object. Consider Super Shuttle, an airport transportation company. If the fleet of vans it owns is the cost object, then the annual van registration and license costs would be variable costs with respect to the number of vans owned. But if a particular van is the cost object, then the registration and license costs for that van are fixed costs with respect to the miles driven during a year.

Time Horizon

Whether a cost is variable or fixed with respect to a particular activity depends on the time horizon being considered in the decision situation. The longer the time horizon, all other things being equal, the more likely that the cost will be variable. For example, inspection costs at Boeing Company are typically fixed in the short run with respect to inspection-hours used because inspectors earn a fixed salary in a given year regardless of the number of inspection-hours of work done. But, in the long run, Boeing's total inspection costs will vary with the inspection-hours required: More inspectors will be hired if more inspection-hours are needed, and some inspectors will be reassigned to other tasks or laid off if fewer inspection-hours are needed.

Relevant Range

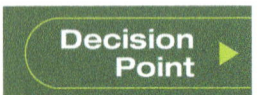

Decision Point ▶

What is a linear cost function and what types of cost behavior can it represent?

Managers should never forget that variable and fixed cost-behavior patterns are valid for linear cost functions only within a given relevant range. Outside the relevant range, variable and fixed cost-behavior patterns change, causing costs to become nonlinear (nonlinear means the plot of the relationship on a graph is not a straight line). For example, Exhibit 10-2 plots the relationship (over several years) between total direct manufacturing labor costs and the number of snowboards produced each year by Ski Authority at its Vermont plant. In this case, the nonlinearities outside the relevant range occur because of labor and other inefficiencies (first because workers are learning to produce snowboards and later because capacity limits are being stretched). Knowing the relevant range is essential to properly classify costs.

Identifying Cost Drivers

Learning Objective 2

Explain the importance of causality in estimating cost functions

. . . only a cause-and-effect relationship establishes an economically plausible relationship between an activity and its costs

The Cannon Services/WWC example illustrates variable-, fixed-, and mixed-cost functions using information about *future* cost structures proposed to Cannon by WWC. Often, however, cost functions are estimated from *past* cost data. Managers use **cost estimation** to measure a relationship based on data from past costs and the related level of an activity. For example, marketing managers at Volkswagen could use cost estimation to understand what causes their marketing costs to change from year to year (for example, the number of new car models introduced or a competitor's sudden recall) and the fixed and variable components of these costs. Managers are interested in estimating past cost-behavior functions primarily because these estimates can help them make more-accurate **cost predictions**, or forecasts, of future costs. Better cost predictions help managers make more-informed planning and control decisions, such as preparing next year's marketing budget. But better management decisions, cost predictions, and estimation of cost functions can be achieved only if managers correctly identify the factors that affect costs.

Exhibit 10-2

Linearity Within Relevant Range for Ski Authority, Inc.

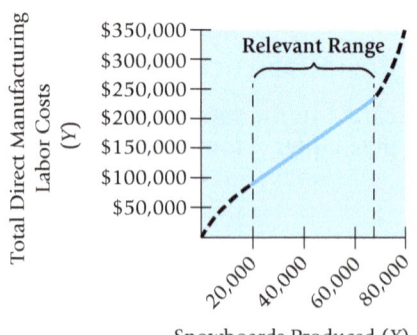

Snowboards Produced (X)

The Cause-and-Effect Criterion

The most important issue in estimating a cost function is determining whether a cause-and-effect relationship exists between the level of an activity and the costs related to that level of activity. Without a cause-and-effect relationship, managers will be less confident about their ability to estimate or predict costs. Recall from Chapter 2 that when a cause-and-effect relationship exists between a change in the level of an activity and a change in the level of total costs, we refer to the activity measure as a *cost driver*. We use the terms *level of activity* and *level of cost driver* interchangeably when estimating cost functions. Understanding the drivers of costs is crucially important for managing costs. The cause-and-effect relationship might arise as a result of the following:

- **A physical relationship between the level of activity and costs.** An example is when units of production are used as the activity that affects direct material costs. Producing more units requires more direct materials, which results in higher total direct material costs.

- **A contractual arrangement.** In alternative 1 of the Cannon Services example described earlier, number of minutes used is specified in the contract as the level of activity that affects the telephone line costs.

- **Knowledge of operations.** An example is when number of parts is used as the activity measure of ordering costs. A product with many parts will incur higher ordering costs than a product with few parts.

Managers must be careful not to interpret a high correlation, or connection, in the relationship between two variables to mean that either variable causes the other. Consider direct material costs and labor costs. For a given product mix, producing more units generally results in higher material costs and higher labor costs. Material costs and labor costs are highly correlated, but neither causes the other. Using labor costs to predict material costs is problematic. Some products require more labor costs relative to material costs, while other products require more material costs relative to labor costs. If the product mix changes toward more labor-intensive products, then labor costs will increase while material costs will decrease. Labor costs are a poor predictor of material costs. By contrast, factors that drive material costs such as product mix, product designs, and manufacturing processes, would have more accurately predicted the changes in material costs.

Only a cause-and-effect relationship—not merely correlation—establishes an economically plausible relationship between the level of an activity and its costs. Economic plausibility is critical because it gives analysts and managers confidence that the estimated relationship will appear again and again in other sets of data from the same situation. Identifying cost drivers also gives managers insights into ways to reduce costs and the confidence that reducing the quantity of the cost drivers will lead to a decrease in costs.

To identify cost drivers on the basis of data gathered over time, always use a long time horizon. Why? Because costs may be fixed in the short run (during which time they have no cost driver), but they are usually variable and have a cost driver in the long run.

Cost Drivers and the Decision-Making Process

Consider Elegant Rugs, which uses state-of-the-art automated weaving machines to produce carpets for homes and offices. Management has made many changes in manufacturing processes and wants to introduce new styles of carpets. It would like to evaluate how these changes have affected costs and what styles of carpets it should introduce. It follows the five-step decision-making process outlined in Chapter 1.

Step 1: Identify the problem and uncertainties. The changes in the manufacturing process were specifically targeted at reducing indirect manufacturing labor costs, and management wants to know whether costs such as supervision, maintenance, and quality control did, in fact, decrease. One option is to simply compare indirect manufacturing labor costs before and after the process change. The problem with this approach is that the volume of activity before and after the process change was very different so costs need to be compared after taking into account the change in activity volume.

Managers were fairly confident about the direct material and direct manufacturing labor costs of the new styles of carpets. They were less certain about the impact that the choice of different styles would have on indirect manufacturing costs.

Step 2: Obtain information. Managers gathered information about potential cost drivers—factors such as machine-hours or direct manufacturing labor-hours that cause indirect manufacturing labor costs to be incurred. They also began considering different techniques (discussed in the next section) such as the industrial engineering method, the conference method, the account analysis method, the high-low method, and the regression method for estimating the magnitude of the effect of the cost driver on indirect manufacturing labor costs. Their goal was to identify the best possible single cost driver.

Step 3: Make predictions about the future. Managers used past data to estimate the relationship between cost drivers and costs and used this relationship to predict future costs.

Step 4: Make decisions by choosing among alternatives. As we will describe later (pp. 353–355), Elegant Rugs chose machine-hours as the cost driver of indirect manufacturing labor costs. Using the regression analysis estimate of indirect manufacturing labor cost per machine-hour, managers estimated the costs of alternative styles of carpets and chose to introduce the most profitable styles.

Step 5: Implement the decision, evaluate performance, and learn. After the managers at Elegant Rugs introduced the new carpet styles, they focused on evaluating the results of their decision. Comparing predicted to actual costs helped managers to learn how accurate the estimates were, to set targets for continuous improvement, and to constantly seek ways to improve efficiency and effectiveness.

> **Decision Point** ▶
>
> What is the most important issue in estimating a cost function?

Cost Estimation Methods

> **Learning Objective 3**
>
> Understand various methods of cost estimation
>
> . . . for example, the regression analysis method determines the line that best fits past data

As we mentioned in Step 2, four methods of cost estimation are the industrial engineering method, the conference method, the account analysis method, and the quantitative analysis method (which takes different forms). These methods differ with respect to how expensive they are to implement, the assumptions they make, and the information they provide about the accuracy of the estimated cost function. They are not mutually exclusive, and many organizations use a combination of these methods.

Industrial Engineering Method

The **industrial engineering method**, also called the **work-measurement method**, estimates cost functions by analyzing the relationship between inputs and outputs in physical terms. Consider Elegant Rugs. It uses inputs of cotton, wool, dyes, direct manufacturing labor, machine time, and power. Production output is square yards of carpet. Time-and-motion studies analyze the time required to perform the various operations to produce the carpet. For example, a time-and-motion study may conclude that to produce 10 square yards of carpet requires one hour of direct manufacturing labor. Standards and budgets transform these physical input measures into costs. The result is an estimated cost function relating direct manufacturing labor costs to the cost driver, square yards of carpet produced.

The industrial engineering method is a very thorough and detailed way to estimate a cost function when there is a physical relationship between inputs and outputs, but it can be very time consuming. Some government contracts mandate its use. Many organizations, such as Bose and Nokia, use it to estimate direct manufacturing costs but find it too costly or impractical for analyzing their entire cost structure. For example, physical relationships between inputs and outputs are difficult to specify for some items, such as indirect manufacturing costs, R&D costs, and advertising costs.

Conference Method

The **conference method** estimates cost functions on the basis of analysis and opinions about costs and their drivers gathered from various departments of a company (purchasing, process engineering, manufacturing, employee relations, etc.). The Cooperative Bank in the United Kingdom has a cost-estimating department that develops cost functions for its retail banking products (checking accounts, VISA cards, mortgages, and so on) based on the consensus of estimates from personnel of the particular departments. Elegant Rugs gathers opinions from supervisors and production engineers about how indirect manufacturing labor costs vary with machine-hours and direct manufacturing labor-hours.

The conference method encourages interdepartmental cooperation. The pooling of expert knowledge from different business functions of the value chain gives the conference method credibility. Because the conference method does not require detailed analysis of data, cost functions and cost estimates can be developed quickly. However, the emphasis on opinions rather than systematic estimation means that the accuracy of the cost estimates depends largely on the care and skill of the people providing the inputs.

Account Analysis Method

The **account analysis method** estimates cost functions by classifying various cost accounts as variable, fixed, or mixed with respect to the identified level of activity. Typically, managers use qualitative rather than quantitative analysis when making these cost-classification decisions. The account analysis approach is widely used because it is reasonably accurate, cost-effective, and easy to use.

Consider indirect manufacturing labor costs for a small production area (or cell) at Elegant Rugs. Indirect manufacturing labor costs include wages paid for supervision, maintenance, quality control, and setups. During the most recent 12-week period, Elegant Rugs ran the machines in the cell for a total of 862 hours and incurred total indirect manufacturing labor costs of $12,501. Using qualitative analysis, the manager and the cost analyst determine that over this 12-week period indirect manufacturing labor costs are mixed costs with only one cost driver—machine-hours. As machine-hours vary, one component of the cost (such as supervision cost) is fixed, whereas another component (such as maintenance cost) is variable. The goal is to use account analysis to estimate a linear cost function for indirect manufacturing labor costs with number of machine-hours as the cost driver. The cost analyst uses experience and judgment to separate total indirect manufacturing labor costs ($12,501) into costs that are fixed ($2,157, based on 950 hours of machine capacity for the cell over a 12-week period) and costs that are variable ($10,344) with respect to the number of machine-hours used. Variable cost per machine-hour is $10,344 ÷ 862 machine-hours = $12 per machine-hour. The linear cost equation, $y = a + bX$, in this example is as follows:

Indirect manufacturing labor costs = $2,157 +
($12 per machine-hour × Number of machine-hours)

Management at Elegant Rugs can use the cost function to estimate the indirect manufacturing labor costs of using, say, 950 machine-hours to produce carpet in the next 12-week period. Estimated costs equal $2,157 + (950 machine-hours × $12 per machine-hour) = $13,557.

To obtain reliable estimates of the fixed and variable components of cost, organizations must take care to ensure that individuals thoroughly knowledgeable about the operations make the cost-classification decisions. Supplementing the account analysis method with the conference method improves credibility.

Quantitative Analysis Method

Quantitative analysis uses a formal mathematical method to fit cost functions to past data observations. Excel is a useful tool for performing quantitative analysis. Columns B and C of Exhibit 10-3 show the breakdown of Elegant Rugs' total machine-hours (862) and total indirect manufacturing labor costs ($12,501) into weekly data for the most recent 12-week period. Note that the data are paired; for each week, there is data for the number of machine-hours and corresponding indirect manufacturing labor costs. For example, week 12 shows 48 machine-hours and indirect manufacturing labor costs of $963. The next section uses the data in Exhibit 10-3 to illustrate how to estimate a cost

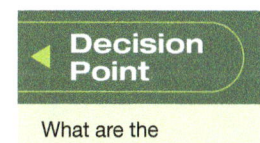

Decision Point

What are the different methods that can be used to estimate a cost function?

Exhibit 10-3

Weekly Indirect
Manufacturing Labor
Costs and Machine-
Hours for Elegant Rugs

	A	B	C
1	Week	Cost Driver: Machine-Hours	Indirect Manufacturing Labor Costs
2		(X)	(Y)
3	1	68	$ 1,190
4	2	88	1,211
5	3	62	1,004
6	4	72	917
7	5	60	770
8	6	96	1,456
9	7	78	1,180
10	8	46	710
11	9	82	1,316
12	10	94	1,032
13	11	68	752
14	12	48	963
15	Total	862	$12,501
16			

function using quantitative analysis. We examine two techniques—the relatively simple high-low method as well as the more common quantitative tool used to examine and understand data, regression analysis.

Steps in Estimating a Cost Function Using Quantitative Analysis

There are six steps in estimating a cost function using quantitative analysis of a past cost relationship. We illustrate the steps as follows using the Elegant Rugs example.

Step 1: Choose the dependent variable. Choice of the **dependent variable** (the cost to be predicted and managed) will depend on the cost function being estimated. In the Elegant Rugs example, the dependent variable is indirect manufacturing labor costs.

Step 2: Identify the independent variable, or cost driver. The **independent variable** (level of activity or cost driver) is the factor used to predict the dependent variable (costs). When the cost is an indirect cost, as it is with Elegant Rugs, the independent variable is also called a cost-allocation base. Although these terms are sometimes used interchangeably, we use the term *cost driver* to describe the independent variable. Frequently, the cost analyst, working with the management team, will cycle through the six steps several times, trying alternative economically plausible cost drivers to identify a cost driver that best fits the data.

A cost driver should be measurable and have an *economically plausible* relationship with the dependent variable. Economic plausibility means that the relationship (describing how changes in the cost driver lead to changes in the costs being considered) is based on a physical relationship, a contract, or knowledge of operations and makes economic sense to the operating manager and the management accountant. As we saw in Chapter 5, all the individual items of costs included in the dependent variable should have the same cost driver, that is, the cost pool should be homogenous. When all items of costs in the dependent variable do not have the same cost driver, the cost analyst should investigate the possibility of creating homogenous cost pools and estimating more than one cost function, one for each cost item/cost driver pair.

Learning Objective 4

Outline six steps in estimating a cost function using quantitative analysis

. . . the end result (Step 6) is to evaluate the cost driver of the estimated cost function

As an example, consider several types of fringe benefits paid to employees and the cost drivers of the benefits:

Fringe Benefit	Cost Driver
Health benefits	Number of employees
Cafeteria meals	Number of employees
Pension benefits	Salaries of employees
Life insurance	Salaries of employees

The costs of health benefits and cafeteria meals can be combined into one homogenous cost pool because they have the same cost driver—the number of employees. Pension benefits and life insurance costs have a different cost driver—the salaries of employees—and, therefore, should not be combined with health benefits and cafeteria meals. Instead, pension benefits and life insurance costs should be combined into a separate homogenous cost pool. The cost pool comprising pension benefits and life insurance costs can be estimated using salaries of employees receiving these benefits as the cost driver.

Step 3: **Collect data on the dependent variable and the cost driver.** This is usually the most difficult step in cost analysis. Cost analysts obtain data from company documents, from interviews with managers, and through special studies. These data may be time-series data or cross-sectional data.

Time-series data pertain to the same entity (organization, plant, activity, and so on) over successive past periods. Weekly observations of indirect manufacturing labor costs and number of machine-hours at Elegant Rugs are examples of time-series data. The ideal time-series database would contain numerous observations for a company whose operations have not been affected by economic or technological change. A stable economy and technology ensure that data collected during the estimation period represent the same underlying relationship between the cost driver and the dependent variable. Moreover, the periods used to measure the dependent variable and the cost driver should be consistent throughout the observations.

Cross-sectional data pertain to different entities during the same period. For example, studies of loans processed and the related personnel costs at 50 individual, yet similar, branches of a bank during March 2012 would produce cross-sectional data for that month. The cross-sectional data should be drawn from entities that, within each entity, have a similar relationship between the cost driver and costs. Later in this chapter, we describe the problems that arise in data collection.

Step 4: **Plot the data.** The general relationship between the cost driver and costs can be readily observed in a graphical representation of the data, which is commonly called a plot of the data. The plot provides insight into the relevant range of the cost function, and reveals whether the relationship between the driver and costs is approximately linear. Moreover, the plot highlights extreme observations (observations outside the general pattern) that analysts should check. Was there an error in recording the data or an unusual event, such as a work stoppage, that makes these observations unrepresentative of the normal relationship between the cost driver and the costs?

Exhibit 10-4 is a plot of the weekly data from columns B and C of the Excel spreadsheet in Exhibit 10-3. This graph provides strong visual evidence of a positive linear relationship between number of machine-hours and indirect manufacturing labor costs (that is, when machine-hours go up, so do indirect manufacturing labor costs). There do not appear to be any extreme observations in Exhibit 10-4. The relevant range is from 46 to 96 machine-hours per week (weeks 8 and 6, respectively).

Step 5: **Estimate the cost function.** We will show two ways to estimate the cost function for our Elegant Rugs data. One uses the high-low method, and the other uses regression analysis, the two most frequently described forms of quantitative analysis. The widespread availability of computer packages such as Excel makes regression analysis much more easy to use. Still, we describe the high-low method to provide some basic intuition for the idea of drawing a line to "fit" a number of data points. We present these methods after Step 6.

Exhibit 10-4

Plot of Weekly Indirect
Manufacturing Labor
Costs and Machine-
Hours for Elegant Rugs

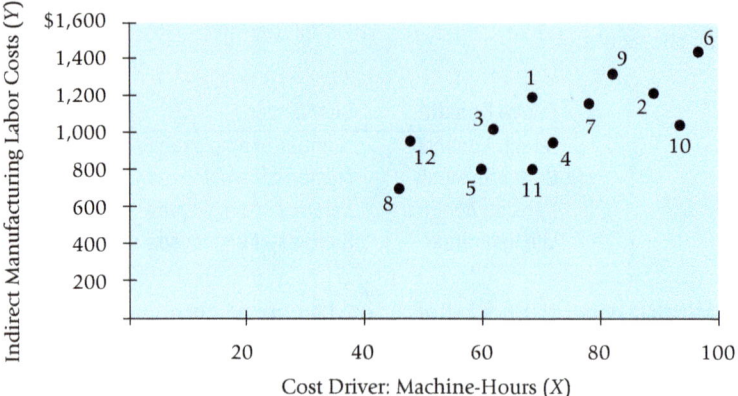

Step 6:   Evaluate the cost driver of the estimated cost function. In this step, we describe criteria for evaluating the cost driver of the estimated cost function. We do this after illustrating the high-low method and regression analysis.

High-Low Method

The simplest form of quantitative analysis to "fit" a line to data points is the **high-low method.** It uses only the highest and lowest observed values of the cost driver within the relevant range and their respective costs to estimate the slope coefficient and the constant of the cost function. It provides a first cut at understanding the relationship between a cost driver and costs. We illustrate the high-low method using data from Exhibit 10-3.

	Cost Driver: Machine-Hours (*X*)	Indirect Manufacturing Labor Costs (*Y*)
Highest observation of cost driver (week 6)	96	$1,456
Lowest observation of cost driver (week 8)	46	710
Difference	50	$ 746

The slope coefficient, *b,* is calculated as follows:

$$\text{Slope coefficient} = \frac{\text{Difference between costs associated with highest and lowest observations of the cost driver}}{\text{Difference between highest and lowest observations of the cost driver}}$$

$$= \$746 \div 50 \text{ machine-hours} = \$14.92 \text{ per machine-hour}$$

To compute the constant, we can use either the highest or the lowest observation of the cost driver. Both calculations yield the same answer because the solution technique solves two linear equations with two unknowns, the slope coefficient and the constant. Because

$$y = a + bX$$
$$a = y - bX$$

At the highest observation of the cost driver, the constant, *a,* is calculated as follows:

$$\text{Constant} = \$1,456 - (\$14.92 \text{ per machine-hour} \times 96 \text{ machine-hours}) = \$23.68$$

And at the lowest observation of the cost driver,

$$\text{Constant} = \$710 - (\$14.92 \text{ per machine-hour} \times 46 \text{ machine-hours}) = \$23.68$$

Thus, the high-low estimate of the cost function is as follows:

$$y = a + bX$$
$$y = \$23.68 + (\$14.92 \text{ per machine-hour} \times \text{Number of machine-hours})$$

The purple line in Exhibit 10-5 shows the estimated cost function using the high-low method (based on the data in Exhibit 10-3). The estimated cost function is a straight line joining the observations with the highest and lowest values of the cost driver (number of machine-hours). Note how this simple high-low line falls "in-between" the data points with three observations on the line, four above it and five below it. The intercept (*a* = $23.68), the point where the dashed extension of the purple line meets the *y*-axis, is the constant component of the equation that provides the best linear approximation of how a cost behaves *within the relevant range* of 46 to 96 machine-hours. The intercept should *not* be interpreted as an estimate of the fixed costs of Elegant Rugs if no machines were run. That's because running no machines and shutting down the plant—that is, using zero machine-hours—is *outside the relevant range.*

Suppose indirect manufacturing labor costs in week 6 were $1,280, instead of $1,456, while 96 machine-hours were used. In this case, the highest observation of the cost driver (96 machine-hours in week 6) will not coincide with the newer highest observation of the costs ($1,316 in week 9). How would this change affect our high-low calculation? Given that the cause-and-effect relationship runs *from* the cost driver *to* the costs in a cost function, we choose the highest and lowest observations of the cost driver (the factor that causes the costs to change). The high-low method would still estimate the new cost function using data from weeks 6 (high) and 8 (low).

There is a danger of relying on only two observations to estimate a cost function. Suppose that because a labor contract guarantees certain minimum payments in week 8, indirect manufacturing labor costs in week 8 were $1,000, instead of $710, when only 46 machine-hours were used. The blue line in Exhibit 10-5 shows the cost function that would be estimated by the high-low method using this revised cost. Other than the two points used to draw the line, all other data lie on or below the line! In this case, choosing the highest and lowest observations for machine-hours would result in an estimated cost function that poorly describes the underlying linear cost relationship between number of machine-hours and indirect manufacturing labor costs. In such situations, the high-low method can be modified so that the two observations chosen to estimate the cost function are a *representative high* and a *representative low.* By using this adjustment, managers can avoid having extreme observations, which arise from abnormal events, influence the estimate of the cost function. The modification allows managers to estimate a cost function that is representative of the relationship between the cost driver and costs and, therefore, is more useful for making decisions (such as pricing and performance evaluation).

The advantage of the high-low method is that it is simple to compute and easy to understand; it gives a quick, initial insight into how the cost driver—number of machine-hours—affects indirect manufacturing labor costs. The disadvantage is that it ignores information from all but two observations when estimating the cost function. We next describe the regression analysis method of quantitative analysis that uses all available data to estimate the cost function.

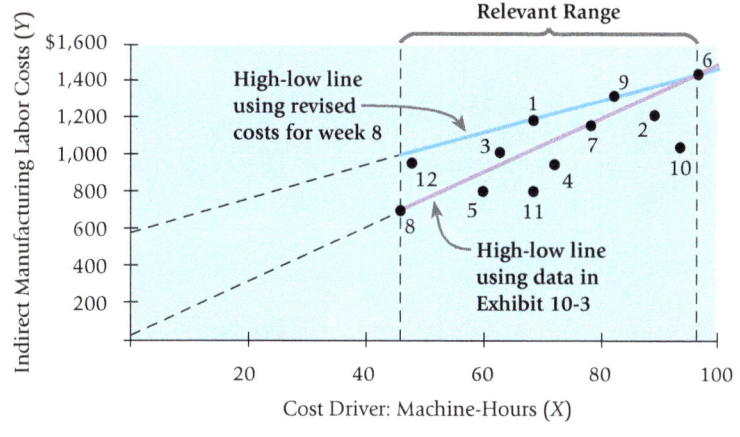

Exhibit 10-5

High-Low Method for Weekly Indirect Manufacturing Labor Costs and Machine-Hours for Elegant Rugs

Regression Analysis Method

Regression analysis is a statistical method that measures the average amount of change in the dependent variable associated with a unit change in one or more independent variables. In the Elegant Rugs example, the dependent variable is total indirect manufacturing labor costs. The independent variable, or cost driver, is number of machine-hours. **Simple regression** analysis estimates the relationship between the dependent variable and *one* independent variable. **Multiple regression** analysis estimates the relationship between the dependent variable and *two or more* independent variables. Multiple regression analysis for Elegant Rugs might use as the independent variables, or cost drivers, number of machine-hours and number of batches. The appendix to this chapter will explore simple regression and multiple regression in more detail.

In later sections, we will illustrate how Excel performs the calculations associated with regression analysis. The following discussion emphasizes how managers interpret and use the output from Excel to make critical strategic decisions. Exhibit 10-6 shows the line developed using regression analysis that best fits the data in columns B and C of Exhibit 10-3. Excel estimates the cost function to be

$$y = \$300.98 + \$10.31X$$

The regression line in Exhibit 10-6 is derived using the least-squares technique. The least-squares technique determines the regression line by minimizing the sum of the squared vertical differences from the data points (the various points in the graph) to the regression line. The vertical difference, called the **residual term**, measures the distance between actual cost and estimated cost for each observation of the cost driver. Exhibit 10-6 shows the residual term for the week 1 data. The line from the observation to the regression line is drawn perpendicular to the horizontal axis, or *x*-axis. The smaller the residual terms, the better the fit between actual cost observations and estimated costs. *Goodness of fit* indicates the strength of the relationship between the cost driver and costs. The regression line in Exhibit 10-6 rises from left to right. The positive slope of this line and small residual terms indicate that, on average, indirect manufacturing labor costs increase as the number of machine-hours increases. The vertical dashed lines in Exhibit 10-6 indicate the relevant range, the range within which the cost function applies.

Instructors and students who want to explore the technical details of estimating the least-squares regression line, can go to the appendix, pages 367–371 and return to this point without any loss of continuity.

The estimate of the slope coefficient, *b*, indicates that indirect manufacturing labor costs vary at the average amount of $10.31 for every machine-hour used within the relevant range. Management can use the regression equation when budgeting for future indirect manufacturing labor costs. For instance, if 90 machine-hours are budgeted for the upcoming week, the predicted indirect manufacturing labor costs would be

$$y = \$300.98 + (\$10.31 \text{ per machine-hour} \times 90 \text{ machine-hours}) = \$1,228.88$$

Exhibit 10-6

Regression Model for
Weekly Indirect
Manufacturing Labor
Costs and Machine-
Hours for Elegant Rugs

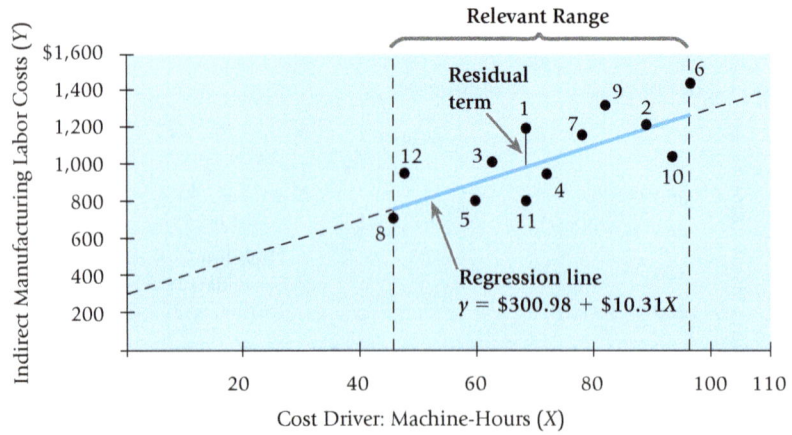

As we have already mentioned, the regression method is more accurate than the high-low method because the regression equation estimates costs using information from all observations, whereas the high-low equation uses information from only two observations. The inaccuracies of the high-low method can mislead managers. Consider the high-low method equation in the preceding section, y = \$23.68 + \$14.92 per machine-hour × Number of machine-hours. For 90 machine-hours, the predicted weekly cost based on the high-low method equation is \$23.68 + (\$14.92 per machine-hour × 90 machine-hours) = \$1,366.48. Suppose that for 7 weeks over the next 12-week period, Elegant Rugs runs its machines for 90 hours each week. Assume average indirect manufacturing labor costs for those 7 weeks are \$1,300. Based on the high-low method prediction of \$1,366.48, Elegant Rugs would conclude it has performed well because actual costs are less than predicted costs. But comparing the \$1,300 performance with the more-accurate \$1,228.88 prediction of the regression model tells a much different story and would probably prompt Elegant Rugs to search for ways to improve its cost performance.

Accurate cost estimation helps managers predict future costs and evaluate the success of cost-reduction initiatives. Suppose the manager at Elegant Rugs is interested in evaluating whether recent strategic decisions that led to changes in the production process and resulted in the data in Exhibit 10-3 have reduced indirect manufacturing labor costs, such as supervision, maintenance, and quality control. Using data on number of machine-hours used and indirect manufacturing labor costs of the previous process (not shown here), the manager estimates the regression equation,

$$y = \$546.26 + (\$15.86 \text{ per machine-hour} \times \text{Number of machine-hours})$$

The constant (\$300.98 versus \$545.26) and the slope coefficient (\$10.31 versus \$15.86) are both smaller for the new process relative to the old process. It appears that the new process has decreased indirect manufacturing labor costs.

Evaluating Cost Drivers of the Estimated Cost Function

How does a company determine the best cost driver when estimating a cost function? In many cases, the choice of a cost driver is aided substantially by understanding both operations and cost accounting.

To see why the understanding of operations is needed, consider the costs to maintain and repair metal-cutting machines at Helix Corporation, a manufacturer of treadmills. Helix schedules repairs and maintenance at a time when production is at a low level to avoid having to take machines out of service when they are needed most. An analysis of the monthly data will then show high repair costs in months of low production and low repair costs in months of high production. Someone unfamiliar with operations might conclude that there is an inverse relationship between production and repair costs. The engineering link between units produced and repair costs, however, is usually clear-cut. Over time, there is a cause-and-effect relationship: the higher the level of production, the higher the repair costs. To estimate the relationship correctly, operating managers and analysts will recognize that repair costs will tend to lag behind periods of high production, and hence, they will use production of prior periods as the cost driver.

In other cases, choosing a cost driver is more subtle and difficult. Consider again indirect manufacturing labor costs at Elegant Rugs. Management believes that both the number of machine-hours and the number of direct manufacturing labor-hours are plausible cost drivers of indirect manufacturing labor costs. However, management is not sure which is the better cost driver. Exhibit 10-7 presents weekly data (in Excel) on indirect manufacturing labor costs and number of machine-hours for the most recent 12-week period from Exhibit 10-3, together with data on the number of direct manufacturing labor-hours for the same period.

◀ **Decision Point**

What are the steps to estimate a cost function using quantitative analysis?

Learning Objective 5

Describe three criteria used to evaluate and choose cost drivers

. . . economically plausible relationships, goodness of fit, and significant effect of the cost driver on costs

Exhibit 10-7

Weekly Indirect
Manufacturing Labor
Costs, Machine-Hours,
and Direct
Manufacturing Labor-
Hours for Elegant Rugs

	Home	Insert	Page Layout	Formulas	Data	Review
	A	B	C	D		
1	Week	Original Cost Driver: Machine-Hours	Alternate Cost Driver: Direct Manufacturing Labor-Hours (X)	Indirect Manufacturing Labor Costs (Y)		
2	1	68	30	$ 1,190		
3	2	88	35	1,211		
4	3	62	36	1,004		
5	4	72	20	917		
6	5	60	47	770		
7	6	96	45	1,456		
8	7	78	44	1,180		
9	8	46	38	710		
10	9	82	70	1,316		
11	10	94	30	1,032		
12	11	68	29	752		
13	12	48	38	963		
14	Total	862	462	$12,501		
15						

Choosing Among Cost Drivers

What guidance do the different cost-estimation methods provide for choosing among cost drivers? The industrial engineering method relies on analyzing physical relationships between cost drivers and costs, relationships that are difficult to specify in this case. The conference method and the account analysis method use subjective assessments to choose a cost driver and to estimate the fixed and variable components of the cost function. In these cases, managers must rely on their best judgment. Managers cannot use these methods to test and try alternative cost drivers. The major advantages of quantitative methods are that they are objective—a given data set and estimation method result in a unique estimated cost function—and managers can use them to evaluate different cost drivers. We use the regression analysis approach to illustrate how to evaluate different cost drivers.

First, the cost analyst at Elegant Rugs enters data in columns C and D of Exhibit 10-7 in Excel and estimates the following regression equation of indirect manufacturing labor costs based on number of direct manufacturing labor-hours:

$$y = \$744.67 + \$7.72X$$

Exhibit 10-8 shows the plot of the data points for number of direct manufacturing labor-hours and indirect manufacturing labor costs, and the regression line that best fits the data. Recall that Exhibit 10-6 shows the corresponding graph when number of machine-hours is the cost driver. To decide which of the two cost drivers Elegant Rugs should choose, the analyst compares the machine-hour regression equation and the direct manufacturing labor-hour regression equation. There are three criteria used to make this evaluation.

1. **Economic plausibility.** Both cost drivers are economically plausible. However, in the state-of-the-art, highly automated production environment at Elegant Rugs, managers familiar with the operations believe that costs such as machine maintenance are likely to be more closely related to number of machine-hours used than to number of direct manufacturing labor-hours used.

2. **Goodness of fit.** Compare Exhibits 10-6 and 10-8. The vertical differences between actual costs and predicted costs are much smaller for the machine-hours regression than for the direct manufacturing labor-hours regression. Number of machine-hours used, therefore, has a stronger relationship—or goodness of fit—with indirect manufacturing labor costs.

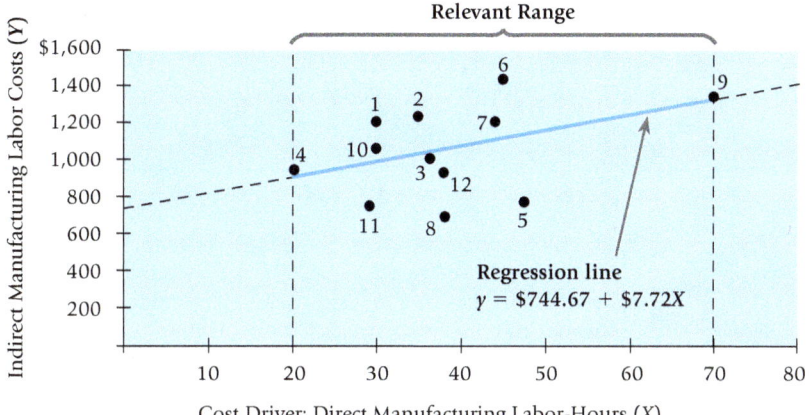

Exhibit 10-8

Regression Model for
Weekly Indirect
Manufacturing Labor
Costs and Direct
Manufacturing Labor-
Hours for Elegant Rugs

3. **Significance of independent variable.** Again compare Exhibits 10-6 and 10-8 (both of which have been drawn to roughly the same scale). The machine-hours regression line has a steep slope relative to the slope of the direct manufacturing labor-hours regression line. *For the same (or more) scatter of observations about the line (goodness of fit), a flat, or slightly sloped regression line indicates a weak relationship between the cost driver and costs.* In our example, changes in direct manufacturing labor-hours appear to have a small influence or effect on indirect manufacturing labor costs.

Based on this evaluation, managers at Elegant Rugs select number of machine-hours as the cost driver and use the cost function y = $300.98 + ($10.31 per machine-hour × Number of machine-hours) to predict future indirect manufacturing labor costs.

Instructors and students who want to explore how regression analysis techniques can be used to choose among different cost drivers can go to the appendix, pages 371–374 and return to this point without any loss of continuity.

Why is choosing the correct cost driver to estimate indirect manufacturing labor costs important? Because identifying the wrong drivers or misestimating cost functions can lead management to incorrect (and costly) decisions along a variety of dimensions. Consider the following strategic decision that management at Elegant Rugs must make. The company is thinking of introducing a new style of carpet that, from a manufacturing standpoint, is similar to the carpets it has manufactured in the past. Prices are set by the market and sales of 650 square yards of this carpet are expected each week. Management estimates 72 machine-hours and 21 direct manufacturing labor-hours would be required per week to produce the 650 square yards of carpet needed. Using the machine-hour regression equation, Elegant Rugs would predict indirect manufacturing labor costs of y = $300.98 + ($10.31 per machine-hour × 72 machine-hours) = $1,043.30. If it used direct manufacturing labor-hours as the cost driver, it would incorrectly predict costs of $744.67 + ($7.72 per labor-hour × 21 labor-hours) = $906.79. If Elegant Rugs chose similarly incorrect cost drivers for other indirect costs as well and systematically underestimated costs, it would conclude that the costs of manufacturing the new style of carpet would be low and basically fixed (fixed because the regression line is nearly flat). But the actual costs driven by number of machine-hours used and other correct cost drivers would be higher. By failing to identify the proper cost drivers, management would be misled into believing the new style of carpet would be more profitable than it actually is. It might decide to introduce the new style of carpet, whereas if Elegant identifies the correct cost driver it might decide not to introduce the new carpet.

Incorrectly estimating the cost function would also have repercussions for cost management and cost control. Suppose number of direct manufacturing labor-hours were used as the cost driver, and actual indirect manufacturing labor costs for the new carpet were $970. Actual costs would then be higher than the predicted costs of $906.79. Management would feel compelled to find ways to cut costs. In fact, on the basis of the preferred machine-hour cost driver, the plant would have actual costs lower than the $1,043.30 predicted costs—a performance that management should seek to replicate, not change!

Concepts in Action

Activity-Based Costing: Identifying Cost and Revenue Drivers

Many cost estimation methods presented in this chapter are essential to service, manufacturing, and retail-sector implementations of activity-based costing across the globe. To determine the cost of an activity in the banking industry, ABC systems often rely on expert analyses and opinions gathered from operating personnel (the conference method). For example, the loan department staff at the Co-operative Bank in the United Kingdom subjectively estimate the costs of the loan processing activity and the quantity of the related cost driver—the number of loans processed, a batch-level cost driver, as distinguished from the amount of the loans, an output unit-level cost driver—to derive the cost of processing a loan.

Elsewhere in the United Kingdom, the City of London police force uses input-output relationships (the industrial engineering method) to identify cost drivers and the cost of an activity. Using a surveying methodology, officials can determine the total costs associated with responding to house robberies, dealing with burglaries, and filling out police reports. In the United States, the Boeing Commercial Airplane Group's Wichita Division used detailed analyses of its commercial airplane-manufacturing methods to support make/buy decisions for complex parts required in airplane assembly. The industrial engineering method is also used by U.S. government agencies such as the U.S. Postal Service to determine the cost of each post office transaction and the U.S. Patent and Trademark Office to identify the costs of each patent examination.

Regression analysis is another helpful tool for determining the cost drivers of activities. Consider how fuel service retailers (that is, gas stations with convenience stores) identify the principal cost driver for labor within their operations. Two possible cost drivers are gasoline sales and convenience store sales. Gasoline sales are batch-level activities because payment transactions occur only once for each gasoline purchase, regardless of the volume of gasoline purchased; whereas convenience store sales are output unit-level activities that vary based on the amount of food, drink, and other products sold. Fuel service retailers generally use convenience store sales as the basis for assigning labor costs because multiple regression analyses confirm that convenience store sales, not gasoline sales, are the major cost driver of labor within their operations.

While popular, these are not the only methods used to evaluate cost drivers. If you recall from chapter five, Charles Schwab is one of the growing number of companies using time-driven activity based costing, which uses time as the cost driver. At Citigroup, the company's internal technology infrastructure group uses time to better manage the labor capacity required to provide reliable, secure, and cost effective technology services to about 60 Citigroup business units around the world.

The trend of using activity-based costing to identify cost and revenue drivers also extends into emerging areas. For example, the U.S. government allocated $19 billion in 2009 to support the adoption of electronic health records. Using the input-output method, many health clinics and doctor's offices are leveraging activity-based costing to identify the cost of adopting this new health information technology tool.

Sources: Barton, T., and J. MacArthur. 2003. Activity-based costing and predatory pricing: The case of the retail industry. *Management Accounting Quarterly* (Spring); Carter, T., A. Sedaghat, and T. Williams. 1998. How ABC changed the post office. *Management Accounting,* (February); The Cooperative Bank. Harvard Business School. Case No. N9-195-196; Federowicz, M., M. Grossman, B. Hayes, and J. Riggs. 2010. A tutorial on activity-based costing of electronic health records. *Quality Management in Health Care* (January–March); Kaplan, Robert, and Steven Anderson. 2008. *Time-driven activity-based costing: A simpler and more powerful path to higher profits.* Boston: Harvard Business School Publishing; Leapman, B. 2006. Police spend £500m filling in forms. *The Daily Telegraph,* January 22; Paduano, Rocco, and Joel Cutcher-Gershenfeld. 2001. Boeing Commercial Airplane Group Wichita Division (Boeing Co.). MIT Labor Aerospace Research Agenda Case Study. Cambridge, MA: MIT; Peckenpaugh, J. 2002. Teaching the ABCs. *Government Executive,* April 1; The United Kingdom Home Office. 2007. *The police service national ABC model: Manual of guidance.* London: Her Majesty's Stationary Office.

Cost Drivers and Activity-Based Costing

Activity-based costing (ABC) systems focus on individual activities—such as product design, machine setup, materials handling, distribution, and customer service—as the fundamental cost objects. To implement ABC systems, managers must identify a cost driver for each activity. For example, using methods described in this chapter, the manager must decide whether the number of loads moved or the weight of loads moved is the cost driver of materials-handling costs.

To choose the cost driver and use it to estimate the cost function in our materials-handling example, the manager collects data on materials-handling costs and the quantities of the two competing cost drivers over a reasonably long period. Why a long period? Because in the short run, materials-handling costs may be fixed and, therefore, will not vary with changes in the level of the cost driver. In the long run, however, there is a clear cause-and-effect relationship between materials-handling costs and the cost driver. Suppose number of loads moved is the cost driver of materials-handling costs. Increases in the number of loads moved will require more materials-handling labor and equipment; decreases will result in equipment being sold and labor being reassigned to other tasks.

ABC systems have a great number and variety of cost drivers and cost pools. That means ABC systems require many cost relationships to be estimated. In estimating the cost function for each cost pool, the manager must pay careful attention to the cost hierarchy. For example, if a cost is a batch-level cost such as setup cost, the manager must only consider batch-level cost drivers like number of setup-hours. In some cases, the costs in a cost pool may have more than one cost driver from different levels of the cost hierarchy. In the Elegant Rugs example, the cost drivers for indirect manufacturing labor costs could be machine-hours and number of production batches of carpet manufactured. Furthermore, it may be difficult to subdivide the indirect manufacturing labor costs into two cost pools and to measure the costs associated with each cost driver. In these cases, companies use multiple regression to estimate costs based on more than one independent variable. The appendix to this chapter discusses multiple regression in more detail.

As the Concepts in Action feature (p. 356) illustrates, managers implementing ABC systems use a variety of methods—industrial engineering, conference, and regression analysis—to estimate slope coefficients. In making these choices, managers trade off level of detail, accuracy, feasibility, and costs of estimating cost functions.

> ◀ **Decision Point**
>
> How should a company evaluate and choose cost drivers?

Nonlinear Cost Functions

In practice, cost functions are not always linear. A **nonlinear cost function** is a cost function for which the graph of total costs (based on the level of a single activity) is not a straight line within the relevant range. To see what a nonlinear cost function looks like, return to Exhibit 10-2 (p. 344). The relevant range is currently set at 20,000 to 65,000 snowboards. But if we extend the relevant range to encompass the region from 0 to 80,000 snowboards produced, it is evident that the cost function over this expanded range is graphically represented by a line that is not straight.

Consider another example. Economies of scale in advertising may enable an advertising agency to produce double the number of advertisements for less than double the costs. Even direct material costs are not always linear variable costs because of quantity discounts on direct material purchases. As shown in Exhibit 10-9 (p. 358), Panel A, total direct material costs rise as the units of direct materials purchased increase. But, because of quantity discounts, these costs rise more slowly (as indicated by the slope coefficient) as the units of direct materials purchased increase. This cost function has b = $25 per unit for 1–1,000 units purchased, b = $15 per unit for 1,001–2,000 units purchased, and b = $10 per unit for 2,001–3,000 units purchased. The direct material cost per unit falls at each price break—that is, the cost per unit decreases with larger purchase orders. If managers are interested in understanding cost behavior over the relevant range from 1 to 3,000 units, the cost function is nonlinear—not a straight line. If, however, managers are only interested in understanding cost behavior over a more narrow relevant range (for example, from 1 to 1,000 units), the cost function is linear.

Step cost functions are also examples of nonlinear cost functions. A **step cost function** is a cost function in which the cost remains the same over various ranges of the level of activity, but the cost increases by discrete amounts—that is, increases in steps—as the level of activity increases from one range to the next. Panel B in Exhibit 10-9 shows a *step variable-cost function*, a step cost function in which cost remains the same over *narrow* ranges of the level of activity in each relevant range. Panel B presents the relationship between units of production and setup costs. The pattern is a step cost function because, as we described in Chapter 5 on activity-based costing, setup costs are

Learning Objective 6

Explain nonlinear cost functions

. . . graph of cost function is not a straight line, for example, because of quantity discounts or costs changing in steps

in particular those arising from learning curve effects

. . . either cumulative average-time learning, where cumulative average time per unit declines by a constant percentage, as units produced double

. . . or incremental unit-time learning, in which incremental time to produce last unit declines by constant percentage, as units produced double

 **Exhibit 10-9** Examples of Nonlinear Cost Functions

PANEL A:
Effects of Quantity Discounts on Slope Coefficient of Direct Material Cost Function

PANEL B:
Step Variable-Cost Function

PANEL C:
Step Fixed-Cost Function

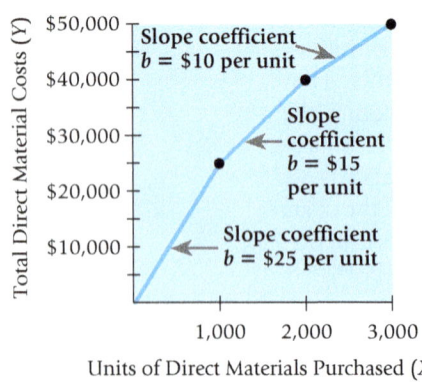

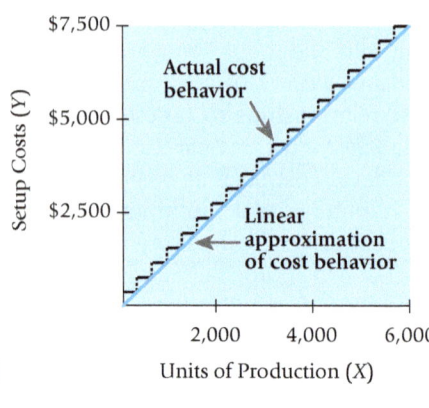

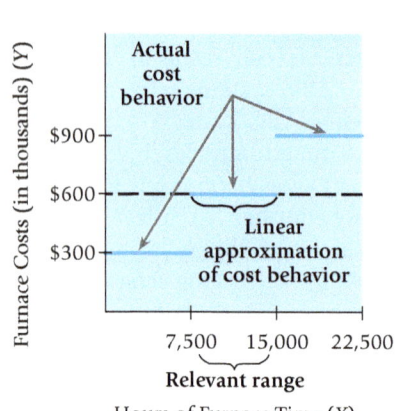

related to each production batch started. If the relevant range is considered to be from 0 to 6,000 production units, the cost function is nonlinear. However, as shown by the blue line in Panel B, managers often approximate step variable costs with a continuously-variable cost function. This type of step cost pattern also occurs when production inputs such as materials-handling labor, supervision, and process engineering labor are acquired in discrete quantities but used in fractional quantities.

Panel C in Exhibit 10-9 shows a *step fixed-cost function* for Crofton Steel, a company that operates large heat-treatment furnaces to harden steel parts. Looking at Panel C and Panel B, you can see that the main difference between a step variable-cost function and a step fixed-cost function is that the cost in a step fixed-cost function remains the same over *wide* ranges of the activity in each relevant range. The ranges indicate the number of furnaces being used (each furnace costs $300,000). The cost increases from one range to the next higher range when the hours of furnace time needed require the use of another furnace. The relevant range of 7,500 to 15,000 hours of furnace time indicates that the company expects to operate with two furnaces at a cost of $600,000. Management considers the cost of operating furnaces as a fixed cost within this relevant range of operation. However, if the relevant range is considered to be from 0 to 22,500 hours, the cost function is nonlinear: The graph in Panel C is not a single straight line; it is three broken lines.

Learning Curves

Nonlinear cost functions also result from learning curves. A **learning curve** is a function that measures how labor-hours per unit decline as units of production increase because workers are learning and becoming better at their jobs. Managers use learning curves to predict how labor-hours, or labor costs, will increase as more units are produced.

The aircraft-assembly industry first documented the effect that learning has on efficiency. In general, as workers become more familiar with their tasks, their efficiency improves. Managers learn how to improve the scheduling of work shifts and how to operate the plant more efficiently. As a result of improved efficiency, unit costs decrease as productivity increases, and the unit-cost function behaves nonlinearly. These nonlinearities must be considered when estimating and predicting unit costs.

Managers have extended the learning-curve notion to other business functions in the value chain, such as marketing, distribution, and customer service, and to costs other than labor costs. The term *experience curve* describes this broader application of the learning curve. An **experience curve** is a function that measures the decline in cost per unit in various business functions of the value chain—marketing, distribution, and so on—as the amount of these activities increases. For companies such as Dell Computer, Wal-Mart, and McDonald's, learning curves and experience curves are key elements of their strategies. These companies use learning curves and experience curves to reduce costs and increase customer satisfaction, market share, and profitability.

We now describe two learning-curve models: the cumulative average-time learning model and the incremental unit-time learning model.

Cumulative Average-Time Learning Model

In the **cumulative average-time learning model,** cumulative average time per unit declines by a constant percentage each time the cumulative quantity of units produced doubles. Consider Rayburn Corporation, a radar systems manufacturer. Rayburn has an 80% learning curve. The 80% means that when the quantity of units produced is doubled from X to $2X$, cumulative average time *per unit* for $2X$ units is 80% of cumulative average time *per unit* for X units. Average time per unit has dropped by 20% (100% − 80%). Exhibit 10-10 is an Excel spreadsheet showing the calculations for the cumulative average-time learning model for Rayburn Corporation. Note that as the number of units produced doubles from 1 to 2 in column A, cumulative average time per unit declines from 100 hours to 80% of 100 hours (0.80 × 100 hours = 80 hours) in column B. As the number of units doubles from 2 to 4, cumulative average time per unit declines to 80% of 80 hours = 64 hours, and so on. To obtain the cumulative total time in column D, multiply cumulative average time per unit by the cumulative number of units produced. For example, to produce 4 cumulative units would require 256 labor-hours (4 units × 64 cumulative average labor-hours per unit).

Exhibit 10-10   Cumulative Average-Time Learning Model for Rayburn Corporation

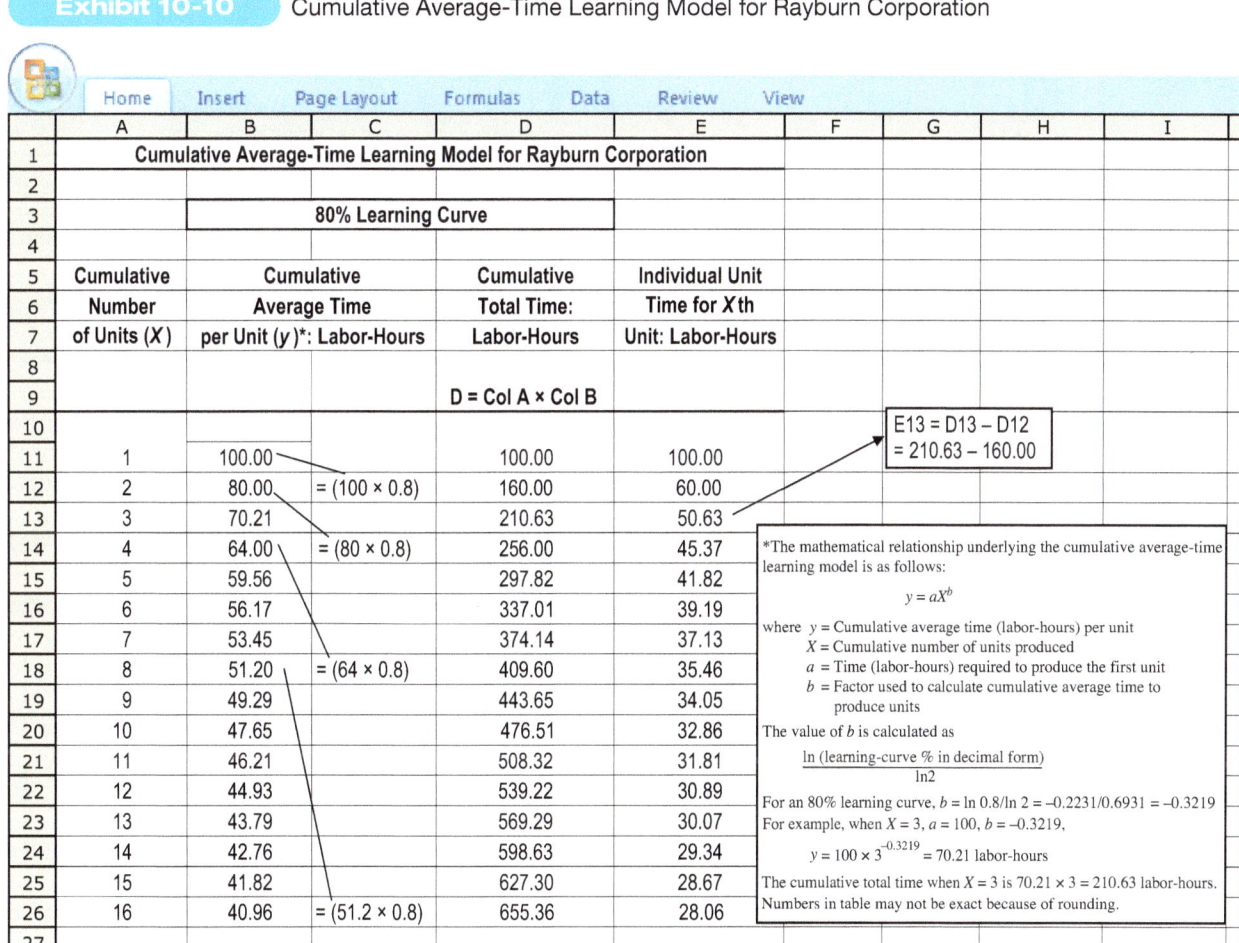

	A	B	C	D	E
1	Cumulative Average-Time Learning Model for Rayburn Corporation				
5	Cumulative	Cumulative		Cumulative	Individual Unit
6	Number	Average Time		Total Time:	Time for X th
7	of Units (X)	per Unit (y)*: Labor-Hours		Labor-Hours	Unit: Labor-Hours
9				D = Col A × Col B	
11	1	100.00		100.00	100.00
12	2	80.00	= (100 × 0.8)	160.00	60.00
13	3	70.21		210.63	50.63
14	4	64.00	= (80 × 0.8)	256.00	45.37
15	5	59.56		297.82	41.82
16	6	56.17		337.01	39.19
17	7	53.45		374.14	37.13
18	8	51.20	= (64 × 0.8)	409.60	35.46
19	9	49.29		443.65	34.05
20	10	47.65		476.51	32.86
21	11	46.21		508.32	31.81
22	12	44.93		539.22	30.89
23	13	43.79		569.29	30.07
24	14	42.76		598.63	29.34
25	15	41.82		627.30	28.67
26	16	40.96	= (51.2 × 0.8)	655.36	28.06

E13 = D13 − D12
= 210.63 − 160.00

*The mathematical relationship underlying the cumulative average-time learning model is as follows:

$$y = aX^b$$

where y = Cumulative average time (labor-hours) per unit
X = Cumulative number of units produced
a = Time (labor-hours) required to produce the first unit
b = Factor used to calculate cumulative average time to produce units

The value of b is calculated as

$$\frac{\ln(\text{learning-curve \% in decimal form})}{\ln 2}$$

For an 80% learning curve, $b = \ln 0.8/\ln 2 = -0.2231/0.6931 = -0.3219$
For example, when $X = 3$, $a = 100$, $b = -0.3219$,

$$y = 100 \times 3^{-0.3219} = 70.21 \text{ labor-hours}$$

The cumulative total time when $X = 3$ is 70.21 × 3 = 210.63 labor-hours. Numbers in table may not be exact because of rounding.

Incremental Unit-Time Learning Model

In the **incremental unit-time learning model,** incremental time needed to produce the last unit declines by a constant percentage each time the cumulative quantity of units produced doubles. Again, consider Rayburn Corporation and an 80% learning curve. The 80% here means that when the quantity of units produced is doubled from X to $2X$, the time needed to produce the last unit when $2X$ total units are produced is 80% of the time needed to produce the last unit when X total units are produced. Exhibit 10-11 is an Excel spreadsheet showing the calculations for the incremental unit-time learning model for Rayburn Corporation based on an 80% learning curve. Note how when units produced double from 2 to 4 in column A, the time to produce unit 4 (the last unit when 4 units are produced) is 64 hours in column B, which is 80% of the 80 hours needed to produce unit 2 (the last unit when 2 units are produced). We obtain the cumulative total time in column D by summing individual unit times in column B. For example, to produce 4 cumulative units would require 314.21 labor-hours (100.00 + 80.00 + 70.21 + 64.00).

Exhibit 10-12 presents graphs using Excel for the cumulative average-time learning model (using data from Exhibit 10-10) and the incremental unit-time learning model (using data from Exhibit 10-11). Panel A graphically illustrates cumulative average time per unit as a function of cumulative units produced for each model (column A in Exhibit 10-10 or 10-11). The curve for the cumulative average-time learning model is plotted using the data from Exhibit 10-10, column B, while the curve for the incremental unit-time learning model is plotted using the data from Exhibit 10-11, column E. Panel B graphically illustrates cumulative total labor-hours, again as a function of cumulative units produced for each model. The curve for the cumulative average-time learning model is plotted using the data from Exhibit 10-10, column D, while that for the incremental unit-time learning model is plotted using the data from Exhibit 10-11, column D.

Exhibit 10-11   Incremental Unit-Time Learning Model for Rayburn Corporation

	A	B	C	D	E	F	G	H	I
1	Incremental Unit-Time Learning Model for Rayburn Corporation								
2									
3			80% Learning Curve						
4									
5	Cumulative	Individual Unit Time		Cumulative	Cumulative				
6	Number	for Xth Unit (y)*:		Total Time:	Average Time				
7	of Units (X)	Labor-Hours		Labor-Hours	per Unit:				
8					Labor-Hours				
9									
10					E = Col D ÷ Col A				
11									
12	1	100.00		100.00	100.00				
13	2	80.00	= (100 × 0.8)	180.00	90.00				
14	3	70.21		250.21	83.40				
15	4	64.00	= (80 × 0.8)	314.21	78.55				
16	5	59.56		373.77	74.75				
17	6	56.17		429.94	71.66				
18	7	53.45		483.39	69.06				
19	8	51.20	= (64 × 0.8)	534.59	66.82				
20	9	49.29		583.89	64.88				
21	10	47.65		631.54	63.15				
22	11	46.21		677.75	61.61				
23	12	44.93		722.68	60.22				
24	13	43.79		766.47	58.96				
25	14	42.76		809.23	57.80				
26	15	41.82		851.05	56.74				
27	16	40.96	= (51.2 × 0.8)	892.01	55.75				
28									

D14 = D13 + B14
= 180.00 + 70.21

*The mathematical relationship underlying the incremental unit-time learning model is as follows:

$$y = aX^b$$

where y = Time (labor-hours) taken to produce the last single unit
X = Cumulative number of units produced
a = Time (labor-hours) required to produce the first unit
b = Factor used to calculate incremental unit time to produce units
$$= \frac{\ln (\text{learning-curve \% in decimal form})}{\ln 2}$$

For an 80% learning curve, $b = \ln 0.8 \div \ln 2 = -0.2231 \div 0.6931 = -0.3219$
For example, when $X = 3$, $a = 100$, $b = -0.3219$,
$$y = 100 \times 3^{-0.3219} = 70.21 \text{ labor-hours}$$
The cumulative total time when $X = 3$ is $100 + 80 + 70.21 = 250.21$ labor-hours.
Numbers in the table may not be exact because of rounding.

Exhibit 10-12 Plots for Cumulative Average-Time Learning Model and Incremental Unit-Time Learning Model for Rayburn Corporation

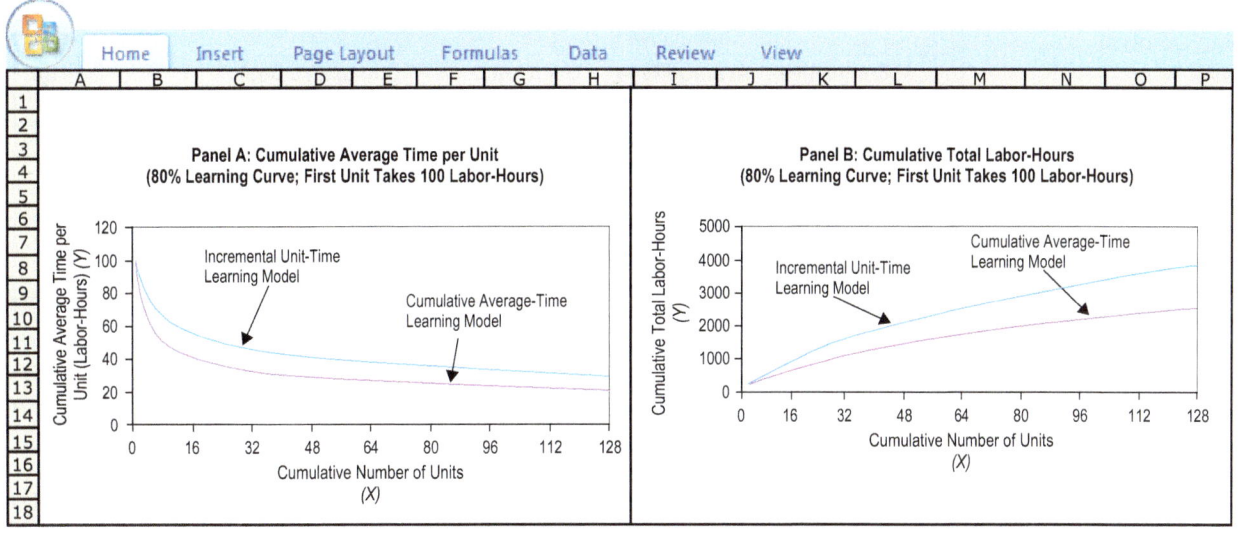

The incremental unit-time learning model predicts a higher cumulative total time to produce 2 or more units than the cumulative average-time learning model, assuming the same learning rate for both models. That is, in Exhibit 10-12, Panel B, the graph for the 80% incremental unit-time learning model lies above the graph for the 80% cumulative average-time learning model. If we compare the results in Exhibit 10-10 (column D) with the results in Exhibit 10-11 (column D), to produce 4 cumulative units, the 80% incremental unit-time learning model predicts 314.21 labor-hours versus 256.00 labor-hours predicted by the 80% cumulative average-time learning model. That's because under the cumulative average-time learning model *average labor-hours needed to produce all 4 units* is 64 hours; the labor-hour amount needed to produce unit 4 is much less than 64 hours—it is 45.37 hours (see Exhibit 10-10). Under the incremental unit-time learning model, the labor-hour amount needed to produce unit 4 is 64 hours, and the labor-hours needed to produce the first 3 units are more than 64 hours, so average time needed to produce all 4 units is more than 64 hours.

How do managers choose which model and what percent learning curve to use? It is important to recognize that managers make their choices on a case-by-case basis. For example, if the behavior of manufacturing labor-hour usage as production levels increase follows a pattern like the one predicted by the 80% learning curve cumulative average-time learning model, then the 80% learning curve cumulative average-time learning model should be used. Engineers, plant managers, and workers are good sources of information on the amount and type of learning actually occurring as production increases. Plotting this information and estimating the model that best fits the data is helpful in selecting the appropriate model.[2]

Incorporating Learning-Curve Effects into Prices and Standards

How do companies use learning curves? Consider the data in Exhibit 10-10 for the cumulative average-time learning model at Rayburn Corporation. Suppose variable costs subject to learning effects consist of direct manufacturing labor, at $20 per hour, and related overhead, at $30 per direct manufacturing labor-hour. Managers should predict the costs shown in Exhibit 10-13.

These data show that the effects of the learning curve could have a major influence on decisions. For example, managers at Rayburn Corporation might set an extremely low selling price on its radar systems to generate high demand. As its production increases to meet this growing demand, cost per unit drops. Rayburn "rides the product down the

[2] For details, see C. Bailey, "Learning Curve Estimation of Production Costs and Labor-Hours Using a Free Excel Add-In," *Management Accounting Quarterly*, (Summer 2000: 25–31). Free software for estimating learning curves is available at Dr. Bailey's Web site, www.profbailey.com.

Exhibit 10-13

Predicting Costs Using
Learning Curves at
Rayburn Corporation

| | Home | Insert | Page Layout | Formulas | Data | Review | View |

	A	B	C	D	E	F
1		Cumulative				
2	Cumulative	Average Time	Cumulative	Cumulative Costs		Additions to
3	Number of	per Unit:	Total Time:	at $50 per		Cumulative
4	Units	Labor-Hours[a]	Labor-Hours[a]	Labor-Hour		Costs
5	1	100.00	100.00	$ 5,000	(100.00 × $50)	$ 5,000
6	2	80.00	160.00	8,000	(160.00 × $50)	3,000
7	4	64.00	256.00	12,800	(256.00 × $50)	4,800
8	8	51.20	409.60	20,480	(409.60 × $50)	7,680
9	16	40.96	655.36	32,768	(655.36 × $50)	12,288
10						
11	[a]Based on the cumulative average-time learning model. See Exhibit 10-10 for the computations					
12	of these amounts.					

learning curve" as it establishes a larger market share. Although it may have earned little operating income on its first unit sold—it may actually have lost money on that unit—Rayburn earns more operating income per unit as output increases.

Alternatively, subject to legal and other considerations, Rayburn's managers might set a low price on just the final 8 units. After all, the total labor and related overhead costs per unit for these final 8 units are predicted to be only $12,288 ($32,768 − $20,480). On these final 8 units, the $1,536 cost per unit ($12,288 ÷ 8 units) is much lower than the $5,000 cost per unit of the first unit produced.

Many companies, such as Pizza Hut and Home Depot, incorporate learning-curve effects when evaluating performance. The Nissan Motor Company expects its workers to learn and improve on the job and evaluates performance accordingly. It sets assembly-labor efficiency standards for new models of cars after taking into account the learning that will occur as more units are produced.

The learning-curve models examined in Exhibits 10-10 to 10-13 assume that learning is driven by a single variable (production output). Other models of learning have been developed (by companies such as Analog Devices and Hewlett-Packard) that focus on how quality—rather than manufacturing labor-hours—will change over time, regardless of whether more units are produced. Studies indicate that factors other than production output, such as job rotation and organizing workers into teams, contribute to learning that improves quality.

Decision Point ▶

What is a nonlinear cost function and in what ways do learning curves give rise to nonlinearities?

Data Collection and Adjustment Issues

The ideal database for estimating cost functions quantitatively has two characteristics:

Learning Objective 7

Be aware of data problems encountered in estimating cost functions

. . . for example, unreliable data and poor record keeping, extreme observations, treating fixed costs as if they are variable, and a changing relationship between a cost driver and cost

1. **The database should contain numerous reliably measured observations of the cost driver (the independent variable) and the related costs (the dependent variable).** Errors in measuring the costs and the cost driver are serious. They result in inaccurate estimates of the effect of the cost driver on costs.

2. **The database should consider many values spanning a wide range for the cost driver.** Using only a few values of the cost driver that are grouped closely considers too small a segment of the relevant range and reduces the confidence in the estimates obtained.

Unfortunately, cost analysts typically do not have the advantage of working with a database having both characteristics. This section outlines some frequently encountered data problems and steps the cost analyst can take to overcome these problems.

1. The time period for measuring the dependent variable (for example, machine-lubricant costs) does not properly match the period for measuring the cost driver. This problem often arises when accounting records are not kept on the accrual basis. Consider a cost function with machine-lubricant costs as the dependent variable and number of machine-hours as the cost driver. Assume that the lubricant is purchased sporadically

and stored for later use. Records maintained on the basis of lubricants purchased will indicate little lubricant costs in many months and large lubricant costs in other months. These records present an obviously inaccurate picture of what is actually taking place. The analyst should use accrual accounting to measure cost of lubricants consumed to better match costs with the machine-hours cost driver in this example.

2. Fixed costs are allocated as if they are variable. For example, costs such as depreciation, insurance, or rent may be allocated to products to calculate cost per unit of output. *The danger is to regard these costs as variable rather than as fixed. They seem to be variable because of the allocation methods used.* To avoid this problem, the analyst should carefully distinguish fixed costs from variable costs and not treat allocated fixed cost per unit as a variable cost.

3. Data are either not available for all observations or are not uniformly reliable. Missing cost observations often arise from a failure to record a cost or from classifying a cost incorrectly. For example, marketing costs may be understated because costs of sales visits to customers may be incorrectly recorded as customer-service costs. Recording data manually rather than electronically tends to result in a higher percentage of missing observations and erroneously entered observations. Errors also arise when data on cost drivers originate outside the internal accounting system. For example, the accounting department may obtain data on testing-hours for medical instruments from the company's manufacturing department and data on number of items shipped to customers from the distribution department. One or both of these departments might not keep accurate records. To minimize these problems, the cost analyst should design data collection reports that regularly and routinely obtain the required data and should follow up immediately whenever data are missing.

4. Extreme values of observations occur from errors in recording costs (for example, a misplaced decimal point), from nonrepresentative periods (for example, from a period in which a major machine breakdown occurred or from a period in which a delay in delivery of materials from an international supplier curtailed production), or from observations outside the relevant range. Analysts should adjust or eliminate unusual observations before estimating a cost relationship.

5. There is no homogeneous relationship between the cost driver and the individual cost items in the dependent variable-cost pool. A homogeneous relationship exists when each activity whose costs are included in the dependent variable has the same cost driver. In this case, a single cost function can be estimated. As discussed in Step 2 for estimating a cost function using quantitative analysis (p. 348), when the cost driver for each activity is different, separate cost functions (each with its own cost driver) should be estimated for each activity. Alternatively, as discussed on pages 372–374, the cost function should be estimated with more than one independent variable using multiple regression.

6. The relationship between the cost driver and the cost is not stationary. That is, the underlying process that generated the observations has not remained stable over time. For example, the relationship between number of machine-hours and manufacturing overhead costs is unlikely to be stationary when the data cover a period in which new technology was introduced. One way to see if the relationship is stationary is to split the sample into two parts and estimate separate cost relationships—one for the period before the technology was introduced and one for the period after the technology was introduced. Then, if the estimated coefficients for the two periods are similar, the analyst can pool the data to estimate a single cost relationship. When feasible, pooling data provides a larger data set for the estimation, which increases confidence in the cost predictions being made.

7. Inflation has affected costs, the cost driver, or both. For example, inflation may cause costs to change even when there is no change in the level of the cost driver. To study the underlying cause-and-effect relationship between the level of the cost driver and costs, the analyst should remove purely inflationary price effects from the data by dividing each cost by the price index on the date the cost was incurred.

In many cases, a cost analyst must expend considerable effort to reduce the effect of these problems before estimating a cost function on the basis of past data.

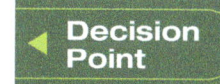

Decision Point

What are the common data problems a company must watch for when estimating costs?

Problem for Self-Study

The Helicopter Division of GLD, Inc., is examining helicopter assembly costs at its Indiana plant. It has received an initial order for eight of its new land-surveying helicopters. GLD can adopt one of two methods of assembling the helicopters:

	Home	Insert	Page Layout	Formulas	Data	Review	View		
	A			B		C		D	E
1				Labor-Intensive Assembly Method				Machine-Intensive Assembly Method	
2	Direct material cost per helicopter			$ 40,000				$36,000	
3	Direct-assembly labor time for first helicopter			2,000	labor-hours			800	labor-hours
4	Learning curve for assembly labor time per helicopter			85%	cumulative average time*			90%	incremental unit time**
5	Direct-assembly labor cost			$ 30	per hour			$ 30	per hour
6	Equipment-related indirect manufacturing cost			$ 12	per direct-assembly labor-hour			$ 45	per direct-assembly labor-hour
7	Material-handling-related indirect manufacturing cost			50%	of direct material cost			50%	of direct material cost
8									
9									
10	*Using the formula (p. 359), for an 85% learning curve, $b = \dfrac{\ln 0.85}{\ln 2} = \dfrac{-0.162519}{0.693147} = -0.234465$								
11									
12									
13									
14									
15	**Using the formula (p. 360), for a 90% learning curve, $b = \dfrac{\ln 0.90}{\ln 2} = \dfrac{-0.105361}{0.693147} = -0.152004$								
16									
17									

Required

1. How many direct-assembly labor-hours are required to assemble the first eight helicopters under (a) the labor-intensive method and (b) the machine-intensive method?
2. What is the total cost of assembling the first eight helicopters under (a) the labor-intensive method and (b) the machine-intensive method?

Solution

1. a. The following calculations show the labor-intensive assembly method based on an 85% cumulative average-time learning model (using Excel):

	Home	Insert	Page Layout	Formulas	Data	Review	View
	G	H	I		J		K
1	Cumulative	Cumulative			Cumulative		Individual
2	Number	Average Time			Total Time:		time for
3	of Units	per Unit (y):			Labor-Hours		Xth unit:
4		Labor-Hours					Labor-Hours
5					Col J = Col G × Col H		
6	1	2,000			2,000		2,000
7	2	1,700	(2,000 × 0.85)		3,400		1,400
8	3	1,546			4,637		1,237
9	4	1,445	(1,700 × 0.85)		5,780		1,143
10	5	1,371			6,857		1,077
11	6	1,314			7,884		1,027
12	7	1,267			8,871		987
13	8	1,228.25	(1,445 × 0.85)		9,826		955
14							

Cumulative average-time per unit for the Xth unit in column H is calculated as $y = aX^b$; see Exhibit 10-10 (p. 359). For example, when $X = 3$, $y = 2{,}000 \times 3^{-0.234465} = 1{,}546$ labor-hours.

b. The following calculations show the machine-intensive assembly method based on a 90% incremental unit-time learning model:

	Home	Insert	Page Layout	Formulas	Data	Review	View	
	G	H	I		J		K	
1	Cumulative	Individual			Cumulative		Cumulative	
2	Number	Unit Time			Total Time:		Average Time	
3	of Units	for *X*th Unit (*y*):			Labor-Hours		Per Unit:	
4		Labor-Hours					Labor-Hours	
5							Col K = Col J ÷ Col G	
6	1	800			800		800	
7	2	720	(800 × 0.9)		1,520		760	
8	3	677			2,197		732	
9	4	648	(720 × 0.9)		2,845		711	
10	5	626			3,471		694	
11	6	609			4,081		680	
12	7	595			4,676		668	
13	8	583	(648 × 0.9)		5,258		657	

Individual unit time for the Xth unit in column H is calculated as $y = aX^b$; see Exhibit 10-11 (p. 360). For example, when $X = 3$, $y = 800 \times 3^{-0.152004} = 677$ labor-hours.

2. Total costs of assembling the first eight helicopters are as follows:

	Home	Insert	Page Layout	Formulas	Data	Review	View	
	O		P	Q
1			Labor-Intensive	Machine-Intensive
2			Assembly Method	Assembly Method
3			(using data from part 1a)	(using data from part 1b)
4	Direct materials:			
5	8 helicopters × $40,000; $36,000 per helicopter		$320,000	$288,000
6	Direct-assembly labor:			
7	9,826 hrs.; 5,258 hrs. × $30/hr.		294,780	157,740
8	Indirect manufacturing costs			
9	Equipment related			
10	9,826 hrs. × $12/hr.; 5,258 hrs. × $45/hr.		117,912	236,610
11	Materials-handling related			
12	0.50 × $320,000; $288,000		160,000	144,000
13	Total assembly costs		$892,692	$826,350

The machine-intensive method's assembly costs are $66,342 lower than the labor-intensive method ($892,692 – $826,350).

Decision Points

The following question-and-answer format summarizes the chapter's learning objectives. Each decision presents a key question related to a learning objective. The guidelines are the answer to that question.

Decision	Guidelines
1. What is a linear cost function and what types of cost behavior can it represent?	A linear cost function is a cost function in which, within the relevant range, the graph of total costs based on the level of a single activity is a straight line. Linear cost functions can be described by a constant, *a*, which represents the estimate of the total cost component that, within the relevant range, does not vary with changes in the level of the activity; and a slope coefficient, *b*, which represents the estimate of the amount by which total costs change for each unit change in the level of the activity within the relevant range. Three types of linear cost functions are variable, fixed, and mixed (or semivariable).
2. What is the most important issue in estimating a cost function?	The most important issue in estimating a cost function is determining whether a cause-and-effect relationship exists between the level of an activity and the costs related to that level of activity. Only a cause-and-effect relationship—not merely correlation—establishes an economically plausible relationship between the level of an activity and its costs.
3. What are the different methods that can be used to estimate a cost function?	Four methods for estimating cost functions are the industrial engineering method, the conference method, the account analysis method, and the quantitative analysis method (which includes the high-low method and the regression analysis method). If possible, the cost analyst should apply more than one method. Each method is a check on the others.
4. What are the steps to estimate a cost function using quantitative analysis?	There are six steps to estimate a cost function using quantitative analysis: (a) Choose the dependent variable; (b) identify the cost driver; (c) collect data on the dependent variable and the cost driver; (d) plot the data; (e) estimate the cost function; and (f) evaluate the cost driver of the estimated cost function. In most situations, working closely with operations managers, the cost analyst will cycle through these steps several times before identifying an acceptable cost function.
5. How should a company evaluate and choose cost drivers?	Three criteria for evaluating and choosing cost drivers are (a) economic plausibility, (b) goodness of fit, and (c) significance of independent variable.
6. What is a nonlinear cost function and in what ways do learning curves give rise to nonlinearities?	A nonlinear cost function is one in which the graph of total costs based on the level of a single activity is not a straight line within the relevant range. Nonlinear costs can arise because of quantity discounts, step cost functions, and learning-curve effects. With learning curves, labor-hours per unit decline as units of production increase. In the cumulative average-time learning model, cumulative average-time per unit declines by a constant percentage each time the cumulative quantity of units produced doubles. In the incremental unit-time learning model, the time needed to produce the last unit declines by a constant percentage each time the cumulative quantity of units produced doubles.
7. What are the common data problems a company must watch for when estimating costs?	The most difficult task in cost estimation is collecting high-quality, reliably measured data on the costs and the cost driver. Common problems include missing data, extreme values of observations, changes in technology, and distortions resulting from inflation.

Appendix

Regression Analysis

This appendix describes estimation of the regression equation, several commonly used regression statistics, and how to choose among cost functions that have been estimated by regression analysis. We use the data for Elegant Rugs presented in Exhibit 10-3 (p. 348) and displayed here again for easy reference.

Week	Cost Driver: Machine-Hours (X)	Indirect Manufacturing Labor Costs (Y)
1	68	$ 1,190
2	88	1,211
3	62	1,004
4	72	917
5	60	770
6	96	1,456
7	78	1,180
8	46	710
9	82	1,316
10	94	1,032
11	68	752
12	48	963
Total	862	$12,501

Estimating the Regression Line

The least-squares technique for estimating the regression line minimizes the sum of the squares of the vertical deviations from the data points to the estimated regression line (also called *residual term* in Exhibit 10-6, p. 352). The objective is to find the values of a and b in the linear cost function $y = a + bX$, where y is the *predicted* cost value as distinguished from the *observed* cost value, which we denote by Y. We wish to find the numerical values of a and b that minimize $\Sigma(Y - y)^2$, the sum of the squares of the vertical deviations between Y and y. Generally, these computations are done using software packages such as Excel. For the data in our example,[3] a = $300.98 and b = $10.31, so that the equation of the regression line is $y = \$300.98 + \$10.31X$.

Goodness of Fit

Goodness of fit measures how well the predicted values, y, based on the cost driver, X, match actual cost observations, Y. The regression analysis method computes a measure of goodness of fit, called the **coefficient of determination**. The coefficient of determination (r^2) measures the percentage of variation in Y explained by X (the independent variable).

---

[3] The formulae for a and b are as follows:

$$a = \frac{(\Sigma Y)(\Sigma X^2) - (\Sigma X)(\Sigma XY)}{n(\Sigma X^2) - (\Sigma X)(\Sigma X)} \text{ and } b = \frac{n(\Sigma XY) - (\Sigma X)(\Sigma Y)}{n(\Sigma X^2) - (\Sigma X)(\Sigma X)}$$

where for the Elegant Rugs data in Exhibit 10-3,

n = number of data points = 12

ΣX = sum of the given X values = 68 + 88 + ... + 48 = 862

ΣX^2 = sum of squares of the X values = $(68)^2 + (88)^2 + ... + (48)^2 + 4,624 + 7,744 + ... + 2,304 = 64,900$

ΣY = sum of given Y values = 1,190 + 1,211 + ... + 963 = 12,501

ΣXY = sum of the amounts obtained by multiplying each of the given X values by the associated observed
Y value = (68)(1,190) + (88)(1,211) + ... + (48)(963)
= 80,920 + 106,568 + ... + 46,224 = 928,716

$$a = \frac{(12,501)(64,900) - (862)(928,716)}{12(64,900) - (862)(862)} = \$300.98$$

$$b = \frac{12(928,716) - (862)(12,501)}{12(64,900) - (862)(862)} = \$10.31$$

It is more convenient to express the coefficient of determination as 1 minus the proportion of total variance that is *not* explained by the independent variable—that is, 1 minus the ratio of unexplained variation to total variation. The unexplained variance arises because of differences between the actual values, Y, and the predicted values, y, which in the Elegant Rugs example is given by[4]

$$r^2 = 1 - \frac{\text{Unexplained variation}}{\text{Total variation}} = 1 - \frac{\Sigma(Y - y)^2}{\Sigma(Y - \bar{Y})^2} = 1 - \frac{290{,}824}{607{,}699} = 0.52$$

The calculations indicate that r^2 increases as the predicted values, y, more closely approximate the actual observations, Y. The range of r^2 is from 0 (implying no explanatory power) to 1 (implying perfect explanatory power). Generally, an r^2 of 0.30 or higher passes the goodness-of-fit test. However, do not rely exclusively on goodness of fit. It can lead to the indiscriminate inclusion of independent variables that increase r^2 but have no economic plausibility as cost drivers. *Goodness of fit has meaning only if the relationship between the cost drivers and costs is economically plausible.*

An alternative and related way to evaluate goodness of fit is to calculate the *standard error of the regression*. The **standard error of the regression** is the variance of the residuals. It is equal to

$$S = \sqrt{\frac{\Sigma(Y - y)^2}{\text{Degrees of freedom}}} = \sqrt{\frac{\Sigma(Y - y)^2}{n - 2}} = \sqrt{\frac{290{,}824}{12 - 2}} = \$170.54$$

Degrees of freedom equal the number of observations, 12, *minus* the number of coefficients estimated in the regression (in this case two, a and b). On average, actual Y and the predicted value, y, differ by \$170.54. For comparison, $\bar{Y}$, the average value of Y, is \$1,041.75. The smaller the standard error of the regression, the better the fit and the better the predictions for different values of X.

Significance of Independent Variables

Do changes in the economically plausible independent variable result in significant changes in the dependent variable? Or alternatively stated, is the slope coefficient, $b = \$10.31$, of the regression line statistically significant (that is, different from \$0)? Recall, for example, that in the regression of number of machine-hours and indirect manufacturing labor costs in the Elegant Rugs illustration, b is estimated from a sample of 12 weekly observations. The estimate, b, is subject to random factors, as are all sample statistics. That is, a different sample of 12 data points would undoubtedly give a different estimate of b. The **standard error of the estimated coefficient** indicates how much the estimated value, b, is likely to be affected by random factors. The *t-value* of the b coefficient measures how large the value of the estimated coefficient is relative to its standard error.

The cutoff *t-value* for making inferences about the b coefficient is a function of the number of degrees of freedom, the significance level, and whether it is a one-sided or two-sided test. A 5% level of significance indicates that there is less than a 5% probability that random factors could have affected the coefficient b. A two-sided test assumes that random factors could have caused the coefficient to be either greater than \$10.31 or less than \$10.31 with equal probability. At a 5% level of significance, this means that there is less than a 2.5% (5% ÷ 2) probability that random factors could have caused the coefficient to be greater than \$10.31 and less than 2.5% probability that random factors could have caused the coefficient to be less than \$10.31. Under the expectation that the coefficient of b is positive, a one-sided test at the 5% level of significance assumes that there is less than 5% probability that random factors would have caused the coefficient to be less than \$10.31. The cutoff *t-value* at the 5% significance level and 10 degrees of freedom for a two-sided test is 2.228. If there were more observations and 60 degrees of freedom, the cutoff *t-value* would be 2.00 at a 5% significance level for a two-sided test.

The *t-value* (called *t* Stat in the Excel output) for the slope coefficient b is the value of the estimated coefficient, \$10.31 ÷ the standard error of the estimated coefficient \$3.12 = 3.30, which exceeds the cutoff *t-value* of 2.228. In other words, a relationship exists between the independent variable, machine-hours, and the dependent variable that cannot be attributed to random chance alone. Exhibit 10-14 shows a convenient format (in Excel) for summarizing the regression results for number of machine-hours and indirect manufacturing labor costs.

---

[4] From footnote 3, $\Sigma Y = 12{,}501$ and $\bar{Y} = 12{,}501 \div 12 = 1{,}041.75$

$$\Sigma(Y - \bar{Y})^2 = (1{,}190 - 1{,}041.75)^2 + (1{,}211 - 1{,}041.75)^2 + \ldots + (963 - 1{,}041.75)^2 = 607{,}699$$

Each value of X generates a predicted value of y. For example, in week 1, $y = \$300.98 + (\$10.31 \times 68) = \$1002.06$; in week 2, $y = \$300.98 + (\$10.31 \times 88) = \$1{,}208.26$; and in week 12, $y = \$300.98 + (\$10.31 \times 48) = \$795.86$. Comparing the predicted and actual values,

$$\Sigma(Y - y)^2 = (1{,}190 - 1{,}002.06)^2 + (1{,}211 - 1208.26)^2 + \ldots + (963 - 795.86)^2 = 290{,}824.$$

Exhibit 10-14	Simple Regression Results with Indirect Manufacturing Labor Costs as Dependent Variable and Machine-Hours as Independent Variable (Cost Driver) for Elegant Rugs

	Home	Insert	Page Layout	Formulas	Data	Review	View		
	A	B		C		D	E	F
1		**Coefficients**		**Standard Error**		**t Stat**		= Coefficient/Standard Error
2		(1)		(2)		(3) = (1) ÷ (2)		= B3/C3
3	Intercept	$300.98		$229.75		1.31 ────────►		= 300.98/229.75
4	Independent Variable: Machine-Hours (X)	$ 10.31		$ 3.12		3.30		
5								
6	**Regression Statistics**							
7	R Square	0.52						
8	Durbin-Watson Statistic	2.05						

An alternative way to test that the coefficient b is significantly different from zero is in terms of a *confidence interval*: There is less than a 5% chance that the true value of the machine-hours coefficient lies outside the range $10.31 ± (2.228 × $3.12), or $10.31 ± $6.95, or from $3.36 to $17.26. Because 0 does not appear in the confidence interval, we conclude that changes in the number of machine-hours do affect indirect manufacturing labor costs. Similarly, using data from Exhibit 10-14, the *t*-value for the constant term a is $300.98 ÷ $229.75 = 1.31, which is less than 2.228. This *t*-value indicates that, within the relevant range, the constant term is *not* significantly different from zero. The Durbin-Watson statistic in Exhibit 10-14 will be discussed in the following section.

Specification Analysis of Estimation Assumptions

Specification analysis is the testing of the assumptions of regression analysis. If the assumptions of (1) linearity within the relevant range, (2) constant variance of residuals, (3) independence of residuals, and (4) normality of residuals all hold, then the simple regression procedures give reliable estimates of coefficient values. This section provides a brief overview of specification analysis. When these assumptions are not satisfied, more-complex regression procedures are necessary to obtain the best estimates.[5]

1. **Linearity within the relevant range.** A common assumption—and one that appears to be reasonable in many business applications—is that a linear relationship exists between the independent variable X and the dependent variable Y within the relevant range. If a linear regression model is used to estimate a nonlinear relationship, however, the coefficient estimates obtained will be inaccurate.

   When there is only one independent variable, the easiest way to check for linearity is to study the data plotted in a scatter diagram, a step that often is unwisely skipped. Exhibit 10-6 (p. 352) presents a scatter diagram for the indirect manufacturing labor costs and machine-hours variables of Elegant Rugs shown in Exhibit 10-3 (p. 348). The scatter diagram reveals that linearity appears to be a reasonable assumption for these data.

   The learning-curve models discussed in this chapter (pp. 358–361) are examples of nonlinear cost functions. Costs increase when the level of production increases, but by lesser amounts than would occur with a linear cost function. In this case, the analyst should estimate a nonlinear cost function that incorporates learning effects.

2. **Constant variance of residuals.** The vertical deviation of the observed value Y from the regression line estimate y is called the *residual term*, *disturbance term*, or *error term*, $u = Y - y$. The assumption of constant variance implies that the residual terms are unaffected by the level of the cost driver. The assumption also implies that there is a uniform scatter, or dispersion, of the data points about the regression line as in Exhibit 10-15, Panel A. This assumption is likely to be violated, for example, in cross-sectional estimation of costs in operations of different sizes. For example, suppose Elegant Rugs has production areas of varying sizes. The company collects data from these different production areas to estimate the relationship between machine-hours and indirect manufacturing labor costs. It is very possible that the residual terms in this regression will be larger for the larger production

[5] For details see, for example, W. H. Greene, *Econometric Analysis*, 6th ed. (Upper Saddle River, NJ: Prentice Hall, 2007).

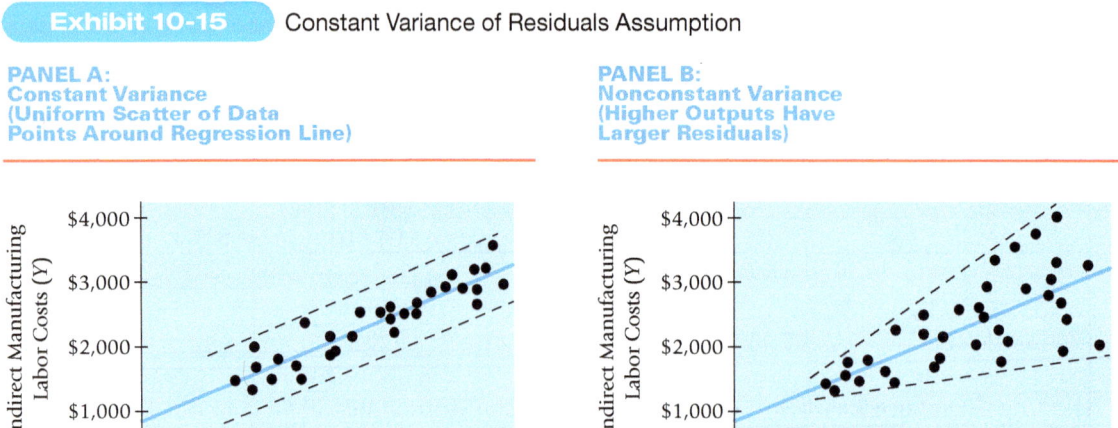

Exhibit 10-15 Constant Variance of Residuals Assumption

PANEL A:
Constant Variance
(Uniform Scatter of Data
Points Around Regression Line)

PANEL B:
Nonconstant Variance
(Higher Outputs Have
Larger Residuals)

areas that have higher machine-hours and higher indirect manufacturing labor costs. There would not be a uniform scatter of data points about the regression line (see Exhibit 10-15, Panel B). Constant variance is also known as *homoscedasticity*. Violation of this assumption is called *heteroscedasticity*.

Heteroscedasticity does not affect the accuracy of the regression estimates a and b. It does, however, reduce the reliability of the estimates of the standard errors and thus affects the precision with which inferences about the population parameters can be drawn from the regression estimates.

3. **Independence of residuals.** The assumption of independence of residuals is that the residual term for any one observation is not related to the residual term for any other observation. The problem of *serial correlation* (also called *autocorrelation*) in the residuals arises when there is a systematic pattern in the sequence of residuals such that the residual in observation n conveys information about the residuals in observations $n + 1$, $n + 2$, and so on. Consider another production cell at Elegant Rugs that has, over a 20-week period, seen an increase in production and hence machine-hours. Exhibit 10-16 Panel B is a scatter diagram of machine-hours and indirect manufacturing labor costs. Observe the systematic pattern of the residuals in Panel B—positive residuals for extreme (high and low) quantities of machine-hours and negative residuals for moderate quantities of machine-hours. One reason for this observed pattern at low values of the cost driver is the "stickiness" of costs. When machine-hours are below 50 hours, indirect manufacturing labor costs do not decline. When machine-hours increase over time as production is ramped up, indirect manufacturing labor costs increase more as managers at Elegant Rugs struggle

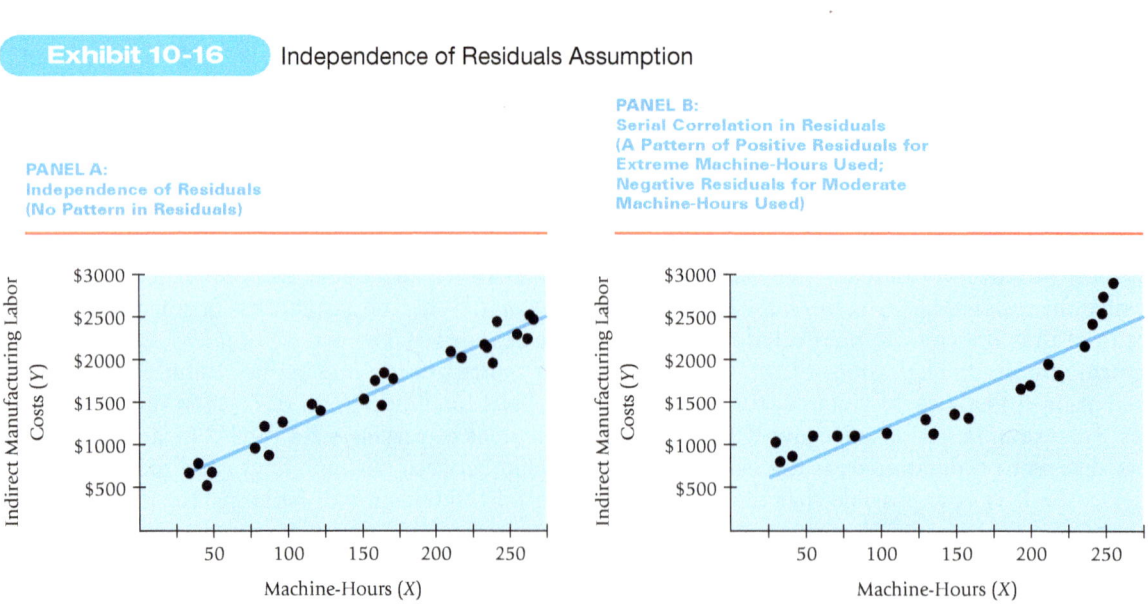

Exhibit 10-16 Independence of Residuals Assumption

PANEL B:
Serial Correlation in Residuals
(A Pattern of Positive Residuals for
Extreme Machine-Hours Used;
Negative Residuals for Moderate
Machine-Hours Used)

PANEL A:
Independence of Residuals
(No Pattern in Residuals)

to manage the higher volume. How would the plot of residuals look if there were no auto-correlation? Like the plot in Exhibit 10-16, Panel A that shows no pattern in the residuals.

Like nonconstant variance of residuals, serial correlation does not affect the accuracy of the regression estimates a and b. It does, however, affect the standard errors of the coefficients, which in turn affect the precision with which inferences about the population parameters can be drawn from the regression estimates.

The Durbin-Watson statistic is one measure of serial correlation in the estimated residuals. For samples of 10 to 20 observations, a Durbin-Watson statistic in the 1.10–2.90 range indicates that the residuals are independent. The Durbin-Watson statistic for the regression results of Elegant Rugs in Exhibit 10-14 is 2.05. Therefore, an assumption of independence in the estimated residuals is reasonable for this regression model.

4. **Normality of residuals.** The normality of residuals assumption means that the residuals are distributed normally around the regression line. The normality of residuals assumption is frequently satisfied when using regression analysis on real cost data. Even when the assumption does not hold, accountants can still generate accurate estimates based on the regression equation, but the resulting confidence interval around these estimates is likely to be inaccurate.

Using Regression Output to Choose Cost Drivers of Cost Functions

Consider the two choices of cost drivers we described earlier in this chapter for indirect manufacturing labor costs (y):

$$y = a + (b \times \text{Number of machine-hours})$$

$$y = a + (b \times \text{Number of direct manufacturing labor-hours})$$

Exhibits 10-6 and 10-8 show plots of the data for the two regressions. Exhibit 10-14 reports regression results for the cost function using number of machine-hours as the independent variable. Exhibit 10-17 presents comparable regression results (in Excel) for the cost function using number of direct manufacturing labor-hours as the independent variable.

On the basis of the material presented in this appendix, which regression is better? Exhibit 10-18 compares these two cost functions in a systematic way. For several criteria, the cost function based on machine-hours is preferable to the cost function based on direct manufacturing labor-hours. The economic plausibility criterion is especially important.

Do not always assume that any one cost function will perfectly satisfy all the criteria in Exhibit 10-18. A cost analyst must often make a choice among "imperfect" cost functions, in the sense that the data of any particular cost function will not perfectly meet one or more of the assumptions underlying regression analysis. For example, both of the cost functions in Exhibit 10-18 are imperfect because, as stated in the section on specification analysis of estimation assumptions, inferences drawn from only 12 observations are not reliable.

Exhibit 10-17   Simple Regression Results with Indirect Manufacturing Labor Costs as Dependent Variable and Direct Manufacturing Labor-Hours as Independent Variable (Cost Driver) for Elegant Rugs

	A	B	C	D	E	F	G	H
		Coefficients	**Standard Error**	**t Stat**				
1								
2		(1)	(2)	(3) = (1) ÷ (2)				
3	Intercept	$744.67	$217.61	3.42				
4	Independent Variable: Direct Manufacturing Labor-Hours (X)	$ 7.72	$ 5.40	1.43		= Coefficient/Standard Error = B4/C4 = 7.72/5.40		
5								
6	**Regression Statistics**							
7	R Square	0.17						
8	Durbin-Watson Statistic	2.26						

Exhibit 10-18	Comparison of Alternative Cost Functions for Indirect Manufacturing Labor Costs Estimated with Simple Regression for Elegant Rugs

Criterion	Cost Function 1: Machine-Hours as Independent Variable	Cost Function 2: Direct Manufacturing Labor-Hours as Independent Variable
Economic plausibility	A positive relationship between indirect manufacturing labor costs (technical support labor) and machine-hours is economically plausible in Elegant Rugs' highly automated plant	A positive relationship between indirect manufacturing labor costs and direct manufacturing labor-hours is economically plausible, but less so than machine-hours in Elegant Rugs' highly automated plant on a week-to-week basis.
Goodness of fit[a]	$r^2 = 0.52$; standard error of regression = $170.50. Excellent goodness of fit.	$r^2 = 0.17$; standard error of regression = $224.60. Poor goodness of fit.
Significance of independent variable(s)	The t-value of 3.30 is significant at the 0.05 level.	The t-value of 1.43 is not significant at the 0.05 level.
Specification analysis of estimation assumptions	Plot of the data indicates that assumptions of linearity, constant variance, independence of residuals (Durbin-Watson statistic = 2.05), and normality of residuals hold, but inferences drawn from only 12 observations are not reliable.	Plot of the data indicates that assumptions of linearity, constant variance, independence of residuals (Durbin-Watson statistic = 2.26), and normality of residuals hold, but inferences drawn from only 12 observations are not reliable.

[a]If the number of observations available to estimate the machine-hours regression differs from the number of observations available to estimate the direct manufacturing labor-hours regression, an *adjusted* r^2 can be calculated to take this difference (in degrees of freedom) into account. Programs such as Excel calculate and present *adjusted* r^2.

Multiple Regression and Cost Hierarchies

In some cases, a satisfactory estimation of a cost function may be based on only one independent variable, such as number of machine-hours. In many cases, however, basing the estimation on more than one independent variable (that is, *multiple regression*) is more economically plausible and improves accuracy. The most widely used equations to express relationships between two or more independent variables and a dependent variable are linear in the form

$$y = a + b_1X_1 + b_2X_2 + \dots + u$$

where,

y = Cost to be predicted

$X_1, X_2, \dots$ = Independent variables on which the prediction is to be based

$a, b_1, b_2, \dots$ = Estimated coefficients of the regression model

u = Residual term that includes the net effect of other factors not in the model as well as measurement errors in the dependent and independent variables

Example: Consider the Elegant Rugs data in Exhibit 10-19. The company's ABC analysis indicates that indirect manufacturing labor costs include large amounts incurred for setup and changeover costs when a new batch of carpets is started. Management believes that in addition to number of machine-hours (an output unit-level cost driver), indirect manufacturing labor costs are also affected by the number of batches of carpet produced during each week (a batch-level driver). Elegant Rugs estimates the relationship between two independent variables, number of machine-hours and number of production batches of carpet manufactured during the week, and indirect manufacturing labor costs.

Exhibit 10-19

Weekly Indirect Manufacturing Labor Costs, Machine-Hours, Direct Manufacturing Labor-Hours, and Number of Production Batches for Elegant Rugs

	Home	Insert	Page Layout	Formulas	Data	Review	View
	A	B	C	D	E
1	Week	Machine-Hours (X_1)	Number of Production Batches (X_2)	Direct Manufacturing Labor-Hours	Indirect Manufacturing Labor Costs (Y)
2	1	68	12	30	$ 1,190
3	2	88	15	35	1,211
4	3	62	13	36	1,004
5	4	72	11	20	917
6	5	60	10	47	770
7	6	96	12	45	1,456
8	7	78	17	44	1,180
9	8	46	7	38	710
10	9	82	14	70	1,316
11	10	94	12	30	1,032
12	11	68	7	29	752
13	12	48	14	38	963
14	Total	862	144	462	$12,501
15					

Exhibit 10-20 presents results (in Excel) for the following multiple regression model, using data in columns B, C, and E of Exhibit 10-19:

$$y = \$42.58 + \$7.60X_1 + \$37.77X_2$$

where X_1 is the number of machine-hours and X_2 is the number of production batches. It is economically plausible that both number of machine-hours and number of production batches would help explain variations in indirect manufacturing labor costs at Elegant Rugs. The r^2 of 0.52 for the simple regression using number of machine-hours (Exhibit 10-14) increases to 0.72 with the multiple regression in Exhibit 10-20. The t-values suggest that the independent variable coefficients of both number of machine-hours ($7.60) and number of production batches ($37.77) are significantly different from zero ($t = 2.74$ is the t-value for number of machine-hours, and $t = 2.48$ is the t-value for number of production batches compared to the cut-off t-value of 2.26). The multiple regression model in Exhibit 10-20 satisfies both economic plausibility and statistical criteria, and it explains much greater variation (that

Exhibit 10-20 Multiple Regression Results with Indirect Manufacturing Labor Costs and Two Independent Variables of Cost Drivers (Machine-Hours and Production Batches) for Elegant Rugs

	Home	Insert	Page Layout	Formulas	Data	Review	View
	A	B	C	D	E	F
1		Coefficients	Standard Error	t Stat		
2		(1)	(2)	(3) = (1) ÷ (2)		
3	Intercept	$42.58	$213.91	0.20		
4	Independent Variable 1: Machine-Hours ($X1$)	$ 7.60	$ 2.77	2.74		= Coefficient/Standard Error = B4/C4 = 7.60/2.77
5	Independent Variable 2: Number of Production Batches ($X2$)	$37.77	$ 15.25	2.48		
6						
7	**Regression Statistics**					
8	R Square	0.72				
9	Durbin-Watson Statistic	2.49				

is, r^2 of 0.72 versus r^2 of 0.52) in indirect manufacturing labor costs than the simple regression model using only number of machine-hours as the independent variable.[6] The standard error of the regression equation that includes number of batches as an independent variable is

$$\sqrt{\frac{\Sigma(Y-y)^2}{n-3}} = \sqrt{\frac{170,156}{9}} = \$137.50$$

which is lower than the standard error of the regression with only machine-hours as the independent variable, $170.50. That is, even though adding a variable reduces the degrees of freedom in the denominator, it substantially improves fit so that the numerator, $\Sigma(Y-y)^2$, decreases even more. Number of machine-hours and number of production batches are both important cost drivers of indirect manufacturing labor costs at Elegant Rugs.

In Exhibit 10-20, the slope coefficients—$7.60 for number of machine-hours and $37.77 for number of production batches—measure the change in indirect manufacturing labor costs associated with a unit change in an independent variable (assuming that the other independent variable is held constant). For example, indirect manufacturing labor costs increase by $37.77 when one more production batch is added, assuming that the number of machine-hours is held constant.

An alternative approach would create two separate cost pools for indirect manufacturing labor costs: one for costs related to number of machine-hours and another for costs related to number of production batches. Elegant Rugs would then estimate the relationship between the cost driver and the costs in each cost pool. The difficult task under this approach is to properly subdivide the indirect manufacturing labor costs into the two cost pools.

Multicollinearity

A major concern that arises with multiple regression is multicollinearity. **Multicollinearity** exists when two or more independent variables are highly correlated with each other. Generally, users of regression analysis believe that a *coefficient of correlation* between independent variables greater than 0.70 indicates multicollinearity. Multicollinearity increases the standard errors of the coefficients of the individual variables. That is, variables that are economically and statistically significant will appear not to be significantly different from zero.

The matrix of correlation coefficients of the different variables described in Exhibit 10-19 are as follows:

	Indirect Manufacturing Labor Costs	Machine-Hours	Number of Production Batches	Direct Manufacturing Labor-Hours
Indirect manufacturing labor costs	1			
Machine-hours	0.72	1		
Number of production batches	0.69	0.4	1	
Direct manufacturing labor-hours	0.41	0.12	0.31	1

These results indicate that multiple regressions using any pair of the independent variables in Exhibit 10-19 are not likely to encounter multicollinearity problems.

When multicollinearity exists, try to obtain new data that do not suffer from multicollinearity problems. Do not drop an independent variable (cost driver) that should be included in a model because it is correlated with another independent variable. Omitting such a variable will cause the estimated coefficient of the independent variable included in the model to be biased away from its true value.

---

[6] Adding another variable always increases r^2. The question is whether adding another variable increases r^2 sufficiently. One way to get insight into this question is to calculate an adjusted r^2 as follows:

Adjusted $r^2 = 1 - (1-r^2)\frac{n-1}{n-p-1}$, where n is the number of observations and p is the number of coefficients estimated. In the model with only machine-hours as the independent variable, adjusted $r^2 = 1 - (1-0.52)\frac{12-1}{12-2-1} = 0.41$. In the model with both machine-hours and number of batches as independent variables, adjusted $r^2 = 1 - (1-0.72)\frac{12-1}{12-3-1} = 0.62$. Adjusted r^2 does not have the same interpretation as r^2 but the increase in adjusted r^2 when number of batches is added as an independent variable suggests that adding this variable significantly improves the fit of the model in a way that more than compensates for the degree of freedom lost by estimating another coefficient.

Terms to Learn

This chapter and the Glossary at the end of this book contain definitions of the following important terms:

account analysis method (**p. 347**)
coefficient of determination (r^2) (**p. 367**)
conference method (**p. 346**)
constant (**p. 343**)
cost estimation (**p. 344**)
cost function (**p. 341**)
cost predictions (**p. 344**)
cumulative average-time learning
  model (**p. 359**)
dependent variable (**p. 348**)
experience curve (**p. 358**)
high-low method (**p. 350**)

incremental unit-time learning model
  (**p. 360**)
independent variable (**p. 348**)
industrial engineering method (**p. 346**)
intercept (**p. 343**)
learning curve (**p. 358**)
linear cost function (**p. 342**)
mixed cost (**p. 343**)
multicollinearity (**p. 374**)
multiple regression (**p. 352**)
nonlinear cost function (**p. 357**)
regression analysis (**p. 352**)

residual term (**p. 352**)
semivariable cost (**p. 343**)
simple regression (**p. 352**)
slope coefficient (**p. 342**)
specification analysis (**p. 369**)
standard error of the estimated
  coefficient (**p. 368**)
standard error of the regression
  (**p. 368**)
step cost function (**p. 357**)
work-measurement method (**p. 346**)

Assignment Material

Questions

10-1 What two assumptions are frequently made when estimating a cost function?

10-2 Describe three alternative linear cost functions.

10-3 What is the difference between a linear and a nonlinear cost function? Give an example of each type of cost function.

10-4 "High correlation between two variables means that one is the cause and the other is the effect." Do you agree? Explain.

10-5 Name four approaches to estimating a cost function.

10-6 Describe the conference method for estimating a cost function. What are two advantages of this method?

10-7 Describe the account analysis method for estimating a cost function.

10-8 List the six steps in estimating a cost function on the basis of an analysis of a past cost relationship. Which step is typically the most difficult for the cost analyst?

10-9 When using the high-low method, should you base the high and low observations on the dependent variable or on the cost driver?

10-10 Describe three criteria for evaluating cost functions and choosing cost drivers.

10-11 Define learning curve. Outline two models that can be used when incorporating learning into the estimation of cost functions.

10-12 Discuss four frequently encountered problems when collecting cost data on variables included in a cost function.

10-13 What are the four key assumptions examined in specification analysis in the case of simple regression?

10-14 "All the independent variables in a cost function estimated with regression analysis are cost drivers." Do you agree? Explain.

10-15 "Multicollinearity exists when the dependent variable and the independent variable are highly correlated." Do you agree? Explain.

Exercises

10-16 Estimating a cost function. The controller of the Ijiri Company wants you to estimate a cost function from the following two observations in a general ledger account called Maintenance:

Month	Machine-Hours	Maintenance Costs Incurred
January	6,000	$4,000
February	10,000	5,400

Required

1. Estimate the cost function for maintenance.
2. Can the constant in the cost function be used as an estimate of fixed maintenance cost per month? Explain.

10-17 Identifying variable-, fixed-, and mixed-cost functions. The Pacific Corporation operates car rental agencies at more than 20 airports. Customers can choose from one of three contracts for car rentals of one day or less:

- Contract 1: $50 for the day
- Contract 2: $30 for the day plus $0.20 per mile traveled
- Contract 3: $1 per mile traveled

Required

1. Plot separate graphs for each of the three contracts, with costs on the vertical axis and miles traveled on the horizontal axis.
2. Express each contract as a linear cost function of the form $y = a + bX$.
3. Identify each contract as a variable-, fixed-, or mixed-cost function.

10-18 Various cost-behavior patterns. (CPA, adapted) Select the graph that matches the numbered manufacturing cost data (requirements 1–9). Indicate by letter which graph best fits the situation or item described.

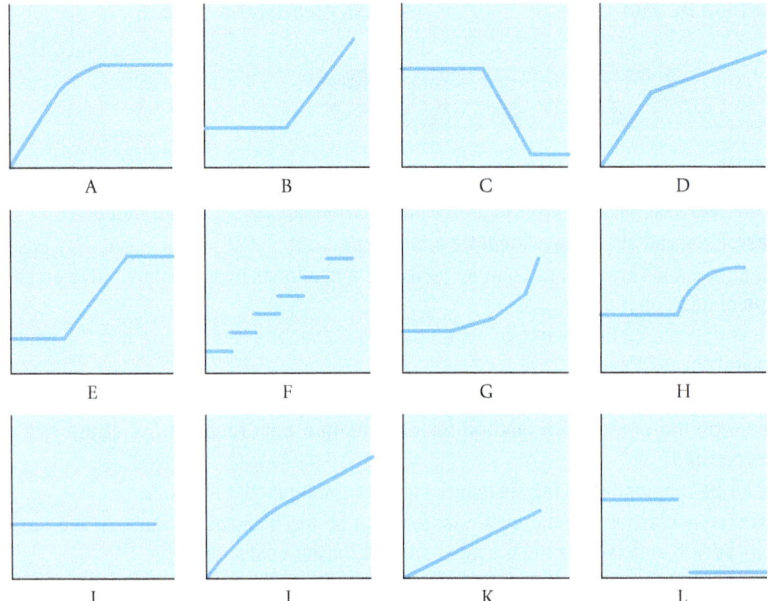

The vertical axes of the graphs represent total cost, and the horizontal axes represent units produced during a calendar year. In each case, the zero point of dollars and production is at the intersection of the two axes. The graphs may be used more than once.

Required

1. Annual depreciation of equipment, where the amount of depreciation charged is computed by the machine-hours method.
2. Electricity bill—a flat fixed charge, plus a variable cost after a certain number of kilowatt-hours are used, in which the quantity of kilowatt-hours used varies proportionately with quantity of units produced.
3. City water bill, which is computed as follows:

First 1,000,000 gallons or less	$1,000 flat fee
Next 10,000 gallons	$0.003 per gallon used
Next 10,000 gallons	$0.006 per gallon used
Next 10,000 gallons	$0.009 per gallon used
and so on	and so on

The gallons of water used vary proportionately with the quantity of production output.

4. Cost of direct materials, where direct material cost per unit produced decreases with each pound of material used (for example, if 1 pound is used, the cost is $10; if 2 pounds are used, the cost is $19.98; if 3 pounds are used, the cost is $29.94), with a minimum cost per unit of $9.20.

5. Annual depreciation of equipment, where the amount is computed by the straight-line method. When the depreciation schedule was prepared, it was anticipated that the obsolescence factor would be greater than the wear-and-tear factor.

6. Rent on a manufacturing plant donated by the city, where the agreement calls for a fixed-fee payment unless 200,000 labor-hours are worked, in which case no rent is paid.

7. Salaries of repair personnel, where one person is needed for every 1,000 machine-hours or less (that is, 0 to 1,000 hours requires one person, 1,001 to 2,000 hours requires two people, and so on).

8. Cost of direct materials used (assume no quantity discounts).

9. Rent on a manufacturing plant donated by the county, where the agreement calls for rent of $100,000 to be reduced by $1 for each direct manufacturing labor-hour worked in excess of 200,000 hours, but a minimum rental fee of $20,000 must be paid.

10-19 Matching graphs with descriptions of cost and revenue behavior. (D. Green, adapted) Given here are a number of graphs.

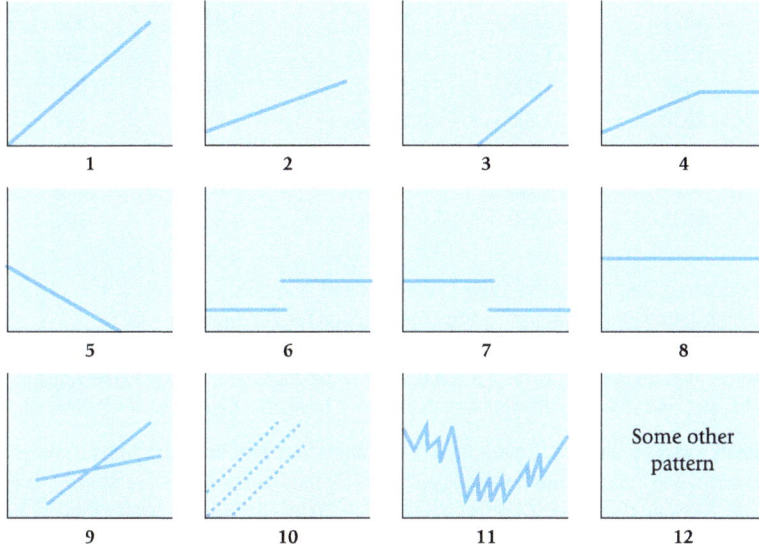

The horizontal axis represents the units produced over the year and the vertical axis represents total cost or revenues. Indicate by number which graph best fits the situation or item described (a–h). Some graphs may be used more than once; some may not apply to any of the situations.

a. Direct material costs
b. Supervisors' salaries for one shift and two shifts
c. A cost-volume-profit graph
d. Mixed costs—for example, car rental fixed charge plus a rate per mile driven
e. Depreciation of plant, computed on a straight-line basis
f. Data supporting the use of a variable-cost rate, such as manufacturing labor cost of $14 per unit produced
g. Incentive bonus plan that pays managers $0.10 for every unit produced above some level of production
h. Interest expense on $2 million borrowed at a fixed rate of interest

10-20 Account analysis method. Lorenzo operates a car wash. Incoming cars are put on an automatic conveyor belt. Cars are washed as the conveyor belt carries them from the start station to the finish station. After a car moves off the conveyor belt, it is dried manually. Workers then clean and vacuum the inside of the car. Lorenzo serviced 80,000 cars in 2012. Lorenzo reports the following costs for 2012:

Account Description	Costs
Car wash labor	$260,000
Soap, cloth, and supplies	42,000
Water	38,000
Electric power to move conveyor belt	72,000
Depreciation	64,000
Salaries	46,000

1. Classify each account as variable or fixed with respect to the number of cars washed. Explain.
2. Suppose Lorenzo washed 90,000 cars in 2012. Use the cost classification you developed in requirement 1 to estimate Lorenzo's total costs in 2012. Depreciation is computed on a straight-line basis.

10-21 Account analysis, high-low. Java Joe Coffees wants to find an equation to estimate monthly utility costs. Java Joe's has been in business for one year and has collected the following cost data for utilities:

Month	Electricity Bill	Kilowatt Hours Used	Telephone Bill	Telephone Minutes Used	Water Bill	Gallons of Water Used
January	$360	1,200	$92.00	1,100	$60	30,560
February	$420	1,400	$91.20	1,060	$60	26,800
March	$549	1,830	$94.80	1,240	$60	31,450
April	$405	1,350	$89.60	980	$60	29,965
May	$588	1,960	$98.00	1,400	$60	30,568
June	$624	2,080	$98.80	1,440	$60	25,540
July	$522	1,740	$93.40	1,170	$60	32,690
August	$597	1,990	$96.20	1,310	$60	31,222
September	$630	2,100	$95.60	1,280	$60	33,540
October	$615	2,050	$93.80	1,190	$60	31,970
November	$594	1,980	$91.00	1,050	$60	28,600
December	$633	2,110	$97.00	1,350	$60	34,100

1. Which of the preceding costs is variable? Fixed? Mixed? Explain.
2. Using the high-low method, determine the cost function for each cost.
3. Combine the preceding information to get a monthly utility cost function for Java Joe's.
4. Next month, Java Joe's expects to use 2,200 kilowatt hours of electricity, make 1,500 minutes of telephone calls, and use 32,000 gallons of water. Estimate total cost of utilities for the month.

10-22 Account analysis method. Gower, Inc., a manufacturer of plastic products, reports the following manufacturing costs and account analysis classification for the year ended December 31, 2012.

Account	Classification	Amount
Direct materials	All variable	$300,000
Direct manufacturing labor	All variable	225,000
Power	All variable	37,500
Supervision labor	20% variable	56,250
Materials-handling labor	50% variable	60,000
Maintenance labor	40% variable	75,000
Depreciation	0% variable	95,000
Rent, property taxes, and administration	0% variable	100,000

Gower, Inc., produced 75,000 units of product in 2012. Gower's management is estimating costs for 2013 on the basis of 2012 numbers. The following additional information is available for 2013.

a. Direct materials prices in 2013 are expected to increase by 5% compared with 2012.
b. Under the terms of the labor contract, direct manufacturing labor wage rates are expected to increase by 10% in 2013 compared with 2012.
c. Power rates and wage rates for supervision, materials handling, and maintenance are not expected to change from 2012 to 2013.
d. Depreciation costs are expected to increase by 5%, and rent, property taxes, and administration costs are expected to increase by 7%.
e. Gower expects to manufacture and sell 80,000 units in 2013.

1. Prepare a schedule of variable, fixed, and total manufacturing costs for each account category in 2013. Estimate total manufacturing costs for 2013.
2. Calculate Gower's total manufacturing cost per unit in 2012, and estimate total manufacturing cost per unit in 2013.
3. How can you obtain better estimates of fixed and variable costs? Why would these better estimates be useful to Gower?

10-23 **Estimating a cost function, high-low method.** Reisen Travel offers helicopter service from suburban towns to John F. Kennedy International Airport in New York City. Each of its 10 helicopters makes between 1,000 and 2,000 round-trips per year. The records indicate that a helicopter that has made 1,000 round-trips in the year incurs an average operating cost of $350 per round-trip, and one that has made 2,000 round-trips in the year incurs an average operating cost of $300 per round-trip.

Required

1. Using the high-low method, estimate the linear relationship $y = a + bX$, where y is the total annual operating cost of a helicopter and X is the number of round-trips it makes to JFK airport during the year.
2. Give examples of costs that would be included in a and in b.
3. If Reisen Travel expects each helicopter to make, on average, 1,200 round-trips in the coming year, what should its estimated operating budget for the helicopter fleet be?

10-24 **Estimating a cost function, high-low method.** Laurie Daley is examining customer-service costs in the southern region of Capitol Products. Capitol Products has more than 200 separate electrical products that are sold with a six-month guarantee of full repair or replacement with a new product. When a product is returned by a customer, a service report is prepared. This service report includes details of the problem and the time and cost of resolving the problem. Weekly data for the most recent 8-week period are as follows:

Week	Customer-Service Department Costs	Number of Service Reports
1	$13,700	190
2	20,900	275
3	13,000	115
4	18,800	395
5	14,000	265
6	21,500	455
7	16,900	340
8	21,000	305

Required

1. Plot the relationship between customer-service costs and number of service reports. Is the relationship economically plausible?
2. Use the high-low method to compute the cost function, relating customer-service costs to the number of service reports.
3. What variables, in addition to number of service reports, might be cost drivers of weekly customer-service costs of Capitol Products?

10-25 **Linear cost approximation.** Terry Lawler, managing director of the Chicago Reviewers Group, is examining how overhead costs behave with changes in monthly professional labor-hours billed to clients. Assume the following historical data:

Total Overhead Costs	Professional Labor-Hours Billed to Clients
$335,000	2,000
400,000	3,000
430,000	4,000
472,000	5,000
533,000	6,500
582,000	7,500

Required

1. Compute the linear cost function, relating total overhead costs to professional labor-hours, using the representative observations of 3,000 and 6,500 hours. Plot the linear cost function. Does the constant component of the cost function represent the fixed overhead costs of the Chicago Reviewers Group? Why?
2. What would be the predicted total overhead costs for (a) 4,000 hours and (b) 7,500 hours using the cost function estimated in requirement 1? Plot the predicted costs and actual costs for 4,000 and 7,500 hours.
3. Lawler had a chance to accept a special job that would have boosted professional labor-hours from 3,000 to 4,000 hours. Suppose Lawler, guided by the linear cost function, rejected this job because it would have brought a total increase in contribution margin of $35,000, before deducting the predicted increase in total overhead cost, $38,000. What is the total contribution margin actually forgone?

10-26 Cost-volume-profit and regression analysis. Goldstein Corporation manufactures a children's bicycle, model CT8. Goldstein currently manufactures the bicycle frame. During 2012, Goldstein made 32,000 frames at a total cost of $1,056,000. Ryan Corporation has offered to supply as many frames as Goldstein wants at a cost of $32.50 per frame. Goldstein anticipates needing 35,000 frames each year for the next few years.

Required

1. **a.** What is the average cost of manufacturing a bicycle frame in 2012? How does it compare to Ryan's offer?
   b. Can Goldstein use the answer in requirement 1a to determine the cost of manufacturing 35,000 bicycle frames? Explain.
2. Goldstein's cost analyst uses annual data from past years to estimate the following regression equation with total manufacturing costs of the bicycle frame as the dependent variable and bicycle frames produced as the independent variable:

$$y = \$435{,}000 + \$19X$$

During the years used to estimate the regression equation, the production of bicycle frames varied from 31,000 to 35,000. Using this equation, estimate how much it would cost Goldstein to manufacture 35,000 bicycle frames. How much more or less costly is it to manufacture the frames rather than to acquire them from Ryan?
3. What other information would you need to be confident that the equation in requirement 2 accurately predicts the cost of manufacturing bicycle frames?

10-27 Regression analysis, service company. (CMA, adapted) Bob Jones owns a catering company that prepares food and beverages for banquets and parties. For a standard party the cost on a per-person basis is as follows:

Food and beverages	$15
Labor (0.5 hour × $10 per hour)	5
Overhead (0.5 hour × $14 per hour)	7
Total cost per person	$27

Jones is quite certain about his estimates of the food, beverages, and labor costs but is not as comfortable with the overhead estimate. The overhead estimate was based on the actual data for the past 12 months, which are presented here. These data indicate that overhead costs vary with the direct labor-hours used. The $14 estimate was determined by dividing total overhead costs for the 12 months by total labor-hours.

Month	Labor-Hours	Overhead Costs
January	2,500	$ 55,000
February	2,700	59,000
March	3,000	60,000
April	4,200	64,000
May	7,500	77,000
June	5,500	71,000
July	6,500	74,000
August	4,500	67,000
September	7,000	75,000
October	4,500	68,000
November	3,100	62,000
December	6,500	73,000
Total	57,500	$805,000

Jones has recently become aware of regression analysis. He estimated the following regression equation with overhead costs as the dependent variable and labor-hours as the independent variable:

$$y = \$48{,}271 + \$3.93X$$

Required

1. Plot the relationship between overhead costs and labor-hours. Draw the regression line and evaluate it using the criteria of economic plausibility, goodness of fit, and slope of the regression line.
2. Using data from the regression analysis, what is the variable cost per person for a standard party?
3. Bob Jones has been asked to prepare a bid for a 200-person standard party to be given next month. Determine the minimum bid price that Jones would be willing to submit to recoup variable costs.

10-28 High-low, regression. Melissa Crupp is the new manager of the materials storeroom for Canton Manufacturing. Melissa has been asked to estimate future monthly purchase costs for part #4599, used in two of Canton's products. Melissa has purchase cost and quantity data for the past nine months as follows:

Month	Cost of Purchase	Quantity Purchased
January	$10,390	2,250 parts
February	10,550	2,350
March	14,400	3,390
April	13,180	3,120
May	10,970	2,490
June	11,580	2,680
July	12,690	3,030
August	8,560	1,930
September	12,450	2,960

Estimated monthly purchases for this part based on expected demand of the two products for the rest of the year are as follows:

Month	Purchase Quantity Expected
October	2,800 parts
November	3,100
December	2,500

Required

1. The computer in Melissa's office is down and Melissa has been asked to immediately provide an equation to estimate the future purchase cost for part # 4599. Melissa grabs a calculator and uses the high-low method to estimate a cost equation. What equation does she get?
2. Using the equation from requirement 1, calculate the future expected purchase costs for each of the last three months of the year.
3. After a few hours Melissa's computer is fixed. Melissa uses the first nine months of data and regression analysis to estimate the relationship between the quantity purchased and purchase costs of part #4599. The regression line Melissa obtains is as follows:

$$y = \$1,779.6 + 3.67X$$

Evaluate the regression line using the criteria of economic plausibility, goodness of fit, and significance of the independent variable. Compare the regression equation to the equation based on the high-low method. Which is a better fit? Why?
4. Use the regression results to calculate the expected purchase costs for October, November, and December. Compare the expected purchase costs to the expected purchase costs calculated using the high-low method in requirement 2. Comment on your results.

10-29 Learning curve, cumulative average-time learning model. Global Defense manufactures radar systems. It has just completed the manufacture of its first newly designed system, RS-32. Manufacturing data for the RS-32 follow:

	Home	Insert	Page Layout	Formulas	Data	Review	View	

	A	B	C
1	Direct material cost	$160,000	per unit of RS-32
2	Direct manufacturing labor time for first unit	6,000	direct manufacturing labor-hours
3	Learning curve for manufacturing labor time per radar system	85%	cumulative average time[a]
4	Direct manufacturing labor cost	$ 30	per direct manufacturing labor-hour
5	Variable manufacturing overhead cost	$ 20	per direct manufacturing labor-hour
6			
7	[a]Using the formula (p. 359), for a 85% learning curve, $b = \dfrac{\ln 0.85}{\ln 2} = \dfrac{-0.162519}{0.693147} = -0.234465$		
8			

Required   Calculate the total variable costs of producing 2, 4, and 8 units.

10-30 Learning curve, incremental unit-time learning model. Assume the same information for Global Defense as in Exercise 10-29, except that Global Defense uses an 85% incremental unit-time learning model as a basis for predicting direct manufacturing labor-hours. (An 85% learning curve means $b = -0.234465$.)

Required

1. Calculate the total variable costs of producing 2, 3, and 4 units.
2. If you solved Exercise 10-29, compare your cost predictions in the two exercises for 2 and 4 units. Why are the predictions different? How should Global Defense decide which model it should use?

Problems

10-31 High-low method. Ken Howard, financial analyst at KMW Corporation, is examining the behavior of quarterly maintenance costs for budgeting purposes. Howard collects the following data on machine-hours worked and maintenance costs for the past 12 quarters:

Quarter	Machine-Hours	Maintenance Costs
1	100,000	$205,000
2	120,000	240,000
3	110,000	220,000
4	130,000	260,000
5	95,000	190,000
6	115,000	235,000
7	105,000	215,000
8	125,000	255,000
9	105,000	210,000
10	125,000	245,000
11	115,000	200,000
12	140,000	280,000

Required

1. Estimate the cost function for the quarterly data using the high-low method.
2. Plot and comment on the estimated cost function.
3. Howard anticipates that KMW will operate machines for 100,000 hours in quarter 13. Calculate the predicted maintenance costs in quarter 13 using the cost function estimated in requirement 1.

10-32 High-low method and regression analysis. Local Harvest, a cooperative of organic family-owned farms outside of Columbus, Ohio, has recently started a fresh produce club to provide support to the group's member farms, and to promote the benefits of eating organic, locally-produced food to the nearby suburban community. Families pay a seasonal membership fee of $50, and place their orders a week in advance for a price of $40 per week. In turn, Local Harvest delivers fresh-picked seasonal local produce to several neighborhood distribution points. Eight hundred families joined the club for the first season, but the number of orders varied from week to week.

Harvey Hendricks has run the produce club for the first 10-week season. Before becoming a farmer, Harvey had been a business major in college, and he remembers a few things about cost analysis. In planning for next year, he wants to know how many orders will be needed each week for the club to break even, but first he must estimate the club's fixed and variable costs. He has collected the following data over the club's first 10 weeks of operation:

Week	Number of Orders per Week	Weekly Total Costs
1	351	$18,795
2	385	21,597
3	410	22,800
4	453	22,600
5	425	21,900
6	486	24,600
7	455	23,900
8	467	22,900
9	525	25,305
10	510	24,500

Required

1. Plot the relationship between number of orders per week and weekly total costs.
2. Estimate the cost equation using the high-low method, and draw this line on your graph.
3. Harvey uses his computer to calculate the following regression formula:

$$\text{Total weekly costs} = \$8,631 + (\$31.92 \times \text{Number of weekly orders})$$

Draw the regression line on your graph. Use your graph to evaluate the regression line using the criteria of economic plausibility, goodness of fit, and significance of the independent variable. Is the cost function estimated using the high-low method a close approximation of the cost function estimated using the regression method? Explain briefly.

4. Did Fresh Harvest break even this season? Remember that each of the families paid a seasonal membership fee of $50.

5. Assume that 900 families join the club next year, and that prices and costs do not change. How many orders, on average, must Fresh Harvest receive each week to break even?

10-33 High-low method; regression analysis. (CIMA, adapted) Anna Martinez, the financial manager at the Casa Real restaurant, is checking to see if there is any relationship between newspaper advertising and sales revenues at the restaurant. She obtains the following data for the past 10 months:

Month	Revenues	Advertising Costs
March	$50,000	$2,000
April	70,000	3,000
May	55,000	1,500
June	65,000	3,500
July	55,000	1,000
August	65,000	2,000
September	45,000	1,500
October	80,000	4,000
November	55,000	2,500
December	60,000	2,500

She estimates the following regression equation:

$$\text{Monthly revenues} = \$39,502 + (\$8.723 \times \text{Advertising costs})$$

Required

1. Plot the relationship between advertising costs and revenues.
2. Draw the regression line and evaluate it using the criteria of economic plausibility, goodness of fit, and slope of the regression line.
3. Use the high-low method to compute the function, relating advertising costs and revenues.
4. Using (a) the regression equation and (b) the high-low equation, what is the increase in revenues for each $1,000 spent on advertising within the relevant range? Which method should Martinez use to predict the effect of advertising costs on revenues? Explain briefly.

10-34 Regression, activity-based costing, choosing cost drivers. Fitzgerald Manufacturing has been using activity-based costing to determine the cost of product X-678. One of the activities, "Inspection," occurs just before the product is finished. Fitzgerald inspects every 10th unit, and has been using "number of units inspected" as the cost driver for inspection costs. A significant component of inspection costs is the cost of the test-kit used in each inspection.

Neela McFeen, the line manager, is wondering if inspection labor-hours might be a better cost driver for inspection costs. Neela gathers information for weekly inspection costs, units inspected, and inspection labor-hours as follows:

Week	Units Inspected	Inspection Labor-Hours	Inspection Costs
1	1,400	190	$3,700
2	400	70	1,800
3	1,700	230	4,500
4	2,400	240	5,900
5	2,100	210	5,300
6	700	90	2,400
7	900	110	2,900

Neela runs regressions on each of the possible cost drivers and estimates these cost functions:

$$\text{Inspection Costs} = \$977 + (\$2.05 \times \text{Number of units inspected})$$
$$\text{Inspection Costs} = \$478 + (\$20.31 \times \text{Inspection labor-hours})$$

Required

1. Explain why number of units inspected and inspection labor-hours are plausible cost drivers of inspection costs.
2. Plot the data and regression line for units inspected and inspection costs. Plot the data and regression line for inspection labor-hours and inspection costs. Which cost driver of inspection costs would you choose? Explain.
3. Neela expects inspectors to work 140 hours next period and to inspect 1,100 units. Using the cost driver you chose in requirement 2, what amount of inspection costs should Neela budget? Explain any implications of Neela choosing the cost driver you did not choose in requirement 2 to budget inspection costs.

10-35 Interpreting regression results, matching time periods. Brickman Apparel produces equipment for the extreme-sports market. It has four peak periods, each lasting two months, for manufacturing the merchandise suited for spring, summer, fall, and winter. In the off-peak periods, Brickman schedules equipment maintenance. Brickman's controller, Sascha Green, wants to understand the drivers of equipment maintenance costs. The data collected is shown in the table as follows:

Month	Machine-Hours	Maintenance Costs
January	5,000	$ 1,300
February	5,600	2,200
March	1,500	12,850
April	6,500	1,665
May	5,820	2,770
June	1,730	15,250
July	7,230	1,880
August	5,990	2,740
September	2,040	15,350
October	6,170	1,620
November	5,900	2,770
December	1,500	14,700

A regression analysis of one year of monthly data yields the following relationships:

$$\text{Maintenance costs} = \$18,552 - (\$2.683 \times \text{Number of machine-hours})$$

Upon examining the results, Green comments, "So, all I have to do to reduce maintenance costs is run my machines longer?! This is hard to believe, but numbers don't lie! I would have guessed just the opposite."

Required

1. Explain why Green made this comment. What is wrong with her analysis?
2. Upon further reflection, Sascha Green reanalyzes the data, this time comparing quarterly machine-hours with quarterly maintenance expenditures. This time, the results are very different. The regression yields the following formula:

$$\text{Maintenance costs} = \$2,622.80 + (\$1.175 \times \text{Number of machine-hours})$$

What caused the formula to change, in light of the fact that the data was the same?

10-36 Cost estimation, cumulative average-time learning curve. The Nautilus Company, which is under contract to the U.S. Navy, assembles troop deployment boats. As part of its research program, it completes the assembly of the first of a new model (PT109) of deployment boats. The Navy is impressed with the PT109. It requests that Nautilus submit a proposal on the cost of producing another six PT109s.

Nautilus reports the following cost information for the first PT109 assembled and uses a 90% cumulative average-time learning model as a basis for forecasting direct manufacturing labor-hours for the next six PT109s. (A 90% learning curve means $b = -0.152004$.)

	A	B	C
	Home Insert Page Layout Formulas Data Review View		
1	Direct material	$200,000	
2	Direct manufacturing labor time for first boat	15,000	labor-hours
3	Direct manufacturing labor rate	$ 40	per direct manufacturing labor-hour
4	Variable manufacturing overhead cost	$ 25	per direct manufacturing labor-hour
5	Other manufacturing overhead	20%	of direct manufacturing labor costs
6	Tooling costs[a]	$280,000	
7	Learning curve for manufacturing labor time per boat	90%	cumulative average time[b]
8			
9	[a]Tooling can be reused at no extra cost because all of its cost has been assigned to the first deployment boat.		
10			
11	[b]Using the formula (p. 359), for a 90% learning curve, $b = \dfrac{\ln 0.9}{\ln 2} = \dfrac{-0.105361}{0.693147} = -0.152004$		
12			

1. Calculate predicted total costs of producing the six PT109s for the Navy. (Nautilus will keep the first deployment boat assembled, costed at $1,575,000, as a demonstration model for potential customers.) **Required**
2. What is the dollar amount of the difference between (a) the predicted total costs for producing the six PT109s in requirement 1, and (b) the predicted total costs for producing the six PT109s, assuming that there is no learning curve for direct manufacturing labor? That is, for (b) assume a linear function for units produced and direct manufacturing labor-hours.

10-37 Cost estimation, incremental unit-time learning model. Assume the same information for the Nautilus Company as in Problem 10-36 with one exception. This exception is that Nautilus uses a 90% incremental unit-time learning model as a basis for predicting direct manufacturing labor-hours in its assembling operations. (A 90% learning curve means $b = -0.152004$.)

1. Prepare a prediction of the total costs for producing the six PT109s for the Navy. **Required**
2. If you solved requirement 1 of Problem 10-36, compare your cost prediction there with the one you made here. Why are the predictions different? How should Nautilus decide which model it should use?

10-38 Regression; choosing among models. Tilbert Toys (TT) makes the popular Floppin' Freddy Frog and Jumpin' Jill Junebug dolls in batches. TT has recently adopted activity-based costing. TT incurs setup costs for each batch of dolls that it produces. TT uses "number of setups" as the cost driver for setup costs.

TT has just hired Bebe Williams, an accountant. Bebe thinks that "number of setup-hours" might be a better cost driver because the setup time for each product is different. Bebe collects the following data.

	A	B	C	D
	Home Insert Page Layout Formulas Data Review View			
1	Month	Number of Setups	Number of Setup Hours	Setup Costs
2	1	300	1,840	$104,600
3	2	410	2,680	126,700
4	3	150	1,160	57,480
5	4	480	3,800	236,840
6	5	310	3,680	178,880
7	6	460	3,900	213,760
8	7	420	2,980	209,620
9	8	300	1,200	90,080
10	9	270	3,280	221,040

Required **1.** Estimate the regression equation for (a) setup costs and number of setups and (b) setup costs and number of setup-hours. You should obtain the following results:

Regression 1: Setup costs = $a + (b \times$ Number of setups)

Variable	Coefficient	Standard Error	t-Value
Constant	$12,890	$61,365	0.21
Independent variable 1: No. of setups	$ 426.77	$ 171	2.49

$r^2 = 0.47$; Durbin-Watson statistic = 1.65

Regression 2: Setup costs = $a + (b \times$ Number of setup-hours)

Variable	Coefficient	Standard Error	t-Value
Constant	$6,573	$ 25,908	0.25
Independent variable 1: No. of setup-hours	$ 56.27	$ 8.90	6.32

$r^2 = 0.85$; Durbin-Watson statistic = 1.50

2. On two different graphs plot the data and the regression lines for each of the following cost functions:
   a. Setup costs = $a + (b \times$ Number of setups)
   b. Setup costs = $a + (b \times$ Number of setup-hours)
3. Evaluate the regression models for "Number of setups" and "Number of setup-hours" as the cost driver according to the format of Exhibit 10-18 (p. 372).
4. Based on your analysis, which cost driver should Tilbert Toys use for setup costs, and why?

10-39 Multiple regression (continuation of 10-38). Bebe Williams wonders if she should run a multiple regression with both number of setups and number of setup-hours, as cost drivers.

Required **1.** Run a multiple regression to estimate the regression equation for setup costs using both number of setups and number of setup-hours as independent variables. You should obtain the following result:

Regression 3: Setup costs = $a (b_1 \times$ No. of setups) + $(b_2 \times$ No. of setup-hours)

Variable	Coefficient	Standard Error	t-Value
Constant	−$2,807	$34,850	−0.08
Independent variable 1: No. of setups	$ 58.62	$ 133.42	0.44
Independent variable 2: No. of setup-hours	$ 52.31	$ 13.08	4.00

$r^2 = 0.86$; Durbin-Watson statistic = 1.38

2. Evaluate the multiple regression output using the criteria of economic plausibility goodness of fit, significance of independent variables, and specification of estimation assumptions. (Assume linearity, constant variance, and normality of residuals.)
3. What difficulties do not arise in simple regression analysis that may arise in multiple regression analysis? Is there evidence of such difficulties in the multiple regression presented in this problem? Explain.
4. Which of the regression models from Problems 10-38 and 10-39 would you recommend Bebe Williams use? Explain.

10-40 Purchasing department cost drivers, activity-based costing, simple regression analysis. Fashion Bling operates a chain of 10 retail department stores. Each department store makes its own purchasing decisions. Barry Lee, assistant to the president of Fashion Bling, is interested in better understanding the drivers of purchasing department costs. For many years, Fashion Bling has allocated purchasing department costs to products on the basis of the dollar value of merchandise purchased. A $100 item is allocated 10 times as many overhead costs associated with the purchasing department as a $10 item.

Lee recently attended a seminar titled "Cost Drivers in the Retail Industry." In a presentation at the seminar, Couture Fabrics, a leading competitor that has implemented activity-based costing, reported number of purchase orders and number of suppliers to be the two most important cost drivers of purchasing department costs. The dollar value of merchandise purchased in each purchase order was not found to be a significant cost driver. Lee interviewed several members of the purchasing department at the Fashion Bling store in Miami. They believed that Couture Fabrics' conclusions also applied to their purchasing department.

Lee collects the following data for the most recent year for Fashion Bling's 10 retail department stores:

	Home	Insert	Page Layout	Formulas	Data	Review	View	
	A		B	C	D	E		
1	Department Store		Purchasing Department Costs (PDC)	Dollar Value of Merchandise Purchased (MP$)	Number of Purchase Orders (No. of POs)	Number of Suppliers (No. of Ss)		
2	Baltimore		$1,522,000	$ 68,307,000	4,345	125		
3	Chicago		1,095,000	33,463,000	2,548	230		
4	Los Angeles		542,000	121,800,000	1,420	8		
5	Miami		2,053,000	119,450,000	5,935	188		
6	New York		1,068,000	33,575,000	2,786	21		
7	Phoenix		517,000	29,836,000	1,334	29		
8	Seattle		1,544,000	102,840,000	7,581	101		
9	St. Louis		1,761,000	38,725,000	3,623	127		
10	Toronto		1,605,000	139,300,000	1,712	202		
11	Vancouver		1,263,000	130,110,000	4,736	196		

Lee decides to use simple regression analysis to examine whether one or more of three variables (the last three columns in the table) are cost drivers of purchasing department costs. Summary results for these regressions are as follows:

Regression 1: PDC = $a + (b \times$ MP$)$

Variable	Coefficient	Standard Error	t-Value
Constant	$1,041,421	$346,709	3.00
Independent variable 1: MP$	0.0031	0.0038	0.83

$r^2 = 0.08$; Durbin-Watson statistic = 2.41

Regression 2: PDC = $a (b \times$ No. of POs$)$

Variable	Coefficient	Standard Error	t-Value
Constant	$722,538	$265,835	2.72
Independent variable 1: No. of POs	$ 159.48	$ 64.84	2.46

$r^2 = 0.43$; Durbin-Watson statistic = 1.97

Regression 3: PDC = $a + (b \times$ No. of Ss$)$

Variable	Coefficient	Standard Error	t-Value
Constant	$828,814	$246,570	3.36
Independent variable 1: No. of Ss	$ 3,816	$ 1,698	2.25

$r^2 = 0.39$; Durbin-Watson statistic = 2.01

1. Compare and evaluate the three simple regression models estimated by Lee. Graph each one. Also, **Required** use the format employed in Exhibit 10-18 (p. 372) to evaluate the information.
2. Do the regression results support the Couture Fabrics' presentation about the purchasing department's cost drivers? Which of these cost drivers would you recommend in designing an ABC system?
3. How might Lee gain additional evidence on drivers of purchasing department costs at each of Fashion Bling's stores?

10-41 Purchasing department cost drivers, multiple regression analysis (continuation of 10-40). Barry Lee decides that the simple regression analysis used in Problem 10-40 could be extended to a multiple regression analysis. He finds the following results for two multiple regression analyses:

Regression 4: PDC = $a + (b_1 \times$ No. of POs) + $(b_2 \times$ No. of Ss)

Variable	Coefficient	Standard Error	t-Value
Constant	$484,522	$256,684	1.89
Independent variable 1: No. of POs	$ 126.66	$ 57.80	2.19
Independent variable 2: No. of Ss	$ 2,903	$ 1,459	1.99

$r^2 = 0.64$; Durbin-Watson statistic = 1.91

Regression 5: PDC = $a + (b_1 \times$ No. of POs) + $(b_2 \times$ No. of Ss) + $(b_3 \times$ MP$)

Variable	Coefficient	Standard Error	t-Value
Constant	$483,560	$312,554	1.55
Independent variable 1: No. of POs	$ 126.58	$ 63.75	1.99
Independent variable 2: No. of Ss	$ 2,901	$ 1,622	1.79
Independent variable 3: MP$	0.00002	0.0029	0.01

$r^2 = 0.64$; Durbin-Watson statistic = 1.91

The coefficients of correlation between combinations of pairs of the variables are as follows:

	PDC	MP$	No. of POs
MP$	0.28		
No. of POs	0.66	0.27	
No. of Ss	0.62	0.30	0.29

Required

1. Evaluate regression 4 using the criteria of economic plausibility, goodness of fit, significance of independent variables and specification analysis. Compare regression 4 with regressions 2 and 3 in Problem 10-40. Which one of these models would you recommend that Lee use? Why?
2. Compare regression 5 with regression 4. Which one of these models would you recommend that Lee use? Why?
3. Lee estimates the following data for the Baltimore store for next year: dollar value of merchandise purchased, $78,000,000; number of purchase orders, 4,000; number of suppliers, 95. How much should Lee budget for purchasing department costs for the Baltimore store for next year?
4. What difficulties do not arise in simple regression analysis that may arise in multiple regression analysis? Is there evidence of such difficulties in either of the multiple regressions presented in this problem? Explain.
5. Give two examples of decisions in which the regression results reported here (and in Problem 10-40) could be informative.

Collaborative Learning Problem

10-42 Interpreting regression results, matching time periods, ethics. Jayne Barbour is working as a summer intern at Mode, a trendy store specializing in clothing for twenty-somethings. Jayne has been working closely with her cousin, Gail Hubbard, who plans promotions for Mode. The store has only been in business for 10 months, and Valerie Parker, the store's owner, has been unsure of the effectiveness of the store's advertising. Wanting to impress Valerie with the regression analysis skills she acquired in a cost accounting course the previous semester, Jayne decides to prepare an analysis of the effect of advertising on revenues. She collects the following data:

	Home	Insert	Page Layout	Formulas
	A	B	C	
1	**Month**	**Advertising Expense**	**Revenue**	
2	October	4,560	$35,400	
3	November	3,285	44,255	
4	December	1,200	56,300	
5	January	4,099	28,764	
6	February	3,452	49,532	
7	March	1,075	43,200	
8	April	4,768	30,600	
9	May	4,775	52,137	
10	June	1,845	49,640	
11	July	1,430	29,542	

Jayne performs a regression analysis, comparing each month's advertising expense with that month's revenue, and obtains the following formula:

$$\text{Revenue} = \$47{,}801 - (1.92 \times \text{Advertising expense})$$

Variable	Coefficient	Standard Error	t-Value
Constant	$47,801.72	7,628.39	6.27
Independent variable: Advertising expense	−1.92	2.26	−0.85

$r^2 = 0.43$; Standard error = 10,340.18

Required

1. Plot the preceding data on a graph and draw the regression line. What does the cost formula indicate about the relationship between monthly advertising expense and monthly revenues? Is the relationship economically plausible?
2. Jayne worries that if she makes her presentation to the owner as planned, it will reflect poorly on her cousin Gail's performance. Is she ethically obligated to make the presentation?
3. Jayne thinks further about her analysis, and discovers a significant flaw in her approach. She realizes that advertising done in a given month should be expected to influence the following month's sales, not necessarily the current month's. She modifies her analysis by comparing, for example, October advertising expense with November sales revenue. The modified regression yields the following:

$$\text{Revenue} = \$23{,}538 + (5.92 \times \text{Advertising expense})$$

Variable	Coefficient	Standard Error	t-Value
Constant	$23,538.45	4,996.60	4.71
Independent variable: Previous month's advertising expense	5.92	1.42	4.18

$r^2 = 0.71$; Standard error = 6,015.67

What does the revised cost formula indicate? Plot the revised data on a graph. (You will need to discard October revenue and July advertising expense from the data set.) Is this relationship economically plausible?

4. Can Jayne conclude that there is a cause and effect relationship between advertising expense and sales revenue? Why or why not?

Decision Making and Relevant Information

How many decisions have you made today?

Maybe you made a big one, such as accepting a job offer. Or maybe your decision was as simple as settling on your plans for the weekend or choosing a restaurant for dinner. Regardless of whether decisions are significant or routine, most people follow a simple, logical process when making them. This process involves gathering information, making predictions, making a choice, acting on the choice, and evaluating results. It also includes deciding what costs and benefits each choice affords. Some costs are irrelevant. For example, once a coffee maker is purchased, its cost is irrelevant when deciding how much money a person saves each time he or she brews coffee at home versus buying it at Starbucks. The cost of the coffee maker was incurred in the past, and the money is spent and can't be recouped. This chapter will explain which costs and benefits are relevant and which are not—and how you should think of them when choosing among alternatives.

Relevant Costs, JetBlue, and Twitter[1]

What does it cost JetBlue to fly a customer on a round-trip flight from New York City to Nantucket? The incremental cost is very small, around $5 for beverages, because the other costs (the plane, pilots, ticket agents, fuel, airport landing fees, and baggage handlers) are fixed. Because most costs are fixed, would it be worthwhile for JetBlue to fill a seat provided it earns at least $5 for that seat? The answer depends on whether the flight is full.

Suppose JetBlue normally charges $330 for this round-trip ticket. If the flight is full, JetBlue would not sell the ticket for anything less than $330, because there are still customers willing to pay this fare for the flight. What if there are empty seats? Selling a ticket for something more than $5 is better than leaving the seat empty and earning nothing.

If a customer uses the Internet to purchase the ticket a month in advance, JetBlue will likely quote $330 because it expects the flight to be full. If, on the Monday before the scheduled Friday departure, JetBlue finds that the plane will not be full, the airline may be willing to lower its prices dramatically in hopes of attracting more customers and earning a profit on the unfilled seats.

---

[1] *Source*: Jones, Charisse. 2009. JetBlue and United give twitter a try to sell airline seats fast. *USA Today*, August 2. www.usatoday.com/travel/flights/2009-08-02-jetblue-united-twitter-airfares_N.htm

Enter Twitter. Like the e-mails that Jet Blue has sent out to customers for years, the widespread messaging service allows JetBlue to quickly connect with customers and fill seats on flights that might otherwise take off less than full. When JetBlue began promoting last-minute fare sales on Twitter in 2009 and Twitter-recipients learned that $330 round-trip tickets from New York City to Nantucket were available for just $18, the flights filled up quickly. JetBlue's Twitter fare sales usually last only eight hours, or until all available seats are sold. To use such a pricing strategy requires a deep understanding of costs in different decision situations.

Just like JetBlue, managers in corporations around the world use a decision process to help them make decisions. Managers at JPMorgan Chase gather information about financial markets, consumer preferences, and economic trends before determining whether to offer new services to customers. Macy's managers examine all the relevant information related to domestic and international clothing manufacturing before selecting vendors. Managers at Porsche gather cost information to decide whether to manufacture a component part or purchase it from a supplier. The decision process may not always be easy, but as Napoleon Bonaparte said, "Nothing is more difficult, and therefore more precious, than to be able to decide."

Information and the Decision Process

Managers usually follow a *decision model* for choosing among different courses of action. A **decision model** is a formal method of making a choice that often involves both quantitative and qualitative analyses. Management accountants analyze and present relevant data to guide managers' decisions.

Consider a strategic decision facing management at Precision Sporting Goods, a manufacturer of golf clubs: Should it reorganize its manufacturing operations to reduce manufacturing labor costs? Precision Sporting Goods has only two alternatives: Do not reorganize or reorganize.

Reorganization will eliminate all manual handling of materials. Current manufacturing labor consists of 20 workers—15 workers operate machines, and 5 workers handle materials. The 5 materials-handling workers have been hired on contracts that

Learning Objective **1**

Use the five-step decision-making process to make decisions

. . . the five steps are identify the problem and uncertainties; obtain information; make predictions about the future; make decisions by choosing among alternatives; and implement the decision, evaluate performance, and learn

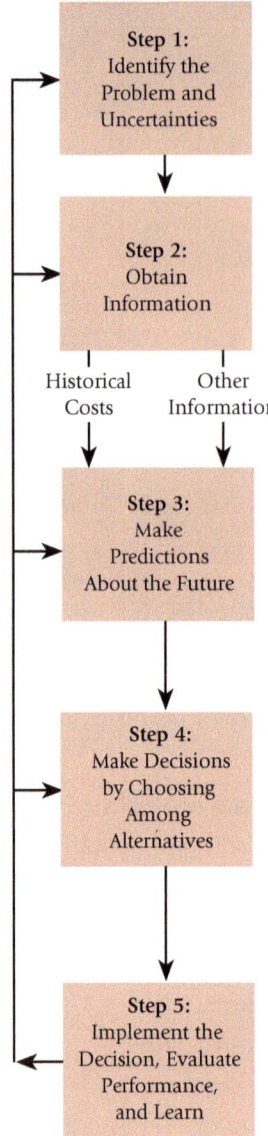

Step 1: Identify the Problem and Uncertainties

Should Precision Sporting Goods reorganize its manufacturing operations to reduce manufacturing labor costs? An important uncertainty is how the reorganization will affect employee morale.

Step 2: Obtain Information

Historical hourly wage rates are $14 per hour. However, a recently negotiated increase in employee benefits of $2 per hour will increase wages to $16 per hour. The reorganization of manufacturing operations is expected to reduce the number of workers from 20 to 15 by eliminating all 5 workers who handle materials. The reorganization is likely to have negative effects on employee morale.

Historical Costs   Other Information

Step 3: Make Predictions About the Future

Managers use information from Step 2 as a basis for predicting future manufacturing labor costs. Under the existing do-not-reorganize alternative, costs are predicted to be $640,000 (20 workers × 2,000 hours per worker per year × $16 per hour), and under the reorganize alternative, costs are predicted to be $480,000 (15 workers × 2,000 hours per worker per year × $16 per hour). Recall, the reorganization is predicted to cost $90,000 per year.

Step 4: Make Decisions by Choosing Among Alternatives

Managers compare the predicted benefits calculated in Step 3 ($640,000 − $480,000 = $160,000—that is, savings from eliminating materials-handling labor costs, 5 workers × 2,000 hours per worker per year × $16 per hour = $160,000) against the cost of the reorganization ($90,000) along with other considerations (such as likely negative effects on employee morale). Management chooses the reorganize alternative because the financial benefits are significant and the effects on employee morale are expected to be temporary and relatively small.

Step 5: Implement the Decision, Evaluate Performance, and Learn

Evaluating performance after the decision is implemented provides critical feedback for managers, and the five-step sequence is then repeated in whole or in part. Managers learn from actual results that the new manufacturing labor costs are $540,000, rather than the predicted $480,000, because of lower-than-expected manufacturing labor productivity. This (now) historical information can help managers make better subsequent predictions that allow for more learning time. Alternatively, managers may improve implementation via employee training and better supervision.

permit layoffs without additional payments. Each worker works 2,000 hours annually. Reorganization is predicted to cost $90,000 each year (mostly for new equipment leases). Production output of 25,000 units as well as the selling price of $250, the direct material cost per unit of $50, manufacturing overhead of $750,000, and marketing costs of $2,000,000 will be unaffected by the reorganization.

Managers use the five-step decision-making process presented in Exhibit 11-1 and first introduced in Chapter 1 to make this decision. Study the sequence of steps in this exhibit and note how Step 5 evaluates performance to provide feedback about actions taken in the previous steps. This feedback might affect future predictions, the prediction methods used, the way choices are made, or the implementation of the decision.

The Concept of Relevance

Much of this chapter focuses on Step 4 in Exhibit 11-1 and on the concepts of relevant costs and relevant revenues when choosing among alternatives.

Relevant Costs and Relevant Revenues

Relevant costs are *expected future costs,* and **relevant revenues** are *expected future revenues* that differ among the alternative courses of action being considered. Revenues and costs that are *not relevant* are said to be *irrelevant*. It is important to recognize that to be relevant costs and relevant revenues they *must*:

Learning Objective 2

Distinguish relevant from irrelevant information in decision situations

. . . only costs and revenues that are expected to occur in the future and differ among alternative courses of action are relevant

- ■ **Occur in the future**—every decision deals with selecting a course of action based on its expected future results.
- ■ **Differ among the alternative courses of action**—costs and revenues that do not differ will not matter and, hence, will have no bearing on the decision being made.

The question is always, "What difference will an action make?"

Exhibit 11-2 presents the financial data underlying the choice between the do-not-reorganize and reorganize alternatives for Precision Sporting Goods. There are two ways to analyze the data. The first considers "All revenues and costs," while the second considers only "Relevant revenues and costs."

The first two columns describe the first way and present *all data*. The last two columns describe the second way and present *only relevant costs*—the $640,000 and $480,000 expected future manufacturing labor costs and the $90,000 expected future reorganization costs that differ between the two alternatives. The revenues, direct materials, manufacturing overhead, and marketing items can be ignored because they will remain the same whether or not Precision Sporting Goods reorganizes. They do not differ between the alternatives and, therefore, are irrelevant.

Note, the past (historical) manufacturing hourly wage rate of $14 and total past (historical) manufacturing labor costs of $560,000 (20 workers × 2,000 hours per worker per year × $14 per hour) do not appear in Exhibit 11-2. *Although they may be a useful basis for making informed predictions of the expected future manufacturing labor costs of $640,000 and $480,000, historical costs themselves are past costs that, therefore, are irrelevant to decision making.* Past costs are also called **sunk costs** because they are unavoidable and cannot be changed no matter what action is taken.

The analysis in Exhibit 11-2 indicates that reorganizing the manufacturing operations will increase predicted operating income by $70,000 each year. Note that the managers at Precision Sporting Goods reach the same conclusion whether they use all data or include only relevant data in the analysis. By confining the analysis to only the relevant data, managers

Exhibit 11-2   Determining Relevant Revenues and Relevant Costs for Precision Sporting Goods

	All Revenues and Costs		Relevant Revenues and Costs	
	Alternative 1: **Do Not Reorganize**	**Alternative 2:** **Reorganize**	**Alternative 1:** **Do Not Reorganize**	**Alternative 2:** **Reorganize**
Revenues[a]	$6,250,000	$6,250,000	—	—
Costs:				
Direct materials[b]	1,250,000	1,250,000	—	—
Manufacturing labor	640,000[c]	480,000[d]	$ 640,000[c]	$ 480,000[d]
Manufacturing overhead	750,000	750,000	—	—
Marketing	2,000,000	2,000,000	—	—
Reorganization costs	—	90,000	—	90,000
Total costs	4,640,000	4,570,000	640,000	570,000
Operating income	$1,610,000	$1,680,000	$(640,000)	$(570,000)

$70,000 Difference $70,000 Difference

[a]25,000 units ×$250 per unit = $6,250,000   [c]20 workers × 2,000 hours per worker × $16 per hour = $640,000

[b]25,000 units × $50 per unit = $1,250,000   [d]15 workers × 2,000 hours per worker × $16 per hour = $480,000

Exhibit 11-3   Key Features of Relevant Information

- Past (historical) costs may be helpful as a basis for making *predictions*. However, past costs themselves are always irrelevant when making *decisions*.
- Different alternatives can be compared by examining differences in expected total future revenues and expected total future costs.
- Not all expected future revenues and expected future costs are relevant. Expected future revenues and expected future costs that do not differ among alternatives are irrelevant and, hence, can be eliminated from the analysis. The key question is always, "What difference will an action make?"
- Appropriate weight must be given to qualitative factors and quantitative nonfinancial factors.

can clear away the clutter of potentially confusing irrelevant data. Focusing on the relevant data is especially helpful when all the information needed to prepare a detailed income statement is unavailable. Understanding which costs are relevant and which are irrelevant helps the decision maker concentrate on obtaining only the pertinent data and is more efficient.

Qualitative and Quantitative Relevant Information

Managers divide the outcomes of decisions into two broad categories: *quantitative* and *qualitative*. **Quantitative factors** are outcomes that are measured in numerical terms. Some quantitative factors are financial; they can be expressed in monetary terms. Examples include the cost of direct materials, direct manufacturing labor, and marketing. Other quantitative factors are nonfinancial; they can be measured numerically, but they are not expressed in monetary terms. Reduction in new product-development time and the percentage of on-time flight arrivals are examples of quantitative nonfinancial factors. **Qualitative factors** are outcomes that are difficult to measure accurately in numerical terms. Employee morale is an example.

Relevant-cost analysis generally emphasizes quantitative factors that can be expressed in financial terms. *But just because qualitative factors and quantitative nonfinancial factors cannot be measured easily in financial terms does not make them unimportant.* In fact, managers must wisely weigh these factors. In the Precision Sporting Goods example, managers carefully considered the negative effect on employee morale of laying-off materials-handling workers, a qualitative factor, before choosing the reorganize alternative. Comparing and trading off nonfinancial and financial considerations is seldom easy.

Exhibit 11-3 summarizes the key features of relevant information.

An Illustration of Relevance: Choosing Output Levels

The concept of relevance applies to all decision situations. In this and the following several sections of this chapter, we present some of these decision situations. Later chapters describe other decision situations that require application of the relevance concept, such as Chapter 12 on pricing, Chapter 16 on joint costs, Chapter 19 on quality and timeliness, Chapter 20 on inventory management and supplier evaluation, Chapter 21 on capital investment, and Chapter 22 on transfer pricing. We start by considering decisions that affect output levels such as whether to introduce a new product or to try to sell more units of an existing product.

One-Time-Only Special Orders

One type of decision that affects output levels is accepting or rejecting special orders when there is idle production capacity and the special orders have no long-run implications. We use the term **one-time-only special order** to describe these conditions.

Example 1: Surf Gear manufactures quality beach towels at its highly automated Burlington, North Carolina, plant. The plant has a production capacity of 48,000 towels each month. Current monthly production is 30,000 towels. Retail department stores account for all existing sales. Expected results for the coming month (August) are shown in Exhibit 11-4. (These amounts are predictions based on past costs.) We assume all costs can be classified as either fixed or variable with respect to a single cost driver (units of output).

As a result of a strike at its existing towel supplier, Azelia, a luxury hotel chain, has offered to buy 5,000 towels from Surf Gear in August at $11 per towel. No subsequent sales to Azelia are anticipated. Fixed manufacturing costs are based on the 48,000-towel production capacity. That is, fixed manufacturing costs relate to the production capacity available and not the actual capacity used. If Surf Gear accepts the special order, it will use existing idle capacity to produce the 5,000 towels, and fixed manufacturing costs will not change. No marketing costs will be necessary for the 5,000-unit one-time-only special order. Accepting this special order is not expected to affect the selling price or the quantity of towels sold to regular customers. Should Surf Gear accept Azelia's offer?

Exhibit 11-4 presents data for this example on an absorption-costing basis (that is, both variable and fixed manufacturing costs are included in inventoriable costs and cost of goods sold). In this exhibit, the manufacturing cost of $12 per unit and the marketing cost of $7 per unit include both variable and fixed costs. The sum of all costs (variable and fixed) in a particular business function of the value chain, such as manufacturing costs or marketing costs, are called **business function costs. Full costs of the product,** in this case $19 per unit, are the sum of all variable and fixed costs in all business functions of the value chain (R&D, design, production, marketing, distribution, and customer service). For Surf Gear, full costs of the product consist of costs in manufacturing and marketing because these are the only business functions. No marketing costs are necessary for the special order, so the manager of Surf Gear will focus

	A	B	C	D
		Total	**Per Unit**	
1				
2	Units sold	30,000		
3				
4	Revenues	$600,000	$20.00	
5	Cost of goods sold (manufacturing costs)			
6	Variable manufacturing costs	225,000	7.50[b]	
7	Fixed manufacturing costs	135,000	4.50[c]	
8	Total cost of goods sold	360,000	12.00	
9	Marketing costs			
10	Variable marketing costs	150,000	5.00	
11	Fixed marketing costs	60,000	2.00	
12	Total marketing costs	210,000	7.00	
13	Full costs of the product	570,000	19.00	
14	Operating income	$ 30,000	$ 1.00	
15				
16	[a]Surf Gear incurs no R&D, product-design, distribution, or customer-service costs			
17	[b]Variable manufacturing = Direct material + Variable direct manufacturing + Variable manufacturing			
18	cost per unit cost per unit labor cost per unit overhead cost per unit			
19	= $6.00 + $0.50 + $1.00 = $7.50			
20	[c]Fixed manufacturing = Fixed direct manufacturing + Fixed manufacturing			
21	cost per unit labor cost per unit overhead cost per unit			
22	= $1.50 + $3.00 = $4.50			

only on manufacturing costs. Based on the manufacturing cost per unit of $12—which is greater than the $11-per-unit price offered by Azelia—the manager might decide to reject the offer.

Exhibit 11-5 separates manufacturing and marketing costs into their variable- and fixed-cost components and presents data in the format of a contribution income statement. The relevant revenues and costs are the expected future revenues and costs that differ as a result of accepting the special offer—revenues of $55,000 ($11 per unit × 5,000 units) and variable manufacturing costs of $37,500 ($7.50 per unit × 5,000 units). The fixed manufacturing costs and all marketing costs (*including variable marketing costs*) are irrelevant in this case because these costs will not change in total whether the special order is accepted or rejected. Surf Gear would gain an additional $17,500 (relevant revenues, $55,000 – relevant costs, $37,500) in operating income by accepting the special order. In this example, comparing total amounts for 30,000 units versus 35,000 units or focusing only on the relevant amounts in the difference column in Exhibit 11-5 avoids a misleading implication—the implication that would result from comparing the $11-per-unit selling price against the manufacturing cost per unit of $12 (Exhibit 11-4), which includes both variable and fixed manufacturing costs.

The assumption of no long-run or strategic implications is crucial to management's analysis of the one-time-only special-order decision. Suppose Surf Gear concludes that the retail department stores (its regular customers) will demand a lower price if it sells towels at $11 apiece to Azelia. In this case, revenues from regular customers will be relevant. Why? Because the future revenues from regular customers will differ depending on whether the special order is accepted or rejected. The relevant-revenue and relevant-cost analysis of the Azelia order would have to be modified to consider both the short-run benefits from accepting the order and the long-run consequences on profitability if prices were lowered to all regular customers.

Exhibit 11-5

One-Time-Only
Special-Order Decision
for Surf Gear:
Comparative
Contribution Income
Statements

	A	B	C	D	E	F	G	H
1		Without the Special Order				With the Special Order		Difference: Relevant Amounts
2		30,000				35,000		for the
3		Units to be Sold				Units to be Sold		5,000
4		Per Unit		Total		Total		Units Special Order
5		(1)		(2) = (1) × 30,000		(3)		(4) = (3) – (2)
6	Revenues	$20.00		$600,000		$655,000		$55,000[a]
7	Variable costs:							
8	Manufacturing	7.50		225,000		262,500		37,500[b]
9	Marketing	5.00		150,000		150,000		0[c]
10	Total variable costs	12.50		375,000		412,500		37,500
11	Contribution margin	7.50		225,000		242,500		17,500
12	Fixed costs:							
13	Manufacturing	4.50		135,000		135,000		0[d]
14	Marketing	2.00		60,000		60,000		0[d]
15	Total fixed costs	6.50		195,000		195,000		0
16	Operating income	$ 1.00		$ 30,000		$ 47,500		$17,500
17								
18	[a]5,000 units × $11.00 per unit = $55,000.							
19	[b]5,000 units × $7.50 per unit = $37,500.							
20	[c]No variable marketing costs would be incurred for the 5,000-unit one-time-only special order.							
21	[d]Fixed manufacturing costs and fixed marketing costs would be unaffected by the special order.							

Potential Problems in Relevant-Cost Analysis

Managers should avoid two potential problems in relevant-cost analysis. First, they must watch for incorrect general assumptions, such as all variable costs are relevant and all fixed costs are irrelevant. In the Surf Gear example, the variable marketing cost of $5 per unit is irrelevant because Surf Gear will incur no extra marketing costs by accepting the special order. But fixed manufacturing costs could be relevant. The extra production of 5,000 towels per month does not affect fixed manufacturing costs because we assumed that the relevant range is from 30,000 to 48,000 towels per month. In some cases, however, producing the extra 5,000 towels might increase fixed manufacturing costs. Suppose Surf Gear would need to run three shifts of 16,000 towels per shift to achieve full capacity of 48,000 towels per month. Increasing the monthly production from 30,000 to 35,000 would require a partial third shift because two shifts could produce only 32,000 towels. The extra shift would increase fixed manufacturing costs, thereby making these additional fixed manufacturing costs relevant for this decision.

Second, unit-cost data can potentially mislead decision makers in two ways:

1. **When irrelevant costs are included.** Consider the $4.50 of fixed manufacturing cost per unit (direct manufacturing labor, $1.50 per unit, plus manufacturing overhead, $3.00 per unit) included in the $12-per-unit manufacturing cost in the one-time-only special-order decision (see Exhibits 11-4 and 11-5). This $4.50-per-unit cost is irrelevant, given the assumptions in our example, so it should be excluded.

2. **When the same unit costs are used at different output levels.** Generally, managers use total costs rather than unit costs because total costs are easier to work with and reduce the chance for erroneous conclusions. Then, if desired, the total costs can be unitized. In the Surf Gear example, total fixed manufacturing costs remain at $135,000 even if Surf Gear accepts the special order and produces 35,000 towels. Including the fixed manufacturing cost per unit of $4.50 as a cost of the special order would lead to the erroneous conclusion that total fixed manufacturing costs would increase to $157,500 ($4.50 per towel × 35,000 towels).

The best way for managers to avoid these two potential problems is to keep focusing on (1) total revenues and total costs (rather than unit revenue and unit cost) and (2) the relevance concept. Managers should always require all items included in an analysis to be expected total future revenues and expected total future costs that differ among the alternatives.

Insourcing-versus-Outsourcing and Make-versus-Buy Decisions

We now apply the concept of relevance to another strategic decision: whether a company should make a component part or buy it from a supplier. We again assume idle capacity.

Outsourcing and Idle Facilities

Outsourcing is purchasing goods and services from outside vendors rather than producing the same goods or providing the same services within the organization, which is **insourcing**. For example, Kodak prefers to manufacture its own film (insourcing) but has IBM do its data processing (outsourcing). Honda relies on outside vendors to supply some component parts but chooses to manufacture other parts internally.

Decisions about whether a producer of goods or services will insource or outsource are also called **make-or-buy decisions.** Surveys of companies indicate that managers consider quality, dependability of suppliers, and costs as the most important factors in the make-or-buy decision. Sometimes, however, qualitative factors dominate management's make-or-buy decision. For example, Dell Computer buys the Pentium chip for its personal computers from Intel because Dell does not have the know-how and technology to make

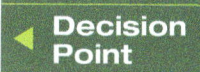

Decision Point

When is a revenue or cost item relevant for a particular decision and what potential problems should be avoided in relevant cost analysis?

Learning Objective 3

Explain the opportunity-cost concept and why it is used in decision making

. . . in all decisions, it is important to consider the contribution to income forgone by choosing a particular alternative and rejecting others

the chip itself. In contrast, to maintain the secrecy of its formula, Coca-Cola does not out-source the manufacture of its concentrate.

Example 2: The Soho Company manufactures a two-in-one video system consisting of a DVD player and a digital media receiver (that downloads movies and video from internet sites such as NetFlix). Columns 1 and 2 of the following table show the expected total and per-unit costs for manufacturing the DVD-player of the video system. Soho plans to manufacture the 250,000 units in 2,000 batches of 125 units each. Variable batch-level costs of $625 per batch vary with the number of batches, not the total number of units produced.

	Expected Total Costs of Producing 250,000 Units in 2,000 Batches Next Year (1)	Expected Cost per Unit (2) = (1) ÷ 250,000
Direct materials ($36 per unit × 250,000 units)	$ 9,000,000	$36.00
Direct manufacturing labor ($10 per unit × 250,000 units)	2,500,000	10.00
Variable manufacturing overhead costs of power and utilities ($6 per unit × 250,000 units)	1,500,000	6.00
Mixed (variable and fixed) batch-level manufacturing overhead costs of materials handling and setup [$750,000 + ($625 per batch × 2,000 batches)]	2,000,000	8.00
Fixed manufacturing overhead costs of plant lease, insurance, and administration	3,000,000	12.00
Total manufacturing cost	$18,000,000	$72.00

Broadfield, Inc., a manufacturer of DVD players, offers to sell Soho 250,000 DVD players next year for $64 per unit on Soho's preferred delivery schedule. Assume that financial factors will be the basis of this make-or-buy decision. Should Soho make or buy the DVD player?

Columns 1 and 2 of the preceding table indicate the expected total costs and expected cost per unit of producing 250,000 DVD players next year. The expected manufacturing cost per unit for next year is $72. At first glance, it appears that the company should buy DVD players because the expected $72-per-unit cost of making the DVD player is more than the $64 per unit to buy it. But a make-or-buy decision is rarely obvious. To make a decision, management needs to answer the question, "What is the difference in relevant costs between the alternatives?"

For the moment, suppose (a) the capacity now used to make the DVD players will become idle next year if the DVD players are purchased and (b) the $3,000,000 of fixed manufacturing overhead will continue to be incurred next year regardless of the decision made. Assume the $750,000 in fixed salaries to support materials handling and setup will not be incurred if the manufacture of DVD players is completely shut down.

Exhibit 11-6 presents the relevant-cost computations. Note that Soho will *save* $1,000,000 by making DVD players rather than buying them from Broadfield. Making DVD players is the preferred alternative.

Note how the key concepts of relevance presented in Exhibit 11-3 apply here:

■ Exhibit 11-6 compares differences in expected total future revenues and expected total future costs. Past costs are always irrelevant when making decisions.

■ Exhibit 11-6 shows $2,000,000 of future materials-handling and setup costs under the make alternative but not under the buy alternative. Why? Because buying DVD players and not manufacturing them will save $2,000,000 in future variable costs per batch and avoidable fixed costs. The $2,000,000 represents future costs that differ between the alternatives and so is relevant to the make-or-buy decision.

Exhibit 11-6

Relevant (Incremental) Items for Make-or-Buy Decision for DVD Players at Soho Company

Relevant Items	Total Relevant Costs		Relevant Cost Per Unit	
	Make	Buy	Make	Buy
Outside purchase of parts ($64 × 250,000 units)		$16,000,000		$64
Direct materials	$ 9,000,000		$36	
Direct manufacturing labor	2,500,000		10	
Variable manufacturing overhead	1,500,000		6	
Mixed (variable and fixed) materials-handling and setup overhead	2,000,000		8	
Total relevant costs[a]	$15,000,000	$16,000,000	$58	$64
Difference in favor of making DVD players	$1,000,000		$4	

[a]The $3,000,000 of plant-lease, plant-insurance, and plant-administration costs could be included under both alternatives. Conceptually, they do not belong in a listing of relevant costs because these costs are irrelevant to the decision. Practically, some managers may want to include them in order to list all costs that will be incurred under each alternative.

■ Exhibit 11-6 excludes the $3,000,000 of plant-lease, insurance, and administration costs under both alternatives. Why? Because these future costs will not differ between the alternatives, so they are irrelevant.

A common term in decision making is *incremental cost*. An **incremental cost** is the additional total cost incurred for an activity. In Exhibit 11-6, the incremental cost of making DVD players is the additional total cost of $15,000,000 that Soho will incur if it decides to make DVD players. The $3,000,000 of fixed manufacturing overhead is not an incremental cost because Soho will incur these costs whether or not it makes DVD players. Similarly, the incremental cost of buying DVD players from Broadfield is the additional total cost of $16,000,000 that Soho will incur if it decides to buy DVD players. A **differential cost** is the difference in total cost between two alternatives. In Exhibit 11-6, the differential cost between the make-DVD-players and buy-DVD-players alternatives is $1,000,000 ($16,000,000 – $15,000,000). Note that *incremental cost* and *differential cost* are sometimes used interchangeably in practice. When faced with these terms, always be sure to clarify what they mean.

We define *incremental revenue* and *differential revenue* similarly to incremental cost and differential cost. **Incremental revenue** is the additional total revenue from an activity. **Differential revenue** is the difference in total revenue between two alternatives.

Strategic and Qualitative Factors

Strategic and qualitative factors affect outsourcing decisions. For example, Soho may prefer to manufacture DVD players in-house to retain control over the design, quality, reliability, and delivery schedules of the DVD players it uses in its video-systems. Conversely, despite the cost advantages documented in Exhibit 11-6, Soho may prefer to outsource, become a leaner organization, and focus on areas of its core competencies—the manufacture and sale of video systems. As an example of focus, advertising companies, such as J. Walter Thompson, only do the creative and planning aspects of advertising (their core competencies), and outsource production activities, such as film, photographs, and illustrations.

Outsourcing is not without risks. As a company's dependence on its suppliers increases, suppliers could increase prices and let quality and delivery performance slip. To minimize these risks, companies generally enter into long-run contracts specifying costs, quality, and delivery schedules with their suppliers. Intelligent managers build close partnerships or alliances with a few key suppliers. Toyota goes so far as to send its own engineers to improve suppliers' processes. Suppliers of companies such as Ford, Hyundai, Panasonic, and Sony have researched and developed innovative products, met demands for increased quantities, maintained quality and on-time delivery, and lowered costs—actions that the companies themselves would not have had the competencies to achieve.

Concepts in Action — Pringles Prints and the Offshoring of Innovation

According to a recent survey, 67% of U.S. companies are engaged in the rapidly-evolving process of "offshoring," which is the outsourcing of business processes and jobs to other countries. Offshoring was initially popular with companies because it yielded immediate labor-cost savings for activities such as software development, call centers, and technical support.

While the practice remains popular today, offshoring has transformed from lowering costs on back-office processes to accessing global talent for innovation. With global markets expanding and domestic talent scarce, companies are now hiring qualified engineers, scientists, inventors, and analysts all over the world for research and development (R&D), new product development (NPD), engineering, and knowledge services.

Innovation Offshoring Services

R&D	NPD	Engineering	Knowledge Services
■ Programming	■ Prototype design	■ Testing	■ Market analysis
■ Code development	■ Product development	■ Reengineering	■ Credit analysis
■ New technologies	■ Systems design	■ Drafting/modeling	■ Data mining
■ New materials/ process research	■ Support services	■ Embedded systems development	■ Forecasting
			■ Risk management

By utilizing offshoring innovation, companies not only continue to reduce labor costs, but cut back-office costs as well. Companies also obtain local market knowledge and access to global best practices in many important areas.

Some companies are leveraging offshore resources by creating global innovation networks. Procter & Gamble (P&G), for instance, established "Connect and Develop," a multi-national effort to create and leverage innovative ideas for product development. When the company wanted to create a new line of Pringles potato chips with pictures and words—trivia questions, animal facts, and jokes—printed on each chip, the company turned to offshore innovation.

Rather than trying to invent the technology required to print images on potato chips in-house, Procter & Gamble created a technology brief that defined the problems it needed to solve, and circulated it throughout the company's global innovation network for possible solutions. As a result, P&G discovered a small bakery in Bologna, Italy, run by a university professor who also manufactured baking equipment. He had invented an ink-jet method for printing edible images on cakes and cookies, which the company quickly adapted for potato chips.

As a result, Pringles Prints were developed in less than a year—as opposed to a more traditional two year process—and immediately led to double-digit product growth.

Sources: Cuoto, Vinay, Mahadeva Mani, Vikas Sehgal, Arie Lewin, Stephan Manning, and Jeff Russell. 2007. *Offshoring 2.0: Contracting knowledge and innovation to expand global capabilities.* Duke University Offshoring Research Network: Durham, NC. Heijmen, Ton, Arie Lewin, Stephan Manning, Nidthida Prem-Ajchariyawong, and Jeff Russell. 2008. *Offshoring reaches the c-suite.* Duke University Offshoring Research Network: Durham, NC. Huston, Larry and Nabil Sakkab. 2006. Connect and develop: Inside Procter & Gamble's new model for innovation. *Harvard Business Review,* March.

Outsourcing decisions invariably have a long-run horizon in which the financial costs and benefits of outsourcing become more uncertain. Almost always, strategic and qualitative factors such as the ones described here become important determinants of the outsourcing decision. Weighing all these factors requires the exercise of considerable management judgment and care.

International Outsourcing

What additional factors would Soho have to consider if the supplier of DVD players was based in Mexico? The most important would be exchange-rate risk. Suppose the Mexican supplier offers to sell Soho 250,000 DVD players for 192,000,000 Pesos. Should Soho make or buy? The answer depends on the exchange rate that Soho expects next year. If Soho forecasts an exchange rate of 12 Pesos per $1, Soho's expected purchase cost equals

$16,000,000 (192,000,000 Pesos/12 Pesos per $) greater than the $15,000,000 relevant costs for making the DVD players in Exhibit 11-6, so Soho would prefer to make DVD players rather than buy them. If, however, Soho anticipates an exchange rate of 13.50 Pesos per $1, Soho's expected purchase cost equals $14,222,222 (192,000,000 Pesos/13.50 Pesos per $), which is less than the $15,000,000 relevant costs for making the DVD players, so Soho would prefer to buy rather than make the DVD players.

Another option is for Soho to enter into a forward contract to purchase 192,000,000 Pesos. A forward contract allows Soho to contract today to purchase pesos next year at a predetermined, fixed cost, thereby protecting itself against exchange rate risk. If Soho decides to go this route, it would make (buy) DVD players if the cost of the contract is greater (less) than $15,000,000. International outsourcing requires companies to evaluate exchange rate risks and to implement strategies and costs for managing them. The Concepts in Action feature (p. 400) describes *offshoring*—the practice of outsourcing services to lower-cost countries.

Opportunity Costs and Outsourcing

In the simple make-or-buy decision in Exhibit 11-6, we assumed that the capacity currently used to make DVD players will remain idle if Soho purchases the parts from Broadfield. Often, however, the released capacity can be used for other, profitable purposes. In this case, the choice Soho's managers are faced with is not whether to make or buy; the choice now centers on how best to use available production capacity.

Example 3: Suppose that if Soho decides to buy DVD players for its video systems from Broadfield, then Soho's best use of the capacity that becomes available is to produce 100,000 Digiteks, a portable, stand-alone DVD player. From a manufacturing standpoint, Digiteks are similar to DVD players made for the video system. With help from operating managers, Soho's management accountant estimates the following future revenues and costs if Soho decides to manufacture and sell Digiteks:

Incremental future revenues		$8,000,000
Incremental future costs		
Direct materials	$3,400,000	
Direct manufacturing labor	1,000,000	
Variable overhead (such as power, utilities)	600,000	
Materials-handling and setup overheads	500,000	
Total incremental future costs		5,500,000
Incremental future operating income		$2,500,000

Because of capacity constraints, Soho can make either DVD players for its video-system unit or Digiteks, but not both. Which of the following two alternatives should Soho choose?

1. Make video-system DVD players and do not make Digiteks
2. Buy video-system DVD players and make Digiteks

Exhibit 11-7, Panel A, summarizes the "total-alternatives" approach—the future costs and revenues for *all* products. Alternative 2, buying video-system DVD players and using the available capacity to make and sell Digiteks, is the preferred alternative. The future incremental costs of buying video-system DVD players from an outside supplier ($16,000,000) exceed the future incremental costs of making video-system DVD players in-house ($15,000,000). Soho can use the capacity freed up by buying video-system DVD players to gain $2,500,000 in operating income (incremental future revenues of $8,000,000 minus total incremental future costs of $5,500,000) by making and selling Digiteks. The *net relevant* costs of buying video-system DVD players and making and selling Digiteks are $16,000,000 – $2,500,000 = $13,500,000.

| Exhibit 11-7 | Total-Alternatives Approach and Opportunity-Cost Approach to Make-or-Buy Decisions for Soho Company |

	Alternatives for Soho	
Relevant Items	**1. Make Video-System DVD Players and Do Not Make Digitek**	**2. Buy Video-System DVD Players and Make Digitek**
PANEL A Total-Alternatives Approach to Make-or-Buy Decisions		
Total incremental future costs of making/buying video-system DVD players (from Exhibit 11-6)	$15,000,000	$16,000,000
Deduct excess of future revenues over future costs from Digitek	0	(2,500,000)
Total relevant costs under total-alternatives approach	$15,000,000	$13,500,000
	1. Make Video-System DVD Players	**2. Buy Video-System DVD Players**
PANEL B Opportunity-Cost Approach to Make-or-Buy Decisions		
Total incremental future costs of making/buying video-system DVD players (from Exhibit 11-6)	$15,000,000	$16,000,000
Opportunity cost: Profit contribution forgone because capacity will not be used to make Digitek, the next-best alternative	2,500,000	0
Total relevant costs under opportunity-cost approach	$17,500,000	$16,000,000

Note that the differences in costs across the columns in Panels A and B are the same: The cost of alternative 3 is $1,500,000 less than the cost of alternative 1, and $2,500,000 less than the cost of alternative 2.

The Opportunity-Cost Approach

Deciding to use a resource in a particular way causes a manager to forgo the opportunity to use the resource in alternative ways. This lost opportunity is a cost that the manager must consider when making a decision. **Opportunity cost** is the contribution to operating income that is forgone by not using a limited resource in its next-best alternative use. For example, the (relevant) cost of going to school for an MBA degree is not only the cost of tuition, books, lodging, and food, but also the income sacrificed (opportunity cost) by not working. Presumably, the estimated future benefits of obtaining an MBA (for example, a higher-paying career) will exceed these costs.

Exhibit 11-7, Panel B, displays the opportunity-cost approach for analyzing the alternatives faced by Soho. *Note that the alternatives are defined differently in the total alternatives approach (1. Make Video-System DVD Players and Do Not Make Digiteks and 2. Buy Video-System DVD Players and Make Digiteks) and the opportunity cost approach (1. Make Video-System DVD Players and 2. Buy Video-System DVD Players), which does not reference Digiteks. Under the opportunity-cost approach, the cost of each alternative includes (1) the incremental costs and (2) the opportunity cost, the profit forgone from not making Digiteks. This opportunity cost arises because Digitek is excluded from formal consideration in the alternatives.*

Consider alternative 1, making video-system DVD players. What are all the costs of making video-system DVD players? Certainly Soho will incur $15,000,000 of incremental costs to make video-system DVD players, but is this the entire cost? No, because by deciding to use limited manufacturing resources to make video-system DVD players, Soho will give up the opportunity to earn $2,500,000 by not using these resources to make Digiteks. Therefore, the relevant costs of making video-system DVD players are the incremental costs of $15,000,000 plus the opportunity cost of $2,500,000.

Next, consider alternative 2, buy video-system DVD players. The incremental cost of buying video-system DVD players will be $16,000,000. The opportunity cost is zero.

Why? Because by choosing this alternative, Soho will not forgo the profit it can earn from making and selling Digiteks.

Panel B leads management to the same conclusion as Panel A: buying video-system DVD players and making Digiteks is the preferred alternative.

Panels A and B of Exhibit 11-7 describe two consistent approaches to decision making with capacity constraints. The total-alternatives approach in Panel A includes all future incremental costs and revenues. For example, under alternative 2, the additional future operating income from *using capacity to make and sell Digiteks* ($2,500,000) is subtracted from the future incremental cost of buying video-system DVD players ($16,000,000). The opportunity-cost analysis in Panel B takes the opposite approach. It focuses only on video-system DVD players. *Whenever capacity is not going to be used to make and sell Digiteks* the future forgone operating income is added as an opportunity cost of making video-system DVD players, as in alternative 1. (Note that when Digiteks are made, as in alternative 2, there is no "opportunity cost of not making Digiteks.") Therefore, whereas Panel A *subtracts* $2,500,000 under alternative 2, Panel B *adds* $2,500,000 under alternative 1. *Panel B highlights the idea that when capacity is constrained, the relevant revenues and costs of any alternative equal (1) the incremental future revenues and costs plus (2) the opportunity cost.* However, when more than two alternatives are being considered simultaneously, it is generally easier to use the total-alternatives approach.

Opportunity costs are not recorded in financial accounting systems. Why? Because historical record keeping is limited to transactions involving alternatives that were *actually selected*, rather than alternatives that were rejected. Rejected alternatives do not produce transactions and so they are not recorded. If Soho makes video-system DVD players, it will not make Digiteks, and it will not record any accounting entries for Digiteks. Yet the opportunity cost of making video-system DVD players, which equals the operating income that Soho forgoes by not making Digiteks, is a crucial input into the make-or-buy decision. Consider again Exhibit 11-7, Panel B. On the basis of only the incremental costs that are systematically recorded in accounting systems, it is less costly for Soho to make rather than buy video-system DVD players. Recognizing the opportunity cost of $2,500,000 leads to a different conclusion: Buying video-system DVD players is preferable.

Suppose Soho has sufficient capacity to make Digiteks even if it makes video-system DVD players. In this case, the opportunity cost of making video-system DVD players is $0 because Soho does not give up the $2,500,000 operating income from making Digiteks even if it chooses to make video-system DVD players. The relevant costs are $15,000,000 (incremental costs of $15,000,000 plus opportunity cost of $0). Under these conditions, Soho would prefer to make video-system DVD players, rather than buy them, and also make Digiteks.

Besides quantitative considerations, the make-or-buy decision should also consider strategic and qualitative factors. If Soho decides to buy video-system DVD players from an outside supplier, it should consider factors such as the supplier's reputation for quality and timely delivery. Soho would also want to consider the strategic consequences of selling Digiteks. For example, will selling Digiteks take Soho's focus away from its video-system business?

Carrying Costs of Inventory

To see another example of an opportunity cost, consider the following data for Soho:

Annual estimated video-system DVD player requirements for next year	250,000 units
Cost per unit when each purchase is equal to 2,500 units	$64.00
Cost per unit when each purchase is equal to or greater than 125,000 units; $64 minus 1% discount	$63.36
Cost of a purchase order	$500

Alternatives under consideration:

    A. Make 100 purchases of 2,500 units each during next year

    B. Make 2 purchases of 125,000 units during the year

Average investment in inventory:

A. (2,500 units × $64.00 per unit) ÷ 2ᵃ ... $80,000

B. (125,000 units × $63.36 per unit) ÷ 2ᵃ ... $3,960,000

Annual rate of return if cash is invested elsewhere (for example, bonds or stocks) at the same level of risk as investment in inventory) 9%

ᵃ The example assumes that video-system-DVD-player purchases will be used uniformly throughout the year. The average investment in inventory during the year is the cost of the inventory when a purchase is received plus the cost of inventory just before the next purchase is delivered (in our example, zero) divided by 2.

Soho will pay cash for the video-system DVD players it buys. Which purchasing alternative is more economical for Soho?

The following table presents the analysis using the total alternatives approach recognizing that Soho has, on average, $3,960,000 of cash available to invest. If Soho invests only $80,000 in inventory as in alternative A, it will have $3,880,000 ($3,960,000 – $80,000) of cash available to invest elsewhere, which at a 9% rate of return will yield a total return of $349,200. This income is subtracted from the ordering and purchasing costs incurred under alternative A. If Soho invests all $3,960,000 in inventory as in alternative B, it will have $0 ($3,960,000 – $3,960,000) available to invest elsewhere and will earn no return on the cash.

	Alternative A: Make 100 Purchases of 2,500 Units Each During the Year and Invest Any Excess Cash (1)	Alternative B: Make 2 Purchases of 125,000 Units Each During the Year and Invest Any Excess Cash (2)	Difference (3) = (1) – (2)
Annual purchase-order costs (100 purch. orders × $500/purch. order; 2 purch. orders × $500/purch. order)	$ 50,000	$ 1,000	$ 49,000
Annual purchase costs (250,000 units × $64.00/unit; 250,000 units × $63.36/unit)	16,000,000	15,840,000	160,000
Deduct annual rate of return earned by investing cash not tied up in inventory elsewhere at the same level of risk [0.09 × ($3,960,000 – $80,000); 0.09 × ($3,960,000 – $3,960,000)	(349,200)	0	(349,200)
Relevant costs	$15,700,800	$15,841,000	$(140,200)

Consistent with the trends toward holding smaller inventories, purchasing smaller quantities of 2,500 units 100 times a year is preferred to purchasing 125,000 units twice a year by $140,200.

The following table presents the two alternatives using the opportunity cost approach. Each alternative is defined only in terms of the two purchasing choices with no explicit reference to investing the excess cash.

	Alternative A: Make 100 Purchases of 2,500 Units Each During the Year (1)	Alternative B: Make 2 Purchases of 125,000 Units Each During the Year (2)	Difference (3) = (1) – (2)
Annual purchase-order costs (100 purch. orders × $500/purch. order; 2 purch. orders × $500/purch. order)	$ 50,000	$ 1,000	$ 49,000
Annual purchase costs (250,000 units × $64.00/unit; 250,000 units × $63.36/unit)	16,000,000	15,840,000	160,000
Opportunity cost: Annual rate of return that could be earned if investment in inventory were invested elsewhere at the same level of risk (0.09 × $80,000; 0.09 × $3,960,000)	7,200	356,400	(349,200)
Relevant costs	$16,057,200	$16,197,400	$(140,200)

Recall that under the opportunity cost approach, the relevant cost of any alternative is (1) the incremental cost of the alternative plus (2) the opportunity cost of the profit forgone from choosing that alternative. The opportunity cost of holding inventory is the income forgone by tying up money in inventory and not investing it elsewhere. The opportunity cost would not be recorded in the accounting system because, once the money is invested in inventory, there is no money available to invest elsewhere, and hence no return related to this investment to record. On the basis of the costs recorded in the accounting system (purchase-order costs and purchase costs), Soho would erroneously conclude that making two purchases of 125,000 units each is the less costly alternative. Column 3, however, indicates that, as in the total alternatives approach, purchasing smaller quantities of 2,500 units 100 times a year is preferred to purchasing 125,000 units twice during the year by $140,200. Why? Because the lower opportunity cost of holding smaller inventory exceeds the higher purchase and ordering costs. If the opportunity cost of money tied up in inventory were greater than 9% per year, or if other incremental benefits of holding lower inventory were considered—such as lower insurance, materials-handling, storage, obsolescence, and breakage costs—making 100 purchases would be even more economical.

Decision Point ◀

What is an opportunity cost and why should it be included when making decisions?

Product-Mix Decisions with Capacity Constraints

We now examine how the concept of relevance applies to **product-mix decisions**—the decisions made by a company about which products to sell and in what quantities. These decisions usually have only a short-run focus, because they typically arise in the context of capacity constraints that can be relaxed in the long run. In the short run, for example, BMW, the German car manufacturer, continually adapts the mix of its different models of cars (for example, 325i, 525i, and 740i) to fluctuations in selling prices and demand.

To determine product mix, a company maximizes operating income, subject to constraints such as capacity and demand. Throughout this section, we assume that as short-run changes in product mix occur, the only costs that change are costs that are variable with respect to the number of units produced (and sold). Under this assumption, the analysis of individual product contribution margins provides insight into the product mix that maximizes operating income.

Learning Objective 4

Know how to choose which products to produce when there are capacity constraints

. . . select the product with the highest contribution margin per unit of the limiting resource

Example 4: Power Recreation assembles two engines, a snowmobile engine and a boat engine, at its Lexington, Kentucky, plant.

	Snowmobile Engine	Boat Engine
Selling price	$800	$1,000
Variable cost per unit	560	625
Contribution margin per unit	$240	$ 375
Contribution margin percentage ($240 ÷ $800; $375 ÷ $1,000)	30%	37.5%

Assume that only 600 machine-hours are available daily for assembling engines. Additional capacity cannot be obtained in the short run. Power Recreation can sell as many engines as it produces. The constraining resource, then, is machine-hours. It takes two machine-hours to produce one snowmobile engine and five machine-hours to produce one boat engine. What product mix should Power Recreation's managers choose to maximize its operating income?

In terms of contribution margin per unit and contribution margin percentage, boat engines are more profitable than snowmobile engines. The product that Power Recreation should produce and sell, however, is not necessarily the product with the higher individual contribution margin per unit or contribution margin percentage. Managers should choose the product with *the highest contribution margin per unit of the constraining resource (factor)*. That's the resource that restricts or limits the production or sale of products.

	Snowmobile Engine	Boat Engine
Contribution margin per unit	$240	$375
Machine-hours required to produce one unit	2 machine-hours	5 machine-hours
Contribution margin per machine-hour		
$240 per unit ÷ 2 machine-hours/unit	$120/machine-hour	
$375 per unit ÷ 5 machine-hours/unit		$75/machine-hour
Total contribution margin for 600 machine-hours		
$120/machine-hour × 600 machine-hours	$72,000	
$75/machine-hour × 600 machine-hours		$45,000

The number of machine-hours is the constraining resource in this example and snow-mobile engines earn more contribution margin per machine-hour ($120/machine-hour) compared to boat engines ($75/machine-hour). Therefore, choosing to produce and sell snowmobile engines maximizes *total* contribution margin ($72,000 versus $45,000 from producing and selling boat engines) and operating income. Other constraints in manufacturing settings can be the availability of direct materials, components, or skilled labor, as well as financial and sales factors. In a retail department store, the con-straining resource may be linear feet of display space. Regardless of the specific con-straining resource, managers should always focus on maximizing *total* contribution margin by choosing products that give the highest contribution margin per unit of the constraining resource.

In many cases, a manufacturer or retailer has the challenge of trying to maximize total operating income for a variety of products, each with more than one constrain-ing resource. Some constraints may require a manufacturer or retailer to stock mini-mum quantities of products even if these products are not very profitable. For example, supermarkets must stock less-profitable products because customers will be willing to shop at a supermarket only if it carries a wide range of products that cus-tomers desire. To determine the most profitable production schedule and the most profitable product mix, the manufacturer or retailer needs to determine the maximum total contribution margin in the face of many constraints. Optimization techniques, such as linear programming discussed in the appendix to this chapter, help solve these more-complex problems.

Finally, there is the question of managing the bottleneck constraint to increase output and, therefore, contribution margin. Can the available machine-hours for assembling engines be increased beyond 600, for example, by reducing idle time? Can the time needed to assemble each snowmobile engine (two machine-hours) and each boat engine (five machine-hours) be reduced, for example, by reducing setup time and processing time of assembly? Can quality be improved so that constrained capacity is used to produce only good units rather than some good and some defective units? Can some of the assem-bly operations be outsourced to allow more engines to be built? Implementing any of these options will likely require Power Recreation to incur incremental costs. Power Recreation will implement only those options where the increase in contribution margins exceeds the increase in costs. *Instructors and students who, at this point, want to explore these issues in more detail can go to the section in Chapter 19, pages 686–688, titled "Theory of Constraints and Throughput Contribution Analysis" and then return to this chapter without any loss of continuity.*

Decision Point ▶

When resources are constrained, how should managers choose which of multiple products to produce and sell?

Learning Objective 5

Discuss factors managers must consider when adding or dropping customers or segments

. . . managers should focus on how total costs differ among alternatives and ignore allocated overhead costs

Customer Profitability, Activity-Based Costing, and Relevant Costs

Not only must companies make choices regarding which products and how much of each product to produce, they must often make decisions about adding or dropping a product line or a business segment. Similarly, if the cost object is a customer, companies must make decisions about adding or dropping customers (analogous to a product line) or a branch office (analogous to a business segment). We illustrate relevant-revenue and relevant-cost analysis for these kinds of decisions using customers rather than products as the cost object.

Example 5: Allied West, the West Coast sales office of Allied Furniture, a wholesaler of specialized furniture, supplies furniture to three local retailers: Vogel, Brenner, and Wisk. Exhibit 11-8 presents expected revenues and costs of Allied West by customer for the upcoming year using its activity-based costing system. Allied West assigns costs to customers based on the activities needed to support each customer. Information on Allied West's costs for different activities at various levels of the cost hierarchy follows:

- Furniture-handling labor costs vary with the number of units of furniture shipped to customers.
- Allied West reserves different areas of the warehouse to stock furniture for different customers. For simplicity, assume that furniture-handling equipment in an area and depreciation costs on the equipment that Allied West has already acquired are identified with individual customers (customer-level costs). Any unused equipment remains idle. The equipment has a one-year useful life and zero disposal value.
- Allied West allocates rent to each customer on the basis of the amount of warehouse space reserved for that customer.
- Marketing costs vary with the number of sales visits made to customers.
- Sales-order costs are batch-level costs that vary with the number of sales orders received from customers; delivery-processing costs are batch-level costs that vary with the number of shipments made.
- Allied West allocates fixed general-administration costs (facility-level costs) to customers on the basis of customer revenues.
- Allied Furniture allocates its fixed corporate-office costs to sales offices on the basis of the square feet area of each sales office. Allied West then allocates these costs to customers on the basis of customer revenues.

In the following sections, we consider several decisions that Allied West's managers face: Should Allied West drop the Wisk account? Should it add a fourth customer, Loral? Should Allied Furniture close down Allied West? Should it open another sales office, Allied South, whose revenues and costs are identical to those of Allied West?

Exhibit 11-8

Customer Profitability Analysis for Allied West

	Customer			
	Vogel	**Brenner**	**Wisk**	**Total**
Revenues	$500,000	$300,000	$400,000	$1,200,000
Cost of goods sold	370,000	220,000	330,000	920,000
Furniture-handling labor	41,000	18,000	33,000	92,000
Furniture-handling equipment cost written off as depreciation	12,000	4,000	9,000	25,000
Rent	14,000	8,000	14,000	36,000
Marketing support	11,000	9,000	10,000	30,000
Sales-order and delivery processing	13,000	7,000	12,000	32,000
General administration	20,000	12,000	16,000	48,000
Allocated corporate-office costs	10,000	6,000	8,000	24,000
Total costs	491,000	284,000	432,000	1,207,000
Operating income	$ 9,000	$ 16,000	$ (32,000)	$ (7,000)

Relevant-Revenue and Relevant-Cost Analysis of Dropping a Customer

Exhibit 11-8 indicates a loss of $32,000 on the Wisk account. Allied West's managers believe the reason for the loss is that Wisk places low-margin orders with Allied, and has relatively high sales-order, delivery-processing, furniture-handling, and marketing costs. Allied West is considering several possible actions with respect to the Wisk account: reducing its own costs of supporting Wisk by becoming more efficient, cutting back on some of the services it offers Wisk; asking Wisk to place larger, less frequent orders; charging Wisk higher prices; or dropping the Wisk account. The following analysis focuses on the operating-income effect of dropping the Wisk account for the year.

To determine what to do, Allied West's managers must answer the question, what are the relevant revenues and relevant costs? Information about the effect of dropping the Wisk account follows:

- Dropping the Wisk account will save cost of goods sold, furniture-handling labor, marketing support, sales-order, and delivery-processing costs incurred on the account.
- Dropping the Wisk account will leave idle the warehouse space and furniture-handling equipment currently used to supply products to Wisk.
- Dropping the Wisk account will have no effect on fixed general-administration costs or corporate-office costs.

Exhibit 11-9, column 1, presents the relevant-revenue and relevant-cost analysis using data from the Wisk column in Exhibit 11-8. Allied West's operating income will be $15,000 lower if it drops the Wisk account—the cost savings from dropping the Wisk account, $385,000, will not be enough to offset the loss of $400,000 in revenues—so Allied West's managers decide to keep the account. Note that there is no opportunity cost of using warehouse space for Wisk because without Wisk, the space and equipment will remain idle.

Depreciation on equipment that Allied West has already acquired is a past cost and therefore irrelevant; rent, general-administration, and corporate-office costs are future costs that will not change if Allied West drops the Wisk account, and hence irrelevant. Overhead costs allocated to the sales office and individual customers are always irrelevant. The only question is, will expected total corporate-office costs decrease as a result of dropping the Wisk account? In our example, they will not, so these costs are irrelevant. *If expected total corporate-office costs* were to decrease by dropping the Wisk account, those savings would be relevant even if *the amount allocated to Allied West did not change.*

Exhibit 11-9

Relevant-Revenue and Relevant-Cost Analysis for Dropping the Wisk Account and Adding the Loral Account

	(Incremental Loss in Revenues) and Incremental Savings in Costs from Dropping Wisk Account (1)	Incremental Revenues and (Incremental Costs) from Adding Loral Account (2)
Revenues	$(400,000)	$400,000
Cost of goods sold	330,000	(330,000)
Furniture-handling labor	33,000	(33,000)
Furniture-handling equipment cost written off as depreciation	0	(9,000)
Rent	0	0
Marketing support	10,000	(10,000)
Sales-order and delivery processing	12,000	(12,000)
General administration	0	0
Corporate-office costs	0	0
Total costs	385,000	(394,000)
Effect on operating income (loss)	$ (15,000)	$ 6,000

Now suppose that if Allied West drops the Wisk account, it could lease the extra warehouse space to Sanchez Corporation for $20,000 per year. Then $20,000 would be Allied's opportunity cost of continuing to use the warehouse to service Wisk. Allied West would gain $5,000 by dropping the Wisk account ($20,000 from lease revenue minus lost operating income of $15,000). Before reaching a decision, Allied West's managers must examine whether Wisk can be made more profitable so that supplying products to Wisk earns more than the $20,000 from leasing to Sanchez. The managers must also consider strategic factors such as the effect of the decision on Allied West's reputation for developing stable, long-run business relationships with its customers.

Relevant-Revenue and Relevant-Cost Analysis of Adding a Customer

Suppose that in addition to Vogel, Brenner, and Wisk, Allied West's managers are evaluating the profitability of adding a customer, Loral. There is no other alternative use of the Allied West facility. Loral has a customer profile much like Wisk's. Suppose Allied West's managers predict revenues and costs of doing business with Loral to be the same as the revenues and costs described under the Wisk column of Exhibit 11-8. In particular, Allied West would have to acquire furniture-handling equipment for the Loral account costing $9,000, with a one-year useful life and zero disposal value. If Loral is added as a customer, warehouse rent costs ($36,000), general-administration costs ($48,000), and *actual total* corporate-office costs will not change. Should Allied West add Loral as a customer?

Exhibit 11-9, column 2, shows incremental revenues exceed incremental costs by $6,000. The opportunity cost of adding Loral is $0 because there is no alternative use of the Allied West facility. On the basis of this analysis, Allied West's managers would recommend adding Loral as a customer. Rent, general-administration, and corporate-office costs are irrelevant because these costs will not change if Loral is added as a customer. However, the cost of new equipment to support the Loral order (written off as depreciation of $9,000 in Exhibit 11-9, column 2), is relevant. That's because this cost can be avoided if Allied West decides not to add Loral as a customer. Note the critical distinction here: *Depreciation cost is irrelevant in deciding whether to drop Wisk as a customer because depreciation on equipment that has already been purchased is a past cost, but the cost of purchasing new equipment in the future, that will then be written off as depreciation, is relevant in deciding whether to add Loral as a customer.*

Relevant-Revenue and Relevant-Cost Analysis of Closing or Adding Branch Offices or Segments

Companies periodically confront decisions about closing or adding branch offices or business segments. For example, given Allied West's expected loss of $7,000 (see Exhibit 11-8), should it be closed for the year? Assume that closing Allied West will have no effect on total corporate-office costs and that there is no alternative use for the Allied West space.

Exhibit 11-10, column 1, presents the relevant-revenue and relevant-cost analysis using data from the "Total" column in Exhibit 11-8. The revenue losses of $1,200,000 will exceed the cost savings of $1,158,000, leading to a decrease in operating income of $42,000. Allied West should not be closed. The key reasons are that closing Allied West will not save depreciation cost or actual total corporate-office costs. Depreciation cost is past or sunk because it represents the cost of equipment that Allied West has already purchased. Corporate-office costs allocated to various sales offices will change *but the total amount of these costs will not decline*. The $24,000 no longer allocated to Allied West will be allocated to other sales offices. Therefore, the $24,000 of allocated corporate-office costs is irrelevant, because it does not represent expected cost savings from closing Allied West.

Now suppose Allied Furniture has the opportunity to open another sales office, Allied South, whose revenues and costs would be identical to Allied West's costs, including a cost of $25,000 to acquire furniture-handling equipment with a one-year useful life and zero disposal value. Opening this office will have no effect on total corporate-office costs.

◄ Decision Point

In deciding to add or drop customers or to add or discontinue branch offices or segments, what should managers focus on and how should they take into account allocated overhead costs?

Exhibit 11-10 Relevant-Revenue and Relevant-Cost Analysis for Closing Allied West and Opening Allied South

	(Incremental Loss in Revenues) and Incremental Savings in Costs from Closing Allied West (1)	Incremental Revenues and (Incremental Costs) from Opening Allied South (2)
Revenues	$(1,200,000)	$1,200,000
Cost of goods sold	920,000	(920,000)
Furniture-handling labor	92,000	(92,000)
Furniture-handling equipment cost written off as depreciation	0	(25,000)
Rent	36,000	(36,000)
Marketing support	30,000	(30,000)
Sales-order and delivery processing	32,000	(32,000)
General administration	48,000	(48,000)
Corporate-office costs	0	0
Total costs	1,158,000	(1,183,000)
Effect on operating income (loss)	$ (42,000)	$ 17,000

Should Allied Furniture open Allied South? Exhibit 11-10, column 2, indicates that it should do so because opening Allied South will increase operating income by $17,000. As before, the cost of new equipment to be purchased in the future (and written off as depreciation) is relevant and *allocated* corporate-office costs should be ignored. Total corporate-office costs will not change if Allied South is opened, therefore these costs are irrelevant.

Irrelevance of Past Costs and Equipment-Replacement Decisions

Learning Objective 6

Explain why book value of equipment is irrelevant in equipment-replacement decisions

. . . it is a past cost

At several points in this chapter, when discussing the concept of relevance, we reasoned that past (historical or sunk) costs are irrelevant to decision making. That's because a decision cannot change something that has already happened. We now apply this concept to decisions about replacing equipment. We stress the idea that **book value**—original cost minus accumulated depreciation—of existing equipment is a past cost that is irrelevant.

Example 6: Toledo Company, a manufacturer of aircraft components, is considering replacing a metal-cutting machine with a newer model. The new machine is more efficient than the old machine, but it has a shorter life. Revenues from aircraft parts ($1.1 million per year) will be unaffected by the replacement decision. Here are the data the management accountant prepares for the existing (old) machine and the replacement (new) machine:

	Old Machine	New Machine
Original cost	$1,000,000	$600,000
Useful life	5 years	2 years
Current age	3 years	0 years
Remaining useful life	2 years	2 years
Accumulated depreciation	$600,000	Not acquired yet
Book value	$400,000	Not acquired yet
Current disposal value (in cash)	$40,000	Not acquired yet
Terminal disposal value (in cash 2 years from now)	$0	$0
Annual operating costs (maintenance, energy, repairs, coolants, and so on)	$800,000	$460,000

Toledo Corporation uses straight-line depreciation. To focus on relevance, we ignore the time value of money and income taxes.[2] Should Toledo replace its old machine?

Exhibit 11-11 presents a cost comparison of the two machines. Consider why each of the four items in Toledo's equipment-replacement decision is relevant or irrelevant:

1. **Book value of old machine, $400,000.** Irrelevant, because it is a past or sunk cost. All past costs are "down the drain." Nothing can change what has already been spent or what has already happened.

2. **Current disposal value of old machine, $40,000.** Relevant, because it is an expected future benefit that will only occur if the machine is replaced.

3. **Loss on disposal, $360,000.** This is the difference between amounts in items 1 and 2. It is a meaningless combination blurring the distinction between the irrelevant book value and the relevant disposal value. Each should be considered separately, as was done in items 1 and 2.

4. **Cost of new machine, $600,000.** Relevant, because it is an expected future cost that will only occur if the machine is purchased.

Exhibit 11-11 should clarify these four assertions. Column 3 in Exhibit 11-11 shows that the book value of the old machine does not differ between the alternatives and could be ignored for decision-making purposes. No matter what the timing of the write-off—whether a lump-sum charge in the current year or depreciation charges over the next two years—the total amount is still $400,000 because it is a past (historical) cost. In contrast, the $600,000 cost of the new machine and the current disposal value of $40,000 for the old machine are relevant because they would not arise if Toledo's managers decided not to replace the machine. Note that the operating income from replacing is $120,000 higher for the two years together.

To provide focus, Exhibit 11-12 concentrates only on relevant items. Note that the same answer—higher operating income as a result of lower costs of $120,000 by replacing the machine—is obtained even though the book value is omitted from the calculations. The only relevant items are the cash operating costs, the disposal value of the old machine, and the cost of the new machine that is represented as depreciation in Exhibit 11-12.

> **Decision Point**
>
> Is book value of existing equipment relevant in equipment replacement decisions?

> **Exhibit 11-11**
>
> Operating Income Comparison: Replacement of Machine, Relevant, and Irrelevant Items for Toledo Company

	Two Years Together		
	Keep (1)	Replace (2)	Difference (3) = (1) – (2)
Revenues	$2,200,000	$2,200,000	—
Operating costs			
Cash operating costs			
($800,000/yr. × 2 years;			
$460,000/yr. × 2 years)	1,600,000	920,000	$ 680,000
Book value of old machine			
Periodic write-off as depreciation or	400,000	—	—
Lump-sum write-off	—	400,000[a]	
Current disposal value of old machine	—	(40,000)[a]	40,000
New machine cost, written off periodically			
as depreciation	—	600,000	(600,000)
Total operating costs	2,000,000	1,880,000	120,000
Operating income	$ 200,000	$ 320,000	$(120,000)

[a]In a formal income statement, these two items would be combined as "loss on disposal of machine" of $360,000.

---

[2] See Chapter 21 for a discussion of time-value-of-money and income-tax considerations in capital investment decisions.

Exhibit 11-12

Cost Comparison:
Replacement of
Machine, Relevant
Items Only, for Toledo
Company

| | Two Years Together | | |
	Keep (1)	Replace (2)	Difference (3) = (1) – (2)
Cash operating costs	$1,600,000	$ 920,000	$680,000
Current disposal value of old machine	—	(40,000)	40,000
New machine, written off periodically as depreciation	—	600,000	(600,000)
Total relevant costs	$1,600,000	$1,480,000	$120,000

Decisions and Performance Evaluation

Consider our equipment-replacement example in light of the five-step sequence in Exhibit 11-1 (p. 392):

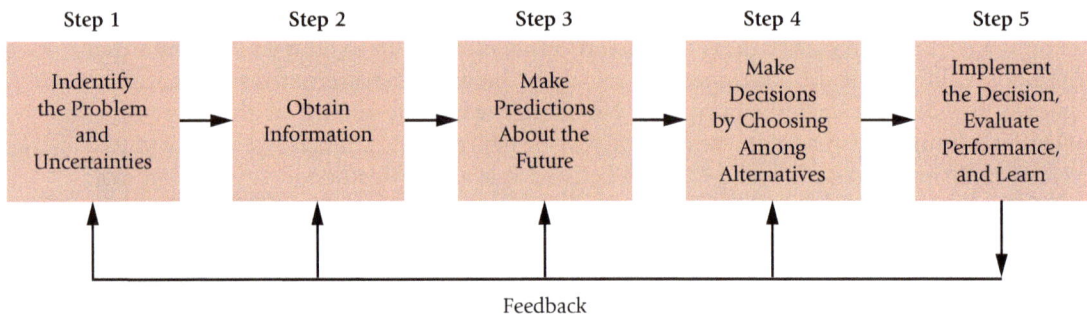

Step 1	Step 2	Step 3	Step 4	Step 5
Indentify the Problem and Uncertainties	Obtain Information	Make Predictions About the Future	Make Decisions by Choosing Among Alternatives	Implement the Decision, Evaluate Performance, and Learn

Feedback

**Learning
Objective 7**

Explain how conflicts
can arise between the
decision model used by
a manager and the
performance-evaluation
model used to evaluate
the manager

. . . tell managers to
take a multiple-year
view in decision making
but judge their
performance only on
the basis of the current
year's operating income

The decision model analysis (Step 4), which is presented in Exhibits 11-11 and 11-12, dictates replacing the machine rather than keeping it. In the real world, however, would the manager replace it? An important factor in replacement decisions is the manager's perception of whether the decision model is consistent with how the manager's performance will be judged after the decision is implemented (the performance-evaluation model in Step 5).

From the perspective of their own careers, it is no surprise that managers tend to favor the alternative that makes their performance look better. If the performance-evaluation model conflicts with the decision model, the performance-evaluation model often prevails in influencing managers' decisions. For example, if the promotion or bonus of the manager at Toledo hinges on his or her first year's operating income performance under accrual accounting, the manager's temptation *not* to replace will be overwhelming. Why? Because the accrual accounting model for measuring performance will show a higher first-year operating income if the old machine is kept rather than replaced (as the following table shows):

First-Year Results: Accrual Accounting	Keep		Replace	
Revenues		$1,100,000		$1,100,000
Operating costs				
Cash-operating costs	$800,000		$460,000	
Depreciation	200,000		300,000	
Loss on disposal	—		360,000	
Total operating costs		1,000,000		1,120,000
Operating income (loss)		$ 100,000		$ (20,000)

Even though top management's goals encompass the two-year period (consistent with the decision model), the manager will focus on first-year results if his or her evaluation is based on short-run measures such as the first-year's operating income.

Resolving the conflict between the decision model and the performance-evaluation model is frequently a baffling problem in practice. In theory, resolving the difficulty seems obvious: Design models that are consistent. Consider our replacement example. Year-by-year effects on operating income of replacement can be budgeted for the two-year planning horizon. The manager then would be evaluated on the expectation that the first year would be poor and the next year would be much better. Doing this for every decision, however, makes the performance evaluation model very cumbersome. As a result of these practical difficulties, accounting systems rarely track each decision separately. Performance evaluation focuses on responsibility centers for a specific period, not on projects or individual items of equipment over their useful lives. Thus, the impacts of many different decisions are combined in a single performance report and evaluation measure, say operating income. Lower-level managers make decisions to maximize operating income, and top management—through the reporting system—is rarely aware of particular desirable alternatives that were *not* chosen by lower-level managers because of conflicts between the decision and performance-evaluation models.

Consider another conflict between the decision model and the performance-evaluation model. Suppose a manager buys a particular machine only to discover shortly thereafter that a better machine could have been purchased instead. The decision model may suggest replacing the machine that was just bought with the better machine, but will the manager do so? Probably not. Why? Because replacing the machine so soon after its purchase will reflect badly on the manager's capabilities and performance. If the manager's bosses have no knowledge of the better machine, the manager may prefer to keep the recently purchased machine rather than alert them to the better machine.

Chapter 23 discusses performance evaluation models in more detail and ways to reduce conflict between the decision model and the performance evaluation model.

Decision Point

How can conflicts arise between the decision model used by a manager and the performance-evaluation model used to evaluate that manager?

Problem for Self-Study

Wally Lewis is manager of the engineering development division of Goldcoast Products. Lewis has just received a proposal signed by all 15 of his engineers to replace the workstations with networked personal computers (networked PCs). Lewis is not enthusiastic about the proposal.

Data on workstations and networked PCs are as follows:

	Workstations	Networked PCs
Original cost	$300,000	$135,000
Useful life	5 years	3 years
Current age	2 years	0 years
Remaining useful life	3 years	3 years
Accumulated depreciation	$120,000	Not acquired yet
Current book value	$180,000	Not acquired yet
Current disposal value (in cash)	$95,000	Not acquired yet
Terminal disposal value (in cash 3 years from now)	$0	$0
Annual computer-related cash operating costs	$40,000	$10,000
Annual revenues	$1,000,000	$1,000,000
Annual noncomputer-related operating costs	$880,000	$880,000

Lewis's annual bonus includes a component based on division operating income. He has a promotion possibility next year that would make him a group vice president of Goldcoast Products.

1. Compare the costs of workstations and networked PCs. Consider the cumulative results **Required** for the three years together, ignoring the time value of money and income taxes.
2. Why might Lewis be reluctant to purchase the networked PCs?

Solution

1. The following table considers all cost items when comparing future costs of workstations and networked PCs:

All Items	Workstations (1)	Networked PCs (2)	Difference (3) = (1) − (2)
	Three Years Together		
Revenues	$3,000,000	$3,000,000	—
Operating costs			
Noncomputer-related operating costs	2,640,000	2,640,000	—
Computer-related cash operating costs	120,000	30,000	$ 90,000
Workstations' book value			
Periodic write-off as depreciation or	180,000	— }	—
Lump-sum write-off	—	180,000 }	
Current disposal value of workstations	—	(95,000)	95,000
Networked PCs, written off periodically			
as depreciation	—	135,000	(135,000)
Total operating costs	2,940,000	2,890,000	50,000
Operating income	$ 60,000	$ 110,000	$ (50,000)

Alternatively, the analysis could focus on only those items in the preceding table that differ between the alternatives.

Relevant Items	Workstations	Networked PCs	Difference
	Three Years Together		
Computer-related cash operating costs	$120,000	$ 30,000	$90,000
Current disposal value of workstations	—	(95,000)	95,000
Networked PCs, written off periodically			
as depreciation	—	135,000	(135,000)
Total relevant costs	$120,000	$ 70,000	$ 50,000

The analysis suggests that it is cost-effective to replace the workstations with the networked PCs.

2. The accrual-accounting operating incomes *for the first year* under the keep workstations versus the buy networked PCs alternatives are as follows:

	Keep Workstations		Buy Networked PCs	
Revenues		$1,000,000		$1,000,000
Operating costs				
Noncomputer-related operating costs	$880,000		$880,000	
Computer-related cash operating costs	40,000		10,000	
Depreciation	60,000		45,000	
Loss on disposal of workstations	—		85,000[a]	
Total operating costs		980,000		1,020,000
Operating income (loss)		$ 20,000		$ (20,000)

[a] $85,000 = Book value of workstations, $180,000 − Current disposal value, $95,000.

Lewis would be less happy with the expected operating loss of $20,000 if the networked PCs are purchased than he would be with the expected operating income of $20,000 if the workstations are kept. Buying the networked PCs would eliminate the component of his bonus based on operating income. He might also perceive the $20,000 operating loss as reducing his chances of being promoted to a group vice president.

Decision Points

The following question-and-answer format summarizes the chapter's learning objectives. Each decision presents a key question related to a learning objective. The guidelines are the answer to that question.

Decision	Guidelines
1. What is the five-step process that managers can use to make decisions?	The five-step decision-making process is (a) identify the problem and uncertainties, (b) obtain information, (c) make predictions about the future, (d) make decisions by choosing among alternatives, and (e) implement the decision, evaluate performance, and learn.
2. When is a revenue or cost item relevant for a particular decision and what potential problems should be avoided in relevant-cost analysis?	To be relevant for a particular decision, a revenue or cost item must meet two criteria: (a) It must be an expected future revenue or expected future cost, and (b) it must differ among alternative courses of action. The outcomes of alternative actions can be quantitative and qualitative. Quantitative outcomes are measured in numerical terms. Some quantitative outcomes can be expressed in financial terms, others cannot. Qualitative factors, such as employee morale, are difficult to measure accurately in numerical terms. Consideration must be given to relevant quantitative and qualitative factors in making decisions.

Two potential problems to avoid in relevant-cost analysis are (a) making incorrect general assumptions—such as all variable costs are relevant and all fixed costs are irrelevant—and (b) losing sight of total amounts, focusing instead on unit amounts. |
3. What is an opportunity cost and why should it be included when making decisions?	Opportunity cost is the contribution to income that is forgone by not using a limited resource in its next-best alternative use. Opportunity cost is included in decision making because the relevant cost of any decision is (1) the incremental cost of the decision plus (2) the opportunity cost of the profit forgone from making that decision.
4. When resources are constrained, how should managers choose which of multiple products to produce and sell?	When resources are constrained, managers should select the product that yields the highest contribution margin per unit of the constraining or limiting resource (factor). In this way, total contribution margin will be maximized.
5. In deciding to add or drop customers or to add or discontinue branch offices or segments, what should managers focus on and how should they take into account allocated overhead costs?	When making decisions about adding or dropping customers or adding or discontinuing branch offices and segments, managers should focus on only those costs that will change and any opportunity costs. Managers should ignore allocated overhead costs.
6. Is book value of existing equipment relevant in equipment-replacement decisions?	Book value of existing equipment is a past (historical or sunk) cost and, therefore, is irrelevant in equipment-replacement decisions.
7. How can conflicts arise between the decision model used by a manager and the performance-evaluation model used to evaluate that manager?	Top management faces a persistent challenge: making sure that the performance-evaluation model of lower-level managers is consistent with the decision model. A common inconsistency is to tell these managers to take a multiple-year view in their decision making but then to judge their performance only on the basis of the current year's operating income.

Appendix

Linear Programming

In this chapter's Power Recreation example (pp. 405–406), suppose both the snowmobile and boat engines must be tested on a very expensive machine before they are shipped to customers. The available machine-hours for testing are limited. Production data are as follows:

Department	Available Daily Capacity in Hours	Use of Capacity in Hours per Unit of Product		Daily Maximum Production in Units	
		Snowmobile Engine	Boat Engine	Snowmobile Engine	Boat Engine
Assembly	600 machine-hours	2.0 machine-hours	5.0 machine-hours	300[a] snow engines	120 boat engines
Testing	120 testing-hours	1.0 machine-hour	0.5 machine-hour	120 snow engines	240 boat engines

[a] For example, 600 machine-hours ÷ 2.0 machine-hours per snowmobile engine = 300, the maximum number of snowmobile engines that the assembly department can make if it works exclusively on snowmobile engines.

Exhibit 11-13 summarizes these and other relevant data. In addition, as a result of material shortages for boat engines, Power Recreation cannot produce more than 110 boat engines per day. How many engines of each type should Power Recreation produce and sell daily to maximize operating income?

Because there are multiple constraints, a technique called *linear programming* or *LP* can be used to determine the number of each type of engine Power Recreation should produce. LP models typically assume that all costs are either variable or fixed with respect to a single cost driver (units of output). As we shall see, LP models also require certain other linear assumptions to hold. When these assumptions fail, other decision models should be considered.[3]

Steps in Solving an LP Problem

We use the data in Exhibit 11-13 to illustrate the three steps in solving an LP problem. Throughout this discussion, S equals the number of units of snowmobile engines produced and sold, and B equals the number of units of boat engines produced and sold.

Step 1: Determine the objective function. The **objective function** of a linear program expresses the objective or goal to be maximized (say, operating income) or minimized (say, operating costs). In our example, the objective is to find the combination of snowmobile engines and boat engines that maximizes total contribution margin. Fixed costs remain the same regardless of the product-mix decision and are irrelevant. The linear function expressing the objective for the total contribution margin (TCM) is as follows:

$$TCM = \$240S + \$375B$$

Step 2: Specify the constraints. A **constraint** is a mathematical inequality or equality that must be satisfied by the variables in a mathematical model. The following linear inequalities express the relationships in our example:

Assembly department constraint	$2S + 5B \leq 600$
Testing department constraint	$1S + 0.5B \leq 120$
Materials-shortage constraint for boat engines	$B \leq 110$
Negative production is impossible	$S \geq 0$ and $B \geq 0$

Exhibit 11-13 Operating Data for Power Recreation

	Department Capacity (per Day) In Product Units		Selling Price	Variable Cost per Unit	Contribution Margin per Unit
	Assembly	Testing			
Only snowmobile engines	300	120	$ 800	$560	$240
Only boat engines	120	240	$1,000	$625	$375

---

[3] Other decision models are described in J. Moore and L. Weatherford, *Decision Modeling with Microsoft Excel*, 6th ed. (Upper Saddle River, NJ: Prentice Hall, 2001); and S. Nahmias, *Production and Operations Analysis*, 6th ed. (New York: McGraw-Hill/Irwin, 2008).

The three solid lines on the graph in Exhibit 11-14 show the existing constraints for assembly and testing and the materials-shortage constraint.[4] The feasible or technically possible alternatives are those combinations of quantities of snowmobile engines and boat engines that satisfy all the constraining resources or factors. The shaded "area of feasible solutions" in Exhibit 11-14 shows the boundaries of those product combinations that are feasible.

Step 3:   Compute the optimal solution. **Linear programming (LP)** is an optimization technique used to maximize the *objective function* when there are multiple *constraints*. We present two approaches for finding the optimal solution using LP: trial-and-error approach and graphic approach. These approaches are easy to use in our example because there are only two variables in the objective function and a small number of constraints. Understanding these approaches provides insight into LP. In most real-world LP applications, managers use computer software packages to calculate the optimal solution.[5]

Trial-and-Error Approach

The optimal solution can be found by trial and error, by working with coordinates of the corners of the area of feasible solutions.

First, select any set of corner points and compute the total contribution margin. Five corner points appear in Exhibit 11-14. It is helpful to use simultaneous equations to obtain the exact coordinates in the graph. To illustrate, the corner point ($S = 75$, $B = 90$) can be derived by solving the two pertinent constraint inequalities as simultaneous equations:

$$2S + 5B = 600 \quad (1)$$

$$1S + 0.5B = 120 \quad (2)$$

Multiplying (2) *by* 2: $\quad 2S + B = 240 \quad (3)$

Subtracting (3) from (1): $\quad 4B = 360$

Therefore, $\quad B = 360 \div 4 = 90$

Substituting for B in (2): $1S + 0.5(90) = 120$

$$S = 120 - 45 = 75$$

Given $S = 75$ snowmobile engines and $B = 90$ boat engines, TCM = ($240 per snowmobile engine × 75 snowmobile engines) + ($375 per boat engine × 90 boat engines) = $51,750.

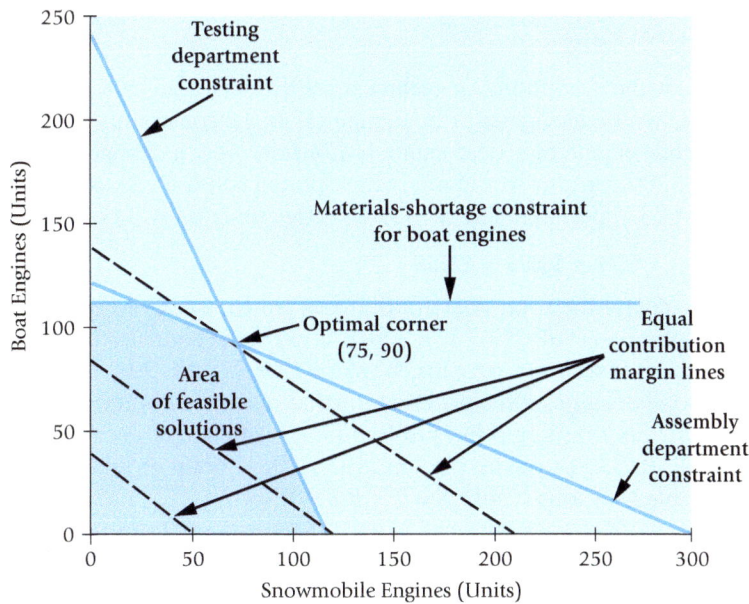

Exhibit 11-14

Linear Programming: Graphic Solution for Power Recreation

---

[4] As an example of how the lines are plotted in Exhibit 11-14, use equal signs instead of inequality signs and assume for the assembly department that $B = 0$; then $S = 300$ (600 machine-hours ÷ 2 machine-hours per snowmobile engine). Assume that $S = 0$; then $B = 120$ (600 machine-hours ÷ 5 machine-hours per boat engine). Connect those two points with a straight line.
[5] Standard computer software packages rely on the simplex method. The *simplex method* is an iterative step-by-step procedure for determining the optimal solution to an LP problem. It starts with a specific feasible solution and then tests it by substitution to see whether the result can be improved. These substitutions continue until no further improvement is possible and the optimal solution is obtained.

Second, move from corner point to corner point and compute the total contribution margin at each corner point.

Trial	Corner Point (S, B)	Snowmobile Engines (S)	Boat Engines (B)	Total Contribution Margin
1	(0, 0)	0	0	$240(0) + $375(0) = $0
2	(0, 110)	0	110	$240(0) + $375(110) = $41,250
3	(25,110)	25	110	$240(25) + $375(110) = $47,250
4	(75, 90)	75	90	$240(75) + $375(90) = $51,750[a]
5	(120, 0)	120	0	$240(120) + $375(0) = $28,800

[a] The optimal solution.

The optimal product mix is the mix that yields the highest total contribution: 75 snowmobile engines and 90 boat engines. To understand the solution, consider what happens when moving from the point (25,110) to (75,90). Power Recreation gives up $7,500 [$375 × (110 − 90)] in contribution margin from boat engines while gaining $12,000 [$240 × (75 − 25)] in contribution margin from snowmobile engines. This results in a net increase in contribution margin of $4,500 ($12,000 − $7,500), from $47,250 to $51,750.

Graphic Approach

Consider all possible combinations that will produce the same total contribution margin of, say, $12,000. That is,

$$\$240S + \$375B = \$12,000$$

This set of $12,000 contribution margins is a straight dashed line through [S = 50 ($12,000 ÷ $240); B = 0)] and [S = 0, B = 32 ($12,000 ÷ $375)] in Exhibit 11-14. Other equal total contribution margins can be represented by lines parallel to this one. In Exhibit 11-14, we show three dashed lines. Lines drawn farther from the origin represent more sales of both products and higher amounts of equal contribution margins.

The optimal line is the one farthest from the origin but still passing through a point in the area of feasible solutions. This line represents the highest total contribution margin. The optimal solution—the number of snowmobile engines and boat engines that will maximize the objective function, total contribution margin—is the corner point (S = 75, B = 90). This solution will become apparent if you put a straight-edge ruler on the graph and move it outward from the origin and parallel with the $12,000 contribution margin line. Move the ruler as far away from the origin as possible—that is, increase the total contribution margin—without leaving the area of feasible solutions. In general, the optimal solution in a maximization problem lies at the corner where the dashed line intersects an extreme point of the area of feasible solutions. Moving the ruler out any farther puts it outside the area of feasible solutions.

Sensitivity Analysis

What are the implications of uncertainty about the accounting or technical coefficients used in the objective function (such as the contribution margin per unit of snowmobile engines or boat engines) or the constraints (such as the number of machine-hours it takes to make a snowmobile engine or a boat engine)? Consider how a change in the contribution margin of snowmobile engines from $240 to $300 per unit would affect the optimal solution. Assume the contribution margin for boat engines remains unchanged at $375 per unit. The revised objective function will be as follows:

$$TCM = \$300S + \$375B$$

Using the trial-and-error approach to calculate the total contribution margin for each of the five corner points described in the previous table, the optimal solution is still (S = 75, B = 90). What if the contribution margin of snowmobile engines falls to $160 per unit? The optimal solution remains the same (S = 75, B = 90). Thus, big changes in the contribution margin per unit of snowmobile engines have no effect on the optimal solution in this case. That's because, although the slopes of the equal contribution margin lines in Exhibit 11-14 change as the contribution margin of snowmobile engines changes from $240 to $300 to $160 per unit, the farthest point at which the equal contribution margin lines intersect the area of feasible solutions is still (S = 75, B = 90).

Terms to Learn

This chapter and the Glossary at the end of the book contain definitions of the following important terms:

book value (p. 410)

business function costs (p. 395)

constraint (p. 416)

decision model (p. 391)

differential cost (p. 399)

differential revenue (p. 399)

full costs of the product (p. 395)

incremental cost (p. 399)

incremental revenue (p. 399)

insourcing (**p. 397**)

linear programming (LP) (**p. 417**)

make-or-buy decisions (**p. 397**)

objective function (**p. 416**)

one-time-only special order (**p. 394**)

opportunity cost (**p. 402**)

outsourcing (**p. 397**)

product-mix decisions (**p. 405**)

qualitative factors (**p. 394**)

quantitative factors (**p. 394**)

relevant costs (**p. 393**)

relevant revenues (**p. 393**)

sunk costs (**p. 393**)

Assignment Material

Questions

11-1 Outline the five-step sequence in a decision process.

11-2 Define relevant costs. Why are historical costs irrelevant?

11-3 "All future costs are relevant." Do you agree? Why?

11-4 Distinguish between quantitative and qualitative factors in decision making.

11-5 Describe two potential problems that should be avoided in relevant-cost analysis.

11-6 "Variable costs are always relevant, and fixed costs are always irrelevant." Do you agree? Why?

11-7 "A component part should be purchased whenever the purchase price is less than its total manufacturing cost per unit." Do you agree? Why?

11-8 Define opportunity cost.

11-9 "Managers should always buy inventory in quantities that result in the lowest purchase cost per unit." Do you agree? Why?

11-10 "Management should always maximize sales of the product with the highest contribution margin per unit." Do you agree? Why?

11-11 "A branch office or business segment that shows negative operating income should be shut down." Do you agree? Explain briefly.

11-12 "Cost written off as depreciation on equipment already purchased is always irrelevant." Do you agree? Why?

11-13 "Managers will always choose the alternative that maximizes operating income or minimizes costs in the decision model." Do you agree? Why?

11-14 Describe the three steps in solving a linear programming problem.

11-15 How might the optimal solution of a linear programming problem be determined?

Exercises

11-16 **Disposal of assets.** Answer the following questions.

1. A company has an inventory of 1,100 assorted parts for a line of missiles that has been discontinued. The inventory cost is $78,000. The parts can be either (a) remachined at total additional costs of $24,500 and then sold for $33,000 or (b) sold as scrap for $6,500. Which action is more profitable? Show your calculations.

2. A truck, costing $101,000 and uninsured, is wrecked its first day in use. It can be either (a) disposed of for $17,500 cash and replaced with a similar truck costing $103,500 or (b) rebuilt for $89,500, and thus be brand-new as far as operating characteristics and looks are concerned. Which action is less costly? Show your calculations.

11-17 **Relevant and irrelevant costs.** Answer the following questions.

1. DeCesare Computers makes 5,200 units of a circuit board, CB76 at a cost of $280 each. Variable cost per unit is $190 and fixed cost per unit is $90. Peach Electronics offers to supply 5,200 units of CB76 for $260. If DeCesare buys from Peach it will be able to save $10 per unit in fixed costs but continue to incur the remaining $80 per unit. Should DeCesare accept Peach's offer? Explain.

2. LN Manufacturing is deciding whether to keep or replace an old machine. It obtains the following information:

	Old Machine	New Machine
Original cost	$10,700	$9,000
Useful life	10 years	3 years
Current age	7 years	0 years
Remaining useful life	3 years	3 years
Accumulated depreciation	$7,490	Not acquired yet
Book value	$3,210	Not acquired yet
Current disposal value (in cash)	$2,200	Not acquired yet
Terminal disposal value (3 years from now)	$0	$0
Annual cash operating costs	$17,500	$15,500

LN Manufacturing uses straight-line depreciation. Ignore the time value of money and income taxes. Should LN Manufacturing replace the old machine? Explain.

11-18 **Multiple choice.** (CPA) Choose the best answer.

1. The Woody Company manufactures slippers and sells them at $10 a pair. Variable manufacturing cost is $4.50 a pair, and allocated fixed manufacturing cost is $1.50 a pair. It has enough idle capacity available to accept a one-time-only special order of 20,000 pairs of slippers at $6 a pair. Woody will not incur any marketing costs as a result of the special order. What would the effect on operating income be if the special order could be accepted without affecting normal sales: (a) $0, (b) $30,000 increase, (c) $90,000 increase, or (d) $120,000 increase? Show your calculations.

2. The Reno Company manufactures Part No. 498 for use in its production line. The manufacturing cost per unit for 20,000 units of Part No. 498 is as follows:

Direct materials	$ 6
Direct manufacturing labor	30
Variable manufacturing overhead	12
Fixed manufacturing overhead allocated	16
Total manufacturing cost per unit	$64

The Tray Company has offered to sell 20,000 units of Part No. 498 to Reno for $60 per unit. Reno will make the decision to buy the part from Tray if there is an overall savings of at least $25,000 for Reno. If Reno accepts Tray's offer, $9 per unit of the fixed overhead allocated would be eliminated. Furthermore, Reno has determined that the released facilities could be used to save relevant costs in the manufacture of Part No. 575. For Reno to achieve an overall savings of $25,000, the amount of relevant costs that would have to be saved by using the released facilities in the manufacture of Part No. 575 would be which of the following: (a) $80,000, (b) $85,000, (c) $125,000, or (d) $140,000? Show your calculations.

11-19 **Special order, activity-based costing.** (CMA, adapted) The Award Plus Company manufactures medals for winners of athletic events and other contests. Its manufacturing plant has the capacity to produce 10,000 medals each month. Current production and sales are 7,500 medals per month. The company normally charges $150 per medal. Cost information for the current activity level is as follows:

Variable costs that vary with number of units produced	
Direct materials	$ 262,500
Direct manufacturing labor	300,000
Variable costs (for setups, materials handling, quality control, and so on)	75,000
that vary with number of batches, 150 batches × $500 per batch	
Fixed manufacturing costs	275,000
Fixed marketing costs	175,000
Total costs	$1,087,500

Award Plus has just received a special one-time-only order for 2,500 medals at $100 per medal. Accepting the special order would not affect the company's regular business. Award Plus makes medals for its existing customers in batch sizes of 50 medals (150 batches × 50 medals per batch = 7,500 medals). The special order requires Award Plus to make the medals in 25 batches of 100 each.

Required

1. Should Award Plus accept this special order? Show your calculations.
2. Suppose plant capacity were only 9,000 medals instead of 10,000 medals each month. The special order must either be taken in full or be rejected completely. Should Award Plus accept the special order? Show your calculations.
3. As in requirement 1, assume that monthly capacity is 10,000 medals. Award Plus is concerned that if it accepts the special order, its existing customers will immediately demand a price discount of $10 in the month in which the special order is being filled. They would argue that Award Plus's capacity costs are now being spread over more units and that existing customers should get the benefit of these lower costs. Should Award Plus accept the special order under these conditions? Show your calculations.

11-20 **Make versus buy, activity-based costing.** The Svenson Corporation manufactures cellular modems. It manufactures its own cellular modem circuit boards (CMCB), an important part of the cellular modem. It reports the following cost information about the costs of making CMCBs in 2011 and the expected costs in 2012:

	Current Costs in 2011	Expected Costs in 2012
Variable manufacturing costs		
Direct material cost per CMCB	$ 180	$ 170
Direct manufacturing labor cost per CMCB	50	45
Variable manufacturing cost per batch for setups, materials handling, and quality control	1,600	1,500
Fixed manufacturing cost		
Fixed manufacturing overhead costs that can be avoided if CMCBs are not made	320,000	320,000
Fixed manufacturing overhead costs of plant depreciation, insurance, and administration that cannot be avoided even if CMCBs are not made	800,000	800,000

Svenson manufactured 8,000 CMCBs in 2011 in 40 batches of 200 each. In 2012, Svenson anticipates needing 10,000 CMCBs. The CMCBs would be produced in 80 batches of 125 each.

The Minton Corporation has approached Svenson about supplying CMCBs to Svenson in 2012 at $300 per CMCB on whatever delivery schedule Svenson wants.

Required

1. Calculate the total expected manufacturing cost per unit of making CMCBs in 2012.
2. Suppose the capacity currently used to make CMCBs will become idle if Svenson purchases CMCBs from Minton. On the basis of financial considerations alone, should Svenson make CMCBs or buy them from Minton? Show your calculations.
3. Now suppose that if Svenson purchases CMCBs from Minton, its best alternative use of the capacity currently used for CMCBs is to make and sell special circuit boards (CB3s) to the Essex Corporation. Svenson estimates the following incremental revenues and costs from CB3s:

Total expected incremental future revenues	$2,000,000
Total expected incremental future costs	$2,150,000

On the basis of financial considerations alone, should Svenson make CMCBs or buy them from Minton? Show your calculations.

11-21 Inventory decision, opportunity costs. Lawn World, a manufacturer of lawn mowers, predicts that it will purchase 264,000 spark plugs next year. Lawn World estimates that 22,000 spark plugs will be required each month. A supplier quotes a price of $7 per spark plug. The supplier also offers a special discount option: If all 264,000 spark plugs are purchased at the start of the year, a discount of 2% off the $7 price will be given. Lawn World can invest its cash at 10% per year. It costs Lawn World $260 to place each purchase order.

Required

1. What is the opportunity cost of interest forgone from purchasing all 264,000 units at the start of the year instead of in 12 monthly purchases of 22,000 units per order?
2. Would this opportunity cost be recorded in the accounting system? Why?
3. Should Lawn World purchase 264,000 units at the start of the year or 22,000 units each month? Show your calculations.

11-22 Relevant costs, contribution margin, product emphasis. The Seashore Stand is a take-out food store at a popular beach resort. Susan Sexton, owner of the Seashore Stand, is deciding how much refrigerator space to devote to four different drinks. Pertinent data on these four drinks are as follows:

	Cola	Lemonade	Punch	Natural Orange Juice
Selling price per case	$18.75	$20.50	$27.75	$39.30
Variable cost per case	$13.75	$15.60	$20.70	$30.40
Cases sold per foot of shelf space per day	22	12	6	13

Sexton has a maximum front shelf space of 12 feet to devote to the four drinks. She wants a minimum of 1 foot and a maximum of 6 feet of front shelf space for each drink.

Required

1. Calculate the contribution margin per case of each type of drink.
2. A coworker of Sexton's recommends that she maximize the shelf space devoted to those drinks with the highest contribution margin per case. Evaluate this recommendation.
3. What shelf-space allocation for the four drinks would you recommend for the Seashore Stand? Show your calculations.

11-23 Selection of most profitable product. Body-Builders, Inc., produces two basic types of weight-lifting equipment, Model 9 and Model 14. Pertinent data are as follows:

	A	B	C
		Per Unit	
1		**Model 9**	**Model 14**
2		**Model 9**	**Model 14**
3	Selling price	$100.00	$70.00
4	Costs		
5	Direct material	28.00	13.00
6	Direct manufacturing labor	15.00	25.00
7	Variable manufacturing overhead*	25.00	12.50
8	Fixed manufacturing overhead*	10.00	5.00
9	Marketing (all variable)	14.00	10.00
10	Total cost	92.00	65.50
11	Operating income	$ 8.00	$ 4.50
12			
13	*Allocated on the basis of machine-hours		

The weight-lifting craze is such that enough of either Model 9 or Model 14 can be sold to keep the plant operating at full capacity. Both products are processed through the same production departments.

Required Which products should be produced? Briefly explain your answer.

11-24 Which center to close, relevant-cost analysis, opportunity costs. Fair Lakes Hospital Corporation has been operating ambulatory surgery centers in Groveton and Stockdale, two small communities each about an hour away from its main hospital. As a cost control measure the hospital has decided that it needs only one of those two centers permanently, so one must be shut down. The decision regarding which center to close will be made on financial considerations alone. The following information is available:

a. The Groveton center was built 15 years ago at a cost of $5 million on land leased from the City of Groveton at a cost of $40,000 per year. The land and buildings will immediately revert back to the city if the center is closed. The center has annual operating costs of $2.5 million, all of which will be saved if the center is closed. In addition, Fair Lakes allocates $800,000 of common administrative costs to the Groveton center. If the center is closed, these costs would be reallocated to other ambulatory centers. If the center is kept open, Fair Lakes plans to invest $1 million in a fixed income note, which will earn the $40,000 that Fair Lakes needs for the lease payments.

b. The Stockdale center was built 20 years ago at a cost of $4.8 million, of which Fair Lakes and the City of Stockdale each paid half, on land donated by a hospital benefactor. Two years ago, Fair Lakes spent $2 million to renovate the facility. If the center is closed, the property will be sold to developers for $7 million. The operating costs of the center are $3 million per year, all of which will be saved if the center is closed. Fair Lakes allocates $1 million of common administrative costs to the Stockdale center. If the center is closed, these costs would be reallocated to other ambulatory centers.

c. Fair Lakes estimates that the operating costs of whichever center remains open will be $3.5 million per year.

Required The City Council of Stockdale has petitioned Fair Lakes to close the Groveton facility, thus sparing the Stockdale center. The Council argues that otherwise the $2 million spent on recent renovations would be wasted. Do you agree with the Stockdale City Council's arguments and conclusions? In your answer, identify and explain all costs that you consider relevant and all costs that you consider irrelevant for the center-closing decision.

11-25 Closing and opening stores. Sanchez Corporation runs two convenience stores, one in Connecticut and one in Rhode Island. Operating income for each store in 2012 is as follows:

	Connecticut Store	**Rhode Island Store**
Revenues	$1,070,000	$860,000
Operating costs		
Cost of goods sold	750,000	660,000
Lease rent (renewable each year)	90,000	75,000
Labor costs (paid on an hourly basis)	42,000	42,000
Depreciation of equipment	25,000	22,000
Utilities (electricity, heating)	43,000	46,000
Allocated corporate overhead	50,000	40,000
Total operating costs	1,000,000	885,000
Operating income (loss)	$ 70,000	$ (25,000)

The equipment has a zero disposal value. In a senior management meeting, Maria Lopez, the management accountant at Sanchez Corporation, makes the following comment, "Sanchez can increase its profitability by closing down the Rhode Island store or by adding another store like it."

Required

1. By closing down the Rhode Island store, Sanchez can reduce overall corporate overhead costs by $44,000. Calculate Sanchez's operating income if it closes the Rhode Island store. Is Maria Lopez's statement about the effect of closing the Rhode Island store correct? Explain.

2. Calculate Sanchez's operating income if it keeps the Rhode Island store open and opens another store with revenues and costs identical to the Rhode Island store (including a cost of $22,000 to acquire equipment with a one-year useful life and zero disposal value). Opening this store will increase corporate overhead costs by $4,000. Is Maria Lopez's statement about the effect of adding another store like the Rhode Island store correct? Explain.

11-26 Choosing customers. Broadway Printers operates a printing press with a monthly capacity of 2,000 machine-hours. Broadway has two main customers: Taylor Corporation and Kelly Corporation. Data on each customer for January follows:

	Taylor Corporation	**Kelly Corporation**	**Total**
Revenues	$120,000	$80,000	$200,000
Variable costs	42,000	48,000	90,000
Contribution margin	78,000	32,000	110,000
Fixed costs (allocated)	60,000	40,000	100,000
Operating income	$ 18,000	$ (8,000)	$ 10,000
Machine-hours required	1,500 hours	500 hours	2,000 hours

Kelly Corporation indicates that it wants Broadway to do an *additional* $80,000 worth of printing jobs during February. These jobs are identical to the existing business Broadway did for Kelly in January in terms of variable costs and machine-hours required. Broadway anticipates that the business from Taylor Corporation in February will be the same as that in January. Broadway can choose to accept as much of the Taylor and Kelly business for February as its capacity allows. Assume that total machine-hours and fixed costs for February will be the same as in January.

What action should Broadway take to maximize its operating income? Show your calculations.

Required

11-27 Relevance of equipment costs. The Auto Wash Company has just today paid for and installed a special machine for polishing cars at one of its several outlets. It is the first day of the company's fiscal year. The machine costs $20,000. Its annual cash operating costs total $15,000. The machine will have a four-year useful life and a zero terminal disposal value.

After the machine has been used for only one day, a salesperson offers a different machine that promises to do the same job at annual cash operating costs of $9,000. The new machine will cost $24,000 cash, installed. The "old" machine is unique and can be sold outright for only $10,000, minus $2,000 removal cost. The new machine, like the old one, will have a four-year useful life and zero terminal disposal value.

Revenues, all in cash, will be $150,000 annually, and other cash costs will be $110,000 annually, regardless of this decision.

For simplicity, ignore income taxes and the time value of money.

Required

1. a. Prepare a statement of cash receipts and disbursements for each of the four years under each alternative. What is the cumulative difference in cash flow for the four years taken together?

b. Prepare income statements for each of the four years under each alternative. Assume straight-line depreciation. What is the cumulative difference in operating income for the four years taken together?

c. What are the irrelevant items in your presentations in requirements a and b? Why are they irrelevant?

2. Suppose the cost of the "old" machine was $1 million rather than $20,000. Nevertheless, the old machine can be sold outright for only $10,000, minus $2,000 removal cost. Would the net differences in requirements 1a and 1b change? Explain.

3. Is there any conflict between the decision model and the incentives of the manager who has just purchased the "old" machine and is considering replacing it a day later?

11-28 Equipment upgrade versus replacement. (A. Spero, adapted) The TechGuide Company produces and sells 7,500 modular computer desks per year at a selling price of $750 each. Its current production equipment, purchased for $1,800,000 and with a five-year useful life, is only two years old. It has a terminal disposal value of $0 and is depreciated on a straight-line basis. The equipment has a current disposal price of $450,000. However, the emergence of a new molding technology has led TechGuide to consider either upgrading or replacing the production equipment. The following table presents data for the two alternatives:

	Home	Insert	Page Layout	Formulas	Data	Review
	A				B	C
1					**Upgrade**	**Replace**
2	One-time equipment costs				$3,000,000	$4,800,000
3	Variable manufacturing cost per desk				$ 150	$ 75
4	Remaining useful life of equipment (years)				3	3
5	Terminal disposal value of equipment				$ 0	$ 0

All equipment costs will continue to be depreciated on a straight-line basis. For simplicity, ignore income taxes and the time value of money.

Required

1. Should TechGuide upgrade its production line or replace it? Show your calculations.
2. Now suppose the one-time equipment cost to replace the production equipment is somewhat negotiable. All other data are as given previously. What is the maximum one-time equipment cost that TechGuide would be willing to pay to replace the old equipment rather than upgrade it?
3. Assume that the capital expenditures to replace and upgrade the production equipment are as given in the original exercise, but that the production and sales quantity is not known. For what production and sales quantity would TechGuide (i) upgrade the equipment or (ii) replace the equipment?
4. Assume that all data are as given in the original exercise. Dan Doria is TechGuide's manager, and his bonus is based on operating income. Because he is likely to relocate after about a year, his current bonus is his primary concern. Which alternative would Doria choose? Explain.

MyAccountingLab

Problems

11-29 Special Order. Louisville Corporation produces baseball bats for kids that it sells for $32 each. At capacity, the company can produce 50,000 bats a year. The costs of producing and selling 50,000 bats are as follows:

	Cost per Bat	Total Costs
Direct materials	$12	$ 600,000
Direct manufacturing labor	3	150,000
Variable manufacturing overhead	1	50,000
Fixed manufacturing overhead	5	250,000
Variable selling expenses	2	100,000
Fixed selling expenses	4	200,000
Total costs	$27	$1,350,000

Required

1. Suppose Louisville is currently producing and selling 40,000 bats. At this level of production and sales, its fixed costs are the same as given in the preceding table. Ripkin Corporation wants to place a one-time special order for 10,000 bats at $25 each. Louisville will incur no variable selling costs for this special order. Should Louisville accept this one-time special order? Show your calculations.

2. Now suppose Louisville is currently producing and selling 50,000 bats. If Louisville accepts Ripkin's offer it will have to sell 10,000 fewer bats to its regular customers. (a) On financial considerations alone, should Louisville accept this one-time special order? Show your calculations. (b) On financial considerations alone, at what price would Louisville be indifferent between accepting the special order and continuing to sell to its regular customers at $32 per bat. (c) What other factors should Louisville consider in deciding whether to accept the one-time special order?

11-30 International outsourcing. Bernie's Bears, Inc., manufactures plush toys in a facility in Cleveland, Ohio. Recently, the company designed a group of collectible resin figurines to go with the plush toy line. Management is trying to decide whether to manufacture the figurines themselves in existing space in the Cleveland facility or to accept an offer from a manufacturing company in Indonesia. Data concerning the decision follows:

Expected annual sales of figurines (in units)	400,000
Average selling price of a figurine	$5
Price quoted by Indonesian company, in Indonesian Rupiah (IDR), for each figurine	27,300 IDR
Current exchange rate	9,100 IDR = $1
Variable manufacturing costs	$2.85 per unit
Incremental annual fixed manufacturing costs associated with the new product line	$200,000
Variable selling and distribution costs[a]	$0.50 per unit
Annual fixed selling and distribution costs[a]	$285,000

[a] Selling and distribution costs are the same regardless of whether the figurines are manufactured in Cleveland or imported.

Required

1. Should Bernie's Bears manufacture the 400,000 figurines in the Cleveland facility or purchase them from the Indonesian supplier? Explain.
2. Bernie's Bears believes that the US dollar may weaken in the coming months against the Indonesian Rupiah and does not want to face any currency risk. Assume that Bernie's Bears can enter into a forward contract today to purchase 27,300 IDRs for $3.40. Should Bernie's Bears manufacture the 400,000 figurines in the Cleveland facility or purchase them from the Indonesian supplier? Explain.
3. What are some of the qualitative factors that Bernie's Bears should consider when deciding whether to outsource the figurine manufacturing to Indonesia?

11-31 Relevant costs, opportunity costs. Larry Miller, the general manager of Basil Software, must decide when to release the new version of Basil's spreadsheet package, Easyspread 2.0. Development of Easyspread 2.0 is complete; however, the diskettes, compact discs, and user manuals have not yet been produced. The product can be shipped starting July 1, 2011.

The major problem is that Basil has overstocked the previous version of its spreadsheet package, Easyspread 1.0. Miller knows that once Easyspread 2.0 is introduced, Basil will not be able to sell any more units of Easyspread 1.0. Rather than just throwing away the inventory of Easyspread 1.0, Miller is wondering if it might be better to continue to sell Easyspread 1.0 for the next three months and introduce Easyspread 2.0 on October 1, 2011, when the inventory of Easyspread 1.0 will be sold out.

The following information is available:

	Easyspread 1.0	Easyspread 2.0
Selling price	$160	$195
Variable cost per unit of diskettes, compact discs, user manuals	25	30
Development cost per unit	70	100
Marketing and administrative cost per unit	35	40
Total cost per unit	130	170
Operating income per unit	$ 30	$ 25

Development cost per unit for each product equals the total costs of developing the software product divided by the anticipated unit sales over the life of the product. Marketing and administrative costs are fixed costs in 2011, incurred to support all marketing and administrative activities of Basil Software. Marketing and administrative costs are allocated to products on the basis of the budgeted revenues of each product. The preceding unit costs assume Easyspread 2.0 will be introduced on October 1, 2011.

Required

1. On the basis of financial considerations alone, should Miller introduce Easyspread 2.0 on July 1, 2011, or wait until October 1, 2011? Show your calculations, clearly identifying relevant and irrelevant revenues and costs.
2. What other factors might Larry Miller consider in making a decision?

11-32 Opportunity costs. (H. Schaefer) The Wild Boar Corporation is working at full production capacity producing 13,000 units of a unique product, Rosebo. Manufacturing cost per unit for Rosebo is as follows:

Direct materials	$ 5
Direct manufacturing labor	1
Manufacturing overhead	7
Total manufacturing cost	$13

Manufacturing overhead cost per unit is based on variable cost per unit of $4 and fixed costs of $39,000 (at full capacity of 13,000 units). Marketing cost per unit, all variable, is $2, and the selling price is $26.

A customer, the Miami Company, has asked Wild Boar to produce 3,500 units of Orangebo, a modification of Rosebo. Orangebo would require the same manufacturing processes as Rosebo. Miami has offered to pay Wild Boar $20 for a unit of Orangebo and share half of the marketing cost per unit.

Required

1. What is the opportunity cost to Wild Boar of producing the 3,500 units of Orangebo? (Assume that no overtime is worked.)
2. The Buckeye Corporation has offered to produce 3,500 units of Rosebo for Wolverine so that Wild Boar may accept the Miami offer. That is, if Wild Boar accepts the Buckeye offer, Wild Boar would manufacture 9,500 units of Rosebo and 3,500 units of Orangebo and purchase 3,500 units of Rosebo from Buckeye. Buckeye would charge Wild Boar $18 per unit to manufacture Rosebo. On the basis of financial considerations alone, should Wild Boar accept the Buckeye offer? Show your calculations.
3. Suppose Wild Boar had been working at less than full capacity, producing 9,500 units of Rosebo at the time the Miami offer was made. Calculate the minimum price Wild Boar should accept for Orangebo under these conditions. (Ignore the previous $20 selling price.)

11-33 Product mix, special order. (N. Melumad, adapted) Pendleton Engineering makes cutting tools for metalworking operations. It makes two types of tools: R3, a regular cutting tool, and HP6, a high-precision cutting tool. R3 is manufactured on a regular machine, but HP6 must be manufactured on both the regular machine and a high-precision machine. The following information is available.

	R3	HP6
Selling price	$ 100	$ 150
Variable manufacturing cost per unit	$ 60	$ 100
Variable marketing cost per unit	$ 15	$ 35
Budgeted total fixed overhead costs	$350,000	$550,000
Hours required to produce one unit on the regular machine	1.0	0.5

Additional information includes the following:

a. Pendleton faces a capacity constraint on the regular machine of 50,000 hours per year.
b. The capacity of the high-precision machine is not a constraint.
c. Of the $550,000 budgeted fixed overhead costs of HP6, $300,000 are lease payments for the high-precision machine. This cost is charged entirely to HP6 because Pendleton uses the machine exclusively to produce HP6. The lease agreement for the high-precision machine can be canceled at any time without penalties.
d. All other overhead costs are fixed and cannot be changed.

Required

1. What product mix—that is, how many units of R3 and HP6—will maximize Pendleton's operating income? Show your calculations.
2. Suppose Pendleton can increase the annual capacity of its regular machines by 15,000 machine-hours at a cost of $150,000. Should Pendleton increase the capacity of the regular machines by 15,000 machine-hours? By how much will Pendleton's operating income increase? Show your calculations.
3. Suppose that the capacity of the regular machines has been increased to 65,000 hours. Pendleton has been approached by Carter Corporation to supply 20,000 units of another cutting tool, S3, for $120 per unit. Pendleton must either accept the order for all 20,000 units or reject it totally. S3 is exactly like R3 except that its variable manufacturing cost is $70 per unit. (It takes one hour to produce one unit of S3 on the regular machine, and variable marketing cost equals $15 per unit.) What product mix should Pendleton choose to maximize operating income? Show your calculations.

11-34 Dropping a product line, selling more units. The Northern Division of Grossman Corporation makes and sells tables and beds. The following estimated revenue and cost information from the division's activity-based costing system is available for 2011.

	4,000 Tables	5,000 Beds	Total
Revenues ($125 × 4,000; $200 × 5,000)	$500,000	$1,000,000	$1,500,000
Variable direct materials and direct manufacturing labor costs			
($75 × 4,000; $105 × 5,000)	300,000	525,000	825,000
Depreciation on equipment used exclusively by each product line	42,000	58,000	100,000
Marketing and distribution costs			
$40,000 (fixed) + ($750 per shipment × 40 shipments)	70,000		
$60,000 (fixed) + ($750 per shipment × 100 shipments)		135,000 }	205,000
Fixed general-administration costs of the division allocated to			
product lines on the basis of revenue	110,000	220,000	330,000
Corporate-office costs allocated to product lines on the basis			
of revenues	50,000	100,000	150,000
Total costs	572,000	1,038,000	1,610,000
Operating income (loss)	$(72,000)	$ (38,000)	$ (110,000)

Additional information includes the following:

a. On January 1, 2011, the equipment has a book value of $100,000, a one-year useful life, and zero disposal value. Any equipment not used will remain idle.

b. Fixed marketing and distribution costs of a product line can be avoided if the line is discontinued.

c. Fixed general-administration costs of the division and corporate-office costs will not change if sales of individual product lines are increased or decreased or if product lines are added or dropped.

1. On the basis of financial considerations alone, should the Northern Division discontinue the tables product line for the year, assuming the released facilities remain idle? Show your calculations.

Required

2. What would be the effect on the Northern Division's operating income if it were to sell 4,000 more tables? Assume that to do so the division would have to acquire additional equipment costing $42,000 with a one-year useful life and zero terminal disposal value. Assume further that the fixed marketing and distribution costs would not change but that the number of shipments would double. Show your calculations.

3. Given the Northern Division's expected operating loss of $110,000, should Grossman Corporation shut it down for the year? Assume that shutting down the Northern Division will have no effect on corporate-office costs but will lead to savings of all general-administration costs of the division. Show your calculations.

4. Suppose Grossman Corporation has the opportunity to open another division, the Southern Division, whose revenues and costs are expected to be identical to the Northern Division's revenues and costs (including a cost of $100,000 to acquire equipment with a one-year useful life and zero terminal disposal value). Opening the new division will have no effect on corporate-office costs. Should Grossman open the Southern Division? Show your calculations.

11-35 Make or buy, unknown level of volume. (A. Atkinson) Oxford Engineering manufactures small engines. The engines are sold to manufacturers who install them in such products as lawn mowers. The company currently manufactures all the parts used in these engines but is considering a proposal from an external supplier who wishes to supply the starter assemblies used in these engines.

The starter assemblies are currently manufactured in Division 3 of Oxford Engineering. The costs relating to the starter assemblies for the past 12 months were as follows:

Direct materials	$200,000
Direct manufacturing labor	150,000
Manufacturing overhead	400,000
Total	$750,000

Over the past year, Division 3 manufactured 150,000 starter assemblies. The average cost for each starter assembly is $5 ($750,000 ÷ 150,000).

Further analysis of manufacturing overhead revealed the following information. Of the total manufacturing overhead, only 25% is considered variable. Of the fixed portion, $150,000 is an allocation of general overhead that will remain unchanged for the company as a whole if production of the starter assemblies is discontinued. A further $100,000 of the fixed overhead is avoidable if production of the starter assemblies is discontinued. The balance of the current fixed overhead, $50,000, is the division manager's salary. If production of the starter assemblies is discontinued, the manager of Division 3 will be transferred to Division 2 at the same salary. This move will allow the company to save the $40,000 salary that would otherwise be paid to attract an outsider to this position.

Required

1. Tidnish Electronics, a reliable supplier, has offered to supply starter-assembly units at $4 per unit. Because this price is less than the current average cost of $5 per unit, the vice president of manufacturing is eager to accept this offer. On the basis of financial considerations alone, should the outside offer be accepted? Show your calculations. (*Hint:* Production output in the coming year may be different from production output in the past year.)
2. How, if at all, would your response to requirement 1 change if the company could use the vacated plant space for storage and, in so doing, avoid $50,000 of outside storage charges currently incurred? Why is this information relevant or irrelevant?

11-36 Make versus buy, activity-based costing, opportunity costs. The Weaver Company produces gas grills. This year's expected production is 20,000 units. Currently, Weaver makes the side burners for its grills. Each grill includes two side burners. Weaver's management accountant reports the following costs for making the 40,000 burners:

	Cost per Unit	Costs for 40,000 Units
Direct materials	$5.00	$200,000
Direct manufacturing labor	2.50	100,000
Variable manufacturing overhead	1.25	50,000
Inspection, setup, materials handling		4,000
Machine rent		8,000
Allocated fixed costs of plant administration, taxes, and insurance		50,000
Total costs		$412,000

Weaver has received an offer from an outside vendor to supply any number of burners Weaver requires at $9.25 per burner. The following additional information is available:

a. Inspection, setup, and materials-handling costs vary with the number of batches in which the burners are produced. Weaver produces burners in batch sizes of 1,000 units. Weaver will produce the 40,000 units in 40 batches.
b. Weaver rents the machine used to make the burners. If Weaver buys all of its burners from the outside vendor, it does not need to pay rent on this machine.

Required

1. Assume that if Weaver purchases the burners from the outside vendor, the facility where the burners are currently made will remain idle. On the basis of financial considerations alone, should Weaver accept the outside vendor's offer at the anticipated volume of 40,000 burners? Show your calculations.
2. For this question, assume that if the burners are purchased outside, the facilities where the burners are currently made will be used to upgrade the grills by adding a rotisserie attachment. (Note: Each grill contains two burners and one rotisserie attachment.) As a consequence, the selling price of grills will be raised by $30. The variable cost per unit of the upgrade would be $24, and additional tooling costs of $100,000 per year would be incurred. On the basis of financial considerations alone, should Weaver make or buy the burners, assuming that 20,000 grills are produced (and sold)? Show your calculations.
3. The sales manager at Weaver is concerned that the estimate of 20,000 grills may be high and believes that only 16,000 grills will be sold. Production will be cut back, freeing up work space. This space can be used to add the rotisserie attachments whether Weaver buys the burners or makes them in-house. At this lower output, Weaver will produce the burners in 32 batches of 1,000 units each. On the basis of financial considerations alone, should Weaver purchase the burners from the outside vendor? Show your calculations.

11-37 Multiple choice, comprehensive problem on relevant costs. The following are the Class Company's unit costs of manufacturing and marketing a high-style pen at an output level of 20,000 units per month:

Manufacturing cost	
Direct materials	$1.00
Direct manufacturing labor	1.20
Variable manufacturing overhead cost	0.80
Fixed manufacturing overhead cost	0.50
Marketing cost	
Variable	1.50
Fixed	0.90

Required

The following situations refer only to the preceding data; there is *no connection* between the situations. Unless stated otherwise, assume a regular selling price of $6 per unit. Choose the best answer to each question. Show your calculations.

1. For an inventory of 10,000 units of the high-style pen presented in the balance sheet, the appropriate unit cost to use is (a) $3.00, (b) $3.50, (c) $5.00, (d) $2.20, or (e) $5.90.

2. The pen is usually produced and sold at the rate of 240,000 units per year (an average of 20,000 per month). The selling price is $6 per unit, which yields total annual revenues of $1,440,000. Total costs are $1,416,000, and operating income is $24,000, or $0.10 per unit. Market research estimates that unit sales could be increased by 10% if prices were cut to $5.80. Assuming the implied cost-behavior patterns continue, this action, if taken, would

a. decrease operating income by $7,200.

b. decrease operating income by $0.20 per unit ($48,000) but increase operating income by 10% of revenues ($144,000), for a net increase of $96,000.

c. decrease fixed cost per unit by 10%, or $0.14, per unit, and thus decrease operating income by $0.06 ($0.20 – $0.14) per unit.

d. increase unit sales to 264,000 units, which at the $5.80 price would give total revenues of $1,531,200 and lead to costs of $5.90 per unit for 264,000 units, which would equal $1,557,600, and result in an operating loss of $26,400.

e. None of these

3. A contract with the government for 5,000 units of the pens calls for the reimbursement of all manufacturing costs plus a fixed fee of $1,000. No variable marketing costs are incurred on the government contract. You are asked to compare the following two alternatives:

Sales Each Month to	Alternative A	Alternative B
Regular customers	15,000 units	15,000 units
Government	0 units	5,000 units

Operating income under alternative B is greater than that under alternative A by (a) $1,000, (b) $2,500, (c) $3,500, (d) $300, or (e) none of these.

4. Assume the same data with respect to the government contract as in requirement 3 except that the two alternatives to be compared are as follows:

Sales Each Month to	Alternative A	Alternative B
Regular customers	20,000 units	15,000 units
Government	0 units	5,000 units

Operating income under alternative B relative to that under alternative A is (a) $4,000 less, (b) $3,000 greater, (c) $6,500 less, (d) $500 greater, or (e) none of these.

5. The company wants to enter a foreign market in which price competition is keen. The company seeks a one-time-only special order for 10,000 units on a minimum-unit-price basis. It expects that shipping costs for this order will amount to only $0.75 per unit, but the fixed costs of obtaining the contract will be $4,000. The company incurs no variable marketing costs other than shipping costs. Domestic business will be unaffected. The selling price to break even is (a) $3.50, (b) $4.15, (c) $4.25, (d) $3.00, or (e) $5.00.

6. The company has an inventory of 1,000 units of pens that must be sold immediately at reduced prices. Otherwise, the inventory will become worthless. The unit cost that is relevant for establishing the minimum selling price is (a) $4.50, (b) $4.00, (c) $3.00, (d) $5.90, or (e) $1.50.

7. A proposal is received from an outside supplier who will make and ship the high-style pens directly to the Class Company's customers as sales orders are forwarded from Class's sales staff. Class's fixed marketing costs will be unaffected, but its variable marketing costs will be slashed by 20%. Class's plant will be idle, but its fixed manufacturing overhead will continue at 50% of present levels. How much per unit would the company be able to pay the supplier without decreasing operating income? (a) $4.75, (b) $3.95, (c) $2.95, (d) $5.35, or (e) none of these.

11-38 Closing down divisions. Belmont Corporation has four operating divisions. The budgeted revenues and expenses for each division for 2011 follows:

	Division			
	A	B	C	D
Sales	$630,000	$ 632,000	$960,000	$1,240,000
Cost of goods sold	550,000	620,000	765,000	925,000
Selling, general, and administrative expenses	120,000	135,000	144,000	210,000
Operating income/loss	$ (40,000)	$(123,000)	$ 51,000	$ 105,000

Further analysis of costs reveals the following percentages of variable costs in each division:

Cost of goods sold	90%	80%	90%	85%
Selling, general, and administrative expenses	50%	50%	60%	60%

Closing down any division would result in savings of 40% of the fixed costs of that division.

Top management is very concerned about the unprofitable divisions (A and B) and is considering closing them for the year.

Required

1. Calculate the increase or decrease in operating income if Belmont closes division A.
2. Calculate the increase or decrease in operating income if Belmont closes division B.
3. What other factors should the top management of Belmont consider before making a decision?

11-39 Product mix, constrained resource. Westford Company produces three products, A110, B382, and C657. Unit data for the three products follows:

	Product		
	A110	**B382**	**C657**
Selling price	$84	$56	70
Variable costs			
Direct materials	24	15	9
Labor and other costs	28	27	40
Quantity of Bistide per unit	8 lb.	5 lb.	3 lb.

All three products use the same direct material, Bistide. The demand for the products far exceeds the direct materials available to produce the products. Bistide costs $3 per pound and a maximum of 5,000 pounds is available each month. Westford must produce a minimum of 200 units of each product.

Required

1. How many units of product A110, B382, and C657 should Westford produce?
2. What is the maximum amount Westford would be willing to pay for another 1,000 pounds of Bistide?

11-40 Optimal product mix. (CMA adapted) Della Simpson, Inc., sells two popular brands of cookies: Della's Delight and Bonny's Bourbon. Della's Delight goes through the Mixing and Baking departments, and Bonny's Bourbon, a filled cookie, goes through the Mixing, Filling, and Baking departments.

Michael Shirra, vice president for sales, believes that at the current price, Della Simpson can sell all of its daily production of Della's Delight and Bonny's Bourbon. Both cookies are made in batches of 3,000. In each department, the time required per batch and the total time available each day are as follows:

	A	B	C	D
1		**Department Minutes**		
2		**Mixing**	**Filling**	**Baking**
3	Della's Delight	30	0	10
4	Bonny's Bourbon	15	15	15
5	Total available per day	660	270	300

Revenue and cost data for each type of cookie are as follows:

	A	B	C
7		Della's	Bonny's
8		Delight	Bourbon
9	Revenue per batch	$ 475	$ 375
10	Variable cost per batch	175	125
11	Contribution margin per batch	$ 300	$ 250
12	Monthly fixed costs		
13	(allocated to each product)	$18,650	$22,350

1. Using *D* to represent the batches of Della's Delight and *B* to represent the batches of Bonny's Bourbon made and sold each day, formulate Shirra's decision as an LP model.
2. Compute the optimal number of batches of each type of cookie that Della Simpson, Inc., should make and sell each day to maximize operating income.

11-41 Dropping a customer, activity-based costing, ethics. Jack Arnoldson is the management accountant for Valley Restaurant Supply (VRS). Bob Gardner, the VRS sales manager, and Jack are meeting to discuss the profitability of one of the customers, Franco's Pizza. Jack hands Bob the following analysis of Franco's activity during the last quarter, taken from Valley's activity-based costing system:

Sales	$15,600
Cost of goods sold (all variable)	9,350
Order processing (25 orders processed at $200 per order)	5,000
Delivery (2,500 miles driven at $0.50 per mile)	1,250
Rush orders (3 rush orders at $110 per rush order)	330
Sales calls (3 sales calls at $100 per call)	300
Profits	($ 630)

Bob looks at the report and remarks, "I'm glad to see all my hard work is paying off with Franco's. Sales have gone up 10% over the previous quarter!"

Jack replies, "Increased sales are great, but I'm worried about Franco's margin, Bob. We were showing a profit with Franco's at the lower sales level, but now we're showing a loss. Gross margin percentage this quarter was 40%, down five percentage points from the prior quarter. I'm afraid that corporate will push hard to drop them as a customer if things don't turn around."

"That's crazy," Bob responds. "A lot of that overhead for things like order processing, deliveries, and sales calls would just be allocated to other customers if we dropped Franco's. This report makes it look like we're losing money on Franco's when we're not. In any case, I am sure you can do something to make its profitability look closer to what we think it is. No one doubts that Franco is a very good customer."

1. Assume that Bob is partly correct in his assessment of the report. Upon further investigation, it is determined that 10% of the order processing costs and 20% of the delivery costs would not be avoidable if VRS were to drop Franco's. Would VRS benefit from dropping Franco's? Show your calculations.
2. Bob's bonus is based on meeting sales targets. Based on the preceding information regarding gross margin percentage, what might Bob have done last quarter to meet his target and receive his bonus? How might VRS revise its bonus system to address this?
3. Should Jack rework the numbers? How should he respond to Bob's comments about making Franco look more profitable?

Collaborative Learning Problem

11-42 Equipment replacement decisions and performance evaluation. Bob Moody manages the Knoxville plant of George Manufacturing. He has been approached by a representative of Darda Engineering regarding the possible replacement of a large piece of manufacturing equipment that George uses in its process with a more efficient model. While the representative made some compelling arguments in favor of replacing the 3-year old equipment, Moody is hesitant. Moody is hoping to be promoted next year to manager of the larger Chicago plant, and he knows that the accrual-basis net operating income of the Knoxville plant will be evaluated closely as part of the promotion decision. The following information is available concerning the equipment replacement decision:

- The historic cost of the old machine is $300,000. It has a current book value of $120,000, two remaining years of useful life, and a market value of $72,000. Annual depreciation expense is $60,000. It is expected to have a salvage value of $0 at the end of its useful life.
- The new equipment will cost $180,000. It will have a two-year useful life and a $0 salvage value. George uses straight-line depreciation on all equipment.
- The new equipment will reduce electricity costs by $35,000 per year, and will reduce direct manufacturing labor costs by $30,000 per year.

For simplicity, ignore income taxes and the time value of money.

1. Assume that Moody's priority is to receive the promotion, and he makes the equipment replacement decision based on next year's accrual-based net operating income. Which alternative would he choose? Show your calculations.
2. What are the relevant factors in the decision? Which alternative is in the best interest of the company over the next two years? Show your calculations.
3. At what cost of the new equipment would Moody be willing to purchase it? Explain.

▶ Learning Objectives

1. Discuss the three major influences on pricing decisions

2. Understand how companies make short-run pricing decisions

3. Understand how companies make long-run pricing decisions

4. Price products using the target-costing approach

5. Apply the concepts of cost incurrence and locked-in costs

6. Price products using the cost-plus approach

7. Use life-cycle budgeting and costing when making pricing decisions

8. Describe two pricing practices in which noncost factors are important when setting prices

9. Explain the effects of antitrust laws on pricing

Most companies make a tremendous effort to analyze their costs and prices.

They know if the price is too high, customers will look elsewhere, too low, and the firm won't be able to cover the cost of making the product. Some companies, however, understand that it is possible to charge a low price to stimulate demand and meet customer needs while relentlessly managing costs to earn a profit. Tata Motors is one such company.

Target Pricing and Tata Motors' $2,500 Car[1]

Despite India's rapid economic growth and growing market for consumer goods, transportation options in the world's most populous country remain limited. Historically, Indians relied on public transportation, bicycles, and motorcycles to get around. Less than 1% owned cars, with most foreign models ill-suited to India's unique traffic conditions. Most cars had unnecessary product features and were priced too high for the vast majority of Indians.

But Ratan Tata, chairman of India's Tata Motors, saw India's dearth of cars as an opportunity. In 2003, after seeing a family riding dangerously on a two-wheel scooter, Mr. Tata set a challenge for his company to build a 'people's car' for the Indian market with three requirements: It should (1) adhere to existing regulatory requirements, (2) achieve certain performance targets for fuel efficiency and acceleration, and (3) cost only $2,500, about the price of the optional DVD player in a new Lexus sport utility vehicle sold in the United States.

The task was daunting: $2,500 was about half the price of the cheapest Indian car. One of Tata's suppliers said, "It's basically throwing out everything the auto industry has thought about cost structures in the past and taking a clean sheet of paper and asking, 'What's possible?'" Mr. Tata and his managers responded with what some analysts have described as "Gandhian engineering"

---

[1] *Sources*: Giridharadas, Anand. 2008. Four wheels for the masses: The $2,500 car. *New York Times*, January 8. http://www.nytimes.com/2008/01/08/business/worldbusiness/08indiacar.html Kripalani, Manjeet. 2008. Inside the Tata Nano Factory. *BusinessWeek*, May 9. http://www.businessweek.com/print/innovate/content/may2008/id2008059_312111.htm

principles: deep frugality with a willingness to challenge conventional wisdom.

At a fundamental level, Tata Motors' engineers created a new category of car by doing more with less. Extracting costs from traditional car development, Tata eschewed traditional long-term supplier relationships, and instead forced suppliers to compete for its business using Internet-based auctions. Engineering innovations led to a hollowed-out steering-wheel shaft, a smaller diameter drive shaft, a trunk with space for a briefcase, one windshield wiper instead of two, and a rear-mounted engine not much more powerful than a high-end riding lawnmower. Moreover, Tata's car has no radio, no power steering, no power windows, and no air conditioning—features standard on most vehicles.

But when Tata Motors introduced the "Nano" in 2008, the company had successfully built a $2,500 entry-level car that is fuel efficient, 50 miles to the gallon; reaches 65 miles per hour; and meets all current Indian emission, pollution, and safety standards. While revolutionizing the Indian automotive marketplace, the "Nano" is also changing staid global automakers. Already, the French-Japanese alliance Renault-Nissan and the Indian-Japanese joint venture Maruti Suzuki are trying to make ultra-cheap cars for India, while Ford recently made India the manufacturing hub for all of its low-cost cars.

Just like Ratan Tata, managers at many innovative companies are taking a fresh look at their strategic pricing decisions. This chapter describes how managers evaluate demand at different prices and manage costs across the value chain and over a product's life cycle to achieve profitability.

Major Influences on Pricing Decisions

Learning Objective 1

Discuss the three major influences on pricing decisions

. . . customers, competitors, and costs

Consider for a moment how managers at Adidas might price their newest line of sneakers, or how decision makers at Microsoft would determine how much to charge for a monthly subscription of MSN Internet service. How companies price a product or a service ultimately depends on the demand and supply for it. Three influences on demand and supply are customers, competitors, and costs.

Customers, Competitors, and Costs

Customers

Customers influence price through their effect on the demand for a product or service, based on factors such as the features of a product and its quality. As the Tata Motors example illustrates, companies must always examine pricing decisions through the eyes of their customers and then manage costs to earn a profit.

Competitors

No business operates in a vacuum. Companies must always be aware of the actions of their competitors. At one extreme, alternative or substitute products of competitors hurt demand and force a company to lower prices. At the other extreme, a company without a competitor is free to set higher prices. When there are competitors, companies try to learn about competitors' technologies, plant capacities, and operating strategies to estimate competitors' costs—valuable information when setting prices.

Because competition spans international borders, fluctuations in exchange rates between different countries' currencies affect costs and pricing decisions. For example, if the yen weakens against the U.S. dollar, Japanese products become cheaper for American consumers and, consequently, more competitive in U.S. markets.

Costs

Costs influence prices because they affect supply. The lower the cost of producing a product, the greater the quantity of product the company is willing to supply. Generally, as companies increase supply, the cost of producing an additional unit initially declines but eventually increases. Companies supply products as long as the revenue from selling additional units exceeds the cost of producing them. Managers who understand the cost of producing products set prices that make the products attractive to customers while maximizing operating income.

Weighing Customers, Competitors, and Costs

Surveys indicate that companies weigh customers, competitors, and costs differently when making pricing decisions. At one extreme, companies operating in a perfectly competitive market sell very similar commodity-type products, such as wheat, rice, steel, and aluminum. These companies have no control over setting prices and must accept the price determined by a market consisting of many participants. Cost information is only helpful in deciding the quantity of output to produce to maximize operating income.

In less-competitive markets, such as those for cameras, televisions, and cellular phones, products are differentiated, and all three factors affect prices: The value customers place on a product and the prices charged for competing products affect demand, and the costs of producing and delivering the product influence supply.

As competition lessens even more, the key factor affecting pricing decisions is the customer's willingness to pay based on the value that customers place on the product or service, not costs or competitors. In the extreme, there are monopolies. A monopolist has no competitors and has much more leeway to set high prices. Nevertheless, there are limits. The higher the price a monopolist sets, the lower the demand for the monopolist's product as customers seek substitute products.

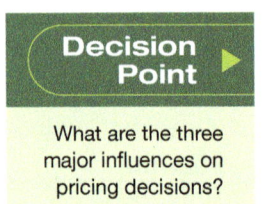

Decision Point ▶

What are the three major influences on pricing decisions?

Costing and Pricing for the Short Run

Short-run pricing decisions typically have a time horizon of less than a year and include decisions such as (a) pricing a *one-time-only special order* with no long-run implications and (b) adjusting product mix and output volume in a competitive market. Long-run pricing decisions have a time horizon of a year or longer and include pricing a product in a market where there is some leeway in setting price.

Consider a short-run pricing decision facing the management team at Astel Computers. Astel manufactures two brands of personal computers (PCs)—Deskpoint, Astel's top-of-the-line product, and Provalue, a less-powerful Pentium chip-based machine. Datatech Corporation has asked Astel to bid on supplying 5,000 Provalue computers over the last three months of 2010. After this three-month period, Datatech is unlikely to place any future sales orders with Astel. Datatech will sell Provalue computers under its own brand name in regions and markets where Astel does not sell Provalue. Whether Astel accepts or rejects this order will not affect Astel's revenues—neither the units sold nor the selling price—from existing sales channels.

Learning Objective **2**

Understand how companies make short-run pricing decisions

. . . consider only incremental costs as relevant and price opportunistically to respond to demand and competition

Relevant Costs for Short-Run Pricing Decisions

Before Astel can bid on Datatech's offer, Astel's managers must estimate how much it will cost to supply the 5,000 computers. Similar to the Surf Gear example in Chapter 11, the relevant costs Astel's managers must focus on include all direct and indirect costs throughout the value chain that will change in total by accepting the one-time-only special order from Datatech. Astel's managers outline the relevant costs as follows:

Direct materials ($460 per computer × 5,000 computers)	$2,300,000
Direct manufacturing labor ($64 per computer × 5,000 computers)	320,000
Fixed costs of additional capacity to manufacture Provalue	250,000
Total costs	$2,870,000*

*No additional costs will be required for R&D, design, marketing, distribution, or customer service.

The relevant cost per computer is $574 ($2,870,000 ÷ 5,000). Therefore, any selling price above $574 will improve Astel's profitability in the short run. What price should Astel's managers bid for the 5,000-computer order?

Strategic and Other Factors in Short-Run Pricing

Based on its market intelligence, Astel believes that competing bids will be between $596 and $610 per computer, so Astel makes a bid of $595 per computer. If it wins this bid, operating income will increase by $105,000 (relevant revenues, $595 × 5,000 = $2,975,000 minus relevant costs, $2,870,000). In light of the extra capacity and strong competition, management's strategy is to bid as high above $574 as possible while remaining lower than competitors' bids.

What if Astel were the only supplier and Datatech could undercut Astel's selling price in Astel's current markets? The relevant cost of the bidding decision would then include the contribution margin lost on sales to existing customers. What if there were many parties eager to bid and win the Datatech contract? In this case, the contribution margin lost on sales to existing customers would be irrelevant to the decision because the existing business would be undercut by Datatech regardless of whether Astel wins the contract.

In contrast to the Astel case, in some short-run situations, a company may experience strong demand for its products or have limited capacity. In these circumstances, a company will strategically increase prices in the short run to as much as the market will bear. We observe high short-run prices in the case of new products or new models of older products, such as microprocessors, computer chips, cellular telephones, and software.

Effect of Time Horizon on Short-Run Pricing Decisions

Two key factors affect short-run pricing.

1. Many costs are irrelevant in short-run pricing decisions. In the Astel example, most of Astel's costs in R&D, design, manufacturing, marketing, distribution, and customer service are irrelevant for the short-run pricing decision, because these costs will not

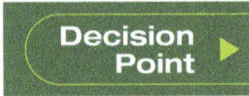

Decision Point ▶

What do companies consider when making short-run pricing decisions?

change whether Astel wins or does not win the Datatech business. These costs will change in the long run and therefore will be relevant.

2. Short-run pricing is opportunistic. Prices are decreased when demand is weak and competition is strong and increased when demand is strong and competition is weak. As we will see, long-run prices need to be set to earn a reasonable return on investment.

Learning Objective 3

Understand how companies make long-run pricing decisions

Consider all future variable and fixed costs as relevant and earn a target return on investment

Costing and Pricing for the Long Run

Long-run pricing is a strategic decision designed to build long-run relationships with customers based on stable and predictable prices. A stable price reduces the need for continuous monitoring of prices, improves planning, and builds long-run buyer–seller relationships. But to charge a stable price and earn the target long-run return, a company must, over the long run, know and manage its costs of supplying products to customers. As we will see, relevant costs for long-run pricing decisions include *all* future fixed and variable costs.

Calculating Product Costs for Long-Run Pricing Decisions

Let's return to the Astel example. However, this time consider the long-run pricing decision for Provalue.

We start by reviewing data for the year just ended, 2011. Astel has no beginning or ending inventory of Provalue and manufactures and sells 150,000 units during the year. Astel uses activity-based costing (ABC) to calculate the manufacturing cost of Provalue. Astel has three direct manufacturing costs, direct materials, direct manufacturing labor, and direct machining costs, and three manufacturing overhead cost pools, ordering and receiving components, testing and inspection of final products, and rework (correcting and fixing errors and defects), in its accounting system. Astel treats machining costs as a direct cost of Provalue because Provalue is manufactured on machines that only make Provalue.[2]

Astel uses a long-run time horizon to price Provalue. Over this horizon, Astel's managers observe the following:

- Direct material costs vary with number of units of Provalue produced.

- Direct manufacturing labor costs vary with number of direct manufacturing labor-hours used.

- Direct machining costs are fixed costs of leasing 300,000 machine-hours of capacity over multiple years. These costs do not vary with the number of machine-hours used each year. Each unit of Provalue requires 2 machine-hours. In 2011, Astel uses the entire machining capacity to manufacture Provalue (2 machine-hours per unit × 150,000 units = 300,000 machine-hours).

- Ordering and receiving, testing and inspection, and rework costs vary with the quantity of their respective cost drivers. For example, ordering and receiving costs vary with the number of orders. In the long run, staff members responsible for placing orders can be reassigned or laid off if fewer orders need to be placed, or increased if more orders need to be processed.

The following Excel spreadsheet summarizes manufacturing cost information to produce 150,000 units of Provalue in 2011.

---

[2] Recall that Astel makes two types of PCs: Deskpoint and Provalue. If Deskpoint and Provalue had shared the same machines, Astel would have allocated machining costs on the basis of the budgeted machine-hours used to manufacture the two products and would have treated these costs as fixed overhead costs.

	Home	Insert	Page Layout	Formulas	Data	Review	View		
	A	B	C	D	E	F	G	H

	A	B	C	D	E	F	G	H
1				Manufacturing Cost Information				
2				to Produce 150,000 Units of Provalue				
3	Cost Category	Cost Driver		Details of Cost Driver Quantities			Total Quantity of Cost Driver	Cost per Unit of Cost Driver
4	(1)	(2)		(3)		(4)	(5) = (3) × (4)	(6)
5	Direct Manufacturing Costs							
6	Direct materials	No. of kits	1	kit per unit	150,000	units	150,000	$460
7	Direct manufacturing labor (DML)	DML hours	3.2	DML hours per unit	150,000	units	480,000	$ 20
8	Direct machining (fixed)	Machine-hours					300,000	$ 38
9	Manufacturing Overhead Costs							
10	Ordering and receiving	No. of orders	50	orders per component	450	components	22,500	$ 80
11	Testing and inspection	Testing-hours	30	testing-hours per unit	150,000	units	4,500,000	$ 2
12	Rework				8%	defect rate		
13		Rework-hours	2.5	rework-hours per defective unit	12,000[a]	defective units	30,000	$ 40
14								
15	[a]8% defect rate × 150,000 units = 12,000 defective units							

Exhibit 12-1 indicates that the total cost of manufacturing Provalue in 2011 is $102 million, and the manufacturing cost per unit is $680. Manufacturing, however, is just one business function in the value chain. To set long-run prices, Astel's managers must calculate the *full cost* of producing and selling Provalue.

For each nonmanufacturing business function, Astel's managers trace direct costs to products and allocate indirect costs using cost pools and cost drivers that measure cause-and-effect relationships (supporting calculations not shown). Exhibit 12-2 summarizes Provalue's 2011 operating income and shows that Astel earned $15 million from Provalue, or $100 per unit sold in 2011.

Alternative Long-Run Pricing Approaches

How should managers at Astel use product cost information to price Provalue in 2012? Two different approaches for pricing decisions are as follows:

1. Market-based
2. Cost-based, which is also called cost-plus

The market-based approach to pricing starts by asking, "Given what our customers want and how our competitors will react to what we do, what price should we charge?" Based on this price, managers control costs to earn a target return on investment. The cost-based approach to pricing starts by asking, "Given what it costs us to make this product, what price should we charge that will recoup our costs and achieve a target return on investment?"

Exhibit 12-1 Manufacturing Costs of Provalue for 2011 Using Activity-Based Costing

	A	B	C
		Total Manufacturing	
1		**Costs for**	**Manufacturing**
2		**150,000 Units**	**Cost per Unit**
3		**(1)**	**(2) = (1) ÷ 150,000**
4			
5	Direct manufacturing costs		
6	Direct material costs		
7	(150,000 kits × $460 per kit)	$ 69,000,000	$460
8	Direct manufacturing labor costs		
9	(480,000 DML-hours × $20 per hour)	9,600,000	64
10	Direct machining costs		
11	(300,000 machine-hours × $38 per machine-hour)	11,400,000	76
12	Direct manufacturing costs	90,000,000	600
13			
14	Manufacturing overhead costs		
15	Ordering and receiving costs		
16	(22,500 orders × $80 per order)	1,800,000	12
17	Testing and inspection costs		
18	(4,500,000 testing-hours × $2 per hour)	9,000,000	60
19	Rework costs		
20	(30,000 rework-hours × $40 per hour)	1,200,000	8
21	Manufacturing overhead cost	12,000,000	80
22	Total manufacturing costs	$102,000,000	$680

Exhibit 12-2 Product Profitability of Provalue for 2011 Using Value-Chain Activity-Based Costing

	A	B	C
1		**Total Amounts**	
2		**for 150,000 Units**	**Per Unit**
3		**(1)**	**(2) = (1) ÷ 150,000**
4	Revenues	$150,000,000	$1,000
5	Costs of goods sold[a] (from Exhibit 12-1)	102,000,000	680
6	Operating costs[b]		
7	R&D costs	5,400,000	36
8	Design cost of product and process	6,000,000	40
9	Marketing costs	15,000,000	100
10	Distribution costs	3,600,000	24
11	Customer-service costs	3,000,000	20
12	Operating costs	33,000,000	220
13	Full cost of the product	135,000,000	900
14	Operating income	$ 15,000,000	$ 100
15			
16	[a]Cost of goods sold = Total manufacturing costs because there is no beginning or ending inventory		
17	of Provalue in 2011		
18	[b]Numbers for operating cost line-items are assumed without supporting calculations		

Companies operating in *competitive* markets (for example, commodities such as steel, oil, and natural gas) use the market-based approach. The items produced or services provided by one company are very similar to items produced or services provided by others. Companies in these markets must accept the prices set by the market.

Companies operating in *less competitive* markets offer products or services that differ from each other (for example, automobiles, computers, management consulting, and legal services), can use either the market-based or cost-based approach as the starting point for pricing decisions. Some companies first look at costs because cost information is more easily available and then consider customers or competitors: the cost-based approach. Others start by considering customers and competitors and then look at costs: the market-based approach. Both approaches consider customers, competitors, and costs. Only their starting points differ. Management must always keep in mind market forces, regardless of which pricing approach it uses. For example, building contractors often bid on a cost-plus basis but then reduce their prices during negotiations to respond to other lower-cost bids.

Companies operating in markets that are *not competitive* favor cost-based approaches. That's because these companies do not need to respond or react to competitors' prices. The margin they add to costs to determine price depends on the value customers place on the product or service.

We consider first the market-based approach.

◄ Decision Point

How do companies make long-run pricing decisions?

Target Costing for Target Pricing

Market-based pricing starts with a target price. A **target price** is the estimated price for a product or service that potential customers are willing to pay. This estimate is based on an understanding of customers' perceived value for a product or service and how competitors will price competing products or services. This understanding of customers and competitors is becoming increasingly important for three reasons:

1. Competition from lower-cost producers is continually restraining prices.
2. Products are on the market for shorter periods of time, leaving less time and opportunity to recover from pricing mistakes, loss of market share, and loss of profitability.
3. Customers are becoming more knowledgeable and incessantly demanding products of higher and higher quality at lower and lower prices.

Learning Objective 4

Price products using the target-costing approach

. . . target costing identifies an estimated price customers are willing to pay and then computes a target cost to earn the desired profit

Understanding Customers' Perceived Value

A company's sales and marketing organization, through close contact and interaction with customers, identifies customer needs and perceptions of product value. Companies such as Apple also conduct market research on features that customers want and the prices they are willing to pay for those features for products such as the iPhone and the Macintosh computer.

Doing Competitor Analysis

To gauge how competitors might react to a prospective price, a company must understand competitors' technologies, products or services, costs, and financial conditions. In general, the more distinctive its product or service, the higher the price a company can charge. Where do companies like Ford Motors or PPG Industries obtain information about their competitors? Usually from former customers, suppliers, and employees of competitors. Another source of information is *reverse engineering*—that is, disassembling and analyzing competitors' products to determine product designs and materials and to become acquainted with the technologies competitors use. At no time should a company resort to illegal or unethical means to obtain information about competitors. For example, a company should never pay off current employees or pose as a supplier or customer in order to obtain competitor information.

Implementing Target Pricing and Target Costing

There are five steps in developing target prices and target costs. We illustrate these steps using our Provalue example.

Step 1: Develop a product that satisfies the needs of potential customers. Customer requirements and competitors' products dictate the product features and design modifications for Provalue for 2012. Astel's market research indicates that customers do not value Provalue's extra features, such as special audio features and designs that accommodate upgrades to make the PC run faster. They want Astel to redesign Provalue into a no-frills but reliable PC and to sell it at a much lower price.

Step 2: Choose a target price. Astel expects its competitors to lower the prices of PCs that compete with Provalue to $850. Astel's management wants to respond aggressively, reducing Provalue's price by 20%, from $1,000 to $800 per unit. At this lower price, Astel's marketing manager forecasts an increase in annual sales from 150,000 to 200,000 units.

Step 3: Derive a target cost per unit by subtracting target operating income per unit from the target price. **Target operating income per unit** is the operating income that a company aims to earn per unit of a product or service sold. **Target cost per unit** is the estimated long-run cost per unit of a product or service that enables the company to achieve its target operating income per unit when selling at the target price.[3] *Target cost per unit* is the target price minus *target operating income per unit* and is often lower than the existing *full cost of the product*. Target cost per unit is really just that—a target—something the company must commit to achieve.

To attain the target return on the capital invested in the business, Astel's management needs to earn 10% target operating income on target revenues.

Total target revenues	= $800 per unit × 200,000 units = $160,000,000
Total target operating income	= 10% × $160,000,000 = $16,000,000
Target operating income per unit	= $16,000,000 ÷ 200,000 units = $80 per unit
Target cost per unit	= Target price – Target operating income per unit
	= $800 per unit – $80 per unit = $720 per unit
Total current full costs of Provalue	= $135,000,000 (from Exhibit 12-2)
Current full cost per unit of Provalue	= $135,000,000 ÷ 150,000 units = $900 per unit

Provalue's $720 target cost per unit is $180 below its existing $900 unit cost. Astel must reduce costs in all parts of the value chain—from R&D to customer service—including achieving lower prices on materials and components, while maintaining quality.

Target costs include *all* future costs, variable costs and costs that are fixed in the short run, because in the long run, a company's prices and revenues must recover all its costs if it is to remain in business. Contrast relevant costs for long-run pricing decisions (all variable and fixed costs) with relevant costs for short-run pricing decisions (costs that change in the short run, mostly but not exclusively variable costs).

Step 4: Perform cost analysis. This step analyzes the specific aspects of a product or service to target for cost reduction. Astel's managers focus on the following elements of Provalue:

- The functions performed by and the current costs of different component parts, such as the motherboard, disc drives, and the graphics and video cards.

- The importance that customers place on different product features. For example, Provalue's customers value reliability more than video quality.

- The relationship and tradeoffs across product features and component parts. For example, choosing a simpler mother board enhances reliability but is unable to support the top-of-the-line video card.

---

[3] For a more-detailed discussion of target costing, see S. Ansari, J. Bell, and The CAM-I Target Cost Core Group, *Target Costing: The Next Frontier in Strategic Cost Management* (Martinsville, IN: Mountain Valley Publishing, 2009). For implementation information, see S. Ansari, L. D. Swenson, and J. Bell, "A Template for Implementing Target Costing," *Cost Management* (September–October 2006): 20–27.

Concepts in Action

Extreme Target Pricing and Cost Management at IKEA

Around the world, IKEA has exploded into a furniture-retailing-industry phenomenon. Known for products named after small Swedish towns, modern design, flat packaging, and do-it-yourself instructions, IKEA has grown from humble beginnings to become the world's largest furniture retailer with 301 stores in 38 countries. How did this happen? Through aggressive target pricing, coupled with relentless cost management. IKEA's prices typically run 30%–50% below its competitors' prices. Moreover, while the prices of other companies' products rise over time, IKEA says it has reduced its retail prices by about 20% over the last four years.

During the conceptualization phase, product developers identify gaps in IKEA's current product portfolio. For example, they might identify the need to create a new flat-screen-television stand. "When we decide about a product, we always start with the consumer need" IKEA Product Developer June Deboehmler said. Second, product developers and their teams survey competitors to determine how much they charge for similar items, if offered, and then select a target price that is 30%–50% less than the competitor's price. With a product and price established, product developers then determine what materials will be used and what manufacturer will do the assembly work—all before the new item is fully designed. For example, a brief describing a new couch's target cost and basic specifications like color and style is submitted for bidding among IKEA's over 1,800 suppliers in more than 50 countries. Suppliers vie to offer the most attractive bid based on price, function, and materials to be used. This value-engineering process promotes volume-based cost efficiencies throughout the design and production process.

Aggressive cost management does not stop there. All IKEA products are designed to be shipped unassembled in flat packages. The company estimates that shipping costs would be at least six times greater if all products were assembled before shipping. To ensure that shipping costs remain low, packaging and shipping technicians work with product developers throughout the product development process. When IKEA recently designed its Lillberg chair, a packaging technician made a small tweak in the angle of the chair's arm. This change allowed more chairs to fit into a single shipping container, which meant a lower cost to the consumer.

What about products that have already been developed? IKEA applies the same cost management techniques to those products, too. For example, one of IKEA's best selling products is the Lack bedside table, which has retailed for the same low price since 1981. How is this possible, you may ask. Since hitting store shelves, more than 100 technical development projects have been performed on the Lack table. Despite the steady increase in the cost of raw materials and wages, IKEA has aggressively sought to reduce product and distribution costs to maintain the Lack table's initial retail price without jeopardizing the company's profit on the product.

As founder Ingvar Kamprad once summarized, "Waste of resources is a mortal sin at IKEA. Expensive solutions are a sign of mediocrity, and an idea without a price tag is never acceptable."

Sources: Baraldi, Enrico and Torkel Strömsten. 2009. Managing product development the IKEA way. Using target costing in inter-organizational networks. Working Paper, December. Margonelli, Lisa. 2002. How IKEA designs its sexy price tags. *Business 2.0,* October. Terdiman, Daniel. 2008. Anatomy of an IKEA product. CNET News.com, April 19.

Step 5: Perform value engineering to achieve target cost. Value engineering is a systematic evaluation of all aspects of the value chain, with the objective of reducing costs and achieving a quality level that satisfies customers. As we describe next, value engineering encompasses improvements in product designs, changes in materials specifications, and modifications in process methods. (See the Concepts in Action feature to learn about IKEA's approach to target pricing and target costing.)

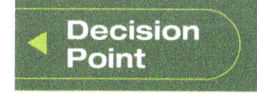

Decision Point

How do companies determine target costs?

Value Engineering, Cost Incurrence, and Locked-In Costs

To implement value engineering, managers distinguish value-added activities and costs from nonvalue-added activities and costs. A **value-added cost** is a cost that, if eliminated, would reduce the actual or perceived value or utility (usefulness) customers experience from using the product or service. Examples are costs of specific product features and attributes desired by customers, such as reliability, adequate memory, preloaded software, clear images, and, in the case of Provalue, prompt customer service.

A **nonvalue-added cost** is a cost that, if eliminated, would not reduce the actual or perceived value or utility (usefulness) customers gain from using the product or service. It is a cost that the customer is unwilling to pay for. Examples of nonvalue-added costs are costs of producing defective products and cost of machine breakdowns. Successful companies keep nonvalue-added costs to a minimum.

Activities and their costs do not always fall neatly into value-added or nonvalue-added categories. Some costs, such as supervision and production control, fall in a gray area because they include mostly value-added but also some nonvalue-added components. Despite these troublesome gray areas, attempts to distinguish value-added from nonvalue-added costs provide a useful overall framework for value engineering.

In the Provalue example, direct materials, direct manufacturing labor, and direct machining costs are value-added costs. Ordering, receiving, testing, and inspection costs fall in the gray area. Rework costs are nonvalue-added costs.

Through value engineering, Astel's managers plan to reduce, and possibly eliminate, nonvalue-added costs and increase the efficiency of value-added activities. They start by distinguishing cost incurrence from locked-in costs. **Cost incurrence** describes when a resource is consumed (or benefit forgone) to meet a specific objective. Costing systems measure cost incurrence. Astel, for example, recognizes direct material costs of Provalue as each unit of Provalue is assembled and sold. But Provalue's direct material cost per unit is *locked in*, or *designed in*, much earlier, when product designers choose Provalue's components. **Locked-in costs**, or **designed-in costs**, are costs that have not yet been incurred but, based on decisions that have already been made, will be incurred in the future.

To manage costs well, a company must identify how design choices lock in costs *before* the costs are incurred. For example, scrap and rework costs incurred during manufacturing are often locked in much earlier by faulty design. Similarly, in the software industry, costly and difficult-to-fix errors that appear during coding and testing are frequently locked in by bad software design and analysis.

Exhibit 12-3 illustrates the locked-in cost curve and the cost-incurrence curve for Provalue. The bottom curve uses information from Exhibit 12-2 to plot the cumulative cost per unit incurred across different business functions of the value chain. The top curve plots how cumulative costs are locked in. (The specific numbers underlying this curve are not presented.) Total cumulative cost per unit for both curves is $900. *Observe, however, the wide divergence between when costs are locked in and when they are incurred*. For example, product design decisions lock in more than 86% ($780 ÷ $900) of the unit cost of Provalue (for example, direct materials, ordering, testing, rework, distribution, and customer service), when only about 8% ($76 ÷ $900) of the unit cost is actually incurred!

Value-Chain Analysis and Cross-Functional Teams

A cross-functional value-engineering team consisting of marketing managers, product designers, manufacturing engineers, purchasing managers, suppliers, dealers, and management accountants redesign Provalue to reduce costs while retaining features that customers value. Some of the team's ideas are as follows:

■ Use a simpler, more-reliable motherboard without complex features to reduce manufacturing and repair costs.

■ Snap-fit rather than solder parts together to decrease direct manufacturing labor-hours and related costs.

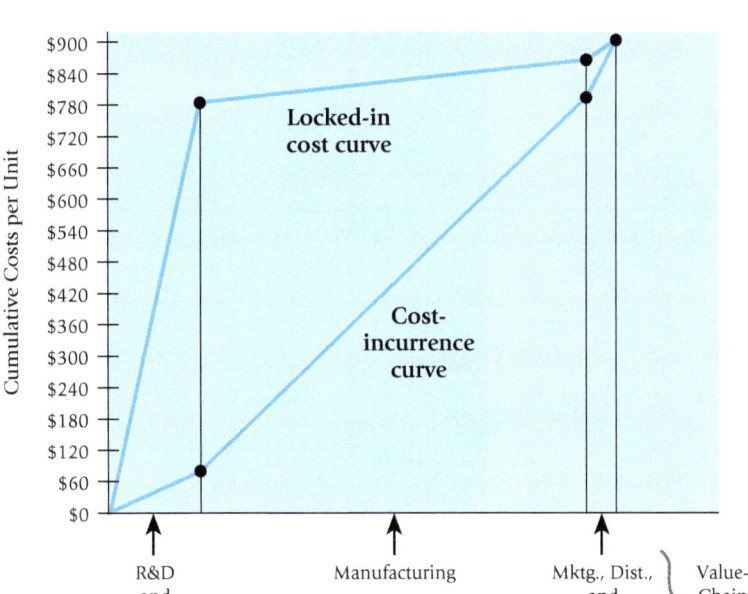

Exhibit 12-3

Pattern of Cost
Incurrence and
Locked-In Costs for
Provalue

■ Use fewer components to decrease ordering, receiving, testing, and inspection costs.

■ Make Provalue lighter and smaller to reduce distribution and packaging costs.

Management accountants use their understanding of the value chain to estimate cost savings.

Not all costs are locked in at the design stage. Managers always have opportunities to reduce costs by improving operating efficiency and productivity. *Kaizen*, or *continuous improvement*, seeks to reduce the time it takes to do a task and to eliminate waste during production and delivery of products.

In summary, the key steps in value-engineering are as follows:

1. Understanding customer requirements, value-added and nonvalue-added costs

2. Anticipating how costs are locked in before they are incurred

3. Using cross-functional teams to redesign products and processes to reduce costs while meeting customer needs

Achieving the Target Cost per Unit for Provalue

Exhibit 12-4 uses an activity-based approach to compare cost-driver quantities and rates for the 150,000 units of Provalue manufactured and sold in 2011 and the 200,000 units of Provalue II budgeted for 2012. Value engineering decreases both value-added costs (by designing Provalue II to reduce direct materials and component costs, direct manufacturing labor-hours, and testing-hours) and nonvalue-added costs (by simplifying Provalue II's design to reduce rework). Value engineering also reduces the machine-hours required to make Provalue II to 1.5 hours per unit. Astel can now use the 300,000 machine-hours of capacity to make 200,000 units of Provalue II (versus 150,000 units for Provalue) reducing machining cost per unit. For simplicity, we assume that value engineering will not reduce the $20 cost per direct manufacturing labor-hour, the $80 cost per order, the $2 cost per testing-hour, or the $40 cost per rework-hour. (The Problem for Self-Study, p. 452, explores how value engineering can also reduce these cost-driver rates.)

Exhibit 12-5 presents the target manufacturing costs of Provalue II, using cost driver and cost-driver rate data from Exhibit 12-4. For comparison, Exhibit 12-5 also shows the actual 2011 manufacturing cost per unit of Provalue from Exhibit 12-1. Astel's managers expect the new design to reduce total manufacturing cost per unit by $140 (from $680 to $540) and cost per unit in other business functions from $220 (Exhibit 12-2) to $180 (calculations not shown) at the budgeted sales quantity of 200,000 units. The budgeted full unit cost of Provalue II is $720 ($540 + $180), the target cost per unit. At the end of 2012,

Exhibit 12-4   Cost-Driver Quantities and Rates for Provalue in 2011 and Provalue II for 2012 Using Activity-Based Costing

						Manufacturing Cost Information for 150,000 Units of Provalue in 2011			Manufacturing Cost Information for 200,000 Units of Provalue II for 2012				
	A	B	C	D	E	F	G	H	I / J	K / L	M	N	
	Cost Category	Cost Driver	Details of Actual Cost Driver Quantities				Actual Total Quantity of Cost Driver	Actual Cost per Unit of Cost Driver (p.437)	Details of Budgeted Cost Driver Quantities		Budgeted Total Quantity of Cost Driver	Budgeted Cost per Unit of Cost Driver (Given)
	(1)	(2)	(3)		(4)		(5)=(3)×(4)	(6)	(7)	(8)	(9)=(7)×(8)	(10)
Direct Manufacturing Costs												
	Direct materials	No. of kits	1	kit per unit	150,000	units	150,000	$460	1 kit per unit	200,000 units	200,000	$385
	Direct manuf. labor (DML)	DML hours	3.2	DML hours per unit	150,000	units	480,000	$ 20	2.65 DML hours per unit	200,000 units	530,000	$ 20
	Direct machining (fixed)	Machine-hours					300,000	$ 38			300,000	$ 38
Manufacturing Overhead Costs												
	Ordering and receiving	No. of orders	50	orders per component	450	compo-nents	22,500	$ 80	50 orders per compo-nent	425 compo-nents	21,250	$ 80
	Testing and inspection	Testing-hours	30	testing-hours per unit	150,000	units	4,500,000	$ 2	15 testing hours per unit	200,000 units	3,000,000	$ 2
	Rework				8%	defect rate				6.5% defect rate		
		Rework-hours	2.5	rework-hours per defective unit	12,000[a]	defective units	30,000	$ 40	2.5 rework-hours per defective unit	13,000[b] defective units	32,500	$ 40

[a] 8% defect rate × 150,000 units = 12,000 defective units

[b] 6.5% defect rate × 200,000 units = 13,000 defective units

Astel's managers will compare actual costs and target costs to gain insight about improvements that can be made in subsequent target-costing efforts.

Unless managed properly, value engineering and target costing can have undesirable effects:

- Employees may feel frustrated if they fail to attain targets.

- The cross-functional team may add too many features just to accommodate the different wishes of team members.

- A product may be in development for a long time as alternative designs are evaluated repeatedly.

- Organizational conflicts may develop as the burden of cutting costs falls unequally on different business functions in the company's value chain, for example, more on manufacturing than on marketing.

Exhibit 12-5   Target Manufacturing Costs of Provalue II for 2012

	A	B	C	D	E	F
		PROVALUE II				PROVALUE
1		Budgeted		Budgeted		Actual Manufacturing
2		Manufacturing Costs		Manufacturing		Cost per Unit
3		for 200,000 Units		Cost per Unit		(Exhibit 12-1)
4		(1)		(2) = (1) ÷ 200,000		(3)
5						
6	Direct manufacturing costs					
7	Direct material costs					
8	(200,000 kits × $385 per kit)	$ 77,000,000		$385.00		$460.00
9	Direct manufacturing labor costs					
10	(530,000 DML-hours × $20 per hour)	10,600,000		53.00		64.00
11	Direct machining costs					
12	(300,000 machine-hours × $38 per machine-hour)	11,400,000		57.00		76.00
13	Direct manufacturing costs	99,000,000		495.00		600.00
14	Manufacturing overhead costs					
15	Ordering and receiving costs					
16	(21,250 orders × $80 per order)	1,700,000		8.50		12.00
17	Testing and inspection costs					
18	(3,000,000 testing-hours × $2 per hour)	6,000,000		30.00		60.00
19	Rework costs					
20	(32,500 rework-hours × $40 per hour)	1,300,000		6.50		8.00
21	Manufacturing overhead costs	9,000,000		45.00		80.00
22	Total manufaturing costs	$108,000,000		$540.00		$680.00

To avoid these pitfalls, target-costing efforts should always (a) encourage employee participation and celebrate small improvements toward achieving the target, (b) focus on the customer, (c) pay attention to schedules, and (d) set cost-cutting targets for all value-chain functions to encourage a culture of teamwork and cooperation.

> ◄ **Decision Point**
>
> Why is it important to distinguish cost incurrence from locked-in costs?

Cost-Plus Pricing

Instead of using the market-based approach for long-run pricing decisions, managers sometimes use a cost-based approach. The general formula for setting a cost-based price adds a markup component to the cost base to determine a prospective selling price. Because a markup is added, cost-based pricing is often called cost-plus pricing, with the plus referring to the markup component. Managers use the cost-plus pricing formula as a starting point. The markup component is rarely a rigid number. Instead, it is flexible, depending on the behavior of customers and competitors. The markup component is ultimately determined by the market.[4]

> **Learning Objective 6**
>
> Price products using the cost-plus approach
>
> . . . cost-plus pricing is based on some measure of cost plus a markup

Cost-Plus Target Rate of Return on Investment

We illustrate a cost-plus pricing formula for Provalue II assuming Astel uses a 12% markup on the full unit cost of the product when computing the selling price.

Cost base (full unit cost of Provalue II)	$720.00
Markup component of 12% (0.12 × $720)	86.40
Prospective selling price	$806.40

---

[4] Exceptions are pricing of electricity and natural gas in many countries, where prices are set by the government on the basis of costs plus a return on invested capital. Chapter 15 discusses the use of costs to set prices in the defense-contracting industry. In these situations, products are not subject to competitive forces and cost accounting techniques substitute for markets as the basis for setting prices.

How is the markup percentage of 12% determined? One way is to choose a markup to earn a *target rate of return on investment*. The **target rate of return on investment** is the target annual operating income divided by invested capital. Invested capital can be defined in many ways. In this chapter, we define it as total assets—that is, long-term assets plus current assets. Suppose Astel's (pretax) target rate of return on investment is 18% and Provalue II's capital investment is $96 million. The target annual operating income for Provalue II is as follows:

Invested capital	$96,000,000
Target rate of return on investment	18%
Target annual operating income (0.18 × $96,000,000)	$17,280,000
Target operating income per unit of Provalue II ($17,280,000 ÷ 200,000 units)	$ 86.40

This calculation indicates that Astel needs to earn a target operating income of $86.40 on each unit of Provalue II. The markup ($86.40) expressed as a percentage of the full unit cost of the product ($720) equals 12% ($86.40 ÷ $720).

Do not confuse the 18% target rate of return on investment with the 12% markup percentage.

- The 18% target rate of return on investment expresses Astel's expected annual operating income as a percentage of investment.

- The 12% markup expresses operating income per unit as a percentage of the full product cost per unit.

Astel uses the target rate of return on investment to calculate the markup percentage.

Alternative Cost-Plus Methods

Computing the specific amount of capital invested in a product is seldom easy because it requires difficult and arbitrary allocations of investments in equipment and buildings to individual products. The following table uses alternative cost bases (without supporting calculations) and assumed markup percentages to set prospective selling prices for Provalue II without explicitly calculating invested capital to set prices.

Cost Base	Estimated Cost per Unit (1)	Markup Percentage (2)	Markup Component (3) = (1) × (2)	Prospective Selling Price (4) = (1) + (3)
Variable manufacturing cost	$475.00	65%	$308.75	$783.75
Variable cost of the product	547.00	45	246.15	793.15
Manufacturing cost	540.00	50	270.00	810.00
Full cost of the product	720.00	12	86.40	806.40

The different cost bases and markup percentages give four prospective selling prices that are close to each other. In practice, a company chooses a reliable cost base and markup percentage to recover its costs and earn a target return on investment. For example, consulting companies often choose the full cost of a client engagement as their cost base because it is difficult to distinguish variable costs from fixed costs.

The markup percentages in the preceding table vary a great deal, from a high of 65% on variable manufacturing cost to a low of 12% on full cost of the product. Why the wide variation? When determining a prospective selling price, a cost base such as variable manufacturing cost (that includes fewer costs) requires a higher markup percentage because the price needs to be set to earn a profit margin *and* to recover costs that have been excluded from the base.

Surveys indicate that most managers use the full cost of the product for cost-based pricing decisions—that is, they include both fixed and variable costs when calculating the cost per unit. Managers include fixed cost per unit in the cost base for several reasons:

1. **Full recovery of all costs of the product.** In the long run, the price of a product must exceed the full cost of the product if a company is to remain in business. Using just the variable cost as a base may tempt managers to cut prices as long as prices are

above variable cost and generate a positive contribution margin. As the experience in the airline industry has shown, variable cost pricing may cause companies to lose money because revenues are too low to recover the full cost of the product.

2. **Price stability.** Managers believe that using the full cost of the product as the basis for pricing decisions promotes price stability, because it limits the ability and temptations of salespersons to cut prices. Stable prices facilitate more-accurate forecasting and planning.

3. **Simplicity.** A full-cost formula for pricing does not require a detailed analysis of cost-behavior patterns to separate product costs into fixed and variable components. Variable and fixed cost components are difficult to identify for many costs such as testing, inspection, and setups.

Including fixed cost per unit in the cost base for pricing is not without problems. Allocating fixed costs to products can be arbitrary. Also, calculating fixed cost per unit requires a denominator level that is based on an estimate of capacity or expected units of future sales. Errors in these estimates will cause actual full cost per unit of the product to differ from the estimated amount.

Cost-Plus Pricing and Target Pricing

The selling prices computed under cost-plus pricing are *prospective* prices. Suppose Astel's initial product design results in a $750 full cost for Provalue II. Assuming a 12% markup, Astel sets a prospective price of $840 [$750 + (0.12 × $750)]. In the competitive personal computer market, customer and competitor reactions to this price may force Astel to reduce the markup percentage and lower the price to, say, $800. Astel may then want to redesign Provalue II to reduce the full cost to $720 per unit, as in our example, and achieve a markup close to 12% while keeping the price at $800. The eventual design and cost-plus price must trade-off cost, markup, and customer reactions.

The target-pricing approach reduces the need to go back and forth among prospective cost-plus prices, customer reactions, and design modifications. In contrast to cost-plus pricing, target pricing first determines product characteristics and target price on the basis of customer preferences and expected competitor responses, and then computes a target cost.

Suppliers who provide unique products and services, such as accountants and management consultants, usually use cost-plus pricing. Professional service firms set prices based on hourly cost-plus billing rates of partners, managers, and associates. These prices are, however, lowered in competitive situations. Professional service firms also take a multiple-year client perspective when deciding prices. Certified public accountants, for example, sometimes charge a client a low price initially and a higher price later.

Service companies such as home repair services, automobile repair services, and architectural firms use a cost-plus pricing method called the *time-and-materials method*. Individual jobs are priced based on materials and labor time. The price charged for materials equals the cost of materials plus a markup. The price charged for labor represents the cost of labor plus a markup. That is, the price charged for each direct cost item includes its own markup. The markups are chosen to recover overhead costs and to earn a profit.

Life-Cycle Product Budgeting and Costing

Companies sometimes need to consider target prices and target costs over a multiple-year product life cycle. The **product life cycle** spans the time from initial R&D on a product to when customer service and support is no longer offered for that product. For automobile companies such as DaimlerChrysler, Ford, and Nissan, the product life cycle is 12 to 15 years to design, introduce, and sell different car models. For pharmaceutical products, the life cycle at companies such as Pfizer, Merck, and Glaxo Smith Kline may be 15 to 20 years. For banks such as Wachovia and Chase Manhattan Bank, a product such as a newly designed savings account with specific privileges can have a life cycle of 10 to 20 years. Personal computers have a shorter life-cycle of 3 to 5 years, because rapid

Decision Point

How do companies price products using the cost-plus approach?

Learning Objective 7

Use life-cycle budgeting and costing when making pricing decisions

. . . accumulate all costs of a product from initial R&D to final customer service for each year of the product's life

innovations in the computing power and speed of microprocessors that run the computers make older models obsolete.

In **life-cycle budgeting**, managers estimate the revenues and business function costs across the entire value chain from a product's initial R&D to its final customer service and support. **Life-cycle costing** tracks and accumulates business function costs across the entire value chain from a product's initial R&D to its final customer service and support. Life-cycle budgeting and life-cycle costing span several years.

Life-Cycle Budgeting and Pricing Decisions

Budgeted life-cycle costs provide useful information for strategically evaluating pricing decisions. Consider Insight, Inc., a computer software company, which is developing a new accounting package, "General Ledger." Assume the following budgeted amounts for General Ledger over a six-year product life cycle:

Years 1 and 2

	Total Fixed Costs
R&D costs	$240,000
Design costs	160,000

Years 3 to 6

	Total Fixed Costs	Variable Cost per Package
Production costs	$100,000	$25
Marketing costs	70,000	24
Distribution costs	50,000	16
Customer-service costs	80,000	30

Exhibit 12-6 presents the six-year life-cycle budget for General Ledger for three alternative selling-price/sales-quantity combinations.

Several features make life-cycle budgeting particularly important:

1. **The development period for R&D and design is long and costly.** When a high percentage of total life-cycle costs are incurred before any production begins and any revenues are received, as in the General Ledger example, the company needs to evaluate revenues and costs over the life-cycle of the product in order to decide whether to begin the costly R&D and design activities.

2. **Many costs are locked in at R&D and design stages, even if R&D and design costs themselves are small.** In our General Ledger example, a poorly designed accounting software package, which is difficult to install and use, would result in higher marketing, distribution, and customer-service costs in several subsequent years. These costs would be even higher if the product failed to meet promised quality-performance levels. A life-cycle revenue-and-cost budget prevents Insight's managers from overlooking these multiple-year relationships among business-function costs. Life-cycle budgeting highlights costs throughout the product's life cycle and, in doing so, facilitates target pricing, target costing, and value engineering at the design stage before costs are locked in. The amounts presented in Exhibit 12-6 are the outcome of value engineering.

Insight decides to sell the General Ledger package for $480 per package because this price maximizes life-cycle operating income. Insight's managers compare actual costs to life-cycle budgets to obtain feedback and to learn about how to estimate costs better for subsequent products. Exhibit 12-6 assumes that the selling price per package is the same over the entire life cycle. For strategic reasons, however, Insight may decide to skim the market by charging higher prices to eager customers when General Ledger is first introduced and then lowering prices later as the product matures. In these later stages, Insight may even add new features to differentiate the product to maintain prices and sales. The life-cycle budget must then incorporate the revenues and costs of these strategies.

Exhibit 12-6   Budgeting Life-Cycle Revenues and Costs for "General Ledger" Software Package of Insight, Inc.[a]

| | Alternative Selling-Price/ Sales-Quantity Combinations | | |
	A	B	C
Selling price per package	$400	$480	$600
Sales quantity in units	5,000	4,000	2,500
Life-cycle revenues ($400 × 5,000; $480 × 4,000; $600 × 2,500)	$2,000,000	$1,920,000	$1,500,000
Life-cycle costs			
R&D costs	240,000	240,000	240,000
Design costs of product/process	160,000	160,000	160,000
Production costs $100,000 + ($25 × 5,000); $100,000 + ($25 × 4,000); $100,000 + ($25 × 2,500)	225,000	200,000	162,500
Marketing costs $70,000 + ($24 × 5,000); $70,000 + ($24 × 4,000); $70,000 + ($24 × 2,500)	190,000	166,000	130,000
Distribution costs $50,000 + ($16 × 5,000); $50,000 + ($16 × 4,000); $50,000 + ($16 × 2,500)	130,000	114,000	90,000
Customer-service costs $80,000 + ($30 × 5,000); $80,000 + ($30 × 4,000); $80,000 + ($30 × 2,500)	230,000	200,000	155,000
Total life-cycle costs	1,175,000	1,080,000	937,500
Life-cycle operating income	$ 825,000	$ 840,000	$ 562,500

[a]This exhibit does not take into consideration the time value of money when computing life-cycle revenues or life-cycle costs. Chapter 21 outlines how this important factor can be incorporated into such calculations.

Management of environmental costs provides another example of life-cycle costing and value engineering. Environmental laws like the U.S. Clean Air Act and the U.S. Superfund Amendment and Reauthorization Act have introduced tougher environmental standards, imposed stringent cleanup requirements, and introduced severe penalties for polluting the air and contaminating subsurface soil and groundwater. Environmental costs that are incurred over several years of the product's life-cycle are often locked in at the product- and process-design stage. To avoid environmental liabilities, companies in industries such as oil refining, chemical processing, and automobiles practice value engineering; they design products and processes to prevent and reduce pollution over the product's life cycle. For example, laptop computer manufacturers like Hewlett Packard and Apple have introduced costly recycling programs to ensure that chemicals from nickel-cadmium batteries do not leak hazardous chemicals into the soil.

Customer Life-Cycle Costing

A different notion of life-cycle costs is *customer life-cycle costs*. **Customer life-cycle costs** focus on the total costs incurred by a customer to acquire, use, maintain, and dispose of a product or service. Customer life-cycle costs influence the prices a company can charge for its products. For example, Ford can charge a higher price and/or gain market share if its cars require minimal maintenance for 100,000 miles. Similarly, Maytag charges higher prices for appliances that save electricity and have low maintenance costs. Boeing Corporation justifies a higher price for the Boeing 777 because the plane's design allows mechanics easier access to different areas of the plane to perform routine maintenance, reduces the time and cost of maintenance, and significantly decreases the life-cycle cost of owning the plane.

◄ **Decision Point**

Describe life-cycle budgeting and life-cycle costing and when companies should use these techniques.

Additional Considerations for Pricing Decisions

Learning Objective 8

Describe two pricing practices in which noncost factors are important when setting prices

. . . price discrimination—charging different customers different prices for the same product—and peak-load pricing—charging higher prices when demand approaches capacity limits

In some cases, cost is *not* a major factor in setting prices. We explore some of the ways that market structures and laws and regulations influence price setting outside of cost.

Price Discrimination

Consider the prices airlines charge for a round-trip flight from Boston to San Francisco. A coach-class ticket for a flight with seven-day advance purchase is $450 if the passenger stays in San Francisco over a Saturday night. It is $1,000 if the passenger returns without staying over a Saturday night. Can this price difference be explained by the difference in the cost to the airline of these round-trip flights? No; it costs the same amount to transport the passenger from Boston to San Francisco and back, regardless of whether the passenger stays in San Francisco over a Saturday night. This difference in price is due to *price discrimination.*

Price discrimination is the practice of charging different customers different prices for the same product or service. How does price discrimination work in the airline example? The demand for airline tickets comes from two main sources: business travelers and pleasure travelers. Business travelers must travel to conduct business for their organizations, so their demand for air travel is relatively insensitive to price. Airlines can earn higher operating incomes by charging business travelers higher prices. Insensitivity of demand to price changes is called *demand inelasticity*. Also, business travelers generally go to their destinations, complete their work, and return home without staying over a Saturday night. Pleasure travelers, in contrast, usually don't need to return home during the week, and prefer to spend weekends at their destinations. Because they pay for their tickets themselves, pleasure travelers' demand is price-elastic, lowering prices stimulates demand. Airlines can earn higher operating incomes by charging pleasure travelers lower prices.

How can airlines keep fares high for business travelers while, at the same time, keeping fares low for pleasure travelers? Requiring a Saturday night stay discriminates between the two customer segments. The airlines price-discriminate to take advantage of different sensitivities to prices exhibited by business travelers and pleasure travelers. Prices differ even though there is no difference in cost in serving the two customer segments.

What if economic conditions weaken such that business travelers become more sensitive to price? The airlines may then need to lower the prices they charge to business travelers. Following the events of September 11, 2001, airlines started offering discounted fares on certain routes without requiring a Saturday night stay to stimulate business travel. Business travel picked up and airlines started filling more seats than they otherwise would have. Unfortunately, travel did not pick up enough, and the airline industry as a whole suffered severe losses over the next few years.

Peak-Load Pricing

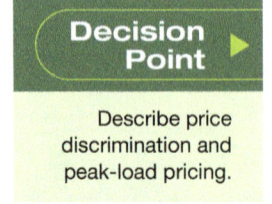

Decision Point ▶

Describe price discrimination and peak-load pricing.

In addition to price discrimination, other noncost factors such as capacity constraints affect pricing decisions. **Peak-load pricing** is the practice of charging a higher price for the same product or service when the demand for the product or service approaches the physical limit of the capacity to produce that product or service. When demand is high and production capacity is limited, customers are willing to pay more to get the product or service. In contrast, slack or excess capacity leads companies to lower prices in order to stimulate demand and utilize capacity. Peak-load pricing occurs in the telephone, telecommunications, hotel, car rental, and electric-utility industries. During the 2008 Summer Olympics in Beijing, for example, hotels charged very high rates and required multiple-night stays. Airlines charged high fares for flights into and out of many cities in the region for roughly a month around the time of the games. Demand far exceeded capacity and the hospitality industry and airlines employed peak-load pricing to increase their profits.

International Considerations

Another example of factors other than costs affecting prices occurs when the same product is sold in different countries. Consider software, books, and medicines produced in one country and sold globally. The prices charged in each country vary much more than the costs of delivering the product to each country. These price differences arise because of differences in the purchasing power of consumers in different countries (a form of price discrimination) and government restrictions that may limit the prices that can be charged.

Antitrust Laws

Legal considerations also affect pricing decisions. Companies are not always free to charge whatever price they like. For example, under the U.S. Robinson-Patman Act, a manufacturer cannot price-discriminate between two customers if the intent is to lessen or prevent competition for customers. Two key features of price-discrimination laws are as follows:

1. Price discrimination is permissible if differences in prices can be justified by differences in costs.
2. Price discrimination is illegal only if the intent is to lessen or prevent competition.

The price discrimination by airline companies described earlier is legal because their practices do not hinder competition.

Learning Objective 9

Explain the effects of antitrust laws on pricing

. . . antitrust laws attempt to counteract pricing below costs to drive out competitors or fixing prices artificially high to harm consumers

Predatory Pricing

To comply with U.S. antitrust laws, such as the Sherman Act, the Clayton Act, the Federal Trade Commission Act, and the Robinson-Patman Act, pricing must not be predatory.[5] A company engages in **predatory pricing** when it deliberately prices below its costs in an effort to drive competitors out of the market and restrict supply, and then raises prices rather than enlarge demand.[6]

The U.S. Supreme Court established the following conditions to prove that predatory pricing has occurred:

■ The predator company charges a price below an appropriate measure of its costs.

■ The predator company has a reasonable prospect of recovering in the future, through larger market share or higher prices, the money it lost by pricing below cost.

The Supreme Court has not specified the "appropriate measure of costs."[7]

Most courts in the United States have defined the "appropriate measure of costs" as the short-run marginal or average variable costs.[8] In *Adjustor's Replace-a-Car* v. *Agency Rent-a-Car,* Adjustor's (the plaintiff) claimed that it was forced to withdraw from the Austin and San Antonio, Texas, markets because Agency had engaged in predatory pricing.[9] To prove predatory pricing, Adjustor pointed to "the net loss from operations" in Agency's income statement, calculated after allocating Agency's headquarters overhead. The judge, however, ruled that Agency had not engaged in predatory

[5] Discussion of the Sherman Act and the Clayton Act is in A. Barkman and J. Jolley, "Cost Defenses for Antitrust Cases," *Management Accounting* 67 (no. 10): 37–40.
[6] For more details, see W. Viscusi, J. Harrington, and J. Vernon, *Economics of Regulation and Antitrust,* 4th ed. (Cambridge, MA: MIT Press, 2006); and J. L. Goldstein, "Single Firm Predatory Pricing in Antitrust Law: The Rose Acre Recoupment Test and the Search for an Appropriate Judicial Standard," *Columbia Law Review* 91 (1991): 1557–1592.
[7] *Brooke Group* v. *Brown & Williamson Tobacco,* 113 S. Ct. (1993); T. J. Trujillo, "Predatory Pricing Standards Under Recent Supreme Court Decisions and Their Failure to Recognize Strategic Behavior as a Barrier to Entry," *Iowa Journal of Corporation Law* (Summer 1994): 809–831.
[8] An exception is *McGahee* v. *Northern Propane Gas Co.* [858 F, 2d 1487 (1988)], in which the Eleventh Circuit Court held that prices below average total cost constitute evidence of predatory intent. For more discussion, see P. Areeda and D. Turner, "Predatory Pricing and Related Practices under Section 2 of Sherman Act," *Harvard Law Review* 88 (1975): 697–733. For an overview of case law, see W. Viscusi, J. Harrington, and J. Vernon, *Economics of Regulation and Antitrust,* 4th ed. (Cambridge, MA: MIT Press, 2006). See also the "Legal Developments" section of the *Journal of Marketing* for summaries of court cases.
[9] *Adjustor's Replace-a-Car, Inc.* v. *Agency Rent-a-Car,* 735 2d 884 (1984).

pricing because the price it charged for a rental car never dropped below its average variable costs.

The Supreme Court decision in *Brooke Group* v. *Brown & Williamson Tobacco* (*BWT*) increased the difficulty of proving predatory pricing. The Court ruled that pricing below average variable costs is not predatory if the company does not have a reasonable chance of later increasing prices or market share to recover its losses.[10] The defendant, BWT, a cigarette manufacturer, sold brand-name cigarettes and had 12% of the cigarette market. The introduction of generic cigarettes threatened BWT's market share. BWT responded by introducing its own version of generics priced below average variable cost, thereby making it difficult for generic manufacturers to continue in business. The Supreme Court ruled that BWT's action was a competitive response and not predatory pricing. That's because, given BWT's small 12% market share and the existing competition within the industry, it would be unable to later charge a monopoly price to recoup its losses.

Dumping

Closely related to predatory pricing is dumping. Under U.S. laws, **dumping** occurs when a non-U.S. company sells a product in the United States at a price below the market value in the country where it is produced, and this lower price materially injures or threatens to materially injure an industry in the United States. If dumping is proven, an antidumping duty can be imposed under U.S. tariff laws equal to the amount by which the foreign price exceeds the U.S. price. Cases related to dumping have occurred in the cement, computer, lumber, paper, semiconductor, steel, sweater, and tire industries. In September 2009, the U.S. Commerce Department said it would place import duties of 25%–35% on imports of automobile and light-truck tires from China.[11] China challenged the decision to the dispute settlement panel of the World Trade Organization (WTO), an international institution created with the goal of promoting and regulating trade practices among countries.

Collusive Pricing

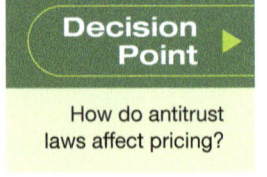

Decision Point ▶

How do antitrust laws affect pricing?

Another violation of antitrust laws is collusive pricing. **Collusive pricing** occurs when companies in an industry conspire in their pricing and production decisions to achieve a price above the competitive price and so restrain trade. In 2008, for example, LG agreed to pay $400 million and Sharp $120 million for colluding to fix prices of LCD picture tubes in the United States.

---

[10]*Brooke Group* v. *Brown & Williamson Tobacco*, 113 S. Ct. (1993).
[11]Edmund Andrews, "U.S. Adds Tariffs on Chinese Tires," *New York Times* (September 11, 2009).

Problem for Self-Study

Reconsider the Astel Computer example (pp. 436–437). Astel's marketing manager realizes that a further reduction in price is necessary to sell 200,000 units of Provalue II. To maintain a target profitability of $16 million, or $80 per unit, Astel will need to reduce costs of Provalue II by $6 million, or $30 per unit. Astel targets a reduction of $4 million, or $20 per unit, in manufacturing costs, and $2 million, or $10 per unit, in marketing, distribution, and customer-service costs. The cross-functional team assigned to this task proposes the following changes to manufacture a different version of Provalue, called Provalue III:

1. Reduce direct materials and ordering costs by purchasing subassembled components rather than individual components.
2. Reengineer ordering and receiving to reduce ordering and receiving costs per order.

3. Reduce testing time and the labor and power required per hour of testing.

4. Develop new rework procedures to reduce rework costs per hour.

No changes are proposed in direct manufacturing labor cost per unit and in total machining costs.

The following table summarizes the cost-driver quantities and the cost per unit of each cost driver for Provalue III compared with Provalue II.

| | Home | Insert | Page Layout | Formulas | Data | Review | View | | | | | | |

	A	B	C	D	E	F	G	H	I	J	K	L	M	N
1			Manufacturing Cost Information							Manufacturing Cost Information				
2			for 200,000 Units of Provalue II for 2012							for 200,000 Units of Provalue III for 2012				
3	Cost Category	Cost Driver	Details of Budgeted Cost Driver Quantities				Budgeted Total Quantity of Cost Driver	Budgeted Cost per Unit of Cost Driver	Details of Budgeted Cost Driver Quantities				Budgeted Total Quantity of Cost Driver	Budgeted Cost per Unit of Cost Driver
4	(1)	(2)	(3)		(4)		(5)=(3)×(4)	(6)	(7)		(8)		(9)=(7)×(8)	(10)
5	Direct materials	No. of kits	1	kit per unit	200,000	units	200,000	$385	1	kit per unit	200,000	units	200,000	$375
6	Direct manuf. labor (DML)	DML hours	2.65	DML hours per unit	200,000	units	530,000	$ 20	2.65	DML hours per unit	200,000	units	530,000	$ 20
7	Direct machining (fixed)	Machine-hours					300,000	$ 38					300,000	$ 38
8	Ordering and receiving	No. of orders	50	orders per component	425	components	21,250	$ 80	50	orders per component	400	components	20,000	$ 60
9	Test and inspection	Testing-hours	15	testing-hours per unit	200,000	units	3,000,000	$ 2	14	testing-hours per unit	200,000	units	2,800,000	$ 1.70
10	Rework				6.5%	defect rate					6.5%	defect rate		
11		Rework-hours	2.5	rework-hours per defective unit	13,000[a]	defective units	32,500	$ 40	2.5	rework-hours per defective unit	13,000[a]	defective units	32,500	$ 32
12														
13	[a]6.5% defect rate × 200,000 units = 13,000 defective units													

Will the proposed changes achieve Astel's targeted reduction of $4 million, or $20 per unit, in manufacturing costs for Provalue III? Show your computations. **Required**

Solution

Exhibit 12-7 presents the manufacturing costs for Provalue III based on the proposed changes. Manufacturing costs will decline from $108 million, or $540 per unit (Exhibit 12-5), to $104 million, or $520 per unit (Exhibit 12-7), and will achieve the target reduction of $4 million, or $20 per unit.

Exhibit 12-7	Target Manufacturing Costs of Provalue III for 2012 Based on Proposed Changes

	A	B	C	D
		Budgeted		**Budgeted**
		Manufacturing Costs		**Manufacturing**
		for 200,000 Units		**Cost per Unit**
		(1)		**(2) = (1) ÷ 200,000**
5	Direct manufacturing costs			
6	Direct material costs			
7	(200,000 kits × $375 per kit)	$ 75,000,000		$375.00
8	Direct manufacturing labor costs			
9	(530,000 DML-hours × $20 per hour)	10,600,000		53.00
10	Direct machining costs			
11	(300,000 machine-hours × $38 per machine-hour)	11,400,000		57.00
12	Direct manufacturing costs	97,000,000		485.00
13				
14	Manufacturing overhead costs			
15	Ordering and receiving costs			
16	(20,000 orders × $60 per order)	1,200,000		6.00
17	Testing and inspection costs			
18	(2,800,000 testing-hours × $1.70 per hour)	4,760,000		23.80
19	Rework costs			
20	(32,500 rework-hours × $32 per hour)	1,040,000		5.20
21	Manufacturing overhead costs	7,000,000		35.00
22	Total manufacturing costs	$104,000,000		$520.00

Decision Points

The following question-and-answer format summarizes the chapter's learning objectives. Each decision presents a key question related to a learning objective. The guidelines are the answers to that question.

Decision	Guidelines
1. What are the three major influences on pricing decisions?	Customers, competitors, and costs influence prices through their effects on demand and supply; customers and competitors affect demand, and costs affect supply.
2. What do companies consider when making short-run pricing decisions?	When making short-run pricing decisions companies only consider those (relevant) costs that will change in total as a result of the decision. Pricing is done opportunistically based on demand and competition.
3. How do companies make long-run pricing decisions?	Companies consider all future variable and fixed costs as relevant and use a market-based or a cost-based pricing approach to earn a target return on investment.
4. How do companies determine target costs?	One approach to long-run pricing is to use a target price. Target price is the estimated price that potential customers are willing to pay for a product or service. Target operating income per unit is subtracted from the target price to determine target cost per unit. Target cost per unit is the estimated long-run cost of a product or service that when sold enables the company to achieve target operating income per unit. The challenge for the company is to make the cost improvements necessary through value-engineering methods to achieve the target cost.

5. Why is it important to distinguish cost incurrence from locked-in costs?

Cost incurrence describes when a resource is sacrificed. Locked-in costs are costs that have not yet been incurred but, based on decisions that have already been made, will be incurred in the future. To reduce costs, techniques such as value engineering are most effective *before* costs are locked in.

6. How do companies price products using the cost-plus approach?

The cost-plus approach to pricing adds a markup component to a cost base as the starting point for pricing decisions. Many different costs, such as full cost of the product or manufacturing cost, can serve as the cost base in applying the cost-plus formula. Prices are then modified on the basis of customers' reactions and competitors' responses. Therefore, the size of the "plus" is determined by the marketplace.

7. Describe life-cycle budgeting and life-cycle costing and when companies should use these techniques.

Life-cycle budgeting estimates and life-cycle costing tracks and accumulates the costs (and revenues) attributable to a product from its initial R&D to its final customer service and support. These life-cycle techniques are particularly important when (a) a high percentage of total life-cycle costs are incurred before production begins and revenues are earned over several years, and (b) a high fraction of the life-cycle costs are locked in at the R&D and design stages.

8. Describe price discrimination and peak-load pricing.

Price discrimination is charging some customers a higher price for a given product or service than other customers. Peak-load pricing is charging a higher price for the same product or service when demand approaches physical-capacity limits. Under price discrimination and peak-load pricing, prices differ among market segments and across time periods even though the cost of providing the product or service is approximately the same.

9. How do antitrust laws affect pricing?

To comply with antitrust laws, a company must not engage in predatory pricing, dumping, or collusive pricing, which lessens competition; puts another company at an unfair competitive disadvantage; or harms consumers.

Terms to Learn

The chapter and the Glossary at the end of the book contain definitions of the following important terms:

collusive pricing (**p. 452**)
cost incurrence (**p. 442**)
customer life-cycle costs (**p. 449**)
designed-in costs (**p. 442**)
dumping (**p. 452**)
life-cycle budgeting (**p. 448**)
life-cycle costing (**p. 448**)

locked-in costs (**p. 442**)
nonvalue-added cost (**p. 442**)
peak-load pricing (**p. 450**)
predatory pricing (**p. 451**)
price discrimination (**p. 450**)
product life cycle (**p. 447**)
target cost per unit (**p. 440**)

target operating income per unit
   (**p. 440**)
target price (**p. 439**)
target rate of return on investment
   (**p. 446**)
value-added cost (**p. 442**)
value engineering (**p. 441**)

Assignment Material

Questions

MyAccountingLab

12-1 What are the three major influences on pricing decisions?

12-2 "Relevant costs for pricing decisions are full costs of the product." Do you agree? Explain.

12-3 Give two examples of pricing decisions with a short-run focus.

12-4 How is activity-based costing useful for pricing decisions?

12-5 Describe two alternative approaches to long-run pricing decisions.

12-6 What is a target cost per unit?

12-7 Describe value engineering and its role in target costing.

12-8 Give two examples of a value-added cost and two examples of a nonvalue-added cost.

12-9 "It is not important for a company to distinguish between cost incurrence and locked-in costs." Do you agree? Explain.

12-10 What is cost-plus pricing?

12-11 Describe three alternative cost-plus pricing methods.

12-12 Give two examples in which the difference in the costs of two products or services is much smaller than the difference in their prices.

12-13 What is life-cycle budgeting?

12-14 What are three benefits of using a product life-cycle reporting format?

12-15 Define predatory pricing, dumping, and collusive pricing.

Exercises

12-16 **Relevant-cost approach to pricing decisions, special order.** The following financial data apply to the DVD production plant of the Dill Company for October 2011:

	Budgeted Manufacturing Cost per DVD Pack
Direct materials	$1.60
Direct manufacturing labor	0.90
Variable manufacturing overhead	0.70
Fixed manufacturing overhead	1.00
Total manufacturing cost	$4.20

Variable manufacturing overhead varies with the number of DVD packs produced. Fixed manufacturing overhead of $1 per pack is based on budgeted fixed manufacturing overhead of $150,000 per month and budgeted production of 150,000 packs per month. The Dill Company sells each pack for $5.

Marketing costs have two components:

- Variable marketing costs (sales commissions) of 5% of revenues
- Fixed monthly costs of $65,000

During October 2011, Lyn Randell, a Dill Company salesperson, asked the president for permission to sell 1,000 packs at $4.00 per pack to a customer not in Dill's normal marketing channels. The president refused this special order because the selling price was below the total budgeted manufacturing cost.

Required

1. What would have been the effect on monthly operating income of accepting the special order?
2. Comment on the president's "below manufacturing costs" reasoning for rejecting the special order.
3. What other factors should the president consider before accepting or rejecting the special order?

12-17 **Relevant-cost approach to short-run pricing decisions.** The San Carlos Company is an electronics business with eight product lines. Income data for one of the products (XT-107) for June 2011 are as follows:

Revenues, 200,000 units at average price of $100 each		$20,000,000
Variable costs		
Direct materials at $35 per unit	$7,000,000	
Direct manufacturing labor at $10 per unit	2,000,000	
Variable manufacturing overhead at $6 per unit	1,200,000	
Sales commissions at 15% of revenues	3,000,000	
Other variable costs at $5 per unit	1,000,000	
Total variable costs		14,200,000
Contribution margin		5,800,000
Fixed costs		5,000,000
Operating income		$ 800,000

Abrams, Inc., an instruments company, has a problem with its preferred supplier of XT-107. This supplier has had a three-week labor strike. Abrams approaches the San Carlos sales representative, Sarah Holtz, about providing 3,000 units of XT-107 at a price of $75 per unit. Holtz informs the XT-107 product manager, Jim McMahon, that she would accept a flat commission of $8,000 rather than the usual 15% of revenues if this special order were accepted. San Carlos has the capacity to produce 300,000 units of XT-107 each month, but demand has not exceeded 200,000 units in any month in the past year.

Required

1. If the 3,000-unit order from Abrams is accepted, how much will operating income increase or decrease? (Assume the same cost structure as in June 2011.)

2. McMahon ponders whether to accept the 3,000-unit special order. He is afraid of the precedent that might be set by cutting the price. He says, "The price is below our full cost of $96 per unit. I think we should quote a full price, or Abrams will expect favored treatment again and again if we continue to do business with it." Do you agree with McMahon? Explain.

12-18 Short-run pricing, capacity constraints. Colorado Mountains Dairy, maker of specialty cheeses, produces a soft cheese from the milk of Holstein cows raised on a special corn-based diet. One kilogram of soft cheese, which has a contribution margin of $10, requires 4 liters of milk. A well-known gourmet restaurant has asked Colorado Mountains to produce 2,600 kilograms of a hard cheese from the same milk of Holstein cows. Knowing that the dairy has sufficient unused capacity, Elise Princiotti, owner of Colorado Mountains, calculates the costs of making one kilogram of the desired hard cheese:

Milk (8 liters × $2.00 per liter)	$16
Variable direct manufacturing labor	5
Variable manufacturing overhead	4
Fixed manufacturing cost allocated	6
Total manufacturing cost	$31

1. Suppose Colorado Mountains can acquire all the Holstein milk that it needs. What is the minimum price per kilogram it should charge for the hard cheese?   **Required**

2. Now suppose that the Holstein milk is in short supply. Every kilogram of hard cheese produced by Colorado Mountains will reduce the quantity of soft cheese that it can make and sell. What is the minimum price per kilogram it should charge to produce the hard cheese?

12-19 Value-added, nonvalue-added costs. The Marino Repair Shop repairs and services machine tools. A summary of its costs (by activity) for 2011 is as follows:

a.	Materials and labor for servicing machine tools	$800,000
b.	Rework costs	75,000
c.	Expediting costs caused by work delays	60,000
d.	Materials-handling costs	50,000
e.	Materials-procurement and inspection costs	35,000
f.	Preventive maintenance of equipment	15,000
g.	Breakdown maintenance of equipment	55,000

1. Classify each cost as value-added, nonvalue-added, or in the gray area between.   **Required**

2. For any cost classified in the gray area, assume 65% is value-added and 35% is nonvalue-added. How much of the total of all seven costs is value-added and how much is nonvalue-added?

3. Marino is considering the following changes: (a) introducing quality-improvement programs whose net effect will be to reduce rework and expediting costs by 75% and materials and labor costs for servicing machine tools by 5%; (b) working with suppliers to reduce materials-procurement and inspection costs by 20% and materials-handling costs by 25%; and (c) increasing preventive-maintenance costs by 50% to reduce breakdown-maintenance costs by 40%. Calculate the effect of programs (a), (b), and (c) on value-added costs, nonvalue-added costs, and total costs. Comment briefly.

12-20 Target operating income, value-added costs, service company. Calvert Associates prepares architectural drawings to conform to local structural-safety codes. Its income statement for 2012 is as follows:

Revenues	$701,250
Salaries of professional staff (7,500 hours × $52 per hour)	390,000
Travel	15,000
Administrative and support costs	171,600
Total costs	576,600
Operating income	$124,650

Following is the percentage of time spent by professional staff on various activities:

Making calculations and preparing drawings for clients	77%
Checking calculations and drawings	3
Correcting errors found in drawings (not billed to clients)	8
Making changes in response to client requests (billed to clients)	5
Correcting own errors regarding building codes (not billed to clients)	7
Total	100%

Assume administrative and support costs vary with professional-labor costs.

Consider each requirement independently.

1. How much of the total costs in 2012 are value-added, nonvalue-added, or in the gray area between? Explain your answers briefly. What actions can Calvert take to reduce its costs?
2. Suppose Calvert could eliminate all errors so that it did not need to spend any time making corrections and, as a result, could proportionately reduce professional-labor costs. Calculate Calvert's operating income for 2012.
3. Now suppose Calvert could take on as much business as it could complete, but it could not add more professional staff. Assume Calvert could eliminate all errors so that it does not need to spend any time correcting errors. Assume Calvert could use the time saved to increase revenues proportionately. Assume travel costs will remain at $15,000. Calculate Calvert's operating income for 2012.

12-21 Target prices, target costs, activity-based costing. Snappy Tiles is a small distributor of marble tiles. Snappy identifies its three major activities and cost pools as ordering, receiving and storage, and shipping, and it reports the following details for 2011:

Activity	Cost Driver	Quantity of Cost Driver	Cost per Unit of Cost Driver
1. Placing and paying for orders of marble tiles	Number of orders	500	$50 per order
2. Receiving and storage	Loads moved	4,000	$30 per load
3. Shipping of marble tiles to retailers	Number of shipments	1,500	$40 per shipment

For 2011, Snappy buys 250,000 marble tiles at an average cost of $3 per tile and sells them to retailers at an average price of $4 per tile. Assume Snappy has no fixed costs and no inventories.

1. Calculate Snappy's operating income for 2011.
2. For 2012, retailers are demanding a 5% discount off the 2011 price. Snappy's suppliers are only willing to give a 4% discount. Snappy expects to sell the same quantity of marble tiles in 2012 as in 2011. If all other costs and cost-driver information remain the same, calculate Snappy's operating income for 2012.
3. Suppose further that Snappy decides to make changes in its ordering and receiving-and-storing practices. By placing long-run orders with its key suppliers, Snappy expects to reduce the number of orders to 200 and the cost per order to $25 per order. By redesigning the layout of the warehouse and reconfiguring the crates in which the marble tiles are moved, Snappy expects to reduce the number of loads moved to 3,125 and the cost per load moved to $28. Will Snappy achieve its target operating income of $0.30 per tile in 2012? Show your calculations.

12-22 Target costs, effect of product-design changes on product costs. Medical Instruments uses a manufacturing costing system with one direct-cost category (direct materials) and three indirect-cost categories:

a. Setup, production order, and materials-handling costs that vary with the number of batches
b. Manufacturing-operations costs that vary with machine-hours
c. Costs of engineering changes that vary with the number of engineering changes made

In response to competitive pressures at the end of 2010, Medical Instruments used value-engineering techniques to reduce manufacturing costs. Actual information for 2010 and 2011 is as follows:

	2010	2011
Setup, production-order, and materials-handling costs per batch	$ 8,000	$ 7,500
Total manufacturing-operations cost per machine-hour	$ 55	$ 50
Cost per engineering change	$12,000	$10,000

The management of Medical Instruments wants to evaluate whether value engineering has succeeded in reducing the target manufacturing cost per unit of one of its products, HJ6, by 10%.

Actual results for 2010 and 2011 for HJ6 are as follows:

	Actual Results for 2010	Actual Results for 2011
Units of HJ6 produced	3,500	4,000
Direct material cost per unit of HJ6	$ 1,200	$ 1,100
Total number of batches required to produce HJ6	70	80
Total machine-hours required to produce HJ6	21,000	22,000
Number of engineering changes made	14	10

1. Calculate the manufacturing cost per unit of HJ6 in 2010.
2. Calculate the manufacturing cost per unit of HJ6 in 2011.

3. Did Medical Instruments achieve the target manufacturing cost per unit for HJ6 in 2011? Explain.
4. Explain how Medical Instruments reduced the manufacturing cost per unit of HJ6 in 2011.

12-23 Cost-plus target return on investment pricing. John Blodgett is the managing partner of a business that has just finished building a 60-room motel. Blodgett anticipates that he will rent these rooms for 15,000 nights next year (or 15,000 room-nights). All rooms are similar and will rent for the same price. Blodgett estimates the following operating costs for next year:

Variable operating costs	$5 per room-night
Fixed costs	
Salaries and wages	$173,000
Maintenance of building and pool	52,000
Other operating and administration costs	150,000
Total fixed costs	$375,000

The capital invested in the motel is $900,000. The partnership's target return on investment is 25%. Blodgett expects demand for rooms to be uniform throughout the year. He plans to price the rooms at full cost plus a markup on full cost to earn the target return on investment.

Required

1. What price should Blodgett charge for a room-night? What is the markup as a percentage of the full cost of a room-night?
2. Blodgett's market research indicates that if the price of a room-night determined in requirement 1 is reduced by 10%, the expected number of room-nights Blodgett could rent would increase by 10%. Should Blodgett reduce prices by 10%? Show your calculations.

12-24 Cost-plus, target pricing, working backward. Road Warrior manufactures and sells a model of motorcycle, XR500. In 2011, it reported the following:

Units produced and sold	1,500
Investment	$8,400,000
Markup percentage on full cost	9%
Rate of return on investment	18%
Variable cost per unit	$8,450

Required

1. What was Road Warrior's operating income on XR500 in 2011? What was the full cost per unit? What was the selling price? What was the percentage markup on variable cost?
2. Road Warrior is considering increasing the annual spending on advertising for the XR500 by $500,000. The company believes that the investment will translate into a 10% increase in unit sales. Should the investment be made? Show your calculations.
3. Refer back to the original data. In 2012, Road Warrior believes that it will only be able to sell 1,400 units at the price calculated in requirement 1. Management has identified $125,000 in fixed cost that can be eliminated. If Road Warrior wants to maintain a 9% markup on full cost, what is the target variable cost per unit?

12-25 Life cycle product costing. Gadzooks, Inc., develops and manufactures toys that it then sells through infomercials. Currently, the company is designing a toy robot that it intends to begin manufacturing and marketing next year. Because of the rapidly changing nature of the toy industry, Gadzooks management projects that the robot will be produced and sold for only three years. At the end of the product's life cycle, Gadzooks plans to sell the rights to the robot to an overseas company for $250,000. Cost information concerning the robot follows:

		Total Fixed Costs over Four Years	Variable Cost per Unit
Year 1	Design costs	$ 650,000	—
Years 2–4	Production costs	$3,560,000	$20 per unit
	Marketing and distribution costs	$2,225,000	$5 per unit

For simplicity, ignore the time value of money.

Required

1. Suppose the managers at Gadzooks price the robot at $50 per unit. How many units do they need to sell to break even?
2. The managers at Gadzooks are thinking of two alternative pricing strategies.
   a. Sell the robot at $50 each from the outset. At this price they expect to sell 500,000 units over its life-cycle.
   b. Boost the selling price of the robot in year 2 when it first comes out to $70 per unit. At this price they expect to sell 100,000 units in year 2. In years 3 and 4 drop the price to $40 per unit. The managers expect to sell 300,000 units each year in years 3 and 4. Which pricing strategy would you recommend? Explain.

Problems

12-26 Relevant-cost approach to pricing decisions. Burst, Inc., cans peaches for sale to food distributors. All costs are classified as either manufacturing or marketing. Burst prepares monthly budgets. The March 2012 budgeted absorption-costing income statement is as follows:

Revenues (1,000 crates × $117 a crate)	$117,000
Cost of goods sold	65,000
Gross margin	52,000
Marketing costs	30,000
Operating income	$ 22,000

Gross margin markup percentage: $52,000 ÷ $65,000
= 80% of cost of goods sold (full manufacturing cost)

Monthly costs are classified as fixed or variable (with respect to the number of crates produced for manufacturing costs and with respect to the number of crates sold for marketing costs):

	Fixed	Variable
Manufacturing	$30,000	$35,000
Marketing	13,000	17,000

Burst has the capacity to can 2,000 crates per month. The relevant range in which monthly fixed manufacturing costs will be "fixed" is from 500 to 2,000 crates per month.

Required

1. Calculate the markup percentage based on total variable costs.
2. Assume that a new customer approaches Burst to buy 200 crates at $55 per crate for cash. The customer does not require any marketing effort. Additional manufacturing costs of $3,000 (for special packaging) will be required. Burst believes that this is a one-time-only special order because the customer is discontinuing business in six weeks' time. Burst is reluctant to accept this 200-crate special order because the $55-per-crate price is below the $65-per-crate full manufacturing cost. Do you agree with this reasoning? Explain.
3. Assume that the new customer decides to remain in business. How would this longevity affect your willingness to accept the $55-per-crate offer? Explain.

12-27 Considerations other than cost in pricing decisions. Executive Suites operates a 100-suite hotel in a busy business park. During April, a 30-day month, Executive Suites experienced a 90% occupancy rate from Monday evening through Thursday evening (weeknights), with business travelers making up virtually all of its guests. On Friday through Sunday evenings (weekend nights), however, occupancy dwindled to 20%. Guests on these nights were all leisure travelers. (There were 18 weeknights and 12 weekend nights in April.) Executive Suites charges $68 per night for a suite. Fran Jackson has recently been hired to manage the hotel, and is trying to devise a way to increase the hotel's profitability. The following information relates to Executive Suites' costs:

	Fixed Cost	Variable Cost
Depreciation	$20,000 per month	
Administrative costs	$35,000 per month	
Housekeeping and supplies	$12,000 per month	$25 per room night
Breakfast	$ 5,000 per month	$5 per breakfast served

Executive Suites offers free breakfast to guests. In April, there were an average of 1.0 breakfasts served per room night on weeknights and 2.5 breakfasts served per room night on weekend nights.

Required

1. Calculate the average cost per guest night for April. What was Executive Suites' operating income or loss for the month?
2. Fran Jackson estimates that if Executive Suites increases the nightly rates to $80, weeknight occupancy will only decline to 85%. She also estimates that if the hotel reduces the nightly rate on weekend nights to $50, occupancy on those nights will increase to 50%. Would this be a good move for Executive Suites? Show your calculations.
3. Why would the $30 price difference per night be tolerated by the weeknight guests?
4. A discount travel clearing-house has approached Executive Suites with a proposal to offer last-minute deals on empty rooms on both weeknights and weekend nights. Assuming that there will be an average of two breakfasts served per night per room, what is the minimum price that Executive Suites could accept on the last-minute rooms?

12-28 Cost-plus, target pricing, working backward. The new CEO of Radco Manufacturing has asked for a variety of information about the operations of the firm from last year. The CEO is given the following information, but with some data missing:

Total sales revenue	?
Number of units produced and sold	500,000 units
Selling price	?
Operating income	$195,000
Total investment in assets	$2,000,000
Variable cost per unit	$3.75
Fixed costs for the year	$3,000,000

1. Find (a) total sales revenue, (b) selling price, (c) rate of return on investment, and (d) markup percentage on full cost for this product.
2. The new CEO has a plan to reduce fixed costs by $200,000 and variable costs by $0.60 per unit while continuing to produce and sell 500,000 units. Using the same markup percentage as in requirement 1, calculate the new selling price.
3. Assume the CEO institutes the changes in requirement 2 including the new selling price. However, the reduction in variable cost has resulted in lower product quality resulting in 10% fewer units being sold compared to before the change. Calculate operating income (loss).

12-29 Target prices, target costs, value engineering, cost incurrence, locked-in costs, activity-based costing. Cutler Electronics makes an MP3 player, CE100, which has 80 components. Cutler sells 7,000 units each month for $70 each. The costs of manufacturing CE100 are $45 per unit, or $315,000 per month. Monthly manufacturing costs are as follows:

Direct material costs	$182,000
Direct manufacturing labor costs	28,000
Machining costs (fixed)	31,500
Testing costs	35,000
Rework costs	14,000
Ordering costs	3,360
Engineering costs (fixed)	21,140
Total manufacturing costs	$315,000

Cutler's management identifies the activity cost pools, the cost driver for each activity, and the cost per unit of the cost driver for each overhead cost pool as follows:

Manufacturing Activity	Description of Activity	Cost Driver	Cost per Unit of Cost Driver
1. Machining costs	Machining components	Machine-hour capacity	$4.50 per machine-hour
2. Testing costs	Testing components and final product (Each unit of CE100 is tested individually.)	Testing-hours	$2 per testing-hour
3. Rework costs	Correcting and fixing errors and defects	Units of CE100 reworked	$20 per unit
4. Ordering costs	Ordering of components	Number of orders	$21 per order
5. Engineering costs	Designing and managing of products and processes	Engineering-hour capacity	$35 per engineering-hour

Cutler's management views direct material costs and direct manufacturing labor costs as variable with respect to the units of CE100 manufactured. Over a long-run horizon, each of the overhead costs described in the preceding table varies, as described, with the chosen cost drivers.

The following additional information describes the existing design:

a. Testing time per unit is 2.5 hours.
b. 10% of the CE100s manufactured are reworked.
c. Cutler places two orders with each component supplier each month. Each component is supplied by a different supplier.
d. It currently takes one hour to manufacture each unit of CE100.

In response to competitive pressures, Cutler must reduce its price to $62 per unit and its costs by $8 per unit. No additional sales are anticipated at this lower price. However, Cutler stands to lose significant sales if it does not reduce its price. Manufacturing has been asked to reduce its costs by $6 per unit. Improvements in manufacturing efficiency are expected to yield a net savings of $1.50 per MP3 player, but that is not enough. The chief engineer has proposed a new modular design that reduces the number of components to 50 and also simplifies testing. The newly designed MP3 player, called "New CE100" will replace CE100.

The expected effects of the new design are as follows:

a. Direct material cost for the New CE100 is expected to be lower by $2.20 per unit.
b. Direct manufacturing labor cost for the New CE100 is expected to be lower by $0.50 per unit.
c. Machining time required to manufacture the New CE100 is expected to be 20% less, but machine-hour capacity will not be reduced.
d. Time required for testing the New CE100 is expected to be lower by 20%.
e. Rework is expected to decline to 4% of New CE100s manufactured.
f. Engineering-hours capacity will remain the same.

Assume that the cost per unit of each cost driver for CE100 continues to apply to New CE100.

Required

1. Calculate Cutler's manufacturing cost per unit of New CE100.
2. Will the new design achieve the per-unit cost-reduction targets that have been set for the manufacturing costs of New CE100? Show your calculations.
3. The problem describes two strategies to reduce costs: (a) improving manufacturing efficiency and (b) modifying product design. Which strategy has more impact on Cutler's costs? Why? Explain briefly.

12-30 Cost-plus, target return on investment pricing. Vend-o-licious makes candy bars for vending machines and sells them to vendors in cases of 30 bars. Although Vend-o-licious makes a variety of candy, the cost differences are insignificant, and the cases all sell for the same price.

Vend-o-licious has a total capital investment of $13,000,000. It expects to produce and sell 500,000 cases of candy next year. Vend-o-licious requires a 10% target return on investment.

Expected costs for next year are as follows:

Variable production costs	$3.50 per case
Variable marketing and distribution costs	$1.50 per case
Fixed production costs	$1,000,000
Fixed marketing and distribution costs	$700,000
Other fixed costs	$500,000

Vend-o-licious prices the cases of candy at full cost plus markup to generate profits equal to the target return on capital.

Required

1. What is the target operating income?
2. What is the selling price Vend-o-licious needs to charge to earn the target operating income? Calculate the markup percentage on full cost.
3. Vend-o-licious's closest competitor has just increased its candy case price to $15, although it sells 36 candy bars per case. Vend-o-licious is considering increasing its selling price to $14 per case. Assuming production and sales decrease by 5%, calculate Vend-o-licious' return on investment. Is increasing the selling price a good idea?

12-31 Cost-plus, time and materials, ethics. R & C Mechanical sells and services plumbing, heating, and air conditioning systems. R & C's cost accounting system tracks two cost categories: direct labor and direct materials. R & C uses a time-and-materials pricing system, with direct labor marked up 100% and direct materials marked up 60% to recover indirect costs of support staff, support materials, and shared equipment and tools, and to earn a profit.

R & C technician Greg Garrison is called to the home of Ashley Briggs on a particularly hot summer day to investigate her broken central air conditioning system. He considers two options: replace the compressor or repair it. The cost information available to Garrison follows:

	Labor	Materials
Repair option	5 hrs.	$100
Replace option	2 hrs.	$200
Labor rate	$30 per hour	

Required

1. If Garrison presents Briggs with the replace or repair options, what price would he quote for each?
2. If the two options were equally effective for the three years that Briggs intends to live in the home, which option would she choose?
3. If Garrison's objective is to maximize profits, which option would he recommend to Briggs? What would be the ethical course of action?

12-32 Cost-plus and market-based pricing. Florida Temps, a large labor contractor, supplies contract labor to building-construction companies. For 2012, Florida Temps has budgeted to supply 84,000 hours of contract labor. Its variable costs are $13 per hour, and its fixed costs are $168,000. Roger Mason, the general manager, has proposed a cost-plus approach for pricing labor at full cost plus 20%.

1. Calculate the price per hour that Florida Temps should charge based on Mason's proposal.   **Required**
2. The marketing manager supplies the following information on demand levels at different prices:

Price per Hour	Demand (Hours)
$16	124,000
17	104,000
18	84,000
19	74,000
20	61,000

Florida Temps can meet any of these demand levels. Fixed costs will remain unchanged for all the demand levels. On the basis of this additional information, calculate the price per hour that Florida Temps should charge to maximize operating income.

3. Comment on your answers to requirements 1 and 2. Why are they the same or different?

12-33 Cost-plus and market-based pricing. (CMA, adapted) Best Test Laboratories evaluates the reaction of materials to extreme increases in temperature. Much of the company's early growth was attributable to government contracts, but recent growth has come from expansion into commercial markets. Two types of testing at Best Test are Heat Testing (HTT) and Arctic-condition Testing (ACT). Currently, all of the budgeted operating costs are collected in a single overhead pool. All of the estimated testing-hours are also collected in a single pool. One rate per test-hour is used for both types of testing. This hourly rate is marked up by 45% to recover administrative costs and taxes, and to earn a profit.

Rick Shaw, Best Test's controller, believes that there is enough variation in the test procedures and cost structure to establish separate costing rates and billing rates at a 45% mark up. He also believes that the inflexible rate structure currently being used is inadequate in today's competitive environment. After analyzing the company data, he has divided operating costs into the following three cost pools:

Labor and supervision	$ 491,840
Setup and facility costs	402,620
Utilities	368,000
Total budgeted costs for the period	$1,262,460

Rick Shaw budgets 106,000 total test-hours for the coming period. This is also the cost driver for labor and supervision. The budgeted quantity of cost driver for setup and facility costs is 800 setup hours. The budgeted quantity of cost driver for utilities is 10,000 machine-hours.

Rick has estimated that HTT uses 60% of the testing hours, 25% of the setup hours, and half the machine-hours.

1. Find the single rate for operating costs based on test-hours and the hourly billing rate for HTT and ACT.   **Required**
2. Find the three activity-based rates for operating costs.
3. What will the billing rate for HTT and ACT be based on the activity-based costing structure? State the rates in terms of testing hours. Referring to both requirements 1 and 2, which rates make more sense for Best Test?
4. If Best Test's competition all charge $20 per hour for arctic testing, what can Best Test do to stay competitive?

12-34 Life-cycle costing. New Life Metal Recycling and Salvage has just been given the opportunity to salvage scrap metal and other materials from an old industrial site. The current owners of the site will sign over the site to New Life at no cost. New Life intends to extract scrap metal at the site for 24 months, and then will clean up the site, return the land to useable condition, and sell it to a developer. Projected costs associated with the project follow:

		Fixed	Variable
Months 1–24	Metal extraction and processing	$4,000 per month	$100 per ton
Months 1–27	Rent on temporary buildings	$2,000 per month	—
	Administration	$5,000 per month	—
Months 25–27	Clean-up	$30,000 per month	—
	Land restoration	$475,000 total	—
	Cost of selling land	$150,000 total	—

Ignore time value of money.

1. Assuming that New Life expects to salvage 50,000 tons of metal from the site, what is the total project life cycle cost?
2. Suppose New Life can sell the metal for $150 per ton and wants to earn a profit (before taxes) of $40 per ton. At what price must New Life sell the land at the end of the project to achieve its target profit per ton?
3. Now suppose New Life can only sell the metal for $140 per ton and the land at $100,000 less than what you calculated in requirement 2. If New Life wanted to maintain the same mark-up percentage on total project life-cycle cost as in requirement 2, by how much would it have to reduce its total project life-cycle cost?

12-35 Airline pricing, considerations other than cost in pricing. Air Eagle is about to introduce a daily round-trip flight from New York to Los Angeles and is determining how it should price its round-trip tickets.

The market research group at Air Eagle segments the market into business and pleasure travelers. It provides the following information on the effects of two different prices on the number of seats expected to be sold and the variable cost per ticket, including the commission paid to travel agents:

		Number of Seats Expected to Be Sold	
Price Charged	**Variable Cost per Ticket**	**Business**	**Pleasure**
$ 500	$ 65	200	100
2,100	175	180	20

Pleasure travelers start their travel during one week, spend at least one weekend at their destination, and return the following week or thereafter. Business travelers usually start and complete their travel within the same work week. They do not stay over weekends.

Assume that round-trip fuel costs are fixed costs of $24,000 and that fixed costs allocated to the round-trip flight for airplane-lease costs, ground services, and flight-crew salaries total $188,000.

1. If you could charge different prices to business travelers and pleasure travelers, would you? Show your computations.
2. Explain the key factor (or factors) for your answer in requirement 1.
3. How might Air Eagle implement price discrimination? That is, what plan could the airline formulate so that business travelers and pleasure travelers each pay the price desired by the airline?

12-36 Ethics and pricing. Apex Art has been requested to prepare a bid on 500 pieces of framed artwork for a new hotel. Winning the bid would be a big boost for sales representative Jason Grant, who works entirely on commission. Sonja Gomes, the cost accountant for Apex, prepares the bid based on the following cost information:

Direct costs		
Artwork		$30,000
Framing materials		40,000
Direct manufacturing labor		20,000
Delivery and installation		7,500
Overhead costs		
Production order	2,000	
Setup	4,000	
Materials handling	5,500	
General and administration	12,000	
Total overhead costs		23,500
Full product costs		$121,000

Based on the company policy of pricing at 125% of full cost, Gomes gives Grant a figure of $151,250 to submit for the job. Grant is very concerned. He tells Gomes that at that price, Apex has no chance of winning the job. He confides in her that he spent $500 of company funds to take the hotel's purchasing agent to a basketball playoff game where the purchasing agent disclosed that a bid of $145,000 would win the job. He hadn't planned to tell Gomes because he was confident that the bid she developed would be below that amount. Gomes reasons that the $500 he spent will be wasted if Apex doesn't capitalize on this valuable information. In any case, the company will still make money if it wins the bid at $145,000 because it is higher than the full cost of $121,000.

Required

1. Is the $500 spent on the basketball tickets relevant to the bid decision? Why or why not?
2. Gomes suggests that if Grant is willing to use cheaper materials for the frame, he can achieve a bid of $145,000. The artwork has already been selected and cannot be changed, so the entire amount of reduction in cost will need to come from framing materials. What is the target cost of framing materials that will allow Grant to submit a bid of $145 assuming a target markup of 25% of full cost?
3. Evaluate whether Gomes' suggestion to Grant to use the purchasing agent's tip is unethical. Would it be unethical for Grant to redo the project's design to arrive at a lower bid? What steps should Grant and Gomes take to resolve this situation?

Collaborative Learning Problem

12-37 Value engineering, target pricing, and locked-in costs. Pacific Décor, Inc., designs, manufactures, and sells contemporary wood furniture. Ling Li is a furniture designer for Pacific. Li has spent much of the past month working on the design of a high-end dining room table. The design has been well-received by Jose Alvarez, the product development manager. However, Alvarez wants to make sure that the table can be priced competitively. Amy Hoover, Pacific's cost accountant, presents Alvarez with the following cost data for the expected production of 200 tables:

Design cost	$ 5,000
Direct materials	120,000
Direct manufacturing labor	142,000
Variable manufacturing overhead	64,000
Fixed manufacturing overhead	46,500
Marketing	15,000

Required

1. Alvarez thinks that Pacific can successfully market the table for $2,000. The company's target operating income is 10% of revenue. Calculate the target full cost of producing the 200 tables. Does the cost estimate developed by Hoover meet Pacific's requirements? Is value engineering needed?
2. Alvarez discovers that Li has designed the table two inches wider than the standard size of wood normally used by Pacific. Reducing the table's size by two inches will lower the cost of direct materials by 40%. However, the redesign will require an additional $6,000 of design cost, and the table will be sold for $1,950. Will this design change allow the table to meet its target cost? Are the costs of materials a locked-in cost?
3. Li insists that the two inches are an absolute necessity in terms of the table's design. She believes that spending an additional $7,000 on better marketing will allow Pacific to sell the tables for $2,200. If this is the case, will the table's target cost be achieved without any value engineering?
4. Compare the total operating income on the 200 tables for requirements 2 and 3. What do you recommend Pacific do, based solely on your calculations? Explain briefly.

Strategy, Balanced Scorecard, and Strategic Profitability Analysis

▶ Learning Objectives

1. Recognize which of two generic strategies a company is using

2. Understand what comprises reengineering

3. Understand the four perspectives of the balanced scorecard

4. Analyze changes in operating income to evaluate strategy

5. Identify unused capacity and how to manage it

Olive Garden wants to know.

So do Barnes and Noble, PepsiCo, and L.L.Bean. Even your local car dealer and transit authority are curious. They all want to know how well they are doing and how they score against the measures they strive to meet. The balanced scorecard can help them answer this question by evaluating key performance measures. Many companies have successfully used the balanced scorecard approach. Infosys Technologies, one of India's leading information technology companies, is one of them.

Balanced Scorecard Helps Infosys Transform into a Leading Consultancy[1]

In the early 2000s, Infosys Technologies was a company in transition. The Bangalore-based company was a market leader in information technology outsourcing, but needed to expand to meet increased client demand. Infosys invested in many new areas including business process outsourcing, project management, and management consulting. This put Infosys in direct competition with established consulting firms, such as IBM and Accenture.

Led by CEO Kris Gopalakrishnan, the company developed an integrated management structure that would help align these new, diverse initiatives. Infosys turned to the balanced scorecard to provide a framework the company could use to formulate and monitor its strategy. The balanced scorecard measures corporate performance along four dimensions—financial, customer, internal business process, and learning and growth.

The balanced scorecard immediately played a role in the transformation of Infosys. The executive team used the scorecard to guide discussion during its meetings. The continual process of adaptation, execution, and management that the scorecard fostered helped the team respond to, and even anticipate, its clients' evolving needs. Eventually, use of the scorecard for performance measurement spread to the rest of the organization, with monetary incentives linked to the company's performance along the different dimensions.

Over time, the balanced scorecard became part of the Infosys culture. In recent years, Infosys has begun using the balanced

---

[1] *Source*: Asis Martinez-Jerez, F., Robert S. Kaplan, and Katherine Miller. 2011. Infosys's relationship scorecard: Measuring transformational partnerships. Harvard Business School Case No. 9-109-006. Boston: Harvard Business School Publishing.

scorecard concept to create "relationship scorecards" for many of its largest clients. Using the scorecard framework, Infosys began measuring its performance for key clients not only on project management and client satisfaction, but also on repeat business and anticipating clients' future strategic needs.

The balanced scorecard helped successfully steer the transformation of Infosys from a technology outsourcer to a leading business consultancy. From 1999 to 2007, the company had a compound annual growth rate of 50%, with sales growing from $120 million in 1999 to more than $3 billion in 2007. Infosys was recognized for its achievements by making the *Wired* 40, *BusinessWeek* IT 100, and *BusinessWeek* Most Innovative Companies lists.

This chapter focuses on how management accounting information helps companies such as Infosys, Merck, Verizon, and Volkswagen implement and evaluate their strategies. Strategy drives the operations of a company and guides managers' short-run and long-run decisions. We describe the balanced scorecard approach to implementing strategy and methods to analyze operating income to evaluate the success of a strategy. We also show how management accounting information helps strategic initiatives, such as productivity improvement, reengineering, and downsizing.

What Is Strategy?

Strategy specifies how an organization matches its own capabilities with the opportunities in the marketplace to accomplish its objectives. In other words, strategy describes how an organization can create value for its customers while differentiating itself from its competitors. For example, Wal-Mart, the retail giant, creates value for its customers by locating stores in suburban and rural areas, and by offering low prices, a wide range of product categories, and few choices within each product category. Consistent with its strategy, Wal-Mart has developed the capability to keep costs down by aggressively negotiating low prices with its suppliers in exchange for high volumes and by maintaining a no-frills, cost-conscious environment.

In formulating its strategy, an organization must first thoroughly understand its industry. Industry analysis focuses on five forces: (1) competitors, (2) potential entrants into the market, (3) equivalent products, (4) bargaining power of customers, and (5) bargaining power of input suppliers.[2] The collective effect of these forces shapes an organization's profit potential. In general, profit potential decreases with greater competition, stronger potential entrants, products that are similar, and more-demanding customers and suppliers. We illustrate these five forces for Chipset, Inc., maker of linear integrated circuit

Learning Objective 1

Recognize which of two generic strategies a company is using

. . . product differentiation or cost leadership

[2] M. Porter, *Competitive Strategy* (New York: Free Press, 1980); M. Porter, *Competitive Advantage* (New York: Free Press, 1985); and M. Porter, "What Is Strategy?" *Harvard Business Review* (November–December 1996): 61–78.

devices (LICDs) used in modems and communication networks. Chipset produces a single specialized product, CX1, a standard, high-performance microchip, which can be used in multiple applications. Chipset designed CX1 with extensive input from customers.

1. **Competitors.** The CX1 model faces severe competition with respect to price, timely delivery, and quality. Companies in the industry have high fixed costs, and persistent pressures to reduce selling prices and utilize capacity fully. Price reductions spur growth because it makes LICDs a cost-effective option in new applications such as digital subscriber lines (DSLs).

2. **Potential entrants into the market.** The small profit margins and high capital costs discourage new entrants. Moreover, incumbent companies such as Chipset are further down the learning curve with respect to lowering costs and building close relationships with customers and suppliers.

3. **Equivalent products.** Chipset tailors CX1 to customer needs and lowers prices by continuously improving CX1's design and processes to reduce production costs. This reduces the risk of equivalent products or new technologies replacing CX1.

4. **Bargaining power of customers.** Customers, such as EarthLink and Verizon, negotiate aggressively with Chipset and its competitors to keep prices down because they buy large quantities of product.

5. **Bargaining power of input suppliers.** To produce CX1, Chipset requires high-quality materials (such as silicon wafers, pins for connectivity, and plastic or ceramic packaging) and skilled engineers, technicians, and manufacturing labor. The skill-sets suppliers and employees bring gives them bargaining power to demand higher prices and wages.

In summary, strong competition and the bargaining powers of customers and suppliers put significant pressure on Chipset's selling prices. To respond to these challenges, Chipset must choose one of two basic strategies: *differentiating its product* or *achieving cost leadership*.

Product differentiation is an organization's ability to offer products or services perceived by its customers to be superior and unique relative to the products or services of its competitors. Apple Inc. has successfully differentiated its products in the consumer electronics industry, as have Johnson & Johnson in the pharmaceutical industry and Coca-Cola in the soft drink industry. These companies have achieved differentiation through innovative product R&D, careful development and promotion of their brands, and the rapid push of products to market. Differentiation increases brand loyalty and the willingness of customers to pay higher prices.

Cost leadership is an organization's ability to achieve lower costs relative to competitors through productivity and efficiency improvements, elimination of waste, and tight cost control. Cost leaders in their respective industries include Wal-Mart (consumer retailing), Home Depot and Lowe's (building products), Texas Instruments (consumer electronics), and Emerson Electric (electric motors). These companies provide products and services that are similar to—not differentiated from—their competitors, but at a lower cost to the customer. Lower selling prices, rather than unique products or services, provide a competitive advantage for these cost leaders.

What strategy should Chipset follow? To help it decide, Chipset develops the customer preference map shown in Exhibit 13-1. The y-axis describes various attributes of the product desired by customers. The x-axis describes how well Chipset and Visilog, a competitor of Chipset that follows a product-differentiation strategy, do along the various attributes desired by customers from 1 (poor) to 5 (very good). The map highlights the trade-offs in any strategy. It shows the advantages CX1 enjoys in terms of price, scalability (the CX1 technology allows Chispet's customer to achieve different performance levels by simply altering the number of CX1 units in their product), and customer service. Visilog's chips, however, are faster and more powerful, and are customized for various applications such as different types of modems and communication networks.

CX1 is somewhat differentiated from competing products. Differentiating CX1 further would be costly, but Chipset may be able to charge a higher price. Conversely, reducing the cost of manufacturing CX1 would allow Chipset to lower price, spur growth, and increase market share. The scalability of CX1 makes it an effective solution for meeting

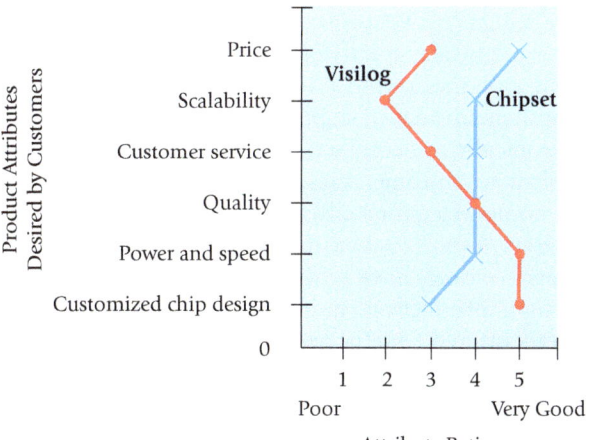

Customer Preference
Map for LICDs

varying customer needs. Also, Chipset's current engineering staff is more skilled at making product and process improvements than at creatively designing new products and technologies. Chipset decides to follow a cost-leadership strategy.

To achieve its cost-leadership strategy, Chipset must improve its own internal capabilities. It must enhance quality and reengineer processes to downsize and eliminate excess capacity. At the same time, Chipset's management team does not want to make cuts in personnel that would hurt company morale and hinder future growth.

Building Internal Capabilities: Quality Improvement and Reengineering at Chipset

To improve product quality—that is, to reduce defect rates and improve yields in its manufacturing process—Chipset must maintain process parameters within tight ranges based on real-time data about manufacturing-process parameters, such as temperature and pressure. Chipset must also train its workers in quality-management techniques to help them identify the root causes of defects and ways to prevent them and empower them to take actions to improve quality.

A second element of Chipset's strategy is reengineering its order-delivery process. Some of Chipset's customers have complained about the lengthening time span between ordering products and receiving them. **Reengineering** is the fundamental rethinking and redesign of business processes to achieve improvements in critical measures of performance, such as cost, quality, service, speed, and customer satisfaction.[3] To illustrate reengineering, consider the order-delivery system at Chipset in 2010. When Chipset received an order from a customer, a copy was sent to manufacturing, where a production scheduler began planning the manufacturing of the ordered products. Frequently, a considerable amount of time elapsed before production began on the ordered product. After manufacturing was complete, CX1 chips moved to the shipping department, which matched the quantities of CX1 to be shipped against customer orders. Often, completed CX1 chips stayed in inventory until a truck became available for shipment. If the quantity to be shipped was less than the number of chips requested by the customer, a special shipment was made for the balance of the chips. Shipping documents moved to the billing department for issuing invoices. Special staff in the accounting department followed up with customers for payments.

The many transfers of CX1 chips and information across departments (sales, manufacturing, shipping, billing, and accounting) to satisfy a customer's order created delays. Furthermore, no single individual was responsible for fulfilling a customer order. To respond to these challenges, Chipset formed a cross-functional team in late 2010 and implemented a reengineered order-delivery process in 2011.

> **Decision Point**
>
> What are two generic strategies a company can use?

> **Learning Objective 2**
>
> Understand what comprises reengineering
>
> . . . redesigning business processes to improve performance by reducing cost and improving quality

[3] See M. Hammer and J. Champy, *Reengineering the Corporation: A Manifesto for Business Revolution* (New York: Harper, 1993); E. Ruhli, C. Treichler, and S. Schmidt, "From Business Reengineering to Management Reengineering—A European Study," *Management International Review* (1995): 361–371; and K. Sandberg, "Reengineering Tries a Comeback—This Time for Growth, Not Just for Cost Savings," *Harvard Management Update* (November 2001).

Under the new system, a customer-relationship manager is responsible for each customer and negotiates long-term contracts specifying quantities and prices. The customer-relationship manager works closely with the customer and with manufacturing to specify delivery schedules for CX1 one month in advance of shipment. The schedule of customer orders and delivery dates is sent electronically to manufacturing. Completed chips are shipped directly from the manufacturing plant to customer sites. Each shipment automatically triggers an electronic invoice and customers electronically transfer funds to Chipset's bank.

Companies, such as AT&T, Banca di America e di Italia, Cigna Insurance, Cisco, PepsiCo, and Siemens Nixdorf, have realized significant benefits by reengineering their processes across design, production, and marketing (just as in the Chipset example). Reengineering has only limited benefits when reengineering efforts focus on only a single activity such as shipping or invoicing rather than the entire order-delivery process. To be successful, reengineering efforts must focus on changing roles and responsibilities, eliminating unnecessary activities and tasks, using information technology, and developing employee skills.

Take another look at Exhibit 13-1 and note the interrelatedness and consistency in Chipset's strategy. To help meet customer preferences for price, quality, and customer service, Chipset decides on a cost-leadership strategy. And to achieve cost leadership, Chipset builds internal capabilities by reengineering its processes. Chipset's next challenge is to effectively implement its strategy

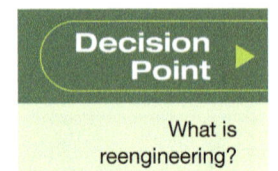

Decision Point

What is reengineering?

Strategy Implementation and the Balanced Scorecard

Many organizations, such as Allstate Insurance, Bank of Montreal, BP, and Dow Chemical, have introduced a *balanced scorecard* approach to track progress and manage the implementation of their strategies.

Learning Objective 3

Understand the four perspectives of the balanced scorecard

. . . financial, customer, internal business process, and learning and growth

The Balanced Scorecard

The **balanced scorecard** translates an organization's mission and strategy into a set of performance measures that provides the framework for implementing its strategy.[4] The balanced scorecard does not focus solely on achieving short-run financial objectives. It also highlights the nonfinancial objectives that an organization must achieve to meet and sustain its financial objectives. The scorecard measures an organization's performance from four perspectives: (1) financial, the profits and value created for shareholders; (2) customer, the success of the company in its target market; (3) internal business processes, the internal operations that create value for customers; and (4) learning and growth, the people and system capabilities that support operations. A company's strategy influences the measures it uses to track performance in each of these perspectives.

Why is this tool called a balanced scorecard? Because it balances the use of financial and nonfinancial performance measures to evaluate short-run and long-run performance in a single report. The balanced scorecard reduces managers' emphasis on short-run financial performance, such as quarterly earnings, because the key strategic nonfinancial and operational indicators, such as product quality and customer satisfaction, measure changes that a company is making for the long run. The financial benefits of these long-run changes may not show up immediately in short-run earnings; however, strong improvement in nonfinancial measures usually indicates the creation of future economic value. For example, an increase in customer satisfaction, as measured by customer surveys and repeat purchases, signals a strong likelihood of higher sales and income in the future. By balancing the mix of financial and nonfinancial measures, the balanced scorecard

---

[4] See R. S. Kaplan and D. P. Norton, *The Balanced Scorecard* (Boston: Harvard Business School Press, 1996); R. S. Kaplan and D. P. Norton, *The Strategy-Focused Organization: How Balanced Scorecard Companies Thrive in the New Business Environment* (Boston: Harvard Business School Press, 2001); R. S. Kaplan and D. P. Norton, *Strategy Maps: Converting Intangible Assets into Tangible Outcomes* (Boston: Harvard Business School Press, 2004); and R. S. Kaplan and D. P. Norton, *Alignment: Using the Balanced Scorecard to Create Corporate Synergies* (Boston: Harvard Business School Press, 2006).

For simplicity, this chapter, and much of the literature, emphasizes long-run financial objectives as the primary goal of for-profit companies. For-profit companies interested in long-run financial, environmental, and social objectives adapt the balanced scorecard to implement all three objectives.

broadens management's attention to short-run *and* long-run performance. *Never lose sight of the key point. In for-profit companies, the primary goal of the balanced scorecard is to sustain long-run financial performance. Nonfinancial measures simply serve as leading indicators for the hard-to-measure long-run financial performance.*

Strategy Maps and the Balanced Scorecard

We use the Chipset example to develop strategy maps and the four perspectives of the balanced scorecard. The objectives and measures Chipset's managers choose for each perspective relates to the action plans for furthering Chipset's cost leadership strategy: *improving quality* and *reengineering processes.*

Strategy Maps

A useful first step in designing a balanced scorecard is a *strategy map*. A **strategy map** is a diagram that describes how an organization creates value by connecting strategic objectives in explicit cause-and-effect relationships with each other in the financial, customer, internal business process, and learning and growth perspectives. Exhibit 13-2 presents Chipset's strategy map. Follow the arrows to see how a strategic objective affects other strategic objectives. For example, empowering the workforce helps align employee and organization goals and improves processes. Employee and organizational alignment also helps improve processes that improve manufacturing quality and productivity, reduce customer delivery time, meet specified delivery dates, and improve post-sales service, all of which increase customer satisfaction. Improving manufacturing quality and productivity

Exhibit 13-2   Strategy Map for Chipset, Inc., for 2011

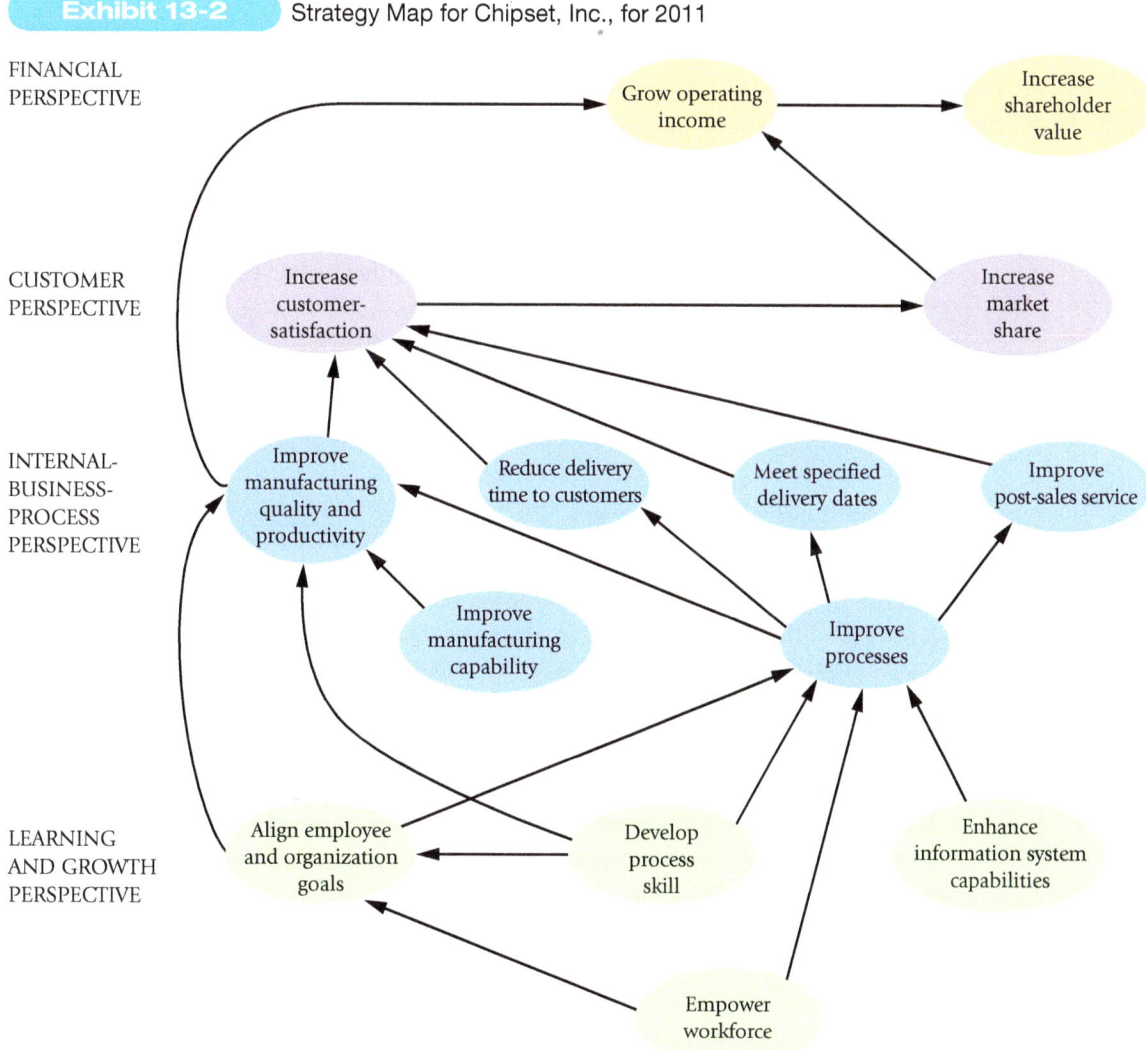

grows operating income and increases customer satisfaction that, in turn, increases market share, operating income, and shareholder value.

Chipset operates in a knowledge-intensive business. To compete successfully, Chipset invests in its employees, implements new technology and process controls, improves quality, and reengineers processes. Doing these activities well enables Chipset to build capabilities and intangible assets, which are not recorded as assets in its financial books. The strategy map helps Chipset evaluate whether these intangible assets are generating financial returns.

Chipset could include many other cause-and-effect relationships in the strategy map in Exhibit 13-2. But, Chipset, like other companies implementing the balanced scorecard, focuses on only those relationships that it believes to be the most significant.

Chipset uses the strategy map from Exhibit 13-2 to build the balanced scorecard presented in Exhibit 13-3. The scorecard highlights the four perspectives of performance: financial, customer, internal business process, and learning and growth. The first column presents the strategic objectives from the strategy map in Exhibit 13-2. At the beginning of 2011, the company's managers specify the strategic objectives, measures, initiatives (the actions necessary to achieve the objectives), and target performance (the first four columns of Exhibit 13-3).

Chipset wants to use the balanced scorecard targets to drive the organization to higher levels of performance. Managers therefore set targets at a level of performance that is achievable, yet distinctly better than competitors. Chipset's managers complete the fifth column, reporting actual performance at the end of 2011. This column compares Chipset's performance relative to target.

Four Perspectives of the Balanced Scorecard

We next describe the perspectives in general terms and illustrate each perspective using the measures chosen by Chipset in the context of its strategy.

1. **Financial perspective.** This perspective evaluates the profitability of the strategy and the creation of shareholder value. Because Chipset's key strategic initiatives are cost reduction relative to competitors' costs and sales growth, the financial perspective focuses on how much operating income results from reducing costs and selling more units of CX1.

2. **Customer perspective.** This perspective identifies targeted customer and market segments and measures the company's success in these segments. To monitor its customer objectives, Chipset uses measures such as market share in the communication-networks segment, number of new customers, and customer-satisfaction ratings.

3. **Internal-business-process perspective.** This perspective focuses on internal operations that create value for customers that, in turn, help achieve financial performance. Chipset determines internal-business-process improvement targets after benchmarking against its main competitors using information from published financial statements, prevailing prices, customers, suppliers, former employees, industry experts, and financial analysts. The internal-business-process perspective comprises three subprocesses:
   - **Innovation process:** Creating products, services, and processes that will meet the needs of customers. This is a very important process for companies that follow a product-differentiation strategy and must constantly design and develop innovative new products to remain competitive in the marketplace. Chipset's innovation focuses on improving its manufacturing capability and process controls to lower costs and improve quality. Chipset measures innovation by the number of improvements in manufacturing processes and percentage of processes with advanced controls.
   - **Operations process:** Producing and delivering existing products and services that will meet the needs of customers. Chipset's strategic initiatives are (a) improving manufacturing quality, (b) reducing delivery time to customers, and (c) meeting specified delivery dates so it measures yield, order-delivery time, and on-time deliveries.
   - **Postsales-service process:** Providing service and support to the customer after the sale of a product or service. Chipset monitors how quickly and accurately it is responding to customer-service requests.

| Exhibit 13-3 | The Balanced Scorecard for Chipset, Inc., for 2011 |

Strategic Objectives	Measures	Initiatives	Target Performance	Actual Performance
Financial Perspective				
Grow operating income	Operating income from productivity gain	Manage costs and unused capacity	$1,850,000	$1,912,500
Increase shareholder value	Operating income from growth	Build strong customer relationships	$2,500,000	$2,820,000
	Revenue growth		9%	10%[a]
Customer Perspective				
Increase market share	Market share in communication-networks segment	Identify future needs of customers	6%	7%
Increase customer satisfaction	Number of new customers	Identify new target-customer segments	1	1[b]
	Customer-satisfaction ratings	Increase customer focus of sales organization	90% of customers give top two ratings	87% of customers give top two ratings
Internal-Business-Process Perspective				
Improve postsales service	Service response time	Improve customer-service process	Within 4 hours	Within 3 hours
Improve manufacturing quality and productivity	Yield	Identify root causes of problems and improve quality	78%	79.3%
Reduce delivery time to customers	Order-delivery time	Reengineer order-delivery process	30 days	30 days
Meet specified delivery dates	On-time delivery	Reengineer order-delivery process	92%	90%
Improve processes	Number of major improvements in manufacturing and business processes	Organize teams from manufacturing and sales to modify processes	5	5
Improve manufacturing capability	Percentage of processes with advanced controls	Organize R&D/manufacturing teams to implement advanced controls	75%	75%
Learning-and-Growth Perspective				
Align employee and organization goals	Employee-satisfaction ratings	Employee participation and suggestions program to build teamwork	80% of employees give top two ratings	88% of employees give top two ratings
Empower workforce	Percentage of line workers empowered to manage processes	Have supervisors act as coaches rather than decision makers	85%	90%
Develop process skill	Percentage of employees trained in process and quality management	Employee training programs	90%	92%
Enhance information-system capabilities	Percentage of manufacturing processes with real-time feedback	Improve online and offline data gathering	80%	80%

[a](Revenues in 2011 − Revenues in 2010) ÷ Revenues in 2010 = ($25,300,000 − $23,000,000) ÷ $23,000,000 = 10%.

[b]Number of customers increased from seven to eight in 2011.

4. **Learning-and-growth perspective.** This perspective identifies the capabilities the organization must excel at to achieve superior internal processes that in turn create value for customers and shareholders. Chipset's learning and growth perspective emphasizes three capabilities: (1) information-system capabilities, measured by the percentage of manufacturing processes with real-time feedback; (2) employee capabilities, measured by the percentage of employees trained in process and quality management; and (3) motivation, measured by employee satisfaction and the percentage of manufacturing and sales employees (line employees) empowered to manage processes.

The arrows in Exhibit 13-3 indicate the *broad* cause-and-effect linkages: how gains in the learning-and-growth perspective lead to improvements in internal business processes, which lead to higher customer satisfaction and market share, and finally lead to superior financial performance. Note how the scorecard describes elements of Chipset's strategy implementation. Worker training and empowerment improve employee satisfaction and lead to manufacturing and business-process improvements that improve quality and reduce delivery time. The result is increased customer satisfaction and higher market share. These initiatives have been successful from a financial perspective. Chipset has earned significant operating income from its cost leadership strategy, and that strategy has also led to growth.

A major benefit of the balanced scorecard is that it promotes causal thinking. Think of the balanced scorecard as a *linked scorecard* or a *causal scorecard*. Managers must search for empirical evidence (rather than rely on faith alone) to test the validity and strength of the various connections. A causal scorecard enables a company to focus on the key drivers that steer the implementation of the strategy. Without convincing links, the scorecard loses much of its value.

Implementing a Balanced Scorecard

To successfully implement a balanced scorecard requires commitment and leadership from top management. At Chipset, the team building the balanced scorecard (headed by the vice president of strategic planning) conducted interviews with senior managers, probed executives about customers, competitors, and technological developments, and sought proposals for balanced scorecard objectives across the four perspectives. The team then met to discuss the responses and to build a prioritized list of objectives.

In a meeting with all senior managers, the team sought to achieve consensus on the scorecard objectives. Senior management was then divided into four groups, with each group responsible for one of the perspectives. In addition, each group broadened the base of inputs by including representatives from the next-lower levels of management and key functional managers. The groups identified measures for each objective and the sources of information for each measure. The groups then met to finalize scorecard objectives, measures, targets, and the initiatives to achieve the targets. Management accountants played an important role in the design and implementation of the balanced scorecard, particularly in determining measures to represent the realities of the business. This required management accountants to understand the economic environment of the industry, Chipset's customers and competitors, and internal business issues such as human resources, operations, and distribution.

Managers made sure that employees understood the scorecard and the scorecard process. The final balanced scorecard was communicated to all employees. Sharing the scorecard allowed engineers and operating personnel, for example, to understand the reasons for customer satisfaction and dissatisfaction and to make suggestions for improving internal processes directly aimed at satisfying customers and implementing Chipset's strategy. Too often, scorecards are seen by only a select group of managers. By limiting the scorecard's exposure, an organization loses the opportunity for widespread organization engagement and alignment.

Chipset (like Cigna Property, Casualty Insurance, and Wells Fargo) also encourages each department to develop its own scorecard that ties into Chipset's main scorecard described in Exhibit 13-3. For example, the quality control department's scorecard has measures that its department managers use to improve yield—number of quality circles, statistical process control charts, Pareto diagrams, and root-cause analyses (see

Chapter 19, pp. 675–677 for more details). Department scorecards help align the actions of each department to implement Chipset's strategy.

Companies frequently use balanced scorecards to evaluate and reward managerial performance and to influence managerial behavior. Using the balanced scorecard for performance evaluation widens the performance management lens and motivates managers to give greater attention to nonfinancial drivers of performance. Surveys indicate, however, that companies continue to assign more weight to the financial perspective (55%) than to the other perspectives—customer (19%), internal business process (12%), and learning and growth (14%). Companies cite several reasons for the relatively smaller weight on nonfinancial measures: difficulty evaluating the relative importance of nonfinancial measures; challenges in measuring and quantifying qualitative, nonfinancial data; and difficulty in compensating managers despite poor financial performance (see Chapter 23 for a more detailed discussion of performance evaluation). Many companies, however, are giving greater weight to nonfinancial measures in promotion decisions because they believe that nonfinancial measures (such as customer satisfaction, process improvements, and employee motivation) better assess a manager's potential to succeed at senior levels of management. For the balanced scorecard to be effective, managers must view it as fairly assessing and rewarding all important aspects of a manager's performance and promotion prospects.

Aligning the Balanced Scorecard to Strategy

Different strategies call for different scorecards. Recall Chipset's competitor Visilog, which follows a product-differentiation strategy by designing custom chips for modems and communication networks. Visilog designs its balanced scorecard to fit its strategy. For example, in the financial perspective, Visilog evaluates how much of its operating income comes from charging premium prices for its products. In the customer perspective, Visilog measures the percentage of its revenues from new products and new customers. In the internal-business-process perspective, Visilog measures the number of new products introduced and new product development time. In the learning-and-growth perspective, Visilog measures the development of advanced manufacturing capabilities to produce custom chips. Visilog also uses some of the measures described in Chipset's balanced scorecard in Exhibit 13-3. For example, revenue growth, customer satisfaction ratings, order-delivery time, on-time delivery, percentage of frontline workers empowered to manage processes, and employee-satisfaction ratings are also important measures under the product-differentiation strategy. The goal is to align the balanced scorecard with company strategy.[5] Exhibit 13-4 presents some common measures found on company scorecards in the service, retail, and manufacturing sectors.

Features of a Good Balanced Scorecard

A well-designed balanced scorecard has several features:

1. It tells the story of a company's strategy, articulating a sequence of cause-and-effect relationships—the links among the various perspectives that align implementation of the strategy. In for-profit companies, each measure in the scorecard is part of a cause-and-effect chain leading to financial outcomes. Not-for-profit organizations design the cause-and-effect chain to achieve their strategic service objectives—for example, number of people no longer in poverty, or number of children still in school.

2. The balanced scorecard helps to communicate the strategy to all members of the organization by translating the strategy into a coherent and linked set of understandable and measurable operational targets. Guided by the scorecard, managers and employees take actions and make decisions to achieve the company's strategy. Companies that have distinct strategic business units (SBUs)—such as consumer

---

[5] For simplicity, we have presented the balanced scorecard in the context of companies that have followed either a cost-leadership or a product-differentiation strategy. Of course, a company may have some products for which cost leadership is critical and other products for which product differentiation is important. The company will then develop separate scorecards to implement the different product strategies. In still other contexts, product differentiation may be of primary importance, but some cost leadership must also be achieved. The balanced scorecard measures would then be linked in a cause-and-effect way to this strategy.

Exhibit 13-4

Frequently Cited
Balanced Scorecard
Measures

Financial Perspective
Income measures: Operating income, gross margin percentage
Revenue and cost measures: Revenue growth, revenues from new products, cost reductions in key areas
Income and investment measures: Economic value added [a](EVA®), return on investment
Customer Perspective
Market share, customer satisfaction, customer-retention percentage, time taken to fulfill customers' requests, number of customer complaints
Internal-Business-Process Perspective
Innovation Process: Operating capabilities, number of new products or services, new-product development times, and number of new patents
Operations Process: Yield, defect rates, time taken to deliver product to customers, percentage of on-time deliveries, average time taken to respond to orders, setup time, manufacturing downtime
Postsales Service Process: Time taken to replace or repair defective products, hours of customer training for using the product
Learning-and-Growth Perspective
Employee measures: Employee education and skill levels, employee-satisfaction ratings, employee turnover rates, percentage of employee suggestions implemented, percentage of compensation based on individual and team incentives
Technology measures: Information system availability, percentage of processes with advanced controls

---

[a]This measure is described in Chapter 23.

products and pharmaceuticals at Johnson & Johnson—develop their balanced scorecards at the SBU level. Each SBU has its own unique strategy and implementation goals; building separate scorecards allows each SBU to choose measures that help implement its distinctive strategy.

3. In for-profit companies, the balanced scorecard must motivate managers to take actions that eventually result in improvements in financial performance. Managers sometimes tend to focus too much on innovation, quality, and customer satisfaction as ends in themselves. For example, Xerox spent heavily to increase customer satisfaction without a resulting financial payoff because higher levels of satisfaction did not increase customer loyalty. Some companies use statistical methods, such as regression analysis, to test the anticipated cause-and-effect relationships among nonfinancial measures and financial performance. The data for this analysis can come from either time series data (collected over time) or cross-sectional data (collected, for example, across multiple stores of a retail chain). In the Chipset example, improvements in non-financial factors have, in fact, already led to improvements in financial factors.

4. The balanced scorecard limits the number of measures, identifying only the most critical ones. Chipset's scorecard, for example, has 16 measures, between 3 and 6 measures for each perspective. Limiting the number of measures focuses managers' attention on those that most affect strategy implementation. Using too many measures makes it difficult for managers to process relevant information.

5. The balanced scorecard highlights less-than-optimal trade-offs that managers may make when they fail to consider operational and financial measures together. For example, a company whose strategy is innovation and product differentiation could achieve superior short-run financial performance by reducing spending on R&D. A good balanced scorecard would signal that the short-run financial performance might have been achieved by taking actions that hurt future financial performance because a leading indicator of that performance, R&D spending and R&D output, has declined.

Pitfalls in Implementing a Balanced Scorecard

Pitfalls to avoid in implementing a balanced scorecard include the following:

1. Managers should not assume the cause-and-effect linkages are precise. They are merely hypotheses. Over time, a company must gather evidence of the strength and timing of the linkages among the nonfinancial and financial measures. With experience,

organizations should alter their scorecards to include those nonfinancial strategic objectives and measures that are the best leading indicators (the causes) of financial performance (a lagging indicator or the effect). Understanding that the scorecard evolves over time helps managers avoid unproductively spending time and money trying to design the "perfect" scorecard at the outset. Furthermore, as the business environment and strategy change over time, the measures in the scorecard also need to change.

2. Managers should not seek improvements across all of the measures all of the time. For example, strive for quality and on-time performance but not beyond the point at which further improvement in these objectives is so costly that it is inconsistent with long-run profit maximization. Cost-benefit considerations should always be central when designing a balanced scorecard.

3. Managers should not use only objective measures in the balanced scorecard. Chipset's balanced scorecard includes both objective measures (such as operating income from cost leadership, market share, and manufacturing yield) and subjective measures (such as customer- and employee-satisfaction ratings). When using subjective measures, though, managers must be careful that the benefits of this potentially rich information are not lost by using measures that are inaccurate or that can be easily manipulated.

4. Despite challenges of measurement, top management should not ignore nonfinancial measures when evaluating managers and other employees. Managers tend to focus on the measures used to reward their performance. Excluding nonfinancial measures when evaluating performance will reduce the significance and importance that managers give to nonfinancial measures.

Evaluating the Success of Strategy and Implementation

Decision Point

How can an organization translate its strategy into a set of performance measures?

To evaluate how successful Chipset's strategy and its implementation have been, its management compares the target- and actual-performance columns in the balanced scorecard (Exhibit 13-3). Chipset met most targets set on the basis of competitor benchmarks in 2011 itself. That's because, in the Chipset context, improvements in the learning and growth perspective quickly ripple through to the financial perspective. Chipset will continue to seek improvements on the targets it did not achieve, but meeting most targets suggests that the strategic initiatives that Chipset identified and measured for learning and growth resulted in improvements in internal business processes, customer measures, and financial performance.

How would Chipset know if it had problems in strategy implementation? If it did not meet its targets on the two perspectives that are more internally focused: learning and growth and internal business processes.

What if Chipset performed well on learning and growth and internal business processes, but customer measures and financial performance in this year and the next did not improve? Chipset's managers would then conclude that Chipset did a good job of implementation (the various internal nonfinancial measures it targeted improved) but that its strategy was faulty (there was no effect on customers or on long-run financial performance and value creation). Management failed to identify the correct causal links. It implemented the wrong strategy well! Management would then reevaluate the strategy and the factors that drive it.

Now what if Chipset performed well on its various nonfinancial measures, and operating income over this year and the next also increased? Chipset's managers might be tempted to declare the strategy a success because operating income increased. Unfortunately, management still cannot conclude with any confidence that Chipset successfully formulated and implemented its strategy. Why? Because operating income can increase simply because entire markets are expanding, not because a company's strategy has been successful. Also, changes in operating income might occur because of factors outside the strategy. For example, a company such as Chipset that has chosen a cost-leadership strategy may find that its operating-income increase actually resulted from, say, some degree of product differentiation. *To evaluate the success of a strategy, managers and management accountants need to link strategy to the sources of operating-income increases.*

For Chipset to conclude that it was successful in implementing its strategy, it must demonstrate that improvements in its financial performance and operating income over time resulted from achieving targeted cost savings and growth in market share. Fortunately, the top two rows of Chipset's balanced scorecard in Exhibit 13-3 show that operating-income gains from productivity ($1,912,500) and growth ($2,820,000) exceeded targets. The next section of this chapter describes how these numbers were calculated. Because its strategy has been successful, Chipset's management can be more confident that the gains will be sustained in subsequent years.

Chipset's management accountants subdivide changes in operating income into components that can be identified with product differentiation, cost leadership, and growth. Why growth? Because successful product differentiation or cost leadership generally increases market share and helps a company to grow. Subdividing the change in operating income to evaluate the success of a strategy is conceptually similar to the variance analysis discussed in Chapters 7 and 8. One difference, however, is that management accountants compare actual operating performance over two different periods, not actual to budgeted numbers in the same time period as in variance analysis.[6]

Strategic Analysis of Operating Income

Learning Objective 4

Analyze changes in operating income to evaluate strategy

. . . growth, price recovery, and productivity

The following illustration explains how to subdivide the change in operating income from one period to *any* future period. The individual components describe company performance with regard to product differentiation, cost leadership, and growth.[7] We illustrate the analysis using data from 2010 and 2011 because Chipset implemented key elements of its strategy in late 2010 and early 2011 and expects the financial consequences of these strategies to occur in 2011. Suppose the financial consequences of these strategies had been expected to affect operating income in only 2012. Then we could just as easily have compared 2010 to 2012. If necessary, we could also have compared 2010 to 2011 and 2012 taken together.

Chipset's data for 2010 and 2011 follow:

	2010	2011
1. Units of CX1 produced and sold	1,000,000	1,150,000
2. Selling price	$23	$22
3. Direct materials (square centimeters of silicon wafers)	3,000,000	2,900,000
4. Direct material cost per square centimeter	$1.40	$1.50
5. Manufacturing processing capacity (in square centimeters of silicon wafer)	3,750,000	3,500,000
6. Conversion costs (all manufacturing costs other than direct material costs)	$16,050,000	$15,225,000
7. Conversion cost per unit of capacity (row 6 ÷ row 5)	$4.28	$4.35

Chipset provides the following additional information:

1. Conversion costs (labor and overhead costs) for each year depend on production processing capacity defined in terms of the quantity of square centimeters of silicon wafers that Chipset can process. These costs do not vary with the actual quantity of silicon wafers processed.

2. Chipset incurs no R&D costs. Its marketing, sales, and customer-service costs are small relative to the other costs. Chipset has fewer than 10 customers, each purchasing roughly the same quantities of CX1. Because of the highly technical nature of the product, Chipset uses a cross-functional team for its marketing, sales, and customer-service activities. This cross-functional approach ensures that, although marketing, sales, and customer-service costs are small, the entire Chipset organization, including manufacturing engineers, remains focused on increasing customer satisfaction and

---

[6] Other examples of focusing on actual performance over two periods rather than comparisons of actuals with budgets can be found in J. Hope and R. Fraser, *Beyond Budgeting* (Boston, MA: Harvard Business School Press, 2003).

[7] For other details, see R. Banker, S. Datar, and R. Kaplan, "Productivity Measurement and Management Accounting," *Journal of Accounting, Auditing and Finance* (1989): 528–554; and A. Hayzen and J. Reeve, "Examining the Relationships in Productivity Accounting," *Management Accounting Quarterly* (2000): 32–39.

market share. (The Problem for Self-Study at the end of this chapter describes a situation in which marketing, sales, and customer-service costs are significant.)

3. Chipset's asset structure is very similar in 2010 and 2011.

4. Operating income for each year is as follows:

	2010	2011
Revenues		
($23 per unit × 1,000,000 units; $22 per unit × 1,150,000 units)	$23,000,000	$25,300,000
Costs		
Direct material costs		
($1.40/sq. cm. × 3,000,000 sq. cm.; $1.50/sq. cm. × 2,900,000 sq. cm.)	4,200,000	4,350,000
Conversion costs		
($4.28/sq. cm. × 3,750,000 sq. cm.; $4.35/sq. cm. × 3,500,000 sq. cm.)	16,050,000	15,225,000
Total costs	20,250,000	19,575,000
Operating income	$ 2,750,000	$ 5,725,000
Change in operating income		$2,975,000 F

The goal of Chipset's managers is to evaluate how much of the $2,975,000 increase in operating income was caused by the successful implementation of the company's cost-leadership strategy. To do this, management accountants start by analyzing three main factors: growth, price recovery, and productivity.

The **growth component** measures the change in operating income attributable solely to the change in the quantity of output sold between 2010 and 2011.

The **price-recovery component** measures the change in operating income attributable solely to changes in Chipset's prices of inputs and outputs between 2010 and 2011. The price-recovery component measures change in output price compared with changes in input prices. A company that has successfully pursued a strategy of product differentiation will be able to increase its output price faster than the increase in its input prices, boosting profit margins and operating income: It will show a large positive price-recovery component.

The **productivity component** measures the change in costs attributable to a change in the quantity of inputs used in 2011 relative to the quantity of inputs that would have been used in 2010 to produce the 2011 output. The productivity component measures the amount by which operating income increases by using inputs efficiently to lower costs. A company that has successfully pursued a strategy of cost leadership will be able to produce a given quantity of output with a lower cost of inputs: It will show a large positive productivity component. Given Chipset's strategy of cost leadership, we expect the increase in operating income to be attributable to the productivity and growth components, not to price recovery. We now examine these three components in detail.

Growth Component of Change in Operating Income

The growth component of the change in operating income measures the increase in revenues minus the increase in costs from selling more units of CX1 in 2011 (1,150,000 units) than in 2010 (1,000,000 units), *assuming nothing else has changed*.

Revenue Effect of Growth

$$\begin{pmatrix} \text{Revenue effect} \\ \text{of growth} \end{pmatrix} = \begin{pmatrix} \text{Actual units of} \\ \text{output sold} \\ \text{in 2011} \end{pmatrix} - \begin{pmatrix} \text{Actual units of} \\ \text{output sold} \\ \text{in 2010} \end{pmatrix} \times \begin{pmatrix} \text{Selling} \\ \text{price} \\ \text{in 2010} \end{pmatrix}$$

$$= (1,150,000 \text{ units} - 1,000,000 \text{ units}) \times \$23 \text{ per unit}$$

$$= \$3,450,000 \text{ F}$$

This component is favorable (F) because the increase in output sold in 2011 increases operating income. Components that decrease operating income are unfavorable (U).

Note that Chipset uses the 2010 price of CX1 and focuses only on the increase in units sold between 2010 and 2011, because the revenue effect of growth component measures how much revenues would have changed in 2010 if Chipset had sold 1,150,000 units instead of 1,000,000 units.

Cost Effect of Growth

The cost effect of growth measures how much costs would have changed in 2010 if Chipset had produced 1,150,000 units of CX1 instead of 1,000,000 units. To measure the cost effect of growth, Chipset's managers distinguish variable costs such as direct material costs from fixed costs such as conversion costs, because as units produced (and sold) increase, variable costs increase proportionately but fixed costs, generally, do not change.

$$\begin{pmatrix} \text{Cost effect of} \\ \text{growth for} \\ \text{variable costs} \end{pmatrix} = \begin{pmatrix} \text{Units of input} & \text{Actual units of} \\ \text{required to} & \text{input used} \\ \text{produce 2011} & - & \text{to produce} \\ \text{output in 2010} & \text{2010 output} \end{pmatrix} \times \begin{matrix} \text{Input} \\ \text{price} \\ \text{in 2010} \end{matrix}$$

$$\begin{matrix} \text{Cost effect of} \\ \text{growth for} \\ \text{direct materials} \end{matrix} = \left(3{,}000{,}000 \text{ sq. cm.} \times \frac{1{,}150{,}000 \text{ units}}{1{,}000{,}000 \text{ units}} - 3{,}000{,}000 \text{ sq. cm.} \right) \times \$1.40 \text{ per sq. cm.}$$

$$= (3{,}450{,}000 \text{ sq. cm.} - 3{,}000{,}000 \text{ sq. cm.}) \times \$1.40 \text{ per sq. cm.} = \$630{,}000 \text{ U}$$

The units of input required to produce 2011 output in 2010 can also be calculated as follows:

$$\text{Units of input per unit of output in 2010} = \frac{3{,}000{,}000 \text{ sq. cm.}}{1{,}000{,}000 \text{ units}} = 3 \text{ sq. cm./unit}$$

Units of input required to produce 2011 output of 1,150,000 units in 2010 = 3 sq. cm. per unit × 1,150,000 units = 3,450,000 sq. cm.

$$\begin{matrix} \text{Cost effect of} \\ \text{growth for} \\ \text{fixed costs} \end{matrix} = \begin{pmatrix} \text{Actual units of capacity in} & \text{Actual units} \\ \text{2010 because adequate capacity} & - & \text{of capacity} \\ \text{exists to produce 2011 output in 2010} & \text{in 2010} \end{pmatrix} \times \begin{matrix} \text{Price per} \\ \text{unit of} \\ \text{capacity} \\ \text{in 2010} \end{matrix}$$

$$\begin{matrix} \text{Cost effect of} \\ \text{growth for} \\ \text{conversion costs} \end{matrix} = (3{,}750{,}000 \text{ sq. cm.} - 3{,}750{,}000 \text{ sq. cm.}) \times \$4.28 \text{ per sq. cm.} = \$0$$

Conversion costs are fixed costs at a given level of capacity. Chipset has manufacturing capacity to process 3,750,000 square centimeters of silicon wafers in 2010 at a cost of $4.28 per square centimeter (rows 5, and 7 of data on p. 478). To produce 1,150,000 units of output in 2010, Chipset needs to process 3,450,000 square centimeters of direct materials, which is less than the available capacity of 3,750,000 sq. cm. Throughout this chapter, we assume adequate capacity exists in the current year (2010) to produce next year's (2011) output. Under this assumption, the cost effect of growth for capacity-related fixed costs is, by definition, $0. Had 2010 capacity been inadequate to produce 2011 output in 2010, we would need to calculate the additional capacity required to produce 2011 output in 2010. These calculations are beyond the scope of the book.

In summary, the net increase in operating income attributable to growth equals the following:

Revenue effect of growth		$3,450,000 F
Cost effect of growth		
Direct material costs	$630,000 U	
Conversion costs	0	630,000 U
Change in operating income due to growth		$2,820,000 F

Price-Recovery Component of Change in Operating Income

Assuming that the 2010 relationship between inputs and outputs continued in 2011, the price-recovery component of the change in operating income measures solely the effect of price changes on revenues and costs to produce and sell the 1,150,000 units of CX1 in 2011.

Revenue Effect of Price Recovery

$$\begin{array}{c}\text{Revenue effect of} \\ \text{price recovery}\end{array} = \left(\begin{array}{c}\text{Selling price} \\ \text{in 2011}\end{array} - \begin{array}{c}\text{Selling price} \\ \text{in 2010}\end{array}\right) \times \begin{array}{c}\text{Actual units} \\ \text{of output} \\ \text{sold in 2011}\end{array}$$

$$= (\$22 \text{ per unit} - \$23 \text{ per unit}) \times 1{,}150{,}000 \text{ units}$$

$$= \$1{,}150{,}000 \text{ U}$$

Note that the calculation focuses on revenue changes caused by changes in the selling price of CX1 between 2010 and 2011.

Cost Effect of Price Recovery

Chipset's management accountants calculate the cost effects of price recovery separately for variable costs and for fixed costs, just as they did when calculating the cost effect of growth.

$$\begin{array}{c}\text{Cost effect of} \\ \text{price recovery for} \\ \text{variable costs}\end{array} = \left(\begin{array}{c}\text{Input price} \\ \text{in 2011}\end{array} - \begin{array}{c}\text{Input price} \\ \text{in 2010}\end{array}\right) \times \begin{array}{c}\text{Units of input} \\ \text{required to} \\ \text{produce 2011} \\ \text{output in 2010}\end{array}$$

$$\begin{array}{c}\text{Cost effect of} \\ \text{price recovery for} \\ \text{direct materials}\end{array} = (\$1.50 \text{ per sq.cm.} - \$1.40 \text{ per sq.cm.}) \times 3{,}450{,}000 \text{ sq.} = \$345{,}000 \text{ U}$$

Recall that the direct materials of 3,450,000 square centimeters required to produce 2011 output in 2010 had already been calculated when computing the cost effect of growth (p. 480).

$$\begin{array}{c}\text{Cost effect of} \\ \text{price recovery for} \\ \text{fixed costs}\end{array} = \left(\begin{array}{c}\text{Price per} \\ \text{unit of} \\ \text{capacity} \\ \text{in 2011}\end{array} - \begin{array}{c}\text{Price per} \\ \text{unit of} \\ \text{capacity} \\ \text{in 2010}\end{array}\right) \times \begin{array}{c}\text{Actual units of capacity in} \\ \text{2010 (because adequate} \\ \text{capacity exists to produce} \\ \text{2011 output in 2010)}\end{array}$$

Cost effect of price recovery for fixed costs is as follows:

Conversion costs: ($4.35 per sq. cm. – $4.28 per sq. cm.) × 3,750,000 sq. cm. = $262,500 U

Note that the detailed analyses of capacities were presented when computing the cost effect of growth (p. 480).

In summary, the net decrease in operating income attributable to price recovery equals the following:

Revenue effect of price recovery		$1,150,000 U
Cost effect of price recovery		
Direct material costs	$345,000 U	
Conversion costs	262,500 U	607,500 U
Change in operating income due to price recovery		$1,757,500 U

The price-recovery analysis indicates that, even as the prices of its inputs increased, the selling prices of CX1 decreased and Chipset could not pass on input-price increases to its customers.

Productivity Component of Change in Operating Income

The productivity component of the change in operating income uses 2011 input prices to measure how costs have decreased as a result of using fewer inputs, a better mix of inputs, and/or less capacity to produce 2011 output, compared with the inputs and capacity that would have been used to produce this output in 2010.

The productivity-component calculations use 2011 prices and output. That's because the productivity component isolates the change in costs between 2010 and 2011 caused solely by the change in the quantities, mix, and/or capacities of inputs.[8]

$$\text{Cost effect of productivity for variable costs} = \left(\begin{array}{c}\text{Actual units of input used to produce 2011 output} - \text{Units of input required to produce 2011 output in 2010}\end{array}\right) \times \text{Input price in 2011}$$

Using the 2011 data given on page 478 and the calculation of units of input required to produce 2011 output in 2010 when discussing the cost effects of growth (p. 480),

$$\text{Cost effect of productivity for direct materials} = (2{,}900{,}000 \text{ sq. cm.} - 3{,}450{,}000 \text{ sq. cm.}) \times \$1.50 \text{ per sq. cm}$$

$$= 550{,}000 \text{ sq. cm.} \times \$1.50 \text{ per sq. cm.} = \$825{,}000 \text{ F}$$

Chipset's quality and yield improvements reduced the quantity of direct materials needed to produce output in 2011 relative to 2010.

$$\text{Cost effect of productivity for fixed costs} = \left(\begin{array}{c}\text{Actual units of capacity in 2011} - \text{Actual units of capacity in 2010 because adequate capacity exists to produce 2011 output in 2010}\end{array}\right) \times \text{Price per unit of capacity in 2011}$$

To calculate the cost effect of productivity for fixed costs, we use the 2011 data given on page 478, and the analyses of capacity required to produce 2011 output in 2010 when discussing the cost effect of growth (p. 480).

Cost effects of productivity for fixed costs are

$$\text{Conversion costs: } (3{,}500{,}000 \text{ sq. cm} - 3{,}750{,}000 \text{ sq. cm.}) \times \$4.35 \text{ per sq. cm.} = \$1{,}087{,}500 \text{ F}$$

Chipset's managers decreased manufacturing capacity in 2011 to 3,500,000 square centimeters by selling off old equipment and laying off workers.

In summary, the net increase in operating income attributable to productivity equals,

Cost effect of productivity	
Direct material costs	$ 825,000 F
Conversion costs	1,087,500 F
Change in operating income due to productivity	1,912,500 F

The productivity component indicates that Chipset was able to increase operating income by improving quality and productivity and eliminating capacity to reduce costs. The appendix to this chapter examines partial and total factor productivity changes between 2010 and 2011 and describes how the management accountant can obtain a deeper understanding of Chipset's cost-leadership strategy. Note that the productivity component focuses exclusively on costs, so there is no revenue effect for this component.

Exhibit 13-5 summarizes the growth, price-recovery, and productivity components of the changes in operating income. Generally, companies that have been successful at cost leadership will show favorable productivity and growth components. Companies that

---

[8] Note that the productivity-component calculation uses actual 2011 input prices, whereas its counterpart, the efficiency variance in Chapters 7 and 8, uses budgeted prices. (In effect, the budgeted prices correspond to 2010 prices). Year 2011 prices are used in the productivity calculation because Chipset wants its managers to choose input quantities to minimize costs in 2011 based on currently prevailing prices. If 2010 prices had been used in the productivity calculation, managers would choose input quantities based on irrelevant input prices that prevailed a year ago! Why does using budgeted prices in Chapters 7 and 8 not pose a similar problem? Because, unlike 2010 prices that describe what happened a year ago, budgeted prices represent prices that are expected to prevail in the current period. Moreover, budgeted prices can be changed, if necessary, to bring them in line with actual current-period prices.

| **Exhibit 13-5** | Strategic Analysis of Profitability |

	Income Statement Amounts in 2010 (1)	Revenue and Cost Effects of Growth Component in 2011 (2)	Revenue and Cost Effects of Price-Recovery Component in 2011 (3)	Cost Effect of Productivity Component in 2011 (4)	Income Statement Amounts in 2011 (5) = (1) + (2) + (3) + (4)
Revenues	$23,000,000	$3,450,000 F	$1,150,000 U	—	$25,300,000
Costs	20,250,000	630,000 U	607,500 U	$1,912,000 F	19,575,000
Operating income	$ 2,750,000	$2,820,000 F	$1,757,500 U	$1,912,500 F	$ 5,725,000

$2,975,000 F

Change in operating income

have successfully differentiated their products will show favorable price-recovery and growth components. In Chipset's case, consistent with its strategy and its implementation, productivity contributed $1,912,500 to the increase in operating income, and growth contributed $2,820,000. Price-recovery contributed a $1,757,500 decrease in operating income, however, because, even as input prices increased, the selling price of CX1 decreased. Had Chipset been able to differentiate its product and charge a higher price, the price-recovery effects might have been less unfavorable or perhaps even favorable. As a result, Chipset's managers plan to evaluate some modest changes in product features that might help differentiate CX1 somewhat more from competing products.

Further Analysis of Growth, Price-Recovery, and Productivity Components

As in all variance and profit analysis, Chipset's managers want to more closely analyze the change in operating income. Chipset's growth might have been helped, for example, by an increase in industry market size. Therefore, at least part of the increase in operating income may be attributable to favorable economic conditions in the industry rather than to any successful implementation of strategy. Some of the growth might relate to the management decision to decrease selling price, made possible by the productivity gains. In this case, the increase in operating income from cost leadership must include operating income from productivity-related growth in market share in addition to the productivity gain.

We illustrate these ideas, using the Chipset example and the following additional information. *Instructors who do not wish to cover these detailed calculations can go to the next section on "Applying the Five-Step Decision-Making Framework to Strategy" without any loss of continuity.*

- The market growth rate in the industry is 8% in 2011. Of the 150,000 (1,150,000 – 1,000,000) units of increased sales of CX1 between 2010 and 2011, 80,000 (0.08 × 1,000,000) units are due to an increase in industry market size (which Chipset should have benefited from regardless of its productivity gains), and the remaining 70,000 units are due to an increase in market share.

- During 2011, Chipset could have maintained the price of CX1 at the 2010 price of $23 per unit. But management decided to take advantage of the productivity gains to reduce the price of CX1 by $1 to grow market share leading to the 70,000-unit increase in sales.

The effect of the industry-market-size factor on operating income (not any specific strategic action) is as follows:

Change in operating income due to growth in industry market size

$2,820,000 (Exhibit 13-5, column 2) $\times \dfrac{80,000 \text{ units}}{150,000 \text{ units}} = \$1,504,000 \text{ F}$

Concepts in Action   **The Growth Versus Profitability Choice at Facebook**

Competitive advantage comes from product differentiation or cost leadership. Successful implementation of these strategies helps a company to be profitable and to grow. Many Internet start-ups pursue a strategy of short-run growth to build a customer base, with the goal of later benefiting from such growth by either charging user fees or sustaining a free service for users supported by advertisers. However, during the 1990s dot-com boom (and subsequent bust), the most spectacular failures occurred in dot-com companies that followed the "get big fast" model but then failed to differentiate their products or reduce their costs.

Today, many social networking companies (Web-based communities that connect friends, colleagues, and groups with shared interests) face this same challenge. At Facebook, the most notable of the social networking sites, users can create personal profiles that allow them to interact with friends through messaging, chat, sharing Web site links, video clips, and more. Additionally, Facebook encourages other companies to build third-party programs, including games and surveys, for its Web site and mobile applications on the iPhone and BlackBerry devices. From 2007 to 2010, Facebook grew from 12 million users to more than 400 million users uploading photos, sharing updates, planning events, and playing games in the Facebook ecosystem.

During this phenomenal growth, the company wrestled with one key question: How could Facebook become profitable? In 2009, experts estimate that Facebook had revenues of $635 million, mostly through advertising and the sale of virtual gifts (as a private company, Facebook does not publicly disclose its financial information). But the company still did not turn a profit. Why not? To keep its global Web site and mobile applications operating, Facebook requires a massive amount of electricity, Internet bandwidth, and storage servers for digital files. In 2009, the company earmarked $100 million to buy 50,000 new servers, along with a new $2 million network storage system per week.

The cost structure of Facebook means that the company must generate tens of millions a month in revenue to sustain its operations over the long term. But how? Facebook has implemented the following popular methods of online revenue generation:

- Additional advertising: To grow its already significant advertising revenue, Facebook recently introduced "Fan Pages" for brands and companies seeking to communicate directly with its users. The company is also working on a tool that will let users share information about their physical whereabouts via the site, which will allow Facebook to sell targeted advertisements for nearby businesses.

- Transactions: Facebook is also testing a feature that would expand Facebook Credits, its transactions platform that allows users to purchase games and gifts, into an Internet-wide "virtual currency," that could be accepted by any Web site integrating the Facebook Connect online identity management platform. Facebook currently gets a 30% cut of all transactions conducted through Facebook Credits.

Despite rampant rumors, Facebook has rejected the idea of charging monthly subscription fees for access to its Web site or for advanced features and premium content.

With increased growth around the world, Facebook anticipates 2010 revenues to exceed $1 billion. Despite the opportunity to become the "world's richest twenty-something," Facebook's 25-year-old CEO Mark Zuckerberg has thus far resisted taking the company public through an initial public offering (IPO). "A lot of companies can go off course because of corporate pressures," says Mr. Zuckerberg. "I don't know what we are going to be building five years from now." With his company's focus on facilitating people's ability to share almost any- and everything with anyone, at any time, via the Internet, mobile phones, and even videogames, Facebook expects to offer users a highly personal and differentiated online experience in the years ahead and expects that this product differentiation will drive its future growth and profitability.

Sources: Vascellaro, Jessica E. 2010. Facebook CEO in no rush to 'friend' wall street. *Wall Street Journal*, March 3. http://online.wsj.com/article/SB10001424052748703787304575075942803630712.html; Eldon, Eric. 2010. Facebook revenues up to $700 million in 2009, on track towards $1.1 billion in 2010. *Inside Facebook*. Blog, March 2. http://www.insidefacebook.com/2010/03/02/facebook-made-up-to-700-million-in-2009-on-track-towards-1-1-billion-in-2010/; Arrington, Michael. 2010. Facebook may be growing too fast. And hitting the capital markets again. *Tech Crunch*. Blog, October 31. http://techcrunch.com/2010/10/31/facebooks-growing-problem/

Lacking a differentiated product, Chipset could have maintained the price of CX1 at $23 per unit even while the prices of its inputs increased.

The effect of product differentiation on operating income is as follows:

Change in prices of inputs (cost effect of price recovery)	607,500 U
Change in operating income due to product differentiation	$607,500 U

To exercise cost and price leadership, Chipset made the strategic decision to cut the price of CX1 by $1. This decision resulted in an increase in market share and 70,000 units of additional sales.

The effect of cost leadership on operating income is as follows:

Productivity component	$1,912,500 F
Effect of strategic decision to reduce price ($1/unit × 1,150,000 units)	1,150,000 U
Growth in market share due to productivity improvement and strategic decision to reduce prices	
$2,820,000 (Exhibit 13-5, column 2) × $\frac{70,000 \text{ units}}{150,000 \text{ units}}$	1,316,000 F
Change in operating income due to cost leadership	$2,078,500 F

A summary of the change in operating income between 2010 and 2011 follows.

Change due to industry market size	$1,504,000 F
Change due to product differentiation	607,500 U
Change due to cost leadership	2,078,500 F
Change in operating income	$2,975,000 F

Consistent with its cost-leadership strategy, the productivity gains of $1,912,500 in 2011 were a big part of the increase in operating income from 2010 to 2011. Chipset took advantage of these productivity gains to decrease price by $1 per unit at a cost of $1,150,000 to gain $1,316,000 in operating income by selling 70,000 additional units. The Problem for Self-Study on page 488 describes the analysis of the growth, price-recovery, and productivity components for a company following a product-differentiation strategy. The Concepts in Action feature (p. 484) describes the unique challenges that dot-com companies face in choosing a profitable strategy.

Under different assumptions about the change in selling price, the analysis will attribute different amounts to the different strategies.

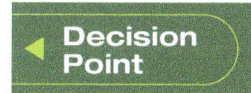

Decision Point

How can a company analyze changes in operating income to evaluate the success of its strategy?

Applying the Five-Step Decision-Making Framework to Strategy

We next briefly describe how the five-step decision-making framework, introduced in Chapter 1, is also useful in making decisions about strategy.

1. *Identify the problem and uncertainties.* Chipset's strategy choice depends on resolving two uncertainties—whether Chipset can add value to its customers that its competitors cannot emulate, and whether Chipset can develop the necessary internal capabilities to add this value.

2. *Obtain information.* Chipset's managers develop customer preference maps to identify various product attributes desired by customers and the competitive advantage or disadvantage it has on each attribute relative to competitors. The managers also gather data on Chipset's internal capabilities. How good is Chipset in designing and developing innovative new products? How good are its process and marketing capabilities?

3. *Make predictions about the future.* Chipset's managers conclude that they will not be able to develop innovative new products in a cost-effective way. They believe that Chipset's strength lies in improving quality, reengineering processes, reducing costs, and delivering products faster to customers.

4. *Make decisions by choosing among alternatives.* Chipset's management decides to follow a cost leadership rather than a product differentiation strategy. It decides to introduce a balanced scorecard to align and measure its quality improvement and process reengineering efforts.

5. *Implement the decision, evaluate performance, and learn.* On its balanced scorecard, Chipset's managers compare actual and targeted performance and evaluate possible cause-and-effect relationships. They learn, for example, that increasing the percentage of processes with advanced controls improves yield. As a result, just as they had anticipated, productivity and growth initiatives result in increases in operating income in 2011. The one change Chipset's managers plan for 2012 is to make modest changes in product features that might help differentiate CX1 somewhat from competing products. In this way, feedback and learning help in the development of future strategies and implementation plans.

Downsizing and the Management of Processing Capacity

Learning Objective 5

Identify unused capacity

. . . capacity available minus capacity used for engineered costs but difficult to determine for discretionary costs

and how to manage it

. . . downsize to reduce capacity

As we saw in our discussion of the productivity component, fixed costs are tied to capacity. Unlike variable costs, fixed costs do not change automatically with changes in activity level (for example, fixed conversion costs do not change with changes in the quantity of silicon wafers started into production). How then can managers reduce capacity-based fixed costs? By measuring and managing unused capacity. **Unused capacity** is the amount of productive capacity available over and above the productive capacity employed to meet consumer demand in the current period. To understand unused capacity, it is necessary to distinguish *engineered costs* from *discretionary costs*.

Engineered and Discretionary Costs

Engineered costs result from a cause-and-effect relationship between the cost driver—output—and the (direct or indirect) resources used to produce that output. Engineered costs have a detailed, physically observable, and repetitive relationship with output. In the Chipset example, direct material costs are *direct engineered costs*. Conversion costs are an example of *indirect engineered costs*. Consider 2011. The output of 1,150,000 units of CX1 and the efficiency with which inputs are converted into outputs result in 2,900,000 square centimeters of silicon wafers being started into production. Manufacturing-conversion-cost resources used equal $12,615,000 ($4.35 per sq. cm. × 2,900,000 sq. cm.), but actual conversion costs ($15,225,000) are higher because Chipset has manufacturing capacity to process 3,500,000 square centimeters of silicon wafer ($4.35 per sq. cm. × 3,500,000 sq. cm. = $15,225,000). Although these costs are fixed in the short run, over the long run there is a cause-and-effect relationship between output and manufacturing capacity required (and conversion costs needed). In the long run, Chipset will try to match its capacity to its needs.

Discretionary costs have two important features: (1) They arise from periodic (usually annual) decisions regarding the maximum amount to be incurred, and (2) they have no measurable cause-and-effect relationship between output and resources used. There is often a delay between when a resource is acquired and when it is used. Examples of discretionary costs include advertising, executive training, R&D, and corporate-staff department costs such as legal, human resources, and public relations. Unlike engineered costs, the relationship between discretionary costs and output is a blackbox because it is nonrepetitive and nonroutine. A noteworthy aspect of discretionary costs is that managers are seldom confident that the "correct" amounts are being spent. The founder of Lever Brothers, an international consumer-products company, once noted, "Half the money I spend on advertising is wasted; the trouble is, I don't know which half!"[9]

Identifying Unused Capacity for Engineered and Discretionary Overhead Costs

Identifying unused capacity is very different for engineered costs compared to discretionary costs. Consider engineered conversion costs.

At the start of 2011, Chipset had capacity to process 3,750,000 square centimeters of silicon wafers. Quality and productivity improvements made during 2011 enabled Chipset to produce 1,150,000 units of CX1 by processing 2,900,000 square centimeters of silicon wafers. Unused manufacturing capacity is 850,000 (3,750,000 – 2,900,000) square centimeters of silicon-wafer processing capacity at the beginning of 2011. At the 2011 conversion cost of $4.35 per square centimeter,

$$\begin{array}{l} \text{Cost of} \\ \text{unused capacity} \end{array} = \begin{array}{l} \text{Cost of capacity} \\ \text{at the beginning} \\ \text{of the year} \end{array} - \begin{array}{l} \text{Manufacturing resources} \\ \text{used during the year} \end{array}$$

$$= (3,750,000 \text{ sq. cm.} \times \$4.35 \text{ per sq. cm.}) - (2,900,000 \text{ sq. cm.} \times \$4.35 \text{ per sq. cm.})$$

$$= \$16,312,500 - \$12,615,000 = \$3,697,500$$

The absence of a cause-and-effect relationship makes identifying unused capacity for discretionary costs difficult. For example, management cannot determine the R&D resources used for the actual output produced. And without a measure of capacity used, it is not possible to compute unused capacity.

Managing Unused Capacity

What actions can Chipset management take when it identifies unused capacity? In general, it has two alternatives: eliminate unused capacity, or grow output to utilize the unused capacity.

In recent years, many companies have *downsized* in an attempt to eliminate unused capacity. **Downsizing** (also called **rightsizing**) is an integrated approach of configuring processes, products, and people to match costs to the activities that need to be performed to operate effectively and efficiently in the present and future. Companies such as AT&T, Delta Airlines, Ford Motor Company, and IBM have downsized to focus on their core businesses and have instituted organization changes to increase efficiency, reduce costs, and improve quality. However, downsizing often means eliminating jobs, which can adversely affect employee morale and the culture of a company.

Consider Chipset's alternatives with respect to its unused manufacturing capacity. Because it needed to process 2,900,000 square centimeters of silicon wafers in 2011, it could have reduced capacity to 3,000,000 square centimeters (Chipset can add or reduce manufacturing capacity in increments of 250,000 sq. cm.), resulting in cost savings of $3,262,500 [(3,750,000 sq. cm. – 3,000,000 sq. cm.) × $4.35 per sq. cm.]. Chipset's strategy, however, is not just to reduce costs but also to grow its business. So early in 2011, Chipset reduces its manufacturing capacity by only 250,000 square centimeters—from 3,750,000 square centimeters to 3,500,000 square centimeters—saving

---

[9] Managers also describe some costs as infrastructure costs—costs that arise from having property, plant, and equipment and a functioning organization. Examples are depreciation, long-run lease rental, and the acquisition of long-run technical capabilities. These costs are generally fixed costs because they are committed to and acquired before they are used. Infrastructure costs can be engineered or discretionary. For instance, manufacturing-overhead cost incurred at Chipset to acquire manufacturing capacity is an infrastructure cost that is an example of an engineered cost. In the long run, there is a cause-and-effect relationship between output and manufacturing-overhead costs needed to produce that output. R&D cost incurred to acquire technical capability is an infrastructure cost that is an example of a discretionary cost. There is no measurable cause-and-effect relationship between output and R&D cost incurred.

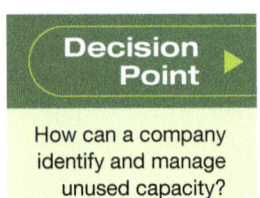

Decision Point ▶

How can a company identify and manage unused capacity?

$1,087,500 ($4.35 per sq. cm. × 250,000 sq. cm.). It retains some extra capacity for future growth. By avoiding greater reductions in capacity, it also maintains the morale of its skilled and capable workforce. The success of this strategy will depend on Chipset achieving the future growth it has projected.

Because identifying unused capacity for discretionary costs, such as R&D costs, is difficult, downsizing or otherwise managing this unused capacity is also difficult. Management must exercise considerable judgment in deciding the level of R&D costs that would generate the needed product and process improvements. Unlike engineered costs, there is no clear-cut way to know whether management is spending too much (or too little) on R&D.

Problem for Self-Study

Following a strategy of product differentiation, Westwood Corporation makes a high-end kitchen range hood, KE8. Westwood's data for 2010 and 2011 follow:

	2010	2011
1. Units of KE8 produced and sold	40,000	42,000
2. Selling price	$100	$110
3. Direct materials (square feet)	120,000	123,000
4. Direct material cost per square foot	$10	$11
5. Manufacturing capacity for KE8	50,000 units	50,000 units
6. Conversion costs	$1,000,000	$1,100,000
7. Conversion cost per unit of capacity (row 6 ÷ row 5)	$20	$22
8. Selling and customer-service capacity	30 customers	29 customers
9. Selling and customer-service costs	$720,000	$725,000
10. Cost per customer of selling and customer-service capacity (row 9 ÷ row 8)	$24,000	$25,000

In 2011, Westwood produced no defective units and reduced direct material usage per unit of KE8. Conversion costs in each year are tied to manufacturing capacity. Selling and customer service costs are related to the number of customers that the selling and service functions are designed to support. Westwood has 23 customers (wholesalers) in 2010 and 25 customers in 2011.

Required ▶

1. Describe briefly the elements you would include in Westwood's balanced scorecard.
2. Calculate the growth, price-recovery, and productivity components that explain the change in operating income from 2010 to 2011.
3. Suppose during 2011, the market size for high-end kitchen range hoods grew 3% in terms of number of units and all increases in market share (that is, increases in the number of units sold greater than 3%) are due to Westwood's product-differentiation strategy. Calculate how much of the change in operating income from 2010 to 2011 is due to the industry-market-size factor, cost leadership, and product differentiation.
4. How successful has Westwood been in implementing its strategy? Explain.

Solution

1. The balanced scorecard should describe Westwood's product-differentiation strategy. Elements that should be included in its balanced scorecard are as follows:
   - **Financial perspective.** Increase in operating income from higher margins on KE8 and from growth
   - **Customer perspective.** Customer satisfaction and market share in the high-end market
   - **Internal business process perspective.** New product features, development time for new products, improvements in manufacturing processes, manufacturing quality, order-delivery time, and on-time delivery
   - **Learning-and-growth perspective.** Percentage of employees trained in process and quality management and employee satisfaction ratings

2. Operating income for each year is as follows:

	2010	2011
Revenues		
($100 per unit × 40,000 units; $110 per unit × 42,000 units)	$4,000,000	$4,620,000
Costs		
Direct material costs		
($10 per sq. ft. × 120,000 sq. ft.; $11 per sq. ft. × 123,000 sq. ft.)	1,200,000	1,353,000
Conversion costs		
($20 per unit × 50,000 units; $22 per unit × 50,000 units)	1,000,000	1,100,000
Selling and customer-service cost		
($24,000 per customer × 30 customers;		
$25,000 per customer × 29 customers)	720,000	725,000
Total costs	2,920,000	3,178,000
Operating income	$1,080,000	$1,442,000
Change in operating income		$362,000 F

Growth Component of Operating Income Change

$$\text{Revenue effect of growth} = \left(\begin{array}{c}\text{Actual units of output sold in 2011} - \text{Actual units of output sold in 2010}\end{array}\right) \times \begin{array}{c}\text{Selling price in 2010}\end{array}$$

$$= (42,000 \text{ units} - 40,000 \text{ units}) \times \$100 \text{ per unit} = \$200,000 \text{ F}$$

$$\text{Cost effect of growth for variable costs} = \left(\begin{array}{c}\text{Units of input required to produce 2011 output in 2010} - \text{Actual units of input used to produce 2010 output}\end{array}\right) \times \begin{array}{c}\text{Input price in 2010}\end{array}$$

$$\text{Cost effect of growth for direct materials} = \left(120,000 \text{ sq. ft.} \times \frac{42,000 \text{ units}}{40,000 \text{ units}} - 120,000 \text{ sq. ft.}\right) \times \$10 \text{ per sq. ft.}$$

$$= (126,000 \text{ sq. ft.} - 120,000 \text{ sq. ft.}) \times \$10 \text{ per sq. ft.} = \$60,000 \text{ U}$$

$$\text{Cost effect of growth for fixed costs} = \left(\begin{array}{c}\text{Actual units of capacity in 2010, because adequate capacity exists to produce 2011 output in 2010} - \text{Actual units of capacity in 2010}\end{array}\right) \times \begin{array}{c}\text{Price per unit of capacity in 2010}\end{array}$$

Cost effects of growth for fixed costs are as follows:

Conversion costs: (50,000 units − 50,000 units) × $20 per unit = $0

Selling and customer-service costs: (30 customers − 30 customers) × $24,000 per customer = $0

In summary, the net increase in operating income attributable to growth equals the following:

Revenue effect of growth		$200,000 F
Cost effect of growth		
Direct material costs	$60,000 U	
Conversion costs	0	
Selling and customer-service costs	0	60,000 U
Change in operating income due to growth		$140,000 F

Price-Recovery Component of Operating-Income Change

$$\begin{matrix} \text{Revenue effect of} \\ \text{price recovery} \end{matrix} = \left(\begin{matrix} \text{Selling price} \\ \text{in 2011} \end{matrix} - \begin{matrix} \text{Selling price} \\ \text{in 2010} \end{matrix} \right) \times \begin{matrix} \text{Actual units} \\ \text{of output} \\ \text{sold in 2011} \end{matrix}$$

$$= (\$110 \text{ per unit} - \$100 \text{ per unit}) \times 42{,}000 \text{ units} = \$420{,}000 \text{ F}$$

$$\begin{matrix} \text{Cost effect of} \\ \text{price recovery} \\ \text{for variable costs} \end{matrix} = \left(\begin{matrix} \text{Input} \\ \text{price} \\ \text{in 2011} \end{matrix} - \begin{matrix} \text{Input} \\ \text{price} \\ \text{in 2010} \end{matrix} \right) \times \begin{matrix} \text{Units of input} \\ \text{required to produce} \\ \text{2011 output in 2010} \end{matrix}$$

Direct material costs: ($11 per sq. ft. − $10 per sq. ft.) × 126,000 sq. ft. = $126,000 U

$$\begin{matrix} \text{Cost effect of} \\ \text{price recovery} \\ \text{for fixed costs} \end{matrix} = \left(\begin{matrix} \text{Price per} \\ \text{unit of} \\ \text{capacity} \\ \text{in 2011} \end{matrix} - \begin{matrix} \text{Price per} \\ \text{unit of} \\ \text{capacity} \\ \text{in 2010} \end{matrix} \right) \times \begin{matrix} \text{Actual units of capacity in} \\ \text{2010, because adequate capacity} \\ \text{exists to produce 2011 output in 2010} \end{matrix}$$

Cost effects of price recovery for fixed costs are as follows:

Conversion costs: ($22 per unit − 20 per unit) × 50,000 units = $100,000 U

Selling and cust.-service costs: ($25,000 per cust. − $24,000 per cust.) × 30 customers = $30,000 U

In summary, the net increase in operating income attributable to price recovery equals the following:

Revenue effect of price recovery		$420,000 F
Cost effect of price recovery		
Direct material costs	$126,000 U	
Conversion costs	100,000 U	
Selling and customer-service costs	30,000 U	256,000 U
Change in operating income due to price recovery		$164,000 F

Productivity Component of Operating-Income Change

$$\begin{matrix} \text{Cost effect of} \\ \text{productivity for} \\ \text{variable costs} \end{matrix} = \left(\begin{matrix} \text{Actual units of} \\ \text{input used to produce} \\ \text{2011 output} \end{matrix} - \begin{matrix} \text{Units of input} \\ \text{required to produce} \\ \text{2011 output in 2010} \end{matrix} \right) \times \begin{matrix} \text{Input} \\ \text{price in} \\ \text{2011} \end{matrix}$$

$$\begin{matrix} \text{Cost effect of} \\ \text{productivity for} \\ \text{direct materials} \end{matrix} = (123{,}000 \text{ sq. ft.} - 126{,}000 \text{ sq. ft.}) \times \$11 \text{ per sq. ft.} = \$33{,}000 \text{ F}$$

$$\begin{matrix} \text{Cost effect of} \\ \text{productivity for} \\ \text{fixed costs} \end{matrix} = \left(\begin{matrix} \text{Actual units} \\ \text{of capacity} \\ \text{in 2011} \end{matrix} - \begin{matrix} \text{Actual units of capacity in} \\ \text{2010, because adequate} \\ \text{capacity exists to produce} \\ \text{2011 output in 2010} \end{matrix} \right) \times \begin{matrix} \text{Price per} \\ \text{unit of} \\ \text{capacity} \\ \text{in 2011} \end{matrix}$$

Cost effects of productivity for fixed costs are as follows:

Conversion costs: (50,000 units − 50,000 units) × $22 per unit = $0

Selling and customer-service costs: (29 customers − 30 customers) × $25,000/customer = $25,000 F

In summary, the net increase in operating income attributable to productivity equals the following:

Cost effect of productivity:	
Direct material costs	$33,000 F
Conversion costs	0
Selling and customer-service costs	25,000 F
Change in operating income due to productivity	$58,000 F

A summary of the change in operating income between 2010 and 2011 follows:

	Income Statement Amounts in 2010 (1)	Revenue and Cost Effects of Growth Component in 2011 (2)	Revenue and Cost Effects of Price-Recovery Component in 2011 (3)	Cost Effect of Productivity Component in 2011 (4)	Income Statement Amounts in 2011 (5) = (1) + (2) + (3) + (4)
Revenue	$4,000,000	$200,000 F	$420,000 F	—	$4,620,000
Costs	2,920,000	60,000 U	256,000 U	$58,000 F	3,178,000
Operating income	$1,080,000	$140,000 F	$164,000 F	$58,000 F	$1,442,000
			362,000 F		

Change in operating income

3. **Effect of the Industry-Market-Size Factor on Operating Income**
   Of the increase in sales from 40,000 to 42,000 units, 3%, or 1,200 units (0.03 × 40,000), is due to growth in market size, and 800 units (2,000 – 1,200) are due to an increase in market share. The change in Westwood's operating income from the industry-market-size factor rather than specific strategic actions is as follows:

$$\$140,000 \text{ (column 2 of preceding table)} \times \frac{1,200 \text{ units}}{2,000 \text{ units}} \qquad \underline{\underline{\$84,000 \text{ F}}}$$

Effect of Product Differentiation on Operating Income

Increase in the selling price of KE8 (revenue effect of the price-recovery component)	$420,000 F
Increase in prices of inputs (cost effect of the price-recovery component)	256,000 U
Growth in market share due to product differentiation	
$\$140,000 \text{ (column 2 of preceding table)} \times \dfrac{800 \text{ units}}{2,000 \text{ units}}$	56,000 F
Change in operating income due to product differentiation	$220,000 F

Effect of Cost Leadership on Operating Income

Productivity component	$ 58,000 F

A summary of the net increase in operating income from 2010 to 2011 follows:

Change due to the industry-market-size factor	$ 84,000 F
Change due to product differentiation	220,000 F
Change due to cost leadership	58,000 F
Change in operating income	$362,000 F

4. The analysis of operating income indicates that a significant amount of the increase in operating income resulted from Westwood's successful implementation of its product-differentiation strategy. The company was able to continue to charge a premium price for KE8 while increasing market share. Westwood was also able to earn additional operating income from improving its productivity.

Decision Points

The following question-and-answer format summarizes the chapter's learning objectives. Each decision presents a key question related to a learning objective. The guidelines are the answer to that question.

Decision	Guidelines
1. What are two generic strategies a company can use?	Two generic strategies are product differentiation and cost leadership. Product differentiation is offering products and services that are perceived by customers as being superior and unique. Cost leadership is achieving low costs relative to competitors. A company chooses its strategy based on an understanding of customer preferences and its own internal capabilities, while differentiating itself from its competitors.
2. What is reengineering?	Reengineering is the rethinking of business processes, such as the order-delivery process, to improve critical performance measures such as cost, quality, and customer satisfaction.
3. How can an organization translate its strategy into a set of performance measures?	An organization can develop a balanced scorecard that provides the framework for a strategic measurement and management system. The balanced scorecard measures performance from four perspectives: (1) financial, (2) customer, (3) internal business processes, and (4) learning and growth. To build their balanced scorecards, organizations often create strategy maps to represent the cause-and-effect relationships across various strategic objectives.
4. How can a company analyze changes in operating income to evaluate the success of its strategy?	To evaluate the success of its strategy, a company can subdivide the change in operating income into growth, price-recovery, and productivity components. The growth component measures the change in revenues and costs from selling more or less units, assuming nothing else has changed. The price-recovery component measures changes in revenues and costs solely as a result of changes in the prices of outputs and inputs. The productivity component measures the decrease in costs from using fewer inputs, a better mix of inputs, and reducing capacity. If a company is successful in implementing its strategy, changes in components of operating income align closely with strategy.
5. How can a company identify and manage unused capacity?	A company must first distinguish engineered costs from discretionary costs. Engineered costs result from a cause-and-effect relationship between output and the resources needed to produce that output. Discretionary costs arise from periodic (usually annual) management decisions regarding the amount of cost to be incurred. Discretionary costs are not tied to a cause-and-effect relationship between inputs and outputs. Identifying unused capacity is easier for engineered costs and more difficult for discretionary costs. Downsizing is an approach to managing unused capacity that matches costs to the activities that need to be performed to operate effectively.

Appendix

Productivity Measurement

Productivity measures the relationship between actual inputs used (both quantities and costs) and actual outputs produced. The lower the inputs for a given quantity of outputs or the higher the outputs for a given quantity of inputs, the higher the productivity. Measuring productivity improvements over time highlights the specific input-output relationships that contribute to cost leadership.

Partial Productivity Measures

Partial productivity, the most frequently used productivity measure, compares the quantity of output produced with the quantity of an individual input used. In its most common form, partial productivity is expressed as a ratio:

$$\text{Partial productivity} = \frac{\text{Quantity of output produced}}{\text{Quantity of input used}}$$

The higher the ratio, the greater the productivity.

Consider direct materials productivity at Chipset in 2011.

$$\frac{\text{Direct materials}}{\text{partial productivity}} = \frac{\text{Quantity of CX1 units produced during 2011}}{\text{Quantity of direct materials used to produce CX1 in 2011}}$$

$$= \frac{1{,}150{,}000 \text{ units of CX1}}{2{,}900{,}000 \text{ sq. cm. of direct materials}}$$

$$= 0.397 \text{ units of CX1 per sq. cm. of direct materials}$$

Note direct materials partial productivity ignores Chipset's other input, manufacturing conversion capacity. Partial-productivity measures become more meaningful when comparisons are made that examine productivity changes over time, either across different facilities or relative to a benchmark. Exhibit 13-6 presents partial-productivity measures for Chipset's inputs for 2011 and the comparable 2010 inputs that would have been used to produce 2011 output, using information from the productivity-component calculations on page 482. These measures compare actual inputs used in 2011 to produce 1,150,000 units of CX1 with inputs that would have been used in 2011 had the input–output relationship from 2010 continued in 2011.

Evaluating Changes in Partial Productivities

Note how the partial-productivity measures differ for variable-cost and fixed-cost components. For variable-cost elements, such as direct materials, productivity improvements measure the reduction in input resources used to produce output (3,450,000 square centimeters of silicon wafers to 2,900,000 square centimeters). For fixed-cost elements such as manufacturing conversion capacity, partial productivity measures the reduction in overall capacity from 2010 to 2011 (3,750,000 square centimeters of silicon wafers to 3,500,000 square centimeters) regardless of the amount of capacity actually used in each period.

An advantage of partial-productivity measures is that they focus on a single input. As a result, they are simple to calculate and easily understood by operations personnel. Managers and operators examine these numbers and try to understand the reasons for the productivity changes—such as, better training of workers, lower labor turnover, better incentives, improved methods, or substitution of materials for labor. Isolating the relevant factors helps Chipset implement and sustain these practices in the future.

For all their advantages, partial-productivity measures also have serious drawbacks. Because partial productivity focuses on only one input at a time rather than on all inputs simultaneously, managers cannot evaluate the effect on overall productivity, if (say) manufacturing-conversion-capacity partial productivity increases while direct materials partial productivity decreases. Total factor productivity (TFP), or total productivity, is a measure of productivity that considers all inputs simultaneously.

Exhibit 13-6   Comparing Chipset's Partial Productivities in 2010 and 2011

Input (1)	Partial Productivity in 2011 (2)	Comparable Partial Productivity Based on 2010 Input–Output Relationships (3)	Percentage Change from 2010 to 2011 (4)
Direct materials	$\dfrac{1{,}150{,}000}{2{,}900{,}000} = 0.397$	$\dfrac{1{,}150{,}000}{3{,}450{,}000} = 0.333$	$\dfrac{0.397 - 0.333}{0.333} = 19.2\%$
Manufacturing conversion capacity	$\dfrac{1{,}150{,}000}{3{,}500{,}000} = 0.329$	$\dfrac{1{,}150{,}000}{3{,}750{,}000} = 0.307$	$\dfrac{0.329 - 0.307}{0.307} = 7.2\%$

Total Factor Productivity

Total factor productivity (TFP) is the ratio of the quantity of output produced to the costs of all inputs used based on current-period prices.

$$\text{Total factor productivity} = \frac{\text{Quantity of output produced}}{\text{Costs of all inputs used}}$$

TFP considers all inputs simultaneously and the trade-offs across inputs based on current input prices. Do not think of all productivity measures as physical measures lacking financial content—how many units of output are produced per unit of input. TFP is intricately tied to minimizing total cost—a financial objective.

Calculating and Comparing Total Factor Productivity

We first calculate Chipset's TFP in 2011, using 2011 prices and 1,150,000 units of output produced (based on information from the first part of the productivity-component calculations on p. 482).

$$\frac{\text{Total factor productivity}}{\text{for 2011 using 2011 prices}} = \frac{\text{Quantity of output produced in 2011}}{\text{Costs of inputs used in 2011 based on 2011 prices}}$$

$$= \frac{1{,}150{,}000}{(2{,}900{,}000 \times \$1.50) + (3{,}500{,}000 \times \$4.35)}$$

$$= \frac{1{,}150{,}000}{\$19{,}575{,}000}$$

$$= 0.058748 \text{ units of output per dollar of input cost}$$

By itself, the 2011 TFP of 0.058748 units of CX1 per dollar of input costs is not particularly helpful. We need something to compare the 2011 TFP against. One alternative is to compare TFPs of other similar companies in 2011. However, finding similar companies and obtaining accurate comparable data are often difficult. Companies, therefore, usually compare their own TFPs over time. In the Chipset example, we use as a benchmark TFP calculated using the inputs that Chipset would have used in 2010 to produce 1,150,000 units of CX1 at 2011 prices (that is, we use the costs calculated from the second part of the productivity-component calculations on p. 482). Why do we use 2011 prices? Because using the current year's prices in both calculations controls for input-price differences and focuses the analysis on adjustments the manager made in quantities of inputs in response to changes in prices.

$$\frac{\text{Benchmark}}{\text{TFP}} = \frac{\text{Quantity of output produced in 2011}}{\begin{array}{c}\text{Costs of inputs at 2011 prices that would have been used in 2010} \\ \text{to produce 2011 output}\end{array}}$$

$$= \frac{1{,}150{,}000}{(3{,}450{,}000 \times \$1.50) + (3{,}750{,}000 \times \$4.35)}$$

$$= \frac{1{,}150{,}000}{\$21{,}487{,}500}$$

$$= 0.053519 \text{ units of output per dollar of input cost}$$

Using 2011 prices, TFP increased 9.8% [(058748 − 0.053519) ÷ 0.053519 = 0.098, or 9.8%] from 2010 to 2011. Note that the 9.8% increase in TFP also equals the $1,912,500 gain (Exhibit 13-5, column 4) divided by the $19,575,000 of actual costs incurred in 2011 (Exhibit 13-5, column 5). Total factor productivity increased because Chipset produced more output per dollar of input cost in 2011 relative to 2010, measured in both years using 2011 prices. The gain in TFP occurs because Chipset increases the partial productivities of individual inputs and, consistent with its strategy, combines inputs to lower costs. Note that increases in TFP cannot be due to differences in input prices because we used 2011 prices to evaluate both the inputs that Chipset would have used in 2010 to produce 1,150,000 units of CX1 and the inputs actually used in 2011.

Using Partial and Total Factor Productivity Measures

A major advantage of TFP is that it measures the combined productivity of all inputs used to produce output and explicitly considers gains from using fewer physical inputs as well as substitution among inputs. Managers can analyze these numbers to understand the reasons for changes in TFP—for example, better human resource management practices, higher quality of materials, or improved manufacturing methods.

Although TFP measures are comprehensive, operations personnel find financial TFP measures more difficult to understand and less useful than physical partial-productivity measures. For example, companies that are more labor intensive than Chipset use manufacturing-labor partial-productivity measures. However, if productivity-based bonuses depend on gains in manufacturing-labor partial productivity alone, workers have incentives to substitute materials (and capital) for labor. This substitution improves their own productivity measure, while possibly decreasing the overall productivity of the company as measured by TFP. To overcome these incentive problems, some companies—for example, TRW, Eaton, and Whirlpool—explicitly adjust bonuses based on manufacturing-labor partial productivity for the effects of other factors such as investments in new equipment and higher levels of scrap. That is, they combine partial productivity with TFP-like measures.

Many companies such as Behlen Manufacturing, a steel fabricator, and Dell Computers use both partial productivity and total factor productivity to evaluate performance. *Partial productivity and TFP measures work best together because the strengths of one offset the weaknesses of the other.*

Terms to Learn

This chapter and the Glossary at the end of the book contain definitions of the following important terms:

balanced scorecard (**p. 470**)

cost leadership (**p. 468**)

discretionary costs (**p. 486**)

downsizing (**p. 487**)

engineered costs (**p. 486**)

growth component (**p. 479**)

partial productivity (**p. 493**)

price-recovery component (**p. 479**)

product differentiation (**p. 468**)

productivity (**p. 492**)

productivity component (**p. 479**)

reengineering (**p. 469**)

rightsizing (**p. 487**)

strategy map (**p. 471**)

total factor productivity (TFP) (**p. 494**)

unused capacity (**p. 486**)

Assignment Material

Questions

13-1   Define strategy.

13-2   Describe the five key forces to consider when analyzing an industry.

13-3   Describe two generic strategies.

13-4   What is a customer preference map and why is it useful?

13-5   What is reengineering?

13-6   What are four key perspectives in the balanced scorecard?

13-7   What is a strategy map?

13-8   Describe three features of a good balanced scorecard.

13-9   What are three important pitfalls to avoid when implementing a balanced scorecard?

13-10 Describe three key components in doing a strategic analysis of operating income.

13-11 Why might an analyst incorporate the industry-market-size factor and the interrelationships among the growth, price-recovery, and productivity components into a strategic analysis of operating income?

13-12 How does an engineered cost differ from a discretionary cost?

13-13 What is downsizing?

13-14 What is a partial-productivity measure?

13-15 "We are already measuring total factor productivity. Measuring partial productivities would be of no value." Do you agree? Comment briefly.

Exercises

13-16 **Balanced scorecard.** Ridgecrest Corporation manufactures corrugated cardboard boxes. It competes and plans to grow by selling high-quality boxes at a low price and by delivering them to customers quickly after receiving customers' orders. There are many other manufacturers who produce similar boxes. Ridgecrest believes that continuously improving its manufacturing processes and having satisfied employees are critical to implementing its strategy in 2012.

1. Is Ridgecrest's 2012 strategy one of product differentiation or cost leadership? Explain briefly.

Required

2. Kearney Corporation, a competitor of Ridgecrest, manufactures corrugated boxes with more designs and color combinations than Ridgecrest at a higher price. Kearney's boxes are of high quality but require more time to produce and so have longer delivery times. Draw a simple customer preference map as in Exhibit 13-1 for Ridgecrest and Kearney using the attributes of price, delivery time, quality, and design.

3. Draw a strategy map as in Exhibit 13-2 with two strategic objectives you would expect to see under each balanced scorecard perspective.

4. For each strategic objective indicate a measure you would expect to see in Ridgecrest's balanced scorecard for 2012.

13-17 Analysis of growth, price-recovery, and productivity components (continuation of 13-16). An analysis of Ridgecrest's operating-income changes between 2011 and 2012 shows the following:

Operating income for 2011	$1,850,000
Add growth component	85,000
Deduct price-recovery component	(72,000)
Add productivity component	150,000
Operating income for 2011	$2,013,000

The industry market size for corrugated cardboard boxes did not grow in 2012, input prices did not change, and Ridgecrest reduced the prices of its boxes.

Required

1. Was Ridgecrest's gain in operating income in 2012 consistent with the strategy you identified in requirement 1 of Exercise 13-16?

2. Explain the productivity component. In general, does it represent savings in only variable costs, only fixed costs, or both variable and fixed costs?

13-18 Strategy, balanced scorecard, merchandising operation. Roberto & Sons buys T-shirts in bulk, applies its own trendsetting silk-screen designs, and then sells the T-shirts to a number of retailers. Roberto wants to be known for its trendsetting designs, and it wants every teenager to be seen in a distinctive Roberto T-shirt. Roberto presents the following data for its first two years of operations, 2010 and 2011.

		2010	2011
1	Number of T-shirts purchased	200,000	250,000
2	Number of T-shirts discarded	2,000	3,300
3	Number of T-shirts sold (row 1 − row 2)	198,000	246,700
4	Average selling price	$25.00	$26.00
5	Average cost per T-shirt	$10.00	$8.50
6	Administrative capacity (number of customers)	4,000	3,750
7	Administrative costs	$1,200,000	$1,162,500
8	Administrative cost per customer (row 8 ÷ row 7)	$300	$310

Administrative costs depend on the number of customers that Roberto has created capacity to support, not on the actual number of customers served. Roberto had 3,600 customers in 2010 and 3,500 customers in 2011.

Required

1. Is Roberto 's strategy one of product differentiation or cost leadership? Explain briefly.

2. Describe briefly the key measures Roberto should include in its balanced scorecard and the reasons it should do so.

13-19 Strategic analysis of operating income (continuation of 13-18). Refer to Exercise 13-18.

Required

1. Calculate Roberto's operating income in both 2010 and 2011.

2. Calculate the growth, price-recovery, and productivity components that explain the change in operating income from 2010 to 2011.

3. Comment on your answers in requirement 2. What does each of these components indicate?

13-20 Analysis of growth, price-recovery, and productivity components (continuation of 13-19). Refer to Exercise 13-19. Suppose that the market for silk-screened T-shirts grew by 10% during 2011. All increases in sales greater than 10% are the result of Roberto's strategic actions.

Required Calculate the change in operating income from 2010 to 2011 due to growth in market size, product differentiation, and cost leadership. How successful has Roberto been in implementing its strategy? Explain.

13-21 Identifying and managing unused capacity (continuation of 13-18). Refer to Exercise 13-18.

Required

1. Calculate the amount and cost of unused administrative capacity at the beginning of 2011, based on the actual number of customers Roberto served in 2011.

2. Suppose Roberto can only add or reduce administrative capacity in increments of 250 customers. What is the maximum amount of costs that Roberto can save in 2011 by downsizing administrative capacity?

3. What factors, other than cost, should Roberto consider before it downsizes administrative capacity?

13-22 Strategy, balanced scorecard. Stanmore Corporation makes a special-purpose machine, D4H, used in the textile industry. Stanmore has designed the D4H machine for 2011 to be distinct from its competitors. It has been generally regarded as a superior machine. Stanmore presents the following data for 2010 and 2011.

	2010	2011
1. Units of D4H produced and sold	200	210
2. Selling price	$40,000	$42,000
3. Direct materials (kilograms)	300,000	310,000
4. Direct material cost per kilogram	$8	$8.50
5. Manufacturing capacity in units of D4H	250	250
6. Total conversion costs	$2,000,000	$2,025,000
7. Conversion cost per unit of capacity (row 6 ÷ row 5)	$8,000	$8,100
8. Selling and customer-service capacity	100 customers	95 customers
9. Total selling and customer-service costs	$1,000,000	$940,500
10. Selling and customer-service capacity cost per customer (row 9 ÷ row 8)	$10,000	$9,900

Stanmore produces no defective machines, but it wants to reduce direct materials usage per D4H machine in 2011. Conversion costs in each year depend on production capacity defined in terms of D4H units that can be produced, not the actual units produced. Selling and customer-service costs depend on the number of customers that Stanmore can support, not the actual number of customers it serves. Stanmore has 75 customers in 2010 and 80 customers in 2011.

1. Is Stanmore's strategy one of product differentiation or cost leadership? Explain briefly. **Required**
2. Describe briefly key measures that you would include in Stanmore's balanced scorecard and the reasons for doing so.

13-23 **Strategic analysis of operating income (continuation of 13-22).** Refer to Exercise 13-22.

1. Calculate the operating income of Stanmore Corporation in 2010 and 2011. **Required**
2. Calculate the growth, price-recovery, and productivity components that explain the change in operating income from 2010 to 2011.
3. Comment on your answer in requirement 2. What do these components indicate?

13-24 **Analysis of growth, price-recovery, and productivity components (continuation of 13-23).** Suppose that during 2011, the market for Stanmore's special-purpose machines grew by 3%. All increases in market share (that is, sales increases greater than 3%) are the result of Stanmore's strategic actions.

Calculate how much of the change in operating income from 2010 to 2011 is due to the industry-market-size factor, product differentiation, and cost leadership. How successful has Stanmore been in implementing its strategy? Explain. **Required**

13-25 **Identifying and managing unused capacity (continuation of 13-22).** Refer to Exercise 13-22.

1. Calculate the amount and cost of (a) unused manufacturing capacity and (b) unused selling and customer-service capacity at the beginning of 2011 based on actual production and actual number of customers served in 2011. **Required**
2. Suppose Stanmore can add or reduce its manufacturing capacity in increments of 30 units. What is the maximum amount of costs that Stanmore could save in 2011 by downsizing manufacturing capacity?
3. Stanmore, in fact, does not eliminate any of its unused manufacturing capacity. Why might Stanmore not downsize?

13-26 **Strategy, balanced scorecard, service company.** Westlake Corporation is a small information-systems consulting firm that specializes in helping companies implement standard sales-management software. The market for Westlake's services is very competitive. To compete successfully, Westlake must deliver quality service at a low cost. Westlake presents the following data for 2010 and 2011.

	2010	2011
1. Number of jobs billed	60	70
2. Selling price per job	$50,000	$48,000
3. Software-implementation labor-hours	30,000	32,000
4. Cost per software-implementation labor-hour	$60	$63
5. Software-implementation support capacity (number of jobs it can do)	90	90
6. Total cost of software-implementation support	$360,000	$369,000
7. Software-implementation support-capacity cost per job (row 6 ÷ row 5)	$4,000	$4,100

Software-implementation labor-hour costs are variable costs. Software-implementation support costs for each year depend on the software-implementation support capacity Westlake chooses to maintain each year (that is the number of jobs it can do each year). It does not vary with the actual number of jobs done that year.

Required

1. Is Westlake Corporation's strategy one of product differentiation or cost leadership? Explain briefly.
2. Describe key measures you would include in Westlake's balanced scorecard and your reasons for doing so.

13-27 Strategic analysis of operating income (continuation of 13-26). Refer to Exercise 13-26.

Required

1. Calculate the operating income of Westlake Corporation in 2010 and 2011.
2. Calculate the growth, price-recovery, and productivity components that explain the change in operating income from 2010 to 2011.
3. Comment on your answer in requirement 2. What do these components indicate?

13-28 Analysis of growth, price-recovery, and productivity components (continuation of 13-27). Suppose that during 2011 the market for implementing sales-management software increases by 5%. Assume that any decrease in selling price and any increase in market share more than 5% are the result of strategic choices by Westlake's management to implement its strategy.

Required

Calculate how much of the change in operating income from 2010 to 2011 is due to the industry-market-size factor, product differentiation, and cost leadership. How successful has Westlake been in implementing its strategy? Explain.

13-29 Identifying and managing unused capacity (continuation of 13-26). Refer to Exercise 13-26.

Required

1. Calculate the amount and cost of unused software-implementation support capacity at the beginning of 2011, based on the number of jobs actually done in 2011.
2. Suppose Westlake can add or reduce its software-implementation support capacity in increments of 15 units. What is the maximum amount of costs that Westlake could save in 2011 by downsizing software-implementation support capacity?
3. Westlake, in fact, does not eliminate any of its unused software-implementation support capacity. Why might Westlake not downsize?

MyAccountingLab

Problems

13-30 Balanced scorecard and strategy. Music Master Company manufactures an MP3 player called the Mini. The company sells the player to discount stores throughout the country. This player is significantly less expensive than similar products sold by Music Master's competitors, but the Mini offers just four giga-bytes of space, compared with eight offered by competitor Vantage Manufacturing. Furthermore, the Mini has experienced production problems that have resulted in significant rework costs. Vantage's model has an excellent reputation for quality, but is considerably more expensive.

Required

1. Draw a simple customer preference map for Music Master and Vantage using the attributes of price, quality, and storage capacity. Use the format of Exhibit 13-1.
2. Is Music Master's current strategy that of product differentiation or cost leadership?
3. Music Master would like to improve quality and decrease costs by improving processes and training workers to reduce rework. Music Master's managers believe the increased quality will increase sales. Draw a strategy map as in Exhibit 13-2 describing the cause-and-effect relationships among the strategic objectives you would expect to see in Music Master's balanced scorecard.
4. For each strategic objective suggest a measure you would recommend in Music Master's balanced scorecard.

13-31 Strategic analysis of operating income (continuation of 13-30). Refer to Problem 13-30. As a result of the actions taken, quality has significantly improved in 2011 while rework and unit costs of the Mini have decreased. Music Master has reduced manufacturing capacity because capacity is no longer needed to support rework. Music Master has also lowered the Mini's selling price to gain market share and unit sales have increased. Information about the current period (2011) and last period (2010) follows:

	2010	2011
1. Units of Mini produced and sold	8,000	9,000
2. Selling price	$45	$43
3. Ounces of direct materials used	32,000	33,000
4. Direct material cost per ounce	$3.50	$3.50
5. Manufacturing capacity in units	12,000	11,000
6. Total conversion costs	$156,000	$143,000
7. Conversion cost per unit of capacity (row 6 ÷ row 5)	$13	$13
8. Selling and customer-service capacity	90 customers	90 customers
9. Total selling and customer-service costs	$45,000	$49,500
10. Selling and customer-service capacity cost per customer (row 9 ÷ row 8)	$500	$550

Conversion costs in each year depend on production capacity defined in terms of units of Mini that can be produced, not the actual units produced. Selling and customer-service costs depend on the number of customers that Music Master can support, not the actual number of customers it serves. Music Master has 70 customers in 2010 and 80 customers in 2011.

1. Calculate operating income of Music Master Company for 2010 and 2011.
2. Calculate the growth, price-recovery, and productivity components that explain the change in operating income from 2010 to 2011.
3. Comment on your answer in requirement 2. What do these components indicate?

Required

13-32 Analysis of growth, price-recovery, and productivity components (continuation of 13-31). Suppose that during 2011, the market for MP3 players grew 3%. All decreases in the selling price of the Mini and increases in market share (that is, sales increases greater than 3%) are the result of Music Master's strategic actions.

Calculate how much of the change in operating income from 2010 to 2011 is due to the industry-market-size factor, product differentiation, and cost leadership. How does this relate to Music Master's strategy and its success in implementation? Explain.

Required

13-33 Identifying and managing unused capacity (continuation of 13-31) Refer to the information for Music Master Company in 13-31.

1. Calculate the amount and cost of (a) unused manufacturing capacity and (b) unused selling and customer-service capacity at the beginning of 2011 based on actual production and actual number of customers served in 2011.
2. Suppose Music Master can add or reduce its selling and customer-service capacity in increments of five customers. What is the maximum amount of costs that Music Master could save in 2011 by downsizing selling and customer-service capacity?
3. Music Master, in fact, does not eliminate any of its unused selling and customer-service capacity. Why might Music Master not downsize?

Required

13-34 Balanced scorecard. Following is a random-order listing of perspectives, strategic objectives, and performance measures for the balanced scorecard.

Perspectives	Performance Measures
Internal business process	Percentage of defective-product units
Customer	Return on assets
Learning and growth	Number of patents
Financial	Employee turnover rate
Strategic Objectives	Net income
Acquire new customers	Customer profitability
Increase shareholder value	Percentage of processes with real-time feedback
Retain customers	Return on sales
Improve manufacturing quality	Average job-related training-hours per employee
Develop profitable customers	Return on equity
Increase proprietary products	Percentage of on-time deliveries by suppliers
Increase information-system capabilities	Product cost per unit
Enhance employee skills	Profit per salesperson
On-time delivery by suppliers	Percentage of error-free invoices
Increase profit generated by each salesperson	Customer cost per unit
Introduce new products	Earnings per share
Minimize invoice-error rate	Number of new customers
	Percentage of customers retained

For each perspective, select those strategic objectives from the list that best relate to it. For each strategic objective, select the most appropriate performance measure(s) from the list.

Required

13-35 Balanced scorecard. (R. Kaplan, adapted) Caltex, Inc., refines gasoline and sells it through its own Caltex Gas Stations. On the basis of market research, Caltex determines that 60% of the overall gasoline market consists of "service-oriented customers," medium- to high-income individuals who are willing to pay a higher price for gas if the gas stations can provide excellent customer service, such as a clean facility, a convenience store, friendly employees, a quick turnaround, the ability to pay by credit card, and high-octane premium gasoline. The remaining 40% of the overall market are "price shoppers" who look to buy the cheapest gasoline available. Caltex's strategy is to focus on the 60% of service-oriented customers. Caltex's balanced scorecard for 2011 follows. For brevity, the initiatives taken under each objective are omitted.

Objectives	Measures	Target Performance	Actual Performance
Financial Perspective			
Increase shareholder value	Operating-income changes from price recovery	$90,000,000	$95,000,000
	Operating-income changes from growth	$65,000,000	$67,000,000
Customer Perspective			
Increase market share	Market share of overall gasoline market	10%	9.8%
Internal-Business-Process Perspective			
Improve gasoline quality	Quality index	94 points	95 points
Improve refinery performance	Refinery-reliability index (%)	91%	91%
Ensure gasoline availability	Product-availability index (%)	99%	100%
Learning-and-Growth Perspective			
Increase refinery process capability	Percentage of refinery processes with advanced controls	88%	90%

Required

1. Was Caltex successful in implementing its strategy in 2011? Explain your answer.
2. Would you have included some measure of employee satisfaction and employee training in the learning-and-growth perspective? Are these objectives critical to Caltex for implementing its strategy? Why or why not? Explain briefly.
3. Explain how Caltex did not achieve its target market share in the total gasoline market but still exceeded its financial targets. Is "market share of overall gasoline market" the correct measure of market share? Explain briefly.
4. Is there a cause-and-effect linkage between improvements in the measures in the internal business-process perspective and the measure in the customer perspective? That is, would you add other measures to the internal-business-process perspective or the customer perspective? Why or why not? Explain briefly.
5. Do you agree with Caltex's decision not to include measures of changes in operating income from productivity improvements under the financial perspective of the balanced scorecard? Explain briefly.

13-36 Balanced scorecard. Lee Corporation manufactures various types of color laser printers in a highly automated facility with high fixed costs. The market for laser printers is competitive. The various color laser printers on the market are comparable in terms of features and price. Lee believes that satisfying customers with products of high quality at low costs is key to achieving its target profitability. For 2011, Lee plans to achieve higher quality and lower costs by improving yields and reducing defects in its manufacturing operations. Lee will train workers and encourage and empower them to take the necessary actions. Currently, a significant amount of Lee's capacity is used to produce products that are defective and cannot be sold. Lee expects that higher yields will reduce the capacity that Lee needs to manufacture products. Lee does not anticipate that improving manufacturing will automatically lead to lower costs because Lee has high fixed costs. To reduce fixed costs per unit, Lee could lay off employees and sell equipment, or it could use the capacity to produce and sell more of its current products or improved models of its current products.

Lee's balanced scorecard (initiatives omitted) for the just-completed fiscal year 2011 follows:

Objectives	Measures	Target Performance	Actual Performance
Financial Perspective			
Increase shareholder value	Operating-income changes from productivity improvements	$1,000,000	$400,000
	Operating-income changes from growth	$1,500,000	$600,000
Customer Perspective			
Increase market share	Market share in color laser printers	5%	4.6%
Internal-Business-Process Perspective			
Improve manufacturing quality	Yield	82%	85%
Reduce delivery time to customers	Order-delivery time	25 days	22 days
Learning-and-Growth Perspective			
Develop process skills	Percentage of employees trained in process and quality management	90%	92%
Enhance information-system capabilities	Percentage of manufacturing processes with real-time feedback	85%	87%

Required

1. Was Lee successful in implementing its strategy in 2011? Explain.
2. Is Lee's balanced scorecard useful in helping the company understand why it did not reach its target market share in 2011? If it is, explain why. If it is not, explain what other measures you might want to add under the customer perspective and why.
3. Would you have included some measure of employee satisfaction in the learning-and-growth perspective and new-product development in the internal-business-process perspective? That is, do you think employee satisfaction and development of new products are critical for Lee to implement its strategy? Why or why not? Explain briefly.
4. What problems, if any, do you see in Lee improving quality and significantly downsizing to eliminate unused capacity?

13-37 Partial productivity measurement. Gerhart Company manufactures wallets from fabric. In 2011, Gerhart made 2,520,000 wallets using 2,000,000 yards of fabric. In 2011, Gerhart has capacity to make 3,307,500 wallets and incurs a cost of $9,922,500 for this capacity. In 2012, Gerhart plans to make 2,646,000 wallets, make fabric use more efficient, and reduce capacity.

Suppose that in 2012 Gerhart makes 2,646,000 wallets, uses 1,764,000 yards of fabric, and reduces capacity to 2,700,000 wallets, incurring a cost of $8,370,000 for this capacity.

Required

1. Calculate the partial-productivity ratios for materials and conversion (capacity costs) for 2012, and compare them to a benchmark for 2011 calculated based on 2012 output.
2. How can Gerhart Company use the information from the partial-productivity calculations?

13-38 Total factor productivity (continuation of 13-37). Refer to the data for Problem 13-37. Assume the fabric costs $3.70 per yard in 2012 and $3.85 per yard in 2011.

Required

1. Compute Gerhart Company's total factor productivity (TFP) for 2012.
2. Compare TFP for 2012 with a benchmark TFP for 2011 inputs based on 2012 prices and output.
3. What additional information does TFP provide that partial productivity measures do not?

Collaborative Learning Problem

13-39 Strategic analysis of operating income. Halsey Company sells women's clothing. Halsey's strategy is to offer a wide selection of clothes and excellent customer service and to charge a premium price. Halsey presents the following data for 2010 and 2011. For simplicity, assume that each customer purchases one piece of clothing.

	2010	2011
1. Pieces of clothing purchased and sold	40,000	40,000
2. Average selling price	$60	$59
3. Average cost per piece of clothing	$40	$41
4. Selling and customer-service capacity	51,000 customers	43,000 customers
5. Selling and customer-service costs	$357,000	$296,700
6. Selling and customer-service capacity cost per customer (row 5 ÷ row 4)	$7 per customer	$6.90 per customer
7. Purchasing and administrative capacity	980 designs	850 designs
8. Purchasing and administrative costs	$245,000	$204,000
9. Purchasing and administrative capacity cost per distinct design (row 8 ÷ row 7)	$250 per design	$240 per design

Total selling and customer-service costs depend on the number of customers that Halsey has created capacity to support, not the actual number of customers that Halsey serves. Total purchasing and administrative costs depend on purchasing and administrative capacity that Halsey has created (defined in terms of the number of distinct clothing designs that Halsey can purchase and administer). Purchasing and administrative costs do not depend on the actual number of distinct clothing designs purchased. Halsey purchased 930 distinct designs in 2010 and 820 distinct designs in 2011.

At the start of 2010, Halsey planned to increase operating income by 10% over operating income in 2011.

1. Is Halsey's strategy one of product differentiation or cost leadership? Explain.
2. Calculate Halsey's operating income in 2010 and 2011.
3. Calculate the growth, price-recovery, and productivity components of changes in operating income between 2010 and 2011.
4. Does the strategic analysis of operating income indicate Halsey was successful in implementing its strategy in 2011? Explain.

Required

14 Cost Allocation, Customer-Profitability Analysis, and Sales-Variance Analysis

▶ Learning Objectives

1. Identify four purposes for allocating costs to cost objects

2. Understand criteria to guide cost-allocation decisions

3. Discuss decisions faced when collecting costs in indirect-cost pools

4. Discuss why a company's revenues and costs can differ across customers

5. Identify the importance of customer-profitability profiles

6. Subdivide the sales-volume variance into the sales-mix variance and the sales-quantity variance

Companies desperately want to make their customers happy.

But how far should they go to please them, and at what price? At what point are you better off not doing business with some customers at all? The following article explains why it's so important for managers to be able to figure out how profitable each of their customers is.

Minding the Store: Analyzing Customers, Best Buy Decides Not All Are Welcome[1]

As the former CEO of Best Buy, Brad Anderson decided to implement a rather unorthodox approach to retail: to separate his 1.5 million daily customers into "angels" and "devils."

The angels, customers who increase profits by purchasing high-definition televisions, portable electronics, and newly released DVDs without waiting for markdowns or rebates, are favored over the devils, who buy products, apply for rebates, return the purchases, and then buy them back at returned-merchandise discounts. These devils focus their spending on "loss leaders," discounted merchandise designed to encourage store traffic, but then flip the goods at a profit on sites like eBay.com.

Best Buy found that its most desirable customers fell into five distinct groups: upper-income men, suburban mothers, small-business owners, young family men, and technology enthusiasts. Male technology enthusiasts, nicknamed Buzzes, are early adopters, interested in buying and showing off the latest gadgets. Each store analyzes the demographics of its local market, and then focuses on two of these groups. For example, at stores popular with Buzzes, Best Buy sets up videogame areas with leather chairs and game players hooked to mammoth, plasma-screen televisions.

Best Buy also began working on ways to deter customers who drove profits down. It couldn't bar them from its stores. Starting in 2004, however, it began taking steps to put a stop to their most damaging practices by enforcing a restocking fee of 15% of the purchase price on returned merchandise. To discourage customers who return items with the intention of repurchasing them at an "open-box" discount, Best Buy started reselling the returned items

---

[1] *Sources*: Bustillo, Miguel. 2009. Best Buy confronts newer nemesis. *Wall Street Journal*, March 16; McWilliams, Gary. 2004. Minding the store: Analyzing customers, Best Buy decides not all are welcome. *Wall Street Journal*, November 8.

over the Internet, so the goods didn't reappear in the store where they were originally purchased.

This strategy stimulated growth for several years at Best Buy and helped the company survive the economic downturn while Circuit City, its leading competitor, went bankrupt. But Best Buy's angels and devils strategy now must confront a new competitor, Walmart. With Walmart's focus on consumers seeking no-frills bargains, Best Buy intends to match its new competitor's prices while leveraging its tech-savvy sales force to help consumers navigate increasingly complicated technology.

To determine which product, customer, program, or department is profitable, organizations must decide how to allocate costs. Best Buy analyzed its operations and chose to allocate costs towards serving its most profitable customers. In this chapter and the next, we provide insight into cost allocation. The emphasis in this chapter is on macro issues in cost allocation: allocation of costs into divisions, plants, and customers. Chapter 15 describes micro issues in cost allocation—allocating support-department costs to operating departments and allocating costs to various cost objects—as well as revenue allocations.

Purposes of Cost Allocation

Recall that *indirect costs* of a particular cost object are costs that are related to that cost object but cannot be traced to it in an economically feasible (cost-effective) way. These costs often comprise a large percentage of the overall costs assigned to such cost objects as products, customers, and distribution channels. Why do managers allocate indirect costs to these cost objects? Exhibit 14-1 illustrates four purposes of cost allocation.

Different sets of costs are appropriate for different purposes described in Exhibit 14-1. Consider costs in different business functions of the value chain illustrated as follows:

Learning Objective 1

Identify four purposes for allocating costs to cost objects

. . . to provide information for decisions, motivate managers, justify costs, and measure income

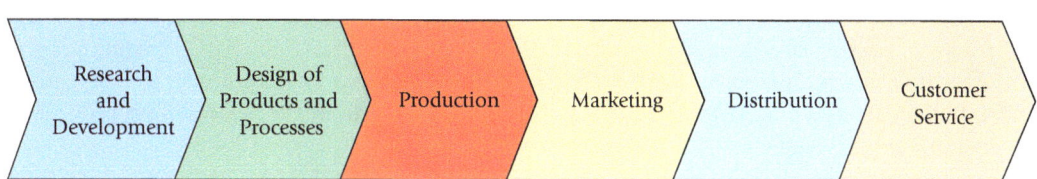

Research and Development | Design of Products and Processes | Production | Marketing | Distribution | Customer Service

For some decisions related to the economic-decision purpose (for example, long-run product pricing), the costs in all six functions are relevant. For other decisions, particularly short-run economic decisions (for example, make or buy decisions), costs from only one or two functions, such as design and manufacturing, might be relevant.

Exhibit 14-1

Purposes of Cost Allocation

Purpose	Examples
1. To provide information for economic decisions	To decide whether to add a new airline flight To decide whether to manufacture a component part of a television set or to purchase it from another manufacturer To decide on the selling price for a customized product or service To evaluate the cost of available capacity used to support different products
2. To motivate managers and other employees	To encourage the design of products that are simpler to manufacture or less costly to service To encourage sales representatives to emphasize high-margin products or services
3. To justify costs or compute reimbursement amounts	To cost products at a "fair" price, often required by law and government defense contracts To compute reimbursement for a consulting firm based on a percentage of the cost savings resulting from the implementation of its recommendations
4. To measure income and assets	To cost inventories for reporting to external parties To cost inventories for reporting to tax authorities

For the motivation purpose, costs from more than one but not all business functions are often included to emphasize to decision makers how costs in different functions are related to one another. For example, to estimate product costs, product designers at companies such as Hitachi and Toshiba include costs of production, distribution, and customer service. The goal is to focus designers' attention on how different product-design alternatives affect total costs.

For the cost-reimbursement purpose, a particular contract will often stipulate what costs will be reimbursed. For instance, cost-reimbursement rules for U.S. government contracts explicitly exclude marketing costs.

For the purpose of income and asset measurement for reporting to external parties under GAAP, only manufacturing costs, and in some cases product-design costs, are inventoriable and allocated to products. In the United States, R&D costs in most industries, marketing, distribution, and customer-service costs are period costs that are expensed as they are incurred. Under International Financial Reporting Standards (IFRS), research costs must be expensed as incurred but development costs must be capitalized if a product/process has reached technical feasibility and the firm has the intention and ability to use or sell the future asset.

Criteria to Guide Cost-Allocation Decisions

After identifying the purposes of cost allocation, managers and management accountants must decide how to allocate costs.

Exhibit 14-2 presents four criteria used to guide cost-allocation decisions. These decisions affect both the number of indirect-cost pools and the cost-allocation base for each indirect-cost pool. We emphasize the superiority of the cause-and-effect and the benefits-received criteria, especially when the purpose of cost allocation is to provide information for economic decisions or to motivate managers and employees.[2] Cause and effect is the primary criterion used in activity-based costing (ABC) applications. ABC systems use the concept of a cost hierarchy to identify the cost drivers that best demonstrate the cause-and-effect relationship between each activity and the costs in the related cost pool. The cost drivers are then chosen as cost-allocation bases.

Fairness and ability-to-bear are less-frequently-used and more problematic criteria than cause-and-effect or benefits-received. Fairness is a difficult criterion on which to

Decision Point ▶

What are four purposes for allocating costs to cost objects?

Learning Objective 2

Understand criteria to guide cost-allocation decisions

. . . such as identifying factors that cause resources to be consumed

---

[2] The Federal Accounting Standards Advisory Board (which sets standards for management accounting for U.S. government departments and agencies) recommends the following: "Cost assignments should be performed by: (a) directly tracing costs whenever feasible and economically practicable, (b) assigning costs on a cause-and-effect basis, and (c) allocating costs on a reasonable and consistent basis" (*FASAB*, 1995, p. 12).

Exhibit 14-2

Criteria for Cost-Allocation Decisions

1. Cause and Effect. Using this criterion, managers identify the variables that cause resources to be consumed. For example, managers may use hours of testing as the variable when allocating the costs of a quality-testing area to products. Cost allocations based on the cause-and-effect criterion are likely to be the most credible to operating personnel.

2. Benefits Received. Using this criterion, managers identify the beneficiaries of the outputs of the cost object. The costs of the cost object are allocated among the beneficiaries in proportion to the benefits each receives. Consider a corporatewide advertising program that promotes the general image of the corporation rather than any individual product. The costs of this program may be allocated on the basis of division revenues; the higher the revenues, the higher the division's allocated cost of the advertising program. The rationale behind this allocation is that divisions with higher revenues apparently benefited from the advertising more than divisions with lower revenues and, therefore, ought to be allocated more of the advertising costs.

3. Fairness or Equity. This criterion is often cited in government contracts when cost allocations are the basis for establishing a price satisfactory to the government and its suppliers. Cost allocation here is viewed as a "reasonable" or "fair" means of establishing a selling price in the minds of the contracting parties. For most allocation decisions, fairness is a matter of judgment rather than an operational criterion.

4. Ability to Bear. This criterion advocates allocating costs in proportion to the cost object's ability to bear costs allocated to it. An example is the allocation of corporate executive salaries on the basis of division operating income. The presumption is that the more-profitable divisions have a greater ability to absorb corporate headquarters' costs.

obtain agreement. What one party views as fair, another party may view as unfair.[3] For example, a university may view allocating a share of general administrative costs to government contracts as fair because general administrative costs are incurred to support all activities of the university. The government may view the allocation of such costs as unfair because the general administrative costs would have been incurred by the university regardless of whether the government contract existed. Perhaps the fairest way to resolve this issue is to understand, as well as possible, the cause-and-effect relationship between the government contract activity and general administrative costs. In other words, fairness is more a matter of judgment than an easily implementable choice criterion.

To get a sense of the issues that arise when using the ability-to-bear criterion, consider a product that consumes a large amount of indirect costs and currently sells for a price below its direct costs. This product has no ability to bear any of the indirect costs it uses. However, if the indirect costs it consumes are allocated to other products, these other products are subsidizing the product that is losing money. An integrated airline, for example, might allocate fewer costs to its activities in a highly contested market such as freight transportation, thereby subsidizing it via passenger transport. Some airports cross-subsidize costs associated with serving airline passengers through sales of duty-free goods. Such practices provide a distorted view of relative product and service profitability, and have the potential to invite both regulatory scrutiny as well as competitors attempting to undercut artificially higher-priced services.

Most importantly, companies must weigh the costs and benefits when designing and implementing their cost allocations. Companies incur costs not only in collecting data but also in taking the time to educate managers about cost allocations. In general, the more complex the cost allocations, the higher these education costs.

The costs of designing and implementing complex cost allocations are highly visible. Unfortunately, the benefits from using well-designed cost allocations, such as enabling managers to make better-informed sourcing decisions, pricing decisions, cost-control decisions, and so on, are difficult to measure. Nevertheless, when making cost allocations, managers should consider the benefits as well as the costs. As costs of collecting and processing information decrease, companies are building more-detailed cost allocations.

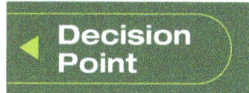

◀ Decision Point

What criteria should managers use to guide cost-allocation decisions?

---

[3] Kaplow and Shavell, in a review of the legal literature, note that "notions of fairness are many and varied. They are analyzed and rationalized by different writers in different way, and they also typically depend upon the circumstances under consideration. Accordingly, it is not possible to identify and consensus view on these notions..." See L. Kaplow and S. Shavell, "Fairness Versus Welfare," *Harvard Law Review* (February 2001); and L. Kaplow and S. Shavell, *Fairness Versus Welfare* (Boston: Harvard University Press, 2002).

Cost Allocation Decisions

Learning Objective 3

Discuss decisions faced when collecting costs in indirect-cost pools

. . . determining the number of cost pools and the costs to be included in each cost pool

In this section, we focus on the first purpose of cost allocation: to provide information for economic decisions, such as pricing, by measuring the full costs of delivering products based on an ABC system.

Chapter 5 described how ABC systems define indirect-cost pools for different activities and use cost drivers as allocation bases to assign costs of indirect-cost pools to products (the second stage of cost allocation). In this section, we focus on the first stage of cost allocation, the assignment of costs to indirect-cost pools.

We will use Consumer Appliances, Inc. (CAI), to illustrate how costs incurred in different parts of a company can be assigned, and then reassigned, for costing products, services, customers, or contracts. CAI has two divisions; each has its own manufacturing plant. The refrigerator division has a plant in Minneapolis, and the clothes dryer division has a plant in St. Paul. CAI's headquarters is in a separate location in Minneapolis. Each division manufactures and sells multiple products that differ in size and complexity.

CAI's management team collects costs at the following levels:

- **Corporate costs**—There are three major categories of corporate costs:
  1. **Treasury costs**—$900,000 of costs incurred for financing the construction of new assembly equipment in the two divisions. The cost of new assembly equipment is $5,200,000 in the refrigerator division and $3,800,000 in the clothes dryer division.
  2. **Human resource management costs**—recruitment and ongoing employee training and development, $1,600,000.
  3. **Corporate administration costs**—executive salaries, rent, and general administration costs, $5,400,000.

- **Division costs**—Each division has two direct-cost categories (direct materials and direct manufacturing labor) and seven indirect-cost pools—one cost pool each for the five activities (design, setup, manufacturing, distribution, and administration), one cost pool to accumulate facility costs, and one cost pool for the allocated corporate treasury costs. Exhibit 14-3 presents data for six of the division indirect-cost pools and cost-allocation bases. (In a later section, we describe how corporate treasury

Exhibit 14-3   Division Indirect-Cost Pools and Cost-Allocation Bases, CAI, for Refrigerator Division (R) and Clothes Dryer Division (CD)

Division Indirect-Cost Pools	Example of Costs		Total Indirect Costs	Cost Hierarchy Category	Cost-Allocation Base	Cause-and-Effect Relationship That Motivates Management's Choice of Allocation Base
Design	Design engineering salaries	(R) (CD)	$6,000,000 4,250,000	Product sustaining	Parts times cubic feet	Complex products (more parts and larger size) require greater design resources.
Setup of machines	Setup labor and equipment cost	(R) (CD)	$3,000,000 2,400,000	Batch level	Setup-hours	Overhead costs of the setup activity increase as setup-hours increase.
Manufacturing operations	Plant and equipment, energy	(R) (CD)	$25,000,000 18,750,000	Output unit level	Machine-hours	Manufacturing-operations overhead costs support machines and, hence, increase with machine usage.
Distribution	Shipping labor and equipment	(R) (CD)	$8,000,000 5,500,000	Output unit level	Cubic feet	Distribution-overhead costs increase with cubic feet of product shipped.
Administration	Division executive salaries	(R) (CD)	$1,000,000 800,000	Facility sustaining	Revenues	Weak relationship between division executive salaries and revenues, but justified by CAI on a benefits-received basis.
Facility	Annual building and space costs	(R) (CD)	$4,500,000 3,500,000	All	Square feet	Facility costs increase with square feet of space.

costs are allocated to each division to create the seventh division indirect-cost pool.) CAI identifies the cost hierarchy category for each cost pool: output-unit level, batch level, product sustaining level, and facility-sustaining level (as described in Chapter 5, p. 149).

Exhibit 14-4 presents an overview diagram of the allocation of corporate and division indirect costs to products of the refrigerator division. Note: The clothes dryer division has its own seven indirect-cost pools used to allocate costs to products. These cost pools and cost-allocation bases parallel the indirect-cost pools and allocation bases for the refrigerator division.

Look first at the middle row of the exhibit, where you see "Division Indirect-Cost Pools," and scan the lower half. It is similar to Exhibit 5-3 (p. 150), which illustrates ABC

Exhibit 14-4 Overview Diagram of Allocation of Corporate and Division Indirect Costs to Products of the Refrigerator Division, CAI

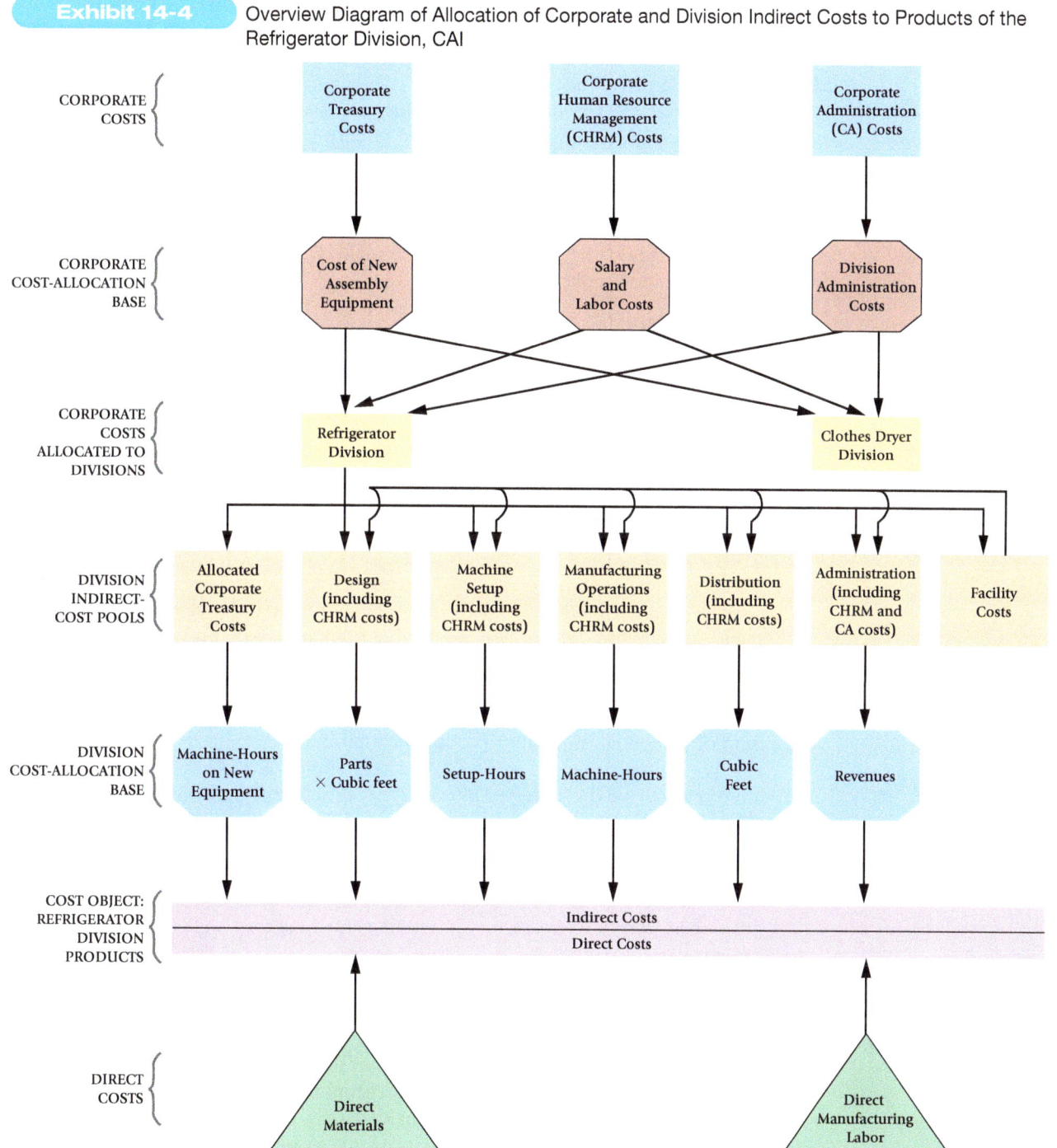

systems using indirect-cost pools and cost drivers for different activities. A major difference in the lower half of Exhibit 14-4 is the cost pool called Facility Costs (far right, middle row), which accumulates all annual costs of buildings and furnishings (such as depreciation) incurred in the division. The arrows in Exhibit 14-4 indicate that CAI allocates facility costs to the five activity-cost pools. Recall from Exhibit 14-3 that CAI uses square feet area required for various activities (design, setup, manufacturing, distribution, and administration) to allocate these facility costs. These activity-cost pools then include the costs of the building and facilities needed to perform the various activities.

The costs in the six remaining indirect-cost pools (that is, after costs of the facility cost pool have been allocated to other cost pools) are allocated to products on the basis of cost drivers described in Exhibit 14-3. These cost drivers are chosen as the cost-allocation bases because there is a cause-and-effect relationship between the cost drivers and the costs in the indirect-cost pool. A cost rate per unit is calculated for each cost-allocation base. Indirect costs are allocated to products on the basis of the total quantity of the cost allocation base for each activity used by the product.

Next focus on the upper half of Exhibit 14-4: how corporate costs are allocated to divisions and then to indirect-cost pools.

Before getting into the details of the allocations, let's first consider some broader choices that CAI faces regarding the allocation of corporate costs.

Allocating Corporate Costs to Divisions and Products

CAI's management team has several choices to make when accumulating and allocating corporate costs to divisions.

1. Which corporate-cost categories should CAI allocate as indirect costs of the divisions? Should CAI allocate all corporate costs or only some of them?
   - Some companies allocate all corporate costs to divisions because corporate costs are incurred to support division activities. Allocating all corporate costs motivates division managers to examine how corporate costs are planned and controlled. Also, companies that want to calculate the full cost of products must allocate all corporate costs to indirect-cost pools of divisions.
   - Other companies do not allocate corporate costs to divisions because these costs are not controllable by division managers.
   - Still other companies allocate only those corporate costs, such as corporate human resources, that are widely perceived as causally related to division activities or that provide explicit benefits to divisions. These companies exclude corporate costs such as corporate donations to charitable foundations because division managers often have no say in making these decisions and because the benefits to the divisions are less evident or too remote. If a company decides not to allocate some or all corporate costs, this results in total company profitability being less than the sum of individual division or product profitabilities.

     For some decision purposes, allocating some but not all corporate costs to divisions may be the preferred alternative. Consider the performance evaluation of division managers. The controllability notion (see p. 200) is frequently used to justify excluding some corporate costs from division reports. For example, salaries of the top management at corporate headquarters are often excluded from responsibility accounting reports of division managers. Although divisions tend to benefit from these corporate costs, division managers argue they have no say in ("are not responsible for") how much of these corporate resources they use or how much they cost. The contrary argument is that full allocation is justified because the divisions receive benefits from all corporate costs.

2. When allocating corporate costs to divisions, should CAI allocate only costs that vary with division activity or should the company assign fixed costs as well? Companies allocate both variable and fixed costs to divisions and then to products, because the resulting product costs are useful for making long-run strategic decisions, such as which products to sell and at what price. To make good long-run decisions, managers

need to know the cost of all resources (whether variable or fixed) required to produce products. Why? Because in the long run, firms can manage the levels of virtually all of their costs; very few costs are truly fixed. Moreover, to survive and prosper in the long run, firms must ensure that the prices charged for products exceed the total resources consumed to produce them, regardless of whether these costs are variable or fixed in the short run.

Companies that allocate corporate costs to divisions must carefully identify relevant costs for specific decisions. Suppose a division is profitable before any corporate costs are allocated but "unprofitable" after allocation of corporate costs. Should the division be closed down? The relevant corporate costs in this case are not the allocated corporate costs but those corporate costs that will be saved if the division is closed. If division profits exceed the relevant corporate costs, the division should not be closed.

3. If CAI allocates corporate costs to divisions, how many cost pools should it use? One extreme is to aggregate all corporate costs into a single cost pool. The other extreme is to have numerous individual corporate cost pools. As discussed in Chapter 5, a major consideration is to construct **homogeneous cost pools** so that all of the costs in the cost pool have the same or a similar cause-and-effect or benefits-received relationship with the cost-allocation base.

For example, when allocating corporate costs to divisions, CAI can combine corporate administration costs and corporate human-resource-management costs into a single cost pool if both cost categories have the same or similar cause-and-effect relationship with the same cost-allocation base (such as the number of employees in each division). If, however, each cost category has a cause-and-effect relationship with a different cost-allocation base (for example, number of employees in each division affects corporate human-resource-management costs, whereas revenues of each division affect corporate administration costs), CAI will prefer to maintain separate cost pools for each of these costs. Determining homogeneous cost pools requires judgment and should be revisited on a regular basis.

The benefit of using a multiple cost-pool system must be balanced against the costs of implementing it. Advances in information-gathering technology make it more likely that multiple cost-pool systems will pass the cost-benefit test.

Implementing Corporate Cost Allocations

After much discussion and debate, CAI's management team chooses to allocate all corporate costs to divisions. We now illustrate the allocation of corporate costs to divisions in CAI's ABC system.

The demands for corporate resources by the refrigerator division and the clothes dryer division depend on the demands that each division's products place on these resources. The top half of Exhibit 14-4 graphically represents the allocations.

1. CAI allocates treasury costs to each division on the basis of the cost of new assembly equipment installed in each division (the cost driver of treasury costs). It allocates the $900,000 of treasury costs as follows (using information from p. 506):

$$\text{Refrigerator Division: } \$900,000 \times \frac{\$5,200,000}{\$5,200,000 + \$3,800,000} = \$520,000$$

$$\text{Clothes Dryer Division: } \$900,000 \times \frac{\$3,800,000}{\$5,200,000 + \$3,800,000} = \$380,000$$

Each division then creates a *separate cost pool* consisting of the allocated corporate treasury costs and reallocates these costs to products on the basis of machine-hours used on the new equipment. Treasury costs are an output unit-level cost because they represent resources used on activities performed on each individual unit of a product.

2. CAI's analysis indicates that the demand for corporate human resource management (CHRM) costs for recruitment and training varies with total salary and labor costs in

each division. Suppose salary and labor costs are $44,000,000 in the refrigerator division and $36,000,000 in the clothes dryer division. Then CHRM costs are allocated to the divisions as follows:

$$\text{Refrigerator Division: } \$1,600,000 \times \frac{\$44,000,000}{\$44,000,000 + \$36,000,000} = \$880,000$$

$$\text{Clothes Dryer Division: } \$1,600,000 \times \frac{\$36,000,000}{\$44,000,000 + \$36,000,000} = \$720,000$$

Each division reallocates the CHRM costs allocated to it to the indirect-cost pools—design, machine setup, manufacturing operations, distribution, and division administration (the allocated-corporate-treasury cost pool and the facility costs pool have no salary and labor costs, so no CHRM costs are allocated to them)—on the basis of total salary and labor costs of each indirect-cost pool. CHRM costs that are added to division indirect-cost pools are then allocated to products using the cost driver for the respective cost pool. Therefore, CHRM costs are product-sustaining costs (for the portion of CHRM costs allocated to the design cost pool), batch-level costs (for the portion of CHRM costs allocated to the machine-setup cost pool), output unit-level costs (for the portions of CHRM costs allocated to the manufacturing-operations and distribution cost pools), and facility-sustaining costs (for the portion of CHRM costs allocated to the division-administration cost pool).

3. CAI allocates corporate administration costs to each division on the basis of division-administration costs (Exhibit 14-3 shows the amounts of division-administration costs) because corporate administration's main role is to support division administration.

$$\text{Refrigerator Division: } \$5,400,000 \times \frac{\$1,000,000}{\$1,000,000 + \$800,000} = \$3,000,000$$

$$\text{Clothes Dryer Division: } \$5,400,000 \times \frac{\$800,000}{\$1,000,000 + \$800,000} = \$2,400,000$$

Decision Point ▶

What are two key decisions managers must make when collecting costs in indirect-cost pools?

Each division adds the allocated corporate-administration costs to the division-administration cost pool. The costs in this cost pool are facility-sustaining costs and do not have a cause-and-effect relationship with individual products produced and sold by each division. CAI's policy, however, is to allocate all costs to products so that CAI's division managers become aware of all costs incurred at CAI in their pricing and other decisions. It allocates the division-administration costs (including allocated corporate-administration costs) to products on the basis of product revenues (a benefits-received criterion).

The issues discussed in this section regarding divisions and products apply nearly identically to customers, as we shall show next. *Instructors and students who, at this point, want to explore more-detailed issues in cost allocation rather than focusing on how activity-based costing extends to customer profitability can skip ahead to Chapter 15.*

Learning Objective 4

Discuss why a company's revenues and costs can differ across customers

. . . revenues can differ because of differences in the quantity purchased and the price discounts given, while costs can differ because different customers place different demands on a company's resources

Customer-Profitability Analysis

Customer-profitability analysis is the reporting and assessment of revenues earned from customers and the costs incurred to earn those revenues. An analysis of customer differences in revenues and costs can provide insight into why differences exist in the operating income earned from different customers. Managers use this information to ensure that customers making large contributions to the operating income of a company receive a high level of attention from the company.

Consider Spring Distribution Company, which sells bottled water. It has two distribution channels: (1) a wholesale distribution channel, in which the wholesaler sells to supermarkets, drugstores, and other stores, and (2) a retail distribution channel for a small number of business customers. We focus mainly on customer-profitability analysis in Spring's retail distribution channel. The list selling price in this channel is $14.40 per case

(24 bottles). The full cost to Spring is $12 per case. If every case is sold at list price in this distribution channel, Spring would earn a gross margin of $2.40 per case.

Customer-Revenue Analysis

Consider revenues from 4 of Spring's 10 retail customers in June 2012:

	A	B	C	D	E
			CUSTOMER		
1		A	B	G	J
2					
3	Cases sold	42,000	33,000	2,900	2,500
4	List selling price	$ 14.40	$ 14.40	$ 14.40	$ 14.40
5	Price discount	$ 0.96	$ 0.24	$ 1.20	$ 0.00
6	Invoice price	$ 13.44	$ 14.16	$ 13.20	$ 14.40
7	Revenues (Row 3 × Row 6)	$564,480	$467,280	$38,280	$36,000

Two variables explain revenue differences across these four customers: (1) the number of cases they purchased and (2) the magnitude of price discounting. A **price discount** is the reduction in selling price below list selling price to encourage customers to purchase more. Companies that record only the final invoice price in their information system cannot readily track the magnitude of their price discounting.[4]

Price discounts are a function of multiple factors, including the volume of product purchased (higher-volume customers receive higher discounts) and the desire to sell to a customer who might help promote sales to other customers. Discounts could also be because of poor negotiating by a salesperson or the unwanted effect of an incentive plan based only on revenues. At no time should price discounts run afoul of the law by way of price discrimination, predatory pricing, or collusive pricing (pp. 451–452).

Tracking price discounts by customer and by salesperson helps improve customer profitability. For example, Spring Distribution may decide to strictly enforce its volume-based price discounting policy. It may also require its salespeople to obtain approval for giving large discounts to customers who do not normally qualify for such discounts. In addition, the company could track the future sales of customers who its salespeople have given sizable price discounts to because of their "high growth potential." For example, Spring should track future sales to customer G to see if the $1.20-per-case discount translates into higher future sales.

Customer revenues are one element of customer profitability. The other element that is equally important to understand is the cost of acquiring, serving, and retaining customers. We study this topic next.

Customer-Cost Analysis

We apply to customers the cost hierarchy discussed in the previous section and in Chapter 5 (page 149). A **customer-cost hierarchy** categorizes costs related to customers into different cost pools on the basis of different types of cost drivers, or cost-allocation bases, or different degrees of difficulty in determining cause-and-effect or benefits-received relationships. Spring's ABC system focuses on customers rather than products. It has one direct cost, the cost of bottled water, and multiple indirect-cost pools. Spring identifies five categories of indirect costs in its customer-cost hierarchy:

1. **Customer output unit-level costs**—costs of activities to sell each unit (case) to a customer. An example is product-handling costs of each case sold.

---

[4] Further analysis of customer revenues could distinguish gross revenues from net revenues. This approach highlights differences across customers in sales returns. Additional discussion of ways to analyze revenue differences across customers is in R. S. Kaplan and R. Cooper, *Cost and Effect* (Boston, MA: Harvard Business School Press, 1998, Chapter 10); and G. Cokins, *Activity-Based Cost Management: An Executive's Guide* (New York: John Wiley & Sons, 2001, Chapter 3).

2. **Customer batch-level costs**—costs of activities related to a group of units (cases) sold to a customer. Examples are costs incurred to process orders or to make deliveries.

3. **Customer-sustaining costs**—costs of activities to support individual customers, regardless of the number of units or batches of product delivered to the customer. Examples are costs of visits to customers or costs of displays at customer sites.

4. **Distribution-channel costs**—costs of activities related to a particular distribution channel rather than to each unit of product, each batch of product, or specific customers. An example is the salary of the manager of Spring's retail distribution channel.

5. **Corporate-sustaining costs**—costs of activities that cannot be traced to individual customers or distribution channels. Examples are top-management and general-administration costs.

Note from these descriptions that four of the five levels of Spring's cost hierarchy closely parallel the cost hierarchy described in Chapter 5, except that Spring focuses on *customers* whereas the cost hierarchy in Chapter 5 focused on *products*. Spring has one additional cost hierarchy category, distribution-channel costs, for the costs it incurs to support its wholesale and retail distribution channels.

Customer-Level Costs

Spring is particularly interested in analyzing *customer-level indirect costs*—costs incurred in the first three categories of the customer-cost hierarchy: customer output-unit-level costs, customer batch-level costs, and customer-sustaining costs. Spring wants to work with customers to reduce these costs. It believes customer actions will have less impact on distribution-channel and corporate-sustaining costs. The following table shows five activities (in addition to cost of goods sold) that Spring identifies as resulting in customer-level costs. The table indicates the cost drivers and cost-driver rates for each activity, as well as the cost-hierarchy category for each activity.

| | Home | Insert | Page Layout | Formulas | Data | Review | View |

	G	H	I	J
1	**Activity Area**	**Cost Driver and Rate**		**Cost-Hierarchy Category**
2	Product handling	$0.50	per case sold	Customer output-unit-level costs
3	Order taking	$ 100	per purchase order	Customer batch-level costs
4	Delivery vehicles	$ 2	per delivery mile traveled	Customer batch-level costs
5	Rush deliveries	$ 300	per expedited delivery	Customer batch-level costs
6	Visits to customers	$ 80	per sales visit	Customer-sustaining costs

Information on the quantity of cost drivers used by each of four customers is as follows:

| | Home | Insert | Page Layout | Formulas | Data | Review |

	A	B	C	D	E
10			**CUSTOMER**		
11		A	B	G	J
12	Number of purchase orders	30	25	15	10
13	Number of deliveries	60	30	20	15
14	Miles traveled per delivery	5	12	20	6
15	Number of rush deliveries	1	0	2	0
16	Number of visits to customers	6	5	4	3

Exhibit 14-5 shows a customer-profitability analysis for the four retail customers using information on customer revenues previously presented (p. 511) and customer-level costs from the ABC system.

Spring Distribution can use the information in Exhibit 14-5 to work with customers to reduce the quantity of activities needed to support them. Consider a comparison of customer G and customer A. Customer G purchases only 7% of the cases that customer A purchases (2,900 versus 42,000). Yet, compared with customer A, customer G uses one-half as many purchase orders, two-thirds as many visits to customers, one-third as many deliveries, and twice as many rush deliveries. By implementing charges for each of these services, Spring might be able to induce customer G to make fewer but larger purchase orders, and require fewer customer visits, deliveries, and rush deliveries while looking to increase sales in the future.

Consider Owens and Minor, a distributor of medical supplies to hospitals. It strategically prices each of its services separately. For example, if a hospital wants a rush delivery or special packaging, Owens and Minor charges the hospital an additional price for each particular service. How have Owens and Minor's customers reacted? Hospitals that value these services continue to demand and pay for them while hospitals that do not value these services stop asking for them, saving Owens and Minor some costs. Owens and Minor's pricing strategy influences customer behavior in a way that increases its revenues or decreases its costs.

The ABC system also highlights a second opportunity for cost reduction. Spring can seek to reduce the costs of each activity. For example, improving the efficiency of the ordering process (such as by having customers order electronically) can reduce costs even if customers place the same number of orders.

Exhibit 14-6 shows a monthly operating income statement for Spring Distribution. The customer-level operating income of customers A and B in Exhibit 14-5 are shown in columns 8 and 9 of Exhibit 14-6. The format of Exhibit 14-6 is based on Spring's cost hierarchy. All costs incurred to serve customers are not included in customer-level costs and therefore are not allocated to customers in Exhibit 14-6. For example, distribution-channel costs such as the salary of the manager of the retail distribution channel are not included in customer-level costs and are not allocated to customers. Instead, these costs are identified as costs of the retail channel as a whole, because Spring's management believes that changes in customer behavior will not affect distribution-channel costs. These costs will be affected only by decisions pertaining to the whole channel, such as a decision to discontinue retail distribution. Another reason Spring does not allocate distribution-channel costs to customers is motivation. Spring's managers contend that

Exhibit 14-5   Customer-Profitability Analysis for Four Retail Channel Customers of Spring Distribution for June 2012

	A	B	C	D	E
1		CUSTOMER			
2		A	B	G	J
3	Revenues at list price: $14.40 × 42,000; 33,000; 2,900; 2,500	$604,800	$475,200	$41,760	$36,000
4	Price discount: $0.96 x 42,000; $0.24 × 33,000; $1.20 × 2,900; $0 × 2,500	40,320	7,920	3,480	0
5	Revenues (at actual price)	564,480	467,280	38,280	36,000
6	Cost of goods sold: $12 × 42,000; 33,000; 2,900; 2,500	504,000	396,000	34,800	30,000
7	Gross margin	60,480	71,280	3,480	6,000
8	Customer-level operating costs				
9	Product handling $0.50 × 42,000; 33,000; 2,900; 2,500	21,000	16,500	1,450	1,250
10	Order taking $100 × 30; 25; 15; 10	3,000	2,500	1,500	1,000
11	Delivery vehicles $2 × (5 × 60); (12 × 30); (20 × 20); (6 × 15)	600	720	800	180
12	Rush deliveries $300 × 1; 0; 2; 0	300	0	600	0
13	Visits to customers $80 × 6; 5; 4; 3	480	400	320	240
14	Total customer-level operating costs	25,380	20,120	4,670	2,670
15	Customer-level operating income	$ 35,100	$ 51,160	$(1,190)	$ 3,330

Exhibit 14-6 Income Statement of Spring Distribution for June 2012

	A	B	C	D	E	F	G	H	I	J	K	L	M
1					CUSTOMER DISTRIBUTION CHANNELS								
2				Wholesale Customers						Retail Customers			
3		Total	Total	A1	A2	A3	▪		Total	A^a	B^a	C	▪
4		(1) = (2) + (7)	(2)	(3)	(4)	(5)	(6)		(7)	(8)	(9)	(10)	(11)
5	Revenues (at actual prices)	$12,138,120	$10,107,720	$1,946,000	$1,476,000	▪	▪		$2,030,400	$564,480	$467,280	▪	▪
6	Customer-level costs	11,633,760	9,737,280	1,868,000	1,416,000	▪	▪		1,896,480	529,380^b	416,120^b	▪	▪
7	Customer-level operating income	504,360	370,440	$ 78,000	$ 60,000	▪	▪		133,920	$ 35,100	$ 51,160	▪	▪
8	Distribution-channel costs	160,500	102,500						58,000				
9	Distribution-channel-level operating income	343,860	$ 267,940						$ 75,920				
10	Corporate-sustaining costs	263,000											
11	Operating income	$ 80,860											
12													
13	^{a}Full details are presented in Exhibit 14-5.												
14	^{b}Cost of goods sold + Total customer-level operating costs from Exhibit 14-5.												

salespersons responsible for managing individual customer accounts would lose motivation if their bonuses were affected by the allocation to customers of distribution-channel costs over which they had minimal influence.

Next, consider corporate-sustaining costs such as top-management and general-administration costs. Spring's managers have concluded that there is no cause-and-effect or benefits-received relationship between any cost-allocation base and corporate-sustaining costs. Consequently, allocation of corporate-sustaining costs serves no useful purpose in decision making, performance evaluation, or motivation. For example, suppose Spring allocated the $263,000 of corporate-sustaining costs to its distribution channels: $173,000 to the wholesale channel and $90,000 to the retail channel. Using information from Exhibit 14-6, the retail channel would then show a loss of $14,080 ($75,920 – $90,000).

If this same situation persisted in subsequent months, should Spring shut down the retail distribution channel? No, because if retail distribution were discontinued, corporate-sustaining costs would be unaffected. Allocating corporate-sustaining costs to distribution channels could give the misleading impression that the potential cost savings from discontinuing a distribution channel would be greater than the likely amount.

Some managers and management accountants advocate fully allocating all costs to customers and distribution channels so that (1) the sum of operating incomes of all customers in a distribution channel (segment) equals the operating income of the distribution channel and (2) the sum of the distribution-channel operating incomes equals company-wide operating income. These managers and management accountants argue that customers and products must eventually be profitable on a full-cost basis. In the previous example, CAI allocated all corporate and division-level costs to its refrigerator and clothes dryer products (see pp. 509–510). For some decisions, such as pricing, allocating all costs ensures that long-run prices are set at a level to cover the cost of all resources used to produce and sell products. Nevertheless, the value of the hierarchical format in Exhibit 14-6 is that it distinguishes among various degrees of objectivity when allocating costs, and it dovetails with the different levels at which decisions are made and performance is evaluated. The issue of when and what costs to allocate is another example of the "different costs for different purposes" theme emphasized throughout this book.

> **Decision Point** ▶
>
> How can a company's revenues and costs differ across customers?

Learning Objective 5

Identify the importance of customer-profitability profiles

. . . highlight that a small percentage of customers contributes a large percentage of operating income.

Customer-Profitability Profiles

Customer-profitability profiles provide a useful tool for managers. Exhibit 14-7 ranks Spring's 10 retail customers based on customer-level operating income. (Four of these customers are analyzed in Exhibit 14-5.)

Column 4, computed by adding the individual amounts in column 1, shows the cumulative customer-level operating income. For example, customer C has a cumulative

Exhibit 14-7   Customer-Profitability Analysis for Retail Channel Customers: Spring Distribution, June 2012

	Home	Insert	Page Layout	Formulas	Data	Review	View	
	A	B	C	D	E	F		
1	**Customers Ranked on Customer-Level Operating Income**							
2						**Cumulative**		
3						**Customer-Level**		
4						**Operating Income**		
5				**Customer-Level**	**Cumulative**	**as a % of Total**		
6	**Retail**	**Customer-Level**	**Customer**	**Operating Income**	**Customer-Level**	**Customer-Level**		
7	**Customer**	**Operating Income**	**Revenue**	**Divided by Revenue**	**Operating Income**	**Operating Income**		
8	**Code**	**(1)**	**(2)**	**(3) = (1) ÷ (2)**	**(4)**	**(5) = (4) ÷ $133,920**		
9	B	$ 51,160	$ 467,280	10.9%	$ 51,160	38%		
10	A	35,100	564,480	6.2%	86,260	64%		
11	C	27,070	295,640	9.2%	113,330	85%		
12	D	20,580	277,000	7.4%	133,910	100%		
13	F	12,504	143,500	8.7%	146,414	109%		
14	J	3,330	41,000	8.1%	149,744	112%		
15	E	176	123,000	0.1%	149,920	112%		
16	G	−1,190	38,280	−3.1%	148,730	111%		
17	H	−5,690	38,220	−14.9%	143,040	107%		
18	I	−9,120	42,000	−21.7%	133,920	100%		
19		$133,920	$2,030,400					
20								

income of $113,330 in column 4. This $113,330 is the sum of $51,160 for customer B, $35,100 for customer A, and $27,070 for customer C.

Column 5 shows what percentage the $113,330 *cumulative* total for customers B, A, and C is of the total customer-level operating income of $133,920 earned in the retail distribution channel from all 10 customers. The three most profitable customers contribute 85% of total customer-level operating income. These customers deserve the highest service and priority. Companies try to keep their best customers happy in a number of ways: special phone numbers and upgrade privileges for elite-level frequent flyers, free usage of luxury hotel suites and big credit limits for high-rollers at casinos, and so on. In many companies, it is common for a small number of customers to contribute a high percentage of operating income. Microsoft uses the phrase "not all revenue dollars are endowed equally in profitability" to stress this point.

Column 3 shows the profitability per dollar of revenue by customer. This measure of customer profitability indicates that, although customer A contributes the second-highest operating income, the profitability per dollar of revenue is lower because of high price discounts. Spring's goal is to increase profit margins for customer A by decreasing the price discounts or saving customer-level costs while maintaining or increasing sales. Customer J has a higher profit margin but has lower total sales. Spring's challenge with customer J is to maintain margins while increasing sales.

Presenting Profitability Analysis

There are two common ways of presenting the results of customer-profitability analysis. Managers often find the bar chart presentation in Exhibit 14-8, Panel A, to be an intuitive way to visualize customer profitability. The highly profitable customers clearly stand out. Moreover, the number of "unprofitable" customers and the magnitude of their losses are apparent. A popular alternative way to express customer profitability is

Exhibit 14-8

Panel A: Bar Chart of Customer-Level Operating Income for Spring Distribution's Retail Channel Customers in June 2012

Panel B: The Whale Curve of Cumulative Profitability for Spring Distribution's Retail Channel Customers in June 2012

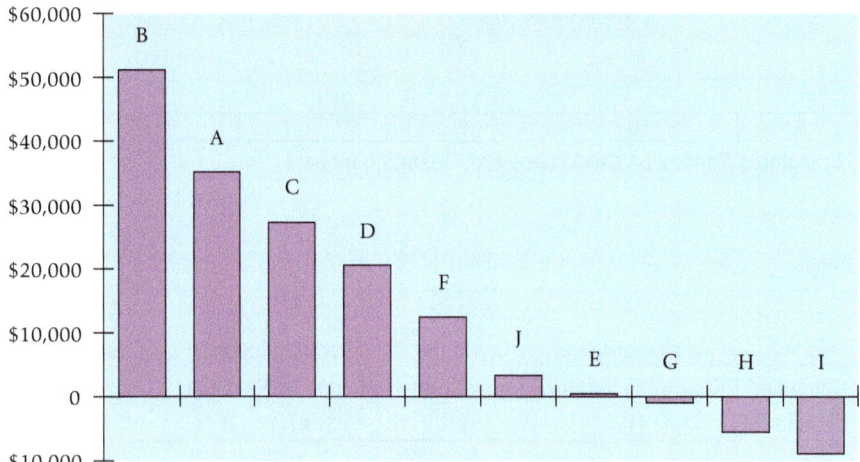

Customer-Level Operating Income

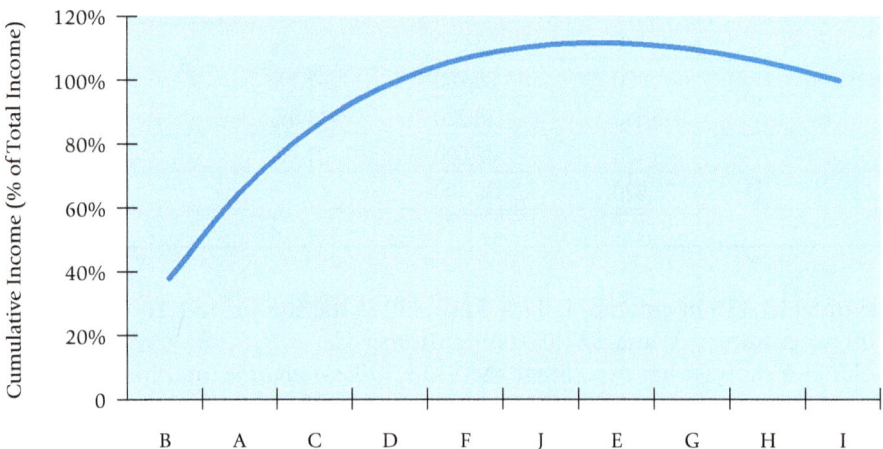

The Whale Curve of Cumulative Profitability for Spring Distribution's Retail Channel Customers in June 2012

by plotting the contents of column 5 of Exhibit 14-7. This chart is called the **whale curve** since it is backward bending at the point where customers start to become unprofitable, and thus resembles a humpback whale.[5]

Spring's managers must explore ways to make unprofitable customers profitable. Exhibits 14-5 to 14-8 emphasize short-run customer profitability. Other factors managers should consider in deciding how to allocate resources among customers include the following:

■ **Likelihood of customer retention.** The more likely a customer will continue to do business with a company, the more valuable the customer. Customers differ in their loyalty and their willingness to frequently "shop their business."

■ **Potential for sales growth.** The higher the likely growth of the customer's industry and the customer's sales, the more valuable the customer. Customers to whom a company can cross-sell other products are more desirable.

■ **Long-run customer profitability.** This factor will be influenced by the first two factors specified and the cost of customer-support staff and special services required to retain customer accounts.

---

[5] In practice, the curve of the chart can be quite steep. The whale curve for cumulative profitability usually reveals that the most profitable 20% of customers generate between 150% and 300% of total profits, the middle 70% of customers break even, and the least profitable 10% of customers lose from 50% to 200% of total profits (see Robert Kaplan and V.G. Narayanan, *Measuring and Managing Customer Profitability, Journal of Cost Management,* Sept/Oct 2001, pp. 1–11).

- **Increases in overall demand from having well-known customers.** Customers with established reputations help generate sales from other customers through product endorsements.
- **Ability to learn from customers.** Customers who provide ideas about new products or ways to improve existing products are especially valuable.

Managers should be cautious when deciding to discontinue customers. In Exhibit 14-7, the current unprofitability of customer G, for example, may provide misleading signals about G's profitability in the long-run. Moreover, as in any ABC-based system, the costs assigned to customer G are not all variable. In the short run, it may well have been efficient for Spring to use its spare capacity to serve G on a contribution-margin basis. Discontinuing customer G will not eliminate all the costs assigned to that customer, and will leave the firm worse off than before.

Of course, particular customers might be chronically unprofitable and hold limited future prospects. Or they might fall outside a firm's target market or require unsustainably high levels of service relative to the firm's strategies and capabilities. In such cases, organizations are becoming increasingly aggressive in severing customer relationships. For example, ING Direct, the largest direct lender and fastest growing financial services organization in the United States, asks 10,000 "high maintenance" customers to close their accounts each month.[6] The Concepts in Action feature on page 518 provides an example of a company that is struggling with the question of how to manage its resources and profitability without affecting the satisfaction of its customers.

Using the Five-Step Decision-Making Process to Manage Customer Profitability

The different types of customer analyses that we have just covered provide companies with key information to guide the allocation of resources across customers. Use the five-step decision-making process, introduced in Chapter 1, to think about how managers use these analyses to make customer-management decisions.

1. *Identify the problem and uncertainties.* The problem is how to manage and allocate resources across customers.
2. *Obtain information.* Managers identify past revenues generated by each customer and customer-level costs incurred in the past to support each customer.
3. *Make predictions about the future.* Managers estimate the revenues they expect from each customer and the customer-level costs they will incur in the future. In making these predictions, managers consider the effects that future price discounts will have on revenues, the effect that pricing for different services (such as rush deliveries) will have on the demand for these services by customers, and ways to reduce the cost of providing services. For example, Deluxe, Corp., a leading check printer, initiated process reductions to rein in its cost to serve customers by opening an electronic channel to shift customers from paper to automated ordering.
4. *Make decisions by choosing among alternatives.* Managers use the customer-profitability profiles to identify the small set of customers who deserve the highest service and priority. They also identify ways to make less-profitable customers (such as Spring's customer G) more profitable. Banks, for example, often impose minimum balance requirements on customers. Distribution firms may require minimum order quantities or levy a surcharge for smaller or customized orders. In making resource-allocation decisions, managers also consider long-term effects, such as the potential for future sales growth and the opportunity to leverage a particular customer account to make sales to other customers.
5. *Implement the decision, evaluate performance, and learn.* After the decision is implemented, managers compare actual results to predicted outcomes to evaluate the decision they made, its implementation, and ways in which they might improve profitability.

Decision Point

How do customer-profitability profiles help managers?

[6] See, for example, "The New Math of Customer Relationships" at http://hbswk.hbs.edu/item/5884.html.

Concepts in Action

iPhone "Apps" Challenge Customer Profitability at AT&T

AT&T is the second largest wireless provider in the United States. The company provides mobile telephone and data access to more than 85 million individuals, businesses, and government agencies. AT&T uses cost accounting to price its various wireless service plans and calculate overall profitability for its customers, including more than 10 million owners of Apple's iPhone. AT&T is the exclusive wireless provider for the popular iPhone smart phone.

Traditionally, the cost of serving different wireless customers varied. Most business customers, for example, required reliable service during business hours and large amounts of data bandwidth for e-mail and Internet access. In contrast, many individuals use their wireless devices extensively on nights and weekends and use features such as text messages and music ringtones. Accordingly, wireless providers considered the costs for these services when developing pricing plans and calculating customer profitability. Therefore, individuals using their phone service sparingly could select a less-expensive plan with fewer minutes, for use mostly at night and on weekends, whereas more-demanding individuals and lucrative business customers chose plans with more telephone minutes, large amounts of wireless data bandwidth, and guaranteed reliability . . . for a higher price.

When AT&T began selling the iPhone in mid-2007, cost accountants projected the profitability for its new customers, and new plans were designed accordingly. Similar to traditional wireless plans, iPhone buyers were offered subscription options with different amounts of telephone minutes at different price points. For example, 450 telephone minutes cost $59.99, while 1,350 minutes were $99.99. However, to showcase the iPhone's wireless and Internet capabilities, Apple insisted that AT&T offer only one data package, an unlimited plan.

While the unlimited data package proved initially lucrative, technology developments added significant costs to AT&T. When Apple introduced the iPhone 3G in 2008, the third-generation data capabilities encouraged software developers to build new programs for the iPhone platform. Within two years, nearly 140,000 applications, ranging from Pandora's mobile music player to Mint's on-the-go budgeting program, were downloaded more than 3 billion times by iPhone users. Each of the applications, however, uses a lot of data bandwidth.

Recall that AT&T does not charge iPhone subscribers for marginal bandwidth use. As a result, subscribers who download and use many iPhone applications quickly became unprofitable for the company. With each 100MB of bandwidth costing AT&T $1, the company is currently considering cost-reducing options, such as limiting data access and changing its all-you-can-eat data subscription plan, but it is very concerned about alienating its customers.

iPhone application usage has also created a bigger cost problem for the company. With data bandwidth on the AT&T wireless network increasing by 5,000% between 2006 and 2009, the company's network is showing signs of strain and poor performance. To act on these concerns, AT&T will spend $18–19 billion making improvements to its data network in 2010, and more in the years to come. As a result, AT&T will need to balance customer satisfaction with ensuring that its iPhone customers remain profitable for the carrier.

Sources: AT&T Inc. and Apple Inc. 2007. AT&T and Apple announce simple, affordable service plans for iPhone. AT&T Inc. and Apple Inc. Press Release, June 26. http://www.apple.com/pr/library/2007/06/26plans.html; Fazard, Roben. 2010. AT&T's iPhone mess. *Business Week*, February 3; Sheth, Niraj. 2010. AT&T, boosted and stressed by iPhone, lays out network plans. *Wall Street Journal*, January 29; Sheth, Niraj. 2010. For wireless carriers, iPad signals further loss of clout. *Wall Street Journal*, January 28.

Sales Variances

The customer-profitability analysis in the previous section focused on the actual profitability of individual customers within a distribution channel (retail, for example) and their effect on Spring Distribution's profitability for June 2012. At a more-strategic level, however, recall that Spring operates in two different markets: wholesale and retail. The operating margins in the retail market are much higher than the operating margins in the wholesale market. In June 2012, Spring had budgeted to sell 80% of its cases to wholesalers and 20% to retailers. It sold more cases in total than it had budgeted, but its actual sales mix (in cases) was 84% to wholesalers and 16% to retailers. Regardless of the profitability of sales to individual customers within each of the retail and wholesale channels, Spring's actual operating income, relative to the master budget, is likely to be positively affected by the higher sales of cases and negatively affected by the shift in mix away from the more-profitable retail customers. Sales-quantity and sales-mix variances can identify the effect of each of these factors on Spring's profitability. Companies such as Cisco, GE, and Hewlett-Packard perform similar analyses because they sell their products through multiple distribution channels like the Internet, over the telephone, and retail stores.

Spring classifies all customer-level costs as variable costs and distribution-channel and corporate-sustaining costs as fixed costs. To simplify the sales-variances analysis and calculations, we assume that all of the variable costs are variable with respect to units (cases) sold. (This means that average batch sizes remain the same as the total cases sold vary.) Without this assumption, the analysis would become more complex and would have to be done using the ABC-variance analysis approach described in Chapter 8, page 281–285. The basic insights, however, would not change.

Budgeted and actual operating data for June 2012 are as follows:

Learning Objective **6**

Subdivide the sales-volume variance into the sales-mix variance

. . . the variance arises because actual sales mix differs from budgeted sales mix

and the sales-quantity variance

. . . this variance arises because actual total unit sales differ from budgeted total unit sales

Budget Data for June 2012

	Selling Price (1)	Variable Cost per Unit (2)	Contribution Margin per Unit (3) = (1) − (2)	Sales Volume in Units (4)	Sales Mix (Based on Units) (5)	Contribution Margin (6) = (3) × (4)
Wholesale channel	$13.37	$12.88	$0.49	712,000	80%[a]	$348,880
Retail channel	14.10	13.12	0.98	178,000	20%	174,440
Total				890,000	100%	$523,320

[a] Percentage of unit sales to wholesale channel = 712,000 units ÷ 890,000 total unit = 80%.

Actual Results for June 2012

	Selling Price (1)	Variable Cost per Unit (2)	Contribution Margin per Unit (3) = (1) − (2)	Sales Volume in Units (4)	Sales Mix (Based on Units) (5)	Contribution Margin (6) = (3) × (4)
Wholesale channel	$13.37	$12.88	$0.49	756,000	84%[a]	$370,440
Retail channel	14.10	13.17	0.93	144,000	16%	133,920
Total				900,000	100%	$504,360

[a] Percentage of unit sales to wholesale channel = 756,000 units ÷ 900,000 total unit = 84%.

The budgeted and actual fixed distribution-channel costs and corporate-sustaining costs are $160,500 and $263,000, respectively (see Exhibit 14-6, p. 514).

Recall that the levels of detail introduced in Chapter 7 (pages 230–233) included the static-budget variance (level 1), the flexible-budget variance (level 2), and the sales-volume variance (level 2). The sales-quantity and sales-mix variances are level 3 variances that subdivide the sales-volume variance.[7]

---

[7] The presentation of the variances in this chapter and the appendix draws on teaching notes prepared by J. K. Harris.

Static-Budget Variance

The *static-budget variance* is the difference between an actual result and the corresponding budgeted amount in the static budget. Our analysis focuses on the difference between actual and budgeted contribution margins (column 6 in the preceding tables). The total static-budget variance is $18,960 U (actual contribution margin of $504,360 – budgeted contribution margin of $523,320). Exhibit 14-9 (columns 1 and 3) uses the columnar format introduced in Chapter 7 to show detailed calculations of the static-budget variance. Managers can gain more insight about the static-budget variance by subdividing it into the flexible-budget variance and the sales-volume variance.

Flexible-Budget Variance and Sales-Volume Variance

The *flexible-budget variance* is the difference between an actual result and the corresponding flexible-budget amount based on actual output level in the budget period. The flexible budget contribution margin is equal to budgeted contribution margin per unit times actual units sold of each product. Exhibit 14-9, column 2, shows the flexible-budget calculations. The flexible budget measures the contribution margin that Spring would have budgeted for the actual quantities of cases sold. The flexible-budget variance is the difference between columns 1 and 2 in Exhibit 14-9. The only difference between columns 1 and 2 is that actual units sold of each product is multiplied by actual contribution margin per unit in column 1 and budgeted contribution margin per unit in column 2. The $7,200 U flexible-budget variance arises because actual contribution margin on retail sales of $0.93 per case is lower than the budgeted amount of $0.98 per case. Spring's management is aware that this difference of $0.05 per case resulted from excessive price discounts, and it has put in place action plans to reduce discounts in the future.

The *sales-volume variance* is the difference between a flexible-budget amount and the corresponding static-budget amount. In Exhibit 14-9, the sales-volume variance shows the effect on budgeted contribution margin of the difference between actual quantity of units sold and budgeted quantity of units sold. The sales-volume variance of $11,760 U is the difference between columns 2 and 3 in Exhibit 14-9. In this case, it is unfavorable overall because while wholesale unit sales were higher than budgeted, retail sales, which are expected to be twice as profitable on a per unit basis, were below budget. Spring's

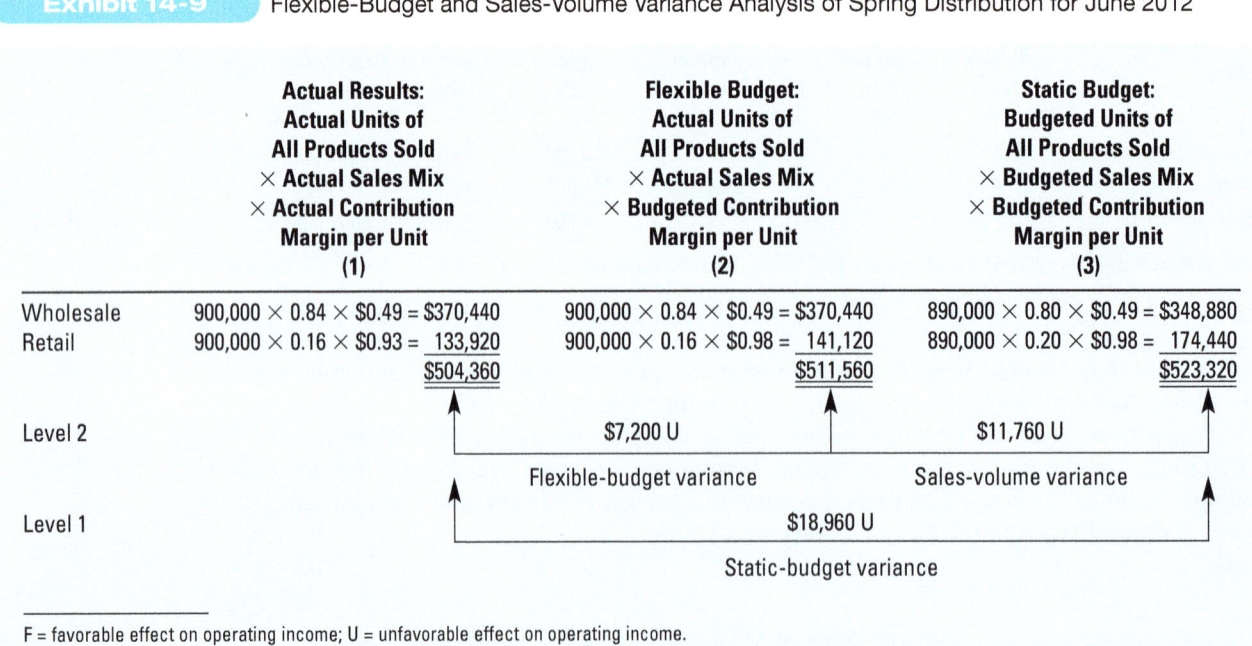

Exhibit 14-9   Flexible-Budget and Sales-Volume Variance Analysis of Spring Distribution for June 2012

	Actual Results: Actual Units of All Products Sold × Actual Sales Mix × Actual Contribution Margin per Unit (1)	Flexible Budget: Actual Units of All Products Sold × Actual Sales Mix × Budgeted Contribution Margin per Unit (2)	Static Budget: Budgeted Units of All Products Sold × Budgeted Sales Mix × Budgeted Contribution Margin per Unit (3)
Wholesale	900,000 × 0.84 × $0.49 = $370,440	900,000 × 0.84 × $0.49 = $370,440	890,000 × 0.80 × $0.49 = $348,880
Retail	900,000 × 0.16 × $0.93 = 133,920	900,000 × 0.16 × $0.98 = 141,120	890,000 × 0.20 × $0.98 = 174,440
	$504,360	$511,560	$523,320
Level 2		$7,200 U	$11,760 U
		Flexible-budget variance	Sales-volume variance
Level 1		$18,960 U	
		Static-budget variance	

F = favorable effect on operating income; U = unfavorable effect on operating income.

managers can gain substantial insight into the sales-volume variance by subdividing it into the sales-mix variance and the sales-quantity variance.

Sales-Mix Variance

The **sales-mix variance** is the difference between (1) budgeted contribution margin for the *actual sales mix* and (2) budgeted contribution margin for the *budgeted sales mix*. The formula and computations (using data from p. 519) are as follows:

	Actual Units of All Products Sold	×	(Actual Sales - Mix Percentage − Budgeted Sales - Mix Percentage)	×	Budgeted Contribution Margin per Unit	=	Sales-Mix Variance
Wholesale	900,000 units	×	(0.84 − 0.80)	×	$0.49 per unit	=	$17,640 F
Retail	900,000 units	×	(0.16 − 0.20)	×	$0.98 per unit	=	35,280 U
Total sales-mix variance							$17,640 U

A favorable sales-mix variance arises for the wholesale channel because the 84% actual sales-mix percentage exceeds the 80% budgeted sales-mix percentage. In contrast, the retail channel has an unfavorable variance because the 16% actual sales-mix percentage is less than the 20% budgeted sales-mix percentage. The sales-mix variance is unfavorable because actual sales mix shifted toward the less-profitable wholesale channel relative to budgeted sales mix.

The concept underlying the sales-mix variance is best explained in terms of composite units. A **composite unit** is a hypothetical unit with weights based on the mix of individual units. Given the budgeted sales for June 2012, the composite unit consists of 0.80 units of sales to the wholesale channel and 0.20 units of sales to the retail channel. Therefore, the budgeted contribution margin per composite unit for the budgeted sales mix is as follows:

$$(0.80) \times (\$0.49) + (0.20) \times (\$0.98) = \$0.5880.[8]$$

Similarly, for the actual sales mix, the composite unit consists of 0.84 units of sales to the wholesale channel and 0.16 units of sales to the retail channel. The budgeted contribution margin per composite unit for the actual sales mix is therefore as follows:

$$(0.84) \times (\$0.49) + (0.16) \times (\$0.98) = \$0.5684.$$

The impact of the shift in sales mix is now evident. Spring obtains a lower budgeted contribution margin per composite unit of $0.0196 ($0.5880 − $0.5684). For the 900,000 units actually sold, this decrease translates to a $17,640 U sales-mix variance ($0.0196 per unit × 900,000 units).

Managers should probe why the $17,640 U sales-mix variance occurred in June 2012. Is the shift in sales mix because, as the analysis in the previous section showed, profitable retail customers proved to be more difficult to find? Is it because of a competitor in the retail channel providing better service at a lower price? Or is it because the initial sales-volume estimates were made without adequate analysis of the potential market?

Exhibit 14-10 uses the columnar format to calculate the sales-mix variance and the sales-quantity variances.

Sales-Quantity Variance

The **sales-quantity variance** is the difference between (1) budgeted contribution margin based on *actual units sold of all products* at the budgeted mix and (2) contribution margin in the static budget (which is based on *budgeted units of all products to*

---

[8] Budgeted contribution margin per composite unit can be computed in another way by dividing total budgeted contribution margin of $523,320 by total budgeted units of 890,000 (p. 519): $523,320 ÷ 890,000 units = $0.5880 per unit.

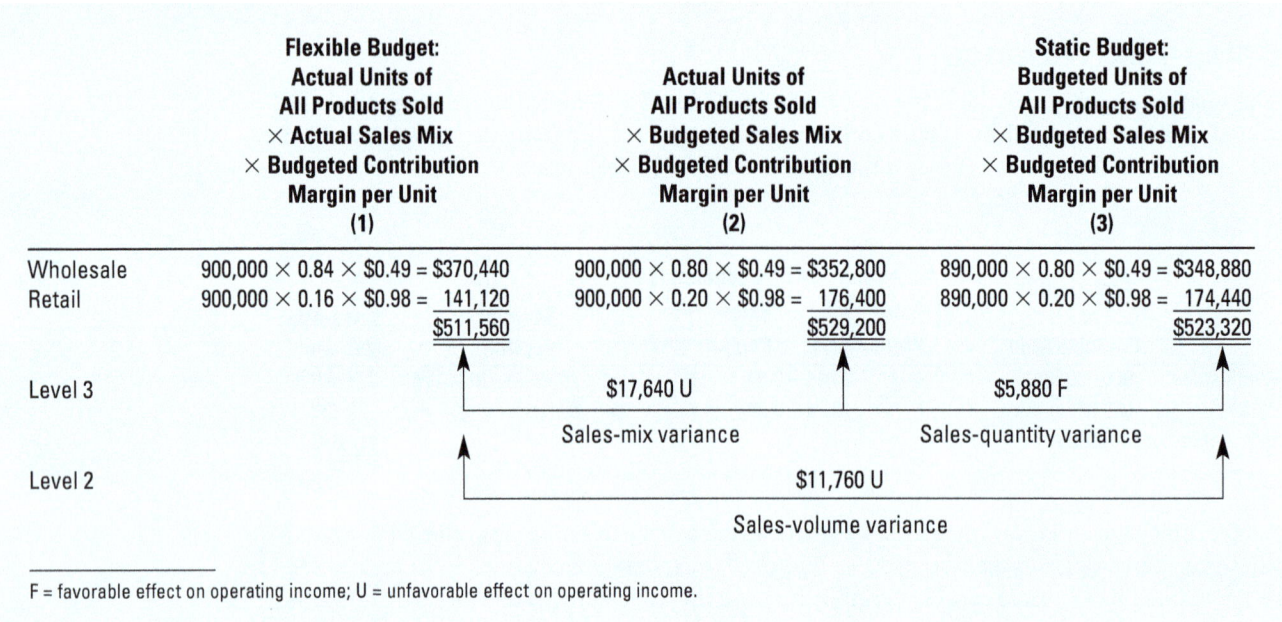

Exhibit 14-10   Sales-Mix and Sales-Quantity Variance Analysis of Spring Distribution for June 2012

F = favorable effect on operating income; U = unfavorable effect on operating income.

be sold at budgeted mix). The formula and computations (using data from p. 519) are as follows:

			Budgeted Sales-Mix Percentages		Budgeted Contribution Margin per Unit		Sales-Quantity Variance
Wholesale	(900,000 units − 890,000 units)	×	0.80	×	$0.49 per unit	=	$3,920 F
Retail	(900,000 units − 890,000 units)	×	0.20	×	$0.98 per unit	=	1,960 F
Total sales-quantity variance							$5,880 F

This variance is favorable when actual units of all products sold exceed budgeted units of all products sold. Spring sold 10,000 more cases than were budgeted, resulting in a $5,880 F sales-quantity variance (also equal to budgeted contribution margin per composite unit for the budgeted sales mix times additional cases sold, $0.5880 × 10,000). Managers would want to probe the reasons for the increase in sales. Did higher sales come as a result of a competitor's distribution problems? Better customer service? Or growth in the overall market? Additional insight into the causes of the sales-quantity variance can be gained by analyzing changes in Spring's share of the total industry market and in the size of that market. The sales-quantity variance can be decomposed into market-share and market-size variances, as illustrated in the appendix to Chapter 7.[9]

Exhibit 14-11 presents an overview of the sales-mix and sales-quantity variances for the Spring example. The sales-mix variance and sales-quantity variance can also be calculated in a multiproduct company, in which each individual product has a different contribution margin per unit. The Problem for Self-Study takes you through such a setting, and also demonstrates the link between these sales variances and the market-share and market-size variances studied earlier. The appendix to this chapter describes mix and quantity variances for production inputs.

Decision Point ▶

What are the two components of the sales-volume variance?

---

[9] Recall that the market-share and market-size variances in the appendix to Chapter 7 (pp. 248–249) were computed for Webb Company, which sold a single product (jackets) using a single distribution channel. The calculation of these variances is virtually unaffected when multiple distribution channels exist, as in the Spring example. The only change required is to replace the phrase "Budgeted Contribution Margin per Unit" in the market-share and market-size variance formulas with "Budgeted Contribution Margin per Composite Unit for Budgeted Sales Mix" (which equals $0.5880 in the Spring example). For additional details and an illustration, see the Problem for Self-Study for this chapter.

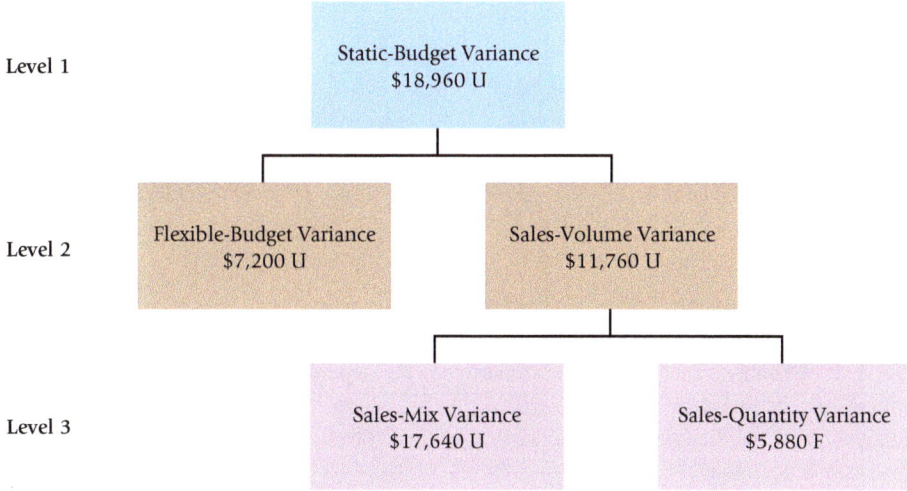

F = favorable effect on operating income; U = unfavorable effect on operating income

Problem for Self-Study

The Payne Company manufactures two types of vinyl flooring. Budgeted and actual operating data for 2012 are as follows:

	Static Budget			Actual Results		
	Commercial	**Residential**	**Total**	**Commercial**	**Residential**	**Total**
Unit sales in rolls	20,000	60,000	80,000	25,200	58,800	84,000
Contribution margin	$10,000,000	$24,000,000	$34,000,000	$11,970,000	$24,696,000	$36,666,000

In late 2011, a marketing research firm estimated industry volume for commercial and residential vinyl flooring for 2012 at 800,000 rolls. Actual industry volume for 2012 was 700,000 rolls.

Required

1. Compute the sales-mix variance and the sales-quantity variance by type of vinyl flooring and in total. (Compute all variances in terms of contribution margins.)
2. Compute the market-share variance and the market-size variance (see Chapter 7, pp. 248–249).
3. What insights do the variances calculated in requirements 1 and 2 provide about Payne Company's performance in 2012?

Solution

1. Actual sales-mix percentage:

$$\text{Commercial} = 25,200 \div 84,000 = 0.30, \text{ or } 30\%$$

$$\text{Residential} = 58,800 \div 84,000 = 0.70, \text{ or } 70\%$$

Budgeted sales-mix percentage:

$$\text{Commercial} = 20,000 \div 80,000 = 0.25, \text{ or } 25\%$$

$$\text{Residential} = 60,000 \div 80,000 = 0.75, \text{ or } 75\%$$

Budgeted contribution margin per unit:

$$\text{Commercial} = \$10,000,000 \div 20,000 \text{ units} = \$500 \text{ per unit}$$

$$\text{Residential} = \$24,000,000 \div 60,000 \text{ units} = \$400 \text{ per unit}$$

	Actual Units of All Products Sold	×	$\left(\begin{array}{c}\text{Actual Sales-Mix Percentage}\end{array} - \begin{array}{c}\text{Budgeted Sales-Mix Percentage}\end{array}\right)$	×	Budgeted Contribution Margin per Unit	=	Sales-Mix Variance
Commercial	84,000 units	×	(0.30 − 0.25)	×	$500 per unit	=	$2,100,000 F
Residential	84,000 units	×	(0.70 − 0.75)	×	$400 per unit	=	1,680,000 U
Total sales-mix variance							$ 420,000 F

	$\left(\begin{array}{c}\text{Actual Units of All Products Sold}\end{array} - \begin{array}{c}\text{Budgeted Units of All Products Sold}\end{array}\right)$	×	Budgeted Sales-Mix Percentage	×	Budgeted Contribution Margin per Unit	=	Sales-Quantity Variance
Commercial	(84,000 units − 80,000 units)	×	0.25	×	$500 per unit	=	$ 500,000 F
Residential	(84,000 units − 80,000 units)	×	0.75	×	$400 per unit	=	1,200,000 F
Total sales-quantity variance							$1,700,000 F

2. Actual market share = 84,000 ÷ 700,000 = 0.12, or 12%
   Budgeted market share = 80,000 ÷ 800,000 units = 0.10, or 10%

$$\begin{array}{c}\text{Budgeted contribution margin}\\\text{per composite unit}\\\text{of budgeted mix}\end{array} = \$34{,}000{,}000 \div 80{,}000 \text{ units} = \$425 \text{ per unit}$$

Budgeted contribution margin per composite unit of budgeted mix can also be calculated as follows:

Commercial: $500 per unit × 0.25	=	$125
Residential: $400 per unit × 0.75	=	300
Budgeted contribution margin per composite unit	=	$425

$$\begin{array}{c}\text{Market-share}\\\text{variance}\end{array} = \begin{array}{c}\text{Actual}\\\text{market size}\\\text{in units}\end{array} \times \left(\begin{array}{c}\text{Actual}\\\text{market}\\\text{share}\end{array} - \begin{array}{c}\text{Budgeted}\\\text{market}\\\text{share}\end{array}\right) \times \begin{array}{c}\text{Budgeted}\\\text{contribution margin}\\\text{per composite unit}\\\text{for budgeted mix}\end{array}$$

$$= 700{,}000 \text{ units} \times (0.12 - 0.10) \times \$425 \text{ per unit}$$

$$= \$5{,}950{,}000 \text{ F}$$

$$\begin{array}{c}\text{Market-size}\\\text{variance}\end{array} = \left(\begin{array}{c}\text{Actual}\\\text{market size}\\\text{in units}\end{array} - \begin{array}{c}\text{Budgeted}\\\text{market size}\\\text{in units}\end{array}\right) \times \begin{array}{c}\text{Budgeted}\\\text{market}\\\text{share}\end{array} \times \begin{array}{c}\text{Budgeted}\\\text{contribution margin}\\\text{per composite unit}\\\text{for budgeted mix}\end{array}$$

$$= (700{,}000 \text{ units} - 800{,}000 \text{ units}) \times 0.10 \times \$425 \text{ per unit}$$

$$= \$4{,}250{,}000 \text{ U}$$

Note that the algebraic sum of the market-share variance and the market-size variance is equal to the sales-quantity variance: $5,950,000 F + $4,250,000 U = $1,700,000 F.

3. Both the total sales-mix variance and the total sales-quantity variance are favorable. The favorable sales-mix variance occurred because the actual mix comprised more of the higher-margin commercial vinyl flooring. The favorable total sales-quantity variance occurred because the actual total quantity of rolls sold exceeded the budgeted amount.

The company's large favorable market-share variance is due to a 12% actual market share compared with a 10% budgeted market share. The market-size variance is unfavorable because the actual market size was 100,000 rolls less than the budgeted market size. Payne's performance in 2012 appears to be very good. Although overall market size declined, the company sold more units than budgeted and gained market share.

Decision Points

The following question-and-answer format summarizes the chapter's learning objectives. Each decision presents a key question related to a learning objective. The guidelines are the answer to that question.

Decision	Guidelines
1. What are four purposes for allocating costs to cost objects?	Four purposes of cost allocation are (a) to provide information for economic decisions, (b) to motivate managers and other employees, (c) to justify costs or compute reimbursement amounts, and (d) to measure income and assets for reporting to external parties. Different cost allocations are appropriate for different purposes.
2. What criteria should managers use to guide cost-allocation decisions?	Managers should use the cause-and-effect and the benefits-received criteria to guide most cost-allocation decisions. Other criteria are fairness or equity and ability to bear.
3. What are two key decisions managers must make when collecting costs in indirect-cost pools?	Two key decisions related to indirect-cost pools are the number of indirect-cost pools to form and the individual cost items to be included in each cost pool to make homogeneous cost pools.
4. How can a company's revenues and costs differ across customers?	Revenues can differ because of differences in the quantity purchased and price discounts given from the list selling price. Costs can differ as different customers place different demands on a company's resources in terms of processing purchase orders, making deliveries, and customer support.
5. How do customer-profitability profiles help managers?	Companies should be aware of and devote sufficient resources to maintaining and expanding relationships with customers who contribute significantly to profitability. Customer-profitability profiles often highlight that a small percentage of customers contributes a large percentage of operating income.
6. What are the two components of the sales-volume variance?	The two components of sales-volume variance are (a) the difference between actual sales mix and budgeted sales mix (the sales-mix variance) and (b) the difference between actual unit sales and budgeted unit sales (the sales-quantity variance).

Appendix

Mix and Yield Variances for Substitutable Inputs

The framework for calculating the sales-mix variance and the sales-quantity variance can also be used to analyze production-input variances in cases in which managers have some leeway in combining and substituting inputs. For example, Del Monte can combine material inputs (such as pineapples, cherries, and grapes) in varying proportions for its cans of fruit cocktail. Within limits, these individual fruits are *substitutable inputs* in making the fruit cocktail.

We illustrate how the efficiency variance discussed in Chapter 7 (pp. 236–237) can be subdivided into variances that highlight the financial impact of input mix and input yield when inputs are substitutable. Consider Delpino Corporation, which makes tomato ketchup. Our example focuses on direct material inputs and substitution among three of these inputs. The same approach can also be used to examine substitutable direct manufacturing labor inputs.

To produce ketchup of a specified consistency, color, and taste, Delpino mixes three types of tomatoes grown in different regions: Latin American tomatoes (Latoms), California tomatoes (Caltoms), and Florida tomatoes

(Flotoms). Delpino's production standards require 1.60 tons of tomatoes to produce 1 ton of ketchup; 50% of the tomatoes are budgeted to be Latoms, 30% Caltoms, and 20% Flotoms. The direct material inputs budgeted to produce 1 ton of ketchup are as follows:

0.80 (50% of 1.6) ton of Latoms at $70 per ton	$ 56.00
0.48 (30% of 1.6) ton of Caltoms at $80 per ton	38.40
0.32 (20% of 1.6) ton of Flotoms at $90 per ton	28.80
Total budgeted cost of 1.6 tons of tomatoes	$123.20

Budgeted average cost per ton of tomatoes is $123.20 ÷ 1.60 tons = $77 per ton.

Because Delpino uses fresh tomatoes to make ketchup, no inventories of tomatoes are kept. Purchases are made as needed, so all price variances relate to tomatoes purchased and used. Actual results for June 2012 show that a total of 6,500 tons of tomatoes were used to produce 4,000 tons of ketchup:

3,250 tons of Latoms at actual cost of $70 per ton	$227,500
2,275 tons of Caltoms at actual cost of $82 per ton	186,550
975 tons of Flotoms at actual cost of $96 per ton	93,600
6,500 tons of tomatoes	507,650
Budgeted cost of 4,000 tons of ketchup at $123.20 per ton	492,800
Flexible-budget variance for direct materials	$ 14,850 U

Given the standard ratio of 1.60 tons of tomatoes to 1 ton of ketchup, 6,400 tons of tomatoes should be used to produce 4,000 tons of ketchup. At standard mix, quantities of each type of tomato required are as follows:

Latoms:	0.50 × 6,400 = 3,200 tons
Caltoms:	0.30 × 6,400 = 1,920 tons
Flotoms:	0.20 × 6,400 = 1,280 tons

Direct Materials Price and Efficiency Variances

Exhibit 14-12 presents in columnar format the analysis of the flexible-budget variance for direct materials discussed in Chapter 7. The materials price and efficiency variances are calculated separately for each input material and then added together. The variance analysis prompts Delpino to investigate the unfavorable price and efficiency variances. Why did it pay more for tomatoes and use greater quantities than it had budgeted? Were actual market prices of tomatoes higher, in general, or could the purchasing department have negotiated lower prices? Did the inefficiencies result from inferior tomatoes or from problems in processing?

Exhibit 14-12 Direct Materials Price and Efficiency Variances for the Delpino Corporation June 2012

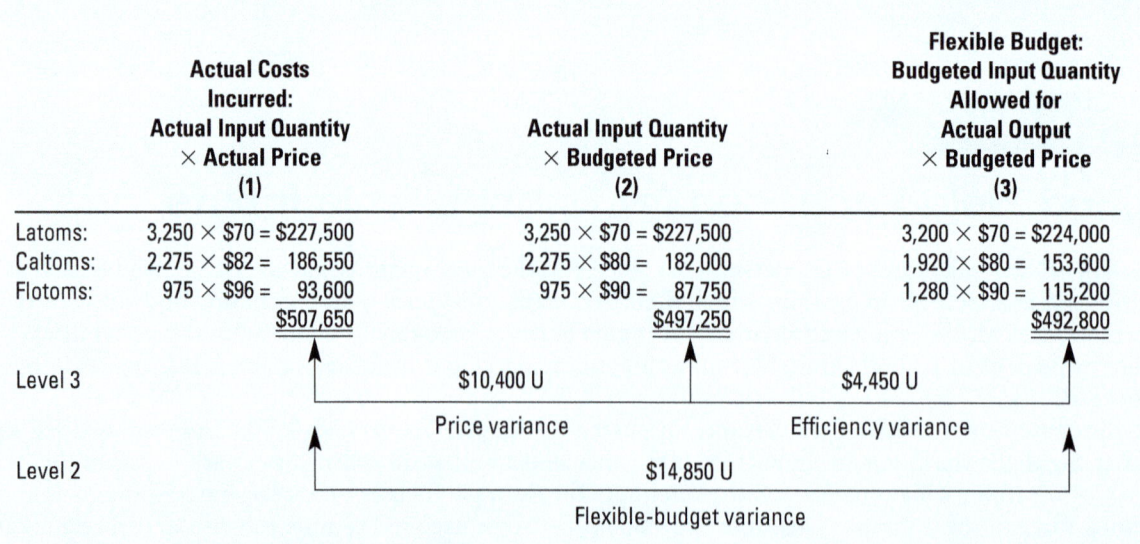

F = favorable effect on operating income; U = unfavorable effect on operating income.

Direct Materials Mix and Direct Materials Yield Variances

Managers sometimes have discretion to substitute one material for another. The manager of Delpino's ketchup plant has some leeway in combining Latoms, Caltoms, and Flotoms without affecting the ketchup's quality. We will assume that to maintain quality, mix percentages of each type of tomato can only vary up to 5% from standard mix. For example, the percentage of Caltoms in the mix can vary between 25% and 35% (30% ± 5%). When inputs are substitutable, direct materials efficiency improvement relative to budgeted costs can come from two sources: (1) using a cheaper mix to produce a given quantity of output, measured by the direct materials mix variance, and (2) using less input to achieve a given quantity of output, measured by the direct materials yield variance.

Holding actual total quantity of all direct materials inputs used constant, the total **direct materials mix variance** is the difference between (1) budgeted cost for actual mix of actual total quantity of direct materials used and (2) budgeted cost of budgeted mix of actual total quantity of direct materials used. Holding budgeted input mix constant, the **direct materials yield variance** is the difference between (1) budgeted cost of direct materials based on actual total quantity of direct materials used and (2) flexible-budget cost of direct materials based on budgeted total quantity of direct materials allowed for actual output produced. Exhibit 14-13 presents the direct materials mix and yield variances for the Delpino Corporation.

Direct Materials Mix Variance

The total direct materials mix variance is the sum of the direct materials mix variances for each input:

$$\begin{array}{c} \text{Direct} \\ \text{materials} \\ \text{mix variance} \\ \text{for each input} \end{array} = \begin{array}{c} \text{Actual total} \\ \text{quantity of all} \\ \text{direct materials} \\ \text{inputs used} \end{array} \times \left(\begin{array}{c} \text{Actual} \\ \text{direct materials} \\ \text{input mix} \\ \text{percentage} \end{array} - \begin{array}{c} \text{Budgeted} \\ \text{direct materials} \\ \text{input mix} \\ \text{percentage} \end{array} \right) \times \begin{array}{c} \text{Budgeted} \\ \text{price of} \\ \text{direct materials} \\ \text{input} \end{array}$$

The direct materials mix variances are as follows:

Latoms:	6,500 tons × (0.50 − 0.50) × $70 per ton = 6,500 × 0.00 × $70	= $ 0
Caltoms:	6,500 tons × (0.35 − 0.30) × $80 per ton = 6,500 × 0.05 × $80	= 26,000 U
Flotoms:	6,500 tons × (0.15 − 0.20) × $90 per ton = 6,500 × −0.05 × $90	= 29,250 F
Total direct materials mix variance		$ 3,250 F

The total direct materials mix variance is favorable because relative to the budgeted mix, Delpino substitutes 5% of the cheaper Caltoms for 5% of the more-expensive Flotoms.

Exhibit 14-13 Total Direct Materials Yield and Mix Variances for the Delpino Corporation for June 2012

	Actual Total Quantity of All Inputs Used × Actual Input Mix × Budgeted Price (1)	Actual Total Quantity of All Inputs Used × Budgeted Input Mix × Budgeted Price (2)	Flexible Budget: Budgeted Total Quantity of All Inputs Allowed for Actual Output × Budgeted Input Mix × Budgeted Price (3)
Latoms:	6,500 × 0.50 × $70 = $227,500	6,500 × 0.50 × $70 = $227,500	6,400 × 0.50 × $70 = $224,500
Caltoms:	6,500 × 0.35 × $80 = 182,000	6,500 × 0.30 × $80 = 156,000	6,400 × 0.30 × $80 = 153,600
Flotoms:	6,500 × 0.15 × $90 = 87,750	6,500 × 0.20 × $90 = 117,000	6,400 × 0.20 × $90 = 115,200
	$497,250	$500,500	$492,800

Level 4 ↑ $3,250 F ↑ $7,700 U ↑

Mix variance   Yield variance

Level 3 ↑ $4,450 U ↑

Efficiency variance

F = favorable effect on operating income; U = unfavorable effect on operating income.

Direct Materials Yield Variance

The direct materials yield variance is the sum of the direct materials yield variances for each input:

$$\begin{array}{c}\text{Direct}\\\text{materials}\\\text{yield variance}\\\text{for each input}\end{array} = \left(\begin{array}{c}\text{Actual total}\\\text{quantity of}\\\text{all direct}\\\text{materials}\\\text{inputs used}\end{array} - \begin{array}{c}\text{Budgeted total}\\\text{quantity of all}\\\text{direct materials}\\\text{inputs allowed}\\\text{for actual output}\end{array}\right) \times \begin{array}{c}\text{Budgeted}\\\text{direct materials}\\\text{input mix}\\\text{percentage}\end{array} \times \begin{array}{c}\text{Budgeted}\\\text{price of}\\\text{direct materials}\\\text{input}\end{array}$$

The direct materials yield variances are as follows:

Latoms: (6,500 – 6,400) tons × 0.50 × $70 per ton = 100 × 0.50 × $70 = $3,500 U
Caltoms: (6,500 – 6,400) tons × 0.30 × $80 per ton = 100 × 0.30 × $80 = 2,400 U
Flotoms: (6,500 – 6,400) tons × 0.20 × $90 per ton = 100 × 0.20 × $90 = 1,800 U
Total direct materials yield variance $7,700 U

The total direct materials yield variance is unfavorable because Delpino used 6,500 tons of tomatoes rather than the 6,400 tons that it should have used to produce 4,000 tons of ketchup. Holding the budgeted mix and budgeted prices of tomatoes constant, the budgeted cost per ton of tomatoes in the budgeted mix is $77 per ton. The unfavorable yield variance represents the budgeted cost of using 100 more tons of tomatoes, (6,500 – 6,400) tons × $77 per ton = $7,700 U. Delpino would want to investigate reasons for this unfavorable yield variance. For example, did the substitution of the cheaper Caltoms for Flotoms that resulted in the favorable mix variance also cause the unfavorable yield variance?

The direct materials variances computed in Exhibits 14-12 and 14-13 can be summarized as follows:

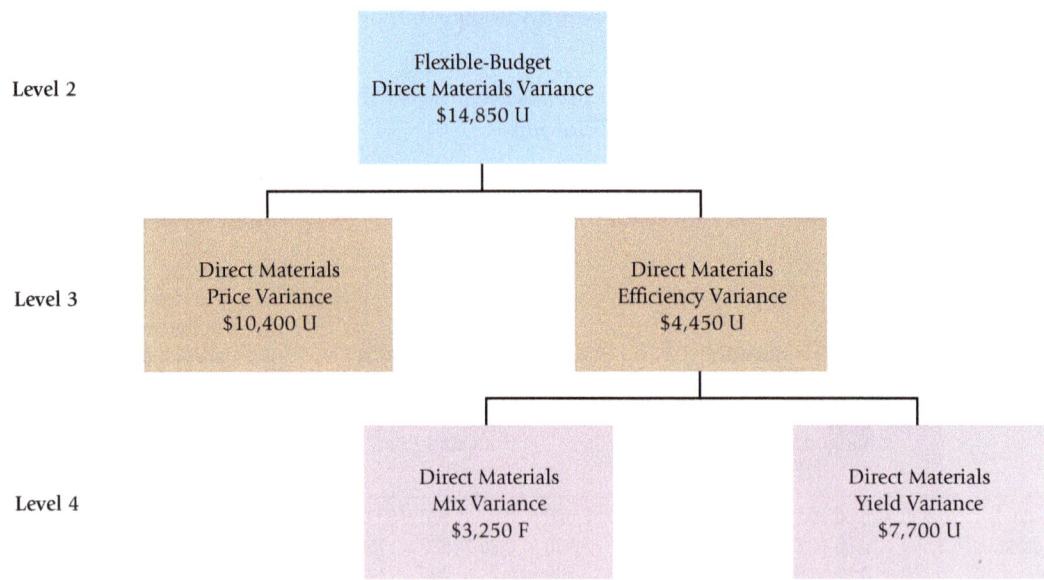

Terms to Learn

This chapter and the Glossary at the end of the book contain definitions of the following important terms:

composite unit **(p. 521)**

customer-cost hierarchy **(p. 511)**

customer-profitability analysis **(p. 510)**

direct materials mix variance **(p. 527)**

direct materials yield variance **(p. 527)**

homogeneous cost pool **(p. 509)**

price discount **(p. 511)**

sales-mix variance **(p. 521)**

sales-quantity variance **(p. 521)**

whale curve **(p. 516)**

Assignment Material

Questions

14-1 "I am going to focus on the customers of my business and leave cost-allocation issues to my accountant." Do you agree with this comment by a division president? Why?

14-2 A given cost may be allocated for one or more purposes. List four purposes.

14-3 What criteria might be used to guide cost-allocation decisions? Which are the dominant criteria?

14-4 "A company should not allocate all of its corporate costs to its divisions." Do you agree? Explain.

14-5 "Once a company allocates corporate costs to divisions, these costs should not be reallocated to the indirect-cost pools of the division." Do you agree? Explain.

14-6 Why is customer-profitability analysis a vitally important topic to managers?

14-7 How can the extent of price discounting be tracked on a customer-by-customer basis?

14-8 "A customer-profitability profile highlights those customers who should be dropped to improve profitability." Do you agree? Explain.

14-9 Give examples of three different levels of costs in a customer-cost hierarchy.

14-10 What information does the whale curve provide?

14-11 Show how managers can gain insight into the causes of a sales-volume variance by subdividing the components of this variance.

14-12 How can the concept of a composite unit be used to explain why an unfavorable total sales-mix variance of contribution margin occurs?

14-13 Explain why a favorable sales-quantity variance occurs.

14-14 How can the sales-quantity variance be decomposed further?

14-15 Explain how the direct materials mix and yield variances provide additional information about the direct materials efficiency variance.

Exercises

14-16 Cost allocation in hospitals, alternative allocation criteria. Dave Meltzer vacationed at Lake Tahoe last winter. Unfortunately, he broke his ankle while skiing and spent two days at the Sierra University Hospital. Meltzer's insurance company received a $4,800 bill for his two-day stay. One item that caught Meltzer's attention was an $11.52 charge for a roll of cotton. Meltzer is a salesman for Johnson & Johnson and knows that the cost to the hospital of the roll of cotton is in the $2.20 to $3.00 range. He asked for a breakdown of the $11.52 charge. The accounting office of the hospital sent him the following information:

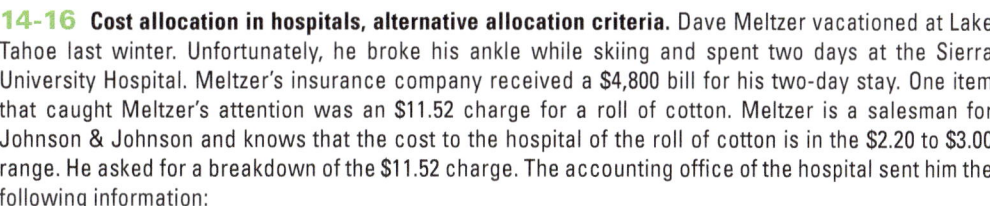

a.	Invoiced cost of cotton roll	$ 2.40
b.	Cost of processing of paperwork for purchase	0.60
c.	Supplies-room management fee	0.70
d.	Operating-room and patient-room handling costs	1.60
e.	Administrative hospital costs	1.10
f.	University teaching-related costs	0.60
g.	Malpractice insurance costs	1.20
h.	Cost of treating uninsured patients	2.72
i.	Profit component	0.60
	Total	$11.52

Meltzer believes the overhead charge is obscene. He comments, "There was nothing I could do about it. When they come in and dab your stitches, it's not as if you can say, 'Keep your cotton roll. I brought my own.'"

Required

1. Compute the overhead rate Sierra University Hospital charged on the cotton roll.
2. What criteria might Sierra use to justify allocation of the overhead items **b–i** in the preceding list? Examine each item separately and use the allocation criteria listed in Exhibit 14-2 (p. 505) in your answer.
3. What should Meltzer do about the $11.52 charge for the cotton roll?

14-17 Cost allocation and decision making. Greenbold Manufacturing has four divisions named after its locations: Arizona, Colorado, Delaware, and Florida. Corporate headquarters is in Minnesota. Greenbold corporate headquarters incurs $5,600,000 per period, which is an indirect cost of the divisions. Corporate headquarters currently allocates this cost to the divisions based on the revenues of each division. The CEO has asked each division manager to suggest an allocation base for the indirect headquarters costs from among revenues, segment margin, direct costs, and number of employees. The following is relevant information about each division:

	Arizona	Colorado	Delaware	Florida
Revenues	$7,800,000	$8,500,000	$6,200,000	$5,500,000
Direct costs	5,300,000	4,100,000	4,300,000	4,600,000
Segment margin	$2,500,000	$4,400,000	$1,900,000	$ 900,000
Number of employees	2,000	4,000	1,500	500

Required

1. Allocate the indirect headquarters costs of Greenbold Manufacturing to each of the four divisions using revenues, direct costs, segment margin, and number of employees as the allocation bases. Calculate operating margins for each division after allocating headquarters costs.
2. Which allocation base do you think the manager of the Florida division would prefer? Explain.
3. What factors would you consider in deciding which allocation base Greenbold should use?
4. Suppose the Greenbold CEO decides to use direct costs as the allocation base. Should the Florida division be closed? Why or why not?

14-18 Cost allocation to divisions. Rembrandt Hotel & Casino is situated on beautiful Lake Tahoe in Nevada. The complex includes a 300-room hotel, a casino, and a restaurant. As Rembrandt's new controller, you are asked to recommend the basis to be used for allocating fixed overhead costs to the three divisions in 2012. You are presented with the following income statement information for 2011:

	Hotel	Restaurant	Casino
Revenues	$16,425,000	$5,256,000	$12,340,000
Direct costs	9,819,260	3,749,172	4,248,768
Segment margin	$ 6,605,740	$1,506,828	$ 8,091,232

You are also given the following data on the three divisions:

	Hotel	Restaurant	Casino
Floor space (square feet)	80,000	16,000	64,000
Number of employees	200	50	250

You are told that you may choose to allocate indirect costs based on one of the following: direct costs, floor space, or the number of employees. Total fixed overhead costs for 2011 was $14,550,000.

Required

1. Calculate division margins in percentage terms prior to allocating fixed overhead costs.
2. Allocate indirect costs to the three divisions using each of the three allocation bases suggested. For each allocation base, calculate division operating margins after allocations in dollars and as a percentage of revenues.
3. Discuss the results. How would you decide how to allocate indirect costs to the divisions? Why?
4. Would you recommend closing any of the three divisions (and possibly reallocating resources to other divisions) as a result of your analysis? If so, which division would you close and why?

14-19 Cost allocation to divisions. Lenzig Corporation has three divisions: pulp, paper, and fibers. Lenzig's new controller, Ari Bardem, is reviewing the allocation of fixed corporate-overhead costs to the three divisions. He is presented with the following information for each division for 2012:

	A	B	C	D
		Pulp	Paper	Fibers
1				
2	Revenues	$8,500,000	$17,500,000	$24,000,000
3	Direct manufacturing costs	4,100,000	8,600,000	11,300,000
4	Division administrative costs	2,000,000	1,800,000	3,200,000
5	Division margin	$2,400,000	$ 7,100,000	$ 9,500,000
6				
7	Number of employees	350	250	400
8	Floor space (square feet)	35,000	24,000	66,000

Until now, Lenzig Corporation has allocated fixed corporate-overhead costs to the divisions on the basis of division margins. Bardem asks for a list of costs that comprise fixed corporate overhead and suggests the following new allocation bases:

	Home	Insert	Page Layout	Formulas	Data	Review	View
		F		G		H	
1	**Fixed Corporate Overhead Costs**				**Suggested Allocation Bases**		
2	Human resource management			$1,800,000	Number of employees		
3	Facility			2,700,000	Floor space (square feet)		
4	Corporate Administration			4,500,000	Division administrative costs		
5	Total			$9,000,000			

Required

1. Allocate 2012 fixed corporate-overhead costs to the three divisions using division margin as the allocation base. What is each division's operating margin percentage (division margin minus allocated fixed corporate-overhead costs as a percentage of revenues)?
2. Allocate 2012 fixed costs using the allocation bases suggested by Bardem. What is each division's operating margin percentage under the new allocation scheme?
3. Compare and discuss the results of requirements 1 and 2. If division performance is linked to operating margin percentage, which division would be most receptive to the new allocation scheme? Which division would be the least receptive? Why?
4. Which allocation scheme should Lenzig Corporation use? Why? How might Bardem overcome any objections that may arise from the divisions?

14-20 Customer profitability, customer-cost hierarchy. Orsack Electronics has only two retail and two wholesale customers. Information relating to each customer for 2012 follows (in thousands):

	Home	Insert	Page Layout	Formulas	Data	Review	View
	A		B	C	D	E	
1			**Wholesale Customers**		**Retail Customers**		
2			**North America Wholesaler**	**South America Wholesaler**	**Big Sam Stereo**	**World Market**	
3	Revenues at list price		$435,000	$550,000	$150,000	$115,000	
4	Discounts from list prices		30,000	44,000	7,200	520	
5	Cost of goods sold		330,000	475,000	123,000	84,000	
6	Delivery costs		475	690	220	130	
7	Order processing costs		750	1,020	175	120	
8	Costs of sales visits		5,400	2,500	2,500	1,400	

Orsack's annual distribution-channel costs are $34 million for wholesale customers and $5 million for retail customers. Its annual corporate-sustaining costs, such as salary for top management and general-administration costs, are $61 million. There is no cause-and-effect or benefits-received relationship between any cost-allocation base and corporate-sustaining costs. That is, corporate-sustaining costs could be saved only if Orsack Electronics were to completely shut down.

Required

1. Calculate customer-level operating income using the format in Exhibit 14-5.
2. Prepare a customer-cost hierarchy report, using the format in Exhibit 14-6.
3. Orsack's management decides to allocate all corporate-sustaining costs to distribution channels: $48 million to the wholesale channel and $13 million to the retail channel. As a result, distribution channel costs are now $82 million ($34 million + $48 million) for the wholesale channel and $18 million ($5 million + $13 million) for the retail channel. Calculate the distribution-channel-level operating income. On the basis of these calculations, what actions, if any, should Orsack's managers take? Explain.

14-21 Customer profitability, service company. Instant Service (IS) repairs printers and photocopiers for five multisite companies in a tristate area. IS's costs consist of the cost of technicians and equipment that are directly traceable to the customer site and a pool of office overhead. Until recently, IS estimated customer profitability by allocating the office overhead to each customer based on share of revenues. For 2012, IS reported the following results:

	A	B	C	D	E	F	G
1		**Avery**	**Okie**	**Wizard**	**Grainger**	**Duran**	**Total**
2	Revenues	$260,000	$200,000	$322,000	$122,000	$212,000	$1,116,000
3	Technician and equipment cost	182,000	175,000	225,000	107,000	178,000	867,000
4	Office overhead allocated	31,859	24,507	39,457	14,949	25,978	136,750
5	Operating income	$ 46,141	$ 493	$ 57,543	$ 51	$ 8,022	$ 112,250

Tina Sherman, IS's new controller, notes that office overhead is more than 10% of total costs, so she spends a couple of weeks analyzing the consumption of office overhead resources by customers. She collects the following information:

	I	J	K
1	**Activity Area**		**Cost Driver Rate**
2	Service call handling	$75	per service call
3	Parts ordering	$80	per Web-base parts order
4	Billing and collection	$50	per bill (or reminder)
5	Customer database maintenance	$10	per service call

	A	B	C	D	E	F
8		**Avery**	**Okie**	**Wizard**	**Grainger**	**Duran**
9	Number of service calls	150	240	40	120	180
10	Number of Web-based parts orders	120	210	60	150	150
11	Number of bills (or reminders)	30	90	90	60	120

Required

1. Compute customer-level operating income using the new information that Sherman has gathered.
2. Prepare exhibits for IS similar to Exhibits 14-7 and 14-8. Comment on the results.
3. What options should IS consider, with regard to individual customers, in light of the new data and analysis of office overhead?

14-22 Customer profitability, distribution. Figure Four is a distributor of pharmaceutical products. Its ABC system has five activities:

Activity Area	Cost Driver Rate in 2012
1. Order processing	$40 per order
2. Line-item ordering	$3 per line item
3. Store deliveries	$50 per store delivery
4. Carton deliveries	$1 per carton
5. Shelf-stocking	$16 per stocking-hour

Rick Flair, the controller of Figure Four, wants to use this ABC system to examine individual customer profitability within each distribution market. He focuses first on the Ma and Pa single-store distribution market. Two customers are used to exemplify the insights available with the ABC approach. Data pertaining to these two customers in August 2012 are as follows:

	Charleston Pharmacy	Chapel Hill Pharmacy
Total orders	13	10
Average line items per order	9	18
Total store deliveries	7	10
Average cartons shipped per store delivery	22	20
Average hours of shelf-stocking per store delivery	0	0.5
Average revenue per delivery	$2,400	$1,800
Average cost of goods sold per delivery	$2,100	$1,650

Required

1. Use the ABC information to compute the operating income of each customer in August 2012. Comment on the results and what, if anything, Flair should do.
2. Flair ranks the individual customers in the Ma and Pa single-store distribution market on the basis of monthly operating income. The cumulative operating income of the top 20% of customers is $55,680. Figure Four reports operating losses of $21,247 for the bottom 40% of its customers. Make four recommendations that you think Figure Four should consider in light of this new customer-profitability information.

14-23 Variance analysis, multiple products. The Detroit Penguins play in the American Ice Hockey League. The Penguins play in the Downtown Arena (owned and managed by the City of Detroit), which has a capacity of 15,000 seats (5,000 lower-tier seats and 10,000 upper-tier seats). The Downtown Arena charges the Penguins a per-ticket charge for use of its facility. All tickets are sold by the Reservation Network, which charges the Penguins a reservation fee per ticket. The Penguins' budgeted contribution margin for each type of ticket in 2012 is computed as follows:

	Lower-Tier Tickets	Upper-Tier Tickets
Selling price	$35	$14
Downtown Arena fee	10	6
Reservation Network fee	5	3
Contribution margin per ticket	$20	$ 5

The budgeted and actual average attendance figures per game in the 2012 season are as follows:

	Budgeted Seats Sold	Actual Seats Sold
Lower tier	4,000	3,300
Upper tier	6,000	7,700
Total	10,000	11,000

There was no difference between the budgeted and actual contribution margin for lower-tier or upper-tier seats.

The manager of the Penguins was delighted that actual attendance was 10% above budgeted attendance per game, especially given the depressed state of the local economy in the past six months.

Required

1. Compute the sales-volume variance for each type of ticket and in total for the Detroit Penguins in 2012. (Calculate all variances in terms of contribution margins.)
2. Compute the sales-quantity and sales-mix variances for each type of ticket and in total in 2012.
3. Present a summary of the variances in requirements 1 and 2. Comment on the results.

14-24 Variance analysis, working backward. The Jinwa Corporation sells two brands of wine glasses: Plain and Chic. Jinwa provides the following information for sales in the month of June 2011:

Static-budget total contribution margin	$11,000
Budgeted units to be sold of all glasses	2,000 units
Budgeted contribution margin per unit of Plain	$4 per unit
Budgeted contribution margin per unit of Chic	$10 per unit
Total sales-quantity variance	$2,200 U
Actual sales-mix percentage of Plain	60%

All variances are to be computed in contribution-margin terms.

Required

1. Calculate the sales-quantity variances for each product for June 2011.
2. Calculate the individual-product and total sales-mix variances for June 2011. Calculate the individual-product and total sales-volume variances for June 2011.
3. Briefly describe the conclusions you can draw from the variances.

14-25 Variance analysis, multiple products. Soda-King manufactures and sells three soft drinks: Kola, Limor, and Orlem. Budgeted and actual results for 2011 are as follows:

	Budget for 2011			Actual for 2011		
Product	Selling Price	Variable Cost per Carton	Cartons Sold	Selling Price	Variable Cost per Carton	Cartons Sold
Kola	$8.00	$5.00	480,000	$8.20	$5.50	467,500
Limor	$6.00	$3.80	720,000	$5.75	$3.75	852,500
Orlem	$7.50	$5.50	1,200,000	$7.80	$5.60	1,430,000

Required

1. Compute the total sales-volume variance, the total sales-mix variance, and the total sales-quantity variance. (Calculate all variances in terms of contribution margin.) Show results for each product in your computations.
2. What inferences can you draw from the variances computed in requirement 1?

14-26 Market-share and market-size variances (continuation of 14-25). Soda-King prepared the budget for 2011 assuming a 12% market share based on total sales in the western region of the United States. The total soft drinks market was estimated to reach sales of 20 million cartons in the region. However, actual total sales volume in the western region was 27.5 million cartons.

Required Calculate the market-share and market-size variances for Soda-King in 2011. (Calculate all variances in terms of contribution margin.) Comment on the results.

MyAccountingLab

Problems

14-27 Allocation of corporate costs to divisions. Dusty Rhodes, controller of Richfield Oil Company, is preparing a presentation to senior executives about the performance of its four divisions. Summary data (dollar amounts in millions) related to the four divisions for the most recent year are as follows:

	Home	Insert	Page Layout	Formulas	Data	Review	View
	A	B	C	D	E	F	
1			DIVISIONS				
2		Oil & Gas Upstream	Oil & Gas Downstream	Chemical Products	Copper Mining	Total	
3	Revenues	$ 8,000	$16,000	$4,800	$3,200	$32,000	
4	Operating Costs	3,000	15,000	3,800	3,500	25,300	
5	Operating Income	$ 5,000	$ 1,000	$1,000	$ (300)	$ 6,700	
6							
7	Identifiable assets	$14,000	$ 6,000	$3,000	$2,000	$25,000	
8	Number of employees	9,000	12,000	6,000	3,000	30,000	

Under the existing accounting system, costs incurred at corporate headquarters are collected in a single cost pool ($3,228 million in the most recent year) and allocated to each division on the basis of its actual revenues. The top managers in each division share in a division-income bonus pool. Division income is defined as operating income less allocated corporate costs.

Rhodes has analyzed the components of corporate costs and proposes that corporate costs be collected in four cost pools. The components of corporate costs for the most recent year (dollar amounts in millions) and Rhodes' suggested cost pools and allocation bases are as follows:

	Home	Insert	Page Layout	Formulas	Data	Review	View	
	A		B	C	D	E		F
11	**Corporate Cost Category**		**Amount**	**Suggested Cost Pool**	**Suggested Allocation Base**			
12	Interest on debt		$2,000	Cost Pool 1	Identifiable assets			
13	Corporate salaries		150	Cost Pool 2				
14	Accounting and control		110	Cost Pool 2				
15	General marketing		200	Cost Pool 2	Division revenues			
16	Legal		140	Cost Pool 2				
17	Research and development		200	Cost Pool 2				
18	Public affairs		203	Cost Pool 3	Positive operating income*			
19	Personnel and payroll		225	Cost Pool 4	Number of employees			
20	Total		$3,228					
21								
22	*Since public affairs cost includes the cost of public relations staff, lobbyists, and donations to							
23	environmental charities, Rhodes proposes that this cost be allocated using operating income (if positive)							
24	of divisions, with only divisions with positive operating income included in the allocation base.							

Required

1. Discuss two reasons why Richfield Oil should allocate corporate costs to each division.
2. Calculate the operating income of each division when all corporate costs are allocated based on revenues of each division.
3. Calculate the operating income of each division when all corporate costs are allocated using the four cost pools.
4. How do you think the new proposal will be received by the division managers? What are the strengths and weaknesses of Rhodes' proposal relative to the existing single-cost-pool method?

14-28 Cost allocation to divisions. Forber Bakery makes baked goods for grocery stores, and has three divisions: bread, cake, and doughnuts. Each division is run and evaluated separately, but the main headquarters incurs costs that are indirect costs for the divisions. Costs incurred in the main headquarters are as follows:

Human resources (HR) costs	$1,900,000
Accounting department costs	1,400,000
Rent and depreciation	1,200,000
Other	600,000
Total costs	$5,100,000

The Forber upper management currently allocates this cost to the divisions equally. One of the division managers has done some research on activity-based costing and proposes the use of different allocation bases for the different indirect costs—number of employees for HR costs, total revenues for accounting department costs, square feet of space for rent and depreciation costs, and equal allocation among the divisions of "other" costs. Information about the three divisions follows:

	Bread	Cake	Doughnuts
Total revenues	$20,900,000	$4,500,000	$13,400,000
Direct costs	14,500,000	3,200,000	7,250,000
Segment margin	$ 6,400,000	$1,300,000	$ 6,150,000
Number of employees	400	100	300
Square feet of space	10,000	4,000	6,000

Required

1. Allocate the indirect costs of Forber to each division equally. Calculate division operating income after allocation of headquarter costs.

2. Allocate headquarter costs to the individual divisions using the proposed allocation bases. Calculate the division operating income after allocation. Comment on the allocation bases used to allocate headquarter costs.

3. Which division manager do you think suggested this new allocation. Explain briefly. Which allocation do you think is "better?"

14-29 Customer profitability. Ring Delights is a new company that manufactures custom jewelry. Ring Delights currently has six customers referenced by customer number: 01, 02, 03, 04, 05, and 06. Besides the costs of making the jewelry, the company has the following activities:

1. Customer orders. The salespeople, designers, and jewelry makers spend time with the customer. The cost driver rate is $40 per hour spent with a customer.

2. Customer fittings. Before the jewelry piece is completed the customer may come in to make sure it looks right and fits properly. Cost driver rate is $25 per hour.

3. Rush orders. Some customers want their jewelry quickly. The cost driver rate is $100 per rush order.

4. Number of customer return visits. Customers may return jewelry up to 30 days after the pickup of the jewelry to have something refitted or repaired at no charge. The cost driver rate is $30 per return visit.

Information about the six customers follows. Some customers purchased multiple items. The cost of the jewelry is 70% of the selling price.

Customer number	01	02	03	04	05	06
Sales revenue	$600	$4,200	$300	$2,500	$4,900	$700
Cost of item(s)	$420	$2,940	$210	$1,750	$3,430	$490
Hours spent on customer order	2	7	1	5	20	3
Hours on fittings	1	2	0	0	4	1
Number of rush orders	0	0	1	1	3	0
Number of returns visits	0	1	0	1	5	1

Required

1. Calculate the customer-level operating income for each customer. Rank the customers in order of most to least profitable and prepare a customer-profitability analysis, as in Exhibit 14-7.

2. Are any customers unprofitable? What is causing this? What should Ring Delights do with respect to these customers?

14-30 Customer profitability, distribution. Spring Distribution has decided to analyze the profitability of five new customers (see pp. 510–517). It buys bottled water at $12 per case and sells to retail customers at a list price of $14.40 per case. Data pertaining to the five customers are as follows:

	Customer				
	P	Q	R	S	T
Cases sold	2,080	8,750	60,800	31,800	3,900
List selling price	$14.40	$14.40	$14.40	$14.40	$14.40
Actual selling price	$14.40	$14.16	$13.20	$13.92	$12.96
Number of purchase orders	15	25	30	25	30
Number of customer visits	2	3	6	2	3
Number of deliveries	10	30	60	40	20
Miles traveled per delivery	14	4	3	8	40
Number of expedited deliveries	0	0	0	0	1

Its five activities and their cost drivers are as follows:

Activity	Cost Driver Rate
Order taking	$100 per purchase order
Customer visits	$80 per customer visit
Deliveries	$2 per delivery mile traveled
Product handling	$0.50 per case sold
Expedited deliveries	$300 per expedited delivery

Required

1. Compute the customer-level operating income of each of the five retail customers now being examined (P, Q, R, S, and T). Comment on the results.

2. What insights are gained by reporting both the list selling price and the actual selling price for each customer?

3. What factors should Spring Distribution consider in deciding whether to drop one or more of the five customers?

14-31 Customer profitability in a manufacturing firm. Bizzan Manufacturing makes a component called P14-31. This component is manufactured only when ordered by a customer, so Bizzan keeps no inventory of P14-31. The list price is $100 per unit, but customers who place "large" orders receive a 10% discount on price. Currently, the salespeople decide whether an order is large enough to qualify for the discount. When the product is finished, it is packed in cases of 10. When a customer order is not a multiple of 10, Bizzan uses a full case to pack the partial amount left over (e.g., if customer C orders 25 units, three cases will be required). Customers pick up the order so Bizzan incurs costs of holding the product in the warehouse until customer pick up. The customers are manufacturing firms; if the component needs to be exchanged or repaired, customers can come back within 10 days for free exchange or repair.

The full cost of manufacturing a unit of P14-31 is $80. In addition, Bizzan incurs customer-level costs. Customer-level cost-driver rates are as follows:

Order taking	$390 per order
Product handling	$10 per case
Warehousing (holding finished product)	$55 per day
Rush order processing	$540 per rush order
Exchange and repair costs	$45 per unit

Information about Bizzan's five biggest customers follows:

	A	B	C	D	E
Number of units purchased	6,000	2,500	1,300	4,200	7,800
Discounts given	10%	0	10%	0	10% on half the units
Number of orders	10	12	52	18	12
Number of cases	600	250	120	420	780
Days in warehouse (total for all orders)	14	18	0	12	140
Number of rush orders	0	3	0	0	6
Number of units exchanged/repaired	0	25	4	25	80

The salesperson gave customer C a price discount because, although customer C ordered only 1,300 units in total, 52 orders (one per week) were placed. The salesperson wanted to reward customer C for repeat business. All customers except E ordered units in the same order size. Customer E's order quantity varied, so E got a discount part of the time but not all the time.

1. Calculate the customer-level operating income for these five customers. Use the format in Exhibit 14-5. Prepare a customer-profitability analysis by ranking the customers from most to least profitable, as in Exhibit 14-7 [Required]

2. Discuss the results of your customer-profitability analysis. Does Bizzan have unprofitable customers? Is there anything Bizzan should do differently with its five customers?

14-32 Variance analysis, sales-mix and sales-quantity variances. Chicago Infonautics, Inc., produces handheld Windows CE™-compatible organizers. Chicago Infonautics markets three different handheld models: PalmPro is a souped-up version for the executive on the go, PalmCE is a consumer-oriented version, and PalmKid is a stripped-down version for the young adult market. You are Chicago Infonautics' senior vice president of marketing. The CEO has discovered that the total contribution margin came in lower than budgeted, and it is your responsibility to explain to him why actual results are different from the budget. Budgeted and actual operating data for the company's third quarter of 2012 are as follows:

Budgeted Operating Data, Third Quarter 2012

	Selling Price	Variable Cost per Unit	Contribution Margin per Unit	Sales Volume in Units
PalmPro	$374	$185	$189	13,580
PalmCE	272	96	176	35,890
PalmKid	144	66	78	47,530
				97,000

Actual Operating Data, Third Quarter 2012

	Selling Price	Variable Cost per Unit	Contribution Margin per Unit	Sales Volume in Units
PalmPro	$365	$175	$190	10,120
PalmCE	288	94	194	32,200
PalmKid	110	75	35	49,680
				92,000

1. Compute the actual and budgeted contribution margins in dollars for each product and in total for the third quarter of 2012.
2. Calculate the actual and budgeted sales mixes for the three products for the third quarter of 2012.
3. Calculate total sales-volume, sales-mix, and sales-quantity variances for the third quarter of 2012. (Calculate all variances in terms of contribution margins.)
4. Given that your CEO is known to have temper tantrums, you want to be well prepared for this meeting. In order to prepare, write a paragraph or two comparing actual results to budgeted amounts.

14-33 Market-share and market-size variances (continuation of 14-32). Chicago Infonautics' senior vice president of marketing prepared his budget at the beginning of the third quarter assuming a 25% market share based on total sales. The total handheld-organizer market was estimated by Foolinstead Research to reach sales of 388,000 units worldwide in the third quarter. However, actual sales in the third quarter were 400,000 units.

1. Calculate the market-share and market-size variances for Chicago Infonautics in the third quarter of 2012 (calculate all variances in terms of contribution margins).
2. Explain what happened based on the market-share and market-size variances.
3. Calculate the actual market size, in units, that would have led to no market-size variance (again using budgeted contribution margin per unit). Use this market-size figure to calculate the actual market share that would have led to a zero market-share variance.

14-34 Variance analysis, multiple products. The Split Banana, Inc., operates a chain of Italian gelato stores. Although the Split Banana charges customers the same price for all flavors, production costs vary, depending on the type of ingredients. Budgeted and actual operating data of its three Washington, DC, stores for August 2011 are as follows:

Budget for August 2011

	Selling Price per Pint	Variable Cost per Pint	Contribution Margin per Pints	Sales Volume in Pints
Mint chocolate chip	$9.00	$4.80	$4.20	25,000
Vanilla	9.00	3.20	5.80	35,000
Rum Raisin	9.00	5.00	4.00	5,000
Peach	9.00	5.40	3.60	15,000
Coffee	9.00	3.90	5.10	20,000
				100,000

Actual for August 2011

	Selling Price per Pint	Variable Cost per Pound	Contribution Margin per Pound	Sales Volume in Pounds
Mint chocolate chip	$9.00	$4.60	$4.40	30,800
Vanilla	9.00	3.25	5.75	27,500
Rum Raisin	9.00	5.15	3.85	8,800
Peach	9.00	5.40	3.60	14,300
Coffee	9.00	4.00	5.00	28,600
				110,000

The Split Banana focuses on contribution margin in its variance analysis.

1. Compute the total sales-volume variance for August 2011.
2. Compute the total sales-mix variance for August 2011.
3. Compute the total sales-quantity variance for August 2011.
4. Comment on your results in requirements 1, 2, and 3.

14-35 **Direct materials efficiency, mix, and yield variances.** Nature's Best Nuts produces specialty nut products for the gourmet and natural foods market. Its most popular product is Zesty Zingers, a mixture of roasted nuts that are seasoned with a secret spice mixture, and sold in one-pound tins. The direct materials used in Zesty Zingers are almonds, cashews, pistachios, and seasoning. For each batch of 100 tins, the budgeted quantities and budgeted prices of direct materials are as follows:

	Quantity for One Batch	Price of Input
Almonds	180 cups	$1 per cup
Cashews	300 cups	$2 per cup
Pistachios	90 cups	$3 per cup
Seasoning	30 cups	$6 per cup

Changing the standard mix of direct material quantities slightly does not significantly affect the overall end product, particularly for the nuts. In addition, not all nuts added to production end up in the finished product, as some are rejected during inspection.

In the current period, Nature's Best made 2,500 tins of Zesty Zingers in 25 batches with the following actual quantity, cost and mix of inputs:

	Actual Quantity	Actual Cost	Actual Mix
Almonds	5,280 cups	$ 5,280	33%
Cashews	7,520 cups	15,040	47%
Pistachios	2,720 cups	8,160	17%
Seasoning	480 cups	2,880	3%
Total actual	16,000 cups	$31,360	100%

Required

1. What is the budgeted cost of direct materials for the 2,500 tins?
2. Calculate the total direct materials efficiency variance.
3. Why is the total direct materials price variance zero?
4. Calculate the total direct materials mix and yield variances. What are these variances telling you about the 2,500 tins produced this period? Are the variances large enough to investigate?

14-36 **Direct labor variances: price, efficiency, mix, and yield.** Trevor Joseph employs two workers in his guitar-making business. The first worker, George, has been making guitars for 20 years and is paid $30 per hour. The second worker, Earl, is less experienced, and is paid $20 per hour. One guitar requires, on average, 10 hours of labor. The budgeted direct labor quantities and prices for one guitar are as follows:

	Quantity	Price per Hour of Labor	Cost for One Guitar
George	6 hours	$30 per hour	$180
Earl	4 hours	$20 per hour	80

That is, each guitar is budgeted to require 10 hours of direct labor, comprised of 60% of George's labor and 40% of Earl's, although sometimes Earl works more hours on a particular guitar and George less, or vice versa, with no obvious change in the quality or function of the guitar.

During the month of August, Joseph manufactures 25 guitars. Actual direct labor costs are as follows:

George (145 hours)	$4,350
Earl (108 hours)	2,160
Total actual direct labor cost	$6,510

Required

1. What is the budgeted cost of direct labor for 25 guitars?
2. Calculate the total direct labor price and efficiency variances.
3. For the 25 guitars, what is the total actual amount of direct labor used? What is the actual direct labor input mix percentage? What is the budgeted amount of George's and Earl's labor that should have been used for the 25 guitars?
4. Calculate the total direct labor mix and yield variances. How do these numbers relate to the total direct labor efficiency variance? What do these variances tell you?

14-37 **Purposes of cost allocation.** Sarah Reynolds recently started a job as an administrative assistant in the cost accounting department of Mize Manufacturing. New to the area of cost accounting, Sarah is puzzled by the fact that one of Mize's manufactured products, SR460, seem to have a different cost, depending on who asks for it. When the marketing department requested the cost of SR460 in order to determine pricing for the new catalog, Sarah was told to report one amount, but when a request came in the very next day from the financial reporting department, the cost of SR460, she was told the cost was very different. Sarah runs a report using Mize's cost accounting system, which produces the following cost elements for one unit of SR460:

Direct materials	$28.50
Direct manufacturing labor	16.35
Variable manufacturing overhead	8.76
Allocated fixed manufacturing overhead	32.84
Research and development costs specific to SR460[a]	6.20
Marketing costs[a]	5.95
Sales commissions[a]	11.40
Allocated administrative costs of production department	5.38
Allocated administrative costs of corporate headquarters	18.60
Customer service costs[a]	3.05
Distribution costs[a]	8.80

[a]These costs are specific to SR460, but would not be eliminated if SR460 were purchased from an outside supplier.

Required

1. Explain to Sarah why the cost given to the marketing and financial reporting departments would be different.
2. Calculate the cost of one unit of SR460 to determine the following:
   a. The selling price of SR460
   b. The cost of inventory for financial reporting
   c. Whether to continue manufacturing SR460, or to purchase it from an outside source (Assume that SR460 is used as a component in one of Mize's other products.)
   d. The ability of Mize's production manager to control costs

14-38 Customer-cost hierarchy, customer profitability. Denise Nelson operates Interiors by Denise, an interior design consulting and window treatment fabrication business. Her business is made up of two different distribution channels, a consulting business in which Denise serves two architecture firms (Attractive Abodes and Better Buildings), and a commercial window treatment business in which Denise designs and constructs window treatments for three commercial clients (Cheery Curtains, Delightful Drapes, and Elegant Extras). Denise would like to evaluate the profitability of her two architecture firm clients and three commercial window treatment clients, as well as evaluate the profitability of each of the two divisions, and the business as a whole. Information about her most recent quarter follow:

Gross revenue from Attractive Abodes (AA)	$58,500
Gross revenue from Better Buildings (BB)	47,200
Gross revenue from Cheery Curtains (CC)	89,345
Gross revenue from Delightful Drapes (DD)	36,960
Gross revenue from Elegant Extras (EE)	18,300
Costs specific to AA	36,750
Costs specific to BB	29,300
Costs specific to CC	54,645
Costs specific to DD	28,930
Costs specific to EE	14,260
Overhead costs[a]	85,100

[a]Denise has determined that 25% of her overhead costs relate directly to her architectural business, 40% relate directly to her window treatment business, and the remainder is general in nature.

Denise gave a 10% discount to Attractive Abodes in order to lure it away from a competitor, and gave a 5% discount to Elegant Extras for advance payment in cash.

Required

1. Prepare a customer-cost hierarchy report for Interiors by Denise, using the format in Exhibit 14-6.
2. Prepare a customer-profitability analysis for the five customers, using the format in Exhibit 14-7.
3. Comment on the results of the preceding reports. What recommendations would you give Denise?

Collaborative Learning Problem

14-39 Customer profitability and ethics. Snark Corporation manufactures a product called the snark, which it sells to merchandising firms such as Snark Republic (SR), Snarks-R-Us (SRU), Neiman Snark-us (NS), Snark Buy (SB), Snark-Mart (SM), and Wal-Snark (WS). The list price of a snark is $50, and the full manufacturing costs are $35. Salespeople receive a commission on sales, but the commission is based on number of orders taken, not on sales revenue generated or number of units sold. Salespeople receive a commission of $25 per order (in addition to regular salary).

Snark Corporation makes products based on anticipated demand. Snark Corporation carries an inventory of snarks so rush orders do not result in any extra manufacturing costs over and above the $35 per snark. Snark Corporation ships finished product to the customer at no additional charge to the customer for either regular or expedited delivery. Snark incurs significantly higher costs for expedited deliveries than for regular deliveries. Customers occasionally return shipments to Snark, and these returns are subtracted from gross revenue. The customers are not charged a restocking fee for returns

Budgeted (expected) customer-level cost driver rates are as follows:

Order taking (excluding sales commission)	$30 per order
Product handling	$2 per unit
Delivery	$0.50 per mile driven
Expedited (rush) delivery	$325 per shipment
Restocking	$100 per returned shipment
Visits to customers	$150 per customer

Because salespeople are paid $25 per order, they often break up large orders into multiple smaller orders. This practice reduces the actual order taking cost by $16 per smaller order (from $30 per order to $14 per order) because the smaller orders are all written at the same time. This lower cost rate is not included in budgeted rates because salespeople create smaller orders without telling management or the accounting department. All other actual costs are the same as budgeted costs.

Information about Snark's clients follows:

	SR	SRU	NS	SB	SM	WS
Total number of units purchased	250	550	320	130	450	1,200
Number of actual orders	3	15	3	4	5	15
Number of written orders	6	15*	8	7	20	30
Total number of miles driven to deliver all products	420	620	470	280	806	900
Total number of units returned	20	35	0	0	40	60
Number of returned shipments	2	1	0	0	2	6
Number of expedited deliveries	0	6	0	0	2	5

*Because SRU places 15 separate orders, its order costs are $30 per order. All other orders are multiple smaller orders and so have actual order costs of $14 each.

1. Classify each of the customer-level operating costs as a customer output-unit-level, customer batch-level, or customer-sustaining cost. **Required**
2. Using the preceding information, calculate the expected customer-level operating income for the six customers of Snark Corporation. Use the number of written orders at $30 each to calculate expected order costs.
3. Recalculate the customer-level operating income using the number of written orders but at their actual $14 cost per order instead of $30 (except for SRU, whose actual cost is $30 per order). How will Snark Corporation evaluate customer-level operating cost performance this period?
4. Recalculate the customer-level operating income if salespeople had not broken up actual orders into multiple smaller orders. Don't forget to also adjust sales commissions.
5. How is the behavior of the salespeople affecting the profit of Snark Corporation? Is their behavior ethical? What could Snark Corporation do to change the behavior of the salespeople?

15 Allocation of Support-Department Costs, Common Costs, and Revenues

▶ Learning Objectives

1. Distinguish the single-rate method from the dual-rate method

2. Understand how divisional incentives are affected by the choice between allocation based on budgeted and actual rates, and budgeted and actual usage

3. Allocate multiple support-department costs using the direct method, the step-down method, and the reciprocal method

4. Allocate common costs using the stand-alone method and the incremental method

5. Explain the importance of explicit agreement between contracting parties when the reimbursement amount is based on costs incurred

6. Understand how bundling of products gives rise to revenue allocation issues and the methods for doing so

How a company allocates its overhead and internal support costs—costs related to marketing, advertising, and other internal services—among its various production departments or projects, can have a big impact on how profitable those departments or projects are.

While the allocation won't affect the firm's profit as a whole, if the allocation isn't done properly, it can make some departments and projects (and their managers) look better or worse than they should profit-wise. As the following article shows, the method of allocating costs for a project affects not just the firm but also the consumer. Based on the method used, consumers may spend more, or less, for the same service.

Cost Allocation and the Future of "Smart Grid" Energy Infrastructure[1]

Across the globe, countries are adopting alternative methods of generating and distributing energy. In the United States, government leaders and companies ranging from GE to Google are advocating the movement towards a "Smart Grid"—that is, making transmission and power lines operate and communicate in a more effective and efficient manner using technology, computers, and software. This proposed system would also integrate with emerging clean energy sources, such as solar farms and geothermal systems, to help create a more sustainable electricity supply that reduces carbon emissions.

According to the Electric Power Resource Institute, the cost of developing the "Smart Grid" is $165 billion over the next two decades. These costs include new infrastructure and technology improvements—mostly to power lines—as well as traditional indirect costs for the organizations upgrading the power system, which include traditional support-department costs and common costs. Private utilities and the U.S. government will pay for the upfront costs of "Smart Grid" development, but those costs will be recouped over time by charging energy consumers. But one question remains: How should those costs be allocated for reimbursement?

A controversy has emerged as two cost allocation methods are being debated by the U.S. government. One method is

---

[1] *Sources*: Garthwaite, Josie. 2009. The $160B question: Who should foot the bill for transmission buildout?" Salon.com, March 12; Jaffe, Mark. 2010. Cost of Smart-Grid projects shocks consumer advocates. *The Denver Post*, February 14.

interconnection-wide cost allocation. Under this system, everybody in the region where a new technology is deployed would have to help pay for it. For example, if new power lines and "smart" energy meters are deployed in Denver, everybody in Colorado would help pay for them. Supporters argue that this method would help lessen the costs consumers would be charged by utilities for the significant investments in new technology.

Another competing proposal would only allocate costs to utility ratepayers that actually benefit from the new "Smart Grid" system. Using the previous example, only utility customers in Denver would be charged for the new power lines and energy meters (likely through additional monthly utility costs). Supporters of this method believe that customers with new "Smart Grid" systems should not be subsidized by those not receiving any of the benefits.

Regardless of the method selected, cost allocation is going to play a key role in the future of the U.S. energy generation and distribution system. The same allocation dilemmas apply to the costs of corporate support departments and the apportionment of revenues when products are sold in bundles. These concerns are common to managers at manufacturing companies such as Nestle, service companies such as Comcast, merchandising companies such as Trader Joe's, and academic institutions such as Auburn University. This chapter focuses on several challenges that arise with regard to cost and revenue allocations.

Allocating Support Department Costs Using the Single-Rate and Dual-Rate Methods

Learning Objective 1

Distinguish the single-rate method

. . . one rate for allocating costs in a cost pool

from the dual-rate method

. . . two rates for allocating costs in a cost pool—one for variable costs and one for fixed costs

Companies distinguish operating departments (and operating divisions) from support departments. An **operating department**, also called a **production department**, directly adds value to a product or service. A **support department**, also called a **service department**, provides the services that assist other internal departments (operating departments and other support departments) in the company. Examples of support departments are information systems and plant maintenance. Managers face two questions when allocating the costs of a support department to operating departments or divisions: (1) Should fixed costs of support departments be allocated to operating divisions? (2) If fixed costs are allocated, should variable and fixed costs be allocated in the same way? With regard to the first question, most companies believe that fixed costs of support departments should be allocated because the support department needs to incur fixed costs to provide operating divisions with the services they require. Depending on the answer to the second question, there are two approaches to allocating support-department costs: the *single-rate cost-allocation method* and the *dual-rate cost-allocation method*.

Single-Rate and Dual-Rate Methods

The **single-rate method** makes no distinction between fixed and variable costs. It allocates costs in each cost pool (support department in this section) to cost objects (operating divisions in this section) using the same rate per unit of a single allocation base. By contrast, the **dual-rate method** partitions the cost of each support department into two pools, a variable-cost pool and a fixed-cost pool, and allocates each pool using a different cost-allocation base. When using either the single-rate method or the dual-rate method, managers can allocate support-department costs to operating divisions based on either a *budgeted* rate or the eventual *actual* cost rate. The latter approach is neither conceptually preferred nor widely used in practice (we explain why in the next section). Accordingly, we illustrate the single-rate and dual-rate methods next based on the use of *budgeted* rates.

Consider the central computer department of Sand Hill Company (SHC). This support department has two users, both operating divisions: the microcomputer division and the peripheral equipment division. The following data relate to the 2012 budget:

Practical capacity	18,750 hours
Fixed costs of operating the computer facility in the 6,000-hour to 18,750-hour relevant range	$3,000,000
Budgeted long-run usage (quantity) in hours:	
Microcomputer division	8,000 hours
Peripheral equipment division	4,000 hours
Total	12,000 hours
Budgeted variable cost per hour in the 6,000-hour to 18,750-hour relevant range	$200 per hour used
Actual usage in 2012 in hours:	
Microcomputer division	9,000 hours
Peripheral equipment division	3,000 hours
Total	12,000 hours

The budgeted rates for central computer department costs can be computed based on either the demand for computer services or the supply of computer services. We consider the allocation of central computer department costs based first on the demand for (or usage of) computer services and then on the supply of computer services.

Allocation Based on the Demand for (or Usage of) Computer Services

We present the single-rate method followed by the dual-rate method.

Single-Rate Method

In this method, a combined budgeted rate is used for fixed and variable costs. The rate is calculated as follows:

Budgeted usage	12,000 hours
Budgeted total cost pool: $3,000,000 + (12,000 hours × $200/hour)	$5,400,000
Budgeted total rate per hour: $5,400,000 ÷ 12,000 hours	$450 per hour used
Allocation rate for microcomputer division	$450 per hour used
Allocation rate for peripheral equipment division	$450 per hour used

Note that the budgeted rate of $450 per hour is substantially higher than the $200 budgeted *variable* cost per hour. That's because the $450 rate includes an allocated amount of $250 per hour (budgeted fixed costs, $3,000,000, ÷ budgeted usage, 12,000 hours) for the *fixed* costs of operating the facility.

Under the single-rate method, divisions are charged the budgeted rate for each hour of *actual* use of the central facility. Applying this to our example, SHC allocates central computer department costs based on the $450 per hour budgeted rate and actual hours used by the operating divisions. The support costs allocated to the two divisions under this method are as follows:

Microcomputer division: 9,000 hours × $450 per hour	$4,050,000
Peripheral equipment division: 3,000 hours × $450 per hour	$1,350,000

Dual-Rate Method

When the dual-rate method is used, allocation bases must be chosen for both the variable and fixed cost pools of the central computer department. As in the single-rate method, variable costs are assigned based on the *budgeted* variable cost per hour of $200 for *actual* hours used by each division. However, fixed costs are assigned based on *budgeted* fixed costs per hour and the *budgeted* number of hours for each division. Given the budgeted usage of 8,000 hours for the microcomputer division and 4,000 hours for the peripheral equipment division, the budgeted fixed-cost rate is $250 per hour ($3,000,000 ÷ 12,000 hours), as before. Since this rate is charged on the basis of the *budgeted* usage, however, the fixed costs are effectively allocated in advance as a lump-sum based on the relative proportions of the central computing facilities expected to be used by the operating divisions.

The costs allocated to the microcomputer division in 2012 under the dual-rate method would be as follows:

Fixed costs: $250 per hour × 8,000 (budgeted) hours	$2,000,000
Variable costs: $200 per hour × 9,000 (actual) hours	1,800,000
Total costs	$3,800,000

The costs allocated to the peripheral equipment division in 2012 would be as follows:

Fixed costs: $250 per hour × 4,000 (budgeted) hours	$1,000,000
Variable costs: $200 per hour × 3,000 (actual) hours	600,000
Total costs	$1,600,000

Note that each operating division is charged the same amount for variable costs under the single-rate and dual-rate methods ($200 per hour multiplied by the actual hours of use). However, the overall assignment of costs differs under the two methods because the single-rate method allocates fixed costs of the support department based on actual usage of computer resources by the operating divisions, whereas the dual-rate method allocates fixed costs based on budgeted usage.

We next consider the alternative approach of allocating central computer department costs based on the capacity of computer services supplied.

Allocation Based on the Supply of Capacity

We illustrate this approach using the 18,750 hours of practical capacity of the central computer department. The budgeted rate is then determined as follows:

Budgeted fixed-cost rate per hour, $3,000,000 ÷ 18,750 hours	$160 per hour
Budgeted variable-cost rate per hour	200 per hour
Budgeted total-cost rate per hour	$360 per hour

Using the same procedures for the single-rate and dual-rate methods as in the previous section, the support cost allocations to the operating divisions are as follows:

Single-Rate Method

Microcomputer division: $360 per hour × 9,000 (actual) hours	$3,240,000
Peripheral equipment division: $360 per hour × 3,000 (actual) hours	1,080,000
Fixed costs of unused computer capacity:	
$160 per hour × 6,750 hours[a]	1,080,000

[a]6,750 hours = Practical capacity of 18,750 – (9,000 hours used by microcomputer division + 3,000 hours used by peripheral equipment division).

Dual-Rate Method

Microcomputer division

Fixed costs: $160 per hour × 8,000 (budgeted) hours	$1,280,000
Variable costs: $200 per hour × 9,000 (actual) hours	1,800,000
Total costs	$3,080,000

Peripheral equipment division

Fixed costs: $160 per hour × 4,000 (budgeted) hours	$ 640,000
Variable costs: $200 per hour × 3,000 (actual) hours	600,000
Total costs	$1,240,000

Fixed costs of unused computer capacity:

$160 per hour × 6,750 hours[b]	$1,080,000

[b]6,750 hours = Practical capacity of 18,750 hours − (8,000 hours budgeted to be used by microcomputer division + 4,000 hours budgeted to be used by peripheral equipment division).

When practical capacity is used to allocate costs, the single-rate method allocates only the actual fixed-cost resources used by the microcomputer and peripheral equipment divisions, while the dual-rate method allocates the budgeted fixed-cost resources to be used by the operating divisions. Unused central computer department resources are highlighted but usually not allocated to the divisions.[2]

The advantage of using practical capacity to allocate costs is that it focuses management's attention on managing unused capacity (described in Chapter 9, pp. 317–318, and Chapter 13, pp. 486–487). Using practical capacity also avoids burdening the user divisions with the cost of unused capacity of the central computer department. In contrast, when costs are allocated on the basis of the demand for computer services, all $3,000,000 of budgeted fixed costs, including the cost of unused capacity, are allocated to user divisions. If costs are used as a basis for pricing, then charging user divisions for unused capacity could result in the downward demand spiral (see p. 316).

Single-Rate Versus Dual-Rate Method

There are benefits and costs of both the single-rate and dual-rate methods. One benefit of the single-rate method is the low cost to implement it. The single-rate method avoids the often-expensive analysis necessary to classify the individual cost items of a department into fixed and variable categories. Also, by conditioning the final allocations on the actual usage of central facilities, rather than basing them solely on uncertain forecasts of expected demand, it offers the user divisions some operational control over the charges they bear.

A problem with the single-rate method is that it makes the allocated fixed costs of the support department appear as variable costs to the operating divisions. Consequently, the single-rate method may lead division managers to make outsourcing decisions that are in their own best interest but that may be inefficient from the standpoint of the organization as a whole. Consider the setting where allocations are made on the basis of the demand for computer services. In this case, each user division is charged $450 per hour under the single-rate method (recall that $250 of this charge relates to the allocated fixed costs of the central computer department). Suppose an external vendor offers the microcomputer division computer services at a rate of $340 per hour, at a time when the central computer department has unused capacity. The microcomputer division's managers would be tempted to use this vendor because it would lower the division's costs ($340 per hour instead of the $450 per hour internal charge for computer services). In the short run, however, the fixed costs of the central computer department remain unchanged in the relevant range (between 6,000 hours of usage and the practical capacity of 18,750 hours). SHC will therefore incur an additional cost of $140 per hour if the managers were to take this offer—the difference between the $340 external purchase price and the true internal variable cost of $200 of using the central computer department.

---

[2] In our example, the cost of unused capacity under the single-rate and the dual-rate methods coincide (each equals $1,080,000). This occurs because the total actual usage of the facility matches the total expected usage of 12,000 hours. The budgeted cost of unused capacity (in the dual-rate method) can be either greater or lower than the actual cost (in the single-rate method), depending on whether the total actual usage is lower or higher than the budgeted usage.

The divergence created under the single-rate method between SHC's interests and those of its division managers is lessened when allocation is done on the basis of practical capacity. The variable cost per hour perceived by the operating division managers is now $360 (rather than the $450 rate when allocation is based on budgeted usage). However, any external offer above $200 (SHC's true variable cost) and below $360 (the single-rate charge per hour) will still result in the user manager preferring to outsource the service at the expense of SHC's overall profits.

A benefit of the dual-rate method is that it signals to division managers how variable costs and fixed costs behave differently. This information guides division managers to make decisions that benefit the organization as a whole, as well as each division. For example, using a third-party computer provider that charges more than $200 per hour would result in SHC's being worse off than if its own central computer department were used, because the latter has a variable cost of $200 per hour. Under the dual-rate method, neither division manager has an incentive to pay more than $200 per hour for an external provider because the internal charge for computer services is precisely that amount. By charging the fixed costs of resources budgeted to be used by the divisions as a lump-sum, the dual-rate method succeeds in removing fixed costs from the division managers' consideration when making marginal decisions regarding the outsourcing of services. It thus avoids the potential conflict of interest that can arise under the single-rate method.

Recently, the dual-rate method has been receiving more attention. Resource Consumption Accounting (RCA), an emerging management accounting system, employs an allocation procedure akin to a dual-rate system. For each cost/resource pool, cost assignment rates for fixed costs are based on practical capacity supplied, while rates for proportional costs (i.e., costs that vary with regard to the output of the resource pool) are based on planned quantities.[3]

Decision Point

When should managers use the dual-rate method over the single-rate method?

Budgeted Versus Actual Costs, and the Choice of Allocaton Base

The allocation methods previously outlined follow specific procedures in terms of the support department costs that are considered as well as the manner in which costs are assigned to the operating departments. In this section, we examine these choices in greater detail and consider the impact of alternative approaches. We show that the decision whether to use actual or budgeted costs, as well as the choice between actual and budgeted usage as allocation base, has a significant impact on the cost allocated to each division and the incentives of the division managers.

Budgeted Versus Actual Rates

In both the single-rate and dual-rate methods, we use budgeted rates to assign support department costs (fixed as well as variable costs). An alternative approach would involve using the actual rates based on the support costs realized during the period. This method is much less common because of the level of uncertainty it imposes on user divisions. When allocations are made using budgeted rates, managers of divisions to which costs are allocated know with certainty the rates to be used in that budget period. Users can then determine the amount of the service to request and—if company policy allows—whether to use the internal source or an external vendor. In contrast, when actual rates are used for cost allocation, user divisions are kept unaware of their charges until the end of the budget period.

Budgeted rates also help motivate the manager of the support (or supplier) department (for example, the central computer department) to improve efficiency. During the

Learning Objective 2

Understand how divisional incentives are affected by the choice between allocation based on budgeted and actual rates,

. . . budgeted rates provide certainty to users about charges and motivate the support division to engage in cost control

and budgeted and actual usage

. . . budgeted usage helps in planning and efficient utilization of fixed resources, actual usage controls consumption of variable resources

[3] Other salient features of Resource Consumption Accounting (RCA) include the selective use of activity-based costing, the nonassignment of fixed costs when causal relationships cannot be established, and the depreciation of assets based on their replacement cost. RCA has its roots in the nearly fifty-year-old German cost accounting system called Grenzplankostenrechnung (GPK), which is used by organizations such as Mercedes-Benz, Porsche, and Stihl. For further details, as well as illustrations of the use of RCA and GPK in organizations, see S. Webber and B. Clinton, "Resource Consumption Accounting Applied: The Clopay Case," *Management Accounting Quarterly* (Fall 2004) and B. Mackie, "Merging GPK and ABC on the Road to RCA," *Strategic Finance* (November 2006).

budget period, the support department, not the user divisions, bears the risk of any unfavorable cost variances. That's because user divisions do not pay for any costs or inefficiencies of the supplier department that cause actual rates to exceed budgeted rates.

The manager of the supplier department would likely view the budgeted rates negatively if unfavorable cost variances occur due to price increases outside of his or her control. Some organizations try to identify these uncontrollable factors and relieve the support department manager of responsibility for these variances. In other organizations, the supplier department and the user division agree to share the risk (through an explicit formula) of a large, uncontrollable increase in the prices of inputs used by the supplier department. This procedure avoids imposing the risk completely on either the supplier department (as when budgeted rates are used) or the user division (as in the case of actual rates).

For the rest of this chapter, we will continue to consider only allocation methods that are based on the budgeted cost of support services.

Budgeted Versus Actual Usage

In both the single-rate and dual-rate methods, the variable costs are assigned on the basis of budgeted rates and actual usage. Since the variable costs are directly and causally linked to usage, charging them as a function of the actual usage is appropriate. Moreover, allocating variable costs on the basis of budgeted usage would provide the user departments with no incentive to control their consumption of support services.

What about the fixed costs? Consider the budget of $3,000,000 fixed costs at the central computer department of SHC. Recall that budgeted usage is 8,000 hours for the microcomputer division and 4,000 hours for the peripheral equipment division. Assume that actual usage by the microcomputer division is always equal to budgeted usage. We consider three cases: when actual usage by the peripheral equipment division equals (Case 1), is greater than (Case 2), and is less than (Case 3) budgeted usage.

Fixed Cost Allocation Based on Budgeted Rates and Budgeted Usage

This is the dual-rate procedure outlined in the previous section. When budgeted usage is the allocation base, regardless of the actual usage of facilities (i.e., whether Case 1, 2, or 3 occurs), user divisions receive a preset lump-sum fixed cost charge. If rates are based on expected demand ($250 per hour), the microcomputer division is assigned $2,000,000 and the peripheral equipment division, $1,000,000. If rates are set using practical capacity ($160 per hour), the microcomputer division is charged $1,280,000, the peripheral equipment division is allocated $640,000, and the remaining $1,080,000 is the unallocated cost of excess capacity.

The advantage of knowing the allocations in advance is that it helps the user divisions with both short-run and long-run planning. Companies commit to infrastructure costs (such as the fixed costs of a support department) on the basis of a long-run planning horizon; budgeted usage measures the long-run demands of the user divisions for support-department services.

Allocating fixed costs on the basis of budgeted long-run usage may tempt some managers to underestimate their planned usage. Underestimating will result in their divisions bearing a lower percentage of fixed costs (assuming all other managers do not similarly underestimate their usage). To discourage such underestimates, some companies offer bonuses or other rewards—the "carrot" approach—to managers who make accurate forecasts of long-run usage. Other companies impose cost penalties—the "stick" approach—for underestimating long-run usage. For instance, a higher cost rate is charged after a division exceeds its budgeted usage.

Fixed Cost Allocation Based on Budgeted Rates and Actual Usage

Column 2 of Exhibit 15-1 provides the allocations when the budgeted rate is based on expected demand ($250 per hour), while column 3 shows the allocations when practical capacity is used to derive the rate ($160 per hour). Note that each operating division's

Exhibit 15-1 Effect of Variations in Actual Usage on Fixed Cost Allocation to Operating Divisions

	(1) Actual Usage		(2) Budgeted Rate Based on Expected Demand[a]		(3) Budgeted Rate Based on Practical Capacity[b]		(4) Allocation of Budgeted Total Fixed Cost	
Case	Micro. Div.	Periph. Div.	Micro. Div.	Periph. Div.	Micro. Div.	Periph. Div.	Micro. Div.	Periph. Div.
1	8,000 hours	4,000 hours	$2,000,000	$1,000,000	$1,280,000	$ 640,000	$2,000,000[c]	$1,000,000[d]
2	8,000 hours	7,000 hours	$2,000,000	$1,750,000	$1,280,000	$1,120,000	$1,600,000[e]	$1,400,000[f]
3	8,000 hours	2,000 hours	$2,000,000	$ 500,000	$1,280,000	$ 320,000	$2,400,000[g]	$ 600,000[h]

$$^a \frac{\$3,000,000}{(8,000 + 4,000)\ \text{hours}} = \$250\ \text{per hour} \qquad ^b \frac{\$3,000,000}{18,750\ \text{hours}} = \$160\ \text{per hour} \qquad ^c \frac{8,000}{(8,000 + 4,000)} \times \$3,000,000 \qquad ^d \frac{4,000}{(8,000 + 4,000)} \times \$3,000,000$$

$$^e \frac{8,000}{(8,000 + 7,000)} \times \$3,000,000 \qquad ^f \frac{7,000}{(8,000 + 7,000)} \times \$3,000,000 \qquad ^g \frac{8,000}{(8,000 + 2,000)} \times \$3,000,000 \qquad ^h \frac{2,000}{(8,000 + 2,000)} \times \$3,000,000$$

fixed cost allocation varies based on its actual usage of support facilities. However, variations in actual usage in one division do not affect the costs allocated to the other division. The microcomputer division is allocated either $2,000,000 or $1,280,000, depending on the budgeted rate chosen, independent of the peripheral equipment division's actual usage. Therefore, combining actual usage as the allocation base with budgeted rates provides user divisions with advanced knowledge of rates, as well as control over the costs charged to them.[4]

Note, however, that this allocation procedure for fixed costs is exactly the same as that under the single-rate method. As such, the procedure shares the disadvantages of the single-rate method discussed in the previous section, such as charging excessively high costs, including the cost of unused capacity, when rates are based on expected usage. Moreover, even when rates are based on practical capacity, recall that allocating fixed cost rates based on actual usage induces conflicts of interest between the user divisions and the firm when evaluating outsourcing possibilities.

Allocating Budgeted Fixed Costs Based on Actual Usage

Finally, consider the impact of having actual usage as the allocation base when the firm assigns total budgeted fixed costs to operating divisions (rather than specifying budgeted fixed cost rates, as we have thus far). If the budgeted fixed costs of $3,000,000 are allocated using budgeted usage, we are back in the familiar dual-rate setting. On the other hand, if the actual usage of the facility is the basis for allocation, the charges would equal the amounts in Exhibit 15-1, column 4. In Case 1, the fixed-cost allocation equals the budgeted amount (which is also the same as the charge under the dual-rate method). In Case 2, the fixed-cost allocation is $400,000 less to the microcomputer division than the amount based on budgeted usage ($1,600,000 versus $2,000,000). In Case 3, the fixed-cost allocation is $400,000 more to the microcomputer division than the amount based on budgeted usage ($2,400,000 versus $2,000,000). Why does the microcomputer division receive $400,000 more in costs in Case 3, even though its actual usage equals its budgeted usage? Because the total fixed costs of $3,000,000 are now spread over 2,000 fewer hours of actual total usage. In other words, the lower usage by the peripheral equipment division leads to an increase in the fixed costs allocated to the microcomputer division. When budgeted fixed costs are allocated based on actual usage, user divisions will not know their fixed cost allocations until the end of the budget period. This method therefore shares the same flaw as those that rely on the use of actual cost realizations rather than budgeted cost rates.

To summarize, there are excellent economic and motivational reasons to justify the precise forms of the single-rate and dual-rate methods considered in the previous section, and in particular, to recommend the dual-rate allocation procedure.

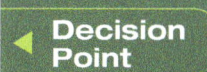

Decision Point

What factors should managers consider when deciding between allocation based on budgeted and actual rates, and budgeted and actual usage?

---

[4] The total amount of fixed costs allocated to divisions will in general not equal the actual realized costs. Adjustments for over-allocations and underallocations would then be made using the methods discussed previously in chapters 4, 7 and 8.

Allocating Costs of Multiple Support Departments

Learning Objective 3

Allocate multiple support-department costs using the direct method,

. . . allocates support-department costs directly to operating departments

the step-down method,

. . . partially allocates support-department costs to other support departments

and the reciprocal method

. . . fully allocates support-department costs to other support departments

We just examined general issues that arise when allocating costs from one support department to operating divisions. In this section, we examine the special cost-allocation problems that arise when two or more of the support departments whose costs are being allocated provide reciprocal support to each other as well as to operating departments. An example of reciprocal support is a firm's human resource department providing recruiting, training, and performance management services to all employees of a firm, including those who work in the legal department, while also utilizing the services of the legal department for compliance activities, drafting of contracts, checking stock option plan documents, etc. More accurate support-department cost allocations result in more accurate product, service, and customer costs.

Consider Castleford Engineering, which operates at practical capacity to manufacture engines used in electric-power generating plants. Castleford has two support departments and two operating departments in its manufacturing facility:

Support Departments	Operating Departments
Plant (and equipment) maintenance	Machining
Information systems	Assembly

The two support departments at Castleford provide reciprocal support to each other as well as support to the two operating departments. Costs are accumulated in each department for planning and control purposes. Exhibit 15-2 displays the data for this example. To understand the percentages in this exhibit, consider the plant maintenance department. This support department provides a total of 20,000 hours of support work: 20% (4,000 ÷ 20,000 = 0.20) for the information systems department, 30% (6,000 ÷ 20,000 = 0.30) for the machining department, and 50% (10,000 ÷ 20,000 = 0.50) for the assembly department.

We now examine three methods of allocating the costs of reciprocal support departments: *direct*, *step-down*, and *reciprocal*. To simplify the explanation and to focus on concepts, we use the single-rate method to allocate the costs of each support department using budgeted rates and budgeted hours used by the other departments. (The Problem for Self-Study illustrates the dual-rate method for allocating reciprocal support-department costs.)

Direct Method

The **direct method** allocates each support department's costs to operating departments only. The direct method does not allocate support-department costs to other support departments. Exhibit 15-3 illustrates this method using the data in Exhibit 15-2. The

---

Exhibit 15-2   Data for Allocating Support-Department Costs at Castleford Engineering for 2012

	A	B	C	D	E	F	G
		SUPPORT DEPARTMENTS			**OPERATING DEPARTMENTS**		
2		Plant Maintenance	Information Systems		Machining	Assembly	Total
3	Budgeted overhead costs						
4	before any interdepartment cost allocations	$6,300,000	$1,452,150		$4,000,000	$2,000,000	$13,752,150
5	Support work furnished:						
6	By plant maintenance						
7	Budgeted labor-hours	—	4,000		6,000	10,000	20,000
8	Percentage	—	20%		30%	50%	100%
9	By information systems						
10	Budgeted computer hours	500	—		4,000	500	5,000
11	Percentage	10%	—		80%	10%	100%

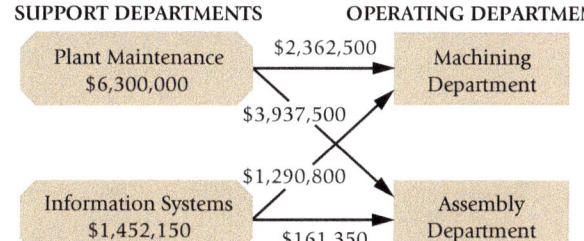

Exhibit 15-3

Direct Method of
Allocating Support-
Department Costs at
Castleford Engineering
for 2012

	A	B	C	D	E	F	G
1		**SUPPORT DEPARTMENTS**			**OPERATING DEPARTMENTS**		
2		**Plant Maintenance**	**Information Systems**		**Machining**	**Assembly**	**Total**
3	Budgeted overhead costs						
4	before any interdepartment cost allocations	$6,300,000	$1,452,150		$4,000,000	$2,000,000	$13,752,150
5	Allocation of plant maintenance (3/8, 5/8)[a]	(6,300,000)			2,362,500	3,937,500	
6	Allocation of information systems (8/9, 1/9)[b]		(1,452,150)		1,290,800	161,350	
7							
8	Total budgeted overhead of operating departments	$ 0	$ 0		$7,653,300	$6,098,850	$13,752,150
9							
10	[a] Base is (6,000 + 10,000), or 16,000 hours; 6,000 ÷ 16,000 = 3/8; 10,000 ÷ 16,000 = 5/8.						
11	[b] Base is (4,000 + 500), or 4,500 hours; 4,000 ÷ 4,500 = 8/9; 500 ÷ 4,500 = 1/9.						

base used to allocate plant maintenance costs to the operating departments is the budgeted total maintenance labor-hours worked in the operating departments: 6,000 + 10,000 = 16,000 hours. This amount excludes the 4,000 hours of budgeted support time provided by plant maintenance to information systems. Similarly, the base used for allocation of information systems costs to the operating departments is 4,000 + 500 = 4,500 budgeted hours of computer time, which excludes the 500 hours of budgeted support time provided by information systems to plant maintenance.

An equivalent approach to implementing the direct method involves calculating a budgeted rate for each support department's costs. For example, the rate for plant maintenance department costs is $6,300,000 ÷ 16,000 hours, or $393.75 per hour. The machining department is then allocated $2,362,500 ($393.75 per hour × 6,000 hours) while the assembly department is assigned $3,937,500 ($393.75 per hour × 10,000 hours). For ease of explanation throughout this section, we will use the fraction of the support-department services used by other departments, rather than calculate budgeted rates, to allocate support-department costs.

The direct method is widely practiced because of its ease of use. The benefit of the direct method is simplicity. There is no need to predict the usage of support-department services by other support departments. A disadvantage of the direct method is that it ignores information about reciprocal services provided among support departments and can therefore lead to inaccurate estimates of the cost of operating departments. We now examine a second approach, which partially recognizes the services provided among support departments.

Step-Down Method

Some organizations use the **step-down method,** also called the **sequential allocation method,** which allocates support-department costs to other support departments and to operating departments in a sequential manner that partially recognizes the mutual services provided among all support departments.

Exhibit 15-4 shows the step-down method. The plant maintenance costs of $6,300,000 are allocated first. Exhibit 15-2 shows that plant maintenance provides 20% of its services

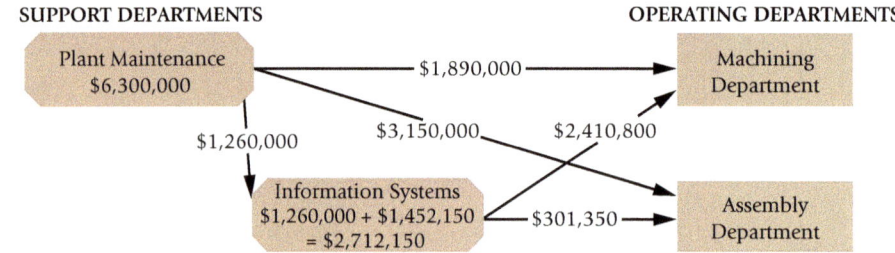

Exhibit 15-4

Step-Down Method of Allocating Support-Department Costs at Castleford Engineering for 2012

	Plant Maintenance	Information Systems	Machining	Assembly	Total
	SUPPORT DEPARTMENTS		OPERATING DEPARTMENTS		
3 Budgeted overhead costs before any					
4 interdepartment cost allocations	$6,300,000	$1,452,150	$4,000,000	$2,000,000	$13,752,150
5 Allocation of plant maintenance (2/10, 3/10, 5/10)[a]	(6,300,000)	1,260,000	1,890,000	3,150,000	
6		2,712,150			
7 Allocation of information systems (8/9, 1/9)[b]		(2,712,150)	2,410,800	301,350	
8					
9 Total budgeted overhead of operating departments	$ 0	$ 0	$8,300,800	$5,451,350	$13,752,150
10					
11 [a] Base is (4,000 + 6,000 + 10,000), or 20,000 hours; 4,000 ÷ 20,000 = 2/10; 6,000 ÷ 20,000 = 3/10; 10,000 ÷ 20,000 = 5/10.					
12 [b] Base is (4,000 + 500), or 4,500 hours; 4,000 ÷ 4,500 = 8/9; 500 ÷ 4,500 = 1/9.					

to information systems, 30% to machining, and 50% to assembly. Therefore, $1,260,000 is allocated to information systems (20% of $6,300,000), $1,890,000 to machining (30% of $6,300,000), and $3,150,000 to assembly (50% of $6,300,000). The information systems costs now total $2,712,150: budgeted costs of the information systems department before any interdepartmental cost allocations, $1,452,150, plus $1,260,000 from the allocation of plant maintenance costs to the information systems department. The $2,712,150 is then only allocated between the two operating departments based on the proportion of the information systems department services provided to machining and assembly. From Exhibit 15-2, the information systems department provides 80% of its services to machining and 10% to assembly, so $2,410,800 (8/9 × $2,712,150) is allocated to machining and $301,350 (1/9 × $2,712,150) is allocated to assembly.

Note that this method requires the support departments to be ranked (sequenced) in the order that the step-down allocation is to proceed. In our example, the costs of the plant maintenance department were allocated first to all other departments, including the information systems department. The costs of the information systems support department were allocated second, but only to the two operating departments. If the information systems department costs had been allocated first and the plant maintenance department costs second, the resulting allocations of support-department costs to operating departments would have been different. A popular step-down sequence begins with the support department that renders the highest percentage of its total services to *other support departments*. The sequence continues with the department that renders the next-highest percentage, and so on, ending with the support department that renders the lowest percentage.[5] In our example, costs of the plant maintenance department were allocated first because it provides 20% of its services to the information systems department, whereas the information systems department provides only 10% of its services to the plant maintenance department (see Exhibit 15-2).

[5] An alternative approach to selecting the sequence of allocations is to begin with the support department that renders the highest dollar amount of services to other support departments. The sequence ends with the allocation of the costs of the department that renders the lowest dollar amount of services to other support departments.

Under the step-down method, once a support department's costs have been allocated, no subsequent support-department costs are allocated back to it. Once the plant maintenance department costs are allocated, it receives no further allocation from other (lower-ranked) support departments. The result is that the step-down method does not recognize the total services that support departments provide to one another. The reciprocal method fully recognizes all such services, as you will see next.

Reciprocal Method

The **reciprocal method** allocates support-department costs to operating departments by fully recognizing the mutual services provided among all support departments. For example, the plant maintenance department maintains all the computer equipment in the information systems department. Similarly, information systems provide database support for plant maintenance. The reciprocal method fully incorporates interdepartmental relationships into the support-department cost allocations.

One way to understand the reciprocal method is as an extension of the step-down method. This approach is illustrated in Exhibit 15-5. As in the step-down procedure, plant maintenance costs are first allocated to all other departments, including the information systems support department: information systems, 20%; machining, 30%; assembly, 50%. The costs in the information systems department then total $2,712,150 ($1,452,150 + $1,260,000 from the first-round allocation), as in Exhibit 15-4. Under the step-down method, these costs are allocated directly to the operating departments alone. But the reciprocal method recognizes that a portion of the information systems department costs arises

Exhibit 15-5 Reciprocal Method of Allocating Support-Department Costs Using Repeated Iterations at Castleford Engineering for 2012

| | | Home | Insert | Page Layout | Formulas | Data | Review | View | | | | |

	A	B	C	D	E	F	G
1		SUPPORT DEPARTMENTS			OPERATING DEPARTMENTS		
2		Plant Maintenance	Information Systems		Machining	Assembly	Total
3	Budgeted overhead costs before any						
4	interdepartment cost allocations	$6,300,000	$1,452,150		$4,000,000	$2,000,000	$13,752,150
5	First allocation of plant maintenance (2/10, 3/10, 5/10)ᵃ	(6,300,000)	1,260,000		1,890,000	3,150,000	
6			2,712,150				
7	First allocation of information systems (1/10, 8/10, 1/10)ᵇ	271,215	(2,712,150)		2,169,720	271,215	
8	Second allocation of plant maintenance (2/10, 3/10, 5/10)ᵃ	(271,215)	54,243		81,364	135,608	
9	Second allocation of information systems (1/10, 8/10, 1/10)ᵇ	5,424	(54,243)		43,395	5,424	
10	Third allocation of plant maintenance (2/10, 3/10, 5/10)ᵃ	(5,424)	1,085		1,627	2,712	
11	Third allocation of information systems (1/10, 8/10, 1/10)ᵇ	109	(1,085)		867	109	
12	Fourth allocation of plant maintenance (2/10, 3/10, 5/10)ᵃ	(109)	22		33	54	
13	Fourth allocation of information systems (1/10, 8/10, 1/10)ᵇ	2	(22)		18	2	
14	Fourth allocation of plant maintenance (2/10, 3/10, 5/10)ᵃ	(2)	0		1	1	
15							
16	Total budgeted overhead of operating departments	$ 0	$ 0		$8,187,025	$5,565,125	$13,752,150
17							
18	Total support department amounts allocated and reallocated (the numbers in parentheses in the first two columns):						
19	Plant Maintenance: $6,300,000 + $271,215 + $5,424 + $109 + $2 = $6,576,750						
20	Information Systems: $2,712,150 + $54,243 + $1,085 + $22 = $2,767,500						
21							
22	ᵃ Base is (4,000 + 6,000 + 10,000), or 20,000 hours; 4,000 ÷ 20,000 = 2/10; 6,000 ÷ 20,000 = 3/10; 10,000 ÷ 20,000 = 5/10.						
23	ᵇ Base is (500 + 4,000 + 500), or 5,000 hours; 500 ÷ 5,000 = 1/10; 4,000 ÷ 5,000 = 8/10; 500 ÷ 5,000 = 1/10.						

because of the support it provides to plant maintenance. Accordingly, the $2,712,150 is allocated to all departments supported by the information systems department, including the plant maintenance department: plant maintenance, 10%; machining, 80%; and assembly, 10% (see Exhibit 15-2). The plant maintenance costs that had been brought down to $0 now have $271,215 from the information systems department allocation. In the next step, these costs are again reallocated to all other departments, including information systems, in the same ratio that the plant maintenance costs were previously assigned. Now the information systems department costs that had been brought down to $0 have $54,243 from the plant maintenance department allocations. These costs are again allocated in the same ratio that the information systems department costs were previously assigned. Successive rounds result in smaller and smaller amounts being allocated to and reallocated from the support departments until eventually all support-department costs are allocated to the operating departments. The final budgeted overhead costs for the operating departments under the reciprocal method are given by the amounts in line 16 of Exhibit 15-5.

An alternative way to implement the reciprocal method is to formulate and solve linear equations. This process requires three steps.

Step 1: Express Support Department Costs and Reciprocal Relationships in the Form of Linear Equations. We will use the term **complete reciprocated costs** or **artificial costs** to mean the support department's own costs plus any interdepartmental cost allocations. Let PM be the *complete reciprocated costs* of plant maintenance and IS be the *complete reciprocated costs* of information systems. We can then express the data in Exhibit 15-2 as follows:

$$PM = \$6,300,000 + 0.1IS \quad (1)$$
$$IS = \$1,452,150 + 0.2PM \quad (2)$$

The $0.1IS$ term in equation 1 is the percentage of the information systems services *used by* plant maintenance. The $0.2PM$ term in equation 2 is the percentage of plant maintenance services *used by* information systems.

Step 2: Solve the Set of Linear Equations to Obtain the Complete Reciprocated Costs of Each Support Department. Substituting equation 1 into 2,

$$IS = \$1,452,150 + [0.2(\$6,300,000 + 0.1IS)]$$
$$IS = \$1,452,150 + \$1,260,000 + 0.02IS$$
$$0.98IS = \$2,712,150$$
$$IS = \$2,767,500$$

Substituting this into equation 1,

$$PM = \$6,300,000 + 0.1(\$2,767,500)$$
$$PM = \$6,300,000 + \$276,750 = \$6,576,750$$

The complete reciprocated costs or artificial costs for plant maintenance and information systems are $6,576,750 and $2,767,500, respectively. Note that these are the same amounts that appear at the bottom of Exhibit 15-5 (lines 19 and 20) as the total support department costs allocated and reallocated during the iterative process. By setting up the system of simultaneous equations, we are able to solve for these amounts directly. When there are more than two support departments with reciprocal relationships, software such as Excel or Matlab is required to compute the complete reciprocated costs of each support department. Since the calculations involve finding the inverse of a matrix, the reciprocal method is also sometimes referred to as the **matrix method**.[6]

Step 3: Allocate the Complete Reciprocated Costs of Each Support Department to All Other Departments (Both Support Departments and Operating Departments) on the Basis of the Usage Percentages (Based on Total Units of Service Provided to All Departments).

---

[6] If there are n support departments, then Step 1 will yield n linear equations. Solving the equations to calculate the complete reciprocated costs then requires finding the inverse of an n-by-n matrix.

Consider the information systems department. The complete reciprocated costs of $2,767,500 are allocated as follows:

To plant maintenance (1/10) × $2,767,500	=$ 276,750
To machining (8/10) × $2,767,500	= 2,214,000
To assembly (1/10) × $2,767,500	= 276,750
Total	$2,767,500

Exhibit 15-6 presents summary data pertaining to the reciprocal method.

Castleford's $9,344,250 complete reciprocated costs of the support departments exceed the budgeted amount of $7,752,150.

Support Department	Complete Reciprocated Costs	Budgeted Costs	Difference
Plant maintenance	$6,576,750	$6,300,000	$ 276,750
Information systems	2,767,500	1,452,150	1,315,350
Total	$9,344,250	$7,752,150	$1,592,100

Each support department's complete reciprocated cost is greater than the budgeted amount to take into account that the support costs will be allocated to all departments using its services and not just to operating departments. This step ensures that the reciprocal method fully recognizes all interrelationships among support departments, as well as relationships between support and operating departments. The difference between complete

Exhibit 15-6 Reciprocal Method of Allocating Support-Department Costs Using Linear Equations at Castleford Engineering for 2012

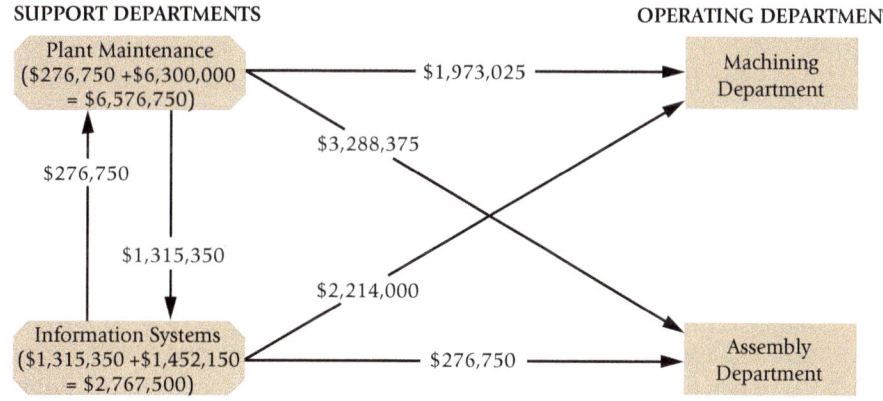

		SUPPORT DEPARTMENTS			OPERATING DEPARTMENTS		
	A	B	C	D	E	F	G
		Plant Maintenance	Information Systems		Machining	Assembly	Total
3	Budgeted overhead costs before any						
4	interdepartment cost allocations	$6,300,000	$1,452,150		$4,000,000	$2,000,000	$13,752,150
5	Allocation of plant maintenance (2/10, 3/10, 5/10)[a]	(6,576,750)	1,315,350		1,973,025	3,288,375	
6	Allocation of information systems (1/10, 8/10, 1/10)[b]	276,750	(2,767,500)		2,214,000	276,750	
7							
8	Total budgeted overhead of operating departments	$ 0	$ 0		$8,187,025	$5,565,125	$13,752,150
9							
10	[a] Base is (4,000 + 6,000 + 10,000), or 20,000 hours; 4,000 ÷ 20,000 = 2/10; 6,000 ÷ 20,000 = 3/10; 10,000 ÷ 20,000 = 5/10.						
11	[b] Base is (500 + 4,000 + 500), or 5,000 hours; 500 ÷ 5,000 = 1/10; 4,000 ÷ 5,000 = 8/10; 500 ÷ 5,000 = 1/10.						

reciprocated costs and budgeted costs for each support department reflects the costs allocated among support departments. The total costs allocated to the operating departments under the reciprocal method are still only $7,752,150.

Overview of Methods

Assume that Castleford reallocates the total budgeted overhead costs of each operating department in Exhibits 15-3 through 15-6 to individual products on the basis of budgeted machine-hours for the machining department (18,000 hours) and budgeted direct labor-hours for the assembly department (25,000 hours). The budgeted overhead allocation rates (to the nearest dollar) for each operating department by allocation method are as follows:

Support Department Cost-Allocation Method	Total Budgeted Overhead Costs After Allocation of All Support-Department Costs		Budgeted Overhead Rate per Hour for Product-Costing Purposes	
	Machining	Assembly	Machining (18,000 machine-hours)	Assembly (25,000 labor-hours)
Direct	$7,653,300	$6,098,850	$425	$244
Step-down	8,300,800	5,451,350	461	218
Reciprocal	8,187,025	5,565,125	455	223

These differences in budgeted overhead rates under the three support-department cost-allocation methods can, for example, affect the amount of costs Castleford is reimbursed for engines it manufactures under cost-reimbursement contracts. Consider a cost-reimbursement contract for a project that uses 200 machine-hours in the machining department and 50 direct labor-hours in the assembly department. The overhead costs allocated to this contract under the three methods would be as follows:

Direct: $97,200 ($425 per hour × 200 hours + $244 per hour × 50 hours)
Step-down: 103,100 ($461 per hour × 200 hours + $218 per hour × 50 hours)
Reciprocal: 102,150 ($455 per hour × 200 hours + $223 per hour × 50 hours)

The amount of cost reimbursed to Castleford will differ depending on the method used to allocate support-department costs to the contract. Differences among the three methods' allocations increase (1) as the magnitude of the reciprocal allocations increases and (2) as the differences across operating departments' usage of each support department's services increase. Note that while the final allocations under the reciprocal method are in between those under the direct and step-down methods in our example, this is not true in general. To avoid disputes in cost-reimbursement contracts that require allocation of support-department costs, managers should always clarify the method to be used for allocation. For example, Medicare reimbursements and federal contracts with universities that pay for the recovery of indirect costs typically mandate use of the step-down method, with explicit requirements about the costs that can be included in the indirect cost pools.

The reciprocal method is conceptually the most precise method because it considers the mutual services provided among all support departments. The advantage of the direct and step-down methods is that they are simple to compute and understand relative to the reciprocal method. However, as computing power to perform repeated iterations (as in Exhibit 15-5) or to solve sets of simultaneous equations (as on pp. 554–555) increases, more companies find the reciprocal method easier to implement.

Another advantage of the reciprocal method is that it highlights the complete reciprocated costs of support departments and how these costs differ from budgeted or actual costs of the departments. Knowing the complete reciprocated costs of a support department is a key input for decisions about whether to outsource all the services that the support department provides.

Suppose all of Castleford's support-department costs are variable over the period of a possible outsourcing contract. Consider a third party's bid to provide, say, all the information systems services currently provided by Castleford's information systems department. Do not compare the bid to the $1,452,150 costs reported for the information systems department. The complete reciprocated costs of the information systems department, which include the services the plant maintenance department provides the information systems department, are $2,767,500 to deliver 5,000 hours of computer time to all other departments at Castleford. The complete reciprocated costs for computer time are $553.50 per hour ($2,767,500 ÷ 5,000 hours). Other things being equal, a third party's bid to provide the same information services as Castleford's internal department at less than $2,767,500, or $553.50 per hour (even if much greater than $1,452,150) would improve Castleford's operating income.

To see this point, note that the relevant savings from shutting down the information systems department are $1,452,150 of information systems department costs *plus* $1,315,350 of plant maintenance department costs. By closing down the information systems department, Castleford will no longer incur the 20% of reciprocated plant maintenance department costs (equal to $1,315,350) that were incurred to support the information systems department. Therefore, the total cost savings are $2,767,500 ($1,452,150 + $1,315,350).[7] Neither the direct nor the step-down methods can provide this relevant information for outsourcing decisions.

We now consider common costs, another special class of costs for which management accountants have developed specific allocation methods.

Allocating Common Costs

A **common cost** is a cost of operating a facility, activity, or like cost object that is shared by two or more users. Common costs exist because each user obtains a lower cost by sharing than the separate cost that would result if such a user were an independent entity.

The goal is to allocate common costs to each user in a reasonable way. Consider Jason Stevens, a graduating senior in Seattle who has been invited to a job interview with an employer in Albany. The round-trip Seattle–Albany airfare costs $1,200. A week later, Stevens is also invited to an interview with an employer in Chicago. The Seattle–Chicago round-trip airfare costs $800. Stevens decides to combine the two recruiting trips into a Seattle–Albany–Chicago–Seattle trip that will cost $1,500 in airfare. The $1,500 is a common cost that benefits both prospective employers. Two methods of allocating this common cost between the two prospective employers are the stand-alone method and the incremental method.

Stand-Alone Cost-Allocation Method

The **stand-alone cost-allocation method** determines the weights for cost allocation by considering each user of the cost as a separate entity. For the common-cost airfare of $1,500, information about the separate (stand-alone) round-trip airfares ($1,200 and $800) is used to determine the allocation weights:

$$\text{Albany employer:} \quad \frac{\$1,200}{\$1,200 + \$800} \times \$1,500 = 0.60 \times \$1,500 = \$900$$

$$\text{Chicago employer:} \quad \frac{\$800}{\$800 + \$1,200} \times \$1,500 = 0.40 \times \$1,500 = \$600$$

Advocates of this method often emphasize the fairness or equity criterion described in Exhibit 14-2 (p. 504). The method is viewed as reasonable because each employer bears a proportionate share of total costs in relation to the individual stand-alone costs.

Incremental Cost-Allocation Method

The **incremental cost-allocation method** ranks the individual users of a cost object in the order of users most responsible for the common cost and then uses this ranking to allocate cost among those users. The first-ranked user of the cost object is the *primary user* (also called the *primary party*) and is allocated costs up to the costs of the primary user as a stand-alone user. The second-ranked user is the *first-incremental user* (*first-incremental party*) and

[7] Technical issues when using the reciprocal method in outsourcing decisions are discussed in R. S. Kaplan and A. A. Atkinson, *Advanced Management Accounting*, 3rd ed. (Upper Saddle River, NJ: Prentice Hall, 1998), 73–81.

is allocated the additional cost that arises from two users instead of only the primary user. The third-ranked user is the *second-incremental user* (*second-incremental party*) and is allocated the additional cost that arises from three users instead of two users, and so on.

To see how this method works, consider again Jason Stevens and his $1,500 airfare cost. Assume the Albany employer is viewed as the primary party. Stevens' rationale is that he had already committed to go to Albany before accepting the invitation to interview in Chicago. The cost allocations would be as follows:

Party	Costs Allocated	Cumulative Costs Allocated
Albany (primary)	$1,200	$1,200
Chicago (incremental)	300 ($1,500 – $1,200)	$1,500
Total	$1,500	

The Albany employer is allocated the full Seattle–Albany airfare. The unallocated part of the total airfare is then allocated to the Chicago employer. If the Chicago employer had been chosen as the primary party, the cost allocations would have been Chicago $800 (the stand-alone round-trip Seattle–Chicago airfare) and Albany $700 ($1,500 – $800). When there are more than two parties, this method requires them to be ranked from first to last (such as by the date on which each employer invited the candidate to interview).

Under the incremental method, the primary party typically receives the highest allocation of the common costs. If the incremental users are newly formed companies or subunits, such as a new product line or a new sales territory, the incremental method may enhance their chances for short-run survival by assigning them a low allocation of the common costs. The difficulty with the method is that, particularly if a large common cost is involved, every user would prefer to be viewed as the incremental party!

One approach to sidestep disputes in such situations is to use the stand-alone cost-allocation method. Another approach is to use the *Shapley value*, which considers each party as first the primary party and then the incremental party. From the calculations shown earlier, the Albany employer is allocated $1,200 as the primary party and $700 as the incremental party, for an average of $950 [($1,200 + $700) ÷ 2]. The Chicago employer is allocated $800 as the primary party and $300 as the incremental party, for an average of $550 [($800 + 300) ÷ 2]. The Shapley value method allocates, to each employer, the average of the costs allocated as the primary party and as the incremental party: $950 to the Albany employer and $550 to the Chicago employer.[8]

As our discussion suggests, allocating common costs is not clear-cut and can generate disputes. Whenever feasible, the rules for such allocations should be agreed on in advance. If this is not done, then, rather than blindly follow one method or another, managers should exercise judgment when allocating common costs. For instance, Stevens must choose an allocation method for his airfare cost that is acceptable to each prospective employer. He cannot, for example, exceed the maximum reimbursable amount of airfare for either firm. The next section discusses the role of cost data in various types of contracts, another area where disputes about cost allocation frequently arise.

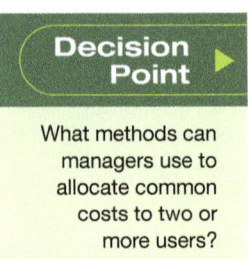

Decision Point ▶

What methods can managers use to allocate common costs to two or more users?

Learning Objective 5

Explain the importance of explicit agreement between contracting parties when the reimbursement amount is based on costs incurred

. . . to avoid disputes regarding allowable cost items and how indirect costs should be allocated

Cost Allocations and Contract Disputes

Many commercial contracts include clauses based on cost accounting information. Examples include the following:

■ A contract between the Department of Defense and a company designing and assembling a new fighter plane specifies that the price paid for the plane is to be based on the contractor's direct and overhead costs plus a fixed fee.

■ A contract between an energy-consulting firm and a hospital specifies that the consulting firm receive a fixed fee plus a share of the energy-cost savings that arise from implementing the consulting firm's recommendations.

[8] For further discussion of the Shapley value, see J. Demski, "Cost Allocation Games," in *Joint Cost Allocations*, ed. S. Moriarity (University of Oklahoma Center for Economic and Management Research, 1981); L. Kruz and P. Bronisz, "Cooperative Game Solution Concepts to a Cost Allocation Problem," *European Journal of Operations Research* 122 (2000): 258–271.

Contract disputes often arise with respect to cost allocation. The areas of dispute between the contracting parties can be reduced by making the "rules of the game" explicit and in writing at the time the contract is signed. Such rules of the game include the definition of allowable cost items; the definitions of terms used, such as what constitutes direct labor; the permissible cost-allocation bases; and how to account for differences between budgeted and actual costs.

Contracting with the U.S. Government

The U.S. government reimburses most contractors in one of two main ways:

1. **The contractor is paid a set price without analysis of actual contract cost data.** This approach is used, for example, when there is competitive bidding, when there is adequate price competition, or when there is an established catalog with prices quoted for items sold in substantial quantities to the general public.

2. **The contractor is paid after analysis of actual contract cost data.** In some cases, the contract will explicitly state that the reimbursement amount is based on actual allowable costs plus a fixed fee.[9] This arrangement is called a *cost-plus contract*.

All contracts with U.S. government agencies must comply with cost accounting standards issued by the **Cost Accounting Standards Board (CASB)**. For government contracts, the CASB has the exclusive authority to make, put into effect, amend, and rescind cost accounting standards and interpretations. The standards are designed to achieve *uniformity and consistency* in regard to measurement, assignment, and allocation of costs to government contracts within the United States.[10]

In government contracting, there is a complex interplay of political considerations and accounting principles. Terms such as "fairness" and "equity," as well as cause and effect and benefits received, are often used in government contracts.

Fairness of Pricing

In many defense contracts, there is great uncertainty about the final cost to produce a new weapon or equipment. Such contracts are rarely subject to competitive bidding. The reason is that no contractor is willing to assume all the risk of receiving a fixed price for the contract and subsequently incurring high costs to fulfill it. Hence, setting a market-based fixed price for the contract fails to attract contractors, or requires a contract price that is too high from the government's standpoint. To address this issue, the government typically assumes a major share of the risk of the potentially high costs of completing the contract. Rather than relying on selling prices as ordinarily set by suppliers in the marketplace, the government negotiates contracts on the basis of *costs plus a fixed fee*. In costs-plus-fixed-fee contracts, which often involve billions of dollars, the allocation of a specific cost may be difficult to defend on the basis of any cause-and-effect reasoning. Nonetheless, the contracting parties may still view it as a "reasonable" or "fair" means to help establish a contract amount.

Some costs are "allowable;" others are "unallowable." An **allowable cost** is a cost that the contract parties agree to include in the costs to be reimbursed. Some contracts specify how allowable costs are to be determined. For example, only economy-class airfares are allowable in many U.S. government contracts. Other contracts identify cost categories that are unallowable. For example, the costs of lobbying activities and alcoholic beverages are not allowable costs in U.S. government contracts. However, the set of allowable costs is not always clear-cut. Contract disputes and allegations about overcharging the government arise from time to time (see Concepts in Action, p. 560).

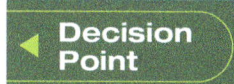

◄ Decision Point

How can contract disputes over reimbursement amounts based on costs be reduced?

---

[9] The Federal Acquisition Regulation (FAR), issued in March 2005 (see https://www.acquisition.gov/far/current/pdf/FAR.pdf) includes the following definition of "allocability" (in FAR 31.201-4): "A cost is allocable if it is assignable or chargeable to one or more cost objectives on the basis of relative benefits received or other equitable relationship. Subject to the foregoing, a cost is allocable to a Government contract if it:
(a) Is incurred specifically for the contract;
(b) Benefits both the contract and other work, and can be distributed to them in reasonable proportion to the benefits received; or
(c) Is necessary to the overall operation of the business, although a direct relationship to any particular cost objective cannot be shown."

[10] Details on the Cost Accounting Standards Board are available at www.whitehouse.gov/omb/procurement/casb.html. The CASB is part of the Office of Federal Procurement Policy, U.S. Office of Management and Budget.

Concepts in Action

Contract Disputes over Reimbursable Costs for the U.S. Department of Defense

For 2011, United States combat activities in Afghanistan are budgeted to cost $159 billion. As in prior years, a portion of this money is allocated to private companies to carry out specific contracted services for the U.S. Department of Defense. In recent years, the U.S. government has pursued cases against several contractors for overcharging for services provided in the combat zone. The following four examples are from cases pursued by the U.S. Department of Justice's Civil Division, who did so on behalf of the federal government. These recent examples illustrate several types of cost disputes that arise in practice.

1. Eagle Global Logistics agreed to pay $4 million to settle allegations of allegedly inflating invoices for military cargo shipments to Iraq. The complaint alleged that a company executive added an extra 50 cents per kilogram "war risk surcharge" to invoices for flights between Dubai and Iraq. This bogus surcharge, which was not part of Eagle's U.S. Department of Defense contract, was applied 379 times between 2003 and 2004.

2. In another shipping case, APL Limited paid the federal government $26.3 million to resolve claims of knowingly overcharging and double-billing the U.S. Department of Defense to transport thousands of containers to destinations in Afghanistan and Iraq. APL was accused of inflating invoices in several ways: marking up electricity costs for containers with perishable cargo, billing in excess of the contractual rate to maintain the operation of refrigerated containers in the port of Karachi, Pakistan, and billing for non-reimbursable services performed by an APL subcontractor at a Kuwaiti port.

3. L-3 communications, a leading defense contractor, paid $4 million to settle a complaint that it overbilled for hours worked by the firm's employees on a contract supporting military operations by the United States in Iraq. The company allegedly submitted false time records and inflated claims for personnel hours as part of an ongoing contract with the U.S. Army to provide helicopter maintenance services at Camp Taji, Iraq.

4. In late 2009, Public Warehousing Company—a principal food supplier for the U.S. military in Iraq, Kuwait, and Jordan since 2003—was sued by the U.S. government for presenting false claims for payment under the company's multibillion dollar contract with the Defense Logistics Agency. The complaint alleged that the company overcharged the U.S. for locally available fresh fruits and vegetables and failed to disclose pass through rebates and discounts it obtained from U.S.-based suppliers, as required by its contracts.

Source: Press releases from the United States Department of Justice, Civil Division (2006–2009).

Learning Objective 6

Understand how bundling of products

. . . two or more products sold for a single-price

gives rise to revenue allocation issues

. . . allocating revenues to each product in the bundle to evaluate managers of individual products

and the methods for doing so

. . . using the stand-alone method or the incremental method

Bundled Products and Revenue Allocation Methods

Allocation issues can also arise when revenues from multiple products (for example, different software programs or cable and internet packages) are bundled together and sold at a single price. The methods for revenue allocation parallel those described for common-cost allocations.

Bundling and Revenue Allocation

Revenues are inflows of assets (almost always cash or accounts receivable) received for products or services provided to customers. Similar to cost allocation, **revenue allocation** occurs when revenues are related to a particular *revenue object* but cannot be traced to it in an economically feasible (cost-effective) way. A **revenue object** is anything for which a separate measurement of revenue is desired. Examples of revenue objects include products, customers, and divisions. We illustrate revenue-allocation issues for Dynamic Software Corporation, which develops, sells, and supports three software programs:

1. WordMaster, a word-processing program, released 36 months ago
2. DataMaster, a spreadsheet program, released 18 months ago
3. FinanceMaster, a budgeting and cash-management program, released six months ago with a lot of favorable media attention

Dynamic Software sells these three products individually as well as together as bundled products.

A **bundled product** is a package of two or more products (or services) that is sold for a single price but whose individual components may be sold as separate items at their own "stand-alone" prices. The price of a bundled product is typically less than the sum of the prices of the individual products sold separately. For example, banks often provide individual customers with a bundle of services from different departments (checking, safety-deposit box, and investment advisory) for a single fee. A resort hotel may offer, for a single amount per customer, a weekend package that includes services from its lodging (the room), food (the restaurant), and recreational (golf and tennis) departments. When department managers have revenue or profit responsibilities for individual products, the bundled revenue must be allocated among the individual products in the bundle.

Dynamic Software allocates revenues from its bundled product sales (called "suite sales") to individual products. Individual-product profitability is used to compensate software engineers, outside developers, and product managers responsible for developing and managing each product.

How should Dynamic Software allocate suite revenues to individual products? Consider information pertaining to the three "stand-alone" and "suite" products in 2012:

	Selling Price	Manufacturing Cost per Unit
Stand-alone		
WordMaster	$125	$18
DataMaster	150	20
FinanceMaster	225	25
Suite		
Word + Data	$220	
Word + Finance	280	
Finance + Data	305	
Word + Finance + Data	380	

Just as we saw in the section on common-cost allocations, the two main revenue-allocation methods are the stand-alone method and the incremental method.

Stand-Alone Revenue-Allocation Method

The **stand-alone revenue-allocation method** uses product-specific information on the products in the bundle as weights for allocating the bundled revenues to the individual products. The term *stand-alone* refers to the product as a separate (nonsuite) item. Consider the Word + Finance suite, which sells for $280. Three types of weights for the stand-alone method are as follows:

1. **Selling prices.** Using the individual selling prices of $125 for WordMaster and $225 for FinanceMaster, the weights for allocating the $280 suite revenues between the products are as follows:

$$\text{WordMaster: } \frac{\$125}{\$125 + \$225} \times \$280 = 0.357 \times \$280 = \$100$$

$$\text{FinanceMaster: } \frac{\$225}{\$125 + \$225} \times \$280 = 0.643 \times \$280 = \$180$$

2. **Unit costs.** This method uses the costs of the individual products (in this case, manufacturing cost per unit) to determine the weights for the revenue allocations.

$$\text{WordMaster: } \frac{\$18}{\$18 + \$25} \times \$280 = 0.419 \times \$280 = \$117$$

$$\text{FinanceMaster: } \frac{\$25}{\$18 + \$25} \times \$280 = 0.581 \times \$280 = \$163$$

3. **Physical units.** This method gives each product unit in the suite the same weight when allocating suite revenue to individual products. Therefore, with two products in the Word + Finance suite, each product is allocated 50% of the suite revenues.

$$\text{WordMaster: } \frac{1}{1+1} \times \$280 = 0.50 \times \$280 = \$140$$

$$\text{FinanceMaster: } \frac{1}{1+1} \times \$280 = 0.50 \times \$280 = \$140$$

These three approaches to determining weights for the stand-alone method result in very different revenue allocations to the individual products:

Revenue-Allocation Weights	WordMaster	FinanceMaster
Selling prices	$100	$180
Unit costs	117	163
Physical units	140	140

Which method is preferred? The selling prices method is best, because the weights explicitly consider the prices customers are willing to pay for the individual products. Weighting approaches that use revenue information better capture "benefits received" by customers than unit costs or physical units.[11] The physical-units revenue-allocation method is used when any of the other methods cannot be used (such as when selling prices are unstable or unit costs are difficult to calculate for individual products).

Incremental Revenue-Allocation Method

The **incremental revenue-allocation method** ranks individual products in a bundle according to criteria determined by management—such as the product in the bundle with the most sales—and then uses this ranking to allocate bundled revenues to individual products. The first-ranked product is the *primary product* in the bundle. The second-ranked product is the *first-incremental product*, the third-ranked product is the *second-incremental product*, and so on.

How do companies decide on product rankings under the incremental revenue-allocation method? Some organizations survey customers about the importance of each of the individual products to their purchase decision. Others use data on the recent stand-alone sales performance of the individual products in the bundle. A third approach is for top managers to use their knowledge or intuition to decide the rankings.

Consider again the Word + Finance suite. Assume WordMaster is designated as the primary product. If the suite selling price exceeds the stand-alone price of the primary product, the primary product is allocated 100% of its *stand-alone* revenue. Because the suite price of $280 exceeds the stand-alone price of $125 for WordMaster, WordMaster is allocated revenues of $125, with the remaining revenue of $155 ($280 – $125) allocated to FinanceMaster:

Product	Revenue Allocated	Cumulative Revenue Allocated
WordMaster	$125	$125
FinanceMaster	155 ($280 – $125)	$280
Total	$280	

If the suite price is less than or equal to the stand-alone price of the primary product, the primary product is allocated 100% of the *suite* revenue. All other products in the suite receive no allocation of revenue.

[11] Revenue-allocation issues also arise in external reporting. The AICPA's Statement of Position 97-2 (Software Revenue Recognition) states that with bundled products, revenue allocation "based on vendor-specific objective evidence (VSOE) of fair value" is required. The "price charged when the element is sold separately" is said to be "objective evidence of fair value" (see "Statement of Position 97-2," Jersey City, NJ: AICPA, 1998). In September 2009, the FASB ratified Emerging Issues Task Force (EITF) Issue 08-1, specifying that with no VSOE or third-party evidence of selling price for all units of accounting in an arrangement, the consideration received for the arrangement should be allocated to the separate units based upon their relative selling prices.

Now suppose FinanceMaster is designated as the primary product and WordMaster as the first-incremental product. Then, the incremental revenue-allocation method allocates revenues of the Word + Finance suite as follows:

Product	Revenue Allocated	Cumulative Revenue Allocated
FinanceMaster	$225	$225
WordMaster	55 ($280 − $225)	$280
Total	$280	

If Dynamic Software sells equal quantities of WordMaster and FinanceMaster, then the Shapley value method allocates to each product the average of the revenues allocated as the primary and first-incremental products:

WordMaster:	($125 + $ 55) ÷ 2 = $180 ÷ 2 = $ 90
FinanceMaster:	($225 + $155) ÷ 2 = $380 ÷ 2 = 190
Total	$280

But what if, in the most recent quarter, the firm sells 80,000 units of WordMaster and 20,000 units of FinanceMaster. Because Dynamic Software sells four times as many units of WordMaster, its managers believe that the sales of the Word + Finance suite are four times more likely to be driven by WordMaster as the primary product. The *weighted Shapley value method* takes this fact into account. It assigns four times as much weight to the revenue allocations when WordMaster is the primary product as when FinanceMaster is the primary product, resulting in the following allocations:

WordMaster:	($125 × 4 + $ 55 × 1) ÷ (4 + 1) = $555 ÷ 5 = $111
FinanceMaster:	($225 × 1 + $155 × 4) ÷ (4 + 1) = $845 ÷ 5 = 169
Total	$280

When there are more than two products in the suite, the incremental revenue-allocation method allocates suite revenues sequentially. Assume WordMaster is the primary product in Dynamic Software's three-product suite (Word + Finance + Data). FinanceMaster is the first-incremental product, and DataMaster is the second-incremental product. This suite sells for $380. The allocation of the $380 suite revenues proceeds as follows:

Product	Revenue Allocated	Cumulative Revenue Allocated
WordMaster	$125	$125
FinanceMaster	155 ($280 − $125)	$280 (price of Word + Finance suite)
DataMaster	100 ($380 − $280)	$380 (price of Word + Finance + Data suite)
Total	$380	

Now suppose WordMaster is the primary product, DataMaster is the first-incremental product, and FinanceMaster is the second-incremental product.

Product	Revenue Allocated	Cumulative Revenue Allocated
WordMaster	$125	$125
DataMaster	95 ($220 − $125)	$220 (price of Word + Data suite)
FinanceMaster	160 ($380 − $220)	$380 (price of Word + Data + Finance suite)
Total	$380	

The ranking of the individual products in the suite determines the revenues allocated to them. Product managers at Dynamic Software likely would differ on how they believe their individual products contribute to sales of the suite products. In fact, each product manager would claim to be responsible for the primary product in the Word + Finance + Data suite![12]

Decision Point

What is product bundling and how can managers allocate revenues of a bundled product to individual products in the package?

---

[12]Calculating the Shapley value mitigates this problem because each product is considered as a primary, first-incremental, and second-incremental product. Assuming equal weights on all products, the revenue allocated to each product is an average of the revenues calculated for the product under these different assumptions. In the preceding example, the interested reader can verify that this will result in the following revenue assignments: FinanceMaster, $180; WordMaster, $87.50; and DataMaster, $112.50.

Because the stand-alone revenue-allocation method does not require rankings of individual products in the suite, this method is less likely to cause debates among product managers.

Problem for Self-Study

This problem illustrates how costs of two corporate support departments are allocated to operating divisions using the dual-rate method. Fixed costs are allocated using budgeted costs and budgeted hours used by other departments. Variable costs are allocated using actual costs and actual hours used by other departments.

Computer Horizons budgets the following amounts for its two central corporate support departments (legal and personnel) in supporting each other and the two manufacturing divisions, the laptop division (LTD) and the work station division (WSD):

		SUPPORT			OPERATING		
	A	Legal Department (B)	Personnel Department (C)	D	LTD (E)	WSD (F)	Total (G)
1							
3	**BUDGETED USAGE**						
4	Legal (hours)	—	250		1,500	750	2,500
5	(Percentages)	—	10%		60%	30%	100%
6	Personnel (hours)	2,500	—		22,500	25,000	50,000
7	(Percentages)	5%	—		45%	50%	100%
8							
9	**ACTUAL USAGE**						
10	Legal (hours)	—	400		400	1,200	2,000
11	(Percentages)	—	20%		20%	60%	100%
12	Personnel (hours)	2,000	—		26,600	11,400	40,000
13	(Percentages)	5%	—		66.50%	28.5%	100%
14	Budgeted fixed overhead costs before any						
15	interdepartment cost allocations	$360,000	$475,000		—	—	$835,000
16	Actual variable overhead costs before any						
17	interdepartment cost allocations	$200,000	$600,000		—	—	$800,000

Required What amount of support-department costs for legal and personnel will be allocated to LTD and WSD using (a) the direct method, (b) the step-down method (allocating the legal department costs first), and (c) the reciprocal method using linear equations?

Solution

Exhibit 15-7 presents the computations for allocating the fixed and variable support-department costs. A summary of these costs follows:

	Laptop Division (LTD)	Work Station Division (WSD)
(a) Direct Method		
Fixed costs	$465,000	$370,000
Variable costs	470,000	330,000
	$935,000	$700,000
(b) Step-Down Method		
Fixed costs	$458,053	$376,947
Variable costs	488,000	312,000
	$946,053	$688,947
(c) Reciprocal Method		
Fixed costs	$462,513	$372,487
Variable costs	476,364	323,636
	$938,877	$696,123

Exhibit 15-7 Alternative Methods of Allocating Corporate Support-Department Costs to Operating Divisions of Computer Horizons: Dual-Rate Method

	A	B	C	D	E	F	G
		CORPORATE SUPPORT DEPARTMENTS			OPERATING DIVISIONS		
20							
21	**Allocation Method**	**Legal Department**	**Personnel Department**		**LTD**	**WSD**	**Total**
22	**A. DIRECT METHOD**						
23	Fixed costs	$360,000	$475,000				
24	Legal (1,500 ÷ 2,250; 750 ÷ 2,250)	(360,000)			$240,000	$120,000	
25	Personnel (22,500 ÷ 47,500; 25,000 ÷ 47,500)		(475,000)		225,000	250,000	
26	Fixed support dept. cost allocated to operating divisions	$ 0	0		$465,000	$370,000	$835,000
27	Variable costs	$200,000	$600,000				
28	Legal (400 ÷ 1,600; 1,200 ÷ 1,600)	(200,000)			$ 50,000	$150,000	
29	Personnel (26,600 ÷ 38,000; 11,400 ÷ 38,000)		(600,000)		420,000	180,000	
30	Variable support dept. cost allocated to operating divisions	$ 0	0		$470,000	$330,000	$800,000
31	**B. STEP-DOWN METHOD**						
32	(Legal department first)						
33	Fixed costs	$360,000	$475,000				
34	Legal (250 ÷ 2,500; 1,500 ÷ 2,500; 750 ÷ 2,500)	(360,000)	36,000		$216,000	$108,000	
35	Personnel (22,500 ÷ 47,500; 25,000 ÷ 47,500)		(511,000)		242,053	268,947	
36	Fixed support dept. cost allocated to operating divisions	$ 0	0		$458,053	$376,947	$835,000
37	Variable costs	$200,000	$600,000				
38	Legal (400 ÷ 2,000; 400 ÷ 2,000; 1,200 ÷ 2,000)	(200,000)	40,000		$ 40,000	$120,000	
39	Personnel (26,600 ÷ 38,000; 11,400 ÷ 38,000)		(640,000)		448,000	192,000	
40	Variable support dept. cost allocated to operating divisions	$ 0	0		$488,000	$312,000	$800,000
41	**C. RECIPROCAL METHOD**						
42	Fixed costs	$360,000	$475,000				
43	Legal (250 ÷ 2,500; 1,500 ÷ 2,500; 750 ÷ 2,500)	(385,678)[a]	38,568		$231,407	$115,703	
44	Personnel (2,500 ÷ 50,000; 22,500 ÷ 50,000; 25,000 ÷ 50,000)	25,678	(513,568)[a]		231,106	256,784	
45	Fixed support dept. cost allocated to operating divisions	$ 0	$ 0		$462,513	$372,487	$835,000
46	Variable costs	$200,000	$600,000				
47	Legal (400 ÷ 2,000; 400 ÷ 2,000; 1,200 ÷ 2,000)	(232,323)[b]	46,465		$ 46,465	$139,393	
48	Personnel (2,000 ÷ 40,000; 26,600 ÷ 40,000; 11,400 ÷ 40,000)	32,323	(646,465)[b]		429,899	184,243	
49	Variable support dept. cost allocated to operating divisions	$ 0	$ 0		$476,364	$323,636	$800,000
50							
51	[a] FIXED COSTS	[b] VARIABLE COSTS					

[a] FIXED COSTS

Letting LF = Legal department fixed costs, and PF = Personnel department fixed costs, the simultaneous equations for the reciprocal method for fixed costs are

$LF = \$360,000 + 0.05 PF$
$PF = \$475,000 + 0.10 LF$
$LF = \$360,000 + 0.05 (\$475,000 + 0.10 LF)$
$LF = \$385,678$
$PF = \$475,000 + 0.10 (\$385,678) = \$513,568$

[b] VARIABLE COSTS

Letting LF = Legal department variable costs, and PV = Personnel department variable costs, the simultaneous equations for the reciprocal method for variable costs are

$LV = \$200,000 + 0.05 PV$
$PV = \$600,000 + 0.20 LV$
$LV = \$200,000 + 0.05 (\$600,000 + 0.20 LV)$
$LV = \$232,323$
$PV = \$600,000 + 0.20 (\$232,323) = \$646,465$

Decision Points

The following question-and-answer format summarizes the chapter's learning objectives. Each decision presents a key question related to a learning objective. The guidelines are the answer to that question.

Decision	Guidelines
1. When should managers use the dual-rate method over the single-rate method?	The single-rate method aggregates fixed and variable costs and allocates them to objects using a single allocation base and rate. Under the dual-rate method, costs are grouped into separate variable cost and fixed cost pools; each pool uses a different cost-allocation base and rate. If costs can be easily separated into variable and fixed costs, the dual-rate method should be used because it provides better information for making decisions.
2. What factors should managers consider when deciding between allocation based on budgeted and actual rates, and budgeted and actual usage?	The use of budgeted rates enables managers of user departments to have certainty about the costs allocated to them, and insulates users from inefficiencies in the supplier department. Charging budgeted variable cost rates to users based on actual usage is causally appropriate and promotes control of resource consumption. Charging fixed cost rates on the basis of budgeted usage helps user divisions with planning, and leads to goal congruence when considering outsourcing decisions.
3. What methods can managers use to allocate costs of multiple support departments to operating departments?	The three methods managers can use are the direct, the step-down, and the reciprocal methods. The direct method allocates each support department's costs to operating departments without allocating a support department's costs to other support departments. The step-down method allocates support-department costs to other support departments and to operating departments in a sequential manner that partially recognizes the mutual services provided among all support departments. The reciprocal method fully recognizes mutual services provided among all support departments.
4. What methods can managers use to allocate common costs to two or more users?	Common costs are the costs of a cost object (such as operating a facility or performing an activity) that are shared by two or more users. The stand-alone cost-allocation method uses information pertaining to each user of the cost object to determine cost-allocation weights. The incremental cost-allocation method ranks individual users of the cost object and allocates common costs first to the primary user and then to the other incremental users. The Shapley value method considers each user, in turn, as the primary and the incremental user.
5. How can contract disputes over reimbursement amounts based on costs be reduced?	Disputes can be reduced by making the cost-allocation rules as explicit as possible and in writing at the time the contract is signed. These rules should include details such as the allowable cost items, the acceptable cost-allocation bases, and how differences between budgeted and actual costs are to be accounted for.
6. What is product bundling and how can managers allocate revenues of a bundled product to individual products in the package?	Bundling occurs when a package of two or more products (or services) is sold for a single price. Revenue allocation of the bundled price is required when managers of the individual products in the bundle are evaluated on product revenue or product operating income. Revenues can be allocated for a bundled product using the stand-alone method, the incremental method, or the Shapley value method.

Terms to Learn

This chapter and the Glossary at the end of the book contain definitions of the following important terms:

allowable cost (**p. 559**)
artificial costs (**p. 554**)
bundled product (**p. 561**)

common cost (**p. 557**)
complete reciprocated costs (**p. 554**)

Cost Accounting Standards Board
(CASB) (**p. 559**)

direct method (**p. 550**)

dual-rate method (**p. 544**)

incremental cost-allocation method (**p. 557**)

incremental revenue-allocation method (**p. 562**)

matrix method (**p. 554**)

operating department (**p. 543**)

production department (**p. 543**)

reciprocal method (**p. 553**)

revenue allocation (**p. 561**)

revenue object (**p. 561**)

service department (**p. 543**)

single-rate method (**p. 544**)

sequential allocation method (**p. 552**)

stand-alone cost-allocation method (**p. 557**)

stand-alone revenue-allocation method (**p. 561**)

step-down method (**p. 552**)

support department (**p. 543**)

Assignment Material

Questions

15-1 Distinguish between the single-rate and the dual-rate methods.

15-2 Describe how the dual-rate method is useful to division managers in decision making.

15-3 How do budgeted cost rates motivate the support-department manager to improve efficiency?

15-4 Give examples of allocation bases used to allocate support-department cost pools to operating departments.

15-5 Why might a manager prefer that budgeted rather than actual cost-allocation rates be used for costs being allocated to his or her department from another department?

15-6 "To ensure unbiased cost allocations, fixed costs should be allocated on the basis of estimated long-run use by user-department managers." Do you agree? Why?

15-7 Distinguish among the three methods of allocating the costs of support departments to operating departments.

15-8 What is conceptually the most defensible method for allocating support-department costs? Why?

15-9 Distinguish between two methods of allocating common costs.

15-10 What role does the Cost Accounting Standards Board play when companies contract with the U.S. government?

15-11 What is one key way to reduce cost-allocation disputes that arise with government contracts?

15-12 Describe how companies are increasingly facing revenue-allocation decisions.

15-13 Distinguish between the stand-alone and the incremental revenue-allocation methods.

15-14 Identify and discuss arguments that individual product managers may put forward to support their preferred revenue-allocation method.

15-15 How might a dispute over the allocation of revenues of a bundled product be resolved?

Exercises

MyAccountingLab

15-16 **Single-rate versus dual-rate methods, support department.** The Chicago power plant that services all manufacturing departments of MidWest Engineering has a budget for the coming year. This budget has been expressed in the following monthly terms:

Manufacturing Department	Needed at Practical Capacity Production Level (Kilowatt-Hours)	Average Expected Monthly Usage (Kilowatt-Hours)
Rockford	10,000	8,000
Peoria	20,000	9,000
Hammond	12,000	7,000
Kankakee	8,000	6,000
Total	50,000	30,000

The expected monthly costs for operating the power plant during the budget year are $15,000: $6,000 variable and $9,000 fixed.

Required

1. Assume that a single cost pool is used for the power plant costs. What budgeted amounts will be allocated to each manufacturing department if (a) the rate is calculated based on practical capacity and costs are allocated based on practical capacity, and (b) the rate is calculated based on expected monthly usage and costs are allocated based on expected monthly usage?

2. Assume the dual-rate method is used with separate cost pools for the variable and fixed costs. Variable costs are allocated on the basis of expected monthly usage. Fixed costs are allocated on the basis of practical capacity. What budgeted amounts will be allocated to each manufacturing department? Why might you prefer the dual-rate method?

15-17 Single-rate method, budgeted versus actual costs and quantities. Chocolat Inc. is a producer of premium chocolate based in Palo Alto. The company has a separate division for each of its two products: dark chocolate and milk chocolate. Chocolat purchases ingredients from Wisconsin for its dark chocolate division and from Louisiana for its milk chocolate division. Both locations are the same distance from Chocolat's Palo Alto plant.

Chocolat Inc. operates a fleet of trucks as a cost center that charges the divisions for variable costs (drivers and fuel) and fixed costs (vehicle depreciation, insurance, and registration fees) of operating the fleet. Each division is evaluated on the basis of its operating income. For 2012, the trucking fleet had a practical capacity of 50 round-trips between the Palo Alto plant and the two suppliers. It recorded the following information:

	Home	Insert	Page Layout	Formulas	Data	Review	View
			A		B	C	
1					**Budgeted**	**Actual**	
2	Costs of truck fleet				$115,000	$96,750	
3	Number of round-trips for dark chocolate division (Palo Alto plant—Wisconsin)				30	30	
4	Number of round-trips for milk chocolate division (Palo Alto plant—Louisiana)				20	15	

Required

1. Using the single-rate method, allocate costs to the dark chocolate division and the milk chocolate division in these three ways.
   a. Calculate the budgeted rate per round-trip and allocate costs based on round-trips budgeted for each division.
   b. Calculate the budgeted rate per round-trip and allocate costs based on actual round-trips used by each division.
   c. Calculate the actual rate per round-trip and allocate costs based on actual round-trips used by each division.
2. Describe the advantages and disadvantages of using each of the three methods in requirement 1. Would you encourage Chocolat Inc. to use one of these methods? Explain and indicate any assumptions you made.

15-18 Dual-rate method, budgeted versus actual costs and quantities (continuation of 15-17). Chocolat Inc. decides to examine the effect of using the dual-rate method for allocating truck costs to each round-trip. At the start of 2012, the budgeted costs were as follows:

Variable cost per round-trip	$ 1,350
Fixed costs	$47,500

The actual results for the 45 round-trips made in 2012 were as follows:

Variable costs	$58,500
Fixed costs	38,250
	$96,750

Assume all other information to be the same as in Exercise 15-17.

Required

1. Using the dual-rate method, what are the costs allocated to the dark chocolate division and the milk chocolate division when (a) variable costs are allocated using the budgeted rate per round-trip and actual round-trips used by each division and when (b) fixed costs are allocated based on the budgeted rate per round-trip and round-trips budgeted for each division?
2. From the viewpoint of the dark chocolate division, what are the effects of using the dual-rate method rather than the single-rate methods?

15-19 Support-department cost allocation; direct and step-down methods. Phoenix Partners provides management consulting services to government and corporate clients. Phoenix has two support departments—administrative services (AS) and information systems (IS)—and two operating departments—government consulting (GOVT) and corporate consulting (CORP). For the first quarter of 2012, Phoenix's cost records indicate the following:

	A	B	C	D	E	F	G
	Home Insert Page Layout Formulas Data Review View						
1		SUPPORT			OPERATING		
2		AS	IS		GOVT	CORP	Total
3	Budgeted overhead costs before any						
4	interdepartment cost allocations	$600,000	$2,400,000		$8,756,000	$12,452,000	$24,208,000
5	Support work supplied by AS (budgeted head count)	—	25%		40%	35%	100%
6	Support work supplied by IS (budgeted computer time)	10%	—		30%	60%	100%

1. Allocate the two support departments' costs to the two operating departments using the following methods: **Required**
   a. Direct method
   b. Step-down method (allocate AS first)
   c. Step-down method (allocate IS first)
2. Compare and explain differences in the support-department costs allocated to each operating department.
3. What approaches might be used to decide the sequence in which to allocate support departments when using the step-down method?

15-20 Support-department cost allocation, reciprocal method (continuation of 15-19). Refer to the data given in Exercise 15-19.

1. Allocate the two support departments' costs to the two operating departments using the reciprocal **Required**
   method. Use (a) linear equations and (b) repeated iterations.
2. Compare and explain differences in requirement 1 with those in requirement 1 of Exercise 15-19. Which method do you prefer? Why?

15-21 Direct and step-down allocation. E-books, an online book retailer, has two operating departments—corporate sales and consumer sales—and two support departments—human resources and information systems. Each sales department conducts merchandising and marketing operations independently. E-books uses number of employees to allocate human resources costs and processing time to allocate information systems costs. The following data are available for September 2012:

	A	B	C	D	E	F
	Home Insert Page Layout Formulas Data Review View					
1		SUPPORT DEPARTMENTS			OPERATING DEPARTMENTS	
2		Human Resources	Information Systems		Corporate Sales	Consumer Sales
3	Budgeted costs incurred before any					
4	interdepartment cost allocations	$72,700	$234,400		$998,270	$489,860
5	Support work supplied by human resources department					
6	Budgeted number of employees	—	21		42	28
7	Support work supplied by information systems department					
8	Budgeted processing time (in minutes)	320	—		1,920	1,600

1. Allocate the support departments' costs to the operating departments using the direct method. **Required**
2. Rank the support departments based on the percentage of their services provided to other support departments. Use this ranking to allocate the support departments' costs to the operating departments based on the step-down method.
3. How could you have ranked the support departments differently?

15-22 Reciprocal cost allocation (continuation of 15-21). Consider E-books again. The controller of E-books reads a widely used textbook that states that "the reciprocal method is conceptually the most defensible." He seeks your assistance.

Required

1. Describe the key features of the reciprocal method.
2. Allocate the support departments' costs (human resources and information systems) to the two operating departments using the reciprocal method.
3. In the case presented in this exercise, which method (direct, step-down, or reciprocal) would you recommend? Why?

15-23 Allocation of common costs. Ben and Gary are students at Berkeley College. They share an apartment that is owned by Gary. Gary is considering subscribing to an Internet provider that has the following packages available:

Package	Per Month
A. Internet access	$60
B. Phone services	15
C. Internet access + phone services	65

Ben spends most of his time on the Internet ("everything can be found online now"). Gary prefers to spend his time talking on the phone rather than using the Internet ("going online is a waste of time"). They agree that the purchase of the $65 total package is a "win–win" situation.

Required

1. Allocate the $65 between Ben and Gary using (a) the stand-alone cost-allocation method, (b) the incremental cost-allocation method, and (c) the Shapley value method.
2. Which method would you recommend they use and why?

15-24 Allocation of common costs. Sunny Gunn, a self-employed consultant near Sacramento, received an invitation to visit a prospective client in Baltimore. A few days later, she received an invitation to make a presentation to a prospective client in Chicago. She decided to combine her visits, traveling from Sacramento to Baltimore, Baltimore to Chicago, and Chicago to Sacramento.

Gunn received offers for her consulting services from both companies. Upon her return, she decided to accept the engagement in Chicago. She is puzzled over how to allocate her travel costs between the two clients. She has collected the following data for regular round-trip fares with no stopovers:

Sacramento to Baltimore	$1,200
Sacramento to Chicago	$ 800

Gunn paid $1,600 for her three-leg flight (Sacramento–Baltimore, Baltimore–Chicago, Chicago–Sacramento). In addition, she paid $40 each way for limousines from her home to Sacramento Airport and back when she returned.

Required

1. How should Gunn allocate the $1,600 airfare between the clients in Baltimore and Chicago using (a) the stand-alone cost-allocation method, (b) the incremental cost-allocation method, and (c) the Shapley value method?
2. Which method would you recommend Gunn use and why?
3. How should Gunn allocate the $80 limousine charges between the clients in Baltimore and Chicago?

15-25 Revenue allocation, bundled products. Yves Parfum Company blends and sells designer fragrances. It has a Men's Fragrances Division and a Women's Fragrances Division, each with different sales strategies, distribution channels, and product offerings. Yves is now considering the sale of a bundled product consisting of a men's cologne and a women's perfume. For the most recent year, Yves reported the following:

	Home	Insert	Page Layout	Formulas
		A		B
1		**Product**		**Retail Price**
2	Monaco (men's cologne)			$ 48
3	Innocence (women's perfume)			112
4	L'Amour (Monaco + Innocence)			130

Required

1. Allocate revenue from the sale of each unit of L'Amour to Monaco and Innocence using the following:
   a. The stand-alone revenue-allocation method based on selling price of each product
   b. The incremental revenue-allocation method, with Monaco ranked as the primary product
   c. The incremental revenue-allocation method, with Innocence ranked as the primary product
   d. The Shapley value method, assuming equal unit sales of Monaco and Innocence
2. Of the four methods in requirement 1, which one would you recommend for allocating L'Amour's revenues to Monaco and Innocence? Explain.

15-26 Allocation of common costs. Jim Dandy Auto Sales uses all types of media to advertise its products (television, radio, newspaper, etc.). At the end of 2011, the company president, Jim Dandridge, decided that all advertising costs would be incurred by corporate headquarters and allocated to each of the company's three sales locations based on number of vehicles sold. Jim was confident that his corporate purchasing manager could negotiate better advertising contracts on a corporate-wide basis than each of the sales managers could on their own. Dandridge budgeted total advertising cost for 2012 to be $1.8 million. He introduced the new plan to his sales managers just before the New Year.

The manager of the east sales location, Tony Snider, was not happy. He complained that the new allocation method was unfair and would increase his advertising costs significantly over the prior year. The east location sold high volumes of low-priced used cars and most of the corporate advertising budget was related to new car sales.

Following Tony's complaint, Jim decided to take another hard look at what each of the divisions were paying for advertising before the new allocation plan. The results were as follows:

Sales Location	Actual Number of Cars Sold in 2011	Actual Advertising Cost Incurred in 2011
East	3,150	$ 324,000
West	1,080	432,000
North	2,250	648,000
South	2,520	756,000
	9,000	$2,160,000

Required

1. Using 2011 data as the cost bases, show the amount of the 2012 advertising cost ($1,800,000) that would be allocated to each of the divisions under the following criteria:
   a. Dandridge's allocation method based on number of cars sold
   b. The stand-alone method
   c. The incremental-allocation method, with divisions ranked on the basis of dollars spent on advertising in 2011
2. Which method do you think is most equitable to the divisional sales managers? What other options might President Jim Dandridge have for allocating the advertising costs?

Problems

MyAccountingLab

15-27 Single-rate, dual-rate, and practical capacity allocation. Perfection Department Store has a new promotional program that offers a free gift-wrapping service for its customers. Perfection's customer-service department has practical capacity to wrap 7,000 gifts at a budgeted fixed cost of $6,650 each month. The budgeted variable cost to gift wrap an item is $0.40. Although the service is free to customers, a gift-wrapping service cost allocation is made to the department where the item was purchased. The customer-service department reported the following for the most recent month:

	Department	Actual Number of Gifts Wrapped	Budgeted Number of Gifts to Be Wrapped	Practical Capacity Available for Gift-Wrapping
2	Women's face wash	2,020	2,470	2,640
3	Men's face wash	730	825	945
4	Fragrances	1,560	1,805	1,970
5	Body wash	545	430	650
6	Hair products	1,495	1,120	795
7	Total	6,350	6,650	7,000

Required

1. Using the single-rate method, allocate gift-wrapping costs to different departments in these three ways.
   a. Calculate the budgeted rate based on the budgeted number of gifts to be wrapped and allocate costs based on the budgeted use (of gift-wrapping services).
   b. Calculate the budgeted rate based on the budgeted number of gifts to be wrapped and allocate costs based on actual usage.
   c. Calculate the budgeted rate based on the practical gift-wrapping capacity available and allocate costs based on actual usage.

2. Using the dual-rate method, compute the amount allocated to each department when (a) the fixed-cost rate is calculated using budgeted costs and the practical gift-wrapping capacity, (b) fixed costs are allocated based on budgeted usage of gift-wrapping services, and (c) variable costs are allocated using the budgeted variable-cost rate and actual usage.

3. Comment on your results in requirements 1 and 2. Discuss the advantages of the dual-rate method.

15-28 Revenue allocation. Lee Shu-yu Inc. produces and sells DVDs to business people and students who are planning extended stays in China. It has been very successful with two DVDs: Beginning Mandarin and Conversational Mandarin. It is introducing a third DVD, Reading Chinese Characters. It has decided to market its new DVD in two different packages grouping the Reading Chinese Characters DVD with each of the other two language DVDs. Information about the separate DVDs and the packages follow.

DVD	Selling Price
Beginning Mandarin (BegM)	$ 50
Conversational Mandarin (ConM)	$ 90
Reading Chinese Characters (RCC)	$ 30
BegM + RCC	$ 60
ConM + RCC	$100

Required

1. Using the selling prices, allocate revenues from the BegM + RCC package to each DVD in that package using (a) the stand-alone method; (b) the incremental method, in either order; and (c) the Shapley value method.

2. Using the selling prices, allocate revenues from the ConM + RCC package to each DVD in that package using (a) the stand-alone method; (b) the incremental method, in either order; and (c) the Shapley value method.

3. Which method is most appropriate for allocating revenues among the DVDs? Why?

15-29 Fixed cost allocation. State University completed construction of its newest administrative building at the end of 2011. The University's first employees moved into the building on January 1, 2012. The building consists of office space, common meeting rooms (including a conference center), a cafeteria and even a workout room for its exercise enthusiasts. The total 2012 building space of 125,000 square feet was utilized as follows:

Usage of Space	% of Total Building Space
Office space (occupied)	52%
Vacant office space	8%
Common meeting space	25%
Workout room	5%
Cafeteria	10%

The new building cost the university $30 million and was depreciated using the straight-line method over 20 years. At the end of 2012 three departments occupied the building: executive offices of the president, accounting, and human resources. Each department's usage of its assigned space was as follows:

Department	Actual Office Space Used (sq. ft.)	Planned Office Space Used (sq. ft.)	Practical Capacity Office Space (sq. ft.)
Executive	16,250	12,400	18,000
Accounting	26,000	26,040	33,000
Human resources	22,750	23,560	24,000

Required

1. How much of the total building cost will be allocated in 2012 to each of the departments, if allocated on the basis of the following?
   a. Actual usage
   b. Planned usage
   c. Practical capacity

2. Assume that State University allocates the total annual building cost in the following manner:
   a. All vacant office space is absorbed by the university and is not allocated to the departments.
   b. All occupied office space costs are allocated on the basis of actual square footage used.
   c. All common costs are allocated on the basis of a department's practical capacity.
   Calculate the cost allocated to each department in 2012 under this plan. Do you think the allocation method used here is appropriate? Explain.

15-30 Allocating costs of support departments; step-down and direct methods. The Central Valley Company has prepared department overhead budgets for budgeted-volume levels before allocations as follows:

Support departments:		
Building and grounds	$10,000	
Personnel	1,000	
General plant administration	26,090	
Cafeteria: operating loss	1,640	
Storeroom	2,670	$ 41,400
Operating departments:		
Machining	$34,700	
Assembly	48,900	83,600
Total for support and operating departments		$125,000

Management has decided that the most appropriate inventory costs are achieved by using individual-department overhead rates. These rates are developed after support-department costs are allocated to operating departments.

Bases for allocation are to be selected from the following:

Department	Direct Manufacturing Labor-Hours	Number of Employees	Square Feet of Floor Space Occupied	Manufacturing Labor-Hours	Number of Requisitions
Building and grounds	0	0	0	0	0
Personnel[a]	0	0	2,000	0	0
General plant administration	0	35	7,000	0	0
Cafeteria: operating loss	0	10	4,000	1,000	0
Storeroom	0	5	7,000	1,000	0
Machining	5,000	50	30,000	8,000	2,000
Assembly	15,000	100	50,000	17,000	1,000
Total	20,000	200	100,000	27,000	3,000

[a]Basis used is number of employees.

Required

1. Using the step-down method, allocate support-department costs. Develop overhead rates per direct manufacturing labor-hour for machining and assembly. Allocate the costs of the support departments in the order given in this problem. Use the allocation base for each support department you think is most appropriate.
2. Using the direct method, rework requirement 1.
3. Based on the following information about two jobs, determine the total overhead costs for each job by using rates developed in (a) requirement 1 and (b) requirement 2.

	Direct Manufacturing Labor-Hours	
	Machining	**Assembly**
Job 88	18	2
Job 89	3	17

4. The company evaluates the performance of the operating department managers on the basis of how well they managed their total costs, including allocated costs. As the manager of the machining department, which allocation method would you prefer from the results obtained in requirements 1 and 2? Explain.

15-31 Support-department cost allocations; single-department cost pools; direct, step-down, and reciprocal methods. The Manes Company has two products. Product 1 is manufactured entirely in department X. Product 2 is manufactured entirely in department Y. To produce these two products, the Manes Company has two support departments: A (a materials-handling department) and B (a power-generating department).

An analysis of the work done by departments A and B in a typical period follows:

	Used By			
Supplied By	**A**	**B**	**X**	**Y**
A	—	100	250	150
B	500	—	100	400

The work done in department A is measured by the direct labor-hours of materials-handling time. The work done in department B is measured by the kilowatt-hours of power. The budgeted costs of the support departments for the coming year are as follows:

	Department A (Materials Handling)	Department B (Power Generation)
Variable indirect labor and indirect materials costs	$ 70,000	$10,000
Supervision	10,000	10,000
Depreciation	20,000	20,000
	$100,000	$40,000
	+Power costs	+Materials-handling costs

The budgeted costs of the operating departments for the coming year are $1,500,000 for department X and $800,000 for department Y.

Supervision costs are salary costs. Depreciation in department B is the straight-line depreciation of power-generation equipment in its 19th year of an estimated 25-year useful life; it is old, but well-maintained, equipment.

Required

1. What are the allocations of costs of support departments A and B to operating departments X and Y using (a) the direct method, (b) the step-down method (allocate department A first), (c) the step-down method (allocate department B first), and (d) the reciprocal method?
2. An outside company has offered to supply all the power needed by the Manes Company and to provide all the services of the present power department. The cost of this service will be $40 per kilowatt-hour of power. Should Manes accept? Explain.

15-32 Common costs. Wright Inc. and Brown Inc. are two small clothing companies that are considering leasing a dyeing machine together. The companies estimated that in order to meet production, Wright needs the machine for 800 hours and Brown needs it for 200 hours. If each company rents the machine on its own, the fee will be $50 per hour of usage. If they rent the machine together, the fee will decrease to $42 per hour of usage.

Required

1. Calculate Wright's and Brown's respective share of fees under the stand-alone cost-allocation method.
2. Calculate Wright's and Brown's respective share of fees using the incremental cost-allocation method. Assume Wright to be the primary party.
3. Calculate Wright's and Brown's respective share of fees using the Shapley value method.
4. Which method would you recommend Wright and Brown use to share the fees?

15-33 Stand-alone revenue allocation. MaxSystems, Inc., sells computer hardware to end consumers. Its most popular model, the CX30 is sold as a "bundle," which includes three hardware products: a personal computer (PC) tower, a 23-inch monitor, and a color laser printer. Each of these products is made in a separate manufacturing division of MaxSystems and can be purchased individually, as well as in a bundle. The individual selling prices and per unit costs are as follows:

Computer Component	Individual Selling Price per Unit	Cost per Unit
PC tower	$ 840	$300
Monitor	$ 280	$180
Color laser printer	$ 480	$270
Computer bundle purchase price	$1,200	

Required

1. Allocate the revenue from the computer bundle purchase to each of the hardware products using the stand-alone method based on the individual selling price per unit.
2. Allocate the revenue from the computer bundle purchase to each of the hardware products using the stand-alone method based on cost per unit.
3. Allocate the revenue from the computer bundle purchase to each of the hardware products using the stand-alone method based on physical units (that is, the number of individual units of product sold per bundle).
4. Which basis of allocation makes the most sense in this situation? Explain your answer.

15-34 Support-department cost allocations; single-department cost pools; direct, step-down, and reciprocal methods. Spirit Training, Inc., manufactures athletic shoes and athletic clothing for both amateur and professional athletes. The company has two product lines (clothing and shoes), which are produced in separate manufacturing facilities; however, both manufacturing facilities share the same support services for information technology and human resources. The following shows total costs for each manufacturing facility and for each support department.

	Variable Costs	Fixed Costs	Total Costs by Department (in thousands)
Information technology (IT)	$ 500	$ 1,500	$ 2,000
Human resources (HR)	$ 100	$ 900	$ 1,000
Clothing	$3,000	$ 7,000	$10,000
Shoes	$2,500	$ 5,500	$ 8,000
Total costs	$7,100	$16,900	$24,000

The total costs of the support departments (IT and HR) are allocated to the production departments (clothing and shoes) using a single rate based on the following:

Information technology: Number of IT labor hours worked by department
Human resources: Number of employees supported by department

Data on the bases, by department, are given as follows:

Department	IT Hours Used	Number of Employees
Clothing	5,000	120
Shoes	3,000	40
Information technology	-	40
Human resources	2,000	-

Required

1. What are the total costs of the production departments (clothing and shoes) **after** the support department costs of information technology and human resources have been allocated using (a) the direct method, (b) the step-down method (allocate information technology first), (c) the step-down method (allocate human resources first), and (d) the reciprocal method?
2. Assume that all of the work of the IT department could be outsourced to an independent company for $97.50 per hour. If Spirit Training no longer operated its own IT department, 30% of the fixed costs of the IT department could be eliminated. Should Spirit outsource its IT services?

Collaborative Learning Problem

15-35 Revenue allocation, bundled products. Exclusive Resorts (ER) operates a five-star hotel with a championship golf course. ER has a decentralized management structure, with three divisions:

- Lodging (rooms, conference facilities)
- Food (restaurants and in-room service)
- Recreation (golf course, tennis courts, swimming pool, etc.)

Starting next month, ER will offer a two-day, two-person "getaway package" for $1,000.
This deal includes the following:

	As Priced Separately
Two nights' stay for two in an ocean-view room	$ 800 ($400 per night)
Two rounds of golf (can be used by either guest)	$ 375 ($187.50 per round)
Candlelight dinner for two at ER's finest restaurant	$ 200 ($100 per person)
Total package value	$1,375

Jenny Lee, president of the recreation division, recently asked the CEO of ER how her division would share in the $1,000 revenue from the getaway package. The golf course was operating at 100% capacity. Currently, anyone booking the package was guaranteed access to the golf course. Lee noted that every "getaway" booking would displace $375 of other golf bookings not related to the package. She emphasized that the high demand reflected the devotion of her team to keeping the golf course rated one of the "Best 10 Courses in the World" by *Golf Monthly*. As an aside, she also noted that the lodging and food divisions had to turn away customers during only "peak-season events such as the New Year's period."

Required

1. Using selling prices, allocate the $1,000 getaway-package revenue to the three divisions using:
   a. The stand-alone revenue-allocation method
   b. The incremental revenue-allocation method (with recreation first, then lodging, and then food)
2. What are the pros and cons of the two methods in requirement 1?
3. Because the recreation division is able to book the golf course at 100% capacity, the company CEO has decided to revise the getaway package to only include the lodging and food offerings shown previously. The new package will sell for $900. Allocate the revenue to the lodging and food divisions using the following:
   a. The Shapley value method.
   b. The weighted Shapley value method, assuming that lodging is three times as likely to sell as the food.

Cost Allocation: Joint Products and Byproducts

▶ Learning Objectives

1. Identify the splitoff point in a joint-cost situation and distinguish joint products from byproducts

2. Explain why joint costs are allocated to individual products

3. Allocate joint costs using four methods

4. Explain when the sales value at splitoff method is preferred when allocating joint costs

5. Explain why joint costs are irrelevant in a sell-or-process-further decision

6. Account for byproducts using two methods

Many companies, such as petroleum refiners, produce and sell two or more products simultaneously.

Similarly, some companies, such as health care providers, sell or provide multiple services. The question is, "How should these companies allocate costs to 'joint' products and services?" Knowing how to allocate joint product costs isn't something that only companies need to understand. It's something that farmers have to deal with, too, especially when it comes to the lucrative production of corn to make billions of gallons of ethanol fuel.

Joint Cost Allocation and the Production of Ethanol Fuel[1]

The increased global demand for oil has driven prices higher and forced countries to look for environmentally-sustainable alternatives. In the United States, the largest source of alternative fuel comes from corn-based ethanol. In 2009, the U.S. produced 10.75 billion gallons of ethanol, or 55% of the world's production, up from 1.7 billion gallons per year in 2001.

Producing ethanol requires a significant amount of corn. In 2011, the U.S. Department of Agriculture predicts that more than one-third of U.S. domestic corn production will be used to create ethanol fuel. But not all of that corn winds up in the ethanol that gets blended into gasoline and sold at service station.

Most biotechnology operations, such as making ethanol, produce two or more products. While distilling corn into ethanol, cell mass from the process—such as antibiotic and yeast fermentations—separates from the liquid and becomes a separate product, which is often sold as animal feed. This separation point, where outputs become distinctly identifiable, is called the splitoff point. Similarly, the residues from corn processing plants create secondary products including distillers' dried grains and gluten.

Accountants refer to these secondary products as byproducts. Ethanol byproducts like animal feed and gluten are accounted for by deducting the income from selling these products from the cost of ethanol fuel, the major product. With ethanol production costing

[1] *Sources:* Hacking, Andrew. 1987. *Economic aspects of biotechnology.* Cambridge, United Kingdom: Cambridge University Press; Leber, Jessica. 2010. Economics improve for first commercial cellulosic ethanol plants. *New York Times*, February 16; *USDA Agricultural Predictions to 2019.* 2010. Washington, DC: Government Printing Office; PBS. 2006. Glut of ethanol byproducts coming. *The Environmental Report*, Spring; *Entrepreneur.* 2007. Edible ethanol byproduct is source of novel foods. August.

around $2 per gallon and byproducts selling for a few cents per pound, most of the costs of production are allocated to the ethanol fuel itself, the main product. Since manufacturers would otherwise have to pay to dispose of their ethanol byproducts, most just try to "break even" on byproduct revenue.

In the coming years, however, this may change. With ethanol production growing, corn-based animal feed byproducts are becoming more plentiful. Some ethanol manufacturers are working together to create a market for ethanol feed, which is cheaper and higher in protein than plain corn. This allows ranchers' animals to gain weight faster and at a lower cost per pound. Additionally, scientists are trying to create an edible byproduct from distillers' dry grains, which could become a low-calorie, low-carbohydrate substitute in foods like breads and pastas.

Accounting concerns similar to those in the ethanol example also arise when traditional energy companies like ExxonMobil simultaneously produce crude oil, natural gas, and raw liquefied petroleum gas (LPS) from petroleum, in a single process. This chapter examines methods for allocating costs to joint products. We also examine how cost numbers appropriate for one purpose, such as external reporting, may not be appropriate for other purposes, such as decisions about the further processing of joint products.

Joint-Cost Basics

Joint costs are the costs of a production process that yields multiple products simultaneously. Consider the distillation of coal, which yields coke, natural gas, and other products. The costs of this distillation are joint costs. The **splitoff point** is the juncture in a joint production process when two or more products become separately identifiable. An example is the point at which coal becomes coke, natural gas, and other products. **Separable costs** are all costs—manufacturing, marketing, distribution, and so on—incurred beyond the splitoff point that are assignable to each of the specific products identified at the splitoff point. At or beyond the splitoff point, decisions relating to the sale or further processing of each identifiable product can be made independently of decisions about the other products.

Industries abound in which a production process simultaneously yields two or more products, either at the splitoff point or after further processing. Exhibit 16-1 presents examples of joint-cost situations in diverse industries. In each of these examples, no individual product can be produced without the accompanying products appearing, although in some cases the proportions can be varied. The focus of joint costing is on allocating costs to individual products at the splitoff point.

The outputs of a joint production process can be classified into two general categories: outputs with a positive sales value and outputs with a zero sales value.[2] For

---

[2] Some outputs of a joint production process have "negative" revenue when their disposal costs (such as the costs of handling nonsalable toxic substances that require special disposal procedures) are considered. These disposal costs should be added to the joint production costs that are allocated to joint or main products.

Industry	Separable Products at the Splitoff Point
Agriculture and	
Food Processing Industries	
Cocoa beans	Cocoa butter, cocoa powder, cocoa drink mix, tanning cream
Lambs	Lamb cuts, tripe, hides, bones, fat
Hogs	Bacon, ham, spare ribs, pork roast
Raw milk	Cream, liquid skim
Lumber	Lumber of varying grades and shapes
Turkeys	Breast, wings, thighs, drumsticks, digest, feather meal, and poultry meal
Extractive Industries	
Coal	Coke, gas, benzol, tar, ammonia
Copper ore	Copper, silver, lead, zinc
Petroleum	Crude oil, natural gas
Salt	Hydrogen, chlorine, caustic soda
Chemical Industries	
Raw LPG (liquefied petroleum gas)	Butane, ethane, propane
Crude oil	Gasoline, kerosene, benzene, naphtha
Semiconductor Industry	
Fabrication of silicon-wafer chips	Memory chips of different quality (as to capacity), speed, life expectancy, and temperature tolerance

example, offshore processing of hydrocarbons yields oil and natural gas, which have positive sales value, and it also yields water, which has zero sales value and is recycled back into the ocean. The term **product** describes any output that has a positive total sales value (or an output that enables a company to avoid incurring costs, such as an intermediate chemical product used as input in another process). The total sales value can be high or low.

When a joint production process yields one product with a high total sales value, compared with total sales values of other products of the process, that product is called a **main product**. When a joint production process yields two or more products with high total sales values compared with the total sales values of other products, if any, those products are called **joint products**. The products of a joint production process that have low total sales values compared with the total sales value of the main product or of joint products are called **byproducts**.

Consider some examples. If timber (logs) is processed into standard lumber and wood chips, standard lumber is a main product and wood chips are the byproduct, because standard lumber has a high total sales value compared with wood chips. If, however, logs are processed into fine-grade lumber, standard lumber, and wood chips, fine-grade lumber and standard lumber are joint products, and wood chips are the byproduct. That's because both fine-grade lumber and standard lumber have high total sales values when compared with wood chips.

Distinctions among main products, joint products, and byproducts are not so definite in practice. For example, some companies may classify kerosene obtained when refining crude oil as a byproduct because they believe kerosene has a low total sales value relative to the total sales values of gasoline and other products. Other companies may classify kerosene as a joint product because they believe kerosene has a high total sales value relative to the total sales values of gasoline and other products. Moreover, the classification of products—main, joint, or byproduct—can change over time, especially for products such as lower-grade semiconductor chips, whose market prices may increase or decrease by 30% or more in a year. When prices of lower-grade chips are high, they are considered joint products together with higher-grade chips; when prices of lower-grade chips fall considerably, they are considered byproducts. In practice, it is important to understand how a specific company chooses to classify its products.

Decision Point

What do the terms joint cost and splitoff point mean, and how do joint products differ from byproducts?

Allocating Joint Costs

Before a manager is able to allocate joint costs, she must first look at the context for doing so. There are several contexts in which joint costs are required to be allocated to individual products or services. These include the following:

- Computation of inventoriable costs and cost of goods sold. Recall from Chapter 9 that absorption costing is required for financial accounting and tax reporting purposes. This necessitates the allocation of joint manufacturing or processing costs to products for calculating ending inventory values.
- Computation of inventoriable costs and cost of goods sold for internal reporting purposes. Many firms use internal accounting data based on joint cost allocations for the purpose of analyzing divisional profitability and in order to evaluate division managers' performance.
- Cost reimbursement for companies that have a few, but not all, of their products or services reimbursed under cost-plus contracts with, say, a government agency. In this case, stringent rules typically specify the manner in which joint costs are assigned to the products or services covered by the cost-plus agreement. That said, fraud in defense contracting, which is often done via cost-plus contracts, remains one of the most active areas of false claim litigation under the Federal False Claims Act. A common practice is "cross-charging," where a contractor shifts joint costs from "fixed-price" defense contracts to those that are done on a cost-plus basis. Defense contractors have also attempted to secure contracts from private businesses or foreign governments by allocating an improper share of joint costs onto the cost-plus agreements they have with the United States government.[3]
- Rate or price regulation for one or more of the jointly produced products or services. This issue is conceptually related to the previous point, and is of great importance in the extractive and energy industries where output prices are regulated to yield a fixed return on a cost basis that includes joint cost allocations. In telecommunications, for example, it is often the case that a firm with significant market power has some products subject to price regulation (e.g., interconnection) and other activities that are unregulated (such as end-user equipment rentals). In this case, it is critical in allocating joint costs to ensure that costs are not transferred from unregulated services to regulated ones.[4]

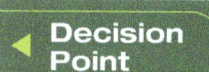

- Insurance-settlement computations for damage claims made on the basis of cost information of jointly produced products. In this case, the joint cost allocations are essential in order to provide a cost-based analysis of the loss in value.
- More generally, any commercial litigation situation in which costs of joint products or services are key inputs requires the allocation of joint costs.

Approaches to Allocating Joint Costs

Two approaches are used to allocate joint costs.

- **Approach 1.** Allocate joint costs using *market-based* data such as revenues. This chapter illustrates three methods that use this approach:
  1. Sales value at splitoff method
  2. Net realizable value (NRV) method
  3. Constant gross-margin percentage NRV method
- **Approach 2.** Allocate joint costs using *physical measures*, such as the weight, quantity (physical units), or volume of the joint products.

In preceding chapters, we used the cause-and-effect and benefits-received criteria for guiding cost-allocation decisions (see Exhibit 14-2, p. 505). Joint costs do not have a cause-and-effect relationship with individual products because the production process simultaneously yields multiple products. Using the benefits-received criterion leads to a preference for methods under approach 1 because revenues are, in general, a better

---

[3] See, for example, www.dodig.mil/iginformation/IGInformationReleases/3eSettlementPR.pdf
[4] For details, see the International Telecommunication Union's ICT Regulation Toolkit at www.ictregulationtoolkit.org/en/Section.3497.html.

indicator of benefits received than physical measures. Mining companies, for example, receive more benefits from 1 ton of gold than they do from 10 tons of coal.

In the simplest joint production process, the joint products are sold at the splitoff point without further processing. Example 1 illustrates the two methods that apply in this case: the sales value at splitoff method and the physical-measure method. Then we introduce joint production processes that yield products that require further processing beyond the splitoff point. Example 2 illustrates the NRV method and the constant-gross margin percentage NRV method. To help you focus on key concepts, we use numbers and amounts that are smaller than the numbers that are typically found in practice.

The exhibits in this chapter use the following symbols to distinguish a joint or main product from a byproduct:

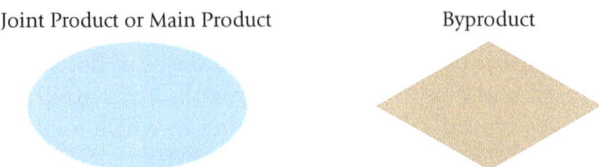

Joint Product or Main Product   Byproduct

To compare methods, we report gross-margin percentages for individual products under each method.

> Example 1: Farmers' Dairy purchases raw milk from individual farms and processes it until the splitoff point, when two products—cream and liquid skim—emerge. These two products are sold to an independent company, which markets and distributes them to supermarkets and other retail outlets.
>
> In May 2012, Farmers' Dairy processes 110,000 gallons of raw milk. During processing, 10,000 gallons are lost due to evaporation and spillage, yielding 25,000 gallons of cream and 75,000 gallons of liquid skim. Summary data follow:

	A	B	C
1		**Joint Costs**	
2	Joint costs (costs of 110,000 gallons raw milk and processing to splitoff point)	$400,000	
3			
4		**Cream**	**Liquid Skim**
5	Beginnning inventory (gallons)	0	0
6	Production (gallons)	25,000	75,000
7	Sales (gallons)	20,000	30,000
8	Ending inventory (gallons)	5,000	45,000
9	Selling price per gallon	$ 8	$ 4

Exhibit 16-2 depicts the basic relationships in this example.

How much of the $400,000 joint costs should be allocated to the cost of goods sold of 20,000 gallons of cream and 30,000 gallons of liquid skim, and how much should be allocated to the ending inventory of 5,000 gallons of cream and 45,000 gallons of liquid skim? We begin by illustrating the two methods that use the properties of the products at the splitoff point, the sales value at splitoff method and the physical-measure method.

Sales Value at Splitoff Method

The **sales value at splitoff method** allocates joint costs to joint products produced during the accounting period on the basis of the relative total sales value at the splitoff point. Using this method for Example 1, Exhibit 16-3, Panel A, shows how joint costs

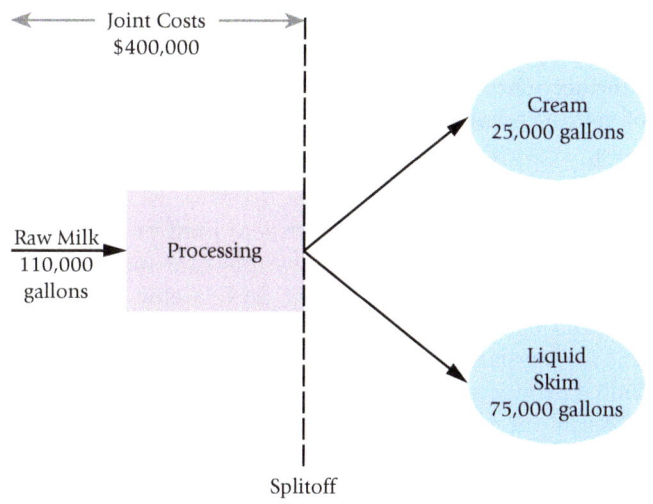

Exhibit 16-2

Example 1: Overview of
Farmers' Dairy

are allocated to individual products to calculate cost per gallon of cream and liquid skim for valuing ending inventory. This method uses the sales value of the *entire production of the accounting period* (25,000 gallons of cream and 75,000 gallons of liquid skim), not just the quantity sold (20,000 gallons of cream and 30,000 gallons of liquid skim). The reason this method does not rely solely on the quantity sold is that the joint costs were incurred on all units produced, not just the portion sold during the current period. Exhibit 16-3, Panel B, presents the product-line income statement using the sales value at splitoff method. Note that the gross-margin percentage for each product is 20%, because the sales value at splitoff method allocates joint costs to each product in proportion to the sales value of total production (cream: $160,000 ÷ $200,000 = 80%; liquid skim: $240,000 ÷ $300,000 = 80%). Therefore, the gross-margin percentage for each product manufactured in May 2012 is the same: 20%.[5]

Note how the sales value at splitoff method follows the benefits-received criterion of cost allocation: Costs are allocated to products in proportion to their revenue-generating

Exhibit 16-3 Joint-Cost Allocation and Product-Line Income Statement Using Sales Value at Splitoff Method: Farmers' Dairy for May 2012

Home	Insert	Page Layout	Formulas	Data	Review	View			
	A						B	C	D
1	PANEL A: Allocation of Joint Costs Using Sales Value at Splitoff Method						Cream	Liquid Skim	Total
2	Sales value of total production at splitoff point								
3	(25,000 gallons × $8 per gallon; 75,000 gallons × $4 per gallon)						$200,000	$300,000	$500,000
4	Weighting ($200,000 ÷ $500,000; $300,000 ÷ 500,000)						0.40	0.60	
5	Joint costs allocated (0.40 × $400,000; 0.60 × $400,000)						$160,000	$240,000	$400,000
6	Joint production cost per gallon								
7	($160,000 ÷ 25,000 gallons; $240,000 ÷ 75,000 gallons)						$ 6.40	$ 3.20	
8									
9	PANEL B: Product-Line Income Statement Using Sales Value at Splitoff Method for May 2012						Cream	Liquid Skim	Total
10	Revenues (20,000 gallons × $8 per gallon; 30,000 gallons × $4 per gallon)						$160,000	$120,000	$280,000
11	Cost of goods sold (joint costs)								
12	Production costs (0.40 × $400,000; 0.60 × $400,000)						160,000	240,000	400,000
13	Deduct ending inventory (5,000 gallons × $6.40 per gallon; 45,000 gallons × $3.20 per gallon)						32,000	144,000	176,000
14	Cost of goods sold (joint costs)						128,000	96,000	224,000
15	Gross margin						$ 32,000	$ 24,000	$ 56,000
16	Gross margin percentage ($32,000 ÷ $160,000; $24,000 ÷ $120,000; $56,000 ÷ $280,000)						20%	20%	20%

---

[5] Suppose Farmers' Dairy has beginning inventory of cream and liquid milk in May 2012 and when this inventory is sold, Farmers' earns a gross margin different from 20%. Then the gross-margin percentage for cream and liquid skim will not be the same. The relative gross-margin percentages will depend on how much of the sales of each product came from beginning inventory and how much came from current-period production.

power (their expected revenues). The cost-allocation base (total sales value at splitoff) is expressed in terms of a common denominator (the amount of revenues) that is systematically recorded in the accounting system. To use this method, selling prices must exist for all products at the splitoff point.

Physical-Measure Method

The **physical-measure method** allocates joint costs to joint products produced during the accounting period on the basis of a *comparable* physical measure, such as the relative weight, quantity, or volume at the splitoff point. In Example 1, the $400,000 joint costs produced 25,000 gallons of cream and 75,000 gallons of liquid skim. Using the number of gallons produced as the physical measure, Exhibit 16-4, Panel A, shows how joint costs are allocated to individual products to calculate the cost per gallon of cream and liquid skim.

Because the physical-measure method allocates joint costs on the basis of the number of gallons, cost per gallon is the same for both products. Exhibit 16-4, Panel B, presents the product-line income statement using the physical-measure method. The gross-margin percentages are 50% for cream and 0% for liquid skim.

Under the benefits-received criterion, the physical-measure method is much less desirable than the sales value at splitoff method, because the physical measure of the individual products may have no relationship to their respective revenue-generating abilities. Consider a gold mine that extracts ore containing gold, silver, and lead. Use of a common physical measure (tons) would result in almost all costs being allocated to lead, the product that weighs the most but has the lowest revenue-generating power. In the case of metals, the method of cost allocation is inconsistent with the main reason that the mining company is incurring mining costs—to earn revenues from gold and silver, not lead. When a company uses the physical-measure method in a product-line income statement, products that have a high sales value per ton, like gold and silver, would show a large "profit," and products that have a low sales value per ton, like lead, would show sizable losses.

Obtaining comparable physical measures for all products is not always straightforward. Consider the joint costs of producing oil and natural gas; oil is a liquid and gas is a vapor. To use a physical measure, the oil and gas need to be converted to the energy equivalent for oil and gas, British thermal units (BTUs). Using some physical measures to allocate joint costs may require assistance from technical personnel outside of accounting.

Determining which products of a joint process to include in a physical-measure computation can greatly affect the allocations to those products. Outputs with no sales value

Exhibit 16-4 Joint-Cost Allocation and Product-Line Income Statement Using Physical-Measure Method: Farmers' Dairy for May 2012

	A	B	C	D
	Home Insert Page Layout Formulas Data Review View			
1	PANEL A: Allocation of Joint Costs Using Physical-Measure Method	Cream	Liquid Skim	Total
2	Physical measure of total production (gallons)	25,000	75,000	100,000
3	Weighting (25,000 gallons ÷ 100,000 gallons; 75,000 gallons ÷ 100,000 gallons)	0.25	0.75	
4	Joint costs allocated (0.25 × $400,000; 0.75 × $400,000)	$100,000	$300,000	$400,000
5	Joint production cost per gallon ($100,000 ÷ 25,000 gallons; $300,000 ÷ 75,000 gallons)	$ 4.00	$ 4.00	
6				
7	PANEL B: Product-Line Income Statement Using Physical-Measure Method for May 2012	Cream	Liquid Skim	Total
8	Revenues (20,000 gallons × $8 per gallon; 30,000 gallons × $4 per gallon)	$160,000	$120,000	$280,000
9	Cost of goods sold (joint costs)			
10	Production costs (0.25 × $400,000; 0.75 × $400,000)	100,000	300,000	400,000
11	Deduct ending inventory (5,000 gallons × $4 per gallon; 45,000 gallons × $4 per gallon)	20,000	180,000	200,000
12	Cost of goods sold (joint costs)	80,000	120,000	200,000
13	Gross margin	$ 80,000	$ 0	$ 80,000
14	Gross margin percentage ($80,000 ÷ $160,000; $0 ÷ $120,000; $80,000 ÷ $280,000)	50%	0%	28.6%

(such as dirt in gold mining) are always excluded. Although many more tons of dirt than gold are produced, costs are not incurred to produce outputs that have zero sales value. Byproducts are also often excluded from the denominator used in the physical-measure method because of their low sales values relative to the joint products or the main product. The general guideline for the physical-measure method is to include only the joint-product outputs in the weighting computations.

Net Realizable Value Method

In many cases, products are processed beyond the splitoff point to bring them to a marketable form or to increase their value above their selling price at the splitoff point. For example, when crude oil is refined, the gasoline, kerosene, benzene, and naphtha must be processed further before they can be sold. To illustrate, let's extend the Farmers' Dairy example.

> Example 2: Assume the same data as in Example 1 except that both cream and liquid skim can be processed further:
>
> ■ Cream → Buttercream: 25,000 gallons of cream are further processed to yield 20,000 gallons of buttercream at additional processing costs of $280,000. Buttercream, which sells for $25 per gallon, is used in the manufacture of butter-based products.
>
> ■ Liquid Skim → Condensed Milk: 75,000 gallons of liquid skim are further processed to yield 50,000 gallons of condensed milk at additional processing costs of $520,000. Condensed milk sells for $22 per gallon.
>
> ■ Sales during May 2012 are 12,000 gallons of buttercream and 45,000 gallons of condensed milk.

Exhibit 16-5, Panel A, depicts how (a) raw milk is converted into cream and liquid skim in the joint production process, and (b) how cream is separately processed into buttercream and liquid skim is separately processed into condensed milk. Panel B shows the data for Example 2.

The **net realizable value (NRV) method** allocates joint costs to joint products produced during the accounting period on the basis of their relative NRV—final sales value minus separable costs. The NRV method is typically used in preference to the sales value at splitoff method only when selling prices for one or more products at splitoff do not exist. Using this method for Example 2, Exhibit 16-6, Panel A, shows how joint costs are allocated to individual products to calculate cost per gallon of buttercream and condensed milk.

Exhibit 16-6, Panel B presents the product-line income statement using the NRV method. Gross-margin percentages are 22.0% for buttercream and 26.4% for condensed milk.

The NRV method is often implemented using simplifying assumptions. For example, even when selling prices of joint products vary frequently, companies implement the

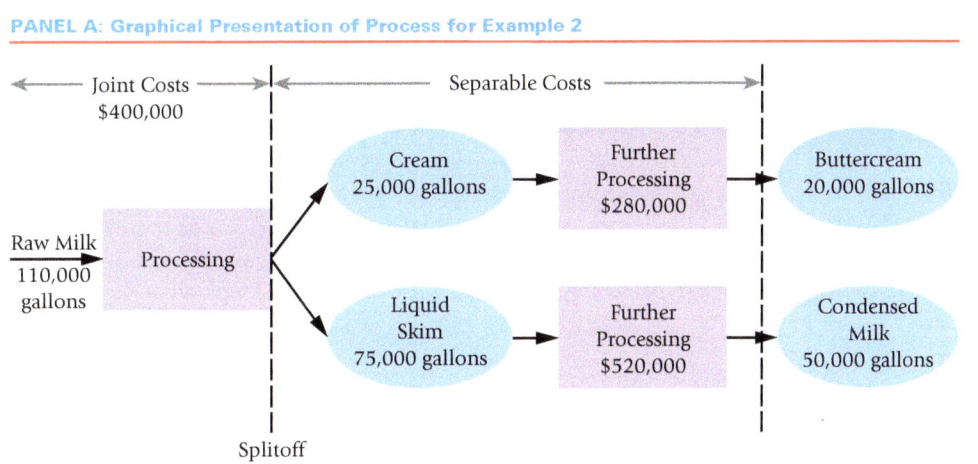

PANEL A: Graphical Presentation of Process for Example 2

Exhibit 16-5

Example 2: Overview of Farmers' Dairy

Exhibit 16-5   Example 2: Overview of Farmers' Dairy (*continued*)

PANEL B: Data for Example 2

	A	B	C	D	E
			Joint Costs	**Buttercream**	**Condensed Milk**
1					
2	Joint costs (costs of 110,000 gallons raw milk and processing to splitoff point)		$400,000		
3	Separable cost of processing 25,000 gallons cream into 20,000 gallons buttercream			$280,000	
4	Separable cost of processing 75,000 gallons liquid skim into 50,000 gallons condensed milk				$520,000
5					
6		**Cream**	**Liquid Skim**	**Buttercream**	**Condensed Milk**
7	Beginning inventory (gallons)	0	0	0	0
8	Production (gallons)	25,000	75,000	20,000	50,000
9	Transfer for further processing (gallons)	25,000	75,000		
10	Sales (gallons)			12,000	45,000
11	Ending inventory (gallons)	0	0	8,000	5,000
12	Selling price per gallon	$ 8	$ 4	$ 25	$ 22

Exhibit 16-6   Joint-Cost Allocation and Product-Line Income Statement Using NRV Method: Farmers' Dairy for May 2012

	A	B	C	D
1	**PANEL A: Allocation of Joint Costs Using Net Realizable Value Method**	**Buttercream**	**Condensed Milk**	**Total**
2	Final sales value of total production during accounting period			
3	(20,000 gallons × $25 per gallon; 50,000 gallons × $22 per gallon)	$500,000	$1,100,000	$1,600,000
4	Deduct separable costs	280,000	520,000	800,000
5	Net realizable value at splitoff point	$220,000	$ 580,000	$ 800,000
6	Weighting ($220,000 ÷ $800,000; $580,000 ÷ $800,000)	0.275	0.725	
7	Joint costs allocated (0.275 × $400,000; 0.725 × $400,000)	$110,000	$ 290,000	$ 400,000
8	Production cost per gallon			
9	([$110,000 + $280,000] ÷ 20,000 gallons; [$290,000 + $520,000] ÷ 50,000 gallons)	$ 19.50	$ 16.20	
10				
11	**PANEL B: Product-Line Income Statement Using Net Realizable Value Method for May 2012**	**Buttercream**	**Condensed Milk**	**Total**
12	Revenues (12,000 gallons × $25 per gallon; 45,000 gallons × $22 per gallon)	$300,000	$ 990,000	$1,290,000
13	Cost of goods sold			
14	Joint costs (0.275 × $400,000; 0.725 × $400,000)	110,000	290,000	400,000
15	Separable costs	280,000	520,000	800,000
16	Production costs	390,000	810,000	1,200,000
17	Deduct ending inventory (8,000 gallons × $19.50 per gallon; 5,000 gallons × $16.20 per gallon)	156,000	81,000	237,000
18	Cost of goods sold	234,000	729,000	963,000
19	Gross margin	$ 66,000	$ 261,000	$ 327,000
20	Gross margin percentage ($66,000 ÷ $300,000; $261,000 ÷ $990,000; $327,000 ÷ $1,290,000)	22.0%	26.4%	25.3%

NRV method using a given set of selling prices throughout the accounting period. Similarly, even though companies may occasionally change the number or sequence of processing steps beyond the splitoff point in order to adjust to variations in input quality or local conditions, they assume a specific constant set of such steps when implementing the NRV method.

Constant Gross-Margin Percentage NRV Method

The **constant gross-margin percentage NRV method** allocates joint costs to joint products produced during the accounting period in such a way that each individual product achieves an identical gross-margin percentage. The method works backward in that the overall gross margin is computed first. Then, for each product, this gross-margin percentage and any separable costs are deducted from the final sales value of production in order to back into the joint cost allocation for that product. The method can be broken down into three discrete steps. Exhibit 16-7, Panel A, shows these steps for allocating the $400,000 joint costs between buttercream and condensed milk in the Farmers' Dairy example. As we describe each step, refer to Exhibit 16-7, Panel A, for an illustration of the step.

Step 1: Compute overall gross margin percentage. The overall gross-margin percentage for all joint products together is calculated first. This is based on the final sales value of *total production* during the accounting period, not the *total revenues* of the period. Note, Exhibit 16-7, Panel A, uses $1,600,000, the final expected sales value of the entire output of buttercream and condensed milk, not the $1,290,000 in actual sales revenue for the month of May.

Step 2: Compute total production costs for each product. The gross margin (in dollars) for each product is computed by multiplying the overall gross-margin percentage by the product's final sales value of total production. The difference between the final sales value of total production and the gross margin then yields the total production costs that the product must bear.

Step 3: Compute allocated joint costs. As the final step, the separable costs for each product are deducted from the total production costs that the product must bear to obtain the joint-cost allocation for that product.

Exhibit 16-7, Panel B, presents the product-line income statement for the constant gross-margin percentage NRV method.

Exhibit 16-7 Joint-Cost Allocation and Product-Line Income Statement Using Constant Gross-Margin Percentage NRV Method: Farmers' Dairy for May 2012

	A	B	C	D
1	**PANEL A: Allocation of Joint Costs Using Constant Gross-Margin Percentage NRV Method**			
2	**Step 1**			
3	Final sales value of total production during accounting period: (20,000 gallons × $25 per gallon) + (50,000 gallons × $22 per gallon)	$1,600,000		
4	Deduct joint and separable costs ($400,000 + $280,000 + $520,000)	1,200,000		
5	Gross margin	$ 400,000		
6	Gross margin percentage ($400,000 ÷ $1,600,000)	25%		
7		**Buttercream**	**Condensed Milk**	**Total**
8	**Step 2**			
9	Final sales value of total production during accounting period: (20,000 gallons × $25 per gallon; 50,000 gallons × $22 per gallon)	$ 500,000	$1,100,000	$1,600,000
10	Deduct gross margin, using overall gross-margin percentage (25% × $500,000; 25% × $1,100,000)	125,000	275,000	400,000
11	Total production costs	375,000	825,000	1,200,000
12	**Step 3**			
13	Deduct separable costs	280,000	520,000	800,000
14	Joint costs allocated	$ 95,000	$ 305,000	$ 400,000
15				
16	**PANEL B: Product-Line Income Statement Using Constant Gross-Margin Percentage NRV Method for May 2012**	**Buttercream**	**Condensed Milk**	**Total**
17	Revenues (12,000 gallons × $25 per gallon; 45,000 gallons × $22 per gallon)	$ 300,000	$ 990,000	$1,290,000
18	Cost of goods sold			
19	Joint costs (from Panel A)	95,000	305,000	400,000
20	Separable costs	280,000	520,000	800,000
21	Production costs	375,000	825,000	1,200,000
22	Deduct ending inventory			
23	(8,000 gallons × $18.75 per gallon[a]; 5,000 gallons × $16.50 per gallon[b])	150,000	82,500	232,500
24	Cost of goods sold	225,000	742,500	967,500
25	Gross margin	$ 75,000	$ 247,500	$ 322,500
26	Gross margin percentage ($75,000 ÷ 300,000; $247,500 ÷ $990,000; $322,500 ÷ $1,290,000)	25%	25%	25%
27				
28	[a]Total production costs of buttercream ÷ Total production of buttercream = $375,000 ÷ 20,000 gallons = $18.75 per gallon.			
29	[b]Total production costs of condensed milk ÷ Total production of condensed milk = $825,000 ÷ 50,000 gallons = $16.50 per gallon.			

Decision Point ▶

What methods can be used to allocate joint costs to individual products?

The constant gross-margin percentage NRV method is the only method of allocating joint costs under which products may receive negative allocations. This may be required in order to bring the gross-margin percentages of relatively unprofitable products up to the overall average. The constant gross-margin percentage NRV method also differs from the other two market-based joint-cost-allocation methods described earlier in another fundamental way. Neither the sales value at splitoff method nor the NRV method takes account of profits earned either before or after the splitoff point when allocating the joint costs. In contrast, the constant gross-margin percentage NRV method allocates both joint costs and profits: Gross margin is allocated to the joint products in order to determine the joint-cost allocations so that the resulting gross-margin percentage for each product is the same.

Choosing an Allocation Method

Learning Objective 4

Explain when the sales value at splitoff method is preferred when allocating joint costs

. . . because it objectively measures the benefits received by each product

Which method of allocating joint costs should be used? The sales value at splitoff method is preferable when selling-price data exist at splitoff (even if further processing is done). Reasons for using the sales value at splitoff method include the following:

1. **Measurement of the value of the joint products at the splitoff point.** Sales value at splitoff is the best measure of the benefits received as a result of joint processing relative to all other methods of allocating joint costs. It is a meaningful basis for allocating joint costs because generating revenues is the reason why a company incurs joint costs in the first place. It is also sometimes possible to vary the physical mix of final output and thereby produce more or less market value by incurring more joint costs. In such cases, there is a clear causal link between total cost and total output value, thereby further validating the use of the sales value at splitoff method.[6]

2. **No anticipation of subsequent management decisions.** The sales value at splitoff method does not require information on the processing steps after splitoff if there is further processing. In contrast, the NRV and constant gross-margin percentage NRV methods require information on (a) the specific sequence of further processing decisions, (b) the separable costs of further processing, and (c) the point at which individual products will be sold.

3. **Availability of a common basis to allocate joint costs to products.** The sales value at splitoff method (as well as other market-based methods) has a common basis to allocate joint costs to products, which is revenue. In contrast, the physical-measure at splitoff method may lack an easily identifiable common basis to allocate joint costs to individual products.

4. **Simplicity.** The sales value at splitoff method is simple. In contrast, the NRV and constant gross-margin percentage NRV methods can be complex for processing operations having multiple products and multiple splitoff points. This complexity increases when management makes frequent changes in the specific sequence of post-splitoff processing decisions or in the point at which individual products are sold.

When selling prices of all products at the splitoff point are unavailable, the NRV method is commonly used because it attempts to approximate sales value at splitoff by subtracting from selling prices separable costs incurred after the splitoff point. The NRV method assumes that all the markup or profit margin is attributable to the joint process and none of the markup is attributable to the separable costs. Profit, however, is attributable to all phases of production and marketing, not just the joint process. More of the profit may be attributable to the joint process if the separable process is relatively routine, whereas more of the profit may be attributable to the separable process if the separable process uses a special patented technology. Despite its complexities, the NRV method is used when selling prices at splitoff are not available as it provides a better measure of benefits received compared with the constant gross-margin percentage NRV method or the physical-measure method.

---

[6] In the semiconductor industry, for example, the use of cleaner facilities, higher quality silicon wafers, and more sophisticated equipment (all of which require higher joint costs) shifts the distribution of output to higher-quality memory devices with more market value. For details, see J. F. Gatti and D. J. Grinnell, "Joint Cost Allocations: Measuring and Promoting Productivity and Quality Improvements," *Journal of Cost Management* (2000). The authors also demonstrate that joint cost allocations based on market value are preferable for promoting quality and productivity improvements.

The constant gross-margin percentage NRV method makes the simplifying assumption of treating the joint products as though they comprise a single product. This method calculates the aggregate gross-margin percentage, applies this gross-margin percentage to each product, and views the residual after separable costs are accounted for as the implicit amount of joint costs assigned to each product. An advantage of this method is that it avoids the complexities inherent in the NRV method to measure the benefits received by each of the joint products at the splitoff point. The main issue with the constant gross-margin percentage NRV method is the assumption that all products have the same ratio of cost to sales value. Recall from our discussion of activity-based costing (ABC) in Chapter 5 that such a situation is very uncommon when companies offer a diverse set of products.

Although there are difficulties in using the physical-measure method—such as lack of congruence with the benefits-received criterion—there are instances when it may be preferred. Consider rate or price regulation. Market-based measures are difficult to use in this context because using selling prices as a basis for setting prices (rates) and at the same time using selling prices to allocate the costs on which prices (rates) are based leads to circular reasoning. To avoid this dilemma, the physical-measure method is useful in rate regulation.

Not Allocating Joint Costs

Some companies choose to not allocate joint costs to products. The usual rationale given by these firms is the complexity of their production or extraction processes and the difficulty of gathering sufficient data for carrying out the allocations correctly. For example, a recent survey of nine sawmills in Norway revealed that none of them allocated joint costs. The study's authors noted that the "interviewed sawmills considered the joint cost problem very interesting, but pointed out that the problem is not easily solved. For example, there is clearly a shortcoming in management systems designed for handling joint cost allocation."[7]

In the absence of joint cost allocation, some firms simply subtract the joint costs directly from total revenues in the management accounts. If substantial inventories exist, then firms that do not allocate joint costs often carry their product inventories at NRV. Industries that use variations of this approach include meatpacking, canning, and mining. Accountants do not ordinarily record inventories at NRV because this practice results in recognizing income on each product at the time production is completed and *before* sales are made. In response, some companies using this no-allocation approach carry their inventories at NRV minus an estimated operating income margin. When any end-of-period inventories are sold in the next period, the cost of goods sold then equals this carrying value. This approach is akin to the "production method" of accounting for byproducts, which we describe in detail later in this chapter.

> ◀ **Decision Point**
>
> When is the sales value at splitoff method considered preferable for allocating joint costs to individual products and why?

Irrelevance of Joint Costs for Decision Making

Chapter 11 introduced the concepts of *relevant revenues*, expected future revenues that differ among alternative courses of action, and *relevant costs*, expected future costs that differ among alternative courses of action. These concepts can be applied to decisions on whether a joint product or main product should be sold at the splitoff point or processed further.

> **Learning Objective 5**
>
> Explain why joint costs are irrelevant in a sell-or-process-further decision
>
> . . . because joint costs are the same whether or not further processing occurs

Sell-or-Process-Further Decisions

Consider Farmers' Dairy's decision to either sell the joint products, cream and liquid skim, at the splitoff point or to further process them into buttercream and condensed milk. The decision to incur additional costs for further processing should be based on the incremental operating income attainable beyond the splitoff point. Example 2 assumed it was profitable for both cream and liquid skim to be further processed into buttercream

---

[7] For further details, see T. Tunes, A. Nyrud, and B. Eikenes, "Cost and Performance Management in the Sawmill Industry," *Scandinavian Forest Economics* (2006).

and condensed milk, respectively. The incremental analysis for the decision to process further is as follows:

Further Processing Cream into Buttercream

Incremental revenues	
($25/gallon × 20,000 gallons) − ($8/gallon × 25,000 gallons)	$300,000
Deduct incremental processing costs	280,000
Increase in operating income from buttercream	$ 20,000

Further Processing Liquid Skim into Condensed Milk

Incremental revenues	
($22/gallon × 50,000 gallons) − ($4/gallon × 75,000 gallons)	$800,000
Deduct incremental processing costs	520,000
Increase in operating income from condensed milk	$280,000

In this example, operating income increases for both products, so the manager decides to process cream into buttercream and liquid skim into condensed milk. *The $400,000 joint costs incurred before the splitoff point are irrelevant in deciding whether to process further.* Why? Because the joint costs of $400,000 are the same whether the products are sold at the splitoff point or processed further.

Incremental costs are the additional costs incurred for an activity, such as further processing. *Do not assume all separable costs in joint-cost allocations are always incremental costs.* Some separable costs may be fixed costs, such as lease costs on buildings where the further processing is done; some separable costs may be sunk costs, such as depreciation on the equipment that converts cream into buttercream; and some separable costs may be allocated costs, such as corporate costs allocated to the condensed milk operations. None of these costs will differ between the alternatives of selling products at the splitoff point or processing further; therefore, they are irrelevant.

Joint-Cost Allocation and Performance Evaluation

The potential conflict between cost concepts used for decision making and cost concepts used for evaluating the performance of managers could also arise in sell-or-process-further decisions. To see how, let us continue with Example 2. Suppose *allocated* fixed corporate and administrative costs of further processing cream into buttercream equal $30,000 and that these costs will be allocated only to buttercream and to the manager's product-line income statement if buttercream is produced. How might this policy affect the decision to process further?

As we have seen, on the basis of incremental revenues and incremental costs, Farmers' operating income will increase by $20,000 if it processes cream into buttercream. However, producing the buttercream also results in an additional charge for allocated fixed costs of $30,000. If the manager is evaluated on a full-cost basis (that is, after allocating all costs), processing cream into buttercream will lower the manager's performance-evaluation measure by $10,000 (incremental operating income, $20,000 − allocated fixed costs, $30,000). Therefore, the manager may be tempted to sell cream at splitoff and not process it into buttercream.

A similar conflict can also arise with respect to production of joint products. Consider again Example 1. Suppose Farmers' Dairy has the option of selling raw milk at a profit of $20,000. From a decision-making standpoint, Farmers' would maximize operating income by processing raw milk into cream and liquid skim because the total revenues from selling both joint products ($500,000, see Exhibit 16-3, p. 581) exceed the joint costs ($400,000, p. 580) by $100,000. (This amount is greater than the $20,000 Farmers' Dairy would make if it sold the raw milk instead of processing it.) Suppose, however, the cream and liquid-skim product lines are managed by different managers, each of whom is evaluated based on a product-line income statement. If the physical-measure method of joint-cost allocation is used and the selling price per gallon of liquid skim falls below $4.00 per gallon, the liquid-skim product line will show a loss (from Exhibit 16-4, p. 582, revenues will be less than $120,000, but cost of goods sold will be unchanged at $120,000). The manager of the liquid-skim line will prefer, from his or her performance-evaluation standpoint, to not produce liquid skim but rather to sell the raw milk.

This conflict between decision making and performance evaluation is less severe if Farmers' Dairy uses any of the market-based methods of joint-cost allocations—sales value at splitoff, NRV, or constant gross-margin percentage NRV—because each of these methods allocates costs using revenues, which generally leads to a positive income for each joint product.

Pricing Decisions

Firms should be wary of using the full cost of a joint product (that is, the cost after joint costs are allocated) as the basis for making pricing decisions. Why? Because in many situations, there is no direct cause-and-effect relationship that identifies the resources demanded by each joint product that can then be used as a basis for pricing. In fact, the use of the sales value at splitoff or the net realizable value method to allocate joint costs results in a reverse effect—selling prices of joint products drive joint-cost allocations, rather than cost allocations serving as the basis for the pricing of joint products! Of course, the principles of pricing covered in Chapter 12 apply to the joint process taken as a whole. Even if the firm cannot alter the mix of products generated by the joint process, it must ensure that the joint products generate sufficient combined revenue in the long run to cover the joint costs of processing.

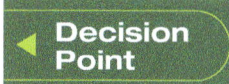

Decision Point

Are joint costs relevant in a sell-or-process-further decision?

Accounting for Byproducts

Joint production processes may yield not only joint products and main products but also byproducts. Although byproducts have relatively low total sales values, the presence of byproducts in a joint production process can affect the allocation of joint costs. Let's consider a two-product example consisting of a main product and a byproduct (also see the Concepts in Action feature on p. 590).

Learning Objective 6

Account for byproducts using two methods

. . . recognize in financial statements at time of production or at time of sale

> Example 3: The Westlake Corporation processes timber into fine-grade lumber and wood chips that are used as mulch in gardens and lawns. Information about these products follows:
>
> ■ Fine-Grade lumber (the main product)—sells for $6 per board foot (b.f.)
>
> ■ Wood chips (the byproduct)—sells for $1 per cubic foot (c.f.)
>
> Data for July 2012 are as follows:

	Beginning Inventory	Production	Sales	Ending Inventory
Fine-Grade lumber (b.f.)	0	50,000	40,000	10,000
Wood chips (c.f.)	0	4,000	1,200	2,800

Joint manufacturing costs for these products in July 2012 are $250,000, comprising $150,000 for direct materials and $100,000 for conversion costs. Both products are sold at the splitoff point without further processing, as Exhibit 16-8 shows.

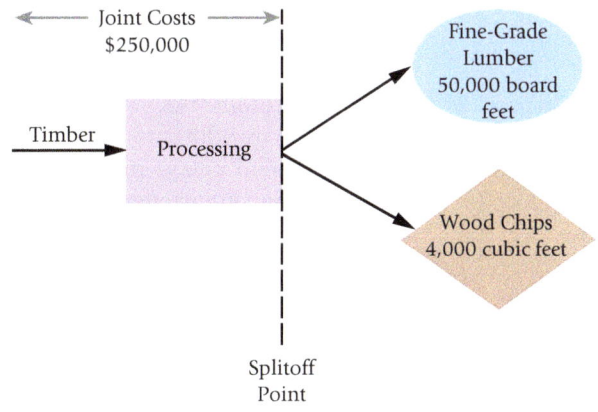

Exhibit 16-8

Example 3: Overview of Westlake Corporation

Concepts in Action

Byproduct Costing Keeps Wendy's Chili Profitable . . . and on the Menu

There are many examples in which joint and byproduct costing issues arise, including coal mining, semiconductor manufacturing, and Wendy's chili. You may be asking yourself, "chili from Wendy's?" Yes! The primary ingredient in chili at Wendy's, one of the largest fast-food chains in the United States, is a byproduct of overcooked, unsellable hamburger patties.

The most important product that Wendy's offers its customers is an "old-fashioned" hamburger, which is a hamburger served from the grill in accordance with individual customer orders. Operationally, the only way to serve hamburgers this way is to anticipate customer demand and have a sufficient supply of hamburgers already cooking when the customers arrive at the restaurant. The problem with this approach, however, is the fate of the extra hamburgers that become too well done whenever the cooks overestimate customer demand. Throwing them away would be too costly and wasteful, but serving them as "old-fashioned" hamburgers would likely result in considerable customer dissatisfaction.

For Wendy's, the solution to this dilemma involved finding a product that was unique to the fast-food industry and required ground beef as one of the major ingredients. Thus, Wendy's "rich and meaty" chili became one of its original menu items. For each batch of chili, which is prepared daily in each restaurant, Wendy's needs 48 quarter-pound cooked ground-beef patties along with crushed tomatoes, tomato juice, red beans, and seasoning. Only 10% of the time is it necessary for Wendy's to cook meat specifically for use in making chili.

Several years ago, Wendy's management considered eliminating some of its traditional menu items. Chili, composing only about 5% of total restaurant sales, was targeted for possible elimination, and at $0.99 for an eight-ounce serving, it brought in far less revenue than a product like a single hamburger, which sold for $1.89. When Wendy's compared the cost of making chili to its sale price, however, the product remained on the menu. How? The beef in Wendy's chili recipe was a byproduct of hamburger patties, its main product, which affected the allocation of joint costs.

Excluding ground beef, the costs to produce Wendy's chili are around $0.37 per eight-ounce serving, which includes labor. When Wendy's has to cook meat for its chili, again only 10% of the time, the recipe calls for ground beef that costs around $0.73 per serving. Under those circumstances, the chili costs Wendy's $1.10 to make, and each $.99 serving sells at a $0.11 loss. However, the 90% of the time Wendy's uses precooked ground beef for its chili, most of those costs have already been allocated to hamburgers, the primary product. As a result, each eight-ounce serving of chili Wendy's sells using precooked ground beef is sold at a significant profit. With a lucrative profit margin for each serving sold, customers are likely to find chili on the Wendy's menu for a long time to come.

Source: Brownlee, E. Richard. 2005. Wendy's chili: A costing conundrum. The University of Virginia Darden School of Business Case No. UVA-C-2206. Charlottesville, VA: Darden Business Publishing.

We present two byproduct accounting methods: the production method and the sales method. The production method recognizes byproducts in the financial statements at the time production is completed. The sales method delays recognition of byproducts until the time of sale.[8] Exhibit 16-9 presents the income statement of Westlake Corporation under both methods.

---

[8] For a discussion of joint cost allocation and byproduct accounting methods, see P. D. Marshall and R. F. Dombrowski, "A Small Business Review of Accounting for Primary Products, Byproducts and Scrap," *The National Public Accountant* (February/March 2003): 10–13.

Exhibit 16-9

Income Statements of
Westlake Corporation
for July 2012 Using the
Production and Sales
Methods for Byproduct
Accounting

	Production Method	Sales Method
Revenues		
Main product: Fine-grade lumber (40,000 b.f. × $6 per b.f.)	$240,000	$240,000
Byproduct: Wood chips (1,200 c.f. × $1 per c.f.)	—	1,200
Total revenues	240,000	241,200
Cost of goods sold		
Total manufacturing costs	250,000	250,000
Deduct byproduct revenue (4,000 c.f. × $1 per c.f.)	(4,000)	—
Net manufacturing costs	246,000	250,000
Deduct main-product inventory	(49,200)[a]	(50,000)[b]
Cost of goods sold	196,800	200,000
Gross margin	$ 43,200	$ 41,200
Gross-margin percentage ($43,200 ÷ $240,000; $41,200 ÷ $241,200)	18.00%	17.08%
Inventoriable costs (end of period):		
Main product: Fine-grade lumber	$ 49,200	$ 50,000
Byproduct: Wood chips (2,800 c.f. × $1 per c.f.)[c]	2,800	0

[a](10,000 ÷ 50,000) × net manufacturing cost = (10,000 ÷ 50,000) × $246,000 = $49,200.

[b](10,000 ÷ 50,000) × total manufacturing cost = (10,000 ÷ 50,000) × $250,000 = $50,000.

[c]Recorded at selling prices.

Production Method: Byproducts Recognized at Time Production Is Completed

This method recognizes the byproduct in the financial statements—the 4,000 cubic feet of wood chips—in the month it is produced, July 2012. The NRV from the byproduct produced is offset against the costs of the main product. The following journal entries illustrate the production method:

1. Work in Process	150,000	
Accounts Payable		150,000
To record direct materials purchased and used in production during July.		
2. Work in Process	100,000	
Various accounts such as Wages Payable and Accumulated Depreciation		100,000
To record conversion costs in the production process during July; examples include energy, manufacturing supplies, all manufacturing labor, and plant depreciation.		
3. Byproduct Inventory—Wood Chips (4,000 c.f. × $1 per c.f.)	4,000	
Finished Goods—Fine-Grade Lumber ($250,000 − $4,000)	246,000	
Work in Process ($150,000 + $100,000)		250,000
To record cost of goods completed during July.		
4a. Cost of Goods Sold [(40,000 b.f. ÷ 50,000 b.f.) × $246,000]	196,800	
Finished Goods—Fine-Grade Lumber		196,800
To record the cost of the main product sold during July.		
4b. Cash or Accounts Receivable (40,000 b.f. × $6 per b.f.)	240,000	
Revenues—Fine-Grade Lumber		240,000
To record the sales of the main product during July.		
5. Cash or Accounts Receivable (1,200 c.f. × $1 per c.f.)	1,200	
Byproduct Inventory—Wood Chips		1,200
To record the sales of the byproduct during July.		

The production method reports the byproduct inventory of wood chips in the balance sheet at its $1 per cubic foot selling price [(4,000 cubic feet − 1,200 cubic feet) × $1 per cubic foot = $2,800].

One variation of this method would be to report byproduct inventory at its NRV reduced by a normal profit margin ($2,800 − 20% × $2,800 = $2,240, assuming a normal profit margin of 20%).[9] When byproduct inventory is sold in a subsequent period, the income statement will match the selling price, $2,800, with the "cost" reported for the byproduct inventory, $2,240, resulting in a byproduct operating income of $560 ($2,800 − $2,240).

Sales Method: Byproducts Recognized at Time of Sale

This method makes no journal entries for byproducts until they are sold. Revenues of the byproduct are reported as a revenue item in the income statement at the time of sale. These revenues are either grouped with other sales, included as other income, or are deducted from cost of goods sold. In the Westlake Corporation example, byproduct revenues in July 2012 are $1,200 (1,200 cubic feet × $1 per cubic foot) because only 1,200 cubic feet of wood chips are sold in July (of the 4,000 cubic feet produced). The journal entries are as follows:

1. and 2.	*Same as for the production method.*		
	Work in Process	150,000	
	Accounts Payable		150,000
	Work in Process	100,000	
	Various accounts such as Wages Payable and Accumulated Depreciation		100,000
3.	Finished Goods—Fine-Grade Lumber	250,000	
	Work in Process		250,000
	To record cost of main product completed during July.		
4a.	Cost of Goods Sold [(40,000 b.f. ÷ 50,000 b.f.) × $250,000]	200,000	
	Finished Goods—Fine-Grade Lumber		200,000
	To record the cost of the main product sold during July.		
4b.	Same as for the production method.		
	Cash or Accounts Receivable (40,000 b.f. × $6 per b.f.)	240,000	
	Revenues—Fine-Grade Lumber		240,000
5.	Cash or Accounts Receivable	1,200	
	Revenues—Wood Chips		1,200
	To record the sales of the byproduct during July.		

Decision Point

What methods can be used to account for byproducts and which of them is preferable?

Which method should a company use? The production method is conceptually correct in that it is consistent with the matching principle. This method recognizes byproduct inventory in the accounting period in which it is produced and simultaneously reduces the cost of manufacturing the main or joint products, thereby better matching the revenues and expenses from selling the main product. However, the sales method is simpler and is often used in practice, primarily on the grounds that the dollar amounts of byproducts are immaterial. Then again, the sales method permits managers to "manage" reported earnings by timing when they sell byproducts. Managers may store byproducts for several periods and give revenues and income a "small boost" by selling byproducts accumulated over several periods when revenues and profits from the main product or joint products are low.

Problem for Self-Study

Inorganic Chemicals (IC) processes salt into various industrial products. In July 2012, IC incurred joint costs of $100,000 to purchase salt and convert it into two products: caustic soda and chlorine. Although there is an active outside market for chlorine, IC processes all 800 tons of chlorine it produces into 500 tons of PVC (polyvinyl chloride), which is

---

[9] One way to make this calculation is to assume all products have the same "normal" profit margin like the constant gross-margin percentage NRV method. Alternatively, the company might allow products to have different profit margins based on an analysis of the margins earned by other companies that sell these products individually.

then sold. There were no beginning or ending inventories of salt, caustic soda, chlorine, or PVC in July. Information for July 2012 production and sales follows:

	Home	Insert	Page Layout	Formulas	Data	Review	View	
	A				B	C	D	
1					Joint Costs		PVC	
2	Joint costs (costs of salt and processing to splitoff point)				$100,000			
3	Separable cost of processing 800 tons chlorine into 500 tons PVC						$20,000	
4								
5					Caustic Soda	Chlorine	PVC	
6	Beginning inventory (tons)				0	0	0	
7	Production (tons)				1,200	800	500	
8	Transfer for further processing (tons)					800		
9	Sales (tons)				1,200		500	
10	Ending inventory (tons)				0	0	0	
11	Selling price per ton in active outside market (for products not actually sold)					$ 75		
12	Selling price per ton for products sold				$ 50		$ 200	

Required

1. Allocate the joint costs of $100,000 between caustic soda and PVC under (a) the sales value at splitoff method and (b) the physical-measure method.
2. Allocate the joint costs of $100,000 between caustic soda and PVC under the NRV method.
3. Under the three allocation methods in requirements 1 and 2, what is the gross-margin percentage of (a) caustic soda and (b) PVC?
4. Lifetime Swimming Pool Products offers to purchase 800 tons of chlorine in August 2012 at $75 per ton. Assume all other production and sales data are the same for August as they were for July. This sale of chlorine to Lifetime would mean that no PVC would be produced by IC in August. How would accepting this offer affect IC's August 2012 operating income?

Solution

The following picture provides a visual illustration of the main facts in this problem.

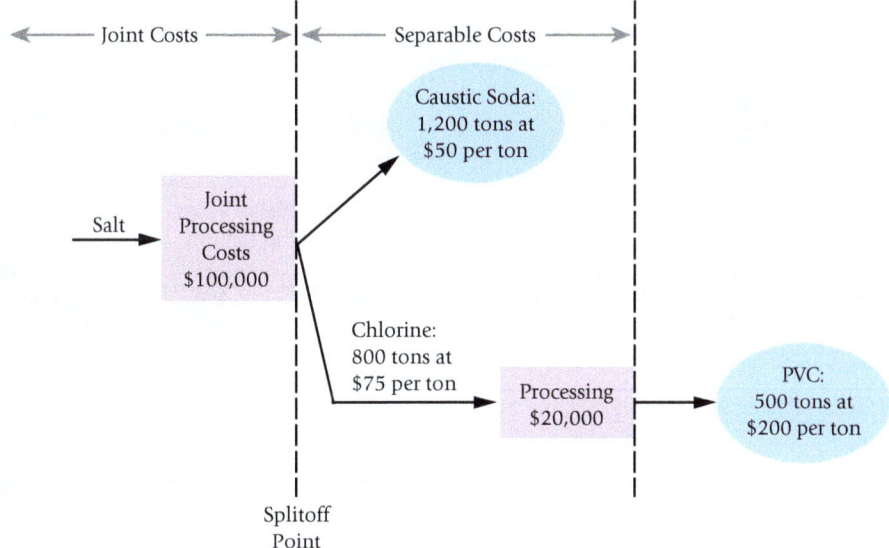

Note that caustic soda is sold as is while chlorine, despite having a market value at split-off, is sold only in processed form as PVC. The goal is to allocate the joint costs of $100,000 to the final products—caustic soda and PVC. However, since PVC exists only in the form of chlorine at the splitoff point, we use chlorine's sales value and physical measure as the basis for allocating joint costs to PVC under the sales value at splitoff and physical measure at splitoff methods. Detailed calculations are shown next.

1a. Sales value at splitoff method

	A	B	C	D
1	**Allocation of Joint Costs Using Sales Value at Splitoff Method**	**Caustic Soda**	**PVC / Chlorine**	**Total**
2	Sales value of total production at splitoff point			
3	(1,200 tons × $50 per ton; 800 × $75 per ton)	$60,000	$60,000	$120,000
4	Weighting ($60,000 ÷ $120,000; $60,000 ÷ $120,000)	0.50	0.50	
5	Joint costs allocated (0.50 × $100,000; 0.50 × $100,000)	$50,000	$50,000	$100,000

1b. Physical-measure method

	A	B	C	D
8	**Allocation of Joint Costs Using Physical-Measure Method**	**Caustic Soda**	**PVC / Chlorine**	**Total**
9	Physical measure of total production (tons)	1,200	800	2,000
10	Weighting (1,200 tons ÷ 2,000 tons; 800 tons ÷ 2,000 tons)	0.60	0.40	
11	Joint cost allocated (0.60 × $100,000; 0.40 × $100,000)	$60,000	$40,000	$100,000

2. Net realizable value (NRV) method

	A	B	C	D
14	**Allocation of Joint Costs Using Net Realizable Value Method**	**Caustic Soda**	**PVC**	**Total**
15	Final sales value of total production during accounting period			
16	(1,200 tons × $50 per ton; 500 tons × $200 per ton)	$60,000	$100,000	$160,000
17	Deduct separable costs to complete and sell	0	20,000	20,000
18	Net realizable value at splitoff point	$60,000	$ 80,000	$140,000
19	Weighting ($60,000 ÷ $140,000; $80,000 ÷ $140,000)	3/7	4/7	
20	Joint costs allocated (3/7 × $100,000; 4/7 × $100,000)	$42,857	$ 57,143	$100,000

3a. Gross-margin percentage of caustic soda

	A	B	C	D
23	**Caustic Soda**	**Sales Value at Splitoff Point**	**Physical Measure**	**NRV**
24	Revenues (1,200 tons × $50 per ton)	$60,000	$60,000	$60,000
25	Cost of goods sold (joint costs)	50,000	60,000	42,857
26	Gross margin	$10,000	$ 0	$17,143
27	Gross margin percentage ($10,000 ÷ $60,000; $0 ÷ $60,000; $17,143 ÷ $60,000)	16.67%	0.00%	28.57%

3b. Gross-margin percentage of PVC

	A	B	C	D
		Sales Value at Splitoff Point	**Physical Measure**	**NRV**
30	**PVC**			
31	Revenues (500 tons × $200 per ton)	$100,000	$100,000	$100,000
32	Cost of goods sold			
33	Joint costs	50,000	40,000	57,143
34	Separable costs	20,000	20,000	20,000
35	Cost of goods sold	70,000	60,000	77,143
36	Gross margin	$ 30,000	$ 40,000	$ 22,857
37	Gross margin percentage ($30,000 ÷ $100,000; $40,000 ÷ $100,000; $22,857 ÷ $100,000)	30.00%	40.00%	22.86%

4. Sale of chlorine versus processing into PVC

	A	B
40	Incremental revenue from processing 800 tons of chlorine into 500 tons of PVC	
41	(500 tons × $200 per ton) − (800 tons × $75 per ton)	$40,000
42	Incremental cost of processing 800 tons of chlorine into 500 tons of PVC	20,000
43	Incremental operating income from further processing	$ 20,000

If IC sells 800 tons of chlorine to Lifetime Swimming Pool Products instead of further processing it into PVC, its August 2012 operating income will be reduced by $20,000.

Decision Points

The following question-and-answer format summarizes the chapter's learning objectives. Each decision presents a key question related to a learning objective. The guidelines are the answer to that question.

Decision	Guidelines
1. What do the terms joint cost and splitoff point mean, and how do joint products differ from byproducts?	A joint cost is the cost of a single production process that yields multiple products simultaneously. The splitoff point is the juncture in a joint production process when the products become separately identifiable. Joint products have high total sales values at the splitoff point. A byproduct has a low total sales value at the splitoff point compared with the total sales value of a joint or main product.
2. Why are joint costs allocated to individual products?	The purposes for allocating joint costs to products include inventory costing for financial accounting and internal reporting, cost reimbursement, insurance settlements, rate regulation, and product-cost litigation.
3. What methods can be used to allocate joint costs to individual products?	The methods to allocate joint costs to products are the sales value at splitoff, NRV, constant gross-margin percentage NRV, and physical-measure methods.

4. When is the sales value at splitoff method considered preferable for allocating joint costs to individual products and why?

The sales value at splitoff method is preferable when market prices exist at splitoff because using revenues is consistent with the benefits-received criterion; further, the method does not anticipate subsequent management decisions on further processing, and is simple.

5. Are joint costs relevant in a sell-or-process-further decision?

No, joint costs and how they are allocated are irrelevant in deciding whether to process further because joint costs are the same regardless of whether further processing occurs.

6. What methods can be used to account for byproducts and which of them is preferable?

The production method recognizes byproducts in financial statements at the time of production, whereas the sales method recognizes byproducts in financial statements at the time of sale. The production method is conceptually superior, but the sales method is often used in practice because dollar amounts of byproducts are immaterial.

Terms to Learn

This chapter and the Glossary at the end of the book contain definitions of the following important terms:

byproducts **(p. 578)**

constant gross-margin percentage NRV method **(p. 584)**

joint costs **(p. 577)**

joint products **(p. 578)**

main product **(p. 578)**

net realizable value (NRV) method **(p. 583)**

physical-measure method **(p. 582)**

product **(p. 578)**

sales value at splitoff method **(p. 580)**

separable costs **(p. 577)**

splitoff point **(p. 577)**

Assignment Material

Questions

16-1 Give two examples of industries in which joint costs are found. For each example, what are the individual products at the splitoff point?

16-2 What is a joint cost? What is a separable cost?

16-3 Distinguish between a joint product and a byproduct.

16-4 Why might the number of products in a joint-cost situation differ from the number of outputs? Give an example.

16-5 Provide three reasons for allocating joint costs to individual products or services.

16-6 Why does the sales value at splitoff method use the sales value of the total production in the accounting period and not just the revenues from the products sold?

16-7 Describe a situation in which the sales value at splitoff method cannot be used but the NRV method can be used for joint-cost allocation.

16-8 Distinguish between the sales value at splitoff method and the NRV method.

16-9 Give two limitations of the physical-measure method of joint-cost allocation.

16-10 How might a company simplify its use of the NRV method when final selling prices can vary sizably in an accounting period and management frequently changes the point at which it sells individual products?

16-11 Why is the constant gross-margin percentage NRV method sometimes called a "joint-cost-allocation and a profit-allocation" method?

16-12 "Managers must decide whether a product should be sold at splitoff or processed further. The sales value at splitoff method of joint-cost allocation is the best method for generating the information managers need for this decision." Do you agree? Explain.

16-13 "Managers should consider only additional revenues and separable costs when making decisions about selling at splitoff or processing further." Do you agree? Explain.

16-14 Describe two major methods to account for byproducts.

16-15 Why might managers seeking a monthly bonus based on attaining a target operating income prefer the sales method of accounting for byproducts rather than the production method?

Exercises

16-16 **Joint-cost allocation, insurance settlement.** Quality Chicken grows and processes chickens. Each chicken is disassembled into five main parts. Information pertaining to production in July 2012 is as follows:

Parts	Pounds of Product	Wholesale Selling Price per Pound When Production Is Complete
Breasts	100	$0.55
Wings	20	0.20
Thighs	40	0.35
Bones	80	0.10
Feathers	10	0.05

Joint cost of production in July 2012 was $50.

A special shipment of 40 pounds of breasts and 15 pounds of wings has been destroyed in a fire. Quality Chicken's insurance policy provides reimbursement for the cost of the items destroyed. The insurance company permits Quality Chicken to use a joint-cost-allocation method. The splitoff point is assumed to be at the end of the production process.

Required

1. Compute the cost of the special shipment destroyed using the following:
   a. Sales value at splitoff method
   b. Physical-measure method (pounds of finished product)
2. What joint-cost-allocation method would you recommend Quality Chicken use? Explain.

16-17 Joint products and byproducts (continuation of 16-16). Quality Chicken is computing the ending inventory values for its July 31, 2012, balance sheet. Ending inventory amounts on July 31 are 15 pounds of breasts, 4 pounds of wings, 6 pounds of thighs, 5 pounds of bones, and 2 pounds of feathers.

Quality Chicken's management wants to use the sales value at splitoff method. However, management wants you to explore the effect on ending inventory values of classifying one or more products as a byproduct rather than a joint product.

Required

1. Assume Quality Chicken classifies all five products as joint products. What are the ending inventory values of each product on July 31, 2012?
2. Assume Quality Chicken uses the production method of accounting for byproducts. What are the ending inventory values for each joint product on July 31, 2012, assuming breasts and thighs are the joint products and wings, bones, and feathers are byproducts?
3. Comment on differences in the results in requirements 1 and 2.

16-18 Net realizable value method. Convad Company is one of the world's leading corn refiners. It produces two joint products—corn syrup and corn starch—using a common production process. In July 2012, Convad reported the following production and selling-price information:

	Home	Insert	Page Layout	Formulas	Data	Review	View		
	A						B	C	D
1							Corn Syrup	Corn Starch	Joint Costs
2	Joint costs (costs of processing corn to splitoff point)								$325,000
3	Separable cost of processing beyond splitoff point						$375,000	$93,750	
4	Beginning inventory (cases)						0	0	
5	Production and Sales (cases)						12,500	6,250	
6	Ending inventory (cases)						0	0	
7	Selling price per case						50	$ 25	

Required

Allocate the $325,000 joint costs using the NRV method.

16-19 Alternative joint-cost-allocation methods, further-process decision. The Wood Spirits Company produces two products—turpentine and methanol (wood alcohol)—by a joint process. Joint costs amount to $120,000 per batch of output. Each batch totals 10,000 gallons: 25% methanol and 75% turpentine. Both products are processed further without gain or loss in volume. Separable processing costs are methanol, $3 per gallon; turpentine, $2 per gallon. Methanol sells for $21 per gallon. Turpentine sells for $14 per gallon.

Required

1. How much of the joint costs per batch will be allocated to turpentine and to methanol, assuming that joint costs are allocated based on the number of gallons at splitoff point?
2. If joint costs are allocated on an NRV basis, how much of the joint costs will be allocated to turpentine and to methanol?
3. Prepare product-line income statements per batch for requirements 1 and 2. Assume no beginning or ending inventories.
4. The company has discovered an additional process by which the methanol (wood alcohol) can be made into a pleasant-tasting alcoholic beverage. The selling price of this beverage would be $60 a gallon. Additional processing would increase separable costs $9 per gallon (in addition to the $3 per gallon separable cost

required to yield methanol). The company would have to pay excise taxes of 20% on the selling price of the beverage. Assuming no other changes in cost, what is the joint cost applicable to the wood alcohol (using the NRV method)? Should the company produce the alcoholic beverage? Show your computations.

16-20 Alternative methods of joint-cost allocation, ending inventories. The Evrett Company operates a simple chemical process to convert a single material into three separate items, referred to here as X, Y, and Z. All three end products are separated simultaneously at a single splitoff point.

Products X and Y are ready for sale immediately upon splitoff without further processing or any other additional costs. Product Z, however, is processed further before being sold. There is no available market price for Z at the splitoff point.

The selling prices quoted here are expected to remain the same in the coming year. During 2012, the selling prices of the items and the total amounts sold were as follows:

- X—75 tons sold for $1,800 per ton
- Y—225 tons sold for $1,300 per ton
- Z—280 tons sold for $800 per ton

The total joint manufacturing costs for the year were $328,000. Evrett spent an additional $120,000 to finish product Z.

There were no beginning inventories of X, Y, or Z. At the end of the year, the following inventories of completed units were on hand: X, 175 tons; Y, 75 tons; Z, 70 tons. There was no beginning or ending work in process.

Required

1. Compute the cost of inventories of X, Y, and Z for balance sheet purposes and the cost of goods sold for income statement purposes as of December 31, 2012, using the following joint cost allocation methods:
   a. NRV method
   b. Constant gross-margin percentage NRV method
2. Compare the gross-margin percentages for X, Y, and Z using the two methods given in requirement 1.

16-21 Joint-cost allocation, process further. Sinclair Oil & Gas, a large energy conglomerate, jointly processes purchased hydrocarbons to generate three nonsaleable intermediate products: ICR8, ING4, and XGE3. These intermediate products are further processed separately to produce crude oil, natural gas liquids (NGL), and natural gas (measured in liquid equivalents). An overview of the process and results for August 2012 are shown here. (Note: The numbers are small to keep the focus on key concepts.)

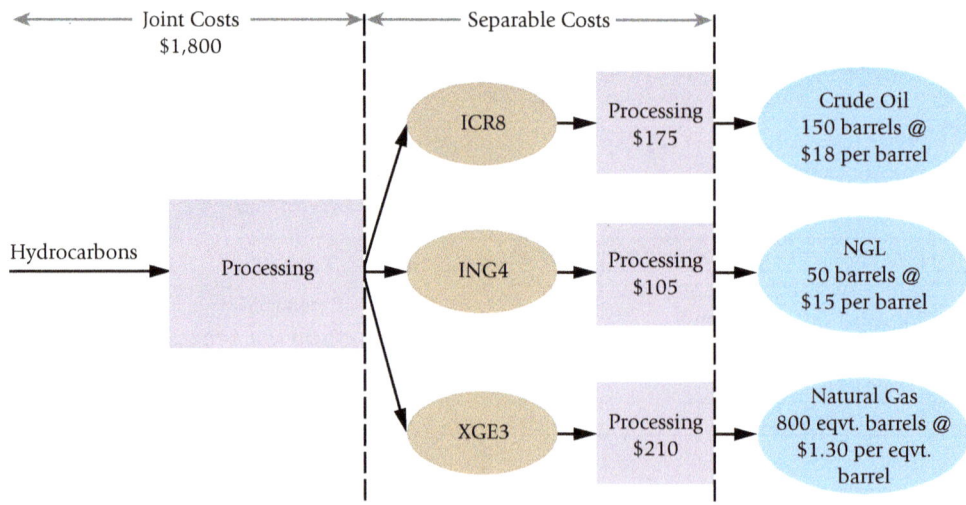

A new federal law has recently been passed that taxes crude oil at 30% of operating income. No new tax is to be paid on natural gas liquid or natural gas. Starting August 2012, Sinclair Oil & Gas must report a separate product-line income statement for crude oil. One challenge facing Sinclair Oil & Gas is how to allocate the joint cost of producing the three separate saleable outputs. Assume no beginning or ending inventory.

Required

1. Allocate the August 2012 joint cost among the three products using the following:
   a. Physical-measure method
   b. NRV method
2. Show the operating income for each product using the methods in requirement 1.
3. Discuss the pros and cons of the two methods to Sinclair Oil & Gas for making decisions about product emphasis (pricing, sell-or-process-further decisions, and so on).
4. Draft a letter to the taxation authorities on behalf of Sinclair Oil & Gas that justifies the joint-cost-allocation method you recommend Sinclair use.

16-22 Joint-cost allocation, sales value, physical measure, NRV methods. Instant Foods produces two types of microwavable products—beef-flavored ramen and shrimp-flavored ramen. The two products share common inputs such as noodle and spices. The production of ramen results in a waste product referred to as stock, which Instant dumps at negligible costs in a local drainage area. In June 2012, the following data were reported for the production and sales of beef-flavored and shrimp-flavored ramen:

	Home	Insert	Page Layout	Formulas	Data	Review	
	A					B	C
1						**Joint Costs**	
2	Joint costs (costs of noodles, spices, and other inputs and processing to splitoff point)					$240,000	
3							
4						**Beef Ramen**	**Shrimp Ramen**
5	Beginning inventory (tons)					0	0
6	Production (tons)					10,000	20,000
7	Sales (tons)					10,000	20,000
8	Selling price per ton					$ 10	$ 15

Due to the popularity of its microwavable products, Instant decides to add a new line of products that targets dieters. These new products are produced by adding a special ingredient to dilute the original ramen and are to be sold under the names Special B and Special S, respectively. The following is the monthly data for all the products:

	Home	Insert	Page Layout	Formulas	Data	Review	View		
	A				B	C		D	E
11					**Joint Costs**			**Special B**	**Special S**
12	Joint costs (costs of noodles, spices, and other inputs and processing to splitoff point)				$240,000				
13	Separable costs of processing 10,000 tons of Beef Ramen into 12,000 tons of Special B							$48,000	
14	Separable cost of processing 20,000 tons of Shrimp Ramen into 24,000 tons of Special S								$168,000
15									
16					**Beef Ramen**	**Shrimp Ramen**		**Special B**	**Special S**
17	Beginning inventory (tons)				0	0		0	0
18	Production (tons)				10,000	20,000		12,000	24,000
19	Transfer for further processing (tons)				10,000	20,000			
20	Sales (tons)							12,000	24,000
21	Selling price per ton				$ 10	$ 15		$ 18	$ 25

Required

1. Calculate Instant's gross-margin percentage for Special B and Special S when joint costs are allocated using the following:
   a. Sales value at splitoff method
   b. Physical-measure method
   c. Net realizable value method
2. Recently, Instant discovered that the stock it is dumping can be sold to cattle ranchers at $5 per ton. In a typical month with the production levels shown, 4,000 tons of stock are produced and can be sold by incurring marketing costs of $10,800. Sherrie Dong, a management accountant, points out that treating the stock as a joint product and using the sales value at splitoff method, the stock product would lose about $2,228 each month, so it should not be sold. How did Dong arrive at that final number, and what do you think of her analysis? Should Instant sell the stock?

16-23 Joint cost allocation: sell immediately or process further. Iowa Soy Products (ISP) buys soy beans and processes them into other soy products. Each ton of soy beans that ISP purchases for $300 can be converted for an additional $200 into 500 pounds of soy meal and 100 gallons of soy oil. A pound of soy meal can be sold at splitoff for $1 and soy oil can be sold in bulk for $4 per gallon.

ISP can process the 500 pounds of soy meal into 600 pounds of soy cookies at an additional cost of $300. Each pound of soy cookies can be sold for $2 per pound. The 100 gallons of soy oil can be packaged at a cost of $200 and made into 400 quarts of Soyola. Each quart of Soyola can be sold for $1.25.

Required

1. Allocate the joint cost to the cookies and the Soyola using the following:
   a. Sales value at splitoff method
   b. NRV method
2. Should ISP have processed each of the products further? What effect does the allocation method have on this decision?

16-24 Accounting for a main product and a byproduct. (Cheatham and Green, adapted) Tasty, Inc., is a producer of potato chips. A single production process at Tasty, Inc., yields potato chips as the main product and a byproduct that can also be sold as a snack. Both products are fully processed by the splitoff point, and there are no separable costs.

For September 2012, the cost of operations is $500,000. Production and sales data are as follows:

	Production (in pounds)	Sales (in pounds)	Selling Price per Pound
Main Product:			
Potato Chips	52,000	42,640	$16
Byproduct	8,500	6,500	$10

There were no beginning inventories on September 1, 2012.

1. What is the gross margin for Tasty, Inc., under the production method and the sales method of byproduct accounting?
2. What are the inventory costs reported in the balance sheet on September 30, 2012, for the main product and byproduct under the two methods of byproduct accounting in requirement 1?

16-25 Joint costs and byproducts. (W. Crum adapted) Royston, Inc., is a large food processing company. It processes 150,000 pounds of peanuts in the peanuts department at a cost of $180,000 to yield 12,000 pounds of product A, 65,000 pounds of product B, and 16,000 pounds of product C.

- Product A is processed further in the salting department to yield 12,000 pounds of salted peanuts at a cost of $27,000 and sold for $12 per pound.
- Product B (raw peanuts) is sold without further processing at $3 per pound.
- Product C is considered a byproduct and is processed further in the paste department to yield 16,000 pounds of peanut butter at a cost of $12,000 and sold for $6 per pound.

The company wants to make a gross margin of 10% of revenues on product C and needs to allow 20% of revenues for marketing costs on product C. An overview of operations follows:

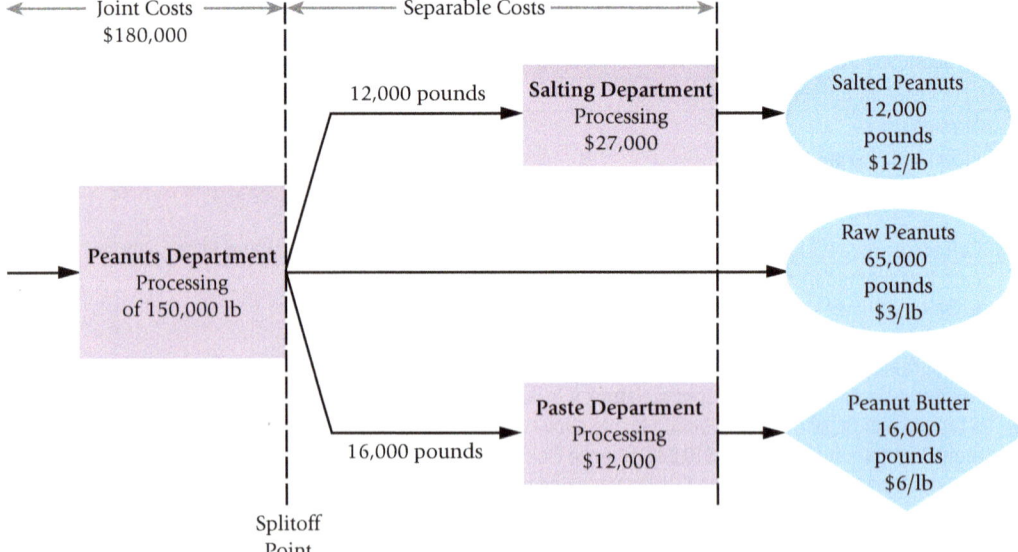

1. Compute unit costs per pound for products A, B, and C, treating C as a byproduct. Use the NRV method for allocating joint costs. Deduct the NRV of the byproduct produced from the joint cost of products A and B. **Required**
2. Compute unit costs per pound for products A, B, and C, treating all three as joint products and allocating joint costs by the NRV method.

Problems

MyAccountingLab

16-26 Accounting for a byproduct. Sunny Day Juice Company produces oranges from various organic growers in Florida. The juice is extracted from the oranges and the pulp and peel remain. Sunny Day considers the pulp and peel byproducts of its juice production and can sell them to a local farmer for $2.00 per pound. During the most recent month, Sunny Day purchased 4,000 pounds of oranges and produced 1,500 gallons of juice and 900 pounds of pulp and peel at a joint cost of $7,200. The selling price for a half-gallon of orange juice is $2.50. Sunny Day sold 2,800 half-gallons of juice and 860 pounds of pulp and peel during the most recent month. The company had no beginning inventories.

1. Assuming Sunny Day accounts for the byproduct using the production method, what is the inventoriable cost for each product and Sunny Day's gross margin? **Required**
2. Assuming Sunny Day accounts for the byproduct using the sales method, what is the inventoriable cost for each product and Sunny Day's gross margin?
3. Discuss the difference between the two methods of accounting for byproducts.

16-27 Alternative methods of joint-cost allocation, product-mix decisions. The Southern Oil Company buys crude vegetable oil. Refining this oil results in four products at the splitoff point: A, B, C, and D. Product C is fully processed by the splitoff point. Products A, B, and D can individually be further refined into Super A, Super B, and Super D. In the most recent month (December), the output at the splitoff point was as follows:

- Product A, 322,400 gallons
- Product B, 119,600 gallons
- Product C, 52,000 gallons
- Product D, 26,000 gallons

The joint costs of purchasing and processing the crude vegetable oil were $96,000. Southern had no beginning or ending inventories. Sales of product C in December were $24,000. Products A, B, and D were further refined and then sold. Data related to December are as follows:

	Separable Processing Costs to Make Super Products	Revenues
Super A	$249,600	$300,000
Super B	102,400	160,000
Super D	152,000	160,000

Southern had the option of selling products A, B, and D at the splitoff point. This alternative would have yielded the following revenues for the December production:

- Product A, $84,000
- Product B, $72,000
- Product D, $60,000

1. Compute the gross-margin percentage for each product sold in December, using the following methods for allocating the $96,000 joint costs: **Required**
   a. Sales value at splitoff
   b. Physical-measure
   c. NRV
2. Could Southern have increased its December operating income by making different decisions about the further processing of products A, B, or D? Show the effect on operating income of any changes you recommend.

16-28 Comparison of alternative joint-cost-allocation methods, further-processing decision, chocolate products. The Chocolate Factory manufactures and distributes chocolate products. It purchases cocoa beans and processes them into two intermediate products: chocolate-powder liquor base and milk-chocolate liquor base. These two intermediate products become separately identifiable at a single splitoff point. Every 1,500 pounds of cocoa beans yields 60 gallons of chocolate-powder liquor base and 90 gallons of milk-chocolate liquor base.

The chocolate-powder liquor base is further processed into chocolate powder. Every 60 gallons of chocolate-powder liquor base yield 600 pounds of chocolate powder. The milk-chocolate liquor base is further processed into milk chocolate. Every 90 gallons of milk-chocolate liquor base yield 1,020 pounds of milk chocolate.

Production and sales data for August 2012 are as follows (assume no beginning inventory):

- Cocoa beans processed, 15,000 pounds
- Costs of processing cocoa beans to splitoff point (including purchase of beans), $30,000

	Production	Sales	Selling Price	Separable Processing Costs
Chocolate powder	6,000 pounds	6,000 pounds	$4 per pound	$12,750
Milk chocolate	10,200 pounds	10,200 pounds	$5 per pound	$26,250

Chocolate Factory fully processes both of its intermediate products into chocolate powder or milk chocolate. There is an active market for these intermediate products. In August 2012, Chocolate Factory could have sold the chocolate-powder liquor base for $21 a gallon and the milk-chocolate liquor base for $26 a gallon.

Required

1. Calculate how the joint costs of $30,000 would be allocated between chocolate powder and milk chocolate under the following methods:
   a. Sales value at splitoff
   b. Physical-measure (gallons)
   c. NRV
   d. Constant gross-margin percentage NRV
2. What are the gross-margin percentages of chocolate powder and milk chocolate under each of the methods in requirement 1?
3. Could Chocolate Factory have increased its operating income by a change in its decision to fully process both of its intermediate products? Show your computations.

16-29 Joint-cost allocation, process further or sell. (CMA, adapted) Sonimad Sawmill, Inc., (SSI) purchases logs from independent timber contractors and processes the logs into three types of lumber products:

- Studs for residential buildings (walls, ceilings)
- Decorative pieces (fireplace mantels, beams for cathedral ceilings)
- Posts used as support braces (mine support braces, braces for exterior fences on ranch properties)

These products are the result of a joint sawmill process that involves removal of bark from the logs, cutting the logs into a workable size (ranging from 8 to 16 feet in length), and then cutting the individual products from the logs.

The joint process results in the following costs of products for a typical month:

Direct materials (rough timber logs)	$ 500,000
Debarking (labor and overhead)	50,000
Sizing (labor and overhead)	200,000
Product cutting (labor and overhead)	250,000
Total joint costs	$1,000,000

Product yields and average sales values on a per-unit basis from the joint process are as follows:

Product	Monthly Output of Materials at Splitoff Point	Fully Processed Selling Price
Studs	75,000 units	$ 8
Decorative pieces	5,000 units	100
Posts	20,000 units	20

The studs are sold as rough-cut lumber after emerging from the sawmill operation without further processing by SSI. Also, the posts require no further processing beyond the splitoff point. The decorative pieces must be planed and further sized after emerging from the sawmill. This additional processing costs $100,000 per month and normally results in a loss of 10% of the units entering the process. Without this planing and sizing process, there is still an active intermediate market for the unfinished decorative pieces in which the selling price averages $60 per unit.

Required

1. Based on the information given for Sonimad Sawmill, allocate the joint processing costs of $1,000,000 to the three products using:
   a. Sales value at splitoff method
   b. Physical-measure method (volume in units)
   c. NRV method
2. Prepare an analysis for Sonimad Sawmill that compares processing the decorative pieces further, as it currently does, with selling them as a rough-cut product immediately at splitoff.

3. Assume Sonimad Sawmill announced that in six months it will sell the unfinished decorative pieces at splitoff due to increasing competitive pressure. Identify at least three types of likely behavior that will be demonstrated by the skilled labor in the planing-and-sizing process as a result of this announcement. Include in your discussion how this behavior could be influenced by management.

16-30 Joint-cost allocation. Elsie Dairy Products Corp. buys one input, full-cream milk, and refines it in a churning process. From each gallon of milk Elsie produces three cups of butter and nine cups of buttermilk. During May 2010, Elsie bought 12,000 gallons of milk for $22,250. Elsie spent another $9,430 on the churning process to separate the milk into butter and buttermilk. Butter could be sold immediately for $2.20 per pound and buttermilk could be sold immediately for $1.20 per quart (note: two cups = one pound; four cups = one quart).

Elsie chooses to process the butter further into spreadable butter by mixing it with canola oil, incurring an additional cost of $1.60 per pound. This process results in two tubs of spreadable butter for each pound of butter processed. Each tub of spreadable butter sells for $2.30.

1. Allocate the $31,680 joint cost to the spreadable butter and the buttermilk using the following:　　　Required
　　a. Physical-measure method (using cups) of joint cost allocation
　　b. Sales value at splitoff method of joint cost allocation
　　c. NRV method of joint cost allocation
　　d. Constant gross margin percentage NRV method of joint cost allocation
2. Each of these measures has advantages and disadvantages; what are they?
3. Some claim that the sales value at split off method is the best method to use. Discuss the logic behind this claim.

16-31 Further processing decision (continuation of 16-30). Elsie has decided that buttermilk may sell better if it was marketed for baking and sold in pints. This would involve additional packaging at an incremental cost of $0.35 per pint. Each pint could be sold for $0.75 (note: one quart = two pints).
1. If Elsie uses the sales value at splitoff method, what combination of products should Elsie sell to maximize profits?
2. If Elsie uses the physical-measure method, what combination of products should Elsie sell to maximize profits?
3. Explain the effect that the different cost allocation methods have on the decision to sell the products at split off or to process them further.

16-32 Joint-cost allocation with a byproduct. Mat Place purchases old tires and recycles them to produce rubber floor mats and car mats. The company washes, shreds, and molds the recycled tires into sheets. The floor and car mats are cut from these sheets. A small amount of rubber shred remains after the mats are cut. The rubber shreds can be sold to use as cover for paths and playgrounds. The company can produce 25 floor mats, 75 car mats, and 40 pounds of rubber shreds from 100 old tires.

In May, Mat Place, which had no beginning inventory, processed 125,000 tires and had joint production costs of $600,000. Mat Place sold 25,000 floor mats, 85,000 car mats, and 43,000 pounds of rubber shreds. The company sells each floor mat for $12 and each car mat for $6. The company treats the rubber shreds as a byproduct that can be sold for $0.70 per pound.

1. Assume that Mat Place allocates the joint costs to floor mats and car mats using the sales value at　　　Required
splitoff method and accounts for the byproduct using the production method. What is the ending inventory cost for each product and gross margin for Mat Place?
2. Assume that Mat Place allocates the joint costs to floor mats and car mats using the sales value at splitoff method and accounts for the byproduct using the sales method. What is the ending inventory cost for each product and gross margin for Mat Place?
3. Discuss the difference between the two methods of accounting for byproducts, focusing on what conditions are necessary to use each method.

16-33 Byproduct-costing journal entries (continuation of 16-32). The Mat Place's accountant needs to record the information about the joint and byproducts in the general journal, but is not sure what the entries should be. The company has hired you as a consultant to help its accountant.

1. Show journal entries at the time of production and at the time of sale assuming the Mat Place accounts　　　Required
for the byproduct using the production method.
2. Show journal entries at the time of production and at the time of sale assuming the Mat Place accounts for the byproduct using the sales method.

16-34 Process further or sell, byproduct. (CMA, adapted) Rochester Mining Company (RMC) mines coal, puts it through a one-step crushing process, and loads the bulk raw coal onto river barges for shipment to customers.

RMC's management is currently evaluating the possibility of further processing the raw coal by sizing and cleaning it and selling it to an expanded set of customers at higher prices. The option of building a new sizing and cleaning plant is ruled out as being financially infeasible. Instead, Amy Kimbell, a mining engineer, is asked to explore outside-contracting arrangements for the cleaning and sizing process. Kimbell puts together the following summary:

	A	B	C
1	Selling price of raw coal	$ 27 per ton	
2	Cost of producing raw coal	$ 21 per ton	
3	Selling price of sized and cleaned coal	$ 35 per ton	
4	Annual raw coal output	9,800,000 tons	
5	Percentage of material weight loss in sizing/cleaning coal	10%	
6			
7		**Incremental Costs of Sizing & Cleaning Processes**	
8	Direct labor	$ 820,000 per year	
9	Supervisory personnel	$ 225,000 per year	
10	Heavy equipment: rental, operating, maintenance costs	$ 15,000 per month	
11	Contract sizing and cleaning	$ 3.60 per ton of raw coal	
12	Outbound rail freight	$ 210 per 60-ton rail car	
13			
14	Percentage of sizing/cleaning waste that can be salvaged for coal fines	75%	
15	Range of costs per ton for preparing coal fine for sale	$2	$4
16	Range of coal fine selling prices (per ton)	$16	$27

Kimbell also learns that 75% of the material loss that occurs in the cleaning and sizing process can be salvaged as coal fines, which can be sold to steel manufacturers for their furnaces. The sale of coal fines is erratic and RMC may need to stockpile it in a protected area for up to one year. The selling price of coal fine ranges from $16 to $27 per ton and costs of preparing coal fines for sale range from $2 to $4 per ton.

Required

1. Prepare an analysis to show whether it is more profitable for RMC to continue selling raw bulk coal or to process it further through sizing and cleaning. (Ignore coal fines in your analysis.)
2. How would your analysis be affected if the cost of producing raw coal could be held down to $17 per ton?
3. Now consider the potential value of the coal fines and prepare an addendum that shows how their value affects the results of your analysis prepared in requirement 1.

16-35 Joint Cost Allocation. Memory Manufacturing Company (MMC) produces memory modules in a two-step process: chip fabrication and module assembly.

In chip fabrication, each batch of raw silicon wafers yields 400 *standard* chips and 600 *deluxe* chips. Chips are classified as standard or deluxe on the basis of their density (the number of memory bits on each chip). Standard chips have 500 memory bits per chip, and deluxe chips have 1,000 memory bits per chip. Joint costs to process each batch are $28,900.

In module assembly, each batch of standard chips is converted into standard memory modules at a separately identified cost of $1,050 and then sold for $14,000. Each batch of deluxe chips is converted into deluxe memory modules at a separately identified cost of $2,450 and then sold for $26,500.

Required

1. Allocate joint costs of each batch to deluxe modules and standard modules using (a) the NRV method, (b) the constant gross-margin percentage NRV method, and (c) the physical-measure method, based on the number of memory bits. Which method should MMC use?
2. MMC can process each batch of 400 standard memory modules to yield 350 DRAM modules at an additional cost of $1,600. The selling price per DRAM module would be $46. Assume MMC uses the physical-measure method. Should MMC sell the standard memory modules or the DRAM modules?

16-36 Joint cost allocation, ending work in process inventories. Tastee Freez, Inc., produces two specialty ice cream mix flavors for soft serve ice cream machines. The two flavors, Extreme Chocolate and Very Strawberry, both start with a vanilla base. The vanilla base can be sold for $2 per gallon. The company did not have any beginning inventories but produced 8,000 gallons of the vanilla base during the most recent month at a cost of $5,200. The 8,000 gallons of base was used to begin production of 5,000 gallons of Extreme Chocolate and 3,000 gallons of Very Strawberry.

At the end of the month, the company had some of its ice cream mix still in process. There were 1,200 gallons of Extreme Chocolate 30% complete and 200 gallons of Very Strawberry 80% complete. Processing costs during the month for Extreme Chocolate and Very Strawberry were $9,152 and $8,880, respectively. The selling prices for Extreme Chocolate and Very Strawberry are $4 and $5, respectively.

1. Allocate the joint costs to Extreme Chocolate and Very Strawberry under the following methods:
   a. Sales value at splitoff
   b. Net realizable value
   c. Constant gross margin percentage NRV
2. Compute the gross margin percentages for Extreme Chocolate and Very Strawberry under each of the methods in requirement 1.

Required

Collaborative Learning Problem

16-37 Joint Cost Allocation, processing further and ethics. Unified Chemical Company has a joint production process that converts Zeta into two chemicals: Alpha and Beta. The company purchases Zeta for $12 per pound and incurs a cost of $30 per pound to process it into Alpha and Beta. For every 10 pounds of Zeta, the company can produce 8 pounds of Alpha and 2 pounds of Beta. The selling price for Alpha and Beta are $76.50 and $144.00, respectively.

Unified Chemical generally processes Alpha and Beta further in separable processes to produce more refined products. Alpha is processed separately into Alphalite at a cost of $25.05 per pound. Beta is processed separately into Betalite at a cost of $112.80 per pound. Alphalite and Betalite sell for $105 and $285 per pound, respectively. In the most recent month, Unified Chemical purchased 15,000 pounds of Zeta. The company had no beginning or ending inventory of Zeta.

1. Allocate the joint costs to Alphalite and Betalite under the following methods:
   a. Sales value at splitoff
   b. Physical measure (pounds)
   c. Net realizable value
   d. Constant gross margin percentage NRV

Required

2. Unified Chemical is considering an opportunity to process Betalite further into a new product called Ultra-Betalite. The separable processing will cost $85 per pound and expects an additional $15 per pound packaging cost for Ultra-Betalite. The expected selling price would be $360 per pound. Should Unified Chemical sell Betalite or Ultra-Betalite? What selling price for Ultra-Betalite would make Unified Chemical indifferent between selling Betalite and Ultra-Betalite?
3. Independent of your answer to requirement (2), suppose Danny Dugard, the assistant controller, has completed an analysis that shows Ultra-Betalite should not be produced. Before presenting his results to top management, he received a visit from Sally Kemper. Sally had been personally responsible for developing Ultra-Betalite and was upset to learn that it would not be manufactured.

Sally: The company is making a big mistake by passing up this opportunity. Ultra-Betalite will be a big seller and will get us into new markets.
Danny: But the analysis shows that we would be losing money on every pound of Ultra-Betalite we manufacture.
Sally: But that is a temporary problem. Eventually the cost of processing will be reduced.
Danny: Do you have any estimates on the cost reductions you expect?
Sally: There is no way of knowing that right now. Can't you just fudge the numbers a little to help me get approval to produce Ultra-Betalite. I am confident that cost reductions will follow.

Comment on the ethical issues in this scenario. What should Danny do?

Learning Objectives

1. Identify the situations in which process-costing systems are appropriate

2. Understand the basic concepts of process-costing and compute average unit costs

3. Describe the five steps in process costing and calculate equivalent units

4. Use the weighted-average method and first-in, first-out (FIFO) method of process costing

5. Apply process-costing methods to situations with transferred-in costs

6. Understand the need for hybrid-costing systems such as operation-costing

Companies that produce identical or similar units of a product or service (for example, an oil-refining company) often use process costing.

A key part of process costing is valuing inventory, which entails determining how many units of the product the firm has on hand at the end of an accounting reporting period, evaluating the units' stages of completion, and assigning costs to the units. There are different methods for doing this, each of which can result in different profits. At times, variations in international rules and customs make it difficult to compare inventory costs across competitors. In the case of ExxonMobil, differences in accounting rules between the United States and Europe also reduce the company's profits and tax liability.

ExxonMobil and Accounting Differences in the Oil Patch[1]

In 2010, ExxonMobil was number two on the *Fortune* 500 annual ranking of the largest U.S. companies. In 2009, the company had $284 billion dollars in revenue with more than $19 billion in profits. Believe it or not, however, by one measure ExxonMobil's profits are *understated*.

ExxonMobil, like most U.S. energy companies, uses last-in, first-out (LIFO) accounting. Under this treatment, ExxonMobil records its cost of inventory at the latest price paid for crude oil in the open market, even though it is often selling oil produced at a much lower cost. This increases the company's cost of goods sold, which in turn reduces profit. The benefit of using LIFO accounting for financial reporting is that ExxonMobil is then permitted to use LIFO for tax purposes as well, thereby lowering its payments to the tax authorities.

In contrast, International Financial Reporting Standards (IFRS) do not permit the use of LIFO accounting. European oil companies such as Royal Dutch Shell and British Petroleum use the first-in, first-out (FIFO) methodology instead when accounting for inventory. Under FIFO, oil companies use the cost of the oldest crude in their inventory to calculate the cost of barrels of oil sold. This reduces costs on the income statement, therefore increasing gross margins.

Assigning costs to inventory is a critical part of process costing, and a company's choice of method can result in substantially different

---

[1] *Source:* Exxon Mobil Corporation. 2010. 2009 Annual Report. Irving, TX: Exxon Mobil Corporation; Kaminska, Izabella. 2010. Shell, BP, and the increasing cost of inventory. *Financial Times.* "FT Alphaville" blog, April 29; Reilly, David. 2006. Big oil's accounting methods fuel criticism. *Wall Street Journal*, August 8.

profits. For instance, ExxonMobil's 2009 net income would have been $7.1 billion higher under FIFO. Moreover, at the end of fiscal 2009, the cumulative difference—or "LIFO Reserve"—between the value of inventory ExxonMobil was carrying on its balance sheet based on the initial cost versus the current replacement cost of that inventory was $17.1 billion. This number takes on special relevance in the context of current efforts to achieve convergence between U.S. GAAP and IFRS. Should that happen, and if U.S. firms are forced to adopt FIFO for financial and tax reporting, they would have to pay additional taxes on the cumulative savings to date from showing a higher cost of goods sold in LIFO. As an approximation, applying a marginal tax rate of 35% to ExxonMobil's LIFO Reserve of $17.1 billion suggests an incremental tax burden of almost $6 billion.

Companies such as ExxonMobil, Coca-Cola, and Novartis produce many identical or similar units of a product using mass-production techniques. The focus of these companies on individual production processes gives rise to process costing. This chapter describes how companies use process costing methods to determine the costs of products or services and to value inventory and cost of goods sold (using methods like FIFO).

Illustrating Process Costing

Before we examine process costing in more detail, let's briefly compare job costing and process costing. Job-costing and process-costing systems are best viewed as ends of a continuum:

Learning Objective **1**

Identify the situations in which process-costing systems are appropriate

. . . when masses of identical or similar units are produced

Job-costing system	Process-costing system
Distinct, identifiable units of a product or service (for example, custom-made machines and houses)	Masses of identical or similar units of a product or service (for example, food or chemical processing)

In a *process-costing system*, the unit cost of a product or service is obtained by assigning total costs to many identical or similar units of output. In other words, unit costs are calculated by dividing total costs incurred by the number of units of output from the production process. In a manufacturing process-costing setting, each unit receives the same or similar amounts of direct material costs, direct manufacturing labor costs, and indirect manufacturing costs (manufacturing overhead).

The main difference between process costing and job costing is the *extent of averaging* used to compute unit costs of products or services. In a job-costing system, individual jobs use different quantities of production resources, so it would be incorrect to cost each job at the same average production cost. In contrast, when identical or similar units of products or services are mass-produced, not processed as individual jobs, process costing is used to calculate an average production cost for all units produced. Some processes such as clothes manufacturing have aspects of both process costing (cost per unit of each operation, such as cutting or sewing, is identical) and job costing (different materials are used in different batches of clothing, say, wool versus cotton). The final section in this chapter describes "hybrid" costing systems that combine elements of both job and process costing.

Consider the following illustration of process costing: Suppose that Pacific Electronics manufactures a variety of cell phone models. These models are assembled in the assembly department. Upon completion, units are transferred to the testing department. We focus on the assembly department process for one model, SG-40. All units of SG-40 are identical and must meet a set of demanding performance specifications. The process-costing system for SG-40 in the assembly department has a single direct-cost category—direct materials— and a single indirect-cost category—conversion costs. Conversion costs are all manufacturing costs other than direct material costs, including manufacturing labor, energy, plant depreciation, and so on. Direct materials are added at the beginning of the assembly process. Conversion costs are added evenly during assembly.

The following graphic represents these facts:

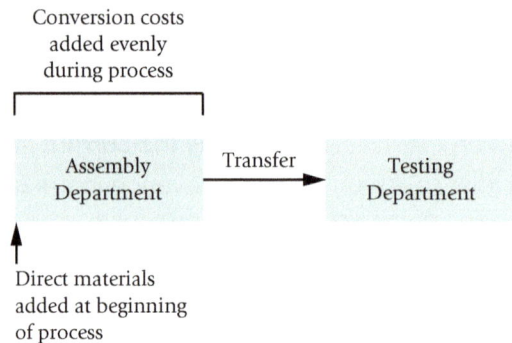

Process-costing systems separate costs into cost categories according to *when costs are introduced into the process*. Often, as in our Pacific Electronics example, only two cost classifications—direct materials and conversion costs—are necessary to assign costs to products. Why only two? Because *all* direct materials are added to the process at one time and all conversion costs generally are added to the process evenly through time. If, however, two different direct materials were added to the process at different times, two different direct-materials categories would be needed to assign these costs to products. Similarly, if manufacturing labor costs were added to the process at a different time from when the other conversion costs were added, an additional cost category—direct manufacturing labor costs—would be needed to separately assign these costs to products.

We will use the production of the SG-40 component in the assembly department to illustrate process costing in three cases, starting with the simplest case and introducing additional complexities in subsequent cases:

■ **Case 1**—Process costing with zero beginning and zero ending work-in-process inventory of SG-40. (That is, all units are started and fully completed within the accounting period.) *This case presents the most basic concepts of process costing and illustrates the feature of averaging of costs.*

■ **Case 2**—Process costing with zero beginning work-in-process inventory and some ending work-in-process inventory of SG-40. (That is, some units of SG-40 started during the accounting period are incomplete at the end of the period.) *This case introduces the five steps of process costing and the concept of equivalent units.*

■ **Case 3**—Process costing with both some beginning and some ending work-in-process inventory of SG-40. *This case adds more complexity and illustrates the effect of weighted-average and first-in, first-out (FIFO) cost flow assumptions on cost of units completed and cost of work-in-process inventory.*

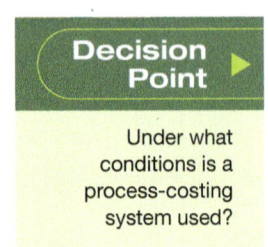

Decision Point ▶

Under what conditions is a process-costing system used?

Case 1: Process Costing with No Beginning or Ending Work-in-Process Inventory

On January 1, 2012, there was no beginning inventory of SG-40 units in the assembly department. During the month of January, Pacific Electronics started, completely assembled, and transferred out to the testing department 400 units.

Data for the assembly department for January 2012 are as follows:

Physical Units for January 2012

Work in process, beginning inventory (January 1)	0 units
Started during January	400 units
Completed and transferred out during January	400 units
Work in process, ending inventory (January 31)	0 units

Learning Objective 2

Understand the basic concepts of process-costing and compute average unit costs

. . . divide total costs by total units in a given accounting period

Physical units refer to the number of output units, whether complete or incomplete. In January 2012, all 400 physical units started were completed.

Total Costs for January 2012

Direct material costs added during January	$32,000
Conversion costs added during January	24,000
Total assembly department costs added during January	$56,000

Pacific Electronics records direct material costs and conversion costs in the assembly department as these costs are incurred. By averaging, assembly cost of SG-40 is $56,000 ÷ 400 units = $140 per unit, itemized as follows:

Direct material cost per unit ($32,000 ÷ 400 units)	$ 80
Conversion cost per unit ($24,000 ÷ 400 units)	60
Assembly department cost per unit	$140

Case 1 shows that in a process-costing system, average unit costs are calculated by dividing total costs in a given accounting period by total units produced in that period. Because each unit is identical, we assume all units receive the same amount of direct material costs and conversion costs. Case 1 applies whenever a company produces a homogeneous product or service but has no incomplete units when each accounting period ends, which is a common situation in service-sector organizations. For example, a bank can adopt this process-costing approach to compute the unit cost of processing 100,000 customer deposits, each similar to the other, made in a month.

Decision Point

How are average unit costs computed when no inventories are present?

Case 2: Process Costing with Zero Beginning and Some Ending Work-in-Process Inventory

In February 2012, Pacific Electronics places another 400 units of SG-40 into production. Because all units placed into production in January were completely assembled, there is no beginning inventory of partially completed units in the assembly department on February 1. Some customers order late, so not all units started in February are completed by the end of the month. Only 175 units are completed and transferred to the testing department.

Data for the assembly department for February 2012 are as follows:

	Physical Units (SG-40s) (1)	Direct Materials (2)	Conversion Costs (3)	Total Costs (4) = (2) + (3)
Work in process, beginning inventory (February 1)	0			
Started during February	400			
Completed and transferred out during February	175			
Work in process, ending inventory (February 29)	225			
Degree of completion of ending work in process		100%	60%	
Total costs added during February		$32,000	$18,600	$50,600

The 225 partially assembled units as of February 29, 2012, are fully processed with respect to direct materials, because all direct materials in the assembly department are added at the beginning of the assembly process. Conversion costs, however, are added evenly during assembly. Based on the work completed relative to the total work required

Learning
Objective 3

Describe the five steps
in process costing

. . . to assign total
costs to units completed
and to units in work
in process

and calculate
equivalent units

. . . output units adjusted
for incomplete units

to complete the SG-40 units still in process at the end of February, an assembly depart-ment supervisor estimates that the partially assembled units are, on average, 60% com-plete with respect to conversion costs.

The accuracy of the completion estimate of conversion costs depends on the care, skill, and experience of the estimator and the nature of the conversion process. Estimating the degree of completion is usually easier for direct material costs than for conversion costs, because the quantity of direct materials needed for a completed unit and the quantity of direct materials in a partially completed unit can be measured more accurately. In contrast, the conversion sequence usually consists of a number of operations, each for a specified period of time, at various steps in the production process.[2] The degree of completion for conversion costs depends on the proportion of the total conversion costs needed to com-plete one unit (or a batch of production) that has already been incurred on the units still in process. It is a challenge for management accountants to make this estimate accurately.

Because of these uncertainties, department supervisors and line managers—individuals most familiar with the process—often make conversion cost estimates. Still, in some industries, such as semiconductor manufacturing, no exact estimate is possible; in other settings, such as the textile industry, vast quantities in process make the task of estimation too costly. In these cases, it is necessary to assume that all work in process in a department is complete to some preset degree with respect to conversion costs (for example, one-third, one-half, or two-thirds complete).

The point to understand here is that a partially assembled unit is not the same as a fully assembled unit. Faced with some fully assembled units and some partially assembled units, we require a common metric that will enable us to compare the work done in each category and, more important, obtain a total measure of work done. The concept we will use in this regard is that of *equivalent units*. We will explain this notion in greater detail next as part of the set of five steps required to calculate (1) the cost of fully assembled units in February 2012 and (2) the cost of partially assembled units still in process at the end of that month, for Pacific Electronics. The five steps of process costing are as follows:

Step 1:   Summarize the flow of physical units of output.

Step 2:   Compute output in terms of equivalent units.

Step 3:   Summarize total costs to account for.

Step 4:   Compute cost per equivalent unit.

Step 5:   Assign total costs to units completed and to units in ending work in process.

Physical Units and Equivalent Units (Steps 1 and 2)

Step 1 tracks physical units of output. Recall that physical units are the number of out-put units, whether complete or incomplete. Where did physical units come from? Where did they go? The physical-units column of Exhibit 17-1 tracks where the physical units came from (400 units started) and where they went (175 units completed and transferred out, and 225 units in ending inventory). Remember, when there is no opening inventory, units started must equal the sum of units transferred out and ending inventory.

Because not all 400 physical units are fully completed, output in **Step 2** is computed in *equivalent units*, not in *physical units*. To see what we mean by equivalent units, let's say that during a month, 50 physical units were started but not completed by the end of the month. These 50 units in ending inventory are estimated to be 70% complete with respect to conversion costs. Let's examine those units from the perspective of the conversion costs already incurred to get the units to be 70% complete. Suppose we put all the conversion costs represented in the 70% into making fully completed units. How many units could have been 100% complete by the end of the month? The answer is 35 units. Why? Because 70% of conversion costs incurred on 50 incomplete units could have been incurred to make 35 (0.70×50) complete units by the end of the month. That is, if all the conversion-cost input in the 50 units in inventory had been used to make completed output units, the com-pany would have produced 35 completed units (also called *equivalent units*) of output.

---
[2] For example, consider the conventional tanning process for converting hide to leather. Obtaining 250–300 kg of leather requires putting one metric ton of raw hide through as many as 15 steps: from soaking, liming, and pickling to tanning, dye-ing, and fatliquoring, the step in which oils are introduced into the skin before the leather is dried.

Exhibit 17-1

Steps 1 and 2:
Summarize Output in
Physical Units and
Compute Output in
Equivalent Units for
Assembly Department
of Pacific Electronics
for February 2012

	Home Insert Page Layout Formulas Data Review View			
	A	B	C	D
1		(Step 1)	(Step 2)	
2			Equivalent Units	
3	**Flow of Production**	**Physical Units**	**Direct Materials**	**Conversion Costs**
4	Work in process, beginning	0		
5	Started during current period	400		
6	To account for	400		
7	Completed and transferred out during current period	175	175	175
8	Work in process, ending[a]	225		
9	(225 × 100%; 225 × 60%)		225	135
10	Accounted for	400		
11	Equivalent units of work done in current period		400	310
12				
13	[a]Degree of completion in this department; direct materials, 100%; conversion costs, 60%.			

Equivalent units is a derived amount of output units that (1) takes the quantity of each input (factor of production) in units completed and in incomplete units of work in process and (2) converts the quantity of input into the amount of completed output units that could be produced with that quantity of input. Note that equivalent units are calculated separately for each input (such as direct materials and conversion costs). Moreover, every completed unit, by definition, is composed of one equivalent unit of each input required to make it. This chapter focuses on equivalent-unit calculations in manufacturing settings. Equivalent-unit concepts are also found in nonmanufacturing settings. For example, universities convert their part-time student enrollments into "full-time student equivalents."

When calculating equivalent units in Step 2, focus on quantities. Disregard dollar amounts until after equivalent units are computed. In the Pacific Electronics example, all 400 physical units—the 175 fully assembled units and the 225 partially assembled units— are 100% complete with respect to direct materials because all direct materials are added in the assembly department at the start of the process. Therefore, Exhibit 17-1 shows output as 400 *equivalent units* for direct materials: 175 equivalent units for the 175 physical units assembled and transferred out, and 225 equivalent units for the 225 physical units in ending work-in-process inventory.

The 175 fully assembled units are also completely processed with respect to conversion costs. The partially assembled units in ending work in process are 60% complete (on average). Therefore, conversion costs in the 225 partially assembled units are *equivalent* to conversion costs in 135 (60% of 225) fully assembled units. Hence, Exhibit 17-1 shows output as 310 *equivalent units* with respect to conversion costs: 175 equivalent units for the 175 physical units assembled and transferred out and 135 equivalent units for the 225 physical units in ending work-in-process inventory.

Calculation of Product Costs (Steps 3, 4, and 5)

Exhibit 17-2 shows Steps 3, 4, and 5. Together, they are called the *production cost worksheet*.

Step 3 summarizes total costs to account for. Because the beginning balance of work-in-process inventory is zero on February 1, total costs to account for (that is, the total charges or debits to the Work in Process—Assembly account) consist only of costs added during February: direct materials of $32,000 and conversion costs of $18,600, for a total of $50,600.

Step 4 in Exhibit 17-2 calculates cost per equivalent unit separately for direct materials and for conversion costs by dividing direct material costs and conversion costs added during February by the related quantity of equivalent units of work done in February (as calculated in Exhibit 17-1).

To see the importance of using equivalent units in unit-cost calculations, compare conversion costs for January and February 2012. Total conversion costs of $18,600 for the 400 units worked on during February are lower than the conversion costs of

Exhibit 17-2 Steps 3, 4, and 5: Summarize Total Costs to Account For, Compute Cost per Equivalent Unit, and Assign Total Costs to Units Completed and to Units in Ending Work in Process for Assembly Department of Pacific Electronics for February 2012

	Home	Insert	Page Layout	Formulas	Data	Review	View			

	A	B	C	D	E
1			Total Production Costs	Direct Materials	Conversion Costs
2	(Step 3)	Costs added during February	$50,600	$32,000	$18,600
3		Total costs to account for	$50,600	$32,000	$18,600
4					
5	(Step 4)	Costs added in current period	$50,600	$32,000	$18,600
6		Divide by equivalent units of work done in current period (Exhibit 17-1)		÷ 400	÷ 310
7		Cost per equivalent unit		$ 80	$ 60
8					
9	(Step 5)	Assignment of costs:			
10		Completed and transferred out (175 units)	$24,500	$(175^a \times \$80)$ +	$(175^a \times \$60)$
11		Work in process, ending (225 units):	26,100	$(225^b \times \$80)$ +	$(135^b \times \$60)$
12		Total costs accounted for	$50,600	$32,000 +	$18,600
13					
14	[a] Equivalent units completed and transferred out from Exhibit 17-1, step 2.				
15	[b] Equivalent units in ending work in process from Exhibit 17-1, step 2.				

$24,000 for the 400 units worked on in January. However, in this example, the conversion costs to fully assemble a unit are $60 in both January and February. Total conversion costs are lower in February because fewer equivalent units of conversion-costs work were completed in February (310) than in January (400). Using physical units instead of equivalent units in the per-unit calculation would have led to the erroneous conclusion that conversion costs per unit declined from $60 in January to $46.50 ($18,600 ÷ 400 units) in February. This incorrect costing might have prompted Pacific Electronics to presume that greater efficiencies in processing had been achieved and to lower the price of SG-40, for example, when in fact costs had not declined.

Step 5 in Exhibit 17-2 assigns these costs to units completed and transferred out and to units still in process at the end of February 2012. The idea is to attach dollar amounts to the equivalent output units for direct materials and conversion costs of (a) units completed and (b) ending work in process, as calculated in Exhibit 17-1, Step 2. *Equivalent output units for each input are multiplied by cost per equivalent unit, as calculated in Step 4 of Exhibit 17-2.* For example, costs assigned to the 225 physical units in ending work-in-process inventory are as follows:

Direct material costs of 225 equivalent units (Exhibit 17-1, Step 2) ×	
$80 cost per equivalent unit of direct materials calculated in Step 4	$18,000
Conversion costs of 135 equivalent units (Exhibit 17-1, Step 2) ×	
$60 cost per equivalent unit of conversion costs calculated in Step 4	8,100
Total cost of ending work-in-process inventory	$26,100

Note that total costs to account for in Step 3 ($50,600) equal total costs accounted for in Step 5.

Journal Entries

Journal entries in process-costing systems are similar to the entries made in job-costing systems with respect to direct materials and conversion costs. The main difference is that, in process costing, there is one Work in Process account for each process. In our example, there are accounts for Work in Process—Assembly and Work in Process—Testing. Pacific Electronics purchases direct materials as needed. These materials are delivered directly to the assembly department. Using amounts from Exhibit 17-2, summary journal entries for February are as follows:

1. Work in Process—Assembly	32,000	
Accounts Payable Control		32,000
To record direct materials purchased and used in production during February.		
2. Work in Process—Assembly	18,600	
Various accounts such as Wages Payable Control and Accumulated Depreciation		18,600
To record conversion costs for February; examples include energy, manufacturing supplies, all manufacturing labor, and plant depreciation.		
3. Work in Process—Testing	24,500	
Work in Process—Assembly		24,500
To record cost of goods completed and transferred from assembly to testing during February.		

Exhibit 17-3 shows a general framework for the flow of costs through T-accounts. Notice how entry 3 for $24,500 follows the physical transfer of goods from the assembly to the testing department. The T-account Work in Process—Assembly shows February 2012's ending balance of $26,100, which is the beginning balance of Work in Process—Assembly in March 2012. It is important to ensure that all costs have been accounted for and that the ending inventory of the current month is the beginning inventory of the following month.

▶ **Decision Point**

What are the five steps in a process-costing system and how are equivalent units calculated?

Case 3: Process Costing with Some Beginning and Some Ending Work-in-Process Inventory

At the beginning of March 2012, Pacific Electronics had 225 partially assembled SG-40 units in the assembly department. It started production of another 275 units in March. Data for the assembly department for March are as follows:

	A	B	C	D	E
		Physical Units (SG-40s) (1)	**Direct Materials** (2)	**Conversion Costs** (3)	**Total Costs** (4) = (2) + (3)
2	Work in process, beginning inventory (March 1)	225	$18,000[a]	$8,100[a]	$26,100
3	Degree of completion of beginning work in process		100%	60%	
4	Started during March	275			
5	Completed and transferred out during March	400			
6	Work in process, ending inventory (March 31)	100			
7	Degree of completion of ending work in process		100%	50%	
8	Total costs added during March		$19,800	$16,380	$36,180
9					
10					
11	[a]Work in process, beginning inventory (equals work in process, ending inventory for February)				
12	Direct materials: 225 physical units × 100% completed × $80 per unit = $18,000				
13	Conversion costs: 225 physical units × 60% completed × $60 per unit = $8,100				

Pacific Electronics now has incomplete units in both beginning work-in-process inventory and ending work-in-process inventory for March 2012. We can still use the five steps described earlier to calculate (1) cost of units completed and transferred out and (2) cost of ending work in process. To assign costs to each of these categories, however, we first need to choose an inventory-valuation method. We next describe the five-step approach for two important methods—the *weighted-average method* and the *first-in, first-out method*. These different valuation methods produce different amounts for cost of units completed and for ending work in process when the unit cost of inputs changes from one period to the next.

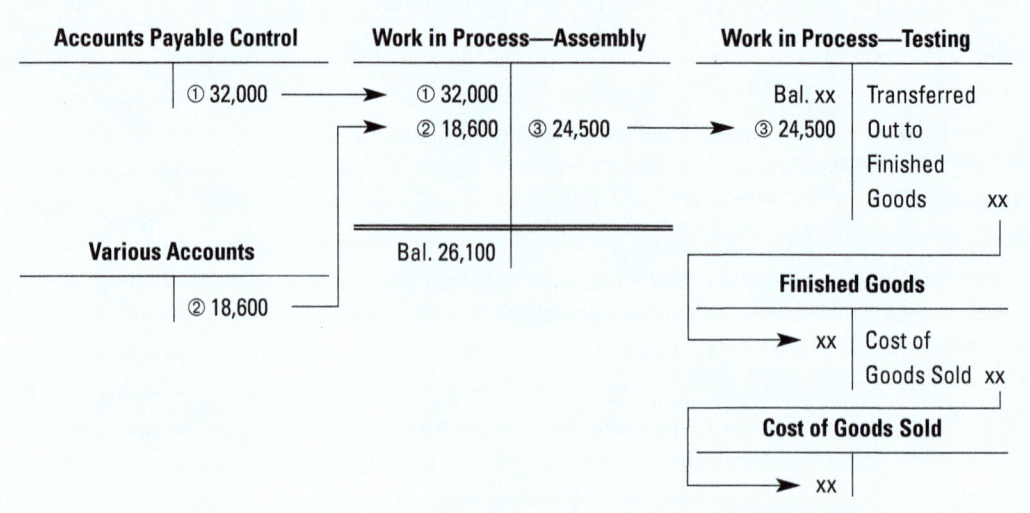

Weighted-Average Method

The **weighted-average process-costing method** calculates cost per equivalent unit of all *work done to date* (regardless of the accounting period in which it was done) and assigns this cost to equivalent units completed and transferred out of the process and to equivalent units in ending work-in-process inventory. The weighted-average cost is the total of all costs entering the Work in Process account (whether the costs are from beginning work in process or from work started during the current period) divided by total equivalent units of work done to date. We now describe the weighted-average method using the five-step procedure introduced on page 610.

Step 1: Summarize the Flow of Physical Units of Output. The physical-units column of Exhibit 17-4 shows where the units came from—225 units from beginning inventory and 275 units started during the current period—and where they went—400 units completed and transferred out and 100 units in ending inventory.

Step 2: Compute Output in Terms of Equivalent Units. The weighted-average cost of inventory is calculated by merging together the costs of beginning inventory and the manufacturing costs of a period and dividing by the total number of units in beginning inventory and units produced during the accounting period. We apply the same concept here

	A	B	C	D
		(Step 1)	(Step 2)	
1				
2			Equivalent Units	
3	**Flow of Production**	**Physical Units**	**Direct Materials**	**Conversion Costs**
4	Work in process, beginning (given, p. 613)	225		
5	Started during current period (given, p. 613)	275		
6	To account for	500		
7	Completed and transferred out during current period	400	400	400
8	Work in process, ending[a] (given, p. 613)	100		
9	(100 × 100%; 100 × 50%)		100	50
10	Accounted for	500		
11	Equivalent units of work done to date		500	450
12				
13	[a]Degree of completion in this department; direct materials, 100%; conversion costs, 50%.			

except that calculating the units—in this case equivalent units—is done differently. We use the relationship shown in the following equation:

$$\begin{array}{c}\text{Equivalent units}\\\text{in beginning work}\\\text{in process}\end{array} + \begin{array}{c}\text{Equivalent units}\\\text{of work done in}\\\text{current period}\end{array} = \begin{array}{c}\text{Equivalent units}\\\text{completed and transferred}\\\text{out in current period}\end{array} + \begin{array}{c}\text{Equivalent units}\\\text{in ending work}\\\text{in process}\end{array}$$

Although we are interested in calculating the left-hand side of the preceding equation, it is easier to calculate this sum using the equation's right-hand side: (1) equivalent units completed and transferred out in the current period plus (2) equivalent units in ending work in process. *Note that the stage of completion of the current-period beginning work in process is not used in this computation.*

The equivalent-units columns in Exhibit 17-4 show equivalent units of work done to date: 500 equivalent units of direct materials and 450 equivalent units of conversion costs. All completed and transferred-out units are 100% complete as to both direct materials and conversion costs. Partially completed units in ending work in process are 100% complete as to direct materials because direct materials are introduced at the beginning of the process, and 50% complete as to conversion costs, based on estimates made by the assembly department manager.

Step 3: Summarize Total Costs to Account For. Exhibit 17-5 presents Step 3. Total costs to account for in March 2012 are described in the example data on page 615: beginning work in process, $26,100 (direct materials, $18,000, plus conversion costs, $8,100), plus costs added during March, $36,180 (direct materials, $19,800, plus conversion costs, $16,380). The total of these costs is $62,280.

Step 4: Compute Cost per Equivalent Unit. Exhibit 17-5, Step 4, shows the computation of weighted-average cost per equivalent unit for direct materials and conversion costs. Weighted-average cost per equivalent unit is obtained by dividing the sum of costs for beginning work in process plus costs for work done in the current period by total

Exhibit 17-5	Steps 3, 4, and 5: Summarize Total Costs to Account For, Compute Cost per Equivalent Unit, and Assign Total Costs to Units Completed and to Units in Ending Work in Process Using Weighted-Average Method of Process Costing for Assembly Department of Pacific Electronics for March 2012

	Home	Insert	Page Layout	Formulas	Data	Review	View		
	A		B				C	D	E
1							Total Production Costs	Direct Materials	Conversion Costs
2	(Step 3)	Work in process, beginning (given, p. 613)					$26,100	$18,000	$ 8,100
3		Costs added in current period (given, p. 613)					36,180	19,800	16,380
4		Total costs to account for					$62,280	$37,800	$24,480
5									
6	(Step 4)	Costs incurred to date						$37,800	$24,480
7		Divide by equivalent units of work done to date (Exhibit 17-4)						÷ 500	÷ 450
8		Cost per equivalent unit of work done to date						$ 75.60	$ 54.40
9									
10	(Step 5)	Assignment of costs:							
11		Completed and transferred out (400 units)					$52,000	(400[a] × $75.60) +	(400[a] × $54.40)
12		Work in process, ending (100 units):					10,280	(100[b] × $75.60) +	(50[b] × $54.40)
13		Total costs accounted for					$62,280	$37,800 +	$24,480
14									
15	[a]Equivalent units completed and transferred out from Exhibit 17-4, Step 2.								
16	[b]Equivalent units in ending work in process from Exhibit 17-4, Step 2.								

equivalent units of work done to date. When calculating weighted-average conversion cost per equivalent unit in Exhibit 17-5, for example, we divide total conversion costs, $24,480 (beginning work in process, $8,100, plus work done in current period, $16,380), by total equivalent units of work done to date, 450 (equivalent units of conversion costs in beginning work in process and in work done in current period), to obtain weighted-average cost per equivalent unit of $54.40.

Step 5:   Assign Total Costs to Units Completed and to Units in Ending Work in Process. Step 5 in Exhibit 17-5 takes the equivalent units completed and transferred out and equivalent units in ending work in process calculated in Exhibit 17-4, Step 2, and assigns dollar amounts to them using the weighted-average cost per equivalent unit for direct materials and conversion costs calculated in Step 4. For example, total costs of the 100 physical units in ending work in process are as follows:

Direct materials:	
100 equivalent units × weighted-average cost per equivalent unit of $75.60	$ 7,560
Conversion costs:	
50 equivalent units × weighted-average cost per equivalent unit of $54.40	2,720
Total costs of ending work in process	$10,280

The following table summarizes total costs to account for ($62,280) and how they are accounted for in Exhibit 17-5. The arrows indicate that the costs of units completed and transferred out and units in ending work in process are calculated using weighted-average total costs obtained after merging costs of beginning work in process and costs added in the current period.

Costs to Account For		**Costs Accounted for Calculated on a Weighted-Average Basis**	
Beginning work in process	$26,100	Completed and transferred out	$52,000
Costs added in current period	36,180	Ending work in process	10,280
Total costs to account for	$62,280	Total costs accounted for	$62,280

Before proceeding, review Exhibits 17-4 and 17-5 to check your understanding of the weighted-average method. Note: Exhibit 17-4 deals with only physical and equivalent units, not costs. Exhibit 17-5 shows the cost amounts.

Using amounts from Exhibit 17-5, the summary journal entries under the weighted-average method for March 2012 at Pacific Electronics are as follows:

1. Work in Process—Assembly   19,800
     Accounts Payable Control   19,800
    To record direct materials purchased and used in production during March.

2. Work in Process—Assembly   16,380
     Various accounts such as Wages Payable Control and Accumulated
     Depreciation   16,380
    To record conversion costs for March; examples include energy,
    manufacturing supplies, all manufacturing labor, and plant depreciation.

3. Work in Process—Testing   52,000
     Work in Process—Assembly   52,000
    To record cost of goods completed and transferred from assembly to
    testing during March.

The T-account Work in Process—Assembly, under the weighted-average method, is as follows:

Work in Process—Assembly			
Beginning inventory, March 1	26,100	③ Completed and transferred	52,000
① Direct materials	19,800	out to Work in Process—	
② Conversion costs	16,380	Testing	
Ending inventory, March 31	10,280		

First-In, First-Out Method

The **first-in, first-out (FIFO) process-costing method** (1) assigns the cost of the previous accounting period's equivalent units in beginning work-in-process inventory to the first units completed and transferred out of the process, and (2) assigns the cost of equivalent units worked on during the *current* period first to complete beginning inventory, next to start and complete new units, and finally to units in ending work-in-process inventory. The FIFO method assumes that the earliest equivalent units in work in process are completed first.

A distinctive feature of the FIFO process-costing method is that work done on beginning inventory before the current period is kept separate from work done in the current period. Costs incurred and units produced in the current period are used to calculate cost per equivalent unit of work done in the current period. In contrast, equivalent-unit and cost-per-equivalent-unit calculations under the weighted-average method *merge* units and costs in beginning inventory with units and costs of work done in the current period.

We now describe the FIFO method using the five-step procedure introduced on page 610.

Step 1: Summarize the Flow of Physical Units of Output. Exhibit 17-6, Step 1, traces the flow of physical units of production. The following observations help explain the calculation of physical units under the FIFO method for Pacific Electronics.

- The first physical units assumed to be completed and transferred out during the period are 225 units from beginning work-in-process inventory.

- The March data on page 613 indicate that 400 physical units were completed during March. The FIFO method assumes that of these 400 units, 175 units (400 units − 225 units from beginning work-in-process inventory) must have been started and completed during March.

- Ending work-in-process inventory consists of 100 physical units—the 275 physical units started minus the 175 units that were started and completed.

- The physical units "to account for" equal the physical units "accounted for" (500 units).

Step 2: Compute Output in Terms of Equivalent Units. Exhibit 17-6 also presents the computations for Step 2 under the FIFO method. *The equivalent-unit calculations for each cost category focus on equivalent units of work done in the current period (March) only.*

Under the FIFO method, equivalent units of work done in March on the beginning work-in-process inventory equal 225 physical units times *the percentage of work remaining to be done in March to complete these units*: 0% for direct materials, because beginning work in process is 100% complete with respect to direct materials, and 40% for conversion costs, because beginning work in process is 60% complete with respect to conversion costs. The results are 0 (0% × 225) equivalent units of work for direct materials and 90 (40% × 225) equivalent units of work for conversion costs.

The equivalent units of work done on the 175 physical units started and completed equals 175 units times 100% for both direct materials and conversion costs, because all work on these units is done in the current period.

The equivalent units of work done on the 100 units of ending work in process equal 100 physical units times 100% for direct materials (because all direct materials for these units are added in the current period) and 50% for conversion costs (because 50% of the conversion-costs work on these units is done in the current period).

Step 3: Summarize Total Costs to Account For. Exhibit 17-7 presents Step 3 and summarizes total costs to account for in March 2012 (beginning work in process and costs added in the current period) of $62,280, as described in the example data (p. 613).

Step 4: Compute Cost per Equivalent Unit. Exhibit 17-7 shows the Step 4 computation of cost per equivalent unit for *work done in the current period only* for direct materials and conversion costs. For example, conversion cost per equivalent unit of $52 is obtained by dividing current-period conversion costs of $16,380 by current-period conversion-costs equivalent units of 315.

Step 5: Assign Total Costs to Units Completed and to Units in Ending Work in Process. Exhibit 17-7 shows the assignment of costs under the FIFO method. Costs of work done in the current period are assigned (1) first to the additional work done to complete the beginning

	Home	Insert	Page Layout	Formulas	Data	Review	View		
			A			B	C		D
1						(Step 1)	(Step 2)		
2							Equivalent Units		
3			**Flow of Production**			Physical Units	Direct Materials		Conversion Costs
4	Work in process, beginning (given, p. 613)					225	(work done before current period)		
5	Started during current period (given, p. 613)					275			
6	To account for					500			
7	Completed and transferred out during current period:								
8	From beginning work in process[a]					225			
9	[225 × (100% – 100%); 225 × (100% – 60%)]						0		90
10	Started and completed					175[b]			
11	(175 × 100%; 175 × 100%)						175		175
12	Work in process, ending[c] (given, p. 613)					100			
13	(100 × 100%; 100 × 50%)						100		50
14	Accounted for					500			
15	Equivalent units of work done in current period						275		315
16									
17	[a]Degree of completion in this department; direct materials, 100%; conversion costs, 60%.								
18	[b]400 physical units completed and transferred out minus 225 physical units completed and								
19	transferred out from beginning work-in-process inventory.								
20	[c]Degree of completion in this department: direct materials, 100%; conversion costs, 50%.								

work in process, then (2) to work done on units started and completed during the current period, and finally (3) to ending work in process. *Step 5 takes each quantity of equivalent units calculated in Exhibit 17-6, Step 2, and assigns dollar amounts to them (using the cost-per-equivalent-unit calculations in Step 4).* The goal is to use the cost of work done in the current period to determine total costs of all units completed from beginning inventory and from work started and completed in the current period, and costs of ending work in process.

Of the 400 completed units, 225 units are from beginning inventory and 175 units are started and completed during March. The FIFO method starts by assigning the costs of beginning work-in-process inventory of $26,100 to the first units completed and transferred out. As we saw in Step 2, an additional 90 equivalent units of conversion costs are needed to complete these units in the current period. Current-period conversion cost per equivalent unit is $52, so $4,680 (90 equivalent units × $52 per equivalent unit) of additional costs are incurred to complete beginning inventory. Total production costs for units in beginning inventory are $26,100 + $4,680 = $30,780. The 175 units started and completed in the current period consist of 175 equivalent units of direct materials and 175 equivalent units of conversion costs. These units are costed at the cost per equivalent unit in the current period (direct materials, $72, and conversion costs, $52) for a total production cost of $21,700 [175 × ($72 + $52)].

Under FIFO, ending work-in-process inventory comes from units that were started but not fully completed during the current period. Total costs of the 100 partially assembled physical units in ending work in process are as follows:

Direct materials:		
100 equivalent units × $72 cost per equivalent unit in March	$7,200	
Conversion costs:		
50 equivalent units × $52 cost per equivalent unit in March	2,600	
Total cost of work in process on March 31	$9,800	

The following table summarizes total costs to account for and costs accounted for of $62,280 in Exhibit 17-7. Notice how under the FIFO method, the layers of beginning work in process and costs added in the current period are kept separate. The arrows

Exhibit 17-7   Steps 3, 4, and 5: Summarize Total Costs to Account For, Compute Cost per Equivalent Unit, and Assign Total Costs to Units Completed and to Units in Ending Work in Process Using FIFO Method of Process Costing for Assembly Department of Pacific Electronics for March 2012

	Home Insert Page Layout Formulas Data Review View			
	A	B	C	D	E
1			Total Production Costs	Direct Material	Conversion Costs
2	**(Step 3)**	Work in process, beginning (given, p. 613)	$26,100	$18,000	$ 8,100
3		Costs added in current period (given, p. 613)	36,180	19,800	16,380
4		Total costs to account for	$62,280	$37,800	$24,480
5					
6	**(Step 4)**	Costs added in current period		$19,800	$16,380
7		Divide by equivalent units of work done in current period (Exhibit 17-6)		÷ 275	÷ 315
8		Cost per equivalent unit of work done in current period		$ 72	$ 52
9					
10	**(Step 5)**	Assignment of costs:			
11		Completed and transferred out (400 units):			
12		Work in process, beginning (225 units)	$26,100	$18,000 + $8,100	
13		Costs added to beginning work in process in current period	4,680	$(0^a \times \$72) + (90^a \times \$52)$	
14		Total from beginning inventory	30,780		
15		Started and completed (175 units)	21,700	$(175^b \times \$72) + (175^b \times \$52)$	
16		Total costs of units completed and transferred out	52,480		
17		Work in process, ending (100 units):	9,800	$(100^c \times \$72) + (50^c \times \$52)$	
18		Total costs accounted for	$62,280	$37,800 + $24,480	
19					
20	[a]Equivalent units used to complete beginning work in process from Exhibit 17-6, Step 2.				
21	[b]Equivalent units started and completed from Exhibit 17-6, Step 2.				
22	[c]Equivalent units in ending work in process from Exhibit 17-6, Step 2.				

indicate where the costs in each layer go—that is, to units completed and transferred out or to ending work in process. Be sure to include costs of beginning work in process ($26,100) when calculating costs of units completed from beginning inventory.

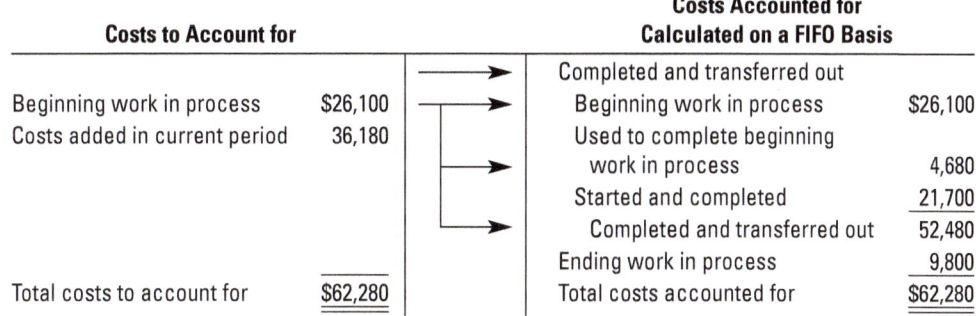

Costs to Account for			Costs Accounted for Calculated on a FIFO Basis	
			Completed and transferred out	
Beginning work in process	$26,100	→	Beginning work in process	$26,100
Costs added in current period	36,180		Used to complete beginning work in process	4,680
			Started and completed	21,700
			Completed and transferred out	52,480
			Ending work in process	9,800
Total costs to account for	$62,280		Total costs accounted for	$62,280

Before proceeding, review Exhibits 17-6 and 17-7 to check your understanding of the FIFO method. Note: Exhibit 17-6 deals with only physical and equivalent units, not costs. Exhibit 17-7 shows the cost amounts.

The journal entries under the FIFO method are identical to the journal entries under the weighted-average method except for one difference. The entry to record the cost of goods completed and transferred out would be $52,480 under the FIFO method instead of $52,000 under the weighted-average method.

Keep in mind that FIFO is applied within each department to compile the cost of units *transferred out*. As a practical matter, however, units *transferred in* during a given period usually are carried at a single average unit cost. For example, the assembly department uses FIFO in the preceding example to distinguish between monthly batches of production. The resulting average cost of units transferred out of the assembly department is $52,480 ÷ 400 units = $131.20 per SG-40 unit. The succeeding department, testing, however, costs these units (which consist of costs incurred in both February and March) at one average unit cost ($131.20 in this illustration). If this averaging were not done, the attempt to track costs on a pure FIFO basis throughout a series of processes would be cumbersome. As a result, the FIFO method should really be called a *modified* or *department* FIFO method.

Comparison of Weighted-Average and FIFO Methods

Consider the summary of the costs assigned to units completed and to units still in process under the weighted-average and FIFO process-costing methods in our example for March 2012:

	Weighted Average (from Exhibit 17-5)	FIFO (from Exhibit 17-7)	Difference
Cost of units completed and transferred out	$52,000	$52,480	+ $480
Work in process, ending	10,280	9,800	− $480
Total costs accounted for	$62,280	$62,280	

The weighted-average ending inventory is higher than the FIFO ending inventory by $480, or 4.9% ($480 ÷ $9,800 = 0.049, or 4.9%). This would be a significant difference when aggregated over the many thousands of products that Pacific Electronics makes. When completed units are sold, the weighted-average method in our example leads to a lower cost of goods sold and, therefore, higher operating income and higher income taxes than the FIFO method. To see why the weighted-average method yields a lower cost of units completed, recall the data on page 613. Direct material cost per equivalent unit in beginning work-in-process inventory is $80, and conversion cost per equivalent unit in beginning work-in-process inventory is $60. These costs are greater, respectively, than the $72 direct materials cost and the $52 conversion cost per equivalent unit of work done during the current period. The current-period costs could be lower due to a decline in the prices of direct materials and conversion-cost inputs, or as a result of Pacific Electronics becoming more efficient in its processes by using smaller quantities of inputs per unit of output, or both.

For the assembly department, FIFO assumes that (1) all the higher-cost units from the previous period in beginning work in process are the first to be completed and transferred out of the process and (2) ending work in process consists of only the lower-cost current-period units. The weighted-average method, however, smooths out cost per equivalent unit by assuming that (1) more of the lower-cost units are completed and transferred out and (2) some of the higher-cost units are placed in ending work in process. The decline in the current-period cost per equivalent unit results in a lower cost of units completed and transferred out and a higher ending work-in-process inventory under the weighted-average method compared with FIFO.

Cost of units completed and, hence, operating income can differ materially between the weighted-average and FIFO methods when (1) direct material or conversion cost per equivalent unit varies significantly from period to period and (2) physical-inventory levels of work in process are large in relation to the total number of units transferred out of the process. As companies move toward long-term procurement contracts that reduce differences in unit costs from period to period and reduce inventory levels, the difference in cost of units completed under the weighted-average and FIFO methods will decrease.[3]

---

[3] For example, suppose beginning work-in-process inventory for March were 125 physical units (instead of 225), and suppose costs per equivalent unit of work done in the current period (March) were direct materials, $75, and conversion costs, $55. Assume that all other data for March are the same as in our example. In this case, the cost of units completed and transferred out would be $52,833 under the weighted-average method and $53,000 under the FIFO method. The work-in-process ending inventory would be $10,417 under the weighted-average method and $10,250 under the FIFO method (calculations not shown). These differences are much smaller than in the chapter example. The weighted-average ending inventory is higher than the FIFO ending inventory by only $167 ($10,417 – $10,250), or 1.6% ($167 ÷ $10,250 = 0.016, or 1.6%), compared with 4.9% higher in the chapter example.

Managers use information from process-costing systems to aid them in pricing and product-mix decisions and to provide them with feedback about their performance. FIFO provides managers with information about changes in costs per unit from one period to the next. Managers can use this information to adjust selling prices based on current conditions (for example, based on the $72 direct material cost and $52 conversion cost in March). They can also more easily evaluate performance in the current period compared with a budget or relative to performance in the previous period (for example, recognizing the decline in both unit direct material and conversion costs relative to the prior period). By focusing on work done and costs of work done during the current period, the FIFO method provides useful information for these planning and control purposes.

The weighted-average method merges unit costs from different accounting periods, obscuring period-to-period comparisons. For example, the weighted-average method would lead managers at Pacific Electronics to make decisions based on the $75.60 direct materials and $54.40 conversion costs, rather than the costs of $72 and $52 prevailing in the current period. Advantages of the weighted-average method, however, are its relative computational simplicity and its reporting of a more-representative average unit cost when input prices fluctuate markedly from month to month.

Activity-based costing plays a significant role in our study of job costing, but how is activity-based costing related to process costing? Each process—assembly, testing, and so on—can be considered a different (production) activity. However, no additional activities need to be identified within each process. That's because products are homogeneous and use resources of each process in a uniform way. The bottom line is that activity-based costing has less applicability in process-costing environments. *The appendix illustrates the use of the standard costing method for the assembly department.*

◀ **Decision Point**

What are the weighted-average and first-in, first-out (FIFO) methods of process costing? Under what conditions will they yield different levels of operating income?

Transferred-In Costs in Process Costing

Many process-costing systems have two or more departments or processes in the production cycle. As units move from department to department, the related costs are also transferred by monthly journal entries. **Transferred-in costs** (also called **previous-department costs**) are costs incurred in previous departments that are carried forward as the product's cost when it moves to a subsequent process in the production cycle.

We now extend our Pacific Electronics example to the testing department. As the assembly process is completed, the assembly department of Pacific Electronics immediately transfers SG-40 units to the testing department. Conversion costs are added evenly during the testing department's process. At the *end of the process* in testing, units receive additional direct materials, including crating and other packing materials to prepare units for shipment. As units are completed in testing, they are immediately transferred to Finished Goods. Computation of testing department costs consists of transferred-in costs, as well as direct materials and conversion costs that are added in testing.

The following diagram represents these facts:

Learning Objective 5

Apply process-costing methods to situations with transferred-in costs

. . . using weighted-average and FIFO methods

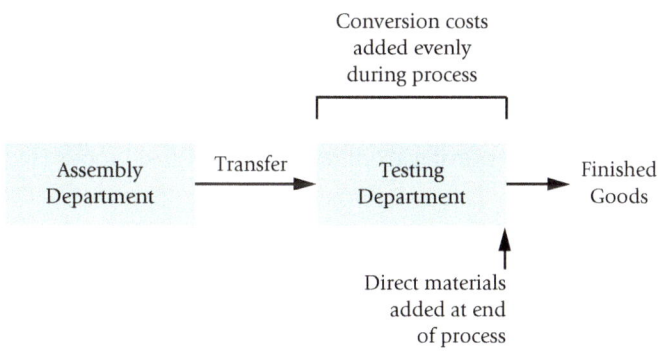

Data for the testing department for March 2012 are as follows:

	Home Insert Page Layout Formulas Data Review View				
	A	B	C	D	E
1		Physical Units (SG-40s)	Transferred-In Costs	Direct Materials	Conversion Costs
2	Work in process, beginning inventory (March 1)	240	$33,600	$ 0	$18,000
3	Degree of completion of beginning work in process		100%	0%	62.5%
4	Transferred in during March	400			
5	Completed and transferred out during March	440			
6	Work in process, ending inventory (March 31)	200			
7	Degree of completion of ending work in process		100%	0%	80%
8	Total costs added during March				
9	Direct materials and conversion costs			$13,200	$48,600
10	Transferred in (Weighted-average from Exhibit 17-5)[a]		$52,000		
11	Transferred in (FIFO from Exhibit 17-7)[a]		$52,480		
12					
13	[a]The transferred-in costs during March are different under the weighted-average method (Exhibit 17-5) and the FIFO method (Exhibit 17-7). In our example, beginning work-in-process inventory, $51,600 ($33,600 + $0 + $18,000) is the same under both the weighted-average and FIFO inventory methods because we assume costs per equivalent unit to be the same in both January and February. If costs per equivalent unit had been different in the two months, work-in-process inventory at the end of February (beginning of March) would be costed differently under the weighted-average and FIFO methods. The basic approach to process costing with transferred-in costs, however, would still be the same as what we describe in this section.				

Transferred-in costs are treated as if they are a separate type of direct material added at the beginning of the process. That is, transferred-in costs are always 100% complete as of the beginning of the process in the new department. When successive departments are involved, transferred units from one department become all or a part of the direct materials of the next department; however, they are called transferred-in costs, not direct material costs.

Transferred-In Costs and the Weighted-Average Method

To examine the weighted-average process-costing method with transferred-in costs, we use the five-step procedure described earlier (p. 610) to assign costs of the testing department to units completed and transferred out and to units in ending work in process.

Exhibit 17-8 shows Steps 1 and 2. The computations are similar to the calculations of equivalent units under the weighted-average method for the assembly department in Exhibit 17-4. The one difference here is that we have transferred-in costs as an additional input. All units, whether completed and transferred out during the period or in ending work in process, are always fully complete with respect to transferred-in costs. The reason is that the transferred-in costs refer to costs incurred in the assembly department, and any units received in the testing department must have first been completed in the assembly department. However, direct material costs have a zero degree of completion in both beginning and ending work-in-process inventories because, in testing, direct materials are introduced at the *end* of the process.

Exhibit 17-9 describes Steps 3, 4, and 5 for the weighted-average method. Beginning work in process and work done in the current period are combined for purposes of computing cost per equivalent unit for transferred-in costs, direct material costs, and conversion costs.

The journal entry for the transfer from testing to Finished Goods (see Exhibit 17-9) is as follows:

Finished Goods Control	120,890	
Work in Process—Testing		120,890
To record cost of goods completed and transferred from testing to Finished Goods.		

Entries in the Work in Process—Testing account (see Exhibit 17-9) are as follows:

Work in Process—Testing

Beginning inventory, March 1	51,600	Transferred out	120,890
Transferred-in costs	52,000		
Direct materials	13,200		
Conversion costs	48,600		
Ending inventory, March 31	44,510		

Exhibit 17-8 Steps 1 and 2: Summarize Output in Physical Units and Compute Output in Equivalent Units Using Weighted-Average Method of Process Costing for Testing Department of Pacific Electronics for March 2012

| Home | Insert | Page Layout | Formulas | Data | Review | View |

	A	B	C	D	E
		(Step 1)		**(Step 2)**	
2				**Equivalent Units**	
3	**Flow of Production**	**Physical Units**	**Transferred-In Costs**	**Direct Materials**	**Conversion Costs**
4	Work in process, beginning (given, p. 622)	240			
5	Transferred in during current period (given, p. 622)	400			
6	To account for	640			
7	Completed and transferred out during current period	440	440	440	440
8	Work in process, ending[a] (given, p. 622)	200			
9	(200 × 100%; 200 × 0%; 200 × 80%)		200	0	160
10	Accounted for	640			
11	Equivalent units of work done to date		640	440	600
12					
13	[a]Degree of completion in this department; transferred-in costs, 100%; direct materials, 0%; conversion costs, 80%.				

Exhibit 17-9 Steps 3, 4, and 5: Summarize Total Costs to Account For, Compute Cost per Equivalent Unit, and Assign Total Costs to Units Completed and to Units in Ending Work in Process Using Weighted-Average Method of Process Costing for Testing Department of Pacific Electronics for March 2012

| Home | Insert | Page Layout | Formulas | Data | Review | View |

	A	B	C	D	E	F
1			**Total Production Costs**	**Transferred-In Costs**	**Direct Materials**	**Conversion Costs**
2	(Step 3)	Work in process, beginning (given, p. 622)	$ 51,600	$33,600	$ 0	$18,000
3		Costs added in current period (given, p. 622)	113,800	52,000	13,200	48,600
4		Total costs to account for	$165,400	$85,600	$13,200	$66,600
5						
6	(Step 4)	Costs incurred to date		$85,600	$13,200	$66,600
7		Divide by equivalent units of work done to date (Exhibit 17-8)		÷ 640	÷ 440	÷ 600
8		Cost per equivalent unit of work done to date		$133.75	$ 30.00	$111.00
9						
10	(Step 5)	Assignment of costs:				
11		Completed and transferred out (440 units)	$120,890	(440[a] × $133.75) +	(440[a] × $30) +	(440[a] × $111)
12		Work in process, ending (200 units):	44,510	(200[b] × $133.75) +	(0[b] × $30) +	(160[b] × $111)
13		Total costs accounted for	$165,400	$85,600 +	$13,200 +	$66,600
14						
15	[a]Equivalent units completed and transferred out from Exhibit 17-8, Step 2.					
16	[b]Equivalent units in ending work in process from Exhibit 17-8, Step 2.					

Transferred-In Costs and the FIFO Method

To examine the FIFO process-costing method with transferred-in costs, we again use the five-step procedure. Exhibit 17-10 shows Steps 1 and 2. Other than considering transferred-in costs, computations of equivalent units are the same as under the FIFO method for the assembly department shown in Exhibit 17-6.

Exhibit 17-11 describes Steps 3, 4, and 5. In Step 3, total costs to account for of $165,880 under the FIFO method differs from the corresponding amount under the weighted-average method of $165,400. The reason is the difference in cost of completed units transferred in from the assembly department under the two methods—$52,480 under FIFO and $52,000 under weighted average. Cost per equivalent unit for the current period in Step 4 is calculated on the basis of costs transferred in and work done in the current period only. Step 5 then accounts for the total costs of $165,880 by assigning them to the units transferred out and those in ending work in process. Again, other than considering transferred-in costs, the calculations mirror those under the FIFO method for the assembly department shown in Exhibit 17-7.

Remember that in a series of interdepartmental transfers, each department is regarded as separate and distinct for accounting purposes. The journal entry for the transfer from testing to Finished Goods (see Exhibit 17-11) is as follows:

Finished Goods Control	122,360	
Work in Process—Testing		122,360
To record cost of goods completed and		
transferred from testing to Finished Goods.		

Exhibit 17-10	Steps 1 and 2: Summarize Output in Physical Units and Compute Output in Equivalent Units Using FIFO Method of Process Costing for Testing Department of Pacific Electronics for March 2012

	A	B	C	D	E
		(Step 1)		(Step 2)	
2				Equivalent Units	
3	**Flow of Production**	**Physical Units**	**Transferred-In Costs**	**Direct Materials**	**Conversion Costs**
4	Work in process, beginning (given, p. 622)	240	(work done before current period)		
5	Transferred in during current period (given, p. 622)	400			
6	To account for	640			
7	Completed and transferred out during current period:				
8	From beginning work in process[a]	240			
9	[240 × (100% – 100%); 240 × (100% – 0%); 240 × (100% – 62.5%)]		0	240	90
10	Started and completed	200[b]			
11	(200 × 100%; 200 × 100%; 200 × 100%)		200	200	200
12	Work in process, ending[c] (given, p. 000)	200			
13	(200 × 100%; 200 × 0%; 200 × 80%)		200	0	160
14	Accounted for	640			
15	Equivalent units of work done in current period		400	440	450
16					
17	[a]Degree of completion in this department: transferred-in costs, 100%; direct materials, 0%; conversion costs, 62.5%.				
18	[b]440 physical units completed and transferred out minus 240 physical units completed and transferred out from beginning				
19	work-in-process inventory.				
20	[c]Degree of completion in this department: transferred-in costs, 100%; direct materials, 0%; conversion costs, 80%.				

Exhibit 17-11   Steps 3, 4, and 5: Summarize Total Costs to Account For, Compute Cost per Equivalent Unit, and Assign Total Costs to Units Completed and to Units in Ending Work in Process Using FIFO Method of Process Costing for Testing Department of Pacific Electronics for March 2012

		Home Insert Page Layout Formulas Data Review View				
	A	B	C	D	E	F
1			Total Production Costs	Transferred-In Cost	Direct Material	Conversion Costs
2	(Step 3)	Work in process, beginning (given, p. 622)	$ 51,600	$33,600	$ 0	$18,000
3		Costs added in current period (given, p. 622)	114,280	52,480	13,200	48,600
4		Total costs to account for	$165,880	$86,080	$13,200	$66,600
5						
6	(Step 4)	Costs added in current period		$52,480	$13,200	$48,600
7		Divide by equivalent units of work done in current period (Exhibit 17-10)		÷ 400	÷ 440	÷ 450
8		Cost per equivalent unit of work done in current period		$131.20	$ 30	$ 108
9						
10	(Step 5)	Assignment of costs:				
11		Completed and transferred out (440 units)				
12		Work in process, beginning (240 units)	$ 51,600	$33,600 +	$0 +	$18,000
13		Costs added to beginning work in process in current period	16,920	(0ᵃ × $131.20) +	(240ᵃ × $30) +	(90ᵃ × $108)
14		Total from beginning inventory	68,520			
15		Started and completed (200 units)	53,840	(200ᵇ × $131.20)+	(200ᵇ × $30) +	(200ᵇ × $108)
16		Total costs of units completed and transferred out	122,360			
17		Work in process, ending (200 units):	43,520	(200ᶜ × $131.20)+	(0ᶜ × $30) +	(160ᶜ × $108)
18		Total costs accounted for	$165,880	$86,080 +	$13,200 +	$66,600
19						
20	ᵃEquivalent units used to complete beginning work in process from Exhibit 17-10, Step 2.					
21	ᵇEquivalent units started and completed from Exhibit 17-10, Step 2.					
22	ᶜEquivalent units in ending work in process from Exhibit 17-10, Step 2.					

Entries in the Work in Process—Testing account (see Exhibit 17-11) are as follows:

Work in Process—Testing

Beginning inventory, March 1	51,600	Transferred out	122,360
Transferred-in costs	52,480		
Direct materials	13,200		
Conversion costs	48,600		
Ending inventory, March 31	43,520		

Points to Remember About Transferred-In Costs

Some points to remember when accounting for transferred-in costs are as follows:

1. Be sure to include transferred-in costs from previous departments in your calculations.
2. In calculating costs to be transferred on a FIFO basis, do not overlook costs assigned in the previous period to units that were in process at the beginning of the current period but are now included in the units transferred. For example, do not overlook the $51,600 in Exhibit 17-11.
3. Unit costs may fluctuate between periods. Therefore, transferred units may contain batches accumulated at different unit costs. For example, the 400 units transferred in

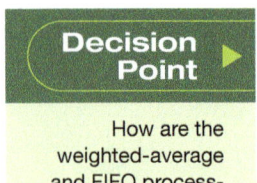

Decision Point ▶

How are the weighted-average and FIFO process-costing methods applied to transferred-in costs?

at $52,480 in Exhibit 17-11 using the FIFO method consist of units that have different unit costs of direct materials and conversion costs when these units were worked on in the assembly department (see Exhibit 17-7). Remember, however, that when these units are transferred to the testing department, they are costed at *one average unit cost* of $131.20 ($52,480 ÷ 400 units), as in Exhibit 17-11.

4. Units may be measured in different denominations in different departments. Consider each department separately. For example, unit costs could be based on kilograms in the first department and liters in the second department. Accordingly, as units are received in the second department, their measurements must be converted to liters.

Hybrid Costing Systems

Learning Objective 6

Understand the need for hybrid-costing systems such as operation-costing

. . . when product-costing does not fall into job-costing or process-costing categories

Product-costing systems do not always fall neatly into either job-costing or process-costing categories. Consider Ford Motor Company. Automobiles may be manufactured in a continuous flow (suited to process costing), but individual units may be customized with a special combination of engine size, transmission, music system, and so on (which requires job costing). A **hybrid-costing system** blends characteristics from both job-costing and process-costing systems. Product-costing systems often must be designed to fit the particular characteristics of different production systems. Many production systems are a hybrid: They have some features of custom-order manufacturing and other features of mass-production manufacturing. Manufacturers of a relatively wide variety of closely related standardized products (for example, televisions, dishwashers, and washing machines) tend to use hybrid-costing systems. The Concepts in Action feature (p. 627) describes a hybrid-costing system at Adidas. The next section explains *operation costing*, a common type of hybrid-costing system.

Overview of Operation-Costing Systems

An **operation** is a standardized method or technique that is performed repetitively, often on different materials, resulting in different finished goods. Multiple operations are usually conducted within a department. For instance, a suit maker may have a cutting operation and a hemming operation within a single department. The term *operation*, however, is often used loosely. It may be a synonym for a department or process. For example, some companies may call their finishing department a finishing process or a finishing operation.

An **operation-costing system** is a hybrid-costing system applied to batches of similar, but not identical, products. Each batch of products is often a variation of a single design, and it proceeds through a sequence of operations. Within each operation, all product units are treated exactly alike, using identical amounts of the operation's resources. A key point in the operation system is that each batch does not necessarily move through the same operations as other batches. Batches are also called production runs.

In a company that makes suits, management may select a single basic design for every suit to be made, but depending on specifications, each batch of suits varies somewhat from other batches. Batches may vary with respect to the material used or the type of stitching. Semiconductors, textiles, and shoes are also manufactured in batches and may have similar variations from batch to batch.

An operation-costing system uses work orders that specify the needed direct materials and step-by-step operations. Product costs are compiled for each work order. Direct materials that are unique to different work orders are specifically identified with the appropriate work order, as in job costing. However, each unit is assumed to use an identical amount of conversion costs for a given operation, as in process costing. A single average conversion cost per unit is calculated for each operation, by dividing total conversion costs for that operation by the number of units that pass through it. This average cost is then assigned to each unit passing through the operation. Units that do not pass through an operation are not allocated any costs of that

Concepts in Action

Hybrid Costing for Customized Shoes at Adidas

Adidas has been designing and manufacturing athletic footwear for nearly 90 years. Although shoemakers have long individually crafted shoes for professional athletes like Reggie Bush of the New Orleans Saints, Adidas took this concept a step further when it initiated the *mi adidas* program. *Mi adidas* gives customers the opportunity to create shoes to their exact personal specifications for function, fit, and aesthetics. *Mi adidas* is available in retail stores around the world, and in special *mi adidas* "Performance Stores" in cities such as New York, Chicago, and San Francisco.

The process works as follows: The customer goes to a *mi adidas* station, where a salesperson develops an in-depth customer profile, a 3-D computer scanner develops a scan of the customer's feet, and the customer selects from among 90 to 100 different styles and colors for his or her modularly designed shoe. During the three-step, 30-minute high-tech process, *mi adidas* experts take customers through the "mi fit," "mi performance," and "mi design" phases, resulting in a customized shoe to fit their needs. The resulting data are transferred to an Adidas plant, where small, multiskilled teams produce the customized shoe. The measuring and fitting process is free, but purchasing your own specially made shoes costs between $40 and $65 on top of the normal retail price, depending on the style.

Historically, costs associated with individually customized products have fallen into the domain of job costing. Adidas, however, uses a hybrid-costing system—job costing for the material and customizable components that customers choose and process costing to account for the conversion costs of production. The cost of making each pair of shoes is calculated by accumulating all production costs and dividing by the number of shoes made. In other words, even though each pair of shoes is different, the conversion cost of each pair is assumed to be the same.

The combination of customization with certain features of mass production is called mass customization. It is the consequence of being able to digitize information that individual customers indicate is important to them. Various products that companies are now able to customize within a mass-production setting (for example, personal computers, blue jeans, bicycles) still require job costing of materials and considerable human intervention. However, as manufacturing systems become flexible, companies are also using process costing to account for the standardized conversion costs.

Sources: Adidas. 2010. New Orleans Saints running back Reggie Bush designs custom Adidas shoes to aid in Haiti relief efforts. AG press release. Portland, OR: February 5; Kamenev, Marina. 2006. Adidas' high tech footwear. *BusinessWeek.com*, November 3; Seifert, Ralf. 2003. The "mi adidas" mass customization initiative. IMD No. 159. Lausanne, Switzerland: International Institute for Management Development.

operation. Our examples assume only two cost categories—direct materials and conversion costs—but operation costing can have more than two cost categories. Costs in each category are identified with specific work orders using job-costing or process-costing methods as appropriate.

Managers find operation costing useful in cost management because operation costing focuses on control of physical processes, or operations, of a given production system. For example, in clothing manufacturing, managers are concerned with fabric waste, how many fabric layers that can be cut at one time, and so on. Operation costing measures, in financial terms, how well managers have controlled physical processes.

Illustration of an Operation-Costing System

The Baltimore Clothing Company, a clothing manufacturer, produces two lines of blazers for department stores: those made of wool and those made of polyester. Wool blazers use better-quality materials and undergo more operations than polyester blazers do.

Operations information on work order 423 for 50 wool blazers and work order 424 for 100 polyester blazers is as follows:

	Work Order 423	Work Order 424
Direct materials	Wool	Polyester
	Satin full lining	Rayon partial lining
	Bone buttons	Plastic buttons
Operations		
1. Cutting cloth	Use	Use
2. Checking edges	Use	Do not use
3. Sewing body	Use	Use
4. Checking seams	Use	Do not use
5. Machine sewing of collars and lapels	Do not use	Use
6. Hand sewing of collars and lapels	Use	Do not use

Cost data for these work orders, started and completed in March 2012, are as follows:

	Work Order 423	Work Order 424
Number of blazers	50	100
Direct material costs	$ 6,000	$3,000
Conversion costs allocated:		
Operation 1	580	1,160
Operation 2	400	—
Operation 3	1,900	3,800
Operation 4	500	—
Operation 5	—	875
Operation 6	700	—
Total manufacturing costs	$10,080	$8,835

As in process costing, all product units in any work order are assumed to consume identical amounts of conversion costs of a particular operation. Baltimore's operation-costing system uses a budgeted rate to calculate the conversion costs of each operation. The budgeted rate for Operation 1 (amounts assumed) is as follows:

$$\text{Operation 1 budgeted conversion-cost rate for 2012} = \frac{\text{Operation 1 budgeted conversion costs for 2012}}{\text{Operation 1 budgeted product units for 2012}}$$

$$= \frac{\$232,000}{20,000 \text{ units}}$$

$$= \$11.60 \text{ per unit}$$

Budgeted conversion costs of Operation 1 include labor, power, repairs, supplies, depreciation, and other overhead of this operation. If some units have not been completed (so all units in Operation 1 have not received the same amounts of conversion costs), the conversion-cost rate is computed by dividing budgeted conversion costs by *equivalent units* of conversion costs, as in process costing.

As goods are manufactured, conversion costs are allocated to the work orders processed in Operation 1 by multiplying the $11.60 conversion cost per unit by the number of units processed. Conversion costs of Operation 1 for 50 wool blazers (work order 423) are $11.60 per blazer × 50 blazers = $580, and for 100 polyester blazers (work order 424) are $11.60 per blazer × 100 blazers = $1,160. When equivalent units are used to calculate the conversion-cost rate, costs are allocated to work orders by multiplying conversion cost per equivalent unit by number of equivalent units in the work order. Direct material costs of $6,000 for the 50 wool blazers (work order 423) and $3,000 for the 100 polyester blazers (work order 424) are specifically identified with each order, as in job costing. Remember the basic point in operation costing: Operation unit costs are assumed to be the same regardless of the work order, but direct material costs vary across orders when the materials for each work order vary.

Journal Entries

Actual conversion costs for Operation 1 in March 2012—assumed to be $24,400, including actual costs incurred for work order 423 and work order 424—are entered into a Conversion Costs Control account:

1. Conversion Costs Control	24,400	
Various accounts (such as Wages Payable		
Control and Accumulated Depreciation)		24,400

Summary journal entries for assigning costs to polyester blazers (work order 424) follow. Entries for wool blazers would be similar. Of the $3,000 of direct materials for work order 424, $2,975 are used in Operation 1, and the remaining $25 of materials are used in another operation. The journal entry to record direct materials used for the 100 polyester blazers in March 2012 is as follows:

2. Work in Process, Operation 1	2,975	
Materials Inventory Control		2,975

The journal entry to record the allocation of conversion costs to products uses the budgeted rate of $11.60 per blazer times the 100 polyester blazers processed, or $1,160:

3. Work in Process, Operation 1	1,160	
Conversion Costs Allocated		1,160

The journal entry to record the transfer of the 100 polyester blazers (at a cost of $2,975 + $1,160) from Operation 1 to Operation 3 (polyester blazers do not go through Operation 2) is as follows:

4. Work in Process, Operation 3	4,135	
Work in Process, Operation 1		4,135

After posting these entries, the Work in Process, Operation 1, account appears as follows:

Work in Process, Operation 1

② Direct materials	2,975	④ Transferred to Operation 3	4,135
③ Conversion costs allocated	1,160		
Ending inventory, March 31	0		

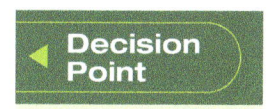

◄ **Decision Point**

What is an operation-costing system and when is it a better approach to product-costing?

Costs of the blazers are transferred through the operations in which blazers are worked on and then to finished goods in the usual manner. Costs are added throughout the fiscal year in the Conversion Costs Control account and the Conversion Costs Allocated account. Any overallocation or underallocation of conversion costs is disposed of in the same way as overallocated or underallocated manufacturing overhead in a job-costing system (see pp. 117–122).

Problem for Self-Study

Allied Chemicals operates a thermo-assembly process as the second of three processes at its plastics plant. Direct materials in thermo-assembly are added at the end of the process. Conversion costs are added evenly during the process. The following data pertain to the thermo-assembly department for June 2012:

	Home	Insert	Page Layout	Formulas	Data	Review	View	
	A			B	C	D	E	
1				Physical Units	Transferred-In Costs	Direct Materials	Conversion Costs	
2	Work in process, beginning inventory			50,000				
3	Degree of completion of beginning work in process				100%	0%	80%	
4	Transferred in during current period			200,000				
5	Completed and transferred out during current period			210,000				
6	Work in process, ending inventory			?				
7	Degree of completion of ending work in process				100%	0%	40%	

Required Compute equivalent units under (1) the weighted-average method and (2) the FIFO method.

Solution

1. The weighted-average method uses equivalent units of work done to date to compute cost per equivalent unit. The calculations of equivalent units follow:

	Home	Insert	Page Layout	Formulas	Data	Review	View	
	A		B	C	D	E	
1			(Step 1)		(Step 2)		
2					Equivalent Units		
3	Flow of Production		Physical Units	Transferred-In Costs	Direct Materials	Conversion Costs	
4	Work in process, beginning (given)		50,000				
5	Transferred in during current period (given)		200,000				
6	To account for		250,000				
7	Completed and transferred out during current period		210,000	210,000	210,000	210,000	
8	Work in process, ending[a]		40,000[b]				
9	(40,000 × 100%; 40,000 × 0%; 40,000 × 40%)			40,000	0	16,000	
10	Accounted for		250,000				
11	Equivalent units of work done to date			250,000	210,000	226,000	
12							
13	[a]Degree of completion in this department: transferred-in costs, 100%; direct materials, 0%; conversion costs, 40%.						
14	[b]250,000 physical units to account for minus 210,000 physical units completed and transferred out.						

2. The FIFO method uses equivalent units of work done in the current period only to compute cost per equivalent unit. The calculations of equivalent units follow:

	A	B	C	D	E
		(Step 1)		(Step 2)	
				Equivalent Units	
	Flow of Production	Physical Units	Transferred-In Costs	Direct Materials	Conversion Costs
4	Work in process, beginning (given)	50,000			
5	Transferred in during current period (given)	200,000			
6	To account for	250,000			
7	Completed and transferred out during current period:				
8	From beginning work in process^a	50,000			
9	[50,000 × (100% − 100%); 50,000 × (100% − 0%); 50,000 × (100% − 80%)]		0	50,000	10,000
10	Started and completed	160,000^b			
11	(160,000 × 100%; 160,000 × 100%; 160,000 × 100%)		160,000	160,000	160,000
12	Work in process, ending^c	40,000^d			
13	(40,000 × 100%; 40,000 × 0%; 40,000 × 40%)		40,000	0	16,000
14	Accounted for	250,000			
15	Equivalent units of work done in current period		200,000	210,000	186,000
16					
17	^aDegree of completion in this department: transferred-in costs, 100%; direct materials, 0%; conversion costs, 80%.				
18	^b210,000 physical units completed and transferred out minus 50,000 physical units completed and transferred out from beginning work-in-process inventory.				
19	^cDegree of completion in this department: transferred-in costs, 100%; direct materials, 0%; conversion costs, 40%.				
20	^d250,000 physical units to account for minus 210,000 physical units completed and transferred out.				

Decision Points

The following question-and-answer format summarizes the chapter's learning objectives. Each decision presents a key question related to a learning objective. The guidelines are the answer to that question.

Decision | Guidelines

1. Under what conditions is a process-costing system used?

A process-costing system is used to determine cost of a product or service when masses of identical or similar units are produced. Industries using process-costing systems include food, textiles, and oil refining.

2. How are average unit costs computed when no inventories are present?

Average unit costs are computed by dividing total costs in a given accounting period by total units produced in that period.

3. What are the five steps in a process-costing system and how are equivalent units calculated?

The five steps in a process-costing system are (1) summarize the flow of physical units of output, (2) compute output in terms of equivalent units, (3) summarize total costs to account for, (4) compute cost per equivalent unit, and (5) assign total costs to units completed and to units in ending work in process.

Equivalent units is a derived amount of output units that (a) takes the quantity of each input (factor of production) in units completed or in incomplete units in work in process and (b) converts the quantity of input into the amount of completed output units that could be made with that quantity of input.

4. What are the weighted-average and first-in, first-out methods of process costing? Under what conditions will they yield different levels of operating income?

The weighted-average method computes unit costs by dividing total costs in the Work in Process account by total equivalent units completed to date, and assigns this average cost to units completed and to units in ending work-in-process inventory.

The first-in, first-out (FIFO) method computes unit costs based on costs incurred during the current period and equivalent units of work done in the current period.

Operating income can differ materially between the two methods when (1) direct material or conversion cost per equivalent unit varies significantly from period to period and (2) physical-inventory levels of work in process are large in relation to the total number of units transferred out of the process.

5. How are the weighted-average and FIFO process-costing methods applied to transferred-in costs?

The weighted-average method computes transferred-in costs per unit by dividing total transferred-in costs to date by total equivalent transferred-in units completed to date, and assigns this average cost to units completed and to units in ending work-in-process inventory. The FIFO method computes transferred-in costs per unit based on costs transferred in during the current period and equivalent units of transferred-in costs of work done in the current period. The FIFO method assigns transferred-in costs in beginning work in process to units completed and costs transferred in during the current period first to complete beginning inventory, next to start and complete new units, and finally to units in ending work-in-process inventory.

6. What is an operation-costing system and when is it a better approach to product-costing?

Operation-costing is a hybrid-costing system that blends characteristics from both job-costing and process-costing systems. It is a better approach to product-costing when production systems share some features of custom-order manufacturing and other features of mass-production manufacturing.

Appendix

Standard-Costing Method of Process Costing

Chapter 7 described accounting in a standard-costing system. Recall that this involves making entries using standard costs and then isolating variances from these standards in order to support management control. This appendix describes how the principles of standard costing can be employed in process-costing systems.

Benefits of Standard Costing

Companies that use process-costing systems produce masses of identical or similar units of output. In such companies, it is fairly easy to set standards for quantities of inputs needed to produce output. Standard cost per input unit can then be multiplied by input quantity standards to develop standard cost per output unit.

The weighted-average and FIFO methods become very complicated when used in process industries that produce a wide variety of similar products. For example, a steel-rolling mill uses various steel alloys and produces sheets of various sizes and finishes. The different types of direct materials used and the operations performed are few, but used in various combinations, they yield a wide variety of products. Similarly, complex conditions are frequently found, for example, in plants that manufacture rubber products, textiles, ceramics, paints, and packaged food products. In each of these cases, if the broad averaging procedure of *actual* process costing were used, the result would be inaccurate costs for each product. Therefore, the standard-costing method of process costing is widely used in these industries.

Under the standard-costing method, teams of design and process engineers, operations personnel, and management accountants work together to determine *separate* standard costs per equivalent unit on the basis of different technical processing specifications for each product. Identifying standard costs for each product overcomes the disadvantage of costing all products at a single average amount, as under actual costing.

Computations Under Standard Costing

We return to the assembly department of Pacific Electronics, but this time we use standard costs. Assume the same standard costs apply in February and March of 2012. Data for the assembly department are as follows:

	Physical Units (SG-40s) (1)	Direct Materials (2)	Conversion Costs (3)	Total Costs (4) = (2) + (3)
2 Standard cost per unit		$ 74	$ 54	
3 Work in process, beginning inventory (March 1)	225			
4 Degree of completion of beginning work in process		100%	60%	
5 Beginning work in process inventory at standard costs		$16,650[a]	$ 7,290[a]	$23,940
6 Started during March	275			
7 Completed and transferred out during March	400			
8 Work in process, ending inventory (March 31)	100			
9 Degree of completion of ending work in process		100%	50%	
10 Actual total costs added during March		$19,800	$16,380	$36,180
11				
12 [a]Work in process, beginning inventory at standard costs				
13 Direct materials: 225 physical units × 100% completed × $74 per unit = $16,650				
14 Conversion costs: 225 physical units × 60% completed × $54 per unit = $7,290				

We illustrate the standard-costing method of process costing using the five-step procedure introduced earlier (p. 610).

Exhibit 17-12 presents Steps 1 and 2. These steps are identical to the steps described for the FIFO method in Exhibit 17-6 because, as in FIFO, the standard-costing method also assumes that the earliest equivalent units in beginning work in process are completed first. Work done in the current period for direct materials is 275 equivalent units. Work done in the current period for conversion costs is 315 equivalent units.

Exhibit 17-13 describes Steps 3, 4, and 5. In Step 3, total costs to account for (that is, the total debits to Work in Process—Assembly) differ from total debits to Work in Process—Assembly under the actual-cost-based weighted-average

Exhibit 17-12

Steps 1 and 2: Summarize Output in Physical Units and Compute Output in Equivalent Units Using Standard-Costing Method of Process Costing for Assembly Department of Pacific Electronics for March 2012

		(Step 1)	(Step 2)	
			Equivalent Units	
3	Flow of Production	Physical Units	Direct Materials	Conversion Costs
4	Work in process, beginning (given, p. 633)	225		
5	Started during current period (given, p. 633)	275		
6	To account for	500		
7	Completed and transferred out during current period:			
8	From beginning work in process[a]	225		
9	[225 × (100% − 100%); 225 × (100% − 60%)]		0	90
10	Started and completed	175[b]		
11	(175 × 100%; 175 × 100%)		175	175
12	Work in process, ending[c] (given, p. 633)	100		
13	(100 × 100%; 100 × 50%)		100	50
14	Accounted for	500		
15	Equivalent units of work done in current period		275	315
16				
17	[a]Degree of completion in this department: direct materials, 100%; conversion costs, 60%.			
18	[b]400 physical units completed and transferred out minus 225 physical units completed and transferred out from beginning work-in-process inventory.			
19	[c]Degree of completion in this department: direct materials, 100%; conversion costs, 50%.			

Exhibit 17-13	Steps 3, 4, and 5: Summarize Total Costs to Account For, Compute Cost per Equivalent Unit, and Assign Total Costs to Units Completed and to Units in Ending Work in Process Using Standard-Costing Method of Process Costing for Assembly Department of Pacific Electronics for March 2012

	A	B	C	D	E	F	G
1			Total Production Costs	Direct Materials		Conversion Costs	
2	(Step 3)	Work in process, beginning (given, p. 633)					
3		Direct materials, 225 × $74; Conversion costs, 135 × $54	$23,940	$16,650		$ 7,290	
4		Costs added in current period at standard costs					
5		Direct materials, 275 × $74; Conversion costs, 315 × $54	37,360	20,350		17,010	
6		Total costs to account for	$61,300	$37,000		$24,300	
7							
8	(Step 4)	Standard cost per equivalent unit (given, p. 633)		$ 74		$ 54	
9							
10	(Step 5)	Assignment of costs at standard costs:					
11		Completed and transferred out (400 units):					
12		Work in process, beginning (225 units)	$23,940	$16,650	+	$ 7,290	
13		Costs added to beginning work in process in current period	4,860	(0[a] × $74)	+	(90[a] × $54)	
14		Total from beginning inventory	28,800				
15		Started and completed (175 units)	22,400	(175[b] × $74)	+	(175[b] × $54)	
16		Total costs of units completed and transferred out	51,200				
17		Work in process, ending (100 units):	10,100	(100[c] × $74)	+	(50[c] × $54)	
18		Total costs accounted for	$61,300	$37,000	+	$24,300	
19							
20	Summary of variances for current performance:						
21	Costs added in current period at standard costs (see step 3)			$20,350		$17,010	
22	Actual costs incurred (given, p. 633)			$19,800		$16,380	
23	Variance			$ 550	F	$ 630	F
24							
25	[a]Equivalent units used to complete beginning work in process from Exhibit 17-12, Step 2.						
26	[b]Equivalent units started and completed from Exhibit 17-12, Step 2.						
27	[c]Equivalent units in ending work in process from Exhibit 17-12, Step 2.						

and FIFO methods. That's because, as in all standard-costing systems, the debits to the Work in Process account are at standard costs, rather than actual costs. These standard costs total $61,300 in Exhibit 17-13. In Step 4, costs per equivalent unit are standard costs: direct materials, $74, and conversion costs, $54. *Therefore, costs per equivalent unit do not have to be computed as they were for the weighted-average and FIFO methods.*

Exhibit 17-13, Step 5, assigns total costs to units completed and transferred out and to units in ending work-in-process inventory, as in the FIFO method. Step 5 assigns amounts of standard costs to equivalent units calculated in Exhibit 17-12. These costs are assigned (1) first to complete beginning work-in-process inventory, (2) next to start and complete new units, and (3) finally to start new units that are in ending work-in-process inventory. Note how the $61,300 total costs accounted for in Step 5 of Exhibit 17-13 equal total costs to account for.

Accounting for Variances

Process-costing systems using standard costs record actual direct material costs in Direct Materials Control and actual conversion costs in Conversion Costs Control (similar to Variable and Fixed Overhead Control in Chapter 8). In the journal entries that follow, the first two record these *actual costs*. In entries 3 and 4a, the Work-in-Process—Assembly account accumulates direct material costs and conversion costs at *standard costs*. Entries 3 and 4b isolate total variances. The final entry transfers out completed goods at standard costs.

1. Assembly Department Direct Materials Control (at actual costs)   19,800
       Accounts Payable Control   19,800
     To record direct materials purchased and used in production during March. This cost control account is debited with actual costs.

2. Assembly Department Conversion Costs Control (at actual costs)   16,380

     Various accounts such as Wages Payable Control and Accumulated Depreciation   16,380

    To record assembly department conversion costs for March. This cost control account is debited with actual costs.

Entries 3, 4, and 5 use standard cost amounts from Exhibit 17-13.

3. Work in Process—Assembly (at standard costs)   20,350

     Direct Materials Variances   550

     Assembly Department Direct Materials Control   19,800

    To record standard costs of direct materials assigned to units worked on and total direct materials variances.

4a. Work in Process—Assembly (at standard costs)   17,010

     Assembly Department Conversion Costs Allocated   17,010

    To record conversion costs allocated at standard rates to the units worked on during March.

4b. Assembly Department Conversion Costs Allocated   17,010

     Conversion Costs Variances   630

     Assembly Department Conversion Costs Control   16,380

    To record total conversion costs variances.

5. Work in Process—Testing (at standard costs)   51,200

     Work in Process—Assembly (at standard costs)   51,200

    To record standard costs of units completed and transferred out from assembly to testing.

Variances arise under standard costing, as in entries 3 and 4b. That's because the standard costs assigned to products on the basis of work done in the current period do not equal actual costs incurred in the current period. Recall that variances that result in higher income than expected are termed favorable, while those that reduce income are unfavorable. From an accounting standpoint, favorable cost variances are credit entries, while unfavorable ones are debits. In the preceding example, both direct materials and conversion cost variances are favorable. This is also reflected in the "F" designations for both variances in Exhibit 17-13.

Variances can be analyzed in little or great detail for planning and control purposes, as described in Chapters 7 and 8. Sometimes direct materials price variances are isolated at the time direct materials are purchased and only efficiency variances are computed in entry 3. Exhibit 17-14 shows how the costs flow through the general-ledger accounts under standard costing.

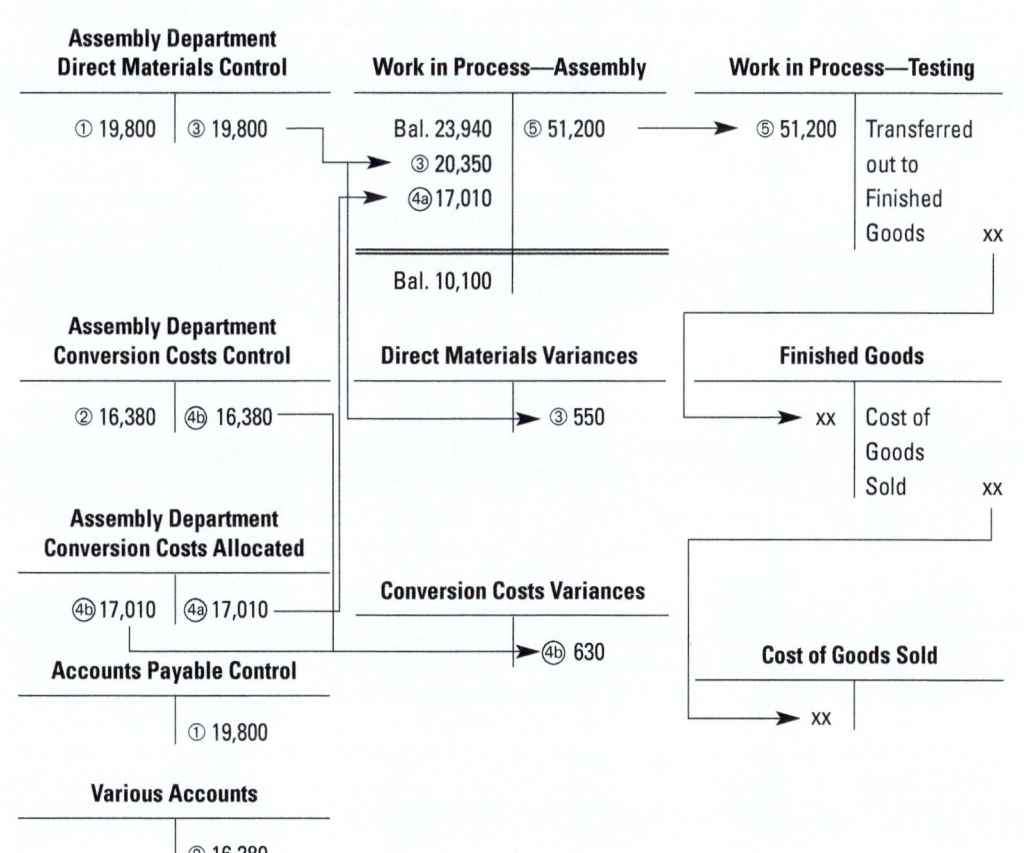

Exhibit 17-14

Flow of Standard Costs in a Process-Costing System for Assembly Department of Pacific Electronics for March 2012

Terms to Learn

This chapter and the Glossary at the end of the book contain definitions of the following important terms:

equivalent units (**p. 611**)

first-in, first-out (FIFO) process-costing
method (**p. 617**)

hybrid-costing system (**p. 626**)

operation (**p. 626**)

operation-costing system (**p. 626**)

previous-department costs (**p. 621**)

transferred-in costs (**p. 621**)

weighted-average process-costing
method (**p. 614**)

Assignment Material

Questions

17-1 Give three examples of industries that use process-costing systems.

17-2 In process costing, why are costs often divided into two main classifications?

17-3 Explain equivalent units. Why are equivalent-unit calculations necessary in process costing?

17-4 What problems might arise in estimating the degree of completion of semiconductor chips in a semiconductor plant?

17-5 Name the five steps in process costing when equivalent units are computed.

17-6 Name the three inventory methods commonly associated with process costing.

17-7 Describe the distinctive characteristic of weighted-average computations in assigning costs to units completed and to units in ending work in process.

17-8 Describe the distinctive characteristic of FIFO computations in assigning costs to units completed and to units in ending work in process.

17-9 Why should the FIFO method be called a modified or department FIFO method?

17-10 Identify a major advantage of the FIFO method for purposes of planning and control.

17-11 Identify the main difference between journal entries in process costing and job costing.

17-12 "The standard-costing method is particularly applicable to process-costing situations." Do you agree? Why?

17-13 Why should the accountant distinguish between transferred-in costs and additional direct material costs for each subsequent department in a process-costing system?

17-14 "Transferred-in costs are those costs incurred in the preceding accounting period." Do you agree? Explain.

17-15 "There's no reason for me to get excited about the choice between the weighted-average and FIFO methods in my process-costing system. I have long-term contracts with my materials suppliers at fixed prices." Do you agree with this statement made by a plant controller? Explain.

Exercises

17-16 Equivalent units, zero beginning inventory. Nihon, Inc., is a manufacturer of digital cameras. It has two departments: assembly and testing. In January 2012, the company incurred $750,000 on direct materials and $798,000 on conversion costs, for a total manufacturing cost of $1,548,000.

Required

1. Assume there was no beginning inventory of any kind on January 1, 2012. During January, 10,000 cameras were placed into production and all 10,000 were fully completed at the end of the month. What is the unit cost of an assembled camera in January?

2. Assume that during February 10,000 cameras are placed into production. Further assume the same total assembly costs for January are also incurred in February, but only 9,000 cameras are fully completed at the end of the month. All direct materials have been added to the remaining 1,000 cameras. However, on average, these remaining 1,000 cameras are only 50% complete as to conversion costs. (a) What are the equivalent units for direct materials and conversion costs and their respective costs per equivalent unit for February? (b) What is the unit cost of an assembled camera in February 2012?

3. Explain the difference in your answers to requirements 1 and 2.

17-17 **Journal entries (continuation of 17-16).** Refer to requirement 2 of Exercise 17-16.

Prepare summary journal entries for the use of direct materials and incurrence of conversion costs. Also prepare a journal entry to transfer out the cost of goods completed. Show the postings to the Work in Process account. **Required**

17-18 **Zero beginning inventory, materials introduced in middle of process.** Roary Chemicals has a mixing department and a refining department. Its process-costing system in the mixing department has two direct materials cost categories (chemical P and chemical Q) and one conversion costs pool. The following data pertain to the mixing department for July 2012:

Units	
Work in process, July 1	0
Units started	50,000
Completed and transferred to refining department	35,000
Costs	
Chemical P	$250,000
Chemical Q	70,000
Conversion costs	135,000

Chemical P is introduced at the start of operations in the mixing department, and chemical Q is added when the product is three-fourths completed in the mixing department. Conversion costs are added evenly during the process. The ending work in process in the mixing department is two-thirds complete.

1. Compute the equivalent units in the mixing department for July 2012 for each cost category. **Required**
2. Compute (a) the cost of goods completed and transferred to the refining department during July and (b) the cost of work in process as of July 31, 2012.

17-19 **Weighted-average method, equivalent units.** Consider the following data for the assembly division of Fenton Watches, Inc.:

The assembly division uses the weighted-average method of process costing.

	Physical Units (Watches)	Direct Materials	Conversion Costs
Beginning work in process (May 1)[a]	80	$ 493,360	$ 91,040
Started in May 2012	500		
Completed during May 2012	460		
Ending work in process (May 31)[b]	120		
Total costs added during May 2012		$3,220,000	$1,392,000

[a]Degree of completion: direct materials, 90%; conversion costs, 40%.
[b]Degree of completion: direct materials, 60%; conversion costs, 30%.

Compute equivalent units for direct materials and conversion costs. Show physical units in the first column of your schedule. **Required**

17-20 **Weighted-average method, assigning costs (continuation of 17-19).**

For the data in Exercise 17-19, summarize total costs to account for, calculate cost per equivalent unit for direct materials and conversion costs, and assign total costs to units completed (and transferred out) and to units in ending work in process. **Required**

17-21 **FIFO method, equivalent units.** Refer to the information in Exercise 17-19. Suppose the assembly division at Fenton Watches, Inc., uses the FIFO method of process costing instead of the weighted-average method.

Compute equivalent units for direct materials and conversion costs. Show physical units in the first column of your schedule. **Required**

17-22 **FIFO method, assigning costs (continuation of 17-21).**

For the data in Exercise 17-19, use the FIFO method to summarize total costs to account for, calculate cost per equivalent unit for direct materials and conversion costs, and assign total costs to units completed (and transferred out) and to units in ending work in process. **Required**

17-23 **Operation Costing.** Whole Goodness Bakery needs to determine the cost of two work orders for the month of June. Work order 215 is for 1,200 packages of dinner rolls and work order 216 is for 1,400 loaves of multigrain bread. Dinner rolls are mixed and cut into individual rolls before being baked and then packaged. Multigrain loaves are mixed and shaped before being baked, sliced, and packaged. The following information applies to work order 215 and work order 216:

	Work Order 215	Work Order 216
Quantity (packages)	1,200	1,400
Operations		
1. Mix	Use	Use
2. Shape loaves	Do not use	Use
3. Cut rolls	Use	Do not use
4. Bake	Use	Use
5. Slice loaves	Do not use	Use
6. Package	Use	Use

Selected budget information for June follows:

	Dinner Rolls	Multigrain Loaves	Total
Packages	4,800	6,500	11,300
Direct material costs	$2,640	$5,850	$ 8,490

Budgeted conversion costs for each operation for June follow:

Mixing	$9,040
Shaping	1,625
Cutting	720
Baking	7,345
Slicing	650
Packaging	8,475

Required

1. Using budgeted number of packages as the denominator, calculate the budgeted conversion-cost rates for each operation.
2. Using the information in requirement 1, calculate the budgeted cost of goods manufactured for the two June work orders.
3. Calculate the cost per package of dinner rolls and multigrain loaves for work order 215 and 216.

17-24 Weighted-average method, assigning costs. Bio Doc Corporation is a biotech company based in Milpitas. It makes a cancer-treatment drug in a single processing department. Direct materials are added at the start of the process. Conversion costs are added evenly during the process. Bio Doc uses the weighted-average method of process costing. The following information for July 2011 is available.

		Equivalent Units	
	Physical Units	Direct Materials	Conversion Costs
Work in process, July 1	8,500[a]	8,500	1,700
Started during July	35,000		
Completed and transferred out during July	33,000	33,000	33,000
Work in process, July 31	10,500[b]	10,500	6,300

[a]Degree of completion: direct materials, 100%; conversion costs, 20%.
[b]Degree of completion: direct materials, 100%; conversion costs, 60%.

Total Costs for July 2008		
Work in process, beginning		
Direct materials	$63,100	
Conversion costs	45,510	$108,610
Direct materials added during July		284,900
Conversion costs added during July		485,040
Total costs to account for		$878,550

Required

1. Calculate cost per equivalent unit for direct materials and conversion costs.
2. Summarize total costs to account for, and assign total costs to units completed (and transferred out) and to units in ending work in process.

17-25 FIFO method, assigning costs.

Do Exercise 17-24 using the FIFO method. Note that you first need to calculate the equivalent units of work done in the current period (for direct materials and conversion costs) to complete beginning work in process, to start and complete new units, and to produce ending work in process.

Required

17-26 Standard-costing method, assigning costs. Refer to the information in Exercise 17-24. Suppose Bio Doc determines standard costs of $8.25 per equivalent unit for direct materials and $12.70 per equivalent unit for conversion costs for both beginning work in process and work done in the current period.

Required

1. Do Exercise 17-24 using the standard-costing method. Note that you first need to calculate the equivalent units of work done in the current period (for direct materials and conversion costs) to complete beginning work in process, to start and complete new units, and to produce ending work in process.
2. Compute the total direct materials and conversion costs variances for July 2011.

17-27 Transferred-in costs, weighted-average method. Asaya Clothing, Inc., is a manufacturer of winter clothes. It has a knitting department and a finishing department. This exercise focuses on the finishing department. Direct materials are added at the end of the process. Conversion costs are added evenly during the process. Asaya uses the weighted-average method of process costing. The following information for June 2012 is available.

Home	Insert	Page Layout	Formulas	Data	Review	View	
	A		B	C	D	E	
1			Physical Units (tons)	Transferred-In Costs	Direct Materials	Conversion Costs	
2	Work in process, beginning inventory (June 1)		75	$ 75,000	$ 0	$30,000	
3	Degree of completion, beginning work in process			100%	0%	60%	
4	Transferred in during June		135				
5	Completed and transferred out during June		150				
6	Work in process, ending inventory (June 30)		60				
7	Degree of completion, ending work in process			100%	0%	75%	
8	Total costs added during June			$142,500	$37,500	$78,000	

Required

1. Calculate equivalent units of transferred-in costs, direct materials, and conversion costs.
2. Summarize total costs to account for, and calculate the cost per equivalent unit for transferred-in costs, direct materials, and conversion costs.
3. Assign total costs to units completed (and transferred out) and to units in ending work in process.

17-28 Transferred-in costs, FIFO method. Refer to the information in Exercise 17-27. Suppose that Asaya uses the FIFO method instead of the weighted-average method in all of its departments. The only changes to Exercise 17-27 under the FIFO method are that total transferred-in costs of beginning work in process on June 1 are $60,000 (instead of $75,000) and total transferred-in costs added during June are $130,800 (instead of $142,500).

Do Exercise 17-27 using the FIFO method. Note that you first need to calculate equivalent units of work done in the current period (for transferred-in costs, direct materials, and conversion costs) to complete beginning work in process, to start and complete new units, and to produce ending work in process.

Required

17-29 Operation Costing. UB Healthy Company manufactures three different types of vitamins: vitamin A, vitamin B, and a multivitamin. The company uses four operations to manufacture the vitamins: mixing, tableting, encapsulating, and bottling. Vitamins A and B are produced in tablet form (in the tableting department) and the multivitamin is produced in capsule form (in the encapsulating department). Each bottle contains 200 vitamins, regardless of the product.

Conversion costs are applied based on the number of bottles in the tableting and encapsulating departments. Conversion costs are applied based on labor hours in the mixing department. It takes 1.5 minutes to mix the ingredients for a 200-unit bottle for each product. Conversion costs are applied based on machine hours in the bottling department. It takes 1 minute of machine time to fill a 200-unit bottle, regardless of the product.

UB Healthy is planning to complete one batch of each type of vitamin in July. The budgeted number of bottles and expected direct material cost for each type of vitamin is as follows:

	Vitamin A	Vitamin B	Multivitamin
Number of 200 unit bottles	12,000	9,000	18,000
Direct material cost	$23,040	$21,600	$47,520

The budgeted conversion costs for each department for July are as follows:

Department	Budgeted Conversion Cost
Mixing	$ 8,190
Tableting	24,150
Encapsulating	25,200
Bottling	3,510

Required

1. Calculate the conversion cost rates for each department.
2. Calculate the budgeted cost of goods manufactured for vitamin A, vitamin B, and the multivitamin for the month of July.
3. Calculate the cost per 200-unit bottle for each type of vitamin for the month of July.

Problems

17-30 Weighted-average method. Larsen Company manufactures car seats in its San Antonio plant. Each car seat passes through the assembly department and the testing department. This problem focuses on the assembly department. The process-costing system at Larsen Company has a single direct-cost category (direct materials) and a single indirect-cost category (conversion costs). Direct materials are added at the beginning of the process. Conversion costs are added evenly during the process. When the assembly department finishes work on each car seat, it is immediately transferred to testing.

Larsen Company uses the weighted-average method of process costing. Data for the assembly department for October 2012 are as follows:

	Physical Units (Car Seats)	Direct Materials	Conversion Costs
Work in process, October 1[a]	5,000	$1,250,000	$ 402,750
Started during October 2012	20,000		
Completed during October 2012	22,500		
Work in process, October 31[b]	2,500		
Total costs added during October 2012		$4,500,000	$2,337,500

[a]Degree of completion: direct materials, ?%; conversion costs, 60%.
[b]Degree of completion: direct materials, ?%; conversion costs, 70%.

Required

1. For each cost category, compute equivalent units in the assembly department. Show physical units in the first column of your schedule.
2. For each cost category, summarize total assembly department costs for October 2012 and calculate the cost per equivalent unit.
3. Assign total costs to units completed and transferred out and to units in ending work in process.

17-31 Journal entries (continuation of 17-30).

Required Prepare a set of summarized journal entries for all October 2012 transactions affecting Work in Process—Assembly. Set up a T-account for Work in Process—Assembly and post your entries to it.

17-32 FIFO method (continuation of 17-30).

Required Do Problem 17-30 using the FIFO method of process costing. Explain any difference between the cost per equivalent unit in the assembly department under the weighted-average method and the FIFO method.

17-33 Transferred-in costs, weighted-average method (related to 17-30 to 17-32). Larsen Company, as you know, is a manufacturer of car seats. Each car seat passes through the assembly department and testing department. This problem focuses on the testing department. Direct materials are added when the testing department process is 90% complete. Conversion costs are added evenly during the testing department's process. As work in assembly is completed, each unit is immediately transferred to testing. As each unit is completed in testing, it is immediately transferred to Finished Goods.

Larsen Company uses the weighted-average method of process costing. Data for the testing department for October 2012 are as follows:

	Physical Units (Car Seats)	Transferred-In Costs	Direct Materials	Conversion Costs
Work in process, October 1[a]	7,500	$2,932,500	$ 0	$ 835,460
Transferred in during October 2012	?			
Completed during October 2012	26,300			
Work in process, October 31[b]	3,700			
Total costs added during October 2012		$7,717,500	$9,704,700	$3,955,900

[a]Degree of completion: transferred-in costs, ?%; direct materials, ?%; conversion costs, 70%.
[b]Degree of completion: transferred-in costs, ?%; direct materials, ?%; conversion costs, 60%.

1. What is the percentage of completion for (a) transferred-in costs and direct materials in beginning work-in-process inventory, and (b) transferred-in costs and direct materials in ending work-in-process inventory? **Required**
2. For each cost category, compute equivalent units in the testing department. Show physical units in the first column of your schedule.
3. For each cost category, summarize total testing department costs for October 2012, calculate the cost per equivalent unit, and assign total costs to units completed (and transferred out) and to units in ending work in process.
4. Prepare journal entries for October transfers from the assembly department to the testing department and from the testing department to Finished Goods.

17-34 Transferred-in costs, FIFO method (continuation of 17-33). Refer to the information in Problem 17-33. Suppose that Larsen Company uses the FIFO method instead of the weighted-average method in all of its departments. The only changes to Problem 17-33 under the FIFO method are that total transferred-in costs of beginning work in process on October 1 are $2,881,875 (instead of $2,932,500) and that total transferred-in costs added during October are $7,735,250 (instead of $7,717,500).

Using the FIFO process-costing method, complete Problem 17-33. **Required**

17-35 Weighted-average method. Ashworth Handcraft is a manufacturer of picture frames for large retailers. Every picture frame passes through two departments: the assembly department and the finishing department. This problem focuses on the assembly department. The process-costing system at Ashworth has a single direct-cost category (direct materials) and a single indirect-cost category (conversion costs). Direct materials are added when the assembly department process is 10% complete. Conversion costs are added evenly during the assembly department's process.

Ashworth uses the weighted-average method of process costing. Consider the following data for the assembly department in April 2012:

	Physical Unit (Frames)	Direct Materials	Conversion Costs
Work in process, April 1[a]	95	$ 1,665	$ 988
Started during April 2012	490		
Completed during April 2012	455		
Work in process, April 30[b]	130		
Total costs added during April 2012		$17,640	$11,856

[a]Degree of completion: direct materials, 100%; conversion costs, 40%.
[b]Degree of completion: direct materials, 100%; conversion costs, 30%.

Summarize total assembly department costs for April 2012, and assign total costs to units completed (and transferred out) and to units in ending work in process. **Required**

17-36 Journal entries (continuation of 17-35).

Prepare a set of summarized journal entries for all April transactions affecting Work in Process—Assembly. Set up a T-account for Work in Process—Assembly and post your entries to it. **Required**

17-37 FIFO method (continuation of 17-35).

Do Problem 17-35 using the FIFO method of process costing. If you did Problem 17-35, explain any difference between the cost of work completed and transferred out and the cost of ending work in process in the assembly department under the weighted-average method and the FIFO method. **Required**

17-38 Transferred-in costs, weighted-average method. Bookworm, Inc., has two departments: printing and binding. Each department has one direct-cost category (direct materials) and one indirect-cost category (conversion costs). This problem focuses on the binding department. Books that have undergone the printing process are immediately transferred to the binding department. Direct material is added when the binding process is 80% complete. Conversion costs are added evenly during binding operations. When those operations are done, the books are immediately transferred to Finished Goods. Bookworm, Inc., uses the weighted-average method of process costing. The following is a summary of the April 2012 operations of the binding department.

	A	B	C	D	E
1		Physical Units (books)	Transferred-In Costs	Direct Materials	Conversion Costs
2	Beginning work in process	1,050	$ 32,550	$ 0	$13,650
3	Degree of completion, beginning work in process		100%	0%	50%
4	Transferred in during April 2012	2,400			
5	Completed and transferred out during April	2,700			
6	Ending work in process (April 30)	750			
7	Degree of completion, ending work in process		100%	0%	70%
8	Total costs added during April		$129,600	$23,490	$70,200

Required

1. Summarize total binding department costs for April 2012, and assign these costs to units completed (and transferred out) and to units in ending work in process.
2. Prepare journal entries for April transfers from the printing department to the binding department and from the binding department to Finished Goods.

17-39 Transferred-in costs, FIFO method. Refer to the information in Problem 17-38. Suppose that Bookworm, Inc., uses the FIFO method instead of the weighted-average method in all of its departments. The only changes to Problem 17-38 under the FIFO method are that total transferred-in costs of beginning work in process on April 1 are $36,750 (instead of $32,550) and that total transferred-in costs added during April are $124,800 (instead of $129,600).

Required

1. Using the FIFO process-costing method, complete Problem 17-38.
2. If you did Problem 17-38, explain any difference between the cost of work completed and transferred out and the cost of ending work in process in the binding department under the weighted-average method and the FIFO method.

17-40 Transferred-in costs, weighted-average and FIFO methods. Frito-Lay, Inc., manufactures convenience foods, including potato chips and corn chips. Production of corn chips occurs in four departments: cleaning, mixing, cooking, and drying and packaging. Consider the drying and packaging department, where direct materials (packaging) are added at the end of the process. Conversion costs are added evenly during the process. The accounting records of a Frito-Lay plant provide the following information for corn chips in its drying and packaging department during a weekly period (week 37):

	Physical Units (Cases)	Transferred-In Costs	Direct Materials	Conversion Costs
Beginning work in process[a]	1,200	$26,750	$ 0	$ 4,020
Transferred in during week 37 from cooking department	4,200			
Completed during week 37	4,000			
Ending work in process, week 37[b]	1,400			
Total costs added during week 37		$91,510	$23,000	$27,940

[a]Degree of completion: transferred-in costs, 100%; direct materials, ?%; conversion costs, 25%.
[b]Degree of completion: transferred-in costs, 100%; direct materials, ?%; conversion costs, 50%.

Required

1. Using the weighted-average method, summarize the total drying and packaging department costs for week 37, and assign total costs to units completed (and transferred out) and to units in ending work in process.
2. Assume that the FIFO method is used for the drying and packaging department. Under FIFO, the transferred-in costs for work-in-process beginning inventory in week 37 are $28,920 (instead of $26,750 under the weighted-average method), and the transferred-in costs during week 37 from the cooking department are $93,660 (instead of $91,510 under the weighted-average method). All other data are unchanged. Summarize the total drying and packaging department costs for week 37, and assign total costs to units completed and transferred out and to units in ending work in process using the FIFO method.

17-41 Standard-costing with beginning and ending work in process. Penelope's Pearls Company (PPC) is a manufacturer of knock off jewelry. Penelope attends Fashion Week in New York City every September and February to gauge the latest fashion trends in jewelry. She then makes trendy jewelry at a fraction of the cost of those designers who participate in Fashion Week. This Fall's biggest item is triple-stranded pearl necklaces. Because of her large volume, Penelope uses process costing to account for her production. In October, she had started some of the triple strands. She continued to work on those in November. Costs and output figures are as follows:

Penelope's Pearls Company
Process Costing
For the Month Ended November 30, 2012

	Units	Direct Materials	Conversion Costs
Standard cost per unit		$3.00	$10.50
Work in process, beginning inventory (Nov. 1)	24,000	$72,000	$176,400
Degree of completion of beginning work in process		100%	70%
Started during November	124,400		
Completed and transferred out	123,000		
Work in process, ending inventory (Nov. 30)	25,400		
Degree of completion of ending work in process		100%	50%
Total costs added during November		$329,000	$1,217,000

Required

1. Compute equivalent units for direct materials and conversion costs. Show physical units in the first column of your schedule.
2. Compute the total standard costs of pearls transferred out in November and the total standard costs of the November 30 inventory of work in process.
3. Compute the total November variances for direct materials and conversion costs.

Collaborative Learning Problem

17-42 Standard-costing method. Ozumo's Gardening makes several different kinds of mulch. Its busy period is in the summer months. In August, the controller suddenly quit due to a stress-related disorder. He took with him the standard costing results for RoseBark, Ozumo's highest quality mulch. The controller had already completed the assignment of costs to finished goods and work in process, but Ozumo does not know standard costs or the completion levels of inventory. The following information is available:

Physical and Equivalent Units for RoseBark
For the Month Ended August 31, 2012

	Physical Units (Yards of Mulch)	Equivalent Units (yards) Direct Materials	Equivalent Units (yards) Conversion Costs
Completion of beginning work in process	965,000	—	434,250
Started and completed	845,000	845,000	845,000
Work on ending work in process	1,817,000	1,817,000	1,090,200
		2,662,000	2,369,450
Units to account for	3,627,000		

	Costs
Cost of units completed from beginning work in process	$ 7,671,750
Cost of new units started and completed	6,717,750
Cost of units completed in August	14,389,500
Cost of ending work in process	12,192,070
Total costs accounted for	$26,581,570

Required

1. Calculate the completion percentages of beginning work in process with respect to the two inputs.
2. Calculate the completion percentages of ending work in process with respect to the two inputs.
3. What are the standard costs per unit for the two inputs?
4. What is the total cost of work-in-process inventory as of August 1, 2012?

18 Spoilage, Rework, and Scrap

▶ Learning Objectives

1. Understand the definitions of spoilage, rework, and scrap

2. Identify the differences between normal and abnormal spoilage

3. Account for spoilage in process costing using the weighted-average method and the first-in, first-out (FIFO) method

4. Account for spoilage at various stages of completion in process costing

5. Account for spoilage in job costing

6. Account for rework in job costing

7. Account for scrap

When a product doesn't meet specification but is subsequently repaired and sold, it is called rework.

Firms try to minimize rework, as well as spoilage and scrap, during production. Why? Because higher-than-normal levels of spoilage and scrap can have a significant negative effect on a company's profits. Rework can also cause substantial production delays, as the following article about Boeing shows.

Rework Delays the Boeing Dreamliner by Three Years[1]

In 2007, Boeing was scheduled to introduce its newest airplane, the Dreamliner 787. Engineered to be the most fuel-efficient commercial plane, the Dreamliner received nearly 600 customer orders, making it the fastest selling commercial airplane in history.

By 2010, however, the first Dreamliner still had not rolled off the production line. The design and assembly process was riddled with production snafus, parts shortages, and supply-chain bottlenecks. The Dreamliner was Boeing's first major attempt at giving suppliers and partners far-ranging responsibility for designing and building the wings, fuselage, and other critical components to be shipped to Boeing for final assembly. The approach did not work as planned, with many of the 787's components delivered unfinished, with flaws, and lacking parts.

As a result, the Boeing Dreamliner aircraft required significant rework. The company's engineers had to redesign structural flaws in the airplane's wings, repair cracks in the composite materials used to construct the airplane, and fix faulty software among many other problems. In 2009, one of Boeing's unions calculated that half of its members' time was spent doing rework.

This rework led to costly delays for Boeing. Many of its customers, including Virgin Atlantic and Japan's All Nippon Airways, asked the company to compensate them for keeping less fuel-efficient planes in the air. Other customers cancelled their orders. Australia's Quantas Airways and a Dubai-based aircraft leasing firm each cancelled its

---

[1] *Sources:* Lunsford, J. Lynn. 2009. Dubai firm cancels 16 of Boeing's Dreamliners. *Wall Street Journal*, February 5; Matlack, Carol. 2009. More Boeing 787 woes as Quantas drops order. *BusinessWeek*, June 26; Sanders, Peter. 2009. At Boeing, Dreamliner fix turns up new glitch. *Wall Street Journal*, November 13; West, Karen. 2009. Boeing has much to prove with 787. *MSNBC.com*, December 16; Wilhelm, Steve. 2009. Boeing engineers seek credit for fixing goofs. *Puget Sound Business Journal*, August 17.

orders for 15 airplanes, which cost Boeing at least $4.5 billion. The company also took a $2.5 billion charge in 2009 related to development costs on the Dreamliner program.

Like Boeing, companies are increasingly focused on improving the quality of, and reducing defects in, their products, services, and activities. A rate of defects regarded as normal in the past is no longer tolerable. In this chapter, we focus on three types of costs that arise as a result of defects—spoilage, rework, and scrap—and ways to account for them. We also describe how to determine (1) cost of products, (2) cost of goods sold, and (3) inventory values when spoilage, rework, and scrap occur.

Defining Spoilage, Rework and Scrap

While the terms used in this chapter may seem familiar, be sure you understand them in the context of management accounting.

Spoilage is units of production—whether fully or partially completed—that do not meet the specifications required by customers for good units and that are discarded or sold at reduced prices. Some examples of spoilage are defective shirts, jeans, shoes, and carpeting sold as "seconds," or defective aluminum cans sold to aluminum manufacturers for remelting to produce other aluminum products.

Rework is units of production that do not meet the specifications required by customers but that are subsequently repaired and sold as good finished units. For example, defective units of products (such as pagers, computers, and telephones) detected during or after the production process but before units are shipped to customers can sometimes be reworked and sold as good products.

Scrap is residual material that results from manufacturing a product. Examples are short lengths from woodworking operations, edges from plastic molding operations, and frayed cloth and end cuts from suit-making operations. Scrap can sometimes be sold for relatively small amounts. In that sense, scrap is similar to byproducts, which we studied in Chapter 16. The difference is that scrap arises as a residual from the manufacturing process, and is not a product targeted for manufacture or sale by the firm.

Some amounts of spoilage, rework, or scrap are inherent in many production processes. For example, semiconductor manufacturing is so complex and delicate that some spoiled units are commonly produced; usually, the spoiled units cannot be reworked. In the manufacture of high-precision machine tools, spoiled units can be reworked to meet standards, but only at a considerable cost. And in the mining industry, companies process ore that contains varying amounts of valuable metals and rock. Some amount of rock, which is scrap, is inevitable.

Learning Objective 1

Understand the definitions of spoilage,

. . . unacceptable units of production

rework,

. . . unacceptable units of production subsequently repaired

and scrap

. . . leftover material

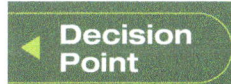

Decision Point

What are spoilage, rework, and scrap?

Learning Objective 2

Identify the differences between normal spoilage

. . . spoilage inherent in an efficient production process

and abnormal spoilage

. . . spoilage that would not arise under efficient operation

Two Types of Spoilage

Accounting for spoilage aims to determine the magnitude of spoilage costs and to distinguish between costs of normal and abnormal spoilage.[2] To manage, control, and reduce spoilage costs, companies need to highlight them, not bury them as an unidentified part of the costs of good units manufactured.

To illustrate normal and abnormal spoilage, consider Mendoza Plastics, which makes casings for the iMac computer using plastic injection molding. In January 2012, Mendoza incurs costs of $615,000 to produce 20,500 units. Of these 20,500 units, 20,000 are good units and 500 are spoiled units. Mendoza has no beginning inventory and no ending inventory that month. Of the 500 spoiled units, 400 units are spoiled because the injection molding machines are unable to manufacture good casings 100% of the time. That is, these units are spoiled even though the machines were run carefully and efficiently. The remaining 100 units are spoiled because of machine breakdowns and operator errors.

Normal Spoilage

Normal spoilage is spoilage inherent in a particular production process. In particular, it arises even when the process is operated in an efficient manner. The costs of normal spoilage are typically included as a component of the costs of good units manufactured, because good units cannot be made without also making some units that are spoiled. There is a tradeoff between the speed of production and the normal spoilage rate. Management makes a conscious decision about how many units to produce per hour with the understanding that, at the rate decided on, a certain level of spoilage is almost unavoidable. For this reason, the cost of normal spoilage is included in the cost of the good units completed. At Mendoza Plastics, the 400 units spoiled because of the limitations of injection molding machines and despite efficient operating conditions are considered normal spoilage. The calculations are as follows:

Manufacturing cost per unit, $615,000 ÷ 20,500 units = $30	
Manufacturing costs of good units alone, $30 per unit × 20,000 units	$600,000
Normal spoilage costs, $30 per unit × 400 units	12,000
Manufacturing costs of good units completed (includes normal spoilage)	$612,000

$$\text{Manufacturing cost per good unit} = \frac{\$612,000}{20,000 \text{ units}} = \$30.60$$

Because normal spoilage is the spoilage related to the good units produced, normal spoilage rates are computed by dividing units of normal spoilage by total *good units completed*, not total *actual units started* in production. At Mendoza Plastics, the normal spoilage rate is therefore computed as 400 ÷ 20,000 = 2%.

Abnormal Spoilage

Abnormal spoilage is spoilage that is not inherent in a particular production process and would not arise under efficient operating conditions. If a firm has 100% good units as its goal, then any spoilage would be considered abnormal. At Mendoza, the 100 units spoiled due to machine breakdowns and operator errors are abnormal spoilage. Abnormal spoilage is usually regarded as avoidable and controllable. Line operators and other plant personnel generally can decrease or eliminate abnormal spoilage by identifying the reasons for machine breakdowns, operator errors, etc., and by taking steps to prevent their recurrence. To highlight the effect of abnormal spoilage costs, companies calculate the units of abnormal spoilage and record the cost in the Loss from Abnormal Spoilage account, which appears as a separate line item in the income statement. At Mendoza, the loss from abnormal spoilage is $3,000 ($30 per unit × 100 units).

Issues about accounting for spoilage arise in both process-costing and job-costing systems. We discuss both instances next, beginning with spoilage in process-costing.

Decision Point ▶

What is the distinction between normal and abnormal spoilage?

---

[2] The helpful suggestions of Samuel Laimon, University of Saskatchewan, are gratefully acknowledged.

Spoilage in Process Costing Using Weighted-Average and FIFO

How do process-costing systems account for spoiled units? We have already said that units of abnormal spoilage should be counted and recorded separately in a Loss from Abnormal Spoilage account. But what about units of normal spoilage? The correct method is to count these units when computing output units—physical or equivalent—in a process-costing system. The following example and discussion illustrate this approach.

Learning Objective 3

Account for spoilage in process costing using the weighted-average method

. . . spoilage cost based on total costs and equivalent units completed to date

and the first-in, first-out (FIFO) method

. . . spoilage cost based on costs of current period and equivalent units of work done in current period

Count All Spoilage

Example 1: Chipmakers, Inc., manufactures computer chips for television sets. All direct materials are added at the beginning of the production process. To highlight issues that arise with normal spoilage, we assume no beginning inventory and focus only on direct material costs. The following data are available for May 2012.

	Home Insert Page Layout Formulas Data Review View		
	A	B	C
1		Physical Units	Direct Materials
2	Work in process, beginning inventory (May 1)	0	
3	Started during May	10,000	
4	Good units completed and transferred out during May	5,000	
5	Units spoiled (all normal spoilage)	1,000	
6	Work in process, ending inventory (May 31)	4,000	
7	Direct material costs added in May		$270,000

Spoilage is detected upon completion of the process and has zero net disposal value.

An **inspection point** is the stage of the production process at which products are examined to determine whether they are acceptable or unacceptable units. Spoilage is typically assumed to occur at the stage of completion where inspection takes place. As a result, the spoiled units in our example are assumed to be 100% complete with respect to direct materials.

Exhibit 18-1 calculates and assigns cost per unit of direct materials. Overall, Chipmakers generated 10,000 equivalent units of output: 5,000 equivalent units in good units completed (5,000 physical units × 100%), 4,000 units in ending work in process

	Home Insert Page Layout Formulas Data Review View	
	A	B
1		Approach Counting Spoiled Units When Computing Output in Equivalent Units
2	Costs to account for	$270,000
3	Divide by equivalent units of output	÷ 10,000
4	Cost per equivalent unit of output	$ 27
5	Assignment of costs:	
6	Good units completed (5,000 units × $27 per unit)	$135,000
7	Add normal spoilage (1,000 units × $27 per unit)	27,000
8	Total costs of good units completed and transferred out	162,000
9	Work in process, ending (4,000 units × $27 per unit)	108,000
10	Costs accounted for	$270,000

Exhibit 18-1

Effect of Recognizing Equivalent Units in Spoilage for Direct Material Costs for Chipmakers, Inc., for May 2012

(4,000 physical units × 100%), and 1,000 equivalent units in normal spoilage (1,000 physical units × 100%). Given total direct material costs of $270,000 in May, this yields an equivalent-unit cost of $27. The total cost of good units completed and transferred out, which includes the cost of normal spoilage, is then $162,000 (6,000 equivalent units × $27), while the ending work in process is assigned a cost of $108,000 (4,000 equivalent units × $27).

There are two noteworthy features of this approach. First, the 4,000 units in ending work in process are not assigned any of the costs of normal spoilage. This is appropriate because the units have not yet been inspected. While the units in ending work in process undoubtedly include some that will be detected as spoiled when inspected, these units will only be identified when the units are completed in the subsequent accounting period. At that time, costs of normal spoilage will be assigned to the good units completed in that period. Second, the approach used in Exhibit 18-1 delineates the cost of normal spoilage as $27,000. By highlighting the magnitude of this cost, the approach helps to focus management's attention on the potential economic benefits of reducing spoilage.

Five-Step Procedure for Process Costing with Spoilage

Example 2: Anzio Company manufactures a recycling container in its forming department. Direct materials are added at the beginning of the production process. Conversion costs are added evenly during the production process. Some units of this product are spoiled as a result of defects, which are detectable only upon inspection of finished units. Normally, spoiled units are 10% of the finished output of good units. That is, for every 10 good units produced, there is 1 unit of normal spoilage. Summary data for July 2012 are as follows:

	Physical Units (1)	Direct Materials (2)	Conversion Costs (3)	Total Costs (4) = (2) + (3)
Work in process, beginning inventory (July 1)	1,500	$12,000	$ 9,000	$ 21,000
Degree of completion of beginning work in process		100%	60%	
Started during July	8,500			
Good units completed and transferred out during July	7,000			
Work in process, ending inventory (July 31)	2,000			
Degree of completion of ending work in process		100%	50%	
Total costs added during July		$76,500	$89,100	$165,600
Normal spoilage as a percentage of good units	10%			
Degree of completion of normal spoilage		100%	100%	
Degree of completion of abnormal spoilage		100%	100%	

The five-step procedure for process costing used in Chapter 17 needs only slight modification to accommodate spoilage.

Step 1: Summarize the Flow of Physical Units of Output. Identify the number of units of both normal and abnormal spoilage.

$$\text{Total Spoilage} = \left(\begin{array}{c}\text{Units in beginning} \\ \text{work-in-process inventory}\end{array} + \begin{array}{c}\text{Units} \\ \text{started}\end{array}\right) - \left(\begin{array}{c}\text{Good units} \\ \text{completed and} + \\ \text{transferred out}\end{array} \begin{array}{c}\text{Units in ending} \\ \text{work-in-process inventory}\end{array}\right)$$

$$= (1,500 + 8,500) - (7,000 + 2,000)$$
$$= 10,000 - 9,000$$
$$= 1,000 \text{ units}$$

Recall that normal spoilage is 10% of good output at Anzio Company. Therefore, normal spoilage = 10% of the 7,000 units of *good* output = 700 units.

$$\text{Abnormal spoilage} = \text{Total spoilage} - \text{Normal spoilage}$$

$$= 1{,}000 \text{ units} - 700 \text{ units}$$

$$= 300 \text{ units}$$

Step 2: Compute Output in Terms of Equivalent Units. Compute equivalent units for spoilage in the same way we compute equivalent units for good units. As illustrated previously, all spoiled units are included in the computation of output units. Because Anzio's inspection point is at the completion of production, the same amount of work will have been done on each spoiled and each completed good unit.

Step 3: Summarize Total Costs to Account For. The total costs to account for are all the costs debited to Work in Process. The details for this step are similar to Step 3 in Chapter 17.

Step 4: Compute Cost per Equivalent Unit. This step is similar to Step 4 in Chapter 17.

Step 5: Assign Total Costs to Units Completed, to Spoiled Units, and to Units in Ending Work in Process. This step now includes computation of the cost of spoiled units and the cost of good units.

We illustrate these five steps of process costing for the weighted-average and FIFO methods next. *The standard-costing method is illustrated in the appendix to this chapter.*

Weighted-Average Method and Spoilage

Exhibit 18-2, Panel A, presents Steps 1 and 2 to calculate equivalent units of work done to date and includes calculations of equivalent units of normal and abnormal spoilage. Exhibit 18-2, Panel B, presents Steps 3, 4, and 5 (together called the production-cost worksheet).

Step 3 summarizes total costs to account for. Step 4 presents cost-per-equivalent-unit calculations using the weighted-average method. Note how, for each cost category, costs of beginning work in process and costs of work done in the current period are totaled and divided by equivalent units of all work done to date to calculate the weighted-average cost per equivalent unit. Step 5 assigns total costs to completed units, normal and abnormal spoiled units, and ending inventory by multiplying the equivalent units calculated in Step 2 by the cost per equivalent unit calculated in Step 4. Also note that the $13,825 costs of normal spoilage are added to the costs of the related good units completed and transferred out.

$$\begin{array}{c}\text{Cost per good unit} \\ \text{completed and transferred} \\ \text{out of the process}\end{array} = \frac{\text{Total costs transferred out (including normal spoilage)}}{\text{Number of good units produced}}$$

$$= \$152{,}075 \div 7{,}000 \text{ good units} = \$21.725 \text{ per good unit}$$

This amount is not equal to $19.75 per good unit, the sum of the $8.85 cost per equivalent unit of direct materials plus the $10.90 cost per equivalent unit of conversion costs. That's because the cost per good unit equals the sum of the direct material and conversion costs per equivalent unit, $19.75, plus a share of normal spoilage, $1.975 ($13,825 ÷ 7,000 good units), for a total of $21.725 per good unit. The $5,925 costs of abnormal spoilage are charged to the Loss from Abnormal Spoilage account and do not appear in the costs of good units.[3]

FIFO Method and Spoilage

Exhibit 18-3, Panel A, presents Steps 1 and 2 using the FIFO method, which focuses on equivalent units of work done in the current period. Exhibit 18-3, Panel B, presents Steps 3, 4, and 5. Note how when assigning costs, the FIFO method keeps the costs of

---

[3] The actual costs of spoilage (and rework) are often greater than the costs recorded in the accounting system because the opportunity costs of disruption of the production line, storage, and lost contribution margins are not recorded in accounting systems. Chapter 19 discusses these opportunity costs from the perspective of cost management.

Exhibit 18-2	Weighted-Average Method of Process Costing with Spoilage for Forming Department of the Anzio Company for July 2012

PANEL A: Steps 1 and 2—Summarize Output in Physical Units and Compute Equivalent Units

	A	B	C	D	E
			(Step 1)	(Step 2)	
1				Equivalent Units	
2					
3		**Flow of Production**	**Physical Units**	**Direct Materials**	**Conversion Costs**
4		Work in process, beginning (given, p. 648)	1,500		
5		Started during current period (given, p. 648)	8,500		
6		To account for	10,000		
7		Good units completed and transferred out during current period	7,000	7,000	7,000
8		Normal spoilage[a]	700		
9		(700 × 100%; 700 × 100%)		700	700
10		Abnormal spoilage[b]	300		
11		(300 × 100%; 300 × 100%)		300	300
12		Work in process, ending[c] (given, p. 648)	2,000		
13		(2,000 × 100%; 2,000 × 50%)		2,000	1,000
14		Accounted for	10,000		
15		Equivalent units of work done to date		10,000	9,000
16					
17		[a]Normal spoilage is 10% of good units transferred out: 10% × 7,000 = 700 units. Degree of completion of normal spoilage			
18		in this department: direct materials, 100%; conversion costs, 100%.			
19		[b]Abnormal spoilage = Total spoilage – Normal spoilage = 1,000 – 700 = 300 units. Degree of completion of abnormal spoilage			
20		in this department: direct materials, 100%; conversion costs, 100%.			
21		[c]Degree of completion in this department: direct materials, 100%; conversion costs, 50%.			

PANEL B: Steps 3, 4, and 5—Summarize Total Costs to Account For, Compute Cost per Equivalent Unit, and Assign Total Costs to Units Completed, to Spoiled Units, and to Units in Ending Work Process

			Total Production Costs	**Direct Materials**	**Conversion Costs**
23					
24	(Step 3)	Work in process, beginning (given, p. 648)	$ 21,000	$12,000	$ 9,000
25		Costs added in current period (given, p. 648)	165,600	76,500	89,100
26		Total costs to account for	$186,600	$88,500	$98,100
27	(Step 4)	Costs incurred to date		$88,500	$98,100
28		Divide by equivalent units of work done to date (Panel A)		÷10,000	÷ 9,000
29		Cost per equivalent unit		$ 8.85	$ 10.90
30	(Step 5)	Assignment of costs:			
31		Good units completed and transferred out (7,000 units)			
32		Costs before adding normal spoilage	$138,250	(7,000[d] × $8.85) +	(7,000[d] × $10.90)
33		Normal spoilage (700 units)	13,825	(700[d] × $8.85) +	(700[d] × $10.90)
34	(A)	Total costs of good units completed and transferred out	152,075		
35	(B)	Abnormal spoilage (300 units)	5,925	(300[d] × $8.85) +	(300[d] × $10.90)
36	(C)	Work in process, ending (2,000 units)	28,600	(2,000[d] × $8.85) +	(1,000[d] × $10.90)
37	(A)+(B)+(C)	Total costs accounted for	$186,600	$88,500 +	$98,100
38					
39		[d]Equivalent units of direct materials and conversion costs calculated in Step 2 in Panel A.			

PANEL A: Steps 1 and 2—Summarize Output in Physical Units and Compute Equivalent Units

Exhibit 18-3

First-In, First-Out (FIFO) Method of Process Costing with Spoilage for Forming Department of the Anzio Company for July 2012

		(Step 1)	(Step 2)	
			Equivalent Units	
	Flow of Production	**Physical Units**	**Direct Materials**	**Conversion Costs**
	Work in process, beginning (given, p. 648)	1,500		
	Started during current period (given, p. 648)	8,500		
	To account for	10,000		
	Good units completed and transferred out during current period:			
	From beginning work in process[a]	1,500		
	[1,500 × (100% − 100%); 1,500 × (100% − 60%)]		0	600
	Started and completed	5,500[b]		
	(5,500 × 100%; 5,500 × 100%)		5,500	5,500
	Normal spoilage[c]	700		
	(700 × 100%; 700 × 100%)		700	700
	Abnormal spoilage[d]	300		
	(300 × 100%; 300 × 100%)		300	300
	Work in process, ending[e] (given, p. 648)	2,000		
	(2,000 × 100%; 2,000 × 50%)		2,000	1,000
	Accounted for	10,000		
	Equivalent units of work done in current period		8,500	8,100

[a]Degree of completion in this department: direct materials, 100%; conversion costs, 60%.
[b]7,000 physical units completed and transferred out minus 1,500 physical units completed and transferred out from beginning work-in-process inventory.
[c]Normal spoilage is 10% of good units transferred out: 10% × 7,000 = 700 units. Degree of completion of normal spoilage in this department: direct materials, 100%; conversion costs, 100%.
[d]Abnormal spoilage = Actual spoilage − Normal spoilage = 1,000 − 700 = 300 units. Degree of completion of abnormal spoilage in this department: direct materials, 100%; conversion costs, 100%.
[e]Degree of completion in this department: direct materials, 100%; conversion costs, 50%.

PANEL B: Steps 3, 4, and 5—Summarize Total Costs to Account for, Compute Cost per Equivalent Unit, and Assign Total Costs to Units Completed, to Spoiled Units, and to Units in Ending Work in Process

		Total Production Costs	**Direct Materials**	**Conversion Costs**
(Step 3)	Work in process, beginning (given, p. 648)	$ 21,000	$12,000	$ 9,000
	Costs added in current period (given, p. 648)	165,600	76,500	89,100
	Total costs to account for	$186,600	$88,500	$98,100
(Step 4)	Costs added in current period		$76,500	$89,100
	Divide by equivalent units of work done in current period (Panel A)		÷ 8,500	÷ 8,100
	Cost per equivalent unit		$ 9.00	$ 11.00
(Step 5)	Assignment of costs:			
	Good units completed and transferred out (7,000 units)			
	Work in process, beginning (1,500 units)	$ 21,000	$12,000 +	$9,000
	Costs added to beginning work in process in current period	6,600	(0[f] × $9) +	(600[f] × $11)
	Total from beginning inventory before normal spoilage	27,600		
	Started and completed before normal spoilage (5,500 units)	110,000	(5,500[f] × $9) +	(5,500[f] × $11)
	Normal spoilage (700 units)	14,000	(700[f] × $9) +	(700[f] × $11)
(A)	Total costs of good units completed and transferred out	151,600		
(B)	Abnormal spoilage (300 units)	6,000	(300[f] × $9) +	(300[f] × $11)
(C)	Work in process, ending (2,000 units)	29,000	(2,000[f] × $9) +	(1,000[f] × $11)
(A)+(B)+(C)	Total costs accounted for	$186,600	$88,500 +	$98,100

[f]Equivalent units of direct materials and conversion costs calculated in Step 2 in Panel A.

the beginning work in process separate and distinct from the costs of work done in the current period. All spoilage costs are assumed to be related to units completed during this period, using the unit costs of the current period.[4]

Journal Entries

The information from Panel B in Exhibits 18-2 and 18-3 supports the following journal entries to transfer good units completed to finished goods and to recognize the loss from abnormal spoilage.

	Weighted Average		FIFO	
Finished Goods	152,075		151,600	
Work in Process—Forming		152,075		151,600
To record transfer of good units completed in July.				
Loss from Abnormal Spoilage	5,925		6,000	
Work in Process—Forming		5,925		6,000
To record abnormal spoilage detected in July.				

Inspection Points and Allocating Costs of Normal Spoilage

Our Anzio Company example assumes inspection occurs upon completion of the units. Although spoilage is typically detected only at one or more inspection points, it might actually occur at various stages of a production process. The cost of spoiled units is assumed to equal all costs incurred in producing spoiled units up to the point of inspection. When spoiled goods have a disposal value (for example, carpeting sold as "seconds"), the net cost of spoilage is computed by deducting the disposal value from the costs of the spoiled goods that have been accumulated up to the inspection point.

The unit costs of normal and abnormal spoilage are the same when the two are detected at the same inspection point. However, situations may arise when abnormal spoilage is detected at a different point from normal spoilage. Consider shirt manufacturing. Normal spoilage in the form of defective shirts is identified upon inspection at the end of the production process. Now suppose a faulty machine causes many defective shirts to be produced at the halfway point of the production process. These defective shirts are abnormal spoilage and occur at a different point in the production process from normal spoilage. In such cases, the unit cost of abnormal spoilage, which is based on costs incurred up to the halfway point of the production process, differs from the unit cost of normal spoilage, which is based on costs incurred through the end of the production process.

Costs of abnormal spoilage are separately accounted for as losses of the accounting period in which they are detected. However, recall that normal spoilage costs are added to the costs of good units, which raises an additional issue: Should normal spoilage costs be allocated between completed units and ending work-in-process inventory? *The common approach is to presume that normal spoilage occurs at the inspection point in the production cycle and to allocate its cost over all units that have passed that point during the accounting period.*

In the Anzio Company example, spoilage is assumed to occur when units are inspected at the end of the production process, so no costs of normal spoilage are allocated to ending work in process. If the units in ending work in process have passed the inspection point, however, the costs of normal spoilage are allocated to units in ending work in process as well as to completed units. For example, if the inspection point is at the halfway point of production, then any ending work in process that is at least 50% complete would be allocated a full measure of normal spoilage costs, and those spoilage costs would be calculated on the basis of all costs incurred up to the inspection point. If ending work in process is less than 50% complete, however, no normal spoilage costs would be allocated to it.

To better understand these issues, let us now assume that inspection at Anzio Company occurs at various stages in the production process. How does this affect the

---

[4] To simplify calculations under FIFO, spoiled units are accounted for as if they were started in the current period. Although some of the beginning work in process probably did spoil, all spoilage is treated as if it came from current production.

amount of normal and abnormal spoilage? As before, consider the forming department, and recall that direct materials are added at the start of production, while conversion costs are added evenly during the process.

Consider three different cases: Inspection occurs at (1) the 20%, (2) the 55%, or (3) the 100% completion stage. The last option is the one we have analyzed so far (see Exhibit 18-2). Assume that normal spoilage is 10% of the good units passing inspection. A total of 1,000 units are spoiled in all three cases. Normal spoilage is computed on the basis of the number of *good units* that pass the inspection point *during the current period*. The following data are for July 2012. Note how the number of units of normal and abnormal spoilage changes, depending on when inspection occurs.

	Home Insert Page Layout Formulas Data Review View			
	A	B	C	D
1		Physical Units: Stage of Completion at Which Inspection Occurs		
2	**Flow of Production**	20%	55%	100%
3	Work in process, beginning[a]	1,500	1,500	1,500
4	Started during July	8,500	8,500	8,500
5	To account for	10,000	10,000	10,000
6	Good units completed and transferred out			
7	(10,000 – 1,000 spoiled – 2,000 ending)	7,000	7,000	7,000
8	Normal spoilage	750[c]	550[d]	700[e]
9	Abnormal spoilage (1,000 – normal spoilage)	250	450	300
10	Work in process, ending[b]	2,000	2,000	2,000
11	Accounted for	10,000	10,000	10,000
12				
13	[a]Degree of completion in this department: direct materials, 100%; conversion costs, 60%.			
14	[b]Degree of completion in this department: direct materials, 100%; conversion costs, 50%.			
15	[c]10% × (8,500 units started – 1,000 units spoiled), because only the units started passed the 20% completion			
16	inspection point in the current period. Beginning work in process is excluded from this calculation because,			
17	being 60% complete at the start of the period, it passed the inspection point in the previous period.			
18	[d]10% × (8,500 units started – 1,000 units spoiled – 2,000 units in ending work in process). Both beginning and			
19	ending work in process are excluded since neither was inspected this period.			
20	[e]10% × 7,000, because 7,000 units are fully completed and inspected in the current period.			

The following diagram shows the flow of physical units for July and illustrates the normal spoilage numbers in the table. Note that 7,000 good units are completed and transferred out—1,500 from beginning work in process and 5,500 started and completed during the period—while 2,000 units are in ending work in process.

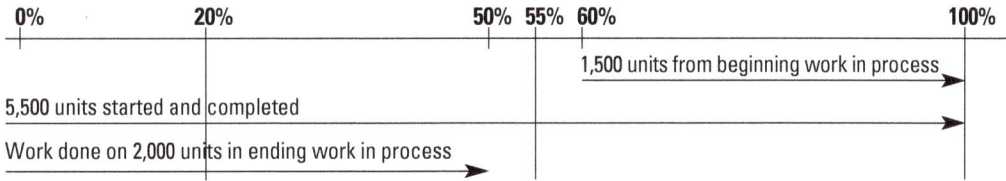

To see the number of units passing each inspection point, consider in the diagram the vertical lines at the 20%, 55%, and 100% inspection points. Note that the vertical line at 20% crosses two horizontal lines—5,500 good units started and completed and 2,000 units in ending work in process—for a total of 7,500 good units. (The 20% vertical line does not cross the line representing work done on the 1,500 good units completed from beginning work in process, because these units are already 60% complete at the start of the period and, hence, are not inspected this period.) Normal spoilage equals 10% of 7,500 = 750 units. On the other hand, the vertical line at the 55% point crosses just the second horizontal line, indicating that only 5,500 good units pass this point. Normal spoilage in this case is 10% of 5,500 = 550 units. At the 100% point, normal spoilage = 10% of 7,000 (1,500 + 5,500) good units = 700 units.

Exhibit 18-4 shows the computation of equivalent units under the weighted-average method, assuming inspection at the 20% completion stage. The calculations depend on the direct materials and conversion costs incurred to get the units to this inspection point. The spoiled units have a full measure of direct materials and a 20% measure of conversion costs. Calculations of costs per equivalent unit and the assignment of total costs to units completed and to ending work in process are similar to calculations in previous illustrations in this chapter. Because ending work in process has passed the inspection point, these units bear normal spoilage costs, just like the units that have been completed and transferred out. For example, conversion costs for units completed and transferred out include conversion costs for 7,000 good units produced plus 20% × (10% × 5,500) = 110 equivalent units of normal spoilage. *We multiply by 20% to obtain equivalent units of normal spoilage because conversion costs are only 20% complete at the inspection point.* Conversion costs of ending work in process include conversion costs of 50% of 2,000 = 1,000 equivalent good units plus 20% × (10% × 2,000) = 40 equivalent units of normal spoilage. Thus, the equivalent units of normal spoilage accounted for are 110 equivalent units related to units completed and transferred out plus 40 equivalent units related to units in ending work in process, for a total of 150 equivalent units, as shown in Exhibit 18-4.

Early inspections can help prevent any further direct materials and conversion costs being wasted on units that are already spoiled. For example, if inspection can occur when units are 70% (rather than 100%) complete as to conversion costs and spoilage occurs prior to the 70% point, a company can avoid incurring the final 30% of conversion costs on the spoiled units. The downside to conducting inspections at too early a stage is that spoilage that happens at later stages of the process may go undetected. It is for these reasons that firms often conduct multiple inspections and also empower workers to identify and resolve defects on a timely basis.

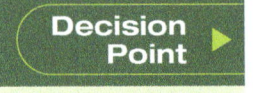

Decision Point

How does inspection at various stages of completion affect the amount of normal and abnormal spoilage?

Exhibit 18-4

Computing Equivalent Units with Spoilage Using Weighted-Average Method of Process Costing with Inspection at 20% of Completion for Forming Department of Anzio Company for July 2012

	A	B	C	D
		(Step 1)	**(Step 2)**	
2			**Equivalent Units**	
3	**Flow of Production**	**Physical Units**	**Direct Materials**	**Conversion Costs**
4	Work in process, beginning[a]	1,500		
5	Started during current period	8,500		
6	To account for	10,000		
7	Good units completed and transferred out:	7,000	7,000	7,000
8	Normal spoilage	750		
9	(750 × 100%; 750 × 20%)		750	150
10	Abnormal spoilage	250		
11	(250 × 100%; 250 × 20%)		250	50
12	Work in process, ending[b]	2,000		
13	(2,000 × 100%; 2,000 × 50%)		2,000	1,000
14	Accounted for	10,000		
15	Equivalent units of work done to date		10,000	8,200
16				
17	[a]Degree of completion: direct materials, 100%; conversion costs, 60%.			
18	[b]Degree of completion: direct materials, 100%; conversion costs, 50%.			

Job Costing and Spoilage

The concepts of normal and abnormal spoilage also apply to job-costing systems. Abnormal spoilage is separately identified so companies can work to eliminate it altogether. Costs of abnormal spoilage are not considered to be inventoriable costs and are written off as costs of the accounting period in which the abnormal spoilage is detected. Normal spoilage costs in job-costing systems—as in process-costing systems—are inventoriable costs, although increasingly companies are tolerating only small amounts of spoilage as normal. When assigning costs, job-costing systems generally distinguish *normal spoilage attributable to a specific job from normal spoilage common to all jobs.*

We describe accounting for spoilage in job costing using the following example.

> Example 3: In the Hull Machine Shop, 5 aircraft parts out of a job lot of 50 aircraft parts are spoiled. Costs assigned prior to the inspection point are $2,000 per part. When the spoilage is detected, the spoiled goods are inventoried at $600 per part, the net disposal value.

Our presentation here and in subsequent sections focuses on how the $2,000 cost per part is accounted for.

Learning Objective 5

Account for spoilage in job costing

. . . normal spoilage assigned directly or indirectly to job; abnormal spoilage written off as a loss of the period

Normal Spoilage Attributable to a Specific Job

When normal spoilage occurs because of the specifications of a particular job, that job bears the cost of the spoilage minus the disposal value of the spoilage. The journal entry to recognize disposal value (items in parentheses indicate subsidiary ledger postings) is as follows:

Materials Control (spoiled goods at current net disposal value): 5 units × $600 per unit	3,000	
Work-in-Process Control (specific job): 5 units × $600 per unit		3,000

Note, the Work-in-Process Control (specific job) has already been debited (charged) $10,000 for the spoiled parts (5 spoiled parts × $2,000 per part). The net cost of normal spoilage = $7,000 ($10,000 − $3,000), which is an additional cost of the 45 (50 − 5) good units produced. Therefore, total cost of the 45 good units is $97,000: $90,000 (45 units × $2,000 per unit) incurred to produce the good units plus the $7,000 net cost of normal spoilage. Cost per good unit is $2,155.56 ($97,000 ÷ 45 good units).

Normal Spoilage Common to All Jobs

In some cases, spoilage may be considered a normal characteristic of the production process. The spoilage inherent in production will, of course, occur when a specific job is being worked on. But the spoilage is not attributable to, and hence is not charged directly to, the specific job. Instead, the spoilage is allocated indirectly to the job as manufacturing overhead because the spoilage is common to all jobs. The journal entry is as follows:

Materials Control (spoiled goods at current disposal value): 5 units × $600 per unit	3,000	
Manufacturing Overhead Control (normal spoilage): ($10,000 − $3,000)	7,000	
Work-in-Process Control (specific job): 5 units × $2,000 per unit		10,000

When normal spoilage is common to all jobs, the budgeted manufacturing overhead rate includes a provision for normal spoilage cost. Normal spoilage cost is spread, through overhead allocation, over all jobs rather than allocated to a specific job.[5] For example, if Hull produced 140 good units from all jobs in a given month, the $7,000 of normal spoilage overhead costs would be allocated at the rate of $50 per good unit ($7,000 ÷ 140 good units). Normal spoilage overhead costs allocated to the 45 good units in the job would be $2,250 ($50 × 45 good units). Total cost of the 45 good units is $92,250: $90,000 (45 units × $2,000 per unit) incurred to produce the good units plus $2,250 of normal spoilage overhead costs. Cost per good unit is $2,050 ($92,250 ÷ 45 good units).

---

[5] Note that costs already assigned to products are charged back to Manufacturing Overhead Control, which generally accumulates only costs incurred, not both costs incurred and costs already assigned.

Abnormal Spoilage

If the spoilage is abnormal, the net loss is charged to the Loss from Abnormal Spoilage account. Unlike normal spoilage costs, abnormal spoilage costs are not included as a part of the cost of good units produced. Total cost of the 45 good units is $90,000 (45 units × $2,000 per unit). Cost per good unit is $2,000 ($90,000 ÷ 45 good units).

Materials Control (spoiled goods at current disposal value): 5 units × $600 per unit	3,000	
Loss from Abnormal Spoilage ($10,000 − $3,000)	7,000	
Work-in-Process Control (specific job): 5 units × $2,000 per unit		10,000

Even though, for external reporting purposes, abnormal spoilage costs are written off in the accounting period and are not linked to specific jobs or units, companies often identify the particular reasons for abnormal spoilage, and, when appropriate, link abnormal spoilage with specific jobs or units for cost management purposes.

Job Costing and Rework

Rework is units of production that are inspected, determined to be unacceptable, repaired, and sold as acceptable finished goods. We again distinguish (1) normal rework attributable to a specific job, (2) normal rework common to all jobs, and (3) abnormal rework.

Consider the Hull Machine Shop data in Example 3 on page 655. Assume the five spoiled parts are reworked. The journal entry for the $10,000 of total costs (the details of these costs are assumed) assigned to the five spoiled units before considering rework costs is as follows:

Work-in-Process Control (specific job)	10,000	
Materials Control		4,000
Wages Payable Control		4,000
Manufacturing Overhead Allocated		2,000

Assume the rework costs equal $3,800 (comprising $800 direct materials, $2,000 direct manufacturing labor, and $1,000 manufacturing overhead).

Normal Rework Attributable to a Specific Job

If the rework is normal but occurs because of the requirements of a specific job, the rework costs are charged to that job. The journal entry is as follows:

Work-in-Process Control (specific job)	3,800	
Materials Control		800
Wages Payable Control		2,000
Manufacturing Overhead Allocated		1,000

Normal Rework Common to All Jobs

When rework is normal and not attributable to a specific job, the costs of rework are charged to manufacturing overhead and are spread, through overhead allocation, over all jobs.

Manufacturing Overhead Control (rework costs)	3,800	
Materials Control		800
Wages Payable Control		2,000
Manufacturing Overhead Allocated		1,000

Abnormal Rework

If the rework is abnormal, it is recorded by charging abnormal rework to a loss account.

Loss from Abnormal Rework	3,800	
Materials Control		800
Wages Payable Control		2,000
Manufacturing Overhead Allocated		1,000

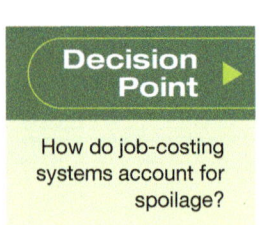

Decision Point

How do job-costing systems account for spoilage?

Learning Objective 6

Account for rework in job costing

... normal rework assigned directly or indirectly to job; abnormal rework written off as a loss of the period

Accounting for rework in a process-costing system also requires abnormal rework to be distinguished from normal rework. Process costing accounts for abnormal rework in the same way as job costing. Accounting for normal rework follows the accounting described for normal rework common to all jobs (units) because masses of identical or similar units are being manufactured.

Costing rework focuses managers' attention on the resources wasted on activities that would not have to be undertaken if the product had been made correctly. The cost of rework prompts managers to seek ways to reduce rework, for example, by designing new products or processes, training workers, or investing in new machines. To eliminate rework and to simplify the accounting, some companies set a standard of zero rework. All rework is then treated as abnormal and is written off as a cost of the current period.

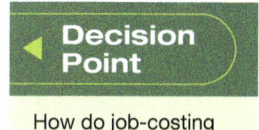

Decision Point

How do job-costing systems account for rework?

Accounting for Scrap

Scrap is residual material that results from manufacturing a product; it has low total sales value compared with the total sales value of the product. No distinction is made between normal and abnormal scrap because no cost is assigned to scrap. The only distinction made is between scrap attributable to a specific job and scrap common to all jobs.

There are two aspects of accounting for scrap:

1. Planning and control, including physical tracking
2. Inventory costing, including when and how scrap affects operating income

Learning Objective 7

Account for scrap

. . . reduces cost of job either at time of sale or at time of production

Initial entries to scrap records are commonly expressed in physical terms. In various industries, companies quantify items such as stamped-out metal sheets or edges of molded plastic parts by weighing, counting, or some other measure. Scrap records not only help measure efficiency, but also help keep track of scrap, and so reduce the chances of theft. Companies use scrap records to prepare periodic summaries of the amounts of actual scrap compared with budgeted or standard amounts. Scrap is either sold or disposed of quickly or it is stored for later sale, disposal, or reuse.

Careful tracking of scrap often extends into the accounting records. Many companies maintain a distinct account for scrap costs somewhere in their accounting system. The issues here are similar to the issues in Chapter 16 regarding the accounting for byproducts:

- When should the value of scrap be recognized in the accounting records—at the time scrap is produced or at the time scrap is sold?
- How should revenues from scrap be accounted for?

To illustrate, we extend our Hull example. Assume the manufacture of aircraft parts generates scrap and that the scrap from a job has a net sales value of $900.

Recognizing Scrap at the Time of Its Sale

When the dollar amount of scrap is immaterial, the simplest accounting is to record the physical quantity of scrap returned to the storeroom and to regard scrap sales as a separate line item in the income statement. In this case, the only journal entry is as follows:

Sale of scrap:	Cash or Accounts Receivable	900	
	Scrap Revenues		900

When the dollar amount of scrap is material and the scrap is sold quickly after it is produced, the accounting depends on whether the scrap is attributable to a specific job or is common to all jobs.

Scrap Attributable to a Specific Job

Job-costing systems sometimes trace scrap revenues to the jobs that yielded the scrap. This method is used only when the tracing can be done in an economically feasible way. For example, the Hull Machine Shop and its customers, such as the U.S. Department of Defense, may reach an agreement that provides for charging specific jobs with all rework or spoilage costs and then crediting these jobs with all scrap revenues that arise from the jobs. The journal entry is as follows:

Scrap returned to storeroom:	No journal entry. [Notation of quantity received and related job entered in the inventory record]		
Sale of scrap:	Cash or Accounts Receivable	900	
	Work-in-Process Control		900
	Posting made to specific job cost record.		

Unlike spoilage and rework, there is no cost assigned to the scrap, so no distinction is made between normal and abnormal scrap. All scrap revenues, whatever the amount, are credited to the specific job. Scrap revenues reduce the costs of the job.

Scrap common to all jobs

The journal entry in this case is as follows:

Scrap returned to storeroom:	No journal entry. [Notation of quantity received and related job entered in the inventory record]		
Sale of scrap:	Cash or Accounts Receivable	900	
	Manufacturing Overhead Control		900
	Posting made to subsidiary ledger—"Sales of Scrap" column on department cost record.		

Scrap is not linked with any particular job or product. Instead, all products bear production costs without any credit for scrap revenues except in an indirect manner: Expected scrap revenues are considered when setting the budgeted manufacturing overhead rate. Thus, the budgeted overhead rate is lower than it would be if the overhead budget had not been reduced by expected scrap revenues. This method of accounting for scrap is also used in process costing when the dollar amount of scrap is immaterial, because the scrap in process costing is common to the manufacture of all the identical or similar units produced (and cannot be identified with specific units).

Recognizing Scrap at the Time of Its Production

Our preceding illustrations assume that scrap returned to the storeroom is sold quickly, so it is not assigned an inventory cost figure. Sometimes, as in the case with edges of molded plastic parts, the value of scrap is not immaterial, and the time between storing it and selling or reusing it can be long and unpredictable. In these situations, the company assigns an inventory cost to scrap at a conservative estimate of its net realizable value so that production costs and related scrap revenues are recognized in the same accounting period. Some companies tend to delay sales of scrap until its market price is considered attractive. Volatile price fluctuations are typical for scrap metal. In these cases, it's not easy to determine some "reasonable inventory value."

Scrap Attributable to a Specific Job

The journal entry in the Hull example is as follows:

Scrap returned to storeroom:	Materials Control	900	
	Work-in-Process Control		900

Scrap Common to All Jobs

The journal entry in this case is as follows:

Scrap returned to storeroom:	Materials Control	900	
	Manufacturing Overhead Control		900

Observe that the Materials Control account is debited in place of Cash or Accounts Receivable. When the scrap is sold, the journal entry is as follows:

Sale of scrap:	Cash or Accounts Receivable	900	
	Materials Control		900

Concepts in Action | Managing Waste and Environmental Costs at KB Home

KB Home is one of the largest home builders in the United States. In recent years, public awareness of environmental issues and interest in environmentally-friendly products and services has led to increased demand for sustainable home construction. KB Home has responded by increasing the sustainability of its homebuilding operations, which includes reducing its waste and environmental costs.

Through its "My Home. My Earth." program, launched in 2007, KB Home has established environmental sustainability as top-priority management issue. It developed core principles to guide its efforts including using "innovation and our process-driven approach to reduce waste and natural resource usage throughout our organization." Much of that focus involves reducing scrap, the residual materials that result from its homebuilding processes. These materials pose additional problems for companies like KB Home, because many federal and state environmental laws dictate that scrap materials be deposed of in an environmentally friendly way; therefore, they add to the cost of generating waste.

To reduce these costs during the homebuilding process, all new homes are built with pre-engineered roof trusses, while 90% also use preconstructed panels. These preconstructed materials are cut offsite for greater precision, which reduces wood waste. Further, these precut materials are made of engineered wood products, which reduce the use of long solid boards that require larger trees to be cut. Beyond scrap reduction, these trusses and panels also eliminate the need for costly job-site rework, or the repair of defective materials during construction.

Similarly, all new homes use oriented strand board, which is made from wood chip rather than plywood. Wood chip is both cheaper and more environmentally sustainable than traditional construction materials. These sustainable practices helped KB Home reduce the cost, exclusive of land, of each home manufactured in 2009 by nearly 39% over the previous year, while increasing profit margins by 13% despite the broader U.S. housing market collapse.

Beyond the construction process, KB Home also includes earth-friendly standard features in all of its homes, at no cost to homebuyers, including energy-efficient windows, recyclable carpets, programmable thermostats, and faucets that reduce water usage. Beyond cutting costs, KB Home's efforts to effectively manage waste and environmental costs have helped the company partially stabilize revenues in a difficult real-estate market. Chief executive Jeffrey Mazger said, "Less than 2% of customers a few years ago were asking about energy-efficient options. Since we introduced 'My Home. My Earth.' in April 2007, it's gone up to 75%." This has helped KB Home differentiate itself within a very competitive market for homebuilders.

Sources: KB Home. 2010. 2009 annual report. Los Angeles: KB Home; KB Home. 2010. 2009 sustainability report. Los Angeles: KB Home; Tischler, Linda. 2008. The green housing boom. *Fast Company*, June 23.

Scrap is sometimes reused as direct material rather than sold as scrap. In this case, Materials Control is debited at its estimated net realizable value and then credited when the scrap is reused. For example, the entries when the scrap is common to all jobs are as follows:

Scrap returned to storeroom:	Materials Control	900	
	Manufacturing Overhead Control		900
Reuse of scrap:	Work-in-Process Control	900	
	Materials Control		900

Accounting for scrap under process costing is similar to accounting under job costing when scrap is common to all jobs. That's because the scrap in process costing is common to the manufacture of masses of identical or similar units.

Managers focus their attention on ways to reduce scrap and to use it more profitably, especially when the cost of scrap is high (see Concepts in Action on p. 659). For example, General Motors has redesigned its plastic injection molding processes to reduce the scrap plastic that must be broken away from its molded products. General Motors also regrinds and reuses the plastic scrap as direct material, saving substantial input costs.

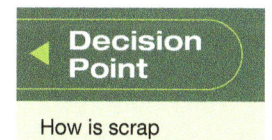

◄ **Decision Point**

How is scrap accounted for?

Problem for Self-Study

Burlington Textiles has some spoiled goods that had an assigned cost of $40,000 and zero net disposal value.

Required Prepare a journal entry for each of the following conditions under (a) process costing (department A) and (b) job costing:
1. Abnormal spoilage of $40,000
2. Normal spoilage of $40,000 regarded as common to all operations
3. Normal spoilage of $40,000 regarded as attributable to specifications of a particular job

Solution

	(a) Process Costing			(b) Job Costing		
1.	Loss from Abnormal Spoilage	40,000		Loss from Abnormal Spoilage	40,000	
	Work in Process—Dept. A		40,000	Work-in-Process Control		40,000
				(specific job)		
2.	No entry until units are completed			Manufacturing Overhead Control	40,000	
	and transferred out. Then the normal			Work-in-Process Control		40,000
	spoilage costs are transferred as			(specific job)		
	part of the cost of good units.					
	Work in Process—Dept. B	40,000				
	Work in Process—Dept. A		40,000			
3.	Not applicable			No entry. Normal spoilage cost		
				remains in		
				Work-in-Process Control		
				(specific job)		

Decision Points

The following question-and-answer format summarizes the chapter's learning objectives. Each decision presents a key question related to a learning objective. The guidelines are the answer to that question.

Decision	Guidelines
1. What are spoilage, rework, and scrap?	Spoilage is units of production that do not meet the specifications required by customers for good units and that are discarded or sold at reduced prices. Spoilage is generally divided into normal spoilage, which is inherent to a particular production process, and abnormal spoilage, which arises because of inefficiency in operations. Rework is unacceptable units that are subsequently repaired and sold as acceptable finished goods. Scrap is residual material that results from manufacturing a product; it has low total sales value compared with the total sales value of the product.
2. What is the distinction between normal and abnormal spoilage?	Normal spoilage is inherent in a particular production process and arises when the process is operated in an efficient manner. Abnormal spoilage on the other hand is not inherent in a particular production process and would not arise under efficient operating conditions. Abnormal spoilage is usually regarded as avoidable and controllable.
3. How do the weighted-average and FIFO methods of process costing calculate the costs of good units and spoilage?	The weighted-average method combines costs in beginning inventory with costs of the current period when determining the costs of good units, which include normal spoilage, and the costs of abnormal spoilage, which are written off as a loss of the accounting period.

The FIFO method keeps separate the costs in beginning inventory from the costs of the current period when determining the costs of good units (which include normal spoilage) and the costs of abnormal spoilage, which are written off as a loss of the accounting period.

4. How does inspection at various stages of completion affect the amount of normal and abnormal spoilage?

The cost of spoiled units is assumed to equal all costs incurred in producing spoiled units up to the point of inspection. Spoilage costs therefore vary based on different inspection points.

5. How do job-costing systems account for spoilage?

Normal spoilage specific to a job is assigned to that job, or when common to all jobs, is allocated as part of manufacturing overhead. Cost of abnormal spoilage is written off as a loss of the accounting period.

6. How do job-costing systems account for rework?

Completed reworked units should be indistinguishable from non-reworked good units. Normal rework specific to a job is assigned to that job, or when common to all jobs, is allocated as part of manufacturing overhead. Cost of abnormal rework is written off as a loss of the accounting period.

7. How is scrap accounted for?

Scrap is recognized in the accounting records either at the time of its sale or at the time of its production. Sale of scrap, if immaterial, is often recognized as other revenue. If not immaterial, sale of scrap or its net realizable value reduces the cost of a specific job or, when common to all jobs, reduces Manufacturing Overhead Control.

Appendix

Standard-Costing Method and Spoilage

The standard-costing method simplifies the computations for normal and abnormal spoilage. To illustrate, we return to the Anzio Company example in the chapter. Suppose Anzio develops the following standard costs per unit for work done in the forming department in July 2012:

Direct materials	$ 8.50
Conversion costs	10.50
Total manufacturing cost	$19.00

Assume the same standard costs per unit also apply to the beginning inventory: 1,500 (1,500 × 100%) equivalent units of direct materials and 900 (1,500 × 60%) equivalent units of conversion costs. Hence, the beginning inventory at standard costs is as follows:

Direct materials, 1,500 units × $8.50 per unit	$12,750
Conversion costs, 900 units × $10.50 per unit	9,450
Total manufacturing costs	$22,200

Exhibit 18-5, Panel A, presents Steps 1 and 2 for calculating physical and equivalent units. These steps are the same as for the FIFO method described in Exhibit 18-3. Exhibit 18-5, Panel B, presents Steps 3, 4, and 5.

The costs to account for in Step 3 are at standard costs and, hence, they differ from the costs to account for under the weighted-average and FIFO methods, which are at actual costs. In Step 4, cost per equivalent unit is simply the standard cost: $8.50 per unit for direct materials and $10.50 per unit for conversion costs. The standard-costing method makes calculating equivalent-unit costs unnecessary, so it simplifies process costing. Step 5 assigns standard costs to units completed (including normal spoilage), to abnormal spoilage, and to ending work-in-process inventory by multiplying the equivalent units calculated in Step 2 by the standard costs per equivalent unit presented in Step 4. Variances can then be measured and analyzed in the manner described in the appendix to Chapter 17 (pp. 634–635).[6]

---

[6] For example, from Exhibit 18-5, Panel B, the standard costs for July are direct materials used, 8,500 × $8.50 = $72,250, and conversion costs, 8,100 × $10.50 = $85,050. From page 648, the actual costs added during July are direct materials, $76,500, and conversion costs, $89,100, resulting in a direct materials variance of $72,250 – $76,500 = $4,250 U and a conversion costs variance of $85,050 – $89,100 = $4,050 U. These variances could then be subdivided further as in Chapters 7 and 8; the abnormal spoilage would be part of the efficiency variance.

Exhibit 18-5	Standard-Costing Method of Process Costing with Spoilage for Forming Department of the Anzio Company for July 2012

PANEL A: Steps 1 and 2—Summarize Output in Physical Units and Compute Equivalent Units

	A	B	C	D	E
			(Step 1)	**(Step 2)**	
1				Equivalent Units	
2					
3		**Flow of Production**	**Physical Units**	**Direct Materials**	**Conversion Costs**
4		Work in process, beginning (given, p. 648)	1,500		
5		Started during current period (given, p. 648)	8,500		
6		To account for	10,000		
7		Good units completed and transferred out during current period:			
8		From beginning work in process[a]	1,500		
9		[1,500 × (100% −100%); 1,500 × (100% −60%)]		0	600
10		Started and completed	5,500[b]		
11		(5,500 × 100%; 5,500 × 100%)		5,500	5,500
12		Normal spoilage[c]	700		
13		(700 × 100%; 700 × 100%)		700	700
14		Abnormal spoilage[d]	300		
15		(300 × 100%; 300 × 100%)		300	300
16		Work in process, ending[e] (given, p. 648)	2,000		
17		(2,000 × 100%; 2,000 × 50%)		2,000	1,000
18		Accounted for	10,000		
19		Equivalent units of work done in current period		8,500	8,100
20					
21	[a]Degree of completion in this department: direct materials, 100%; conversion costs, 60%.				
22	[b]7,000 physical units completed and transferred out minus 1,500 physical units completed and transferred out from beginning				
23	work-in-process inventory.				
24	[c]Normal spoilage is 10% of good units transferred out: 10% × 7,000 = 700 units. Degree of completion of normal spoilage in this				
25	department: direct materials, 100%; conversion costs, 100%.				
26	[d]Abnormal spoilage = Actual spoilage − Normal spoilage = 1,000 − 700 = 300 units. Degree of completion of abnormal spoilage in this				
27	department: direct materials, 100%; conversion costs, 100%.				
28	[e]Degree of completion in this department: direct materials, 100%; conversion costs, 50%.				

PANEL B: Steps 3, 4, and 5—Summarize Total Costs to Account for, Compute Cost per Equivalent Unit, and Assign Total Costs to Units Completed, to Spoiled Units, and to Units in Ending Work in Process

	A	B	C	D	E
30			**Total Production Costs**	**Direct Materials**	**Conversion Costs**
31	(Step 3)	Work in process, beginning (given, p. 661)	$ 22,200	(1,500 × $8.50)	(900 × $10.50)
32		Costs added in current period at standard prices	157,300	(8,500 × $8.50)	(8,100 × $10.50)
33		Total costs to account for	$179,500	$85,000	$94,500
34	(Step 4)	Standard costs per equivalent unit (given, p. 661)	$ 19.00	$ 8.50	$ 10.50
35	(Step 5)	Assignment of costs at standard costs:			
36		Good units completed and transferred out (7,000 units)			
37		Work in process, beginning (1,500 units)	$ 22,200	(1,500 × $8.50) +	(900 × $10.50)
38		Costs added to beginning work in process in current period	6,300	(0[f] × $8.50) +	(600[f] × $10.50)
39		Total from beginning inventory before normal spoilage	28,500		
40		Started and completed before normal spoilage (5,500 units)	104,500	(5,500[f] × $8.50) +	(5,500[f] × $10.50)
41		Normal spoilage (700 units)	13,300	(700[f] × $8.50) +	(700[f] × $10.50)
42	(A)	Total costs of good units completed and transferred out	146,300		
43	(B)	Abnormal spoilage (300 units)	5,700	(300[f] × $8.50) +	(300[f] × $10.50)
44	(C)	Work in process, ending (2,000 units)	27,500	(2,000[f] × $8.50) +	(1,000[f] × $10.50)
45	(A)+(B)+(C)	Total costs accounted for	$179,500	$85,000 +	$94,500
46					
47	[f]Equivalent units of direct materials and conversion costs calculated in Step 2 in Panel A.				

Finally, note that the journal entries corresponding to the amounts calculated in Step 5 are as follows:

Finished Goods	146,300	
Work in Process—Forming		146,300
To record transfer of good units completed in July.		
Loss from Abnormal Spoilage	5,700	
Work in Process—Forming		5,700
To record abnormal spoilage detected in July.		

Terms to Learn

This chapter and the Glossary at the end of the book contain definitions of the following important terms:

abnormal spoilage (**p. 646**)   normal spoilage (**p. 646**)   scrap (**p. 645**)

inspection point (**p. 647**)   rework (**p. 645**)   spoilage (**p. 645**)

Assignment Material

Questions

18-1 Why is there an unmistakable trend in manufacturing to improve quality?

18-2 Distinguish among spoilage, rework, and scrap.

18-3 "Normal spoilage is planned spoilage." Discuss.

18-4 "Costs of abnormal spoilage are losses." Explain.

18-5 "What has been regarded as normal spoilage in the past is not necessarily acceptable as normal spoilage in the present or future." Explain.

18-6 "Units of abnormal spoilage are inferred rather than identified." Explain.

18-7 "In accounting for spoiled units, we are dealing with cost assignment rather than cost incurrence." Explain.

18-8 "Total input includes abnormal as well as normal spoilage and is, therefore, inappropriate as a basis for computing normal spoilage." Do you agree? Explain.

18-9 "The inspection point is the key to the allocation of spoilage costs." Do you agree? Explain.

18-10 "The unit cost of normal spoilage is the same as the unit cost of abnormal spoilage." Do you agree? Explain.

18-11 "In job costing, the costs of normal spoilage that occur while a specific job is being done are charged to the specific job." Do you agree? Explain.

18-12 "The costs of rework are always charged to the specific jobs in which the defects were originally discovered." Do you agree? Explain.

18-13 "Abnormal rework costs should be charged to a loss account, not to manufacturing overhead." Do you agree? Explain.

18-14 When is a company justified in inventorying scrap?

18-15 How do managers use information about scrap?

Exercises

18-16 Normal and abnormal spoilage in units. The following data, in physical units, describe a grinding process for January:

Work in process, beginning	19,000
Started during current period	150,000
To account for	169,000
Spoiled units	12,000
Good units completed and transferred out	132,000
Work in process, ending	25,000
Accounted for	169,000

Inspection occurs at the 100% completion stage. Normal spoilage is 5% of the good units passing inspection.

1. Compute the normal and abnormal spoilage in units.

2. Assume that the equivalent-unit cost of a spoiled unit is $10. Compute the amount of potential savings if all spoilage were eliminated, assuming that all other costs would be unaffected. Comment on your answer.

Required

18-17 Weighted-average method, spoilage, equivalent units. (CMA, adapted) Consider the following data for November 2012 from Gray Manufacturing Company, which makes silk pennants and uses a process-costing system. All direct materials are added at the beginning of the process, and conversion costs are added evenly during the process. Spoilage is detected upon inspection at the completion of the process. Spoiled units are disposed of at zero net disposal value. Gray Manufacturing Company uses the weighted-average method of process costing.

	Physical Units (Pennants)	Direct Materials	Conversion Costs
Work in process, November 1[a]	1,000	$ 1,423	$ 1,110
Started in November 2012	?		
Good units completed and transferred out during November 2012	9,000		
Normal spoilage	100		
Abnormal spoilage	50		
Work in process, November 30[b]	2,000		
Total costs added during November 2012		$12,180	$27,750

[a]Degree of completion: direct materials, 100%; conversion costs, 50%.
[b]Degree of completion: direct materials, 100%; conversion costs, 30%.

Required Compute equivalent units for direct materials and conversion costs. Show physical units in the first column of your schedule.

18-18 Weighted-average method, assigning costs (continuation of 18-17).

Required For the data in Exercise 18-17, summarize total costs to account for; calculate the cost per equivalent unit for direct materials and conversion costs; and assign total costs to units completed and transferred out (including normal spoilage), to abnormal spoilage, and to units in ending work in process.

18-19 FIFO method, spoilage, equivalent units. Refer to the information in Exercise 18-17. Suppose Gray Manufacturing Company uses the FIFO method of process costing instead of the weighted-average method.

Required Compute equivalent units for direct materials and conversion costs. Show physical units in the first column of your schedule.

18-20 FIFO method, assigning costs (continuation of 18-19).

Required For the data in Exercise 18-17, use the FIFO method to summarize total costs to account for; calculate the cost per equivalent unit for direct materials and conversion costs; and assign total costs to units completed and transferred out (including normal spoilage), to abnormal spoilage, and to units in ending work in process.

18-21 Weighted-average method, spoilage. Appleton Company makes wooden toys in its forming department, and it uses the weighted-average method of process costing. All direct materials are added at the beginning of the process, and conversion costs are added evenly during the process. Spoiled units are detected upon inspection at the end of the process and are disposed of at zero net disposal value. Summary data for August 2012 are as follows:

	A	B	C	D
		Physical Units	Direct Materials	Conversion Costs
1				
2	Work in process, beginning inventory (August 1)	2,000	$17,700	$10,900
3	Degree of completion of beginning work in process		100%	50%
4	Started during August	10,000		
5	Good units completed and transferred out during August	9,000		
6	Work in process, ending inventory (August 31)	1,800		
7	Degree of completion of ending work in process		100%	75%
8	Total costs added during August		$81,300	$93,000
9	Normal spoilage as a percentage of good units	10%		
10	Degree of completion of normal spoilage		100%	100%
11	Degree of completion of abnormal spoilage		100%	100%

1. For each cost category, calculate equivalent units. Show physical units in the first column of your schedule.
2. Summarize total costs to account for; calculate cost per equivalent unit for each cost category; and assign total costs to units completed and transferred out (including normal spoilage), to abnormal spoilage, and to units in ending work in process.

18-22 Standard costing method, spoilage, journal entries. Jordan, Inc., is a manufacturer of vents for water heaters. The company uses a process-costing system to account for its work-in-process inventories. When Job 512 was being processed in the machining department, a piece of sheet metal was off center in the bending machine and two vents were spoiled. Because this problem occurs periodically, it is considered normal spoilage and is consequently recorded as an overhead cost. Because this step comes first in the procedure for making the vents, the only costs incurred were $475 for direct materials. Assume the sheet metal cannot be sold, and its cost has been recorded in work-in-process inventory.

Prepare the journal entries to record the spoilage incurred.

18-23 Recognition of loss from spoilage. Arokia Electronics manufactures cell phone models in its Walnut Creek plant. Suppose the company provides you with the following information regarding operations for September 2011:

Total cell phones manufactured	8,000
Phones rejected as spoiled units	300
Total manufacturing cost	$320,000

Assume the spoiled units have no disposal value.

1. What is the unit cost of making the 8,000 cell phones?
2. What is the total cost of the 300 spoiled units?
3. If the spoilage is considered normal, what is the increase in the unit cost of good phones manufactured as a result of the spoilage?
4. If the spoilage is considered abnormal, prepare the journal entries for the spoilage incurred.

18-24 Weighted-average method, spoilage. Chipcity is a fast-growing manufacturer of computer chips. Direct materials are added at the start of the production process. Conversion costs are added evenly during the process. Some units of this product are spoiled as a result of defects not detectable before inspection of finished goods. Spoiled units are disposed of at zero net disposal value. Chipcity uses the weighted-average method of process costing.

Summary data for September 2011 are as follows:

	A	B Physical Units (Computer Chips)	C Direct Materials	D Conversion Costs
2	Work in process, beginning inventory (September 1)	600	$ 96,000	$ 15,300
3	Degree of completion of beginning work in process		100%	30%
4	Started during September	2,550		
5	Good units completed and transferred out during September	2,100		
6	Work in process, ending inventory (September 30)	450		
7	Degree of completion of ending work in process		100%	40%
8	Total costs added during September		$567,000	$230,400
9	Normal spoilage as a percentage of good units	15%		
10	Degree of completion of normal spoilage		100%	100%
11	Degree of completion of abnormal spoilage		100%	100%

1. For each cost category, compute equivalent units. Show physical units in the first column of your schedule.
2. Summarize total costs to account for; calculate cost per equivalent unit for each cost category; and assign total costs to units completed and transferred out (including normal spoilage), to abnormal spoilage, and to units in ending work in process.

18-25 FIFO method, spoilage. Refer to the information in Exercise 18-24.

Do Exercise 18-24 using the FIFO method of process costing.

18-26 Standard-costing method, spoilage. Refer to the information in Exercise 18-24. Suppose Chipcity determines standard costs of $200 per equivalent unit for direct materials and $75 per equivalent unit for conversion costs for both beginning work in process and work done in the current period.

Do Exercise 18-24 using the standard-costing method.

18-27 Spoilage and job costing. (L. Bamber) Barrett Kitchens produces a variety of items in accordance with special job orders from hospitals, plant cafeterias, and university dormitories. An order for 2,100 cases of mixed vegetables costs $9 per case: direct materials, $4; direct manufacturing labor, $3; and manufacturing overhead allocated, $2. The manufacturing overhead rate includes a provision for normal spoilage. Consider each requirement independently.

1. Assume that a laborer dropped 420 cases. Suppose part of the 420 cases could be sold to a nearby prison for $420 cash. Prepare a journal entry to record this event. Calculate and explain briefly the unit cost of the remaining 1,680 cases.
2. Refer to the original data. Tasters at the company reject 420 of the 2,100 cases. The 420 cases are disposed of for $840. Assume that this rejection rate is considered normal. Prepare a journal entry to record this event, and do the following:
   a. Calculate the unit cost if the rejection is attributable to exacting specifications of this particular job.
   b. Calculate the unit cost if the rejection is characteristic of the production process and is not attributable to this specific job.
   c. Are unit costs the same in requirements 2a and 2b? Explain your reasoning briefly.
3. Refer to the original data. Tasters rejected 420 cases that had insufficient salt. The product can be placed in a vat, salt can be added, and the product can be reprocessed into jars. This operation, which is considered normal, will cost $420. Prepare a journal entry to record this event and do the following:
   a. Calculate the unit cost of all the cases if this additional cost was incurred because of the exacting specifications of this particular job.
   b. Calculate the unit cost of all the cases if this additional cost occurs regularly because of difficulty in seasoning.
   c. Are unit costs the same in requirements 3a and 3b? Explain your reasoning briefly.

18-28 Reworked units, costs of rework. White Goods assembles washing machines at its Auburn plant. In February 2012, 60 tumbler units that cost $44 each (from a new supplier who subsequently went bankrupt) were defective and had to be disposed of at zero net disposal value. White Goods was able to rework all 60 washing machines by substituting new tumbler units purchased from one of its existing suppliers. Each replacement tumbler cost $50.

1. What alternative approaches are there to account for the material cost of reworked units?
2. Should White Goods use the $44 tumbler or the $50 tumbler to calculate the cost of materials reworked? Explain.
3. What other costs might White Goods include in its analysis of the total costs of rework due to the tumbler units purchased from the (now) bankrupt supplier?

18-29 Scrap, job costing. The Morgan Company has an extensive job-costing facility that uses a variety of metals. Consider each requirement independently.

1. Job 372 uses a particular metal alloy that is not used for any other job. Assume that scrap is material in amount and sold for $520 quickly after it is produced. Prepare the journal entry.
2. The scrap from Job 372 consists of a metal used by many other jobs. No record is maintained of the scrap generated by individual jobs. Assume that scrap is accounted for at the time of its sale. Scrap totaling $4,400 is sold. Prepare two alternative journal entries that could be used to account for the sale of scrap.
3. Suppose the scrap generated in requirement 2 is returned to the storeroom for future use, and a journal entry is made to record the scrap. A month later, the scrap is reused as direct material on a subsequent job. Prepare the journal entries to record these transactions.

Problems

18-30 Weighted-average method, spoilage. The Boston Company is a food-processing company based in San Francisco. It operates under the weighted-average method of process costing and has two departments: cleaning and packaging. For the cleaning department, conversion costs are added evenly during the process, and direct materials are added at the beginning of the process. Spoiled units are detected upon inspection at the end of the process and are disposed of at zero net disposal value. All completed work is transferred to the packaging department. Summary data for May follow:

	Home	Insert	Page Layout	Formulas	Data	Review	View		

	A	B	C	D
1	The Boston Company: Cleaning Department	Physical Units	Direct Materials	Conversion Costs
2	Work in process, beginning inventory (May 1)	3,000	$ 4,500	$ 2,700
3	Degree of completion of beginning work in process		100%	60%
4	Started during May	25,000		
5	Good units completed and transferred out during May	20,500		
6	Work in process, ending inventory (May 31)	4,200		
7	Degree of completion of ending work in process		100%	30%
8	Total costs added during May		$46,250	$37,216
9	Normal spoilage as a percentage of good units	10%		
10	Degree of completion of normal spoilage		100%	100%
11	Degree of completion of abnormal spoilage		100%	100%

Required

For the cleaning department, summarize total costs to account for and assign total costs to units completed and transferred out (including normal spoilage), to abnormal spoilage, and to units in ending work in process. Carry unit-cost calculations to four decimal places when necessary. Calculate final totals to the nearest dollar. (Problem 18-32 explores additional facets of this problem.)

18-31 **FIFO method, spoilage.** Refer to the information in Problem 18-30.

Required

Do Problem 18-30 using the FIFO method of process costing. (Problem 18-33 explores additional facets of this problem.)

18-32 **Weighted-average method, packaging department (continuation of 18-30).** In Boston Company's packaging department, conversion costs are added evenly during the process, and direct materials are added at the end of the process. Spoiled units are detected upon inspection at the end of the process and are disposed of at zero net disposal value. All completed work is transferred to the next department. The transferred-in costs for May equal the total cost of good units completed and transferred out in May from the cleaning department, which were calculated in Problem 18-30 using the weighted-average method of process costing. Summary data for May follow.

	Home	Insert	Page Layout	Formulas	Data	Review	View			

	A	B	C	D	E
1	The Boston Company: Packaging Department	Physical Units	Transferred-In Costs	Direct Materials	Conversion Costs
2	Work in process, beginning inventory (May 1)	10,500	$39,460	$ 0	$14,700
3	Degree of completion of beginning work in process		100%	0%	70%
4	Started during May	20,500			
5	Good units completed and transferred out during May	22,000			
6	Work in process, ending inventory (May 31)	7,000			
7	Degree of completion of ending work in process		100%	0%	40%
8	Total costs added during May		?	$4,800	$38,900
9	Normal spoilage as a percentage of good units	8%			
10	Degree of completion of normal spoilage			100%	100%
11	Degree of completion of abnormal spoilage			100%	100%

Required

For the packaging department, use the weighted-average method to summarize total costs to account for and assign total costs to units completed and transferred out (including normal spoilage), to abnormal spoilage, and to units in ending work in process.

18-33 **FIFO method, packaging department (continuation of 18-31).** Refer to the information in Problem 18-32 except for the transferred-in costs for May, which equal the total cost of good units completed and transferred out in May from the cleaning department, which were calculated in Problem 18-31 using the FIFO method of process costing.

For the packaging department, use the FIFO method to summarize total costs to account for and assign total costs to units completed and transferred out (including normal spoilage), to abnormal spoilage, and to units in ending work in process.

18-34 Job-costing spoilage and scrap. MetalWorks, Inc., manufactures various metal parts in batches as ordered by customers, and accounts for them using job costing. Job 2346-8, a large job for customer X, incurred $240,000 of direct materials costs and $620,000 of direct labor costs. MetalWorks applies overhead at a rate of 150% of direct labor cost. MetalWorks quoted customer X a fixed price for the job of $2,000,000. The job consisted of 90,000 good units and 10,000 spoiled units with no rework or disposal value. The job also created 200 pounds of scrap which can be sold for $3 per pound.

1. Calculate the gross margin MetalWorks will earn for this job, assuming the scrap sale is treated as material, and
   a. all spoilage is considered abnormal.
   b. normal spoilage is 8% of good units.
   c. normal spoilage is 12% of good units.
2. How would your answer to number 1 differ if the scrap sale is treated as immaterial?

18-35 Spoilage in job costing. Crystal Clear Machine Shop is a manufacturer of motorized carts for vacation resorts.

Peter Cruz, the plant manager of Crystal Clear, obtains the following information for Job #10 in August 2010. A total of 32 units were started, and 7 spoiled units were detected and rejected at final inspection, yielding 25 good units. The spoiled units were considered to be normal spoilage. Costs assigned prior to the inspection point are $1,450 per unit. The current disposal price of the spoiled units is $230 per unit. When the spoilage is detected, the spoiled goods are inventoried at $230 per unit.

Required

1. What is the normal spoilage rate?
2. Prepare the journal entries to record the normal spoilage, assuming the following:
   a. The spoilage is related to a specific job.
   b. The spoilage is common to all jobs.
   c. The spoilage is considered to be abnormal spoilage.

18-36 Rework in job costing, journal entry (continuation of 18-35). Assume that the 7 spoiled units of Whitefish Machine Shop's Job #10 can be reworked for a total cost of $1,700. A total cost of $10,150 associated with these units has already been assigned to Job #10 before the rework.

Required Prepare the journal entries for the rework, assuming the following:

   a. The rework is related to a specific job.
   b. The rework is common to all jobs.
   c. The rework is considered to be abnormal.

18-37 Scrap at time of sale or at time of production, journal entries (continuation of 18-35). Assume that Job #10 of Crystal Clear Machine Shop generates normal scrap with a total sales value of $650 (it is assumed that the scrap returned to the storeroom is sold quickly).

Required Prepare the journal entries for the recognition of scrap, assuming the following:

   a. The value of scrap is immaterial and scrap is recognized at the time of sale.
   b. The value of scrap is material, is related to a specific job, and is recognized at the time of sale.
   c. The value of scrap is material, is common to all jobs, and is recognized at the time of sale.
   d. The value of scrap is material, and scrap is recognized as inventory at the time of production and is recorded at its net realizable value.

18-38 Physical units, inspection at various stages of completion. Fantastic Furniture manufactures plastic lawn furniture in a continuous process. The company pours molten plastic into molds and then cools the plastic. Materials are added at the beginning of the process, and conversion is considered uniform through the period. Occasionally, the plastic does not completely fill a mold because of air pockets, and the chair is then considered spoiled. Normal spoilage is 6% of the good units that pass inspection. The following information pertains to March, 2011:

Beginning inventory	1,400 units (100% complete for materials; 20% complete for conversion costs)
Units started	12,000
Units in ending work in process	1,100 (100% complete for materials; 70% complete for conversion costs)

Fantastic Furniture had 1,000 spoiled units in March, 2011.

Required Using the format on page 653, compute the normal and abnormal spoilage in units, assuming the inspection point is at (a) the 15% stage of completion, (b) the 40% stage of completion, and (c) the 100% stage of completion.

18-39 Weighted-average method, inspection at 80% completion. (A. Atkinson) The Kim Company is a furniture manufacturer with two departments: molding and finishing. The company uses the weighted-average method of process costing. In August, the following data were recorded for the finishing department:

Units of beginning work in process inventory	12,500
Percentage completion of beginning work in process units	25%
Cost of direct materials in beginning work in process	$0
Units started	87,500
Units completed	62,500
Units in ending inventory	25,000
Percentage completion of ending work in process units	95%
Spoiled units	12,500
Total costs added during current period:	
Direct materials	$819,000
Direct manufacturing labor	$794,500
Manufacturing overhead	$770,000
Work in process, beginning:	
Transferred-in costs	$103,625
Conversion costs	$52,500
Cost of units transferred in during current period	$809,375

Conversion costs are added evenly during the process. Direct material costs are added when production is 90% complete. The inspection point is at the 80% stage of production. Normal spoilage is 10% of all good units that pass inspection. Spoiled units are disposed of at zero net disposal value.

For August, summarize total costs to account for and assign these costs to units completed and transferred out (including normal spoilage), to abnormal spoilage, and to units in ending work in process.   **Required**

18-40 Job costing, rework. Riposte Corporation manufactures a computer chip called XD1. Manufacturing costs of one XD1 chip, excluding rework costs, are direct materials, $60; direct manufacturing labor, $12; and manufacturing overhead, $38. At the inspection point, defective units are sent back for rework. Rework costs per XD1 chip are direct materials, $12; direct manufacturing labor, $9; and manufacturing overhead, $15.

In August 2011, Riposte manufactured 1,000 XD1 chips, 80 of which required rework. Of these 80 chips, 50 were considered normal rework common to all jobs and the other 30 were considered abnormal rework.

1. Prepare journal entries to record the accounting for both the normal and abnormal rework.   **Required**
2. What were the total rework costs of XD1 chips in August 2011?
3. Now assume instead that the normal rework is attributable entirely to job #3879, for 200 units of XD1. In this case, what would be the total and unit cost of the good units produced for that job in August 2011? Prepare journal entries for the manufacture of the 200 units, as well as the normal rework costs.

Collaborative Learning Problem

18-41 Physical units, inspection at various levels of completion, weighted-average process costing report. Lester Company makes metal products and has a forging department. In this department, materials are added at the beginning of the process and conversion takes place uniformly. At the start of November 2011, the forging department had 20,000 units in beginning work in process, which are 100% complete for materials and 40% complete for conversion costs. An additional 100,000 units are started in the department in November, and 30,000 units remain in work in process at the end of the month. These unfinished units are 100% complete for materials and 70% complete for conversion costs.

The forging department had 15,000 spoiled units in November. Normal spoilage is 12% of good units. The department's costs for the month of November are as follows:

	Beginning WIP	Costs Incurred During Period
Direct materials costs	$ 64,000	$ 200,000
Conversion costs	102,500	1,000,000

1. Using the format on page 653, compute the normal and abnormal spoilage in units for November, assuming the inspection point is at (a) the 30% stage of completion, (b) the 60% stage of completion, and (c) the 100% stage of completion.   **Required**
2. Refer to your answer in requirement 1. Why are there different amounts of normal and abnormal spoilage at different inspection points?
3. Now assume that the forging department inspects at the 60% stage of completion. Using the weighted-average method, calculate the cost of units transferred out, the cost of abnormal spoilage, and the cost of ending inventory for the forging department in November.

▶ Learning Objectives

1. Explain the four cost categories in a costs-of-quality program

2. Develop nonfinancial measures and methods to improve quality

3. Combine financial and nonfinancial measures to make decisions and evaluate quality performance

4. Describe customer-response time and explain why delays happen and their costs

5. Explain how to manage bottlenecks

To satisfy ever-increasing customer expectations, managers need to find cost-effective ways to continuously improve the quality of their products and services and shorten response times.

This requires trading off the costs of achieving these improvements and the benefits from higher performance on these dimensions. When companies do not meet customer expectations, the losses can be substantial, as the following article about Toyota Motor Corporation shows.

Toyota Plans Changes After Millions of Defective Cars Are Recalled[1]

Toyota Motor Corporation, the Japanese automaker, built its reputation on manufacturing reliable cars. In 2002, Toyota executives set an ambitious goal to gain 15% of the global auto industry by 2010, meaning it would surpass General Motors as the world's largest carmaker. In the subsequent years, Toyota grew sales by 50% and managed to win bragging rights as the world's biggest car company. But the company's focus on rapid growth appears to have come at a cost to its reputation for quality.

Between November 2009 and January 2010, Toyota was forced to recall 9 million vehicles worldwide because gas pedals began to stick and were causing unwanted acceleration on eight Toyota models. After months of disagreements with government safety officials, the company ultimately recalled 12 models and suspended the production and sales of eight new Toyota and Lexus models, including its popular Camry and Corolla sedans. While most cars were quickly returned to the sales floor, some industry analysts estimated that the loss of revenue to Toyota could have been as much as $500 million each week.

Beyond lost revenue, Toyota's once-vaunted image took a serious hit. As the crisis unfolded, Toyota was slow to take responsibility for manufacturing problems. The company then faced the long and difficult task of restoring its credibility and assuring

[1] *Sources*: Kaufman, Wendy. 2010. Can Toyota recover its reputation for quality? Morning Edition, National Public Radio, February 9. http://www.npr.org/templates/story/story.php?storyId=123519027&ps=rs; Linebaugh, Kate and Norihiko Shirouzu. 2010. Toyota heir faces crisis at the wheel. *Wall Street Journal*, January 27. http://online.wsj.com/article/SB10001424052748704094304575029493222357402.html; Maynard, Micheline and Hiroko Tabuchi. 2010. Rapid growth has its perils, Toyota learns. *New York Times*, January 27. http://www.nytimes.com/2010/01/28/business/28toyota.html; Kageyama, Yuri. 2010. Toyota holds quality meeting to help repair reputation; promises quicker complaint response. *Associated Press*, March 29. http://abcnews.go.com/International/wireStory?id=10238266

owners and new-car shoppers that it had fixed the problems.

It established a quality committee led by Akio Toyoda, the company's chief executive; announced plans to add a brake override system to all new models; added four new quality training facilities; and promised faster decisions on future recall situations. "Listening to consumer voices is most important in regaining credibility from our customers," Mr. Toyoda said.

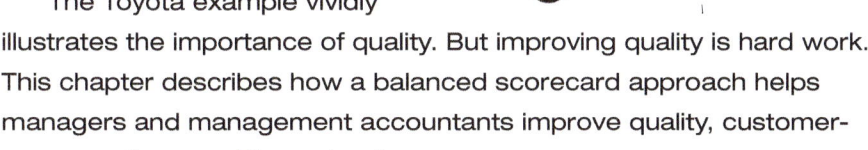

The Toyota example vividly illustrates the importance of quality. But improving quality is hard work. This chapter describes how a balanced scorecard approach helps managers and management accountants improve quality, customer-response time, and throughput.

This chapter covers three topics. The first topic addresses quality as a competitive tool, looking at quality from the financial perspective, the customer perspective, the internal business process perspective, and the learning-and-growth perspective before discussing the evaluation of quality performance. The second topic addresses time as a competitive tool and focuses on customer response time, on-time performance, time drivers, and the cost of time. The third topic looks closely at the theory of constraints and throughput-margin analysis, covering the management of bottlenecks and nonfinancial measures of time. The presentation is modular so you can omit a topic or explore it in any order.

Quality as a Competitive Tool

The American Society for Quality defines **quality** as the total features and characteristics of a product or a service made or performed according to specifications to satisfy customers at the time of purchase and during use. Many companies throughout the world—like Cisco Systems and Motorola in the United States and Canada, British Telecom in the United Kingdom, Fujitsu and Honda in Japan, Crysel in Mexico, and Samsung in South Korea—emphasize quality as an important strategic initiative. These companies have found that focusing on the quality of a product or service generally builds expertise in producing it, lowers the costs of providing it, creates higher satisfaction for customers using it, and generates higher future revenues for the company selling it. Several high-profile awards, such as the Malcolm Baldrige National Quality Award in the United States, the Deming Prize in Japan, and the Premio Nacional de Calidad in Mexico, are given to companies that have produced high-quality products and services.

International quality standards have also emerged. ISO 9000, developed by the International Organization for Standardization, is a set of five international standards for quality management adopted by more than 85 countries. ISO 9000 enables companies to effectively document and certify the elements of their production processes that lead to quality. To ensure that their suppliers deliver high-quality products at competitive costs, companies such as DuPont and General Electric require their suppliers to obtain ISO 9000 certification. Documenting evidence of quality through ISO 9000 has become a necessary condition for competing in the global marketplace.

As corporations' responsibilities toward the environment grow, managers are applying the quality management and measurement practices discussed in this chapter to find cost-effective ways to reduce the environmental and economic costs of air pollution, wastewater, oil spills, and hazardous waste disposal. An environmental management standard, ISO 14000, encourages organizations to pursue environmental goals vigorously by developing (1) environmental management systems to reduce environmental costs and (2) environmental auditing and performance-evaluation systems to review and provide feedback on environmental goals. Nowhere has the issue of quality and the environment come together in a bigger way than at the British Petroleum (BP) Deepwater Horizon oil rig in the Gulf of Mexico. An explosion on the oil-drilling platform in April of 2010 resulted in millions of gallons of oil spilling out in the Gulf, causing environmental damage over thousands of square miles and resulting in billions of dollars of clean up costs for BP.

We focus on two basic aspects of quality: design quality and conformance quality. **Design quality** refers to how closely the characteristics of a product or service meet the needs and wants of customers. **Conformance quality** is the performance of a product or service relative to its design and product specifications. Apple Inc. has built a reputation for design quality by developing many innovative products such as the iPod, iPhone, and iPad that have uniquely met customers' music, telephone, entertainment, and business needs. Apple's products have also had excellent conformance quality; the products did what they were supposed to do. In the case of the iPhone 4, however, many customers complained about very weak signal receptions on their phones. The enthusiastic customer response to the iPhone 4 when it was launched in the summer of 2010 indicates good design quality, as customers liked what the iPhone 4 had to offer. The problem with its antenna that caused signals not to be received is a problem of conformance quality, because the phone did not do what it was designed to do. The following diagram illustrates that actual performance can fall short of customer satisfaction because of design-quality failure and because of conformance-quality failure.

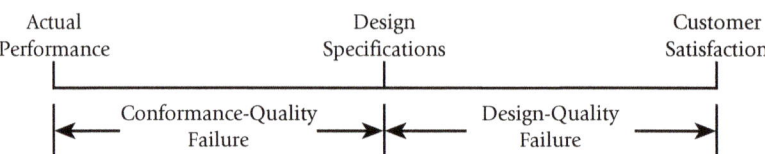

We illustrate the issues in managing quality—computing the costs of quality, identifying quality problems, and taking actions to improve quality—using Photon Corporation. While Photon makes many products, we will focus only on Photon's photocopying machines, which earned an operating income of $24 million on revenues of $300 million (from sales of 20,000 copiers) in 2011.

Quality has both financial and nonfinancial components relating to customer satisfaction, improving internal quality processes, reducing defects, and the training and empowering of workers. To provide some structure, we discuss quality from the four perspectives of the balanced scorecard: financial, customer, internal business process, and learning and growth.

Learning Objective **1**

Explain the four cost categories in a costs-of-quality program

. . . prevention, appraisal, internal failure, and external failure costs

The Financial Perspective: Costs of Quality

The financial perspective of Photon's balanced scorecard includes measures such as revenue growth and operating income, financial measures that are impacted by quality. The most direct financial measure of quality, however, is *costs of quality*. **Costs of quality (COQ)**

are the costs incurred to prevent, or the costs arising as a result of, the production of a low-quality product. Costs of quality are classified into four categories; examples for each category are listed in Exhibit 19-1.

1. **Prevention costs**—costs incurred to preclude the production of products that do not conform to specifications

2. **Appraisal costs**—costs incurred to detect which of the individual units of products do not conform to specifications

3. **Internal failure costs**—costs incurred on defective products *before* they are shipped to customers

4. **External failure costs**—costs incurred on defective products *after* they have been shipped to customers

The items in Exhibit 19-1 come from all business functions of the value chain, and they are broader than the internal failure costs of spoilage, rework, and scrap described in Chapter 18.

An important role for management accountants is preparing COQ reports for managers. Photon determines the COQ of its photocopying machines by adapting the seven-step activity-based costing approach described in Chapter 5.

Step 1: Identify the Chosen Cost Object. The cost object is the quality of the photocopying machine that Photon made and sold in 2011. Photon's goal is to calculate the total costs of quality of these 20,000 machines.

Step 2: Identify the Direct Costs of Quality of the Product. The photocopying machines have no direct costs of quality because there are no resources such as inspection or repair workers dedicated to managing the quality of the photocopying machines.

Step 3: Select the Activities and Cost-Allocation Bases to Use for Allocating Indirect Costs of Quality to the Product. Column 1 of Exhibit 19-2, Panel A, classifies the activities that result in prevention, appraisal, and internal and external failure costs of quality at Photon Corporation and the business functions of the value chain in which these costs occur. For example, the quality-inspection activity results in appraisal costs and occurs in the manufacturing function. Photon identifies the total number of inspection-hours (across all products) as the cost-allocation base for the inspection activity. (To avoid details not needed to explain the concepts here, we do not show the total quantities of each cost-allocation base.)

Step 4: Identify the Indirect Costs of Quality Associated with Each Cost-Allocation Base. These are the total costs (variable and fixed) incurred for each of the costs-of-quality activities, such as inspections, across all of Photon's products. (To avoid details not needed to understand the points described here, we do not present these total costs.)

Step 5: Compute the Rate per Unit of Each Cost-Allocation Base. For each activity, total costs (identified in Step 4) are divided by total quantity of the cost-allocation base (calculated in Step 3) to compute the rate per unit of each cost-allocation base. Column 2 of Exhibit 19-2, Panel A, shows these rates (without supporting calculations).

Prevention Costs	Appraisal Costs	Internal Failure Costs	External Failure Costs
Design engineering	Inspection	Spoilage	Customer support
Process engineering	Online product	Rework	Manufacturing/
Supplier evaluations	manufacturing	Scrap	process
Preventive equipment	and process	Machine repairs	engineering
maintenance	inspection	Manufacturing/	for external
Quality training	Product testing	process	failures
Testing of new		engineering on	Warranty repair
materials		internal failures	costs
			Liability claims

Exhibit 19-1

Items Pertaining to Costs-of-Quality Reports

Exhibit 19-2 Analysis of Activity-Based Costs of Quality (COQ) for Photocopying Machines at Photon Corporation

Home	Insert	Page Layout	Formulas	Data	Review	View

	A	B	C	D	E	F	G
1	**PANEL A: ACCOUNTING COQ REPORT**						**Percentage of**
2		**Cost Allocation**		**Quantity of Cost**		**Total**	**Revenues**
3	**Cost of Quality and Value-Chain Category**	**Rate**[a]		**Allocation Base**		**Costs**	**(5) = (4) ÷**
4	(1)	(2)		(3)		**(4) = (2) x (3)**	**$300,000,000**
5	*Prevention costs*						
6	Design engineering (R&D/Design)	$ 80	per hour	40,000	hours	$ 3,200,000	1.1%
7	Process engineering (R&D/Design)	$ 60	per hour	45,000	hours	2,700,000	0.9%
8	Total prevention costs					5,900,000	2.0%
9	*Appraisal costs*						
10	Inspection (Manufacturing)	$ 40	per hour	240,000	hours	9,600,000	3.2%
11	Total appraisal costs					9,600,000	3.2%
12	*Internal failure costs*						
13	Rework (Manufacturing)	$100	per hour	100,000	hours	10,000,000	3.3%
14	Total internal failure costs					10,000,000	3.3%
15	*External failure costs*						
16	Customer support (Marketing)	$ 50	per hour	12,000	hours	600,000	0.2%
17	Transportation (Distribution)	$240	per load	3,000	loads	720,000	0.2%
18	Warranty repair (Customer service)	$110	per hour	120,000	hours	13,200,000	4.4%
19	Total external failure costs					14,520,000	4.8%
20	Total costs of quality					$40,020,000	13.3%
21							
22	[a]Calculations not shown.						
23							
24	**PANEL B: OPPORTUNITY COST ANALYSIS**						
25						**Total Estimated**	**Percentage**
26						**Contribution**	**of Revenues**
27	**Cost of Quality Category**					**Margin Lost**	**(3) = (2) ÷**
28	(1)					(2)	**$300,000,000**
29	*External failure costs*						
30	Estimated forgone contribution margin						
31	and income on lost sales					$12,000,000[b]	4.0%
32	Total external failure costs					$12,000,000	4.0%
33							
34	[b]Calculated as total revenues minus all variable costs (whether output-unit, batch, product-sustaining, or facility-sustaining) on						
35	lost sales in 2011. If poor quality causes Photon to lose sales in subsequent years as well, the opportunity costs will be						
36	even greater.						

Step 6: Compute the Indirect Costs of Quality Allocated to the Product. The indirect costs of quality of the photocopying machines, shown in Exhibit 19-2, Panel A, column 4, equal the cost-allocation rate from Step 5 (column 2) multiplied by the total quantity of the cost-allocation base used by the photocopying machines for each activity (column 3). For example, inspection costs for assuring the quality of the photocopying machines are $9,600,000 ($40 per hour × 240,000 inspection-hours).

Step 7: Compute the Total Costs of Quality by Adding All Direct and Indirect Costs of Quality Assigned to the Product. Photon's total costs of quality in the COQ report for photocopying machines is $40.02 million (Exhibit 19-2, Panel A, column 4) or 13.3% of current revenues (column 5).

As we have seen in Chapter 11, opportunity costs are not recorded in financial accounting systems. Yet, a very significant component of costs of quality is the opportunity cost of the contribution margin and income forgone from lost sales, lost production, and lower prices resulting from poor design and conformance quality. Photon's market research department estimates that design and conformance quality problems experienced by some customers resulted in lost sales of 2,000 photocopying machines in 2011 and forgone contribution margin and operating income of $12 million (Exhibit 19-2, Panel B). Total costs of quality, including opportunity costs, equal $52.02 million ($40.02 million recorded in the accounting system and shown in Panel A + $12 million of opportunity costs shown in Panel B), or 17.3% of current revenues. Opportunity costs account for 23.1% ($12 million ÷ $52.02 million) of Photon's total costs of quality.

We turn next to the leading indicators of the costs of quality, the nonfinancial measures of customer satisfaction about the quality of Photon's photocopiers.

The Customer Perspective: Nonfinancial Measures of Customer Satisfaction

Similar to Unilever, Federal Express, and TiVo, Photon tracks the following measures of customer satisfaction:

- Market research information on customer preferences for and customer satisfaction with specific product features (to measure design quality)
- Market share
- Percentage of highly satisfied customers
- Number of defective units shipped to customers as a percentage of total units shipped
- Number of customer complaints (Companies estimate that for every customer who actually complains, there are 10–20 others who have had bad experiences with the product or service but did not complain.)
- Percentage of products that fail soon after delivery
- Average delivery delays (difference between the scheduled delivery date and the date requested by the customer)
- On-time delivery rate (percentage of shipments made on or before the scheduled delivery date)

Photon's management monitors whether these numbers improve or deteriorate over time. Higher customer satisfaction should lead to lower costs of quality and higher future revenues from greater customer retention, loyalty, and positive word-of-mouth advertising. Lower customer-satisfaction indicates that costs of quality will likely increase in the future. We next turn to the driver of customer satisfaction, the internal business processes to identify and analyze quality problems and to improve quality.

The Internal-Business-Process Perspective: Analyzing Quality Problems and Improving Quality

We present three techniques for identifying and analyzing quality problems: control charts, Pareto diagrams, and cause-and-effect diagrams.

Control Charts

Statistical quality control (SQC), also called statistical process control (SPC), is a formal means of distinguishing between random and nonrandom variations in an operating process. Random variations occur, for example, when chance fluctuations in the speed of equipment cause defective products to be produced such as copiers that produce fuzzy and unclear copies or copies that are too light or too dark. Nonrandom variations occur when defective products are produced as a result of a systematic problem such as an incorrect speed setting, a flawed part design, or mishandling of a component part. A **control chart**, an important tool in SQC, is a graph of a series of successive observations of a particular step, procedure, or operation taken at regular intervals of time. Each observation is plotted relative to specified ranges that represent the limits within which

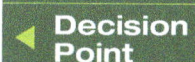
Decision Point

What are the four cost categories of a costs-of-quality program?

Learning Objective 2

Develop nonfinancial measures

. . . customer satisfaction measures such as number of customer complaints, internal-business process measures such as percentage of defective and reworked products, and learning and growth measures such as employee empowerment and training

and methods to improve quality

. . . control charts, Pareto diagrams, and cause-and-effect diagrams

observations are expected to fall. Only those observations outside the control limits are ordinarily regarded as nonrandom and worth investigating.

Exhibit 19-3 presents control charts for the daily defect rates (defective copiers divided by the total number of copiers produced) observed at Photon's three photocopying-machine production lines. Defect rates in the prior 60 days for each production line were assumed to provide a good basis from which to calculate the distribution of daily defect rates. The arithmetic mean (μ, read as mu) and standard deviation (σ, read as sigma, how much an observation deviates from the mean) are the two parameters of the distribution that are used in the control charts in Exhibit 19-3. On the basis of experience, the company decides that any observation outside the $\mu \pm 2\sigma$ range should be investigated.

For production line A, all observations are within the range of $\mu \pm 2\sigma$, so management believes no investigation is necessary. For production line B, the last two observations signal that a much higher percentage of copiers are not performing as they should, indicating that the problem is probably because of a nonrandom, out-of-control occurrence such as an incorrect speed setting or mishandling of a component part. Given the $\pm 2\sigma$ rule, both observations would be investigated. Production line C illustrates a process that would not prompt an investigation under the $\pm 2\sigma$ rule but that may well be out of control, because the last eight observations show a clear direction, and over the last six days, the percentage of defective copiers are increasing and getting further and further away from the mean. The pattern of observations moving away from the mean could be due, for example, to the tooling on a machine beginning to wear out, resulting in poorly machined parts. As the tooling deteriorates further, the trend in producing defective copiers is likely to persist until the production line is no longer in statistical control. Statistical procedures have been developed using the trend as well as the variation to evaluate whether a process is out of control.

Pareto Diagrams

Observations outside control limits serve as inputs for Pareto diagrams. A **Pareto diagram** is a chart that indicates how frequently each type of defect occurs, ordered from the most frequent to the least frequent. Exhibit 19-4 presents a Pareto diagram of quality problems for all observations outside the control limits at the final inspection point in 2011. Fuzzy and unclear copies are the most frequently recurring problem. Fuzzy and unclear copies result in high rework costs. Sometimes fuzzy and unclear copies occur at customer sites and result in high warranty and repair costs and low customer satisfaction.

Cause-and-Effect Diagrams

The most frequently recurring and costly problems identified by the Pareto diagram are analyzed using cause-and-effect diagrams. A **cause-and-effect diagram** identifies potential causes of defects using a diagram that resembles the bone structure of a fish (hence, cause-and-effect diagrams are also called *fishbone diagrams*).[2] Exhibit 19-5 presents the

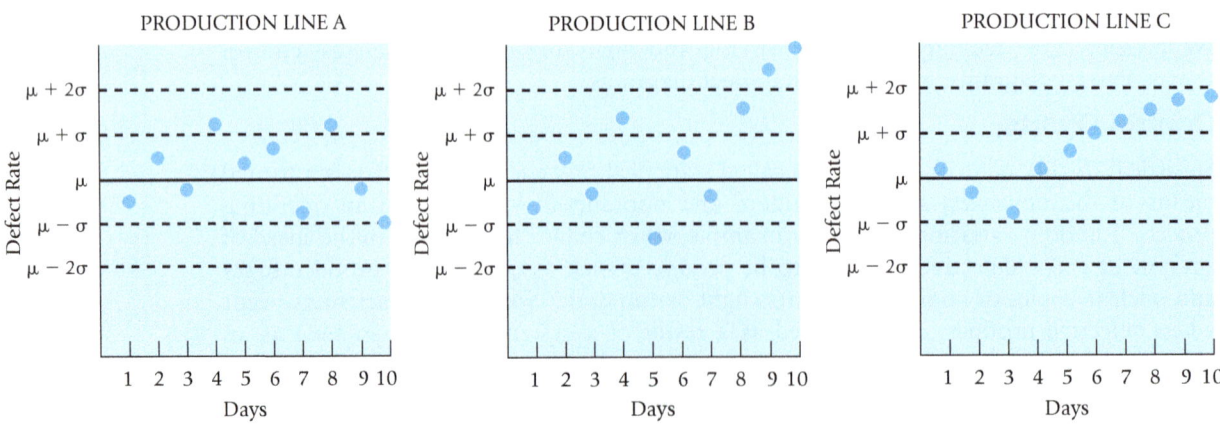

| Exhibit 19-3 | Statistical Quality Control Charts: Daily Defect Rate for Photocopying Machines at Photon Corporation |

――――――――――
[2] See P. Clark, "Getting the Most from Cause-and-Effect Diagrams," *Quality Progress* (June 2000).

cause-and-effect diagram describing potential reasons for fuzzy and unclear copies. The "backbone" of the diagram represents the problem being examined. The large "bones" coming off the backbone represent the main categories of potential causes of failure. The exhibit identifies four of these: human factors, methods and design factors, machine-related factors, and materials and components factors. Photon's engineers identify the materials and components factor as an important reason for the fuzzy and unclear copies. Additional arrows or bones are added to provide more-detailed reasons for each higher-level cause. For example, the engineers determine that two potential causes of material and component problems are variation in purchased components and incorrect component specification. They quickly settle on variation in purchased components as the likely cause and focus on the use of multiple suppliers and mishandling of purchased parts as the root causes of variation in purchased components. Further analysis leads them to conclude that mishandling of the steel frame that holds in place various components of the copier such as drums, mirrors, and lenses results in the misalignment of these components, causing fuzzy and unclear copies.

The analysis of quality problems is aided by automated equipment and computers that record the number and types of defects and the operating conditions that existed at the time the defects occurred. Using these inputs, computer programs simultaneously and iteratively prepare control charts, Pareto diagrams, and cause-and-effect diagrams with the goal of continuously reducing the mean defect rate, μ, and the standard deviation, σ.

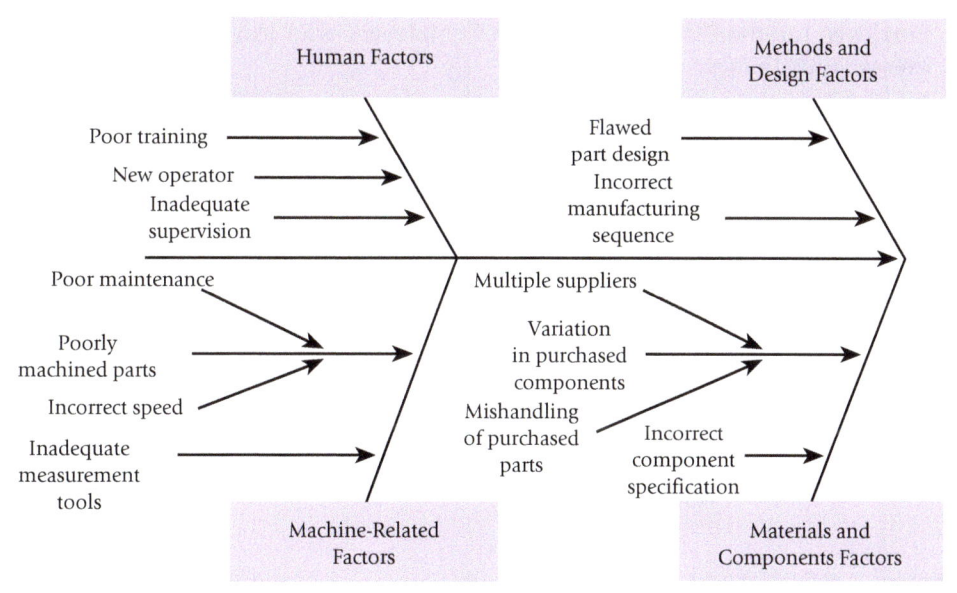

Six Sigma Quality

The ultimate goal of quality programs at companies such as Motorola, Honeywell, and General Electric is to achieve Six Sigma quality.[3] This means that the process is so well-understood and tightly controlled that the mean defect rate, μ, and the standard deviation, σ, are both very small. As a result, the upper and lower control limits in Exhibit 19-3 can be set at a distance of 6σ (six sigma) from the mean (μ). The implication of controlling a process at a Six Sigma level is that the process produces only 3.4 defects per million products produced.

To implement Six Sigma, companies use techniques such as control charts, Pareto diagrams, and cause-and-effect diagrams to define, measure, analyze, improve, and control processes to minimize variability in manufacturing and achieve almost zero defects. Critics of Six Sigma argue that it emphasizes incremental rather than dramatic or disruptive innovation. Nevertheless, companies report substantial benefits from Six Sigma initiatives.

Companies routinely use nonfinancial measures to track the quality improvements they are making.

Nonfinancial Measures of Internal-Business-Process Quality

Photon uses the following measures of internal-business-process quality:

- Percentage of defective products
- Percentage of reworked products
- Number of different types of defects analyzed using control charts, Pareto diagrams, and cause-and-effect diagrams
- Number of design and process changes made to improve design quality or reduce costs of quality

Photon's managers believe that improving these measures will lead to greater customer satisfaction, lower costs of quality, and better financial performance.

The Learning-and-Growth Perspective: Quality Improvements

What are the drivers of internal-business-process quality? Photon believes that recruiting outstanding design engineers, providing more employee training, and lowering employee turnover as a result of greater employee empowerment and satisfaction will reduce the number of defective products and increase customer satisfaction, leading to better financial performance. Photon measures the following factors in the learning-and-growth perspective in the balanced scorecard:

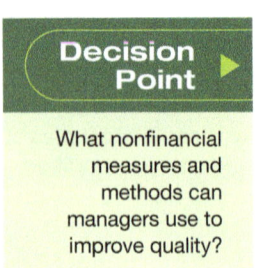

Decision Point ▶

What nonfinancial measures and methods can managers use to improve quality?

- Experience and qualifications of design engineers
- Employee turnover (ratio of number of employees who leave the company to the average total number of employees)
- Employee empowerment (ratio of the number of processes in which employees have the right to make decisions without consulting supervisors to the total number of processes)
- Employee satisfaction (ratio of employees indicating high satisfaction ratings to the total number of employees surveyed)
- Employee training (percentage of employees trained in different quality-enhancing methods)

Making Decisions and Evaluating Quality Performance

Relevant Costs and Benefits of Quality Improvement

When making decisions and evaluating performance, companies combine financial and nonfinancial information. We use the Photon example to illustrate relevant revenues and relevant costs in the context of decisions to improve quality.

---

[3] Six Sigma is a registered trademark of Motorola Inc.

Recall that Photon's cause-and-effect diagram reveals that the steel frame (or chassis) of the copier is often mishandled as it travels from a supplier's warehouse to Photon's plant. The frame must meet very precise specifications or else copier components (such as drums, mirrors, and lenses) will not fit exactly on the frame. Mishandling frames during transport causes misalignment and results in fuzzy and unclear copies.

A team of engineers offers two solutions: (1) inspect the frames immediately on delivery or (2) redesign and strengthen the frames and their shipping containers to withstand mishandling during transportation. The cost structure for 2012 is expected to be the same as the cost structure for 2011 presented in Exhibit 19-2.

To evaluate each alternative versus the status quo, management identifies the relevant costs and benefits for each solution by focusing on *how total costs and total revenues will change under each alternative*. As explained in Chapter 11, relevant-cost and relevant-revenue analysis ignores allocated amounts.

Photon uses only a one-year time horizon (2012) for the analysis because it plans to introduce a completely new line of copiers at the end of 2012. The new line is so different that the choice of either the inspection or the redesign alternative will have no effect on the sales of copiers in future years.

Exhibit 19-6 shows the relevant costs and benefits for each alternative.

Learning Objective 3

Combine financial and nonfinancial measures to make decisions and evaluate quality performance

. . . Identify relevant incremental and opportunity costs to evaluate tradeoffs across costs of quality and nonfinancial measures to identify problem areas and to highlight leading indicators of future performance

1. **Estimated incremental costs:** $400,000 for the inspection alternative; $460,000 for the redesign alternative.

2. **Cost savings from less rework, customer support, and repairs:** Exhibit 19-6, line 10, shows that reducing rework results in savings of $40 per hour. Exhibit 19-2, Panel A, column 2, line 13, shows total rework cost per hour of $100. Why the difference? Because as it improves quality, Photon will only save the $40 variable cost per rework-hour, not the $60 fixed cost per rework-hour. Exhibit 19-6, line 10, shows total savings of $960,000 ($40 per hour × 24,000 rework-hours saved) if it inspects the frames and $1,280,000 ($40 per rework-hour × 32,000 rework-hours saved) if it redesigns the frames. Exhibit 19-6 also shows expected variable-cost savings in customer support, transportation, and warranty repair for the two alternatives.

3. **Increased contribution margin from higher sales as a result of building a reputation for quality and performance (Exhibit 19-6, line 14):** $1,500,000 for 250 copiers under the inspection alternative and $1,800,000 for 300 copiers under the redesign alternative. Management should always look for opportunities to generate higher revenues, not just cost reductions, from quality improvements.

Exhibit 19-6 Estimated Effects of Quality-Improvement Actions on Costs of Quality for Photocopying Machines at Photon Corporation

	A	B	C	D	E	F	G	H	I	J
1						Relevant Costs and Benefits of				
2				Further Inspecting Incoming Frames				Redesigning Frames		
3	Relevant Items	Relevant Benefit per Unit		Quantity		Total Benefits		Quantity		Total Benefits
4	(1)	(2)		(3)		(4)		(5)		(6)
5	Additional inspection and testing costs					$ (400,000)				
6	Additional process engineering costs									$ (300,000)
7	Additional design engineering costs									(160,000)
8										
9						(2) × (3)				(2) × (5)
10	Savings in rework costs	$ 40	per hour	24,000	hours	$ 960,000		32,000	hours	$1,280,000
11	Savings in customer-support costs	$ 20	per hour	2,000	hours	40,000		2,800	hours	56,000
12	Savings in transportation costs for repair parts	$ 180	per load	500	loads	90,000		700	loads	126,000
13	Savings in warranty repair costs	$ 45	per hour	20,000	hours	900,000		28,000	hours	1,260,000
14	Total contribution margin from additional sales	$6,000	per copier	250	copiers	1,500,000		300	copiers	1,800,000
15										
16	Net cost savings and additional contribution margin					$3,090,000				$4,062,000
17										
18	Difference in favor of redesigning frames (J16) – (F16)						$972,000			

Exhibit 19-6 shows that both the inspection and the redesign alternatives yield net benefits relative to the status quo. However, the net benefits from the redesign alternative are expected to be $972,000 greater.

Note how making improvements in internal business processes affects the COQ numbers reported in the financial perspective. In our example, redesigning the frame increases prevention costs (design and process engineering), decreases internal failure costs (rework), and decreases external failure costs (customer support and warranty repairs). COQ reports provide more insight about quality improvements when managers compare trends over time. In successful quality programs, companies decrease costs of quality and, in particular, internal and external failure costs, as a percentage of revenues. Many companies, such as Hewlett-Packard, go further and believe they should eliminate all failure costs and have zero defects.

How should Photon use financial and nonfinancial measures to evaluate quality performance? They should utilize both types of measures because financial (COQ) and nonfinancial measures of quality have different advantages.

Advantages of COQ Measures

- Consistent with the attention-directing role of management accounting, COQ measures focus managers' attention on the costs of poor quality.
- Total COQ provides a measure of quality performance for evaluating trade-offs among prevention costs, appraisal costs, internal failure costs, and external failure costs.
- COQ measures assist in problem solving by comparing costs and benefits of different quality-improvement programs and setting priorities for cost reduction.

Advantages of Nonfinancial Measures of Quality

- Nonfinancial measures of quality are often easy to quantify and understand.
- Nonfinancial measures direct attention to physical processes and hence help managers identify the precise problem areas that need improvement.
- Nonfinancial measures, such as number of defects, provide immediate short-run feedback on whether quality-improvement efforts are succeeding.
- Nonfinancial measures such as measures of customer satisfaction and employee satisfaction are useful indicators of long-run performance.

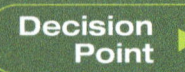

Decision Point ▶

How do managers identify the relevant costs and benefits of quality improvement programs and use financial and nonfinancial measures to evaluate quality?

COQ measures and nonfinancial measures complement each other. Without financial quality measures, companies could be spending more money on improving nonfinancial quality measures than it is worth. Without nonfinancial quality measures, quality problems might not be identified until it is too late. Most organizations use both types of measures to gauge quality performance. McDonald's, for example, evaluates employees and individual franchisees on multiple measures of quality and customer satisfaction. A mystery shopper, an outside party contracted by McDonald's to evaluate restaurant performance, scores individual restaurants on quality, cleanliness, service, and value. A restaurant's performance on these dimensions is evaluated over time and against other restaurants. In its balanced scorecard, Photon evaluates whether improvements in various nonfinancial quality measures eventually lead to improvements in financial measures.

Time as a Competitive Tool

Companies increasingly view time as a driver of strategy.[4] For example, CapitalOne has increased business on its Web site by promising home-loan approval decisions in 30 minutes or less. Companies such as AT&T, General Electric, and Wal-Mart attribute not only higher revenues but also lower costs to doing things faster and on time. They cite, for example, the need to carry less inventory due to their ability to respond rapidly to customer demands.

---

[4] See K. Eisenhardt and S. Brown, "Time Pacing: Competing in Strategic Markets That Won't Stand Still," *Harvard Business Review* (March–April 1998); and T. Willis and A. Jurkus, "Product Development: An Essential Ingredient of Time-Based Competition," *Review of Business* (2001).

Companies need to measure time to manage it properly. In this section, we focus on two *operational measures of time*: *customer-response time*, which reveals how quickly companies respond to customers' demands for their products and services, and *on-time performance*, which indicates how reliably they meet scheduled delivery dates. We also show how companies measure the causes and costs of delays.

Customer-Response Time and On-Time Performance

Customer-response time is how long it takes from the time a customer places an order for a product or service to the time the product or service is delivered to the customer. Fast responses to customers are of strategic importance in industries such as construction, banking, car rental, and fast food. Some companies, such as Airbus, have to pay penalties to compensate their customers (airline companies) for lost revenues and profits (from being unable to operate flights) as a result of delays in delivering aircraft to them.

Exhibit 19-7 describes the components of customer-response time. *Receipt time* is how long it takes the marketing department to specify to the manufacturing department the exact requirements in the customer's order. **Manufacturing cycle time** (also called **manufacturing lead time**) is how long it takes from the time an order is received by manufacturing to the time a finished good is produced. Manufacturing cycle time is the sum of waiting time and manufacturing time for an order. For example, an aircraft order received by Airbus may need to wait before the equipment required to process it becomes available. *Delivery time* is how long it takes to deliver a completed order to a customer.

Some companies evaluate their response time improvement efforts using a measure called **manufacturing cycle efficiency (MCE):**

$$\text{MCE} = (\text{Value-added manufacturing time} \div \text{Manufacturing cycle time})$$

As discussed in Chapter 12, value-added manufacturing activities are activities that customers perceive as adding value or utility to a product. The time actually spent assembling the product is value-added manufacturing time. The rest of manufacturing cycle time, such as the time the product spends waiting for parts or for the next stage in the production process, and being repaired, represents nonvalue-added manufacturing time. Identifying and minimizing the sources of nonvalue-added manufacturing time increases customer responsiveness and reduces costs.

Similar measures apply to service-sector companies. Consider a 40-minute doctor's office visit, of which 9 minutes is spent on administrative tasks such as filling out forms, 20 minutes is spent waiting in the reception area and examination room, and 11 minutes is spent with a nurse or doctor. The service cycle efficiency for this visit equals $11 \div 40$, or 0.275. In other words, only 27.5% of the time in the office added value to the customer. Minimizing nonvalue-added service time in their medical delivery processes has allowed hospitals such as Alle-Kiski Medical Center in Pennsylvania to treat more patients in less time.

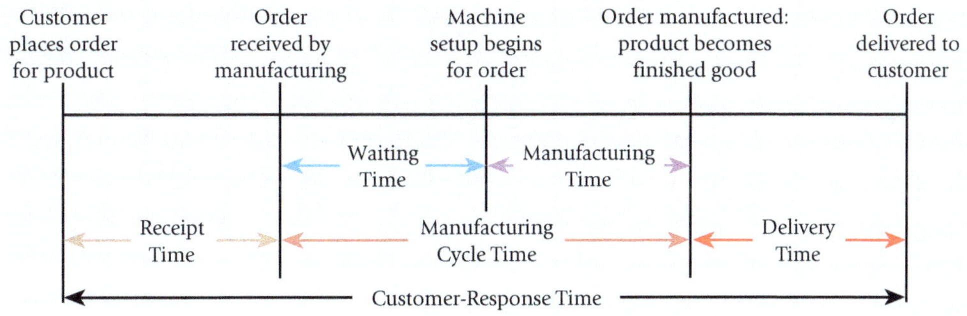

Learning Objective 4

Describe customer-response time

. . . time between receipt of customer order and product delivery

and explain why delays happen and their costs

. . . uncertainty about the timing of customer orders and limited capacity lead to lower revenues and higher inventory carrying costs

Exhibit 19-7

Components of Customer-Response Time

On-time performance is delivery of a product or service by the time it is scheduled to be delivered. Consider Federal Express, which specifies a price per package and a next-day delivery time of 10:30 A.M. for its overnight courier service. Federal Express measures on-time performance by how often it meets its stated delivery time of 10:30 A.M. On-time performance increases customer satisfaction. For example, commercial airlines gain loyal passengers as a result of consistent on-time service. But there is a trade-off between a customer's desire for shorter customer-response time and better on-time performance. Scheduling longer customer-response times, such as airlines lengthening scheduled arrival times, displeases customers on the one hand but increases customer satisfaction on the other hand by improving on-time performance.

Bottlenecks and Time Drivers

Managing customer-response time and on-time performance requires understanding the causes and costs of delays that occur, for example, at a machine in a manufacturing plant or at a checkout counter in a store.

A **time driver** is any factor that causes a change in the speed of an activity when the factor changes. Two time drivers are as follows:

1. **Uncertainty about when customers will order products or services.** For example, the more randomly Airbus receives orders for its airplanes, the more likely queues will form and delays will occur.

2. **Bottlenecks due to limited capacity.** A **bottleneck** occurs in an operation when the work to be performed approaches or exceeds the capacity available to do it. For example, a bottleneck results and causes delays when products that must be processed at a particular machine arrive while the machine is being used to process other products. Bottlenecks also occur on the Internet, for example, when many users try to operate wireless mobile devices at the same time (see Concepts in Action, p. 684). Many banks, such as Bank of China; grocery stores, such as Krogers; and entertainment parks, such as Disneyland, actively work to reduce queues and delays to better serve their customers.

Consider Falcon Works (FW), which uses one turning machine to convert steel bars into a special gear for planes. FW makes this gear, which is its sole product, only after customers have ordered it. To focus on manufacturing cycle time, we assume FW's receipt time and delivery time are minimal. FW's strategy is to differentiate itself from competitors by offering faster delivery. The company's manager is examining opportunities to sell other products to increase profits without sacrificing the competitive advantage provided by short customer-response times. The manager examines these opportunities using the five-step decision-making process introduced in Chapter 1.

Step 1: Identify the problem and uncertainties. FW's manager is considering introducing a second product, a piston for pumps. The primary uncertainty is how the introduction of a second product will affect manufacturing cycle times for gears.

Step 2: Obtain information. The manager gathers data on the number of orders for gears FW has received in the past, the time it takes to manufacture gears, the available capacity, and the average manufacturing cycle time for gears. FW typically receives 30 orders for gears, but it could receive 10, 30, or 50 orders. Each order is for 1,000 units and takes 100 hours of manufacturing time (8 hours of setup time to clean and prepare the machine, and 92 hours of processing time). Annual capacity of the machine is 4,000 hours. If FW receives the 30 orders it expects, the total amount of manufacturing time required on the machine is 3,000 hours (100 hours per order × 30 orders), which is within the available machine capacity of 4,000 hours. Even though capacity utilization is not strained, queues and delays still occur, because uncertainty about when FW's customers place their orders causes an order to be received while the machine is processing an earlier order.

Average waiting time, the average amount of time that an order waits in line before the machine is set up and the order is processed, equals,[5]

$$\frac{\left(\begin{array}{c}\text{Annual average}\\\text{number of}\\\text{orders for gears}\end{array}\times\left(\begin{array}{c}\text{Manufacturing}\\\text{time per order}\\\text{for gears}\end{array}\right)^2\right)}{2\times\left[\begin{array}{c}\text{Annual machine}\\\text{capacity}\end{array}-\left(\begin{array}{c}\text{Annual average number}\\\text{of orders for gears}\end{array}\times\begin{array}{c}\text{Manufacturing}\\\text{time per order for gears}\end{array}\right)\right]}$$

$$=\frac{30\times(100)^2}{2\times[4{,}000-(30\times100)]}=\frac{30\times10{,}000}{2\times(4{,}000-3{,}000)}=\frac{300{,}000}{2\times1{,}000}=\frac{300{,}000}{2{,}000}=150\text{ hours per order (for gears)}$$

Therefore, the average manufacturing cycle time for an order is 250 hours (150 hours of average waiting time + 100 hours of manufacturing time). Note that manufacturing time per order is a squared term in the numerator. It indicates the disproportionately large impact manufacturing time has on waiting time. As the manufacturing time lengthens, there is a much greater chance that the machine will be in use when an order arrives, leading to longer delays. The denominator in this formula is a measure of the unused capacity, or cushion. As the unused capacity becomes smaller, the chance that the machine is processing an earlier order becomes more likely, leading to greater delays.

The formula describes only the *average* waiting time. A particular order might arrive when the machine is free, in which case manufacturing will start immediately. In another situation, FW may receive an order while two other orders are waiting to be processed, which means the delay will be longer than 150 hours.

Step 3: Make predictions about the future. The manager makes the following predictions about pistons: FW expects to receive 10 orders for pistons, each order for 800 units, in the coming year. Each order will take 50 hours of manufacturing time, comprising 3 hours for setup and 47 hours of processing. Expected demand for FW's gears will be unaffected by whether FW introduces pistons.

Average waiting time *before* machine setup begins is expected to be (the formula is an extension of the preceding formula for the single-product case) as follows:

$$\frac{\left[\begin{array}{c}\text{Annual average number}\\\text{of orders for gears}\end{array}\times\left(\begin{array}{c}\text{Manufacturing}\\\text{time per order}\\\text{for gears}\end{array}\right)^2\right]+\left[\begin{array}{c}\text{Annual average number}\\\text{of orders for pistons}\end{array}\times\left(\begin{array}{c}\text{Manufacturing}\\\text{time per order}\\\text{for pistons}\end{array}\right)^2\right]}{2\times\left[\begin{array}{c}\text{Annual machine}\\\text{capacity}\end{array}-\left(\begin{array}{c}\text{Annual average number}\\\text{of orders for gears}\end{array}\times\begin{array}{c}\text{Manufacturing}\\\text{time per order}\\\text{for gears}\end{array}\right)-\left(\begin{array}{c}\text{Annual average number}\\\text{of orders for pistons}\end{array}\times\begin{array}{c}\text{Manufacturing}\\\text{time per order}\\\text{for pistons}\end{array}\right)\right]}$$

$$=\frac{[30\times(100)^2]+[10\times(50)^2]}{2\times[4{,}000-(30\times100)-(10\times50)]}=\frac{(30\times10{,}000)+(10\times2{,}500)}{2\times(4{,}000-3{,}000-500)}$$

$$=\frac{300{,}000+25{,}000}{2\times500}=\frac{325{,}000}{1{,}000}=325\text{ hours per order (for gears \textit{and} pistons)}$$

Introducing pistons will cause average waiting time for an order to more than double, from 150 hours to 325 hours. Waiting time increases because introducing pistons will cause unused capacity to shrink, increasing the probability that new orders will arrive while current orders are being manufactured or waiting to be manufactured. Average waiting time is very sensitive to the shrinking of unused capacity.

If the manager decides to make pistons, average manufacturing cycle time will be 425 hours for a gear order (325 hours of average waiting time + 100 hours of manufacturing time), and 375 hours for a piston order (325 hours of average waiting time + 50 hours

[5] The technical assumptions are (a) that customer orders for the product follow a Poisson distribution with a mean equal to the expected number of orders (30 in our example), and (b) that orders are processed on a first-in, first-out (FIFO) basis. The Poisson arrival pattern for customer orders has been found to be reasonable in many real-world settings. The FIFO assumption can be modified. Under the modified assumptions, the basic queuing and delay effects will still occur, but the precise formulas will be different.

Concepts in Action   Overcoming Wireless Data Bottlenecks

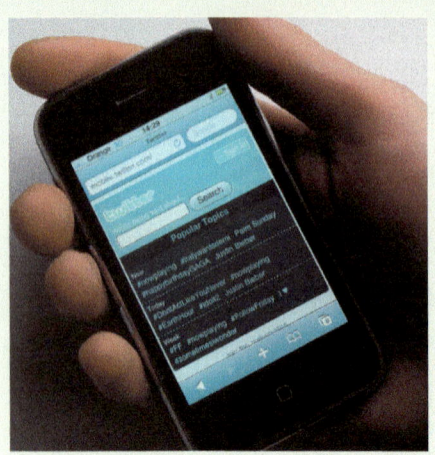

The wired world is quickly going wireless. In 2010, sales of smartphones—such as the Apple iPhone and BlackBerry—in the United States were predicted to be 53 million units. In addition to the smartphone boom, emerging devices including e-book readers and machine-to-machine appliances (the so-called "Internet of things") will add to rapidly growing data traffic.

With every new device that lets users browse the Internet, and every new business that taps into the convenience and speed of the wireless world, the invisible information superhighway gets a little more crowded. Cisco recently forecast that data traffic will grow at a compound rate of 108% from 90,000 terabytes per month in 2009 to 3.6 million terabytes per month by 2014.

This astronomical growth already causes many users to suffer from mobile bottlenecks caused by too many users trying to transfer mobile data at the same time in a given area. These bottlenecks are most harmful to companies buying and selling products and services over the mobile Internet. Without access, Amazon.com Kindle owners cannot download new e-books and mobile brokerage users cannot buy and sell stocks "on the go."

To relieve mobile bottlenecks, wireless providers and other high-tech companies are working on more efficient mobile broadband networks, such as LTE, that make use of complementary technologies to automatically choose the best available wireless network to increase capacity. Technology providers are also deploying Wi-Fi direct, which allows mobile users to freely transfer video, digital music, and photos between mobile devices without choking up valuable bandwidth. Companies and government agencies around the world are also trying to increase the wireless broadband spectrum. In the United States, for example, current holders of spectrum—such as radio stations—are being encouraged to sell their excess capacity to wireless providers in exchange for a share of the profits.

Sources: Edwards, Cliff. 2010. Wi-fi direct seen as way to alleviate network congestion. *BusinessWeek*, January 7. www.businessweek.com/technology/content/jan2010/tc2010017_884186.htm; Morris, John. 2010. CTIA: More spectrum, and other ways to break the wireless data bottleneck. *ZDNet*. "Laptops & Desktops," blog March 24. http://www.zdnet.com/blog/computers/ctia-more-spectrum-and-other-ways-to-break-the-wireless-data-bottleneck/1877; Pyle, George. 2010. Wireless growth leading to bottlenecks. *Buffalo News*, May 9. www.buffalonews.com/2010/05/09/1044893/wireless-growth-leading-to-bottlenecks.html.

of manufacturing time). A gear order will spend 76.5% (325 hours ÷ 425 hours) of its manufacturing cycle time just waiting for manufacturing to start!

Step 4: Make decisions by choosing among alternatives. Given the anticipated effects on manufacturing cycle time of adding pistons, should FW's manager introduce pistons? To help the manager make a decision, the management accountant identifies and analyzes the relevant revenues and relevant costs of adding the piston product and, in particular, the cost of delays on all products. The rest of this section focuses on Step 4. While we do not cover Step 5 in this example, we discuss later in the chapter how the balanced scorecard can be a useful tool to evaluate and learn about time-based performance.

Relevant Revenues and Relevant Costs of Time

To determine the relevant revenues and costs of adding pistons under Step 4, the management accountant prepares the following additional information:

Product	Annual Average Number of Orders	Average Selling Price per Order If Average Manufacturing Cycle Time per Order Is		Direct Material Cost per Order	Inventory Carrying Cost per Order per Hour
		Less Than 300 Hours	More Than 300 Hours		
Gears	30	$22,000	$21,500	$16,000	$1.00
Pistons	10	10,000	9,600	8,000	0.50

Manufacturing cycle times affect both revenues and costs. Revenues are affected because customers are willing to pay a higher price for faster delivery. On the cost side, direct material costs and inventory carrying costs are the only relevant costs of introducing pistons (all other costs are unaffected and hence irrelevant). Inventory carrying costs equal the opportunity costs of investment tied up in inventory (see Chapter 11, pp. 403–405) and the relevant costs of storage, such as space rental, spoilage, deterioration, and materials handling. Usually, companies calculate inventory carrying costs on a per-unit, per-year basis. To simplify calculations, the management accountant calculates inventory carrying costs on a per-order, per-hour basis. Also, FW acquires direct materials at the time the order is received by manufacturing and, therefore, calculates inventory carrying costs for the duration of the manufacturing cycle time.

Exhibit 19-8 presents relevant revenues and relevant costs for the "introduce pistons" and "do not introduce pistons" alternatives. Based on the analysis, FW's managers decide not to introduce pistons, even though pistons have a positive contribution margin of $1,600 ($9,600 − $8,000) per order and FW has the capacity to process pistons. If it produces pistons, FW will, on average, use only 3,500 (Gears: 100 hours per order × 30 orders + Pistons: 50 hours per order × 10 orders) of the available 4,000 machine-hours. So why is FW better off not introducing pistons? *Because of the negative effects that producing pistons will have on the existing product, gears.* The following table presents the *costs of time,* the expected loss in revenues and expected increase in carrying costs as a result of delays caused by using machine capacity to manufacture pistons.

| | Effect of Increasing Average Manufacturing Cycle Time | | Expected Loss in Revenues Plus |
| | Expected Loss in Revenues for Gears | Expected Increase in Carrying Costs for All Products | Expected Increase in Carrying Costs of Introducing Pistons |
Product	(1)	(2)	(3) = (1) + (2)
Gears	$15,000[a]	$5,250[b]	$20,250
Pistons	—	1,875[c]	1,875
Total	$15,000	$7,125	$22,125

[a]($22,000 − $21,500) per order × 30 expected orders = $15,000.
[b](425 − 250) hours per order × $1.00 per hour × 30 expected orders = $5,250.
[c](375 − 0) hours per order × $0.50 per hour × 10 expected orders = $1,875.

Introducing pistons causes the average manufacturing cycle time of gears to increase from 250 hours to 425 hours. Longer manufacturing cycle times increases inventory carrying costs of gears and decreases gear revenues (average manufacturing cycle time for gears exceeds 300 hours so the average selling price per order decreases from $22,000 to $21,500). Together

Relevant Items	Alternative 1: Introduce Pistons (1)	Alternative 2: Do Not Introduce Pistons (2)	Difference (3) = (1) − (2)
Expected revenues	741,000[a]	$660,000[b]	$ 81,000
Expected variable costs	560,000[c]	480,000[d]	(80,000)
Expected inventory carrying costs	14,625[e]	7,500[f]	(7,125)
Expected total costs	574,625	487,500	(87,125)
Expected revenues minus expected costs	$166,375	$172,500	$ (6,125)

[a]($21,500 × 30) + ($9,600 × 10) = $741,000; average manufacturing cycle time will be more than 300 hours.
[b]($22,000 × 30) = $660,000; average manufacturing cycle time will be less than 300 hours.
[c]($16,000 × 30) + ($8,000 × 10) = $560,000.
[d]$16,000 × 30 = $480,000.
[e](Average manufacturing cycle time for gears × Unit carrying cost per order for gears × Expected number of orders for gears) + (Average manufacturing cycle time for pistons × Unit carrying cost per order for pistons × Expected number of orders for pistons) = (425 × $1.00 × 30) + (375 × $0.50 × 10) = $12,750 + $1,875 = $14,625.
[f]Average manufacturing cycle time for gears × Unit carrying cost per order for gears × Expected number of orders for gears = 250 × $1.00 × 30 = $7,500.

with the inventory carrying cost of pistons, the expected costs of introducing pistons, $22,125, exceeds the expected contribution margin of $16,000 ($1,600 per order × 10 expected orders) from selling pistons by $6,125 (the difference calculated in Exhibit 19-8).

This simple example illustrates that when demand uncertainty is high, some unused capacity is desirable.[6] Increasing the capacity of a bottleneck resource reduces manufacturing cycle times and delays. One way to increase capacity is to reduce the time required for setups and processing via more-efficient setups and processing. Another way to increase capacity is to invest in new equipment, such as flexible manufacturing systems that can be programmed to switch quickly from producing one product to producing another. Delays can also be reduced through careful scheduling of orders on machines, such as by batching similar jobs together for processing.

Decision Point ▶

What is customer-response time? What are the reasons for and the costs of delays?

Theory of Constraints and Throughput-Margin Analysis

In this section, we consider products that are made from multiple parts and processed on multiple machines. With multiple parts and machines, dependencies arise among operations—that is, some operations cannot be started until parts from the preceding operation are available. Furthermore, some operations are bottlenecks (have limited capacity), and others are not.

Managing Bottlenecks

Learning Objective 5

Explain how to manage bottlenecks

. . . keep bottlenecks busy and increase their efficiency and capacity by increasing throughput margin

The **theory of constraints (TOC)** describes methods to maximize operating income when faced with some bottleneck and some nonbottleneck operations.[7] The TOC defines three measures as follows:

1. **Throughput margin** equals revenues minus the direct material costs of the goods sold.
2. *Investments* equal the sum of material costs in direct materials, work-in-process, and finished goods inventories; R&D costs; and costs of equipment and buildings.
3. *Operating costs* equal all costs of operations (other than direct materials) incurred to earn throughput margin. Operating costs include salaries and wages, rent, utilities, depreciation, and the like.

The objective of the TOC is to increase throughput margin while decreasing investments and operating costs. *The TOC considers a short-run time horizon and assumes operating costs are fixed.* It focuses on managing bottleneck operations as explained in the following steps:

Step 1: Recognize that the bottleneck operation determines throughput margin of the entire system.

Step 2: Identify the bottleneck operation by identifying operations with large quantities of inventory waiting to be worked on.

Step 3: Keep the bottleneck operation busy and subordinate all nonbottleneck operations to the bottleneck operation. That is, the needs of the bottleneck operation determine the production schedule of the nonbottleneck operations.

Step 3 represents one of the key concepts described in Chapter 11: To maximize operating income, the manager must maximize contribution margin (in this case, throughput margin) of the constrained or bottleneck resource (see pp. 405–406). The bottleneck machine must always be kept running; it should not be waiting for jobs. To achieve this objective, companies often maintain a small buffer inventory of jobs at the bottleneck machine. The bottleneck machine sets the pace for all nonbottleneck machines. Workers at nonbottleneck machines do not produce more output than can be

---

[6] Other complexities, such as analyzing a network of machines, priority scheduling, and allowing for uncertainty in processing times, are beyond the scope of this book. In these cases, the basic queuing and delay effects persist, but the precise formulas are more complex.

[7] See E. Goldratt and J. Cox, *The Goal* (New York: North River Press, 1986); E. Goldratt, *The Theory of Constraints* (New York: North River Press, 1990); E. Noreen, D. Smith, and J. Mackey, *The Theory of Constraints and Its Implications for Management Accounting* (New York: North River Press, 1995); and M. Woeppel, *Manufacturers' Guide to Implementing the Theory of Constraints* (Boca Raton, FL: Lewis Publishing, 2000).

processed by the bottleneck machine, because producing more nonbottleneck output only creates excess inventory; it does not increase throughput margin.

Step 4: Take actions to increase the efficiency and capacity of the bottleneck operation as long as throughput margin exceeds the incremental costs of increasing efficiency and capacity.

We illustrate Step 4 using data from Cardinal Industries (CI). CI manufactures car doors in two operations: stamping and pressing.

	Stamping	Pressing
Capacity per hour	20 units	15 units
Annual capacity (6,000 hours of capacity available in each operation)		
6,000 hours × 20 units/hour; 6,000 hours × 15 units/hour)	120,000 units	90,000 units
Annual production and sales	90,000 units	90,000 units
Other fixed operating costs (excluding direct materials)	$720,000	$1,080,000
Other fixed operating costs per unit produced		
($720,000 ÷ 90,000 units; $1,080,000 ÷ 90,000 units)	$8 per unit	$12 per unit

Each door sells for $100 and has a direct material cost of $40. Variable costs in other functions of the value chain—design of products and processes, marketing, distribution, and customer service—are negligible. CI's output is constrained by the capacity of 90,000 units in the pressing operation. What can CI do to relieve the bottleneck constraint of the pressing operation?

Desirable actions include the following:

1. **Eliminate idle time at the bottleneck operation (time when the pressing machine is neither being set up to process products nor actually processing products).** CI's manager is evaluating permanently positioning two workers at the pressing operation to unload finished units as soon as one batch of units is processed and to set up the machine to begin processing the next batch. This action will cost $48,000 and bottleneck output will increase by 1,000 doors per year. Should CI incur the additional costs? Yes, because CI's throughput margin will increase by $60,000 [(selling price per door, $100 − direct material cost per door, $40) × 1,000 doors], which is greater than the incremental cost of $48,000. All other costs are irrelevant.

2. **Process only those parts or products that increase throughput margin, not parts or products that will be placed in finished goods or spare parts inventories.** Making products that remain in inventory will not increase throughput margin.

3. **Shift products that do not have to be made on the bottleneck machine to nonbottleneck machines or to outside processing facilities.** Suppose Spartan Corporation, an outside contractor, offers to press 1,500 doors at $15 per door from stamped parts that CI supplies. Spartan's quoted price is greater than CI's own operating costs in the pressing department of $12 per door. Should CI accept the offer? Yes, because pressing is the bottleneck operation. Getting additional doors pressed by Spartan will increase throughput margin by $90,000 [($100 − $40) per door × 1,500 doors], while the relevant cost of increasing capacity will be $22,500 ($15 per door × 1,500 doors). The fact that CI's unit cost is less than Spartan's quoted price is irrelevant.

   Suppose Gemini Industries, another outside contractor, offers to stamp 2,000 doors from direct materials that CI supplies at $6 per door. Gemini's price is lower than CI's operating cost of $8 per door in the stamping department. Should CI accept the offer? No, because other operating costs are fixed costs. CI will not save any costs by subcontracting the stamping operations. Instead, its costs will increase by $12,000 ($6 per door × 2,000 doors) with no increase in throughput margin, which is constrained by pressing capacity.

4. **Reduce setup time and processing time at bottleneck operations (for example, by simplifying the design or reducing the number of parts in the product).** Suppose CI can press 2,500 more doors at a cost of $55,000 a year by reducing setup time at the pressing operation. Should CI incur this cost? Yes, because throughput margin will increase by $150,000 [($100 − $40) per door × 2,500 doors], which is greater than

the incremental costs of $55,000. Will CI find it worthwhile to incur costs to reduce machining time at the nonbottleneck stamping operation? No. Other operating costs will increase, while throughput margin will remain unchanged because bottleneck capacity of the pressing operation will not increase.

5. **Improve the quality of parts or products manufactured at the bottleneck operation.** Poor quality is more costly at a bottleneck operation than at a nonbottleneck operation. The cost of poor quality at a nonbottleneck operation is the cost of materials wasted. If CI produces 1,000 defective doors at the stamping operation, the cost of poor quality is $40,000 (direct material cost per door, $40, × 1,000 doors). No throughput margin is forgone because stamping has unused capacity. Despite the defective production, stamping can produce and transfer 90,000 good-quality doors to the pressing operation. At a bottleneck operation, the cost of poor quality is the cost of materials wasted *plus* the opportunity cost of lost throughput margin. Bottleneck capacity not wasted in producing defective units could be used to generate additional throughput margin. If CI produces 1,000 defective units at the pressing operation, the cost of poor quality is the lost revenue of $100,000, or alternatively stated, direct material costs of $40,000 (direct material cost per door, $40, × 1,000 doors) plus forgone throughput margin of $60,000 [($100 − $40) per door × 1,000 doors].

The high cost of poor quality at the bottleneck operation means that bottleneck time should not be wasted processing units that are defective. That is, parts should be inspected before the bottleneck operation to ensure that only good-quality parts are processed at the bottleneck operation. Furthermore, quality-improvement programs should place special emphasis on minimizing defects at bottleneck machines.

If successful, the actions in Step 4 will increase the capacity of the pressing operation until it eventually exceeds the capacity of the stamping operation. The bottleneck will then shift to the stamping operation. CI would then focus continuous-improvement actions on increasing stamping efficiency and capacity. For example, the contract with Gemini Industries to stamp 2,000 doors at $6 per door from direct material supplied by CI will become attractive because throughput margin will increase by ($100 − $40) per door × 2,000 doors = $120,000, which is greater than the incremental costs of $12,000 ($6 per door × 2,000 doors).

The theory of constraints emphasizes management of bottleneck operations as the key to improving performance of production operations as a whole. It focuses on short-run maximization of throughput margin, revenues minus direct material costs of goods sold. Because TOC regards operating costs as difficult to change in the short run, it does not identify individual activities and drivers of costs. TOC is, therefore, less useful for the long-run management of costs. In contrast, activity-based costing (ABC) systems take a long-run perspective and focus on improving processes by eliminating nonvalue-added activities and reducing the costs of performing value-added activities. ABC systems, therefore, are more useful for long-run pricing, cost control, and capacity management. The short-run TOC emphasis on maximizing throughput margin by managing bottlenecks complements the long-run strategic-cost-management focus of ABC.[8]

Balanced Scorecard and Time-Related Measures

In this section, we focus on the final step of the five-step decision-making process by tracking changes in time-based measures, evaluating and learning whether these changes affect financial performance, and modifying decisions and plans to achieve the company's goals. We use the structure of the balanced scorecard perspectives—financial, customer, internal business processes, and learning and growth—to summarize how financial and nonfinancial measures of time relate to one another, reduce delays, and increase output of bottleneck operations.

Financial measures
    Revenue losses or price discounts attributable to delays
    Carrying cost of inventories
    Throughput margin minus operating costs

---

[8] For an excellent evaluation of TOC, operations management, cost accounting, and the relationship between TOC and activity-based costing, see A. Atkinson, "Cost Accounting, the Theory of Constraints, and Costing," (Issue Paper, CMA Canada, December 2000).

Customer measures

    Customer-response time (the time it takes to fulfill a customer order)

    On-time performance (delivering a product or service by the scheduled time)

Internal-business-process measures

    Average manufacturing time for key products

    Manufacturing cycle efficiency for key processes

    Idle time at bottleneck operations

    Defective units produced at bottleneck operations

    Average reduction in setup time and processing time at bottleneck operations

Learning-and-growth measures

    Employee satisfaction

    Number of employees trained in managing bottleneck operations

To see the cause-and-effect linkages across these balanced scorecard perspectives, consider the example of the Bell Group, a designer and manufacturer of equipment for the jewelry industry. Based on TOC analysis, the company determined that a key financial measure was improving throughput margin by 18% for a specific product line. In the customer perspective, the company set a goal of a two-day turn-around time on all orders for the product. To achieve this goal, the internal-business-process measure was the amount of time a bottleneck machine operated, with a goal of running 22 hours per day, six days a week. Finally, in the learning perspective, the company focused on training new employees to carry out nonbottleneck operations in order to free experienced employees to operate the bottleneck machine. The Bell Group's emphasis on time-related measures in its balanced scorecard has allowed the company to substantially increase manufacturing throughput and slash response times, leading to higher revenues and increased profits.[9]

Decision Point

What are the steps managers can take to manage bottlenecks?

Problem for Self-Study

The Sloan Moving Corporation transports household goods from one city to another within the continental United States. It measures quality of service in terms of (a) time required to transport goods, (b) on-time delivery (within two days of agreed-upon delivery date), and (c) number of lost or damaged items. Sloan is considering investing in a new scheduling-and-tracking system costing $160,000 per year, which should help it improve performance with respect to items (b) and (c). The following information describes Sloan's current performance and the expected performance if the new system is implemented:

	Current Performance	Expected Future Performance
On-time delivery performance	85%	95%
Variable cost per carton lost or damaged	$60	$60
Fixed cost per carton lost or damaged	$40	$40
Number of cartons lost or damaged per year	3,000 cartons	1,000 cartons

Sloan expects each percentage point increase in on-time performance to increase revenue by $20,000 per year. Sloan's contribution margin percentage is 45%.

Required

1. Should Sloan acquire the new system? Show your calculations.
2. Sloan is very confident about the cost savings from fewer lost or damaged cartons as a result of introducing the new system but unsure about the increase in revenues. Calculate the minimum amount of increase in revenues needed to make it worthwhile for Sloan to invest in the new system.

---

[9] Management Roundtable, "The Bell Group Uses the Balanced Scorecard with the Theory of Constraints to Keep Strategic Focus," FastTrack.roundtable.com, fasttrack.roundtable.com/app/content/knowledgesource/item/197 (accessed May 15, 2007).

Solution

1. Additional costs of the new scheduling-and-tracking system are $160,000 per year. Additional annual benefits of the new scheduling-and-tracking system are as follows:

Additional annual revenues from a 10% improvement in on-time performance, from 85% to 95%, $20,000 per 1% × 10 percentage points	$200,000
45% contribution margin from additional annual revenues (0.45 × $200,000)	$ 90,000
Decrease in costs per year from fewer cartons lost or damaged (only variable costs are relevant)[$60 per carton × (3,000 − 1,000) cartons]	120,000
Total additional benefits	$210,000

Because the benefits of $210,000 exceed the costs of $160,000, Sloan should invest in the new system.

2. As long as Sloan earns a contribution margin of $40,000 (to cover incremental costs of $160,000 minus relevant variable-cost savings of $120,000) from additional annual revenues, investing in the new system is beneficial. This contribution margin corresponds to additional revenues of $40,000 ÷ 0.45 = $88,889.

Decision Points

The following question-and-answer format summarizes the chapter's learning objectives. Each decision presents a key question related to a learning objective. The guidelines are the answer to that question.

Decision	Guidelines
1. What are the four cost categories of a costs-of-quality program?	Four cost categories in a costs-of-quality program are prevention costs (costs incurred to preclude the production of products that do not conform to specifications), appraisal costs (costs incurred to detect which of the individual units of products do not conform to specifications), internal failure costs (costs incurred on defective products before they are shipped to customers), and external failure costs (costs incurred on defective products after they are shipped to customers).
2. What nonfinancial measures and methods can managers use to improve quality?	Nonfinancial quality measures managers can use include customer satisfaction measures such as number of customer complaints and percentage of defective units shipped to customers; internal-business process measures such as percentage of defective and reworked products; and learning and growth measures such as percentage of employees trained in and empowered to use quality principles.
	Three methods to identify quality problems and to improve quality are (a) control charts, to distinguish random from nonrandom variations in an operating process; (b) Pareto diagrams, to indicate how frequently each type of failure occurs; and (c) cause-and-effect diagrams, to identify and respond to potential causes of failure.
3. How do managers identify the relevant costs and benefits of quality improvement programs and use financial and nonfinancial measures to evaluate quality?	The relevant costs of quality improvement programs are the expected incremental costs to implement the program. The relevant benefits are the cost savings and the estimated increase in contribution margin from the higher revenues expected from quality improvements.
	Financial measures are helpful to evaluate trade-offs among prevention costs, appraisal costs, and failure costs. Nonfinancial measures identify problem areas that need improvement and serve as indicators of future long-run performance.

4. What is customer-response time? What are the reasons for and the costs of delays?

Customer-response time is how long it takes from the time a customer places an order for a product or service to the time the product or service is delivered to the customer. Delays occur because of (a) uncertainty about when customers will order products or services and (b) bottlenecks due to limited capacity. Bottlenecks are operations at which the work to be performed approaches or exceeds available capacity. Costs of delays include lower revenues and increased inventory carrying costs.

5. What are the steps managers can take to manage bottlenecks?

The four steps in managing bottlenecks are (1) recognize that the bottleneck operation determines throughput margin, (2) identify the bottleneck, (3) keep the bottleneck busy and subordinate all nonbottleneck operations to the bottleneck operation, and (4) increase bottleneck efficiency and capacity.

Terms to Learn

This chapter and the Glossary at the end of the book contain definitions of the following important terms:

appraisal costs (**p. 673**)
average waiting time (**p. 683**)
bottleneck (**p. 682**)
cause-and-effect diagram (**p. 676**)
conformance quality (**p. 672**)
control chart (**p. 675**)
costs of quality (COQ) (**p. 672**)
customer-response time (**p. 681**)

design quality (**p. 672**)
external failure costs (**p. 673**)
internal failure costs (**p. 673**)
manufacturing cycle efficiency (MCE) (**p. 681**)
manufacturing cycle time (**p. 681**)
manufacturing lead time (**p. 681**)

on-time performance (**p. 682**)
Pareto diagram (**p. 676**)
prevention costs (**p. 673**)
quality (**p. 671**)
theory of constraints (TOC) (**p. 686**)
throughput margin (**p. 686**)
time driver (**p. 682**)

Assignment Material

Questions

19-1 Describe two benefits of improving quality.
19-2 How does conformance quality differ from design quality? Explain.
19-3 Name two items classified as prevention costs.
19-4 Distinguish between internal failure costs and external failure costs.
19-5 Describe three methods that companies use to identify quality problems.
19-6 "Companies should focus on financial measures of quality because these are the only measures of quality that can be linked to bottom-line performance." Do you agree? Explain.
19-7 Give two examples of nonfinancial measures of customer satisfaction relating to quality.
19-8 Give two examples of nonfinancial measures of internal-business-process quality.
19-9 Distinguish between customer-response time and manufacturing cycle time.
19-10 "There is no trade-off between customer-response time and on-time performance." Do you agree? Explain.
19-11 Give two reasons why delays occur.
19-12 "Companies should always make and sell all products whose selling prices exceed variable costs." Assuming fixed costs are irrelevant, do you agree? Explain.
19-13 Describe the three main measures used in the theory of constraints.
19-14 Describe the four key steps in managing bottleneck operations.
19-15 Describe three ways to improve the performance of a bottleneck operation.

Exercises

19-16 **Costs of quality.** (CMA, adapted) Costen, Inc., produces cell phone equipment. Jessica Tolmy, Costen's president, decided to devote more resources to the improvement of product quality after learning that her company had been ranked fourth in product quality in a 2009 survey of cell phone users. Costen's quality-improvement program has now been in operation for two years, and the cost report shown here has recently been issued.

	A	B	C	D	E
		Home Insert Page Layout Formulas Data Review View			
1	**Semi-Annual COQ Report, Costen, Inc.**				
2	**(in thousands)**				
3		6/30/2010	12/31/2010	6/30/2011	12/31/2011
4	Prevention costs				
5	Machine maintenance	$ 440	$ 440	$ 390	$ 330
6	Supplier training	20	100	50	40
7	Design reviews	50	214	210	200
8	Total prevention costs	510	754	650	570
9	Appraisal costs				
10	Incoming inspections	108	123	90	63
11	Final testing	332	332	293	203
12	Total appraisal costs	440	455	383	266
13	Internal failure costs				
14	Rework	231	202	165	112
15	Scrap	124	116	71	67
16	Total internal failure costs	355	318	236	179
17	External failure costs				
18	Warranty repairs	165	85	72	68
19	Customer returns	570	547	264	188
20	Total external failure costs	735	632	336	256
21	Total quality costs	$2,040	$2,159	$1,605	$1,271
22					
23	Total revenues	$8,240	$9,080	$9,300	$9,020

Required

1. For each period, calculate the ratio of each COQ category to revenues and to total quality costs.
2. Based on the results of requirement 1, would you conclude that Costen's quality program has been successful? Prepare a short report to present your case.
3. Based on the 2009 survey, Jessica Tolmy believed that Costen had to improve product quality. In making her case to Costen management, how might Tolmy have estimated the opportunity cost of not implementing the quality-improvement program?

19-17 Costs of quality analysis. Dream Rider produces car seats for children from newborn to two years old. The company is worried because one of its competitors has recently come under public scrutiny because of product failure. Historically, Dream Rider's only problem with its car seats was stitching in the straps. The problem can usually be detected and repaired during an internal inspection. The cost of the inspection is $4, and the repair cost is $0.75. All 250,000 car seats were inspected last year and 9% were found to have problems with the stitching in the straps during the internal inspection. Another 3% of the 250,000 car seats had problems with the stitching, but the internal inspection did not discover them. Defective units that were sold and shipped to customers needed to be shipped back to Dream Rider and repaired. Shipping costs are $7, and repair costs are $0.75. However, the out-of-pocket costs (shipping and repair) are not the only costs of defects not discovered in the internal inspection. For 20% of the external failures, negative word of mouth will result in a loss of sales, lowering the following year's profits by $300 for each of the 20% of units with external failures.

Required

1. Calculate appraisal cost.
2. Calculate internal failure cost.
3. Calculate out-of-pocket external failure cost.
4. Determine the opportunity cost associated with the external failures.
5. What are the total costs of quality?
6. Dream Rider is concerned with the high up-front cost of inspecting all 250,000 units. It is considering an alternative internal inspection plan that will cost only $1.00 per car seat inspected. During the internal inspection, the alternative technique will detect only 5.0% of the 250,000 car seats that have stitching problems. The other 7.0% will be detected after the car seats are sold and shipped. What are the total costs of quality for the alternative technique?
7. What factors other than cost should Dream Rider consider before changing inspection techniques?

19-18 Costs of quality, ethical considerations. Refer to information in Exercise 19-17 in answering this question. Dream Rider has discovered a more serious problem with the plastic core of its car seats. An accident can cause the plastic in some of the seats to crack and break, resulting in serious injuries to the occupant. It is estimated that this problem will affect about 175 car seats in the next year. This problem could be corrected by using a higher quality of plastic that would increase the cost of every car seat produced by $15. If this problem is not corrected, Dream Rider estimates that out of the 175 accidents, customers will realize that the problem is due to a defect in the seats in only three cases. Dream Rider's legal team has estimated that each of these three accidents would result in a lawsuit that could be settled for about $775,000. All lawsuits settled would include a confidentiality clause, so Dream Rider's reputation would not be affected.

1. Assuming that Dream Rider expects to sell 250,000 car seats next year, what would be the cost of increasing the quality of all 250,000 car seats? **Required**
2. What will be the total cost of the lawsuits next year if the problem is not corrected?
3. Suppose Dream Rider has decided not to increase the quality of the plastic because the cost of increasing the quality exceeds the benefits (saving the cost of lawsuits). What do you think of this decision? (Note: Because of the confidentiality clause, the decision will have no effect on Dream Rider's reputation.)
4. Are there any other costs or benefits that Dream Rider should consider?

19-19 Nonfinancial measures of quality and time. Worldwide Cell Phones (WCP) has developed a cell phone that can be used anywhere in the world (even countries like Japan that have a relatively unique cell phone system). WCP has been receiving complaints about the phone. For the past two years, WCP has been test marketing the phones and gathering nonfinancial information related to actual and perceived aspects of the phone's quality. The company expects that, given the lack of competition in this market, increasing the quality of the phone will result in higher sales and thereby higher profits.

Quality data for 2010 and 2011 include the following:

	2010	2011
Cell phones produced and shipped	2,000	10,000
Number of defective units shipped	100	400
Number of customer complaints	150	250
Units reworked before shipping	120	700
Manufacturing cycle time	15 days	16 days
Average customer response time	30 days	28 days

1. For each year, 2010 and 2011, calculate the following: **Required**
   a. Percentage of defective units shipped
   b. Customer complaints as a percentage of units shipped
   c. Percentage of units reworked during production
   d. Manufacturing cycle time as a percentage of total time from order to delivery
2. Referring to the information computed in requirement 1, explain whether WCP's quality and timeliness have improved.
3. Why would manufacturing cycle time have increased while customer response time decreased? (It may be useful to first describe what is included in each time measurement—see Exhibit 19-7, p. 681.)

19-20 Quality improvement, relevant costs, relevant revenues. SpeedPrint manufactures and sells 18,000 high-technology printing presses each year. The variable and fixed costs of rework and repair are as follows:

	Variable Cost	Fixed Cost	Total Cost
Rework cost per hour	$ 79	$115	$194
Repair costs			
Customer support cost per hour	35	55	90
Transportation cost per load	350	115	465
Warranty repair cost per hour	89	150	239

SpeedPrint's current presses have a quality problem that causes variations in the shade of some colors. Its engineers suggest changing a key component in each press. The new component will cost $70 more than the old one. In the next year, however, SpeedPrint expects that with the new component it will (1) save 14,000 hours of rework, (2) save 850 hours of customer support, (3) move 225 fewer loads, (4) save

8,000 hours of warranty repairs, and (5) sell an additional 140 printing presses, for a total contribution margin of $1,680,000. SpeedPrint believes that even as it improves quality, it will not be able to save any of the fixed costs of rework or repair. SpeedPrint uses a one-year time horizon for this decision because it plans to introduce a new press at the end of the year.

Required

1. Should SpeedPrint change to the new component? Show your calculations.
2. Suppose the estimate of 140 additional printing presses sold is uncertain. What is the minimum number of additional printing presses that SpeedPrint needs to sell to justify adopting the new component?

19-21 Quality improvement, relevant costs, relevant revenues. Flagstar Conference Center and Catering is a conference center and restaurant facility that hosts over 300 national and international events each year attended by 50,000 professionals. Due to increased competition and soaring customer expectations, the company has been forced to revisit its quality standards. In the company's 25 year history, customer demand has never been greater for high quality products and services. Flagstar has the following budgeted fixed and variable costs for 2011:

	Total Conference Center Fixed Cost	Variable Cost per Conference Attendee
Building and facilities	$3,600,000	
Management salaries	$1,400,000	
Customer support and service personnel		$ 55
Food and drink		$100
Conference materials		$ 35
Incidental products and services		$ 15

The company's budgeted operating income is $3,500,000.

After conducting a survey of 3,000 conference attendees, the company has learned that its customers would most like to see the following changes in the quality of the company's products and services: 1) more menu options and faster service, 2) more incidental products and services (wireless access in all meeting rooms, computer stations for internet use, free local calling, etc.), and 3) upscale and cleaner meeting facilities. To satisfy these customer demands, the company would be required to increase fixed costs by 50% per year and increase variable costs by $10 per attendee as follows:

	Additional Variable Cost per Conference Attendee
Customer support and service personnel	$3
Food and drink	$5
Conference materials	$0
Incidental products and services	$2

Flagstar believes that the preceding improvements in product and service quality would increase overall conference attendance by 40%.

Required

1. What is the budgeted revenue per conference attendee?
2. Assuming budgeted revenue per conference attendee is unchanged, should Flagstar implement the proposed changes?
3. Assuming budgeted revenue per conference attendee is unchanged, what is the variable cost per conference attendee at which Flagstar would be indifferent between implementing and not implementing the proposed changes?

19-22 Waiting time, service industry. The registration advisors at a small midwestern university (SMU) help 4,200 students develop each of their class schedules and register for classes each semester. Each advisor works for 10 hours a day during the registration period. SMU currently has 10 advisors. While advising an individual student can take anywhere from 2 to 30 minutes, it takes an average of 12 minutes per student. During the registration period, the 10 advisors see an average of 300 students a day on a first-come, first-served basis.

Required

1. Using the formula on page 683, calculate how long the average student will have to wait in the advisor's office before being advised.

2. The head of the registration advisors would like to increase the number of students seen each day, because at 300 students a day it would take 14 working days to see all of the students. This is a problem because the registration period lasts for only two weeks (10 working days). If the advisors could advise 420 students a day, it would take only two weeks (10 days). However, the head advisor wants to make sure that the waiting time is not excessive. What would be the average waiting time if 420 students were seen each day?

3. SMU wants to know the effect of reducing the average advising time on the average wait time. If SMU can reduce the average advising time to 10 minutes, what would be the average waiting time if 420 students were seen each day?

19-23 Waiting time, cost considerations, customer satisfaction. Refer to the information presented in Exercise 19-22. The head of the registration advisors at SMU has decided that the advisors must finish their advising in two weeks and therefore must advise 420 students a day. However, the average waiting time given a 12-minute advising period will result in student complaints, as will reducing the average advising time to 10 minutes. SMU is considering two alternatives:

A. Hire two more advisors for the two-week (10-working day) advising period. This will increase the available number of advisors to 12 and therefore lower the average waiting time.

B. Increase the number of days that the advisors will work during the two-week registration period to six days a week. If SMU increases the number of days worked to six per week, then the 10 advisors need only see 350 students a day to advise all of the students in two weeks.

1. What would the average wait time be under alternative A and under alternative B?   **Required**
2. If advisors earn $100 per day, which alternative would be cheaper for SMU (assume that if advisors work six days in a given work week, they will be paid time and a half for the sixth day)?
3. From a student satisfaction point of view, which of the two alternatives would be preferred? Why?

19-24 Nonfinancial measures of quality, manufacturing cycle efficiency. (CMA, adapted) Torrance Manufacturing evaluates the performance of its production managers based on a variety of factors, including cost, quality, and cycle time. The following are nonfinancial measures for quality and time for 2010 and 2011 for its only product:

Nonfinancial Quality Measures	2010	2011
Number of returned goods	385	462
Number of defective units reworked	1,122	834
Annual hours spent on quality training per employee	32	36
Number of units delivered on time	12,438	14,990

Annual Totals	2010	2011
Units of finished goods shipped	14,240	16,834
Average total hours worked per employee	2,000	2,000

The following information relates to the average amount of time needed to complete an order:

Time to Complete an Order	2010	2011
Wait time		
From order being placed to start of production	8	6
From start of production to completion	6	7
Inspection time	2	1
Process time	4	4
Move time	2	2

1. Compute the manufacturing cycle efficiency for an order for 2010 and 2011.   **Required**
2. For each year 2010 and 2011, calculate the following:
    a. Percentage of goods returned
    b. Defective units reworked as a percentage of units shipped
    c. Percentage of on-time deliveries
    d. Percentage of hours spent by each employee on quality training
3. Evaluate management's performance on quality and timeliness over the two years.

19-25 Theory of constraints, throughput margin, relevant costs. The Mayfield Corporation manufactures filing cabinets in two operations: machining and finishing. It provides the following information:

	Machining	Finishing
Annual capacity	100,000 units	80,000 units
Annual production	80,000 units	80,000 units
Fixed operating costs (excluding direct materials)	$640,000	$400,000
Fixed operating costs per unit produced ($640,000 ÷ 80,000; $400,000 ÷ 80,000)	$8 per unit	$5 per unit

Each cabinet sells for $72 and has direct material costs of $32 incurred at the start of the machining operation. Mayfield has no other variable costs. Mayfield can sell whatever output it produces. The following requirements refer only to the preceding data. There is no connection between the requirements.

Required

1. Mayfield is considering using some modern jigs and tools in the finishing operation that would increase annual finishing output by 1,000 units. The annual cost of these jigs and tools is $30,000. Should Mayfield acquire these tools? Show your calculations.
2. The production manager of the machining department has submitted a proposal to do faster setups that would increase the annual capacity of the machining department by 10,000 units and would cost $5,000 per year. Should Mayfield implement the change? Show your calculations.
3. An outside contractor offers to do the finishing operation for 12,000 units at $10 per unit, double the $5 per unit that it costs Mayfield to do the finishing in-house. Should Mayfield accept the subcontractor's offer? Show your calculations.
4. The Hunt Corporation offers to machine 4,000 units at $4 per unit, half the $8 per unit that it costs Mayfield to do the machining in-house. Should Mayfield accept Hunt's offer? Show your calculations.

19-26 Theory of constraints, throughput margin, quality. Refer to the information in Exercise 19-25 in answering the following requirements. There is no connection between the requirements.

Required

1. Mayfield produces 2,000 defective units at the machining operation. What is the cost to Mayfield of the defective items produced? Explain your answer briefly.
2. Mayfield produces 2,000 defective units at the finishing operation. What is the cost to Mayfield of the defective items produced? Explain your answer briefly.

MyAccountingLab

Problems

19-27 Quality improvement, relevant costs, and relevant revenues. The Thomas Corporation sells 300,000 V262 valves to the automobile and truck industry. Thomas has a capacity of 110,000 machine-hours and can produce 3 valves per machine-hour. V262's contribution margin per unit is $8. Thomas sells only 300,000 valves because 30,000 valves (10% of the good valves) need to be reworked. It takes one machine-hour to rework 3 valves, so 10,000 hours of capacity are used in the rework process. Thomas's rework costs are $210,000. Rework costs consist of the following:

- Direct materials and direct rework labor (variable costs): $3 per unit
- Fixed costs of equipment, rent, and overhead allocation: $4 per unit

Thomas's process designers have developed a modification that would maintain the speed of the process and ensure 100% quality and no rework. The new process would cost $315,000 per year. The following additional information is available:

- The demand for Thomas's V262 valves is 370,000 per year.
- The Jackson Corporation has asked Thomas to supply 22,000 T971 valves (another product) if Thomas implements the new design. The contribution margin per T971 valve is $10. Thomas can make two T971 valves per machine-hour with 100% quality and no rework.

Required

1. Suppose Thomas's designers implement the new design. Should Thomas accept Jackson's order for 22,000 T971 valves? Show your calculations.
2. Should Thomas implement the new design? Show your calculations.
3. What nonfinancial and qualitative factors should Thomas consider in deciding whether to implement the new design?

19-28 Quality improvement, relevant costs, and relevant revenues. The Tan Corporation uses multicolor molding to make plastic lamps. The molding operation has a capacity of 200,000 units per year. The demand for lamps is very strong. Tan will be able to sell whatever output quantities it can produce at $40 per lamp.

Tan can start only 200,000 units into production in the molding department because of capacity constraints on the molding machines. If a defective unit is produced at the molding operation, it must be scrapped at a net disposal value of zero. Of the 200,000 units started at the molding operation, 30,000 defective units (15%) are produced. The cost of a defective unit, based on total (fixed and variable) manufacturing costs incurred up to the molding operation, equals $25 per unit, as follows:

Direct materials (variable)	$16 per unit
Direct manufacturing labor, setup labor, and materials-handling labor (variable)	3 per unit
Equipment, rent, and other allocated overhead, including inspection and testing costs on scrapped parts (fixed)	6 per unit
Total	$25 per unit

Tan's designers have determined that adding a different type of material to the existing direct materials would result in no defective units being produced, but it would increase the variable costs by $4 per lamp in the molding department.

1. Should Tan use the new material? Show your calculations.
2. What nonfinancial and qualitative factors should Tan consider in making the decision?

Required

19-29 Statistical quality control. Keltrex Cereals produces a wide variety of breakfast products. The company's three best selling breakfast cereals are Double Bran Bits, Honey Wheat Squares, and Sugar King Pops. Each box of a particular type of cereal is required to meet pre-determined weight specifications, so that no single box contains more or less cereal than another. The company measures the mean weight per production run to determine if there are variances over or under the company's specified upper and lower level control limits. A production run that falls outside of the specified control limit does not meet quality standards and is investigated further by management to determine the cause of the variance. The three Keltrex breakfast cereals had the following weight standards and production run data for the month of March:

Quality Standard: Mean Weight per Production Run

Double Bran Bits	Honey Wheat Squares	Sugar King Pops
17.97 ounces	14 ounces	16.02 ounces

Actual Mean Weight per Production Run (Ounces)

Production Run	Double Bran Bits	Honey Wheat Squares	Sugar King Pops
1	18.23	14.11	15.83
2	18.14	14.13	16.11
3	18.22	13.98	16.24
4	18.30	13.89	15.69
5	18.10	13.91	15.95
6	18.05	14.01	15.50
7	17.84	13.94	15.86
8	17.66	13.99	16.23
9	17.60	14.03	16.15
10	17.52	13.97	16.60
Standard Deviation	0.28	0.16	0.21

Required

1. Using the $\pm 2\sigma$ rule, what variance investigation decisions would be made?
2. Present control charts for each of the three breakfast cereals for March. What inferences can you draw from the charts?
3. What are the costs of quality in this example? How could Keltrex employ Six Sigma programs to improve quality?

19-30 Compensation linked with profitability, waiting time, and quality measures. East Coast Healthcare operates two medical groups, one in Philadelphia and one in Baltimore. The semi-annual bonus plan for each medical group's president has three components:

a. Profitability performance. Add 0.75% of operating income.
b. Average patient waiting time. Add $40,000 if the average waiting time for a patient to see a doctor after the scheduled appointment time is less than 10 minutes. If average patient waiting time is more than 10 minutes, add nothing.
c. Patient satisfaction performance. Deduct $40,000 if patient satisfaction (measured using a survey asking patients about their satisfaction with their doctor and their overall satisfaction with East Coast Healthcare) falls below 65 on a scale from 0 (lowest) to 100 (highest). No additional bonus is awarded for satisfaction scores of 65 or more.

Semi-annual data for 2011 for the Philadelphia and Baltimore groups are as follows:

	January–June	July–December
Philadelphia		
Operating income	$11,150,000	$10,500,000
Average waiting time	13 minutes	12 minutes
Patient satisfaction	74	72
Baltimore		
Operating income	$ 9,500,000	$ 5,875,000
Average waiting time	12 minutes	9.5 minutes
Patient satisfaction	59	68

Required

1. Compute the bonuses paid in each half year of 2011 to the Philadelphia and Baltimore medical group presidents.
2. Discuss the validity of the components of the bonus plan as measures of profitability, waiting time performance, and patient satisfaction. Suggest one shortcoming of each measure and how it might be overcome (by redesign of the plan or by another measure).
3. Why do you think East Coast Healthcare includes measures of both operating income and waiting time in its bonus plan for group presidents? Give one example of what might happen if waiting time was dropped as a performance measure.

19-31 Waiting times, manufacturing cycle times. The Seawall Corporation uses an injection molding machine to make a plastic product, Z39, after receiving firm orders from its customers. Seawall estimates that it will receive 50 orders for Z39 during the coming year. Each order of Z39 will take 80 hours of machine time. The annual machine capacity is 5,000 hours.

Required

1. Calculate (a) the average amount of time that an order for Z39 will wait in line before it is processed and (b) the average manufacturing cycle time per order for Z39.
2. Seawall is considering introducing a new product, Y28. The company expects it will receive 25 orders of Y28 in the coming year. Each order of Y28 will take 20 hours of machine time. Assuming the demand for Z39 will not be affected by the introduction of Y28, calculate (a) the average waiting time for an order received and (b) the average manufacturing cycle time per order for each product, if Seawall introduces Y28.

19-32 Waiting times, relevant revenues, and relevant costs (continuation of 19-31). Seawall is still debating whether it should introduce Y28. The following table provides information on selling prices, variable costs, and inventory carrying costs for Z39 and Y28:

Product	Annual Average Number of Orders	Selling Price per Order if Average Manufacturing Cycle Time per Order Is — Less Than 320 Hours	Selling Price per Order if Average Manufacturing Cycle Time per Order Is — More Than 320 Hours	Variable Cost per Order	Inventory Carrying Cost per Order per Hour
Z39	50	$27,000	$26,500	$15,000	$0.75
Y28	25	8,400	8,000	5,000	0.25

Required

1. Using the average manufacturing cycle times calculated in Problem 19-31, requirement 2, should Seawall manufacture and sell Y28? Show your calculations.
2. Should Seawall manufacture and sell Y28 if the data are changed as follows:

Product	Annual Average Number of Orders	Selling Price per Order if Average Manufacturing Cycle Time per Order Is — Less Than 320 Hours	Selling Price per Order if Average Manufacturing Cycle Time per Order Is — More Than 320 Hours	Variable Cost per Order	Inventory Carrying Cost per Order per Hour
Z39	50	$27,000	$26,500	$15,000	$0.75
Y28	25	6,400	6,000	5,000	0.25

19-33 Manufacturing cycle times, relevant revenues, and relevant costs. The Brandt Corporation makes wire harnesses for the aircraft industry only upon receiving firm orders form its customers. Brandt has recently purchased a new machine to make two types of wire harnesses, one for Boeing airplanes (B7) and the other for Airbus Industries airplanes (A3). The annual capacity of the new machine is 6,000 hours. The following information is available for next year:

Customer	Annual Average Number of Orders	Manufacturing Time Required	Selling Price per Order if Average Manufacturing Cycle Time per Order Is		Variable Cost per Order	Inventory Carrying Cost per Order per Hour
			Less Than 200 Hours	More Than 200 Hours		
B7	125	40 hours	$15,000	$14,400	$10,000	$0.50
A3	10	50 hours	13,500	12,960	9,000	0.45

Required

1. Calculate the average manufacturing cycle times per order (a) if Brandt manufactures only B7 and (b) if Brandt manufactures both B7 and A3.
2. Even though A3 has a positive contribution margin, Brandt's managers are evaluating whether Brandt should (a) make and sell only B7 or (b) make and sell both B7 and A3. Which alternative will maximize Brandt's operating income? Show your calculations.
3. What other factors should Brandt consider in choosing between the alternatives in requirement 2?

19-34 Theory of constraints, throughput margin, and relevant costs. Nevada Industries manufactures electronic testing equipment. Nevada also installs the equipment at customers' sites and ensures that it functions smoothly. Additional information on the manufacturing and installation departments is as follows (capacities are expressed in terms of the number of units of electronic testing equipment):

	Equipment Manufactured	Equipment Installed
Annual capacity	400 units per year	250 units per year
Equipment manufactured and installed	250 units per year	250 units per year

Nevada manufactures only 250 units per year because the installation department has only enough capacity to install 250 units. The equipment sells for $60,000 per unit (installed) and has direct material costs of $35,000. All costs other than direct material costs are fixed. The following requirements refer only to the preceding data. There is no connection between the requirements.

Required

1. Nevada's engineers have found a way to reduce equipment manufacturing time. The new method would cost an additional $60 per unit and would allow Nevada to manufacture 20 additional units a year. Should Nevada implement the new method? Show your calculations.
2. Nevada's designers have proposed a change in direct materials that would increase direct material costs by $3,000 per unit. This change would enable Nevada to install 280 units of equipment each year. If Nevada makes the change, it will implement the new design on all equipment sold. Should Nevada use the new design? Show your calculations.
3. A new installation technique has been developed that will enable Nevada's engineers to install 7 additional units of equipment a year. The new method will increase installation costs by $45,000 each year. Should Nevada implement the new technique? Show your calculations.
4. Nevada is considering how to motivate workers to improve their productivity (output per hour). One proposal is to evaluate and compensate workers in the manufacturing and installation departments on the basis of their productivities. Do you think the new proposal is a good idea? Explain briefly.

19-35 Theory of constraints, throughput margin, quality, and relevant costs. Aardee Industries manufactures pharmaceutical products in two departments: mixing and tablet making. Additional information on the two departments follows. Each tablet contains 0.5 gram of direct materials.

	Mixing	Tablet Making
Capacity per hour	150 grams	200 tablets
Monthly capacity (2,000 hours available in each department)	300,000 grams	400,000 tablets
Monthly production	200,000 grams	390,000 tablets
Fixed operating costs (excluding direct materials)	$16,000	$39,000
Fixed operating cost per unit ($16,000 ÷ 200,000 grams; $39,000 ÷ 390,000 tablets)	$0.08 per gram	$0.10 per tablet

The mixing department makes 200,000 grams of direct materials mixture (enough to make 400,000 tablets) because the tablet-making department has only enough capacity to process 400,000 tablets. All direct material costs of $156,000 are incurred in the mixing department. The tablet-making department manufactures only 390,000 tablets from the 200,000 grams of mixture processed; 2.5% of the direct materials mixture is lost in the tablet-making process. Each tablet sells for $1. All costs other than direct material costs are fixed costs. The following requirements refer only to the preceding data. There is no connection between the requirements.

Required

1. An outside contractor makes the following offer: If Aardee will supply the contractor with 10,000 grams of mixture, the contractor will manufacture 19,500 tablets for Aardee (allowing for the normal 2.5% loss of the mixture during the tablet-making process) at $0.12 per tablet. Should Aardee accept the contractor's offer? Show your calculations.
2. Another company offers to prepare 20,000 grams of mixture a month from direct materials Aardee supplies. The company will charge $0.07 per gram of mixture. Should Aardee accept the company's offer? Show your calculations.
3. Aardee's engineers have devised a method that would improve quality in the tablet-making department. They estimate that the 10,000 tablets currently being lost would be saved. The modification would cost $7,000 a month. Should Aardee implement the new method? Show your calculations.
4. Suppose that Aardee also loses 10,000 grams of mixture in its mixing department. These losses can be reduced to zero if the company is willing to spend $9,000 per month in quality-improvement methods. Should Aardee adopt the quality-improvement method? Show your calculations.
5. What are the benefits of improving quality in the mixing department compared with improving quality in the tablet-making department?

19-36 Theory of constraints, contribution margin, sensitivity analysis. Fun Time Toys (FTT) produces dolls in two processes: molding and assembly. FTT is currently producing two models: Chatty Chelsey and Talking Tanya. Production in the molding department is limited by the amount of materials available. Production in the assembly department is limited by the amount of trained labor available. The only variable costs are materials in the molding department and labor in the assembly department. Following are the requirements and limitations by doll model and department:

	Molding Materials	Assembly Time	Selling Price
Chatty Chelsey	1.5 pounds per doll	20 minutes per doll	$39 per doll
Talking Tanya	2 pounds per doll	30 minutes per doll	$51 per doll
Materials/Labor Available	30,000 pounds	8,500 hours	
Cost	$12 per pound	$18 per hour	

Required

1. If there were enough demand for either doll, which doll would FTT produce? How many of these dolls would it make and sell?
2. If FTT sells two Chatty Chelseys for each Talking Tanya, how many dolls of each type would it produce and sell? What would be the total contribution margin?
3. If FTT sells two Chatty Chelseys for each Talking Tanya, how much would production and contribution margin increase if the molding department could buy 15 more pounds of materials for $12 per pound?
4. If FTT sells two Chatty Chelseys for each Talking Tanya, how much would production and contribution margin increase if the assembly department could get 10 more labor hours at $18 per hour?

19-37 Quality improvement, Pareto diagram, cause-and-effect diagram. Pauli's Pizza has recently begun collecting data on the quality of its customer order processing and delivery. Pauli's made 1,800 deliveries during the first quarter of 2012. The following quality data pertains to first quarter deliveries:

Type of Quality Failure	Quality Failure Incidents First Quarter 2012
Late delivery	50
Damaged or spoiled product delivered	5
Incorrect order delivered	12
Service complaints by customer of delivery personnel	8
Failure to deliver incidental items with order (drinks, side items, etc.)	18

Required

1. Draw a Pareto diagram of the quality failures experienced by Pauli's Pizza.
2. Give examples of prevention activities that could reduce the failures experienced by Pauli's.
3. Draw a cause-and-effect diagram of possible causes for late deliveries.

19-38 Ethics and quality. Wainwright Corporation manufactures auto parts for two leading Japanese automakers. Nancy Evans is the management accountant for one of Wainwright's largest manufacturing plants. The plant's General Manager, Chris Sheldon, has just returned from a meeting at corporate headquarters where quality expectations were outlined for 2012. Chris calls Nancy into his office to relay the corporate quality objective that total quality costs will not exceed 10% of total revenues by plant under any circumstances. Chris asks Nancy to provide him with a list of options for meeting corporate headquarter's quality objective. The plant's initial budgeted revenues and quality costs for 2012 are as follows:

Revenue	3,400,000
Quality Costs:	
Testing of purchased materials	32,000
Quality control training for production staff	5,000
Warranty repairs	82,000
Quality design engineering	48,000
Customer support	37,000
Materials scrap	12,000
Product inspection	102,000
Engineering redesign of failed parts	21,000
Rework of failed parts	18,000

Prior to receiving the new corporate quality objective, Nancy had collected information for all of the plant's possible options for improving both product quality and costs of quality. She was planning to introduce the idea of reengineering the manufacturing process at a one-time cost of $75,000, which would decrease product inspection costs by approximately 25% per year and was expected to reduce warranty repairs and customer support by an estimated 40% per year. After seeing the new corporate objective, Nancy is reconsidering the reengineering idea.

Nancy returns to her office and crunches the numbers again to look for other alternatives. She concludes that by increasing the cost of quality control training for production staff by $15,000 per year, the company would reduce inspection costs by 10% annually and reduce warranty repairs and customer support costs by 20% per year, as well. She is leaning toward only presenting this latter option to Chris, the general manager, since this is the only option that meets the new corporate quality objective.

1. Calculate the ratio of each costs-of-quality category (prevention, appraisal, internal failure, and external failure) to revenues for 2012. Are the total costs of quality as a percentage of revenues currently less than 10%?
2. Which of the two quality options should Nancy propose to the general manager, Chris Sheldon? Show the two-year outcome for each option: (a) reengineer the manufacturing process for $75,000 and (b) increase quality training expenditure by $15,000 per year.
3. Suppose Nancy decides not to present the reengineering option to Chris. Is Nancy's action unethical? Explain.

Required

Collaborative Learning Problem

19-39 Quality improvement, theory of constraints. The Wellesley Corporation makes printed cloth in two departments: weaving and printing. Currently, all product first moves through the weaving department and then through the printing department before it is sold to retail distributors for $1,250 per roll. Wellesley provides the following information:

	Weaving	Printing
Monthly capacity	10,000 rolls	15,000 rolls
Monthly production	9,500 rolls	8,550 rolls
Direct material cost per roll of cloth processed at each operation	$500	$100
Fixed operating costs	$2,850,000	$427,500

Wellesley can start only 10,000 rolls of cloth in the weaving department because of capacity constraints of the weaving machines. Of the 10,000 rolls of cloth started in the weaving department, 500 (5%) defective rolls are scrapped at zero net disposal value. The good rolls from the weaving department (called gray cloth) are sent to the printing department. Of the 9,500 good rolls started at the printing operation, 950 (10%) defective rolls are scrapped at zero net disposal value. The Wellesley Corporation's total monthly sales of printed cloth equal the printing department's output.

1. The printing department is considering buying 5,000 additional rolls of gray cloth from an outside supplier at $900 per roll, which is much higher than Wellesley's cost to manufacture the roll. The printing department expects that 10% of the rolls obtained from the outside supplier will result in defective products. Should the printing department buy the gray cloth from the outside supplier? Show your calculations.
2. Wellesley's engineers have developed a method that would lower the printing department's rate of defective products to 6% at the printing operation. Implementing the new method would cost $350,000 per month. Should Wellesley implement the change? Show your calculations.
3. The design engineering team has proposed a modification that would lower the weaving department's rate of defective products to 3%. The modification would cost the company $175,000 per month. Should Wellesley implement the change? Show your calculations.

Required

20 Inventory Management, Just-in-Time, and Simplified Costing Methods

Suppose you could receive a large quantity discount for a product that you regularly use, but the discount requires you to buy a year's supply and necessitates a large up-front expenditure.

Would you take the quantity discount? Companies face similar decisions because firms pay a price for tying up money in inventory sitting on their shelves or elsewhere. Money tied up in inventory is a particularly serious problem when times are tough. When faced with these circumstances, companies like Costco work very hard to better manage their inventories.

Costco Aggressively Manages Inventory to Thrive in Tough Times[1]

When consumers reduced their spending in 2008, traditional stalwarts like Circuit City and Linens 'n Things wilted under the weight of their own massive inventories. They could not turn their inventories quickly enough to pay suppliers and were forced to close their doors when cash ran out.

At the same time, Costco continued to thrive! How? By intentionally stocking *fewer* items than its competitors—and employing inventory management practices that successfully reduced costs throughout its operations. While the average grocery store carries around 40,000 items, Costco limits its offerings to about 4,000 products, or 90% less! Limiting the number of products on its shelves reduces Costco's costs of carrying inventory.

Costco also employs a just-in-time inventory management system, which includes sharing data directly with many of its largest suppliers. Companies like Kimberly-Clark calculate re-order points in real time and send new inventory, as needed, to replenish store shelves. Costco also works to redesign product packaging to squeeze more bulky goods onto trucks and shelves, reducing the number of orders Costco needs to place with suppliers.

Occasionally, the company leverages its 75 million square feet of warehouse space to reduce purchasing costs. For example, when Procter & Gamble recently announced a 6% price increase for its paper goods, Costco bought 258 truckloads of paper towels at the old rate and stored them using available capacity in its distribution centers and warehouses.

---

[1] *Source*: McGregor, Jena. 2008. Costco's artful discounts. *BusinessWeek*, October 20.

These inventory management techniques have allowed Costco to succeed in tough times while others have failed. Costco turns its inventory nearly 12 times a year, far more often than other retailers. With many suppliers agreeing to be paid 30 days after delivery, Costco often sells many of its goods before it even has to pay for them!

Inventory management is important because materials costs often account for more than 40% of total costs of manufacturing companies and more than 70% of total costs in merchandising companies. In this chapter, we describe the components of inventory costs, relevant costs for different inventory-related decisions, and planning and control systems for managing inventory.

Inventory Management in Retail Organizations

Inventory management includes planning, coordinating, and controlling activities related to the flow of inventory into, through, and out of an organization. Consider this breakdown of operations for three major retailers for which cost of goods sold constitutes their largest cost item.

	Kroger	Costco	Wal-Mart
Revenues	100.0%	100.0%	100.0%
Deduct costs:			
Cost of goods sold	76.8%	87.2%	74.7%
Selling and administration costs	21.7%	10.2%	19.5%
Other costs, interest, and taxes	1.4%	1.1%	2.3%
Total costs	99.9%	98.5%	96.5%
Net income	0.1%	1.5%	3.5%

The low percentages of net income to revenues mean that improving the purchase and management of goods for sale can cause dramatic percentage increases in net income.

Costs Associated with Goods for Sale

Managing inventories to increase net income requires companies to effectively manage costs that fall into the following six categories:

1. **Purchasing costs** are the cost of goods acquired from suppliers, including incoming freight costs. These costs usually make up the largest cost category of goods for sale. Discounts for various purchase-order sizes and supplier payment terms affect purchasing costs.

Learning Objective 1

Identify six categories of costs associated with goods for sale

. . . purchasing, ordering, carrying, stockout, quality, and shrinkage

2. **Ordering costs** arise in preparing and issuing purchase orders, receiving and inspecting the items included in the orders, and matching invoices received, purchase orders, and delivery records to make payments. Ordering costs include the cost of obtaining purchase approvals, as well as other special processing costs.

3. **Carrying costs** arise while holding an inventory of goods for sale. Carrying costs include the opportunity cost of the investment tied up in inventory (see Chapter 11, pp. 403–405) and the costs associated with storage, such as space rental, insurance, obsolescence, and spoilage.

4. **Stockout costs** arise when a company runs out of a particular item for which there is customer demand, a *stockout*. The company must act quickly to replenish inventory to meet that demand or suffer the costs of not meeting it. A company may respond to a stockout by expediting an order from a supplier, which can be expensive because of additional ordering costs plus any associated transportation costs. Or the company may lose sales due to the stockout. In this case, the opportunity cost of the stockout includes lost contribution margin on the sale not made plus any contribution margin lost on future sales due to customer ill will.

5. **Costs of quality** result when features and characteristics of a product or service are not in conformance with customer specifications. There are four categories of quality costs (prevention costs, appraisal costs, internal failure costs, and external failure costs), as described in Chapter 19.

6. **Shrinkage costs** result from theft by outsiders, embezzlement by employees, misclassifications, and clerical errors. Shrinkage is measured by the difference between (a) the cost of the inventory recorded on the books in the absence of theft and other incidents just mentioned, and (b) the cost of inventory when physically counted. Shrinkage can often be an important measure of management performance. Consider, for example, the grocery business, where operating income percentages hover around 2%. With such small margins, it is easy to see why one of a store manager's prime responsibilities is controlling inventory shrinkage. A $1,000 increase in shrinkage will erase the operating income from sales of $50,000 (2% × $50,000 = $1,000).

Note that not all inventory costs are available in financial accounting systems. For example, opportunity costs are not recorded in these systems and are a significant component in several of these cost categories.

Information-gathering technology increases the reliability and timeliness of inventory information and reduces costs in the six cost categories. For example, barcoding technology allows a scanner to record purchases and sales of individual units. As soon as a unit is scanned, an instantaneous record of inventory movements is created that helps in the management of purchasing, carrying, and stockout costs. In the next several sections, we consider how relevant costs are computed for different inventory-related decisions in merchandising companies.

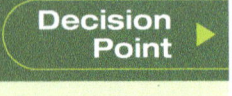

Decision Point

What are the six categories of costs associated with goods for sale?

Learning Objective 2

Balance ordering costs with carrying costs using the economic-order-quantity (EOQ) decision model

. . . choose the inventory quantity per order to minimize these costs

Economic-Order-Quantity Decision Model

The first decision in managing goods for sale is *how much to order* of a given product. The **economic order quantity** (EOQ) is a decision model that, under a given set of assumptions, calculates the optimal quantity of inventory to order.

■ The simplest version of an EOQ model assumes there are only ordering and carrying costs.

■ The same quantity is ordered at each reorder point.

■ Demand, ordering costs, and carrying costs are known with certainty. The **purchase-order lead time**, the time between placing an order and its delivery, is also known with certainty.

■ Purchasing cost per unit is unaffected by the order quantity. This assumption makes purchasing costs irrelevant to determining EOQ, because the purchase price is the same, whatever the order size.

■ No stockouts occur. The basis for this assumption is that the costs of stockouts are so high that managers maintain adequate inventory to prevent them.

■ In deciding on the size of a purchase order, managers consider costs of quality and shrinkage costs only to the extent that these costs affect ordering or carrying costs.

Given these assumptions, EOQ analysis ignores purchasing costs, stockout costs, costs of quality, and shrinkage costs. EOQ is the order quantity that minimizes the relevant ordering and carrying costs (that is, the ordering and carrying costs affected by the quantity of inventory ordered):

$$\text{Relevant total costs} = \text{Relevant ordering costs} + \text{Relevant carrying costs}$$

We use the following notations:

$$D = \text{Demand in units for a specified period (one year in this example)}$$

$$Q = \text{Size of each order (order quantity)}$$

$$\text{Number of purchase orders per period (one year)} = \frac{\text{Demand in units for a period (one year)}}{\text{Size of each order (order quantity)}} = \frac{D}{Q}$$

Average inventory in units $= \dfrac{Q}{2}$, because each time the inventory goes down to 0, an order for Q units is received. The inventory varies from Q to 0 so the average inventory is $\dfrac{0 + Q}{2}$.

$$P = \text{Relevant ordering cost per purchase order}$$

$$C = \text{Relevant carrying cost of one unit in stock for the time period used for } D \text{ (one year)}$$

For any order quantity, Q,

$$\text{Annual relevant ordering costs} = \left(\begin{array}{ccc} \text{Number of} & & \text{Relevant ordering} \\ \text{purchase orders} & \times & \text{cost per} \\ \text{per year} & & \text{purchase order} \end{array} \right) = \left(\frac{D}{Q} \times P \right)$$

$$\text{Annual relevant carrying costs} = \left(\begin{array}{ccc} & & \text{Annual} \\ \text{Average inventory} & \times & \text{relevant carrying} \\ \text{in units} & & \text{cost per unit} \end{array} \right) = \left(\frac{Q}{2} \times C \right)$$

$$\text{Annual relevant total costs} = \begin{array}{c} \text{Annual} \\ \text{relevant ordering} \\ \text{costs} \end{array} + \begin{array}{c} \text{Annual} \\ \text{relevant carrying} \\ \text{costs} \end{array} = \left(\frac{D}{Q} \times P \right) + \left(\frac{Q}{2} \times C \right)$$

The order quantity that minimizes annual relevant total costs is

$$EOQ = \sqrt{\frac{2DP}{C}}$$

The EOQ model is solved using calculus but the key intuition is that relevant total costs are minimized when relevant ordering costs equal relevant carrying costs. If carrying costs are less (greater) than ordering costs, total costs can be reduced by increasing (decreasing) the order quantity. To solve for EOQ, we set

$$\left(\frac{Q}{2} \times C \right) = \left(\frac{D}{Q} \times P \right)$$

Multiplying both sides by $\dfrac{2Q}{C}$, we get $Q^2 = \dfrac{2DP}{C}$

$$Q = \sqrt{\frac{2DP}{C}}$$

The formula indicates that EOQ increases with higher demand and/or higher ordering costs and decreases with higher carrying costs.

Let's consider an example to see how EOQ analysis works. CD World is an independent electronics store that sells blank compact disks. CD World purchases the CDs from

Sontek at $14 a package (each package contains 20 disks). Sontek pays for all incoming freight. No inspection is necessary at CD World because Sontek supplies quality merchandise. CD World's annual demand is 13,000 packages, at a rate of 250 packages per week. CD World requires a 15% annual rate of return on investment. The purchase-order lead time is two weeks. Relevant ordering cost per purchase order is $200.

Relevant carrying cost per package per year is as follows:

Required annual return on investment, 0.15 × $14	$2.10
Relevant costs of insurance, materials handling, breakage, shrinkage, and so on, per year	3.10
Total	$5.20

What is the EOQ of packages of disks?

Substituting D = 13,000 packages per year, P = $200 per order, and C = $5.20 per package per year, in the EOQ formula, we get,

$$EOQ = \sqrt{\frac{2 \times 13{,}000 \times \$200}{\$5.20}} = \sqrt{1{,}000{,}000} = 1{,}000 \text{ packages}$$

Purchasing 1,000 packages per order minimizes total relevant ordering and carrying costs. Therefore, the number of deliveries each period (one year in this example) is as follows:

$$\frac{D}{EOQ} = \frac{13{,}000}{1{,}000} = 13 \text{ deliveries}$$

Recall the annual relevant total costs (RTC) = $\left(\dfrac{D}{Q} \times P\right) + \left(\dfrac{Q}{2} \times C\right)$
For Q = 1,000 units,

$$RTC = \frac{13{,}000 \times \$200}{1{,}000} + \frac{1{,}000 \times \$5.20}{2}$$

$$= \$2{,}600 + \$2{,}600 = \$5{,}200$$

Exhibit 20-1 graphs the annual relevant total costs of ordering (DP/Q) and carrying inventory ($QC/2$) under various order sizes (Q), and it illustrates the trade-off between these two types of costs. The larger the order quantity, the lower the annual relevant ordering costs, but the higher the annual relevant carrying costs. *Annual relevant total costs are at a minimum at the EOQ at which the relevant ordering and carrying costs are equal.*

Exhibit 20-1 Graphic Analysis of Ordering Costs and Carrying Costs for Compact Disks at CD World

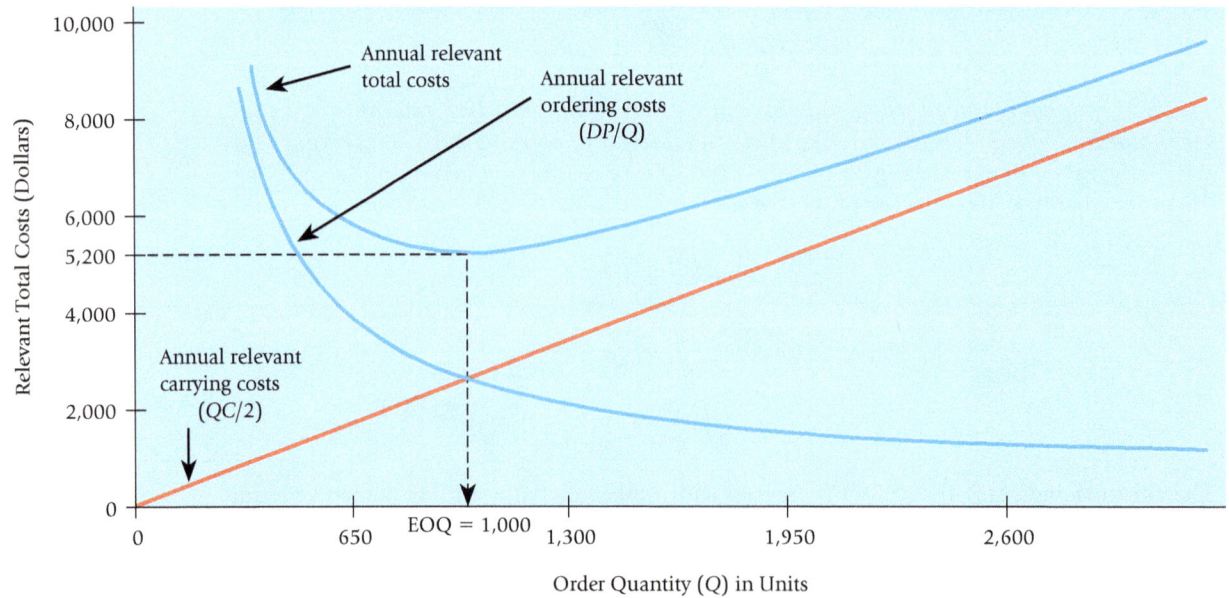

When to Order, Assuming Certainty

The second decision in managing goods for sale is *when to order* a given product. The **reorder point** is the quantity level of inventory on hand that triggers a new purchase order. The reorder point is simplest to compute when both demand and purchase-order lead time are known with certainty:

$$\text{Reorder point} = \frac{\text{Number of units sold}}{\text{per time period}} \times \frac{\text{Purchase-order}}{\text{lead time}}$$

In our CD World example, we choose one week as the time period in the reorder-point formula:

Economic order quantity	1,000 packages
Number of units sold per week	250 packages per week (13,000 packages ÷ 52 weeks)
Purchase-order lead time	2 weeks

$$\text{Reorder point} = 250 \text{ packages per week} \times 2 \text{ weeks} = 500 \text{ packages}$$

CD World will order 1,000 packages each time inventory stock falls to 500 packages.[2] The graph in Exhibit 20-2 shows the behavior of the inventory level of compact disk packages, assuming demand occurs uniformly during each week. If purchase-order lead time is two weeks, a new order will be placed when the inventory level falls to 500 packages, so the 1,000 packages ordered will be received at the precise time that inventory reaches zero.

Safety Stock

We have assumed that demand and purchase-order lead time are known with certainty. Retailers who are uncertain about demand, lead time, or the quantity that suppliers can provide, hold safety stock. **Safety stock** is inventory held at all times regardless of the quantity of inventory ordered using the EOQ model. Safety stock is used as a buffer against unexpected increases in demand, uncertainty about lead time, and unavailability of stock from suppliers. Suppose that in the CD World example, the only uncertainty is about demand. CD World's managers will have some notion (usually based on experience) of the range of weekly demand. CD World's managers expect demand to be 250 packages per week, but they feel that a maximum demand of 400 packages per week

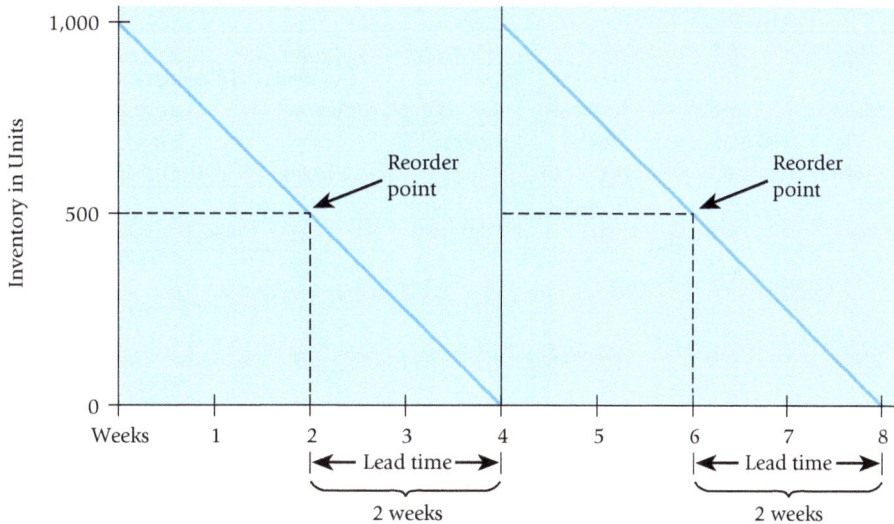

Exhibit 20-2

Inventory Level of Compact Disks at CD World[a]

[a] This exhibit assumes that demand and purchase-order lead time are certain:
   Demand = 250 CD packages per week
   Purchase-order lead time = 2 weeks

---

[2] This handy but special formula does not apply when receipt of the order fails to increase inventory to the reorder-point quantity (for example, when lead time is three weeks and the order is a one-week supply). In these cases, orders will overlap.

may occur. If stockout costs are very high, CD World will hold a safety stock of 300 packages and incur higher carrying costs. The 300 packages equal the maximum excess demand of 150 (400 − 250) packages per week times the two weeks of purchase-order lead time. If stockout costs are minimal, CD World will hold no safety stocks and avoid incurring the additional carrying costs.

A frequency distribution based on prior daily or weekly levels of demand forms the basis for computing safety-stock levels. Assume that one of the following levels of demand will occur over the two-week purchase-order lead time at CD World.

Total Demand for 2 Weeks	200 Units	300 Units	400 Units	500 Units	600 Units	700 Units	800 Units
Probability (sums to 1.00)	0.06	0.09	0.20	0.30	0.20	0.09	0.06

We see that 500 units is the most likely level of demand for two weeks because it has the highest probability of occurrence. We see also a 0.35 probability that demand will be 600, 700, or 800 packages (0.20 + 0.09 + 0.06 = 0.35).

If a customer wants to buy compact disks and the store has none in stock, CD World can "rush" them to the customer at an additional cost to CD World of $4 per package. The relevant stockout costs in this case are $4 per package. The optimal safety-stock level is the quantity of safety stock that minimizes the sum of annual relevant stockout and carrying costs. Note that CD World will place 13 orders per year and will incur the same ordering costs whatever level of safety stock it chooses. Therefore, ordering costs are irrelevant for the safety-stock decision. Recall that the relevant carrying cost for CD World is $5.20 per package per year.

Exhibit 20-3 tabulates annual relevant total stockout and carrying costs when the reorder point is 500 units. Over the two-week purchase-order lead time, stockouts can occur if demand is 600, 700, or 800 units because these levels of demand exceed the 500 units in stock at the time CD World places the purchase orders. Consequently, CD World only evaluates safety stock levels of 0, 100, 200, and 300 units. If safety stock is 0 units, CD World will

Exhibit 20-3 Computation of Safety Stock for CD World When Reorder Point Is 500 Units

	A	B	C	D	E	F	G	H	I
	Home	Insert	Page Layout	Formulas	Data	Review	View		
	A	B	C	D	E	F	G	H	I
1	Safety	Demand							
2	Stock	Levels			Relevant	Number of	Expected	Relevant	Relevant
3	Level	Resulting	Stockout	Probability	Stockout	Orders	Stockout	Carrying	Total
4	in Units	in Stockouts	in Units[a]	of Stockout	Costs[b]	per Year[c]	Costs[d]	Costs[e]	Costs
5	(1)	(2)	(3) = (2) − 500 − (1)	(4)	(5) = (3) × $4	(6)	(7) = (4) × (5) × (6)	(8) = (1) × $5.20	(9) = (7) + (8)
6	0	600	100	0.20	$ 400	13	$1,040		
7		700	200	0.09	800	13	936		
8		800	300	0.06	1,200	13	936		
9							$2,912	$ 0	$2,912
10	100	700	100	0.09	400	13	$ 468		
11		800	200	0.06	800	13	624		
12							$1,092	$ 520	$1,612
13	200	800	100	0.06	400	13	$ 312	$1,040	$1,352
14	300	-	-	-	-	-	$ 0[f]	$1,560	$1,560
15									
16	[a]Demand level resulting in stockouts − Inventory available during lead time (excluding safety stock), 500 units − Safety stock.								
17	[b]Stockout in units × Relevant stockout costs of $4.00 per unit.								
18	[c]Annual demand, 13,000 ÷ 1,000 EOQ = 13 orders per year.								
19	[d]Probability of stockout × Relevant stockout costs × Number of orders per year.								
20	[e]Safety stock × Annual relevant carrying costs of $5.20 per unit (assumes that safety stock is on hand at all times and that there is no overstocking								
21	caused by decreases in expected usage).								
22	[f]At a safety stock level of 300 units, no stockout will occur and, hence, expected stockout costs = $0.								

incur stockout costs if demand is 600, 700, or 800 units but will have no additional carrying costs. At the other extreme, if safety stock is 300 units, CD World will never incur stockout costs but will have higher carrying costs. As Exhibit 20-3 shows, annual relevant total stockout and carrying costs would be the lowest ($1,352) when a safety stock of 200 packages is maintained. Therefore, 200 units is the optimal safety-stock level. Consider the 200 units of safety stock as extra stock that CD World maintains. For example, CD World's total inventory of compact disks at the time of reordering its EOQ of 1,000 units would be 700 units (the reorder point of 500 units plus safety stock of 200 units).

◄ Decision Point

What does the EOQ decision model help managers do and how do managers decide on the level of safety stocks?

Estimating Inventory-Related Relevant Costs and Their Effects

Just as we did in earlier chapters, we need to determine which costs are relevant when making and evaluating inventory management decisions. We next describe the estimates that need to be made to calculate the annual relevant carrying costs of inventory, stockout costs, and ordering costs.

Learning Objective 3

Identify the effect of errors that can arise when using the EOQ decision model

. . . errors in predicting parameters have a small effect on costs

and ways to reduce conflicts between the EOQ model and models used for performance evaluation

. . . by making the two models congruent

Considerations in Obtaining Estimates of Relevant Costs

Relevant inventory carrying costs consist of the *relevant incremental costs* plus the *relevant opportunity cost of capital*.

What are the *relevant incremental costs* of carrying inventory? Only those costs of the purchasing company, such as warehouse rent, warehouse workers' salaries, costs of obsolescence, costs of shrinkage, and costs of breakage, that change with the quantity of inventory held. Salaries paid to clerks, stock keepers, and materials handlers are irrelevant if they are unaffected by changes in inventory levels. Suppose, however, that as inventories increase (decrease), total salary costs increase (decrease) as clerks, stock keepers, and materials handlers are added (transferred to other activities or laid off). In this case, salaries paid are relevant costs of carrying inventory. Similarly, costs of storage space owned that cannot be used for other profitable purposes when inventories decrease are irrelevant. But if the space has other profitable uses, or if total rental cost is tied to the amount of space occupied, storage costs are relevant costs of carrying inventory.

What is the *relevant opportunity cost of capital*? It is the return forgone by investing capital in inventory rather than elsewhere. It is calculated as the required rate of return multiplied by the per-unit costs such as the purchase price of units, incoming freight, and incoming inspection. Opportunity costs are not computed on investments (say, in buildings) if these investments are unaffected by changes in inventory levels.

In the case of stockouts, the relevant incremental cost is the cost of expediting an order from a supplier. The relevant opportunity cost is (1) the lost contribution margin on sales forgone because of the stockout and (2) lost contribution margin on future sales forgone as a result of customer ill will.

Relevant ordering costs are only those ordering costs that change with the number of orders placed (for example, costs of preparing and issuing purchase orders and receiving and inspecting materials).

Cost of a Prediction Error

Predicting relevant costs is difficult and seldom flawless, which raises the question, "What is the cost when actual relevant costs differ from the estimated relevant costs used for decision making?"

Let's revisit the CD World example. Suppose relevant ordering costs per purchase order are $100, while the manager predicts them to be $200 at the time of calculating the order quantity. We can calculate the cost of this "prediction" error using a three-step approach.

Step 1: Compute the Monetary Outcome from the Best Action That Could Be Taken, Given the *Actual* Amount of the Cost Input (Cost per Purchase Order). This is the benchmark, the decision the manager would have made if the manager had known the correct ordering cost against which actual performance can be measured. Using D = 13,000 packages per year, P = \$100, and C = \$5.20 per package per year,

$$EOQ = \sqrt{\frac{2DP}{C}}$$

$$= \sqrt{\frac{2 \times 13,000 \times \$100}{\$5.20}} = \sqrt{500,000}$$

$$= 707 \text{ packages (rounded)}$$

Annual relevant total costs when EOQ = 707 packages are as follows:

$$RTC = \frac{DP}{Q} + \frac{QC}{2}$$

$$= \frac{13,000 \times \$100}{707} + \frac{707 \times \$5.20}{2}$$

$$= \$1,839 + \$1,838 = \$3,677$$

Step 2:   Compute the Monetary Outcome from the Best Action Based on the Incorrect *Predicted* **Amount of the Cost Input (Cost per Purchase Order).** In this step, the manager calculates the order quantity based on the prediction (that later proves to be wrong) that the ordering cost is \$200. If the relevant ordering cost per purchase order is predicted to be \$200, the best action is to purchase 1,000 packages in each order (p. 706). The actual cost of the purchase order turns out to be \$100 so the actual annual relevant total costs when D = 13,000 packages per year, Q = 1,000 packages, P = \$100, and C = \$5.20 per package per year are as follows:

$$RTC = \frac{13,000 \times \$100}{1,000} + \frac{1,000 \times \$5.20}{2}$$

$$= \$1,300 + \$2,600 = \$3,900$$

Step 3:   Compute the Difference Between the Monetary Outcomes from Step 1 and Step 2.

	Monetary Outcome
Step 1	\$3,677
Step 2	3,900
Difference	\$ (223)

The cost of the prediction error, \$223, is less than 7% of the relevant total costs of \$3,677. Note that the annual relevant-total-costs curve in Exhibit 20-1 is somewhat flat over the range of order quantities from 650 to 1,300 units. *The square root in the EOQ model dampens the effect of errors in predicting parameters because taking square roots results in the incorrect numbers becoming smaller.*

In the next section, we consider a planning-and-control and performance-evaluation issue that frequently arises when managing inventory.

Decision Point ▶

What is the effect on costs of errors in predicting parameters of the EOQ model? How can companies reduce the conflict between the EOQ decision model and models used for performance evaluation?

Conflict Between the EOQ Decision Model and Managers' Performance Evaluation

What happens if the order quantity calculated based on the EOQ decision model differs from the order quantity that managers making inventory management decisions would choose to make their own performance look best? For example, because there are no opportunity costs recorded in financial accounting systems, conflicts may arise between the EOQ model's optimal order quantity and the order quantity that purchasing managers (who are evaluated on financial accounting numbers) will regard as optimal. As a result of ignoring some carrying costs (the opportunity costs), managers will be inclined to purchase larger lot sizes of materials than the lot sizes calculated according to the EOQ model. To achieve congruence between the EOQ decision model and managers' performance evaluations, companies such as Wal-Mart design performance-evaluation models that charge managers responsible for managing inventory levels with carrying costs that include a required return on investment.

Just-in-Time Purchasing

Just-in-time (JIT) purchasing is the purchase of materials (or goods) so that they are delivered just as needed for production (or sales). Consider JIT purchasing for Hewlett-Packard's (HP's) manufacture of computer printers. HP has long-term agreements with suppliers for the major components of its printers. Each supplier is required to make frequent deliveries of small orders directly to the production floor, based on the production schedule that HP gives its suppliers. Suppliers work hard to keep their commitments because failure to deliver components on time, or to meet agreed-upon quality standards, can cause an HP assembly plant not to meet its own scheduled deliveries for printers.

Learning Objective 4

Describe why companies are using just-in-time purchasing

. . . high carrying costs, low ordering costs, high-quality suppliers, and reliable supply chains

JIT Purchasing and EOQ Model Parameters

Companies moving toward JIT purchasing to reduce their costs of carrying inventories (parameter C in the EOQ model) say that, in the past, carrying costs have actually been much greater than estimated because costs of warehousing, handling, shrinkage, and investment have not been fully identified. At the same time, the cost of placing a purchase order (parameter P in the EOQ model) is decreasing because of the following:

- Companies are establishing long-term purchasing agreements that define price and quality terms over an extended period. Individual purchase orders covered by those agreements require no additional negotiation regarding price or quality.
- Companies are using electronic links to place purchase orders at a cost that is estimated to be a small fraction of the cost of placing orders by telephone or by mail.
- Companies are using purchase-order cards (similar to consumer credit cards such as VISA and MasterCard). As long as purchasing personnel stay within preset total and individual-transaction dollar limits, traditional labor-intensive procurement-approval procedures are not required.

Exhibit 20-4 tabulates the sensitivity of CD World's EOQ (p. 705) to changes in carrying and ordering costs. Exhibit 20-4 supports JIT purchasing because, as relevant carrying costs increase and relevant ordering costs per purchase order decrease, EOQ decreases and ordering frequency increases.

Relevant Costs of JIT Purchasing

JIT purchasing is not guided solely by the EOQ model. The EOQ model is designed only to emphasize the trade-off between relevant carrying and ordering costs. However, inventory management also includes purchasing costs, stockout costs, costs of quality, and shrinkage costs. We next present the calculation of relevant costs in a JIT purchasing decision.

Exhibit 20-4

Sensitivity of EOQ to Variations in Relevant Ordering and Carrying Costs for CD World

Home Insert Page Layout Formulas Data Review View						
A	B	C	D	E	F	G
1			Economic Order Quantity in Units			
2			At Different Ordering and Carrying Costs			
3 Annual Demand (D) =	13,000	units				
4						
5 Relevant Carrying Costs			Relevant Ordering Costs per Purchase Order (P)			
6 Per Package per Year (C)			$ 200	$150	$100	$ 30
7 $ 5.20			1,000	866	707	387
8 7.00			862	746	609	334
9 10.00			721	624	510	279
10 15.00			589	510	416	228

Exhibit 20-5 Annual Relevant Costs of Current Purchasing Policy and JIT Purchasing Policy for CD World

	A	B		C	D	E	F	G		H	I	J
1						Relevant Costs Under						
2				Current Purchasing Policy						JIT Purchasing Policy		
3	Relevant Items	Relevant Cost Per Unit			Quantity Per Year	Total Costs		Relevant Cost Per Unit			Quantity Per Year	Total Costs
4	(1)	(2)			(3)	(4) = (2) × (3)		(5)			(6)	(7) = (5) × (6)
5	Purchasing costs	$14.00	per unit		13,000	$182,000		$14.02	per unit		13,000	$182,260
6	Ordering costs	2.00	per order		13	26		2.00	per order		130	260
7	Opportunity carrying costs	2.10[a]	per unit of average inventory per year		500[b]	1,050		2.10[a]	per unit of average inventory per year		50[c]	105
8	Other carrying costs (insurance, materials handling, and so on)	3.10	per unit of average inventory per year		500[b]	1,550		3.10	per unit of average inventory per year		50[c]	155
9	Stockout costs	4.00	per unit		0	0		4.00	per unit		150	600
10	Total annual relevant costs					$184,626						$183,380
11	Annual difference in favor of JIT purchasing						$1,246					
12												
13	[a]Purchasing cost per unit × 0.15 per year											
14	[b]Order quantity ÷ 2 = 1,000 ÷ 2 = 500 units											
15	[c]Order quantity ÷ 2 = 100 ÷ 2 = 50 units											

CD World has recently established an Internet business-to-business purchase-order link with Sontek. CD World triggers a purchase order for compact disks by a single computer entry. Payments are made electronically for batches of deliveries, rather than for each individual delivery. These changes reduce the ordering cost from $200 to only $2 per purchase order! CD World will use the Internet purchase-order link whether or not it shifts to JIT purchasing. CD World is negotiating to have Sontek deliver 100 packages of disks 130 times per year (5 times every 2 weeks), instead of delivering 1,000 packages 13 times per year, as shown in Exhibit 20-1. Sontek is willing to make these frequent deliveries, but it would add $0.02 to the price per package. As before, CD World's required rate of return on investment is 15% and the annual relevant carrying cost of insurance, materials handling, shrinkage, breakage, and the like is $3.10 per package per year.

Also assume that CD World incurs no stockout costs under its *current* purchasing policy, because demand and purchase-order lead times during each four-week period are known with certainty. CD World is concerned that lower inventory levels from implementing JIT purchasing will lead to more stockouts, because demand variations and delays in supplying disks are more likely in the short time intervals between orders delivered under JIT purchasing. Sontek has flexible manufacturing processes that enable it to respond rapidly to changing demand patterns. Nevertheless, CD World expects to incur stockout costs on 150 compact disk packages per year under the JIT purchasing policy. When a stockout occurs, CD World must rush-order compact disk packages from another supplier at an additional cost of $4 per package. Should CD World implement the JIT purchasing option of 130 deliveries per year? Exhibit 20-5 compares CD World's relevant total costs under the current purchasing policy and the JIT policy, and it shows net cost savings of $1,246 per year by shifting to a JIT purchasing policy.

Supplier Evaluation and Relevant Costs of Quality and Timely Deliveries

Companies that implement JIT purchasing choose their suppliers carefully and develop long-term supplier relationships. Some suppliers are better positioned than others to support JIT purchasing. For example, Frito-Lay, a supplier of potato chips and other snack foods, has a corporate strategy that emphasizes service, consistency, freshness, and quality of the delivered products. As a result, the company makes deliveries to retail outlets more frequently than many of its competitors.

Exhibit 20-6 Annual Relevant Costs of Purchasing from Sontek and Denton

	Home	Insert	Page Layout	Formulas	Data	Review	View			
	A	B	C	D	E	F	G	H	I	J
1				Relevant Cost of Purchasing From						
2			Sontek				Denton			
3	**Relevant Items**	**Relevant Cost Per Unit**		**Quantity Per Year**	**Total Costs**		**Relevant Cost Per Unit**		**Quantity Per Year**	**Total Costs**
4	(1)	(2)		(3)	(4) = (2) × (3)		(5)		(6)	(7) = (5) × (6)
5	Purchasing costs	$14.02	per unit	13,000	$182,260		$13.80	per unit	13,000	$179,400
6	Ordering costs	2.00	per order	130	260		2.00	per order	130	260
7	Inspection costs	0.05	per unit	0	0		0.05	per unit	13,000	650
8	Opportunity carrying costs	2.10[a]	per unit of average inventory per year	50[b]	105		2.07[a]	per unit of average inventory per year	50[b]	103
9	Other carrying costs (insurance, materials handling, and so on)	3.10	per unit of average inventory per year	50[b]	155		3.00	per unit of average inventory per year	50[b]	150
10	Customer return costs	10.00	per unit returned	0	0		10.00	per unit returned	325[c]	3,250
11	Stockout costs	4.00	per unit	150	600		4.00	per unit	360	1,440
12	Total annual relevant costs				$183,380					$185,253
13	Annual difference in favor of Sontek					$1,873				
14										
15	[a]Purchasing cost per unit × 0.15 per year									
16	[b]Order quantity ÷ 2 = 100 ÷ 2 = 50 units									
17	[c]2.5% of units returned × 13,000 units									

What are the relevant total costs when choosing suppliers? Consider again CD World. Denton Corporation, another supplier of disks, offers to supply all of CD World's compact disk needs at a price of $13.80 per package, less than Sontek's price of $14.02, under the same JIT delivery terms that Sontek offers. Denton proposes an Internet purchase-order link identical to Sontek's link, making CD World's ordering cost $2 per purchase order. CD World's relevant cost of insurance, materials handling, breakage, and the like would be $3.00 per package per year if it purchases from Denton, versus $3.10 if it purchases from Sontek. Should CD World buy from Denton? To answer this, we need to consider the relevant costs of quality and delivery performance.

CD World has used Sontek in the past and knows that Sontek will deliver quality disks on time. In fact, CD World does not even inspect the compact disk packages that Sontek supplies and therefore incurs zero inspection costs. Denton, however, does not enjoy such a sterling reputation for quality. CD World anticipates the following negative aspects of using Denton:

- Inspection cost of $0.05 per package.
- Average stockouts of 360 packages per year requiring rush orders at an additional cost of $4 per package.
- Product returns of 2.5% of all packages sold due to poor compact disk quality. CD World estimates an additional cost of $10 to handle each returned package.

Exhibit 20-6 shows the relevant total costs of purchasing from Sontek and Denton. Even though Denton is offering a lower price per package, there is a net cost savings of $1,873 per year by purchasing disks from Sontek. Selling Sontek's high-quality compact disks also enhances CD World's reputation and increases customer goodwill, which could lead to higher sales and profitability in the future.

JIT Purchasing, Planning and Control, and Supply-Chain Analysis

The levels of inventories held by retailers are influenced by the demand patterns of their customers and supply relationships with their distributors and manufacturers, the suppliers to their manufacturers, and so on. The *supply chain* describes the flow of goods, services, and information from the initial sources of materials and services to the delivery of products to consumers, regardless of whether those activities occur in the same company or in other companies. Retailers can purchase inventories on a JIT basis only if activities throughout the supply chain are properly planned, coordinated, and controlled.

Procter and Gamble's (P&G's) experience with its Pampers product illustrates the gains from supply-chain coordination. Retailers selling Pampers encountered variability in weekly demand because families purchased disposable diapers randomly. Anticipating even more demand variability and lacking information about available inventory with P&G, retailers' orders to P&G became more variable that, in turn, increased variability of orders at P&G's suppliers, resulting in high levels of inventory at all stages in the supply chain.

How did P&G respond to these problems? By sharing information and planning and coordinating activities throughout the supply chain among retailers, P&G, and P&G's suppliers. Sharing sales information reduced the level of uncertainty that P&G and its suppliers had about retail demand for Pampers and led to (1) fewer stockouts at the retail level, (2) reduced manufacture of Pampers not immediately needed by retailers, (3) fewer manufacturing orders that had to be "rushed" or "expedited," and (4) lower inventories held by each company in the supply chain. The benefits of supply chain coordination at P&G have been so great that retailers such as Wal-Mart have contracted with P&G to manage Wal-Mart's retail inventories on a just-in-time basis. This practice is called *supplier- or vendor-managed inventory*. Supply-chain management, however, has challenges in sharing accurate, timely, and relevant information about sales, inventory, and sales forecasts caused by problems of communication, trust, incompatible information systems, and limited people and financial resources.

Inventory Management, MRP and JIT Production

We now turn our attention away from purchasing to managing production inventories in manufacturing companies. Managers at manufacturing companies have developed numerous systems to plan and implement inventory activities within their plants. We consider two widely used types of systems: materials requirements planning (MRP) and just-in-time (JIT) production.

Materials Requirements Planning

**Learning
Objective 5**

Distinguish materials
requirements planning
(MRP) systems

. . . manufacturing
products based on
demand forecasts

from just-in-time (JIT)
systems for
manufacturing

. . . manufacturing
products only
upon receiving
customer orders

Materials requirements planning (MRP) is a "push-through" system that manufactures finished goods for inventory on the basis of demand forecasts. To determine outputs at each stage of production, MRP uses (1) demand forecasts for final products; (2) a bill of materials detailing the materials, components, and subassemblies for each final product; and (3) available inventories of materials, components, and products. Taking into account the lead time required to purchase materials and to manufacture components and finished products, a master production schedule specifies the quantity and timing of each item to be produced. Once production starts as scheduled, the output of each department is pushed through the production line. This "push through" can sometimes result in an accumulation of inventory when workstations receive work they are not yet ready to process.

Maintaining accurate inventory records and costs is critical in an MRP system. For example, after becoming aware of the full costs of carrying finished goods inventory in its MRP system, National Semiconductor contracted with Federal Express to airfreight its microchips from a central location in Singapore to customer sites worldwide, instead of storing products at geographically dispersed warehouses. This change enabled National to move products from plant to customer in 4 days rather than 45 days and to reduce distribution costs from 2.6% to 1.9% of revenues. These benefits subsequently led National to outsource all its shipping activities to Federal Express.

MRP is a push-through approach. We now consider JIT production, a "demand-pull" approach, which is used by companies such as Toyota in the automobile industry, Dell in the computer industry, and Braun in the appliance industry.

JIT Production

Just-in-time (JIT) production, which is also called **lean production,** is a "demand-pull" manufacturing system that manufactures each component in a production line as soon as, and only when, needed by the next step in the production line. In a JIT production line, manufacturing activity at any particular workstation is prompted by the need for that workstation's output at the following workstation. Demand triggers each step of the production process, starting with customer demand for a finished product at the end of the process and working all the way back to the demand for direct materials at the beginning of the process. In this way, demand pulls an order through the production line. The demand-pull feature of JIT production systems achieves close coordination among workstations. It smooths the flow of goods, despite low quantities of inventory. JIT production systems aim to simultaneously (1) meet customer demand in a timely manner (2) with high-quality products and (3) at the lowest possible total cost.

Decision Point

How do materials requirements planning (MRP) systems differ from just-in-time (JIT) production systems?

Features of JIT Production Systems

A JIT production system has these features:

- Production is organized in **manufacturing cells,** groupings of all the different types of equipment used to make a given product. Materials move from one machine to another, and various operations are performed in sequence, minimizing materials-handling costs.

- Workers are hired and trained to be multiskilled and capable of performing a variety of operations and tasks, including minor repairs and routine equipment maintenance.

- Defects are aggressively eliminated. Because of the tight links between workstations in the production line and the minimal inventories at each workstation, defects arising at one workstation quickly affect other workstations in the line. JIT creates an urgency for solving problems immediately and eliminating the root causes of defects as quickly as possible. Low levels of inventories allow workers to trace problems to and solve problems at earlier workstations in the production process, where the problems likely originated.

- *Setup time,* the time required to get equipment, tools, and materials ready to start the production of a component or product, and *manufacturing cycle time,* the time from when an order is received by manufacturing until it becomes a finished good, are reduced. Setup costs correspond to the ordering costs *P* in the EOQ model. Reducing setup time and costs makes production in smaller batches economical, which in turn reduces inventory levels. Reducing manufacturing cycle time enables a company to respond faster to changes in customer demand (see also Concepts in Action, p. 717).

- Suppliers are selected on the basis of their ability to deliver quality materials in a timely manner. Most companies implementing *JIT production* also implement *JIT purchasing.* JIT plants expect JIT suppliers to make timely deliveries of high-quality goods directly to the production floor.

We next present a relevant-cost analysis for deciding whether to implement a JIT production system.

Learning Objective 6

Identify the features and benefits of a just-in-time production system

. . . for example, organizing work in manufacturing cells, improving quality, and reducing manufacturing lead time to reduce costs and earn higher margins

Financial Benefits of JIT and Relevant Costs

Early advocates saw the benefit of JIT production as lower carrying costs of inventory. But there are other benefits of lower inventories: heightened emphasis on improving quality by eliminating the specific causes of rework, scrap, and waste, and lower manufacturing cycle times. In computing the relevant benefits and costs of reducing inventories in JIT production systems, the cost analyst should take into account all benefits and all costs.

Consider Hudson Corporation, a manufacturer of brass fittings. Hudson is considering implementing a JIT production system. To implement JIT production, Hudson must incur $100,000 in annual tooling costs to reduce setup times. Hudson expects that JIT will reduce average inventory by $500,000 and that relevant costs of insurance, storage, materials handling, and setup will decline by $30,000 per year. The company's required rate of return on inventory investments is 10% per year. Should Hudson implement a JIT production system? On the basis of the information provided, we would be tempted to say "no," because annual relevant total cost savings amount to $80,000 [(10% of $500,000) + $30,000)], which is less than the additional annual tooling costs of $100,000.

Our analysis, however, is incomplete. We have not considered the other benefits of lower inventories in JIT production. Hudson estimates that implementing JIT will improve quality and reduce rework on 500 units each year, resulting in savings of $50 per unit. Also, better quality and faster delivery will allow Hudson to charge $2 more per unit on the 20,000 units that it sells each year.

The annual relevant benefits and costs from implementing JIT equal the following:

Incremental savings in insurance, storage, materials handling, and set up	$ 30,000
Incremental savings in inventory carrying costs (10% × $500,000)	50,000
Incremental savings from reduced rework ($50 per unit × 500 units)	25,000
Additional contribution margin from better quality and faster delivery ($2 per unit × 20,000 units)	40,000
Incremental annual tooling costs	(100,000)
Net incremental benefit	$ 45,000

Therefore, Hudson *should* implement a JIT production system.

JIT in Service Industries

JIT purchasing and production methods can be applied in service industries as well. For example, inventories and supplies, and the associated labor costs to manage them, represent more than a third of the costs in most hospitals. By implementing a JIT purchasing and distribution system, Eisenhower Memorial Hospital in Palm Springs, California, reduced its inventories and supplies by 90% in 18 months. McDonald's has adapted JIT production practices to making hamburgers.[3] Before, McDonald's precooked a batch of hamburgers that were placed under heat lamps to stay warm until ordered. If the hamburgers didn't sell within a specified period of time, they were discarded resulting in high inventory holding costs and spoilage costs. Moreover, the quality of hamburgers deteriorated the longer they sat under the heat lamps. Finally, customers placing a special order for a hamburger (such as a hamburger with no cheese) had to wait for the hamburger to be cooked. Today, the use of new technology (including an innovative bun toaster) and JIT production practices allow McDonald's to cook hamburgers only when they are ordered, significantly reducing inventory holding and spoilage costs. More importantly, JIT has improved customer satisfaction by increasing the quality of hamburgers and reducing the time needed for special orders.

We next turn our attention to planning and control in JIT production systems.

Enterprise Resource Planning (ERP) Systems[4]

The success of a JIT production system hinges on the speed of information flows from customers to manufacturers to suppliers. Information flows are a problem for large companies that have fragmented information systems spread over dozens of unlinked computer systems. Enterprise Resource Planning (ERP) systems improve these information flows. An ERP system is an integrated set of software modules covering accounting, distribution, manufacturing, purchasing, human resources, and other functions. ERP uses a single database to collect and feed data into all software applications, allowing integrated, real-time information sharing and providing visibility to the company's business processes as a whole. For example, using an ERP system, a salesperson can

---

[3] Charles Atkinson, "McDonald's, A Guide to the Benefits of JIT," *Inventory Management Review*, www.inventorymanagementreview.org/2005/11/mcdonalds_a_gui.html (accessed May 2, 2007).

[4] For an excellent discussion, see T. H. Davenport, "Putting the Enterprise into the Enterprise System," *Harvard Business Review*, (July–August 1998); also see A. Cagilo, "Enterprise Resource Planning Systems and Accountants: Towards Hybridization?" *European Accounting Review*, (May 2003).

Concepts in Action — After the Encore: Just-in-Time Live Concert Recordings

Each year, millions of music fans flock to concerts to see artists ranging from Lady Gaga to rock-band O.A.R. Although many of them stop by the merchandise stand to pick up a t-shirt or poster after the show ends, they increasingly have another option: buying a professional recording of the concert they just saw! Just-in-time production, enabled by recent advances in audio and computer technology, now allows fans to relive the live concert experience just a few minutes after the final chord is played.

Live concert recordings have long been hampered by production and distribution difficulties. Traditionally, fans could only hear these recordings via unofficial "bootleg" cassettes or CDs. Occasionally, artists would release official live albums between studio releases. Further, live albums typically sold few copies, and retail outlets that profit from volume-driven merchandise turnover, like Best Buy, were somewhat reluctant to carry them.

Enter instant concert recordings. Organizations such as Adreea, Concert Live, and Live Nation employ microphones, recording and audio mixing hardware and software, and an army of high-speed computers to produce concert recordings during the show. As soon as each song is complete, engineers burn that track onto hundreds of CDs or USB drives. At the end of the show, they have to burn only one last song. Once completed, the CDs or USB drives are packaged and rushed to merchandise stands throughout the venue for instant sale.

There are, of course, some limitations to this technology. With such a quick turnaround time, engineers cannot edit or remaster any aspect of the show. Also, although just-in-time live recordings work successfully in smaller venues, the logistics for arenas, amphitheatres, and stadiums are much more difficult. Despite these concerns, the benefits of this new technology include sound-quality assurance, near-immediate production turnaround, and low finished-goods carrying costs. These recordings can also be distributed through Apple's iTunes platform and artist Web sites, making live recordings more accessible than ever. With such opportunities, it's no wonder that bands like O.A.R. augment their existing CD sales with just-in-time recordings.

Sources: Buskirk, Eliot Van. 2009. Apple unveils 'live music' in iTunes. *Wired.* "Epicenter," blog November 24. www.wired.com/epicenter/2009/11/apple-unveils-live-music-in-itunes/ Chartrand, Sabra. 2004. How to take the concert home. *New York Times,* May 3. www.nytimes.com/2004/05/03/technology/03patent.html *Daily Telegraph.* 2009. Online exclusive: How Concert Live co-founders overcame barriers. February 3. www.telegraph.co.uk/sponsored/business/businesstruth/diary_of_a/4448290/Online-Exclusive-How-Concert-Live-co-founders-overcame-barriers.html Humphries, Stephen. 2003. Get your official 'bootleg' here. *Christian Science Monitor,* November 21. www.csmonitor.com/2003/1121/p16s01-almp.html *Websites*: Live O.A.R. http://liveoar.com/store/first_index.php Aderra. www.aderra.net/ Concert Live. www.concertlive.co.uk/

generate a contract for a customer in Germany, verify the customer's credit limits, and place a production order. The system then uses this same information to schedule manufacturing in, say, Brazil, requisition materials from inventory, order components from suppliers, and schedule shipments. At the same time, it credits sales commissions to the salesperson and records all the costing and financial accounting information.

ERP systems give lower-level managers, workers, customers, and suppliers access to detailed and timely operating information. This benefit, coupled with tight coordination across business functions of the value chain, enables ERP systems to shift manufacturing and distribution plans rapidly in response to changes in supply and demand. Companies believe that an ERP system is essential to support JIT initiatives because of the effect it has on lead times. Using an ERP system, Autodesk, a maker of computer-aided design software, reduced order lead time from two weeks to one day; and Fujitsu reduced lead time from 18 days to 1.5 days.

ERP systems are large and unwieldy. Because of its complexity, suppliers of ERP systems such as SAP and Oracle provide software packages that are standard but that can be customized, although at considerable cost. Without some customization, unique and distinctive features that confer strategic advantage will not be available. The challenge when implementing ERP systems is to strike the proper balance between the lower cost of standardized systems and the strategic benefits that accrue from customization.

Performance Measures and Control in JIT Production

In addition to personal observation, managers use financial and nonfinancial measures to evaluate and control JIT production. We describe these measures and indicate the effect that JIT systems are expected to have on these measures.

1. Financial performance measures, such as inventory turnover ratio (Cost of goods sold ÷ Average inventory), which is expected to increase
2. Nonfinancial performance measures of inventory, quality, and time such as the following:
   - Number of days of inventory on hand, expected to decrease
   - Units produced per hour, expected to increase
   - $\dfrac{\text{Number of units scrapped or requiring rework}}{\text{Total number of units started and completed}}$, expected to decrease
   - Manufacturing cycle time, expected to decrease
   - $\dfrac{\text{Total setup time for machines}}{\text{Total manufacturing time}}$, expected to decrease

Personal observation and nonfinancial performance measures provide the most timely, intuitive, and easy to understand measures of manufacturing performance. Rapid, meaningful feedback is critical because the lack of inventories in a demand-pull system makes it urgent to detect and solve problems quickly. JIT measures can also be incorporated into the four perspectives of the balanced scorecard (financial, customer, internal business process, and learning and growth). The logic is as follows: Multiskilled, and well-trained employees (learning and growth measures) improve internal business processes measured by the preceding inventory, quality, and time measures. As operational performance improves, customer satisfaction also increases because of greater flexibility, responsiveness, and quality resulting in better financial performance from lower purchasing, inventory holding, and quality costs, and higher revenues.

Effect of JIT Systems on Product Costing

Decision Point ▶

What are the features and benefits of a JIT production system?

By reducing materials handling, warehousing, and inspection, JIT systems reduce overhead costs. JIT systems also aid in direct tracing of some costs usually classified as indirect. For example, the use of manufacturing cells makes it cost-effective to trace materials handling and machine operating costs to specific products or product families made in these cells. These costs then become direct costs of those products. Also, the use of multiskilled workers in these cells allows the costs of setup, maintenance, and quality inspection to be traced as direct costs. These changes have prompted some companies using JIT to adopt simplified product costing methods that dovetail with JIT production and that are less costly to operate than the traditional costing systems described in Chapters 4, 7, 8, and 17. We examine two of these methods next: backflush costing and lean accounting.

Backflush Costing

Learning Objective 7

Describe different ways backflush costing can simplify traditional inventory-costing systems

. . . for example, by not recording journal entries for work in process, purchase of materials, or production of finished goods

Organizing manufacturing in cells, reducing defects and manufacturing cycle time, and ensuring timely delivery of materials enables purchasing, production, and sales to occur in quick succession with minimal inventories. The absence of inventories makes choices about cost-flow assumptions (such as weighted average or first-in, first-out) or inventory-costing methods (such as absorption or variable costing) unimportant: All manufacturing costs of the accounting period flow directly into cost of goods sold. The rapid conversion of direct materials into finished goods that are immediately sold greatly simplifies the costing system.

Simplified Normal or Standard Costing Systems

Traditional normal or standard-costing systems (Chapters 4, 7, 8, and 17) use **sequential tracking**, which is a costing system in which recording of the journal entries occurs in the same order as actual purchases and progress in production. Costs are tracked sequentially as products pass through each of the following four stages:

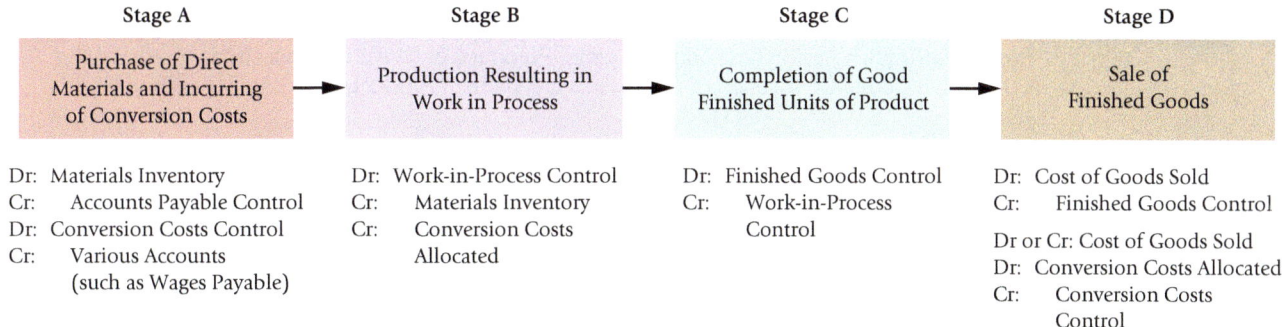

Stage A	Stage B	Stage C	Stage D
Purchase of Direct Materials and Incurring of Conversion Costs	Production Resulting in Work in Process	Completion of Good Finished Units of Product	Sale of Finished Goods

Stage A:
Dr: Materials Inventory
Cr: Accounts Payable Control
Dr: Conversion Costs Control
Cr: Various Accounts
      (such as Wages Payable)

Stage B:
Dr: Work-in-Process Control
Cr: Materials Inventory
Cr: Conversion Costs
      Allocated

Stage C:
Dr: Finished Goods Control
Cr: Work-in-Process
      Control

Stage D:
Dr: Cost of Goods Sold
Cr: Finished Goods Control

Dr or Cr: Cost of Goods Sold
Dr: Conversion Costs Allocated
Cr: Conversion Costs
      Control

A sequential-tracking costing system has four *trigger points*, corresponding to Stages A, B, C, and D. A **trigger point** is a stage in the cycle, from purchase of direct materials and incurring of conversion costs (Stage A) to sale of finished goods (Stage D), at which journal entries are made in the accounting system. The journal entries (with Dr. representing debits and Cr. representing credits) for each stage are displayed below the box for that stage (as described in Chapter 4).

An alternative approach to sequential tracking is backflush costing. **Backflush costing** is a costing system that omits recording some of the journal entries relating to the stages from purchase of direct materials to the sale of finished goods. When journal entries for one or more stages are omitted, the journal entries for a subsequent stage use normal or standard costs to work backward to "flush out" the costs in the cycle for which journal entries were *not* made. When inventories are minimal, as in JIT production systems, backflush costing simplifies costing systems without losing much information.

Consider the following data for the month of April for Silicon Valley Computer (SVC), which produces keyboards for personal computers.

- There are no beginning inventories of direct materials and no beginning or ending work-in-process inventories.

- SVC has only one direct manufacturing cost category (direct materials) and one indirect manufacturing cost category (conversion costs). All manufacturing labor costs are included in conversion costs.

- From its bill of materials and an operations list (description of operations to be undergone), SVC determines that the standard direct material cost per keyboard unit is $19 and the standard conversion cost is $12.

- SVC purchases $1,950,000 of direct materials. To focus on the basic concepts, we assume SVC has no direct materials variances. Actual conversion costs equal $1,260,000. SVC produces 100,000 good keyboard units and sells 99,000 units.

- Any underallocated or overallocated conversion costs are written off to cost of goods sold at the end of April.

We use three examples to illustrate backflush costing. *They differ in the number and placement of trigger points.*

Example 1: The three trigger points for journal entries are Purchase of direct materials and incurring of conversion costs (Stage A), Completion of good finished units of product (Stage C), and Sale of finished goods (Stage D).

Note that there is no journal entry for Production resulting in work in process (Stage B) because JIT production has minimal work in process.

SVC records two inventory accounts:

Type	Account Title
Combined materials inventory and materials in work in process	Materials and In-Process Inventory Control
Finished goods	Finished Goods Control

Exhibit 20-7, Panel A, summarizes the journal entries for Example 1 with three trigger points: Purchase of direct materials and incurring of conversion costs, Completion of good

| Exhibit 20-7 | Journal Entries and General Ledger Overview for Backflush Costing and Journal Entries for Sequential Tracking with Three Trigger Points: Purchase of Direct Materials and Incurring of Conversion Costs, Completion of Good Finished Units of Product, and Sale of Finished Goods |

PANEL A: Journal Entries

Backflush Costing			Sequential Tracking		

Stage A: Record Purchase of Direct Materials and Incurring of Conversion Costs

1. Record Direct Materials Purchased.

| Entry (A1) | Materials and In-Process Inventory Control | 1,950,000 | | Materials Inventory Control | 1,950,000 | |
| | Accounts Payable Control | | 1,950,000 | Accounts Payable Control | | 1,950,000 |

2. Record Conversion Costs Incurred.

Entry (A2)	Conversion Costs Control	1,260,000		Conversion Costs Control	1,260,000	
	Various accounts (such as Wages			Various accounts (such as Wages		1,260,000
	Payable Control)		1,260,000	Payable Control)		

Stage B: Record Production Resulting in Work in Process.

Entry (B1)	No Entry Recorded			Work-in-Process Control	3,100,000	
				Materials Inventory Control		1,900,000
				Conversion Costs Allocated		1,200,000

Stage C: Record Cost of Good Finished Units Completed.

Entry (C1)	Finished Goods Control	3,100,000		Finished Goods Control	3,100,000	
	Materials and In-Process Inventory Control		1,900,000	Work-in-Process Control		3,100,000
	Conversion Costs Allocated		1,200,000			

Stage D: Record Cost of Finished Goods Sold (and Under- or Overallocated Conversion Costs).

1. Record Cost of Finished Goods Sold.

| Entry (D1) | Cost of Goods Sold | 3,069,000 | | Cost of Goods Sold | 3,069,000 | |
| | Finished Goods Control | | 3,069,000 | Finished Goods Control | | 3,069,000 |

2. Record Underallocated or Overallocated Conversion Costs.

Entry (D2)	Conversion Costs Allocated	1,200,000		Conversion Costs Allocated	1,200,000	
	Cost of Goods Sold	60,000		Cost of Goods Sold	60,000	
	Conversion Costs Control		1,260,000	Conversion Costs Control		1,260,000

PANEL B: General Ledger Overview for Backflush Costing

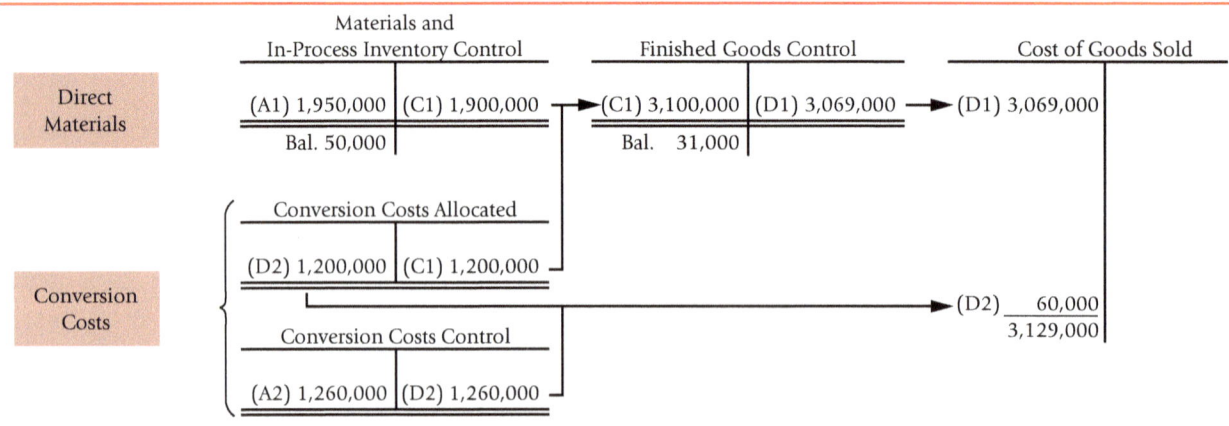

The coding that appears in parentheses for each entry indicates the stage in the production process that the entry relates to as presented in the text.

finished units of product, and Sale of finished goods (and recognizing under- or overallocated costs). For each stage, the backflush costing entries for SVC are shown on the left. The comparable entries under sequential tracking (costing) are shown on the right.

Consider first the entries for purchase of direct materials and incurring of conversion costs (Stage A). As described earlier, the inventory account under backflush costing combines direct materials and work in process. When materials are purchased, these costs increase (are debited to) Materials and In-Process Inventory Control. Under the sequential tracking approach, the direct materials and work in process accounts are separate, so the purchase of direct materials is debited to Materials Inventory Control. Actual conversion costs are recorded as incurred under backflush costing, just as in sequential tracking, and they increase (are debited to) Conversion Costs Control.

Next consider the entries for production resulting in work in process (Stage B). Recall that 100,000 units were started into production in April and that the standard cost for the units produced is $31 ($19 direct materials + $12 conversion costs) per unit. Under backflush costing, no entry is recorded in Stage B because work-in-process inventory is minimal and all units are quickly converted to finished goods. Under sequential tracking, work-in-process inventory is increased as manufacturing occurs and later decreased as manufacturing is completed and the product becomes a finished good.

The entries to record completion of good finished units of product (Stage C) gives backflush costing its name. Costs have not been recorded sequentially with the flow of product along its production route through work in process and finished goods. Instead, the output trigger point reaches *back* and pulls ("*flushes*") the standard direct material costs from Materials and In-Process Inventory Control and the standard conversion costs for manufacturing the finished goods. Under the sequential tracking approach, Finished Goods Control is debited (increased) and Work-in-Process Control is credited (decreased) as manufacturing is completed and finished goods are produced. The net effect of Stages B and C under sequential tracking is the same as the effect under backflush costing (except for the name of the inventory account).

Finally consider entries to record the sale of finished goods (and under- or overallocated conversion costs) (Stage D). The standard cost of 99,000 units sold in April equals $3,069,000 (99,000 units × $31 per unit). The entries to record the cost of finished goods sold are exactly the same under backflush costing and sequential tracking.

Actual conversion costs may be underallocated or overallocated in an accounting period. Chapter 4 (pp. 117–122) discussed various ways to dispose of underallocated or overallocated manufacturing overhead costs. Companies that use backflush costing typically have low inventories, so proration of underallocated or overallocated conversion costs between work in process, finished goods, and cost of goods sold is seldom necessary. Many companies write off underallocated or overallocated conversion costs to cost of goods sold only at the end of the fiscal year. Other companies, like SVC, record the write-off monthly. The journal entry to dispose of the difference between actual conversion costs incurred and standard conversion costs allocated is exactly the same under backflush costing and sequential tracking.

The April 30 ending inventory balances under backflush costing are as follows:

Materials and In-Process Inventory Control ($1,950,000 − $1,900,000)	$50,000
Finished Goods Control, 1,000 units × $31/unit ($3,100,000 − $3,069,000)	31,000
Total	$81,000

The April 30 ending inventory balances under sequential tracking would be exactly the same except that the inventory account would be Materials Inventory Control. Exhibit 20-7, Panel B (p. 720), provides a general-ledger overview of this version of backflush costing.

The elimination of the typical Work-in-Process Control account reduces the amount of detail in the accounting system. Units on the production line may still be tracked in physical terms, but there is "no assignment of costs" to specific work orders while they are in the production cycle. In fact, there are no work orders or labor-time records in the accounting system.

The three trigger points to make journal entries in Example 1 will lead SVC's backflush costing system to report costs that are similar to the costs reported under sequential tracking when SVC has minimal work-in-process inventory. In Example 1, any inventories of direct materials or finished goods are recognized in SVC's backflush costing system when they first appear (as would be done in a costing system using sequential tracking). International Paper Company uses a method similar to Example 1 in its specialty papers plant.

Accounting for Variances Accounting for variances between actual and standard costs is basically the same under all standard-costing systems. The procedures are described in Chapters 7 and 8. Suppose that in Example 1, SVC had an unfavorable direct materials price variance of $42,000. Then the journal entry would be as follows:

Materials and In-Process Inventory Control	1,950,000	
Direct Materials Price Variance	42,000	
Accounts Payable Control		1,992,000

Direct material costs are often a large proportion of total manufacturing costs, sometimes well over 60%. Consequently, many companies will at least measure the direct materials efficiency variance in total by physically comparing what remains in direct materials inventory against what should remain based on the output of finished goods for the accounting period. In our example, suppose that such a comparison showed an unfavorable materials efficiency variance of $30,000. The journal entry would be as follows:

Direct Materials Efficiency Variance	30,000	
Materials and In-Process Inventory Control		30,000

The underallocated or overallocated conversion costs are split into various overhead variances (spending variance, efficiency variance, and production-volume variance), as explained in Chapter 8. Each variance is closed to cost of goods sold, if it is immaterial in amount.

Example 2: The two trigger points are Purchase of direct materials and incurring of conversion costs (Stage A) and Sale of finished goods (Stage D).

This example uses the SVC data to illustrate a backflush costing that differs more from sequential tracking than the backflush costing in Example 1. This example and Example 1 have the same first trigger point, purchase of direct materials and incurring of conversion costs. But the second trigger point in Example 2 is the sale, not the completion, of finished goods. *Note that in this example, there is no journal entry for Production resulting in work in progress (Stage B) and Completion of good finished units of product (Stage C) because there are minimal work in process and finished goods inventories.*

In this example, there is only one inventory account: direct materials, whether they are in storerooms, in process, or in finished goods.

Type	Account Title
Combines direct materials inventory and any direct materials in work-in-process and finished goods inventories	Inventory Control

Exhibit 20-8, Panel A, summarizes the journal entries for Example 2 with two trigger points: Purchase of direct materials and incurring of conversion costs, and Sale of finished goods (and recognizing under- or overallocated costs). As in Example 1, for each stage, the backflush costing entries for SVC are shown on the left. The comparable entries under sequential tracking are shown on the right.

The entries for direct materials purchased and conversion costs incurred (Stage A) are the same as in Example 1, except that the inventory account is called Inventory Control. As in Example 1, no entry is made to record production of work-in-process inventory (Stage B) because work-in-process inventory is minimal. When finished goods are completed (Stage C), no entry is recorded because the completed units are expected to be sold quickly and finished goods inventory is expected to be minimal. As finished goods are sold (Stage D), the cost of goods sold is calculated as 99,000 units sold × $31 per unit = $3,069,000, which is composed of direct material costs (99,000 units × $19 per unit = $1,881,000) and conversion costs allocated (99,000 units × $12 per unit = $1,188,000). This is the same Cost of Goods Sold calculated under sequential tracking as described in Example 1.

Exhibit 20-8	Journal Entries and General Ledger Overview for Backflush Costing and Journal Entries for Sequential Tracking with Two Trigger Points: Purchase of Direct Materials and Incurring of Conversion Costs and Sale of Finished Goods

PANEL A: Journal Entries

	Backflush Costing			**Sequential Tracking**		
Stage A: Record Purchase of Direct Materials and Incurring of Conversion Costs						
1. Record Direct Materials Purchased.						
Entry (A1)	Inventory: Control	1,950,000		Materials Inventory Control	1,950,000	
	Accounts Payable Control		1,950,000	Accounts Payable Control		1,950,000
2. Record Conversion Costs Incurred.						
Entry (A2)	Conversion Costs Control	1,260,000		Conversion Costs Control	1,260,000	
	Various accounts (such as Wages			Various accounts (such as Wages		1,260,000
	Payable Control)		1,260,000	Payable Control)		
Stage B: Record Production Resulting in Work in Process.						
Entry (B1)	No Entry Recorded			Work-in-Process Control	3,100,000	
				Materials Inventory Control		1,900,000
				Conversion Costs Allocated		1,200,000
Stage C: Record Cost of Good Finished Units Completed.						
Entry (C1)	No Entry Recorded			Finished Goods Control	3,100,000	
				Work-in-Process Control		3,100,000
Stage D: Record Cost of Finished Goods Sold (and Under- or Overallocated Conversion Costs).						
1. Record Cost of Finished Goods Sold.						
Entry (D1)	Cost of Goods Sold	3,069,000		Cost of Goods Sold	3,069,000	
	Inventory Control		1,881,000	Finished Goods Control		3,069,000
	Conversion Costs Allocated		1,188,000			
2. Record Underallocated or Overallocated Conversion Costs.						
Entry (D2)	Conversion Costs Allocated	1,188,000		Conversion Costs Allocated	1,200,000	
	Cost of Goods Sold	72,000		Cost of Goods Sold	60,000	
	Conversion Costs Control		1,260,000	Conversion Costs Control		1,260,000

PANEL B: General Ledger Overview for Backflush Costing

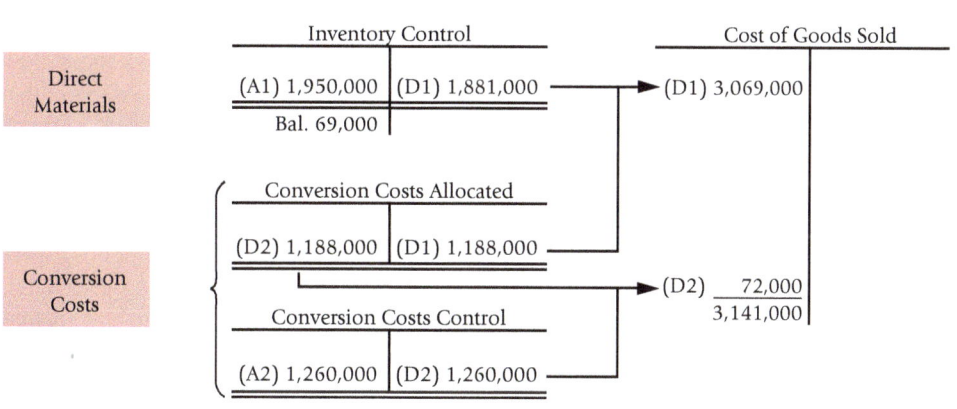

The coding that appears in parentheses for each entry indicates the stage in the production process that the entry relates to as presented in the text.

Under this method of backflush costing, conversion costs are not inventoried because no entries are recorded when finished goods are produced in Stage C. That is, compared with sequential tracking, Example 2 does not assign $12,000 ($12 per unit × 1,000 units) of conversion costs to finished goods inventory produced but not sold. Of the $1,260,000 in conversion costs, $1,188,000 is allocated at standard cost to the units sold. The remaining $72,000 ($1,260,000 − $1,188,000) of conversion costs is underallocated. Entry (D2) presents the journal entry if SVC, like many companies, writes off these under-allocated costs monthly as additions to cost of goods sold.

The April 30 ending balance of Inventory Control is $69,000 ($1,950,000 − $1,881,000). This balance represents the $50,000 direct materials still on hand + $19,000 direct materials embodied in the 1,000 good finished units manufactured but not sold during the period. Exhibit 20-8, Panel B, provides a general-ledger overview of Example 2. The approach described in Example 2 closely approximates the costs computed using sequential tracking when a company holds minimal work-in-process and finished goods inventories.

Toyota's cost accounting system at its Kentucky plant is similar to this example. Two advantages of this system are (1) it removes the incentive for managers to produce for inventory because conversion costs are recorded as period costs instead of inventoriable costs and (2) it focuses managers on sales.

Example 3: The two trigger points are Completion of good finished units of product (Stage C) and Sale of finished goods (Stage D).

This example has two trigger points. In contrast to Example 2, the first trigger point in Example 3 is delayed until Stage C, SVC's completion of good finished units of product. *Note that in this example, there are no journal entries for Purchase of direct materials and incurring of conversion costs (Stage A) and Production resulting in work in process (Stage B) because there are minimal direct materials and work-in-process inventories.*

Exhibit 20-9, Panel A, summarizes the journal entries for Example 3 with two trigger points: Completion of good finished units of product and Sale of finished goods (and recognizing under- or overallocated costs). As in Examples 1 and 2, for each stage, the backflush costing entries for SVC are shown on the left. The comparable entries under sequential tracking are shown on the right.

No entry is made for direct materials purchases of $1,950,000 (Stage A) because the acquisition of direct materials is not a trigger point in this form of backflush costing. As in Examples 1 and 2, actual conversion costs are recorded as incurred and no entry is made to record production resulting in work-in-process inventory (Stage B). The cost of 100,000 good finished units completed (Stage C) is recorded at standard cost of $31 ($19 direct materials + $12 conversion costs) per unit as in Example 1 except that Accounts Payable Control is credited (instead of Materials and In-Process Inventory Control) because no entry had been made when direct materials were purchased in Stage A. Note that at the end of April, $50,000 of direct materials purchased have not yet been placed into production ($1,950,000 − $1,900,000 = $50,000), nor have the cost of those direct materials been entered into the inventory-costing system. The Example 3 version of backflush costing is suitable for a JIT production system in which both direct materials inventory and work-in-process inventory are minimal. As finished goods are sold (Stage D), the cost of goods sold is calculated as 99,000 units sold × $31 per unit = $3,069,000. This is the same Cost of Goods sold calculated under sequential tracking. Finished Goods Control has a balance of $31,000 under both this form of backflush costing and sequential tracking. The journal entry to dispose of the difference between actual conversion costs incurred and standard conversion costs allocated is the same under backflush costing and sequential tracking. The only difference between this form of backflush costing and sequential tracking is that direct materials inventory of $50,000 (and the corresponding Accounts Payable Control) is not recorded, which is no problem if direct materials inventories are minimal. Exhibit 20-9, Panel B, provides a general-ledger overview of Example 3.

Exhibit 20-9 Journal Entries and General Ledger Overview for Backflush Costing and Journal Entries for Sequential Tracking with Two Trigger Points: Completion of Good Finished Units of Product and Sale of Finished Goods

PANEL A: Journal Entries

	Backflush Costing			Sequential Tracking		

Stage A: Record Purchase of Direct Materials and Incurring of Conversion Costs.

1. Record Direct Materials Purchased.

| Entry (A1) | No Entry Recorded | | | Materials Inventory Control | 1,950,000 | |
| | | | | Accounts Payable Control | | 1,950,000 |

2. Record Conversion Costs Incurred.

| Entry (A2) | Conversion Costs Control | 1,260,000 | | Conversion Costs Control | 1,260,000 | |
| | Various accounts (such as Wages Payable Control) | | 1,260,000 | Various accounts (such as Wages Payable Control) | | 1,260,000 |

Stage B: Record Production Resulting in Work in Process.

Entry (B1)	No Entry Recorded			Work-in-Process Control	3,100,000	
				Materials Inventory Control		1,900,000
				Conversion Costs Allocated		1,200,000

Stage C: Record Cost of Good Finished Units Completed.

Entry (C1)	Finished Goods Control	3,100,000		Finished Goods Control	3,100,000	
	Accounts Payable Control		1,900,000	Work-in-Process Control		3,100,000
	Conversion Costs Allocated		1,200,000			

Stage D: Record Cost of Finished Goods Sold (and Under- or Overallocated Conversion Costs).

1. Record Cost of Finished Goods Sold.

| Entry (D1) | Cost of Goods Sold | 3,069,000 | | Cost of Goods Sold | 3,069,000 | |
| | Finished Goods Control | | 3,069,000 | Finished Goods Control | | 3,069,000 |

2. Record Underallocated or Overallocated Conversion Costs.

Entry (D2)	Conversion Costs Allocated	1,200,000		Conversion Costs Allocated	1,200,000	
	Cost of Goods Sold	60,000		Cost of Goods Sold	60,000	
	Conversion Costs Control		1,260,000	Conversion Costs Control		1,260,000

PANEL B: General Ledger Overview for Backflush Costing

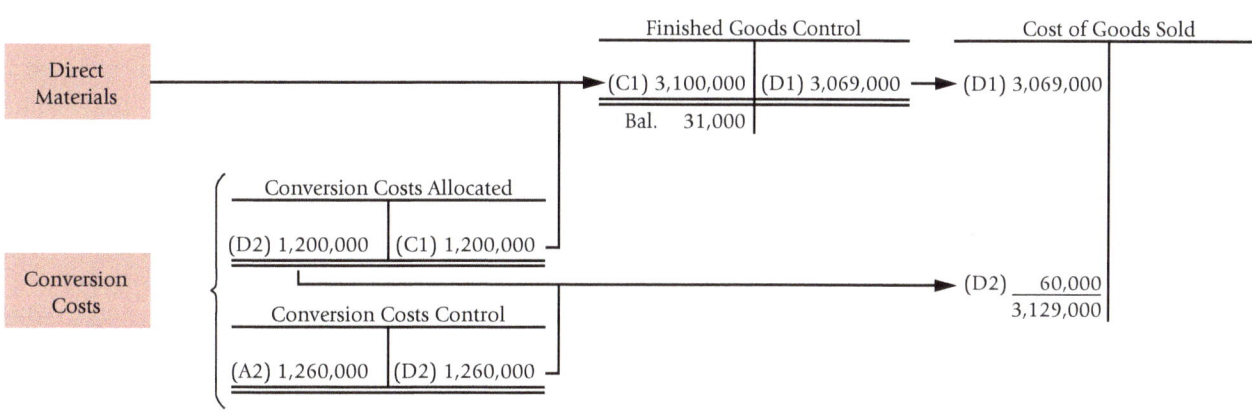

The coding that appears in parentheses for each entry indicates the stage in the production process that the entry relates to as presented in the text.

Extending Example 3, backflush costing systems could use the sale of finished goods as the only trigger point. This version of backflush costing is most suitable for a JIT production system with minimal direct materials, work-in-process, and finished goods inventories. That's because this backflush costing system maintains no inventory accounts.

Special Considerations in Backflush Costing

The accounting procedures illustrated in Examples 1, 2, and 3 do not strictly adhere to generally accepted accounting principles (GAAP). For example, work in process inventory, which is an asset, exists although it is not recognized in the financial accounting system. Advocates of backflush costing, however, cite the generally accepted accounting principle of materiality in support of the various versions of backflush costing. As the three examples illustrate, backflush costing can approximate the costs that would be reported under sequential tracking by varying the number of trigger points and where they are located. If significant amounts of direct materials inventory or finished goods inventory exist, adjusting entries can be incorporated into backflush costing (as explained next).

Suppose there are material differences in operating income and inventories based on a backflush costing system and a conventional standard-costing system. A journal entry can be recorded to adjust the backflush number to satisfy GAAP. For example, the backflush entries in Example 2 would result in expensing all conversion costs to Cost of Goods Sold ($1,188,000 at standard costs + $72,000 write-off of underallocated conversion costs = $1,260,000). But suppose conversion costs were regarded as sufficiently material in amount to be included in Inventory Control. Then entry (D2) in Example 2, closing the Conversion Costs accounts, would change as follows:

Original entry (D2)	Conversion Costs Allocated	1,188,000	
	Cost of Goods Sold	72,000	
	Conversion Costs Control		1,260,000
Revised entry (D2)	Conversion Costs Allocated	1,188,000	
	Inventory Control (1,000 units × $12)	12,000	
	Cost of Goods Sold	60,000	
	Conversion Costs Control		1,260,000

Critics say backflush costing leaves no audit trails—the ability of the accounting system to pinpoint the uses of resources at each step of the production process. However, the absence of sizable amounts of materials inventory, work-in-process inventory, and finished goods inventory means managers can keep track of operations by personal observations, computer monitoring, and nonfinancial measures.

What are the implications of JIT and backflush costing systems for activity-based costing (ABC) systems? Simplifying the production process, as in a JIT system, makes more of the costs direct and reduces the extent of overhead cost allocations. Simple ABC systems are often adequate for companies implementing JIT. These simple ABC systems work well with backflush costing. Costs from ABC systems yield more-accurate budgeted conversion cost per unit for different products in the backflush costing system. The activity-based cost information is also useful for product costing, decision making, and cost management.

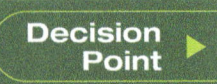

Decision Point

How does backflush costing simplify traditional inventory costing?

Lean Accounting

Another approach for simplified product costing in JIT (or lean production) systems is *lean accounting*. Successful JIT production requires companies to focus on the entire value chain of business functions (from suppliers to manufacturing to customers) in order to reduce inventories, lead times, and waste. The emphasis on improvements throughout the value chain has led some JIT companies to develop organization structures and costing systems that focus on **value streams**, which are all the value-added activities needed to design, manufacture, and deliver a given product or product line to customers. For example, a value stream can include the activities needed to develop and engineer products, advertise and market those products, process orders, purchase and receive materials, manufacture and ship orders, bill customers, and collect payments. The focus on value streams is aided by the use of manufacturing cells in JIT systems that group together the operations needed to make a given product or product line.

Learning Objective 8

Understand the principles of lean accounting

. . . focus on costing value streams rather than products, and limit arbitrary allocations

Lean accounting is a costing method that supports creating value for customers by costing the value streams, as distinguished from individual products or departments, thereby eliminating waste in the accounting process.[5] If multiple, related products are made in a single value stream, product costs for the individual products are not computed. Actual costs are directly traced to the value stream and standard costs and variances are not computed. Tracing direct costs to value streams is simple because companies using lean accounting dedicate resources to individual value streams.

Consider the following product costs for Allston Company that makes two models of designer purses in one manufacturing cell and two models of designer wallets in another manufacturing cell.

	Purses		Wallets	
	Model A	Model B	Model C	Model D
Revenues	$600,000	$700,000	$800,000	$550,000
Direct materials	340,000	400,000	410,000	270,000
Direct manufacturing labor	70,000	78,000	105,000	82,000
Manufacturing overhead costs (e.g., equipment lease, supervision, and unused facility costs)	112,000	130,000	128,000	103,000
Rework costs	15,000	17,000	14,000	10,000
Design costs	20,000	21,000	24,000	18,000
Marketing and sales costs	30,000	33,000	40,000	28,000
Total costs	587,000	679,000	721,000	511,000
Operating income	$ 13,000	$ 21,000	$ 79,000	$ 39,000
Direct materials purchased	$350,000	$420,000	$430,000	$285,000
Unused facility costs	$ 22,000	$ 38,000	$ 18,000	$ 15,000

Using lean accounting principles, Allston calculates value-stream operating costs and operating income for purses and wallets, not individual models, as follows:

	Purses	Wallets
Revenues ($600,000 + $700,000; $800,000 + $550,000)	$1,300,000	$1,350,000
Direct material purchases ($350,000 + $420,000; $430,000 + $285,000)	770,000	715,000
Direct manufacturing labor (70,000 + $78,000; $105,000 + $82,000)	148,000	187,000
Manufacturing overhead (after deducting unused facility costs) ($112,000 – $22,000) + ($130,000 – $38,000); ($128,000 – $18,000) + $103,000 – $15,000)	182,000	198,000
Design costs ($20,000 + $21,000; $24,000 + $18,000)	41,000	42,000
Marketing and sales costs ($30,000 + $33,000; $40,000 + $28,000)	63,000	68,000
Total value stream operating costs	1,204,000	1,210,000
Value stream operating income	$ 96,000	$ 140,000

Allston Company, like many lean accounting systems, expenses the costs of all purchased materials in the period in which they are bought to signal that direct material and work-in-process inventory need to be reduced. In our example, the cost of direct material purchases under lean accounting exceeds the cost of direct materials used in the operating income statement.

Facility costs (such as depreciation, property taxes, and leases) are allocated to value streams based on the square footage used by each value stream to encourage managers to use less space for holding and moving inventory. Note that unused facility costs are subtracted when calculating manufacturing overhead costs of value streams. These costs are instead treated as plant or business unit expenses. Excluding unused facility costs from value stream costs means that only those costs that add value are included in value-stream costs.

[5] See B. Baggaley, "Costing by Value Stream," *Journal of Cost Management* (May–June 2003).

Moreover, increasing the visibility of unused capacity costs creates incentives to reduce these costs or to find alternative uses for capacity. Allston Company excludes rework costs when calculating value-stream costs and operating income because these costs are nonvalue-added costs. Companies also exclude from value stream costs common costs such as corporate or support department costs that cannot reasonably be assigned to value streams.

The analysis indicates that while total cost for purses is $1,266,000 ($587,000 + $679,000), the value stream cost using lean accounting is $1,204,000 (95.1% of $1,266,000), indicating significant opportunities for improving profitability by reducing unused facility and rework costs, and by purchasing direct materials only as needed for production. Wallets portray a different picture. Total cost for wallets is $1,232,000 ($721,000 + $511,000) while the value-stream cost using lean accounting is $1,210,000 (98.2% of $1,232,000). The wallets value stream has low unused facility and rework costs and is more efficient.

Lean accounting is much simpler than traditional product costing. Why? Because calculating actual product costs by value streams requires less overhead allocation. Compared to traditional product costing methods, the focus on value streams and costs is consistent with the emphasis of JIT and lean production on improvements in the value chain from suppliers to customers. Moreover, the practices that lean accounting encourages (such as reducing direct material and work-in-process inventories, improving quality, using less space, and eliminating unused capacity) reflect the goals of JIT production.

A potential limitation of lean accounting is that it does not compute costs for individual products. Critics charge that this limits its usefulness for decision making. Proponents of lean accounting argue that the lack of individual product costs is not a problem because most decisions are made at the product line level rather than the individual product level, and that pricing decisions are based on the value created for the customer (market prices) and not product costs.

Another criticism is that lean accounting excludes certain support costs and unused capacity costs. As a result, the decisions based on only value stream costs will look profitable because they do not consider all costs. Supporters argue that lean accounting overcomes this problem by adding a larger markup on value stream costs to compensate for some of these excluded costs. Moreover, in a competitive market, prices will eventually settle at a level that represents a reasonable markup above value stream costs because customers will be unwilling to pay for nonvalue-added costs. The goal must therefore be to eliminate nonvalue-added costs. A final criticism is that lean accounting, like backflush costing, does not correctly account for inventories under generally accepted accounting principles (GAAP). However, proponents are quick to point out that in lean accounting environments, work in process and finished goods inventories are immaterial from an accounting perspective.

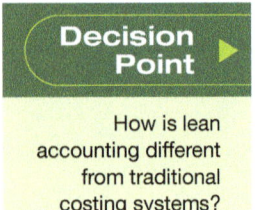

Decision Point ▶

How is lean accounting different from traditional costing systems?

Problems for Self-Study

Problem 1

Lee Company has a Singapore plant that manufactures MP3 players. One component is an XT chip. Expected demand is for 5,200 of these chips in March 2011. Lee estimates the ordering cost per purchase order to be $250. The monthly carrying cost for one unit of XT in stock is $5.

Required ▶ 1. Compute the EOQ for the XT chip.
2. Compute the number of deliveries of XT in March 2011.

Solution

$$EOQ = \sqrt{\frac{2 \times 5,200 \times \$250}{\$5}}$$

$$= 721 \text{ chips (rounded)}$$

$$\text{Number of deliveries} = \frac{5,200}{721}$$

$$= 8 \text{ (rounded)}$$

Problem 2

Littlefield Company uses a backflush costing system with three trigger points:

■ Purchase of direct materials

■ Completion of good finished units of product

■ Sale of finished goods

There are no beginning inventories. Information for April 2011 is as follows:

Direct materials purchased	$880,000	Conversion costs allocated	$ 400,000
Direct materials used	$850,000	Costs transferred to finished goods	$1,250,000
Conversion costs incurred	$422,000	Cost of goods sold	$1,190,000

Required

1. Prepare journal entries for April (without disposing of underallocated or overallocated conversion costs). Assume there are no direct materials variances.
2. Under an ideal JIT production system, how would the amounts in your journal entries differ from the journal entries in requirement 1?

Solution

1. Journal entries for April are as follows:

Entry (A1)	Materials and In-Process Inventory Control	880,000	
	Accounts Payable Control		880,000
	(direct materials purchased)		
Entry (A2)	Conversion Costs Control	422,000	
	Various accounts (such as Wages Payable Control)		422,000
	(conversion costs incurred)		
Entry (C1)	Finished Goods Control	1,250,000	
	Materials and In-Process Inventory Control		850,000
	Conversion Costs Allocated		400,000
	(standard cost of finished goods completed)		
Entry (D1)	Cost of Goods Sold	1,190,000	
	Finished Goods Control		1,190,000
	(standard costs of finished goods sold)		

2. Under an ideal JIT production system, if the manufacturing lead time per unit is very short, there would be zero inventories at the end of each day. Entry (C1) would be $1,190,000 finished goods production [to match finished goods sold in entry (D1)], not $1,250,000. If the marketing department could only sell goods costing $1,190,000, the JIT production system would call for direct materials purchases and conversion costs of lower than $880,000 and $422,000, respectively, in entries (A1) and (A2).

Decision Points

The following question-and-answer format summarizes the chapter's learning objectives. Each decision presents a key question related to a learning objective. The guidelines are the answer to that question.

Decision	Guidelines
1. What are the six categories of costs associated with goods for sale?	The six categories are purchasing costs (costs of goods acquired from suppliers), ordering costs (costs of preparing a purchase order and receiving goods), carrying costs (costs of holding inventory of goods for sale), stockout costs (costs arising when a customer demands a unit of product and that unit is not on hand), costs of quality (prevention, appraisal, internal failure, and external failure costs), and shrinkage costs (the costs resulting from theft by outsiders, embezzlement by employees, misclassifications, and clerical errors).

2. What does the EOQ decision model help managers do and how do managers decide on the level of safety stocks?

The economic-order-quantity (EOQ) decision model helps managers to calculate the optimal quantity of inventory to order by balancing ordering costs and carrying costs. The larger the order quantity, the higher the annual carrying costs and the lower the annual ordering costs. The EOQ model includes costs recorded in the financial accounting system as well as opportunity costs not recorded in the financial accounting system. Managers choose a level of safety stocks to minimize stock out costs and carrying costs of holding more inventory.

3. What is the effect on costs of errors in predicting parameters of the EOQ model? How can companies reduce the conflict between the EOQ decision model and models used for performance evaluation?

The cost of prediction errors when using the EOQ model is small. To reduce the conflict between the EOQ decision model and the performance evaluation model, companies should include the opportunity cost of investment when evaluating managers. The opportunity cost of investment tied up in inventory is a key input in the EOQ decision model that is often ignored in the performance-evaluation model.

4. Why are companies using just-in-time purchasing?

Just-in-time (JIT) purchasing is making purchases in small order quantities just as needed for production (or sales). JIT purchasing is a response to high carrying costs and low ordering costs. JIT purchasing increases the focus of companies and suppliers on quality and timely deliveries. Companies coordinate their activities and reduce inventories throughout the supply chain, from the initial sources of materials and services to the delivery of products to consumers.

5. How do materials requirements planning (MRP) systems differ from just-in-time (JIT) production systems?

Materials requirements planning (MRP) systems use a "push-through" approach that manufactures finished goods for inventory on the basis of demand forecasts. Just-in-time (JIT) production systems use a "demand-pull" approach in which goods are manufactured only to satisfy customer orders.

6. What are the features and benefits of a JIT production system?

JIT production systems (a) organize production in manufacturing cells, (b) hire and train multiskilled workers, (c) emphasize total quality management, (d) reduce manufacturing lead time and setup time, and (e) build strong supplier relationships. The benefits of JIT production include lower costs and higher margins from better flow of information, higher quality, and faster delivery.

7. How does backflush costing simplify traditional inventory costing?

Traditional inventory-costing systems use sequential tracking, in which recording of the journal entries occurs in the same order as actual purchases and progress in production. Most backflush costing systems do not record journal entries for the work-in-process stage of production. Some backflush costing systems also do not record entries for either the purchase of direct materials or the completion of finished goods.

8. How is lean accounting different from traditional costing systems?

Lean accounting costs value streams rather than products. Nonvalue-added costs, unused capacity costs and costs that cannot be easily traced to value streams are not allocated but instead expensed.

Terms to Learn

This chapter and the Glossary at the end of the book contain definitions of the following important terms:

backflush costing (**p. 719**)	lean production (**p. 715**)	reorder point (**p. 707**)
carrying costs (**p. 704**)	manufacturing cells (**p. 715**)	safety stock (**p. 707**)
economic order quantity (EOQ) (**p. 704**)	materials requirements planning	sequential tracking (**p. 718**)
inventory management (**p. 703**)	(MRP) (**p. 714**)	shrinkage costs (**p. 704**)
just-in-time (JIT) production (**p. 715**)	ordering costs (**p. 704**)	stockout costs (**p. 704**)
just-in-time (JIT) purchasing (**p. 711**)	purchase-order lead time (**p. 704**)	trigger point (**p. 719**)
lean accounting (**p. 727**)	purchasing costs (**p. 703**)	value streams (**p. 726**)

Assignment Material

Questions

20-1 Why do better decisions regarding the purchasing and managing of goods for sale frequently cause dramatic percentage increases in net income?

20-2 Name six cost categories that are important in managing goods for sale in a retail company.

20-3 What assumptions are made when using the simplest version of the economic-order-quantity (EOQ) decision model?

20-4 Give examples of costs included in annual carrying costs of inventory when using the EOQ decision model.

20-5 Give three examples of opportunity costs that typically are not recorded in accounting systems, although they are relevant when using the EOQ model in the presence of demand uncertainty.

20-6 What are the steps in computing the cost of a prediction error when using the EOQ decision model?

20-7 Why might goal-congruence issues arise when an EOQ model is used to guide decisions on how much to order?

20-8 Describe JIT purchasing and its benefits.

20-9 What are three factors causing reductions in the cost to place purchase orders for materials?

20-10 "You should always choose the supplier who offers the lowest price per unit." Do you agree? Explain.

20-11 What is supply-chain analysis, and how can it benefit manufacturers and retailers?

20-12 What are the main features of JIT production?

20-13 Distinguish inventory-costing systems using sequential tracking from those using backflush costing.

20-14 Describe three different versions of backflush costing.

20-15 Discuss the differences between lean accounting and traditional cost accounting.

Exercises

20-16 Economic order quantity for retailer. Fan Base (FB) operates a megastore featuring sports merchandise. It uses an EOQ decision model to make inventory decisions. It is now considering inventory decisions for its Los Angeles Galaxy soccer jerseys product line. This is a highly popular item. Data for 2011 are as follows:

Expected annual demand for Galaxy jerseys	10,000
Ordering cost per purchase order	$200
Carrying cost per year	$7 per jersey

Each jersey costs FB $40 and sells for $80. The $7 carrying cost per jersey per year comprises the required return on investment of $4.80 (12% $\times$ $40 purchase price) plus $2.20 in relevant insurance, handling, and theft-related costs. The purchasing lead time is 7 days. FB is open 365 days a year.

Required

1. Calculate the EOQ.
2. Calculate the number of orders that will be placed each year.
3. Calculate the reorder point.

20-17 Economic order quantity, effect of parameter changes (continuation of 20-16). Athletic Textiles (AT) manufactures the Galaxy jerseys that Fan Base (FB) sells to its customers. AT has recently installed computer software that enables its customers to conduct "one-stop" purchasing using state-of-the-art Web site technology. FB's ordering cost per purchase order will be $30 using this new technology.

Required

1. Calculate the EOQ for the Galaxy jerseys using the revised ordering cost of $30 per purchase order. Assume all other data from Exercise 20-16 are the same. Comment on the result.
2. Suppose AT proposes to "assist" FB. AT will allow FB customers to order directly from the AT Web site. AT would ship directly to these customers. AT would pay $10 to FB for every Galaxy jersey purchased by one of FB's customers. Comment qualitatively on how this offer would affect inventory management at FB. What factors should FB consider in deciding whether to accept AT's proposal?

20-18 EOQ for a retailer. The Denim World sells fabrics to a wide range of industrial and consumer users. One of the products it carries is denim cloth, used in the manufacture of jeans and carrying bags. The supplier for the denim cloth pays all incoming freight. No incoming inspection of the denim is necessary because the supplier has a track record of delivering high-quality merchandise. The purchasing officer of the Denim World has collected the following information:

Annual demand for denim cloth	26,400 yards
Ordering cost per purchase order	$165
Carrying cost per year	20% of purchase costs
Safety-stock requirements	None
Cost of denim cloth	$9 per yard

The purchasing lead time is 2 weeks. The Denim World is open 250 days a year (50 weeks for 5 days a week).

Required

1. Calculate the EOQ for denim cloth.
2. Calculate the number of orders that will be placed each year.
3. Calculate the reorder point for denim cloth.

20-19 EOQ for manufacturer. Lakeland Company produces lawn mowers and purchases 18,000 units of a rotor blade part each year at a cost of $60 per unit. Lakeland requires a 15% annual rate of return on investment. In addition, the relevant carrying cost (for insurance, materials handling, breakage, and so on) is $6 per unit per year. The relevant ordering cost per purchase order is $150.

Required

1. Calculate Lakeland's EOQ for the rotor blade part.
2. Calculate Lakeland's annual relevant ordering costs for the EOQ calculated in requirement 1.
3. Calculate Lakeland's annual relevant carrying costs for the EOQ calculated in requirement 1.
4. Assume that demand is uniform throughout the year and known with certainty so that there is no need for safety stocks. The purchase-order lead time is half a month. Calculate Lakeland's reorder point for the rotor blade part.

20-20 Sensitivity of EOQ to changes in relevant ordering and carrying costs, cost of prediction error. Alpha Company's annual demand for its only product, XT-590, is 10,000 units. Alpha is currently analyzing possible combinations of relevant carrying cost per unit per year and relevant ordering cost per purchase order, depending on the company's choice of supplier and average levels of inventory. This table presents three possible combinations of carrying and ordering costs.

Relevant Carrying Cost per Unit per Year	Relevant Ordering Cost per Purchase Order
$10	$400
$20	$200
$40	$100

Required

1. For each of the relevant ordering and carrying-cost alternatives, determine (a) EOQ and (b) annual relevant total costs.
2. How does your answer to requirement 1 give insight into the impact of changes in relevant ordering and carrying costs on EOQ and annual relevant total costs? Explain briefly.
3. Suppose the relevant carrying cost per unit per year was $20 and the relevant ordering cost per purchase order was $200. Suppose further that Alpha calculates EOQ after incorrectly estimating relevant carrying cost per unit per year to be $10 and relevant ordering cost per purchase order to be $400. Calculate the actual annual relevant total costs of Alpha's EOQ decision. Compare this cost to the annual relevant total costs that Alpha would have incurred if it had correctly estimated the relevant carrying cost per unit per year of $20 and the relevant ordering cost per purchase order of $200 that you have already calculated in requirement 1. Calculate and comment on the cost of the prediction error.

20-21 Inventory management and the balanced scorecard. Devin Sports Cars (DSC) has implemented a balanced scorecard to measure and support its just-in-time production system. In the learning and growth category, DSC measures the percentage of employees who are cross-trained to perform a wide variety of production tasks. Internal business process measures are inventory turns and on-time delivery. The customer perspective is measured using a customer satisfaction measure and financial performance using operating income. DSC estimates that if it can increase the percentage of cross-trained employees by 5%, the resulting increase in labor productivity will reduce inventory-related costs by $100,000 per year and shorten delivery times by 10%. The 10% reduction in delivery times, in turn, is expected to increase customer satisfaction by 5%, and each 1% increase in customer satisfaction is expected to increase revenues by 2% due to higher prices.

Required

1. Assume that budgeted revenues in the coming year are $5,000,000. Ignoring the costs of training, what is the expected increase in operating income in the coming year if the number of cross-trained employees is increased by 5%?
2. What is the most DSC would be willing to pay to increase the percentage of cross-trained employees if it is only interested in maximizing operating income in the coming year?
3. What factors other than short-term profits should DSC consider when assessing the benefits from employee cross-training?

20-22 JIT production, relevant benefits, relevant costs. The Champion Hardware Company manufactures specialty brass door handles at its Lynchburg plant. Champion is considering implementing a JIT production system. The following are the estimated costs and benefits of JIT production:

a. Annual additional tooling costs would be $100,000.
b. Average inventory would decline by 80% from the current level of $1,000,000.

c. Insurance, space, materials-handling, and setup costs, which currently total $300,000 annually, would decline by 25%.

d. The emphasis on quality inherent in JIT production would reduce rework costs by 30%. Champion currently incurs $200,000 in annual rework costs.

e. Improved product quality under JIT production would enable Champion to raise the price of its product by $4 per unit. Champion sells 40,000 units each year.

Champion's required rate of return on inventory investment is 15% per year.

Required

1. Calculate the net benefit or cost to Champion if it adopts JIT production at the Lynchburg plant.

2. What nonfinancial and qualitative factors should Champion consider when making the decision to adopt JIT production?

3. Suppose Champion implements JIT production at its Lynchburg plant. Give examples of performance measures Champion could use to evaluate and control JIT production. What would be the benefit of Champion implementing an enterprise resource planning (ERP) system?

20-23 Backflush costing and JIT production. Road Warrior Corporation assembles handheld computers that have scaled-down capabilities of laptop computers. Each handheld computer takes six hours to assemble. Road Warrior uses a JIT production system and a backflush costing system with three trigger points:

■ Purchase of direct materials and incurring of conversion costs
■ Completion of good finished units of product
■ Sale of finished goods

There are no beginning inventories of materials or finished goods and no beginning or ending work-in-process inventories. The following data are for August 2011:

Direct materials purchased	$2,754,000	Conversion costs incurred	$723,600
Direct materials used	$2,733,600	Conversion costs allocated	$750,400

Road Warrior records direct materials purchased and conversion costs incurred at actual costs. It has no direct materials variances. When finished goods are sold, the backflush costing system "pulls through" standard direct material cost ($102 per unit) and standard conversion cost ($28 per unit). Road Warrior produced 26,800 finished units in August 2011 and sold 26,400 units. The actual direct material cost per unit in August 2011 was $102, and the actual conversion cost per unit was $27.

Required

1. Prepare summary journal entries for August 2011 (without disposing of under- or overallocated conversion costs).

2. Post the entries in requirement 1 to T-accounts for applicable Materials and In-Process Inventory Control, Finished Goods Control, Conversion Costs Control, Conversion Costs Allocated, and Cost of Goods Sold.

3. Under an ideal JIT production system, how would the amounts in your journal entries differ from those in requirement 1?

20-24 Backflush costing, two trigger points, materials purchase and sale (continuation of 20-23). Assume the same facts as in Exercise 20-23, except that Road Warrior now uses a backflush costing system with the following two trigger points:

■ Purchase of direct materials and incurring of conversion costs
■ Sale of finished goods

The Inventory Control account will include direct materials purchased but not yet in production, materials in work in process, and materials in finished goods but not sold. No conversion costs are inventoried. Any under- or overallocated conversion costs are written off monthly to Cost of Goods Sold.

Required

1. Prepare summary journal entries for August, including the disposition of under- or overallocated conversion costs.

2. Post the entries in requirement 1 to T-accounts for Inventory Control, Conversion Costs Control, Conversion Costs Allocated, and Cost of Goods Sold.

20-25 Backflush costing, two trigger points, completion of production and sale (continuation of 20-23). Assume the same facts as in Exercise 20-23, except now Road Warrior uses only two trigger points, Completion of good finished units of product and Sale of finished goods. Any under- or overallocated conversion costs are written off monthly to Cost of Goods Sold.

Required

1. Prepare summary journal entries for August, including the disposition of under- or overallocated conversion costs.

2. Post the entries in requirement 1 to T-accounts for Finished Goods Control, Conversion Costs Control, Conversion Costs Allocated, and Cost of Goods Sold.

Problems

20-26 Effect of different order quantities on ordering costs and carrying costs, EOQ. Soothing Meadow, a retailer of bed and bath linen, sells 380,000 packages of Mona Lisa designer sheets each year. Soothing Meadow incurs an ordering cost of $57 per purchase order placed with Mona Lisa Enterprises and an annual carrying cost of $12.00 per package. Liv Carrol, purchasing manager at Soothing Meadow, seeks your help: She wants to understand how ordering and carrying costs vary with order quantity.

	Scenario				
	1	2	3	4	5
Annual demand (packages)	380,000	380,000	380,000	380,000	380,000
Cost per purchase order	$ 57	$ 57	$ 57	$ 57	$ 57
Carrying cost per package per year	$ 12.00	$ 12.00	$ 12.00	$ 12.00	$ 12.00
Quantity (packages) per purchase order	760	1,000	1,900	3,800	4,750
Number of purchase orders per year					
Annual relevant ordering costs					
Annual relevant carrying costs					
Annual relevant total costs of ordering and carrying inventory					

Required

1. Complete the table for Liv Carrol. What is the EOQ? Comment on your results.
2. Mona Lisa is about to introduce a Web-based ordering system for its customers. Liv Carrol estimates that Soothing Meadow's ordering costs will reduce to $30 per purchase order. Calculate the new EOQ and the new annual relevant costs of ordering and carrying inventory.
3. Liv Carrol estimates that Soothing Meadow will incur a cost of $2,150 to train its two purchasing assistants to use the new Mona Lisa system. Will Soothing Meadow recoup its training costs within the first year of adoption?

20-27 EOQ, uncertainty, safety stock, reorder point. Chadwick Shoe Co. produces and sells an excellent quality walking shoe. After production, the shoes are distributed to 20 warehouses around the country. Each warehouse services approximately 100 stores in its region. Chadwick uses an EOQ model to determine the number of pairs of shoes to order for each warehouse from the factory. Annual demand for Warehouse OR2 is approximately 120,000 pairs of shoes. The ordering cost is $250 per order. The annual carrying cost of a pair of shoes is $2.40 per pair.

Required

1. Use the EOQ model to determine the optimal number of pairs of shoes per order.
2. Assume each month consists of approximately 4 weeks. If it takes 1 week to receive an order, at what point should warehouse OR2 reorder shoes?
3. Although OR2's average weekly demand is 2,500 pairs of shoes (120,000 ÷ 12 months ÷ 4 weeks), demand each week may vary with the following probability distribution:

Total demand for 1 week	2,000 pairs	2,250 pairs	2,500 pairs	2,750 pairs	3,000 pairs
Probability (sums to 1.00)	0.04	0.20	0.52	0.20	0.04

If a store wants shoes and OR2 has none in stock, OR2 can "rush" them to the store at an additional cost of $2 per pair. How much safety stock should Warehouse OR2 hold? How will this affect the reorder point and reorder quantity?

20-28 MRP, EOQ, and JIT. Global Tunes Corp. produces J-Pods, music players that can download thousands of songs. Global Tunes forecasts that demand in 2011 will be 48,000 J-Pods. The variable production cost of each J-Pod is $54. Due to the large $10,000 cost per setup, Global Tunes plans to produce J-Pods once a month in batches of 4,000 each. The carrying cost of a unit in inventory is $17 per year.

Required

1. Using an MRP system, what is the annual cost of producing and carrying J-Pods in inventory? (Assume that, on average, half of the units produced in a month are in inventory.)
2. A new manager at Global Tunes has suggested that the company use the EOQ model to determine the optimal batch size to produce. (To use the EOQ model, Global Tunes needs to treat the setup cost in the same way it would treat ordering cost in a traditional EOQ model.) Determine the optimal batch size and number of batches. Round up the number of batches to the nearest whole number. What would be the annual cost of producing and carrying J-Pods in inventory if it uses the optimal batch size? Compare this cost to the cost calculated in requirement 1. Comment briefly.
3. Global Tunes is also considering switching from an MRP system to a JIT system. This will result in producing J-Pods in batch sizes of 600 J-Pods and will reduce obsolescence, improve quality, and result in a higher selling price. The frequency of production batches will force Global Tunes to reduce setup

time and will result in a reduction in setup cost. The new setup cost will be $500 per setup. What is the annual cost of producing and carrying J-Pods in inventory under the JIT system?

4. Compare the models analyzed in the previous parts of the problem. What are the advantages and disadvantages of each?

20-29 Effect of management evaluation criteria on EOQ model. Computers 4 U purchases one model of computer at a wholesale cost of $200 per unit and resells it to end consumers. The annual demand for the company's product is 500,000 units. Ordering costs are $800 per order and carrying costs are $50 per computer, including $20 in the opportunity cost of holding inventory.

1. Compute the optimal order quantity using the EOQ model.
2. Compute a) the number of orders per year and b) the annual relevant total cost of ordering and carrying inventory.
3. Assume that when evaluating the manager, the company excludes the opportunity cost of carrying inventory. If the manager makes the EOQ decision excluding the opportunity cost of carrying inventory, the relevant carrying cost would be $30 not $50. How would this affect the EOQ amount and the actual annual relevant cost of ordering and carrying inventory?
4. What is the cost impact on the company of excluding the opportunity cost of carrying inventory when making EOQ decisions? Why do you think the company currently excludes the opportunity costs of carrying inventory when evaluating the manager's performance? What could the company do to encourage the manager to make decisions more congruent with the goal of reducing total inventory costs?

Required

20-30 JIT purchasing, relevant benefits, relevant costs. (CMA, adapted) The Margro Corporation is an automotive supplier that uses automatic turning machines to manufacture precision parts from steel bars. Margro's inventory of raw steel averages $600,000. John Oates, president of Margro, and Helen Gorman, Margro's controller, are concerned about the costs of carrying inventory. The steel supplier is willing to supply steel in smaller lots at no additional charge. Gorman identifies the following effects of adopting a JIT inventory program to virtually eliminate steel inventory:

- Without scheduling any overtime, lost sales due to stockouts would increase by 35,000 units per year. However, by incurring overtime premiums of $40,000 per year, the increase in lost sales could be reduced to 20,000 units per year. This would be the maximum amount of overtime that would be feasible for Margro.
- Two warehouses currently used for steel bar storage would no longer be needed. Margro rents one warehouse from another company under a cancelable leasing arrangement at an annual cost of $60,000. The other warehouse is owned by Margro and contains 12,000 square feet. Three-fourths of the space in the owned warehouse could be rented for $1.50 per square foot per year. Insurance and property tax costs totaling $14,000 per year would be eliminated.

Margro's required rate of return on investment is 20% per year. Margro's budgeted income statement for the year ending December 31, 2011 (in thousands) is as follows:

Revenues (900,000 units)		$10,800
Cost of goods sold		
Variable costs	$4,050	
Fixed costs	1,450	
Total costs of goods sold		5,500
Gross margin		5,300
Marketing and distribution costs		
Variable costs	$ 900	
Fixed costs	1,500	
Total marketing and distribution costs		2,400
Operating income		$ 2,900

1. Calculate the estimated dollar savings (loss) for the Margro Corporation that would result in 2011 from the adoption of JIT purchasing.
2. Identify and explain other factors that Margro should consider before deciding whether to adopt JIT purchasing.

Required

20-31 Supply chain effects on total relevant inventory cost. Cow Spot Computer Co. outsources the production of motherboards for its computers. It is currently deciding which of two suppliers to use: Maji or Induk. Due to differences in the product failure rates across the two companies, 5% of motherboards purchased from Maji will be inspected and 25% of motherboards purchased from Induk will be inspected. The following data refers to costs associated with Maji and Induk.

	Maji	Induk
Number of orders per year	50	50
Annual motherboards demanded	10,000	10,000
Price per motherboard	$93	$90
Ordering cost per order	$10	$8
Inspection cost per unit	$5	$5
Average inventory level	100 units	100 units
Expected number of stockouts	100	300
Stockout cost (cost of rush order) per stockout	$5	$8
Units returned by customers for replacing motherboards	50	500
Cost of replacing each motherboard	$25	$25
Required annual return on investment	10%	10%
Other carrying cost per unit per year	$2.50	$2.50

Required

1. What is the relevant cost of purchasing from Maji and Induk?
2. What factors other than cost should Cow Spot consider?

20-32 Backflush costing and JIT production. The Rippel Corporation manufactures electrical meters. For August, there were no beginning inventories of direct materials and no beginning or ending work in process. Rippel uses a JIT production system and backflush costing with three trigger points for making entries in the accounting system:

■ Purchase of direct materials and incurring of conversion costs
■ Completion of good finished units of product
■ Sale of finished goods

Rippel's August standard cost per meter is direct material, $26, and conversion cost, $19. Rippel has no direct materials variances. The following data apply to August manufacturing:

Direct materials purchased	$546,000	Number of finished units manufactured	20,000
Conversion costs incurred	$399,000	Number of finished units sold	19,000

Required

1. Prepare summary journal entries for August (without disposing of under- or overallocated conversion costs). Assume no direct materials variances.
2. Post the entries in requirement 1 to T-accounts for Materials and In-Process Inventory Control, Finished Goods Control, Conversion Costs Control, Conversion Costs Allocated, and Cost of Goods Sold.

20-33 Backflush, two trigger points, materials purchase and sale (continuation of 20-32). Assume that the second trigger point for Rippel Corporation is the sale—rather than the completion—of finished goods. Also, the inventory account is confined solely to direct materials, whether these materials are in a store-room, in work in process, or in finished goods. No conversion costs are inventoried. They are allocated to the units sold at standard costs. Any under- or overallocated conversion costs are written off monthly to Cost of Goods Sold.

Required

1. Prepare summary journal entries for August, including the disposition of under- or overallocated conversion costs. Assume no direct materials variances.
2. Post the entries in requirement 1 to T-accounts for Inventory Control, Conversion Costs Control, Conversion Costs Allocated, and Cost of Goods Sold.

20-34 Backflush, two trigger points, completion of production and sale (continuation of 20-32). Assume the same facts as in Problem 20-32 except now there are only two trigger points: Completion of good finished units of product and Sale of finished goods.

Required

1. Prepare summary journal entries for August, including the disposition of under- or overallocated conversion costs. Assume no direct materials variances.
2. Post the entries in requirement 1 to T-accounts for Finished Goods Control, Conversion Costs Control, Conversion Costs Allocated, and Cost of Goods Sold.

20-35 Lean Accounting. Flexible Security Devices (FSD) has introduced a just-in-time production process and is considering the adoption of lean accounting principles to support its new production philosophy. The company has two product lines: Mechanical Devices and Electronic Devices. Two individual products are made in each line. Product-line manufacturing overhead costs are traced directly to product lines, and then allocated to the two individual products in each line. The company's traditional cost accounting system allocates all plant-level facility costs and some corporate overhead costs to individual products. The latest accounting report using traditional cost accounting methods included the following information (in thousands of dollars).

	Mechanical Devices		Electronic Devices	
	Product A	**Product B**	**Product C**	**Product D**
Sales	$700	$500	$900	$450
Direct material (based on quantity used)	200	100	250	75
Direct manufacturing labor	150	75	200	60
Manufacturing overhead (equipment lease, supervision, production control)	90	120	200	95
Allocated plant-level facility costs	50	40	80	30
Design and marketing costs	95	50	105	42
Allocated corporate overhead costs	15	10	20	8
Operating income	$100	$105	$ 45	$140

FSD has determined that each of the two product lines represents a distinct value stream. It has also determined that out of the $200,000 ($50,000 + $40,000 + $80,000 + $30,000) plant-level facility costs, product A occupies 22% of the plant's square footage, product B occupies 18%, product C occupies 36%, and product D occupies 14%. The remaining 10% of square footage is not being used. Finally, FSD has decided that direct material should be expensed in the period it is purchased, rather than when the material is used. According to purchasing records, direct material purchase costs during the period were as follows:

	Mechanical Devices		Electronic Devices	
	Product A	**Product B**	**Product C**	**Product D**
Direct material (purchases)	$210	$120	$250	$90

Required

1. What are the cost objects in FSD's lean accounting system?
2. Compute operating income for the cost objects identified in requirement 1 using lean accounting principles. Why does operating income differ from the operating income computed using traditional cost accounting methods? Comment on your results.

Collaborative Learning Problem

20-36 JIT production, relevant benefits, relevant costs, ethics. Parson Container Corporation is considering implementing a JIT production system. The new system would reduce current average inventory levels of $2,000,000 by 75%, but would require a much greater dependency on the company's core suppliers for on-time deliveries and high quality inputs. The company's operations manager, Jim Ingram, is opposed to the idea of a new JIT system. He is concerned that the new system will be too costly to manage; will result in too many stockouts; and will lead to the layoff of his employees, several of whom are currently managing inventory. He believes that these layoffs will affect the morale of his entire production department. The plant controller, Sue Winston is in favor of the new system, due to the likely cost savings. Jim wants Sue to rework the numbers because he is concerned that top management will give more weight to financial factors and not give due consideration to nonfinancial factors such as employee morale. In addition to the reduction in inventory described previously, Sue has gathered the following information for the upcoming year regarding the JIT system:

■ Annual insurance and warehousing costs for inventory would be reduced by 60% of current budgeted level of $350,000.
■ Payroll expenses for current inventory management staff would be reduced by 15% of the budgeted total of $600,000.
■ Additional annual costs for JIT system implementation and management, including personnel costs, would equal $220,000.
■ The additional number of stockouts under the new JIT system is estimated to be 5% of the total number of shipments annually. 10,000 shipments are budgeted for the upcoming year. Each stockout would result in an average additional cost of $250.
■ Parson's required rate of return on inventory investment is 10% per year.

Required

1. From a financial perspective should Parson adopt the new JIT system?
2. Should Sue Winston rework the numbers?
3. How should she manage Jim Ingram's concerns?

Management Control Systems, Transfer Pricing, and Multinational Considerations

Transfer pricing is the price one subunit of a company charges for the services it provides another subunit of the same company.

Top management uses transfer prices (1) to focus managers' attention on the performance of their own subunits and (2) to plan and coordinate the actions of different subunits to maximize the company's income as a whole. While transfer pricing is productive, it can also be contentious, because managers of different subunits often have very different preferences about how transfer prices should be set. For example, some managers prefer the prices be based on market prices. Others prefer the prices be based on costs alone. Controversy also arises when multinational corporations seek to reduce their overall income tax burden by charging high transfer prices to units located in countries with high tax rates. Many countries, including the United States, attempt to restrict this practice, as the following article shows.

Symantec Wins $545 million Opinion in Transfer Pricing Dispute with the IRS[1]

Symantec Corp., a large U.S. software company, won a significant court decision in December 2009, potentially saving it $545 million in contested back taxes. The Internal Revenue Service (IRS) had been seeking back taxes it alleged were owed by Veritas Software Corp., a company acquired by Symantec in 2005. The dispute was over the company's formula for "transfer pricing," a complex set of rules determining how companies set prices, fees, and cost-allocation arrangements between their operations in different tax jurisdictions.

At issue were the fees and cost-allocation arrangements between Veritas and its Irish subsidiary. Ireland has emerged as a popular tax haven for U.S. technology companies. Veritas granted rights to Veritas Ireland to conduct research and development on various intangibles (such as computer programs and manufacturing process technologies) related to data storage software and related devices. Under the agreement in effect, Veritas Ireland paid $160 million for this grant of rights from 1999 to 2001. Based on a discounted cash flow analysis, the IRS contended that the true value of the transferred rights was closer to $1.675 billion. As a consequence, it claimed that the transaction artificially increased the income of Veritas Ireland at the

[1] *Source*: Chinnis, Cabell et al. 2009. Tax court upends IRS's billion dollar buy-in valuation adjustment in "Veritas." Mondaq Business Briefing, December 17; Letzing, John. 2009. Symantec wins $545M opinion in tax case. *Dow Jones News Service*, December 11.

expense of income in the U.S. parent corporation, consequently lowering the U.S. tax bills during this period.

Veritas, however, maintained that it acted appropriately. The company testified that the $160 million figure was based on royalty rates it had received from seven original equipment manufacturers (OEMs) for rights to incorporate Veritas United States' software and technologies into an operating system, with adjustments made for purposes of comparability. At trial, the United States Tax Court supported this position, and called the IRS's valuation of the intangibles "arbitrary, capricious, and unreasonable." Among other things, the court took issue with the discount and growth rates used in the IRS expert's analysis, and disagreed with his assumption that the transferred intangibles had a perpetual useful life.

Though not all companies face multinational tax concerns, transfer-pricing issues are common to many companies. In these companies, transfer pricing is part of the larger management control system. This chapter develops the links among strategy, organization structure, management control systems, and accounting information. We'll examine the benefits and costs of centralized and decentralized organization structures, and we'll look at the pricing of products or services transferred between subunits of the same company. We emphasize how accounting information, such as costs, budgets, and prices, helps in planning and coordinating actions of subunits.

Management Control Systems

A **management control system** is a means of gathering and using information to aid and coordinate the planning and control decisions throughout an organization and to guide the behavior of its managers and other employees. Some companies design their management control system around the concept of the balanced scorecard. For example, ExxonMobil's management control system contains financial and nonfinancial information in each of the four perspectives of the balanced scorecard (see Chapter 13 for details). Well-designed management control systems use information both from within the company, such as net income and employee satisfaction, and from outside the company, such as stock price and customer satisfaction.

Formal and Informal Systems

Management control systems consist of formal and informal control systems. The formal management control system of a company includes explicit rules, procedures, performance measures, and incentive plans that guide the behavior of its managers and other employees. The formal control system is comprised of several systems, such as the

Learning Objective 1

Describe a management control system

. . . gathers information for planning and control decisions

and its three key properties

. . . aligns with strategy, supports organizational responsibility of managers, and motivates employees

management accounting system, which provides information regarding costs, revenues, and income; the human resources systems, which provide information on recruiting, training, absenteeism, and accidents; and the quality systems, which provide information on yield, defective products, and late deliveries to customers.

The informal management control system includes shared values, loyalties, and mutual commitments among members of the organization, company culture, and the unwritten norms about acceptable behavior for managers and other employees. Examples of company slogans that reinforce values and loyalties are "At Ford, Quality Is Job 1," and "At Home Depot, Low Prices Are Just the Beginning."

Effective Management Control

To be effective, management control systems should be closely aligned with the organization's strategies and goals. Two examples of strategies at ExxonMobil are (1) providing innovative products and services to increase market share in key customer segments (by targeting customers who are willing to pay more for faster service, better facilities, and well-stocked convenience stores) and (2) reducing costs and targeting price-sensitive customers. Suppose ExxonMobil decides to pursue the former strategy. The management control system must then reinforce this goal, and ExxonMobil should tie managers' rewards to achieving the targeted measures.

Management control systems should also be designed to support the organizational responsibilities of individual managers. Different levels of management at ExxonMobil need different kinds of information to perform their tasks. For example, top management needs stock-price information to evaluate how much shareholder value the company has created. Stock price, however, is less important for line managers supervising individual refineries. They are more concerned with obtaining information about on-time delivery of gasoline, equipment downtime, product quality, number of days lost to accidents and environmental problems, cost per gallon of gasoline, and employee satisfaction. Similarly, marketing managers are more concerned with information about service at gas stations, customer satisfaction, and market share.

Effective management control systems should also motivate managers and other employees. **Motivation** is the desire to attain a selected goal (the *goal-congruence* aspect) combined with the resulting pursuit of that goal (the *effort* aspect).

Goal congruence exists when individuals and groups work toward achieving the organization's goals—that is, managers working in their own best interest take actions that align with the overall goals of top management. Suppose the goal of ExxonMobil's top management is to maximize operating income. If the management control system evaluates the refinery manager *only* on the basis of costs, the manager may be tempted to make decisions that minimize cost but overlook product quality or timely delivery to retail stations. This oversight is unlikely to maximize operating income of the company as a whole. In this case, the management control system will not achieve goal congruence.

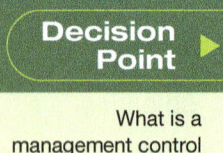

Decision Point ▶

What is a management control system and how should it be designed?

Effort is the extent to which managers strive or endeavor in order to achieve a goal. Effort goes beyond physical exertion, such as a worker producing at a faster rate, to include mental actions as well. For example, effort includes the diligence or acumen with which a manager gathers and analyzes data before authorizing a new investment. It is impossible to directly observe or reward effort. As a result, management control systems motivate employees to exert effort by rewarding them for the achievement of observable goals, such as profit targets or stock returns. This induces managers to exert effort because higher levels of effort increase the likelihood that the goals are achieved. The rewards can be monetary (such as cash, shares of company stock, use of a company car, or membership in a club) or nonmonetary (such as a better title, greater responsibility, or authority over a larger number of employees).

Decentralization

Management control systems must fit an organization's structure. An organization whose structure is decentralized has additional issues to consider for its management control system to be effective.

Decentralization is the freedom for managers at lower levels of the organization to make decisions. **Autonomy** is the degree of freedom to make decisions. The greater the freedom, the greater the autonomy. As we discuss the issues of decentralization and autonomy, we use the term "subunit" to refer to any part of an organization. A subunit may be a large division, such as the refining division of ExxonMobil, or a small group, such as a two-person advertising department of a local clothing chain.

Until the mid-twentieth century, many firms were organized in a centralized, hierarchical fashion. Power was concentrated at the top and there was relatively little freedom for managers at the lower levels to make decisions. Perhaps the most famous example of a highly centralized structure is the Soviet Union, prior to its collapse in the late 1980s. Today, organizations are far more decentralized and many companies have pushed decision-making authority down to subunit managers. Examples of firms with decentralized structures include Nucor, the U.S. steel giant, which allows substantial operational autonomy to the general managers of its plants, and Tesco, Britain's largest retailer, which offers great latitude to its store managers. Of course, no firm is completely decentralized. At Nucor headquarters management still retains responsibility for overall strategic planning, company financing, setting base salary levels and bonus targets, purchase of steel scrap, etc. How much decentralization is optimal? Companies try to choose the degree of decentralization that maximizes benefits over costs. From a practical standpoint, top management can seldom quantify either the benefits or the costs of decentralization. Still, the cost-benefit approach helps management focus on the key issues.

Learning Objective 2

Describe the benefits of decentralization

. . . responsiveness to customers, faster decision making, management development

and the costs of decentralization

. . . loss of control, duplication of activities

Benefits of Decentralization

Supporters of decentralizing decision making and granting responsibilities to managers of subunits advocate the following benefits:

1. **Creates greater responsiveness to needs of a subunit's customers, suppliers, and employees.** Good decisions cannot be made without good information. Compared with top managers, subunit managers are better informed about their customers, competitors, suppliers, and employees, as well as about local factors that affect performance, such as ways to decrease costs, improve quality, and be responsive to customers. Eastman Kodak reports that two advantages of decentralization are an "increase in the company's knowledge of the marketplace and improved service to customers."

2. **Leads to gains from faster decision making by subunit managers.** Decentralization speeds decision making, creating a competitive advantage over centralized organizations. Centralization slows decision making as responsibility for decisions creeps upward through layer after layer of management. Interlake, a manufacturer of materials handling equipment, cites this benefit of decentralization: "We have distributed decision-making powers more broadly to the cutting edge of product and market opportunity." Interlake's materials-handling equipment must often be customized to fit customers' needs. Delegating decision making to the sales force allows Interlake to respond faster to changing customer requirements.

3. **Increases motivation of subunit managers.** Subunit managers are more motivated and committed when they can exercise initiative. Hawei & Hawei, a highly decentralized company, maintains that "Decentralization = Creativity = Productivity."

4. **Assists management development and learning.** Giving managers more responsibility helps develop an experienced pool of management talent to fill higher-level management positions. The company also learns which people are unlikely to be successful top managers. According to Tektronix, an electronics instruments company, "Decentralized units provide a training ground for general managers and a visible field of combat where product champions can fight for their ideas."

5. **Sharpens the focus of subunit managers, broadens the reach of top management.** In a decentralized setting, the manager of a subunit has a concentrated focus. The head of Yahoo Japan, for example, can develop country-specific knowledge and expertise (local advertising trends, cultural norms, payment forms, etc.) and focus attention on maximizing Yahoo's profits in Japan. At the same time, this relieves Yahoo's top

management in Sunnyvale, CA from the burden of controlling day-to-day operating decisions in Japan. The American managers can now spend more time and effort on strategic planning for the entire organization.

Costs of Decentralization

Advocates of more-centralized decision making point to the following costs of decentralizing decision making:

1. **Leads to suboptimal decision making.** This cost arises because top management has given up control over decision making. If the subunit managers do not have the necessary expertise or talent to handle this responsibility, the company, as a whole, is worse off.

   Even if subunit managers are sufficiently skilled, **suboptimal decision making**—also called **incongruent decision making** or **dysfunctional decision making**—occurs when a decision's benefit to one subunit is more than offset by the costs to the organization as a whole. This is most prevalent when the subunits in the company are highly interdependent, such as when the end product of one subunit is used or sold by another subunit. For example, suppose that Nintendo's marketing group receives an order for additional Wii consoles in Australia following the release of some unexpectedly popular new games. A manufacturing manager in Japan who is evaluated on the basis of costs may be unwilling to arrange this rush order since altering production schedules invariably increases manufacturing costs. From Nintendo's viewpoint, however, supplying the consoles may be optimal, both because the Australian customers are willing to pay a premium price and because the current shipment is expected to stimulate orders for other Nintendo games and consoles in the future.

2. **Focuses manager's attention on the subunit rather than the company as a whole.** Individual subunit managers may regard themselves as competing with managers of other subunits in the same company as if they were external rivals. This pushes them to view the relative performance of the subunit as more important than the goals of the company. Consequently, managers may be unwilling to assist when another subunit faces an emergency (as in the Nintendo example) or share important information. In the recent Congressional hearings on the recall of Toyota vehicles, it was revealed that it was common for Toyota's Japan unit to not share information about engineering problems or reported defects between its United States, Asian, and European operations. Toyota has since asserted that this dysfunctional behavior will no longer be tolerated.

3. **Results in duplication of output.** If subunits provide similar products or services, their internal competition could lead to failure in the external markets. The reason is that divisions may find it easier to steal market share from one another, by mimicking each other's successful products, rather than from outside firms. Eventually, this leads to confusion in the minds of customers, and the loss of each division's distinctive strengths. The classic example is General Motors, which has had to wind down its Oldsmobile, Pontiac, and Saturn divisions and is now in bankruptcy reorganization. Similarly, Condé Nast Publishing's initially distinct (and separately run) food magazines, *Bon Appétit* and *Gourmet*, eventually ended up chasing the same readers and advertisers, to the detriment of both. *Gourmet* magazine stopped publication in November 2009.[2]

4. **Results in duplication of activities.** Even if the subunits operate in distinct markets, several individual subunits of the company may undertake the same activity separately. In a highly decentralized company, each subunit may have personnel to carry out staff functions such as human resources or information technology. Centralizing these functions helps to streamline and use fewer resources for these activities, and eliminates wasteful duplication. For example, ABB (Switzerland), a global leader in power and automation technology, is decentralized but has generated significant cost savings of late by centralizing its sourcing decisions across business units for parts, such as pipe pumps and fittings, as well as engineering and erection services. The

---

[2] For an intriguing comparison of the failure of decentralization in these disparate settings, see Jack Shafer's article, "How Condé Nast is Like General Motors: The Magazine Empire as Car Wreck," Slate, October 5, 2009, www.slate.com/id/2231177/.

growing popularity of the "shared service center" model, especially for financial transactions and human resources, is predicated on the 30%–40% savings enabled by the consolidation of such functions, rather than allowing them to be controlled by the subunits.[3]

Comparison of Benefits and Costs

To choose an organization structure that will implement a company's strategy, top managers must compare the benefits and costs of decentralization, often on a function-by-function basis. Surveys of U.S. and European companies report that the decisions made most frequently at the decentralized level are related to product mix and product advertising. In these areas, subunit managers develop their own operating plans and performance reports and make faster decisions based on local information. Decisions related to the type and source of long-term financing and income taxes are made least frequently at the decentralized level. Corporate managers have better information about financing terms in different markets and can obtain the best terms. Centralizing income tax strategies allows the organization to trade off and manage income in a subunit with losses in others. The benefits of decentralization are generally greater when companies face uncertainties in their environments, require detailed local knowledge for performing various jobs, and have few interdependencies among divisions.

Decentralization in Multinational Companies

Multinational companies—companies that operate in multiple countries—are often decentralized because centralized control of a company with subunits around the world is often physically and practically impossible. Also, language, customs, cultures, business practices, rules, laws, and regulations vary significantly across countries. Decentralization enables managers in different countries to make decisions that exploit their knowledge of local business and political conditions and enables them to deal with uncertainties in their individual environments. For example, Philips, a global electronics company headquartered in the Netherlands, delegates marketing and pricing decisions for its television business in the Indian and Singaporean markets to the managers in those countries. Multinational corporations often rotate managers between foreign locations and corporate headquarters. Job rotation combined with decentralization helps develop managers' abilities to operate in the global environment.

There are drawbacks to decentralizing multinational companies. One of the most important is the lack of control and the resulting risks. Barings PLC, a British investment banking firm, went bankrupt and had to be sold when one of its traders in Singapore caused the firm to lose more than £1 billion on unauthorized trades that were not detected until after the trades were made. Similarly, a trader at Sumitomo Corporation racked up $2.6 billion in copper-trading losses because poor controls failed to detect the magnitude of the trader's activities. Multinational corporations that implement decentralized decision making usually design their management control systems to measure and monitor division performance. Information and communications technology helps the flow of information for reporting and control.

Choices About Responsibility Centers

Recall from Chapter 6 that a responsibility center is a segment or subunit of the organization whose manager is accountable for a specified set of activities. To measure the performance of subunits in centralized or decentralized companies, the management control system uses one or a mix of the four types of responsibility centers:

1. *Cost center*—the manager is accountable for costs only.
2. *Revenue center*—the manager is accountable for revenues only.
3. *Profit center*—the manager is accountable for revenues and costs.
4. *Investment center*—the manager is accountable for investments, revenues, and costs.

Centralization or decentralization is not mentioned in the descriptions of these centers because each type of responsibility center can be found in either centralized or decentralized companies.

---

[3] For more on this topic, see http://www.sap.com/solutions/business-suite/erp/pdf/BWP_WP_Shared_Services.pdf.

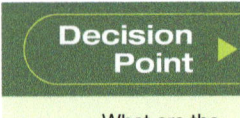

Decision Point ▶

What are the benefits and costs of decentralization?

A common misconception is that *profit center*—and, in some cases, *investment center*—is a synonym for a decentralized subunit, and *cost center* is a synonym for a centralized subunit. *Profit centers can be coupled with a highly centralized organization, and cost centers can be coupled with a highly decentralized organization.* For example, managers in a division organized as a profit center may have little freedom in making decisions. They may need to obtain approval from corporate headquarters for introducing new products and services, or to make expenditures over some preset limit. When Michael Eisner ran Walt Disney Co., the giant media and entertainment conglomerate, the strategic-planning division applied so much scrutiny to business proposals that managers were reluctant to even pitch new ideas.[4] In other companies, divisions such as Information Technology may be organized as cost centers, but their managers may have great latitude with regard to capital expenditures and the purchase of materials and services. In short, the labels "profit center" and "cost center" are independent of the degree of centralization or decentralization in a company.

Transfer Pricing

Learning Objective 3

Explain transfer prices

. . . price one subunit charges another for product

and four criteria used to evaluate alternative transfer-pricing methods

. . . goal congruence, management effort, subunit performance evaluation, and subunit autonomy

In decentralized organizations, much of the decision-making power resides in its individual subunits. In these cases, the management control system often uses *transfer prices* to coordinate the actions of the subunits and to evaluate their performance.

As you may recall from the opener, a **transfer price** is the price one subunit (department or division) charges for a product or service supplied to another subunit of the same organization. If, for example, a car manufacturer has a separate division that manufactures engines, the transfer price is the price the engine division charges when it transfers engines to the car assembly division. The transfer price creates revenues for the selling subunit (the engine division in our example) and purchase costs for the buying subunit (the assembly division in our example), affecting each subunit's operating income. These operating incomes can be used to evaluate subunits' performances and to motivate their managers. The product or service transferred between subunits of an organization is called an **intermediate product**. This product may either be further worked on by the receiving subunit (as in the engine example) or, if transferred from production to marketing, sold to an external customer.

In one sense, transfer pricing is a curious phenomenon. Activities within an organization are clearly nonmarket in nature; products and services are not bought and sold as they are in open-market transactions. Yet, establishing prices for transfers among subunits of a company has a distinctly market flavor. The rationale for transfer prices is that subunit managers (such as the manager of the engine division), when making decisions, need only focus on how their decisions will affect their subunit's performance without evaluating their impact on company-wide performance. In this sense, transfer prices ease the subunit managers' information-processing and decision-making tasks. In a well-designed transfer-pricing system, a manager focuses on optimizing subunit performance (the performance of the engine division) and in so doing optimizes the performance of the company as a whole.

Criteria for Evaluating Transfer Prices

As in all management control systems, transfer prices should help achieve a company's strategies and goals and fit its organization structure. We describe four criteria to evaluate transfer pricing: (1) Transfer prices should promote goal congruence. (2) They should induce managers to exert a high level of effort. Subunits selling a product or service should be motivated to hold down their costs; subunits buying the product or service should be motivated to acquire and use inputs efficiently. (3) The transfer price should help top management evaluate the performance of individual subunits. (4) If top management favors a high degree of decentralization, transfer prices should preserve a high degree of subunit autonomy in decision making. That is, a subunit manager seeking to maximize the operating income of the subunit should have the freedom to transact with other subunits of the company (on the basis of transfer prices) or to transact with external parties.

---

[4] When Robert Iger replaced Eisner as CEO in 2005, one of his first acts was to disassemble the strategic-planning division, thereby giving more authority to Disney's business units (parks and resorts, consumer products, and media networks).

Calculating Transfer Prices

There are three broad categories of methods for determining transfer prices. They are as follows:

1. **Market-based transfer prices.** Top management may choose to use the price of a similar product or service publicly listed in, say, a trade association Web site. Also, top management may select, for the internal price, the external price that a subunit charges to outside customers.

2. **Cost-based transfer prices.** Top management may choose a transfer price based on the cost of producing the product in question. Examples include variable production cost, variable and fixed production costs, and full cost of the product. Full cost of the product includes all production costs plus costs from other business functions (R&D, design, marketing, distribution, and customer service). The cost used in cost-based transfer prices can be actual cost or budgeted cost. Sometimes, the cost-based transfer price includes a markup or profit margin that represents a return on subunit investment.

3. **Hybrid transfer prices.** Hybrid transfer prices take into account both cost and market information. Top management may administer such prices, for example by specifying a transfer price that is an average of the cost of producing and transporting the product internally and the market price for comparable products. At other times, a hybrid transfer price may take the form where the revenue recognized by the selling unit is different from the cost recognized by the buying unit. The most common form of hybrid prices arise via negotiation—the subunits of a company are asked to negotiate the transfer price between them and to decide whether to buy and sell internally or deal with external parties. The eventual transfer price is then the outcome of a bargaining process between selling and buying subunits. Even though there is no requirement that the chosen transfer price bear any specific relationship to cost or market-price data, information regarding costs and prices plays a critical role in the negotiation process. Negotiated transfer prices are often employed when market prices are volatile and change constantly.

To see how each of the three transfer-pricing methods works and to see the differences among them, we examine transfer pricing at Horizon Petroleum against the four criteria of promoting goal congruence, motivating management effort, evaluating subunit performance, and preserving subunit autonomy (if desired).

An Illustration of Transfer Pricing

Horizon Petroleum has two divisions, each operating as a profit center. The transportation division purchases crude oil in Matamoros, Mexico, and transports it from Matamoros to Houston, Texas. The refining division processes crude oil into gasoline. For simplicity, we assume gasoline is the only salable product the Houston refinery makes and that it takes two barrels of crude oil to yield one barrel of gasoline.

Variable costs in each division are variable with respect to a single cost driver: barrels of crude oil transported by the transportation division, and barrels of gasoline produced by the refining division. The fixed cost per unit is based on the budgeted annual fixed costs and practical capacity of crude oil that can be transported by the transportation division, and the budgeted fixed costs and practical capacity of gasoline that can be produced by the refining division. Horizon Petroleum reports all costs and revenues of its non-U.S. operations in U.S. dollars using the prevailing exchange rate.

- The transportation division has obtained rights to certain oil fields in the Matamoros area. It has a long-term contract to purchase crude oil produced from these fields at $72 per barrel. The division transports the oil to Houston and then "sells" it to the refining division. The pipeline from Matamoros to Houston has the capacity to carry 40,000 barrels of crude oil per day.

- The refining division has been operating at capacity (30,000 barrels of crude oil a day), using oil supplied by Horizon's transportation division (an average of 10,000 barrels per day) and oil bought from another producer and delivered to the Houston refinery (an average of 20,000 barrels per day at $85 per barrel).

- The refining division sells the gasoline it produces to outside parties at $190 per barrel.

Exhibit 22-1 summarizes Horizon Petroleum's variable and fixed costs per barrel of crude oil in the transportation division and variable and fixed costs per barrel of gasoline in the refining division, the external market prices of buying crude oil, and the external market price of selling gasoline. What's missing in the exhibit is the actual transfer price from the transportation division to the refining division. This transfer price will vary depending on the transfer-pricing method used. Transfer prices from the transportation division to the refining division under each of the three methods are as follows:

1. Market-based transfer price of $85 per barrel of crude oil based on the competitive market price in Houston.
2. Cost-based transfer prices at, say, 105% of full cost, where full cost is the cost of the crude oil purchased in Matamoros plus the transportation division's own variable and fixed costs (from Exhibit 22-1): 1.05 × ($72 + $1 + $3) = $79.80.
3. Hybrid transfer price of, say, $82 per barrel of crude oil, which is between the market-based and cost-based transfer prices. We describe later in this section the various ways in which hybrid prices can be determined.

Exhibit 22-2 presents division operating incomes per 100 barrels of crude oil purchased under each transfer-pricing method. Transfer prices create income for the selling division and corresponding costs for the buying division that cancel out when division results are consolidated for the company as a whole. The exhibit assumes all three transfer-pricing methods yield transfer prices that are in a range that does not cause division managers to change the business relationships shown in Exhibit 22-1. That is, Horizon Petroleum's total operating income from purchasing, transporting, and refining the 100 barrels of crude oil and selling the 50 barrels of gasoline is the same, $1,200, *regardless of the internal transfer prices used.*

$$\begin{array}{l} \text{Operating} \\ \text{income} \end{array} = \text{Revenues} - \begin{array}{c} \text{Cost of crude} \\ \text{oil purchases} \\ \text{in Matamoros} \end{array} - \begin{array}{c} \text{Transportation} \\ \text{Division} \\ \text{costs} \end{array} - \begin{array}{c} \text{Refining} \\ \text{Division} \\ \text{costs} \end{array}$$

$$= (\$190 \times 50 \text{ barrels of gasoline}) - (\$72 \times 100 \text{ barrels of crude oil})$$

$$- (\$4 \times 100 \text{ barrels of crude oil}) - (\$14 \times 50 \text{ barrels of gasoline})$$

$$= \$9,500 - \$7,200 - \$400 - \$700 = \$1,200$$

Note further that under all three methods, summing the two division operating incomes equals Horizon Petroleum's total operating income of $1,200. By keeping total operating

Exhibit 22-1 Operating Data for Horizon Petroleum

	A	B	C	D	E	F	G	H
1								
2				**Transportation Division**				
3	Contract price per barrel of crude oil supplied in Matamoros	=	$72	Variable cost per barrel of crude oil	$1			
4				Fixed cost per barrel of crude oil	3			
5				Full cost per barrel of crude oil	$4			
6								
7								
8				Barrels of crude oil transferred				
9								
10								
11				**Refining Division**				
12	Market price per barrel of crude oil supplied to Houston refinery	=	$85	Variable cost per barrel of gasoline	$ 8		Market price per barrel of gasoline sold to external parties	
13				Fixed cost per barrel of gasoline	6			= $190
14				Full cost per barrel of gasoline	$14			
15								

Exhibit 22-2 Division Operating Income of Horizon Petroleum for 100 Barrels of Crude Oil Under Alternative Transfer-Pricing Methods

	A	B	C	D	E	F	G	H
	Home Insert Page Layout Formulas Data Review View							
1	Production and Sales Data							
2	Barrels of crude oil transferred =	100						
3	Barrels of gasoline sold =	50						
4								
5		Internal Transfers at			Internal Transfers at			
6		Market Price =			105% of Full Cost =		Hybrid Price =	
7		$85 per Barrel			$79.80 per Barrel		$82 per Barrel	
8	Transportation Division							
9	Revenues, $85, $79.80, $82 × 100 barrels of crude oil	$8,500			$7,980		$8,200	
10	Costs							
11	Crude oil purchase costs, $72 × 100 barrels of crude oil	7,200			7,200		7,200	
12	Division variable costs, $1 × 100 barrels of crude oil	100			100		100	
13	Division fixed costs, $3 × 100 barrels of crude oil	300			300		300	
14	Total division costs	7,600			7,600		7,600	
15	Division operating income	$ 900			$ 380		$ 600	
16								
17	Refining Division							
18	Revenues, $190 × 50 barrels of gasoline	$9,500			$9,500		$9,500	
19	Costs							
20	Transferred-in costs, $85, $79.80, $82							
21	× 100 barrels of crude oil	8,500			7,980		8,200	
22	Division variable costs, $8 × 50 barrels of gasoline	400			400		400	
23	Division fixed costs, $6 × 50 barrels of gasoline	300			300		300	
24	Total division costs	9,200			8,680		8,900	
25	Division operating income	$ 300			$ 820		$ 600	
26	Operating income of both divisions together	$1,200			$1,200		$1,200	

income the same, we focus attention on the effects of different transfer-pricing methods on the operating income of each division. Subsequent sections of this chapter show that different transfer-pricing methods can cause managers to take different actions leading to different total operating incomes.

Consider the two methods in the first two columns of Exhibit 22-2. The operating income of the transportation division is $520 more ($900 − $380) if transfer prices are based on market prices rather than on 105% of full cost. The operating income of the refining division is $520 more ($820 − $300) if transfer prices are based on 105% of full cost rather than market prices. If the transportation division's sole criterion were to maximize its own division operating income, it would favor transfer prices at market prices. In contrast, the refining division would prefer transfer prices at 105% of full cost to maximize its own division operating income. The hybrid transfer price of $82 is between the 105% of full cost and market-based transfer prices. It splits the $1,200 of operating income equally between the divisions, and could arise as a result of negotiations between the transportation and refining division managers.

It's not surprising that subunit managers, especially those whose compensation or promotion directly depends on subunit operating income, take considerable interest in setting transfer prices. To reduce the excessive focus of subunit managers on their own subunits, many companies compensate subunit managers on the basis of both subunit and company-wide operating incomes.

We next examine market-based, cost-based, and hybrid transfer prices in more detail. We show how the choice of transfer-pricing method combined with managers' sourcing decisions can determine the size of the company-wide operating-income pie itself.

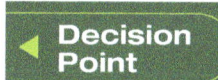

Decision Point

What are alternative ways of calculating transfer prices, and what criteria should be used to evaluate them?

Market-Based Transfer Prices

Learning Objective 4

Illustrate how market-based transfer prices promote goal congruence in perfectly competitive markets

. . . division managers transacting internally are motivated to take the same actions as if they were transacting externally

Transferring products or services at market prices generally leads to optimal decisions when three conditions are satisfied: (1) The market for the intermediate product is perfectly competitive, (2) interdependencies of subunits are minimal, and (3) there are no additional costs or benefits to the company as a whole from buying or selling in the external market instead of transacting internally.

Perfectly-Competitive-Market Case

A **perfectly competitive market** exists when there is a homogeneous product with buying prices equal to selling prices and no individual buyers or sellers can affect those prices by their own actions. By using market-based transfer prices in perfectly competitive markets, a company can (1) promote goal congruence, (2) motivate management effort, (3) evaluate subunit performance, and (4) preserve subunit autonomy.

Consider Horizon Petroleum again. Assume there is a perfectly competitive market for crude oil in the Houston area. As a result, the transportation division can sell and the refining division can buy as much crude oil as each wants at $85 per barrel. Horizon would prefer its managers to buy or sell crude oil internally. Think about the decisions that Horizon's division managers would make if each had the autonomy to sell or buy crude oil externally. If the transfer price between Horizon's transportation and refining divisions is set below $85, the manager of the transportation division will be motivated to sell all crude oil to external buyers in the Houston area at $85 per barrel. If the transfer price is set above $85, the manager of the refining division will be motivated to purchase all crude oil requirements from external suppliers. Only an $85 transfer price will motivate the transportation division and the refining division to buy and sell internally. That's because neither division profits by buying or selling in the external market.

Suppose Horizon evaluates division managers on the basis of their individual division's operating income. The transportation division will sell, either internally or externally, as much crude oil as it can profitably transport, and the refining division will buy, either internally or externally, as much crude oil as it can profitably refine. An $85-per-barrel transfer price achieves goal congruence—the actions that maximize each division's operating income are also the actions that maximize operating income of Horizon Petroleum as a whole. Furthermore, because the transfer price is not based on costs, it motivates each division manager to exert management effort to maximize his or her own division's operating income. Market prices also serve to evaluate the economic viability and profitability of each division individually. For example, Koch Industries, the second-largest private company in the United States, uses market-based pricing for all internal transfers. As their CFO, Steve Feilmeier, notes, "We believe that the alternative for any given asset should always be considered in order to best optimize the profitability of the asset. If you simply transfer price between two different divisions at cost, then you may be subsidizing your whole operation and not know it." Returning to our Horizon example, suppose that under market-based transfer prices, the refining division consistently shows small or negative profits. Then, Horizon may consider shutting down the refining division and simply transport and sell the oil to other refineries in the Houston area.

Distress Prices

When supply outstrips demand, market prices may drop well below their historical averages. If the drop in prices is expected to be temporary, these low market prices are sometimes called "distress prices." Deciding whether a current market price is a distress price is often difficult. Prior to the worldwide spike in commodity prices in the 2006–2008 period, the market prices of several mineral and agricultural commodities, including nickel, uranium, and wheat, stayed for many years at what people initially believed were temporary distress levels!

Which transfer price should be used for judging performance if distress prices prevail? Some companies use the distress prices themselves, but others use long-run average prices, or "normal" market prices. In the short run, the manager of the selling subunit should supply the product or service at the distress price as long as it exceeds the *incremental costs* of supplying the product or service. If the distress price is used as the transfer price, the selling division will show a loss because the distress price will not exceed the *full cost* of the division. If the long-run average market price is used, forcing the manager to buy internally at a price above the current market price will hurt the buying division's short-run operating income. But the long-run average market price will provide a better measure of the long-run profitability and viability of the supplier division. Of course, if the price remains low in the long run, the company should use the low market price as the transfer price. If this price is lower than the variable and fixed costs that can be saved if manufacturing facilities are shut down, the production facilities of the selling subunit should be sold, and the buying subunit should purchase the product from an external supplier.

Imperfect Competition

If markets are not perfectly competitive, selling prices affect the quantity of product sold. If the selling division sells its product in the external market, the selling division manager would choose a price and quantity combination that would maximize the division's operating income. If the transfer price is set at this selling price, the buying division may find that acquiring the product is too costly and results in a loss. It may decide not to purchase the product. Yet, from the point of view of the company as a whole, it may well be that profits are maximized if the selling division transfers the product to the buying division for further processing and sale. For this reason, when the market for the intermediate good is imperfectly competitive, the transfer price must generally be set below the external market price (but above the selling division's variable cost) in order to induce efficient transfers.[5]

Cost-Based Transfer Prices

Cost-based transfer prices are helpful when market prices are unavailable, inappropriate, or too costly to obtain, such as when markets are not perfectly competitive, when the product is specialized, or when the internal product is different from the products available externally in terms of quality and customer service.

Full-Cost Bases

In practice, many companies use transfer prices based on full cost. To approximate market prices, cost-based transfer prices are sometimes set at full cost plus a margin. These transfer prices, however, can lead to suboptimal decisions. Suppose Horizon Petroleum makes internal transfers at 105% of full cost. Recall that the refining division purchases, on average, 20,000 barrels of crude oil per day from a local Houston supplier, who delivers the crude oil to the refinery at a price of $85 per barrel. To reduce crude oil costs, the refining division has located an independent producer in Matamoros—Gulfmex Corporation— that is willing to sell 20,000 barrels of crude oil per day at $79 per barrel, delivered to Horizon's pipeline in Matamoros. Given Horizon's organization structure, the transportation division would purchase the 20,000 barrels of crude oil in Matamoros from Gulfmex, transport it to Houston, and then sell it to the refining division. The pipeline has unused capacity and can ship the 20,000 barrels per day at its variable cost of $1 per barrel without affecting the shipment of the 10,000 barrels of crude oil per day acquired under its existing long-term contract arrangement. Will Horizon Petroleum incur lower costs by

---

[5] Consider a firm where division S produces the intermediate product. S has a capacity of 15 units and a variable cost per unit of $2. The imperfect competition is reflected in a downward-sloping demand curve for the intermediate product—if S wants to sell Q units, it has to lower the market price to $P = 20 - Q$. The division's profit function is therefore given by $Q \times (20 - Q) - 2Q = 18Q - Q^2$. Simple calculus reveals that it is optimal for S to sell 9 units of the intermediate product at a price of $11, thereby making a profit of $81. Now, suppose that division B in the same firm can take the intermediate product, incur an additional variable cost of $4 and sell it in the external market for $12. Since S has surplus capacity (it only uses 9 of its 15 units of capacity), it is clearly in the firm's interest to have S make additional units and transfer them to B. The firm makes an incremental profit of $12 − $2 − $4 = $6 for each transferred unit. However, if the transfer price for the intermediate product were set equal to the market price of $11, B would reject the transaction since it would lose money on it ($12 − $11 − $4 = − $3 per unit).

To resolve this conflict, the transfer price should be set at a suitable *discount* to the external price in order to induce the buying division to seek internal transfers. In our example, the selling price must be greater than S's variable cost of $2, but less than B's contribution margin of $8. That is, the transfer price has to be discounted relative to the market price ($11) by a minimum of $3. We explore the issue of feasible transfer pricing ranges further in the section on hybrid transfer prices.

purchasing crude oil from Gulfmex in Matamoros or by purchasing crude oil from the Houston supplier? Will the refining division show lower crude oil purchasing costs by acquiring oil from Gulfmex or by acquiring oil from its current Houston supplier?

The following analysis shows that Horizon Petroleum's operating income would be maximized by purchasing oil from Gulfmex. The analysis compares the incremental costs in both divisions under the two alternatives. The analysis assumes the fixed costs of the transportation division will be the same regardless of the alternative chosen. That is, the transportation division cannot save any of its fixed costs if it does not transport Gulfmex's 20,000 barrels of crude oil per day.

- **Alternative 1:** Buy 20,000 barrels from the Houston supplier at $85 per barrel. Total costs to Horizon Petroleum are 20,000 barrels × $85 per barrel = $1,700,000.
- **Alternative 2:** Buy 20,000 barrels in Matamoros at $79 per barrel and transport them to Houston at a variable cost of $1 per barrel. Total costs to Horizon Petroleum are 20,000 barrels × ($79 + $1) per barrel = $1,600,000.

There is a reduction in total costs to Horizon Petroleum of $100,000 ($1,700,000 − $1,600,000) by acquiring oil from Gulfmex.

Suppose the transportation division's transfer price to the refining division is 105% of full cost. The refining division will see its reported division costs increase if the crude oil is purchased from Gulfmex:

$$\text{Transfer price} = 1.05 \times \left(\begin{array}{ccc} \text{Purchase price} & & \text{Variable cost per unit} & & \text{Fixed cost per unit} \\ \text{from} & + & \text{of Transportation} & + & \text{of Transportation} \\ \text{Gulfmex} & & \text{Division} & & \text{Division} \end{array} \right)$$

$$= 1.05 \times (\$79 + \$1 + \$3) = 1.05 \times \$83 = \$87.15 \text{ per barrel}$$

- **Alternative 1:** Buy 20,000 barrels from Houston supplier at $85 per barrel. Total costs to refining division are 20,000 barrels × $85 per barrel = $1,700,000.
- **Alternative 2:** Buy 20,000 barrels from the transportation division of Horizon Petroleum that were purchased from Gulfmex. Total costs to refining division are 20,000 barrels × $87.15 per barrel = $1,743,000.

As a profit center, the refining division can maximize its short-run division operating income by purchasing from the Houston supplier at $1,700,000.

The refining division looks at each barrel that it obtains from the transportation division as a variable cost of $87.15 per barrel; if 10 barrels are transferred, it costs the refining division $871.50; if 100 barrels are transferred, it costs $8,715. In fact, the variable cost per barrel is $80 ($79 to purchase the oil from Gulfmex plus $1 to transport it to Houston). The remaining $7.15 ($87.15 − $80) per barrel is the transportation division's fixed cost and markup. *The full cost plus a markup transfer-pricing method causes the refining division to regard the fixed cost (and the 5% markup) of the transportation division as a variable cost and leads to goal incongruence.*

Should Horizon's top management interfere and force the refining division to buy from the transportation division? Top management interference would undercut the philosophy of decentralization, so Horizon's top management would probably view the decision by the refining division to purchase crude oil from external suppliers as an inevitable cost of decentralization and not interfere. Of course, some interference may occasionally be necessary to prevent costly blunders. But recurring interference and constraints would simply transform Horizon from a decentralized company into a centralized company.

What transfer price will promote goal congruence for both the transportation and refining divisions? The minimum transfer price is $80 per barrel. A transfer price below $80 does not provide the transportation division with an incentive to purchase crude oil from Gulfmex in Matamoros because it is below the transportation division's incremental costs. The maximum transfer price is $85 per barrel. A transfer price above $85 will cause the refining division to purchase crude oil from the external market rather than from the transportation division. A transfer price between the minimum and maximum transfer prices of $80 and $85 will promote goal congruence: Each division will increase its own reported operating income while increasing Horizon Petroleum's operating income if the refining division purchases crude oil from Gulfmex in Matamoros.

In the absence of a market-based transfer price, senior management at Horizon Petroleum cannot easily determine the profitability of the investment made in the transportation division and hence whether Horizon should keep or sell the pipeline. Furthermore, if the transfer price had been based on the actual costs of the transportation division, it would provide the division with no incentive to control costs. That's because all cost inefficiencies of the transportation division would get passed along as part of the actual full-cost transfer price. In fact, every additional dollar of cost arising from wastefulness in the transportation division would generate an additional five cents in profit for the division under the "105% of full cost" rule!

Surveys indicate that, despite the limitations, managers generally prefer to use fullcost-based transfer prices. That's because these transfer prices represent relevant costs for long-run decisions, they facilitate external pricing based on variable and fixed costs, and they are the least costly to administer. However, full-cost transfer pricing does raise many issues. How are each subunit's indirect costs allocated to products? Have the correct activities, cost pools, and cost-allocation bases been identified? Should the chosen fixedcost rates be actual or budgeted? The issues here are similar to the issues that arise in allocating fixed costs, which were introduced in Chapter 14. Many companies determine the transfer price based on budgeted rates and practical capacity because it overcomes the problem of inefficiencies in actual costs and costs of unused capacity getting passed along to the buying division.

Variable-Cost Bases

Transferring 20,000 barrels of crude oil from the transportation division to the refining division at the variable cost of $80 per barrel achieves goal congruence, as shown in the preceding section. The refining division would buy from the transportation division because the transportation division's variable cost is less than the $85 price charged by external suppliers. Setting the transfer price equal to the variable cost has other benefits. Knowledge of the variable cost per barrel of crude oil is very helpful to the refining division for many decisions such as the short-run pricing decisions discussed in Chapters 11 and 12. However, at the $80-per-barrel transfer price, the transportation division would record an operating loss, and the refining division would show large profits because it would be charged only for the variable costs of the transportation division. One approach to addressing this problem is to have the refining division make a lump-sum transfer payment to cover fixed costs and generate some operating income for the transportation division while the transportation division continues to make transfers at variable cost. The fixed payment is the price the refining division pays for using the capacity of the transportation division. The income earned by each division can then be used to evaluate the performance of each division and its manager.

Hybrid Transfer Prices

Consider again Horizon Petroleum. As we saw earlier, the transportation division has unused capacity it can use to transport oil from Matamoros to Houston at an incremental cost of $80 per barrel of crude oil. Horizon Petroleum, as a whole, maximizes operating income if the refining division purchases crude oil from the transportation division rather than from the Houston market (incremental cost per barrel of $80 versus price per barrel of $85). Both divisions would be interested in transacting with each other (and the firm achieves goal congruence) if the transfer price is between $80 and $85.

For any internal transaction, there is generally a minimum transfer price the selling division will not go below, based on its cost structure. In the Horizon Petroleum example, the minimum price acceptable to the transportation division is $80. There is also a maximum price the buying division will not wish to exceed, given by the lower of two quantities—the eventual contribution it generates from an internal transaction and the price of purchasing a comparable intermediate product from an outside party. For the

Decision Point

What problems can arise when full cost plus a markup is used as the transfer price?

Learning Objective 6

Describe the range of feasible transfer prices when there is unused capacity

. . . from variable cost to market price of the product transferred

refining division, each barrel of gasoline sold to external parties generates $182 in contribution (the $190 price less the $8 variable cost of refining). Since it takes two barrels of crude oil to generate a barrel of gasoline, this is equivalent to a contribution of $91 per barrel of crude. For any price higher than $91, the refining division would lose money for each barrel of crude it takes from the transportation division. On the other hand, the refining division can purchase crude oil on the open market for $85 rather than having it transported internally. The maximum feasible transfer price is thus the lower of $91 and $85, or $85 in this instance. We saw previously that a transfer price between the minimum price ($80) and the maximum ($85) would promote goal congruence. We now describe three different ways in which firms attempt to determine the specific transfer price within these bounds.

Prorating the Difference Between Maximum and Minimum Transfer Prices

One approach that Horizon Petroleum could pursue is to choose a transfer price that splits, on some fair basis, the $5 difference between the $85-per-barrel market-based maximum price the refining division is willing to pay and the $80-per-barrel variable cost-based minimum price the transportation division wants to receive. An easy solution is to split the difference equally, resulting in a transfer price of $82.50. However, this solution ignores the relative costs incurred by the two divisions and might lead to disparate profit margins on the work contributed by each division to the final product. As an alternative approach, Horizon Petroleum could allocate the $5 difference on the basis of the variable costs of the two divisions. Using the data in Exhibit 22-1 (p. 782), variable costs are as follows:

Transportation division's variable costs to transport 100 barrels of crude oil ($1 × 100)	$100
Refining division's variable costs to refine 100 barrels of crude oil and produce 50 barrels of gasoline ($8 × 50)	400
Total variable costs	$500

Of the $5 difference, the transportation division gets to keep ($100 ÷ $500) × $5.00 = $1.00, and the refining division gets to keep ($400 ÷ $500) × $5.00 = $4.00. That is, the transfer price is $81 per barrel of crude oil ($79 purchase cost + $1 variable cost + $1 that the transportation division gets to keep). In effect, this approach results in a budgeted variable-cost-plus transfer price. The "plus" indicates the setting of a transfer price above variable cost.

To decide on the $1 and $4 allocations of the $5 incremental benefit to total company operating income per barrel, the divisions must share information about their variable costs. In effect, each division does not operate (at least for this transaction) in a totally decentralized manner. Furthermore, each division has an incentive to overstate its variable costs to receive a more-favorable transfer price. In the preceding example, suppose the transportation division claims a cost of $2 per barrel to ship crude oil from Gulfmex to Houston. This increased cost raises the variable cost-based minimum price to $79 + $2 = $81 per barrel; the maximum price remains $85. Of the $4 difference between the minimum and maximum, the transportation division now gets to keep ($200 ÷ ($200 + $400)) × $4.00 = $1.33, resulting in a higher transfer price of $82.33. The refining division similarly benefits from asserting that its variable cost to refine 100 barrels of crude oil is greater than $400. As a consequence, proration methods either require a high degree of trust and information exchange among divisions or include provisions for objective audits of cost information in order to be successful.

Negotiated Pricing

This is the most common hybrid method. Under this approach, top management does not administer a specific split of the eventual profits across the transacting divisions. Rather, the eventual transfer price results from a bargaining process between the selling and buying subunits. In the Horizon Petroleum case, for example, the transportation division and the refining division would be free to negotiate a price that is mutually acceptable to both.

As described earlier, the minimum and maximum feasible transfer prices are $80 and $85, respectively, per barrel of crude oil. Where between $80 and $85 will the transfer price per barrel be set? Under a negotiated transfer price, the answer depends on several things: the bargaining strengths of the two divisions; information the transportation division has about the price minus incremental marketing costs of supplying crude oil to outside refineries; and the information the refining division has about its other available sources of crude oil. Negotiations become particularly sensitive because Horizon Petroleum can now evaluate each division's performance on the basis of division operating income. The price negotiated by the two divisions will, in general, have no specific relationship to either costs or market price. But cost and price information is often the starting point in the negotiation process.

Consider the following situation: Suppose the refining division receives an order to supply specially processed gasoline. The incremental cost to purchase and supply crude oil is still $80 per barrel. However, suppose the refining division will profit from this order only if the transportation division can supply crude oil at a price not exceeding $82 per barrel.[6] In this case, the transfer price that would benefit both divisions must be greater than $80 but less than $82. Negotiations would allow the two divisions to achieve an acceptable transfer price. By contrast, a rule-based transfer price, such as a market-based price of $85 or a 105% of full-cost-based price of $87.15, would result in Horizon passing up a profitable opportunity.

A negotiated transfer price strongly preserves division autonomy. It also has the advantage that each division manager is motivated to put forth effort to increase division operating income. Surveys have found that approximately 15%–20% of firms set transfer prices based on negotiation among divisions. The key reason cited by firms that do not use negotiated prices is the cost of the bargaining process, that is, the time and energy spent by managers haggling over transfer prices.

Dual Pricing

There is seldom a single transfer price that simultaneously meets the criteria of promoting goal congruence, motivating management effort, evaluating subunit performance, and preserving subunit autonomy. As a result, some companies choose **dual pricing**, using two separate transfer-pricing methods to price each transfer from one subunit to another. An example of dual pricing arises when the selling division receives a full-cost-based price and the buying division pays the market price for the internally transferred products. Assume Horizon Petroleum purchases crude oil from Gulfmex in Matamoros at $79 per barrel. One way of recording the journal entry for the transfer between the transportation division and the refining division is as follows:

1. Debit the refining division (the buying division) with the market-based transfer price of $85 per barrel of crude oil.

2. Credit the transportation division (the selling division) with the 105%-of-full-cost transfer price of $87.15 per barrel of crude oil.

3. Debit a corporate cost account for the $2.15 ($87.15 − $85) per barrel difference between the two transfer prices.

The dual-pricing system promotes goal congruence because it makes the refining division no worse off if it purchases the crude oil from the transportation division rather than from the external supplier at $85 per barrel. The transportation division receives a corporate subsidy. In dual pricing, the operating income for Horizon Petroleum as a whole is less than the sum of the operating incomes of the divisions.

Dual pricing is not widely used in practice even though it reduces the goal incongruence associated with a pure cost-based transfer-pricing method. One concern with dual pricing is that it leads to problems in computing the taxable income of subunits located in different tax jurisdictions, such as in our example, where the transportation division is taxed in Mexico while the refining division is taxed in the United States. A second concern is that dual pricing insulates managers from the frictions of the marketplace because costs, not market prices, affect the revenues of the supplying division.

Decision Point

Within a range of feasible transfer prices, what are alternative ways for firms to arrive at the eventual price?

---

[6] For example, suppose a barrel of specially processed gasoline could be sold for $200 but also required a higher variable cost of refining of $36 per barrel. In this setting, the incremental contribution to the refining division is $164 per barrel of gasoline, which implies that it will pay at most $82 for a barrel of crude oil (since two barrels of crude are required for one barrel of gasoline).

A General Guideline for Transfer-Pricing Situations

Learning Objective 7

Apply a general guideline for determining a minimum transfer price

. . . incremental cost plus opportunity cost of supplying division

Exhibit 22-3 summarizes the properties of market-based, cost-based, and negotiated transfer-pricing methods using the criteria described in this chapter. As the exhibit indicates, it is difficult for a transfer-pricing method to meet all criteria. Market conditions, the goal of the transfer-pricing system, and the criteria of promoting goal congruence, motivating management effort, evaluating subunit performance, and preserving subunit autonomy (if desired) must all be considered simultaneously. The transfer price a company will eventually choose depends on the economic circumstances and the decision at hand. Surveys of company practice indicate that the full-cost-based transfer price is generally the most frequently used transfer-pricing method around the world, followed by market-based transfer price and negotiated transfer price.

Our discussion thus far highlight that, barring settings in which a perfectly competitive market exists for the intermediate product, there is generally a range of possible transfer prices that would induce goal congruence. We now provide a general guideline for determining the minimum price in that range. The following formula is a helpful first step in setting the minimum transfer price in many situations:

$$\text{Minimum transfer price} = \begin{matrix}\text{Incremental cost} \\ \text{per unit} \\ \text{incurred up} \\ \text{to the point of transfer}\end{matrix} + \begin{matrix}\text{Opportunity cost} \\ \text{per unit} \\ \text{to the selling subunit}\end{matrix}$$

Incremental cost in this context means the additional cost of producing and transferring the product or service. Opportunity cost here is the maximum contribution margin forgone by the selling subunit if the product or service is transferred internally. For example, if the selling subunit is operating at capacity, the opportunity cost of transferring a unit internally rather than selling it externally is equal to the market price minus variable cost. That's because by transferring a unit internally, the subunit forgoes the contribution margin it could have obtained by selling the unit in the external market. We distinguish incremental cost from opportunity cost because financial accounting systems record incremental cost but do not record opportunity cost. The guideline measures a *minimum* transfer price because it represents the selling unit's cost of transferring the product. We illustrate the general guideline in some specific situations using data from Horizon Petroleum.

1. **A perfectly competitive market for the intermediate product exists, and the selling division has no unused capacity.** If the market for crude oil in Houston is perfectly

Exhibit 22-3

Comparison of Different Transfer-Pricing Methods

Criteria	Market-Based	Cost-Based	Negotiated
Achieves goal congruence	Yes, when markets are competitive	Often, but not always	Yes
Motivates management effort	Yes	Yes, when based on budgeted costs; less incentive to control costs if transfers are based on actual costs	Yes
Useful for evaluating subunit performance	Yes, when markets are competitive	Difficult unless transfer price exceeds full cost and even then is somewhat arbitrary	Yes, but transfer prices are affected by bargaining strengths of the buying and selling divisions
Preserves subunit autonomy	Yes, when markets are competitive	No, because it is rule-based	Yes, because it is based on negotiations between subunits
Other factors	Market may not exist, or markets may be imperfect or in distress	Useful for determining full cost of products and services; easy to implement	Bargaining and negotiations take time and may need to be reviewed repeatedly as conditions change

competitive, the transportation division can sell all the crude oil it transports to the external market at $85 per barrel, and it will have no unused capacity. The transportation division's incremental cost (as shown in Exhibit 22-1, p. 782) is $73 per barrel (purchase cost of $72 per barrel plus variable transportation cost of $1 per barrel) for oil purchased under the long-term contract or $80 per barrel (purchase cost of $79 plus variable transportation cost of $1) for oil purchased at current market prices from Gulfmex. The transportation division's opportunity cost per barrel of transferring the oil internally is the contribution margin per barrel forgone by not selling the crude oil in the external market: $12 for oil purchased under the long-term contract (market price, $85, minus variable cost, $73) and $5 for oil purchased from Gulfmex (market price, $85, minus variable cost, $80). In either case,

$$\frac{\text{Minimum transfer price}}{\text{per barrel}} = \frac{\text{Incremental cost}}{\text{per barrel}} + \frac{\text{Opportunity cost}}{\text{per barrel}}$$

$$= \$73 + \$12 = \$85$$

$$\text{or}$$

$$= \$80 + \$5 = \$85$$

2. **An intermediate market exists that is not perfectly competitive, and the selling division has unused capacity.** In markets that are not perfectly competitive, capacity utilization can only be increased by decreasing prices. Unused capacity exists because decreasing prices is often not worthwhile—it decreases operating income.

   If the transportation division has unused capacity, its opportunity cost of transferring the oil internally is zero because the division does not forgo any external sales or contribution margin from internal transfers. In this case,

$$\frac{\text{Minimum transfer price}}{\text{per barrel}} = \frac{\text{Incremental cost}}{\text{per barrel}} = \begin{array}{l}\text{\$73 per barrel for oil purchased under the}\\\text{long-term contract or \$80 per barrel for}\\\text{oil purchased from Gulfmex in Matamoros}\end{array}$$

   In general, when markets are not perfectly competitive, the potential to influence demand and operating income through prices complicates the measurement of opportunity costs. The transfer price depends on constantly changing levels of supply and demand. There is not just one transfer price. Rather, the transfer prices for various quantities supplied and demanded depend on the incremental costs and opportunity costs of the units transferred.

3. **No market exists for the intermediate product.** This situation would occur for the Horizon Petroleum case if the crude oil transported by the transportation division could be used only by the Houston refinery (due to, say, its high tar content) and would not be wanted by external parties. Here, the opportunity cost of supplying crude oil internally is zero because the inability to sell crude oil externally means no contribution margin is forgone. For the transportation division of Horizon Petroleum, the minimum transfer price under the general guideline is the incremental cost per barrel (either $73 or $80). As in the previous case, any transfer price between the incremental cost and $85 will achieve goal congruence.

Multinational Transfer Pricing and Tax Considerations

Transfer pricing is an important accounting priority for managers around the world. A 2007 Ernst & Young survey of multinational enterprises in 24 countries found that 74% of parent firms and 81% of subsidiary respondents believed that transfer pricing was "absolutely critical" or "very important" to their organizations. The reason is that parent companies identify transfer pricing as the single most important tax issue they face. The sums of money involved are often staggering. Google, for example, has a 90% market share of UK internet searches and earned £1.6 billion in advertising revenues last year in Britain; yet, Google UK reported a pretax loss of £26 million. The reason is that revenues from customers in Britain are transferred to Google's European headquarters in Dublin. By paying the low Irish corporate tax rate of 12.5%, Google saved £450 million in UK taxes in 2009 alone. Transfer prices affect not just income taxes, but

> **Decision Point**
>
> What is the general guideline for determining a minimum transfer price?

> **Learning Objective 8**
>
> Incorporate income tax considerations in multinational transfer pricing
>
> . . . set transfer prices to minimize tax payments to the extent permitted by tax authorities

also payroll taxes, customs duties, tariffs, sales taxes, value-added taxes, environment-related taxes, and other government levies. Our aim here is to highlight tax factors, and in particular income taxes, as important considerations in determining transfer prices.

Transfer Pricing for Tax Minimization

Consider the Horizon Petroleum data in Exhibit 22-2 (p. 783). Assume that the transportation division based in Mexico pays Mexican income taxes at 30% of operating income and that the refining division based in the United States pays income taxes at 20% of operating income. Horizon Petroleum would minimize its total income tax payments with the 105%-of-full-cost transfer-pricing method, as shown in the following table, because this method minimizes income reported in Mexico, where income is taxed at a higher rate than in the United States.

Transfer-Pricing Method	Operating Income for 100 Barrels of Crude Oil			Income Tax on 100 Barrels of Crude Oil		
	Transportation Division (Mexico) (1)	Refining Division (United States) (2)	Total (3) = (1) + (2)	Transportation Division (Mexico) (4) = 0.30 × (1)	Refining Division (United States) (5) = 0.20 × (2)	Total (6) = (4) + (5)
Market price	$900	$300	$1,200	$270	$ 60	$330
105% of full costs	380	820	1,200	114	164	278
Hybrid price	600	600	1,200	180	120	300

Income tax considerations raise additional issues. Tax issues may conflict with other objectives of transfer pricing. Suppose the market for crude oil in Houston is perfectly competitive. In this case, the market-based transfer price achieves goal congruence, provides incentives for management effort, and helps Horizon to evaluate the economic profitability of the transportation division. But it is costly from the perspective of income taxes. To minimize income taxes, Horizon would favor using 105% of full cost for tax reporting. Tax laws in the United States and Mexico, however, constrain this option. In particular, the Mexican tax authorities, aware of Horizon's incentives to minimize income taxes by reducing the income reported in Mexico, would challenge any attempts to shift income to the refining division through an unreasonably low transfer price (see also Concepts in Action, p. 793).

Section 482 of the U.S. Internal Revenue Code governs taxation of multinational transfer pricing. Section 482 requires that transfer prices between a company and its foreign division or subsidiary, for both tangible and intangible property, equal the price that would be charged by an unrelated third party in a comparable transaction. Regulations related to Section 482 recognize that transfer prices can be market-based or cost-plus-based, where the plus represents margins on comparable transactions.[7]

If the market for crude oil in Houston is perfectly competitive, Horizon would be required to calculate taxes using the market price of $85 for transfers from the transportation division to the refining division. Horizon might successfully argue that the transfer price should be set below the market price because the transportation division incurs no marketing and distribution costs when selling crude oil to the refining division. For example, if marketing and distribution costs equal $2 per barrel, Horizon could set the transfer price at $83 ($85 – $2) per barrel, the selling price net of marketing and distribution costs. Under the U.S. Internal Revenue Code, Horizon could obtain advanced approval of the transfer-pricing arrangements from the tax authorities, called an *advanced pricing agreement* (APA). The APA is a binding agreement for a specified number of years. The goal of the APA program is to avoid costly transfer-pricing disputes between taxpayers and tax authorities. In 2007, there were 81 APAs executed, of which 54 were bilateral agreements with other tax treaty countries. Included in this was the completion of the first bilateral APA between the United States and China, involving Wal-Mart Stores.

The current global recession has pushed governments around the world to impose tighter trading rules and more aggressively pursue tax revenues. The number of countries

---

[7] J. Styron, "Transfer Pricing and Tax Planning: Opportunities for US Corporations Operating Abroad," *CPA Journal Online* (November 2007); R. Feinschreiber (Ed.), *Transfer Pricing Handbook*, 3rd ed. (New York: John Wiley & Sons, 2002).

Concepts in Action

Transfer Pricing Dispute Temporarily Stops the Flow of Fiji Water

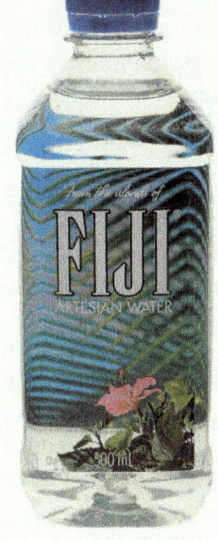

Tax authorities and government officials across the globe pay close attention to taxes paid by multinational companies operating within their boundaries. At the heart of the issue are the transfer prices that companies use to transfer products from one country to another. Since 2008, Fiji Water, LLC, a U.S.-based company that markets its famous brand of bottled water in more than a dozen counties, has been engaged in a fierce transfer-pricing dispute with the government of the Fiji Islands, where its water bottling plant is located.

While Fiji Water is produced in the Fiji Islands, all other activities in the company's value chain—importing, distributing, and retailing—occur in the countries where Fiji Water is sold. Over time, the Fiji Islands government became concerned that Fiji Water was engaging in transfer price manipulations, selling the water shipments produced in the Fiji Islands at a very low price to the company headquarters in Los Angeles. It was feared that very little of the wealth generated by Fiji Water, the country's second largest exporter, was coming into the Fiji Islands as foreign reserves from export earnings, which Fiji badly needed to fund its imports. To the Fiji Islands government, Fiji Water was funneling most of its cash to the United States.

As a result of these concerns, the Fiji Islands Revenue and Customs Authority (FIRCA) decided to take action against Fiji Water. FIRCA halted exports in January 2008 at ports in the Fiji Islands by putting 200 containers loaded with Fiji Water bottled under armed guard, and issuing a statement accusing Fiji Water of transfer price manipulations. FIRCA's chief executive, Jitoko Tikolevu, said, "The wholly U.S.-owned Fijian subsidiary sold its water exclusively to its U.S. parent at the declared rate, in Fiji, of $4 a carton. In the U.S., though, the same company then sold it for up to $50 a carton."

Fiji Water immediately filed a lawsuit against FIRCA with the High Court of Fiji. The court issued an interim order, allowing the company to resume shipment of the embargoed containers upon payment of a bond to the court. In the media and subsequent court filings, the company stated that on a global basis it sold each carton of water for $20–28, and it did not make a profit due to "heavy investments in assets, employees, and marketing necessary to aggressively grow a successful branded product."

The dispute between FICRA and Fiji Water remains unresolved in the Fiji Islands court system. In the interim, Fiji Water has maintained its previous transfer price of $4 for water produced at its bottling plant in the Fiji Islands. To pressure the company to change its transfer pricing practices, the Fiji Islands government considered adding a 20-cents-per-litre excise tax on water produced in the country, but the tax was ultimately rejected as too draconian. As this high-profile case demonstrates, transfer pricing formulas and taxation details remain a contentious issue for governments and countries around the globe.

Source: Matau, Robert. 2008. Fiji water explains saga. *Fiji Times*, February 9; McMaster, James and Jan Novak. 2009. Fiji water and corporate social responsibility—Green makeover or 'green-washing'? The University of Western Ontario Richard Ivey School of Business No. 909A08, London, Ontario: Ivey Publishing.

that have imposed transfer pricing regulations has approximately quadrupled from 1995 to 2007, according to a 2008 KPMG report. Officials in China, where foreign businesses enjoyed favorable treatment until last year, recently issued new rules requiring multinationals to submit extensive transfer-pricing documentation. Countries such as India, Canada, Turkey, and Greece have brought greater scrutiny to bear on transfer pricing, focusing in particular on intellectual-property values, costs of back-office functions and losses of any type. In the United States, the Obama administration plans to shrink a "tax gap" the IRS estimates may be as high as $345 billion by restricting or closing several widely used tax loopholes. While the plan does not directly address transfer pricing practice, the IRS has become even more aggressive with enforcement. The agency added 1,200 people to its international staff in 2009, and the 2010 budget called for hiring another 800.

Transfer Prices Designed for Multiple Objectives

To meet multiple transfer-pricing objectives, such as minimizing income taxes, achieving goal congruence, and motivating management effort, a company may choose to keep one set of accounting records for tax reporting and a second set for internal management reporting.

Of course, it is costly to maintain two sets of books and companies such as Case New Holland, a world leader in the agricultural and construction equipment business, also oppose it for conceptual reasons. However, a survey by the AnswerThink Consulting Group of large companies (more than $2 billion in revenues) found that 77% used separate reporting systems to track internal pricing information, compared with about 25% of large companies outside that "best practices" group. Microsoft, for example, believes in "delinking" transfer pricing and employs an internal measurement system (Microsoft Accounting Principles, or MAPs) that uses a separate set of company-designed rules and accounts.[8] A key aspect of management control at Microsoft is the desire to hold local managers accountable for product profitability and to establish appropriate sales and marketing spending levels for every product line. To establish these sales and spending levels, the firm creates a profitability statement for every product in every region, and allocates G&A and R&D costs across sales divisions in ways that aren't necessarily the most tax efficient.

Even if a company does not have such formal separated reporting systems, it can still informally adjust transfer prices to satisfy the tradeoff between tax minimization and incentive provision. Consider a multinational firm that makes semiconductor products that it sells through its sales organization in a higher-tax country. To minimize taxes, the parent sets a high transfer price, thereby lowering the operating income of the foreign sales organization. It would be inappropriate to penalize the country sales manager for this low income since the sales organization has no say in determining the transfer price. As an alternative, the company can evaluate the sales manager on the direct contribution (revenues minus marketing costs) incurred in the country. That is, the transfer price incurred to acquire the semiconductor products is omitted for performance-evaluation purposes. Of course, this is not a perfect solution. By ignoring the cost of acquiring the products, the sales manager is given incentives to overspend on local marketing relative to what would be optimal from the firm's overall perspective. If the dysfunctional effects of this are suitably large, corporate managers must then step in and dictate specific operational decisions and goals for the manager based on the information available to them. More generally, adoption of a tax-compliant transfer pricing policy creates a need for nonfinancial performance indicators at lower management levels in order to better evaluate and reward performance.[9]

Additional Issues in Transfer Pricing

Additional factors that arise in multinational transfer pricing include tariffs and customs duties levied on imports of products into a country. The issues here are similar to income tax considerations; companies will have incentives to lower transfer prices for products imported into a country to reduce tariffs and customs duties charged on those products.

In addition to the motivations for choosing transfer prices already described, multinational transfer prices are sometimes influenced by restrictions that some countries place on dividend- or income-related payments to parties outside their national borders. By increasing the prices of goods or services transferred into divisions in these countries, companies can seek to increase the cash paid out of these countries without violating dividend- or income-related restrictions.

Decision Point

How do income tax considerations affect transfer pricing in multinationals?

Problem for Self-Study

The Pillercat Corporation is a highly decentralized company. Each division manager has full authority for sourcing decisions and selling decisions. The machining division of Pillercat has been the major supplier of the 2,000 crankshafts that the tractor division needs each year.

The tractor division, however, has just announced that it plans to purchase all its crankshafts in the forthcoming year from two external suppliers at $200 per crankshaft.

---

[8] For further details, see I. Springsteel, "Separate but Unequal," *CFO Magazine*, August 1999.

[9] Cools et al. "Management control in the transfer pricing tax compliant multinational enterprise," *Accounting, Organizations and Society*, August 2008 provides an illustrative case study of this issue in the context of a semiconductor product division of a multinational firm.

The machining division of Pillercat recently increased its selling price for the forthcoming year to $220 per unit (from $200 per unit in the current year).

Juan Gomez, manager of the machining division, feels that the 10% price increase is justified. It results from a higher depreciation charge on some new specialized equipment used to manufacture crankshafts and an increase in labor costs. Gomez wants the president of Pillercat Corporation to force the tractor division to buy all its crankshafts from the machining division at the price of $220. The following table summarizes the key data.

	A	B
1	Number of crankshafts purchased by tractor division	2,000
2	External supplier's market price per crankshaft	$ 200
3	Variable cost per crankshaft in machining division	$ 190
4	Fixed cost per crankshaft in machining division	$ 20

1. Compute the advantage or disadvantage in terms of annual operating income to the Pillercat Corporation as a whole if the tractor division buys crankshafts internally from the machining division under each of the following cases:

   a. The machining division has no alternative use for the facilities used to manufacture crankshafts.

   b. The machining division can use the facilities for other production operations, which will result in annual cash operating savings of $29,000.

   c. The machining division has no alternative use for its facilities, and the external supplier drops the price to $185 per crankshaft.

2. As the president of Pillercat, how would you respond to Juan Gomez's request that you force the tractor division to purchase all of its crankshafts from the machining division? Would your response differ according to the three cases described in requirement 1? Explain.

Required

Solution

1. Computations for the tractor division buying crankshafts internally for one year under cases **a**, **b**, and **c** are as follows:

	A	B	C	D
1			Case	
2		a	b	c
3	Number of crankshafts purchased by tractor division	2,000	2,000	2,000
4	External supplier's market price per crankshaft	$ 200	$ 200	$ 185
5	Variable cost per crankshaft in machining division	$ 190	$ 190	$ 190
6	Opportunity costs of the machining division supplying crankshafts to the tractor division	-	$ 29,000	-
7				
8	Total purchase costs if buying from an external supplier			
9	(2,000 shafts × $200, $200, $185 per shaft)	$400,000	$400,000	$370,000
10	Incremental cost of buying from the machining division			
11	(2,000 shafts × $190 per shaft)	380,000	380,000	380,000
12	Total opportunity costs of the machining division	-	29,000	-
13	Total relevant costs	380,000	409,000	380,000
14	Annual operating income advantage (disadvantage) to			
15	Pillercat of buying from the machining division	$ 20,000	$ (9,000)	$ (10,000)

The general guideline that was introduced in the chapter (p. 790) as a first step in setting a transfer price can be used to highlight the alternatives:

	Home	Insert	Page Layout	Formulas	Data	Review	View	
	A	B	C	D	E	F	G
1	Case	Incremental Cost per Unit Incurred to Point of Transfer	+	Opportunity Cost per Unit to the Supplying Division	=	Transfer Price	External Market Price
2	a	$190	+	$0	=	$190.00	$200
3	b	$190	+	$14.50[a]	=	$204.50	$200
4	c	$190	+	$0	=	$190.00	$185
5							
6	[a]Opportunity cost per unit	=	Total opportunity costs	÷	Number of crankshafts	= $29,000 ÷ 2,000 = $14.50	
7							

Comparing transfer price to external-market price, the tractor division will maximize annual operating income of Pillercat Corporation as a whole by purchasing from the machining division in case **a** and by purchasing from the external supplier in cases **b** and **c**.

2. Pillercat Corporation is a highly decentralized company. If no forced transfer were made, the tractor division would use an external supplier, a decision that would be in the best interest of the company as a whole in cases **b** and **c** of requirement 1 but not in case **a**.

   Suppose in case **a**, the machining division refuses to meet the price of $200. This decision means that the company will be $20,000 worse off in the short run. Should top management interfere and force a transfer at $200? This interference would undercut the philosophy of decentralization. Many top managers would not interfere because they would view the $20,000 as an inevitable cost of a suboptimal decision that can occur under decentralization. But how high must this cost be before the temptation to interfere would be irresistible? $30,000? $40,000?

   Any top management interference with lower-level decision making weakens decentralization. Of course, Pillercat's management may occasionally interfere to prevent costly mistakes. But recurring interference and constraints would hurt Pillercat's attempts to operate as a decentralized company.

Decision Points

The following question-and-answer format summarizes the chapter's learning objectives. Each decision presents a key question related to a learning objective. The guidelines are the answer to that question.

Decision	Guidelines
1. What is a management control system and how should it be designed?	A management control system is a means of gathering and using information to aid and coordinate the planning and control decisions throughout the organization and to guide the behavior of managers and other employees. Effective management control systems (a) are closely aligned to the organization's strategy, (b) support the organizational responsibilities of individual managers, and (c) motivate managers and other employees to give effort to achieve the organization's goals.

2. What are the benefits and costs of decentralization?

The benefits of decentralization include (a) greater responsiveness to local needs, (b) gains from faster decision making, (c) increased motivation of subunit managers, (d) greater management development and learning, and (e) sharpened focus of subunit managers. The costs of decentralization include (a) suboptimal decision making, (b) excessive focus on the subunit rather than the company as a whole, (c) increased costs of information gathering, and (d) duplication of activities.

3. What are alternative ways of calculating transfer prices, and what criteria should be used to evaluate them?

A transfer price is the price one subunit charges for a product or service supplied to another subunit of the same organization. Transfer prices can be (a) market-based, (b) cost-based, or (c) hybrid. Different transfer-pricing methods produce different revenues and costs for individual subunits, and hence, different operating incomes for the subunits. Transfer prices seek to (a) promote goal congruence, (b) motivate management effort, (c) help evaluate subunit performance, and (d) preserve subunit autonomy (if desired).

4. Under what market conditions do market-based transfer prices promote goal congruence?

In perfectly competitive markets, there is no unused capacity, and division managers can buy and sell as much of a product or service as they want at the market price. In such settings, using the market price as the transfer price motivates division managers to transact internally and to take exactly the same actions as they would if they were transacting in the external market.

5. What problems can arise when full cost plus a markup is used as the transfer price?

A transfer price based on full cost plus a markup may lead to suboptimal decisions because it leads the buying division to regard the fixed costs and the markup of the selling division as a variable cost. The buying division may then purchase products from an external supplier expecting savings in costs that, in fact, will not occur.

6. Within a range of feasible transfer prices, what are alternative ways for firms to arrive at the eventual price?

When there is unused capacity, the transfer-price range lies between the minimum price at which the selling division is willing to sell (its variable cost per unit) and the maximum price the buying division is willing to pay (the lower of its contribution or price at which the product is available from external suppliers). Methods for arriving at a price in this range include proration (such as splitting the difference equally or on the basis of relative variable costs), negotiation between divisions, and dual pricing.

7. What is the general guideline for determining a minimum transfer price?

The general guideline states that the minimum transfer price equals the incremental cost per unit incurred up to the point of transfer plus the opportunity cost per unit to the selling division resulting from transferring products or services internally.

8. How do income tax considerations affect transfer pricing in multinationals?

Transfer prices can reduce income tax payments by reporting more income in low-tax-rate countries and less income in high-tax-rate countries. However, tax regulations of different countries restrict the transfer prices that companies can use.

Terms to Learn

This chapter and the Glossary at the end of the book contain definitions of the following important terms:

autonomy (**p. 777**)
decentralization (**p. 777**)
dual pricing (**p. 789**)
dysfunctional decision making (**p. 778**)
effort (**p. 776**)

goal congruence (**p. 776**)
incongruent decision making (**p. 778**)
intermediate product (**p. 780**)
management control system (**p. 775**)

motivation (**p. 776**)
perfectly competitive market (**p. 784**)
suboptimal decision making (**p. 778**)
transfer price (**p. 780**)

Assignment Material

Questions

22-1 What is a management control system?

22-2 Describe three criteria you would use to evaluate whether a management control system is effective.

22-3 What is the relationship among motivation, goal congruence, and effort?

22-4 Name three benefits and two costs of decentralization.

22-5 "Organizations typically adopt a consistent decentralization or centralization philosophy across all their business functions." Do you agree? Explain.

22-6 "Transfer pricing is confined to profit centers." Do you agree? Explain.

22-7 What are the three methods for determining transfer prices?

22-8 What properties should transfer-pricing systems have?

22-9 "All transfer-pricing methods give the same division operating income." Do you agree? Explain.

22-10 Under what conditions is a market-based transfer price optimal?

22-11 What is one potential limitation of full-cost-based transfer prices?

22-12 Give two reasons why the dual-pricing system of transfer pricing is not widely used.

22-13 "Cost and price information play no role in negotiated transfer prices." Do you agree? Explain.

22-14 "Under the general guideline for transfer pricing, the minimum transfer price will vary depending on whether the supplying division has unused capacity or not." Do you agree? Explain.

22-15 How should managers consider income tax issues when choosing a transfer-pricing method?

MyAccountingLab

Exercises

22-16 Evaluating management control systems, balanced scorecard. Adventure Parks Inc. (API) operates ten theme parks throughout the United States. The company's slogan is "Name Your Adventure," and its mission is to offer an exciting theme park experience to visitors of all ages. API's corporate strategy supports this mission by stressing the importance of sparkling clean surroundings, efficient crowd management and, above all, cheerful employees. Of course, improved shareholder value drives this strategy.

Required

1. Assuming that API uses a balanced scorecard approach (see Chapter 13) to formulating its management control system. List three measures that API might use to evaluate each of the four balanced scorecard perspectives: financial perspective, customer perspective, internal-business-process perspective, and learning-and-growth perspective.

2. How would the management controls related to financial and customer perspectives at API differ between the following three managers: a souvenir shop manager, a park general manager, and the corporation's CEO?

22-17 Cost centers, profit centers, decentralization, transfer prices. Fenster Corporation manufactures windows with wood and metal frames. Fenster has three departments: glass, wood, and metal. The glass department makes the window glass and sends it to either the wood or metal department where the glass is framed. The window is then sold. Upper management sets the production schedules for the three departments and evaluates them on output quantity, cost variances, and product quality.

Required

1. Are the three departments cost centers, revenue centers, or profit centers?
2. Are the three departments centralized or decentralized?
3. Can a centralized department be a profit center? Why or why not?
4. Suppose the upper management of Fenster Corporation decides to let the three departments set their own production schedules, buy and sell products in the external market, and have the wood and metal departments negotiate with the glass department for the glass panes using a transfer price.
   a. Will this change your answers to requirements 1 and 2?
   b. How would you recommend upper management evaluate the three departments if this change is made?

22-18 Benefits and costs of decentralization. Jackson Markets, a chain of traditional supermarkets, is interested in gaining access to the organic and health food retail market by acquiring a regional company in that sector. Jackson intends to operate the newly-acquired stores independently from its supermarkets.

One of the prospects is Health Source, a chain of twenty stores in the mid-Atlantic. Buying for all twenty stores is done by the company's central office. Store managers must follow strict guidelines for all aspects of store management in an attempt to maintain consistency among stores. Store managers are evaluated on the basis of achieving profit goals developed by the central office.

The other prospect is Harvest Moon, a chain of thirty stores in the Northeast. Harvest Moon managers are given significant flexibility in product offerings, allowing them to negotiate purchases with local organic farmers. Store managers are rewarded for exceeding self-developed return on investment goals with company stock options. Some managers have become significant shareholders in the company, and have even decided on their own to open additional store locations to improve market penetration. However, the increased autonomy has led to competition and price cutting among Harvest Moon stores within the same geographic market, resulting in lower margins.

Required

1. Would you describe Health Source as having a centralized or a decentralized structure? Explain.
2. Would you describe Harvest Moon as having a centralized or a decentralized structure? Discuss some of the benefits and costs of that type of structure.

3. Would stores in each chain be considered cost centers, revenue centers, profit centers, or investment centers? How does that tie into the evaluation of store managers?

4. Assume that Jackson chooses to acquire Harvest Moon. What steps can Jackson take to improve goal congruence between store managers and the larger company?

22-19 Multinational transfer pricing, effect of alternative transfer-pricing methods, global income tax minimization. Tech Friendly Computer, Inc., with headquarters in San Francisco, manufactures and sells a desktop computer. Tech Friendly has three divisions, each of which is located in a different country:

a. China division—manufactures memory devices and keyboards

b. South Korea division—assembles desktop computers using locally manufactured parts, along with memory devices and keyboards from the China division

c. U.S. division—packages and distributes desktop computers

Each division is run as a profit center. The costs for the work done in each division for a single desktop computer are as follows:

China division:	Variable cost =	900 yuan
	Fixed cost =	1,980 yuan
South Korea division:	Variable cost =	350,000 won
	Fixed cost =	470,000 won
U.S. division:	Variable cost =	$125
	Fixed cost =	$325

■ Chinese income tax rate on the China division's operating income: 40%
■ South Korean income tax rate on the South Korea division's operating income: 20%
■ U.S. income tax rate on the U.S. division's operating income: 30%

Each desktop computer is sold to retail outlets in the United States for $3,800. Assume that the current foreign exchange rates are as follows:

$$9 \text{ yuan} = \$1 \text{ U.S.}$$

$$1,000 \text{ won} = \$1 \text{ U.S.}$$

Both the China and the South Korea divisions sell part of their production under a private label. The China division sells the comparable memory/keyboard package used in each Tech Friendly desktop computer to a Chinese manufacturer for 4,500 yuan. The South Korea division sells the comparable desktop computer to a South Korean distributor for 1,340,000 won.

1. Calculate the after-tax operating income per unit earned by each division under the following transfer-pricing methods: (a) market price, (b) 200% of full cost, and (c) 350% of variable cost. (Income taxes are not included in the computation of the cost-based transfer prices.)   **Required**

2. Which transfer-pricing method(s) will maximize the after-tax operating income per unit of Tech Friendly Computer?

22-20 Transfer-pricing methods, goal congruence. British Columbia Lumber has a raw lumber division and a finished lumber division. The variable costs are as follows:

■ Raw lumber division: $100 per 100 board-feet of raw lumber
■ Finished lumber division: $125 per 100 board-feet of finished lumber

Assume that there is no board-feet loss in processing raw lumber into finished lumber. Raw lumber can be sold at $200 per 100 board-feet. Finished lumber can be sold at $275 per 100 board-feet.

1. Should British Columbia Lumber process raw lumber into its finished form? Show your calculations.   **Required**

2. Assume that internal transfers are made at 110% of variable cost. Will each division maximize its division operating-income contribution by adopting the action that is in the best interest of British Columbia Lumber as a whole? Explain.

3. Assume that internal transfers are made at market prices. Will each division maximize its division operating-income contribution by adopting the action that is in the best interest of British Columbia Lumber as a whole? Explain.

22-21 Effect of alternative transfer-pricing methods on division operating income. (CMA, adapted) Ajax Corporation has two divisions. The mining division makes toldine, which is then transferred to the metals division. The toldine is further processed by the metals division and is sold to customers at a price of $150 per unit. The mining division is currently required by Ajax to transfer its total yearly output of

200,000 units of toldine to the metals division at 110% of full manufacturing cost. Unlimited quantities of toldine can be purchased and sold on the outside market at $90 per unit.

The following table gives the manufacturing cost per unit in the mining and metals divisions for 2012:

	Mining Division	Metals Division
Direct material cost	$12	$ 6
Direct manufacturing labor cost	16	20
Manufacturing overhead cost	32[a]	25[b]
Total manufacturing cost per unit	$60	$51

[a]Manufacturing overhead costs in the mining division are 25% fixed and 75% variable.
[b]Manufacturing overhead costs in the metals division are 60% fixed and 40% variable.

Required

1. Calculate the operating incomes for the mining and metals divisions for the 200,000 units of toldine transferred under the following transfer-pricing methods: (a) market price and (b) 110% of full manufacturing cost.
2. Suppose Ajax rewards each division manager with a bonus, calculated as 1% of division operating income (if positive). What is the amount of bonus that will be paid to each division manager under the transfer-pricing methods in requirement 1? Which transfer-pricing method will each division manager prefer to use?
3. What arguments would Brian Jones, manager of the mining division, make to support the transfer-pricing method that he prefers?

22-22 Transfer pricing, general guideline, goal congruence. (CMA, adapted). Quest Motors, Inc., operates as a decentralized multidivision company. The Vivo division of Quest Motors purchases most of its airbags from the airbag division. The airbag division's incremental cost for manufacturing the airbags is $90 per unit. The airbag division is currently working at 80% of capacity. The current market price of the airbags is $125 per unit.

Required

1. Using the general guideline presented in the chapter, what is the minimum price at which the airbag division would sell airbags to the Vivo division?
2. Suppose that Quest Motors requires that whenever divisions with unused capacity sell products internally, they must do so at the incremental cost. Evaluate this transfer-pricing policy using the criteria of goal congruence, evaluating division performance, motivating management effort, and preserving division autonomy.
3. If the two divisions were to negotiate a transfer price, what is the range of possible transfer prices? Evaluate this negotiated transfer-pricing policy using the criteria of goal congruence, evaluating division performance, motivating management effort, and preserving division autonomy.
4. Instead of allowing negotiation, suppose that Quest specifies a hybrid transfer price that "splits the difference" between the minimum and maximum prices from the divisions' standpoint. What would be the resulting transfer price for airbags?

22-23 Multinational transfer pricing, global tax minimization. The Mornay Company manufactures telecommunications equipment at its plant in Toledo, Ohio. The company has marketing divisions throughout the world. A Mornay marketing division in Vienna, Austria, imports 10,000 units of Product 4A36 from the United States. The following information is available:

U.S. income tax rate on the U.S. division's operating income	35%
Austrian income tax rate on the Austrian division's operating income	40%
Austrian import duty	15%
Variable manufacturing cost per unit of Product 4A36	$ 550
Full manufacturing cost per unit of Product 4A36	$ 800
Selling price (net of marketing and distribution costs) in Austria	$1,150

Suppose the United States and Austrian tax authorities only allow transfer prices that are between the full manufacturing cost per unit of $800 and a market price of $950, based on comparable imports into Austria. The Austrian import duty is charged on the price at which the product is transferred into Austria. Any import duty paid to the Austrian authorities is a deductible expense for calculating Austrian income taxes due.

Required

1. Calculate the after-tax operating income earned by the United States and Austrian divisions from transferring 10,000 units of Product 4A36 (a) at full manufacturing cost per unit and (b) at market price of comparable imports. (Income taxes are not included in the computation of the cost-based transfer prices.)
2. Which transfer price should the Mornay Company select to minimize the total of company import duties and income taxes? Remember that the transfer price must be between the full manufacturing cost per unit of $800 and the market price of $950 of comparable imports into Austria. Explain your reasoning.

22-24 Multinational transfer pricing, goal congruence (continuation of 22-23). Suppose that the U.S. division could sell as many units of Product 4A36 as it makes at $900 per unit in the U.S. market, net of all marketing and distribution costs.

Required

1. From the viewpoint of the Mornay Company as a whole, would after-tax operating income be maximized if it sold the 10,000 units of Product 4A36 in the United States or in Austria? Show your computations.
2. Suppose division managers act autonomously to maximize their division's after-tax operating income. Will the transfer price calculated in requirement 2 of Exercise 22-23 result in the U.S. division manager taking the actions determined to be optimal in requirement 1 of this exercise? Explain.
3. What is the minimum transfer price that the U.S. division manager would agree to? Does this transfer price result in the Mornay Company as a whole paying more import duty and taxes than the answer to requirement 2 of Exercise 22-23? If so, by how much?

22-25 Transfer-pricing dispute. The Allison-Chambers Corporation, manufacturer of tractors and other heavy farm equipment, is organized along decentralized product lines, with each manufacturing division operating as a separate profit center. Each division manager has been delegated full authority on all decisions involving the sale of that division's output both to outsiders and to other divisions of Allison-Chambers. Division C has in the past always purchased its requirement of a particular tractor-engine component from division A. However, when informed that division A is increasing its selling price to $150, division C's manager decides to purchase the engine component from external suppliers.

Division C can purchase the component for $135 per unit in the open market. Division A insists that, because of the recent installation of some highly specialized equipment and the resulting high depreciation charges, it will not be able to earn an adequate return on its investment unless it raises its price. Division A's manager appeals to top management of Allison-Chambers for support in the dispute with division C and supplies the following operating data:

C's annual purchases of the tractor-engine component	1,000 units
A's variable cost per unit of the tractor-engine component	$120
A's fixed cost per unit of the tractor-engine component	$ 20

Required

1. Assume that there are no alternative uses for internal facilities of division A. Determine whether the company as a whole will benefit if division C purchases the component from external suppliers for $135 per unit. What should the transfer price for the component be set at so that division managers acting in their own divisions' best interests take actions that are also in the best interest of the company as a whole?
2. Assume that internal facilities of division A would not otherwise be idle. By not producing the 1,000 units for division C, division A's equipment and other facilities would be used for other production operations that would result in annual cash-operating savings of $18,000. Should division C purchase from external suppliers? Show your computations.
3. Assume that there are no alternative uses for division A's internal facilities and that the price from outsiders drops $20. Should division C purchase from external suppliers? What should the transfer price for the component be set at so that division managers acting in their own divisions' best interests take actions that are also in the best interest of the company as a whole?

22-26 Transfer-pricing problem (continuation of 22-25). Refer to Exercise 22-25. Assume that division A can sell the 1,000 units to other customers at $155 per unit, with variable marketing cost of $5 per unit.

Determine whether Allison-Chambers will benefit if division C purchases the 1,000 units from external suppliers at $135 per unit. Show your computations.

Required

Problems

MyAccountingLab

22-27 General guideline, transfer pricing. The Slate Company manufactures and sells television sets. Its assembly division (AD) buys television screens from the screen division (SD) and assembles the TV sets. The SD, which is operating at capacity, incurs an incremental manufacturing cost of $65 per screen. The SD can sell all its output to the outside market at a price of $100 per screen, after incurring a variable marketing and distribution cost of $8 per screen. If the AD purchases screens from outside suppliers at a price of $100 per screen, it will incur a variable purchasing cost of $7 per screen. Slate's division managers can act autonomously to maximize their own division's operating income.

Required

1. What is the minimum transfer price at which the SD manager would be willing to sell screens to the AD?
2. What is the maximum transfer price at which the AD manager would be willing to purchase screens from the SD?
3. Now suppose that the SD can sell only 70% of its output capacity of 20,000 screens per month on the open market. Capacity cannot be reduced in the short run. The AD can assemble and sell more than 20,000 TV sets per month.
   a. What is the minimum transfer price at which the SD manager would be willing to sell screens to the AD?

b. From the point of view of Slate's management, how much of the SD output should be transferred to the AD?

c. If Slate mandates the SD and AD managers to "split the difference" on the minimum and maximum transfer prices they would be willing to negotiate over, what would be the resulting transfer price? Does this price achieve the outcome desired in requirement 3b?

22-28 Pertinent transfer price. Europa, Inc., has two divisions, A and B, that manufacture expensive bicycles. Division A produces the bicycle frame, and division B assembles the rest of the bicycle onto the frame. There is a market for both the subassembly and the final product. Each division has been designated as a profit center. The transfer price for the subassembly has been set at the long-run average market price. The following data are available for each division:

Selling price for final product	$300
Long-run average selling price for intermediate product	200
Incremental cost per unit for completion in division B	150
Incremental cost per unit in division A	120

The manager of division B has made the following calculation:

Selling price for final product		$300
Transferred-in cost per unit (market)	$200	
Incremental cost per unit for completion	150	350
Contribution (loss) on product		$(50)

Required

1. Should transfers be made to division B if there is no unused capacity in division A? Is the market price the correct transfer price? Show your computations.
2. Assume that division A's maximum capacity for this product is 1,000 units per month and sales to the intermediate market are now 800 units. Should 200 units be transferred to division B? At what transfer price? Assume that for a variety of reasons, division A will maintain the $200 selling price indefinitely. That is, division A is not considering lowering the price to outsiders even if idle capacity exists.
3. Suppose division A quoted a transfer price of $150 for up to 200 units. What would be the contribution to the company as a whole if a transfer were made? As manager of division B, would you be inclined to buy at $150? Explain.

22-29 Pricing in imperfect markets (continuation of 22-28). Refer to Problem 22-28.

Required

1. Suppose the manager of division A has the option of (a) cutting the external price to $195, with the certainty that sales will rise to 1,000 units or (b) maintaining the external price of $200 for the 800 units and transferring the 200 units to division B at a price that would produce the same operating income for division A. What transfer price would produce the same operating income for division A? Is that price consistent with that recommended by the general guideline in the chapter so that the resulting decision would be desirable for the company as a whole?
2. Suppose that if the selling price for the intermediate product were dropped to $195, sales to external parties could be increased to 900 units. Division B wants to acquire as many as 200 units if the transfer price is acceptable. For simplicity, assume that there is no external market for the final 100 units of division A's capacity.
   a. Using the general guideline, what is (are) the minimum transfer price(s) that should lead to the correct economic decision? Ignore performance-evaluation considerations.
   b. Compare the total contributions under the alternatives to show why the transfer price(s) recommended lead(s) to the optimal economic decision.

22-30 Effect of alternative transfer-pricing methods on division operating income. Crango Products is a cranberry cooperative that operates two divisions, a harvesting division and a processing division. Currently, all of harvesting's output is converted into cranberry juice by the processing division, and the juice is sold to large beverage companies that produce cranberry juice blends. The processing division has a yield of 500 gallons of juice per 1,000 pounds of cranberries. Cost and market price data for the two divisions are as follows:

	Home	Insert	Page Layout	Formulas	Data	Review	View	

	A	B	C	D	E
1	**Harvesting Division**			**Processing Division**	
2	Variable cost per pound of cranberries	$0.10		Variable processing cost per gallon of juice produced	$0.20
3	Fixed cost per pound of cranberries	$0.25		Fixed cost per gallon of juice produced	$0.40
4	Selling price per pound of cranberries in outside market	$0.60		Selling price per gallon of juice	$2.10

1. Compute Crango's operating income from harvesting 400,000 pounds of cranberries during June 2012 and processing them into juice.

2. Crango rewards its division managers with a bonus equal to 5% of operating income. Compute the bonus earned by each division manager in June 2012 for each of the following transfer pricing methods:
   a. 200% of full cost
   b. Market price

3. Which transfer-pricing method will each division manager prefer? How might Crango resolve any conflicts that may arise on the issue of transfer pricing?

22-31 Goal-congruence problems with cost-plus transfer-pricing methods, dual-pricing system (continuation of 22-30). Assume that Pat Borges, CEO of Crango, had mandated a transfer price equal to 200% of full cost. Now he decides to decentralize some management decisions and sends around a memo that states the following: "Effective immediately, each division of Crango is free to make its own decisions regarding the purchase of direct materials and the sale of finished products."

1. Give an example of a goal-congruence problem that will arise if Crango continues to use a transfer price of 200% of full cost and Borges's decentralization policy is adopted.

2. Borges feels that a dual transfer-pricing policy will improve goal congruence. He suggests that transfers out of the harvesting division be made at 200% of full cost and transfers into the processing division be made at market price. Compute the operating income of each division under this dual transfer pricing method when 400,000 pounds of cranberries are harvested during June 2012 and processed into juice.

3. Why is the sum of the division operating incomes computed in requirement 2 different from Crango's operating income from harvesting and processing 400,000 pounds of cranberries?

4. Suggest two problems that may arise if Crango implements the dual transfer prices described in requirement 2.

22-32 Multinational transfer pricing, global tax minimization. Industrial Diamonds, Inc., based in Los Angeles, has two divisions:

■ South African mining division, which mines a rich diamond vein in South Africa
■ U.S. processing division, which polishes raw diamonds for use in industrial cutting tools

The processing division's yield is 50%: It takes 2 pounds of raw diamonds to produce 1 pound of top-quality polished industrial diamonds. Although all of the mining division's output of 8,000 pounds of raw diamonds is sent for processing in the United States, there is also an active market for raw diamonds in South Africa. The foreign exchange rate is 6 ZAR (South African Rand) = $1 U.S. The following information is known about the two divisions:

	Home	Insert	Page Layout	Formulas	Data	Review
	A	B	C	D	F	G
1	South African Mining Division					
2	Variable cost per pound of raw diamonds				600	ZAR
3	Fixed cost per pound of raw diamonds				1,200	ZAR
4	Market price per pound of raw diamonds				3,600	ZAR
5	Tax rate				25%	
6						
7	U.S. Processing Division					
8	Variable cost per pound of polished diamonds				220	U.S. dollars
9	Fixed cost per pound of polished diamonds				850	U.S. dollars
10	Market price per pound of polished diamonds				3,500	U.S. dollars
11	Tax rate				40%	

1. Compute the annual pretax operating income, in U.S. dollars, of each division under the following transfer-pricing methods: (a) 250% of full cost and (b) market price.

2. Compute the after-tax operating income, in U.S. dollars, for each division under the transfer-pricing methods in requirement 1. (Income taxes are not included in the computation of cost-based transfer price, and Industrial Diamonds does not pay U.S. income tax on income already taxed in South Africa.)

3. If the two division managers are compensated based on after-tax division operating income, which transfer-pricing method will each prefer? Which transfer-pricing method will maximize the total after-tax operating income of Industrial Diamonds?

4. In addition to tax minimization, what other factors might Industrial Diamonds consider in choosing a transfer-pricing method?

22-33 International transfer pricing, taxes, goal congruence. Argone division of Gemini Corporation is located in the United States. Its effective income tax rate is 30%. Another division of Gemini, Calcia, is located in Canada, where the income tax rate is 42%. Calcia manufactures, among other things, an intermediate product for Argone called IP-2007. Calcia operates at capacity and makes 15,000 units of IP-2007 for Argone each period, at a variable cost of $60 per unit. Assume that there are no outside customers for IP-2007. Because the IP-2007 must be shipped from Canada to the United States, it costs Calcia an additional $4 per unit to ship the IP-2007 to Argone. There are no direct fixed costs for IP-2007. Calcia also manufactures other products.

A product similar to IP-2007 that Argone could use as a substitute is available in the United States for $75 per unit.

Required

1. What is the minimum and maximum transfer price that would be acceptable to Argone and Calcia for IP-2007, and why?
2. What transfer price would minimize income taxes for Gemini Corporation as a whole? Would Calcia and Argone want to be evaluated on operating income using this transfer price?
3. Suppose Gemini uses the transfer price from requirement 2, and each division is evaluated on its own after-tax division operating income. Now suppose Calcia has an opportunity to sell 8,000 units of IP-2007 to an outside customer for $68 each. Calcia will not incur shipping costs because the customer is nearby and offers to pay for shipping. Assume that if Calcia accepts the special order, Argone will have to buy 8,000 units of the substitute product in the United States at $75 per unit.
   a. Will accepting the special order maximize after-tax operating income for Gemini Corporation as a whole?
   b. Will Argone want Calcia to accept this special order? Why or why not?
   c. Will Calcia want to accept this special order? Explain.
   d. Suppose Gemini Corporation wants to operate in a decentralized manner. What transfer price should Gemini set for IP-2007 so that each division acting in its own best interest takes actions with respect to the special order that are in the best interests of Gemini Corporation as a whole?

22-34 Transfer pricing, goal congruence. The Bosh Corporation makes and sells 20,000 multisystem music players each year. Its assembly division purchases components from other divisions of Bosh or from external suppliers and assembles the multisystem music players. In particular, the assembly division can purchase the CD player from the compact disc division of Bosh or from Hawei Corporation. Hawei agrees to meet all of Bosh's quality requirements and is currently negotiating with the assembly division to supply 20,000 CD players at a price between $44 and $52 per CD player.

A critical component of the CD player is the head mechanism that reads the disc. To ensure the quality of its multisystem music players, Bosh requires that if Hawei wins the contract to supply CD players, it must purchase the head mechanism from Bosh's compact disc division for $24 each.

The compact disc division can manufacture at most 22,000 CD players annually. It also manufactures as many additional head mechanisms as can be sold. The incremental cost of manufacturing the head mechanism is $18 per unit. The incremental cost of manufacturing a CD player (including the cost of the head mechanism) is $30 per unit, and any number of CD players can be sold for $45 each in the external market.

Required

1. What are the incremental costs minus revenues from sale to external buyers for the company as a whole if the compact disc division transfers 20,000 CD players to the assembly division and sells the remaining 2,000 CD players on the external market?
2. What are the incremental costs minus revenues from sales to external buyers for the company as a whole if the compact disc division sells 22,000 CD players on the external market and the assembly division accepts Hawei's offer at (a) $44 per CD player or (b) $52 per CD player?
3. What is the minimum transfer price per CD player at which the compact disc division would be willing to transfer 20,000 CD players to the assembly division?
4. Suppose that the transfer price is set to the minimum computed in requirement 3 plus $2, and the division managers at Bosh are free to make their own profit-maximizing sourcing and selling decisions. Now, Hawei offers 20,000 CD players for $52 each.
   a. What decisions will the managers of the compact disc division and assembly division make?
   b. Are these decisions optimal for Bosh as a whole?
   c. Based on this exercise, at what price would you recommend the transfer price be set?

22-35 Transfer pricing, goal congruence, ethics. Jeremiah Industries manufactures high-grade aluminum luggage made from recycled metal. The company operates two divisions: metal recycling and luggage fabrication. Each division operates as a decentralized entity. The metal recycling division is free to sell sheet aluminum to outside buyers, and the luggage fabrication division is free to purchase recycled sheet aluminum from other sources. Currently, however, the recycling division sells all of its output to the fabrication division, and the fabrication division does not purchase materials from any outside suppliers.

Aluminum is transferred from the recycling division to the fabrication division at 110% of full cost. The recycling division purchases recyclable aluminum for $0.50 per pound. The division's other variable costs equal $2.80 per pound, and fixed costs at a monthly production level of 50,000 pounds are $1.50 per pound.

During the most recent month, 50,000 pounds of aluminum were transferred between the two divisions. The recycling division's capacity is 70,000 pounds.

Due to increased demand, the fabrication division expects to use 60,000 pounds of aluminum next month. Metalife Corporation has offered to sell 10,000 pounds of recycled aluminum next month to the fabrication division for $5.00 per pound.

Required

1. Calculate the transfer price per pound of recycled aluminum. Assuming that each division is considered a profit center, would the fabrication manager choose to purchase 10,000 pounds next month from Metalife?
2. Is the purchase in the best interest of Jeremiah Industries? Show your calculations. What is the cause of this goal incongruence?
3. The fabrication division manager suggests that $5.00 is now the market price for recycled sheet aluminum, and that this should be the new transfer price. Jeremiah's corporate management tends to agree. The metal recycling manager is suspicious. Metalife's prices have always been considerably higher than $5.00 per pound. Why the sudden price cut? After further investigation by the recycling division manager, it is revealed that the $5.00 per pound price was a one-time-only offer made to the fabrication division due to excess inventory at Metalife. Future orders would be priced at $5.50 per pound. Comment on the validity of the $5.00 per pound market price and the ethics of the fabrication manager. Would changing the transfer price to $5.00 matter to Jeremiah Industries?

Collaborative Learning Problem

22-36 Transfer pricing, utilization of capacity. (J. Patell, adapted) The California Instrument Company (CIC) consists of the semiconductor division and the process-control division, each of which operates as an independent profit center. The semiconductor division employs craftsmen who produce two different electronic components: the new high-performance Super-chip and an older product called Okay-chip. These two products have the following cost characteristics:

	Super-chip	Okay-chip
Direct materials	$ 5	$ 2
Direct manufacturing labor, 3 hours × $20; 1 hour × $20	60	20

Due to the high skill level necessary for the craftsmen, the semiconductor division's capacity is set at 45,000 hours per year.

Maximum demand for the Super-chip is 15,000 units annually, at a price of $80 per chip. There is unlimited demand for the Okay-chip at $26 per chip.

The process-control division produces only one product, a process-control unit, with the following cost structure:

- Direct materials (circuit board): $70
- Direct manufacturing labor (3 hours × $15): $45

The current market price for the control unit is $132 per unit.

A joint research project has just revealed that a single Super-chip could be substituted for the circuit board currently used to make the process-control unit. Direct labor cost of the process-control unit would be unchanged. The improved process-control unit could be sold for $145.

Required

1. Calculate the contribution margin per direct-labor hour of selling Super-chip and Okay-chip. If no transfers of Super-chip are made to the process-control division, how many Super-chips and Okay-chips should the semiconductor division manufacture and sell? What would be the division's annual contribution margin? Show your computations.
2. The process-control division expects to sell 5,000 process-control units this year. From the viewpoint of California Instruments as a whole, should 5,000 Super-chips be transferred to the process-control division to replace circuit boards? Show your computations.
3. What transfer price, or range of prices, would ensure goal congruence among the division managers? Show your calculations.
4. If labor capacity in the semiconductor division were 60,000 hours instead of 45,000, would your answer to requirement 3 differ? Show your calculations.

23

Performance Measurement, Compensation, and Multinational Considerations

At the end of this school term, you're going to receive a grade that represents a measure of your performance in this course.

Your grade will likely consist of four elements—homework, quizzes, exams, and class participation. Do some of these elements better reflect your knowledge of the material than others? Would the relative weights placed on the various elements when determining your final grade influence how much effort you expend to improve performance on the different elements? Would it be fair if you received a good grade regardless of your performance? The following article about former AIG chief executive Martin Sullivan examines that very situation in a corporate context. Sullivan continued to receive performance bonuses despite pushing AIG to the brink of bankruptcy. By failing to link pay to performance, the AIG board of directors rewarded behavior that led to a government takeover of the firm.

Misalignment Between CEO Compensation and Performance at AIG[1]

After the September 2008 collapse of AIG, many shareholders and observers focused on the company's executive compensation. Many believed that the incentive structures for executives helped fuel the real estate bubble. Though people were placing long-term bets on mortgage-backed securities, much of their compensation was in the form of short-term bonuses. This encouraged excessive risk without the fear of significant repercussions.

Executive compensation at AIG had been under fire for many years. The Corporate Library, an independent research firm specializing in corporate governance, called the company "a serial offender in the category of outrageous CEO compensation."

Judging solely by company financial measures, AIG's 2007 results were a failure. Driven by the write-down of $11.1 billion in fixed income guarantees, the company's revenue was down 56% from 2006 results. AIG also reported $5 billion in losses in the final quarter of 2007 and warned of possible future losses due to ill-advised investments. Despite this, AIG chief executive Martin Sullivan earned $14.3 million in salary, bonus, stock options, and other long-term

---

[1] *Source:* Blair, Nathan. 2009. AIG – Blame for the bailout. Stanford Graduate School of Business No. A-203, Stanford, CA: Stanford Graduate School of Business; Son, Hugh. 2008. AIG chief Sullivan's compensation fell 32 percent. *Bloomberg.com*, April 4; Son, Hugh and Erik Holm. 2008. AIG's former chief Sullivan gets $47 million package. *Bloomberg.com*, July 1.

incentives. Sullivan's compensation was in the 90th percentile for CEOs of S&P 500 firms for 2007.

On June 15, 2008, AIG replaced Sullivan as CEO. By then, AIG reported cumulative losses totaling $20 billion. During Sullivan's three-year tenure at the helm, AIG lost 46% of its market value. At the time of his dismissal, the AIG board of directors agreed to give the ousted CEO about $47 million in severance pay, bonus, and long-term compensation.

Two months later, on the verge of bankruptcy, the U.S. government nationalized AIG. At a Congressional hearing in the aftermath of AIG's failure, one witness testified on Sullivan's compensation stating, "I think it is fair to say by any standard of measurement that this pay plan is as uncorrelated to performance as it is possible to be."

Companies measure reward and performance to motivate managers to achieve company strategies and goals. As the AIG example illustrates, however, if the measures are inappropriate or not connected to sustained performance, managers may improve their performance evaluations and increase compensation without achieving company goals. This chapter discusses the general design, implementation, and uses of performance measures, part of the final step in the decision-making process.

Financial and Nonfinancial Performance Measures

Many organizations are increasingly presenting financial and nonfinancial performance measures for their subunits in a single report called the *balanced scorecard* (Chapter 13). Different organizations stress different measures in their scorecards, but the measures are always derived from a company's strategy. Consider the case of Hospitality Inns, a chain of hotels. Hospitality Inns' strategy is to provide excellent customer service and to charge a higher room rate than its competitors. Hospitality Inns uses the following measures in its balanced scorecard:

Learning Objective 1

Select financial performance measures

. . . such as return on investment, residual income

and nonfinancial performance measures to use in a balanced scorecard

. . . such as customer-satisfaction, number of defects

1. **Financial perspective**—stock price, net income, return on sales, return on investment, and economic value added
2. **Customer perspective**—market share in different geographic locations, customer satisfaction, and average number of repeat visits
3. **Internal-business-process perspective**—customer-service time for making reservations, for check-in, and in restaurants; cleanliness of hotel and room, quality of room service; time taken to clean rooms; quality of restaurant experience; number of new services provided to customers (fax, wireless Internet, video games); time taken to plan and build new hotels

4. **Learning-and-growth perspective**—employee education and skill levels, employee satisfaction, employee turnover, hours of employee training, and information-system availability

As in all balanced scorecard implementations, the goal is to make improvements in the learning-and-growth perspective that will lead to improvements in the internal-business-process perspective that, in turn, will result in improvements in the customer and financial perspectives. Hospitality Inns also uses balanced scorecard measures to evaluate and reward the performance of its managers.

Some performance measures, such as the time it takes to plan and build new hotels, have a long time horizon. Other measures, such as time taken to check in or quality of room service, have a short time horizon. In this chapter, we focus on *organization subunits'* most widely used performance measures that cover an intermediate-to-long time horizon. These are internal financial measures based on accounting numbers routinely reported by organizations. In later sections, we describe why companies use both financial and nonfinancial measures to evaluate performance.

Designing accounting-based performance measures requires several steps:

Step 1: Choose Performance Measures That Align with Top Management's Financial Goals. For example, is operating income, net income, return on assets, or revenues the best measure of a subunit's financial performance?

Step 2: Choose the Details of Each Performance Measure in Step 1. Once a firm has chosen a specific performance measure, it must make a variety of decisions about the precise way in which various components of the measure are to be calculated. For example, if the chosen performance measure is return on assets, should it be calculated for one year or for a multiyear period? Should assets be defined as total assets or net assets (total assets minus total liabilities)? Should assets be measured at historical cost or current cost?

Step 3: Choose a Target Level of Performance and Feedback Mechanism for Each Performance Measure in Step 1. For example, should all subunits have identical targets, such as the same required rate of return on assets? Should performance reports be sent to top management daily, weekly, or monthly?

These steps need not be done sequentially. The issues considered in each step are interdependent, and top management will often proceed through these steps several times before deciding on one or more accounting-based performance measures. The answers to the questions raised at each step depend on top management's beliefs about how well each alternative measure fulfills the behavioral criteria discussed in Chapter 22: promoting goal congruence, motivating management effort, evaluating subunit performance, and preserving subunit autonomy.

Accounting-Based Measures for Business Units

Companies commonly use four measures to evaluate the economic performance of their subunits. We illustrate these measures for Hospitality Inns.

Hospitality Inns owns and operates three hotels: one each in San Francisco, Chicago, and New Orleans. Exhibit 23-1 summarizes data for each hotel for 2012. At present, Hospitality Inns does not allocate the total long-term debt of the company to the three separate hotels. The exhibit indicates that the New Orleans hotel generates the highest operating income, $510,000, compared with Chicago's $300,000 and San Francisco's $240,000. But does this comparison mean the New Orleans hotel is the most "successful"? The main weakness of comparing operating incomes alone is that differences in *the size of the investment* in each hotel are ignored. **Investment** refers to the resources or assets used to generate income. It is not sufficient to compare operating incomes alone. The real question is whether a division generates sufficient operating income relative to the investment made to earn it.

Three of the approaches to measuring performance include a measure of investment: return on investment, residual income, and economic value added. A fourth approach, return on sales, does not measure investment.

Decision Point

What financial and nonfinancial performance measures do companies use in their balanced scorecards?

Learning Objective 2

Examine accounting-based measures for evaluating business unit performance, including return on investment (ROI),

. . . return on sales times investment turnover

residual income (RI),

. . . income minus a dollar amount for required return on investment

and economic value added (EVA®)

. . . a variation of residual income

Exhibit 23-1

Financial Data for
Hospitality Inns for
2012 (in thousands)

	A	B	C	D	E
	Home Insert Page Layout Formulas Data Review View				
1		San Francisco Hotel	Chicago Hotel	New Orleans Hotel	Total
2	Hotel revenues	$1,200,000	$1,400,000	$3,185,000	$5,785,000
3	Hotel variable costs	310,000	375,000	995,000	1,680,000
4	Hotel fixed costs	650,000	725,000	1,680,000	3,055,000
5	Hotel operating income	$ 240,000	$ 300,000	$ 510,000	1,050,000
6	Interest costs on long-term debt at 10%				450,000
7	Income before income taxes				600,000
8	Income taxes at 30%				180,000
9	Net income				$ 420,000
10	Net book value at the end of 2012:				
11	Current assets	$ 400,000	$ 500,000	$ 660,000	$1,560,000
12	Long-term assets	600,000	1,500,000	2,340,000	4,440,000
13	Total assets	$1,000,000	$2,000,000	$3,000,000	$6,000,000
14	Current liabilities	$ 50,000	$ 150,000	$ 300,000	$ 500,000
15	Long-term debt				4,500,000
16	Stockholders' equity				1,000,000
17	Total liabilities and stockholders' equity				$6,000,000
18					

Return on Investment

Return on investment (ROI) is an accounting measure of income divided by an accounting measure of investment.

$$\text{Return on investment} = \frac{\text{Income}}{\text{Investment}}$$

Return on investment is the most popular approach to measure performance. ROI is popular for two reasons: it blends all the ingredients of profitability—revenues, costs, and investment—into a single percentage; and it can be compared with the rate of return on opportunities elsewhere, inside or outside the company. Like any single performance measure, however, ROI should be used cautiously and in conjunction with other measures.

ROI is also called the *accounting rate of return* or the *accrual accounting rate of return* (Chapter 21, pp. 749–750). Managers usually use the term "ROI" when evaluating the performance of an organization's subunit and the term "accrual accounting rate of return" when using an ROI measure to evaluate a project. Companies vary in the way they define income in the numerator and investment in the denominator of the ROI calculation. Some companies use operating income for the numerator; others prefer to calculate ROI on an after-tax basis and use net income. Some companies use total assets in the denominator; others prefer to focus on only those assets financed by long-term debt and stockholders' equity and use total assets minus current liabilities.

Consider the ROIs of each of the three Hospitality hotels in Exhibit 23-1. For our calculations, we use the operating income of each hotel for the numerator and total assets of each hotel for the denominator.

Using these ROI figures, the San Francisco hotel appears to make the best use of its total assets.

Hotel	Operating Income	÷	Total Assets	=	ROI
San Francisco	$240,000	÷	$1,000,000	=	24%
Chicago	$300,000	÷	$2,000,000	=	15%
New Orleans	$510,000	÷	$3,000,000	=	17%

Each hotel manager can increase ROI by increasing revenues or decreasing costs (each of which increases the numerator), or by decreasing investment (which decreases the denominator). A hotel manager can increase ROI even when operating income decreases by reducing total assets by a greater percentage. Suppose, for example, that operating income of the Chicago hotel decreases by 4% from $300,000 to $288,000 [$300,000 × (1 − 0.04)] and total assets decrease by 10% from $2,000,000 to $1,800,000 [$2,000,000 × (1 − 0.10)]. The ROI of the Chicago hotel would then increase from 15% to 16% ($288,000 ÷ $1,800,000).

ROI can provide more insight into performance when it is represented as two components:

$$\frac{\text{Income}}{\text{Investment}} = \frac{\text{Income}}{\text{Revenues}} \times \frac{\text{Revenues}}{\text{Investment}}$$

which is also written as,

$$ROI = \text{Return on sales} \times \text{Investment turnover}$$

This approach is known as the *DuPont method of profitability analysis*. The DuPont method recognizes the two basic ingredients in profit-making: increasing income per dollar of revenues and using assets to generate more revenues. An improvement in either ingredient without changing the other increases ROI.

Assume that top management at Hospitality Inns adopts a 30% target ROI for the San Francisco hotel. How can this return be attained? We illustrate the DuPont method for the San Francisco hotel and show how this method can be used to describe three alternative ways in which the San Francisco hotel can increase its ROI from 24% to 30%.

	Operating Income (1)	Revenues (2)	Total Assets (3)	Operating Income / Revenues (4) = (1) ÷ (2)	×	Revenues / Total Assets (5) = (2) ÷ (3)	=	Operating Income / Total Assets (6) = (4) × (5)
Current ROI	$240,000	$1,200,000	$1,000,000	20%	×	1.2	=	24%
Alternatives								
A. Decrease assets (such as receivables), keeping revenues and operating income per dollar of revenue constant	$240,000	$1,200,000	$800,000	20%	×	1.5	=	30%
B. Increase revenues (via higher occupancy rate), keeping assets and operating income per dollar of revenue constant	$300,000	$1,500,000	$1,000,000	20%	×	1.5	=	30%
C. Decrease costs (via, say, efficient maintenance) to increase operating income per dollar of revenue, keeping revenue and assets constant	$300,000	$1,200,000	$1,000,000	25%	×	1.2	=	30%

Other alternatives, such as increasing the selling price per room, could increase both the revenues per dollar of total assets and the operating income per dollar of revenues. ROI makes clear the benefits managers can obtain by reducing their investment in current or long-term assets. Some managers know the need to boost revenues or to control costs, but they pay less attention to reducing their investment base. Reducing the investment base involves decreasing idle cash, managing credit judiciously, determining proper inventory levels, and spending carefully on long-term assets.

Residual Income

Residual income (RI) is an accounting measure of income minus a dollar amount for required return on an accounting measure of investment.

$$\text{Residual income } (RI) = \text{Income} - (\text{Required rate of return} \times \text{Investment})$$

Required rate of return multiplied by the investment is the *imputed cost of the investment*. The **imputed cost** of the investment is a cost recognized in particular situations but not recorded in financial accounting systems because it is an opportunity cost. In this situation, the imputed cost refers to the return Hospitality Inns could have obtained by making an alternative investment with similar risk characteristics.

Assume each hotel faces similar risks, and that Hospitality Inns has a required rate of return of 12%. The RI for each hotel is calculated as the operating income minus the required rate of return of 12% of total assets:

Hotel	Operating Income	−	Required Rate of Return	×	Investment	=	Residual Income
San Francisco	$240,000	−	(12%	×	$1,000,000)	=	$120,000
Chicago	$300,000	−	(12%	×	$2,000,000)	=	$ 60,000
New Orleans	$510,000	−	(12%	×	$3,000,000)	=	$150,000

Note that the New Orleans hotel has the best RI.

Some companies favor the RI measure because managers will concentrate on maximizing an absolute amount, such as dollars of RI, rather than a percentage, such as ROI. The objective of maximizing RI means that as long as a subunit earns a return in excess of the required return for investments, that subunit should continue to invest.

The objective of maximizing ROI may induce managers of highly profitable subunits to reject projects that, from the viewpoint of the company as a whole, should be accepted. Suppose Hospitality Inns is considering upgrading room features and furnishings at the San Francisco hotel. The upgrade will increase operating income of the San Francisco hotel by $70,000 and increase its total assets by $400,000. The ROI for the expansion is 17.5% ($70,000 ÷ $400,000), which is attractive to Hospitality Inns because it exceeds the required rate of return of 12%. By making this expansion, however, the San Francisco hotel's ROI will decrease:

$$\text{Pre-upgrade } ROI = \frac{\$240,000}{\$1,000,000} = 0.24, \text{ or } 24\%$$

$$\text{Post-upgrade } ROI = \frac{\$240,000 + \$70,000}{\$1,000,000 + \$400,000} = \frac{\$310,000}{\$1,400,000} = 0.221, \text{ or } 22.1\%$$

The annual bonus paid to the San Francisco manager may decrease if ROI affects the bonus calculation and the upgrading option is selected. Consequently, the manager may shun the expansion. In contrast, if the annual bonus is a function of RI, the San Francisco manager will favor the expansion:

$$\text{Pre-upgrade } RI = \$240,000 - (0.12 \times \$1,000,000) = \$120,000$$

$$\text{Post-upgrade } RI = \$310,000 - (0.12 \times \$1,400,000) = \$142,000$$

Goal congruence (ensuring that subunit managers work toward achieving the company's goals) is thus more likely using RI rather than ROI as a measure of the subunit manager's performance.

To see that this is a general result, observe that the post-upgrade ROI is a weighted average of the pre-upgrade ROI and the ROI of the project under consideration. Therefore, whenever a new project has a return higher than the required rate of return (12% in our example) but below the current ROI of the division (24% in our example), the division manager is tempted to reject it even though it is a project the shareholders would like to pursue.[2] On the other hand, RI is a measure that aggregates linearly. Therefore, the post-upgrade RI always equals the pre-upgrade RI plus the RI of the project under consideration (in the preceding example, the project's RI is $70,000 – 12% × $400,000 = $22,000, which is the difference between the post-upgrade and pre-upgrade RI amounts). As a result, a manager who is evaluated on residual income will choose a new project if and only if it has a positive RI. But this is exactly the criterion shareholders want the manager to employ; in other words, RI achieves goal congruence.

---

[2] Analogously, the manager of an underperforming division with an ROI of 7%, say, may wish to accept projects with returns between 7% and 12% even though these opportunities do not meet the shareholders' required rate of return.

Economic Value Added[3]

Economic value added is a specific type of RI calculation that is used by many companies. **Economic value added (EVA®)** equals after-tax operating income *minus* the (after-tax) weighted-average cost of capital *multiplied* by total assets minus current liabilities.

$$\begin{array}{c} \text{Economic value} \\ \text{added (EVA)} \end{array} = \begin{array}{c} \text{After-tax} \\ \text{operating income} \end{array} - \left[\begin{array}{c} \text{Weighted-} \\ \text{average} \\ \text{cost of capital} \end{array} \times \left(\begin{array}{c} \text{Total} \\ \text{assets} \end{array} - \begin{array}{c} \text{Current} \\ \text{liabilities} \end{array} \right) \right]$$

EVA substitutes the following numbers in the RI calculations: (1) income equal to after-tax operating income, (2) required rate of return equal to the (after-tax) weighted-average cost of capital, and (3) investment equal to total assets minus current liabilities.[4]

We use the Hospitality Inns data in Exhibit 23-1 to illustrate the basic EVA calculations. The weighted-average cost of capital (WACC) equals the *after-tax* average cost of all the long-term funds used by Hospitality Inns. The company has two sources of long-term funds: (a) long-term debt with a market value and book value of $4.5 million issued at an interest rate of 10%, and (b) equity capital that also has a market value of $4.5 million (but a book value of $1 million).[5] Because interest costs are tax-deductible and the income tax rate is 30%, the after-tax cost of debt financing is $0.10 \times (1 - \text{Tax rate}) = 0.10 \times (1 - 0.30) = 0.10 \times 0.70 = 0.07$, or 7%. The cost of equity capital is the opportunity cost to investors of not investing their capital in another investment that is similar in risk to Hospitality Inns. Hospitality Inns' cost of equity capital is 14%.[6] The WACC computation, which uses market values of debt and equity, is as follows:

$$WACC = \frac{(7\% \times \text{Market value of debt}) + (14\% \times \text{Market value of equity})}{\text{Market value of debt} + \text{Market value of equity}}$$

$$= \frac{(0.07 \times \$4,500,000) + (0.14 \times \$4,500,000)}{\$4,500,000 + \$4,500,000}$$

$$= \frac{\$945,000}{\$9,000,000} = 0.105, \text{ or } 10.5\%$$

The company applies the same WACC to all its hotels because each hotel faces similar risks. Total assets minus current liabilities (see Exhibit 23-1) can also be computed as follows:

$$\text{Total assets} - \text{Current liabilities} = \text{Long-term assets} + \text{Current assets} - \text{Current liabilities}$$

$$= \text{Long-term assets} + \text{Working capital}$$

where

$$\text{Working capital} = \text{Current assets} - \text{Current liabilities}$$

After-tax hotel operating income is:

$$\begin{array}{c} \text{Hotel operating} \\ \text{income} \end{array} \times (1 - \text{Tax rate}) = \begin{array}{c} \text{Hotel operating} \\ \text{income} \end{array} \times (1 - 0.30) = \begin{array}{c} \text{Hotel operating} \\ \text{income} \end{array} \times 0.70$$

---

[3] S. O'Byrne and D. Young, *EVA and Value-Based Management: A Practical Guide to Implementation* (New York: McGraw-Hill, 2000); J. Stein, J. Shiely, and I. Ross, *The EVA Challenge: Implementing Value Added Change in an Organization* (New York: John Wiley and Sons, 2001).

[4] When implementing EVA, companies make several adjustments to the operating income and asset numbers reported under generally accepted accounting principles (GAAP). For example, when calculating EVA, costs such as R&D, restructuring costs, and leases that have long-run benefits are recorded as assets (which are then amortized), rather than as current operating costs. The goal of these adjustments is to obtain a better representation of the economic assets, particularly intangible assets, used to earn income. Of course, the specific adjustments applicable to a company will depend on its individual circumstances.

[5] The market value of Hospitality Inns' equity exceeds book value because book value, based on historical cost, does not measure the current value of the company's assets and because various intangible assets, such as the company's brand name, are not shown at current value in the balance sheet under GAAP.

[6] In practice, the most common method of calculating the cost of equity capital is by applying the capital asset pricing model (CAPM). For details, see J. Berk and P. DeMarzo, *Corporate Finance*, 2nd ed. (Upper Saddle River, NJ: Prentice Hall, 2010).

EVA calculations for Hospitality Inns are as follows:

Hotel	After-Tax Operating Income	−	[WACC ×	(Total Assets − Current Liabilities)]	=	EVA
San Francisco	$240,000 × 0.70	−	[10.50% ×	($1,000,000 − $ 50,000)]	=	$68,250
Chicago	$300,000 × 0.70	−	[10.50% ×	($2,000,000 − $150,000)]	=	$15,750
New Orleans	$510,000 × 0.70	−	[10.50% ×	($3,000,000 − $300,000)]	=	$73,500

The New Orleans hotel has the highest EVA. Economic value added, like residual income, charges managers for the cost of their investments in long-term assets and working capital. Value is created only if after-tax operating income exceeds the cost of investing the capital. To improve EVA, managers can, for example, (a) earn more after-tax operating income with the same capital, (b) use less capital to earn the same after-tax operating income, or (c) invest capital in high-return projects.[7]

Managers in companies such as Briggs and Stratton, Coca-Cola, CSX, Equifax, and FMC use the estimated impact on EVA to guide their decisions. Division managers find EVA helpful because it allows them to incorporate the cost of capital, which is generally only available at the company-wide level, into decisions at the division level. Comparing the actual EVA achieved to the estimated EVA is useful for evaluating performance and providing feedback to managers about performance. CSX, a railroad company, credits EVA for decisions such as to run trains with three locomotives instead of four and to schedule arrivals just in time for unloading rather than having trains arrive at their destination several hours in advance. The result? Higher income because of lower fuel costs and lower capital investments in locomotives.

Return on Sales

The income-to-revenues ratio (or sales ratio), often called *return on sales* (ROS), is a frequently used financial performance measure. As we have seen, ROS is one component of ROI in the DuPont method of profitability analysis. To calculate ROS for each of Hospitality's hotels, we divide operating income by revenues:

Hotel	Operating Income	÷	Revenues (Sales)	=	ROS
San Francisco	$240,000	÷	$1,200,000	=	20.0%
Chicago	$300,000	÷	$1,400,000	=	21.4%
New Orleans	$510,000	÷	$3,185,000	=	16.0%

The Chicago hotel has the highest ROS, but its performance is rated worse than the other hotels using measures such as ROI, RI, and EVA.

Comparing Performance Measures

The following table summarizes the performance of each hotel and ranks it (in parentheses) under each of the four performance measures:

Hotel	ROI	RI	EVA	ROS
San Francisco	24% (1)	$120,000 (2)	$68,250 (2)	20.0% (2)
Chicago	15% (3)	$ 60,000 (3)	$15,750 (3)	21.4% (1)
New Orleans	17% (2)	$150,000 (1)	$73,500 (1)	16.0% (3)

The RI and EVA rankings are the same. They differ from the ROI and ROS rankings. Consider the ROI and RI rankings for the San Francisco and New Orleans hotels. The New Orleans hotel has a smaller ROI. Although its operating income is only slightly more than

---

[7] Observe that the sum of the divisional after-tax operating incomes used in the EVA calculation, ($240,000 + $300,000 + $510,000) × 0.7 = $735,000, exceeds the firm's net income of $420,000. The difference is due to the firm's after-tax interest expense on its long-term debt, which amounts to $450,000 × 0.7 = $315,000. Because the EVA measure includes a charge for the weighted average cost of capital, which includes the after-tax cost of debt, the income figure used in computing EVA should reflect the after-tax profit before interest payments on debt are considered. After-tax operating income (often referred to in practice as NOPAT, or net operating profit after taxes) is thus the relevant measure of divisional profit for EVA calculations.

twice the operating income of the San Francisco hotel—$510,000 versus $240,000—its total assets are three times as large—$3 million versus $1 million. The New Orleans hotel has a higher RI because it earns a higher income after covering the required rate of return on investment of 12%. The high ROI of the San Francisco hotel indicates that its assets are being used efficiently. Even though each dollar invested in the New Orleans hotel does not give the same return as the San Francisco hotel, this large investment creates considerable value because its return exceeds the required rate of return. The Chicago hotel has the highest ROS but the lowest ROI. The high ROS indicates that the Chicago hotel has the lowest cost structure per dollar of revenues of all of Hospitality Inns' hotels. The reason for Chicago's low ROI is that it generates very low revenues per dollar of assets invested. Is any method better than the others for measuring performance? No, because each evaluates a different aspect of performance.

ROS measures how effectively costs are managed. To evaluate overall aggregate performance, ROI, RI, or EVA measures are more appropriate than ROS because they consider both income and investment. ROI indicates which investment yields the highest return. RI and EVA measures overcome some of the goal-congruence problems of ROI. Some managers favor EVA because of the accounting adjustments related to the capitalization of investments in intangibles. Other managers favor RI because it is easier to calculate and because, in most cases, it leads to the same conclusions as EVA. Generally, companies use multiple financial measures to evaluate performance.

Choosing the Details of the Performance Measures

It is not sufficient for a company to identify the set of performance measures it wishes to use. The company has to make several choices regarding the specific details of how the measures are computed. These range from decisions regarding the time frame over which the measures are computed, to the definition of key terms such as "investment" and the calculation of particular components of each performance measure.

Alternative Time Horizons

An important element in designing accounting-based performance measures is choosing the time horizon of the performance measures. The ROI, RI, EVA, and ROS calculations represent the results for a single period, one year in our example. Managers could take actions that cause short-run increases in these measures but that conflict with the long-run interest of the company. For example, managers may curtail R&D and plant maintenance in the last three months of a fiscal year to achieve a target level of annual operating income. For this reason, many companies evaluate subunits on the basis of ROI, RI, EVA, and ROS over multiple years.

Another reason to evaluate subunits over multiple years is that the benefits of actions taken in the current period may not show up in short-run performance measures, such as the current year's ROI or RI. For example, an investment in a new hotel may adversely affect ROI and RI in the short run but benefit ROI and RI in the long run.

A multiyear analysis highlights another advantage of the RI measure: Net present value of all cash flows over the life of an investment equals net present value of the RIs.[8]

[8] This equivalence, often referred to as the "Conservation Property" of residual income, was originally articulated by Gabriel Preinreich in 1938. To see the equivalence, suppose the $400,000 investment in the San Francisco hotel increases operating income by $70,000 per year as follows: Increase in operating cash flows of $150,000 each year for 5 years minus depreciation of $80,000 ($400,000 ÷ 5) per year, assuming straight-line depreciation and $0 terminal disposal value. Depreciation reduces the investment amount by $80,000 each year. Assuming a required rate of return of 12%, net present values of cash flows and residual incomes are as follows:

Year	0	1	2	3	4	5	Net Present Value
(1) Cash flow	−$400,000	$150,000	$150,000	$150,000	$150,000	$150,000	
(2) Present value of $1 discounted at 12%	1	0.89286	0.79719	0.71178	0.63552	0.56743	
(3) Present value: (1) × (2)	−$400,000	$133,929	$119,578	$106,767	$95,328	$85,114	$140,716
(4) Operating income		$70,000	$70,000	$70,000	$70,000	$70,000	
(5) Assets at start of year		$400,000	$320,000	$240,000	$160,000	$80,000	
(6) Capital charge: (5) × 12%		$48,000	$38,400	$28,800	$19,200	$9,600	
(7) Residual income: (4) − (6)		$22,000	$31,600	$41,200	$50,800	$60,400	
(8) Present value of RI: (7) × (2)		$19,643	$25,191	$29,325	$32,284	$34,273	$140,716

This characteristic means that if managers use the net present value method to make investment decisions (as advocated in Chapter 21), then using multiyear RI to evaluate managers' performances achieves goal congruence.

Another way to motivate managers to take a long-run perspective is by compensating them on the basis of changes in the market price of the company's stock, because stock prices incorporate the expected future effects of current decisions.

Alternative Definitions of Investment

Companies use a variety of definitions for measuring investment in divisions. Four common alternative definitions used in the construction of accounting-based performance measures are as follows:

1. **Total assets available**—includes all assets, regardless of their intended purpose.
2. **Total assets employed**—total assets available minus the sum of idle assets and assets purchased for future expansion. For example, if the New Orleans hotel in Exhibit 23-1 has unused land set aside for potential expansion, total assets employed by the hotel would exclude the cost of that land.
3. **Total assets employed minus current liabilities**—total assets employed, excluding assets financed by short-term creditors. One negative feature of defining investment in this way is that it may encourage subunit managers to use an excessive amount of short-term debt because short-term debt reduces the amount of investment.
4. **Stockholders' equity**—calculated by assigning liabilities among subunits and deducting these amounts from the total assets of each subunit. One drawback of this method is that it combines operating decisions made by hotel managers with financing decisions made by top management.

Companies that use ROI or RI generally define investment as the total assets available. When top management directs a subunit manager to carry extra or idle assets, total assets employed can be more informative than total assets available. Companies that adopt EVA define investment as total assets employed minus current liabilities. The most common rationale for using total assets employed minus current liabilities is that the subunit manager often influences decisions on current liabilities of the subunit.

Alternative Asset Measurements

To design accounting-based performance measures, we must consider different ways to measure assets included in the investment calculations. Should assets be measured at historical cost or current cost? Should gross book value (that is, original cost) or net book value (original cost minus accumulated depreciation) be used for depreciable assets?

Current Cost

Current cost is the cost of purchasing an asset today identical to the one currently held, or the cost of purchasing an asset that provides services like the one currently held if an identical asset cannot be purchased. Of course, measuring assets at current costs will result in different ROIs than the ROIs calculated on the basis of historical costs.

We illustrate the current-cost ROI calculations using the data for Hospitality Inns (Exhibit 23-1) and then compare current-cost-based ROIs and historical-cost-based ROIs. Assume the following information about the long-term assets of each hotel:

	San Francisco	Chicago	New Orleans
Age of facility in years (at end of 2012)	8	4	2
Gross book value (original cost)	$1,400,000	$2,100,000	$2,730,000
Accumulated depreciation	$ 800,000	$ 600,000	$ 390,000
Net book value (at end of 2012)	$ 600,000	$1,500,000	$2,340,000
Depreciation for 2012	$ 100,000	$ 150,000	$ 195,000

Hospitality Inns assumes a 14-year estimated useful life, zero terminal disposal value for the physical facilities, and straight-line depreciation.

An index of construction costs indicating how the cost of construction has changed over the eight-year period that Hospitality Inns has been operating (2004 year-end = 100) is as follows:

Year	2005	2006	2007	2008	2009	2010	2011	2012
Construction cost index	110	122	136	144	152	160	174	180

Earlier in this chapter, we computed an ROI of 24% for San Francisco, 15% for Chicago, and 17% for New Orleans (p. 809). One possible explanation of the high ROI for the San Francisco hotel is that its long-term assets are expressed in 2004 construction-price levels—prices that prevailed eight years ago—and the long-term assets for the Chicago and New Orleans hotels are expressed in terms of higher, more-recent construction-price levels, which depress ROIs for these two hotels.

Exhibit 23-2 illustrates a step-by-step approach for incorporating current-cost estimates of long-term assets and depreciation expense into the ROI calculation. We make these calculations to approximate what it would cost today to obtain assets that would produce the same expected operating income that the subunits currently earn. (Similar adjustments to represent the current costs of capital employed and depreciation expense can also be made in the RI and EVA calculations.) The current-cost adjustment reduces the ROI of the San Francisco hotel by more than half.

	Historical-Cost ROI	Current-Cost ROI
San Francisco	24%	10.8%
Chicago	15%	11.1%
New Orleans	17%	14.7%

Adjusting assets to recognize current costs negates differences in the investment base caused solely by differences in construction-price levels. Compared with historical-cost ROI, current-cost ROI better measures the current economic returns from the investment. If Hospitality Inns were to invest in a new hotel today, investing in one like the New Orleans hotel offers the best ROI.

Current cost estimates may be difficult to obtain for some assets. Why? Because the estimate requires a company to consider, in addition to increases in price levels, technological advances and processes that could reduce the current cost of assets needed to earn today's operating income.

Long-Term Assets: Gross or Net Book Value?

Historical cost of assets is often used to calculate ROI. There has been much discussion about whether gross book value or net book value of assets should be used. Using the data in Exhibit 23-1 (p. 809), we calculate ROI using net and gross book values of plant and equipment as follows:

	Operating Income (from Exhibit 23-1) (1)	Net Book Value of Total Assets (from Exhibit 23-1) (2)	Accumulated Depreciation (from p. 815) (3)	Gross Book Value of Total Assets (4) = (2) + (3)	2012 ROI Using Net Book Value of Total Assets (calculated earlier) (5) = (1) ÷ (2)	2012 ROI Using Gross Book Value of Total Assets (6) = (1) ÷ (4)
San Francisco	$240,000	$1,000,000	$800,000	$1,800,000	24%	13.3%
Chicago	$300,000	$2,000,000	$600,000	$2,600,000	15%	11.5%
New Orleans	$510,000	$3,000,000	$390,000	$3,390,000	17%	15.0%

Using gross book value, the 13.3% ROI of the older San Francisco hotel is lower than the 15.0% ROI of the newer New Orleans hotel. Those who favor using gross book value claim it enables more accurate comparisons of ROI across subunits. For example, using

Exhibit 23-2 ROI for Hospitality Inns: Computed Using Current-Cost Estimates as of the End of 2012 for Depreciation Expense and Long-Term Assets

	A	B	C	D	E	F	G	H	I	J
1	**Step 1:** Restate long-term assets from gross book value at historical cost to gross book value at current cost as of the end of 2012.									
2		**Gross book value of long-term assets at historical cost**	×	**Construction cost index in 2012**	÷	**Construction cost index in year of construction**	=	**Gross book value of long-term assets at current cost at end of 2012**		
3	San Francisco	$1,400,000	×	(180	÷	100)	=	$2,520,000		
4	Chicago	$2,100,000	×	(180	÷	144)	=	$2,625,000		
5	New Orleans	$2,730,000	×	(180	÷	160)	=	$3,071,250		
6										
7	**Step 2:** Derive net book value of long-term assets at current cost as of the end of 2012. (Assume estimated useful life of each hotel is 14 years.)									
8		**Gross book value of long-term assets at current cost at end of 2012**	×	**Estimated remaining useful life**	÷	**Estimated total useful life**	=	**Net book value of long-term assets at current cost at end of 2012**		
9	San Francisco	$2,520,000	×	(6	÷	14)	=	$1,080,000		
10	Chicago	$2,625,000	×	(10	÷	14)	=	$1,875,000		
11	New Orleans	$3,071,250	×	(12	÷	14)	=	$2,632,500		
12										
13	**Step 3:** Compute current cost of total assets in 2012. (Assume current assets of each hotel are expressed in 2012 dollars.)									
14		**Current assets at end of 2012 (from Exhibit 23-1)**	+	**Long-term assets from Step 2**	=	**Current cost of total assets at end of 2012**				
15	San Francisco	$400,000	+	$1,080,000	=	$1,480,000				
16	Chicago	$500,000	+	$1,875,000	=	$2,375,000				
17	New Orleans	$660,000	+	$2,632,500	=	$3,292,500				
18										
19	**Step 4:** Compute current-cost depreciation expense in 2012 dollars.									
20		**Gross book value of long-term assets at current cost at end of 2012 (from Step 1)**	÷	**Estimated total useful life**	=	**Current-cost depreciation expense in 2012 dollars**				
21	San Francisco	$2,520,000	÷	14	=	$180,000				
22	Chicago	$2,625,000	÷	14	=	$187,500				
23	New Orleans	$3,071,250	÷	14	=	$219,375				
24										
25	**Step 5:** Compute 2012 operating income using 2012 current-cost depreciation expense.									
26		**Historical-cost operating income**	−	**Current-cost depreciation expense in 2012 dollars (from Step 4)**	−	**Historical-cost depreciation expense**	=	**Operating income for 2012 using current-cost depreciation expense in 2012 dollars**		
27	San Francisco	$240,000	−	($180,000	−	$100,000)	=	$160,000		
28	Chicago	$300,000	−	($187,500	−	$150,000)	=	$262,500		
29	New Orleans	$510,000	−	($219,375	−	$195,000)	=	$485,625		
30										
31	**Step 6:** Compute ROI using current-cost estimates for long-term assets and depreciation expense.									
32		**Operating income for 2012 using current-cost depreciation expense in 2012 dollars (from Step 5)**	÷	**Current cost of total assets at end of 2012 (from Step 3)**	=	**ROI using current-cost estimate**				
33	San Francisco	$160,000	÷	$1,480,000	=	10.8%				
34	Chicago	$262,500	÷	$2,375,000	=	11.1%				
35	New Orleans	$485,625	÷	$3,292,500	=	14.7%				

Decision Point ▶

Over what time frame should companies measure performance, and what are the alternative choices for calculating the components of each performance measure?

gross-book-value calculations, the return on the original plant-and-equipment investment is higher for the newer New Orleans hotel than for the older San Francisco hotel. This difference probably reflects the decline in earning power of the San Francisco hotel. Using the net book value masks this decline in earning power because the constantly decreasing investment base results in a higher ROI for the San Francisco hotel—24% in this example. This higher rate may mislead decision makers into thinking that the earning power of the San Francisco hotel has not decreased.

The proponents of using net book value as an investment base maintain that it is less confusing because (1) it is consistent with the amount of total assets shown in the conventional balance sheet, and (2) it is consistent with income computations that include deductions for depreciation expense. Surveys report net book value to be the dominant measure of assets used by companies for internal performance evaluation.

Target Levels of Performance and Feedback

Now that we have covered the different types of measures and how to choose them, let us turn our attention to how mangers set and measure target levels of performance.

Learning Objective 4

Study the choice of performance targets and design of feedback mechanisms

. . . carefully crafted budgets and sufficient feedback for timely corrective action

Choosing Target Levels of Performance

We next consider target-setting for accounting-based measures of performance against which actual performance can be compared. Historical-cost-based accounting measures are usually inadequate for evaluating economic returns on new investments, and in some cases, they create disincentives for expansion. Despite these problems, historical-cost ROIs can be used to evaluate current performance by establishing *target* ROIs. For Hospitality Inns, we need to recognize that the hotels were built in different years, which means they were built at different construction-price levels. Top management could adjust the target historical-cost-based ROIs accordingly, say, by setting San Francisco's ROI at 26%, Chicago's at 18%, and New Orleans' at 19%.

This useful alternative of comparing actual results with target or budgeted performance is frequently overlooked. The budget should be carefully negotiated with full knowledge of historical-cost accounting pitfalls. *Companies should tailor a budget to a particular subunit, a particular accounting system, and a particular performance measure.* For example, many problems of asset valuation and income measurement can be resolved if top management can get subunit managers to focus on what is attainable in the forthcoming budget period—whether ROI, RI, or EVA is used and whether the financial measures are based on historical cost or some other measure, such as current cost.

A popular way to establish targets is to set continuous improvement targets. If a company is using EVA as a performance measure, top management can evaluate operations on year-to-year changes in EVA, rather than on absolute measures of EVA. Evaluating performance on the basis of *improvements* in EVA makes the initial method of calculating EVA less important.

In establishing targets for financial performance measures, companies using the balanced scorecard simultaneously determine targets in the customer, internal-business-process, and learning-and-growth perspectives. For example, Hospitality Inns will establish targets for employee training and employee satisfaction, customer-service time for reservations and check-in, quality of room service, and customer satisfaction that each hotel must reach to achieve its ROI and EVA targets.

Choosing the Timing of Feedback

A final critical step in designing accounting-based performance measures is the timing of feedback. Timing of feedback depends largely on (a) how critical the information is for the success of the organization, (b) the specific level of management receiving the feedback, and (c) the sophistication of the organization's information technology. For example, hotel managers responsible for room sales want information on the number of rooms sold (rented) on a daily or weekly basis, because a large percentage of hotel costs are fixed costs. Achieving high room sales and taking quick action to reverse any declining sales trends are critical to the financial success of each hotel. Supplying managers with daily information about room sales is much easier if Hospitality Inns has a computerized room-reservation and check-in system. Top management, however, may look at information about daily room sales only on a monthly basis. In some instances, for example, because of concern about the low sales-to-total-assets ratio of the Chicago hotel, management may want the information weekly.

The timing of feedback for measures in the balanced scorecard varies. For example, human resources managers at each hotel measure employee satisfaction annually because satisfaction is best measured over a longer horizon. However, housekeeping department managers measure the quality of room service over much shorter time horizons, such as a week, because poor levels of performance in these areas for even a short period of time can harm a hotel's reputation for a long period. Moreover, housekeeping problems can be detected and resolved over a short time period.

Performance Measurement in Multinational Companies

Our discussion so far has focused on performance evaluation of different divisions of a company operating within a single country. We next discuss the additional difficulties created when the performance of divisions of a company operating in different countries is compared. Several issues arise.[9]

- The economic, legal, political, social, and cultural environments differ significantly across countries.

- Governments in some countries may limit selling prices of, and impose controls on, a company's products. For example, some countries in Asia, Latin America, and Eastern Europe impose tariffs and custom duties to restrict imports of certain goods.

- Availability of materials and skilled labor, as well as costs of materials, labor, and infrastructure (power, transportation, and communication), may also differ significantly across countries.

- Divisions operating in different countries account for their performance in different currencies. Issues of inflation and fluctuations in foreign-currency exchange rates affect performance measures.

As a result of these differences, adjustments need to be made to compare performance measures across countries.

Calculating the Foreign Division's ROI in the Foreign Currency

Suppose Hospitality Inns invests in a hotel in Mexico City. The investment consists mainly of the costs of buildings and furnishings. Also assume the following:

- The exchange rate at the time of Hospitality's investment on December 31, 2011, is 10 pesos = $1.

- During 2012, the Mexican peso suffers a steady decline in its value. The exchange rate on December 31, 2012, is 15 pesos = $1.

- The average exchange rate during 2012 is [(10 + 15) ÷ 2] = 12.5 pesos = $1.

- The investment (total assets) in the Mexico City hotel is 30,000,000 pesos.

- The operating income of the Mexico City hotel in 2012 is 6,000,000 pesos.

What is the historical-cost-based ROI for the Mexico City hotel in 2012?

To answer this question, Hospitality Inns' managers first have to determine if they should calculate the ROI in pesos or in dollars. If they calculate the ROI in dollars, what exchange rate should they use? The managers may also be interested in how the

Decision Point

What targets should companies use and when should they give feedback to managers regarding their performance relative to these targets?

Learning Objective 5

Indicate the difficulties that occur when the performance of divisions operating in different countries is compared

. . . adjustments needed for differences in inflation rates and changes in exchange rates

---

[9] See M. Z. Iqbal, *International Accounting—A Global Perspective* (Cincinnati: South-Western College Publishing, 2002).

ROI of Hospitality Inns Mexico City (HIMC) compares with the ROI of Hospitality Inns New Orleans (HINO), which is also a relatively new hotel of approximately the same size. The answers to these questions yield information that will be helpful when making future investment decisions.

$$\text{HIMC's } ROI \text{ (calculated using pesos)} = \frac{\text{Operating income}}{\text{Total assets}} = \frac{6,000,000 \text{ pesos}}{30,000,000 \text{ pesos}} = 0.20, \text{ or } 20\%$$

HIMC's ROI of 20% is higher than HINO's ROI of 17% (p. 809). Does this mean that HIMC outperformed HINO based on the ROI criterion? Not necessarily. That's because HIMC operates in a very different economic environment than HINO.

The peso has declined in value relative to the dollar in 2012. This decline has led to higher inflation in Mexico than in the United States. As a result of the higher inflation in Mexico, HIMC will charge higher prices for its hotel rooms, which will increase HIMC's operating income and lead to a higher ROI. Inflation clouds the real economic returns on an asset and makes historical-cost-based ROI higher. Differences in inflation rates between the two countries make a direct comparison of HIMC's peso-denominated ROI with HINO's dollar-denominated ROI misleading.

Calculating the Foreign Division's ROI in U.S. Dollars

One way to make a comparison of historical-cost-based ROIs more meaningful is to restate HIMC's performance in U.S. dollars. But what exchange rate should be used to make the comparison meaningful? Assume operating income was earned evenly throughout 2012. Hospitality Inns' managers should use the average exchange rate of 12.5 pesos = $1 to convert operating income from pesos to dollars: 6,000,000 pesos ÷ 12.5 pesos per dollar = $480,000. The effect of dividing the operating income in pesos by the higher pesos-to-dollar exchange rate prevailing during 2012, rather than the 10 pesos = $1 exchange rate prevailing on December 31, 2011, is that any increase in operating income in pesos as a result of inflation during 2012 is eliminated when converting back to dollars.

At what rate should HIMC's total assets of 30,000,000 pesos be converted? The 10 pesos = $1 exchange rate prevailing when the assets were acquired on December 31, 2011, because HIMC's assets are recorded in pesos at the December 31, 2011, cost, and they are not revalued as a result of inflation in Mexico in 2012. Because the cost of assets in HIMC's financial accounting records is unaffected by subsequent inflation, the exchange rate prevailing when the assets were acquired should be used to convert the assets into dollars. Using exchange rates after December 31, 2011, would be incorrect because these exchange rates incorporate the higher inflation in Mexico in 2012. Total assets are converted to 30,000,000 pesos ÷ 10 pesos per dollar = $3,000,000.

Then,

$$\text{HIMC's } ROI \text{ (calculated using dollars)} = \frac{\text{Operating income}}{\text{Total assets}} = \frac{\$480,000}{\$3,000,000} = 0.16, \text{ or } 16\%$$

As we have discussed, these adjustments make the historical-cost-based ROIs of the Mexico City and New Orleans hotels comparable because they negate the effects of any differences in inflation rates between the two countries. HIMC's ROI of 16% is less than HINO's ROI of 17%.

Residual income calculated in pesos suffers from the same problems as ROI calculated using pesos. Calculating HIMC's RI in dollars adjusts for changes in exchange rates and makes for more-meaningful comparisons with Hospitality's other hotels:

$$\text{HIMC's } RI = \$480,000 - (0.12 \times \$3,000,000)$$
$$= \$480,000 - \$360,000 = \$120,000$$

which is also less than HINO's RI of $150,000. In interpreting HIMC's and HINO's ROI and RI, keep in mind that they are historical-cost-based calculations. They do, however, pertain to relatively new hotels.

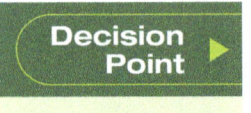

Decision Point ▶

How can companies compare the performance of divisions operating in different countries?

Distinction Between Managers and Organization Units[10]

Our focus has been on how to evaluate the performance of a subunit of a company, such as a division. However, is evaluating the performance of a subunit manager the same as evaluating the performance of the subunit? If the subunit performed well, does it mean the manager performed well? In this section, we argue that the performance evaluation of a *manager* should be distinguished from the performance evaluation of that manager's *subunit*. For example, companies often put the most skillful division manager in charge of the division producing the poorest economic return in an attempt to improve it. The division may take years to show improvement. Furthermore, the manager's efforts may result merely in bringing the division up to a minimum acceptable ROI. The division may continue to be a poor performer in comparison with other divisions, but it would be a mistake to conclude from the poor performance of the division that the manager is performing poorly. The division's performance may be adversely affected by economic conditions over which the manager has no control.

As another example, consider again the Hospitality Inns Mexico City (HIMC) hotel. Suppose, despite the high inflation in Mexico, HIMC could not increase room prices because of price-control regulations imposed by the government. HIMC's performance in dollar terms would be very poor because of the decline in the value of the peso. But should top management conclude from HIMC's poor performance that the HIMC manager performed poorly? Probably not. Most likely, the poor performance of HIMC is largely the result of regulatory factors beyond the manager's control.

In the following sections, we show the basic principles for evaluating the performance of an individual subunit manager. These principles apply to managers at all organization levels. Later sections consider examples at the individual-worker level and the top-management level. We illustrate these principles using the RI performance measure.

The Basic Trade-Off: Creating Incentives Versus Imposing Risk

How the performance of managers and other employees is measured and evaluated affects their rewards. Compensation arrangements range from a flat salary with no direct performance-based incentive (or bonus), as in the case of many government employees, to rewards based on only performance, as in the case of real estate agents who are compensated only via commissions paid on the properties they sell. Most managers' total compensation includes some combination of salary and performance-based incentive. In designing compensation arrangements, we need to consider the *trade-off between creating incentives and imposing risk*. We illustrate this trade-off in the context of our Hospitality Inns example.

Sally Fonda owns the Hospitality Inns chain of hotels. Roger Brett manages the Hospitality Inns San Francisco (HISF) hotel. Assume Fonda uses RI to measure performance. To improve RI, Fonda would like Brett to increase sales, control costs, provide prompt and courteous customer service, and reduce working capital. But even if Brett did all those things, high RI is not guaranteed. HISF's RI is affected by many factors beyond Fonda's and Brett's control, such as a recession in the San Francisco economy, an earthquake that might negatively affect HISF, or even road construction near competing hotels which would drive customers to HISF. Uncontrollable factors make HISF's profitability uncertain and, therefore, risky.

As an entrepreneur, Fonda expects to bear risk. But Brett does not like being subject to risk. One way of "insuring" Brett against risk is to pay Brett a flat salary, regardless of the actual amount of RI earned. All the risk would then be borne by Fonda. This arrangement creates a problem, however, because Brett's effort is difficult to monitor. The absence of performance-based compensation means that Brett has no direct incentive to work harder or to undertake extra physical and mental effort beyond what is necessary to retain his job or to uphold his own personal values.

---
[10]The presentations here draw (in part) from teaching notes prepared by S. Huddart, N. Melumad, and S. Reichelstein.

Learning Objective 6

Understand the roles of salaries and incentives when rewarding managers

. . . balancing risk and performance-based rewards

Moral hazard describes a situation in which an employee prefers to exert less effort (or to report distorted information) compared with the effort (or accurate information) desired by the owner, because the employee's effort (or validity of the reported information) cannot be accurately monitored and enforced.[11] In some repetitive jobs, such as in electronic assembly, a supervisor can monitor the workers' actions, and the moral-hazard problem may not arise. However, a manager's job is to gather and interpret information and to exercise judgment on the basis of the information obtained. Monitoring a manager's effort is more difficult.

Paying no salary and rewarding Brett *only* on the basis of some performance measure— RI in our example—raises different concerns. In this case, Brett would be motivated to strive to increase RI because his rewards would increase with increases in RI. But compensating Brett on RI also subjects him to risk, because HISF's RI depends not only on Brett's effort, but also on factors such as local economic conditions over which Brett has no control.

Brett does not like being subject to risk. To compensate Brett for taking risk, Fonda must pay him extra compensation. That is, using performance-based bonuses will cost Fonda more money, *on average*, than paying Brett a flat salary. Why "on average"? Because Fonda's compensation payment to Brett will vary with RI outcomes. When averaged over these outcomes, the RI-based compensation will cost Fonda more than paying Brett a flat salary. The motivation for having some salary and some performance-based bonus in compensation arrangements is to balance the benefit of incentives against the extra cost of imposing risk on the manager.

Intensity of Incentives and Financial and Nonfinancial Measurements

What affects the intensity of incentives? That is, how large should the incentive component of a manager's compensation be relative to the salary component? To answer these questions, we need to understand how much the performance measure is affected by actions the manager takes to further the owner's objectives.

Preferred performance measures are those that are sensitive to or that change significantly with the manager's performance. They do not change much with changes in factors that are beyond the manager's control. Sensitive performance measures motivate the manager as well as limit the manager's exposure to risk, reducing the cost of providing incentives. Less-sensitive performance measures are not affected by the manager's performance and fail to induce the manager to improve. The more that owners have sensitive performance measures available to them, the more they can rely on incentive compensation for their managers.

The salary component of compensation dominates when performance measures that are sensitive to managers' actions are not available. This is the case, for example, for some corporate staff and government employees. A high salary component, however, does not mean incentives are completely absent. Promotions and salary increases do depend on some overall measure of performance, but the incentives are less direct. The incentive component of compensation is high when sensitive performance measures are available and when monitoring the employee's effort is difficult, such as in real estate agencies.

In evaluating Brett, Fonda uses measures from multiple perspectives of the balanced scorecard because nonfinancial measures on the balanced scorecard—employee satisfaction and the time taken for check-in, cleaning rooms, and providing room service—are more sensitive to Brett's actions. Financial measures such as RI are less sensitive to Brett's actions because they are affected by external factors such as local economic conditions beyond Brett's control. Residual income may be a very good measure of the economic viability of the hotel, but it is only a partial measure of Brett's performance.

Another reason for using nonfinancial measures in the balanced scorecard is that these measures follow Hospitality Inns' strategy and are drivers of future performance. Evaluating managers on these nonfinancial measures motivates them to take actions that will sustain long-run performance. Therefore, evaluating performance in all four perspectives of the balanced scorecard promotes both short- and long-run actions.

---

[11] The term *moral hazard* originated in insurance contracts to represent situations in which insurance coverage caused insured parties to take less care of their properties than they might otherwise. One response to moral hazard in insurance contracts is the system of deductibles (that is, the insured parties pay for damages below a specified amount).

Benchmarks and Relative Performance Evaluation

Owners often use financial and nonfinancial benchmarks to evaluate performance. Benchmarks representing "best practice" may be available inside or outside an organization. For HISF, benchmarks could be from similar hotels, either within or outside the Hospitality Inns chain. Suppose Brett has responsibility for revenues, costs, and investments. In evaluating Brett's performance, Fonda would want to use as a benchmark a hotel of a similar size influenced by the same uncontrollable factors, such as location, demographic trends, or economic conditions, that affect HISF. If all these factors were the same, *differences* in performances of the two hotels would occur only because of differences in the two managers' performances. Benchmarking, which is also called *relative performance evaluation*, filters out the effects of the common uncontrollable factors.

Can the performance of two managers responsible for running similar operations within a company be benchmarked against each other? Yes, but this approach could create a problem: The use of these benchmarks may reduce incentives for these managers to help one another, because a manager's performance-evaluation measure improves either by doing a better job or as a result of the other manager doing poorly. When managers do not cooperate, the company suffers. In this case, using internal benchmarks for performance evaluation may not lead to goal congruence.

Performance Measures at the Individual Activity Level

There are two issues when evaluating performance at the individual-activity level:

1. Designing performance measures for activities that require multiple tasks
2. Designing performance measures for activities done in teams

Performing Multiple Tasks

Most employees perform more than one task as part of their jobs. Marketing representatives sell products, provide customer support, and gather market information. Manufacturing workers are responsible for both the quantity and quality of their output. Employers want employees to allocate their time and effort intelligently among various tasks or aspects of their jobs.

Consider mechanics at an auto repair shop. Their jobs have two distinct aspects: repair work—performing more repair work generates more revenues for the shop—and customer satisfaction—the higher the quality of the job, the more likely the customer will be pleased. If the employer wants an employee to focus on both aspects, then the employer must measure and compensate performance on both aspects.

Suppose that the employer can easily measure the quantity, but not the quality, of auto repairs. If the employer rewards workers on a by-the-job rate, which pays workers only on the basis of the number of repairs actually performed, mechanics will likely increase the number of repairs they make and quality will likely suffer. Sears experienced this problem when it introduced by-the-job rates for its mechanics. To resolve the problem, Sears' managers took three steps to motivate workers to balance both quantity and quality: (1) They dropped the by-the-job rate system and paid mechanics an hourly salary, a step that deemphasized the quantity of repairs. Management determined mechanics' bonuses, promotions, and pay increases on the basis of an assessment of each mechanic's overall performance regarding quantity and quality of repairs. (2) Sears evaluated employees, in part, using data such as customer-satisfaction surveys, the number of dissatisfied customers, and the number of customer complaints. (3) Finally, Sears used staff from an independent outside agency to randomly monitor whether the repairs performed were of high quality.

Team-Based Compensation Arrangements

Many manufacturing, marketing, and design problems can be resolved when employees with multiple skills, knowledge, experiences, and perceptions pool their talents. A team achieves better results than individual employees acting alone.[12] Companies reward

---

[12] *Teams That Click: The Results-Driven Manager Series* (Boston: Harvard Business School Press, 2004).

individuals on a team based on team performance. Such team-based incentives encourage individuals to help one another as they strive toward a common goal.

The specific forms of team-based compensation vary across companies. Colgate-Palmolive rewards teams on the basis of each team's performance. Novartis, the Swiss pharmaceutical company, rewards teams on company-wide performance; a certain amount of team-based bonuses are paid only if the company reaches certain goals. To encourage the development of team skills, Eastman Chemical Company rewards team members using a checklist of team skills, such as communication and willingness to help one another. Whether team-based compensation is desirable depends, to a large extent, on the culture and management style of a particular organization. For example, one criticism of team-based compensation, especially in the United States, is that incentives for individual employees to excel are diminished, harming overall performance. Another problem is how to manage team members who are not productive contributors to the team's success but who, nevertheless, share in the team's rewards.

Executive Performance Measures and Compensation

The principles of performance evaluation described in the previous sections also apply to executive compensation plans. These plans are based on both financial and nonfinancial performance measures and consist of a mix of (1) base salary; (2) annual incentives, such as a cash bonus based on achieving a target annual RI; (3) long-run incentives, such as stock options (described later in this section) based on stock performance over, say, a five-year period; and (4) other benefits, such as medical benefits, pensions plans, and life insurance.

Well-designed plans use a compensation mix that balances risk (the effect of uncontrollable factors on the performance measure and hence compensation) with short-run and long-run incentives to achieve the organization's goals. For example, evaluating performance on the basis of annual EVA sharpens an executive's short-run focus. And using EVA and stock option plans over, say, five years motivates the executive to take a long-run view as well.

Stock options give executives the right to buy company stock at a specified price (called the exercise price) within a specified period. Suppose that on September 16, 2011, Hospitality Inns gave its CEO the option to buy 200,000 shares of the company's stock at any time before June 30, 2019, at the September 16, 2011, market price of $49 per share. Let's say Hospitality Inns' stock price rises to $69 per share on March 24, 2017, and the CEO exercises his options on all 200,000 shares. The CEO would earn $20 ($69 − $49) per share on 200,000 shares, or $4 million. If Hospitality Inns' stock price stays below $49 during the entire period, the CEO will simply forgo his right to buy the shares. By linking CEO compensation to increases in the company's stock price, the stock option plan motivates the CEO to improve the company's long-run performance and stock price. (See also the Concepts in Action feature, p. 825.)[13]

The Securities and Exchange Commission (SEC) requires detailed disclosures of the compensation arrangements of top-level executives. In complying with these rules in 2010, Starwood Hotels and Resorts, for example, disclosed a compensation table showing the salaries, bonuses, stock options, other stock awards, and other compensation earned by its top five executives during the 2007, 2008, and 2009 fiscal years. Starwood, whose brands include Sheraton, Westin, and the W Hotels, also disclosed the peer companies that it uses to set executive pay and conduct performance comparisons. These include competitors in the hotel and hospitality industry (such as Host, Marriott, and Wyndham), as well as companies with similar revenues in other industries relevant to key talent recruitment needs (including Colgate-Palmolive, Nike, and Starbucks). Investors use this information to evaluate the relationship between compensation and performance across companies generally, and across companies operating in similar industries.

---

[13] Although stock options can improve incentives by linking CEO pay to improvements in stock price, they have been criticized for promoting improper or illegal activities by CEOs to increase the options' value. See J. Fox, "Sleazy CEOs Have Even More Options Tricks," www.money.cnn.com/2006/11/13/magazines/fortune/options_scandals.fortune/index.htm (accessed September 5, 2007).

Concepts in Action

Government Bailouts, Record Profits, and the 2009 Wall Street Compensation Dilemma

Wall Street firms paid out near-record bonuses to their employees for 2009 and many in the public were furious, given Wall Street's role in triggering the recent economic crisis. After losing $42.8 billion in 2008 and requiring a government bailout, Wall Street firms recorded $55 billion in 2009 profits, a sum nearly three times greater than the previous record. These results begged a serious question for managers at Goldman Sachs, Morgan Stanley, JPMorgan Chase, and leading financial institutions: After requiring public support just a year earlier, just how big should bankers' paydays be?

Highly paid executives on Wall Street are virtually always investment bankers or the top executives of the firms that employ them. Wall Street firms traditionally paid their investment bankers a share of the total revenue garnered by their unit. While this system worked in previous years, many argued it led to bankers taking the excessive risks that pushed the U.S. financial system to the brink of collapse.

Moreover, 2008 Wall Street bonuses infuriated the public. Just months after government intervention totaling $700 billion, the largest Wall Street banks paid out $56.9 billion in bonuses, or 45.4% of their 2008 revenues. As a result, President Barack Obama laid out strict new regulations on compensation for the 100 highest-paid employees at firms that the government deemed "exceptional assistance recipients" (i.e., firms receiving the largest bailouts). Further, there is little question that without the government intervening to save the financial sector in late 2008, the investment banks would have had a much worse year in 2009. This created a difficult situation for the banks. As one observer noted, "It is fair to say that some of the pay schemes promoted bad behavior and led to excessive risk, but you still need some sort of short-term incentive" for good performance, which Wall Street produced in 2009.

Wall Street firms tried to find some middle ground in 2009 by reducing bonus pools, or the amount of revenues allocated to bonuses, and introducing more long-term compensation into the bonus mix. At Goldman Sachs, for example, top executives received no cash bonuses in 2009, and instead received shares in the company that must be held for five years. For investment bankers and other employees, the company reduced its bonus pool to 36% of company revenue (down from 44% in 2008) and increased the stock-to-cash compensation ratio. Despite these changes, the average Wall Street bonus jumped 25% in 2009 to $123,850. At Goldman Sachs, where profits hit an all-time high, employees made an average of $500,000 each in 2009, including salary and bonus.

While many observers lauded the movement towards having a higher-percentage of bonuses be deferred, the size of 2009 Wall Street bonuses outraged others and ensured that investment banker compensation will remain a hot-button issue on Wall Street, Main Street, and in Washington, DC, for many years to come.

Source: Corkery, Michael. 2009. Goldman bows to pressure, makes changes to compensation. *Wall Street Journal* "Deal Journal," blog December 10; Elliott, Douglas J. 2010. *Wall Street Pay: A Primer.* Washington, DC: The Brookings Institution; Gandel, Stephen. 2009. Wall Street, meet Ken Feinberg, the pay czar. *Time,* November 2; Phillips, Matt. 2010. Goldman: Employees don't mind record low pay ratios. *Wall Street Journal.* "MarketBeat," blog February 3; Shell, Adam. 2010. Despite recession, average Wall Street bonus leaps 25%. *USA,* February 24; *Wall Street Journal.* 2010. The easy guide to Wall Street pay and bonuses. January 20; Weisman, Jonathan and Joanna S. Lublin. 2009. Obama lays out limits on executive pay. *Wall Street Journal,* February 5.

The SEC rules also require companies to disclose the principles underlying their executive compensation plans and the performance criteria—such as profitability, revenue growth, and market share—used in determining compensation. In its financial statements, Starwood described some of these principles as promoting the company's competitive position, providing a balanced approach to incentivizing and retaining employees, and aligning senior management's interests with those of shareholders. Starwood uses earnings per share and EBITDA as performance criteria to determine annual incentives for all of its executives. In addition, each executive has an individual scorecard of financial and nonfinancial performance measures. The company's board of directors creates the overall strategic direction of the company. Individual and strategic goals for executives are then established to support the overall company goals but are tailored to each executive's area of control.

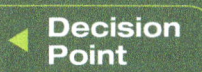

Decision Point

Why are managers compensated based on a mix of salary and incentives?

Strategy and Levers of Control[14]

Learning Objective 7

Describe the four levers of control and why they are necessary

. . . boundary, belief, and interactive control systems counterbalance diagnostic control systems

Given the management accounting focus of this book, this chapter has emphasized the role of quantitative financial and nonfinancial performance-evaluation measures that companies use to implement their strategies. These measures, such as ROI, RI, EVA, customer satisfaction, and employee satisfaction, monitor critical performance variables that help managers track progress toward achieving a company's strategic goals. Because these measures help diagnose whether a company is performing to expectations, they are collectively called **diagnostic control systems.** Companies motivate managers to achieve goals by holding them accountable for and by rewarding them for meeting these goals. The concern, however, is that the pressure to perform may cause managers to cut corners and misreport numbers to make their performance look better than it is, as happened at companies such as Enron, WorldCom, Tyco, and Health South. To prevent unethical and outright fraudulent behavior, companies need to balance the push for performance resulting from diagnostic control systems, the first of four levers of control, with three other levers: *boundary systems, belief systems,* and *interactive control systems.*

Boundary Systems

Boundary systems describe standards of behavior and codes of conduct expected of all employees, especially actions that are off-limits. Ethical behavior on the part of managers is paramount. In particular, numbers that subunit managers report should not be tainted by "cooking the books." They should be free of, for example, overstated assets, understated liabilities, fictitious revenues, and understated costs.

Codes of business conduct signal appropriate and inappropriate individual behaviors. The following are excerpts from Caterpillar's "Worldwide Code of Conduct":

> *While we conduct our business within the framework of applicable laws and regulations, for us, mere compliance with the law is not enough. We strive for more than that. . . . We must not engage in activities that create, or even appear to create, conflict between our personal interests and the interests of the company.*

Division managers often cite enormous pressure from top management "to make the budget" as excuses or rationalizations for not adhering to legal or ethical accounting policies and procedures. A healthy amount of motivational pressure is desirable, as long as the "tone from the top" and the code of conduct simultaneously communicate the absolute need for all managers to behave ethically at all times. Managers should train employees to behave ethically. They should promptly and severely reprimand unethical conduct, regardless of the benefits that might accrue to the company from unethical actions. Some companies, such as Lockheed-Martin, emphasize ethical behavior by routinely evaluating employees against a business code of ethics.

Many organizations also set explicit boundaries precluding actions that harm the environment. Environmental violations (such as water and air pollution) carry heavy fines and prison terms under the laws of the United States and other countries. But in many companies, environmental responsibilities extend beyond legal requirements.

Socially responsible companies set aggressive environmental goals and measure and report their performance against them. German, Swiss, Dutch, and Scandinavian companies report on environmental performance as part of a larger set of social responsibility disclosures (such as employee welfare and community development activities). Some companies, such as DuPont, make environmental performance a line item on every employee's salary appraisal report. Duke Power Company appraises employees on their performance in reducing solid waste, cutting emissions and discharges, and implementing environmental plans. The result? Duke Power has met all of its environmental goals.

---

[14]For a more-detailed discussion see R. Simons, *Levers of Control: How Managers Use Innovative Control Systems to Drive Strategic Renewal* (Boston: Harvard Business School Press, 1995).

Belief Systems

Belief systems articulate the mission, purpose, and core values of a company. They describe the accepted norms and patterns of behavior expected of all managers and other employees with respect to one another, shareholders, customers, and communities. For example, Johnson & Johnson describes its values and norms in a credo statement that is intended to inspire all managers and other employees to do their best.[15] Belief systems play to employees' *intrinsic motivation*, the desire to achieve self-satisfaction from good performance regardless of external rewards such as bonuses or promotion. Intrinsic motivation comes from being given greater responsibility, doing interesting and creative work, having pride in doing that work, establishing commitment to the organization, and developing personal bonds with coworkers. High intrinsic motivation enhances performance because managers and workers have a sense of achievement in doing something important, feel satisfied with their jobs, and see opportunities for personal growth.

Interactive Control Systems

Interactive control systems are formal information systems that managers use to focus the company's attention and learning on key strategic issues. Managers use interactive control systems to create an ongoing dialogue around these key issues and to personally involve themselves in subordinates' decision-making activities. An excessive focus on diagnostic control systems and critical performance variables can cause an organization to ignore emerging threats and opportunities—changes in technology, customer preferences, regulations, and industry competition that can undercut a business. Interactive control systems help prevent this problem by highlighting and tracking strategic uncertainties that businesses face, such as the emergence of digital imaging in the case of Kodak and Fujifilm, airline deregulation in the case of American Airlines, and the shift in customer preferences for mini- and microcomputers in the case of IBM. The key to this control lever is frequent face-to-face communications regarding these critical uncertainties. The result is ongoing discussion and debate about assumptions and action plans. New strategies emerge from the dialogue and debate surrounding the interactive process. Interactive control systems force busy managers to step back from the actions needed to manage the business today and to shift their focus forward to positioning the organization for the opportunities and threats of tomorrow.

Measuring and rewarding managers for achieving critical performance variables is an important driver of corporate performance. But these diagnostic control systems must be counterbalanced by the other levers of control, boundary systems, belief systems, and interactive control systems, to ensure that proper business ethics, inspirational values, and attention to future threats and opportunities are not sacrificed while achieving business results.

◄ Decision Point

What are the four levers of control, and why does a company need to implement them?

Problems for Self-Study

The baseball division of Home Run Sports manufactures and sells baseballs. Assume production equals sales. Budgeted data for February 2011 are as follows:

Current assets	$ 400,000
Long-term assets	600,000
Total assets	$1,000,000
Production output	200,000 baseballs per month
Target ROI (Operating income ÷ Total assets)	30%
Fixed costs	$400,000 per month
Variable cost	$4 per baseball

1. Compute the minimum selling price per baseball necessary to achieve the target ROI of 30%.   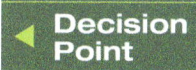 **Required**

2. Using the selling price from requirement 1, separate the target ROI into its two components using the DuPont method.
3. Compute the RI of the baseball division for February 2011, using the selling price from requirement 1. Home Run Sports uses a required rate of return of 12% on total division assets when computing division RI.
4. In addition to her salary, Pamela Stephenson, the division manager, receives 3% of the monthly RI of the baseball division as a bonus. Compute Stephenson's bonus. Why do you think Stephenson is rewarded using both salary and a performance-based bonus? Stephenson does not like bearing risk.

Solution

1.

$$\text{Target operating income} = 30\% \text{ of } \$1,000,000 \text{ of total assets}$$
$$= \$300,000$$
$$\text{Let } P = \text{Selling price}$$
$$\text{Revenues} - \text{Variable costs} - \text{Fixed costs} = \text{Operating income}$$
$$200,000P - (200,000 \times \$4) - \$400,000 = \$300,000$$
$$200,000P = \$300,000 + \$800,000 + \$400,000$$
$$= \$1,500,000$$
$$P = \$7.50 \text{ per baseball}$$

Proof:

Revenues, 200,000 baseballs × $7.50/baseball	$1,500,000
Variable costs, 200,000 baseballs × $4/baseball	800,000
Contribution margin	700,000
Fixed costs	400,000
Operating income	$ 300,000

2. The DuPont method describes ROI as the product of two components: return on sales (income ÷ revenues) and investment turnover (revenues ÷ investment).

$$\frac{\text{Income}}{\text{Revenues}} \times \frac{\text{Revenues}}{\text{Investment}} = \frac{\text{Income}}{\text{Investment}}$$

$$\frac{\$300,000}{\$1,500,000} \times \frac{\$1,500,000}{\$1,000,000} = \frac{\$300,000}{\$1,000,000}$$

$$0.2 \times 1.5 = 0.30, \text{ or } 30\%$$

3. RI = Operating income − Required return on investment
= $300,000 − (0.12 × $1,000,000)
= $300,000 − $120,000
= $180,000

4. Stephensons bonus = 3% of RI
= 0.03 × $180,000 = $5,400

The baseball division's RI is affected by many factors, such as general economic conditions, beyond Stephenson's control. These uncontrollable factors make the baseball division's profitability uncertain and risky. Because Stephenson does not like bearing risk, paying her a flat salary, regardless of RI, would shield her from this risk. But there is a moral-hazard problem with this compensation arrangement. Because Stephenson's effort is difficult to monitor, the absence of performance-based compensation will provide her with no incentive to undertake extra physical and mental effort beyond what is necessary to retain her job or to uphold her personal values.

Paying no salary and rewarding Stephenson only on the basis of RI provides her with incentives to work hard but also subjects her to excessive risk because of uncontrollable factors that will affect RI and hence Stephenson's compensation. A compensation arrangement based only on RI would be more costly for Home Run Sports because it would have to compensate Stephenson for taking on uncontrollable risk. A compensation arrangement that consists of both a salary and an RI-based performance bonus balances the benefits of incentives against the extra costs of imposing uncontrollable risk

Decision Points

The following question-and-answer format summarizes the chapter's learning objectives. Each decision presents a key question related to a learning objective. The guidelines are the answer to that question.

Decision	Guidelines
1. What financial and nonfinancial performance measures do companies use in their balanced scorecards?	Financial measures such as return on investment and residual income measure aspects of both manager performance and organization-subunit performance. In many cases, financial measures are supplemented with nonfinancial measures of performance from the customer, internal-business-process, and learning-and-growth perspectives of the balanced scorecard—for example, customer-satisfaction, quality of products and services, and employee satisfaction.
2. What are the relative merits of return on investment (ROI), residual income (RI), and economic-value added (EVA) as performance measures for subunit managers?	Return on investment (ROI) is the product of two components: income divided by revenues (return on sales) and revenues divided by investment (investment turnover). Managers can increase ROI by increasing revenues, decreasing costs, and decreasing investment. But, ROI may induce managers of highly profitable divisions to reject projects that are in the firm's best interest because accepting the project reduces divisional ROI.

Residual income (RI) is income minus a dollar amount of required return on investment. RI is more likely than ROI to promote goal congruence. Evaluating managers on RI is also consistent with the use of discounted cash flow to choose long-term projects.

Economic value added (EVA) is a variation of the RI calculation. It equals after-tax operating income minus the product of (after-tax) weighted-average cost of capital and total assets minus current liabilities. |
3. Over what timeframe should companies measure performance, and what are the alternative choices for calculating the components of each performance measure?	A multiyear perspective induces managers to consider the long-term consequences of their actions and prevents a myopic focus on short-run profits. When constructing accounting-based performance measures, firms must first decide on a definition of investment. They must also choose whether assets included in the investment calculations are measured at historical cost or current cost, and whether depreciable assets are calculated at gross or net book value.
4. What targets should companies use and when should they give feedback to managers regarding their performance relative to these targets?	Companies should tailor a budget to a particular subunit, a particular accounting system, and a particular performance measure. In general, problems of asset valuation and income measurement in a performance measure can be overcome by emphasizing budgets and targets that stress continuous improvement. Timely feedback is critical to enable managers to implement actions that correct deviations from target performance.
5. How can companies compare the performance of divisions operating in different countries?	Comparing the performance of divisions operating in different countries is difficult because of legal, political, social, economic, and currency differences. ROI and RI calculations for subunits operating in different countries need to be adjusted for differences in inflation between the two countries and changes in exchange rates.
6. Why are managers compensated based on a mix of salary and incentives?	Companies create incentives by rewarding managers on the basis of performance. But managers face risks because factors beyond their control may also affect their performance. Owners choose a mix of salary and incentive compensation to trade off the incentive benefit against the cost of imposing risk.
7. What are the four levers of control, and why does a company need to implement them?	The four levers of control are diagnostic control systems, boundary systems, belief systems, and interactive control systems. Implementing the four levers of control helps a company simultaneously strive for performance, behave ethically, inspire employees, and respond to strategic threats and opportunities.

Terms to Learn

This chapter and the Glossary at the end of the book contain definitions of the following important terms:

belief systems (**p. 827**)

boundary systems (**p. 826**)

current cost (**p. 815**)

diagnostic control systems (**p. 826**)

economic value added (EVA®) (**p. 812**)

imputed cost (**p. 810**)

interactive control systems (**p. 827**)

investment (**p. 808**)

moral hazard (**p. 822**)

residual income (RI) (**p. 810**)

return on investment (ROI) (**p. 809**)

Assignment Material

Questions

23-1 Give examples of financial and nonfinancial performance measures that can be found in each of the four perspectives of the balanced scorecard.

23-2 What are the three steps in designing accounting-based performance measures?

23-3 What factors affecting ROI does the DuPont method of profitability analysis highlight?

23-4 "RI is not identical to ROI, although both measures incorporate income and investment into their computations." Do you agree? Explain.

23-5 Describe EVA.

23-6 Give three definitions of investment used in practice when computing ROI.

23-7 Distinguish between measuring assets based on current cost and historical cost.

23-8 What special problems arise when evaluating performance in multinational companies?

23-9 Why is it important to distinguish between the performance of a manager and the performance of the organization subunit for which the manager is responsible? Give an example.

23-10 Describe moral hazard.

23-11 "Managers should be rewarded only on the basis of their performance measures. They should be paid no salary." Do you agree? Explain.

23-12 Explain the role of benchmarking in evaluating managers.

23-13 Explain the incentive problems that can arise when employees must perform multiple tasks as part of their jobs.

23-14 Describe two disclosures required by the SEC with respect to executive compensation.

23-15 Describe the four levers of control.

Exercises

23-16 ROI, comparisons of three companies. (CMA, adapted) Return on investment (ROI) is often expressed as follows:

$$\frac{\text{Income}}{\text{Investment}} = \frac{\text{Income}}{\text{Revenues}} \times \frac{\text{Revenues}}{\text{Investment}}$$

Required

1. What advantages are there in the breakdown of the computation into two separate components?
2. Fill in the following blanks:

	Companies in Same Industry		
	A	B	C
Revenues	$1,000,000	$500,000	?
Income	$ 100,000	$ 50,000	?
Investment	$ 500,000	?	$5,000,000
Income as a percentage of revenues	?	?	0.5%
Investment turnover	?	?	2
ROI	?	1%	?

After filling in the blanks, comment on the relative performance of these companies as thoroughly as the data permit.

23-17 Analysis of return on invested assets, comparison of two divisions, DuPont method. Global Data, Inc., has two divisions: Test Preparation and Language Arts. Results (in millions) for the past three years are partially displayed here:

	A	B	C	D	E	F	G
1		Operating Income	Operating Revenues	Total Assets	Operating Income/ Operating Revenues	Operating Revenues/ Total Assets	Operating Income/ Total Assets
2	Test Preparation Division						
3	2011	$ 720	$ 9,000	$1,800	?	?	?
4	2012	920	?	?	11.5%	?	46%
5	2013	1,140	?	?	9.5%	6	?
6	Language Arts Division						
7	2011	$ 660	$ 3,000	$2,000	?	?	?
8	2012	?	3,525	2,350	20%	?	?
9	2013	?	?	2,900	?	1.6	20%
10	Global Data, Inc.						
11	2011	$1,380	$12,000	$3,800	?	?	?
12	2012	?	?	?	?	?	?
13	2013	?	?	?	?	?	?

1. Complete the table by filling in the blanks.
2. Use the DuPont method of profitability analysis to explain changes in the operating-income-to-total-assets ratios over the 2011–2013 period for each division and for Global Data as a whole. Comment on the results.

23-18 ROI and RI. (D. Kleespie, adapted) The Outdoor Sports Company produces a wide variety of outdoor sports equipment. Its newest division, Golf Technology, manufactures and sells a single product—AccuDriver, a golf club that uses global positioning satellite technology to improve the accuracy of golfers' shots. The demand for AccuDriver is relatively insensitive to price changes. The following data are available for Golf Technology, which is an investment center for Outdoor Sports:

Total annual fixed costs	$30,000,000
Variable cost per AccuDriver	$ 500
Number of AccuDrivers sold each year	150,000
Average operating assets invested in the division	$48,000,000

1. Compute Golf Technology's ROI if the selling price of AccuDrivers is $720 per club.
2. If management requires an ROI of at least 25% from the division, what is the minimum selling price that the Golf Technology Division should charge per AccuDriver club?
3. Assume that Outdoor Sports judges the performance of its investment centers on the basis of RI rather than ROI. What is the minimum selling price that Golf Technology should charge per AccuDriver if the company's required rate of return is 20%?

23-19 ROI and RI with manufacturing costs. Superior Motor Company makes electric cars and has only two products, the Simplegreen and the Superiorgreen. To produce the Simplegreen, Superior Motor employed assets of $13,500,000 at the beginning of the period, and $13,400,000 of assets at the end of the period. Other costs to manufacture the Simplegreen include the following:

Direct materials	$3,000 per unit
Setup	$1,300 per setup-hour
Production	$415 per machine-hour

General administration and selling costs total $7,340,000 for the period. In the current period, Superior Motor produced 10,000 Simplegreen cars using 6,000 setup-hours and 175,200 machine-hours. Superior Motor sold these cars for $12,000 each.

1. Assuming that Superior Motor defines investment as average assets during the period, what is the return on investment for the Simplegreen division?
2. Calculate the residual income for the Simplegreen if Superior Motor has a required rate of return of 12% on investments.

23-20 Financial and nonfinancial performance measures, goal congruence. (CMA, adapted) Summit Equipment specializes in the manufacture of medical equipment, a field that has become increasingly competitive. Approximately two years ago, Ben Harrington, president of Summit, decided to revise the bonus plan (based, at the time, entirely on operating income) to encourage division managers to focus on areas that were important to customers and that added value without increasing cost. In addition to a profitability incentive, the revised plan includes incentives for reduced rework costs, reduced sales returns, and on-time deliveries. Bonuses are calculated and awarded semiannually on the following basis: A base bonus is calculated at 2% of operating income; this amount is then adjusted as follows:

a. (i) Reduced by excess of rework costs over and above 2% of operating income
   (ii) No adjustment if rework costs are less than or equal to 2% of operating income
b. (i) Increased by $5,000 if more than 98% of deliveries are on time, and by $2,000 if 96% to 98% of deliveries are on time
   (ii) No adjustment if on-time deliveries are below 96%
c. (i) Increased by $3,000 if sales returns are less than or equal to 1.5% of sales
   (ii) Decreased by 50% of excess of sales returns over 1.5% of sales

Note: If the calculation of the bonus results in a negative amount for a particular period, the manager simply receives no bonus, and the negative amount is not carried forward to the next period.

Results for Summit's Charter division and Mesa division for 2012, the first year under the new bonus plan, follow. In 2011, under the old bonus plan, the Charter division manager earned a bonus of $27,060 and the Mesa division manager, a bonus of $22,440.

	Charter Division		Mesa Division	
	January 1, 2012, to June 30, 2012	July 1, 2012, to Dec. 31, 2012	January 1, 2012, to June 30, 2012	July 1, 2012, to Dec. 31, 2012
Revenues	$4,200,000	$4,400,000	$2,850,000	$2,900,000
Operating income	$462,000	$440,000	$342,000	$406,000
On-time delivery	95.4%	97.3%	98.2%	94.6%
Rework costs	$11,500	$11,000	$6,000	$8,000
Sales returns	$84,000	$70,000	$44,750	$42,500

Required

1. Why did Harrington need to introduce these new performance measures? That is, why does Harrington need to use these performance measures in addition to the operating-income numbers for the period?
2. Calculate the bonus earned by each manager for each six-month period and for 2012.
3. What effect did the change in the bonus plan have on each manager's behavior? Did the new bonus plan achieve what Harrington desired? What changes, if any, would you make to the new bonus plan?

23-21 Goal incongruence and ROI. Bleefl Corporation manufactures furniture in several divisions, including the patio furniture division. The manager of the patio furniture division plans to retire in two years. The manager receives a bonus based on the division's ROI, which is currently 11%.

One of the machines that the patio furniture division uses to manufacture the furniture is rather old, and the manager must decide whether to replace it. The new machine would cost $30,000 and would last 10 years. It would have no salvage value. The old machine is fully depreciated and has no trade-in value. Bleefl uses straight-line depreciation for all assets. The new machine, being new and more efficient, would save the company $5,000 per year in cash operating costs. The only difference between cash flow and net income is depreciation. The internal rate of return of the project is approximately 11%. Bleefl Corporation's weighted average cost of capital is 6%. Bleefl is not subject to any income taxes.

Required

1. Should Bleefl Corporation replace the machine? Why or why not?
2. Assume that "investment" is defined as average net long-term assets after depreciation. Compute the project's ROI for each of its first five years. If the patio furniture manager is interested in maximizing his or her bonus, would the manager replace the machine before he or she retires? Why or why not?
3. What can Bleefl do to entice the manager to replace the machine before retiring?

23-22 ROI, RI, EVA. Performance Auto Company operates a new car division (that sells high performance sports cars) and a performance parts division (that sells performance improvement parts for family cars). Some division financial measures for 2011 are as follows:

	A	B	C
		New Car Division	Performance Parts Division
1			
2	Total assets	$33,000,000	$28,500,000
3	Current liabilities	$ 6,600,000	$ 8,400,000
4	Operating income	$ 2,475,000	$ 2,565,000
5	Required rate of return	12%	12%

Required

1. Calculate return on investment (ROI) for each division using operating income as a measure of income and total assets as a measure of investment.
2. Calculate residual income (RI) for each division using operating income as a measure of income and total assets minus current liabilities as a measure of investment.
3. William Abraham, the New Car Division manager, argues that the performance parts division has "loaded up on a lot of short-term debt" to boost its RI. Calculate an alternative RI for each division that is not sensitive to the amount of short-term debt taken on by the performance parts division. Comment on the result.
4. Performance Auto Company, whose tax rate is 40%, has two sources of funds: long-term debt with a market value of $18,000,000 at an interest rate of 10%, and equity capital with a market value of $12,000,000 and a cost of equity of 15%. Applying the same weighted-average cost of capital (WACC) to each division, calculate EVA for each division.
5. Use your preceding calculations to comment on the relative performance of each division.

23-23 ROI, RI, measurement of assets. (CMA, adapted) Carter Corporation recently announced a bonus plan to be awarded to the manager of the most profitable division. The three division managers are to choose whether ROI or RI will be used to measure profitability. In addition, they must decide whether investment will be measured using gross book value or net book value of assets. Carter defines income as operating income and investment as total assets. The following information is available for the year just ended:

Division	Gross Book Value of Assets	Accumulated Depreciation	Operating Income
Radnor	$1,200,000	$645,000	$142,050
Easttown	1,140,000	615,000	137,550
Marion	750,000	420,000	92,100

Carter uses a required rate of return of 10% on investment to calculate RI.

Required

Each division manager has selected a method of bonus calculation that ranks his or her division number one. Identify the method for calculating profitability that each manager selected, supporting your answer with appropriate calculations. Comment on the strengths and weaknesses of the methods chosen by each manager.

23-24 Multinational performance measurement, ROI, RI. The Seaside Corporation manufactures similar products in the United States and Norway. The U.S. and Norwegian operations are organized as decentralized divisions. The following information is available for 2012; ROI is calculated as operating income divided by total assets:

	U.S. Division	Norwegian Division
Operating income	?	6,840,000 kroner
Total assets	$7,500,000	72,000,000 kroner
ROI	9.3%	?

Both investments were made on December 31, 2011. The exchange rate at the time of Seaside's investment in Norway on December 31, 2011, was 9 kroner = $1. During 2012, the Norwegian kroner decreased steadily in value so that the exchange rate on December 31, 2012, is 10 kroner = $1. The average exchange rate during 2012 is [(9 + 10) ÷ 2] = 9.5 kroner = $1.

Required

1a. Calculate the U.S. division's operating income for 2012.
 b. Calculate the Norwegian division's ROI for 2012 in kroner.
 2. Top management wants to know which division earned a better ROI in 2012. What would you tell them? Explain your answer.
 3. Which division do you think had the better RI performance? Explain your answer. The required rate of return on investment (calculated in U.S. dollars) is 8%.

23-25 ROI, RI, EVA and Performance Evaluation. Eva Manufacturing makes fashion products and competes on the basis of quality and leading-edge designs. The company has $3,000,000 invested in assets in its clothing manufacturing division. After-tax operating income from sales of clothing this year is $600,000. The cosmetics division has $10,000,000 invested in assets and an after-tax operating income this year of $1,600,000. Income for the clothing division has grown steadily over the last few years. The weighted-average cost of capital for Eva is 10% and the previous period's after-tax return on investment for each division was 15%. The CEO of Eva has told the manager of each division that the division that "performs best" this year will get a bonus.

Required

1. Calculate the ROI and residual income for each division of Eva Manufacturing, and briefly explain which manager will get the bonus. What are the advantages and disadvantages of each measure?
2. The CEO of Eva Manufacturing has recently heard of another measure similar to residual income called EVA. The CEO has the accountant calculate EVA adjusted incomes of clothing and cosmetics, and finds that the adjusted after-tax operating incomes are $720,000 and $1,430,000, respectively. Also, the clothing division

has $400,000 of current liabilities, while the cosmetics division has only $200,000 of current liabilities. Using the preceding information, calculate EVA, and discuss which division manager will get the bonus.

3. What nonfinancial measures could Eva use to evaluate divisional performances?

23-26 Risk sharing, incentives, benchmarking, multiple tasks. The Dexter division of AMCO sells car batteries. AMCO's corporate management gives Dexter management considerable operating and investment autonomy in running the division. AMCO is considering how it should compensate Jim Marks, the general manager of the Dexter division. Proposal 1 calls for paying Marks a fixed salary. Proposal 2 calls for paying Marks no salary and compensating him only on the basis of the division's ROI, calculated based on operating income before any bonus payments. Proposal 3 calls for paying Marks some salary and some bonus based on ROI. Assume that Marks does not like bearing risk.

Required

1. Evaluate the three proposals, specifying the advantages and disadvantages of each.
2. Suppose that AMCO competes against Tiara Industries in the car battery business. Tiara is approximately the same size as the Dexter division and operates in a business environment that is similar to Dexter's. The top management of AMCO is considering evaluating Marks on the basis of Dexter's ROI minus Tiara's ROI. Marks complains that this approach is unfair because the performance of another company, over which he has no control, is included in his performance-evaluation measure. Is Marks' complaint valid? Why or why not?
3. Now suppose that Marks has no authority for making capital-investment decisions. Corporate management makes these decisions. Is ROI a good performance measure to use to evaluate Marks? Is ROI a good measure to evaluate the economic viability of the Dexter division? Explain.
4. Dexter's salespersons are responsible for selling and providing customer service and support. Sales are easy to measure. Although customer service is important to Dexter in the long run, it has not yet implemented customer-service measures. Marks wants to compensate his sales force only on the basis of sales commissions paid for each unit of product sold. He cites two advantages to this plan: (a) It creates strong incentives for the sales force to work hard, and (b) the company pays salespersons only when the company itself is earning revenues. Do you like his plan? Why or why not?

Problems

23-27 Residual Income and EVA; timing issues. Doorchime Company makes doorbells. It has a weighted average cost of capital of 9%, and total assets of $5,550,000. Doorchime has current liabilities of $800,000. Its operating income for the year was $630,000. Doorchime does not have to pay any income taxes. One of the expenses for accounting purposes was a $90,000 advertising campaign. The entire amount was deducted this year, although the Doorchime CEO believes the beneficial effects of this advertising will last four years.

Required

1. Calculate residual income, assuming Doorchime defines investment as total assets.
2. Calculate EVA for the year. Adjust both the assets and operating income for advertising assuming that for the purposes of economic value added the advertising is capitalized and amortized on a straight-line basis over four years.
3. Discuss the difference between the outcomes of requirements 1 and 2 and which measure is preferred.

23-28 ROI performance measures based on historical cost and current cost. Nature's Elixir Corporation operates three divisions that process and bottle natural fruit juices. The historical-cost accounting system reports the following information for 2011:

	Passion Fruit Division	Kiwi Fruit Division	Mango Fruit Division
Revenues	$1,000,000	$1,400,000	$2,200,000
Operating costs			
(excluding plant depreciation)	600,000	760,000	1,200,000
Plant depreciation	140,000	200,000	240,000
Operating income	$ 260,000	$ 440,000	$ 760,000
Current assets	$ 400,000	$ 500,000	$ 600,000
Long-term assets—plant	280,000	1,800,000	2,640,000
Total assets	$ 680,000	$2,300,000	$3,240,000

Nature's Elixir estimates the useful life of each plant to be 12 years, with no terminal disposal value. The straight-line depreciation method is used. At the end of 2011, the passion fruit plant is 10 years old, the kiwi fruit plant is 3 years old, and the mango fruit plant is 1 year old. An index of construction costs over the 10-year period that Nature's Elixir has been operating (2001 year-end = 100) is as follows:

2001	2008	2010	2011
100	136	160	170

Given the high turnover of current assets, management believes that the historical-cost and current-cost measures of current assets are approximately the same.

1. Compute the ROI ratio (operating income to total assets) of each division using historical-cost measures. Comment on the results.
2. Use the approach in Exhibit 23-2 (p. 817) to compute the ROI of each division, incorporating current-cost estimates as of 2011 for depreciation expense and long-term assets. Comment on the results.
3. What advantages might arise from using current-cost asset measures as compared with historical-cost measures for evaluating the performance of the managers of the three divisions?

23-29 ROI, measurement alternatives for performance measures P. F. Skidaddle's operates casual dining restaurants in three regions: Denver, Seattle, and Sacramento. Each geographic market is considered a separate division. The Denver division is made up of four restaurants, each built in early 2002. The Seattle division is made up of three restaurants, each built in January 2006. The Sacramento division is the newest, consisting of three restaurants built four years ago. Division managers at P. F. Skidaddle's are evaluated on the basis of ROI. The following information refers to the three divisions at the end of 2012:

	Home	Insert	Page Layout	Formulas	Data	Review	View	

	A	B	C	D	E
1		Denver	Seattle	Sacramento	Total
2	Division revenues	$8,365,000	$6,025,000	$5,445,000	$20,138,000
3	Division expenses	7,945,000	5,521,000	4,979,000	18,445,000
4	Division operating income	723,000	504,000	466,000	1,693,000
5	Gross book value of long-term assets	4,750,000	3,750,000	4,050,000	12,300,000
6	Accumulated depreciation	3,300,000	1,750,000	1,080,000	6,130,000
7	Current assets	999,800	768,200	824,600	2,592,600
8	Depreciation expense	300,000	250,000	270,000	820,000
9	Construction cost index for year of construction	100	110	118	

1. Calculate ROI for each division using net book value of total assets. **Required**
2. Using the technique in Exhibit 23-2, compute ROI using current-cost estimates for long-term assets and depreciation expense. Construction cost index for 2012 is 122. Estimated useful life of operational assets is 15 years.
3. How does the choice of long-term asset valuation affect management decisions regarding new capital investments? Why might this be more significant to the Denver division manager than to the Sacramento division manager?

23-30 ROI, RI, and Multinational Firms. Konekopf Corporation has a division in the United States, and another in France. The investment in the French assets was made when the exchange rate was $1.30 per euro. The average exchange rate for the year was $1.40 per euro. The exchange rate at the end of the fiscal year was $1.45 per euro. Income and investment for the two divisions are as follows:

	United States	France
Investment in assets	$5,450,000	3,800,000 euro
Income for current year	$ 681,250	486,400 euro

1. The required return for Konekopf is 12%. Calculate ROI and RI for the two divisions. For the French division, calculate these measures using both dollars and euro. Which division is doing better? **Required**
2. What are the advantages and disadvantages of translating the French division information from euro to dollars?

23-31 Multinational firms, differing risk, comparison of profit, ROI and RI. Zynga Multinational, Inc., has divisions in the United States, Germany, and New Zealand. The U.S. division is the oldest and most established of the three, and has a cost of capital of 8%. The German division was started three years ago when the exchange rate for euro was 1 euro = $1.25. It is a large and powerful division of Zynga, Inc., with a cost of capital of 12%. The New Zealand division was started this year, when the exchange rate was 1 New Zealand Dollar (NZD) = $0.60. Its cost of capital is 14%. Average exchange rates for the current year are 1 euro = $1.40 and 1 NZD = $0.64. Other information for the three divisions includes the following:

	United States	Germany	New Zealand
Long term assets	$23,246,112	11,939,200 euro	9,400,000 NZD
Operating revenues	$13,362,940	5,250,000 euros	4,718,750 NZD
Operating expenses	$ 8,520,000	3,200,000 euros	3,250,000 NZD
Income tax rate	40%	35%	25%

Required

1. Translate the German and New Zealand information into dollars to make the divisions comparable. Find the after-tax operating income for each division and compare the profits.
2. Calculate ROI using after-tax operating income. Compare among divisions.
3. Use after-tax operating income and the individual cost of capital of each division to calculate residual income and compare.
4. Redo requirement 2 using pretax operating income instead of net income. Why is there a big difference, and what does it mean for performance evaluation?

23-32 ROI, RI, DuPont method, investment decisions, balanced scorecard. Global Event Group has two major divisions: print and Internet. Summary financial data (in millions) for 2011 and 2012 are as follows:

	Operating Income			Revenues			Total Assets	
	2011	2012		2011	2012		2011	2012
Print	$3,740	$6,120		$18,300	$20,400		$18,650	$24,000
Internet	565	780		25,900	30,000		11,200	12,000

The two division managers' annual bonuses are based on division ROI (defined as operating income divided by total assets). If a division reports an increase in ROI from the previous year, its management is automatically eligible for a bonus; however, the management of a division reporting a decline in ROI has to present an explanation to the Global Event Group board and is unlikely to get any bonus.

Carol Mays, manager of the print division, is considering a proposal to invest $960 million in a new computerized news reporting and printing system. It is estimated that the new system's state-of-the-art graphics and ability to quickly incorporate late-breaking news into papers will increase 2013 division operating income by $144 million. Global Event Group uses a 12% required rate of return on investment for each division.

Required

1. Use the DuPont method of profitability analysis to explain differences in 2012 ROIs between the two divisions. Use 2012 total assets as the investment base.
2. Why might Mays be less than enthusiastic about accepting the investment proposal for the new system, despite her belief in the benefits of the new technology?
3. Chris Moreno, CEO of Global Event Group, is considering a proposal to base division executive compensation on division RI.
   a. Compute the 2012 RI of each division.
   b. Would adoption of an RI measure reduce Mays' reluctance to adopt the new computerized system investment proposal?
4. Moreno is concerned that the focus on annual ROI could have an adverse long-run effect on Global Event Group's customers. What other measurements, if any, do you recommend that Moreno use? Explain briefly.

23-33 Division managers' compensation, levers of control (continuation of 23-32). Chris Moreno seeks your advice on revising the existing bonus plan for division managers of Global Event Group. Assume division managers do not like bearing risk. Moreno is considering three ideas:

- Make each division manager's compensation depend on division RI.
- Make each division manager's compensation depend on company-wide RI.
- Use benchmarking, and compensate division managers on the basis of their division's RI minus the RI of the other division.

Required

1. Evaluate the three ideas Moreno has put forth using performance-evaluation concepts described in this chapter. Indicate the positive and negative features of each proposal.
2. Moreno is concerned that the pressure for short-run performance may cause managers to cut corners. What systems might Moreno introduce to avoid this problem? Explain briefly.

3. Moreno is also concerned that the pressure for short-run performance might cause managers to ignore emerging threats and opportunities. What system might Moreno introduce to prevent this problem? Explain briefly.

23-34 Executive compensation, balanced scorecard. Community Bank recently introduced a new bonus plan for its business unit executives. The company believes that current profitability and customer satisfaction levels are equally important to the bank's long-term success. As a result, the new plan awards a bonus equal to 1% of salary for each 1% increase in business unit net income or 1% increase in the business unit's customer satisfaction index. For example, increasing net income from $3 million to $3.3 million (or 10% from its initial value) leads to a bonus of 10% of salary, while increasing the business unit's customer satisfaction index from 70 to 73.5 (or 5% from its initial value) leads to a bonus of 5% of salary. There is no bonus penalty when net income or customer satisfaction declines. In 2011 and 2012, Community Bank's three business units reported the following performance results:

	Retail Banking		Business Banking		Credit Cards	
	2011	2012	2011	2012	2011	2012
Net income	$2,600,000	$2,912,000	$2,800,000	$2,940,000	$2,550,000	$2,499,000
Customer satisfaction	74	75.48	69	75.9	68	78.88

Required

1. Compute the bonus as a percent of salary earned by each business unit executive in 2012.
2. What factors might explain the differences between improvement rates for net income and those for customer satisfaction in the three units? Are increases in customer satisfaction likely to result in increased net income right away?
3. Community Bank's board of directors is concerned that the 2012 bonus awards may not actually reflect the executives' overall performance. In particular, it is concerned that executives can earn large bonuses by doing well on one performance dimension but underperforming on the other. What changes can it make to the bonus plan to prevent this from happening in the future? Explain briefly.

23-35 Ethics, manager's performance evaluation. (A. Spero, adapted) Hamilton Semiconductors manufactures specialized chips that sell for $25 each. Hamilton's manufacturing costs consist of variable cost of $3 per chip and fixed costs of $8,000,000. Hamilton also incurs $900,000 in fixed marketing costs each year.

Hamilton calculates operating income using absorption costing—that is, Hamilton calculates manufacturing cost per unit by dividing total manufacturing costs by actual production. Hamilton costs all units in inventory at this rate and expenses the costs in the income statement at the time when the units in inventory are sold. Next year, 2012, appears to be a difficult year for Hamilton. It expects to sell only 400,000 units. The demand for these chips fluctuates considerably, so Hamilton usually holds minimal inventory.

Required

1. Calculate Hamilton's operating income in 2012 (a) if Hamilton manufactures 400,000 units and (b) if Hamilton manufactures 500,000 units.
2. Would it be unethical for Randy Jones, the general manager of Hamilton Semiconductors, to produce more units than can be sold in order to show better operating results? Jones' compensation has a bonus component based on operating income. Explain your answer.
3. Would it be unethical for Jones to ask distributors to buy more product than they need? Hamilton follows the industry practice of booking sales when products are shipped to distributors. Explain your answer.

23-36 Ethics, levers of control. Monroe Moulding is a large manufacturer of wood picture frame moulding. The company operates distribution centers in Dallas and Philadelphia. The distribution centers cut frames to size (called "chops") and ship them to custom picture framers. Because of the exacting standards and natural flaws of wood picture frame moulding, the company typically produces a large amount of waste in cutting chops. In recent years, the company's average yield has been 76% of length moulding. The remaining 24% is sent to a wood recycler. Monroe's performance-evaluation system pays its distribution center managers substantial bonuses if the company achieves annual budgeted profit numbers. In the last quarter of 2010, Frank Jessup, Monroe's controller, noted a significant increase in yield percentage of the Dallas distribution center, from 74% to 85%. This increase resulted in a 5% increase in the center's profits.

During a recent trip to the Dallas center, Jessup wandered into the moulding warehouse. He noticed that much of the scrap moulding was being returned to the inventory bins rather than being placed in the discard pile. Upon further inspection, he determined that the moulding was in fact unusable. When he asked one of the workers, he was told that the center's manager had directed workers to stop scrapping all but the very shortest pieces. This practice resulted in the center over-reporting both yield and ending inventory. The overstatement of Dallas inventory will have a significant impact on Monroe's financial statements.

1. What should Jessup do? You may want to refer to the *IMA Statement of Ethical Professional Practice*, p. 16.
2. Which lever of control is Monroe emphasizing? What changes, if any, should be made?

Collaborative Learning Problem

23-37 RI, EVA, Measurement alternatives, Goal congruence. Renewal Resorts, Inc., operates health spas in Ft. Meyers, Florida, Scottsdale, Arizona, and Monterey, California. The Ft. Meyers spa was the company's first, opened in 1986. The Scottsdale spa opened in 1999, and the Monterey spa opened in 2008. Renewal Resorts has previously evaluated divisions based on residual income (RI), but the company is considering changing to an economic value added (EVA) approach. All spas are assumed to face similar risks. Data for 2012 follow:

	A	B	C	D	E
		Ft. Meyers Spa	**Scottsdale Spa**	**Monterey Spa**	**Total**
1					
2	Revenues	$4,100,000	$4,380,000	$3,230,000	$11,710,000
3	Variable costs	1,600,000	1,630,000	955,000	4,185,000
4	Fixed costs	1,280,000	1,560,000	980,000	3,820,000
5	Operating income	1,220,000	1,190,000	1,295,000	3,705,000
6	Interest costs on long-term debt at 8%	368,000	416,000	440,000	1,224,000
5	Income before taxes at 35%	852,000	774,000	855,000	2,481,000
6	Net income	553,800	503,100	555,750	1,612,650
7					
8	Net book value at 2012 year-end:				
9	Current assets	$1,280,000	$ 850,000	$ 600,000	$ 2,730,000
10	Long-term assets	4,875,000	5,462,000	6,835,000	17,172,000
11	Total assets	6,155,000	6,312,000	7,435,000	19,902,000
12	Current liabilities	330,000	265,000	84,000	679,000
13	Long-term debt	4,600,000	5,200,000	5,500,000	15,300,000
14	Stockholders' equity	1,225,000	847,000	1,851,000	3,923,000
15	Total liabilities and stockholders' equity	6,155,000	6,312,000	7,435,000	19,902,000
16					
17	Market value of debt	$4,600,000	$5,200,000	$5,500,000	$15,300,000
18	Market value of equity	2,400,000	2,660,000	2,590,000	7,650,000
19	Cost of equity capital				17%
20	Required rate of return				11%
21	Accumulated depreciation on long-term assets	2,200,000	1,510,000	220,000	

Required

1. Calculate RI for each of the spas based on operating income and using total assets as the measure of investment. Suppose that the Ft. Meyers spa is considering adding a new group of saunas from Finland that will cost $225,000. The saunas are expected to bring in operating income of $22,000. What effect would this project have on the RI of the Ft. Meyers spa? Based on RI, would the Ft. Meyers manager accept or reject this project? Why? Without resorting to calculations, would the other managers accept or reject the project? Why?
2. Why might Renewal Resorts want to use EVA instead of RI for evaluating the performance of the three spas?
3. Refer back to the original data. Calculate the WACC for Renewal Resorts.
4. Refer back to the original data. Calculate EVA for each of the spas, using net book value of long-term assets. Calculate EVA again, this time using gross book value of long-term assets. Comment on the differences between the two methods.
5. How is goal congruence affected by the selection of asset measurement method?

Appendix A

Notes on Compound Interest and Interest Tables

Interest is the cost of using money. It is the rental charge for funds, just as renting a building and equipment entails a rental charge. When the funds are used for a period of time, it is necessary to recognize interest as a cost of using the borrowed ("rented") funds. This requirement applies even if the funds represent ownership capital and if interest does not entail an outlay of cash. Why must interest be considered? Because the selection of one alternative automatically commits a given amount of funds that could otherwise be invested in some other alternative.

Interest is generally important, even when short-term projects are under consideration. Interest looms correspondingly larger when long-run plans are studied. The rate of interest has significant enough impact to influence decisions regarding borrowing and investing funds. For example, $100,000 invested now and compounded annually for 10 years at 8% will accumulate to $215,900; at 20%, the $100,000 will accumulate to $619,200.

Interest Tables

Many computer programs and pocket calculators are available that handle computations involving the time value of money. You may also turn to the following four basic tables to compute interest.

Table 1—Future Amount of $1

Table 1 shows how much $1 invested now will accumulate in a given number of periods at a given compounded interest rate per period. Consider investing $1,000 now for three years at 8% compound interest. A tabular presentation of how this $1,000 would accumulate to $1,259.70 follows:

Year	Interest per Year	Cumulative Interest Called Compound Interest	Total at End of Year
0	$ —	$ —	$1,000.00
1	80.00 (0.08 × $1,000)	80.00	1,080.00
2	86.40 (0.08 × $1,080)	166.40	1,166.40
3	93.30 (0.08 × $1,166.40)	259.70	1,259.70

This tabular presentation is a series of computations that could appear as follows, where S is the future amount and the subscripts 1, 2, and 3 indicate the number of time periods.

$$S_1 = \$1,000(1.08)^1 = \$1,080$$

$$S_2 = \$1,080(1.08) = \$1,000(1.08)^2 = \$1,166.40$$

$$S_3 = \$1,166.40 \times (1.08) = \$1,000(1.08)^3 = \$1,259.70$$

The formula for the "amount of P", often called the "future value of P" or "future amount of P", can be written as follows:

$$S = P(1 + r)^n$$

S is the future value amount; P is the present value, r is the rate of interest; and n is the number of time periods.

When $P = \$1,000$, $n = 3$, $r = 0.08$, $S = \$1,000(1 + .08)^3 = \$1,259.70$

Fortunately, tables make key computations readily available. A facility in selecting the *proper* table will minimize computations. Check the accuracy of the preceding answer using Table 1, page 842.

Table 2—Present Value of $1

In the previous example, if $1,000 compounded at 8% per year will accumulate to $1,259.70 in three years, then $1,000 must be the present value of $1,259.70 due at the end of three years. The formula for the present value can be derived by reversing the process of *accumulation* (finding the future amount) that we just finished.
If

$$S = P(1 + r)^n$$

then

$$P = \frac{S}{(1 + r)^n}$$

In our example, S = $1,259.70, n = 3, r = 0.08, so

$$P = \frac{\$1,259.70}{(1.08)^3} = \$1,000$$

Use Table 2, page 843, to check this calculation.

When accumulating, we advance or roll forward in time. The difference between our original amount and our accumulated amount is called *compound interest*. When discounting, we retreat or roll back in time. The difference between the future amount and the present value is called *compound discount*. Note the following formulas:

$$\text{Compound interest} = P[(1 + r)^n - 1]$$

In our example, P = $1,000, n = 3, r = 0.08, so

$$\text{Compound interest} = \$1,000\,[(1.08)^3 - 1] = \$259.70$$

$$\text{Compound discount} = S\left[1 - \frac{1}{(1 + r)^n}\right]$$

In our example, S = $1,259.70, n = 3, r = 0.08, so

$$\text{Compound discount} = \$1,259.70\left[1 - \frac{1}{(1.08)^3}\right] = \$259.70$$

Table 3—Amount of Annuity of $1

An (ordinary) *annuity* is a series of equal payments (receipts) to be paid (or received) at the end of successive periods of equal length. Assume that $1,000 is invested at the end of each of three years at 8%:

End of Year			Amount
1st payment	$1,000.00 ⟶	$1,080.00 ⟶	$1,166.40, which is $1,000(1.08)²
2nd payment		$1,000.00 ⟶	1,080.00, which is $1,000(1.08)¹
3rd payment			1,000.00
Accumulation (future amount)			$3,246.40

The preceding arithmetic may be expressed algebraically as the amount of an ordinary annuity of $1,000 for 3 years = $1,000(1 + r)² + $1,000(1 + r)¹ + $1,000.

We can develop the general formula for S_n, the amount of an ordinary annuity of $1, by using the preceding example as a basis where n = 3 and r = 0.08:

1.
$$S_3 = 1 + (1 + r)^1 + (1 + r)^2$$

2. Substitute:

$$S_3 = 1 + (1.08)^1 + (1.08)^2$$

3. Multiply (2) by $(1 + r)$:

$$(1.08)S_3 = (1.08)^1 + (1.08)^2 + (1.08)^3$$

4. Subtract (2) from (3): Note that all terms on the right-hand side are removed except $(1.08)^3$ in equation (3) and 1 in equation (2).

$$1.08S_3 - S_3 = (1.08)^3 - 1$$

5. Factor (4):

$$S_3(1.08 - 1) = (1.08)^3 - 1$$

6. Divide (5) by $(1.08 - 1)$:

$$S_3 = \frac{(1.08)^3 - 1}{1.08 - 1} = \frac{(1.08)^3 - 1}{.08} = \frac{0.2597}{0.08} = 3.246$$

7. The general formula for the amount of an ordinary annuity of $1 becomes:

$$S_n = \frac{(1 + r)^n - 1}{r} \text{ or } \frac{\text{Compound interest}}{\text{Rate}}$$

This formula is the basis for Table 3, page 844. Check the answer in the table.

Table 4—Present Value of an Ordinary Annuity of $1

Using the same example as for Table 3, we can show how the formula of P_n, *the present value of an ordinary annuity*, is developed.

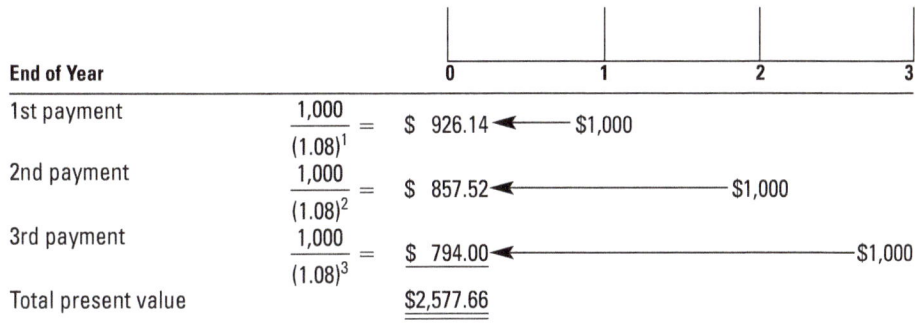

End of Year		0	1	2	3
1st payment	$\dfrac{1{,}000}{(1.08)^1}$ =	$ 926.14 ◄——— $1,000			
2nd payment	$\dfrac{1{,}000}{(1.08)^2}$ =	$ 857.52 ◄———————— $1,000			
3rd payment	$\dfrac{1{,}000}{(1.08)^3}$ =	$ 794.00 ◄———————————— $1,000			
Total present value		$2,577.66			

We can develop the general formula for P_n by using the preceding example as a basis where $n = 3$ and $r = 0.08$:

1.
$$P_3 = \frac{1}{1 + r} + \frac{1}{(1 + r)^2} + \frac{1}{(1 + r)^3}$$

2. Substitute:
$$P_3 = \frac{1}{1.08} + \frac{1}{(1.08)^2} + \frac{1}{(1.08)^3}$$

3. Multiply by $\frac{1}{1.08}$:
$$P_3\frac{1}{1.08} = \frac{1}{(1.08)^2} + \frac{1}{(1.08)^3} + \frac{1}{(1.08)^4}$$

4. Subtract (3) from (2):
$$P_3 - P_3\frac{1}{1.08} = \frac{1}{1.08} - \frac{1}{(1.08)^4}$$

5. Factor (4):
$$P_3\left(1 - \frac{1}{(1.08)}\right) = \frac{1}{1.08}\left[1 - \frac{1}{(1.08)^3}\right]$$

6. or
$$P_3\left(\frac{.08}{1.08}\right) = \frac{1}{1.08}\left[1 - \frac{1}{(1.08)^3}\right]$$

7. Multiply by $\frac{1.08}{.08}$:
$$P_3 = \frac{1}{.08}\left[1 - \frac{1}{(1.08)^3}\right] = \frac{.2062}{.08} = 2.577$$

The general formula for the present value of an annuity of $1.00 is as follows:

$$P_n = \frac{1}{r}\left[1 - \frac{1}{(1 + r)^n}\right] = \frac{\text{Compound discount}}{\text{Rate}}$$

The formula is the basis for Table 4, page 845. Check the answer in the table. The present value tables, Tables 2 and 4, are used most frequently in capital budgeting.

The tables for annuities are not essential. With Tables 1 and 2, compound interest and compound discount can readily be computed. It is simply a matter of dividing either of these by the rate to get values equivalent to those shown in Tables 3 and 4.

Table 1

Compound Amount of $1.00 (The Future Value of $1.00)

$S = P(1 + i)^n$. In this table $P = \$1.00$

Periods	2%	4%	6%	8%	10%	12%	14%	16%	18%	20%	22%	24%	26%	28%	30%	32%	40%	Periods
1	1.020	1.040	1.060	1.080	1.100	1.120	1.140	1.160	1.180	1.200	1.220	1.240	1.260	1.280	1.300	1.320	1.400	1
2	1.040	1.082	1.124	1.166	1.210	1.254	1.300	1.346	1.392	1.440	1.488	1.538	1.588	1.638	1.690	1.742	1.960	2
3	1.061	1.125	1.191	1.260	1.331	1.405	1.482	1.561	1.643	1.728	1.816	1.907	2.000	2.097	2.197	2.300	2.744	3
4	1.082	1.170	1.262	1.360	1.464	1.574	1.689	1.811	1.939	2.074	2.215	2.364	2.520	2.684	2.856	3.036	3.842	4
5	1.104	1.217	1.338	1.469	1.611	1.762	1.925	2.100	2.288	2.488	2.703	2.932	3.176	3.436	3.713	4.007	5.378	5
6	1.126	1.265	1.419	1.587	1.772	1.974	2.195	2.436	2.700	2.986	3.297	3.635	4.002	4.398	4.827	5.290	7.530	6
7	1.149	1.316	1.504	1.714	1.949	2.211	2.502	2.826	3.185	3.583	4.023	4.508	5.042	5.629	6.275	6.983	10.541	7
8	1.172	1.369	1.594	1.851	2.144	2.476	2.853	3.278	3.759	4.300	4.908	5.590	6.353	7.206	8.157	9.217	14.758	8
9	1.195	1.423	1.689	1.999	2.358	2.773	3.252	3.803	4.435	5.160	5.987	6.931	8.005	9.223	10.604	12.166	20.661	9
10	1.219	1.480	1.791	2.159	2.594	3.106	3.707	4.411	5.234	6.192	7.305	8.594	10.086	11.806	13.786	16.060	28.925	10
11	1.243	1.539	1.898	2.332	2.853	3.479	4.226	5.117	6.176	7.430	8.912	10.657	12.708	15.112	17.922	21.199	40.496	11
12	1.268	1.601	2.012	2.518	3.138	3.896	4.818	5.936	7.288	8.916	10.872	13.215	16.012	19.343	23.298	27.983	56.694	12
13	1.294	1.665	2.133	2.720	3.452	4.363	5.492	6.886	8.599	10.699	13.264	16.386	20.175	24.759	30.288	36.937	79.371	13
14	1.319	1.732	2.261	2.937	3.797	4.887	6.261	7.988	10.147	12.839	16.182	20.319	25.421	31.691	39.374	48.757	111.120	14
15	1.346	1.801	2.397	3.172	4.177	5.474	7.138	9.266	11.974	15.407	19.742	25.196	32.030	40.565	51.186	64.359	155.568	15
16	1.373	1.873	2.540	3.426	4.595	6.130	8.137	10.748	14.129	18.488	24.086	31.243	40.358	51.923	66.542	84.954	217.795	16
17	1.400	1.948	2.693	3.700	5.054	6.866	9.276	12.468	16.672	22.186	29.384	38.741	50.851	66.461	86.504	112.139	304.913	17
18	1.428	2.026	2.854	3.996	5.560	7.690	10.575	14.463	19.673	26.623	35.849	48.039	64.072	85.071	112.455	148.024	426.879	18
19	1.457	2.107	3.026	4.316	6.116	8.613	12.056	16.777	23.214	31.948	43.736	59.568	80.731	108.890	146.192	195.391	597.630	19
20	1.486	2.191	3.207	4.661	6.727	9.646	13.743	19.461	27.393	38.338	53.358	73.864	101.721	139.380	190.050	257.916	836.683	20
21	1.516	2.279	3.400	5.034	7.400	10.804	15.668	22.574	32.324	46.005	65.096	91.592	128.169	178.406	247.065	340.449	1171.356	21
22	1.546	2.370	3.604	5.437	8.140	12.100	17.861	26.186	38.142	55.206	79.418	113.574	161.492	228.360	321.184	449.393	1639.898	22
23	1.577	2.465	3.820	5.871	8.954	13.552	20.362	30.376	45.008	66.247	96.889	140.831	203.480	292.300	417.539	593.199	2295.857	23
24	1.608	2.563	4.049	6.341	9.850	15.179	23.212	35.236	53.109	79.497	118.205	174.631	256.385	374.144	542.801	783.023	3214.200	24
25	1.641	2.666	4.292	6.848	10.835	17.000	26.462	40.874	62.669	95.396	144.210	216.542	323.045	478.905	705.641	1033.590	4499.880	25
26	1.673	2.772	4.549	7.396	11.918	19.040	30.167	47.414	73.949	114.475	175.936	268.512	407.037	612.998	917.333	1364.339	6299.831	26
27	1.707	2.883	4.822	7.988	13.110	21.325	34.390	55.000	87.260	137.371	214.642	332.955	512.867	784.638	1192.533	1800.927	8819.764	27
28	1.741	2.999	5.112	8.627	14.421	23.884	39.204	63.800	102.967	164.845	261.864	412.864	646.212	1004.336	1550.293	2377.224	12347.670	28
29	1.776	3.119	5.418	9.317	15.863	26.750	44.693	74.009	121.501	197.814	319.474	511.952	814.228	1285.550	2015.381	3137.935	17286.737	29
30	1.811	3.243	5.743	10.063	17.449	29.960	50.950	85.850	143.371	237.376	389.758	634.820	1025.927	1645.505	2619.996	4142.075	24201.432	30
35	2.000	3.946	7.686	14.785	28.102	52.800	98.100	180.314	327.997	590.668	1053.402	1861.054	3258.135	5653.911	9727.860	16599.217	130161.112	35
40	2.208	4.801	10.286	21.725	45.259	93.051	188.884	378.721	750.378	1469.772	2847.038	5455.913	10347.175	19426.689	36118.865	66520.767	700037.697	40

Table 2 (*Place a clip on this page for easy reference.*)

Present Value of $1.00

$$P = \frac{S}{(1 + r)^n}.$$ In this table $S = \$1.00$.

Periods	2%	4%	6%	8%	10%	12%	14%	16%	18%	20%	22%	24%	26%	28%	30%	32%	40%	Periods
1	0.980	0.962	0.943	0.926	0.909	0.893	0.877	0.862	0.847	0.833	0.820	0.806	0.794	0.781	0.769	0.758	0.714	1
2	0.961	0.925	0.890	0.857	0.826	0.797	0.769	0.743	0.718	0.694	0.672	0.650	0.630	0.610	0.592	0.574	0.510	2
3	0.942	0.889	0.840	0.794	0.751	0.712	0.675	0.641	0.609	0.579	0.551	0.524	0.500	0.477	0.455	0.435	0.364	3
4	0.924	0.855	0.792	0.735	0.683	0.636	0.592	0.552	0.516	0.482	0.451	0.423	0.397	0.373	0.350	0.329	0.260	4
5	0.906	0.822	0.747	0.681	0.621	0.567	0.519	0.476	0.437	0.402	0.370	0.341	0.315	0.291	0.269	0.250	0.186	5
6	0.888	0.790	0.705	0.630	0.564	0.507	0.456	0.410	0.370	0.335	0.303	0.275	0.250	0.227	0.207	0.189	0.133	6
7	0.871	0.760	0.665	0.583	0.513	0.452	0.400	0.354	0.314	0.279	0.249	0.222	0.198	0.178	0.159	0.143	0.095	7
8	0.853	0.731	0.627	0.540	0.467	0.404	0.351	0.305	0.266	0.233	0.204	0.179	0.157	0.139	0.123	0.108	0.068	8
9	0.837	0.703	0.592	0.500	0.424	0.361	0.308	0.263	0.225	0.194	0.167	0.144	0.125	0.108	0.094	0.082	0.048	9
10	0.820	0.676	0.558	0.463	0.386	0.322	0.270	0.227	0.191	0.162	0.137	0.116	0.099	0.085	0.073	0.062	0.035	10
11	0.804	0.650	0.527	0.429	0.350	0.287	0.237	0.195	0.162	0.135	0.112	0.094	0.079	0.066	0.056	0.047	0.025	11
12	0.788	0.625	0.497	0.397	0.319	0.257	0.208	0.168	0.137	0.112	0.092	0.076	0.062	0.052	0.043	0.036	0.018	12
13	0.773	0.601	0.469	0.368	0.290	0.229	0.182	0.145	0.116	0.093	0.075	0.061	0.050	0.040	0.033	0.027	0.013	13
14	0.758	0.577	0.442	0.340	0.263	0.205	0.160	0.125	0.099	0.078	0.062	0.049	0.039	0.032	0.025	0.021	0.009	14
15	0.743	0.555	0.417	0.315	0.239	0.183	0.140	0.108	0.084	0.065	0.051	0.040	0.031	0.025	0.020	0.016	0.006	15
16	0.728	0.534	0.394	0.292	0.218	0.163	0.123	0.093	0.071	0.054	0.042	0.032	0.025	0.019	0.015	0.012	0.005	16
17	0.714	0.513	0.371	0.270	0.198	0.146	0.108	0.080	0.060	0.045	0.034	0.026	0.020	0.015	0.012	0.009	0.003	17
18	0.700	0.494	0.350	0.250	0.180	0.130	0.095	0.069	0.051	0.038	0.028	0.021	0.016	0.012	0.009	0.007	0.002	18
19	0.686	0.475	0.331	0.232	0.164	0.116	0.083	0.060	0.043	0.031	0.023	0.017	0.012	0.009	0.007	0.005	0.002	19
20	0.673	0.456	0.312	0.215	0.149	0.104	0.073	0.051	0.037	0.026	0.019	0.014	0.010	0.007	0.005	0.004	0.001	20
21	0.660	0.439	0.294	0.199	0.135	0.093	0.064	0.044	0.031	0.022	0.015	0.011	0.008	0.006	0.004	0.003	0.001	21
22	0.647	0.422	0.278	0.184	0.123	0.083	0.056	0.038	0.026	0.018	0.013	0.009	0.006	0.004	0.003	0.002	0.001	22
23	0.634	0.406	0.262	0.170	0.112	0.074	0.049	0.033	0.022	0.015	0.010	0.007	0.005	0.003	0.002	0.002	0.000	23
24	0.622	0.390	0.247	0.158	0.102	0.066	0.043	0.028	0.019	0.013	0.008	0.006	0.004	0.003	0.002	0.001	0.000	24
25	0.610	0.375	0.233	0.146	0.092	0.059	0.038	0.024	0.016	0.010	0.007	0.005	0.003	0.002	0.001	0.001	0.000	25
26	0.598	0.361	0.220	0.135	0.084	0.053	0.033	0.021	0.014	0.009	0.006	0.004	0.002	0.002	0.001	0.001	0.000	26
27	0.586	0.347	0.207	0.125	0.076	0.047	0.029	0.018	0.011	0.007	0.005	0.003	0.002	0.001	0.001	0.001	0.000	27
28	0.574	0.333	0.196	0.116	0.069	0.042	0.026	0.016	0.010	0.006	0.004	0.002	0.002	0.001	0.001	0.000	0.000	28
29	0.563	0.321	0.185	0.107	0.063	0.037	0.022	0.014	0.008	0.005	0.003	0.002	0.001	0.001	0.000	0.000	0.000	29
30	0.552	0.308	0.174	0.099	0.057	0.033	0.020	0.012	0.007	0.004	0.003	0.002	0.001	0.001	0.000	0.000	0.000	30
35	0.500	0.253	0.130	0.068	0.036	0.019	0.010	0.006	0.003	0.002	0.001	0.001	0.000	0.000	0.000	0.000	0.000	35
40	0.453	0.208	0.097	0.046	0.022	0.011	0.005	0.003	0.001	0.001	0.000	0.000	0.000	0.000	0.000	0.000	0.000	40

Table 3
Compound Amount of Annuity of $1.00 in Arrears* (Future Value of Annuity)

$$S_n = \frac{(1 + r)^n - 1}{r}$$

Periods	2%	4%	6%	8%	10%	12%	14%	16%	18%	20%	22%	24%	26%	28%	30%	32%	40%	Periods
1	1.000	1.000	1.000	1.000	1.000	1.000	1.000	1.000	1.000	1.000	1.000	1.000	1.000	1.000	1.000	1.000	1.000	1
2	2.020	2.040	2.060	2.080	2.100	2.120	2.140	2.160	2.180	2.200	2.220	2.240	2.260	2.280	2.300	2.320	2.400	2
3	3.060	3.122	3.184	3.246	3.310	3.374	3.440	3.506	3.572	3.640	3.708	3.778	3.848	3.918	3.990	4.062	4.360	3
4	4.122	4.246	4.375	4.506	4.641	4.779	4.921	5.066	5.215	5.368	5.524	5.684	5.848	6.016	6.187	6.362	7.104	4
5	5.204	5.416	5.637	5.867	6.105	6.353	6.610	6.877	7.154	7.442	7.740	8.048	8.368	8.700	9.043	9.398	10.946	5
6	6.308	6.633	6.975	7.336	7.716	8.115	8.536	8.977	9.442	9.930	10.442	10.980	11.544	12.136	12.756	13.406	16.324	6
7	7.434	7.898	8.394	8.923	9.487	10.089	10.730	11.414	12.142	12.916	13.740	14.615	15.546	16.534	17.583	18.696	23.853	7
8	8.583	9.214	9.897	10.637	11.436	12.300	13.233	14.240	15.327	16.499	17.762	19.123	20.588	22.163	23.858	25.678	34.395	8
9	9.755	10.583	11.491	12.488	13.579	14.776	16.085	17.519	19.086	20.799	22.670	24.712	26.940	29.369	32.015	34.895	49.153	9
10	10.950	12.006	13.181	14.487	15.937	17.549	19.337	21.321	23.521	25.959	28.657	31.643	34.945	38.593	42.619	47.062	69.814	10
11	12.169	13.486	14.972	16.645	18.531	20.655	23.045	25.733	28.755	32.150	35.962	40.238	45.031	50.398	56.405	63.122	98.739	11
12	13.412	15.026	16.870	18.977	21.384	24.133	27.271	30.850	34.931	39.581	44.874	50.895	57.739	65.510	74.327	84.320	139.235	12
13	14.680	16.627	18.882	21.495	24.523	28.029	32.089	36.786	42.219	48.497	55.746	64.110	73.751	84.853	97.625	112.303	195.929	13
14	15.974	18.292	21.015	24.215	27.975	32.393	37.581	43.672	50.818	59.196	69.010	80.496	93.926	109.612	127.913	149.240	275.300	14
15	17.293	20.024	23.276	27.152	31.772	37.280	43.842	51.660	60.965	72.035	85.192	100.815	119.347	141.303	167.286	197.997	386.420	15
16	18.639	21.825	25.673	30.324	35.950	42.753	50.980	60.925	72.939	87.442	104.935	126.011	151.377	181.868	218.472	262.356	541.988	16
17	20.012	23.698	28.213	33.750	40.545	48.884	59.118	71.673	87.068	105.931	129.020	157.253	191.735	233.791	285.014	347.309	759.784	17
18	21.412	25.645	30.906	37.450	45.599	55.750	68.394	84.141	103.740	128.117	158.405	195.994	242.585	300.252	371.518	459.449	1064.697	18
19	22.841	27.671	33.760	41.446	51.159	63.440	78.969	98.603	123.414	154.740	194.254	244.033	306.658	385.323	483.973	607.472	1491.576	19
20	24.297	29.778	36.786	45.762	57.275	72.052	91.025	115.380	146.628	186.688	237.989	303.601	387.389	494.213	630.165	802.863	2089.206	20
21	25.783	31.969	39.993	50.423	64.002	81.699	104.768	134.841	174.021	225.026	291.347	377.465	489.110	633.593	820.215	1060.779	2925.889	21
22	27.299	34.248	43.392	55.457	71.403	92.503	120.436	157.415	206.345	271.031	356.443	469.056	617.278	811.999	1067.280	1401.229	4097.245	22
23	28.845	36.618	46.996	60.893	79.543	104.603	138.297	183.601	244.487	326.237	435.861	582.630	778.771	1040.358	1388.464	1850.622	5737.142	23
24	30.422	39.083	50.816	66.765	88.497	118.155	158.659	213.978	289.494	392.484	532.750	723.461	982.251	1332.659	1806.003	2443.821	8032.999	24
25	32.030	41.646	54.865	73.106	98.347	133.334	181.871	249.214	342.603	471.981	650.955	898.092	1238.636	1706.803	2348.803	3226.844	11247.199	25
26	33.671	44.312	59.156	79.954	109.182	150.334	208.333	290.088	405.272	567.377	795.165	1114.634	1561.682	2185.708	3054.444	4260.434	15747.079	26
27	35.344	47.084	63.706	87.351	121.100	169.374	238.499	337.502	479.221	681.853	971.102	1383.146	1968.719	2798.706	3971.778	5624.772	22046.910	27
28	37.051	49.968	68.528	95.339	134.210	190.699	272.889	392.503	566.481	819.223	1185.744	1716.101	2481.586	3583.344	5164.311	7425.699	30866.674	28
29	38.792	52.966	73.640	103.966	148.631	214.583	312.094	456.303	669.447	984.068	1447.608	2128.965	3127.798	4587.680	6714.604	9802.923	43214.343	29
30	40.568	56.085	79.058	113.263	164.494	241.333	356.787	530.312	790.948	1181.882	1767.081	2640.916	3942.026	5873.231	8729.985	12940.859	60501.081	30
35	49.994	73.652	111.435	172.317	271.024	431.663	693.573	1120.713	1816.652	2948.341	4783.645	7750.225	12527.442	20188.966	32422.868	51869.427	325400.279	35
40	60.402	95.026	154.762	259.057	442.593	767.091	1342.025	2360.757	4163.213	7343.858	12936.535	22728.803	39792.982	69377.460	120392.883	207874.272	1750091.741	40

*Payments (or receipts) at the end of each period.

Table 4 (Place a clip on this page for easy reference.)

Present Value of Annuity $1.00 in Arrears*

$$P_n = \frac{1}{r}\left[1 - \frac{1}{(1+r)^n}\right]$$

Periods	2%	4%	6%	8%	10%	12%	14%	16%	18%	20%	22%	24%	26%	28%	30%	32%	40%	Periods
1	0.980	0.962	0.943	0.926	0.909	0.893	0.877	0.862	0.847	0.833	0.820	0.806	0.794	0.781	0.769	0.758	0.714	1
2	1.942	1.886	1.833	1.783	1.736	1.690	1.647	1.605	1.566	1.528	1.492	1.457	1.424	1.392	1.361	1.331	1.224	2
3	2.884	2.775	2.673	2.577	2.487	2.402	2.322	2.246	2.174	2.106	2.042	1.981	1.923	1.868	1.816	1.766	1.589	3
4	3.808	3.630	3.465	3.312	3.170	3.037	2.914	2.798	2.690	2.589	2.494	2.404	2.320	2.241	2.166	2.096	1.849	4
5	4.713	4.452	4.212	3.993	3.791	3.605	3.433	3.274	3.127	2.991	2.864	2.745	2.635	2.532	2.436	2.345	2.035	5
6	5.601	5.242	4.917	4.623	4.355	4.111	3.889	3.685	3.498	3.326	3.167	3.020	2.885	2.759	2.643	2.534	2.168	6
7	6.472	6.002	5.582	5.206	4.868	4.564	4.288	4.039	3.812	3.605	3.416	3.242	3.083	2.937	2.802	2.677	2.263	7
8	7.325	6.733	6.210	5.747	5.335	4.968	4.639	4.344	4.078	3.837	3.619	3.421	3.241	3.076	2.925	2.786	2.331	8
9	8.162	7.435	6.802	6.247	5.759	5.328	4.946	4.607	4.303	4.031	3.786	3.566	3.366	3.184	3.019	2.868	2.379	9
10	8.983	8.111	7.360	6.710	6.145	5.650	5.216	4.833	4.494	4.192	3.923	3.682	3.465	3.269	3.092	2.930	2.414	10
11	9.787	8.760	7.887	7.139	6.495	5.938	5.453	5.029	4.656	4.327	4.035	3.776	3.543	3.335	3.147	2.978	2.438	11
12	10.575	9.385	8.384	7.536	6.814	6.194	5.660	5.197	4.793	4.439	4.127	3.851	3.606	3.387	3.190	3.013	2.456	12
13	11.348	9.986	8.853	7.904	7.103	6.424	5.842	5.342	4.910	4.533	4.203	3.912	3.656	3.427	3.223	3.040	2.469	13
14	12.106	10.563	9.295	8.244	7.367	6.628	6.002	5.468	5.008	4.611	4.265	3.962	3.695	3.459	3.249	3.061	2.478	14
15	12.849	11.118	9.712	8.559	7.606	6.811	6.142	5.575	5.092	4.675	4.315	4.001	3.726	3.483	3.268	3.076	2.484	15
16	13.578	11.652	10.106	8.851	7.824	6.974	6.265	5.668	5.162	4.730	4.357	4.033	3.751	3.503	3.283	3.088	2.489	16
17	14.292	12.166	10.477	9.122	8.022	7.120	6.373	5.749	5.222	4.775	4.391	4.059	3.771	3.518	3.295	3.097	2.492	17
18	14.992	12.659	10.828	9.372	8.201	7.250	6.467	5.818	5.273	4.812	4.419	4.080	3.786	3.529	3.304	3.104	2.494	18
19	15.678	13.134	11.158	9.604	8.365	7.366	6.550	5.877	5.316	4.843	4.442	4.097	3.799	3.539	3.311	3.109	2.496	19
20	16.351	13.590	11.470	9.818	8.514	7.469	6.623	5.929	5.353	4.870	4.460	4.110	3.808	3.546	3.316	3.113	2.497	20
21	17.011	14.029	11.764	10.017	8.649	7.562	6.687	5.973	5.384	4.891	4.476	4.121	3.816	3.551	3.320	3.116	2.498	21
22	17.658	14.451	12.042	10.201	8.772	7.645	6.743	6.011	5.410	4.909	4.488	4.130	3.822	3.556	3.323	3.118	2.498	22
23	18.292	14.857	12.303	10.371	8.883	7.718	6.792	6.044	5.432	4.925	4.499	4.137	3.827	3.559	3.325	3.120	2.499	23
24	18.914	15.247	12.550	10.529	8.985	7.784	6.835	6.073	5.451	4.937	4.507	4.143	3.831	3.562	3.327	3.121	2.499	24
25	19.523	15.622	12.783	10.675	9.077	7.843	6.873	6.097	5.467	4.948	4.514	4.147	3.834	3.564	3.329	3.122	2.499	25
26	20.121	15.983	13.003	10.810	9.161	7.896	6.906	6.118	5.480	4.956	4.520	4.151	3.837	3.566	3.330	3.123	2.500	26
27	20.707	16.330	13.211	10.935	9.237	7.943	6.935	6.136	5.492	4.964	4.524	4.154	3.839	3.567	3.331	3.123	2.500	27
28	21.281	16.663	13.406	11.051	9.307	7.984	6.961	6.152	5.502	4.970	4.528	4.157	3.840	3.568	3.331	3.124	2.500	28
29	21.844	16.984	13.591	11.158	9.370	8.022	6.983	6.166	5.510	4.975	4.531	4.159	3.841	3.569	3.332	3.124	2.500	29
30	22.396	17.292	13.765	11.258	9.427	8.055	7.003	6.177	5.517	4.979	4.534	4.160	3.842	3.569	3.332	3.124	2.500	30
35	24.999	18.665	14.498	11.655	9.644	8.176	7.070	6.215	5.539	4.992	4.541	4.164	3.845	3.571	3.333	3.125	2.500	35
40	27.355	19.793	15.046	11.925	9.779	8.244	7.105	6.233	5.548	4.997	4.544	4.166	3.846	3.571	3.333	3.125	2.500	40

*Payments (or receipts) at the end of each period.

Glossary

Abnormal spoilage. Spoilage that would not arise under efficient operating conditions; it is not inherent in a particular production process. (646)

Absorption costing. Method of inventory costing in which all variable manufacturing costs and all fixed manufacturing costs are included as inventoriable costs. (302)

Account analysis method. Approach to cost function estimation that classifies various cost accounts as variable, fixed, or mixed with respect to the identified level of activity. Typically, qualitative rather than quantitative analysis is used when making these cost-classification decisions. (347)

Accrual accounting rate of return (AARR) method. Capital budgeting method that divides an accrual accounting measure of average annual income of a project by an accrual accounting measure of its investment. See also *return on investment (ROI)*. (749)

Activity. An event, task, or unit of work with a specified purpose. (146)

Activity-based budgeting (ABB). Budgeting approach that focuses on the budgeted cost of the activities necessary to produce and sell products and services. (193)

Activity-based costing (ABC). Approach to costing that focuses on individual activities as the fundamental cost objects. It uses the costs of these activities as the basis for assigning costs to other cost objects such as products or services. (146)

Activity-based management (ABM). Method of management decision-making that uses activity-based costing information to improve customer satisfaction and profitability. (156)

Actual cost. Cost incurred (a historical or past cost), as distinguished from a budgeted or forecasted cost. (27)

Actual costing. A costing system that traces direct costs to a cost object by using the actual direct-cost rates times the actual quantities of the direct-cost inputs and allocates indirect costs based on the actual indirect-cost rates times the actual quantities of the cost allocation bases. (102)

Actual indirect-cost rate. Actual total indirect costs in a cost pool divided by the actual total quantity of the cost-allocation base for that cost pool. (110)

Adjusted allocation-rate approach. Restates all overhead entries in the general ledger and subsidiary ledgers using actual cost rates rather than budgeted cost rates. (118)

Allowable cost. Cost that the contract parties agree to include in the costs to be reimbursed. (559)

Appraisal costs. Costs incurred to detect which of the individual units of products do not conform to specifications. (673)

Artificial costs. See *complete reciprocated costs*. (554)

Autonomy. The degree of freedom to make decisions. (777)

Average cost. See *unit cost*. (35)

Average waiting time. The average amount of time that an order will wait in line before the machine is set up and the order is processed. (683)

Backflush costing. Costing system that omits recording some of the journal entries relating to the stages from purchase of direct material to the sale of finished goods. (719)

Balanced scorecard. A framework for implementing strategy that translates an organization's mission and strategy into a set of performance measures. (470)

Batch-level costs. The costs of activities related to a group of units of products or services rather than to each individual unit of product or service. (149)

Belief systems. Lever of control that articulates the mission, purpose, norms of behaviors, and core values of a company intended to inspire managers and other employees to do their best. (827)

Benchmarking. The continuous process of comparing the levels of performance in producing products and services and executing activities against the best levels of performance in competing companies or in companies having similar processes. (244)

Book value. The original cost minus accumulated depreciation of an asset. (410)

Bottleneck. An operation where the work to be performed approaches or exceeds the capacity available to do it. (682)

Boundary systems. Lever of control that describes standards of behavior and codes of conduct expected of all employees, especially actions that are off-limits. (826)

Breakeven point (BEP). Quantity of output sold at which total revenues equal total costs, that is where the operating income is zero. (68)

Budget. Quantitative expression of a proposed plan of action by management for a specified period and an aid to coordinating what needs to be done to implement that plan. (10)

Budgetary slack. The practice of underestimating budgeted revenues, or overestimating budgeted costs, to make budgeted targets more easily achievable. (201)

Budgeted cost. Predicted or forecasted cost (future cost) as distinguished from an actual or historical cost. (27)

Budgeted indirect-cost rate. Budgeted annual indirect costs in a cost pool divided by the budgeted annual quantity of the cost allocation base. (104)

Budgeted performance. Expected performance or a point of reference to compare actual results. (227)

Bundled product. A package of two or more products (or services) that is sold for a single price, but whose individual components may be sold as separate items at their own "stand-alone" prices. (561)

Business function costs. The sum of all costs (variable and fixed) in a particular business function of the value chain. (395)

Byproducts. Products from a joint production process that have low total sales values compared with the total sales value of the main product or of joint products. (578)

Capital budgeting. The making of long-run planning decisions for investments in projects. (739)

Carrying costs. Costs that arise while holding inventory of goods for sale. (704)

Cash budget. Schedule of expected cash receipts and disbursements. (207)

Cause-and-effect diagram. Diagram that identifies potential causes of defects. Four categories of potential causes of failure are human factors, methods and design factors, machine-related factors, and materials and components factors. Also called a *fishbone diagram*. (676)

Chief financial officer (CFO). Executive responsible for overseeing the financial operations of an organization. Also called *finance director*. (13)

Choice criterion. Objective that can be quantified in a decision model. (84)

Coefficient of determination (r^2). Measures the percentage of variation in a dependent variable explained by one or more independent variables. (367)

Collusive pricing. Companies in an industry conspire in their pricing and production decisions to achieve a price above the competitive price and so restrain trade. (452)

Common cost. Cost of operating a facility, activity, or like cost object that is shared by two or more users. (557)

Complete reciprocated costs. The support department's own costs plus any interdepartmental cost allocations. Also called the *artificial costs* of the support department. (554)

Composite unit. Hypothetical unit with weights based on the mix of individual units. (521)

Conference method. Approach to cost function estimation on the basis of analysis and opinions about costs and their drivers gathered from various departments of a company (purchasing, process engineering, manufacturing, employee relations, and so on). (346)

Conformance quality. Refers to the performance of a product or service relative to its design and product specifications. (672)

Constant. The component of total cost that, within the relevant range, does not vary with changes in the level of the activity. Also called *intercept*. (343)

Constant gross-margin percentage NRV method. Method that allocates joint costs to joint products in such a way that the overall gross-margin percentage is identical for the individual products. (584)

Constraint. A mathematical inequality or equality that must be satisfied by the variables in a mathematical model. (416)

Continuous budget. See *rolling budget*. (188)

Contribution income statement. Income statement that groups costs into variable costs and fixed costs to highlight the contribution margin. (65)

Contribution margin. Total revenues minus total variable costs. (64)

Contribution margin per unit. Selling price minus the variable cost per unit. (65)

Contribution margin percentage. Contribution margin per unit divided by selling price. Also called *contribution margin ratio*. (65)

Contribution margin ratio. See *contribution margin percentage*. (65)

Control. Taking actions that implement the planning decisions, deciding how to evaluate performance, and providing feedback and learning that will help future decision making. (10)

Control chart. Graph of a series of successive observations of a particular step, procedure, or operation taken at regular intervals of time. Each observation is plotted relative to specified ranges that represent the limits within which observations are expected to fall. (675)

Controllability. Degree of influence that a specific manager has over costs, revenues, or related items for which he or she is responsible. (200)

Controllable cost. Any cost that is primarily subject to the influence of a given responsibility center manager for a given period. (200)

Controller. The financial executive primarily responsible for management accounting and financial accounting. Also called *chief accounting officer*. (13)

Conversion costs. All manufacturing costs other than direct material costs. (43)

Cost. Resource sacrificed or forgone to achieve a specific objective. (27)

Cost accounting. Measures, analyzes, and reports financial and nonfinancial information relating to the costs of acquiring or using resources in an organization. It provides information for both management accounting and financial accounting. (4)

Cost Accounting Standards Board (CASB). Government agency that has the exclusive authority to make, put into effect, amend, and rescind cost accounting standards and interpretations thereof designed to achieve uniformity and consistency in regard to measurement, assignment, and allocation of costs to government contracts within the United States. (559)

Cost accumulation. Collection of cost data in some organized way by means of an accounting system. (28)

Cost allocation. Assignment of indirect costs to a particular cost object. (29)

Cost-allocation base. A factor that links in a systematic way an indirect cost or group of indirect costs to a cost object. (100)

Cost-application base. Cost-allocation base when the cost object is a job, product, or customer. (100)

Cost assignment. General term that encompasses both (1) tracing accumulated costs that have a direct relationship to a cost object and (2) allocating accumulated costs that have an indirect relationship to a cost object. (29)

Cost-benefit approach. Approach to decision-making and resource allocation based on a comparison of the expected benefits from attaining company goals and the expected costs. (12)

Cost center. Responsibility center where the manager is accountable for costs only. (199)

Cost driver. A variable, such as the level of activity or volume, that causally affects costs over a given time span. (32)

Cost estimation. The attempt to measure a past relationship based on data from past costs and the related level of an activity. (344)

Cost function. Mathematical description of how a cost changes with changes in the level of an activity relating to that cost. (341)

Cost hierarchy. Categorization of indirect costs into different cost pools on the basis of the different types of cost drivers, or cost-allocation bases, or different degrees of difficulty in determining cause-and-effect (or benefits received) relationships. (149)

Cost incurrence. Describes when a resource is consumed (or benefit forgone) to meet a specific objective. (442)

Cost leadership. Organization's ability to achieve lower costs relative to competitors through productivity and efficiency improvements, elimination of waste, and tight cost control. (468)

Cost management. The approaches and activities of managers to use resources to increase value to customers and to achieve organizational goals. (4)

Cost object. Anything for which a measurement of costs is desired. (27)

Cost of capital. See *required rate of return (RRR)*. (742)

Cost of goods manufactured. Cost of goods brought to completion, whether they were started before or during the current accounting period. (41)

Cost pool. A grouping of individual cost items. (100)

Cost predictions. Forecasts about future costs. (344)

Cost tracing. Describes the assignment of direct costs to a particular cost object. (28)

Costs of quality (COQ). Costs incurred to prevent, or the costs arising as a result of, the production of a low-quality product. (672)

Cost-volume-profit (CVP) analysis. Examines the behavior of total revenues, total costs, and operating income as changes occur in the units sold, the selling price, the variable cost per unit, or the fixed costs of a product. (63)

Cumulative average-time learning model. Learning curve model in which the cumulative average time per unit declines by a constant percentage each time the cumulative quantity of units produced doubles. (359)

Current cost. Asset measure based on the cost of purchasing an asset today identical to the one currently held, or the cost of purchasing an asset that provides services like the one currently held if an identical asset cannot be purchased. (815)

Customer-cost hierarchy. Hierarchy that categorizes costs related to customers into different cost pools on the basis of different types of cost drivers, or cost-allocation bases, or different degrees of difficulty in determining cause-and-effect or benefits-received relationships. (511)

Customer life-cycle costs. Focuses on the total costs incurred by a customer to acquire, use, maintain, and dispose of a product or service. (449)

Customer-profitability analysis. The reporting and analysis of revenues earned from customers and the costs incurred to earn those revenues. (510)

Customer-response time. Duration from the time a customer places an order for a product or service to the time the product or service is delivered to the customer. (681)

Customer service. Providing after-sale support to customers. (6)

Decentralization. The freedom for managers at lower levels of the organization to make decisions. (777)

Decision model. Formal method for making a choice, often involving both quantitative and qualitative analyses. (391)

Decision table. Summary of the alternative actions, events, outcomes, and probabilities of events in a decision model. (85)

Degree of operating leverage. Contribution margin divided by operating income at any given level of sales. (76)

Denominator level. The denominator in the budgeted fixed overhead rate computation. (266)

Denominator-level variance. See *production-volume variance*. (272)

Dependent variable. The cost to be predicted. (348)

Design of products and processes. The detailed planning and engineering of products and processes. (6)

Design quality. Refers to how closely the characteristics of a product or service meet the needs and wants of customers. (672)

Designed-in costs. See *locked-in costs*. (442)

Diagnostic control systems. Lever of control that monitors critical performance variables that help managers track progress toward achieving a company's strategic goals. Managers are held accountable for meeting these goals. (826)

Differential cost. Difference in total cost between two alternatives. (399)

Differential revenue. Difference in total revenue between two alternatives. (399)

Direct costing. See *variable costing*. (302)

Direct costs of a cost object. Costs related to the particular cost object that can be traced to that object in an economically feasible (cost-effective) way. (28)

Direct manufacturing labor costs. Include the compensation of all manufacturing labor that can be traced to the cost object (work in process and then finished goods) in an economically feasible way. (37)

Direct material costs. Acquisition costs of all materials that eventually become part of the cost object (work in process and then finished goods), and that can be traced to the cost object in an economically feasible way. (37)

Direct materials inventory. Direct materials in stock and awaiting use in the manufacturing process. (37)

Direct materials mix variance. The difference between (1) budgeted cost for actual mix of the actual total quantity of direct materials used and (2) budgeted cost of budgeted mix of the actual total quantity of direct materials used. (527)

Direct materials yield variance. The difference between (1) budgeted cost of direct materials based on the actual total quantity of direct materials used and (2) flexible-budget cost of direct materials based on the budgeted total quantity of direct materials allowed for the actual output produced. (527)

Direct method. Cost allocation method that allocates each support department's costs to operating departments only. (550)

Discount rate. See *required rate of return (RRR)*. (742)

Discounted cash flow (DCF) methods. Capital budgeting methods that measure all expected future cash inflows and outflows of a project as if they occurred at the present point in time. (741)

Discounted payback method. Capital budgeting method that calculates the amount of time required for the discounted expected future cash flows to recoup the net initial investment in a project. (748)

Discretionary costs. Arise from periodic (usually annual) decisions regarding the maximum amount to be incurred and have no measurable cause-and-effect relationship between output and resources used. (486)

Distribution. Delivering products or services to customers. (6)

Downsizing. An integrated approach of configuring processes, products, and people to match costs to the activities that need to be performed to operate effectively and efficiently in the present and future. Also called *rightsizing*. (487)

Downward demand spiral. Pricing context where prices are raised to spread capacity costs over a smaller number of output units. Continuing reduction in the demand for products that occurs when the prices of competitors' products are not met and, as demand drops further, higher and higher unit costs result in more and more reluctance to meet competitors' prices. (317)

Dual pricing. Approach to transfer pricing using two separate transfer-pricing methods to price each transfer from one subunit to another. (789)

Dual-rate method. Allocation method that classifies costs in each cost pool into two pools (a variable-cost pool and a fixed-cost pool) with each pool using a different cost-allocation base. (544)

Dumping. Under U.S. laws, it occurs when a non-U.S. company sells a product in the United States at a price below the market value in the country where it is produced, and this lower price materially injures or threatens to materially injure an industry in the United States. (452)

Dysfunctional decision making. See *suboptimal decision making*. (778)

Economic order quantity (EOQ). Decision model that calculates the optimal quantity of inventory to order under a set of assumptions. (704)

Economic value added (EVA®). After-tax operating income minus the (after-tax) weighted-average cost of capital multiplied by total assets minus current liabilities. (812)

Effectiveness. The degree to which a predetermined objective or target is met. (243)

Efficiency. The relative amount of inputs used to achieve a given output level. (243)

Efficiency variance. The difference between actual input quantity used and budgeted input quantity allowed for actual output, multiplied by budgeted price. Also called *usage variance*. (236)

Effort. Exertion toward achieving a goal. (776)

Engineered costs. Costs that result from a cause-and-effect relationship between the cost driver, output, and the (direct or indirect) resources used to produce that output. (486)

Equivalent units. Derived amount of output units that (a) takes the quantity of each input (factor of production) in

units completed and in incomplete units of work in process and (b) converts the quantity of input into the amount of completed output units that could be produced with that quantity of input. (611)

Event. A possible relevant occurrence in a decision model. (84)

Expected monetary value. See *expected value*. (85)

Expected value. Weighted average of the outcomes of a decision with the probability of each outcome serving as the weight. Also called *expected monetary value*. (85)

Experience curve. Function that measures the decline in cost per unit in various business functions of the value chain, such as manufacturing, marketing, distribution, and so on, as the amount of these activities increases. (358)

External failure costs. Costs incurred on defective products after they are shipped to customers. (673)

Facility-sustaining costs. The costs of activities that cannot be traced to individual products or services but support the organization as a whole. (149)

Factory overhead costs. See *indirect manufacturing costs*. (37)

Favorable variance. Variance that has the effect of increasing operating income relative to the budgeted amount. Denoted F. (229)

Finance director. See *chief financial officer (CFO)*. (13)

Financial accounting. Measures and records business transactions and provides financial statements that are based on generally accepted accounting principles. It focuses on reporting to external parties such as investors and banks. (3)

Financial budget. Part of the master budget that focuses on how operations and planned capital outlays affect cash. It is made up of the capital expenditures budget, the cash budget, the budgeted balance sheet, and the budgeted statement of cash flows. (189)

Financial planning models. Mathematical representations of the relationships among operating activities, financial activities, and other factors that affect the master budget. (197)

Finished goods inventory. Goods completed but not yet sold. (37)

First-in, first-out (FIFO) process-costing method. Method of process costing that assigns the cost of the previous accounting period's equivalent units in beginning work-in-process inventory to the first units completed and transferred out of the process, and assigns the cost of equivalent units worked on during the current period first to complete beginning inventory, next to start and complete new units, and finally to units in ending work-in-process inventory. (617)

Fixed cost. Cost that remains unchanged in total for a given time period, despite wide changes in the related level of total activity or volume. (30)

Fixed overhead flexible-budget variance. The difference between actual fixed overhead costs and fixed overhead costs in the flexible budget. (271)

Fixed overhead spending variance. Same as the fixed overhead flexible-budget variance. The difference between actual fixed overhead costs and fixed overhead costs in the flexible budget. (271)

Flexible budget. Budget developed using budgeted revenues and budgeted costs based on the actual output in the budget period. (230)

Flexible-budget variance. The difference between an actual result and the corresponding flexible-budget amount based on the actual output level in the budget period. (231)

Full costs of the product. The sum of all variable and fixed costs in all business functions of the value chain (R&D, design, production, marketing, distribution, and customer service). (395)

Goal congruence. Exists when individuals and groups work toward achieving the organization's goals. Managers working in their own best interest take actions that align with the overall goals of top management. (776)

Gross margin percentage. Gross margin divided by revenues. (82)

Growth component. Change in operating income attributable solely to the change in the quantity of output sold between one period and the next. (479)

High-low method. Method used to estimate a cost function that uses only the highest and lowest observed values of the cost driver within the relevant range and their respective costs. (350)

Homogeneous cost pool. Cost pool in which all the costs have the same or a similar cause-and-effect or benefits-received relationship with the cost-allocation base. (509)

Hurdle rate. See *required rate of return (RRR)*. (742)

Hybrid-costing system. Costing system that blends characteristics from both job-costing systems and process-costing systems. (626)

Idle time. Wages paid for unproductive time caused by lack of orders, machine breakdowns, material shortages, poor scheduling, and the like. (45)

Imputed costs. Costs recognized in particular situations but not incorporated in financial accounting records. (810)

Incongruent decision making. See *suboptimal decision making*. (778)

Incremental cost. Additional total cost incurred for an activity. (399)

Incremental cost-allocation method. Method that ranks the individual users of a cost object in the order of users most responsible for the common cost and then uses this ranking to allocate cost among those users. (557)

Incremental revenue. Additional total revenue from an activity. (399)

Incremental revenue-allocation method. Method that ranks individual products in a bundle according to criteria determined by management (for example, sales), and then uses this ranking to allocate bundled revenues to the individual products. (562)

Incremental unit-time learning model. Learning curve model in which the incremental time needed to produce the last unit declines by a constant percentage each time the cumulative quantity of units produced doubles. (360)

Independent variable. Level of activity or cost driver used to predict the dependent variable (costs) in a cost estimation or prediction model. (348)

Indirect costs of a cost object. Costs related to the particular cost object that cannot be traced to that object in an economically feasible (cost-effective) way. (28)

Indirect manufacturing costs. All manufacturing costs that are related to the cost object (work in process and then finished goods) but that cannot be traced to that cost object in an economically feasible way. Also called *manufacturing overhead costs* and *factory overhead costs*. (37)

Industrial engineering method. Approach to cost function estimation that analyzes the relationship between inputs and outputs in physical terms. Also called *work measurement method*. (346)

Inflation. The decline in the general purchasing power of the monetary unit, such as dollars. (762)

Input-price variance. See *price variance*. (236)

Insourcing. Process of producing goods or providing services within the organization rather than purchasing those same goods or services from outside vendors. (397)

Inspection point. Stage of the production process at which products are examined to determine whether they are acceptable or unacceptable units. (647)

Interactive control systems. Formal information systems that managers use to focus organization attention and learning on key strategic issues. (827)

Intercept. See *constant*. (343)

Intermediate product. Product transferred from one subunit to another subunit of an organization. This product may either be further worked on by the receiving subunit or sold to an external customer. (780)

Internal failure costs. Costs incurred on defective products before they are shipped to customers. (673)

Internal rate-of-return (IRR) method. Capital budgeting discounted cash flow (DCF) method that calculates the discount rate at which the present value of expected cash inflows from a project equals the present value of its expected cash outflows. (743)

Inventoriable costs. All costs of a product that are considered as assets in the balance sheet when they are incurred and that become cost of goods sold only when the product is sold. (37)

Inventory management. Planning, coordinating, and controlling activities related to the flow of inventory into, through, and out of an organization. (703)

Investment. Resources or assets used to generate income. (808)

Investment center. Responsibility center where the manager is accountable for investments, revenues, and costs. (199)

Job. A unit or multiple units of a distinct product or service. (100)

Job-cost record. Source document that records and accumulates all the costs assigned to a specific job, starting when work begins. Also called *job-cost sheet*. (104)

Job-cost sheet. See *job-cost record*. (104)

Job-costing system. Costing system in which the cost object is a unit or multiple units of a distinct product or service called a job. (100)

Joint costs. Costs of a production process that yields multiple products simultaneously. (577)

Joint products. Two or more products that have high total sales values compared with the total sales values of other products yielded by a joint production process. (578)

Just-in-time (JIT) production. Demand-pull manufacturing system in which each component in a production line is produced as soon as, and only when, needed by the next step in the production line. Also called *lean production.* (715)

Just-in-time (JIT) purchasing. The purchase of materials (or goods) so that they are delivered just as needed for production (or sales). (711)

Kaizen budgeting. Budgetary approach that explicitly incorporates continuous improvement anticipated during the budget period into the budget numbers. (203)

Labor-time sheet. Source document that contains information about the amount of labor time used for a specific job in a specific department. (106)

Lean accounting. Costing method that supports creating value for the customer by costing the entire value stream, not individual products or departments, thereby eliminating waste in the accounting process. (727)

Lean production. See *just-in-time (JIT) production.* (715)

Learning. Involves managers examining past performance and systematically exploring alternative ways to make better-informed decisions and plans in the future. (10)

Learning curve. Function that measures how labor-hours per unit decline as units of production increase because workers are learning and becoming better at their jobs. (358)

Life-cycle budgeting. Budget that estimates the revenues and business function costs of the value chain attributable to each product from initial R&D to final customer service and support. (448)

Life-cycle costing. System that tracks and accumulates business function costs of the value chain attributable to each product from initial R&D to final customer service and support. (448)

Line management. Managers (for example, in production, marketing, or distribution) who are directly responsible for attaining the goals of the organization. (13)

Linear cost function. Cost function in which the graph of total costs versus the level of a single activity related to that cost is a straight line within the relevant range. (342)

Linear programming (LP). Optimization technique used to maximize an objective function (for example, contribution margin of a mix of products), when there are multiple constraints. (417)

Locked-in costs. Costs that have not yet been incurred but, based on decisions that have already been made, will be incurred in the future. Also called *designed-in costs.* (442)

Main product. Product from a joint production process that has a high total sales value compared with the total sales values of all other products of the joint production process. (578)

Make-or-buy decisions. Decisions about whether a producer of goods or services will insource (produce goods or services within the firm) or outsource (purchase them from outside vendors). (397)

Management accounting. Measures, analyzes, and reports financial and nonfinancial information that helps managers make decisions to fulfill the goals of an organization. It focuses on internal reporting. (4)

Management by exception. Practice of focusing management attention on areas not operating as expected and giving less attention to areas operating as expected. (227)

Management control system. Means of gathering and using information to aid and coordinate the planning and control decisions throughout an organization and to guide the behavior of its managers and employees. (775)

Manufacturing cells. Grouping of all the different types of equipment used to make a given product. (715)

Manufacturing cycle efficiency (MCE). Value-added manufacturing time divided by manufacturing cycle time. (681)

Manufacturing cycle time. See *manufacturing lead time.* (681)

Manufacturing lead time. Duration between the time an order is received by manufacturing to the time a finished good is produced. Also called *manufacturing cycle time.* (681)

Manufacturing overhead allocated. Amount of manufacturing overhead costs allocated to individual jobs, products, or services based on the budgeted rate multiplied by the actual quantity used of the cost-allocation base. Also called *manufacturing overhead applied.* (113)

Manufacturing overhead applied. See *manufacturing overhead allocated.* (113)

Manufacturing overhead costs. See *indirect manufacturing costs.* (37)

Manufacturing-sector companies. Companies that purchase materials and components and convert them into various finished goods. (36)

Margin of safety. Amount by which budgeted (or actual) revenues exceed breakeven revenues. (74)

Marketing. Promoting and selling products or services to customers or prospective customers. (6)

Market-share variance. The difference in budgeted contribution margin for actual market size in units caused solely by actual market share being different from budgeted market share. (249)

Market-size variance. The difference in budgeted contribution margin at the budgeted market share caused solely by actual market size in units being different from budgeted market size in units. (249)

Master budget. Expression of management's operating and financial plans for a specified period (usually a fiscal year) including a set of budgeted financial statements. Also called *pro forma statements.* (185)

Master-budget capacity utilization. The expected level of capacity utilization for the current budget period (typically one year). (315)

Materials requirements planning (MRP). Push-through system that manufactures finished goods for inventory on the basis of demand forecasts. (714)

Materials-requisition record. Source document that contains information about the cost of direct materials used on a specific job and in a specific department. (105)

Matrix method. See *reciprocal method.* (554)

Merchandising-sector companies. Companies that purchase and then sell tangible products without changing their basic form. (36)

Mixed cost. A cost that has both fixed and variable elements. Also called a *semivariable cost.* (343)

Moral hazard. Describes situations in which an employee prefers to exert less effort (or to report distorted information) compared with the effort (or accurate information) desired by the owner because the employee's effort (or validity of the reported information) cannot be accurately monitored and enforced. (822)

Motivation. The desire to attain a selected goal (the goal-congruence aspect) combined with the resulting pursuit of that goal (the effort aspect). (776)

Multicollinearity. Exists when two or more independent variables in a multiple regression model are highly correlated with each other. (374)

Multiple regression. Regression model that estimates the relationship between the dependent variable and two or more independent variables. (352)

Net income. Operating income plus nonoperating revenues (such as interest revenue) minus nonoperating costs (such as interest cost) minus income taxes. (70)

Net present value (NPV) method. Capital budgeting discounted cash flow (DCF) method that calculates the expected monetary gain or loss from a project by discounting all expected future cash inflows and outflows to the present point in time, using the required rate of return. (742)

Net realizable value (NRV) method. Method that allocates joint costs to joint products on the basis of final sales value minus separable costs of total production of the joint products during the accounting period. (583)

Nominal rate of return. Made up of three elements: (a) a risk-free element when there is no expected inflation, (b) a business-risk element, and (c) an inflation element. (762)

Nonlinear cost function. Cost function in which the graph of total costs based on the level of a single activity is not a straight line within the relevant range. (357)

Nonvalue-added cost. A cost that, if eliminated, would not reduce the actual or perceived value or utility (usefulness) customers obtain from using the product or service. (442)

Normal capacity utilization. The level of capacity utilization that satisfies average customer demand over a period (say, two to three years) that includes seasonal, cyclical, and trend factors. (315)

Normal costing. A costing system that traces direct costs to a cost object by using the actual direct-cost rates times the actual quantities of the direct-cost inputs and that allocates indirect costs based on the budgeted indirect-cost rates times the actual quantities of the cost-allocation bases. (104)

Normal spoilage. Spoilage inherent in a particular production process that arises even under efficient operating conditions. (646)

Objective function. Expresses the objective to be maximized (for example, operating income) or minimized (for example, operating costs) in a decision model (for example, a linear programming model). (416)

On-time performance. Delivering a product or service by the time it is scheduled to be delivered. (682)

One-time-only special order. Orders that have no long-run implications. (394)

Operating budget. Budgeted income statement and its supporting budget schedules. (189)

Operating department. Department that directly adds value to a product or service. Also called a *production department* in manufacturing companies. (543)

Operating income. Total revenues from operations minus cost of goods sold and operating costs (excluding interest expense and income taxes). (42)

Operating-income volume variance. The difference between static-budget operating income and the operating income based on budgeted profit per unit and actual units of output. (281)

Operating leverage. Effects that fixed costs have on changes in operating income as changes occur in units sold and hence in contribution margin. (76)

Operation. A standardized method or technique that is performed repetitively, often on different materials, resulting in different finished goods. (626)

Operation-costing system. Hybrid-costing system applied to batches of similar, but not identical, products. Each batch of products is often a variation of a single design, and it proceeds through a sequence of operations, but each batch does not necessarily move through the same operations as other batches. Within each operation, all product units use identical amounts of the operation's resources. (626)

Opportunity cost. The contribution to operating income that is forgone or rejected by not using a limited resource in its next-best alternative use. (402)

Opportunity cost of capital. See *required rate of return (RRR).* (742)

Ordering costs. Costs of preparing, issuing, and paying purchase orders, plus receiving and inspecting the items included in the orders. (704)

Organization structure. Arrangement of lines of responsibility within the organization. (199)

Outcomes. Predicted economic results of the various possible combinations of actions and events in a decision model. (85)

Output unit-level costs. The costs of activities performed on each individual unit of a product or service. (149)

Outsourcing. Process of purchasing goods and services from outside vendors rather than producing the same goods or providing the same services within the organization. (397)

Overabsorbed indirect costs. See *overallocated indirect costs.* (118)

Overallocated indirect costs. Allocated amount of indirect costs in an accounting period is greater than the actual (incurred) amount in that period. Also called *overapplied indirect costs* and *overabsorbed indirect costs.* (118)

Overapplied indirect costs. See *overallocated indirect costs.* (118)

Overtime premium. Wage rate paid to workers (for both direct labor and indirect labor) in excess of their straight-time wage rates. (44)

Pareto diagram. Chart that indicates how frequently each type of defect occurs, ordered from the most frequent to the least frequent. (676)

Partial productivity. Measures the quantity of output produced divided by the quantity of an individual input used. (493)

Payback method. Capital budgeting method that measures the time it will take to recoup, in the form of expected future cash flows, the net initial investment in a project. (746)

Peak-load pricing. Practice of charging a higher price for the same product or service when the demand for it approaches the physical limit of the capacity to produce that product or service. (450)

Perfectly competitive market. Exists when there is a homogeneous product with buying prices equal to selling prices and no individual buyers or sellers can affect those prices by their own actions. (784)

Period costs. All costs in the income statement other than cost of goods sold. (38)

Physical-measure method. Method that allocates joint costs to joint products on the basis of the relative weight, volume, or other physical measure at the splitoff point of total production of these products during the accounting period. (582)

Planning. Selecting organization goals, predicting results under various alternative ways of achieving those goals, deciding how to attain the desired goals, and communicating the goals and how to attain them to the entire organization. (10)

Practical capacity. The level of capacity that reduces theoretical capacity by unavoidable operating interruptions such as scheduled maintenance time, shutdowns for holidays, and so on. (315)

Predatory pricing. Company deliberately prices below its costs in an effort to drive out competitors and restrict supply and then raises prices rather than enlarge demand. (451)

Prevention costs. Costs incurred to preclude the production of products that do not conform to specifications. (673)

Previous-department costs. See *transferred-in costs*. (621)

Price discount. Reduction in selling price below list selling price to encourage increases in customer purchases. (511)

Price discrimination. Practice of charging different customers different prices for the same product or service. (450)

Price-recovery component. Change in operating income attributable solely to changes in prices of inputs and outputs between one period and the next. (479)

Price variance. The difference between actual price and budgeted price multiplied by actual quantity of input. Also called *input-price variance* or *rate variance*. (236)

Prime costs. All direct manufacturing costs. (43)

Pro forma statements. Budgeted financial statements. (185)

Probability. Likelihood or chance that an event will occur. (84)

Probability distribution. Describes the likelihood (or the probability) that each of the mutually exclusive and collectively exhaustive set of events will occur. (84)

Process-costing system. Costing system in which the cost object is masses of identical or similar units of a product or service. (101)

Product. Any output that has a positive total sales value (or an output that enables an organization to avoid incurring costs). (578)

Product cost. Sum of the costs assigned to a product for a specific purpose. (45)

Product-cost cross-subsidization. Costing outcome where one undercosted (overcosted) product results in at least one other product being overcosted (undercosted). (140)

Product differentiation. Organization's ability to offer products or services perceived by its customers to be superior and unique relative to the products or services of its competitors. (468)

Product life cycle. Spans the time from initial R&D on a product to when customer service and support is no longer offered for that product. (447)

Product-mix decisions. Decisions about which products to sell and in what quantities. (405)

Product overcosting. A product consumes a low level of resources but is reported to have a high cost per unit. (140)

Product-sustaining costs. The costs of activities undertaken to support individual products regardless of the number of units or batches in which the units are produced. (149)

Product undercosting. A product consumes a high level of resources but is reported to have a low cost per unit. (140)

Production. Acquiring, coordinating, and assembling resources to produce a product or deliver a service. (6)

Production-denominator level. The denominator in the budgeted manufacturing fixed overhead rate computation. (266)

Production department. See *operating department*. (543)

Production-volume variance. The difference between budgeted fixed overhead and fixed overhead allocated on the basis of actual output produced. Also called *denominator-level variance*. (272)

Productivity. Measures the relationship between actual inputs used (both quantities and costs) and actual outputs produced; the lower the inputs for a given quantity of outputs or the higher the outputs for a given quantity of inputs, the higher the productivity. (492)

Productivity component. Change in costs attributable to a change in the quantity of inputs used in the current period relative to the quantity of inputs that would have been used in the prior period to produce the quantity of current period output. (479)

Profit center. Responsibility center where the manager is accountable for revenues and costs. (199)

Proration. The spreading of underallocated manufacturing overhead or overallocated manufacturing overhead among ending work in process, finished goods, and cost of goods sold. (119)

Purchase-order lead time. The time between placing an order and its delivery. (704)

Purchasing costs. Cost of goods acquired from suppliers including incoming freight or transportation costs. (703)

PV graph. Shows how changes in the quantity of units sold affect operating income. (70)

Qualitative factors. Outcomes that are difficult to measure accurately in numerical terms. (394)

Quality. The total features and characteristics of a product made or a service performed according to specifications to satisfy customers at the time of purchase and during use. (671)

Quantitative factors. Outcomes that are measured in numerical terms. (394)

Rate variance. See *price variance*. (236)

Real rate of return. The rate of return demanded to cover investment risk (with no inflation). It has a risk-free element and a business-risk element. (762)

Reciprocal method. Cost allocation method that fully recognizes the mutual services provided among all support departments. Also called *matrix method*. (553)

Reengineering. The fundamental rethinking and redesign of business processes to achieve improvements in critical measures of performance, such as cost, quality, service, speed, and customer satisfaction. (469)

Refined costing system. Costing system that reduces the use of broad averages for assigning the cost of resources to cost objects (jobs, products, services) and provides better measurement of the costs of indirect resources used by different cost objects—no matter how differently various cost objects use indirect resources. (145)

Regression analysis. Statistical method that measures the average amount of change in the dependent variable associated with a unit change in one or more independent variables. (352)

Relevant costs. Expected future costs that differ among alternative courses of action being considered. (393)

Relevant range. Band of normal activity level or volume in which there is a specific relationship between the level of activity or volume and the cost in question. (33)

Relevant revenues. Expected future revenues that differ among alternative courses of action being considered. (393)

Reorder point. The quantity level of inventory on hand that triggers a new purchase order. (707)

Required rate of return (RRR). The minimum acceptable annual rate of return on an investment. Also called the *discount rate*, *hurdle rate*, *cost of capital*, or *opportunity cost of capital*. (742)

Research and development. Generating and experimenting with ideas related to new products, services, or processes. (6)

Residual income (RI). Accounting measure of income minus a dollar amount for required return on an accounting measure of investment. (810)

Residual term. The vertical difference or distance between actual cost and estimated cost for each observation in a regression model. (352)

Responsibility accounting. System that measures the plans, budgets, actions, and actual results of each responsibility center. (199)

Responsibility center. Part, segment, or subunit of an organization whose manager is accountable for a specified set of activities. (199)

Return on investment (ROI). An accounting measure of income divided by an accounting measure of investment. See also *accrual accounting rate of return method*. (809)

Revenue allocation. The allocation of revenues that are related to a particular revenue object but cannot be traced to it in an economically feasible (cost-effective) way. (561)

Revenue center. Responsibility center where the manager is accountable for revenues only. (199)

Revenue driver. A variable, such as volume, that causally affects revenues. (68)

Revenue object. Anything for which a separate measurement of revenue is desired. (561)

Revenues. Inflows of assets (usually cash or accounts receivable) received for products or services provided to customers. (38)

Rework. Units of production that do not meet the specifications required by customers for finished units that are subsequently repaired and sold as good finished units. (645)

Rightsizing. See *downsizing*. (487)

Rolling budget. Budget or plan that is always available for a specified future period by adding a period (month, quarter, or year) to the period that just ended. Also called *continuous budget*. (188)

Safety stock. Inventory held at all times regardless of the quantity of inventory ordered using the EOQ model. (707)

Sales mix. Quantities of various products or services that constitute total unit sales. (77)

Sales-mix variance. The difference between (1) budgeted contribution margin for the actual sales mix, and (2) budgeted contribution margin for the budgeted sales mix. (521)

Sales-quantity variance. The difference between (1) budgeted contribution margin based on actual units sold of all products at the budgeted mix and (2) contribution margin in the static budget (which is based on the budgeted units of all products to be sold at the budgeted mix). (521)

Sales value at splitoff method. Method that allocates joint costs to joint products on the basis of the relative total sales value at the splitoff point of the total production of these products during the accounting period. (580)

Sales-volume variance. The difference between a flexible-budget amount and the corresponding static-budget amount. (231)

Scrap. Residual material left over when making a product. (645)

Selling-price variance. The difference between the actual selling price and the budgeted selling price multiplied by the actual units sold. (233)

Semivariable cost. See *mixed cost*. (343)

Sensitivity analysis. A what-if technique that managers use to calculate how an outcome will change if the original predicted data are not achieved or if an underlying assumption changes. (73)

Separable costs. All costs (manufacturing, marketing, distribution, and so on) incurred beyond the splitoff point that are assignable to each of the specific products identified at the splitoff point. (577)

Sequential allocation method. See *step-down method*. (552)

Sequential tracking. Approach in a product-costing system in which recording of the journal entries occurs in the same order as actual purchases and progress in production. (718)

Service department. See *support department*. (543)

Service-sector companies. Companies that provide services or intangible products to their customers. (36)

Service-sustaining costs. The costs of activities undertaken to support individual services. (149)

Shrinkage costs. Costs that result from theft by outsiders, embezzlement by employees, misclassifications, and clerical errors. (704)

Simple regression. Regression model that estimates the relationship between the dependent variable and one independent variable. (352)

Single-rate method. Allocation method that allocates costs in each cost pool to cost objects using the same rate per unit of a single allocation base. (544)

Slope coefficient. Coefficient term in a cost estimation model that indicates the amount by which total cost changes when a one-unit change occurs in the level of activity within the relevant range. (342)

Source document. An original record that supports journal entries in an accounting system. (104)

Specification analysis. Testing of the assumptions of regression analysis. (369)

Splitoff point. The juncture in a joint-production process when two or more products become separately identifiable. (577)

Spoilage. Units of production that do not meet the specifications required by customers for good units and that are discarded or sold at reduced prices. (645)

Staff management. Staff (such as management accountants and human resources managers) who provide advice and assistance to line management. (13)

Stand-alone cost-allocation method. Method that uses information pertaining to each user of a cost object as a separate entity to determine the cost-allocation weights. (557)

Stand-alone revenue-allocation method. Method that uses product-specific information on the products in the bundle as weights for allocating the bundled revenues to the individual products. (561)

Standard. A carefully determined price, cost, or quantity that is used as a benchmark for judging performance. It is usually expressed on a per unit basis. (234)

Standard cost. A carefully determined cost of a unit of output. (235)

Standard costing. Costing system that traces direct costs to output produced by multiplying the standard prices or rates by the standard quantities of inputs allowed for actual outputs produced and allocates overhead costs on the basis of the standard overhead-cost rates times the standard quantities of the allocation bases allowed for the actual outputs produced. (264)

Standard error of the estimated coefficient. Regression statistic that indicates how much the estimated value of the coefficient is likely to be affected by random factors. (368)

Standard error of the regression. Statistic that measures the variance of residuals in a regression analysis. (368)

Standard input. A carefully determined quantity of input required for one unit of output. (235)

Standard price. A carefully determined price that a company expects to pay for a unit of input. (235)

Static budget. Budget based on the level of output planned at the start of the budget period. (229)

Static-budget variance. Difference between an actual result and the corresponding budgeted amount in the static budget. (229)

Step cost function. A cost function in which the cost remains the same over various ranges of the level of activity, but the cost increases by discrete amounts (that is, increases in steps) as the level of activity changes from one range to the next. (357)

Step-down method. Cost allocation method that partially recognizes the mutual services provided among all support departments. Also called *sequential allocation method*. (552)

Stockout costs. Costs that result when a company runs out of a particular item for which there is customer demand. The company must act to meet that demand or suffer the costs of not meeting it. (704)

Strategic cost management. Describes cost management that specifically focuses on strategic issues. (5)

Strategy. Specifies how an organization matches its own capabilities with the opportunities in the marketplace to accomplish its objectives. (5)

Strategy map. A diagram that describes how an organization creates value by connecting strategic objectives in explicit cause-and-effect relationships with each other in the financial, customer, internal business process, and learning and growth perspectives. (471)

Suboptimal decision making. Decisions in which the benefit to one subunit is more than offset by the costs or loss of benefits to the organization as a whole. Also called *incongruent decision making* or *dysfunctional decision making*. (778)

Sunk costs. Past costs that are unavoidable because they cannot be changed no matter what action is taken. (393)

Super-variable costing. See *throughput costing*. (312)

Supply chain. Describes the flow of goods, services, and information from the initial sources of materials and services to the delivery of products to consumers, regardless of whether those activities occur in the same organization or in other organizations. (7)

Support department. Department that provides the services that assist other internal departments (operating departments and other support departments) in the company. Also called a *service department*. (543)

Target cost per unit. Estimated long-run cost per unit of a product or service that enables the company to achieve its target operating income per unit when selling at the target price. Target cost per unit is derived by subtracting the target operating income per unit from the target price. (440)

Target operating income per unit. Operating income that a company aims to earn per unit of a product or service sold. (440)

Target price. Estimated price for a product or service that potential customers will pay. (439)

Target rate of return on investment. The target annual operating income that an organization aims to achieve divided by invested capital. (446)

Theoretical capacity. The level of capacity based on producing at full efficiency all the time. (314)

Theory of constraints (TOC). Describes methods to maximize operating income when faced with some bottleneck and some nonbottleneck operations. (686)

Throughput costing. Method of inventory costing in which only variable direct material costs are included as inventoriable costs. Also called *super-variable costing*. (312)

Throughput margin. Revenues minus the direct material costs of the goods sold. (686)

Time driver. Any factor in which a change in the factor causes a change in the speed of an activity. (682)

Time value of money. Takes into account that a dollar (or any other monetary unit) received today is worth more than a dollar received at any future time. (741)

Total factor productivity (TFP). The ratio of the quantity of output produced to the costs of all inputs used, based on current period prices. (494)

Total-overhead variance. The sum of the flexible-budget variance and the production-volume variance. (278)

Transfer price. Price one subunit (department or division) charges for a product or service supplied to another subunit of the same organization. (780)

Transferred-in costs. Costs incurred in previous departments that are carried forward as the product's costs when it moves to a subsequent process in the production cycle. Also called *previous department costs*. (621)

Trigger point. Refers to a stage in the cycle from purchase of direct materials to sale of finished goods at which journal entries are made in the accounting system. (719)

Uncertainty. The possibility that an actual amount will deviate from an expected amount. (75)

Underabsorbed indirect costs. See *underallocated indirect costs*. (118)

Underallocated indirect costs. Allocated amount of indirect costs in an accounting period is less than the actual (incurred) amount in that period. Also called *underapplied indirect costs* or *underabsorbed indirect costs*. (118)

Underapplied indirect costs. See *underallocated indirect costs*. (118)

Unfavorable variance. Variance that has the effect of decreasing operating income relative to the budgeted amount. Denoted U. (230)

Unit cost. Cost computed by dividing total cost by the number of units. Also called *average cost*. (35)

Unused capacity. The amount of productive capacity available over and above the productive capacity employed to meet consumer demand in the current period. (486)

Usage variance. See *efficiency variance*. (236)

Value-added cost. A cost that, if eliminated, would reduce the actual or perceived value or utility (usefulness) customers obtain from using the product or service. (442)

Value chain. The sequence of business functions in which customer usefulness is added to products or services of a company. (6)

Value engineering. Systematic evaluation of all aspects of the value chain, with the objective of reducing costs and achieving a quality level that satisfies customers. (441)

Value streams. All valued-added activities needed to design, manufacture, and deliver a given product or product line to customers. (726)

Variable cost. Cost that changes in total in proportion to changes in the related level of total activity or volume. (30)

Variable costing. Method of inventory costing in which only all variable manufacturing costs are included as inventoriable costs. Also called *direct costing*. (301)

Variable overhead efficiency variance. The difference between the actual quantity of variable overhead cost-allocation base used and budgeted quantity of variable overhead cost-allocation base that should have been used to produce actual output, multiplied by budgeted variable overhead cost per unit of cost-allocation base. (267)

Variable overhead flexible-budget variance. The difference between actual variable overhead costs incurred and flexible-budget variable overhead amounts. (267)

Variable overhead spending variance. The difference between actual variable overhead cost per unit and budgeted variable overhead cost per unit of the cost-allocation base, multiplied by actual quantity of variable overhead cost-allocation base used for actual output. (269)

Variance. The difference between actual result and expected performance. (227)

Weighted-average process-costing method. Method of process costing that assigns the equivalent-unit cost of the work done to date (regardless of the accounting period in which it was done) to equivalent units completed and transferred out of the process and to equivalent units in ending work-in-process inventory. (614)

Whale curve. A typically backward-bending curve that represents the results from customer profitability analysis by first ranking customers from best to worst and then plotting their cumulative profitability level. (516)

Work-in-process inventory. Goods partially worked on but not yet completed. Also called *work in progress*. (37)

Work in progress. See *work-in-process inventory*. (37)

Work-measurement method. See *industrial engineering method*. (346)

Index

Author

A
Adamy, J., 237
Anderson, S., 146n, 356
Anderson, S. R., 160
Andrews, E., 452
Ansari, S., 440n
Areeda, P., 451n
Arrington, M., 484
Atkinson, A., 688n
Atkinson, A. A., 202n, 557n
Atkinson, C., 716n

B
Baggaley, B., 727n
Bailey, C., 361n
Banker, R., 478n
Baraldi, E., 441
Barkman, A., 451n
Barton, T., 356
Bell, J., 440n
Berk, J., 812n
Biderman, D., 226n
Birger, J., 78
Blair, N., 806n
Borjesson, S., 194n
Boyle, M., 262
Bronisz, P., 558n
Brown, S., 680n
Brownlee, R., 590
Bruno, A., 2n
Bunkley, N., 26n
Bustillo, M., 502n
Buskirk, E., 717

C
Cagilo, A., 716n
Carbone, J., 138n
Carter, T., 356
Champy, J., 469n
Chartrand, S., 717
Chinnis, C., 774n
Clark, P., 676n
Clifford, S., 78
Clinton, B., 547n
Cokins, G., 146n, 511n
Cooper, R., 146n, 511n
Corkery, M., 825
Cox, J., 686n
Cuoto, V., 400
Cutcher-Gershenfeld, J., 356

D
Dash, E., 15
Datar, S., 478n
Davenport, T. H., 716n
Davidson, P., 300n
Day, K., 280
Delmar, E., 183n
DeMarzo, P., 812n

Demski, J., 558n
Dillon, D., 108
Ding, D., 738n
Dombrowski, R.F., 590n

E
Edwards, C., 684
Eikenes, B., 587n
Eisenhardt, K., 680n
Eldon, E., 484
Elliot, D., 825
Erchr, E., 280
Evans, E., 280

F
Fazard, R., 518
Federowicz, M., 356
Fox, J., 824n
Fraser, R., 186n, 478n

G
Gage, J., 198
Gandel, S., 825
Garling, W., 15
Garrity, J., 15
Garthwaite, J., 542n
Gatti, J. F., 586n
Giridharadas, A., 432n
Goff, J., 198
Goldratt, E., 312n, 686n
Goldstein, J. L., 451n
Gollakota, K., 15n
Graham, J., 745n
Green, M., 15
Gregory, A., 226n
Grinnell, D. J., 586n
Grossman, M., 356
Gunderson, E., 62n
Gumbus, A., 15
Gupta, V., 15

H
Hacking, A., 576n
Halpern, S., 280
Hammer, M., 469n
Hansell, S., 319
Harrington, J., 451n
Harris, C., 237
Harris, J. K., 519n
Harvey, C., 745n
Hayzen, A., 478n
Hayes, B., 356
Heijmen, T., 400
Holm, E., 806n
Hope, J., 186n, 478n
Horvath, P., 187n
Huddart, S., 821n
Humphries, S., 717
Huston, L., 400

I
Iqbal, M. X., 819n

J
Jaffe, M., 542n
Jargon, J., 237
Jolley, J., 451n
Jones, C., 390n
Jurkus, A., 680n

K
Kageyama, Y., 670n
Kamenev, M., 627
Kaminska, I., 606n
Kaplan, R., 356
Kaplan, R. S., 146n, 160, 202n, 466n, 470n, 478n, 511n, 516n, 557n
Kaplow, L., 505n
Kapner, S., 262
Kaufman, W., 670n
Keegan, P., 33
Kesmodel, D., 237
Klammer, T., 320n
Knudson, B., 108
Kripalani, M., 432n
Kruz, L., 558n

L
Lacayo, R., 108
Laimon, S., 646n
Lampe, S., 198
Latham, G., 187n
Leapman, B., 356
Leber, J., 576n
Lewin, A., 400
Linebaugh, K., 670n
Loomis, C., 26n
Lublin, J., 825
Lunsford, L., 644n
Lyons, B., 15

M
Macario, A., 264
MacArthur, J., 356
Mackey, J., 312n, 686n
Mackie, B., 547n
Mani, M., 400
Manning, S., 400
Maragonelli, L., 441
Marshall, P. D., 590n
Martinez-Jerez, F. A., 160, 466n
Matau, R., 793
Matlack, C., 644n
Maynard, M., 670n
McGregor, J., 702n
McWilliams, G., 502n
McMaster, J., 793
Melumad, N., 821n
Miller, K., 466n
Misawa, M., 758
Moore, J., 86n, 416n
Moriarity, S., 558n
Morris, J., 684

Company

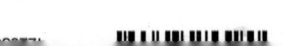